Psychotherapists' Sexual Involvement With Clients: Intervention And Prevention

GARY RICHARD SCHOENER

JEANETTE HOFSTEE MILGROM

JOHN C. GONSIOREK

ELLEN T. LUEPKER

RAY M. CONROE

Foreword by

ANDREW CZAJKOWSKI

WALK-IN COUNSELING CENTER

Minneapolis, Minnesota

The authors gratefully acknowledge permission to include the following material: "The incest analogy..." reprinted from *Incest in the Organizational Family*, by William L. White, published by Lighthouse Training Institute, ©1986; reprinted by permission of William L. White. "Accountability and Consumerism, by Mary Tambornino (nee Work), unpublished, ©1975; reprinted by permission of Mary Tambornino.The excerpt from *Sex in the Forbidden Zone: Sexual Exploitation in Professional Relationships*, by Peter Rutter, to be published by Jeremy P. Tarcher, ©1989; reprinted by permission of Jeremy P. Tarcher, Los Angeles, CA. The excerpt from *Sexual Exploitation in Professional Relationships*, by Glen Gabbard, published by American Psychiatric Press, ©1989; reprinted by permission of Glen Gabbard. The excerpt from *Medical Malpractice Psychiatric Care*, by Joseph Smith, published by Shepard's/McGraw Hill, ©1986; reprinted by permission of Shepard's/McGraw Hill. "Sexual Abuse of Clients in Psychotherapy: A Non-Professional Perspective," by William C. Cliadakis, unpublished, ©1985; reprinted by permission of William C. Cliadakis. *Child Sexual Abuse Within the Catholic Church*, by Kathe Stark, from her unpublished manuscript, 1988; printed by permission of Kathe Stark. *A Victim's Perspective*, by Judith Janssen, from her unpublished text, 1989; printed by permission of Judith Janssen.

Walk-In Counseling Center
2421 Chicago Avenue South
Minneapolis, MN 55404

ISBN 0-9624337-0-5

FIRST EDITION

Table of Contents

PREFACE

The beginning of this book was a series of in-house papers describing our work with people who had been sexually exploited by the therapists and counselors from whom they had sought treatment. They originally came for help to the Walk-In Counseling Center because of its reputation for taking on new issues. Hence, the papers were written for the professionals who volunteered at the center as well as for colleagues in the community.

In 1974 WICC was probably the only organization in the country attempting to provide services for victims of therapists and by the late 1970s our work was well enough known that we received many requests for copies of these papers. By the 1980s requests had increased so much that the cost of copying and mailing the papers became quite significant. In addition, we found it equally difficult to keep up with the demand for other written items, such as the Minnesota statutes dealing with sexual exploitation by therapists.

Several years ago we decided to rewrite our papers and to put them together in a "manual" of perhaps 100 printed pages for inexpensive and easy distribution. The Board of Directors approved the project and we set about the revisions. In order to discuss some key issues which had not been covered in our earlier papers, we included some additional chapters and we expanded the resource materials in the planned appendices.

Despite our limited intentions, the manuscript seemed to take on a life of its own. It kept getting longer and longer. A number of colleagues urged us to cover some critical topics that were receiving scant attention in the literature. Soon it became clear that we were actually producing a major reference work on the subject of therapist-client sexual involvement, and that with a few additional contributions the coverage would be far more comprehensive than any publication then available. We also made the decision that the book could provide a forum for other authors who were doing important work which had not yet made its way into the professional literature.

We sought contributions from our Wisconsin colleagues and were pleased to receive the fine chapters by Andrew Kane and Anthony Kuchan. Estelle Disch graciously developed a chapter on her work with victims in Boston, and Marie Fortune from Seattle contributed a chapter based on her pioneering work on sexual victimization and the church. Bill Cliadakis from New York and Mary Tambornino from Minneapolis allowed us to reprint consumer education papers which they had previously written. Anne List, a former intern, contributed a chapter, and colleagues Laura Brown, Michael O'Brien, and Janet Schank collaborated with other writers to produce key chapters. William White, Kathe Stark, and Judith Janssen allowed us to reprint their fine writings in various appendices. We owe a great debt to all these people; they not only contributed time, energy, and ideas but often paid for typing and long distance phone calls as well.

It has taken about 3-1/2 years to compile the contents of this book. The material has undergone constant revision to keep it current. Each chapter has been reviewed by at least one of us, other than the author, and some by several of us. Schoener reviewed all the chapters and developed the bibliography and appendices, and has overseen the production of the book. He as well as the authors of the chapters take full responsibility for any errors and omissions.

Colleagues and other readers who are familiar with the research literature may note the absence from the list of contributors of some well-known investigators in the field. For example, Nanette Gartrell and her colleagues who have produced a series of fine research articles, and with whom we have collaborated for some time, were not asked for contributions; the reason is that their work has received relatively wide distribution. Indeed we cite their work frequently. Her long-term support and continual sharing of resources has been very helpful to our work at WICC and we are grateful for this assistance.

Although the work of the Task Force on Sexual Exploitation by Counselors and Psychotherapists, in which we all participated, is mentioned on numerous occasions, we elected to limit our discussion of the Task Force's work because of the availability of a fine volume that provides considerable detail.[1] Peggy Spector's translation of our early work into implications for public policy and Barbara Sanderson's extraordinary capacity to run the Task Force contributed greatly to our own work (see Ch. 42). Sanderson's accomplishments, while the most visible, illustrate the sort of broad community involvement and professional support that this work has had in Minnesota. Our own efforts and those of the Task Force received broad support from a great number of professional groups; we are especially appreciative of the support of the Minnesota Psychological Association and the Minnesota Chapter of the National Association of Social Workers.

The work described in this book would not have been possible without the application and dedication of more than a thousand volunteers, most of them mental health professionals, who have staffed the Walk-In Counseling Center for the past 20 years. Also critical to the organization has been the active involvement and support of the Board of Directors of the Walk-In Counseling Center. The Board is made up of WICC volunteers and volunteers from a number of local businesses and corporations. An important buttress for our work and the continued existence of the Walk-In Counseling Center is the support provided by Commissioners, administrators, and staff members of the Mental Health Division and Purchase of Services Department of Hennepin County. We also wish to thank here the corporations and foundations who have provided us with additional funds at critical junctures.

Luepker did much of her early work at the Minneapolis Family and Children's Service with the early encouragement and support of Earl Beatt, the Executive Director, and Minna Shapiro, the Director of Child and Family Treatment. During her years at Family and Children's Service several staff social workers contributed their time to act as co-therapists in the work with groups for victims. Luepker is particularly grateful to Wendy Farrar, LuAnn Gilbert, Donna Johnson, Cindy Libman, and Carol Retsch-Bogart. As part of her collegial work with WICC, Luepker has provided supervision to interns who have co-led groups for victims of sexual exploitation by therapists (see Ch. 15). Luepker appreciates the contributions of Anne List and Ellen Stewart, interns, who co-led groups. Last but not least, in recent years Park Place Clinic has served as a supportive home for Luepker's work with individuals, families and groups, and the Clinic and its staff continue to contribute to this work.

The assistance by colleagues also has been essential in keeping the manuscript up to date. Over the years they have helped us to obtain copies of original dissertations; Hannah Lerman, whose annotated bibliography[2] on this topic is an essential resource, was particularly helpful. In recent months, Debra Borys and Marie Valiquette kindly provided

---

[1] Sanderson, Barbara (Ed.) (1989). It's Never O.K.: A Handbook for Professionals on Sexual Exploitation by Counselors and Psychotherapists.

[2] Lerman, Hannah (1984). *Sexual Intimacies Between Therapists and Patients.* An annotated bibliography of mental health, legal, and public media literature including relevant legal cases.

copies of their Ph.D. dissertations on very short notice and answered questions about their work over the phone. Jacqueline Bouhoutsos generously provided us with data from an unpublished study (Bouhoutsos & Gechtman, 1985) as well as other information. Kenneth Pope, who has continually shared information with us for many years, alerted us to many major recent developments. Dr. Pope always has shared his prepublication manuscripts with us. We are grateful to Dr. Glen Gabbard for permission to quote from his book, *Sexual Exploitation in Professional Relationships*. Dr. Peter Rutter and his publisher, Jeremy P. Tarcher, kindly let us review the manuscript of Dr. Rutter's forthcoming work, *Sex in the Forbidden Zone* (it will be published in Fall, 1989) and granted us permission to quote from the manuscript.

Joseph Smith, MD, JD, has for years exchanged information with us concerning legal issues in therapist-client sex cases. We are grateful to him and his publisher, Shepard's/McGraw-Hill, Inc. for granting permission to reprint material from *Medical Malpractice Psychiatric Care*. Dr. Martin Orne helped locate some key hypnosis-related references, and Dr. Erik Hoencamp provided us with a prepublication copy of his forthcoming article.

Over the years a great many people have provided us with valuable insights, information, and resources. It is impossible to name them all but we would like to acknowledge their contributions. More than 1,500 clients and therapists shared their pain and their stories with us. Countless administrators and attorneys have discussed specific situations and issues with us, and some have developed longer term relations with us. They often are the source of key information. Attorneys Sandra Nye, Jeff Kremers, Philip Getts, James Bliss, Laurel Learmonth, Susan Lentz, and Virginia Marso deserve special note, as do Assistant Attorney Generals John Breviu, Janet Newberg, and Mary Theisen. Lois Mizuno, Executive Director of the Minnesota Board of Psychology, Richard Auld, Assistant Director for Discipline, Minnesota Board of Medical Examiners, and David Mills of the American Psychological Association's national Ethics Committee have provided information on many occasions, something for which we are deeply appreciative.

In a sense, this volume reflects the dedication of the volunteers, Board, and staff members of the Walk-In Counseling Center to our purpose and philosophy. Inasmuch as the work described in this book represents only a small part of the overall activities of the Walk-In Counseling Center, their stellar efforts have been necessary to keep the Center's programs running smoothly while we undertook, over a 15-year period, this work with the therapist-client sex issue. In particular, we are grateful to the following:

Myra Barrett, David Reynolds-Gooch, Lawrence Kutner, Ph.D., and Richard Niemiec, who each served as Board President during the years of production of this book. Dr. Kutner provided invaluable advice and also made available the word processing equipment at Health and Science Communications.

Linda Sue Anderson, former Office Coordinator at WICC, gave considerable time to the early drafts of the manuscript, and Margee Shoshnik, the current Office Coordinator, goodnaturedly handles much of the details entailed in publication.

Martha Hughes, WICC's Clinic and Administrative Coordinator for many years, has smoothed out the financial/busiiness aspects of the entire project and has kept WICC running smoothly.

Stephen Lundberg, an attorney with the Minneapolis firm of Merchant and Gould, handled the various contractual and copyright issues that have arisen.

Larry Ritt, President of Professional Resource Exchange, Sarasota, Florida, Bruce Lansky, President of Meadowbrook Press, graciously provided us with advice on publishing.

WICC volunteer counselors Joachim Roski and Violaine Londe-Tarbès translated German and French language literature.

The project could not have been completed without the ongoing involvement of a number of people who have lived with the project almost as long as we have:

Andrew Czajkowski, President of Blue Cross and Blue Shield of Minnesota; he has encouraged and supported our work, arranged for a major contribution to the project from his organization, and contributed the foreword.

Richard Niemiec, Senior Vice President, Blue Cross and Blue Shield of Minnesota and Carol Doffing, Senior Manager, Office Services, arranged for the contribution of the first printing by Blue Cross.

Sylvia W. Rosen, a Minneapolis-based editor with extensive experience in the mental health and human services fields, for her sensitive and skilled editorial services and consultation. She has spent many long hours helping to clarify our ideas and to shape up the manuscript.

Last but not least, Sharon Anstett. Her unfailing patience, humor, and skills have transformed our manuscripts that were often difficult to decipher into accurate, clean copy.

We also owe thanks to the individuals who agreed to review the manuscript to describe its contents and usefulness for potential readers, and who have permitted us to quote them in the publication notice: Leonard Boche; Annette Brodsky, Ph.D.; Ann Burgess, Ph.D.; Nanette Gartrell, M.D.; Hannah Lerman, Ph.D.; Sandra Nye, J.D., ACSW; Barbara Sanderson, M.A.; Shirley Siegel; Joseph Smith, M.D., J.D.; Drayton Vincent, ACSW; and William White, M.A. Minneapolis designer Barbara Wulf created the notice.

Any proceeds realized from the sale of this book will be used to further the Walk-In Counseling Center's activities on behalf of the victims of sexual exploitation by therapists and counselors.

Gary Richard Schoener
Jeanette Hofstee Milgrom
John C. Gonsiorek
Ellen T. Luepker
Ray M. Conroe

FOREWORD

by Andrew Czajkowski

The Walk-In Counseling Center (WICC) of Minneapolis has become well-known as a place to go for help—anyone who walks in will see a professional therapist within 20 minutes. No identification, no paperwork is necessary. Undoubtedly, it is that informal, no-red-tape format that has made this book possible.

When a person feels exploited by the therapist who was trusted and confided in, to whom does he or she next turn for help? WICC has earned a reputation as a safe and respected place to start.

The first clients came to WICC in 1974 seeking help for problems resulting from sexual involvement with their therapists. Staff and the psychologists, psychiatrists, and other professional counselors who volunteer there, began to work out ways of helping those clients to cope with the problems created by that previous "treatment." Sometimes that meant helping a client to file charges, or to facilitate sessions with the client and the previous therapist. Sometimes it meant forming victim support groups to help those involved to realize they were not alone.

With limited publicity and no advertising, the cases kept coming. By the end of 1975 WICC dropped plans to conduct a prevalence study—it was determined there was no need to prove the problems existed. Eventually, in 1986, the first national conference focusing on the issue was held in Minnesota.

Much of this volume contains information that comes directly from WICC experiences with more than 1,000 clients. With a small staff that coordinates the volunteer hours of 220 professional therapists and provides consultations for many area organizations, it has become impossible to keep up with the requests for information and copies of papers delivered in various forums. Thus, this manual.

WICC has received both local and national recognition. Locally, WICC was responsible for the first conferences on rape (1973), incest and child sexual abuse (1974), and battered women (1974). Nationally, it was the recipient in 1977 of the prestigious Gold Achievement Award in Hospital and Community Psychiatry from the American Psychiatric Association.

Blue Cross and Blue Shield of Minnesota has provided support to WICC throughout my involvement on the Board of Directors for 9 years. I was succeeded by Richard Niemiec, a vice president at our company, who is now the Board's president. We also have assisted by handling production of marketing communication pieces.

WICC operates in areas not covered by Blue Cross and Blue Shield or other third party payers. It provides services before a client has a diagnosable disorder that would be covered under insurance or HMO plans. It also provides services to uninsured individuals or those whose plans do not allow for quick access to services.

So why are we involved? First, our support of WICC stems from our company's commitment to community mental health. Programs like WICC that provide service in an easily accessible format can lead to earlier intervention and can prevent the need for more costly services later. In Minnesota alone, Blue Cross and Blue Shield provided over $29 million in coverage for the treatment of mental health problems during 1987.

Second, we have undertaken to publish this book because it promises to inform and challenge practitioners regarding an issue critical to the profession and to the professional commitment to provide help.

Finally, Blue Cross and Blue Shield of Minnesota has a commitment to pay for quality care and not to pay for inappropriate treatment. Therapists' sexual misconduct not only renders the original treatment invalid but also can create a new iatrogenic disorder. This is disturbing to those of us in the business of arranging for payment for professional services. It is particularly appalling to realize that some of those limited treatment dollars paid for help were detrimental or harmful.

The challenge issued on these pages is twofold. First, the profession must define itself and set standards of conduct. Second, the impaired practitioners need to be identified and reprimanded. Every profession has some bad apples. Every professional at times suffers personal problems that becloud professional judgment. And sometimes counselors may just lose sight of their professional boundaries. The various psychotherapy fields have, as a whole, developed little in the way of evaluative or rehabilitative methodologies for the sexually exploitative therapist. This volume offers some approaches to treatment in Part IX, but it is clear that evaluation and rehabilitation in this domain lag far behind the work done for professionals impaired due to alcoholism or drug dependency. It is clear that the problem of sexual misconduct is not new, but an old problem that the profession has been slow to address.

The phenomenon of therapist-client sexual exploitation is a complex one and may well require a broad community approach. In Minnesota, a broad approach was used to involve people from a range of health professions as well as consumers and legislators. The resulting law passed by the Minnesota legislature in 1985 makes it a felony for a psychotherapist to have sexual contact with a client. It is still too soon to judge the outcome, but clearly Minnesota now has some new useful tools with which to address the problem.

A key facet of both WICC and the state approach to the problem is emphasis on the importance of innovation and the need to evaluate the outcomes of the attempted solutions. Collective efforts by many people can make a difference, and complex problems may require continuous attempts at solutions.

Some alternatives to traditional treatment are proposed. It appears they may actually be preferable to traditional long-term psychotherapy. The nontraditional forms of treatment are cost effective, and it makes sense intuitively that a client who has been victimized in individual therapy may have considerable reluctance to deal with the resulting problems through the same format.

Finally, better standards are needed. The call in the final chapter for the development of clearer standards for the delivery of psychotherapy echoes the experiences of Blue Cross and Blue Shield in attempting to evaluate mental health claims and service needs.

In fact, two concerns common to many plans that provide health care coverage appear and reappear throughout this volume: the need for better accountability through peer review and policing of practitioners who provide mental health services; and the need for better overall standards for the delivery of psychotherapy and other mental health services.

When the standards are clear, providers, consumers, and payers can all fairly judge the service provided. If they are unclear, consumers may be wary of such services and payers will apply additional scrutiny.

AUTHORS' PROFILES

LAURA S. BROWN

Laura S. Brown received her Ph.D. in Clinical Psychology in 1977 from Southern Illinois University at Carbondale. She is a Diplomate in Clinical Psychology of the American Board of Professional Psychology and a Fellow of the American Psychological Association, Divisions 12, 35, 42 and 44. She recently served as President of American Psychological Association Division 44, The Society for the Psychological Study of Lesbian and Gay Issues.

Dr. Brown currently works in private practice in Seattle, Washington. She also serves as Clinical Associate Professor at the Department of Psychology, University of Washington and supervises predoctoral students.

Dr. Brown's areas of expertise include assessment and diagnosis, feminist therapy, evaluation and treatment of victimization and professional ethics. She has served as an expert witness in a variety of legal arenas involving exploitation by health care providers of their patients. She has written extensively in a variety of areas including gay and lesbian issues in psychotherapy, ethics and feminist therapy, assessment in diagnostic issues in feminist therapy and the psychological effects of victimization. In 1987 Dr. Brown received the Distinguished Publication Award from the Association of Women in Psychology for her article on feminist therapy with post traumatic stress disorder. Her mailing address is 4527 1st Ave. N.E., Seattle, Washington 98105.

WILLIAM C. CLIADAKIS

William C. Cliadakis founded the National Committee for Preventing Psychotherapy Abuse (NCPPA) in 1981. He is a former geologist and received an M.S. degree from New York University in 1959. Mr. Cliadakis is currently Director of Research and Founder at William Cliadakis Research, an investment research consulting firm specializing in research for securities firms.

Over the last decade, Mr. Cliadakis has been active in the rights of healthcare consumers. In 1979 he cofounded Peer Support, a currently active self-help group in Manhattan. In 1982 he organized the first nonprofessional conference on public protection from psychotherapy abuse. It was held at the City University of New York Graduate Center. Mr. Cliadakis served as principle negotiator with the National Institute of Health and the New York Academy of Sciences in discussions which led to landmark first inclusion of a panel of electroconvulsive schock therapy (ECT) patients to participate in an ECT conference. He has also been active in a variety of other areas in winning representation for the consumers of healthcare.

Mr. Cliadakis has authored a number of publications on psychotherapy abuse, client rights in the healthcare system, the abuse of electroconvulsive therapy (ECT) and other topics. He has made numerous appearances on radio and television and has been quoted in articles in newspapers nationally. Mr. Cliadakis is also involved in a regular cable television program on mental health issues and client rights. He is currently involved in national distribution of a four-part documentary, on video cassette, about the abuse and ethics of ECT. His work has included involvement with many organizations working for prevention of psychotherapy abuse and the rights of clients in healthcare systems across the country.

Mr. Cliadakis can be reached at 175 W. 93rd St., New York, NY 10025.

ANDREW P. CZAJKOWSKI

Andrew P. Czajkowski is President and Chief Executive Officer of Blue Cross and Blue Shield of Minnesota, a nonprofit corporation and Minnesota's largest health care carrier. He is also Chief Executive Officer of its wholly owned subsidiary, MII, which provides life insurance and flexible spending accounts. He began his career with Blue Cross and Blue Shield of Minnesota in 1966 as Manager of Underwriting, was later made Vice President, and became President in January 1983.

Mr. Czajkowski is a member of the Board and the Executive Committee of the National Blue Cross Association. He is Chairman of the Board of Managers for the Federal Employee Program for the Blue Cross System nationally, and is also Chairman of the Plan Investment Fund, a national Blue Cross organization. He was the founder of the Minnesota Comprehensive Health Association, which provides health care coverage to uninsurable Minnesotans, and served as its President and Board Chairman from 1976 to 1982.

Mr. Czajkowski has also served on the Boards of a number of local organizations including the Walk-In Counseling Center. He currently serves as Chairman of the Board of the St. Paul United Way. He also serves on the Board of the American National Bank in St. Paul.

Mr. Czajkowski speaks locally and nationally on a variety of topics including controlling health care costs, cost containment programs, AIDS, and other health economic issues. He can be contacted at Blue Cross and Blue Shield of Minnesota, 3535 Blue Cross Road, St. Paul, Minnesota 55122.

RAY M. CONROE

Ray M. Conroe received his Ph.D. in Counseling Psychology from the State University of New York at Buffalo in 1970. During his career he has worked on a spinal cord injury service; has coordinated a medical school program for teaching, interviewing and psychological counseling; and has served as Clinic Director at Walk-In Counseling Center. He currently works in private practice and also serves as a Psychology Consultant for Disability Determination Services, Minnesota Department of Jobs and Training and as Clinical Assistant Professor, Department of Psychology, University of Minnesota.

Dr. Conroe has talked, presented and written about a variety of topics: psychological aspects of illness and disabilities; teaching interviewing and counseling in the medical school setting; and ethical issues in counseling, therapy, and clinical supervision. Current professional interests include career development of health care providers, the relationship between work and disability, ethical issues in the practice of psychotherapy, and the efficacy of brief psychotherapeutic interventions. He can be reached at 1528 W. Edgewater Ave., Arden Hills, Minnesota 55112.

ESTELLE DISCH

Estelle Disch received her Ph.D. in Sociology and has pursued a double career teaching sociology and practicing psychology for the past 20 years. She is an Associate Professor of Sociology at the University of Massachusetts at Boston and is a Certified Clinical Sociologist. After working for ten years with a feminist therapy center she has become co-founder of Boston Associates to Stop Therapy Abuse (BASTA).

In the beginning of 1984 Dr. Disch began leading workshops for survivors of sexual abuse by psychotherapists. Her personal experience with a sexually abusive psychotherapist 18 years ago provided an impetus for this work. Dr. Disch runs one-day workshops for survivors and also helps people find support as they go through complaint procedures. She consults to groups of people who have been abused by the same therapist and provides training and consultation to professionals about this and other boundary issues. She can be reached c/o BASTA at 528 Franklin Street, Cambridge, Massachusetts 02139.

MARIE M. FORTUNE

Rev. Marie M. Fortune received her seminary training at Yale Divinity School and was ordained a minister in the United Church of Christ in 1976. After serving as Minister of a local parish she founded the Center for the Prevention of Social and Domestic Violence where she currently serves as Executive Director. The center in Seattle, Washington, is an educational ministry providing training to religious communities in the United States and Canada.

Rev. Fortune is a pastor, educator, as well as a practicing ethicist and theologian. She has written extensively on family violence, sexual abuse prevention, abused women and unethical behavior by clergy. In 1989 Harper & Row published her volume *Is Nothing Sacred? When Sex Enters the Pastoral Relationship*. In 1987, the same publisher published her work *Keeping the Faith: Questions and Answers for Abused Women*. Rev. Fortune can be reached at the Center for the Prevention of Sexual and Domestic Violence, 1914 N. 34th St., Suite 105, Seattle, Washington 98103.

JOHN C. GONSIOREK

John C. Gonsiorek received his Ph.D. in Clinical Psychology in 1978 from the University of Minnesota. He is a Diplomate in Clinical Psychology of the American Board of Professional Psychology and works as Director of Psychological Services at Twin Cities Therapy Clinic in Minneapolis, MN. He previously served as Clinic Director at Walk-In Counseling Center. He is currently on the faculty of the Minneapolis School of Professional Psychology and has served as Clinical Assistant Professor in the Department of Psychology at the University of Minnesota.

Dr. Gonsiorek has published extensively in the areas of psychotherapy with gay and lesbian individuals, professional ethics and boundaries, quality assurance in mental health and other areas. His major publications include *Homosexuality and Psychotherapy: A Practitioner's Handbook of Affirmative Models*, Hayworth Press, 1982; *Homosexuality: Social, Psychological and Biological Issues*, edited by William Paul, James Weinrick, John C. Gonsiorek and Mary Hotvedt, 1982, Sage Publications. Dr. Gonsiorek, along with James Weinrich, is currently revising and updating this later volume for publication in 1990. In addition, Dr. Gonsiorek is working with Laura Brown on a book on psychotherapy with gay and lesbian clients, and with Walter Bera and Don LeTourneau on a book on treatment of male victims.

Dr. Gonsiorek has served as consultant for a variety of organizations locally and nationally on sexual exploitation of clients by healthcare providers and clergy and on sexual identity issues. He has lectured widely on these topics and has served as expert witness in numerous cases. His current areas of interest include assessment and rehabilitation of exploitative therapists and clergy, treatment of male victims, psychotherapy with gay and lesbian clients, sexual identity issues and quality assurance in mental health. He can be reached at Twin Cities Therapy Clinic, Physicians and Surgeons Bldg., Room 506, 63 S. 9th St., Minneapolis, Minnesota 55402.

ANDREW W. KANE

Andrew W. Kane received his Ph.D. in Clinical Psychology in 1971 from the University of Wisconsin at Milwaukee. He is a Licensed Psychologist in private practice in Milwaukee, Wisconsin, and also serves as Clinical Consultant to The Thompson Group, management consultants. He is on the Faculty of the Wisconsin School of Professional Psychology, and the Clinical Faculty of the University of Wisconsin at Milwaukee and the Medical College of Wisconsin. Dr. Kane divides his professional time between psychotherapy with individuals and couples, and forensic issues such as child custody, divorce mediation, personal injury litigation, etc.

Dr. Kane has been involved with the issue of sexual exploitation by psychotherapists and counselors since 1983, and has spoken publicly on this issue numerous times. In 1984, as President of the Wisconsin Psychological Association, he appointed a Task Force on Sexual Misconduct by Psychotherapists and Counselors. In 1987, the Task Force became a Coalition which involves nearly all mental health organizations in Wisconsin. Dr. Kane chaired the Task Force/Coalition from 1985 until April 1989. He has also been actively involved in community mental health programming and in the provision of services for adolescents and drug abusers.

Dr. Kane is listed in the National Register of Health Service Providers in Psychology, and is a Diplomate and Fellow of the American Board of Medical Psychotherapists. He was elected in 1989 as the founding President of the Division of Forensic and Correctional Psychologists of the Wisconsin Psychological Association. In 1987 he was given an award for "Distinguished Contribution to the Practice of Psychology in the Public Interest" by the Wisconsin Psychological Association. He is the author of 17 professional papers and one book, and has a second book scheduled for publication in late 1989 (*Examination of Psychologists in Divorce and Other Civil Actions*).

Dr. Kane can be reached at 2815 North Summit Avenue, Milwaukee, Wisconsin 53211.

ANTHONY M. KUCHAN

Anthony M. Kuchan received his Ph.D. in Clinical Psychology in 1964 from Purdue University. He is an Assistant Professor in the Department of Psychology, Marquette University, in Milwaukee, Wisconsin. He served as Department Chairman from 1977 to 1987, and was Acting Assistant and then Associate Dean of the Graduate School from 1966 to 1972.

Dr. Kuchan has several scholarly publications on topics related to the training of psychologists, treatment program evaluation, and the long-term effects of aftercare services following the residential treatment of delinquent adolescents. He has been active in both University and community affairs, serving on many task forces and committees. He has been a member of the Ethics Committee of the Wisconsin Psychological Assocation, and has served as its Chairman since 1976. From 1981 to 1985 he served on the Professional Education and Credentials Committee of the State of Wisconsin Psychology Examining Board.

Dr. Kuchan has provided a variety of consultation services, and for a number of years has been a Psychological Consultant to both the St. Charles Youth and Family Services and the Wisconsin Province of the Society of Jesus. He is a Consulting Faculty Member of the Wisconsin School of Professional Psychology. He was a charter member of the Wisconsin Psychological Association Task Force on Sexual Misconduct by Therapists and continued his involvement after the Task Force became the Wisconsin Coalition on Sexual Misconduct by Therapists. He is a practicing psychotherapist, and he lectures and consults on the following topics: sexual misconduct, residential treatment, personality theory, ethical issues, and issues in psychology.

Dr. Kuchan can be reached at 5760 W. Green Brook Drive, Milwaukee, Wisconsin 53223.

ANNE L. LIST

Anne L. List received her M.S.W. in 1987 from the University of Minnesota. She currently works as a social worker at the Good Beginnings Program at Minneapolis Children's Medical Center. She previously worked as Family Life Facilitator at Project STEEP at the University of Minnesota. Ms. List interned at Walk-In Counseling Center in the academic year 1986-1987 and has also worked at a University of Minnesota refugee training program in health careers and did a research project on the effects of iron deficiency and iron deficiency anemia on cognitive development of young children. Ms. List has taught classes on assertiveness training for women, burnout, stress, and other topics. She can be reached at 2848 40th Avenue S., Minneapolis, Minnesota 55406.

ELLEN T. LUEPKER

Ellen T. Luepker received her M.S.W. from Smith College in 1966. She is an A.C.S.W. and also a Board Certified Diplomate in Clinical Social Work and a Licensed Psychologist. In 1977 Ms. Luepker received a Bush Fellowship in Early Childhood Education and Development at the University of Minnesota.

Ms. Luepker currently works at Park Place Clinic of Counseling, Minneapolis, Minnesota, providing psychotherapy services to children, adolescents and adults. She has served as Director of Group Treatment at Minneapolis Family and Children's Service, Field Instructor for the Boston University School of Social Work, and Instructor in Psychiatry (Social Work), University of Rochester School of Medicine and Dentistry. Ms. Luepker is Past President of the Minnesota Society for Clinical Social Work and Past Secretary of the National Federation of Societies for Clinical Social Work.

Since 1980 Ms. Luepker has collaborated with Walk-In Counseling Center in providing a range of clinical support services to sexually exploited clients and their families. In addition, she has supervised and trained students at Walk-In Counseling Center and has served as special consultant to the Minnesota Task Force on Sexual Exploitation of Clients by Therapists and Counselors. Ms. Luepker has provided training and consultation on this topic in the United States and Europe. Ms. Luepker has served as an expert witness in a variety of legal proceedings locally and nationally in situations involving complaints of unprofessional conduct against therapists and clergy.

Ms. Luepker can be reached at 4108 Edmund Blvd., Minneapolis, Minnesota 55406.

JEANETTE HOFSTEE MILGROM

Jeanette Hofstee Milgrom currently works as Director of Consultation and Training at Walk-In Counseling Center in Minneapolis, Minnesota. She received her undergraduate degree in Social Work in Groningen, Netherlands and her M.S.W. from the University of Minnesota. She is a Clinical Field Instructor for the School of Social Work, University of Minnesota, supervising graduate interns. Prior to her work at Walk-In Counseling Center, Ms. Milgrom worked in a variety of settings including neighborhood houses, daycare, mental health residential and outpatient programs and both institutional- and community-based correctional programs in the Netherlands, Great Britain and the United States.

While at Walk-In Counseling Center she has worked extensively with clients who were sexually exploited by their counselors, therapists and clergy. Prior to that she also responded to other problems of victimization such as sexual assault, incest and battered women, working with grass roots organizations and involving traditional agencies in the process of social change. She received the first Feminist of the Year Award from Chrysalis Center for Women in 1981 in recognition of her outstanding service to the community.

Her other areas of expertise are training regarding staff/client relationships and professional boundaries, and consultation on ethical dilemmas and staff/organizational conflict resolution. She can be reached at Walk-In Counseling Center, 2421 Chicago Avenue S., Minneapolis, Minnesota 55404.

MICHAEL O'BRIEN

Michael O'Brien received his M.A. degree from the University of Minnesota in 1974 in Educational Psychology. He is currently a Licensed Psychologist and is completing his doctoral work in Educational Psychology at the University of Minnesota. Mr. O'Brien works as Director of Clinical Services at East Communities Family Service, a private, non-profit counseling agency in Maplewood, Minnesota affiliated with Family Service of Greater St. Paul.

Mr. O'Brien is founder and Director of Phase, the Program for Healthy Adolescent Sexual Expression. Phase is an outpatient program for the treatment of adolescent sex offenders which has served over six hundred adolescents since 1981. Mr. O'Brien has authored a number of articles on sexual abuse by adolescents and has lectured and trained widely in the United States and Canada. He is a participating member of the National Task Force on Juvenile Sexual Offending, a national group of experts working to develop standards for assessment, intervention and treatment of this population. He consults to a number of agencies and programs regarding issues of sexuality and sexual abuse. Mr. O'Brien has appeared on the *TODAY Show* and *Larry King Live* TV talk shows discussing these issues.

Mr. O'Brien can be reached at East Communities Family Service, 1709 N. McKnight Road, Maplewood, Minnesota 55109

JANET SCHANK

Janet Schank received her M.A. degree in Counseling and Student Personnel Psychology from the University of Minnesota in 1987. She is currently a doctoral candidate in that program. In the academic year 1985-1986, Ms. Schank worked as an intern at Walk-In Counseling Center where she has been a volunteer mental health professional since 1982. She currently works as a staff psychotherapist at the Macalester College Health Service. She has worked at the University of Minnesota Counseling Service and hte International Student Advisors Office at the University of Minnesota. Her dissertation research explores ethical dilemmas of rural psychologists. Ms. Schank is also active in training and education, especially in the areas of self-esteem and assertiveness.

Ms. Schank can be reached at Macalester College Health Service, 1600 Grand Avenue, St. Paul, Minnesota 55105.

GARY RICHARD SCHOENER

Gary Schoener is a Licensed Psychologist and Executive Director of Walk-In Counseling Center. Mr. Schoener has been at Walk-In Counseling Center for 20 years and its Executive Director since 1973. Previously he worked as a clinical psychologist at the Minneapolis Clinic of Psychiatry and Neurology.

Mr. Schoener is a Ph.D. candidate in clinical psychology at the University of Minnesota. He is also a faculty member for the Chemical Dependency Counselor Training Program and the Independent Study Program in Health Care Administration at the School of Public Health, University of Minnesota. He served as special consultant to the Minnesota Task Force on Sexual Exploitation by Counselors and Psychotherapists and is a member of the Task Force on The Impaired Psychologist of the American Psychological Association.

Mr. Schoener has been a local, state and national consultant for 15 years on issues of intervening with victims, assessment of therapists, professional boundaries and ethics and administrative safeguards. He has served as an expert witness in a variety of proceedings nationally.

In 1987 Mr. Schoener received the Award of Excellence from the National Federation on Therapy Abuse and in 1986 received the Non-Profit Excellence Award for Management of a Non-Profit Organization, as well as other recognitions over the years.

He has authored a number of book chapters and professional articles and has been interviewed extensively by various news media. He was one of the editors of a volume produced by the American Psychological Association in 1988, *Assisting Impaired Psychologists*, by M. Schwebel, J. Skorina and G. Schoener.

He can be reached at Walk-In Counseling Center, 2421 Chicago Avenue S., Minneapolis, Minnesota 55404.

MARY TAMBORNINO

Mary Tambornino, a certified legal assistant, has a Bachelors Degree in English Literature at the University of Minnesota and is currently a private consultant providing legal research/writing services. Previously Ms. Tambornino was the Director of Public Affairs and the Director of tfeh Hennepin County Chapter of the Mental Health Association of Minnesota. She has also worked as a Research Associate for the Independent Republican Caucus of the Minnesota State Senate, as a Management Consultant for United Research, as a Legal Assistant for the law firm of Broeker, Geer, Fletcher and LaFond, and most recently for Fingerhut Corporation.

Ms. Tambornino is active in the GOP Feminist Caucus of Minnesota and the Minnesota Women's Political Caucus where she has functioned respectively as president and chair. She has also been a member of the Minnesota State Board of Nursing, the President of the Mental Health Association of Hennepin County, and the President of Wellspring Therapeutic Community. She can be reached at 3851 Susan Lane, Minnetonka, Minnesota 55345.

PART I

BACKGROUND

Chapter 1 by Schoener describes the Walk-In Counseling Center and the evolution of the Minnesota approach to the problem of sexual exploitation by counselors and psychotherapists. The purpose of the chapter is to explain the development of our interest in and activities relating to the issue, as well as to articulate our underlying philosophical positions.

Chapter 2 by Schoener introduces the area under discussion. It provides a glimpse of the history of responses to the issues by the various psychotherapy professions and some insight to the public's perspective on the problem. It is not meant to be a comprehensive literature review; this book is directed to practical solutions, not academic deliberations.

In Chapter 3, Kuchan discusses previously unpublished data collected in Wisconsin on the incidence of sexual contact with clients. It is unique in that the survey was directed to practitioners in the various psychotherapy professions. It also reports in much greater detail than is usual on the actual types of sexual contact and, also, on the time periods when abuses occurred.

The problem of sexual exploitation of clients by therapists is reviewed in Chapters 4 (Schoener & Luepker) and 5 (Luepker) in different but related frameworks. The first examines sexual exploitation as a type of abuse of power in the therapeutic relationship; it goes beyond the typical analysis, however, by examining the shift in various power roles during different phases of therapy. A rarely discussed aspect of the power relationship is also examined. It is the possibility of the client's becoming very powerful following therapy termination by bringing a complaint against the therapist.

The second framework, explored in Chapter 5, focuses on parallels between sexual exploitation of clients and parent-child incest. Beyond noting the striking similarities, the discussion offers useful suggestions, derived from our experience in dealing with parent-child incest, which may help therapists and others to deal with therapist-client sexual exploitation cases. This chapter is a development of concepts which the author discussed in a chapter in a recent publication (Luepker, 1989).

The final chapter in Part I by Rev. Marie Fortune examines similarities and differences in sexual exploitation by members of the clergy and other types of counselors. Rev. Fortune has been a national leader in raising such issues among clergy; she also was a keynote speaker at the first national conference on sexual exploitation, "It's Never OK," held in Minneapolis in June 1986. She establishes a conceptual framework for her discussion and provides useful suggestions for dealing with sexual exploitation by clergy. Additional suggestions for intervention in such cases are given in a companion piece by Schoener and Milgrom in Part V, Chapter 20.

CHAPTER 1

THE WALK-IN COUNSELING CENTER AND THE MINNESOTA APPROACH TO THE PROBLEM OF SEXUAL EXPLOITATION BY THERAPISTS

Gary Richard Schoener

Early in 1969 a group of psychologists met at the University of Minnesota to organize a chapter of Psychologists for Social Action. One task force set up at that meeting worked on a "free clinic." The decision was made to offer psychological consultation services to the community using volunteer psychologists. In May 1969 the free, no-red-tape counseling program began under the aegis of Teen Age Medical Service (TAMS), a free clinic aimed at alienated adolescents, which had opened its doors in the Fall of 1968.

When both clinics became busier, TAMS moved into other quarters in 1970. Before long the Walk-In Counseling Center (WICC) began seeing adults as well as teenagers and the two programs took somewhat separate pathways. The pediatricians and other personnel who developed TAMS went on to open a pediatric hospital (the Minneapolis Children's Medical Center) in the adjacent block.

In addition to offering free, short-term, no-red-tape professional counseling in the evenings, WICC provided speakers to community groups. Its volunteer force expanded to include social workers and psychiatrists, as well as psychologists. By late 1970 it was clear the services WICC offered were needed by the community and that professionals were willing to continue their volunteer contributions. A paid staff became essential, however, to better organize and coordinate the different activities and services more efficiently. WICC incorporated as a private, non-profit organization in 1971.

From July 1971 through June 1973 a grant from the Governor's Crime Commission provided funding for three staff members. During those years I served as the half-time Community Coordinator and began to develop a very broad consultation program. Its purpose was to assist community groups and agencies and, especially, the developing "street agencies" (community-based mental health programs).

Hennepin County's mental health program office began providing funds for our program in mid-1973. They enabled WICC to expand our staff and to continue providing short-term counseling. I became Executive Director. Jeanette Milgrom, a social worker, was hired as the full-time Director of Consultation & Training. The consultation, education, and training services she provided were directed to the needs of alienated individuals and to problems in the community which were not receiving appropriate attention.

The next year WICC organized the first large-scale workshop on rape and sexual assault in the Twin Cities. It led to improved cooperation among human service providers, police, and the courts. The following year, a similar workshop was held on the subject of incest and the sexual abuse of children. Milgrom then conducted the first workshop on battered women and organized the Consortium on Battered Women. The latter had a dramatic effect on the availability of services to women and to the community. In 1977, WICC was given a Gold Achievement Award in Hospital and Community Psychiatry (see *Hospital and Community Psychiatry*, 1977, for an account of WICC and its activities; for a detailed history of WICC, see Glasscote, Raybin, Reitler, and Kane, 1986, *The Alternate Services: Their Role in Mental Health*).

The professional community continues to give WICC strong support. More than 200 therapists volunteer as counselors or supervisors each year. A smaller number volunteer to act as consultants to other programs, with several hundred clients being served yearly. More than 1,000 have volunteered during the past 19 years along with paraprofessionals who serve as receptionists. Several thousand clients are served each year. Hennepin County continues to provide most of the program funding as part of its community mental health services. The remainder of the program budget comes from client donations, fees from consultation and training activities, and contributions from local businesses and foundations for some capital items. Mental health professionals and business and community members serve on the Board of Directors.

More formal work on the issue of sex between therapist and client began in 1974 when a caller asked for a referral to "a female psychiatrist who could undo the damage done by a male psychiatrist." When pressed for details she revealed that the client in question had been sexually abused by her therapist, a well-known psychiatrist. Dr. Irving Benoist, WICC's Clinic Director at that time, received a separate complaint about this psychiatrist. Then we learned of a third. Because the victims feared taking action, we decided to make a third-party complaint to the Minnesota Board of Medical Examiners and to the local medical society.

Eventually, the clients filed a formal complaint with the Board of Medical Examiners, which led to the prosecution of the psychiatrist by the Board. Both before and after a meeting between a WICC staff member and the psychiatrist (who was supported by a psychologist colleague) to discuss the situation, we were pressured informally by individuals and organizations to drop our involvement. Although the Board took minimal action, the psychiatrist's attorney leaked key documents to the press, which gave the story major coverage.

Meanwhile, WICC staff members received inquiries from victims of other therapists. We helped them to sort out their experiences, to obtain support, and to examine options for complaints or related actions. When this work became known in the professional community we received considerable informal support and even veiled threats. Weren't we worried that an accused therapist might turn on us? Why did we engage in this risky undertaking given that WICC depended on volunteerism from the professional community? We had three responses:

1. There is no "middle ground." One is either part of the problem or part of the solution. To fail to take action is the ultimate "crime of silence."

2. We believe that the majority of professionals abhor such behavior and are pleased that somebody is taking action to deal with it.

3. If people did not want to volunteer because WICC helps clients to protect others from abuse, then we would not want such volunteers anyway.

It is a pleasure to note that over the years our assumptions proved correct. We still receive unsolicited statements of support from many mental health professionals for our work. Volunteerism is as strong as ever, and our volunteer force is much larger than it was in 1974. We have had the great fortune to address this sexual issue in a generally supportive environment.

Minnesota was and still is a very progressive state in terms of dealing with social problems. Its system of programs for the victims of rape, sexual assault, and domestic abuse is extraordinary, especially when one considers the state's population. Government, business, and foundations form an enlightened public-private partnership to bring about change.

Since 1973 WICC has had an extraordinary relation with the Mental Health Division of Hennepin County; it has provided stable funding for us through economically bad as well as good times. Its high-caliber staff members have provided support and guidance of a type rarely seen anywhere, and they have opened the way for innovative programing. To their credit the County Commissioners also have supported the development of innovative programing.

The work on sexual exploitation by therapists is principally done by myself and Jeanette Milgrom, although interns (e.g., Janet Shank, Ch. 23; Anne List, Chs. 15 and 16) and other staff (e.g., Ray Conroe, John Gonsiorek) have played key roles.

Our work on the sexual exploitation of therapy clients has needed funding and professional support, of course, but, in the final analysis, it has depended primarily on three key elements; from the start they have characterized our approach to the issue and the attitudes of the staff members who work with the victims:

1. The willingness to listen to clients, even when they are making distressing statements about our own profession, and the belief that they deserve a hearing and some action.

2. The belief that complex problems such as sexual exploitation by therapists must be viewed in the broader context to be understood or remedied, and that the whole community must be involved in finding solutions.

3. The belief in taking action, even in the face of risks.

We are profoundly impressed by the courage of clients who have taken considerable personal risk to try to protect other clients, even when regulatory bodies are unresponsive. In some cases clients have been willing to "go public" and to educate consumers and the public through radio and television. Clients also have contributed greatly to our knowledge and understanding of the issue. They have critiqued many of our memos and papers to improve the accuracy.

By seeing this problem in a broad context we have been able to address it by many means and to involve many other professionals in the work. We also have avoided the trap of hearing only one side of the story and thus limiting our perspective. We assist everyone who seeks help: clients, therapists, organizations, and governments.

Finally, some comments are in order on risk taking. First of all, after being involved in more than 1,000 cases of sexual exploitation as well as a number of risky situations that were handled in other areas of WICC, the center never has been sued or attacked in any way save for occasional behind-the-back snide comments. Our Board of Directors has provided superb guidance over the years for our programs. At times they elected to put significant restrictions on the news media to protect WICC from being used as a site for filming TV programs.

EVOLUTION OF THE WICC MODEL

Following our first case in 1974 of sexual exploitation of a client by a therapist, WICC staff members not only assisted several clients but also worked with the staff of a licensure board to gain the cooperation of the victims. We provided significant assistance to prosecutors to help them to master the professional literature on the topic and to prepare them to cross examine the experts employed by the defense. Consequently, the licensure boards regarded WICC as a resource to assist other clients who had filed complaints and who needed emotional support or counseling. Other professionals in the community began to call upon WICC staff members for consultation in other cases. Thus WICC staff members became known for assisting clients who had been victimized by therapists.

In addition to seeing more clients, a number of informal discussions were held during 1975 with other concerned mental health professionals. In March of that year, the Julie Roy vs. Renatus Hartogs lawsuit in New York City received national publicity and the problem was moved "out of the closet." By the end of 1975, WICC abandoned the idea of conducting an incidence and prevalence survey; we believed then that the need no longer existed to prove that there was a problem.

By mid-1976 the number of clients seeking our assistance had grown, even without publicity, and WICC decided to offer a support group for victims. (See Ch. 13.) When local therapists privately voiced their disbelief that enough clients could be found for a group, it became clear that educating the professional community was imperative.

The WICC staff produced a paper in Fall 1976 on working with victims of sexual exploitation by therapists and circulated it in the professional community. Several clients read it and found it helpful so the paper also was privately circulated among some victims. The paper prompted calls from therapists in the community who were working with victims of sexually exploitative therapists and WICC's consultation to other professionals increased.

A proposal was submitted to and accepted by the 84th Annual Conference of the Minnesota Social Service Association for a 5-hour workshop on "Eroticism in Therapy." The workshop was presented on March 21, 1977, and attracted 36 professionals. The feedback from the evaluation questionnaire indicated that both professional and public education was essential to bring this problem out into the open.

WICC staff members began to do occasional inservices for other agencies on the topic and to push for its inclusion in local conferences and professional meetings. We had mixed success. In September 1977 a local magazine, *MPLS*, published a dramatic cover story entitled "Sex and the Therapist" (Sundstrom, 1977); it gave the problem considerable public visibility and highlighted WICC's work. One client even walked into WICC with a copy of the article in hand saying that (although the individual was carefully disguised) she recognized the exploitative therapist described in the article and that he had also exploited her. As it turned out, she had correctly guessed his identity.

Betrayal (Freeman & Roy, 1976), the first book by a victim, was published in 1976 but it received little attention or distribution in Minnesota. Only reports of disciplinary action against therapists, which were few and far between, gave the problem public visibility. Discussion in the professional community was not much greater even though WICC already had enough new data to revise the article on working with victims.

Cases continued to increase during 1978 and WICC's advocacy role also grew. It became clear that both professionals and victims needed information on how to file complaints. A guide to filing complaints (see Appendix B) was finished and released in April 1979.

The public and professional discussion of the problem of therapist-client sex was greatly stimulated by a lengthy story in the *Minneapolis Tribune* on March 8, 1979, on a disciplinary proceeding against a psychiatrist. The hearing examiner, Howard L. Kaibel, Jr., sided with the psychiatrist but on appeal, District Court Judge Donald Barbeau affirmed the Board of Medical Examiner's disciplinary order and flatly stated, "Even common sense would condemn the propriety of petitioner's [the psychiatrist's] behavior in this case" (Newlund, 1979). There followed a flood of professional protest aimed at the hearing examiner. Eventually, an in-depth treatment of the general issue, "Some therapists break rule against sex," was published (Newlund, 1979).

By late 1979 (see Milgrom and Luepker, Chs. 13 and 14), Ellen Luepker and her colleagues at the Minneapolis Family and Children's Service were offering groups for victims. Luepker expanded her work during the 1980s, which allowed WICC staff members to focus largely on client advocacy and other types of consultation. When Luepker left the agency in 1986 and joined a private practice group, she continued her work with victims. John Gonsiorek, who, had been clinic director at WICC, continued to provide services to both victims and perpetrators when he went into private practice.

WICC received an increasing number of inquiries during the 1980s from professionals and clients across the country. So too did Luepker and Gonsiorek. These inquiries led to informal case consultations, the supply of reading material, workshops, presentations at professional conferences, and the like. By the mid-1980s WICC was receiving so many letters or phone calls each week that many hours were required to respond to them. By 1986 it had become impossible both to respond to these requests and to keep detailed records; WICC staff members thereupon opted for service delivery over data collection.

At various times during the past 14 years WICC staff and Board members debated the status of our work and its future direction. Considerable debate in 1986-87 led to the decision that WICC would not attempt to put together some sort of national center to deal with the issue but, rather, would focus on the following:

1. Publish a manual (this volume) of up-to-date information on WICC's work with the victims of sexual abuse by therapists, and include relevant contributions from other workers in the field.

2. Train professionals around the United States and Canada to help to develop resources elsewhere and thereby to reduce WICC's national role.

3. Assist the Minnesota State Task Force on Sexual Exploitation by Counselors and Psychotherapists to set up a statewide response network to reduce WICC's role within Minnesota.

Historically, WICC developed and launched innovative programs and then gave the programs to other organizations to continue. With the problems of rape, incest, and battered women, WICC helped to organize community responses and then faded into the background. In the area of therapists' sexual involvement with clients this development has not occurred but we hope to move in such a direction in the years ahead.

WICC's CASE EXPERIENCE

To date WICC staff members provided consultation in well over 1,000 cases of alleged therapist misconduct. The majority have centered on some allegations of sexual contact, sexual harassment (pressure for contact), or seduction. Usually, they also have involved other complaints of therapist misconduct ranging, for example, from financial exploitation and fraud, fraudulent billing practices, violations of confidentiality, dual relationships of other sorts, practicing outside one's area of competence, failure to properly diagnose or treat a given condition, to encouraging extreme dependency.

The consultations may consist of relatively brief phone contacts to involvement spanning several years. Although most consultations are with clients, some are with a subsequent therapist treating the client, a significant other, a family member, or even an attorney. A smaller number involve the therapist, either through a processing session for both therapist and client, a direct contact by the therapist, or a request from the therapist's employer or attorney. Over the years WICC staff members have learned to work very efficiently in these situations.

Given the immense demands on the few people working on this issue, WICC tries, whenever possible, to coach other professionals to do the actual work. In fact, our goal is to train other professionals throughout the country to handle these cases and so to reduce our direct consultation work.

The majority of our clients are from Minnesota, although WICC has always received calls, letters, and visitors from around the country. Whenever a WICC staff member does a presentation on this topic it is inevitable that at least one new client situation will be brought to her/his attention during or after the presentation. Sometimes a professional who is present reveals that he or she is a victim. In some instances multiple cases are brought to our attention by a single clinic or therapist.

Clients also contact former WICC staff members, such as John Gonsiorek, and colleagues who are working in the area, such as Ellen Luepker; they frequently call upon WICC for consultation. The state Task Force on Sexual Exploitation by Counselors and Psychotherapists brought a number of aggrieved clients to our attention through its public hearings. Media coverage of the issue has led to still other contacts.

Were WICC to advertise our services it seems likely that additional cases would turn up. Even now when some clients contact us they regret they had not known about WICC's services years ago.

WICC's SERVICES

A picture is sketched in some detail in this volume of the many services offered by WICC in connection with the sexual exploitation of clients by therapists. The brief overview that is presented here is designed to orient readers to those contents.

For Clients:

1. Intervention and consultation:

    a. Crisis intervention and support
    b. Assistance in identifying needs; referral to other resources
    c. If appropriate, review of options for action, or complaints

    d. If needed, assistance in composing a complaint
    e. If needed, support through a complaint process
    f. Processing sessions, when appropriate and possible, with client and therapist

2. <u>Consultation to significant others</u>

3. <u>Consultation to client's subsequent therapist</u>

4. <u>Testimony in civil suits, criminal actions, etc.</u>

5. <u>Consultation to attorneys handling cases</u>

<u>For Licensure Boards:</u>

1. <u>Support for clients</u> who are referred by a Board

2. <u>Consultation to prosecutors</u>

3. <u>Expert testimony</u>

4. <u>Evaluations of practitioners under discipline; development of recommended rehabilitation plans</u>

<u>For Regulatory and Funding Agencies:</u>

1. <u>Consultation on the evaluation of a complaint</u>

2. <u>Design and effectuation of studies or investigations in cases of multiple allegations against a treatment program</u>

3. <u>Assistance with and consultation on administrative safeguards</u>

<u>For Government:</u>

1. <u>In Minnesota, consultation to legislative and executive bodies</u> on the scope of the problem; remedies, and assistance in locating consumers willing to testify

2. <u>In other states, consultation to governmental units studying possible legislation</u>

3. <u>In Minnesota, involvement in the state Task Force on Sexual Exploitation by Counselors and Psychotherapists</u>

4. <u>In Minnesota, participation in statewide training sponsored by the Department of Corrections</u>

<u>For Human Service Agencies:</u>

1. Same as #1 above (under "For Government") for training institutions

2. <u>Inservices on professional boundaries and sexual contact with clients</u>

3. <u>Workshops for staff members and/or administrators:</u>

    a. <u>Structured workshops on boundaries</u>

    b. <u>Customized workshops, for specific agencies</u>, ranging from 1/2 day to 2 days, on boundaries, dealing with complaints, prevention, etc.

4. <u>Workshops for consortia of agencies, or as part of professional conferences</u>

5. <u>Workshops for administrators or personnel officers</u> on hiring and other administrative safeguards; also, brief phone or mail consultations on these topics

<u>For Therapists</u>:

1. <u>Conducting a processing session</u> requested by the therapist

2. <u>Consultation in cases where boundary problems have developed or the therapy has become eroticized</u>—ranging from consultation to the therapist, or participation in a session with therapist and client

3. <u>Crisis intervention and assessment, with referral for assistance</u>

4. <u>Evaluation and development of rehabilitation plans</u>:

    a. Completely voluntary
    b. Relative to the requirements of a licensure or regulatory body, or employer
    c. As part of a civil settlement

5. <u>In rare instances, service as a consultant or expert witness</u>

<u>For the News Media</u>:

1. <u>Provision of copies of articles and factual background</u>

2. <u>Assistance in locating subjects to interview</u>

3. <u>Some active solicitation of media coverage of the issue</u>

THE FUTURE

A recent review of our own efforts as well as the Minnesota approach to the problem of sexual exploitation by therapists notes that with "on-going evaluation and modification, some of Minnesota's regulations and programs should serve as useful models..." (Gartrell, Herman, Olarte, Feldstein, Localio, 1988). Indeed, much remains to be done in terms of evaluating the model we have helped to develop.

However, over time we hope to decrease the centrality of our role in dealing with the issue of therapist-client sex. We hope also to avoid expanding our national role, save for the training of people in other states. Someday, we hope, there will be services and consultation available to therapists and clients close to their homes.

Our present goal is to turn our attention more to the subtler boundary problems in sexual exploitation and to expanding prevention activities. We hope that the publications germinated by this book will expand on the training tools WICC has conceptualized or developed and that professionals, and professionals-in-training will be better prepared to recognize and prevent abuses and, when necessary, intervene to help both clients and errant professionals.

CHAPTER 2

A LOOK AT THE LITERATURE

Gary Richard Schoener

HISTORICAL BACKGROUND

Sexual exploitation of clients or patients by health professionals is a very old problem. It is mentioned in the Hippocratic Oath, which was written more than 2,200 years ago, and it was an issue in the practice of medicine during the Middle Ages (see Ch. 27 for elaboration).

Erotic feelings between therapist and client also are found in the earliest reported cases of psychotherapy—the "talking cure." Anna O. (to whom "talking cure" is attributed) was treated by hypnosis by Joseph Breuer in 1880; subsequently, the case became one of Freud's most widely discussed models. Jones (1953), Freud's first biographer, reported, on the basis of Freud's account of the case,

> ...that Breuer had developed what we should nowadays call a strong counter-transference to his interesting patient....his wife became bored at listening to no other topic,...jealous....unhappy and morose. It was a long time before Breuer...divined the meaning of her state of mind. It provoked a violent reaction in him, perhaps compounded of love and guilt, and he...[brought] the treatment to an end....that evening he was fetched back to find [Anna O.] in the throes of an hysterical childbirth...the logical termination of a phantom pregnancy....he managed to calm her down...and then fled the house in a cold sweat. The next day he and his wife left for Venice to spend a second honeymoon.... (pp. 224-25)

Although this experience deterred Breuer from further experiments with hypnosis to treat hysterical symptoms, Freud went on to experiment with the "talking cure" and, eventually, to develop psychoanalysis. In his classic *Introductory Lectures in Psychoanalysis*, published in 1917, Freud noted the romantic and erotic feelings his female patients exhibited toward him, labeling it <u>transference</u>. In writing on this topic, Freud (1958) clearly indicated that the therapist should not take advantage of the patient's "longing for love" and should abstain from sexual involvement. Freud also noted that the therapist had to struggle with his own countertransference love feelings.

Despite Freud's warnings of the potentially erotic atmosphere of the psychoanalytic relationship, some of his followers experimented with physical contact with clients. When Freud learned that Ferenczi, one of his followers, had engaged in kissing and other physical contact with clients, he wrote a challenging letter on December 13, 1931, warning Ferenczi about this practice (Jones, 1953).

Wilhelm Reich (1945, pp. 126-7) believed that the therapist should allow the client's overt sexual feelings to develop until they are "concentrated, without ambivalence, in the transference." Although he never advocated sexual relationships between therapist and client, at times "[he] physically manipulated... [some clients] to 'appropriate' responses" (Marmor, 1970, p. 12). Reich (1945, p. 133) cited two measures of whether sensual genital striving was freed from repression: "Phantasies of incest without guilt feeling" and "genital excitation during analysis...." While explaining Reich's theories and behavior as, in part, symptoms of paranoid schizophrenia, Marmor (1970, p. 12) accused Reich's students and followers of using "the prestige of this unfortunate psychoanalytic pioneer to act out their own countertransference needs."

In recent years it has come to light that psychoanalyst Carl Jung had a romantic affair with Sabina Spielrein, whom he treated from 1905 to 1909. She had been 19 years old when she began her analysis. Subsequently she became a physician and in 1912 joined the Vienna Psychoanalytic Society. Her relationship with Jung was discussed in letters between Freud, Jung, and herself and later was reprinted in a book by Aldo Carotenuto, first published in Italy in 1980, and then appeared in English translation (Carotenuto, 1982) as *A Secret Symmetry: Spielrein Between Jung and Freud*. The book generated reviews such as Bettelheim's (1983) "Scandal in the Family." In terms of physical contact the romantic involvement may have gone no further than kissing and talk of love, but Spielrein has been referred to as Jung's "mistress," implying greater sexual involvement.[1] The rumors it generated and the subsequent interchanges between Freud, Jung, Spielrein, and others are discussed by Masson (1988, pp. 170-77).

Such transgressions were not limited to male psychoanalysts. Karen Horney, one of the leading figures in psychoanalysis, who challenged Freud's views on women, was quoted as saying:

> As a rule it is better not to have social relationships with a patient, but I am not terribly rigid about it. Generally, I have none or a restricted relationship. (Wolff, 1956, p. 87)

However, in her biography of Horney, *A Mind of Her Own*, Susan Quinn notes that in her later years she had a romantic relationship with a young man who was in treatment with her, something Quinn (1988, p. 378) attributed to "old impulsive ways [which] survived into middle age." Quinn claims that this relationship, begun during the second half of the 1940s, lasted until the end of Horney's life (1952).

Mainstream psychoanalysis followed Freud's proscription against physical contact with clients, however. Karl Menninger (1958, p. 40), for example, wrote in *Theory of Psychoanalytic Technique*,

> ...the psychoanalysis must <u>try</u> (and it is not easy) to remain neutral and "aseptic." This means that one doesn't <u>chat</u> with patients, touch them (e.g., shake hands) unnecessarily, <u>ask</u> favors of them or accept favors or gifts from them, attend small social engagements where they will be....

In a footnote at the bottom of the same page, he added the comments of his associate, Dr. H. G. van der Waals:

> I think every analyst in Europe, at least every analyst I know, shakes hands with his patient at the beginning and the end of the hour. It gives valuable information about the mood of the patient, his reaction to the hour, etc. In Europe it would be a technical error not to do this; patients would think it very queer.

> As a general rule an analyst should not accept gifts, but he should also know when to make an exception. When a patient who has great difficulty in giving anything is able

---

[1] Gay (1988, p. 396), in his biography of Freud, described Spielrein as "one of the most extraordinary among the younger analysts," who "had gone to Zurich to study medicine and in desperate mental distress, went into psychoanalytic treatment with Jung." "She fell in love with her analyst, and Jung, taking advantage of her dependency, made her his mistress. After a painful struggle in which Freud played a minor but not admirable part, she freed herself from her involvement and became an analyst."

in the course of his treatment to make the analyst a small present, it would be a serious mistake not to accept the gift.

As for sexual contact with clients, Menninger (1958, pp. 117-118), wrote,

...patients sometimes report that they were given physical gratification (or manipulation) by a previous therapist. He may or may not have been a psychoanalyst. He may or may not have regarded his behavior as an irresistible consequence of countertransference. But however he saw it, and whether or not he realized it then, he probably damaged the patient irreparably by this violation of the Hippocratic oath.

THE 1960S

The human potential movement of the 1960s brought with it considerable experimentation with types and practices of psychotherapy. The movement also fostered the development of the sensitivity or "T" group and the marathon group (Bach, 1966; Mintz, 1967). There was considerable experimentation with touch in therapy, and some therapists began testing other traditional boundary areas. Even within the psychoanalytic tradition there was discussion of the use of touch in therapy.

Maslow (1965, p. 160) suggested the possibility of nudity in sensitivity groups:

After all, these training groups are a kind of psychological nudism under careful direction. I wonder, as a matter of fact, what would happen as an experiment, if these T-groups remained exactly as they are but only added a physical nudism. People would go away from there an awful lot freer, a lot more spontaneous, less guarded, less defensive....

Bindrim (1972) summarized the movement as follows:

Over a period of seven years the author noted that there was a growing tendency to disrobe as emotional intimacy and transparency developed between group members. On a few occasions, when a pool or hot baths were available, the participants spontaneously engaged in nude swimming after the marathon had ended. (p. 180)

Most excursions into nudity or erotic interaction in marathons did not find their way into the literature. Bindrim (1972), however, reported on an experimental nude marathon; its sixth ground rule is worthy of note:

6. Refrain from photography or overt sexual expression which might prove offensive to other participants in the group. Overt sexual expression was defined as any activity which would be socially inappropriate in a similar group wearing clothing. For example, hugging and kissing would be permissible, but intercourse or fondling of the genitals would not be considered appropriate behavior in a group setting. (p. 182; emphasis added)

In private conversations, a number of therapists linked their erotic contact with clients to experimentation with touch in the 1960s or 1970s. Some cited demonstrations seen at workshops, others, their personal experiences in encounter or sensitivity groups or marathons, as the initial source of the idea to attempt more physical contact with clients.

During the same period some members of the analytic community were challenging the taboo against touching in psychotherapy. For example, Forer (1969, p. 229), argued for more touch in therapy:

One potential function of the therapist is to become more appetizing or precious to the client than the internal parents have been.

What I have in mind is not gratification for the client's needs but a process by which the therapist changes the structure of the client so that he becomes open to new relationships. I do not believe that orthodox psychoanalytic procedure has the power to do so.

Similarly, Mintz (1969) saw a need to discard the taboo against touching in psychoanalysis; she was in favor of some use of touch as another helpful form of communication in therapy. However, she cautioned that "it would seem always inappropriate to use touch in a way suggesting sexual foreplay or offering the patient realistic grounds for anticipating full sexual satisfaction" (Mintz, 1969, p. 372); she did not, however, discuss the difficulty of predicting a patient's expectations. She was concerned that once the taboo is broken some psychoanalysts may engage in "full sexual indulgence"; yet to her, "it seems absurd that any qualified psychoanalyst should be so carried away by contact with a patient, however attractive, that he (or she) could not refrain from complete gratification" (Mintz, 1969, p. 371).

During the same period some researchers began examining covert seductive or "quasi-courting" behaviors in the clinical interview; they noted the presence of such behaviors in various therapies along with their role in either engaging the client in therapy or discouraging erotic transference (Scheflen, 1965).

In a book widely read in both lay and professional circles, *Games People Play*, Berne posed one hypothetical scenario in which the client seduces the therapist:

One woman played "Gee You're Wonderful Professor" (GYWP) with her psychiatrist without any alleviation of symptoms; she finally left him with many salaams and apologies. She then went to her revered clergyman for help and played GYWP with him. After a few weeks she seduced him into a game of second-degree "Rapo." She then told her neighbor confidentially over the back fence how disappointed she was that so fine a man as Rev. Black could, in a moment of weakness, make a pass at an innocent and unattractive woman like herself. (Berne, 1964, pp. 152-53)

The personnel and guidance counseling literature of the same period contains discussions of intimacy in the counseling relationship, such as "The Challenge of Authentic Behavior" (Cottingham, 1966) and "Humans: A Therapeutic Variable" (Dreyfus, 1967). However, sexual feelings were generally ignored until Feist (1968) described the "erotic-neurotic-symbiotic" relationship:

The client and counselor become sexually attracted to each other. The anxiety and guilt that each experiences over these feelings blocks the building of a growth relationship. The inability of the client to distinguish between sex and love prevents him from building a relationship with the counselor. He fears intimacy because, to him, intimacy means sex, and a sexual relationship with either a male or female counselor is too threatening. He therefore guards himself against a close personal involvement, but at the same time he enjoys the sexual feelings aroused in him by the counselor. The counselor may also have erotic feelings for the client which frighten him away from building an intimate relationship. Close personal involvement, to him, means sexual involvement, and this feeling raises his anxiety to a level that prevents him from operating effectively as a counselor. Counseling is continued, however, since the fantasies stimulated by the encounter prove to be satisfying to both counselor and client. (p. 65)

These discussions helped to generate James McClernan's (1972) doctoral (Ed.D.) dissertation at the University of Southern Mississippi, which was entitled, "Implications of Sexual Attraction (Feeling) in the Counselor-Client Relationship." McClernan reported that male graduate students and female undergraduate clients were conscious of sexual feelings between them in 43.5% of the counseling relationships, and were uncertain or had only weak feelings 22% of the time; only 34% were certain there was no attraction (p. 57). These feelings affected the quality of the counseling relationship (pp. 89-90).

Also of interest is Richard Robertiello's (1969) article, "Encouraging the Patient to Live Out Sexual Fantasies." Robertiello argued the value, in the context of a psychoanalysis, of the analyst's encouraging clients to act out sexual fantasies, for example, sado-masochistic, voyeuristic, and other impulses, including one in which a male client was encouraged to have sex with both a mother and daughter. One case in this article is of particular interest; it reads, in part, as follows:

Example 5: A female patient of 34 had been discussing her feelings about having small breasts and, therefore, being unattractive to men. She was very inhibited about undressing in front of a man and this caused her to avoid men and sex. She was in a group as well as in individual treatment. She began to talk about a fantasy of undressing in front of the group. I encouraged her to live out her fantasy. With great trepidation and with a lot of encouragement from the other group members she did so. (p. 185)

No information on the group is given, so it is not clear whether Robertiello himself was present. Also unclear is the clause, "a lot of encouragement from group members...." The other case examples centered on the analyst's becoming actively involved in encouraging considerable experimentation in the client's sex life.

From our present perspective we can wonder why none of these articles generated any sort of furor. For a decade or more psychotherapists were experimenting with the use of touch and nudity and with breaking related taboos in the treatment of clients yet the literature gives no evidence that much debate was taking place over the propriety of such experimentation.

THE IMPACT OF SEX THERAPY

The publication of Masters and Johnson's classic *Human Sexual Inadequacy* in 1970 inaugurated the development of a new therapy field: sex therapy. A secondary impact of the book was its disclosure that a sizable number of the authors' clients alleged that they had experienced sexual contact with a previous therapist. In an address subsequently to the annual meeting of the American Psychiatric Association, which was widely reported in the press, the two investigators labeled such conduct "rape" (Masters & Johnson, 1975).

This new field of sex therapy received considerable media attention throughout much of the 1970s; unintentionally, it brought about increased confusion among consumers. Because much of the public was unable to distinguish between psychotherapy and sex therapy, it is my impression that many potential consumers of psychotherapy services believed that erotic contact or touching by the therapist was proper if the client was being treated for a sexual problem. Over the past 14 years numerous clients have described this confusion to us.

The use of surrogate partners in sex therapy became the source of considerable conflict and debate among psychotherapists (the arguments are not reviewed here). The practice was given wide visibility in the media which, again, led to some public confusion. It should be noted that from time to time professionals in the field of sex therapy have advocated that the therapist become the sex partner instead of using a surrogate (e.g., "Therapist as Sex Partner Better Than 'Surrogate'," *OB-Gyn News*, Jan. 1976, p. 11).

The discussions of transference/countertransference in sex therapy as opposed to psychotherapy are worth reading (e.g., Singer-Kaplan, 1974, pp. 241-42) but they do not belong in this discussion. The code of ethics for sex therapists is discussed in Chapter 27.

THE DEBATE BEGINS

In 1966 a major debate erupted in psychiatry in response to the publication of J. L. McCartney's (1966) now famous article, "Overt Transference." Of the 1500 psychoanalyses he claimed to have performed over a 40-year career, he reported that a full 30% of his female clients experienced some type of "overt transference," which he defined as holding his hand, sitting on his lap, and hugging or kissing him, and 10% engaged in mutual undressing, genital manipulation, or sexual intercourse (McCartney, 1966, p. 236). It is unclear whether he meant 10% of the total client load or 10% of the 30%. Pope & Bouhoutsos (1986, p. 59) note that it would have been physically impossible for him to have performed 1500 full analyses so the number of clients involved may have been smaller.

McCartney was widely attacked within the profession and expelled from membership in the American Psychiatric Association. Since then, professionals and the media have raised questions about whether McCartney was expelled to protect the reputation of the profession or whether the expulsion was a response to a specific ethics complaint (e.g., Branch, 1969, p. 2; Gaines, 1972, pp. 152, 166; West, 1969, pp. 228-29). It has been noted, however, that none of McCartney's clients filed complaints (Riskin, 1979, pp. 1007-8).

In 1971 New York psychiatrist Martin Shepard completed *The Love Treatment*, a book supposedly based on his interviews with 11 clients who reported sexual relationships with psychotherapists. The therapists in question were all psychiatrists or clinical psychologists and more than half were psychoanalytically trained. He reported that of the 11 clients, 6 labeled the sex as "useful"; 3, as "harmful"; and 2, as a "diversionary waste of time" (Shepard, 1971, pp. 200-201).

Shepard's book was given far more attention than McCartney's article, partly because it was available in book stores and not just to members of the profession, and partly because its publication was followed by articles by Shepard and others in newspapers, women's magazines (e.g., *Vogue*; Weber, 1972), and sexually oriented men's magazines (Shepard, 1972a). This discussion raged on through the late 1970s with both professional responses (e.g., Redlich, 1977) and popular rejoinders (e.g., Romeo, 1978). Illustrative of the situation in the early 1970s was a statement by Gaines (1972, pp. 152, 166) in *Cosmopolitan* that McCartney's expulsion from membership in the American Psychiatric Association was a result "of the static moral climate that preceded America's cultural revolution."

Inasmuch as I agree with Redlich's (1977, p. 150) characterization of Shepard's cases as showing evidence in each instance of "breakdown of trust" as well as hostility and disappointment, I am reluctant to spend much time here examining Shepard's claims. However, a short discussion is in order to clarify what Shepard actually argued in the first place.

Although some authors have characterized his "findings" as showing that sex with a therapist is "beneficial" and that 8 of his 11 cases involved "emotional growth" (e.g., Pope & Bouhoutsos, 1986, pp. 58, 60), Shepard himself concluded that the sex was useful in only 6 cases. In fact, Shepard (1971, p. 201) noted that some of the therapists who regarded the sex as beneficial "had sexual problems of a far greater magnitude than the people they were treating," and, further, that the "instability of many therapists" made him "reluctant to do anything or state anything that would encourage them toward closer contact with their patients."

In his proposed rules for intimacy between client and therapist, Shepard (1971, pp. 204-206) cautioned readers against "needy," "possessive," and "insistent" therapists, and against sexual involvements "where intimacy would repeat a previously bad pattern." He then went on to conclude,

> I suspect that owing to the possessiveness, confusion of roles, guilt, and shame on the part of the therapists, such involvement is, generally speaking, not a good idea. (p. 208)

Probably the most accurate summary of his views regarding sex between therapist and client is that "as many people are aided by intimate involvements with their therapists as are hurt" (Simon, 1988, p. 280).

Shepard and his publisher came out with a sequel to *The Love Treatment* the following year. Entitled, *A Psychiatrist's Head*, it described an orgy during a group therapy session (Shepard, 1972b, p. 87). Shepard indicated, however, that the participants were not patients; in fact, he denied that he engaged in sexual relationships with patients. His license to practice medicine was revoked by the New York licensure board nevertheless (Simon, 1988, p. 280).

OTHER VOICES

McCartney and Shepard, although widely discredited by their own professions, were not alone in suggesting that sexual contact between client and therapist might have a place in therapy or, at least, was worthy of study. An advocate for further study, psychoanalyst Clay Dahlberg, for example, wrote about 9 cases of client-therapist sex of which he had clinical knowledge from his practice. He described them as ranging from "relatively harmless" to "frankly destructive" (Dahlberg, 1970, pp. 107, 111). After noting that he had had great difficulty getting his article published, even in journals in which he had influence, he stated the need for research:

> How many are there who do not complain—who do not feel that they are hurt or perhaps, as in McCartney's cases, even think they were helped by their therapists' sexual intervention? This is a worthwhile question and could be answered, at least in part.

What I am proposing is a Kinsey-type survey of therapists and patients to probe into the circumstances and results of sexual acting out and near acting out. What was the nature of the interpersonal dynamics when temptation was strong but not resisted, and what was the outcome? This would be a tough job, but it could be done. (Dahlberg, 1970, p. 123)

Shepard (1971, p. 2) cited a New York psychologist named Greenwood who, after raising the possibility that the phenomenon of sex between client and therapist could be studied, became the subject of a petition circulated by fellow members asking that he be expelled from the New York Psychological Association. Pope & Bouhoutsos (1986, p. 26) described Forer's survey of the membership of the Los Angeles County Psychological Association in which he found "a high rate of therapist-patient sexual intimacies," and then was told it was "not in the best interests of psychology to present it publicly." According to Pope & Bouhoutsos (1986, p. 26), even when Forer presented his findings in professional meetings he was only allowed to discuss part of his data. However, discussion and study broadened during the 1970s.

Taylor and Wagner (1976, pp. 593-94), after reviewing 34 cases in the professional literature, concluded that the therapeutic outcome in cases of therapist-client sex was positive in 21% of the cases, negative in 47%, and mixed in 32%. Even Masters & Johnson (1976, p. 553), who referred to sex between therapist and client as rape, wrote that up to 5% of therapists who "are sleeping with their patients every day" do so with "integrity and objectivity."

Within the field of sex therapy and education the debate continued. Wagner (1972) reported that 25% of the freshman medical students he studied believed that sexual contact with patients might be acceptable if the physician was "authentic" and "genuine." Dr. Mary Calderone, President of SIECUS, took the position that:

We have only opinions rather than facts with which to determine that it might or might not have value. But until we know more, rather than saying "no" or "it's bad," we should simply say that we don't have enough information to say whether it's good or bad. (Masters, Johnson, & Kolodny, 1977, p. 177)

Lowry & Lowry (1975, pp. 231-32) noted the use of various types of "sexological" examinations among sex therapists, including one type "recommended by a well-known therapy center," that involves a male therapist stimulating the wife sexually, leading at times to "orgasm in the examining room, much to their surprise." They further noted that "it is difficult to assess the efficacy" of this method because the "success rates of this center are not published." In regard to overt sexual activity with clients, Lowry & Lowry (1975, p. 233) stated that "it is inappropriate and indefensible to provide intentional sexual stimulation."

William Masters (1974) wrote a popular article in *Today's Health* warning consumers about fraudulent sex therapy clinics. When the field was developing nationally broad discussions were held on how unethical persons could offer "sex therapy" with the goal of defrauding consumers or obtaining sexual contact. The use of surrogates continued, and in some cases the surrogate was actually a therapist.

For example, an article in *OB-Gyn News* (1976) entitled "Therapist as Sex Partner Better Than 'Surrogate'" reported:

Having the female co-therapist act as the sexual partner during sex therapy makes more sense than using a female "surrogate" who is without professional training for partnerless males, Martin Williams, Ph.D., said at the annual meeting of the Eastern Association for Sex Therapy.

This is the program used at the Berkeley (Calif.) Sex Therapy Group, where 170 men without partners have been treated in the past 4 years, said Dr. Williams, who is associate director of the group.

*****

The intensive 10-day program comprises daily "body work" for several hours with the female co-therapist much along the lines used in the Masters and Johnson program. For the most part, the patient is in a passive role.

*****

There have been no instances in which the patient "fell in love with" the co-therapist, Dr. Williams said. (p. 11)

Given the growth of sex therapy, the proliferation of various schools of traditional psychotherapy, and the experimentation with new techniques, some writers attempted to focus attention on scientific integrity.

...in the interests of scientific integrity any therapist using such techniques should publicly affirm them so that his patients may be fully aware of this technique before they are caught in the emotional web of a positive transference. To patients who will nevertheless choose such a therapist, one can only say, "caveat emptor!" [Let the buyer beware!] Marmor (1970, p. 14)

Psychologist Ned Wagner suggested a similar "truth in advertising" approach when he was interviewed in 1978 on the "Fifty Minutes" episode of the CBS-TV series *Sixty Minutes*. The subject of the episode was therapist-client sex. Leonard Riskin, Professor of Law at the University of Houston College of Law, later proposed a scientific approach to the problem with research controls replacing typical professional controls, which had not worked (Riskin, 1979). An American Psychological Association (1975, p. 1174) study, "Sex Bias and Sex Role Stereotyping in Psychotherapeutic Practice," noted that if sexual intercourse was accepted as "therapy" then it would be necessary to "educate the female public so that they may choose the kind of relationship they wish to pay for before a transference relationship obscures their objectivity."

In an effort to challenge the concept of "therapeutic intercourse," Seagull (1972) presented a list of questions:

(a) Ought one to charge the patient for the hour (fifty minutes) of intercourse? That is, is this therapy for the patient, and thus within the rubric of professional handling, or is this "pleasure" and thus unprofessional interaction?

(b) Ought one to have intercourse with every patient who "needs" him whether or not they "turn him on?"

(c) How does the heterosexual therapist deal with the homosexual patient, whose sexual desire for the same-sex therapist is just as strong as in a cross-sex relationship, and for whom the reasons adduced in support of a therapist-patient sexual relationship are just as valid? Ought a therapist become bi-sexual for his patient's sake? (p. 3)

A similar approach was taken by Rachel Hare-Mustin (1974). She noted both that psychologists are not trained to provide sex and have no claim to expertise in sex, and that sexual acts performed in the therapy context would lack authenticity and, thus, not aid in growth. A column entitled, "Healing in the Hay?" in *Human Behavior* (1975) presented this approach to a broader audience.

However, during the mid-1970s professional discussions of sexual contacts with clients often muddied the distinction between sex therapy, body therapies (e.g., rolfing), and the writings of persons who propose sex with clients in the context of more traditional psychotherapy. For example, Schultz (1975), in the introduction to the report, "A Survey of Social Workers' Attitudes and Use of Body and Sex Psychotherapies," wrote:

> Traditional concepts of transference do not appear to hold now the critical position of yesteryear, so that mismanaged transference concepts do not apply so well, and in some treatment techniques erotized (sic) transference is the very article of treatment.... (p. 90)

The study itself surveyed social worker attitudes toward and the use of a very broad range of approaches, some of which are established techniques and some of which are terms Schultz appears to have created to describe the practices of some therapists. The list includes the following:

Direct Sex Coaching	Clinical Prostitution
Teaching Masturbation	Erotic Body Contact
Mechanical Device Instruction	Infidelity Therapy
Cyentic Exercises	Group Nudism
Explicit Sex Aids	Bi-Sexual Therapy
Sex Surrogates	Sexual Intercourse

(Schultz, 1975, p. 94)

Schultz (1975) found that 83.9% of respondents do not use any of these "therapies" although they approve of many in theory, at least. Nearly 35% responded that they would use some of these techniques, or use them more often, if a client requested it; 25% would increase their use if the agency sanctioned the approach. Legal concerns made a difference for 20%; lack of training, for 17%; and lack of approval by the profession, for nearly 7% (p. 93).

Because Schultz's rankings combine a numerical rating of frequency with the frequency of those indicating approval or use of a technique, absolute incidence figures are not presented. Without clear definitions it is also difficult to know which responses signal actual sexual contact beyond the two items, "Erotic Body Contact" and "Sexual Intercourse." For example, techniques such as "Direct Sex Coaching," "Infidelity Therapy," and "Clinical Prostitution" could include sexual contact with the social worker. Among the 16% (N=10) who reported using sex therapies, sexual intercourse has a "Use Ranking" of only 1.8%, likely indicating that only a single respondent reported use of it. "Erotic Body Contact," however, with a Use Ranking of 19.3%, could indicate an incidence of 3-6% (p. 94).

Len and Fischer (1978) conducted a similar study 3 years later of "Clinicians' Attitudes Toward and Use of Four Body Contact or Sexual Techniques with Clients." They mailed a questionnaire to 155 private practitioners in Hawaii: psychiatrists (61), psychologists (56), social workers (19), and marriage and family therapists (19). Responses were received from 54 practitioners but only 46 of the returns were usable: 28 from males and 18 from females. These 46 respondents do not provide an exact breakdown of professions; 12 had M.D.s (and are thus psychiatrists); 19 had Ph.D.s in psychology; 6 were MSWs, and 5 had Ph.D.s in other fields (p. 40).

Of these respondents, 64% indicated that they did not believe that sexual contact in therapy would be beneficial and 70% indicated that they had not used such contacts; 36% said that it might be beneficial and 30% had used it, although most (25%) had used it with less than 20% of their clients, and only 2 (5%) had used it with 40-50% of clients. Only 9% felt that sexual intercourse could be therapeutically beneficial but none reported using it. It is interesting that 69% believed that the use of partner-surrogates might be helpful in treating sexual problems, but none had used them. (Len & Fischer, 1978, p. 46) Schultz (1975) also found a reasonably high approval for surrogates, but practically no use of them in his sample.

Interestingly enough, the focus on the use of sexual contact as a therapy technique, which we see in Schultz (1975) and Len and Fischer (1978), all but disappeared from the literature by the late 1970s. A number of reasons may be responsible. (a) The feminist counter-offensive (see next section) challenged the classification of these behaviors as "new therapies." (b) The popularity of the "body therapies," which also were part of these studies, reached an asymptote or declined by the late 1970s. (c) Within the sex therapy field considerable debate centered on the use of surrogates.

Quite recently, in a study related to the ethics of practice, Pope, Tabachnick, and Keith-Spiegel (1987) asked psychologists about two of the "sex therapies" surveyed by Schultz (1975): use of sexual surrogates and nude treatment or growth groups. In the case of sexual surrogates, a full third of the sample responded that the question did not apply to their work. Correcting for missing data, it appears that less than 10% use sexual surrogates and only 1% use them fairly often or very often (Pope, Tabachnick, & Keith-Spiegel, 1987, p. 995). About 3/4 of the sample responded to the question about leading nude groups, and only 3.6% (corrected for missing data) indicated that they lead such groups (p. 996).

This study, however, is an exception. The literature from the late 1970s focuses on sexual contact with clients, rather than sexual treatment techniques. The major treatment-related question asked by subsequent researchers is whether the sex was presented as a part of treatment or justified in terms of treatment goals.

THE FEMINIST COUNTER-OFFENSIVE

Phyllis Chesler's (1972) *Women and Madness* contained an entire chapter on the topic of sexual contact between male therapists and female clients, based on interviews with 11 women, 10 of whom reported sex with their psychotherapists. Of the 10, 7 had seen psychiatrists and 3, psychologists, all well-established practitioners in New York. Chesler also interviewed a group of women who had been propositioned by one particular therapist.

While describing past fantasies of love and possible marriage to their therapists, some women were protective of their therapists: they "insisted that they were to blame; they were the real seducers" (Chesler, 1972b, p. 145). They felt abandoned and devastated after the relationship ended. As Chesler (1972b) put it,

Although many of the women described being humiliated and frustrated by their therapists' emotional and sexual coldness or ineptitude, it was the therapist, more often than the patient, who ended the "affair." (pp. 146-47)

Chesler (1972b) characterized these women as fitting the culturally defined traditional norm of "feminine";

They were all conventionally and frantically "attractive"; they were all economically limited and intellectually insecure; they were both sexually fearful and sexually compulsive; they were paralyzed by real and feared loneliness and self-contempt; they all blamed themselves for any "mistreatment" by men; they all confused economic and selfhood needs with romantic "love"; and they were slow to express any anger. (p. 149)

Based on her interviews with two women who had been sexually exploited by the same therapist and a group of women who had been propositioned by a second therapist, Chesler (1972b, p. 150) characterized two of the exploitative therapists as "involved in creating a primal patriarchal family-empire, consisting of one male guru (themselves) and many "wives" (female patients, legal wives, mistresses)." Both were compulsive exploiters; they had sex with numerous clients, pressured clients for sex after observing that the client had "sexual hangups" or "unhealthy... sexual repression" (Chesler, 1972b, pp. 150-51).

The book received broad attention in the professional community and from the public at large. In fact, prior to publication of the book, *New York* magazine printed an excerpt entitled, "The Sensuous Psychiatrists" (Chesler, 1972a), which, as the title suggests, dealt with the issue of sex between therapist and client. Beyond her view that sex between male psychotherapists and female clients derives from the sexual oppression inherent in sex roles in our society, Chesler (1972b, p. 138) was broadly critical of psychotherapy:

The sine qua non of "feminine" identity in patriarchal society is the violation of the incest taboo; i.e., the initial and continued "preference" for Daddy, followed by the approved falling in love with and/or marrying of powerful father figures. There is no real questioning of such feminine identity in psychotherapy.

Belote (1974), in an unpublished Ph.D. dissertation, cited Chesler's pioneering work but criticized her analysis: "these traits are merely Chesler's observations, she had no objective data to support them." Belote sought to test these observations by collecting empirical data.

The study, *Sexual Intimacy Between Female Clients and Male Psychotherapists: Masochistic Sabotage*, sought to test the hypothesis that

Women who are sexually intimate with their male psychotherapists are characterized by masochistic personality traits and attitudes such as: low inner-directedness, low self-regard, low acceptance of their own aggression and high femininity. (Belote, 1974, p. 61)

Belote sought referrals by advertising in San Francisco Bay area newspapers, posting flyers, and sending letters to selected practitioners. Her sample consisted of the first 25 of the total 34 women who responded to the ads. All had engaged in sex with their therapists. She received only two calls from women who had resisted the therapist's advances so she dropped the idea of a control group (Belote, 1974, pp. 52-53).

The findings of the study are best described in the author's "Abstract":

...the majority of study subjects... were in awe of their therapists; felt helpless and were emotionally dependent upon their therapists; were unmarried, separated and living alone; were unemployed either as students or as housewives and mothers; were college graduates or had attended some college; were an average of sixteen and one-half years younger than their therapists; were above average in physical attractiveness, and conventional and feminine in their dress and grooming.

In most cases they sought therapy because they were depressed and did not know where else to turn; were non-orgasmic with their therapists and in all other sexual relationships; had closer emotional relationships with their fathers than with their mothers and viewed them negatively; had historically preferred male to female friendships; and felt that having sex with their therapists meant that they were very "special" and was a validation of their self-worth. These traits are not only characteristics of masochism, but are also traits of the "hysterical personality" as defined by various theoreticians.

The conclusion of the research is that the psychology of masochism and the "hysterical personality" corresponds with the female sex role and/or femininity, which is learned, socially acceptable behavior, rather than merely an intra-psychic conflict. The findings are interpreted as demonstrating the destructiveness of therapists encouraging and rewarding the female sex role, whether or not the therapist and client actually have sex. The implications of the study then, go beyond the behavioral acting out of a sexual involvement between male therapist and a female client and penetrate the very structure of male-female relationships in this culture.

Looking at the effect of the sexual relationship, Belote (1974, pp. 82-83) reported that "Nearly all of the 25 women felt that the relationships they had with their therapists had positive aspects," including, having "made them feel very special at a time in their lives when they were feeling especially low"; "better feelings about their... external attractiveness"; a "loss of naivetè" and development of more sexual sophistication; and having broken "through their pattern of 'setting men up as gods'."

Most of the women also had negative reactions, including,

...feelings that they were "worthless" or had "failed" when their therapists terminated the relationship; that their therapy had come to a halt without resolution of their real problems; that the relationship increased their feelings of distrust toward men; that the sexual contact made them feel "bad," "whorish" and "sneaky"; and that the whole experience increased their dependency. (p. 84)

Belote concluded that "sexual intimacy between male therapists and female clients is debilitating to the client because it encourages and reinforces the core qualities of 'healthy' femininity, which equals masochism and the 'hysterical personality'" (p. 120). More broadly, she concluded,

Thus, it is to be expected that feminine female clients will engage in sexual intimacy with their male psychotherapists, given the therapists' particularly powerful positions and the women's hope of gaining this power and thereby increasing their self-esteem. This dynamic is a natural outgrowth of sexual inequality in this society, and it conforms to male-female sex-role expectations. Within this context, it is obvious that the issue cannot be effectively dealt with by stringent professional ethics or legal prohibitions.

Rather, the issue is a political/therapeutic one which is most clearly seen through feminist analysis and the women's movement. Briefly stated, these goals are: to raise the consciousness of women as to their sexual oppression; to have them take their own power independently of men; and to define for themselves what their particular role, purpose and meaning in life might be. (Belote, 1974, p. 121)

Unfortunately, Belote (1974, p. 53) did not discuss the bias inherent in her sample, almost all of whom were obtained from newspaper and radio announcements, and none of whom was referred by psychotherapists. She judged them to be "above average in physical attractiveness, conventionally and femininely groomed and dressed...," very much fitting "the image of the middle class working woman," although most were not working (Belote, 1974, p. 69). In contrast to our sample, which dates back nearly to the time of Belote's, only a few (3 out of 25) women whom Belote interviewed "felt consciously angry at their therapists and wanted to get revenge" (p. 69). Indeed, "most tended to regard it as 'just another fact of life'" and "A few felt that the experience with the therapist was so 'wonderful' that they wanted to share it with the world" (pp. 69-70).

From the case examples in Belote's dissertation, her sample clearly represents a subset of our sample and is not generally representative. We know of situations in which a former or current client who is sexually involved with her or his psychotherapist has quite positive feelings about the situation but, typically, has not sought assistance at our center. It is difficult to weigh the positive vs. negative effects reported in Belote's study because the subjects were not asked to give overall ratings for their experiences, and no objective evaluations were made of the effects on them.

In the early 1970s feminists also turned their attention to the abuse of women in drug abuse treatment programs. When the nonprofit research group, Women's Health Advocates, was formed and given a send-off benefit by Phyllis Chesler (author of *Women and Madness*) and a grant from the Drug Abuse Council, its investigators embarked on a study, using intensive interviews, of 70 women who had been through treatment programs in New Haven, Connecticut (Ponsor, Soler, & Abod, 1976; Wynne, 1977).

The women (especially lesbian women) reported pressure to reveal personal details of their sex life, and 40 women reported knowing women who had been propositioned by male staff members; in fact, 38 of the 40 women had themselves been propositioned. In many cases women were offered an easier time in the program if they agreed to have sex. Ironically, if the sexual liaison became known, the woman was often labeled a whore or slut and took the brunt of the blame. "The study raises serious questions about sexual and psychological abuse of participants by staff members, including administrators and it documents many of the reasons why drug abuse treatment is a failure..." (Wynne, 1977, p. 5). Unfortunately, the report of this study was never published by the Drug Abuse Council although summaries of its findings received limited distribution (e.g., Ponsor et al., 1976; Wynne, 1977) and its authors presented the findings at symposia and conferences in the late 1970s. The data were well received when Esta Soler and I used them in workshops for drug abuse treatment personnel. The common response during the late 1970s was that such problems were not limited to New Haven. Yet, neither funding agencies nor national organizations were interested in having such data widely disseminated at that time.

BROADER COLLECTION OF DATA

Both Belote (1974, pp. 4-5) and D'Addario (1977, pp. 23-24) cited an unpublished survey by Arlene Daniels (1971) in which she interviewed 98 male psychiatrists (50 in private practice and 48 in organizational practice) about service-related ethical problems.

Among the private practitioners, 12% characterized sexual intimacy with clients as "incompetence" and 26%, as "exploitive"; the corresponding figures for those practicing in organizations were 13% and 19% respectively (Belote, 1974, pp. 4-5). Unfortunately, the source of the respondents' knowledge of cases was not specified so these data only indicate professional awareness of the problem.

Kardener, Fuller, and Mensh (1973) sent an anonymous questionnaire to a random sample of 1000 physicians in Los Angeles County of whom 460 (46%) completed the questionnaires; 115 of the respondents were psychiatrists. Overall from 5% to 13% of all respondents, representing various groups of physicians, self-reported that they engaged in erotic contact (kissing, fondling, manual-genital or oral-genital contact) or sexual intercourse with patients. From 5% to 7.5% acknowledged sexual intercourse with a patient. Among the psychiatrists alone, 10% acknowledged erotic contact with patients but only 5% acknowledged sexual intercourse. Various arguments were made by the respondents defending or challenging this practice (Kardener et al., 1973, p. 1079).

The study played a key role in what was to follow because it established once and for all that a sizable number of licensed and presumably qualified psychotherapists have sexual contact with their clients. These data have been cited countless times in professional debate, as well as in the media, and usually are presented as lower-end estimates. The senior author published a brief theoretical article as a follow-up a year later (Kardener, 1974). All three authors indicated to me in 1975 that they did not plan to continue working on this topic although an additional analysis of their data appeared the following year (Kardener et al., 1976).

In 1975 Sharon Butler submitted a Ph.D. dissertation, *Sexual Contact Between Therapists and Patients*, in which she reported on structured interviews with 20 therapists who had engaged in sexual contact with clients; 8 of their patients; and 8 therapists who had not reported sexual contact with a client. This sample was not random in that most participants were obtained through "the grapevine" after mailed requests for assistance failed to provide an adequate number. The therapists were psychologists and psychiatrists, all practicing in Los Angeles County (Butler, 1975, pp. 31-32).

Like Belote (1974), Butler (1975, pp. 51-52) reported some of the same mixed feelings about the sexualized therapy in her client samples: 65% were ambivalent; 85% had positive feelings, which were related to learning more about themselves; but many reported "feelings of anger, resentment and abandonment, which usually emerged when the relationship was over" (p. 52). An amazing 65% indicated that they had "a continued friendship with the ex-therapist after the end of the relationship" (p. 51). This percentage is radically different from our sample among whom a continued friendship is extremely rare. For the control group, the 8 therapists who had not engaged in sexual contact, Butler (1975, p. 50) concluded that "the study did not yield clear differences between the groups."

In Butler's sample of 20 therapists (18 males and 2 females) who had been involved in sexual contact with clients, 55% claimed to have genuinely cared for the client and reported feeling "in love with" the client (pp. 43-44). "Ninety percent reported having been 'vulnerable,' 'needy,' and/or 'lonely' when the sexual contact occurred" (pp. 44-45). Therapy was "terminated" after the first sexual episode by 25% whereas 30% continued therapy and sex for no more than 2 months and another 30% continued therapy plus sex for the duration (p. 47). Although 95% of the therapists reported "conflicts, fears and guilts" only 40% sought help from a friend or colleague (p. 48). Furthermore, 95% reported "an unwillingness to re-experience sexual contact with patients" yet 75% had sexual contact with other patients: 15% with one additional patient, 20% with three, and 25% with many (from 4 to more than 20) (p. 49).

Perhaps Butler's most striking findings are the following:

Often, therapists described their relationships as 'soul-connections'. This phrase signified the deep emotional and spiritual connection that existed between the two people. Incidentally, this level of interaction has not ordinarily been associated with patient-therapist sexual contact. These soul-connections have an emotional and spiritual quality not often found, even among 'ordinary' relationships.

The opinion of the author is these soul-connections were poignant in light of the disconnectedness which characterizes human relationships. There were no reports of catastrophic experiences (patients who became psychotic or suicidal). Many of the relationships developed into long-lasting friendships and some others developed into marriages. One might infer that the duration of the relationship is an index of success. (pp. 54-55)

Butler (1975, p. 57) went on to propose "conditions that might enhance a positive or negative experience" which bear some similarity to those suggested by Shepard (1971). In a follow-up journal article (Butler & Zelen, 1977) the findings on the neediness of the therapist-perpetrator were reviewed. Unfortunately, neither this article nor the original dissertation contains sufficient data or illustrative material to permit evaluation of the author's observations and conclusions. They seem heavily weighted by the therapists' perceptions of the relationships (which are atypical, compared to our sample) and also appear to be inconsistent with Butler's data on repeated sexual episodes with other clients. If these therapists simply lost control because of situational stressors and loneliness, one would not expect multiple victims. Beyond the obvious sampling bias inherent in such a study, one is left to wonder, consequently, how much the results reflect rationalization and lack of insight by the therapists as opposed to an objective analysis of both the true character and antecedents of the sexual contacts.

RUMORS ABOUT THE VIEWS OF WELL-KNOWN THERAPISTS

During the mid-1970s there was a widely circulated rumor that Albert Ellis, the founder of Rational-Emotive Therapy, had publicly indicated support for sexual involvement between client and therapist. I wrote Ellis in October of 1975 concerning his stand on this issue. His response indicated:

I have given two talks against therapists having sex with clients: one at the APA meetings in Philadelphia in 1964 and one at the Association for Humanistic Psychology meetings in 1974.

*****

In spite of my strong stand in this connection, rumors have persisted over the years that I favor therapists having sex with their clients under certain conditions and that I have personally engaged in such relations. These rumors intensified after People Magazine wrongly quoted me to this effect.   (Ellis, Personal Communication, 1975)

At the same time Martin Shepard, who had become well-known as a result of *The Love Treatment*, wrote a book about Fritz Perls and the development of Gestalt Therapy which presented a picture of him as being "both a dirty old man and a guru" (Shepard, 1975, p. 158). Perls is quoted as having written of himself:

My hands are strong and warm. A dirty old man's hands are cold and clammy. I have affection and love—too much of it. And if I comfort a girl in grief or distress and the sobbing subsides and she presses closer and the stroking gets out of rhythm and slides over the hips and breasts.... (Shepard, 1975, p. 159)

It should be noted that the free-wheeling sexual encounters described at Esalen were with colleagues, trainees, and group members who might well be classified as clients. So, in the case of Perls, it is quite possible that the rumors of sexual contact with clients are accurate. Yet, unlike McCartney (1966) Perls did not publicly espouse sex with clients as a therapy technique.

MORE MEDICAL DATA

The March 1974 issue of *Nursing '74* contained a 73-item questionnaire on ethical standards and conduct. More than 11,000 of the journal's American and Canadian readership (about 10% of the total) completed questionnaires and sent in letters and notes (*Nursing '74*, 1974, p. 35).

The report, which was published in September 1974 (*Nursing '74*), contains a wealth of fascinating information on nurses' views of and relationships with doctors, and on many aspects of their work. Beyond numerical data, the article quotes a number of specific, detailed, individual responses.

When asked about sexual involvement between a nurse and a doctor who work together, nurses varied markedly in their opinions:

16% Nothing wrong with it.
16% It's all right if they share affection.
40% It's all right, but it may hamper their work.
14% It's wrong because it's unprofessional behavior.
14% It's morally wrong.

Age and regional differences and differences related to religious background were noted (p. 42).

Almost all respondents (96%) saw sexual involvement with a patient while on duty as wrong; the remaining 4% felt that it was acceptable. Of the nurses who experienced a sexual advance by a patient, although about 1 in 8 was tempted to respond and 1 in 30 responded nonsexually, 1 in 170 had sexual contact and 1 in 170 had sexual intercourse; 25% never had had a sexual advance from a patient; 43%, only once or twice; 30%, occasionally; and only 2% reported advances as a frequent occurrence. The following data show the responses to sexual advances by patients:

Responses to Sexual Advances

	Female Nurses	Male Nurses
No, because advances never made	22%	29%
Never responded	66%	44%
No, but secretly tempted	9%	21%
Sometimes, but with no sex play	2%	2%
Sometimes, but short of intercourse	0.3%	2%
Yes, including intercourse	0.3%	2%

(Nursing '74, 1974, p. 43)

Nurses were also asked if they knew of any nurses who had engaged in sexual intercourse with their patients. The responses follow:

	Female Nurses	Male Nurses
Yes, many	1%	1%
Yes, several	2%	5%
Yes, one or two	10%	20%
No	87%	75%

(Nursing '74, 1974, p. 44)

The following vignette by one respondent is interesting:

About 8 years ago, I held a position as a charge nurse (11-7) in a small private hospital. In this position, I was the only person on duty during my shift. I found myself drawn to a patient, who was unmarried and largely ignored by his family. He was some 15 years older than me and in a terminal stage of illness. A relationship developed during some of the long hours of the night when I spent time talking to him. This reduced his need for narcotics. You could even call this a sexual relationship, even though intercourse was never done. It ended with his death in a few months. I was married during this time and my husband and I were not getting along, but I suffered greatly during the next few years with feelings of guilt. Only now after some psychotherapy am I able to live with the past. The whole affair was against all my beliefs and ethics both as a woman and a nurse, but it happened. Thank you for the opportunity to share this experience. -- Respondent #8608   *(Nursing '74*, 1974, p. 43)

Perry (1976), stimulated by Kardener et al.'s (1973) study of male physicians, surveyed a random sample of 500 women physicians, half in New York and half in California. Of the 164 responses (33%), 156 were usable. Like Kardener et al., Perry (1976) sampled psychiatrists, general practitioners, and physicians practicing internal medicine. Kardener et al., however, had a large group of OB-Gyns whereas a large portion of Perry's sample was pediatricians, and 13 other specialties were combined in a single group.

In Perry's findings, only 2% of the women physicians believed that erotic contact with patients might be beneficial, and only a single physician—a pediatrician—indicated that she had engaged in erotic contact with a patient which did not, however, include sexual intercourse (p. 840).

When asked about "nonerotic touching," defined as "hugging, kissing, and affectionate touching," women psychiatrists responded as follows: 27% never, 30% rarely, 33% occasionally, and 10% frequently or always (p. 839). In contrast, Kardener et al. (1973, p. 1078) reported the following percentages for male psychiatrists in answer to the same question: 45% never, 41% rarely, 14% occasionally, and 1% frequently or always. This striking difference is statistically significant. For both male and female physicians one must wonder about the classification of "hugging, kissing, and affectionate touching" as "nonerotic." Is this how patients experienced it? The sample of women psychiatrists (N=30) may simply have been too small to include a single "erotic" respondent. One would predict at most one such respondent, given the percentages obtained in later, larger surveys (e.g., 2.2%—Hamilton & DeRosis (1985); 1.9%—Gartrell, Herman, Olarte, Feldstein, & Localio, 1986).

THE MAY 1976 MEETING OF THE AMERICAN PSYCHIATRIC ASSOCIATION

Several key papers on therapist-client sex were presented at the annual meeting of the American Psychiatric Association in May 1976. The one by Grunebaum, Nadelson, and Macht (1976), "Sexual Activity With the Psychiatrist: A District Branch Dilemma," was never published. It reported a survey of 100 members of the Massachusetts Psychiatric Society to which one-third responded. About 50% of the respondents had heard of cases of sexual involvement between psychiatrist and client; in 12 instances the reports came from patients. In all instances the psychiatrists felt that the complaint was justified. The paper discussed the impediments to reporting that were given by the respondents, such as problems of confidentiality, fear of becoming involved, and the belief that no action would be taken.

Dr. Judd Marmor (1976) presented a paper, "Some Psychodynamic Aspects of the Seduction of Patients in Psychotherapy," which was published the same year. He reviewed predisposing factors that contribute to male therapists' sexual involvement with female clients, noting situational factors and characterological ones:

Situational:

1. Being alone in an office with the client sharing her innermost thoughts, resulting in emotional intimacy;

2. Eroticized transference combined with the client's physical attractiveness;

3. Seductiveness or flirtatiousness by the client;

4. Libidinal needs of the therapist—the health of his sex life or marriage.

Characterological:

1. The therapist's countertransference needs to respond as a loving and affectionate "parent;"

2. Unconscious hostility to women, with a sadistic need to exploit, humiliate, and ultimately reject;

3. The "Don Juan complex," a reaction formation against inner feelings of masculine inadequacy or pseudohomosexual fears;

4. Defective superegos—psychopathic personalities or people who border on that category.   (Marmor, 1976, pp. 321-22)

Marmor (1976) concluded:

> The implications of sexual acting-out by the therapist are serious both for the patient and the therapist. Regardless of any "technical" explanations or caveats that a therapist may use to rationalize his behavior to the patient, the fact is that the vast majority of patients invest such intimacies with reality connotations, and develop hopes and expectations that are doomed to disappointment. When a therapist lends reality to a patient's eroticized fantasies of transference love, he fosters a serious confusion between reality and fantasy in the patient, with inevitably antitherapeutic results. I have yet to see a woman patient who became involved in an erotic relationship with a therapist who did not eventually end up feeling exploited and betrayed by him. (pp. 322-23)

Another paper, "Psychiatry's Problem With No Name: Therapist-Patient Sex," was published the following year (Davidson, 1977). This excellent work examined the problem in its broad societal context. For example, she examined the portrayal of the doctor-patient relationship in the popular media:

> One recent example (October 1975) is a cover from *Esquire* magazine which is an excerpt from a short story about a woman whose relationship with her analyst included sex on the couch. Although written by Truman Capote, the vignette has much in common with the clinical histories reported by Chesler, Belote, and Dahlberg. From the cinema is a scene from Igmar Bergman's *Scenes from a Marriage*, shown at the 1975 annual meeting of the American Psychiatric Association; in it the estranged husband asks his wife if she is having sex with her psychiatrist. She matter of factly replies that they have gone to bed a couple of times, but that it was a dead loss. (p. 45)

One also could cite examples from the popular literature, such as F. Scott Fitzgerald's classic novel, *Tender is the Night*, wherein a psychiatrist becomes involved with a patient; the article, "Should You Sleep With Your Therapist?" in *Vogue* (Weber, 1972); from the cinema, *Pretty Maids All In A Row* (Metro Goldwyn-Mayer, 1970) in which Rock Hudson plays a counselor who seduces high school girls in his office, or *What's New Pussycat* in which Peter Sellers plays a psychiatrist who pursues a client.

The other side of the story, however, was finally beginning to reach public attention. From March 10-19 the case of Roy v. Hartogs was tried in New York City; it made headlines in that city's newspapers and received considerable attention elsewhere. The following year *Betrayal* was published. It described the successful lawsuit filed by Julie Roy against Dr. Renatus Hartogs, a psychiatrist who authored a column for *Cosmopolitan* magazine (Freeman & Roy, 1976).

During the 10 years following the publication of *Betrayal* and the broad publicity given Roy v. Hartogs, a large number of lawsuits were filed against psychotherapists for sexual misconduct with a client. Many of these suits gained at least local publicity. In cases involving psychologists, for example, $7,018,165 was paid out in claims for sex cases during that period; the sum was 44.8% of all claims dollars and represented the largest number of cases (Pope, 1987).

Discussion within the profession began to shift toward concern with the identification of "erotic" practitioners. For example, Kardener et al. (1976) offered an additional analysis of their original survey data. The respondents who did and did not report sexual contact with patients did not differ demographically. A significant difference, however, was found in one area: respondents who became sexual with patients also engaged in more "non-erotic" physical contact with patients (p. 1325). Examples of the justifications for erotic contact include the following: "supports and reinforces a patient's sexual appeal"; "stimulating the clitoris helps a patient relax"; "it was originally for my need, but led to better rapport and more durable relationship"; and "with mature patients" (p. 1325).

THE WORK OF LINDA D'ADDARIO

In July 1977 Linda D'Addario's Ph.D. dissertation, *Sexual Relationships Between Female Clients and Male Therapists*, was accepted. We obtained a copy of it within the following year and were impressed by the depth of her examination of the problem. Dr. D'Addario has been quoted on numerous occasions in magazine and newspaper stories since 1977, and appeared on "Sixty Minutes" (CBS, 1978), the Oprah Winfrey Show (Jan. 30, 1987), and has been featured on the Donahue Show several times. (She changed her name to Linnda Durre' a few years after receiving her Ph.D.)

She started her original study by placing ads in several magazines asking for participants. She received 93 inquiries, 66 from *Ms. Magazine*, 22 from *Psychology Today*, 3 from other papers, and 2 from unknown sources. (None came from the California National Organization for Women Bulletin in which she also advertised.) She sent a lengthy questionnaire to the 93 women who inquired, and received 75 returns (D'Addario, 1977, pp. 92, 16).

Of the 75 respondents, 15 reported no sexual contact but 55 reported sexual contact with 1 therapist, and 5, with 2 therapists. The women ranged in age from 16 to 52 when the sex occurred. The 60 women who had had sexual contact with a total of 65 therapists reported the following types of contact:

Embrace	64	98.4%
Kiss	63	96.9%
Fondling	62	95.4%
Intercourse	54	83.1%
Oral/Genital	39	60.0%
Massage	38	58.6%
Other[2]	4	6.2%

Interestingly, only 54 (83.1%) reported handshakes: the same number that reported sexual intercourse but fewer than those who reported embraces and kissing (p. 93).

The length of treatment ranged from 1 month to 10 years. Of the therapists, 40% were psychologists; 35.4%, psychiatrists; 6.2%, social workers; and 18.5%, pastoral counselors and other types of "non-credentialed counselors" (p. 94). One respondent alleged that her father, while in training to be a psychologist, "fondled her and forced her to fondle him," and also "ordered her to masturbate for his viewing" (p. 103).

Twenty-one of the 60 respondents who reported sex with a therapist were interviewed in considerable depth and 4 case studies were chosen for analysis and detailed reporting in the dissertation (D'Addario, 1977, p.124). These accounts are well-written and still worth

---

[2]Included "anal intercourse, mutual masturbation, manual stimulation, verbal enticements, suggestions and/or invitations" (D'Addario, 1977, p. 93).

reading. In the case study of "Tina" chosen for analysis, she had been living with her therapist for 3 years and felt positive about the relationship when she was first contacted but 3 months later, at the time of the interview, her view of the relationship was negative, thus providing an interesting account of the disadvantages of involvement with someone who knows as much about you as your therapist. According to Tina,

> Whenever we had a really big blow up, he hit me below the belt, with things that I had told him while I was in therapy and with what I considered an unfair analysis of my life.... (p. 277)

> ...Whenever he was angry he used anything to hurt me; he used my fantasies against me. He used our sex life together against me. In any relationship with any other man, he found something wrong.... (p. 278)

> He always seemed to twist around what you said, just twists it into what he wants to hear or what he thinks you should be saying.... (p. 278)

In her analysis of the case studies D'Addario (1977) noted harmful consequences for all four women. She also pointed out that "all four women served as 'therapists' for their therapist..." (p. 308). However, each of the four also experienced personal growth and some gains during these relationships. When asked to rate the experience on a 7-point scale, the four checked 1, between 2 and 3, 3.5, and 6 (D'Addario, 1977, pp. 315-18, 324-25).[3] They also noted that the ratings of the experience would have varied greatly at different points in the relationship.

D'Addario also quoted respondents' answers to the question of why they were willing to be interviewed (N=36) and an open-ended question asking for "Other pertinent information" (N=38). In answer to the first, the "majority of comments spoke of the negative, harmful or destructive quality of their experience" (p. 108). For the second question, "Very few statements were positive or even neutral" (p. 123).[4]

THE WORK OF HOLROYD AND BRODSKY

Two California psychologists, Holroyd and Brodsky, replicated the Kardener et al. (1973) study on a national sample of licensed psychologists. In addition to the questions asked in the Kardener et al. survey, Holroyd and Brodsky (1977) asked about the respondent's gender and therapy orientation, and whether sexual contact had occurred during the 3-month period following termination. Questionnaires were sent to 500 male and 500 female psychologists who returned 666 usable questionnaires.

The results included the following information: 10.9% of male psychologists and 1.9% of female psychologists reported erotic contact during treatment; 5.5% of males and 0.6% of females reported sexual intercourse during treatment; and an additional 2.6% of males and 0.3% of females reported intercourse within 3 months of termination of therapy. So, if one considers the 3-month period following termination still part of therapy, 8.1% of males

---

[3]The Experience Evaluation Scale (D'Addario, 1977, p. 83) had only three points identified: 7=major positive changes; 4=median; and 1=negative, destructive changes. These findings have been inaccurately cited as showing only "harmful" as opposed to mixed results (Pope & Bouhoutsos, 1986, p. 58, Table 3, and p. 60).

[4]Vinson (1984) interpreted these responses as indicating that "90% of the 30 women who discussed the impact of the sexual contact judged the impact to have been negative" (p. 15). However, this requires interpretation of responses to a question which did not directly ask about impact, so Vinson's figure should be viewed skeptically.

and 0.9% of females had sexual intercourse with clients. Among the respondents who acknowledged having had sexual intercourse, 80% of the 19 men and 2 women indicated that it had happened with more than one client, in the range of 1-10 (median=2, mean=2.6).

THE CALIFORNIA PSYCHOLOGICAL ASSOCIATION TASK FORCE

To my knowledge, the California Psychological Association's Task Force on Sexual Intimacy Between Psychotherapists and Patients was the first undertaking of its kind. Begun in 1978 and chaired by Bouhoutsos, the task force undertook a large-scale research project, the results of which were published several years later (Bouhoutsos, Holroyd, Herman, Forer, & Greenberg, 1983).

A questionnaire was sent to each of the 4,385 licensed psychologists in California asking a number of questions about cases of reported intimacy between clients and former therapists. Approximately one-sixth, or 704, questionnaires were returned of which 318 contained reports of therapist-client sex. Information was provided on 559 cases. In addition, 21 males (4.8%) and 2 females (0.8%) acknowledged having had sexual contact with clients themselves (Bouhoutsos et al., 1983, p. 187).

The sexually abused clients included 509 females and 33 males (gender was not stated in 17 reports); 96% of the former therapists were male. The following breakdown of therapist-client dyads was found:

male therapist—female client	489	(92.4%)
male therapist—male client	18	(3.4%)
female therapist—male client	13	(2.5%)
female therapist—female client	9	(1.7%)

(Bouhoutsos et al., 1983, p. 188)

Overall the respondents indicated that about 90% of the clients who had experienced sexual contact with a previous therapist were harmed by it in some way; only 10% emerged unscathed. However, although as a result of the sexual intimacies 34% suffered adverse effects on their personalities, 26% had relationships worsen, and 29% had negative feelings about the experience, 16% were rated as having become "healthier" or as having improved "emotionally and/or in sexual relationships." Negative effects on the past and current therapies were more clearly negative (p. 190). Although this study is most frequently cited for the findings related to the harm done by the experience, it is highly recommended to serious students of the issue.

THE DATA EXPANDS

Stone (1980) reports a study on a sample of 46 women who had been in therapy with male therapists whom she classified into four groups: 1. those who had been sexually intimate with their therapists; 2. those who had been propositioned by their therapists; 3. those who had terminated therapy prematurely; and 4. those who had successfully completed therapy. The study found no significant differences between the groups in ego strength or on anxious attachment as measured by Hansburg's Separation Anxiety Test or on the criteria utilized by Hansburg to measure the level of anxious attachment. The study did find some support for the hypothesis that women who had been sexually involved with their therapists had more anxious attachment to therapist, male partner, and mother.

Blackmon (1984), in a study of stresses in the lives of clergy, surveyed 300 pastors from four denominations (Assembly of God, Episcopal, Presbyterian, United Methodist) in Southern California. While sexual contact between pastors and parishoners was not the major focus of this study, 13% of the respondents reported that they had had sexual intercourse with a member of their church (other than their wife). It is further important to note that no information is provided on the women, so there is no way of knowing how many were counselees of the clergyman.

In Washington, Russell (1984) surveyed 298 social workers from King County and the city of Seattle; he received 111 returns (37%). Of the respondents, 28% had interviewed clients who reported sexual contact with a previous therapist, accounting for a total of 51 cases; the respondents also reported knowledge of 95 incidents from other sources. The distribution of reports follows:

	From clients	From other sources
Male therapist/female client	88%	77%
Female therapist/female client	6%	8.5%
Male therapist/male client	6%	8.5%
Female therapist/male client	--	6%

(Russell, 1984, pp. 36, 41)

Clients had been assisted in reporting the abuse by 48% of the respondents (p. 49). When they were asked about the relative importance of various factors in bringing about the abuse, the following factors were rated as playing a role:

Power..82%
Seductiveness of the worker.....................71%
Sexism..66%
Training (deficiencies)...........................58%
Use of sex as a treatment technique............31%
Relaxed social norms 28%
Seductiveness of the client.....................22%

(Russell, 1984, p. 62)

Feldman-Summers and Jones (1984) compared 3 groups of clients: a group of 14 who had had sexual contact with therapists, a group of 7 who had had sexual contact with other health professionals, and a group of 10 who had seen therapists but had not had sexual contact with them. The criterion for "sexual contact" was sexual intercourse or genital stimulation. Of the 32 women who responded, 28 agreed to participate but 7 failed to do so, resulting in a sample of 21. (Of the 11 men, 3 agreed to participate but only 1 did, so he was dropped from the sample.) No significant differences were found between women who had had sexual contact with a therapist and those who had had sexual contact with some other type of health professional. When they were compared with the control group (those who had not had sexual contact) only 2 of 16 comparisons yielded significant differences. Women who had had sexual contact with either a therapist or some other health care professional showed a greater mistrust and anger toward men in general as well as more post-treatment symptoms of distress.

The Women's Committee of the Washington (D.C.) Psychiatric Society conducted a survey during 1980-81 which was not reported until several years later (Hamilton & DeRosis, 1985). The Committee sent out 1,060 questionnaires to the membership of which 621 were returned (58.6%). The following data were supplied: 6.1% of respondents reported sex with clients while they were still in therapy, and an additional 0.5% reported sex with former clients: 6.6% overall; 7.9% of the male and 2.2% of the female respondents acknowledged such sexual contact; 97% of female but only 79% of male psychiatrists felt that sexual contact with clients was "always harmful" (Hamilton & DeRosis, 1985, p. 37). Only 60% of the psychiatrists who acknowledged having had sex with clients felt that sex with clients was "always harmful" (DeRosis, Hamilton, Morrison, & Strauss, 1987, p. 689).

The Wisconsin Psychological Association Task Force began actively studying the problem of therapist-client sex in 1984 (see Ch. 41) and carried out a large-scale study (for the results of the survey, see Ch. 3).

Bouhoutsos and Gechtman finished a national survey of social workers in 1985 but the results were only published. Questionnaires were sent to a random sample of 1,000 social workers, and 54% were returned. Of the respondents, 1.3% admitted sexual contact with a client during therapy and 0.6%, after termination; thus a total of 1.9% acknowledged sexual contact with a client. Only 1% reported sexual intercourse during therapy, and an additional 0.1% after termination, for a total of 1.1% sexual intercourse. 3.6% had sex with a supervisee, and 1.9% with a student, while 1.1% had sexual contact with an employee. Only 0.6% had sex with their own personal therapist. 2.7% had sexual contact with their employer, 1.3% with their supervisor, 1% with their administrator, and 0.6% with a teacher of theirs (Gechtman, 1989). Gechtman (1989) speculated that the relatively low incidence of sexual contact with clients might be due to the fact that 89% of social workers are in institutional settings (compared with 14% of psychologists, or to selection factors as to which men enter the profession.

Vinson (1984) studied client reactions and complaint procedures in client-therapist sex cases. She interviewed 30 representatives from California's state licensing boards and professional organizations and concluded that complaint procedures leave a great deal to be desired given that only a miniscule proportion of cases are reported or adjudicated. She also interviewed 22 women and 6 men who had experienced sexual contact with their psychotherapists; 95% of the females experienced various negative consequences in their interpersonal and emotional lives whereas only 1 male subject (17%) reported severe negative effects and 50% of the males reported only positive consequences. Both the dissertation (Vinson, 1984) and a subsequent journal article (Vinson, 1987) provide a useful look at complaint options and their deficiencies.

Pope, Keith-Spiegel, and Tabachnick (1986) studied therapists' sexual attraction to their clients using a questionnaire sent to 1,000 psychologists who are members of Division 42 (Psychologists in Private Practice) of the American Psychological Association; 585 were returned. The findings showed that 9.4% of men and 2.5% of women acknowledged sexual contact with clients. Rates of attraction for men and women with male and female clients are reported, as are those client characteristics cited by the therapists which play a role in the attraction. The results also explore implications for the training of therapists.

Noel (1986) also surveyed a random sample of 1,000 psychologists but this time members of Division 12 (Clinical Psychology) of the APA and received returns from 40.5%. Sexual intimacy with a client was acknowledged by 2.6% of males and 3% of females; 84% of the males and 82.8% of the females reported having been told—36.4% by a client, 50.7% by a colleague—about a psychologist who had been sexually intimate with clients. Few took action in these cases. Noel (1986) used a series of vignettes to attempt to learn what factors increased the likelihood that a psychologist would take action in a case. A greater likelihood of action occurred as the frequency or intensity of the sexual contact increased. Formal training in ethics, training in human sexuality, and gender all contributed to the likelihood of taking action.

THE WORK OF GARTRELL AND COLLEAGUES

In 1982 the Committee on Women of the American Psychiatric Association began studying the sexual abuse of clients by psychiatrists. The Committee had a difficult time obtaining permission to conduct a national study of the problem, a saga that is recounted in "Institutional Resistance to Self-Study: A Case Report" (Gartrell, Herman, & Olarte, 1986).

The resulting study and five professional articles are of great importance but are far too complex to be summarized here. (See Gartrell et al., 1986; 1987; 1988a and b; Herman, Gartrell, Olarte, Localio, & Feldstein, 1987.)

In terms of incidence, the survey of 5,574 psychiatrists nationally yielded 1,423 usable returns; 7.1% of males and 3.1% of females acknowledged sexual contact with clients: 88% between male psychiatrists and female clients, 7.6% between two males, 3.5% between female psychiatrists and male clients, and only 1.4% between two females; and 4.4% of the women and 0.9% of the men responding had been involved in sexual contact with their personal therapists. (Gartrell et al., 1986, pp. 1128-29)

Of the 1,423 respondents, 65% had treated clients who had been sexually involved with a former therapist. Although they saw these relationships as harmful in 87% of the cases, they reported the abuse in only 8% of the situations. The 920 psychiatrists who reported treating clients who alleged sexual contact with a previous therapist indicated they had seen a total of 3,031 such clients, 91% of whom were women and 9% men. The professions of these previous therapists were psychiatry (48%), psychology (27.4%), clergy (9.1%), social work (7.2%), "lay therapists" (5.7%), and "unspecified" (2.7%). (Gartrell et al., 1987, p. 289)

Eighty-four (6.4%) of the respondents acknowledged sexual contacts with their own clients. Twenty-eight of the 75 males who acknowledged sexual contacts indicated involvement with more than one client, accounting for 108 victims in all. Only 8 women psychiatrists acknowledged sexual contact with a client, and in each case the contact was with a single client. By contrast to psychiatrists who did not report having had sex with a client, respondents who reported sex with a client were more likely to have completed an accredited residency and to have undergone personal psychotherapy or psychoanalysis (Gartrell et al., 1987, p. 289).

One of the most fascinating findings of this study was the differences it found between non-offenders, one-time offenders, and repeat offenders:

	Repeat Offenders (N=28)	One-Time Offenders (N=56)	Non-Offenders (N=1339)
Reported involved therapist to a professional association or legal authority	0	6.7%	8.2%
Treated patients who were sexually involved with previous therapists	100%	80%	63.6%
Assessed previous therapist-patient involvement as always harmful	39.3%	70.4%	88.3%
Know psychiatrists who have been sexually involved with patients	75%	55.4%	37.6%
Favor mandatory reporting	14.8%	45.3%	57%

(Gartrell et al., 1987, p. 290)

Herman et al. (1987) reported on psychiatrists' responses to survey questions about sexual contact with clients, and compared the responses of the 84 psychiatrists who had acknowledged sexual contact with patients with the 1,232 who denied having had such contact. The survey allowed for a response of: always appropriate, sometimes appropriate, always inappropriate, no opinion. (Less than 3% of respondents chose always appropriate for any item in the survey.) The authors present a comparison of offenders (those who reported having sexual contact with clients) and non-offenders as to their rating of factors which can make sexual contact with a patient always or sometimes appropriate:

Factors	Percent agreeing that sexual contact can be appropriate	
	Offenders	Non-Offenders
Setting:		
After termination	74.1%	27.4%
During treatment sessions	9.5%	1.4%
Concurrent with treatment	8.4%	0.6%
Activity:		
Hugging	91.7%	66.7%
Kissing	31.0%	10.7%
Sitting on lap	16.7%	3.1%
Disrobing	9.5%	1.6%
Fondling	6.0%	0.5%
Genital Contact	6.0%	0.4%
Rationale:		
Therapist in love with patient	21.4%	3.5%
Sexual dysfunction	17.9%	3.9%
Enhance self-esteem	10.7%	0.9%
Corrective emotional experience	8.4%	0.5%
Change sexual orientation	7.1%	0.7%
Shorten grief reaction	6.0%	0.8%

(Herman et al., 1987, p. 166)

Offenders and non-offenders showed statistically significant differences on all of these items. The authors report that "Repeat offenders were particularly likely to believe in the therapeutic value of sexual relations with patients" (p. 166).

In September 1986 this team of researchers conducted an additional study (Gartrell et al., 1988a); they sent questionnaires to all 1113 psychiatric residents who were identified as trainees in the AMA master file, of which 1087 were delivered. Of this number 548 (50.4%) were returned. The responses of 74.2% indicated that sexual contact between a psychiatric educator and resident who have an on-going work relationship is inappropriate; 80% felt that it would be harmful to the work relationship. However, 4.9% had experienced such contact (6.3% of the women; 3.9% of the men); and 4 male residents (1.2%) and only 1 female resident (0.4%) acknowledged having sex with a client. (In this case sexual contact must have occurred during treatment or within 11 months of termination.)

RECENT DATA

The Maine Psychological Association reported on some data that had been collected in 1985 on its members' knowledge of various types of impairment in other psychologists (Pelletier & Settin, 1988). Of the 73 respondents (33% return rate), 16% had direct knowledge of sexual contact between a client and a psychologist and 51% had received a complaint from a client about the behavior or work of a psychologist; 41% of the complaints related to sexual conduct.

Akamatsu (1988), in a national survey of intimate relationships with former clients (see also Chapter 24), reported a 40% return rate. Among his sample of 395 members of Division 29 (Psychotherapy) of the American Psychological Association, 3.5% of the men and 2.3% of the women acknowledged sexual contact with a client during therapy. An additional 14.2% of the men and 4.7% of the women reported sex with a former client. (See Ch. 24 for further discussion of these results.)

Pope, Tabachnick, and Keith-Spiegel (1987) reported some extraordinary survey data which they collected from 456 members of APA Division 29 relating to their beliefs and practices in a number of areas. The following items are worthy of note here:

Becoming sexually involved ....10.5% rarely, 0.4% sometimes;
with a former client.....................................0.2% very often

Engaging in erotic activity with a client..........2.4% rarely, 0.2% sometimes

Engaging in sexual contact with a client.........1.5% rarely, 0.2% sometimes
(p. 996)

This article is essential reading and is highly recommended.

For a summary of the research on the frequency of therapist-client sexual contact see Figure 1. The research reported there, which used various definitions of sexual contact, shows varying rates of self-reported sexual contact with clients. However, when data on men and women professionals can be separated, the rates of therapist-client sexual contact are always lower for women therapists.

No.	Professions	Sampling Area	Number of Returns	Return Rate	MALE Intercourse	MALE Sexual Contact	FEMALE Intercourse	FEMALE Sexual Contact
1	Psychologists	LA County	225	70%	—	13.7%[a]	—	0[a]
2	Psychiatrists	LA County	109	55%	5%	5%	—	—
	Other Physicians	LA County	336	42%	7-9%	5-11%	—	—
3	Nurses	National	11,000+	10%	2%	2%	0.3%	0.3%
4	Social Work	National	60	30%	1.8%	3-6%	Not reported separately	
5	Psychiatrists	California & New York	30	?	—	—	0	0
	Other Physicians		156	33%	—	—	0	0
6	Psychologists (Licensed)	National	666	70%	5.5% / 2.6%[b] / 8.1%	10.9%	0.6% / 0.3%[b] / 0.9%	1.9%
7	Psychologists, Psychiatrists, Soc. Workers, Marriage & Fam. Therapists	Hawaii	46	30%	0[c]	30%[c]	Not reported separately Figures combine male & female	
8.	Psychologists - APA Div. 29	National	480	48%	—	12%	—	3%
9.	Psychologists (Licensed)	California	704	16%	—	4.8%	—	0.6%
10.	Clergy	S. California	300	25%	12%	—	—	—
11.	Social Workers	National	540	54%	1% / 0.1%[d] / 1.1%	1.3% / 0.6%[d] / 1.9%	0	0

1. Forer (1968) reported in 1981
2. Kardener, Fuller, & Mensh (1973)
3. Nursing '74 (1974)
4. Schultz (1975)
5. Perry (1976)
6. Holroyd & Brodsky (1977)
7. Len & Fischer (1978)
8. Pope, Levenson, & Schover (1979)
9. Bouhoutsos et al., (1983)
10. Blackman (1984)
11. Bouhoutsos & Gechman (1985)

© 1989 Walk-In Counseling Center

Fig. 1 Self-Report Frequency Studies

[a]Where only sexual contact is reported, this may include intercourse.
[b]Within 3 months of termination.
[c]These are percentages for use of sexual contact in therapy.
[d]Following termination with time period not designated.

No	Professions	Sampling Area	Number of Returns	Return Rate	MALE		FEMALE	
					Intercourse	Sexual Contact	Intercourse	Sexual Contact
12	Psychiatrists	Washington, D.C.	621	59%	—	7.9%[e]	—	2.2%[e]
13	Psychologists — APA Division 12	National	371	41%	—	2.6%	—	3.0%
14	Psychiatrists	National	1423	26%	—	2.6% / 4.5%[f] / 7.1%	—	1.2% / 1.9%[f] / 3.1%
15	Psychologists — APA Division 42	National	585	59%	—	9.4%	—	2.5%
16	Psychiatry Residents	National	542	50%	—	1.2%	—	0.4%
17	Psychologists — APA Division 29	National	395	40%	—	3.5% / 14.2%[f] / 17.7%	—	2.3% / 4.7%[f] / 7.0%
18	Psychiatrists	National	570	26.7%	—	0.8% / 7.0%[f] / 7.8%	Not reported separately. Figures combine male and female	Not reported separately. Figures combine male and female
	Psychologists		904	42.4%	—	1.1% / 11.9%[f] / 13.0%		
	Social Workers		658	31.0%	—	0% / 1.6%[f] / 1.6%		
19	Psychologists (Licensed)	Wisconsin	394	41.1%	—	6.5%[g]	—	0
	School Psychologists (Licensed)		55	31.2%	—	3.1%[g]	—	0

Fig. 1: <u>Self-Report Frequency Studies</u> (Continued)

12. Hamilton & Derosis (1985)
13. Noel (1986)
14. Gartrell et al. (1986)

15. Pope, Keith-Spiegel, Tabachnick (1986)
16. Gartrell et al. (1988)

17. Akamatsu (1988)
18. Borys (1988)
19. Brigham (1989)

[e]6.1% overall had sex with current clients; 0.5% with former clients.
[f]former clients.
[g]4.3% of total sample had sex with former clients; 1.6% with current clients.

Borys (1988) sent out surveys to a random sample of 4,800 psychiatrists, psychologists, and social workers, sampling equal numbers of males and females from each profession. The response rate was 49% (N=2,132), although it varied by profession considerably—psychologists, 42.4% (904); social workers, 31% (658); and psychiatrists, 26.7% (570) (pp. 73-74). More than 91% had done psychotherapy in the past 5 years, and they practiced in the following settings:

> 47.2% in solo private practice
> 23.5% in outpatient clinics
> 15.1% in group private practice
> 9.9% in inpatient settings   (p. 87)

Only the 91% who had done psychotherapy in the past 5 years (N=2,133) were used for the analyses which follow. Approximately half the sample completed a "Therapeutic Practices Survey" which focused on the ethics of various behaviors, while the other half filled out a form of the same name which focused on practices. The ethicality of several behaviors was rated as follows:

	Never Ethical	Ethical Under Rare Conditions	Ethical Under Some Conditions	Ethical Under Most Conditions	Always Ethical	Not Sure
Engaging in sexual activity with a current client	98.3%	0.5%	0	0.1%	0.6%	0.5%
Engaging in sexual activity with a client after termination	68.5%	23.1%	4.1%	0.6%	0.3%	2.7%

(Borys, 1988, pp. 112-13)

In terms of actual practices, respondents reported:

	No Clients	Few Clients	Some Clients	Most Clients	All Clients
Engaged in sexual activity with a current client	99.5%	0.4%	0.1%	0	0
Engaged in sexual activity with a client after termination	81%	3.9%	0	0	0

(Borys, 1988, 00. 114-15)

Borys had hoped to compare therapists who had acknowledged having had sex with non-erotic practitioners, but only 4 in the entire sample acknowledged sex with current clients. She combined these 4 with the 40 who acknowledged sex with former clients and compared this group of 44 with the 827 non-erotic therapists. Dropping an item from the Social Involvement Scale on having engaged in sexual activity with a client after termination, Borys found that she could correctly classify 55% of the erotic and 79.4% of the non-erotic practitioners based on their responses to the following practice items (p. 154):

> Became friends with a client after termination.
> Disclosed details of your current personal stresses to a client.
> Invited clients to an office/clinic open house.
> Went out to eat with a client after a session.
> Invited clients to a personal party or social event.   (p. 71)

Given the fact that 91% of the erotic practitioners engaged in sex only with former clients, some of these items may simply be correlates of the involvement rather than separate boundary violations.

Horst (1988) reported on a study of "Dual Relationships Between Psychologists and Clients" in Minnesota which compared psychologists who were grouped according to their place of residence (Twin Cities and suburbs; other large cities; small cities; rural areas) on self-reported frequency of engaging in dual relationships with clients. Horst's design permitted her to separate situations in which therapists are asked to take on clients with whom they have some other type of prior relationship from those where another relationship is established after therapy has begun. Based on the responses on the 99 questionnaires which were returned (69.7% response rate), Horst concluded:

> The outside relationships in which participants reported they were as likely as not to engage do not involve the same type of role confusion or reversal. These relationships are either fairly distant socially, or involve the therapist's being known to an individual as someone else's therapist. In either case the therapist can remain clearly in the role of therapist. Some therapists, in fact, feel that seeing clients in outside contexts and from others' points of view actually benefits the therapy...

> The factor which psychologists seem to identify as the distinguishing criterion between a dual relationship and an overlapping one, then, is not outside contact per se, but rather the degree to which the outside relationship allows therapist and client to remain in their appropriate roles. (p. 27)

*****

> The evidence... suggests that while psychologists who practice in rural areas do experience more outside contact with clients, they manage to differentiate between true dual (i.e., harmful, conflictual) relationships and relationships which overlap in less harmful ways. (p. 28)

As for entering a romantic relationship with a client, all but two psychologists gave the most negative score possible—"very unlikely." the two remaining psychologists gave the next most negative rating, so respondents overwhelmingly indicated that they were not likely to engage in a romantic relationship with a client.

Brigham (1989), in a study of psychotherapy stressors and sexual misconduct by therapists in Wisconsin, surveyed 785 licensed psychologists and 176 school psychologists. Usable responses were received from 394 (41.4%)—323 psychologists and 55 licensed for the independent practice of school psychology (pp. 46, 49). Sixteen (4.4%), all males, acknowledged having had sex with a client—6.5% of the licensed psychologists, and 3.1% of the licensed school psychologists (p. 61). Five (1.3%) reported sex with a current client seen in private practice; one (0.3%) reported sexual contact with a client seen in an institution; and twelve (3.04%) reported sex with a former private practice client. Comparing those who had been sexual with clients with those who had not, there were no differences in the psychologists' reports of having had training relevant to dealing with sexual intimacy in therapy, nor were there any significant differences in stress between offenders and non-offenders. (p. 89)

Psychologists reported their concerns that mandated reporting would increase frivolous complaints against non-offenders. In order to protect themselves against false complaints, psychologists reported:

63% kept careful notes
31% had secretary in outer office
17% refused to see clients perceived as potentially seductive
8% used the handout "Making Therapy Work For You" (see Appendix Z)

(Brigham, 1988, p. 68)

Knowledge of reports of sexual misconduct by a colleague were a leading source of anxiety for respondents, ranking ahead of excessive workload, frustration with insufficient treatment success, and a sense of responsibility for client's lives (p. 81). In terms of stressful client behaviors, psychologists ranked suicidal gestures well above other items, but ranked a client's report of sex with a previous therapist at the same approximate level as client phone calls at home—ranking numbers 2 and 3 (p. 72). (See Ch. 41 for further discussion of this study.)

Valiquette (1989), in another recent unpublished Ph.D. dissertation, advertised for subjects in Montreal and received responses from 83 women and 16 men (of whom 3 were calling about their wives). Twelve of the women lived too far away, and 7 had experienced verbal advances only. Sixty-two responded to the request to participate, but 6 didn't show up, 3 turned out to still be involved in a therapeutic relationship with the therapist, and 2 reported involvement with women therapists. Of the 51 remaining subjects, 78% had sexual contact during therapy, and 22% at the very end of therapy. Sexual intercourse was reported by 78%, whereas 22% reported erotic kisses, caresses, or masturbation (pp. 28-29).

The subjects were divided into three groups:

Experimental group 1 (N=42) — had sex with a therapist and returned to see another therapist

Experimental group 2 (N=9) — had sex with a therapist but did not return for more therapy

Conrol group   (N=25) — had prior therapy without sex

(p. 30)

The 51 experimental subjects reported the duration of their treatment as follows: 36% less than 1 year; 20%, 1-2 years; 24%, 2-5 years; 20%, 5+ years. A history of prior sexual abuse was reported by 56.9%. The therapeutic relationship continued following the sexual contact in 62.7% of the cases, and 76.5% of the clients reported that they still had some sort of contact with the therapist (Appendix 4, p. 40). The sexual contact was described as follows:

Beginning of the Sexual Contact		Cumulative Percentage
First few sessions	13.7%	13.7%
Within 3 months	27.5%	41.2%
Within 6 months	11.8%	53.0%
Within 1 year	15.7%	68.7%
After 2 or more years	9.8%	78.5%
Just at the end	21.5%	100%
Following Termination:	0	

Who Initiated It?		Who Ended It?
Client	13.7%	60.8%
Therapist	66.7%	27.5%
Both	19.6%	11.8%

Type of Sexual Contact:		
	Sexual intercourse	78.4%
	Erotic kisses	74.5%
	Erotic caresses	68.6%
	Masturbation	54.9%

Filed a Complaint:	17.6%

I expressed surprise to Valiquette (Personal Communication, June 24, 1989) concerning the absence of post-termination sex cases in the sample, and she indicated that it was possible that the wording of the ads for the study may have been the reason for this. I queried her about the 21% who reported that sex occurred at the end of therapy and she indicated that this meant that the first sexual contact occurred during the last session or immediately after it. Two examples of such cases are one therapist who arranged to have a drink with the client following the last session, telling her that this is how he terminates. In another case a therapist and client terminated, and then he phoned her to come back for another therapy session. When she arrived it became clear that it wasn't to be a therapy session.

In a letter dated June 22, 1989, Valiquette generously provided me with data on the time in months between the end of therapy and her September 1987 survey:

Time in Months	Exper. Group 1	Exper. Group 2	Total
Less than 2	1	1	2
3 to 6	0	1	1
7 to 12	4	0	4
13 to 24	10	0	10
25 to 36	2	0	2
37 to 60	5	1	6
61 to 120	7	3	10
121 to 180	8	1	9
180 and more	5	2	7
Longest time	274 (22.8 yrs.)	220 (18.3 yrs.)	

So, there is considerable variability in the sample regarding the time which has elapsed since the sexual contact with the therapist occurred.

Valiquette asked subjects to rate themselves on self-esteem and psychological distress at three points in time: (1) prior to therapy; (2) at the end of therapy; and (3) currently. Subjects also rated themselves on an index of psychiatric symptoms, a questionnaire concerning the effect of various events, a questionnaire evaluating social supports, and a questionnaire concerning the attribution of blame.

Valiquette's findings were that when the client attributed blame to the therapist recovery was better, although a punitive attitude toward the former therapist was related to ineffective coping (p. 72). The combination of good social support and attribution of causality to the therapist decreased the psychological consequences of the sexual contact. The two experimental groups (that is, those who had follow-up therapy and those who didn't), did not differ significantly from each other, so the follow-up therapy was not shown to have made a difference in ameliorating the impact of the sexual misconduct (pp. 61, 106). Great variability was found in the impact of the sexual involvement as estimated by subjects immediately following the therapy and in September 1987, when they filled out the questionnaires (p. 107). This variability washes out many of the differences. At the time of the survey, in terms of psychological distress and self-esteem, the experimental subjects did not differ significantly from the controls. Valiquette noted (Personal Communication, June 24, 1989), however, that 30 of the 51 experimental subjects attended debriefing meetings following the research sessions. Some reported that this was very helpful, and Valiquette believes that some were just then beginning to fully understand and appraise some of the effects of the sexual contact.

CLIENT CHARACTERISTICS

Chapters 7, 9, and 10 in this book discuss the literature on client characteristics so that issue is not reviewed here. There are no data in the literature to show that any client characteristic predicts sexual involvement with a therapist. Although sexual involvement often has some predictable effects on clients, I do not believe that a clear pattern or syndrome can be found across the board in victims and thus I must reject the notion of a "client-therapist sex syndrome" that was proposed by Pope and Bouhoutsos (1986). Many of the characteristics they noted are also characteristics of other syndromes or victims in general, and we see great variability among victims.

I would, however, like to summarize here the various views in the literature on therapist characteristics and dynamics. Our experience and assessments of therapists have yielded a much more diverse picture (see Chs. 32 & 33) than that presented in the literature: either professional or popular.

THERAPIST CHARACTERISTICS AND DYNAMICS

In popular fiction the image of the therapist who becomes sexually involved with a client is that of a reasonably ethical, well-trained, and highly regarded professional who is overcome by lust when he encounters a particularly alluring female client. He may have feet of clay but he is not pathological.

F. Scott Fitzgerald in *Tender is the Night* (1933, p. 174) described Dr. Diver, his psychiatrist protagonist, when his patient asks if he finds her attractive:

He was in for it now, possessed by a vast irrationality. She was so near that he felt his breathing change but again his training came to his aid in a boy's laugh and a trite remark.

In the end Dr. Diver gave in, became involved, and thus sowed the seeds of his own destruction. Kittler observed (1986, p. 49): "Tender is the night, but, oh, so cruel is the blinding light of day."

Dr. Reuben Grayson in *A Kind of Rape* (Kane, 1974, p. 220) "was sexually entrapped" because his patient was "bewitchingly beautiful" and "fairly oozed sex appeal." He had a rough ending—shot to death by a patient's husband.

Then there was Dr. Saul Benjamin (played by Dudley Moore) in *Lovesick*, a 1983 comedy about a psychiatrist who falls in love with a patient despite warnings from the shade of Sigmund Freud and a challenge from a psychoanalyst who asks: "Do you want to throw everything away over a little countertransference?"

In stark contrast to these fictionalized accounts of therapists who sexually exploit their clients are the actual accounts by victims. They reveal an image of exploitative therapists as severely disturbed individuals who are sadistic and even violent at times. Dr. Renatus Hartogs, as described by Julie Roy in the book and movie *Betrayal* (Freeman & Roy, 1976), emerges as both evil and disturbed, and the relationship pictured is nothing like a romance.

Ellen Plasil's description of Dr. Leonard in *Therapist* includes not only sexual abuse but physical assaults on his clients and a hostile attacking approach to clients who challenged him, as in the following vignette: "You're scum," he muttered slowly with quiet venom. "You're real scum" (Plasil, 1985, p. 1).

The psychological testing done on Dr. Parzen, which emerged in the Walker v. Parzen civil suit was interpreted, in part, as follows: "although the patient may appear sociopathic, the possibility of a psychotic or pre-psychotic condition should be considered" (Walker & Young, 1986, p. 243). Sadism and abuse were described throughout this book.

The most recent account by a victim also describes a therapist who has abused multiple clients and is quite likely to be disturbed (Bates & Brodsky, 1988). Although they are presented only from the client's side, these books provide valuable insights into some varieties of therapist-client sexual relationships.

Thus far no exploitative therapist has written such an in-depth account, although McCartney (1966) described briefly his sexual contact with clients using his technique of "overt transference," and Shepard (1972b, p. 87) described an orgy during a group therapy session he was leading, although only briefly. Eigen (1973), describing his struggles with his sexual attraction to a client in an article entitled "The Call and the Lure," was able to muster more restraint than Dr. Benjamin did in *Lovesick*.

Rutter (in press), in *Sex in the Forbidden Zone: When Therapists, Doctors, Clergy, Teachers and Other Men in Power Betray Women's Trust*, provides an excellent account of his own near loss of control with a client. His fifth chapter, "Men in the Forbidden Zone: Snapshots of a Man Crossing the Boundary," has a very useful analysis of the stages in growing intimacy with a client or student, and some illustrative quotes on the experience of losing control. Since Eigen's (1973) early article on this topic little has been written concerning the experience and feelings of the therapist as he or she becomes involved with a client or begins to lose control.

Guy (1987, p. 217), in *The Personal Life of the Psychotherapist*, attempted to categorize under three headings therapist-related factors that contribute to the occurrence of therapist-client sex. They are, (a) pre-disposition; (b) work-related factors; and (c) life events. He cited an unpublished review of the literature by Scruggs in 1986 and concluded that the following were believed to be predisposing personality characteristics: "Don Juan Syndrome," doubts concerning sexuality and sexual identity, curiosity about someone else's sexual performance, masochistic or sadistic tendencies, a history of incest-like experiences, or a tendency to be exploitative.

Marmor (1953) cited a frequent attitude of grandiosity and superiority among therapists to be a causal agent. Holroyd & Brodsky (1977, 1980) and Brodsky (1986) linked these traits, in part, to societal attitudes toward power, status, and sex roles, although these tend to explain the actions of male therapists only. Zelen (1985) noted the tendency for males to take on the role of "father figures." Searles (1979, p. 431) wrote that sexual involvement results from the therapist's succumbing "to the illusion that a magically curative copulation will resolve the patient's illness which has resisted all the more sophisticated psychotherapy techniques...." Gorkin (1987, pp. 115-16) wrote, "Along with Searles, I would agree that when sexual activity does in fact occur, we may be sure that omnipotent and grandiose fantasies have overtaken both patient and therapist."

Goldberg (1986, pp. 201-202), in *On Being a Psychotherapist*, provided three hypotheses: (a) the practitioner's sense of superiority and a feeling of disdain for the client; (b) the therapist "believing that he/she has something of extraordinary value—something others have not been able to give the client"; and (c) that in cases in which the client is unable to pay the therapist, "The therapist, feeling exploited and used, may ask implicitly to be repaid in love for his caring and taking care of the client."

Dahlberg (1970, pp. 118-19), in his early review of nine cases, came up with a theory that combines predisposition and work-related factors. In his cases, the therapists were all in middle age, a time when "men tend to roam," and therapists have less opportunity to meet young women other than their clients. He theorized that these people entered the psychotherapy field when they were withdrawn, shy, and unattractive to the opposite sex, and when they reached middle age they were unable to avoid acting out their fantasies of "having beautiful girls throwing themselves at you without having to take the chance of being rejected...." This thesis is consistent with Holroyd & Brodsky's (1977, 1980) beliefs about societal attitudes.

Kottler (1986, p. 53) speculated on narcissism in the context of the therapist's work environment: "Restraining our egos is a challenge many of us will never quite overcome. What with our diplomas, titles, and carefully appointed chambers, it is hard for us not to take ourselves seriously."

Work-related stress is well documented among psychotherapists (e.g., Guy, 1987; Kottler, 1986) although it is difficult to separate distress related to being a psychotherapist from personal pathology present prior to entry to the field. Guy and Liaboe (1986) noted that there is considerable evidence of both positive and negative consequences to conducting psychotherapy on psychotherapists' interpersonal functioning.

Certainly we have considerable documentation for the incidence of emotional disorder in therapists. Watterson (1982, pp. 30-31), for example, wrote, "Psychiatry is the only field of practice with a significantly high incidence of psychiatric illness and of suicide among both residents and qualified specialists." Kaslow (1984, p. 21), in *Psychotherapy With Psychotherapists*, considered that "although most clinicians probably fall in the 'normal-neurotic' range, our ranks also include schizophrenics, borderline, and psychopathic personalities." Kaslow interviewed eight therapists who treated a number of clinical psychology trainees; half of them suggested that "there is a greater tendency for such students to be borderline narcissistic characters than there is for members of the general population" (Kaslow, 1984, p. 45).

Many commentators cite life events or situational stressors as a causative factor in therapists' sexual exploitation of clients. Dahlberg (1970, p. 119) noted that marital problems are a key issue, as did Guy (1987). Butler and Zelen (1977) found marital problems and recent separation and divorce to be characteristic of the sexual exploitative therapists whom they studied. Butler (1975), who interviewed 20 exploitative therapists found that 90% reported feeling vulnerable, lonely, or needy prior to the sexual involvement. These feelings, of course, could have reflected long-standing problems as opposed to situational distress. It may be worth noting, by way of base rates, that Norcross and Prochaska (1986a) found that about 80% of therapists experienced at least one episode of high distress in the preceding 3 years, and that 28% of them related to relationship problems. Wood, Cross, Lammers and Elliot (1985) are probably quite correct in stating the general belief that for a psychotherapist to engage in sexual misconduct he or she would have to be in emotional distress that is significant enough to cloud the judgment and reduce impulse control.

Last but not least, Sydney Smith (1984) discussed the sadistic element in many cases of therapist sexual exploitation of clients. This element is noteworthy in a number of the well-publicized cases. He posited a sado-masochistic dyad between therapist and client. This hypothesis is interesting given the format of most rape and sexual assault statutes that specify that the attack must be shown to be aimed at satisfying either sexual or aggressive impulses.

IS THIS JUST A NORTH AMERICAN PROBLEM?

Over the years the Walk-In Counseling Center has received inquiries from Europe, Australia, New Zealand, South America, and elsewhere concerning therapist-client sex. During the early 1970s I had several discussions and exchanged correspondence with Dr. Ian Baker, a Jungian analyst in Zurich, about several European cases. In 1986 Luepker, while living in Sweden, was consulted by colleagues concerning three Swedish therapist-client sex cases. Dr. Jacqueline Bouhoutsos (Personal Communication, Feb. 14, 1989), co-author of *Sexual Intimacy Between Therapists and Patients*, a book which has received wide distribution, has received communications from around the world concerning this topic.

Buell (1988), in researching an article for a German magazine, *Quick*, learned of several reports of such misconduct in Germany. In the article psychologist Peter Feldman is quoted as saying that the German Psychological Association has 3 to 4 of these cases each year, but that the real numbers are even higher because the patients are so dependent on their therapists that they don't readily talk about the sexual involvement. Feldman noted that although the psychologists are thrown out of the German Psychological Association, they can still practice as psychotherapists (psychologists aren't licensed). Dr. Reinhart Stalmann, a psychologist in Munich, is quoted as disapproving of such behavior, noting that if therapist and client want to become involved they need to terminate treatment for about 8 weeks and find out if they are really in love.

Besides the cases cited by Smith and Bisbing (1987) from England, there are hypnosis-related cases in Australia (Perry, 1979) and Holland (Hoencamp, in press) cited in the literature. It is quite possible that the international literature contains even more information on this topic. My review covers only American journals.

A FINAL NOTE

In recent years the popular press has covered the topic of therapist-client sex far more frequently, often in response to a civil suit against a therapist or some sort of scandal. Not infrequently the scandal involves either a major figure in the field, at least locally, or someone who holds offices in professional organizations or on a licensure board.

Anti-therapy books, such as Jeffrey Masson's (1988) *Against Therapy*, have no difficulty documenting widespread problems in our field and relatively ineffectual intervention by professional bodies and regulatory agencies. Apologists for professional misconduct, usually members of the profession, include people of good reputation and high visibility. Both Masson (1988) and Herman, Gartrell, Olarte, Feldstein, and Localio (1987) take Bettelheim to task for his defense of Jung's involvement with Sabina Spielrein in the *New York Review of Books* (Bettelheim, 1983) and the paperback edition of *A Secret Symetry: Sabina Spielrein Between Jung and Freud* (Carotenuto, 1984). Bettelheim wrote, in part:

> Whatever may be one's judgment of Jung's behavior toward Spielrein... one must not disregard its most important consequence: he cured her....
>
> In retrospect we ought to ask ourselves: what convincing evidence do we have that the same result would have been achieved if Jung had behaved toward her in the way we must expect a conscientious therapist to behave toward his patient? However questionable Jung's behavior was from a moral point of view—however unorthodox, even disreputable, it may have been—somehow it met the prime obligation of the therapist toward his patient: to cure her. True, Spielrein paid a very high price in unhappiness, confusion, and disillusion for the paticular way in which she got cured, but then this is often true for mental patients who are as sick as she was.
>
> (Carotenuto, 1984, p. 38)

The professional literature itself has meandered through the topic area and documents more in the way of inaction than of active and creative study leading toward solutions. In fact, some of the solutions suggested 20 years ago still have not been tried. Many preventive approaches that seem logical and reasonable are suggested year after year but never carried out. Indeed, there is considerable discontinuity between research and action.

The field itself is still not clear that it has a problem. Prominent psychologist Rogers Wright[5], as recently as 1985, stated that the growing number of allegations of sexual misbehavior by therapists were "motivated by the client/attorney's wish for a quick settlement" and were largely the result of consumer awareness of the "economic rewards of... sexual dalliance between provider and consumer" (Wright, 1985, pp. 112-114). He went on to complain that based on the "myth" that:

> sexual acting-out is most frequently between "older male therapists and younger female patients," ...a number of self-appointed lay and professional champions are, in true vigilante fashion, charging forth to protect young maidens from the importunements

---

[5]Dr. Wright is identified as having practiced for approximately 30 years, having served on the American Psychological Association Board of Directors, Board of Professional Affairs, and a number of committees and task forces. He is a former president of a state association, a member of the APA Insurance Trust, founding member and president of the Council for the Advancement of the Psychological Professions and Sciences, and has published widely (Wright, 1985, p. 118).

and advances of aging male therapists (chanting slogans of the "aha, I knew there was a dirty old man around here somewhere" theme). (pp. 112-13)

He mentioned "unscrupulous consumers" who "recognize the vulnerability of the provider" and who attempt "to exploit that vulnerability for economic gain" (p. 114). He asks of the consumer, "Are they so weak of will and so poorly integrated that they are unable to set limits for themselves or the provider?" (p. 116). Wright, in fact, asserted that "the therapist is every bit as much in the power of the consumer, as the consumer is in the power of the therapist" (p. 117). His solution is discipline by ethics committees and licensure boards. This, he feels, will avoid "the unfortunately, all too frequent, illogic of a court of law" (p. 118).

In the same vein, an assistant professor of psychiatry recently wrote,

The woman reporter on the telephone was determined to write a story portraying women as helpless victims of male psychiatrists' seductions. I'd talked with her for some time, trying to point out that this was a complicated subject with very few heroes or villains. I'd pointed out that no one had a scientifically valid idea of the actual number of such sexual affairs, but that even if we accepted the imaginary numbers of 5% to 13%, that was quite a low incidence that the profession did not need to feel ashamed about, but rather proud of. (emphasis added) (Clements, 1987, p. 556)

The author had little or no influence on the reporter and commented subsequently,

There were liberal quotes from "victims" who relished telling their story of suffering and betrayal. There were addresses of professional organizations to contact to report such outrages. (Clements, 1987, p. 556)

The remainder of Clement's article extolls the virtues of Freud's approach to transference and love.

On a more positive note, research and discussion are not only continuing but show signs of increasing. The December 1988 issue of the *Journal of Counseling and Development* (Vasquez & Kitchener, 1988) was devoted to therapist-client sex, with articles on everything from dual role relationships (Kitchener, 1988) to ethics training (Vasquez, 1988). The program for the 1989 national convention of the American Psychological Association included three programs on this topic as well as a day-long workshop on programs for impaired psychologists. We hope this research and discussion will lead to more constructive approaches to the problem of therapist-client sexual involvement in the near future.

CHAPTER 3

SURVEY OF INCIDENCE OF PSYCHOTHERAPISTS' SEXUAL CONTACT WITH CLIENTS IN WISCONSIN

Anthony Kuchan

The discussion of sexual contact in psychotherapy began well before the publication of the classic study by Kardener, Fuller, and Mensh in 1973; nevertheless their findings, which were reported in a major psychiatric journal, startled the professional world. The impact of their findings derived from the fact that, for the first time, our knowledge of sexual contact between psychotherapists and clients was based on data from a national sample of psychiatrists, who gave first-hand accounts of their own conduct, and not on anecdotal and single-case study information. To the dismay of almost everyone, the incidence of erotic contact between patients and psychiatrists was shown to be far higher than previous guesses would have suggested.

The debate in the professional community that followed the Kardener et al. article led to discussions at professional meetings, especially those of psychiatry (Davidson, 1977) and psychology (Hare-Mustin, 1974). Grunebaum, Nadelson, and Macht (1976) collected additional local survey data for the Massachusetts Psychiatric Society and presented their findings at the annual meeting of the American Psychological Association; these data were never published, however. Holroyd and Brodsky (1977) conducted a national survey of psychologists (modeled on the Kardener et al. study) and their findings evoked additional concern about the relatively high incidence of erotic contact with clients reported by psychologists. Two years later, another survey was conducted by Pope, Levinson, and Schover (1979); they reported similar findings for psychotherapists and also brought to light the fact that many psychologists in training had been sexually exploited by their professors.

Occasional reports of these surveys appeared in the press, and on-going but scattered discussions were held within the professional community; however, public attention to the therapist-client sex issue was intensified only after New York psychiatrist, Renatus Hartogs, author of a column on psychiatry for *Cosmopolitan Magazine*, was sued by several ex-clients for sexual exploitation. The Roy vs. Hartogs (1975) case, the best publicized of the suits, achieved widespread press coverage when, on March 20, 1975, the Associated Press reported that a jury had awarded $350,000 to the defendant (*Montreal Star*, March 20, 1975, p. 1). A year later the story of the trial was recounted by Freeman and Roy (1976) in *Betrayal*, which eventually was made into a TV movie with the same title. Then, in early 1978, the CBS weekly news program, "Sixty Minutes," presented a segment entitled "Fifty Minutes" that focused on the issue of sexual exploitation by therapists. In the succeeding 10 years, both professional and public awareness of the problem increased dramatically.

THE WISCONSIN EXPERIENCE

Like professionals elsewhere in the country, those in various psychotherapy fields and professional organizations in Wisconsin gradually became aware of the growing public debate on the issue of therapist abuse. Local civil suits and criminal actions had raised the issue in Wisconsin and, together with TV interview programs (e.g., the Phil Donahue Show), helped to convince the Chairman of the Judiciary Committee of the Wisconsin State

Assembly, as well as local consumers and practitioners, that something needed to be done. As a result, in 1983 Wisconsin became the first state to criminalize sexual contact between therapist and client. Section 940.22 Wisconsin statutes made it a Class A misdemeanor for any psychotherapist to engage in sexual contact with a therapy client. (See Ch. 42 for a detailed account of these events.)

In June 1984 the Wisconsin Psychological Association, under the leadership of its then-President, Andrew Kane, formed a Task Force on Sexual Misconduct by Psychotherapists and Counselors and appointed Gordon Polder as its first Chair. (See Ch. 41.)

At its first meeting the Task Force decided to obtain a clearer picture of the seriousness of the problem of therapist abuse in Wisconsin in order to set priorities for itself and, if the problem was found to be as widespread as suspected, to convince professionals within the state that it was not "only a California problem." It also would help to discover how the situation in Wisconsin might differ from that in other areas of the country.

Previous surveys, although provocative, had failed to provide a very clear picture of the therapist abuse problem. First of all, they surveyed either psychologists or psychiatrists; none surveyed both or other professional groups, such as the clergy or alcohol and drug counselors. Furthermore, published surveys reported only on sexual intercourse versus a broadly defined category of "erotic contact" instead of on specific and discrete sexual activities (Kardener et al., 1973; Holroyd & Brodsky, 1977; Pope et al., 1979). Thus, after 10 years of study and debate, little was still known about the actual types of sexual contact taking place in psychotherapeutic relationships. Consequently, an important feature of the present survey was to learn more about the various types of sexual behaviors occurring in psychotherapy.

METHOD

Given the serious impediments to obtaining accurate information on therapist abuse from either victims or offenders, the Task Force decided to seek information from all the licensed psychologists in the state through a survey that would ask for reports on the number of such cases that had come to their professional attention during the previous 3 years. I accepted the responsibility of designing a survey instrument that could be completed and distributed quickly and would yield a high return rate. The questionnaire was reviewed and modified at two successive meetings of the Task Force, and it was decided to limit the questionnaire to only fundamental questions in order to prompt a high rate of return.

The final version of the instrument (See Appendix U) was designed to determine how many cases of sexual misconduct had come to the attention of all licensed psychologists in Wisconsin during the period January 1, 1982 and (roughly) October 1, 1984. The psychologists surveyed were asked to identify, by year, (a) the number of clients they had seen who reported having had sexual contact with a previous therapist; (b) the gender of each victim; (c) the professional background of the offending therapists; (d) the gender of the offending therapists; (e) the type of sexual contact experienced and the frequency with which each act occurred; and (f) the responding therapist's opinion regarding the negative effect such experiences had had on each client's well-being. In addition to supplying some standard demographic identifiers (i.e., gender, years of practice, extent of practice), respondents were asked to indicate whether they would be willing to seek the permission of their victimized clients to be contacted by the Task Force for further study.

To encourage a high return rate, the 7 items were printed in loosely composed type to facilitate readability on two pages of Wisconsin Psychological Association letterheads, and were accompanied by a self-addressed, stamped envelope. In addition, respondents were guaranteed anonymity. The questionnaire was mailed to all licensed psychologists of record in Wisconsin. Respondents were given one week to reply, but at least 4 weeks were allowed before the survey period was closed.

After the questionnaire was sent to all licensed psychologists, representatives from other professional groups on the Task Force began to explore the possibility of circulating the questionnaire to members of their organizations as well. Eventually it was sent to a sample of social workers, Protestant clergy, rabbis, AODA (alcohol or drug) counselors, and employees of the Wisconsin Association of Outpatient Mental Health Facilities; the latter included occupational therapists, nurse practitioners, psychiatrists, nonlicensed psychology aides, and a miscellaneous group of counselors with B.A., M.S., M.S.E., and M.A. degrees. The process by which questionnaires were distributed to other professional groups was not as highly controlled as it had been for licensed psychologists. Most often a copy of the questionnaire (without a stamped, addressed, return envelope) was included along with another mailing to the membership or in a newsletter with a request that the completed form be returned to the Task Force. Hence, it was not always possible to determine exactly how many questionnaires had been distributed or the effect of not including a return envelope. The data collected on groups other than licensed psychologists, therefore, must be interpreted with considerable caution.

It is always easy to second-guess the use of a "quick and dirty" survey methodology of the type used in this study. However, it is important to remember that the survey was conducted to bring the problem to the attention of state psychologists without delay and to obtain information quickly so the Task Force could attack this complex and significantly hidden problem. Given the sensitivities of the professional community, a more elaborate and costly method of distribution would have been difficult to fund and could have delayed completion of the study. Furthermore, the Task Force believed that it was still in the exploratory stage of examining this problem and, thus, still within the context of "discovery." It always has been assumed that further research by the Task Force and others would be essential to attain a full understanding of the problem.

RESULTS AND DISCUSSION

The results of the survey are summarized in the following four tables. The discussion of the results accompany the presentation of the data themselves to facilitate interpretation. Inconsistencies in some category totals are due to missing or internally inconsistent data obtained in some responses.

The footnotes to Table 1 show that the clergy sample is composed primarily of Protestants. Of the 37 rabbis in southeastern Wisconsin who were sent questionnaires, only 2 returned them and neither had any cases to report. The Archdiocese of Milwaukee declined to participate as did the Wisconsin Psychiatric Association, although 22 returns were obtained from psychiatrists through different means.

The "Others" category includes various professionals and paraprofessionals whose responses were obtained through the Wisconsin Association of Outpatient Mental Health Facilities. The professional groups represented are occupational therapists, nurse practitioners, psychiatrists, some additional psychologists, workers with MS, MA, and

MSE degrees, and a miscellaneous group of workers with BA degrees (see Table 1, footnote 3).

The exact return rate for the entire survey cannot be calculated because the exact number of questionnaires distributed to groups other than psychologists and clergy is unknown (see Table 1). Overall, however, a total of more than 4,500 copies were distributed to all participating groups. The results are discussed in the order in which the data are presented in the four tables.

Table 1

1. Return Rate

Licensed psychologists and clergy had the highest return rate: 51.0% and 46.6%, respectively. In both cases the survey form was sent to members of the two groups in individual mailings and followed up with reminders. The active involvement of the W.P.A. as the sponsoring organization for the Task Force may well have contributed to the psychologists' high return rate.

Contrary to expectations, there often have been good return rates in surveys of psychologists on the topic of sexual misconduct by therapists and professors. Pope and Bouhoutsos (1986) reported Forer's 1968 unpublished survey of Los Angeles County psychologists which had a 70% return rate. National surveys of psychologists on this subject have had return rates of 70% (Holroyd and Brodsky, 1977), 59% (Pope, Keith-Spiegel, and Tabachnick, 1986), 48% (Pope, Levenson, and Schover, 1979), and 40.5% (Noel, 1987). Similar surveys of psychiatrists, however, have consistently reported lower return rates: Kardener et al. (1973), a 46% return rate from Los Angeles County, Perry (1976), a 33% return rate from New York and California; and Gartrell, Herman, Olarte, Feldstein, and Localio (1986), a low 26% from a national sample.

The study that compares most closely with ours in scope and target population was conducted by Bouhoutsos, Holroyd, Lerman, Forer, and Greenberg (1983). They surveyed California psychologists about a year before the Wisconsin study; their rate of return, however, was only 16%.

When questionnaires were sent in combination with other mailings (e.g., news letters) to social workers, AODA counselors, and others through the Wisconsin Association of Outpatient Mental Health Facilities, no follow-up reminders were mailed. In the cases of social workers and AODA counselors, where the return rates on similar groups in other studies are known, our return rates are quite low: 16.5% and 18.5%, respectively. It is worth noting further that many persons in the field of social work are not engaged in the practice of psychotherapy and, thus, may be less likely to respond to such a survey. Again, there is little comparable data except for the national survey of social workers by Gechtman and Bouhoutsos in 1983 which had a 54% return rate (Pope and Bouhoutsos, 1986). A survey of King County/Seattle area social workers reported a 37% return rate (Russell, 1984).

2. Percentage Reporting Cases

Of the 1,559 therapists in the state who returned questionnaires, 310 or 19.9% reported having encountered one or more persons who had engaged in sexual activity with a previous therapist. The fact that 655 cases were reported for the years 1982, 1983, and 1984 indicates that many therapists reporting such cases had seen more than one exploited

Table 1

Sexual Misconduct by Therapists: Survey Results

	Psychologists	Soc. Wkrs.	Clergy*	AODA** Coun.	Others***	Total
1. Number of surveys distributed:	837	2,000	923	750	Unknown	Unknown
a. Number returned:	427	329	430	139	234	1,559
b. Return percent:	51.0%	16.5%	46.6%	18.5%	Unknown	Unknown
2. No. of respondents reporting cases:	107	80	39	34	50	310
a. Percentage reporting cases:	25.1%	24.3%	9.1%	24.5%	21.4%	19.9%
3. Total number of cases reported:						
a. In 1982	63	55	27	15	33	193
b. In 1983	85	56	24	20	43	228
c. In 1984	74	69	24	24	43	234
d. Total cases reported:	222	180	75	59	119	655
e. Average reported per year	74	60	25	19.7	40	218.3

*	This sample is composed primarily of Protestant clergy. Thirty-seven rabbis from S.E. Wisconsin also were sent surveys; two returned them with no cases to report.

**	Alcohol or Drug Abuse

***	This sample is composed of respondents from a variety of professional orientations, all of whom were surveyed through the auspices of the Wis. Assoc. of Outpt. Mental Health Facil. Professional groups represented (with number of returns/number reporting cases shown in parentheses) are occupational therapists (29/0); nurse practitioners (25/7); psychiatrists (22/8); psychologists who were not polled, for whatever reason, in the licensed psychologist sample (52/15); holders of MS, MSE, and MA degrees who did not identify themselves as social workers or AODA counselors (72/15); and a miscellaneous group of mental health workers who are bachelor degree holders, counselors, etc. (34/5).

person during that 3-year period. Some of the people, however, probably consulted more than one follow-up therapist or counselor during the period of the study. A typical example of the range in number of cases reported is seen in the responses of licensed psychologists: 58 of the 107 practitioners (54.2%) had seen only one case whereas one psychologist had seen as many as 10 in that 3-year period. Of those reporting, 86.9% (93 of 107) saw no more than 3 cases, whereas only 2.8% (3 of 107) saw as many as 8 or more cases.

These data are difficult to compare with other survey data because they focus on specific time periods—something no other survey had done. Thus cases seen earlier in the psychotherapist's career (e.g., prior to 1982) were not included. Furthermore, the nature of this survey made it clear that the therapist reporting a case was expected to have direct knowledge of it whereas other investigators (e.g., Grunebaum, Nadelson, and Macht, 1976) asked respondents to report on the awareness of cases, regardless of source or time period. In that study, about 50% of the therapists surveyed reported knowledge of one or more cases. Noel (1987), in a national survey of psychologists, found 36.4% had been told of an incident by a client but another 50.7% had become aware of cases through colleagues only.

In a survey of social workers in the King County/Seattle area in the state of Washington, Russell (1984) found that 28% of her respondents had worked with clients who had reported sexual contact with a previous therapist. By contrast Gartrell et al. (1987) reported that 65% of the 1,423 psychiatrists who responded to their national survey reported treating patients who had been sexually involved with previous therapists.

The percentages in the Task Force study (Table 1) are comparable to Russell's (1984) 28% but well below those reported by Gartrell et al. (1986). However, it is important to bear in mind that the Wisconsin findings might have included much higher numbers if the survey had not been limited to cases that had come to light within a 3-year period.

The low percentage of clergy reporting cases is difficult to interpret except for the obvious possibility that clients seek out more traditional mental health professionals to deal with the consequences of sexual involvement with a therapist. In fact, as I discuss subsequently, nearly one-third of the cases reported by clergy involved another clergyperson.

As a final note, no relation was evident between return rate and percentage of respondents who reported cases of sexual misconduct.

3. Total Number of Cases Reported

Figures on the total number of cases reported per year show rather clearly that cases of misconduct were coming to light at a steady rate during the 3-year period of the study. It is important to understand that these data do not reveal the incidence of misconduct during these 3 years but rather, the incidence of reports of sexual involvement to a subsequent therapist; these reports bear no necessary relation to the period in the client's life when the abusive activity actually took place. One must understand also, that the 218.3 cases per year reported by therapists is probably an underestimate of the actual number reported in any given year because our survey did not reach all individuals who were engaged in the practice of therapy; surely some therapists received questionnaires but did not return them even though they may have had clients who reported some incidents of exploitation to them. The net effect of these factors is to reduce the actual number of cases reported. We also must understand, however, that overreporting also is likely to have occurred in those cases of a client/patient who consulted more than one follow-up therapist/counselor during the period of the study and thus more than one of these professionals would have reported the same case. Some inflation in reported cases also may have occurred if professionals reported on cases they learned about second-hand and the primary therapist/counselor also reported the same case.

Little data are known on the percentage of clients who return to therapy after having been sexually abused by a previous therapist. Stone (1980) reported that a large percentage of clients who were sexually involved with therapists returned to therapy at some later period. The only empirical information on this matter comes from a small sample study (N=28) by Vinson (1984) in which 79% of the subjects reported that they had sought further therapy. However, only 54% of the sample who sought further therapy actually mentioned the prior sexual relationship. Of those who kept the experience secret, 18% said they were unable to raise the issue and 14% felt that they didn't need to. Of the 21% who did not seek therapy, 7% said they didn't need it whereas 14% said they needed it but could not face it (Vinson, 1984).

An examination of results from available research, including those of our Task Force study, indicates that there is no means of weighing the relative influence of factors that lead to over- or underreporting of cases. For example, <u>one cannot conclude from the figures in Table 1 that 218 cases of sexual misconduct actually occur each year because we do not know how many incidents may have accumulated prior to 1982 and are simply reported in our three-year sample</u>, nor do we have any way of estimating the number of incidents that actually may have occurred but have gone unreported to subsequent therapists because the victim never pursued additional therapy or never reported such misconduct out of shame, fear, or other emotional blocks. We can say, however, that our figures reveal a surprisingly high frequency of sexual involvement, considering that 10 years ago such behavior was regarded as relatively rare.

Table 2

4. Gender of Clients

The results from this section of the study support the findings of a number of other investigators; that is, the victims of therapist-counselors' sexual misconduct are predominantly women. Except for the unusual proportions reported by AODA counselors (only 7 in 10 victims were women) all other professional groups reported essentially the same thing: women are far more subject to sexual exploitation than are men, and this finding is consistent over the entire 3 years of our sample period.

Worthy of note is the fact that AODA counselors reported an atypically high proportion of male victims: about 30% of the sample. Examining the data on the professional affiliation of the offending therapist reported, in Table 3, it may be significant that more than 44% of the cases the AODA counselors reported involved therapists in the "other" category, which includes many paraprofessional counselors and AODA counselors. Such groups are characterized by less professional training, as well as fewer ethical responsibilities, and a more peer-like relationship with clients. Given the influence of such factors, it is quite possible that female counselors are more likely to become involved with male clients. It also appears possible that some unique characteristics of clients and/or counselors show up in such settings and that they render males more susceptible to abuse than in other settings.

Virtually all studies in the literature have focused on the female client victim. Some data exist on the gender of the therapist but most other surveys have not inquired about the gender of the client. One noteworthy exception is the most recent national survey of

Table 2

Gender of Clients and Perpetrators

		Psychologists	Soc. Wkrs.	Clergy	AODA Coun.	Others	Total
4. Gender of Clients:		%	%	%	%	%	%
a. In 1982:	Male:	4 (6.7)	6 (10.9)	0 (0.0)	7 (46.7)	1 (2.9)	18 (9.5)
	Female:	56 (93.3)	49 (89.1)	26 (100)	8 (53.3)	33 (97.1)	172 (90.5)
b. In 1983:	Male:	6 (7.0)	9 (15.8)	1 (4.2)	6 (28.6)	3 (7.0)	25 (10.8)
	Female:	80 (93.0)	48 (84.2)	23 (95.8)	15 (71.4)	40 (93.0)	206 (89.2)
c. In 1984:	Male:	11 (14.9)	8 (11.8)	1 (4.2)	5 (21.7)	4 (9.5)	29 (12.6)
	Female:	63 (85.1)	60 (88.2)	23 (95.8)	18 (78.3)	38 (90.5)	202 (87.4)
d. Total:	Male:	21 (9.6)	23 (12.8)	2 (2.7)	18 (30.5)	8 (6.7)	72 (11.0)
	Female:	199 (90.4)	157 (87.2)	72 (97.3)	41 (69.5)	111 (93.3)	580 (89.0)
e. Grand Total:		220	180	74	59	119	652
5. Gender of offending therapist:		%	%	%	%	%	%
a. In 1982:	Male:	63 (97.0)	53 (94.6)	27 (100)	14 (93.3)	28 (84.8)	185 (94.4)
	Female:	2 (3.0)	3 (5.4)	0 (0.0)	1 (6.7)	5 (15.2)	11 (5.6)
b. In 1983:	Male:	80 (96.4)	47 (83.9)	22 (95.7)	15 (71.4)	40 (97.6)	204 (91.1)
	Female:	3 (3.6)	9 (16.1)	1 (4.3)	6 (28.6)	1 (2.4)	20 (8.9)
c. In 1984:	Male:	73 (98.6)	62 (91.2)	22 (91.7)	21 (87.5)	40 (95.2)	218 (94.0)
	Female:	1 (1.4)	6 (8.9)	2 (8.3)	3 (12.5)	2 (4.8)	14 (6.0)
d. Total:	Male:	216 (97.3)	162 (90.0)	71 (96.0)	50 (83.3)	108 (93.1)	607 (93.1)
	Female:	6 (2.7)	18 (10.0)	3 (4.0)	10 (16.7)	8 (6.9)	45 (6.9)

psychiatrists by Gartrell et al. (1986); they found 89% of the clients to be women and 11% male. These figures are identical to those obtained in our Task Force survey. Schoener and Milgrom (1987) estimated an approximate 93%/7% female-to-male ratio in the more than 800 cases they have seen.

5. Gender of Therapists

Just as women were found in our study to be overwhelmingly more likely than men to report sexual abuse by a past therapist, so it was not surprising to find that male therapists were the perpetrators in such relationships by an even more overwhelming majority—a 93% to 7% margin. These findings were absolutely consistent for all three reporting years and for all responding professional groups; furthermore, they are highly consistent with results from other studies showing approximately a 9 to 1 ratio of male to female offenders.

In the study by Gartrell et al. (1986), 88% of the cases reported by their sample consisted of male therapist/female patient whereas 7.6% were male therapist/male patient, 3.5% were female therapist/male patient and only 1.4% were female therapist/female patient. By contrast, in Schoener and Milgrom's (1987) report that 83% of their cases were of the male therapist/female client type, their second most common relationship was female/female (10% of their cases). Male/male relationships accounted for approximately 5% of their cases and female therapist/male client cases were found in only about 2%. In the psychiatric sample, then, about 95% of the perpetrators were male and only 5% female whereas in the Walk-In Counseling Center sample the proportion was about 88% male and 12% female perpetrators. Russell (1984), whose sample was smaller (N=51), reported 88% male therapist/female client relationships and 6% each for same-sex contacts; thus 94% of the offenders were identified as male.

Table 3

6. Professional Affiliation of Offending Therapists

In what may be one of the more controversial findings of our study, the therapists accounting for a substantial number of the cases of sexual involvement reported were psychiatrists, 33.8%, and psychologists, 18.7%, the two professional groups which enjoy the highest levels of professional autonomy and the clearest degree of social and legal recognition. Except for clergy, who reported a higher incidence of abuse by psychologists than by psychiatrists, all other groups reported a significantly higher rate for psychiatrists by a ratio of nearly two to one. It is also relevant to note that of the 22 psychiatrists who responded to questionnaires received through the Wisconsin mental health centers mailing, 8 reported a total of 24 abuse cases of which 12 were abuses by psychiatrists. Because of the limited size of the sample, these results were not reported separately but were pooled in the category, "Others." Of the 52 psychologists employed in the same mental health centers who were also included in the "Others" category (instead of the major group of licensed psychologists), 15 listed 24 cases of abuse that were almost evenly distributed among psychologists (5), psychiatrists (6), and social workers (6). It also may be noteworthy that, for both clergy and AODA counselors, the likelihood was greater that the abuse would be reported to another counselor of the same type. What cannot be discerned from the data is whether the clients sought help from these counselors or contacted them to complain about the abuse.

Comparable information in the literature on the professional affiliation of perpetrators is scarce. In one of the few studies that includes these data which were collected in a national survey of psychiatrists, the previous therapists who had sexually abused clients were

Table 3

Professional Affiliations of Perpetrators

<u>Source of Report</u>

Perpetrator's Profession:	Psychologists	Social Workers	Clergy	AODA Counselors	Others	Total
	%	%	%	%	%	%
a. Psychologist:	40 (18.3)	40 (22.2)	18 (23.7)	6 (9.8)	18 (15.4)	122 (18.7)
b. Psychiatrist:	96 (43.8)	60 (33.3)	13 (17.1)	13 (21.3)	39 (33.3)	221 (33.8)
c. Physician:	15 (6.8)	6 (3.3)	3 (4.0)	0 (0.0)	12 (10.3)	36 (5.5)
d. Social Worker:	26 (11.9)	26 (14.4)	5 (6.6)	5 (8.2)	21 (17.9)	83 (12.7)
e. Marriage Counselor:	7 (3.2)	5 (2.7)	7 (9.2)	3 (4.9)	1 (.9)	23 (3.5)
f. Clergy:	13 (5.9)	18 (10.0)	24 (31.6)	7 (11.5)	11 (9.4)	73 (11.2)
g. Other:	22 (10.1)	25 (13.9)	6 (7.9)	27 (44.3)	15 (12.8)	95 (14.5)
h. Total:	219	180	76	61	117	653

psychiatrists (48%), psychologists (27.4%), social workers (7.2%), clergy (9.1%), lay therapists (5.7%), and 2.7% unspecified (Gartrell et al., 1987). Russell's (1984) survey of social workers found 25% of perpetrators to be psychiatrists; 23%, psychologists; 18%, MSWs; 6%, pastoral counselors; 18%, others; and 10% unknown. The one consistent finding in both these studies and ours is that psychiatry and psychology account for the largest percentage of cases with psychiatry regularly showing the higher frequency rate.

These comparison figures must not be interpreted to mean that any professional group as a whole is more or less likely to abuse therapy clients sexually by a given numerical factor. Also it should be carefully noted that the number of reported cases does not correspond exactly to the number of offenders in a professional group. From previously published research we know, for example, that offending therapists often are likely to have taken advantage of many different clients; indeed, 80% of these individuals are known to have had more than one victim, which means that one such person probably accounts for a number of the cases reported in our total figure. Nevertheless, these findings suggest that the temptation to engage in sexual contact with clients may be related to the profession's relative freedom from outside supervision and/or to a progressive reduction in self-monitoring that comes from the complacency born of uncritical social support and approbation. Apparently, serious errors of judgment in the management of therapeutic relationships are not prevented and, in some paradoxical way, even may be abetted by the high station and public trust. Obviously, this matter is far from clear and needs more systematic research.

Table 4

7. Type and Frequency of Sexual Contact

The types of sexual contact listed in Table 4 along with the frequency of occurrence for each type are the best estimates our respondents could provide. Unfortunately, the formulation of the question on this subject did not allow clear and unequivocal frequency counts of discrete sexual events. Indeed, it is doubtful that any question, no matter how clearly stated, would elicit an accurate frequency count, given the fact that sexual exchanges varied a great deal across the sample of abused clients and that the descriptions of contact were based upon second-hand information, which itself was likely to have been subjected to memory distortions by client-victims. To complicate matters further, there was no way to distinguish a single incident of erotic hugging from a sexual exchange that included a series of sexual activities within a single episode. Nevertheless, these data are given, despite the problems noted, in order to develop some picture of the patterns of sexual contact that occur between therapists and clients.

Not surprisingly, sexual intercourse, fondling, erotic hugging/kissing, and suggestive behavior were the most commonly reported erotic behaviors. Oral sex, genital exposure, and masturbation were listed far less often by respondents and anal intercourse was reported in only a very small proportion of the cases.

Previous surveys provide little in the way of comparable data. Earlier studies (e.g., Kardener et al., 1973; Holroyd and Brodsky, 1977) asked respondents only about intercourse versus other erotic contacts. In an early dissertation that used the case study method, Belote (1974) reported that in 24 of the 25 cases she studied, sexual intercourse usually was preceded by kissing, petting, or massage, and fellatio and cunnilingus usually were involved also. In another dissertation with a sample of 65, D'Addario (1976) reported the following types of sexual contact: kissing (96.9%), fondling (95.4%), sexual intercourse (83.1%), oral/genital contact (60%), and other, including anal intercourse, masturbation, and verbal enticements (6.2%). Taking a somewhat different approach to classifying sexual conduct, Vinson (1984) reported on the "greatest degree of sexual involvement" between therapist and client as follows: intercourse (75%), oral/genital contact (4%), kissing/fondling (11%), words only (11%).

Gartrell et al. (1986) reported that 74% of the sexual relationships between therapist and patient identified in their study included genital contact, whereas 26% included only kissing, fondling, and/or nudity.

Given the difficulties discussed earlier regarding our current data, exact comparisons are not possible. It is worth noting, however, that our figures for the incidence of sexual intercourse or genital contact seem low in comparison to other studies. Consistent with the other studies, however, we found that the common behaviors were sexual intercourse, fondling, and erotic hugging/kissing. Although more research is needed on the types of sexual contact occurring in therapeutic relationships, some ethical advocates argue that such information is irrelevant because any breach of sexual boundaries, no matter how limited, exposes the client to a rupture of trust and, thus, to the psychic injury it entails.

Table 4

Type of Sexual Contact and Impact on Client

	Psycho-logists	Social Workers	Clergy*	AODA Counselors	Others*	Total
7. Type and frequency of sexual contact:						
a. Intercourse:	111	100	48	24	52	335
b. Fondling:	63	67	36	13	30	209
c. Oral Sex:	21	16	10	10	9	66
d. Masturbation:	19	9	1	5	6	40
e. Erotic Hugging/ Kissing:	63	73	23	15	26	200
f. Suggestive Behavior:	70	75	21	19	30	215
g. Anal Intercourse:	5	2	0	1	1	9
h. Genital Exposure:	5	17	7	1	12	42
8. Degree of respondent endorsement of "negative effect" statement:						
a. Strongly Agree:	120	136	44	39	73	412
b. Agree:	63	32	20	11	30	156
c. Neutral or Uncertain:	27	9	10	5	13	64
d. Disagree:	3	3	2	0	0	8
e. Strongly Disagree:	0	0	0	0	0	0
Total:	213	180	76	55	116	640
9. Weighted scale score by all respondents:	+1.41	+1.67	+1.40	+1.62	+1.51	+1.52

*The inconsistencies in category totals in these tabulations stem primarily from missing or internally inconsistent data obtained in some surveys.

8 & 9. <u>Degree to Which Experience was Harmful</u>

Our figures assess the degree to which the responding mental health professionals believed that sexual contact between therapists and clients produced "a serious and negative effect on the psychological well-being of clients." The weighted scale score was ascertained by assigning a score of +2 to "strongly agree" and +1 to "agree" endorsements of this statement, 0 to "neutral or uncertain" endorsements, and -1 and -2 to "disagree" and "strongly disagree" endorsements, respectively. These scores then were multiplied by the number of endorsements recorded for each category, and the sums were added and divided by the total number of respondents in each professional group to produce the weighted scale score. A score of +2.0, therefore, indicates that every respondent in the group endorsed the "negative effect" statement with a "strongly agree" response, and a -2.0 indicates that everyone answered with a "strongly disagree" response.

The findings show, without exception, that every professional group polled believes that sexual contact between therapists and clients/patients is highly likely to have an injurious effect on the latter; not a single one of our 310 respondents who reported cases of sexual contact "strongly disagreed" with the statement. Among the very small minority who "disagreed," the respondents' explanatory comments indicated that the therapy often had been terminated technically prior to the onset of sexual contact or that the client/patients had not reported any special negative effect from the previous liaison. The majority of respondents, however, were likely to cite effects that were highly destructive to the psychological welfare of their clients.

SUMMARY AND CONCLUSIONS

The findings of this Task Force study seem to show that a much higher incidence of sexual contact is present between client/patients and therapists in the state of Wisconsin than was previously thought. It was the consensus of our respondents that such activity is highly destructive to the well-being of clients in nearly all cases. If true, the fact that 655 such cases in Wisconsin were reported for the 3-year period surveyed amounts to a serious consumer-welfare problem that needs the immediate and concerted attention by all professional groups who are committed to the ethical practice of psychotherapy and counseling. Consistent with data in the professional literature, the Wisconsin data show that although the exploitation of female clients by male therapists is the common type of exploitative relationship, males also may be victims, and female therapists also may be perpetrators. Consistent with other surveys is our finding that therapists from all professional groups contribute to the problem of therapist abuse although the members of the most highly trained and legally protected groups are those cited most frequently.

Our survey, like surveys of impaired practitioners (Schwebel, Skorina, and Schoener, 1988), appears to have contributed significantly to increased awareness of this problem in Wisconsin. Some of the attention it attracted to the work of the early Task Force doubtless helped to foster the growth of the Task Force into a Coalition (see Ch. 41). It also affected people already active in the Task Force by confirming the group's suspicion that therapist abuse was more widespread, even in a conservative state like Wisconsin, than had been believed earlier. This recognition galvanized the group's determination to press its agenda forward out of our enhanced awareness that the welfare of future therapy clients, the recovery of victim/survivors, and the integrity of therapy professionals themselves all required the help that such a Coalition could offer.

The results of the survey received good media coverage, including an extensive article in a major newspaper (Rosenberg, 1984). Much to our surprise, however, there was virtually no response to the publicized results. "Quiet" crimes such as abuse by therapists are, much like incest, accompanied by so much embarrassment and disbelief that public avoidance and denial continue to be the primary response to revelations. If this speculation is correct, it is all the more reason for groups like the Coalition to exist and to strive for more open recognition of the problem by professionals, therapy clients, and society at large.

CHAPTER 4

SEXUAL INVOLVEMENT AND THE ABUSE OF POWER IN PSYCHOTHERAPEUTIC RELATIONSHIPS[1]

Ellen T. Luepker
and
Gary Richard Schoener

Sexual involvement between client and therapist is one example of the abuse of power that occurs in some psychotherapeutic relationships. In developing this theme in this chapter we explore some characteristics of the psychotherapy situation that set the stage for potential abuse and then we examine the evolution of sexual involvement at various stages in the psychotherapeutic relationship. The possible interventions at each stage also are discussed.

BACKGROUND

The growing public and professional discussion of problems in psychotherapy during the past decade have focused on possible harm to the client and on the psychotherapist's power. In 1980, for example, Robitscher published *The Powers of Psychiatry* in which he briefly examined, from a number of perspectives, power issues in the delivery of mental health services. Five years earlier, when Dorothy Tennov's (1975) book, *Psychotherapy: The Hazardous Cure*, was published, she took only scant note of the problem of therapists' sexual involvement with clients. Each book, of course, reflected the time in which it was written.

By 1982, Edelwich and Brodsky (in *Sexual Dilemmas for the Helping Professional*) focused considerable attention on the power dynamics of the psychotherapeutic relationship insofar as they relate to sexual involvement between therapist and client.

Even more recently, Luepker, (1986, 1989) explored the parallels between sexual exploitation of clients by therapists and parent/child incest (see also Ch. 5). White (1986) in his fine book *Incest in the Organizational Family*, also gave a useful analysis of the parallels (see Appendix A).

Unfortunately, other than Edelwich and Brodsky's (1982) brief discussion of a client's potential power after termination of therapy, there has been practically no discussion of how the power relationship can become topsy-turvy when the client decides to file a complaint.[2]

---

[1] The origin of this chapter dates back to 1983 when the two authors collaborated on a paper of the same title for a conference on power issues in the psychotherapeutic relationship. Unfortunately, the conference was cancelled and the paper was not put into final form. The paper was updated for the present publication.

[2] Although it deals with a malpractice case unrelated to sexual misconduct, *Defendant,* by Charles and Kennedy (1985) offers some insight into what it's like to be a psychotherapist on trial. "Family Stress During Malpractice Litigation" (Johnson, 1988), a videotape available from the AMA Auxillary, also provides a useful look at stress related to being on trial.

Gonsiorek's discussion (Ch. 33) on the treatment of sexually exploitative therapists provides examples of the effect on therapists of being confronted or charged with misconduct.

To begin the exposition of our theme, we start by examining the psychotherapeutic relationship and the power of the therapist in that relationship.

THE PSYCHOTHERAPEUTIC RELATIONSHIP

Two cornerstones of the psychotherapeutic relationship provide the basis for either helping or harming a client.

1. The socially defined role of the therapist is that of a skilled and caring helper who, presumably, is emotionally healthy and who can put his/her personal needs aside to assist a client.

2. The socially defined role of the client is that of a person with a problem which he/she cannot solve on his/her own, has faith in and expects the therapist to help him/her to change, and is able to share problems with a degree of candor uncommon in other interpersonal relationships.

In all human relationships, emotional and sexual attractions are likely. In the psychotherapeutic relationship, however, it is assumed that the therapist will not allow such feelings—therapist's, client's, or mutual—to obstruct the efficacy of the therapeutic relationship. Codes of Ethics and some statutes rely on this assumption. Beyond ordinary emotional and sexual attraction, it is not unlikely that the encapsulated intimacy of the intense sharing of feelings and personal/family secrets within a 45-minute to one-hour session will lead to heightened familiarity. Furthermore, it is assumed that the phenomenon of "transference," through which feelings connected with significant persons in a client's life are displaced on the therapist, will further heighten the emotions between client and therapist. The same is true for "countertransference," in which the therapist's own life experience and his or her feelings in reaction to the client become an issue.

The confidentiality inherent in the relationship, which is prescribed by professional ethics and law, may lead to a situation of extreme secrecy in which only the client and therapist know what is transpiring between them. Most client visits are not supervised, of course, which may mean that the only reality testing possible is by the two participants—client and therapist—themselves. Even when there is supervision, the therapist usually decides what to share with the supervisor or case consultant and when to communicate this information.

Furthermore, the psychotherapeutic relationship has other potential pitfalls. To name a few:

1. The therapist's financial rewards, in some senses, are contingent on the client's staying ill or dependent, at least for a time.

2. The client seeks validation as a "good person" from the therapist whereas the therapist looks for validation as a "helper" from the client.

3. Intelligent, emotionally responsive, and otherwise attractive clients often are preferred for outpatient psychotherapy.

4. When a client becomes healthy, he or she may be far more rewarding to talk with, which may lead to the therapist's reluctance to terminate.

5. Because clients use therapists as models, even the client's values may become subservient to those of the therapist; the client may agree to suggestions by the therapist to actions (e.g., sexual contact) that contradict the client's value system.

6. The therapist typically sets most or all the rules in the relationship. Most clients lack even rudimentary knowledge of what is acceptable behavior by a therapist.

7. Clients often come into therapy without the adequate knowledge needed to be a good consumer: how to inquire about a therapist's qualifications; how to shop around for a therapist; and the importance of challenging things that do not seem right.

SEXUAL INVOLVEMENT WITH CLIENTS AS A TYPE OF ABUSE

In our clinical experience, which includes cases illustrating various abuses of power (e.g., financial exploitation, violations of confidentiality and privacy, isolating clients from others, retaining clients too long in therapy, and violence), sexual abuse has been the most common. The reason, in part, may be that it is the most easily identified and best publicized of the abuses, and we are recognized as offering services for those abused in this fashion.

The concern with this problem is a very old one. Many physicians still take the Hippocratic Oath, written more than 2,000 years ago, that admonishes medical practitioners to refrain from the seduction of males or females encountered in the course of their professional work. The ethics codes of various psychotherapeutic professions (social work, psychiatry, psychology, marriage and family counseling) cite some characteristics of the psychotherapeutic relationship that may lead to problems. For example, the "Ethical Standards of Psychologists" (American Psychological Assn., 1981) focuses on the power issue (the underlining is added):

Psychologists are continually cognizant of their own needs and of their inherently powerful position vis-à-vis clients, in order to avoid exploiting their trust and dependency. Psychologists make every effort to avoid dual relationships with clients and/or relationships which might impair their professional judgment or increase the risk of client exploitation.... Sexual intimacies with clients are unethical. (p. 4)

The "Principles of Medical Ethics," as annotated for psychiatry (American Psychiatric Assn., 1985), cites the vulnerability of both client and therapist, and the importance of not abusing power:

Section 1

A physician shall be dedicated to providing competent medical service with compassion and respect for human dignity.

1. The patient may place his/her trust in his/her psychiatrist knowing that the psychiatrist's ethics and professional responsibilities preclude him/her gratifying his/her own needs by exploiting the patient. This becomes particularly important

because of the essentially private, highly personal, and sometimes intensely emotional nature of the relationship established with the psychiatrist.

and

Section 2

A physician shall deal honestly with patients and colleagues, and strive to expose those physicians deficient in character or competence, or to engage in fraud or deception.

1. The requirement that the physician conduct himself with propriety in his/her profession and all the actions of his/her life is especially important in the case of the psychiatrist because the patient tends to model his/her behavior after that of his/her therapist by identification. Further, the necessary intensity of the therapeutic relationship may tend to activate sexual and other needs and fantasies on the part of both patient and therapist, while weakening the objectivity necessary for control. Sexual activity with a patient is unethical.

2. The psychiatrist should diligently guard against exploiting information furnished by the patient and should not use the unique position of power afforded him/her by the psychotherapeutic situation to influence the patient in any way not directly relevant to the treatment goals.

EVOLUTION OF SEXUAL INVOLVEMENT AND INTERVENTION STRATEGIES

Phase I—Seeking Help: Many clients tell us that they do not know how to choose or evaluate therapists. They also are uninformed or unclear about the propriety of touch in therapy and the rules for sexual involvement. Most feel quite vulnerable and are hesitant to trust their "gut" feelings that the sexual touching is improper. Therapists may exploit this vulnerability effectively. For example, after one therapist touched a woman's breast and asked if she felt anxious, which she did, the therapist then steered the discussion to her supposed need to get over her sexual anxiety.

Clearly, consumers need more and broader information, especially on psychotherapeutic services. Such information should include the following: the importance of shopping around for a therapist, how to shop around, questions to ask a potential therapist, how to check on credentials, and the importance of raising doubts or concerns about treatment methods and the fact that sexual involvement with a therapist or counselor is always inappropriate. The brochure, "Making Therapy Work For You," is an excellent example of such information (see Appendix Z).

Phase II—Early Therapy: Some therapists introduce touch during the very first session and even may initiate sexual touching that quickly. At this time the client may go along with anything the therapist suggests or demands. Some clients succumb to flattery by the therapist which might not be taken seriously in another setting with another person. In still other situations there is nothing erotic or sexual, but the client begins to develop considerable dependency on the therapist. In one case involving a psychoanalyst who saw the client four times per week, no sex was initiated until the second year of therapy.

Usually, in early therapy, the client has a sense of relief that finally he or she has gotten to someone who can help and there may be some hope that his or her problems can be resolved. When sex is introduced, a client who lacks a sex life outside of therapy reports initially feeling pleasure or a renewed sense of sexual well-being. A client whose self-esteem is low often reports feeling "high" and "happy," and that the therapist's sexual interest has signalled full acceptance by the therapist. Fantasies even may begin and may center on marriage or longer term involvement with the therapist.

Clients who feel that the sex is inappropriate often go along with it, even if they feel considerable guilt and shame. We have seen clients who either do not trust their "gut feelings" that the sex is wrong or idealize the therapist and his power. In some instances, clients who have become dependent on psychotropic medication tolerate the sex in exchange for the medication.

During the early phase of the therapy, the clients we have interviewed usually have not tried to break off the relationship and may have made only limited efforts to do away with the sex. The majority of early therapy situations that are brought to our attention are those in which the therapy is gradually becoming more and more erotic and is not under anyone's control. The therapist or client or both have become concerned and want help to re-establish proper boundaries. In such situations joint meeting(s) of client, therapist, and a consultant can unravel the problem and help to design a remedy, which usually involves a referral or supervision. Unfortunately, we seldom have the opportunity to do such interventions.

It is important, during an intervention, to carefully re-examine the development of the therapeutic relationship in all its aspects—not just the erotic facets. It is useful to discuss positive as well as negative feelings, as described in Chapters 6, 12, and 28.

Phase III—Middle Therapy: In some instances the sexual involvement begins during this stage of therapy when the client and therapist have gotten to know each other well and the client's trust in the therapist has developed. Sometimes the growing involvement is like a romance, or reflects the increasing attractiveness of the client who is showing improvement and may have changed in physical appearance and/or become more self-confident, or reflects the therapist's feeling of greater safety with the client. Conversely, the sexual involvement may be stimulated by the client's expression of extreme vulnerability; e.g., unresolved grief. And sometimes the involvement is stimulated by events outside of therapy in the client's life, the therapist's life, or in the lives of both (e.g., divorce, separation).

It is important to recognize that sexual relationships frequently occur in the context of other boundary breakdowns, such as the development of a social relationship between the therapist and client, or the therapist's employing the client. These breakdowns, in turn, may have been potentiated by mutual neediness, for example, a lonely client seeing a lonely therapist; a therapist overwhelmed by the demands of family or professional life who employs a client as a housekeeper, handyman, or typist; or a client who needs a job who seeks work from the therapist.

Sometimes when sex is initiated at some mid-point in therapy, a client or therapist or both may realize, after one or two encounters, that sex and therapy do not mix and they may terminate the sex, the therapy, or both. At other times, one or both parties perceive the sex as a healthy development and the involvement continues, fueled by fantasies about future happiness.

Things may be going badly in this phase if the sexual involvement began earlier in therapy. The client and, possibly, the therapist, may be isolated still further from family and friends; the secret of the client's "special" sexual involvement is shared only with the therapist. The client's isolation may be extreme. Meanwhile, spouses and family may perceive the distance but not know how to interpret it. In some cases clients lose motivation to work on their marriages and these suffer deterioration.

At some point, however, the future of the relationship usually becomes an issue. Eventually, fantasies about becoming long-term lovers or marriage partners must be tested. In addition, the therapist may begin to tire of the client or the client's dependency. The therapist may start to fear the client since he or she now is in a position to ruin the therapist's career. Clients may begin to doubt the role and/or propriety of the sex and begin to feel extreme guilt and depression. If breakoff of the relationship is threatened, clients often experience traumatic disillusionment. Suicide attempts or even attacks on the therapist may occur. Clients begin looking for ways to regain their lost sense of personal power and control.

During this phase in the therapy clients who are sexually involved with their therapists sometimes are at their lowest ebb. They are unlikely to be able to assert themselves or to look for outside help. In their desperation some attempt suicide or blurt out information on the sexual relationship in a group session or to a friend.

At this point in therapy some clients call on their reserve strength and begin moving toward leaving the relationship. Sometimes a therapist pushes a client to leave the relationship, although there is rarely a true termination. In some cases a client goes to see another therapist but gives no names or details about the troubled therapy relationship. Often the consultation lasts but one or two sessions, and the client is usually unable to break off the relationship with the first therapist.

In the best of circumstances, friends, family, or outside professionals are able to respond helpfully and the client gets some assistance in trying to disengage from the relationship. However, in many situations the client's report is discounted and the client is then thrust back to the therapist because of confusion, and a sense of alienation from other supports.

Phase IV—End of Therapy: Clients pushed out of or those who decide to leave therapy when their fantasized "life ever after" with the therapist is clearly not about to happen may struggle with a variety of feelings. Loss, grief, and despair over having been rejected by or disconnected from the therapist and over other relationships that may also have been lost tend to predominate. Sadness alternates with anger and the client is confused about what, if anything, was "real" about the therapy. Here again the client is often at risk of suicide.

Clients are uncertain of what to do with their mixed feelings about the therapist and usually are very ambivalent about whether to try to get further help from another therapist. In most instances a true termination does not occur; rather there is an ill-defined departure or agreement not to continue seeing each other. Some clients continue some sort of relationship with the therapist after therapy terminates, via phone, letter, or casual contact. In some cases the therapist quickly terminates the therapy in writing in order to justify having a sexual involvement, hoping thereby for less risk of legal consequences.

Most of our caseload comes out of the subset of clients who have left therapy. Sometimes the termination has been recent, sometimes years earlier. Because of the lack of problem resolution and the absence of a proper termination, even years later the client still may be struggling with the same issues like a client who has just left therapy. This lack of closure with the first therapist interferes with many clients' ability to seek help from a new therapist and to form a therapeutic alliance.

Clients often need individual therapy as described by Luepker (Ch. 12) to clarify the issues remaining from the previous therapy as well as to deal with the personal problems that led them to seek help in the first place. They need to sort out their often mixed feelings, including both the positive and negative feelings about the therapist. They need to develop trust in their own ability to accurately perceive reality and to clarify options for safeguarding themselves in the future. A group of the type described by Luepker (Ch. 14) can be immensely helpful in providing validation.

Advocacy (see Ch. 26) can be very helpful to clients considering complaint options. It is important that they obtain information so they can weigh the various options and make an informed choice of what they want to do.

THE POST-TERMINATION SITUATION

Sexual/romantic relationships between clients and therapists following therapy termination are discussed in Part 6 of this manual. However, a few comments are in order here.

Like all relationships during therapy, the degree of asymmetry in power varies markedly in the post-termination situation. In some instances, clients feel that the therapist still exerts considerable power. In fact, in Minnesota a therapist can be subject to criminal charges or civil suit if it can be shown that the client's level of continuing dependency prevents her or him from fully exercising independent judgment on becoming sexually involved with the therapist.

When client-therapist romantic/sexual relationships develop after termination of therapy, transitions in the balance of power can occur which are not unlike those observed in relationships that begin during therapy. The client initially may idealize the therapist, feel gratitude, and be quite infatuated, making the therapist quite powerful. Even when clients strive for an equal relationship it is difficult if not impossible to attain because the therapist has learned a great deal about the client in the context of an unequal relationship (in therapy). As time passes, the idealized image of the therapist may become tarnished as his/her personal problems become visible to the client. This also happens if the therapist seems to be using the client to meet his or her own needs, or if the therapist tries to remain the dominant figure in the relationship.

Power struggles may develop and the client may make vague threats to report the therapist. Or, the client may demand that the couple see a therapist, something which may be very threatening to the therapist. In the end the therapist may feel quite exposed and helpless and try to bribe the client into silence. The client may decide to take action against the therapist by filing a civil suit, making a licensure complaint, or reporting the therapist to colleagues.

It should be noted that this sort of disintegration in the relationship may occur at any time, even years later. Thus, one must be careful in making judgments of post-therapy relationships that appear to be harmonious. Clinical case data, such as those of Rigby-Weinberg (1986), in which post-termination lesbian relationships between therapist and client were characterized as on-going and satisfying for both parties, should be examined cautiously in this context. At times such relationships may indeed "work out" but it is difficult to weigh outcomes until some time has passed.

A FINAL NOTE

Although the power differential between therapist and client is recognized in ethics codes and laws and is discussed in professional settings, some therapists continue to believe that they are on equal terms with their clients and have little power over them. Some therapists acknowledge the power differential during most of therapy but claim that it is equalized by the time of termination and the post-termination relationship, consequently is one of equals.

A much larger group of therapists seem unaware that the power differential can shift, sometimes dramatically, if professional boundaries are not maintained. Sexual involvement with a client often sets the stage for such a shift in power. Many therapists cannot imagine how helpless and vulnerable they may become if a client decides to file a complaint. They seem unable to picture a dependent and adoring client as angrily turning on them and destroying their careers.

The literature contains numerous examples of clients who have been exploited and harmed by therapists who abuse their power, but not of accounts of the consequences to a therapist when a client files a lawsuit or complaint. Whether a clearer understanding of this contingency would act as a deterrent remains to be seen. We hope that therapists will take note of the risk.

CHAPTER 5

SEXUAL EXPLOITATION OF CLIENTS BY THERAPISTS: PARALLELS WITH PARENT-CHILD INCEST

Ellen T. Luepker

The parallels between parent-child incest and the sexual exploitation of clients by therapists have been noted by a number of investigators (Bates and Brodsky, 1988; D'Addario, 1977; Kardener, 1974; Marmor, 1972; Pope and Bouhoutsos, 1986) as well as Fortune (Ch. 6 in this volume). White's (1986) examination of the organizational context of sexual exploitation even includes a detailed comparison of the incest dynamic in the nuclear vs. the organizational family (see Appendix A).

In studies of sexual exploitation by therapists, some clients characterize their experience as "a kind of incest" (Vinson, 1984, p. 124). D'Addario (1977, p. 346) reported that one woman she interviewed, to whom she referred as "Anne," said:

He was daddy. That's why I didn't want sex with him. He was my father. You don't have sex with your father.

Some of the almost 60 clients (whom I have treated for problems related to sexual exploitation by therapists) characterized the experience as "incestuous"; and they noted that sometimes it had been like a re-enactment of earlier sexual abuse by a parent.

In order to provide clinicians with a frame of reference for work with individuals who have been sexually exploited by therapists, I explore the incest analogy in this chapter. The understanding gained from a problem which clinicians have been addressing for a much longer period helped White (1986) to assist organizational consultants or administrators and offers guidance to us to deal with a newly recognized problem.

This is not to imply, however, that the two problems—parent-child incest, and sexual exploitation of clients by therapists—are identical. The understanding and techniques developed from work with incest victims may prove quite helpful in this "new" domain, nevertheless experience with incest victims does not, by itself, qualify clinicians for work with the victims of therapist-client sex.

RESPONSES TO ALLEGATIONS OF SEXUAL IMPROPRIETY BY CLIENTS AND CHILD VICTIMS

Early in the history of psychotherapy, Freud regarded his adult clients' memories of parent-child incest as probable fantasies and thereby initiated what was to become a widely held belief that influenced a generation of psychoanalysts (Masson, 1984). Until relatively recently many clinicians treated reports of incest as possible fantasies or distortions; this attitude began to change only after broad societal concern with child abuse and neglect surfaced in the United States.

So too with the sexual exploitation of clients by therapists, the tendency to dismiss such allegations as fantasies or "wishful thinking" by clients, especially if an alleged perpetrator was a prominent clinician. All it took was a denial from the accused for the allegation to be promptly dismissed. The prevalence of the problem seemed very low because therapist-client sexual exploitation, like incest, was rarely the subject of routine clinical inquiry. Even when a client hinted at it clinicians typically avoided the issue.

Research in both areas often focused on the characteristics of the victim rather than on those of the perpetrator. Theories of causation tended to give considerable focus to the supposed personal dynamics of victims (see Part II). Even research conducted from an avowed feminist viewpoint focused on the personality characteristics of victims (Belote, 1974). Furthermore, recent publications have proposed classifications of clients "at risk" (Pope & Bouhoutsos, 1986; Smith & Bisbing, 1988); when one examines the purported characteristics, few clients would be excluded. My own work (Luepker & Retsch-Bogart, 1986) and that of other investigators (Schoener, Milgrom & Gonsiorek, 1983; Vinson, 1984), by contrast, has emphasized the heterogeneity of clients.

As with incest, the prevalent professional view of the therapist-client problem has further heightened the sense of isolation and rejection already experienced by victims of therapist sexual exploitation. Although support groups were an obvious treatment of choice for the sense of isolation experienced in both parent-child incest and therapists' sexual exploitation of clients, the initial tendency was to use only individual therapy as an intervention. In both instances, however, both support and therapy groups are increasingly important treatment options currently.

VIEW OF THE PERPETRATOR

With both parents who have sexually abused their children and psychotherapists who have sexually abused their clients, it has been assumed that psychotherapy is a cure-all. In the case of incest, the genesis of the widespread use of specialized sex-offender treatment programs dates only from about a decade ago; the technology is still undergoing considerable change. This volume takes cognizance of the fact that assessment and rehabilitation plans for psychotherapist perpetrators is very recent; even today the common response is to prescribe psychotherapy.

Incest perpetrators fall into categories as diverse as those identified for psychotherapist perpetrators in Part IX. Sexual contact may have a number of underlying determinants. Only recently has it become understood that full rehabilitation for all sexual abusers may not be possible. A supervised probation, long-term scrutiny, and, in the case of psychotherapists, revocation of the license to practice, may be necessary solutions.

POWER IMBALANCE

Many concepts in this part of the volume on the abuse of power in psychotherapy relationships have parallels in the parent-child incest situation. In both instances the more powerful person, the parent or therapist, is supposed to take proper care of the less powerful individual, the child or client.[1] Both parents and therapists are deemed by cultural norms to be trustworthy custodians of this power and thus they tend to go unquestioned.

The consequence of this lopsided power relationship is that American society saw fit, during the late 1960s, to intercede via child protection statutes to require the reporting of incest as well as other types of child abuse and neglect. Likewise, in the case of exploitative psychotherapy, some states now mandate reporting this abuse and others are considering such legislation.

---

[1] See Fortune's remarks on the biblical mandate to protect vulnerable individuals in Chapter 6.

Just as incestuous parents often abuse their power in nonsexual domains, so too may exploitative psychotherapists' abuse their power in various ways. Common examples are breaches of confidentiality, insurance fraud, isolating clients from friends and family.

In both instances the less powerful individual (child or client) may gain some power or the illusion of it by meeting the sexual needs of the more powerful person (parent or therapist). Normally, however, the victim has little or no true power until the relationship ends and he or she regains a sense of self by telling the secret, filing a complaint, receiving validation for feelings, and receiving support and assistance of the authorities.

DIMINISHED CAPACITY TO MAKE DECISIONS IN ONE'S OWN BEST INTEREST

Both lay people and therapists often have difficulty understanding clients' inability to protect themselves from exploitative psychotherapists, especially when the client lacks major emotional problems and/or is in some professional field (including psychotherapy).

This is more easily understood when we examine it through the prism of the incest analogy. Even very bright and independent young people have great difficulty resisting sexual advances or other abuses by their parents. Indeed, Alice Miller (1987, p. 43) wrote: "Our capacity to resist has nothing to do with our intelligence, but with the degree of access to the true self." Abused children lose a sense of their true self due to their vulnerability and to their own need or society's expectation that they see their parents in a favorable light. They set aside their own needs in order to adapt to those of their parents, thereby preserving the image of the idealized parents.

The direct parallel is the client who seeks counseling. He or she is in a vulnerable state and feels somewhat child-like in the inability to manage his/her life without assistance. The therapist or counselor is sought out because that person is expected not only to possess skills but also to be completely trustworthy. When the client seeks help, even a healthy individual may feel that there is nobody he/she can trust completely—except the therapist. Thus, both cultural stereotypes tend to idealize both therapists and parents, which leads to an extremely high level of trust, a desire to preserve the idealization, and a tendency to accede to the demands made upon them. Self-protective instincts are weakened or, at times, ignored in both situations.

DISCOMFORT WITH SEXUAL FEELINGS

Parents often have difficulty accepting the idea that it is normal to experience some sexual feelings toward their children. Some parents protect themselves from acknowledging these feelings by distancing themselves emotionally but others act them out through sexual contact. In the same way therapists too often have trouble dealing with sexual feelings toward clients and usually do not even discuss these feelings with their supervisors. Like parents, they may either distance themselves from their clients or act out the feelings through some sort of sexual contact.

SEX AS A ROLE REVERSAL IN THE CONTEXT OF OTHER ROLE REVERSALS

It is a given fact that the primary needs of parents should be met by persons other than a child; in the same way the primary needs of therapists should be met by persons other than a client. When sexual exploitation occurs, the therapist's need rather than the client's is met. Like incestuous parent-child relationships in which sex is but one of several types of role reversals by which children are "parentified," sex in therapy often occurs within a larger context of role reversals in which the clients are treated as peers. Clients have reported various types of role reversals, such as therapists using them to perform personal services (e.g., shopping or secretarial work).

Among the most striking role reversals are those when a parent or therapist begins to rely on the child or client for emotional support and guidance. The parent who shares his/her marital troubles with the child and asks to be taken care of bears a stark similarity to the therapist who spends the client's session talking about his or her personal problems and then asks the client to fulfill unmet needs.

SECRECY AND ISOLATION

Both parent-child incest and sexual exploitation of clients usually involve secrecy. Consequences may include the loss of trust in one's ability to accurately perceive reality and the disruption of important relationships with family members and other persons. Many clients, like incest survivors, also experience a traumatic disillusionment with the idealized object. In order to recover from this trauma, clients need the opportunity to talk freely about what happened, but the need for secrecy precludes it. Also, when the client has been experiencing some isolation or difficulty in relationships—part of the initial reason for seeking therapy—the secrecy and resulting isolation exacerbate existing relationship problems and create new ones.

FEAR OF EXPLOSIVE DISRUPTIONS IN RELATIONSHIPS WHEN SECRET IS TOLD

Child victims of incest fear explosive disruptions to the family unit should they tell the incest secret. They often take extraordinary measures to conceal the secret of incest to prevent what they feel will be catastrophic damage to their parents and family. They also fear recriminations from other family members and/or the community for telling the secret that leads to such ruptures. In a similar way, clients describe their agony about imagined or real disruptions to their therapists' family relationships and employment should they reveal, or when they have revealed, the secret of inappropriate boundary violations. In both instances delayed disclosure is common.

MIXED FEELINGS ABOUT THE EXPERIENCE

Both types of victims experience complex, intensely mixed feelings toward the parent (or therapist) which range from affection, appreciation, and loyalty to betrayal, distrust, and confusion. They may have a strong sense of responsibility for what happened and a fear of hurting the perpetrator if a complaint is made. They also may fear reprisal from the perpetrator or other people. Both types of incest victims describe great difficulties in integrating such wide-ranging feelings.

People offering support for incest victims often understand that idealization of and loyalty to the parent or family can generate positive feelings in the child toward the perpetrator. But it is harder to understand the positive feelings a client has for an abusive therapist. Just as it is uncommon for the parenting by the incest perpetrator to be "all bad," so it is uncommon for the therapist to have been of no support or assistance. Focusing only on the negative or attempting to portray the situation in black/white terms sabotages the victim's ability to clarify these confusing feelings.

POSSIBILITY OF DEVELOPMENTAL FIXATION AND CONTINUING TRAUMA

The clients who have sought my help for problems stemming from sexual exploitation by therapists or counselors have seemed "stuck" in resolving the issues they were attempting to master at the time the exploitation began. They also have diminished self-esteem, problems forming relationships with others, and problems succeeding in other life tasks (e.g., parenting, school, or career). Sometimes they fear they will exploit others as they themselves have been exploited. These problems are reminiscent of the continuing problems experienced by parent-child incest survivors.

How negatively the boundary violations affect the development of identity seems related to variables such as how young the client was when the exploitation occurred, the extent and duration of the exploitation, and the extent to which other important relationships were disrupted. With clergy or pastoral counselors, clients may suffer additional problems, such as loss of faith in God, alienation from a given church, or an existential crisis (see Fortune's analysis in Ch. 6).

ASSOCIATES' SILENCE IMPLIES CONSENT

Frequently, incestuous family members and mental health colleagues remain silent and do not act to protect the victim of incest or client sexual abuse. Sometimes the fact that incest is occurring is not clear to family members; they may be only vaguely aware that "something is different." Similarly, sometimes it is not clear that the sexual abuse of a client is occurring in a mental health or counseling setting. Colleagues may be aware of warning signals but may not recognize these as symptomatic of sexual exploitation, and may not seek clarification of what is amiss.

Yet sometimes family members do know of the existence of incest in the family—in the same way that mental health colleagues are aware of clients' allegations of sexual exploitation—but still say or do nothing. They may wish to protect the family, organization, or profession at any cost. Sometimes there is fear of ostracism or punishment (in the case of mental health professions it can take the form of loss of referrals), or fear of accusations of slander. The imagined or real costs to the whistle blower sometimes are too threatening.

Silence implies consent. Silence helps to perpetuate the exploitation. Family members as well as mental health colleagues may suffer remorse later for not having acted to protect the victim.

RESPONSE WHEN PERPETRATOR IS WELL-REGARDED

When a parent incest perpetrator is a well-regarded, upstanding community citizen, the child's shame, guilt, and confusion and the community's paralysis are more intense. When sexually seductive therapists are among the community's most highly regarded practitioners, the confusion, disbelief, and paralysis of clients and helping professionals are similarly increased. People ask: "How can such a well-regarded therapist be guilty of this conduct?"

BETRAYAL DUE TO THE INACTION OF OTHERS

Children suffer when family members and others do not protect them from parental sexual abuse. So too do clients feel betrayed when the therapist's colleagues either deny that the abuse has occurred or do not take action when they become aware of the problem. My clients ask, "If they knew, why didn't they do anything?" This betrayal frequently is more painful to the victim than the betrayal experienced in the abuse itself.

NEED FOR OUTSIDERS TO BREAK UP ENMESHMENT

Incestuous families usually require outside help, such as an arm of the government, to break up the unhealthy enmeshment of parent and child. The unhealthy enmeshment between client and therapist also requires intervention by outsiders. For the psychotherapy and counseling professions, "outsiders" include alert peers who identify warning signs, supervisors, licensure boards, professional ethics committees, client support groups, advocates, law enforcement, the courts, and the legislature.

IMPLICATIONS FOR INTERVENTION

Professionals are well aware of the value of education in the prevention of and early intervention in incest, as well as in the treatment of incest survivors. Educational presentations, along with accessible materials about client exploitation by therapists, also create better informed consumers of counseling services. Informed clients may recognize abuse earlier and terminate sexual contacts, or learn how to file complaints. In recent years clients seem to be seeking help earlier for problems stemming from previous therapies. This tendency appears to be related to increased public awareness of the problem of boundary violations by therapists.

•Just as professionals have learned to inquire routinely about incest history, so too is it important to ask about problems in past therapy or counseling. Professionals in Minnesota who make such inquiries find that the questions yield valuable information on both past abuse and dissatisfactions with therapy.

•Just as there was a need for improved assessment techniques in parent-child incest cases, so too must assessment techniques for client sexual exploitation be carefully developed.

•Just as helping professionals have learned not to make assumptions about what children experienced or what meaning the incestuous experience has for children, so too is it equally important to inquire specifically about what clients experienced and its meaning to them. Based upon the assessment of clients' unique needs, helping professionals then can carefully make selections from a range of intervention strategies (e.g., consultation, advocacy, and various treatment modalities).

•Given a client's high level of distrust of therapists following sexual exploitation, and a follow-up therapist's anxiety upon hearing accounts of the abuse, it is important that follow-up therapists avoid unnecessary isolation. This need is even greater when therapists work with clients who have experienced boundary violations in therapy than with victims of parent-child incest; the follow-up therapists' anxiety is higher because they are members of the professional "family" in which the boundary violations occurred. Thus follow-up therapists should obtain professional consultation to maximize their objectivity in considering clients' stories, choosing options for resolution, and, when indicated, protecting other clients.

• To help clients to reduce their isolation, follow-up therapists may suggest that the clients try group counseling, a self-help group, or other opportunities to meet persons who have survived similar exploitative experiences.

• Just as siblings who are victims of the same parent perpetrator can benefit from speaking freely to each other about their respective abuse experiences, it may help sexually exploited clients of the same therapist to participate in group counseling where they have the opportunity to freely discuss their respective experiences.

• Follow-up therapists should also consider the usefulness and availability of advocacy support for clients who wish to make a formal complaint, pursue litigation, or hold a processing session with their former therapists. Just as it is too much to expect incest survivors to confront their perpetrators alone, so it is too much to expect sexually exploited clients to act alone in confronting their therapists.

Conclusion

The similarities between parent-child incest and sexual exploitation of clients by therapists have been discussed to help professionals who intervene in such situations to build on the knowledge of practitioners who have worked with incest victims.

Situations vary in the degree to which the incest analogy fits. Although the use of the term "incest" may be inflammatory and distracting when it is applied to a given case situation, the parallels between incest and sexual exploitation may be quite helpful in conceptualizing intervention approaches.

In sum, it is important to repeat the caution on equating parent-child incest with sexual exploitation by therapists. Granted that the approaches to each are similar, yet they are not identical; sometimes, but not always, a victim of sexual exploitation by a therapist may benefit from being in a group with other types of victims. Training and experience in working with incest victims does not automatically qualify one to work with victims of sexual exploitation by therapists.

Other clinicians and I have found that drawing parallels between incest and exploitation of clients by therapists is useful in meeting the challenges of assessment and intervention in the more recently recognized problem of the sexual exploitation of clients.

CHAPTER 6

BETRAYAL OF THE PASTORAL RELATIONSHIP: SEXUAL CONTACT BY PASTORS AND PASTORAL COUNSELORS

Rev. Marie M. Fortune

Sexual contact in professional relationships by pastors or pastoral counselors with parishioners or clients is a longstanding problem that now is being discussed more openly. It is an issue of professional ethics too long ignored by the church; the issue compromises the integrity of the professional ministry whenever it occurs and causes serious damage to individuals and congregations. Following the lead of professional organizations of secular counselors and consumer activists who have raised the issue of counselor abuse within a counseling relationship, it is important to break the silence that has surrounded this issue within the church for years. Thus the purpose of this article is to name the sin of violation of professional pastoral relationships, to provide a framework for understanding it ethically, and to offer some practical suggestions for action by the church.

Sexual contact by pastors or pastoral counselors in professional relationships is a violation of professional ethics. It is a serious situation of professional misconduct that often is minimized or ignored. It is not an "affair" although it may involve an on-going sexual relationship with a client or parishioner. It is not merely adultery; it may involve adultery, nevertheless, if the pastor or counselor is in a committed relationship. It is not just a momentary lapse of judgment by the pastor. Often it is a recurring pattern of misuse of the pastoral role by a pastor who does not either comprehend or care about the damaging effects it may have on a parishioner or client.

DEFINITION OF THE PROBLEM

Sexual contact by pastors or pastoral counselors with parishioners or clients within a professional relationship is a violation of professional ethics that not only undercuts an effective pastoral relationship but, also, is exploitative and abusive. It is not the sexual contact per se that is problematic but the fact that the sexual activity takes place within the professional relationship. Once sexual activity occurs, the nature of that relationship is violated. The relationship in question may be formal, such as between a pastoral counselor and a client who is seeking psychotherapy through a pastoral counseling agency, or less formal, such as between a parish pastor and a parishioner currently serving on a parish committee or seeking pastoral support during a crisis. Regardless of the particulars, the relationship between a clergyperson (pastor or pastoral counselor) and those whom he or she is called to serve is a professional one within which sexual activity is inappropriate.

The sexual contact or activity may take many different forms: touching the erogenous zones, fondling the breasts or genital areas, kissing, and/or sexual intercourse. It also may include verbal suggestions of sexual activity or requests for sexual favors by the pastor or pastoral counselor. It may become an on-going sexual relationship. It almost always will be secretive.

Sexual contact or activity within a professional relationship creates a dual relationship; that is, both a love relationship and a counselor/client relationship. This dual relationship undercuts any possibility of an effective counseling relationship. Such a relationship is based on a client or parishioner's being able to have confidence in the knowledge and authority that the clergyperson brings as pastor or counselor, and to know that this knowledge and authority will not be misused. The client or parishioner also must be able to trust the pastor to respond to the client's or parishioner's best interest, and not to the pastor's self-interest alone. Sexual contact or activity between the two seriously diminishes these important factors and, hence, the professional relationship itself.

Because the professional relationship is by definition primarily the responsibility of the professional (i.e., the pastor or pastoral counselor) any initiation of or participation in activity that jeopardizes the relationship is unethical. The pastor or pastoral counselor by definition is committed to seeking the well-being of those whom he/she serves, hence any activity threatening that well-being is unethical. Sexual contact between persons who, by nature of their roles in a relationship, do not possess equal power is exploitative and abusive; therefore, such contact within a pastoral relationship is abusive and victimizes the parishioner or client.

We have no current data that reveals the extent of this problem within the religious community. The research on this particular form of abuse has yet to be done. However, there is no reason to assume that the incidence among clergypersons is any less frequent than the estimated 10-15% for other counseling professions (see introduction to this volume). The most glaring gap in our current information is the absence of research data from persons who have been victimized by this unethical professional behavior. A national staff person for the United Church of Christ reported that "90% or more of women in a group discussing this issue had experienced it in their own lives in one form or another" (Breitling, 1984). Somewhere between these two sets of figures lies the reality of a serious problem facing the church and its ministry. Whatever the number of clergy who engage in sexual activity with parishioners or clients, whatever the number of parishioners and clients who are victimized by this problem, it is an issue. One incident is one too many. Whenever this problem occurs, it not only damages the individual victim, but also it compromises the integrity of the ministry and the church.

An Ethical Analysis of Sexual Contact by Ministerial Professionals

An ethical analysis of unethical professional conduct by pastors and pastoral counselors offers insight to the nature of the violation and to the need for a just response. If we make decisions that affect our actions toward others on the basis of ethics, then an ethical analysis of the problem of sexual contact by pastors and pastoral counselors in professional relationships should point to those dimensions that give us the potential to diminish the life of another. They include (a) violation of role, (b) misuse of authority and power, (c) taking advantage of vulnerability, and (d) the absence of meaningful consent.

Violation of Role: A number of parallels can be found between a pastor's being called to serve a congregation and a pastoral counselor being approached by an individual seeking counseling. In each case the pastoral relationship establishes certain role expectations. This role carries with it a power differential and the expectation that the pastor will bring gifts and resources that the congregation or client may need to call upon.

The role does not include an intimate relationship involving sexual contact. The latter characterizes a lover relationship that differs altogether and presupposes a context of mutuality and equality (i.e., both persons mutually consent and can expect needs to be met mutually). Thus, for a pastor to engage in a sexual relationship with one of his/her parishioners or clients creates a dual relationship in which he/she is both pastor/counselor and sexual partner. Given that the expectations for each role are widely divergent, it is not possible for a pastor to carry out both responsibly and simultaneously.

Misuse of Authority and Power: The role of pastor or pastoral counselor carries with it authority and power and the responsibility to use them to benefit the people who have called upon a clergyperson for services. This power comes from knowledge, experience, training, leadership skills and charisma, which are gifts much needed in effective ministry with individuals or groups. They are gifts that can readily be misused to the detriment of persons: for example, authority may be used to mislead someone or to encourage harmful action, especially when a person seeks counsel during time of crisis; that is, when the person is vulnerable to a suggestion from someone who is respected and trusted. This is often when a pastor or counselor may suggest or initiate sexual contact with a parishioner or client and thus misuse authority. When the parishioner or client seeks affirmation and intimacy by initiating sexual contact with a clergyperson whom they see as an authority figure, the clergyperson still retains the power to say "no" to the approach. The need thus expressed by the parishioner or client then becomes the issue for the counseling agenda, and the clergyperson's task is to help the individual to find ways to build relationships with peers in which these needs can be met appropriately. Responding sexually to a client or parishioner who makes a sexual overture is still a misuse of role. The pastoral role is best used to set limits and to retain the pastoral relationship; ultimately this is of greatest benefit to the client or parishioner.

Taking Advantage of Vulnerability: To be vulnerable is to lack adequate power or resources to choose for one's self; consequently, one may be overpowered or exploited by another. A number of factors may make a person vulnerable or powerless: age, physical size, gender, race, role, current situation, and the like. A young teenager who is physically small and emotionally naive is vulnerable to possible exploitation by a teacher, employer, parent, or pastor. A woman in crisis during the serious illness of her husband who seeks support from a pastoral counselor is vulnerable to possible exploitation. When a pastor or pastoral counselor uses this vulnerability to dominate, control, and gain sexual access to a parishioner or client, the latter is exploited to her/his detriment. The Hebrew scriptures speak consistently of the expectation that vulnerable members of the community will be protected in their vulnerability. It names them as the sojourner, the widow, and the orphan. In Biblical times, these persons, due to life circumstances, were powerless to care for themselves and the community was mandated to protect them. Likewise, the life circumstances that result in vulnerability today mandate members of the religious community to protect persons in those circumstances from exploitation and never to take advantage of their vulnerability.

Absence of Meaningful Consent: To be meaningful, consent to sexual activity must take place in a context of mutuality, choice, and equality and in the absence of coercion or fear. These factors are not present when an imbalance of power arises out of life circumstances or role differences between two persons, thus coercion or fear is likely to be employed, overtly or covertly, to achieve sexual access. Such is the case in which a dual relationship exists; that is, a relationship in which one person is both pastor and lover to her/his parishioner or client. Even though both persons initially may "choose" to engage in sexual activity with each other and may see themselves as "consenting adults," the "consent" of the parishioner or client is not authentic because of the difference in role, authority, and power. The lack of authenticity may not be immediately apparent, but as the counseling and sexual relationships progress they lead to increased confusion and conflict of expectations and the effect of coercion will begin to be felt. The person with less power in the relationship realizes that her/his freedom to choose and to give shape to the relationship is limited. Meaningful consent, which is necessary for a just and emotionally satisfying sexual relationship, is absent in relationships that are shaped by a difference in power and role. Hence it is unethical for a pastor to pursue or agree to sexual activity within such a relationship.

RESPONSE OF THE SECULAR PROFESSIONS

The secular counseling professions have been aware of and concerned with sexual abuse by therapists for a number of years. Acting out of this concern, many professional, secular organizations have established policies and procedures to hold their members accountable to a standard of professional conduct and, in so doing, to protect the consumers of their services. (See Ch. 27)

Among religious professionals, similar codes of ethics for pastoral counselors have been established and maintained by professional organizations.

"...Pastoral counselors do not engage in sexual misconduct with their clients." (American Association of Pastoral Counselors, 1981)

"...The CPE supervisor shall maintain supervisory relationships on a professional basis, avoiding exploitation of any kind." (Association for Clinical Pastoral Education, 1980)

The AAPC specifically provides a formal complaint process that is overseen by the Regional Ethics Committee in each region. This body has the option to recommend suspension or dismissal from the organization if a member is found to have engaged in unethical conduct.

Unlike codes of ethics for other professional groups, codes of the American Association of Pastoral Counselors and the Association for Clinical Pastoral Education do not specifically refer to sexual contact with clients as unethical conduct. The AAPC refers to "sexual misconduct" which is undefined and ambiguous.. It suggests that some sexual contact may not be "misconduct" whereas other sexual contact may be. The ACPE does not specify sexual contact at all. This lack of clarity weakens both policy statements.

Clearly all codes of ethics for the secular professions are designed to provide guidelines for professionals in the practice of counseling and to protect the clients they serve from the destructive consequences of unethical behavior. The codes also provide a mechanism for professional groups to monitor themselves and thus to maintain a high standard of service. As such, these policies and procedures reflect a commitment by the professions to provide quality service.

For the pastor who ministers outside a formal counseling setting or professional organization (either parish or specialized ministry), there are far fewer guidelines to assist him/her in dealing with the issue of sexual contact with parishioners or clients. Although some denominations make specific reference to sexual misconduct, the expectation is rarely stated that pastors will not engage in sexual activity with the persons they serve because it violates the pastoral relationship. Likewise, the procedures for responding to a complaint about such unethical behavior vary widely and frequently are nonexistent. Hence a clergyperson lacks specific guidance on this issue and the layperson is not aware that sexual contact with a pastor is unprofessional conduct, or that a means of protection and recourse exist should the problem arise.

Some have suggested that specificity is not necessary in stating that sexual contact with parishioners or clients is unethical for clergy. The clergy is supposed to know better.

Others have said that the Bible is their code of ethics and it addresses the issue adequately. Ideally, both views are true but, unfortunately, neither is adequate for either clergy or laypersons at present.

The following situations illustrate the problem of sexual contact by pastors and pastoral counselors in their professional capacities:

- Marsha was an active laywoman in her congregation. This meant that she regularly served on boards and committees and attended many meetings at the church. She noticed after meetings that her senior pastor was paying unusual attention to her; he then made sexual advances which she refused. His advances continued and included touching and trying to kiss her. She consistently refused his approaches. Initially, she did not tell anyone but her husband about the pastor's behavior. It continued. Two years later, in conversation with a friend in the congregation, she pursued an oblique comment that seemed relevant to her situation. In clarifying the comment, her friend shared her experience with the pastor which mirrored Marsha's. After discovering their common problem, they carefully asked other women friends in the congregation and discovered as many as a dozen other women who had been sexually harassed by the senior pastor. They wrote a letter to the parish council requesting that the pastor be confronted and that if the behavior did not cease, that he be relieved of his position. Immediately following the confrontation, the pastor came to Marsha's workplace, walked up to her, grabbed her shoulders and kissed her on the mouth. Even though she was initially stunned and confused by his action, Marsha returned to the council and requested the pastor's dismissal. The council concurred.

- A local pastor was sued by an 18-year-old member of his church who alleged that he forced her into "obnoxious sexual and abusive physical contact" two years earlier. The young woman commented: "I feel very angry at him for taking my trust and throwing it out the door; he used me." The pastor publicly denied the allegation but in court papers he said that the girl consented to the "alleged assaults and batteries" and understood the nature of her acts. Neither the local church nor the denomination took any disciplinary step in this situation.

- A pastoral counselor, a former police chaplain, was ordered to pay damages to a woman who sued him after he had sexual relations with her when she sought counseling from him. He did not dispute the fact of the sexual contact and admitted that it was wrong, but he denied that any damage had resulted to the woman.

- A pastoral counselor, a former president of his regional profes-sional organization, was sued by four women for malpractice. One woman said that the pastoral counselor told her that the sexual activity with him would be "therapeutically beneficial" for her. The cases were settled out of court and damages were paid to each woman. His professional organization ordered him to resign as president, write a letter of apology to each woman, enter therapy himself, and no longer counsel women. His denomination took no disciplinary action.

- A clergywoman who was a guest speaker at a local church was invited by the parish pastor to stop by his study after her presentation. She did so assuming an occasion for a collegial discussion. The pastor closed the door, grabbed the clergywoman, threw her on the sofa, jumped on top of her and penetrated her vaginally with his fingers. The clergywoman was so shocked, frightened, and confused that she waited two months before reporting her experience to her conference minister. The latter subsequently took action that resulted in the removal of the pastor's standing with the conference. The clergywoman filed a police report alleging attempted rape by the pastor.

- A priest in a local parish engaged some teenagers in the youth group in sexual activity. He would arrange trips with them in order to have the opportunity to approach them sexually. When some teens finally told their parents, the adults confronted the priest who denied the reports. They then went to the bishop and requested his assistance. He chose not to get involved. The priest sought other employment and was hired by a parish in another state. No information about his offending behavior with the youth was passed to his new employers. The bishop refused a request from members of the congregation to meet with them and to deal with their anger and sense of betrayal. A new priest was employed by the parish.

- A young woman went to a Christian counselor seeking help for the recent break-up with her husband. After the first three counseling sessions, the counselor suggested that she needed to be reminded that she was a lovable person and that God still loved her and would show that love through him (the counselor). On this basis, he initiated a sexual relationship that lasted three years until the woman finally indicated that she did not want it to continue. At this point, he threatened her not to tell anyone about the sexual contact. When she told someone in the church he had her committed to a psychiatric ward. She was released only when she agreed that she had lied about his sexual contact with her.

These situations are evidence of the range of abuse from sexual harassment to coercive sexual activity to rape. Also, clearly indicated, is the range of institutional response (or lack of response) by the church.

PARALLELS WITH INCEST

The dynamics of incestuous abuse provide a paradigm for viewing sexual contact by pastors and pastoral counselors in professional relationships and for understanding its consequences. Incestuous abuse takes place within the intimacy and privacy of a family relationship. There is a pre-existing relationship between parent and child or older and younger sibling that establishes the power and authority of roles: the father's or mother's parental role vis-a-vis a child or the older sibling's role based on age, size, and designated authority. In either case, the younger child knows that the parent or sibling has authority over her/him. The child also assumes, until he/she learns otherwise, that the parent or older sibling will protect her/his vulnerability. Trust is central to the relationship. The responsible adults or older sibling should protect the child's vulnerability and not misuse the familial role to the child's detriment. Specifically, this means not engaging in sexual activity with the child in violation of their roles and their trust relationship. This does not mean that they may not have sexual feelings at times in response to the child. However, they do not act on these feelings because of their overriding concern for the child's welfare. When this relationship is betrayed by incestuous abuse, the victim is often sworn to secrecy and the resulting isolation prevents assistance from other family members or persons outside the family. The secrecy also may contribute to the victim's tendency to blame her/himself for the sexual abuse. When the child calls for help by telling someone what is going on, she/he is not likely to be believed. Denial of the reality of incestuous abuse allows avoiding the responsibility for stopping it. Initially, the special attention from the parent or older sibling may be experienced as positive by the child, nevertheless the betrayal of role and trust and subsequent dual relationship takes its toll. The abuse often continues unabated and its victims frequently suffer the long-term consequences of this broken trust, including the unwillingness or inability to ever trust in a relationship again.

Often the church is spoken of as the family of God. As such it is regarded by its members as a series of relationships in which intimacy and trust should abound. Many such relationships are shaped by the particular roles taken by persons and which determine relational expectations. Thus a pastor is called to serve a congregation and, in this capacity, is given power and authority to exercise leadership and provide for the needs of the congregation. A pastoral counselor is called to a specialized ministry of pastoral care for persons. Both roles presuppose responsibility for the persons who are served; both roles carry the potential for betrayal and misuse.

When either pastoral role is betrayed by the initiation of sexual contact with a parishioner or client, secrecy is expected or required and often is upheld by the victim out of fear or shame. She/he is confused: the attention feels good but, at the same time, the blurring of the boundaries of the pastoral relationship feels bad. If and when a victim does speak out, she/he is not likely to be believed or, if believed, is likely to be blamed. The church may not want to know and thus carefully makes itself unavailable to assist the parishioner or client or to call the pastor or counselor to account for his/her actions. Silence begets silence and the family of God becomes for some persons yet another source of pain, fear, confusion, and injustice.

PSYCHOLOGICAL AND SPIRITUAL IMPACT

The psychological effect on a person of sexual exploitation by a clergyperson is profound. Initially, the person may feel flattered by the special attention, especially if she/he has sought counseling at a time of low self-esteem or crisis because of difficulties in a relationship. In fact, sexual attention initially may seem positive and the client even may "consent" to the activity. At the same time, however, the person realizes that she/he is being denied a much-needed pastoral relationship and begins to feel taken advantage of (the consequence of the dual relationship). It is common for persons who have experienced sexual contact with pastors or pastoral counselors to feel that their trust in the pastoral relationship has been betrayed. They also report feeling victimized; that is, made a victim by the experience. To be made a victim is to be made powerless by another. Victims frequently are confused and fearful; as a result, they may not speak to anyone about their experiences. The subsequent isolation then exacerbates the already damaged self-esteem and the tendency to blame themselves for the pastor's actions.

On some level, at some point, most victims of this experience feel anger. It is usually a sign of health when a person begins to respond to exploitation with anger; it can be the primary motivation to try to rectify the situation and to protect others.

Spiritually, victimization by a clergyperson has a profound effect. All the psychological pain is magnified and takes on cosmic proportions. Not only is the victimization experienced as a betrayal of what should have been a trust relationship, but the betrayal is by one who represents God. Thus it is experienced as a betrayal by God. This breach of trust then makes a trusting relationship with anyone difficult. If you cannot trust your pastor, whom can you trust? In addition, the pastor/pastoral counselor by virtue of her/his role has access to the spiritual core of a person's being, perhaps a person's truest self. This access carries with it a dimension of power exceeding that of the secular therapist as well as an even greater potential for abuse. The sexual contact engenders a great deal of guilt and shame for the victim, especially for women who have been taught that any sexual approach by any man is the woman's responsibility. If the client or parishioner currently is in a committed relationship, there is also the guilt associated with the betrayal of that relationship. Thus, the confusion and ambivalence that commonly result take on theological dimensions: "The person to whom I look for spiritual guidance is engaging me in activity which I thought was sinful but he says it is permissible because it is God's love flowing through him to me. This must be God's will for me." This sense quickly turns to self-blame when it becomes apparent that the sexual relationship is not therapeutic and is not helping to resolve the problems the person brought to the counseling relationship but, in fact, has aggravated those problems. Then the interpretation can be made that this painful experience is God's punishment which the person deserved because she initially "consented" to the sexual activity.

Clearly, the spiritual dimensions are easily distorted and convoluted in the midst of a confusing and difficult experience. The potential for damage is great because the stakes are high. If a woman feels betrayed by the person who represents God to her, and that betrayal leads to her feeling betrayed by God, the foundation of her relationship with God is shaken. If, in addition, the church does little or nothing in response to her call for help, then she may readily conclude that neither God nor the church body is available in her suffering. Then, when her anger and rage do surface, not surprisingly they are frequently directed toward God and the church. This emotional crisis is also a crisis of faith that may lead to complete abandonment of a faith life and of anything to do with the institutional church. The way to reconcile the relationship with God or the church is not easy and must be grounded in an experience of justice for the person betrayed.

PREVENTION: PROTECTING THE PROFESSIONAL PASTORAL RELATIONSHIP

It is not unusual for a pastor or pastoral counselor to be sexually attracted to a parishioner or client. If the attraction occurs in a counseling relationship and could compromise the relationship, the pastor should refer the client to another pastor and terminate his/her relationship. As long it is clear that the pastor's priority is to provide for the client's pastoral and counseling needs and to avoid exploiting the counseling relationship, the client need not interpret the referral as rejection but, rather, as a clear indication of concern for the client's well-being.

If a pastor and parishioner experience a mutual attraction, and if they are mutually interested in fostering this attraction and developing an on-going and possibly sexual relationship, then they should terminate the professional pastoral relationship prior to pursuing the possible sexual relationship. For example, the parishioner could transfer membership to another church, or the pastor could resign his/her position and seek employment elsewhere. Such actions would avoid the development of a dual relationship and would insure that the parishioner retains the counseling resources of a pastor. To some people these suggestions may seem extreme. However, they make clear the seriousness of the situation and the importance of a careful and intentional response to it.

When a pastor feels some confusion about his/her feelings and the appropriate action to take, it is useful to seek out a colleague or counselor, one who shares the concern for maintaining professional standards, to assist in clarifying the best course of action. This careful avoidance of a dual relationship protects the integrity of the pastor or pastoral counselor and the welfare of a parishioner or client. Hence it serves the best interests of both.

A parishioner or client and the congregation in which he/she participates also can help to protect and preserve professional, pastoral relationships. Expectations for professional relationships should be made explicit when a pastor is appointed or called: "The congregation expects the pastor not to engage in sexual activity with any of its members but to maintain pastoral relationships in a professional and ethical manner." This kind of clarity not only helps the pastor to set clear boundaries but, also, helps parishioners to know that if those boundaries are crossed, they will have some recourse within the congregation and can call for help. Basically, specific expectations establish the community norm for a pastor's behavior.

So too for a pastoral counselor. A statement of expectations for the counseling relationship (preferably written) protects both counselor and client: "As a pastoral counselor, I will not engage in any sexual activity with a client and will relate only within the boundaries of a professional, pastoral relationship. This commitment reflects both the expectations of my professional association and my own standards of professional conduct."

Clarity of role expectations establishes a point of reference for a parishioner or client and helps individuals to avoid unrealistic expectations of their pastor or counselor as well as providing a basis for recourse should this expectation be violated. Some people may feel that this specificity is clinical and legalistic and, thus, may interfere with a caring, trusting, pastoral relationship. In fact, the clear definition of expectations may well enhance the trust level of a relationship and, thus, enable the development of a more effective pastoral, therapeutic relationship.

EFFECTIVE RESPONSES TO ABUSES OF PASTORAL ROLE

An overview of the goals and principles of effective responses to reports of abuse by pastors or pastoral counselors is the focus of this section. Specific suggestions for policy and procedures are available currently in a 1984 report prepared by the Washington Association of Churches ("Sexual Contact by Pastors and Pastoral Counselors in Professional Relationships: A Study with Recommendations to Denominational Judicatories.")

The primary goal of a response to sexual contact by a pastor or pastoral counselor in a professional relationship is to create justice in the midst of injustice. The basic premise of the justice in this circumstance is the shared understanding by everyone involved that an offense has taken place, a member of the church has been harmed by the actions of another, and the pastor or pastoral counselor is responsible for that harm done. Initially the client or parishioner will need support as he/she makes known the abuse has occurred and the violation of the pastoral relationship. The pastor or pastoral counselor who is responsible must be held accountable for his/her behavior and every effort should be made to insure that the offending behavior is not repeated.

The secondary goals focus on the restoration to wholeness. For the victim, this means support and affirmation to heal her/himself. For the community of faith, this means the opportunity to deal openly with its feelings of betrayal and to have its pain and grief acknowledged as well. For the offender, this means a possible therapeutic intervention that may help her/him to deal with the personal and professional issues that may have contributed to poor judgment, lack of impulse control, loss of professional boundaries, denial of responsibility for behavior, and the like. A context of creating justice is required in order for any secondary goal to be achieved.

Restoration for the victim means regaining a sense of personal and collective power, positive self-esteem, trust in the church and its professionals, and so forth. Restoration for the community of faith may result in a renewed sense of its ability to protect members from exploitation and to be faithful to its theological and ethical foundations, as well as a renewal of its trust in the pastoral ministry. Restoration for the offender may result in his/her ability to carry out an effective ministry and not to threaten the well being of parishioners and clients.

Forgiveness and reconciliation are the theological tools by which restoration is accomplished. However, forgiveness by the victim or the congregation depends on the offender's repentance. "If your brother wrongs you, reprove him; and if he repents, forgive him" (Luke 17:3). Repentance means to take on a new mind; that is, to change, which requires the offender to acknowledge responsibility and to be willing to undertake the necessary work to change his/her behavior. This acknowledgement must be expressed directly to the victim(s). Restitution also may be a part of this acknowledgement and the taking of responsibility for damage done. Financial restitution may make possible payment for medical and counseling expenses incurred by the victim(s) as a result of the offending behavior. When these kinds of actions have taken place, the victim(s) may be able to consider the possibility of forgiveness and the climate for reconciliation, restoration, and healing may develop.

A word of caution: Premature reconciliation should be avoided at all costs. The encouragement of premature reconciliation by a congregation or denomination prior to repentance or restitution undercuts the process of seeking justice and eventually prevents authentic restoration for all persons in the situation.

The church as institution (whether congregation or denomination) is responsible for the actions of its professionals. It ordains ministers to serve on its behalf and in its name. Therefore, it has the responsibility of overseeing the professional behavior of these persons. By and large the professional relationship between an individual clergyperson and the congregation/denomination is less formal than that of a doctor or psychologist with their professions (e.g., it does not involve licensing). It does, however, in some sense involve a covenantal relationship in which an ordained minister is accountable to the church (in whatever form) that ordained him/her. Likewise the church is responsible for its ministers. Thus, when a church learns that one of its ministers is engaged in sexual activity with a parishioner or client, it is the church's responsibility to call this minister to account and thus to protect its members from the abusive professional relationship.

The response is both administrative and pastoral. Administratively, policies and procedures should be developed and implemented so that when a situation of abuse within a professional relationship arises, the mechanism exists through which a congregation or denomination can act. Initially, the response to victim(s) should include information on the process of making a complaint, clarifying of their options in pursuing a complaint (including civil or criminal litigation), advocacy for them within the system, and counseling support to assist personal recovery. The administrative options in response to the offending pastor may range from restrictions on the pastor's counseling ministry with the requirement for rehabilitative therapy to termination of employment to denial of ministerial standing. Depending on the policy of the denomination, these options can be carried out by any designated church body or administrator. If the offense has occurred within a congregation itself, then the congregation also should be recognized as a victim and included in the administrative action. It should be kept informed of the process and involved whenever possible in decision making while respecting the wishes of the victims and their confidentiality.

Pastorally, the response to the victim is the first priority. She/he needs affirmation and support from her/his church in order to even raise this issue. Challenging an institution is never easy but challenging the church and one of its professionals from a position of powerlessness and betrayal is extremely difficult. She/he needs to know that there is both emotional and spiritual support for going through this process. The second pastoral priority is the congregation (if the offense occurred there). Denominational administrators must be sensitive to the pastoral needs of the congregation as a whole and to their sense of betrayal. Careful and sensitive listening and response in an open discussion can be invaluable to the sustenance of the congregation as a whole. The pastoral needs of the offending pastor should also be addressed. The best pastoral response here is refusal to support his/her denial of the behavior or of responsibility for the behavior. A firm and clear expectation of accountability can provide the means for acknowledging responsibility, repenting, and making restitution; thus the possibility of forgiveness and reconciliation may be created. Neither the administrative nor pastoral responses to the offending pastor should be punitive nor should they isolate and ostracize him/her. Likewise, they should not avoid naming the offense and the one responsible for it and taking all steps necessary to see that the offending behavior is not repeated in the church at any level. This is the only way to provide the means to rehabilitation and restoration. The offending professional must recognize that while there is support for him/her as a person and as a fellow pastor, there is no support for the unprofessional and unethical behavior in which he/she has engaged and that it will not be tolerated or excused.

CONCLUSION

Sexual contact by pastors and pastoral counselors in professional relationships is a serious credibility issue for the church today. The unwillingness of the church, by and large, to acknowledge this problem and to address it directly results in a loss of credibility with its people. Hence some people perceive the church, rightly or wrongly, as acting first to protect its own (i.e., the pastors who act unethically in their pastoral role) from the consequences of their behavior. This perception is understandable since some people have experienced an absence of action and support when they reported instances of clergy misconduct, and have seen the church side with an offending pastor in a civil suit. They also may have seen other clergy support a colleague's denial and excuse the behavior by suggesting that "he who is without sin...." Or they have observed the conspiracy of silence within the church when an offending pastor is "moved" to another conference/diocese/synod but no information is shared with the new employer about the offending behavior. Because of the lack of institutional response by the church, individuals frequently feel that their only recourse is civil court. Here, at least, they find a mechanism to seek restitution for damages done to them. It is an indictment of the church's inaction when recourse to the civil court is deemed necessary..

The church is responsible for monitoring the professional behavior of its ministers. But even if it decides conscientiously to do so now, it still will have to build trust with the public. The lack of credibility is such that the concerns by some people within the church with raising this issue and diligently pursuing it is not necessarily supported. Individuals who have been harmed by a pastor and who have not found support from their denomination or congregation do not trust the church to be willing or capable of holding its representatives accountable. Too often this belief results in persons leaving the church altogether, feeling betrayed, and concluding that the church is not a safe place for them.

Certainly the church must take responsibility for the well-being of its members if it is to be a place where we seek to make justice within and without and if it is to be a place of sanctuary and safety for persons who are vulnerable and facing crisis. We cannot overlook or avoid the injustice in our midst when pastors misuse their pastoral role in sexual contact with their parishioners or clients. We must act justly, fairly, and decisively if we are to restore the integrity of the ministry and of the church.

PART II

Assessment And Initial Intervention With Victims

The discussion by Schoener, Milgrom, and Gonsiorek in Chapter 7 of the issues in treating the victims of sexual exploitation by psychotherapists and counselors is an updated revision of a monograph that was widely circulated for over 12 years. Although it focuses largely on adult female victims, many of the observations and suggestions also apply to male victims of sexual exploitation.

Chapter 8 by Gonsiorek presents specific suggestions regarding both male victims and the victims of same-sex contact. Very little discussion of this segment of sexually exploited clients has appeared in the literature to date.

Virtually all professional writings on therapist-client sex have focused, explicitly or implicitly, on the adult client. Chapter 9 by Schoener attends to the child or adolescent victim. The discussion covers a number of different types of cases and, also, the effects of sexual exploitation on younger victims.

Chapter 10, by Schoener, is a supplement, in a sense, to Chapters 7-9. All three are concerned with the effects on clients of sexual abuse by therapists and stress the clients' needs for intervention and treatment. In contrast, Chapter 10 relates predominantly to the assessments of damages suffered by abused clients who are initiating civil suits against their abusers.

False and misleading complaints, an issue that has been grossly neglected in the literature, are central to Chapter 11. The discussion by Schoener and Milgrom includes descriptions of some of the people and complaints that have been dealt with at the Walk-In Counseling Center and offers suggestions for evaluating such complaints. Although the cases are rare, they occur often enough to deserve knowledgeable handling.

CHAPTER 7

THERAPEUTIC RESPONSES TO CLIENTS WHO HAVE BEEN SEXUALLY ABUSED BY PSYCHOTHERAPISTS[1]

Gary Richard Schoener
Jeanette Hofstee Milgrom
John C. Gonsiorek

In order to work with the sexually exploited victims of psychotherapists, a thorough understanding of the victims' experiences is essential. Some valuable background information on such abused clients is provided in different chapters of this volume in Chapter 12 which discusses assessment. Reports of work with support groups can be found in Chapters 13, 14, and 15.

Four books, written at least in part by victim/survivors of therapist-client sex, are now available; they are Bates and Brodsky (1988), Freeman and Roy (1976), Plasil (1985), and Walker and Young (1986). Each presents a different type of situation, and three of the four (Plasil is the exception) focus on civil suits filed against the abusing therapists. Freeman & Roy's book (*Betrayal*, 1976), which was made into a movie of the same title, may some day be commercially available on videotape. A number of national and local TV programs over the past decade also have included interviews with victims of sexual exploitation by therapists.

Sanderson (1989a) presents a number of articles by counselors and psychotherapists on working with victims of sexual exploitation. Pope and Bouhoutsos (1986) focus much of their book on work with victims; their first chapter includes various scenarios of client-therapist sexual involvement. Rasmussen (1987) also offers some useful observations and suggestions on work with victim/survivors.

In the updated version of our work with sexually exploited clients of psychotherapists presented in this chapter, most of our clients were women, and nearly 80% were women who had been sexually abused by a male therapist. Our basic observations, however, also seem to fit the more than 10% female/female exploitative relationships as well as the less frequent male/male and female therapist/male client situations. In addition, Gonsiorek (see Ch. 8), provides some observations vis-à-vis male victims and same-sex situations. Child/adolescent victims also are treated separately (see Ch.9).

---

[1] This chapter is a revision and amplification of the authors' earliest publications on the subject. The initial version was a monograph (Schoener, Milgrom, & Grace) published in Fall 1976 by the Walk-In Counseling Center. It was rewritten in January 1977 and then revised in 1981 and 1983 by Schoener, Milgrom, & Gonsiorek. The work was again revised by Schoener, Milgrom, & Gonsiorek and published in *Women and Mental Health* (Mowbray, Lanir, & Hulce, 1984). More recent versions were produced by Schoener and Milgrom (1987) and Milgrom and Schoener (1987).

Like the earlier versions, this chapter is based primarily on the authors' clinical experiences. At the time of writing they included more than 1,500 client situations spanning well over a decade. This time period has been long enough to give us the benefit of some long-term follow-up and considerable feedback from clients. A number of these clients also have made valuable suggestions for improving our exposition.

VARIETIES OF THERAPIST-CLIENT SEXUAL CONTACT

The ever-broadening variety of therapist-client sexual contact situations that have come to our attention over the past 14 years increase the difficulty of making summary statements about therapeutic responses to clients who have undergone such an experience.

The treatment of this subject in fiction and in the news media has led to images that vary considerably, depending upon what one has read or heard. Furthermore, the growing awareness of sexual exploitation by clergy and religious professionals as well as nonpsychiatric physicians has complicated the picture even further.

In the mid-1970s many clients did not realize that sex with a therapist is unethical and a type of exploitation; today, however, most seem to realize that it is improper.[2] There is still some confusion over seductive game-playing and various types of touching, but it is a very rare client indeed who does not know that the sexual contact is wrong.

Another change today is that more clients come in with a specific need or agenda, such as obtaining assistance in filing a complaint or confronting the therapist, whereas in the past clients often needed all sorts of assistance just to define their needs.

The effect of sexual exploitation on a client varies a great deal depending on the client's strengths and vulnerabilities, the nature of the relationship, support or lack thereof from significant others, how long ago the relationship ended, and many other factors.

To convey a notion of the variety of situations in which we have consulted, we offer, as examples, the following types of relationships:

1. Sexual Touch as Therapy: Regardless of the client's presenting complaint, therapist A manages to focus the therapy, at least in part, on sexual inhibitions. He seems able to find such inhibitions in everyone. He fondles a female's breasts or genitals, in order to help "desensitize" the client to sexual anxiety.

Therapist B uses relaxation techniques with clients who are trying to cope with migraine headaches or tension. Once he has them relaxed on a couch, he kisses them on the neck, touches their breasts, and appears to have an orgasm.

2. "Learning to Love" as Therapy: Therapist C develops a romantic involvement with female clients in a "storybook" fashion, in most cases. In several, however, he "loses control" and has sexual contact with the clients, after which he apologizes, saying he "got carried away." Clients are confused and troubled about all this; some of the greatest upset occurs among clients with whom he was not overtly sexual.

Therapist D sexually arouses clients and has them practice masturbation in front of him. They are instructed to fantasize the therapist when they make love to their spouses. As the marital relationships deteriorate, he blames their spouses'

---

[2]While the psychiatric code of ethics prohibited it in 1973, psychology did not do so until 1977.

"immaturity." He does not have intercourse with the client but seems to get his primary satisfaction from the power and control he wields and from voyeurism.

Therapist E tells clients directly that they need to "learn to love" and that this can be done with him. He even tells them that "transference" means that the client transfers love and affection to the therapist. This situation is similar to that described in *Betrayal* (Freeman & Roy, 1976).

3. Exploring Sexual Identity: A purportedly heterosexual female therapist, F, has questions about her sexual identity which she shares with a female client who is dealing with some of the same issues. The therapist initiates sexual activity as an experiment.

Another heterosexual therapist, G, is flattered by the adoration and attraction of a lesbian adolescent who is just coming out, and engages in seductive games, playing a sort of brinksmanship, which eventually breaks down and sexual activity occurs.

A closeted gay male therapist, H, and a closeted lesbian therapist, I, each engage in sex play and inappropriate closeness with young clients who are in the process of "coming out."

An older female heterosexual therapist, J, attempts to "cure" a young adult gay male of his homosexuality by "teaching" him "normal" heterosexual sex—in vivo.

4. "Fatal Attraction": Therapist and client develop an intense, emotionally charged relationship, starting with their first session together. The transference and countertransference are strong and literally out of control from the outset.

Therapist K, a male, develops an intense involvement with a female client, risking discovery by colleagues and each of their spouses. They take trips together and, at times, are seen together in public. When the relationship goes stale and the therapist attempts to break it off, the client pursues and harasses him, and attempts to destroy him professionally.

A female therapist, L, develops an intense involvement with a bisexual female client. There is hugging and kissing, but the therapist sets the limit at that point and tries to get the therapy going again. The client resists, angrily charging the therapist with abuse and trying to blackmail her into continuing the relationship, all the time charging that the therapist is censoring her true feelings of love and attraction for the client.

5. Romance: Therapist and client insist that they have fallen in love and that since love is not easy to come by in this world they deserve to pursue it. For example:

Therapist M who is married becomes romantically involved with a female client and they end up in an affair that lasts more than a decade. Many of their friends are not even aware that she was initially his client. After many years he finally divorces his wife but does not marry the client; she files charges and a civil suit.

Therapist N engages in erotic contact with many clients over the years until, in one instance, a client's spouse catches him in the act and he is charged with misconduct by a licensure board. Follow-up therapy is aimed at severing the relationship but it is unsuccessful and he and the client end up marrying.

Therapist O calls a number of clients for dates at intervals of from several weeks to several years after termination. He has sexual contact with a number of them and develops a long-term relationship with several. Some of the former clients think he is an exploiter whereas others feel that he genuinely cared for them and they appreciated his interest.

6. Brief Loss of Control: A married but separated female therapist, P, makes a home visit to a young lesbian client who is in extreme crisis. She ends up spending the night and they sleep in the same bed. The client is very confused. Varying accounts are given of how much physical contact took place.

A male therapist, Q, who has always been intrigued by prostitutes, ends up with one as a client. During a session he confesses his fascination, and he indicates that he is too distracted to do any therapy. The client comforts and reassures him. At this point they have sex. He apologizes and cancels the bill for the session.

Therapist R, a gay male, interviews a young and attractive male who is new in town. It turns out that the client does not really want therapy; he simply wants help in getting oriented in finding out about community organizations. The therapist mentions that his lover just left him and the client offers oral sex, which the therapist readily accepts.

7. "Bonding" and Other Types of Closeness: Therapists S and T, male and female, respectively, who work together in an "institute" they founded believe that true change comes about only through regression back to infantile states followed by "bonding" with and "reparenting" of the client by the therapist. A great deal of physical contact is involved, and at times, it is sexual. In one instance T, the female therapist, has a sexual encounter with a young man. Though alarmed at this, both therapists believe other professionals are "backward" and do not appreciate "reparenting." They decide against outside consultation and, within a year, both find themselves sexually involved with a client.

8. Closeness Between Women is "Different": A lesbian therapist, U, convinces herself and her client that there is no way their relationship can be exploitative if they terminate the therapy. Both she and the client see other therapists, and they become involved with each other. They then begin living together. They have been together in a committed relationship for seven years. (Rigby-Weinberg, 1986, describes several relationships of this type.)

9. "Nurturance": V, a female therapist of some prominence, engages in a sort of mock breast-feeding of an adolescent female client. The breast-feeding is represented as a type of "nurturance."

Therapist W, a male, believes that only a great deal of "nurturance" cures borderline personalities, and so he has adult clients sit on his lap while he "cradles and regresses them." Several women clients indicate that he appears to have an erection during the procedure, and that he often brushes the sides of their breasts, although he tries not be too obvious about it.

THE ROLE OF THE FOLLOW-UP HELPER[3]

Working with victims of therapist-client sexual involvement brings with it many challenges, not the least of which are the feelings of the helper. If the involvement is akin to incest (see Chapter 5 and Appendix A) then all subsequent helpers may be seen as family members in an incestuous family.

Before working with victims it is important to explore how one feels about this problem of therapist-client sex. If one is angry about the profession's failure to prevent it, one may be distracted from the client's needs and focus instead on one's reaction. And if one blames and rages against the therapist-perpetrator, the client may be distracted and try to defend the therapist.

Any therapist who has been harassed by a client may have great difficulty dealing with the level of rage many sexually exploited clients experience.

A therapist who is not knowledgeable about various complaint mechanisms may be of little help to a client who is trying to take action. One may project confusion or anxiety, which frequently is an outgrowth of the lack of knowledge, and so communicate to the client that he or she should not pursue a complaint.

SOME BASIC GUIDELINES

Based on our experiences with clients at WICC we repeat the suggestions we have made in earlier versions of this paper, with just a few additions.

1. Explore How the Client Feels About Seeing You and Offer Options

Clients who feel betrayed by a previous therapist are often fearful, uneasy, cautious, and/or ambivalent about seeing another mental health professional. They are understandably uneasy about therapists, often fearing that they will be seduced back into on-going therapy. Sometimes the feelings of distrust are focused on therapists of a particular gender but usually they are generalized to all professionals.

We view this distrust as healthy. In order to facilitate the most effective working relationship, we suggest that the following be made clear at the outset:

(1) The client can see a different helper, or one of a different gender, if it seems desirable.

(2) Sexual contact with clients is wrong in all circumstances.

(3) You yourself do not engage in erotic touching with clients.

We also recommend encouraging clients to set limits within their relationships with subsequent therapists or helpers; for example,

---

[3]We use the term "helper" instead of "therapist" or "advocate" to emphasize our position that clients who have been sexually exploited by psychotherapists often need kinds of assistance which do not necessarily fit into the specific roles of "therapist" or "advocate". Indeed, to automatically assume such clients "need" therapy or advocacy may be inappropriate, intrusive, or counterproductive. We focus in this section instead on the kinds of assistance which may be needed, not on reducing such needs to a specific role.

(1) to raise questions if they do not understand, feel discomfort, or disagree;

(2) to be aware that if discomfort ever becomes problematic, a consultant can be brought in to help sort things out; and

(3) to feel free to break off the sessions at any time or to ask for a referral to another practitioner.

2. Focus Intervention on Crisis Issues

Many clients are in crisis when they first come for help. It is important, therefore, to assess the suicide risk and to intervene in a specific crisis. Often a potential crisis looms because of an impending hearing, deposition, or other complaint-related event. As in other types of crisis situations, it is important to assess the client's support base or lack thereof. Clients often require encouragement and direction to call upon friends and family for support. If the client is in considerable distress and does not have a good support base, one may have to schedule several contacts—either face to face or via phone calls—to help him or her through the crisis.

3. Be Clear on Why the Client is Seeking Help From You

Some clients come in simply for assistance in filing a complaint of some sort whereas others require all types of assistance. It is very helpful to clarify why they decided to come in at this time and what they most hope you can supply. This focus on a client's agenda, besides being generally good clinical practice, is reassuring to most clients in that it exemplifies good professional boundaries.

4. Clarify the Current Status of the Relationship With the Exploitative Therapist

Not all clients who come in for help have broken off the relationship with the abusive therapist. Some, in fact, may imply or state that they have and reveal only later that they have not. For example, there may be upcoming events when they are likely to see the therapist and at other times there may be communication via phone calls, letters, or through third parties (e.g. a friend who is still seeing the therapist). It is important to clarify the situation early in the work with the client.

5. Avoid Making Assumptions About What Sexual Contact Occurred

If and when a client is willing to discuss the sexual contact or sexual advances, carefully explore what specifically occurred. It is common for clients to make general statements such as, "he was sexual with me" or "we got sexual" or "he propositioned me." However, these vague statements can have a wide range of meanings, and until a detailed account is obtained from the client it is impossible to know what happened. Statements about hugs, kisses, touches on the thigh, and the like are easier to understand if the client is specific about the nature of the contact, when it occurred, how long it lasted, and so forth.

6. Avoid Making Assumptions About the Gender of the Therapist or the Sexual Identity of Either Party

Clients sometimes talk about their experiences without revealing a therapist's gender. We recommend using the pronouns "he or she" to refer to the therapist until the client clarifies the gender. It is also very important to refrain from making assumptions about the sexual preferences of each party. Same-sex contact does not necessarily mean that either party is gay or lesbian. Sometimes within the therapeutic context both therapists and clients are involved with partners who are generally atypical for them. The same may be true of specific sexual acts. At times it appears that the therapist is actually experimenting with a client.

7. Refrain From Making Assumptions About How the Sexual Advances or Contact Affected the Client

When the client comes in for consultation his or her feelings about the therapist and the sexual contact may still be in a state of flux and quite changeable, even during one discussion. Subsequent conversation may reveal new layers of feelings that are not immediately accessible when the client is first interviewed.

Some clients are relatively unambivalent and see the relationship as exploitative or see the therapist as disturbed, and they simply want assistance in pressing charges. Some clients may be at the other end of the continuum and still be emotionally and romantically involved with the therapist and unwilling to let go. In between these extremes are clients who have mixed feelings and some confusion. They are angry and feel that the therapist behaved improperly, but they also feel as though they had a "special" romantic or emotional involvement with the therapist and are grieving its loss. Some had wrapped up their lives—or at least dreams of the future—in the relationship, often because they had been led on by the therapist, whereas others experienced the relationship as something they had to put up with to obtain therapeutic help.

In some situations, those in which the therapist broke implicit or explicit promises, a client may be far more focused on abandonment or on having been conned than on the sex. Some clients come in for assistance to recover assets that were given to the therapist at a time when the client believed a personal relationship was developing. They feel more like victims of fraud than sexual exploitation. The sexual transgressions or other aspects of unprofessional conduct that may seem of primary importance to the helper may be of minor importance to the client. The sexual contact may be the "tip of the iceberg" of a pattern of exploitation, and the non-sexual aspects may be the most egregious in some cases.

8. Identify What Issues Still Need Resolution

Clients come in with varying needs. Some persons have resolved most of their feelings about the past relationship with the exploitative therapist but others still have unresolved business. The client should be helped to clarify what has been resolved and what remains to be dealt with before a course of action is considered.

If the client is still actively involved with the abusive therapist, our practice is to agree to only one or two sessions in order not to inadvertently support the destructive relationship. If the client is actively withdrawing from the relationship, we work with her or him for as long as the client appears to be genuinely pulling out of it. If we discontinue seeing a client because he or she still is involved in the destructive relationship, we give a clear rationale for our decision and the assurance that we are available to help at some future date if the client genuinely wants to discontinue the relationship.

9. Evaluate the Client's "Other Problems"

Although a client may seem intent on dealing with the past exploitation, he or she may have current life stresses or problems that require attention. It is important to assess a client's situation fully before focusing on merely the exploitation issues.

10. Provide Advocacy or Refer the Client to an Advocate

Most clients hope for and/or need advocacy. It may mean simply providing support for a client's going ahead with a complaint, accompanying the client to a meeting, or helping the client to put together a formal complaint. Some helpers avoid such a role but in exploitation cases it may be very important. Hence, if one is not in a position to serve as an advocate, one should help the client to locate someone who can. It is important for the helper to understand the complaint procedures so that he or she will have a clear picture of what the client will be facing. Being ignorant of complaint mechanisms gives the client a message that perhaps complaints are useless or even dangerous, or that the helper does not take the complaint process seriously enough to be well-versed in it.

11. Writing Diaries and Complaints

Some clients find keeping journals to be very helpful in understanding and dealing with the abusive relationship. Likewise, many clients find it helpful to write about their experiences, even if they do not file a formal complaint. Many clients report that writing down their stories as part of a complaint process is quite therapeutic, and some have found that accounts written by professionals are helpful. A few clients have written books or short stories as a way of collecting their thoughts.

12. Use of Reading Material

Reading material on sexual exploitation in general, and exploitation by psychotherapists in particular can be very useful in helping to reduce the client's sense of isolation, and also in helping the client to feel "normal." This can also facilitate some understanding of confusing feelings.

We frequently have given clients earlier versions of this chapter (e.g., Schoener, Milgrom, & Grace, 1977; Schoener, Milgrom, & Gonsiorek, 1981, 1983, 1984); though they were written for professional audiences, clients were appreciative of them. We also have frequently passed on an article from a local popular magazine (Sundstrom, 1977).

In addition, we have recommended books written by clients who have been victimized. For many years the only such book was *Betrayal* (Freeman & Roy, 1976). During the last two years we have referred some clients to *Therapist* (Plasil, 1985) and *A Killing Cure* (Walker & Young, 1986); the first gets the best reception and has the advantage of being less expensive and available in paperback. The new book by Bates and Brodsky (1988) is also worth considering, especially because it offers a unique combination of a client's account alongside that of an expert witness.

Serious practitioners should read these books and articles and decide for themselves which would be useful to recommend to clients. After suggesting them, one might solicit client feedback about their use. In addition, one might seek out and make copies of local newspaper or magazine pieces on this topic. In all cases one should forewarn the client that each case differs, but that it is sometimes helpful to read what others have been through. One should be prepared for the possibility that reading such a publication will spark the client's memory and generate the discussion of events that previously had been forgotten or overlooked.

13. Consider a Processing Session

Processing sessions (see Ch. 28) can be very helpful in sorting out what happened between the client and therapist. It is one of the few means of getting the therapist to answer questions about his or her actions. Extensive litigation, sad to say, sometimes fails to reveal answers to the very simple questions many clients have about why their therapist did what he/she did.

14. Support Groups: Very Helpful and At Times Essential

Included in this volume are a number of chapters on support groups and workshops for victims. They are invaluable approaches to breaking down a client's sense of isolation and providing her or him with much-needed support. Group meetings can take the edge off the exploitation experience in a way that individual therapy rarely can.

COMMON CLIENT EXPERIENCES

Pope (1987, p. 16) suggested, "The sequelae of a patient's sexual relatioship with a therapist may form a distinct clinical syndrome with both acute and chronic phases. He describes a "Therapist-Patient Sex Syndrome," which includes:

a. ambivalence...
b. guilt...
c. emptiness and isolation...
d. sexual confusion...
e. identity and boundary disturbance...
f. lability of mood (frequently involving severe depression and anxiety)
g. inability to trust
h. suppressed rage
i. increased suicidal risk (which may be related to the suppressed rage)
j. cognitive dysfunction (especially in the areas of attention and concentration, frequently involving flashbacks, intrusive thoughts, unbidden images, and nightmares)

(Pope, 1987, pp. 16-17)

Apfel and Simon (1986, pp. 146-48) described the following series of psychodynamic themes as emerging in victims of therapist-client sex: (a) Ambivalence toward therapist and therapy; (b) questioning of reality and sanity; (c) replay of pathogenic childhood situations; (d) bondage to a therapist; (e) persistence or worsening of original symptoms; (f) constricted intimacy with men; (g) rage and desire for revenge; (h) excesses of guilt and shame; (i) stifled imagination; and (j) creation of a crisis situation.

From still another perspective, Rasmussen (1987, pp. 15-17) listed the following feeling states as common to victim survivors: (a) denial; (b) confusion; (c) rage (directed at therapist, or global); (d) powerlessness; (e) guilt; (f) shame; (g) depression; (h) betrayal and a sense of abandonment; (i) ambivalence; (j) anxiety and fear; and (k) psychic numbing.

Despite the different perspectives of these authors, they show considerable overlap in what they observed. However, we feel that there is not, in fact, a predictable, unvarying syndrome common to victims; thus we make no attempt to define one. Yet, it is quite useful for clients who have been victimized to learn that many of the feelings they are experiencing have been experienced by others who have been through a like experience. Indeed, we often gave clients copies of the earlier versions of this chapter in hopes that they would reassure the client that others had been through what they were experiencing.

It is important to note that many clients experience only a few of the following feelings or do not experience them to the extent described here:

Deep-Seated Distrust

Most helpers are not accustomed to being mistrusted and, hence, they are not prepared for the level of distrust many exploited clients feel toward professionals in general. Gender is no protection; many clients who have been abused by male therapists come out of the experience with the same distrust for female professionals. These feelings also may generalize to family, friends, men in general, or everyone.

All other things being equal, the more areas in which boundaries were violated, the deeper is the distrust. Clients whose previous therapists violated confidentiality or manipulated their lives in addition to sexually exploiting them, are even more distrustful.

It is important to recognize and to accept the client's distrust. Efforts to win the client's trust are ill-advised and usually unnecessary. It is useful to understand the parameters of the distrust in order to have an idea of their effect. We commend a client for being appropriately guarded and note that the distrust of us should be no problem. We make it clear that we do not have sex with clients or try to run their lives or make their decisions for them, but that does not mean that we, or any other helpers, should be trusted completely.

We invite feedback, both positive and negative, and periodically ask clients how they feel about the direction in which our work with them is moving. We try to clarify our role and to encourage questions.

Ambivalence and Confusion

Clients who have been victimized by their therapists often struggle with contradictory feelings, which leads to considerable confusion and ambivalence. Anger is often felt along with closeness or affectionate feelings. Rage and distrust conflict with feelings of loss and a desire to be in the therapist's good graces again. Memories of feeling in love and fantasies of an on-going relationship or marriage clash with the sense of having been conned and used.

Clients often are confused about what the therapist really felt about them and what his or her true motivations were. A client often feels "special," yet wonders if there were others. The relationship may have seemed like "true love" yet the client is not sure what would have happened if they had met not as therapist and client but as social equals. The client wonders: "Why me?" "What attracted him to me?" "Did he (or she) really care about me?" "Is he (she) evil and exploitative?...or sick?" "What does this say about me?"

Furthermore, clients have difficulty separating the helpful things they learned or the true gains that were made in therapy from those aspects that may have simply been part of a seduction. They come to distrust even the major gains made in therapy, and follow-up work with them must help them to recognize the true gains and, at the same time, to support them in rejecting harmful aspects of the past relationship.

Confusion and ambivalence are especially evident during discussions of what sort of action to take. Many clients have a desire to have further contact with the therapist to obtain answers to questions left unanswered or to confront him/her with feelings that were never expressed. They would like the therapist to suffer consequences; yet, when filing a complaint is discussed, the clients tend to be protective. They feel that a grievous wrong was done to them but are not sure whether it justifies their bringing charges. They would like to protect other clients from harm additionally but are not sure they want to sacrifice themselves additionally to bring it about.

Our major therapeutic suggestions regarding ambivalence is to expect it and to assist the client in exploring the conflicting feelings, noting that they are all important.

Depression and Loss of Self-Esteem

Inasmuch as many people often seek psychotherapy in the first place to deal with depression and self-esteem problems, it is a sorry state of affairs when psychotherapy adds to these problems. When a romantic relationship starts with a psychotherapist, a client may feel a heightened sense of self-esteem. Some even report feeling "higher and happier" than ever before. Then, when the relationship turns sour or ends, the loss of self-esteem and depression may be worse than those experienced previously.

By contrast, in other situations, the client may begin losing self-esteem and developing a depression when the sexual contact begins. He or she may react the way a child incest victim sometimes does, that is, becoming fearful, depressed, and assuming blame for what is happening. The therapist may choose either to ignore the client's obvious distress or to explain it away, rationalizing that the cause of the distress is something other than the sexual contact.

Depression can be potentiated by persistent guilt and self-blame or by anger that is turned inward because the client has no easy avenue for its outward expression. Depression also can be felt in conjunction with grief over the loss of an important relationship or with the end of the fantasy about a long term relationship with the therapist.

Clients are often angry at themselves for having been vulnerable and trusting. One client was very disappointed in herself "...for having been so vulnerable, trusting, and being so emotionally involved with such a venomous creature." She was embarrassed about entries in her diary that portrayed the "school girl" infatuation she felt at the time.

Some exploitative therapists interpret a client's reluctance to become sexually involved as an inability "to love," "to trust," or "to accept love." The client's anxiety about intimacy with the therapist is interpreted as evidence of neurosis. Even after termination clients may fault themselves for not having been able to accept the therapist's love and they give the therapist the benefit of the doubt by assuming that his or her intentions may have been honorable.

Clients are often very hard on themselves for not having terminated the relationship earlier or, at least, at the first moment they sensed that something was wrong with it. This self-criticism can be heightened when a subsequent therapist, attorney, or friend puts them on the spot for not having exited from the situation earlier. The clients do not give themselves credit for terminating the relationship; instead, they criticize themselves for having succumbed in the first place.

In some cases a client may need anti-depressant medication. Facilitating the ventilation of anger can assist in improving his or her self-esteem.

The frequency of exploitation by psychotherapists should be discussed, and so should the fact that all manner of people (including clients who are themselves mental health professionals) have been victimized because of the powerful dynamics that bring the exploitation into being. Clients who still have protective or affectionate feelings toward a therapist especially need such reassurance; they need to know that such feelings do not mean that they are unable to come to grips with the situation.

Anger/Rage

Anger is almost universal among clients who have been sexually exploited by therapists, but the amount of anger varies considerably. Clients feel angry about a variety of things: the violation of trust; exploitation by someone they had paid for help; the waste of time on a relationship with no future; the deprivation of badly needed help; the continuation of their original problems after expending considerable effort in therapy; the emergence of new problems that must be dealt with as a result of therapy; the irretrievable waste of several years of their lives on this relationship; and the like.

Clients are outraged at still feeling sorry for the therapist or still feeling somewhat in his power after the relationship ends. They are angry that the government or professional societies do not do a better job of preventing incompetent and exploitative therapists from practicing. They often deeply resent the effort and energy it takes to file complaints and lawsuits, in terms of both the time involved and the personal exposure to further abuse. They may resent having to pay for therapy to deal with the aftermath of the abuse.

Subsequent helpers must assist clients to ventilate these feelings. Clients often have few people, if any, to whom they can express such anger and rage. However, clients who become fixated on these feelings may need to be challenged. At the same time, a few clients may insist that they feel no anger, only sadness and pity. We see no virtue in pushing them to "get in touch with their underlying anger"; whether it actually is underneath other feelings is not the issue. A client needs to develop self-confidence and to follow her or his own instincts—something that is not fostered by continuous challenge and second guessing from a helper.

Guilt and Shame

Like other victims, sexually exploited clients tend to blame themselves for what happened. Some exploitative therapists are masters of guilt induction, and clients may end up taking complete responsibility for the situation. Clients who have a history of problems with guilt or shame may be almost incapacitated by these feelings and carry them for years.

Specifically, clients often feel that they were seductive or did something to lead the therapist on. They point out that they were attracted to the therapist; they dressed attractively; they jumped at the opportunity for a more personal relationship with the therapist; and so on. They seem to ignore the fact that a therapist is a professional and is supposed to be in charge. They feel guilty about taking actions that may bring some tough consequences for the therapist.

Clients feel ashamed of having been conned or taken in by the therapist's promises, reassurances, or rationalizations. They feel guilty at times because even if they were not totally fooled they went along with the sexual advances anyway.

Clients also may feel guilty for having violated the trust of a spouse or significant other. They feel that they are guilty of infidelity and fault themselves for any deception they engaged in, even including deception in which the therapist provided the direction. The sense of having betrayed a spouse may be further complicated by the spouse's feeling betrayed.

Another area of shame and guilt is one in which the sexual behaviors themselves are sources of the client's disturbance or confusion, such as sexual contact with a gender not typical for that client or certain sexual practices (e.g., anal sex).

Many clients feel guilty because they have introduced or referred friends or relatives to the therapist. In some cases these people still are involved with the therapist and the client fears that they too are being harmed.

It is important to make clear to clients that the therapist alone is responsible for the conduct of the therapy; their readiness to trust and perhaps to go along with the therapist's requests are precisely what is expected of the "good client." Furthermore, a client's seductiveness is irrelevant; what is relevant is that the therapist violated ethical principles. Furthermore, involvement with a therapist is not comparable to an extra-marital affair although, unfortunately, the spouse or significant other may not see it so. As for sexual behaviors that induce guilt, it can be noted that the therapy situation is unique: it is one in which people do things they would not do in a different context.

When the feelings are very strong, shame and guilt may not be easily resolved; to some degree the reactions of significant others play a major role, positive or negative, in the resolution (or lack thereof). Pushing for quick resolution accomplishes little. Furthermore, some clients seem to have resolved these feelings but they reappear in "flashbacks" The subsequent helper should deal with the flashbacks and reassure the client that their reoccurrence is natural and will diminish over time.

Grief

After termination of a relationship with a therapist a client may experience grief; its severity depends on the length, extent, and nature of the involvement with the therapist. In understanding the grief and helping the client to gain insight into it, the roles the therapist has played in the client's life and the hopes and expectations that were tied to the relationship should be carefully examined.

First of all, the therapist may have helped the client through some very difficult times. In the helping role, the therapist may have taken on the mantle of a supportive parent, someone who accepted the client unconditionally.

Second, the therapist may have played the role of a close friend with whom most things could be shared and who stood by the client during crises. In many cases of therapist-client sex, the client has become the therapist's friend and has provided invaluable support when the therapist had a personal crisis. The ability to provide the therapist with this support also may have been of great importance to the client and a source of self-esteem.

Last but not least, the therapist may have been an important lover both emotionally and physically. Even in those situations in which the sexual relationship itself did not go well because of the therapist's problems, the romantic element may have been very important. When it did go well, sometimes it was very pleasurable and intense and, as such, difficult to replace. The client may now find "ordinary" relationships to lack intensity.

We recommend reviewing with the client the hopes, aspirations, and fantasies that were generated by the relationship and separating out the grief associated with their loss. Then the client can be led to examine from his or her perspective the positive aspects of the relationship and to use them to reaffirm his or her search for warmth, affection, support, and the like, however illusory they may have been in the exploitative context. Nonetheless, the losses are real and must be treated supportively, but without losing sight of the degree to which they may have been fantasized.

We reassure clients that grief tends to lessen over time although on occasion, especially when things are not going well and at anniversaries the grief may be temporarily heightened. These recurrences reflect the desire to withdraw from the current rigors of life. The sense of loss diminishes also with the development of new relationships or the reaffirmation of old ones.

Self-Doubt

Although connected with problems of self-esteem and potentiated by ambivalence and confusion, self-doubt is a distinct problem in itself. Experience has led us to believe that the attempts of victims to blame themselves can be healthy if they are part of the effort to attain mastery over the situation. If one believes that one is in part responsible for what happened, then there may be a hope of preventing its reoccurrence. In turn, a sudden collapse of the belief in personal responsibility can precipitate acute grief and depression, during which the client struggles with feelings of helplessness.

Even clients who displayed impressive histories of personal accomplishment and considerable self-confidence prior to the exploitative relationship with the therapist may struggle with self-doubt afterwards. The destruction of self-confidence in an exploitative therapy situation may be the ultimate modern anti-miracle: like the turning of gold into lead.

Sadly, the self-doubt at times may be pervasive and extend far beyond doubts of one's capacity to judge professional relationships to doubting that one can achieve anything on one's own. In one case, while the relationship was still going on, the client—chief counsel for a major firm—became unable to make legal decisions without his therapist's advice. He lost his position when his employer found out whom he was phoning for consultation when he left the conference room.

In dealing with self-doubt, one should first identify the client's past levels of self-confidence and self-doubt. A therapist has many tools to help or hurt, and the expertise to attack self-confidence as well as to challenge self-doubt. A number of historians of the healing arts have described troubling examples of abuse for political purposes in which psychological techniques became key aspects of brainwashing and interrogation. So, if a client was "broken," it may well have been by an "expert."

Second, one should explore with the client the degree and extent to which his or her instincts provided warnings, as well as any efforts that were made to test or challenge the therapist's actions or direction. Then examine the client's actions to get out of the relationship. The client should recognize that some people have more difficulties breaking off and, in fact, some remain involved with the therapist many years later.

As with other feelings, self-doubt will tend to diminish as the client moves ahead in his or her life and successfully tackles new challenges. Sometimes the ability to face the therapist in some sort of confrontation such as the ability to make it through a deposition in a civil suit or follow through on filing charges gives a major boost to self-confidence.

Fear

Fear and anxiety are common experiences of clients who are emerging from sexual relationships with their therapists. There are fears associated with what is ahead, such as fears that they will not be believed if they file a complaint, or fears that family or friends will reject them. They have pervasive fears of loss of privacy and losing other relationships or being humiliated in the process.

There are also often deeper fears that the therapist still has power over them, sometimes a result of subtle terrorization by the therapist; that the therapist may be violent, especially if they have witnessed hostile or aggressive behavior (including violence) expressed toward another client (see for example Plasil, 1985). They also may recall previous attempts to leave the relationship which failed because of the therapist's entreaties and/or intimidation.

Clients sometimes are directly intimidated and threatened by a therapist in subtle or not so subtle ways. This may have occurred by the therapist, by other clients under the therapist's direction (see for example Plasil, 1985), or by "supporters" of the therapist (see for example Olsen, 1989). We have had cases in which clients were terrorized by "mock rape"; being held down or sat on; or by being tickled while they were held down, and the like. When co-therapists and/or group members participate in such activities the level of terror can be extreme and clients then show some of the symptoms of torture victims.

Sadly, many clients do not spontaneously share accounts of this sort of episode, because of feeling considerable shame. The sadism of some exploitative therapists is frightening even in second-hand accounts; a few authors have taken cognizance of it, however (e.g., Smith, 1982).

In our experience therapists rarely have attempted to act on their threats; however, it is noteworthy that in some cases on record they have attempted to bring about a client's suicide (see for example Walker & Young, 1986), threatened clients with murder, or told clients that records can be altered and they can be made to appear crazy (WCCO-TV, 1984). Beyond exploring direct threats and advising a client to contact the authorities about them, it is important to ask about continued terrorization, such as the former therapist driving by the client's house, showing up in places frequented by the client, calling on the telephone, or sending messages through third parties. In the case of psychotherapy cults (see Ch. 19), other clients may participate in such harassment.

We try to help a client assess fears realistically and to take appropriate action. But we also try to provide reassurance when fears appear irrational or overblown; these fears should not be underestimated because they often gain more momentum when the client is contemplating following through on a complaint or similar action.

PRACTICAL PROBLEMS A CLIENT MAY HAVE TO FACE

The unique aspects of the therapist-client sexual relationship lead to some very real, practical problems in various aspects of the recovery process. Some of the common problems follow:

Where to Go for Help

When a therapist who exploited clients is well-known, or is one who was highly recommended by friends, family, or another health care practitioner, the clients have great difficulty ascertaining where to go for help. Often, the therapist has told them that they will not be believed or has emphasized his or her powerful contacts in the professional community. In some instances, a therapist has told clients that he or she was the only one who could provide help.

Perpetrators are very intimidating when they hold offices in professional organizations, have faculty appointments, or consult broadly in the community. Clients, consequently, are not sure where they can find an objective helper, or even a helper who will maintain confidentiality because they often assume that professionals "stick together" and "cover for each other." This is not a groundless concern.

The problem can seem almost insoluble in rural areas, small towns, or within minority communities where few options exist. It is one of the reasons we receive calls from throughout the United States and why clients sometimes travel long distances to participate in groups or workshops (see Chs. 13, 17, and 18).

Being Discounted by Professionals

Clients are quite fearful of not being believed or of being treated as pariahs by the next professional they see. Some clients even wait until they have been in therapy for a period before they reveal the past relationship. Not surprisingly, they are very sensitive to signs of rejection or disbelief.

One practical problem is that the professional to whom a sexually exploited client recounts her or his experience may be sufficiently shocked to the point of having difficulty reacting to it. The client often has considerable difficulty "reading" this reaction and may interpret it as rejection (e.g., reflecting disbelief, or disgust). The helper's anxiety and uneasiness can be similarly interpreted.

In some instances the professional to whom the story is told comes on like an interrogator as he or she tries to focus on the facts of the allegation. This behavior is especially common when the professional has a potential dual role in the case, for example, when he or she is a partner or co-worker at the same facility, chairs an ethics committee or professional organization, or sits on a licensure board. Sadly, many professionals behave improperly in such situations by not immediately clarifying their situation. Friends of the therapist-perpetrator also are in a conflict of interest situation should declare this and refer the client to someone else.

We encounter many incidents of professionals who discount clients' stories, a fact that should not be surprising given the number of prominent professionals who are more suspicious of clients than of colleagues.

Overreaction by Friends or Professionals

Sometimes the professionals who hear the story or complaint of sexual exploitation become upset to the point of overreacting. Instead of providing support for the client, listening to details, and allowing for a careful discussion of options, they demand immediate action. Family members or other victims (including professionals who have themselves been victims) may over-identify with the victim and project their own feelings onto the victim, or they may push for certain responses from the victim.

Clients need the time and freedom to explore diverse and often evolving feelings. Excessive catharsis by family, friends, or professionals can interfere with this process. Professionals need to work out their frustration with unethical practitioners through professional consultation, not during a client session. We do not mean to imply that a professional should not share her or his strong disapproval of the therapist's alleged unethical conduct but that once these feelings have been communicated, they need to be put aside. The client likely is already overburdened by feelings and does not need to be further burdened by someone else's.

How to Express Feelings?

The emotional isolation felt by most clients is often directly related to the difficulty of knowing how or when to share feelings with others. Rasmussen (1987, p. 17) described a "kind of psychic numbing" that may occur in the effort to survive the situation. Unfortunately, friends and family members often are not in a position to fully understand or sympathize with the client's situation. They may be quite angry with or even blame the client.

Family members and other "significant others" must struggle with their own feelings. Revelation of a sexual relationship with a therapist can lead to relationship problems or divorce (see Ch. 22). People often do not understand the extent of the power inequity in a therapeutic relationship and the degree of the client's vulnerability. The victim may not be seen as a victim, which was once the case with victims of rape and incest.

Even when the story can be told to significant others, some aspects often cannot be shared (e.g., the guilt about particular sexual practices). Another problem is discussing positive feelings for the therapist. It is easier for family and friends to accept anger in such situations than positive feelings.

The Difficulties of Taking Action

Reporting acts of exploitation brings with it new burdens for the client. It requires an additional expenditure of time by a client who already resents having wasted time on therapy. Ironically, taking action or complaining will extend for a time the effect of the exploitation on his or her life. Legal action, or filing a licensure complaint, means having to relive painful experiences and to endure the unpleasantness of cross-examination. A client also may need to expend funds to obtain legal advice or assistance, but even then the client may face possible retaliation attempts by the therapist.

Clients typically feel resentment at the sufferings they undergo to protect the public. Many complaint mechanisms are very slow moving. Although the client is only a "witness" and has no independent right to counsel, a good deal is often required of him or her. The client may be cross-examined while the therapist looks on but be excluded from sessions in which the therapist tells his or her story. Even in a civil suit or licensure action, if the finding is against the therapist, legal appeals may keep the matter alive for several years.

<u>Fear of Public Exposure</u>

A major deterrent to client action is the fear of public exposure for the past exploitation. However willingly the client may take the risk personally, he or she may fear embarrassing family members. Some clients may fear professional embarrassment, disrupting progress in a new job, or the effect on a current relationship.

Clients also fear gossip. They refrain from telling family or friends lest the story be passed on and become community knowledge. They worry about confidentiality, loosely guarded records or professional gossip on the "grapevine." They also are reluctant to tell members of their support groups for fear that the story will be repeated outside the group. In a small town or minority community setting, fears of public exposure can be almost overwhelming.

CONCLUSION

The broad range of client responses to sexual exploitation by psychotherapists makes it critical that therapeutic helpers approach such clients with an open mind and flexible response set. The client must define the issues and set the tone for the interaction. Preset rigid approaches based on theories of victimization are a disservice to the client and in some instances can bring about further victimization. Many of the other chapters in this book provide descriptions of a variety of intervention and support strategies—options which may be useful if a therapeutic helper approaches the client in the problem-solving manner suggested in this chapter.

CHAPTER 8

SEXUAL EXPLOITATION BY PSYCHOTHERAPISTS: SOME OBSERVATIONS ON MALE VICTIMS AND SEXUAL ORIENTATION ISSUES

John C. Gonsiorek

This chapter presents observations on men who have been exploited by their psychotherapists (male or female) and on situations in which women have been exploited by female therapists. The ideas presented here are tentative observations based on a limited number of cases.

Such cases are relatively rare. Schoener, Milgrom, and Gonsiorek (1983), describing the sample of cases of sexual exploitation by psychotherapists handled by Walk-In Counseling Center of Minneapolis, reported that in 250 cases, the offender-victim distribution was 208, male psychotherapist with female client; 30, female psychotherapist with female client; 8, male psychotherapist with male client; and 4, female psychotherapist with male client.

In the four years that followed the collection of these data, the Center worked with three times as many cases of sexual exploitation and now shows some increases in male victims. The rough percentages currently are 80% for male therapist-female client; 13% female-female; 5% male-male; and about 2% female therapist-male client.

Two fairly recent studies indicate higher percentages for male-male relationships. Gartrell, Herman, Olarte, Feldstein, and Localio (1986) described a self-report study of psychiatrists in which 88% reported male psychiatrist-female patient sex; 7.6%, male-male sex; 3.5%, female psychiatrist-male patient sex; and only 1.4%, female psychiatrist-female patient sex. In the first attempt at an incidence-prevalence study of which I am aware, the Wisconsin Psychological Association Task Force on Sexual Misconduct by Psychotherapists, reported by Kuchin (see Chapter 3), 89% of the client victims were women and 11%, men. The Wisconsin study also found 6.9% of the offending therapists to be women, whereas Gartrell et al. reported only 4.9%. In contrast, our clinic finds female therapist offenders to account for about 15% of the cases, although most are female-female relationships.

Clearly, the "typical" sexual exploitation is by a male therapist of a female client; at the same time, the "typical" client-victim is female more often than the "typical" perpetrator is male. It is possible that the differences in percentages between these samples relate to differences within each professional group or even geographical areas. For example, the Walk-In Counseling Center sample is less than 25% psychiatric, whereas the Wisconsin sample is 33% psychiatric, and Gartrell's sample, 100% psychiatric. Furthermore, for reasons discussed later in this chapter, male victims are unlikely to report sexual incidents, and, in same-sex involvements, the incidents are even less likely to be reported.

Accounts of same-sex sexual exploitation by psychotherapists are rare in the literature. Burnstein (1986), Olsen (1989), and Oder (1986) described male same-sex cases, and Brown (1984, 1986) and Rigby-Weinberg (1986) described cases in a lesbian community. Brodsky (1986) briefly mentioned same-sex situations; however, she did not cite a data base for supporting the familiar stereotype that lesbian and gay male therapists, and especially the latter, have younger victims. Rigby-Weinberg (1986), in contrast, reported quasi-consensual relationships between mature lesbian women in a number of cases she had examined. My experience is at variance with Brodsky's; I have found no particular trend for lesbian therapists to choose younger victims, and I have observed that male victims, as a group and regardless of sex of therapist, tend to be younger.

One final caveat is in order. It is noted elsewhere in this volume that the sexual activity between client and therapist does not in and of itself define the sexual orientation of either party. Sexual experimentation may occur within the psychotherapeutic context either in terms of specific sexual acts or the gender of the partner.

CHARACTERISTICS OF MALE VICTIMS

The effects of sexual exploitation by psychotherapists (see Luepker & Retsch-Bogart, 1980; Pope & Bouhoutsos, 1986; Schoener, Milgrom & Gonsiorek, 1983, 1984; and Ch. 10) include client guilt, shame, grief, anger, depression, loss of self-esteem, ambivalence, confusion, fear, and distrust. I have observed that male as well as female victims display these characteristics. However, male victims also appear to manifest some unique reactions. Vinson (1984) reported that in her small sample both male victims and victims in same-sex situations described the sexual involvement with their psychotherapists as positive. Nevertheless, this finding differs from the reports of most victims and from my observations.

Male victims tend to have a difficult time perceiving that they have been victimized. My hypothesis is that this reaction is related to male sex-role socialization. It is congruent for a woman socialized in our society to perceive herself as being victimized. Because males tend to assume that any power dynamic operates in their favor, they may have a high level of rationalization and denial that they are powerless and have been victimized. Further, the psychological aftermath experienced by victims of sexual exploitation by psychotherapists appears to be ego-dystonic (i.e., unacceptable to the self) for many male victims. Thus there is erected an initial barrier of denial and rationalization to the occurrence of the victimization and then a second barrier to the effects of that victimization.

In a similar vein, many men tend to view sexual expression as a male prerogative. They tend to view any sexual experience as something they have chosen or created rather than something in which they may have been manipulated, tricked, or forced to participate. It is striking how many male victims—even in the face of much corroborating evidence that their psychotherapists were exploitative and manipulative—retain the belief that the sexual interaction was freely chosen by them and was their prerogative. This is especially true when the psychotherapist is female and the client is a younger heterosexual male. The responses of gay male victims of male psychotherapists tend to fall among those of female victims of male therapists. I hypothesize that if gay males during the process of coming out experienced sexual manipulation by other males, then perhaps they more readily can identify manipulation and react against it.

SEXUAL ORIENTATION AND SEXUAL EXPLOITATION BY PSYCHOTHERAPISTS: SOME INTERACTIONS

The sexual orientation of clients may influence how they will be affected by sexual exploitation by therapists.

When clients are firmly heterosexual, they are apt to view the experience of sexual contact with a therapist of the same sex as highly ego-dystonic. Clients whose orientation is firmly homosexual experience sexual contact with a therapist of the opposite sex as highly ego-dystonic also. This reaction seems to have two very different effects: On the one hand, some individuals may more easily see the exploitation as victimization (precisely because it is ego-dystonic for them). And, on the other hand, some individuals may feel ashamed and confused, and they may have a great deal of difficulty making sense of the experience. For some of the latter, the exploitation can precipitate a crisis about sexual identity that appears to have little or no basis in their histories, but stems directly from the exploitation. My impression, although tentative, is that heterosexual males view sexual contact with a therapist of the same sex as exploitative more easily than do heterosexual females, and that these women tend to be somewhat more confused and disoriented by sexual exploitation by a same-sex therapist. The reason for the difference may be that heterosexual males as a group tend to be more intolerant of homosexuality. They view it as more alien and they distance themselves from it more strenuously. Both sexes, however, present the full range of reactions.

Clients whose sexual orientation is homosexual often present some different issues. They may find it difficult to complain about a therapist of the same sex who has exploited them for fear of being regarded as disloyal to their community. That is, their perception of the exploitative therapist as a member of their oppressed minority group makes for a greater ambivalence in filing a complaint. Client-victims who are homosexual also may have realistic fears: In the process of taking action against the exploitative therapist, their own sexual orientation may become public and they may be victimized consequently by powerful social forces. Although this attitude sometimes may stem to some degree from the client's internalized homophobia (i.e., self-hatred for being gay; see Malyon, 1982), the process of complaining does represent a great risk for homosexual clients. They may well experience discrimination if their sexual orientation becomes public.

The sexual exploitation of a homosexual client by a therapist of the opposite sex often can mobilize internal homophobia and leave the client feeling confused, ashamed, inadequate, and powerless. Such clients also risk disclosure of the sexual orientation during a complaint, even though it may not be germane to the issue. The exploitation may have been especially confusing if it was presented as an effort to "cure" their homosexuality or to "explore their sexual options."

The experience of being exploited by an individual of the same sex may increase the internalized homophobia of a homosexual client if it contributes to a belief that same-sex relationships are untrustworthy, damaging, and improper. I also have the impression of sex differences in this situation. For some gay males perceiving sexual exploitation by a male therapist as victimization is rife with difficulties to the extent that they view sexual contact with many males as part of their gay lifestyle. A segment of the gay male community is in some ways "super male" insofar as they view unrestricted sexual behavior as their prerogative. Such an intensification and crystallization of male attitudes may make it difficult for this subset of individuals to perceive that they have been exploited. On the other hand, some gay men who may have experienced sexual manipulation by other men have understood this as exploitation, and developed the assertiveness skills necessary to avoid being sexually exploited. Paradoxically, this second group of gay men very quickly may label sexual contact with their therapists as exploitative with minimal denial and a clear understanding of the abuse involved.

Lesbian clients, particularly if they are strongly feminist-identified, may be deeply ambivalent toward complaining about a female psychotherapist who has sexually exploited them, especially if that female psychotherapist is also lesbian and/or feminist-identified. The strong sense of cohesion in many lesbian communities may set up covert expectations that women, especially lesbian women, never betray other women. Again, paradoxically, those lesbian clients who are assertive and clear about the nature of exploitation may have an easier time viewing the situation for what it is. However, the pressures toward cohesion in the lesbian community appear to be stronger than those in the gay male community. Further, some lesbian feminist therapists hold the personal and political belief that therapists and clients should be equal. This belief may make it easier for them to rationalize or to deny the beginnings of boundary violation. Brown (1984, 1986) provided an excellent discussion of the particulars of these issues in lesbian communities.

Clients who are confused about their sexual orientation often are thrown into a deeper stage of confusion when they are sexually exploited by their psychotherapists. These individuals frequently display intense ambivalence toward filing a complaint as well as toward their own sexuality. Some clients who are confused about their sexual orientation are exceptionally vulnerable to the prolonged and highly negative effects of sexual exploitation by their psychotherapists regardless of a therapist's gender.

THERAPIST-PERPETRATORS IN SAME-SEX EXPLOITATION

The following description is not meant to substitute for the therapist types described in Chapter 32, but to elaborate on that typology. The therapists who sexually exploit clients of the same sex show some diversity.

Psychotherapists who are in the process of working through their own coming out issues appear to be vulnerable to engaging in the sexual exploitation of same-sex clients. Note that these therapists represent a risk to clients who are gay, lesbian, or confused about their sexual orientation, independent of any direct sexual exploitation per se. Thus such psychotherapists also go through denial, ambivalence, and internalized homophobia, which often may be projected, acted out, or in other ways foisted upon clients. These psychotherapists may be consciously or unconsciously seductive to clients, particularly if the psychotherapists fear taking risks in disclosing their sexual orientation to others. Unconsciously, therefore, they may encourage clients to take poorly planned risks or no risks at all.

Another risky situation is that in which the therapist, whose sexual orientation is more or less stable as gay or lesbian, is socially isolated. The situation may arise out of poor social skills, depression, a series of stresses or setbacks in her or his personal life, or other factors that may be characterological or situational. These psychotherapists may tend to view gay or lesbian clients or clients who are confused about their sexual orientation as peers or as a support system. If these psychotherapists perceive themselves to be powerless, and if they are fearful or unsuccessful in social situations with other gay or lesbian persons, they may begin to socialize with their gay or lesbian clients to maintain the environment in which they can feel respected, successful, and powerful. The situation may then lead to a sexual relationship with the client. In this situation the sexual exploitation per se may be the tip of the iceberg, especially if there is a history of the therapist's using clients for social and personal needs (whether any sexual contact occurs). Although these problems certainly are not unique to gay and lesbian psychotherapists, such therapists actually may have fewer opportunities to reduce their isolation.

Many minority groups, including gay and lesbian communities, have a tradition of tolerance for less well-trained and credentialed professionals. Given the hostile treatment the lesbian and gay communities have endured from "established" mental health professionals until very recently, this tolerance is not surprising. Minorities are more likely to attract more mental health "practitioners" who have no or minimal training and credentials and some of whom have little understanding of professional boundaries and ethical concerns, as well as others who may see standard qualifications as "traditional" and therefore undesirable or irrelevant. Such individuals pose a special risk for boundary violations when they function as therapists within the gay and lesbian communities.

I have noted a few instances of cult-like phenomena in the gay and lesbian communities. For example, a therapist will purport to have special abilities or techniques for helping individuals to come to accept and embrace their same-sex orientation. Such therapists do not differ substantially from the psychotherapy cult phenomena discussed in other chapters (see Ch. 19) in this volume. However, given the external oppression that many gay and lesbian persons continue to face, and the ensuing vulnerability of some members of the community, the appeal of such cults can be especially strong.

Occasionally, one encounters a particular boundary problem in mental health services in the gay and lesbian (or other minority) community, which is not primarily sexual exploitation but may involve sexual behavior. Therapists who are very active in multiple community organizations may develop complicated and overlapping ties within the gay and lesbian community. If great care is not taken to maintain proper professional boundaries, such individuals may blur distinctions among different organizational, social, and therapeutic roles. Typically, this confusion eventuates in confidentiality problems, financial exploitation, and various conflicts of interest and poor boundary situations. Sexual or emotional exploitation also may become part of this picture.

Another situation that I have observed appears to be one that is the most damaging and exploitative. It involves psychotherapists who are deeply ambivalent and profoundly conflicted about their same sex feelings. They often are intensively homophobic and their same sex feelings are fragmented and, at times, split off and not integrated into their emotional life. These individuals may act out sexually with clients of the same sex and treat the situation as a "dirty little secret." Often they project their intense ambivalence and self-hatred onto clients, and they may overtly or covertly blame the clients for the sexual interactions. Clients may receive messages that they are sick and perverted for being involved in same sex situations and that the involvements are all their fault. Such psychotherapists frequently are highly disparaging toward other gay and lesbian individuals, may actively discourage a client from forming a support system in the gay or lesbian community, and subtly label gay/lesbian individuals as pathological. They may even deny that the sexual contact with the client is a homosexual experience; instead, it may be termed a "special friendship" or something similar. My somewhat tentative impression is that this kind of exploitative psychotherapist tends to be found more often among clergy or pastoral counselors. Nevertheless, the effects upon the client often are profoundly damaging because, in addition to the "usual" sequelae of sexual exploitation, there is considerable mobilization of internalized homophobia.

SAME SEX EXPLOITATION BY PSYCHOTHERAPISTS: SPECIAL PROBLEMS

Some unique problem areas are found in situations in which the exploitative therapist and the client-victim are of the same sex.

1. The client may not be believed, particularly if the exploitative psychotherapist is heterosexually married or alleges to be heterosexual. For gay or lesbian clients, their sexual orientation may be pathologized and used as "evidence" against them. A purportedly heterosexual therapist who may be a "pillar of the community" but who sexually acts out with clients of the same sex, is the extreme example. In this situation same-sex behavior does not necessarily indicate gay or lesbian identity in the psychotherapist.

2. Homosexual clients, especially those who are lesbian, are likely to be highly conflicted over issues of loyalty to their minority community when they file complaints. Sometimes there is a realistic component to this ambivalence. It is my impression that psychotherapists who sexually exploit clients of the same sex or who are believed to be gay, lesbian, or bisexual are often treated in fact more harshly than are heterosexual offenders by licensing bodies, ethics committees, the media, and the public. Gay/lesbian clients may be faced with the untenable choice either not to complain and stand up for themselves, or to set in motion a process that may result in yet another action of discrimination against gay or lesbian individuals.

3. Gay and lesbian psychotherapists often are challenged to an unusual degree by situations of potential boundary problems. A few investigations (Anthony, 1982; Brown, 1986, Gonsiorek, 1982) have described such situations as comparable to that of a psychotherapist in a small town. A gay/lesbian psychotherapist is much more likely to operate in the same social sphere as that of a client or ex-client. Hence gay or lesbian psychotherapists who work with gay or lesbian clients must make regular and challenging determinations on appropriate boundaries with them. Such choices are relatively rare for heterosexual psychotherapists, except for those who work in small towns, or psychotherapists who are members of other minority groups, working within their own communities.

4. Minority therapists tend to be more bound up with a community and to have special obligations therein (see Brown, 1987, for a further discussion). Furthermore, those who work within their own communities often are thrust into unusual leadership roles. Within an oppressed community, the power to heal confers special and considerable personal authority. The situation is compounded when the same psychotherapists are called upon to exercise leadership roles in community organizations. This makes violations of the personal power more damaging and appropriate management of boundaries more complex.

5. Many oppressed communities have within them a certain number of "walking wounded"—persons who, for a variety of reasons, have absorbed a much greater-than-average share of self-hate for being a minority member. The concept of "internalized homophobia" is its variant among gay and lesbian people (for a more general discussion of this phenomenon, see Allport, 1954). Open and successful gay and lesbian professionals often are prime targets for such individuals.

6. When boundary problems occur within minority communities the stakes are often higher. Bigots are apt to focus upon failings within the communities, and to use such situations to discredit its members specifically and generally. In turn a defensive "siege mentality" may be set up in the minority communities, and that engenders a variety of unproductive responses (see Gonsiorek, 1982, for further discussion).

RECOMMENDATIONS

1. Although protecting a complaining client is an important issue in many situations, it is especially important when the complaining client is gay or lesbian, or has been involved in a same-sex situation with their psychotherapist.

   Licensing boards, ethics committees, and other agencies should do whatever is possible to guarantee needed anonymity for such clients.

2. Psychotherapists who are confused about their sexual orientation or who are in the process of coming out should not work with gay or lesbian clients or with clients who are confused about their sexual identity, until the personal issues are clearly resolved.

   My personal recommendation is that <u>a gay or lesbian therapist should wait at least two years after "coming out" before working with gay or lesbian clients</u>.

3. Gay and lesbian psychotherapists must develop systems of consultation and support to handle the particularly intense and frequent boundary decisions which they often face. Thus they can make certain that they do not work out any residual coming out issues or internalized homophobia with their clients and that they do not use their clients as support systems, particularly in times of stress.

   <u>Developing a dialogue with peers about the "small town" pressures of being a minority psychotherapist is highly encouraged</u>.

4. <u>Licensing boards and ethics committees should standardize their responses, both in the investigation and disposition of complaints</u>.

   This position is advocated for general reasons of fairness and equitable response but, particularly to prevent homophobic responses to gay and lesbian psychotherapists who have been involved in ethical violations.

5. Many male victims have an especially difficult time recognizing and understanding sexual exploitation.

   <u>Advocates and therapists working with such victims should be prepared for a slower process and for greater denial</u>.

Recognition of the existence and adverse consequences of sexual abuse has been slow to develop in our society. Much remains to be done in this area; one of the major remaining blind spots involves acknowledging the reality of male victims, and their particular reactions to abuse. The uncritical application of victimology information derived from women to male victim experiences is as sexist and empirically unjustifiable as the reverse.

Same-sex client-therapist exploitation situations often elicit the same biased responses as same-sex relationships do in our society. Such cases not only require the same thoughtfulness, sensitivity, and caution in handling both client and therapist as has been described in other chapters of this volume, but also responsiveness to some of the unique factors described in this chapter.

CHAPTER 9

THE CHILD OR ADOLESCENT VICTIM

Gary Richard Schoener

The experience of WICC staff members and our collaborators has been predominantly with adults, in our work with victims of sexual exploitation by therapists. In fact, in a number of our cases involving practitioners who specialize in treating children or adolescents, the misconduct occurred with the parent, not the young person.

So far, child/adolescent victims seem to have been overlooked for the most part. They were given no attention in the far-reaching work of the Minnesota State Task Force on Sexual Exploitation by Counselors and Therapists (Sanderson, 1985). The same lack of attention is seen in the professional literature in general. Yet Bajt and Pope (1989), in their survey of a select group of psychologists found that 24% of their respondents (including this writer) reported cases of sexual intimacy between therapists and underage clients. Chester, Pellauer, and Boyajian (1987) dealt with the sexual abuse of children in their book, which is addressed to clergy and religious professionals, but they gave no information whatsoever on clergy who themselves abuse children sexually, despite the increasing public concern with the problem. Gaylor (1988), in a recent book, *Betrayal of Trust: Clergy Abuse of Children*, provides a remarkable collection of media accounts of abuse of children by clergy. The reader is referred to Chapter 20 and Appendix BB for discussions of child sexual abuse by clergy.

The noteworthy exception to this dearth of discussion is Burgess and Hartman's (1986) *Sexual Exploitation of Patients by Health Professionals*. The chapters include a mother's account of the sexual abuse of her 13-year-old daughter by a pediatrician—a neighbor and friend of the family; the sexual abuse of a 12-year-old girl by an anesthesiologist (by Audrey Mertz); an examination in the community context of a pedophile, a pediatrician who sexually abused young male patients (by Carolyn and Eli Newberger); and the therapy needed by 15 boys who had been molested by two male physicians (by Calvin Frederick).

In his recent book, *DOC—The Rape of the Town of Lovell,* Olsen (1989) describes the sexual abuse of young girls, ages 3 (p. 275), 9, and 15 (pp. 107-108) by a male physician. The same physician reportedly had sexual contact with adult women, including a 75-year-old woman (p. 179). In one instance, the case of the 3-year-old, the child's mother witnessed the abuse (p. 275).

The national media at times have discussed the cases of child or adolescent victims of psychotherapists or counselors. For example, Nemiroff (1983) described the abuse of a young woman by a psychiatrist which began when the client was only 16 years old. Among other abuses, the doctor "...massaged her, working his way down from her shoulders to masturbating her himself" (p. 5). More recent newspaper stories have described civil suits and licensure actions against psychologists, psychiatrists, and clergy who were alleged to have sexually abused a number of young male clients—usually adolescents (e.g., Cox, 1987 a & b; Associated Press, 1987).

A sampling of child/adolescent exploitation cases from our local newspapers is worthy of examination:

A 12-year-old girl who had run away from a private residential treatment center for emotionally disturbed children was found living with her counselor in Florida. She alleged that they had intercourse perhaps 10 times (Oberdorfer, 1982). Although he initially denied the charges, he eventually pleaded guilty and was sentenced to a year in jail followed by 14 years probation. He also was directed to take part in a treatment program (Associated Press, 1983).

Three boys, aged 14, 15, and 17 were sexually abused by their doctor. "He was accused of fondling one boy's penis and of performing oral sodomy on the other youths, committing 10 incidents of abuse in all." In 1980 he pleaded guilty to criminal sexual conduct, and after a civil suit the boys were awarded $240,000 (Phelps, 1983).

Two staff members, aged 48 and 27, were arrested for allegedly performing oral sex on a 16-year-old male patient in a residential facility for treatment of emotional and drug abuse problems (McEnroe, 1983).

A former President of the Psychiatric Association in a neighboring state was charged with 23 counts of sexually assaulting nine children under his psychiatric care over a five year period. One charge involved an 11-year-old girl, another an 18-year-old man.

A psychologist's license was restricted after he admitted engaging in sexual contact with a 16-year-old boy who had begun living with him after he met the boy while doing psychological testing at a residential chemical dependency treatment center (Mpls. *Star Tribune*, 1986).

A 29-year-old child-care counselor was arrested for allegedly taking a 16-year-old girl patient in a residential treatment center for emotionally disturbed young people into a linen closet and having sex with her. The young girl was described as having come to the center because of "long-standing emotional problems, including suicidal tendencies...and depression" (Parry, 1987).

Adolescent victims of therapists also have appeared on local (e.g., in Minneapolis, *I-Team Report* on "The Wilson Center," 1984) and national TV shows (e.g., *Geraldo*, Sept. 19, 1988). Last but not least, numerous reports of children and adolescents of both sexes who have been abused by members of the clergy have been published all across the United States in connection with both civil and criminal actions. (See Ch. 20 and Appendix BB)

INCIDENCE AND PREVALENCE

Despite the accounts of the alleged sexual abuse of young people by professionals that appear in the public media from time to time, no survey data exists so far. In the surveys of therapist-client sex child and adolescent victims are not separated out. Child molestation itself has been under systematic empirical study for only a little more than a decade, although a recent review concluded that it "occurs with alarming frequency" in the general population (Lanyon, 1986).

Early in his career Freud chose to believe his clients when they claimed childhood sexual abuse. He changed his mind subsequently and formulated psychoanalysis, in part, on the thesis that memories of abuse were "only fantasies, or memories of fantasies" (Masson, 1985). Off to this unfortunate start, the psychotherapy field has been catching up ever since. Only in recent years are the allegations of sexual abuse of children widely believed.

Early in my career, a 12-year-old female client I was evaluating shocked me when she reported that a prominent psychiatrist had bounced her on his knee, stroked her hair, told her how pretty she was, and kissed her. My supervisor told me to believe it. He had heard similar allegations about the behavior of the same child psychiatrist from other children. Despite this early sensitization, through much of my career I did not routinely ask young clients about troubling contacts with professionals and so I have no way of knowing how many contacts may have been sexual in nature. In a few cases, however, adolescents volunteered such information.

Consequently, we do not have the vaguest idea how prevalent the sexual abuse of children and adolescents by therapists is. As there surfaces an increasing number of cases of child sexual abuse involving clergy, physicians, and other persons in professional roles, it has become clear that the psychotherapy field needs similar scrutiny.

COUNTERTRANSFERENCE ISSUES

Christ (1964) made what is probably the earliest reference to sexualized countertransference in analysis of a child. This topic has been even more taboo than the discussion of sexual feelings toward adult clients (see Chapter 39). Kohrman, Fineberg, Gelman, and Weiss (1971) provide a very useful examination as to the probable reasons for the neglect of countertransference in child analysis. After examining a number of historical issues, they note:

On the other hand, there are those child analysts who regress and live out infantile longings with the child. They tend to feel anything goes; that as long as the child gets better, whatever is done is justified. (p. 492)

While reading this passage, I was reminded of the case of an adolescent girl in treatment with an eminent female child analyst who had regular sexual contact with her over a period of several years. The description had an "anything goes" aspect to it and the analyst had elaborate rationalizations as to how this would be of help. Now an adult, this woman has considerable documentation concerning the relationship including love notes written to her by the analyst as well as admissions to most of the acts she alleges took place. Many years later she still shows considerable evidence of the damage.

There has been limited mention in the literature of the transference problems male therapists may encounter when treating girls who have reached puberty (e.g., Corday, 1967), but even this topic is rarely discussed. I am unaware of any article dealing with sexual attraction between female therapists and young girls, although I can't claim to have scoured the literature. I know more about the problem from adult women who were victimized as girls than I do from professional writings or workshops.

Kohrman et al. (1971) note that child therapists often point out provocative behavior by child clients which is aimed at making the therapist angry, but that "...few therapists do this in areas of sexual excitement and good mothering (p. 496)." The authors make an intriguing point regarding young children, as opposed to adolescents:

The sexual reactions the analyst experiences are more directly stimulated by the activity of the child. Younger children who feel free to touch the analyst, crawl on his lap, jump on him from heights, kiss him, can create intense reactions regardless of their sex. (p. 496)

REPORTING ISSUES

Reports of sexual exploitation of children and adolescents have a number of complicating aspects that are not found in reports of sexual abuse of adults. Some are as follows:

1. Failure to Ask: Adults are asked to assess past professional services more frequently these days but children and adolescents are seldom asked.

2. "Acting Out" Children: Adults who work with young people, especially those who are labeled "delinquent" or "acting out" tend to discount their complaints under the general assumption that they will make things up to "manipulate the system" or adults, in general. Sometimes a young person's "record" is checked before that of the professional and further inquiries are not made (Newberger & Newberger, 1986, p. 102).

3. Disbelief by Adults: Parents and other adults often just plain do not believe the young person's accounts of abuse by professionals because, often, they do not fit the stereotype of the child molester as a "dirty old man" or marginal individual. Lanyon (1986, p. 177) noted that "the molester is... commonly a respectable, otherwise law-abiding person, who may escape detection for exactly that reason."

4. "Kids Never Lie": On the other side of the coin, many "experts" on child abuse believe and testify that children "never lie" about sexual abuse, or that "victims never lie." "Victims never lie" is a non sequitur because the question is whether someone is a victim. Children, like adults, of course, at times do lie or distort facts. Some writers (Lanyon, 1986, p. 177) have suggested that fabrication is rare and to be found in situations where "there are clear motivations to do so." The literature focuses on self-report by the supposed victim. In reports of abuse by professionals, sometimes one must also deal with the credibility of peers' supportive testimony. Here, at times, peer pressure may play a role and I am aware of several situations in which young people admitted to a fabrication to support a friend.[1]

5. Misconstruing the Report: A follow-up professional may assume that he or she misunderstood a young person's account of the touch or remarks of a previous professional. At times a professional may overreact to or overinterpret statements of young people. Just as with adults, so too with young persons it takes careful interviewing to ascertain what may or may not have happened, and the younger the child the more skill may be needed to clarify what happened. An increasing number of reports of supposedly experienced child abuse interviewers distort the account of a child or adolescent through the misuse of "anatomically correct" dolls, use of leading questions, or inadequate interview techniques.

6. Child Abuse Reporting—The Legal System: Suspected child abuse may generate a report to the authorities before many facts have been sorted out, a situation that has pluses and minuses depending on how well the police and prosecutors do their job. In such cases cover-up or discounting by other health care professionals are prevented. Authorities sometimes drop cases because the person being accused is so prominent or because they believe that the young person won't make a good enough witness. On the other side of the

---

[1] A recent case in Minnesota was dismissed after "it became clear to the court that there was a conspiracy of silence amongst the major witnesses." (Linsley, 1989)

coin, overzealous police or prosecutors sometimes may bring charges without a careful investigation. This situation was evident in several cases and had distressing aftermaths.

7. The Power of Adults: Powerlessness of Young People: Burgess & Hartman (1986) described cases that illustrate the powerlessness of young people. In one case pressure was applied by a local minister; in another the family was pressured by a private detective; and in still another the effect of the major national expert who testified for the defense was overwhelming. In other cases parents actually have petitioned to permit the known abuser to continue to practice so the small town would not lose its doctor. His abuses were community knowledge but parents simply warned their sons to keep the practitioner at bay. Just as children fear reporting their parents for abuses so they may fear reporting a professional like a doctor, minister, or therapist. It sometimes takes people years to gain the objectivity and strength to make a complaint. We have recent reports of abuse that took place 10 or 20 years ago when the client was a child.

8. Informal Solutions—The Fear of Publicity: Although most news media withhold the names of child and adolescent victims, it is not uncommon for parents and other persons to keep an incident quiet in order to protect the young person. They may seek only a private confrontation. Many people believe erroneously that once a perpetrator is confronted, the abusive behavior will not recur. They also believe that if the professional agrees to seek counseling everything will be OK. The problems with such solutions is that they perpetuate the victimization by giving the young persons the message that the offense is not serious, and they do not permit discovering other victims who need help. Last but not least, when solutions are not tied to legal consequences they often have less of a chance of working.

9. Young People in Institutional Settings: Young people in residential or hospital-based treatment for emotional disorders or chemical dependency, or confined to juvenile detention facilities, constitute a very vulnerable group. They often are somewhat at the mercy of the institution's staff and, even worse, susceptible to disbelief. Some come into the facility with a reputation for lying, which makes them an easy target for any perpetrator who has read their charts carefully. By the same token, there are are young people in the group who may distort facts or fabricate incidents to get back at a staff person or to get themselves transferred.

10. The Seriously Disturbed Child: Yates and Musty (1988) describe a 5-year-old boy who told a child protection worker that his mother "bit my penis so hard that I peed in her mouth." He was impulsive, exciteable, aggressive, and sexualized many events. He was placed in a shelter and engaged in exhibitionism, lying, and made attempts to have sexual contact with the other kids. He then:

> ...accused his therapist of molesting him when the therapist helped him out from under a table, and he claimed that his shelter care father walked around with his pants down. (p. 991)

Although in this case there was good reason to disbelieve the charge against the therapist and other staff, it's important to remember that abused and disturbed children are also sometimes abused in treatment by treatment personnel.

CHILD SEXUAL ABUSE

Lanyon (1986) presented a very useful examination of the current state of knowledge regarding child sexual abuse (other than actual rape) in which violence was a factor. He reviewed and synthesized the work of key theorists such as Groth (1982) and Howells (1981) and called attention to the fact that in recent works child molesters have been separated into two groups: preference and situational. In the first, the abuser prefers children as a sex object whereas in the second, the abuser has sexual contact with a child if no adult is available. The preference abuser is similar to the character disorder type of abuser that is conceptualized in the traditional analytic viewpoint.

Using such an analysis in a professional group, one may say that the preference abuser has knowingly entered the profession in order to obtain access to and power over the preferred sex object, in contrast to the situational abuser for whom the professional role is either a convenience or too full of temptation. I have seen professionals who fit the two descriptions.

Like therapists who exploit adult clients, the abusers of children may be psychotic or borderline cases in whom the sexual drive is not the key issue; it is, rather, the unwise physical contact or a lack of boundaries that sets the stage for the behavior. Lanyon (1986), in fact, characterized some child molestation as "sexual behavior in the service of primarily nonsexual needs," including affection, power, and anger.

It is critical that when we look to the existing literature to seek understanding of the problem that we remind ourselves of how much remains to be learned about child molestation in general, and how little we know about those varieties of abuse that occur in the therapeutic or professional context. To illustrate this point, let us examine a single common descriptor of child molesters: that they select victims of a particular age and gender (Newberger & Newberger, 1986). Yet Burgess & Hartman (1986) presented a case of a physician who had sexual contact with young people of both sexes and Mertz (1986) described an anesthesiologist who had sexual contact with a 12-year-old girl as well as adult women. In our clinical experience with therapists there have been several who had sexual contact with both adults and pre-adolescent children and an additional number who have had sex with adolescents as well as with young adults in their twenties.

We have found that the sexual orientation of professionals cannot be judged from the gender of their victims. Male molesters of young boys, for example, tend to state that they are not adult homosexuals and indeed, laboratory studies of sexual arousal bear out their heterosexual preference (Lanyon, 1986; Freund & Langevin, 1976). We know little of female child molesters in the professional ranks and have seen only a few cases of women practitioners who became sexually involved with adolescents. Several, however, have had sex with older male adolescents and others have had sexual contact with young women under the guise of providing them with "nurturance." In the latter cases the therapists rationalized their behavior and denied that it was for their own gratification.

CRIMINAL SEXUAL MISCONDUCT; CHILD ABUSE REPORTING

Although it should be obvious, we need reminding that sexual contact between an adult professional and a minor is criminal sexual misconduct in all jurisdictions. The exact definition of the contact and the age of the minor varies from state to state. No matter where it occurs, such contact is reportable as child abuse in all jurisdictions in the United States. Parents, children, and others should be forewarned that everyone is obligated to report such contacts as child abuse before the story is told so that they can make an informed choice to tell it and they can understand the consequences.

EXAMPLES OF SEXUAL ABUSE OF CHILDREN AND ADOLESCENTS BY THERAPISTS

In addition to the abuse by physicians that was discussed earlier and described in Burgess & Hartman (1986), we have seen various types of abuse by persons acting as therapists.

1. Physician Providing Counseling: Non-psychiatric physicians thus may provide counseling, especially in rural areas, and may develop an on-going relationship with a child or adolescent. Sometimes this alone leads parents to become suspicious as it did in the case described by Burgess & Hartman (1986). In fact, the "counseling" may be a cover for the on-going sexual contact although the physician may not have consciously planned the contact. This type of sexual contact is normally disguised as some sort of regular, repeated physical examination or a treatment of some sort.

2. Physical Exam by Psychiatrist: Psychiatrists are licensed as physicians in all states and thus, are legally and often technically qualified to give physical examinations. These examinations may lead to confusion or upset even when they are legitimate. Consequently, many prudent psychiatrists do not do full examinations on their hospitalized patients but leave the work to other physicians. We have seen cases of male psychiatrists, however, who have performed breast examinations on women patients in both inpatient and outpatient settings where the examinations appeared to be erotically motivated. In addition, we have had cases of male psychiatrists who examined the genitals of adolescent male clients as part of a supposed physical examination.

3. Clergy: In recent years there have surfaced numerous cases of male clergy having sexual contact with young male and female counselees and parishioners (see Appendix BB). The contacts have occurred in a variety of settings and in the context of many different scenarios. We also have consulted in several cases of sexual exploitation of young noviates by nuns. In one such case the sexual contact was introduced as part of a religious rite; when the contact was discovered the order denied the attribution.

4. Therapists Who Abuse Both Adult and Young Women: We have seen several cases in which the same therapist abused both adult women and children or adolescents. In some instances the patterns were similar; in others, the abuses differed, depending on the age of the client. The therapists were loose with professional boundaries and all believed they could act on their impulses. They were quite grandiose and would not accept feedback that these practices were harmful to clients.

In several cases the contact with the children and adolescents involved predominantly hugging and kissing, stroking hair and buttocks, and limited touching of the breast area. By contrast, contact with adult women included attempts at sexual intercourse. The young girls were uneasy, troubled, confused, and fearful of saying "no." The adult women were at first flattered but soon realized that they were being exploited and decided to take action via complaints.

In several of these situations both mothers and daughters were involved, and the major traumatization came about because both felt that the mother had allowed the exploitative contact to take place.

5. <u>Child Being Evaluated for Custody Case or Child Abuse</u>: In several situations a young child who was being evaluated in connection with a custody case or allegations of child abuse alleged that the evaluator had sexual contact with him or her. It is still unclear to us what actually happened.

6. <u>Adolescent in Outpatient Treatment</u>: In this case, reminiscent of the adult situation described elsewhere in this volume, a young person has sexual contact with a therapist. The contact is presented as a therapeutic intervention of some sort (e.g., to deal with anorgasmia), and it is carried out in a subtle fashion as part of other physician contact or as the representation (supposedly) of the feeling of love between therapist and client.

7. <u>Adolescent in Residential Treatment</u>: The variety of cases include a number that are difficult to fully assess. It should be noted that in addition to the problem of contact between therapist and client in such settings there are the related problems of sexual contact by ancillary personnel such as aides and orderlies, and of contact by other clients.

a. Several adolescents claim that a psychologist examined their genitals after they showed him worrisome scars or a rash. One youth had a history of exposing himself to various staff members and clients. The psychologist indicated that he had gone along with them: he wanted to examine these complaints, hoping to maintain rapport, and he had referred the youths to the consulting physician for an exam. This was documented in the notes. The psychologist was inexperienced with kids this disturbed. He was tried criminally and acquitted.

b. Male consulting psychiatrist had adolescent girls sit on his lap during evaluations, at times hugging them or kissing them on the cheek. A psychologist reported this behavior as suspected child abuse, and although there was no prosecution, the faculty demanded that he have no physical contact with clients.

c. Three adolescents in a residential program for delinquents alleged breast fondling and attempts at sexual intercourse by a male nurse. He was dismissed but got his job back on appeal. The other staff members and clients felt that he was guilty.

d. A male psychiatrist performed a physical on an adolescent male client, allegedly spending a lot of time examining his genitals. This was done in his hospital room. The psychiatrist admitted the exam but denied improper contact; he was not disciplined, but decided to avoid doing such physicals himself.

e. A disturbed adolescent who had recently been discharged from a residential treatment program for chemical dependency bragged to another client that he had had sex with an attractive female staff member after discharge. The female staff member admitted to having had follow-up contact with him and inviting him to visit her family and have dinner with them, but vehemently denied any sexual contact whatsoever. The client was re-interviewed and asked for specifics but he was able to come up with only vague statements.

f. An older woman who was both a Board member and volunteer at a chemical dependency treatment program donated the rental for an apartment to a young man who was being discharged from the program. He wanted to live apart from his parents because they had alcohol problems. It turned out that this Board member was visiting the ex-resident and having sexual intercourse and there was some suggestion that some of the intimacy may have begun while the client was still in the program.

8. <u>Contact Outside the Office</u>: Here again we have a range of case examples. Burgess & Hartman (1986) reported the case of a neighbor, a pediatrician, who made frequent home visits to a young girl he was sexually abusing. There are cases of mental health professionals sexually abusing neighborhood children with whom they had no professional relationship. It also has been noted (Newberger & Newberger, 1986) that some abusive professionals may work in schools and summer camps in hopes of having more access to children or adolescents. Some case examples follow:

a. GROUP SOCIAL ACTIVITIES: There are various situations in which a counselor or therapist can be involved with young people in a social situation in which sexual contact may be possible. Examples have included the involvement of clergy in youth activities or mental health staff in field trips (e.g., in connection with residential or day treatment). These can involve overnights (e.g., camping) or situations such as swimming in a lake where sexual contact is possible, either away from the group or out of sight (e.g., underwater fondling of youngsters).

b. INDIVIDUAL SOCIALIZING: A therapist can have contact with a client outside of counseling sessions, presumably to help the person learn to socialize. For example, a middle-aged male counselor began going on what appeared to be "dates" with a teenager and also visiting her home. Her parents were pleased at his interest, noting that he was the first counselor their daughter had really seemed involved with; they held on to this belief even when his agency told them his behavior was out of line. Both client and counselor denied any sexual contact, and they and her parents defended the relationship. The agency fired the counselor for refusing to break off the relationship. Despite the intense fascination and infatuation he described, sexual contact may not have occurred.

c. INVITING THE CLIENT ON FAMILY OUTING: A therapist invited an adolescent male client on a camping trip with him and his sons. He slept in the same tent as the client, and the client claims that the therapist made an attempt to fondle him during the night. The therapist denied this and, because it happened when the client was in a sort of twilight state, disciplinary action was not taken. It also was relevant that the therapist indicated he had ceased the practice of taking clients camping.

d. HOME VISIT: A male therapist made a follow-up visit to a client of limited intelligence in whom he seemed quite interested. When the client exposed himself, the therapist momentarily lost control and touched his penis. He later apologized, sought treatment, and came under licensure board discipline. All evidence suggested this was a one-time loss of control.

What is abundantly clear is that contacts outside the office or outside a professional setting hold additional risks for both therapist and client.

EFFECT ON THE CLIENT

The effects of exploitative behaviors vary as markedly with children and adolescents as they do with adults. The client's personal adjustment, the timing, the nature and duration of the contact, its connection with personal or family history, and how others deal with it all determine the effects. Chapter 7 by Schoener, Milgrom & Gonsiorek is directed to adult victims but applies to some adolescent victims also.

Some children and adolescents are able to see the practitioner as disturbed or sick, to report him, and then to walk away from the situation. Others, like adult victims, blame themselves, are confused and frightened, withdraw, and so forth. Some are grievously injured and may take years to recover fully from the experience. Some consequences of sexual abuse by a therapist may include:

1. Post-Traumatic Stress Syndrome: Frederick (1986) described the assessment of 15 boys, aged 10-17, who were sexually abused by two male physicians (12 were victims of one, 3 of the other). All were diagnosed as suffering from Post-Traumatic Stress Disorder and showed the required criteria: (a) acknowledged severe stressor; (b) replaying or reliving the stressful event; (c) psychic numbing; (d) newly developed symptoms of distress.

2. Typical Signs of Child Molestation: As with sexual abuse in non-therapeutic situations, victims of molestation may show a number of traits or symptoms (Finkelhor, 1985; Frederick, 1986; Burgess, Hartman, McCausland, and Powers, 1984; Sgroi, 1982; Summit, 1985). It should be noted that these symptoms may be attributable to other things also; none in and of itself is proof of sexual abuse. The signs include the following:

   a. Withdrawal from peers and others.
   b. Seeking constant protection from parent or other adult.
   c. Fears of being seen nude; avoidance of group showers.
   d. Suicidal thoughts or acts; sense of worthlessness.
   e. Fear, and/or hatred of the perpetrator.
   f. Psychosomatic symptoms (headaches, stomach aches).
   g. Bedwetting.
   h. Sexual identity questions; remarks about being gay.
   i. Irritable or easily annoyed; tense and uncomfortable.
   j. Risk-taking behavior; hazardous activities or actions.
   k. Significant depression; sense of hopelessness.
   l. Unwillingness to discuss the abuse or trauma associated with it.

3. Wariness and Distrust of Professionals: Even more than adult victims, child and adolescent victims may overgeneralize and assume that all professionals cannot be trusted. They often are very fearful of seeing professionals on their own and it is wise to consider sessions with the parent or someone else present. This measure has the added benefit of reassuring the parent who may have little trust of professionals left also.

4. Distrust of Parents: Parents or the professional doing follow-up work experience considerable pain in observing a young person's distrust of parents that may result from sexual abuse by a therapist. The child may resent the parent for several reasons:

   a. Referring him or her to the professional in the first place.
   b. Disregarding questions or complaints by the child when they were first made.
   c. Observing abusive conduct by the therapist during a session and failing to intervene.

With "c" above there may be significant damage leading to sleep disturbance, bad dreams, and serious difficulty in trusting parents or adults in general. Even after the parents, with the help of a follow-up therapist, try to explain the situation, many children simply cannot understand why the parent was unable to protect them in the therapy sessions. This distrust may take some time and maturation to disappear, even if the child receives follow-up therapy.

Any of the problems or symptoms discussed in this chapter may be short-lived or continue for months or even years, depending on the timing, context, and nature of the abuse. Abuse that has gone on for a long while has a much greater effect. A child's reaction is even more problematic if the therapist is well-known, comes highly recommended, and the parents see him or her apart from the child or adolescent. The more the parental stamp of approval is given a therapist, and the more the parents ignore questions or complaints from the young person, the more trust between child and parents may be damaged.

A FINAL NOTE

I would like to repeat my earlier observations on the tentative nature of these formulations; we have had far less experience with child/adolescent abuse situations.

Let us hope that sexual abuse of children and adolescents by therapists is not so common as the abuse of their elders. If experience with sexual abuse in the broader community or in the home is any measure, however, it is that the victims are not yet reporting the full extent of the abuse and the problem still is largely hidden. Sad though this conclusion may be, we must be willing to face this possibility.

CHAPTER 10

THE ASSESSMENT OF DAMAGES

Gary Richard Schoener

The purpose of this chapter is to provide some framework for the assessment of a client—the plaintiff in a civil suit—to determine the extent of the damages suffered as the result of sexual exploitation by a therapist during treatment. The client so discussed is an adult. The assessments focused on here are those that must be made in connection with some legal or quasi-legal proceedings and are not to be confused with assessments of the clinical treatment itself. The scope of the chapter, consequently, is limited. The chapter is not meant to supplant any of the books on being an expert witness (e.g., Sadoff, 1975; Smith, 1986; Ziskin, 1984b) or the constantly expanding number of videotapes, manuals, and workshops on the topic.

THE ROLE OF THE EXPERT WITNESS

Civil suits brought by clients against therapists for sexual misconduct typically have been malpractice actions, a type of negligence tort in which it must be proved that the therapist had a duty to perform vis-`a-vis the client, that the duty was not performed, and that damages were a direct result of this duty failure. Obviously, it is also possible to sue using an intentional tort theory—that is, that the therapist injured the client through an intentional act—but this approach has the disadvantage that liability insurance typically does not provide coverage for intentional acts.

The expert witness, therefore, usually appears for the client to testify to (a) the existence of a duty; (b) the failure to do that duty (i.e., to render treatment that meets the local "standard of care"); and (c) specific damages that resulted as a direct outcome of the duty failure.

Historically, psychotherapy has been regarded as a field in which the duty of care is difficult to define and, hence, malpractice actions are not easily brought (Smith, 1986). When sexual misconduct occurs, however, the perspective changes.

To date, the mental health profession and the courts have consistently held that engaging in sexual relations by a psychiatrist with a patient is unethical and an actionable breach of a physician's duty of care. The general rationale is that sex with a patient serves no bona fide purpose in treatment and is, instead, an abuse of the fiduciary role and an exploitation of the superior authoritative position assumed by a psychiatrist over a patient. (Smith, 1986, p. 133)

I think that the same generalization applies to case law involving nonpsychiatric psychotherapists. The situation with other types of physicians and sex therapists is not so clear.

In five states (Colorado, Michigan, New Hampshire, Rhode Island, and Wyoming) statutes define as rape physician-patient sexual contact that occurs during the course of "medical treatment or examination" (Bliss, 1986). In these jurisdictions, then, it may be easier to argue that sexual contact within the physician-patient relationship is improper, but not in other states.

Four states (California, Minnesota, North Dakota, and Wisconsin) now have special statutes governing suits filed against therapists for sexual misconduct in the professional relationship. These statutes, in essence, define sexual contact with a client as malpractice. Expert testimony may not be necessary in these states to argue that the sexual conduct violates the standard of care.

In summation, it seems that the role of experts in the future (except, possibly, for post-termination sexual involvement; see Chs. 24 & 25) will be to assess and testify to damages. The expert, of course, may be hired by either side. If retained by the plaintiff (client), he or she will have the job of discovering and testifying to damages. If hired by the defendant (therapist) the task will be to critically examine the alleged damages and to contest their severity or the degree to which they may be attributable to a pre-existing condition or to causes other than the defendant's misconduct.

THE ADVERSE EXAMINATION

Given that most of this chapter focuses on the discovery and assessment of damages usually conducted for the plaintiff's side, let's look first at the other side of the coin. In most cases the defense has the opportunity to retain an expert to conduct an adverse examination of the plaintiff. In fact, the plaintiff should be forewarned of this right before beginning a civil suit.

Pope and Bouhoutsos (1986) present a useful discussion of some of the challenges in such a role, including ethical dilemmas for the examiner, the need to respect client vulnerability, and the difficulties of conducting a valid assessment when rapport with the client is lacking.

Under the best of circumstances, an adverse examination is done in a supportive fashion and focuses on details of the client's personal adjustment before, during, and after the psychotherapeutic misadventure. Rather than challenging, for example, that the client feels in fact as he or she claims, the examination would stress those reports of behavior and life events that may reflect the client's ability to function effectively. For example, if depression is alleged, what are the specific symptoms (e.g., sleep disturbance, loss of appetite)? To what degree can true impairment in functioning be documented, and what were its empirical consequences?

An interview with the client and psychological testing alone cannot establish the extent of problems or their connection to the therapy. It is most useful to be able to examine reports or descriptions that are generated by such third-party observers as family and friends, co-workers, employers, and subsequent therapists.

It is critical that the examiner gain a clear understanding of the client's version of events by directing questions to ambiguities. Cross-examination should be left to the attorney who will be able to take depositions and, perhaps, to test the story in court. Experts who take on the job of determining truthfulness, or who allow attorneys to believe that they have unique powers to judge truthfulness, are making a big mistake and doing their side a major disservice. In my experience defense attorneys appreciate candor and an honest appraisal of the likelihood that damage was done. Questions of client exaggeration or honesty should be presented to the defense attorney with caveats regarding the limitations of the adverse examination, and should be tied to whatever further inquiry the attorney may want to pursue, either through investigations or in the courtroom.

In such arrangements, the temptation to bend the facts or test data are always present. Many practitioners, consequently, avoid appearing for the defense. Those who undertake the task may do so because of prior relationships with defendants, but they find themselves so bent on disapproving the allegations that they do a poor job of evaluating clients. In the best of all possible worlds, experts for each side of a case act on behalf of the court and justice, and their findings and testimony are a product of the best work they can do with the available instruments and tools.

SERVING AS AN EXPERT WITNESS FOR THE PLAINTIFF

Objectivity is also a potential struggle for an expert hired by the plaintiff (client). In Minnesota the performance of expert witnesses in child sex abuse cases has led to so much public discussion and concern that Attorney General Humphrey asked the Minnesota Psychological Association to draw up guidelines for expert witnesses. The result, the "Minnesota Psychological Association Guidelines for the Practice of Psychology in Child Sexual Abuse Cases" (Minnesota Psychologist, 1986), is directed to criminal cases but contains much useful advice for expert witnesses in general. The most important issues raised were (a) the need to be clear on one's role and (b) to limit one's testimony to statements that can be supported by objective readings of the professional literature or unbiased interpretations of test results and other clinical data.

A useful description of the role of an expert witness in a major civil suit against a psychotherapist who sexually exploited a client is presented by Bates and Brodsky (1988). Other descriptions of relevant trials (e.g., Freeman & Roy, 1976; Walker & Young, 1986) actually do not describe in detail the expert testimony on damages. Brodsky's account is well worth reading before undertaking such a task, therefore.

The expert who works for the plaintiff has an easier job because he or she can often interview the plaintiff more than once to clarify ambiguities. The expert for the defense tends to get only one evaluation session in which to do it all. The plaintiff's expert also has a greater responsibility: to suggest to the plaintiff's attorney areas of investigation or inquiry that may help to substantiate changes in the client as a result of the abuse by the therapist. Furthermore, the client may not have a clear grasp of how he or she was damaged by the abuse and so it is up to the expert to structure the inquiry.

THE ASSESSMENT OF DAMAGES

The single most important piece of advice I can give is for the evaluator to focus on assessing the effect of the overall treatment, not just the sexual contact. Not infrequently I find that even experienced attorneys focus narrowly on the sexual acts rather than to take account of other events or actions in the treatment that may constitute therapeutic malpractice or have brought about untoward outcomes.

The fact that the therapist's sexual misconduct instigated the client's distress does not mean that other deficiencies were not present in the treatment. Clients and their attorneys often do not know enough about professional standards to identify the other failings. The behaviors that outrage a client may not have been the most serious problem in the care provided and, therefore, may not be the major source of the damage to the client.

Another important aspect of the examination of damages to the client is to develop clear examples of the practical implications of the damage. For example, a diagnosis of depression is helpful, but equally important is a clear description of the severity and practical consequences of depression for the client.

There follow sources of data for assessing damages to a client:

1. The exploitative therapist's records and reports.

2. Reports from and interviews with any therapist who treated the client before or after the abusive therapist.

3. Results of past psychological testing.

4. Results of current psychological testing (of most use if they can be compared with results of previous testing).

5. Records kept by the client; e.g., diaries, letters to or from the therapist, photographs.

6. Data from the client's employer, including performance evaluations, testimony given in a deposition (if necessary, augmented by interviews with the employer, work supervisor, or co-workers).

7. Testimony of or interviews with co-workers.

8. Testimony of or interviews with family members, spouse, lover.

9. Testimony of or interviews with neighbors, friends, and others.

10. Testimony of client (essential reading although the evaluator conducts the interview).

11. Interview with the client.

12. Miscellaneous data, such as chronologies of attempts to gain employment, data from physicians who have treated the client, data related to involvement in community activities.

A number of authors (e.g., Smith, 1986) have discussed the difficulty in proving psychological injury, yet the frequency and size of damage awards I have seen suggest that in therapist sexual misconduct cases this problem is not insurmountable.

THE CAUSES OF DAMAGES

Damages, I indicated in the previous section, may result from far more than simply the sexual misconduct. In a number of cases I have concluded that the sexual exploitation caused fewer damages than did certain other components of the treatment. A list of some causes of damage in sexual misconduct cases should include the following possibilities:

1. FAILURE TO RENDER TREATMENT: Bouhoutsos, Holroyd, Lerman, Forer, and Greenberg (1983, p. 194) concluded, "When sexual intercourse begins, therapy ends...." This observation echoes our experience. Our typical finding is that the original problem for which the client sought help has not been treated. To the degree that the problem or condition is treatable, the client had to suffer its consequences as a direct result of this

negligence. Because of both impaired judgment and a vested interest in keeping the client dependent, several other therapeutic failures are not unusual.

I. Failure to Diagnose Other Problems: The therapist may have a vested interest in either under- or over-diagnosing the client, or simply to be so involved in the sexual or romantic aspects of the interchange to not pay attention to the client's needs at all.

   A. Underpathologizing: The therapist may be motivated to see the client as quite healthy to justify a romantic involvement with someone who is "healthy" and, therefore, an acceptable object for romance. Or, underpathologizing may be needed to rationalize the involvement as one between "equals" or "two consenting adults." Ignoring problems like chemical addiction or dependency permits the therapist not to make referrals or allows the therapist to support the client in remaining dependent.

   B. Overpathologizing : Exaggeration of the client's problems helps to lower the client's self-esteem and keeps the client dependent on the therapist. The extreme is the therapist's informing the client that nobody else would be willing to treat her or him.

II. Inadequate Treatment of Presenting Complaint: For as long as the problem isn't "fixed" the client stays dependent on the therapist.

   A. Failure to Treat Chemical Dependency: The client is kept dependent on the therapist or even in a "fog."

   B. Failure to Treat Relationship Problems: This failure leads directly to the client's being quite needy and vulnerable to the therapist.

   C. Failure to Treat Loneliness, Shyness, etc.: This too can keep the client dependent on the therapist for social and emotional support, and for romance.

   D. Failure to Intervene With Child-Rearing Problems: When a parent is stressed or distraught because of demands at home, he or she can become and remain very dependent on the therapist who is "the only one who really understands."

   E. Failure to Treat Depression: When a supposedly "neurotic depression" does not lift within a few months and other approaches, including medications, are not tried, the treatment is suspect.

   F. Failure to Address Assertiveness: The non-assertive client is more easily controlled, and thus he or she is not motivated to challenge this failure.

   G. Failure to Examine Vocational Problems: A client trapped in a stressful employment situation remains vulnerable if the therapist pushes the focus on personal issues without examining vocational problems.

   H. Ignoring Financial Dependency: Although one may assume a therapist's vested interest in having clients deal effectively with their financial strains, some therapists ignore the strains so they can continue to magnanimously provide "free" or cut-rate therapy.

2. <u>FAILURE TO REFER</u>: Obviously, a therapist seeking to continue a sexual or romantic relationship with a client typically is very reluctant to refer her or him, fearing discovery of the misconduct by the other therapist. This failure may lead to the client's not receiving the following attentions:

    a. An evaluation for possible psychotropic medications.
    b. An evaluation for possible physical disease or problems.
    c. An evaluation of possible chemical abuse or addiction.
    d. Treatment of relationship or family problems.
    e. Treatment of problems of children in the client's family.

3. <u>TREATMENT OUTSIDE ONE'S AREA OF EXPERTISE</u>: Implicit in the failure to make a referral is the assumption that the therapist is not competent to provide a specific type of treatment, or that there is a conflict of interest for the therapist in providing the treatment (e.g., treating a couple while having an affair with one of them).

4. <u>FAILURE TO HANDLE TRANSFERENCE OR OTHER TREATMENT DYNAMICS</u>: Mishandling transference, even without sexual contact, can lead to damages provable in court. This conclusion is demonstrated by, for example, Landau vs. Werner (Riskin, 1979) and Anclote Manor Foundation vs. Wilkinson (Smith, 1986). Even when sex enters the picture, mishandling transference still may be a key duty failure, as determined in Zipkin vs. Freeman (Smith, 1986). I have seen three related failures:

    a. Failure to handle transference directly, either by ignoring or discounting it, emphasizing to the client that what is occurring is "true love."

    b. Failure to obtain and document outside consultation in a case in which, admittedly, the relationship with the client is clearly troubled. This is a key in cases in which the practitioner has made a point of describing in notes, or elsewhere, problems in transference.

    c. Failure to obtain on-going consultation or supervision, or to have a consultant or supervisor meet directly with client and therapist to resolve the problem.

<u>Another example often seen with 4b and 4c above is the failure to reveal to the consultant or supervisor all details of the relationship or the actual distortion of the details.</u> This practice renders the consultation or supervision valueless or even perverts it by, for example, using the feedback based on the inaccurate account of events to justify to the client what is going on.

5. <u>FAILURE TO OBTAIN INFORMED CONSENT</u>: If, in fact, some unusual or questionable treatment techniques are in use and are being justified as "experimental," did the therapist obtain true informed consent, clearly explaining the "experimental" nature of the treatment and all foreseeable outcomes?

6. <u>CONFIDENTIALITY VIOLATIONS</u>: In many cases therapists who have become sexually involved with clients are overly involved in their lives and, at times, break confidentiality to manipulate events. For example, information, either accurate or false, is passed on to a spouse to manipulate the situation; or the "special" client is provided with details of the treatment of other clients, and learns later that he or she has been the victim of a confidentiality violation.

7. DECEPTION: Actually, deception is a special case of failure to obtain informed consent (#5 above). The client is misled to believe that the sexual contact is a part of or consistent with therapy. In the Minnesota statutes, such practices are termed "therapeutic deception" (see Ch. 43).

8. IMPROPER USE OF HYPNOSIS: The common improper use of hypnosis is to bring about nontherapeutic regression in the client. Hypnosis is inappropriately used when a client is already prone to regression, or in order to bring about regression in the client. In several such cases the hypnosis was far more destructive than the sexual exploitation. (See also Ch. 43.)

9. IMPROPER USE OF MEDICATIONS: The therapist may over-medicate the client or fail to properly monitor the medication. The immediate outcome is the client's docility and excessive dependence on the practitioner. This misuse of medication may occur also when the client is striving to break free of the relationship. In the largest damage award to date in such a case, Walker vs. Parzen (Walker & Young, 1986), it was alleged that the therapist was attempting to bring about a suicide.

10. IMPROPER USE OF ELECTRO-CONVULSIVE SHOCK (ECT): In several cases involving psychiatrists, ECT was used inappropriately in connection with sexual involvements with clients. In one case the ECT was administered in the hospital immediately after sexual episodes and had the effect of erasing the client's memory of these encounters. In several other cases clients who were becoming feisty and threatening to break off the relationships were hospitalized and given ECT.

11. INSTRUCTING CLIENTS TO ACT OUT IMPULSES WITHIN THERAPY: This procedure may involve the verbal or physical expression of strong feelings, such as anger, in a fashion potentially harmful, physically or psychologically, toward the therapist or other clients. It also may include instructions to sexually touch another client.

12. INSTRUCTING CLIENTS TO ENGAGE IN POTENTIALLY HARMFUL BEHAVIORS OUTSIDE OF THERAPY: The instructions can range from physical assault on a spouse or other person to verbal attacks on others. Sometimes clients lose family and friends, not to mention jobs, because of such instructions. The effect, of course, is to make the client more dependent on the therapist (see "Psychotherapy Cults," Ch. 19).

13. INSTRUCTING CLIENTS TO WASTE ASSETS OR TO TURN THEM OVER TO THE THERAPIST: Examples range from outright fraud and rip-off with criminal intent to therapeutic directions to dispose of family heirlooms in order to purge oneself of one's "evil past." In some instances therapists actually have wormed their way into partnership arrangements with clients.

14. USE OF DRUGS OR ALCOHOL WITH CLIENTS: The substances are especially harmful if the client has a history of abuse or dependency on a chemical. With some adolescent cases the effect has been devastating. This practice may reflect a chemical abuse or dependency problem in the therapist or use of the drugs to dis-inhibit the therapist, client, or both.

15. ADVISING AGAINST EDUCATION, TRAINING, OR PROFESSIONAL ADVANCEMENT: Some therapists have longstanding patterns of advising their clients against "moving too fast" or taking steps toward growth or advancement, a practice that also helps to maintain the client in a dependent role.

16. <u>TECHNIQUES THAT LEAD TO EMOTIONAL BREAKDOWN, OR REGRESSION</u>: The issue in this area is two-fold: the techniques that are used and the therapist's failure to screen out vulnerable persons before applying a technique. Examples are "primal scream" sessions and other techniques that generate breakdowns in some individuals. With the "bonding" techniques an active attempt is made to blur personal boundaries, and some techniques are directed to fostering regression in the client to a child-like level of functioning.

17. <u>FAILING TO SET LIMITS ON CLIENTS' BEHAVIOR</u>: Bizarre or dangerous conduct during sessions toward the therapist or other clients should be confronted and appropriate limits set. When these precautions are not taken, the behaviors may become part of the client's customary behavioral repertoire. Furthermore, sexual touching by the client should be challenged and proper limits set. When a therapist argues that the client initiated activities of a sexual nature, it should be noted that it is the therapist's duty is to set proper limits; if unable to do so he or she should obtain consultation. In Minnesota, the failure to set such limits in the sexual area is just as criminal as initiating the contact.

18. <u>PHYSICAL ASSAULT OF CLIENTS</u>: Among these behaviors may be physically pinning down the client to "teach them about power," whipping her or him to "teach them to be tough" or "how to deal with anger," or even a forced rape. Plasil (1985) described such an incident and a number of cases in Minnesota have been litigated on this issue.

19. <u>TERRORIZATION OF CLIENTS</u>: Walker & Young (1986) and Ponsor, Soler, & Abod (1976) described some very threatening behavior toward clients in various settings in which seduction took place. Sometimes the terrorization occurs when the client is trying to break out of the destructive relationship with the therapist and other times, during therapy. It may be presented or later defended as a therapeutic technique. The therapist may claim that he/she was exaggerating to show the client how ridiculous a certain fear is and that there was no intent to terrorize. Or, the technique may be justified as an "implosion" technique—a behavioral method by which the client is flooded with anxiety in hopes that some fear will be extinguished. In one instance we encountered several therapists engaged in a "mock rape" (their words) with a sexual assault victim who was thereby duly terrorized. This "technique" was discussed with a consultant and videotaped, although the tape disappeared before we could view it.

20. <u>SEXUAL CONTACT</u>: The many types of sexual contact and the many situations in which they occur may have a range of effects and may damage a client in various ways. Some variables follow, although this list is far from exhaustive:

    a. Contact that is confusing to the client.

    b. Contact that is physically painful to the client.

    c. Sexual practices that trouble the client, such as anal intercourse, oral sex, etc.

    d. Sexual practices with someone not normally of the gender of choice (e.g., same-sex contact by a heterosexual; cross-sex contact with a gay or lesbian client).

    e. A first sexual experience, or the only sexual experience the client has had, or is having.

f. Sexual contact that is an acting out of questions on sexual identity.

g. Sexual contact that is more intensive than or competes with a sexual relationship in the client's private life (the client may even be instructed to fantasize the therapist while making love to the spouse).

h. Contact that leads to guilt because the client has an exclusive relationship or marriage, or because the therapist is cheating on a relationship.

i. Contact or verbal instructions that convince a client he or she has a sexual problem when one is not present (or which exaggerates sexual dysfunction).

ASSESSMENT

Ideally an expert has comparable before and after data and a means of controlling for intervening variables when he or she assesses the damages to a client in relation to therapeutic events. In fact, however, the ideal seldom occurs.

It is important, when developing a theory of damages, to carefully note the sources of all information and to link all theories and testimony to observables. It is equally important to recognize that the degree of confidence in a given theory may vary considerably, both in the mind of the expert and in the minds of others, such as a jury, who will weigh the testimony.

1. The expert should focus on four distinct time periods when determining damages:

    a. The period of the therapy in question.

    b. The period following therapy termination, up until the client is evaluated.

    c. The client's status when the expert conducts the assessment.

    d. Any projection into the future on the likelihood that the phenomena will persist or that past problems will recur or new ones develop.

2. The expert must develop some sense of baseline measures; that is, how was the client functioning prior to the therapy? Although the tendency is to focus on the client's situation at the time he or she actually entered therapy, it is important to examine the client's usual functioning and life accomplishments in general terms.

3. The expert should inquire about other events that occurred during or subsequent to therapy which are not related to therapy but which may have contributed to the client's problems. It is my practice to ask the client directly about such events and, also, to ask the client to compare and contrast symptoms or functioning at various stages.

4. The expert must focus on demonstrable damages that can be linked to the malpractice and the time frame associated with the damages. Arguments over the value of such damages are the province of the attorney. It is not the expert's role, for example, to try to place a value on two years of depression, but the expert may be asked legitimately to estimate the length and cost of treatment that will be necessary to ameliorate a symptom or condition.

The following list of areas of specific damage and the examples are not exhaustive.

1. PSYCHOLOGICAL DISORDER: A diagnosable disorder results from the malpractice, for example:

   a. Depressive Reaction: A depression, not previously in evidence, results from an abusive therapeutic relationship.

   b. Post-Traumatic Stress Disorder: Vinson (1984) reported that 64% of her female subjects suffered from PTSD. Frederick (1986) reported the same percentage for child and adolescent victims of sexual exploitation by therapists as Pope and Bouhoutsos (1986) did for adult victims.

   c. Atypical Dissociative Disorder: Although we have not seen this disorder in people coming out of psychotherapy cults where one would most expect it, the disorder was apparent in several cases in which the therapist used hypnosis to foster considerable regression and/or the therapy was designed in part to bring about dissociation.

2. EXACERBATION OF EXISTING DISORDER: Sometimes a previously existing psychological problem not only does not improve but may, indeed, get worse. Countless examples could be listed here, but a few should suffice for illustrative purposes:

   a. Deepening of depression: Demonstrated by symptoms not previously experienced, or a worsening of previous symptoms:

      (1) Weight loss, sleep disturbance and difficulty.

      (2) Excessive eating, excessive sleep.

      (3) Stronger subjective feelings of depression, despair, despondency.

      (4) Lowered motivation, lack of energy.

      (5) Suicidal thinking; suicide attempts.

      (6) Need for medications or hospitalization.

   b. Worsening of anxiety: Demonstrated by new symptoms or greater interference with functioning, either in terms of frequency or severity of symptoms:

      (1) Panic attacks—new, worse, or more frequent.
      (2) Free-floating anxiety; general fearfulness.
      (3) Phobias, new or more severe.

   c. Excessive rumination and worry: May occur in persons such as obsessionals who tend to worry, or in persons who typically are not "worriers."

   d. Distrust: Pre-existing distrust of people may worsen in terms of who is included or a lowered threshold to trigger it.

   e. Recurrence or worsening of a pattern of drug or alcohol abuse, including an increase in cigarette smoking.

f. Recurrence or worsening of an eating disorder (e.g., anorexia; bulemia)

3. PROBLEMS IN MARITAL OR FAMILY RELATIONSHIPS: The problems may be new or an exacerbation of pre-existing ones.

a. A marital or love relationship ended as a result of the therapy.

b. Custody of a child was lost or relinquished either directly because of the therapy or as a product of increased dysfunction.

c. Disruption in or deterioration of sexual relationship.

4. DIFFICULTY TRUSTING PROFESSIONALS: This very common consequence leads to a reluctance to get help in the future and, often, increases the difficulty of benefitting from treatment. All authors report this disorder (e.g., Burgess, 1981; Feldman-Summers & Jones, 1984; Pope & Bouhoutsos, 1986). It often generalizes beyond therapists alone to health care practitioners in general. Assuming that it does not prevent the client from receiving help, it is still noteworthy in that a client often experiences considerable anxiety during every professional visit.

5. PSYCHOSOMATIC SYMPTOMS: Reported by Feldman-Summers & Jones (1984); we also have noted that persons with no history of somatizing on occasion develop psychosomatic symptoms.

6. CONCENTRATION PROBLEMS: Some clients report difficulty concentrating or experiencing intrusive memories of the relationship with the therapist; still others report recurrent dreams.

7. IMPAIRED SOCIAL ADJUSTMENT AND WITHDRAWAL: Clients at times lose self-confidence and develop social fears, resulting in decreased social involvement. In some cases this disorder can be documented quite effectively by comparing pre-morbid community and social involvement with that in evidence after the destructive therapy relationship. Feelings of isolation may be quite strong and troubling.

8. MOODINESS: Some clients exhibit far more lability of mood following the abusive relationship. Friends report that the clients are less predictable and, therefore, more difficult to relate to.

9. LACK OF SELF-CONFIDENCE: Many clients display a striking lack of self-confidence. They report this fact and it also is evident in their difficulties at work and in social situations. They often can provide graphic examples of their inability to handle situations that previously presented no problems.

10. ANGER AND RESENTMENT: Free-floating anger is often present and noted not only by the client but, also, by spouses, friends, and co-workers.

11. LOSS OF JOB, OR FAILURE TO PROGRESS VOCATIONALLY: Many problems described above may contribute to difficulties at work.

12. EMOTIONAL BREAKDOWN: When the client exits from the abusive relationship, a breakdown, one that, perhaps, requires psychiatric hospitalization, may occur (Vinson, 1984; Luepker & Retsch-Bogart, 1986). Psychiatric hospitalization, in turn, may lead to some loss of self-esteem as well as to the typical problems that result from stigmatization.

Vinson (1984) reported the following rank-ordered symptoms experienced by her 21 female subjects at the end of the sexually abusive relationship with their therapists:

86% Feeling blue or depressed

81% Feeling less close to friends and family
81% Feeling hopeless about the future

76% Feeling emotionally dead or numb

67% Sudden feeling that the relationship was happening again
67% Upsetting, reoccurring thoughts about the relationship
67% Less interest in activities usually enjoyed
67% Trouble concentrating
67% Feelings of guilt or shame about the relationship

57% Irritability
57% Loss of sexual interest

52% Frequent wishes to move or change lifestyle
52% Feeling upset when reminded of the relationship

48% Difficulty in getting to sleep or staying asleep
48% Needing to avoid activities that remind them of the relationship

43% Taking more pills, drugs, or alcohol than usual

33% Getting very jumpy or easily startled
33% Thoughts of ending life

14% Repeated bad dreams about the relationship

Vinson (1984) also reported on the frequency of events that occurred during the two years following the termination of the relationship which her subjects felt were caused by the relationship:

43% Much more arguing with spouse or lover
43% Major weight gain or loss
43% Much less participation in social activities

38% Friends becoming more distant
38% More distant from family
38% Sexual difficulties

19% Marital separation due to conflict
19% Major personal illness or injury
19% Major financial loss
19% Loss of job
19% Major change in type or amount of recreation

14% Borrowing from $1,000 to $10,000
14% New job
14% Change of residence

10% Trouble with employer (job endangered)

In addition, a divorce, a minor violation of the law (e.g., traffic ticket), and a sex-related physical problem were each reported by one subject.

A FINAL NOTE ON DAMAGES

The nature and extent of damages are related to a client's strength or vulnerability just as much as they are to the therapist's actual behaviors. Some clients who have been the victims of truly outrageous and unconscionable behavior by their therapists emerge with surprisingly little damage whereas others suffer greatly as the result of much more innocuous behavior.

The amount of sexual involvement may have little to do with the damages given the fact that sexual involvement per se may not be the major cause of the damage that occurs. It is important to try to focus on damages, not on the outrageousness of a therapist's alleged conduct. Actual damages should not be equated with seriousness of the offense or punishment. The court may, of course, reach a finding of punitive damages to take into account the level of negligence or willful disregard for professional duty.

A discussion of studies of damages and harm caused by therapist-client sexual involvement is presented in Chapter 2.

CHAPTER 11

FALSE OR MISLEADING COMPLAINTS

Gary Richard Schoener
and
Jeanette Hofstee Milgrom

The literature virtually never mentions the possibility of clients making false or misleading complaints of sexual misconduct against therapists. Stone (1983) assumes all complaints to be truthful, with which almost all the authors who have written on this topic agree. We have had only a few questionable complaints, but we are aware of their possibility.[1] In his book, *Medical Malpractice Psychiatric Care*, Smith (1987) raised the possibility of false complaints, and licensure boards and ethics committees certainly dismiss some cases of alleged sexual misconduct by therapists (Sell, Gottlieb, & Schoenfeld, 1986), which suggests that all complaints are not considered valid. Gerson (1989) describes a case in which a couple allegedly charged him with sexual misconduct to avoid paying their bill.

In a recent article Gutheil (1989, p. 597), although asserting that "False accusations represent a miniscule fraction of total allegations..." of therapist-patient sexual involvement, claims that "Patients with borderline disorder apparently constitute the majority of those patients who falsely accuse therapists of sexual involvement." The latter conclusion is based on cases Gutheil reviewed in connection with malpractice litigation or the provision of forensic consultations. It is noteworthy that Gutheil (1989, p. 599) classified as false complaints where "...either the patient retracted the claim and identified it as false or the patient admitted to a disinterested third party that the claim was specious." He provided two such examples in the article.

Over the past 14 or so years, our experience with more than 1,000 cases of sexual exploitation has yielded only a few in which, we believe, misleading or false information was presented by a complainant or someone assisting the complainant. Such cases have increased in number in recent years but still they are comparatively rare. In reviewing malpractice claims against psychologists, Cummings and Sobel (1985) state:

An interesting statistic is that of all the sexual malpractice cases that have been filed, only one person has been exonerated. This would suggest that those individuals who have been accused have been violators in more than one instance and that the data are quite clear. (p. 187)

The situation may change, however. Although it often is quite traumatic for a victim to come forward with a complaint, a person without a legitimate grievance actually may find the public accusation easier to make than would a bona fide victim. It should be further noted that greater awareness in our community of sexual exploitation as well as of mandatory reporting has brought out complaints that otherwise would not have been made, and in some of these complaints the client has not been willing to back them up.

---

[1] A judge recently dismissed charges against convicted rapist Gary Dotson after his accuser, Cathleen Webb, recanted (Johnson, 1989). Her book, *Forgive Me*, (Webb, 1987) describes the case.

Although there has been some discussion and research of lying and distortion by children (see Ch. 9), there has been very little study of the phenomenon in adults. The reader is referred to an interesting article on this subject entitled "Lies and Liars: Psychiatric Aspects of Prevarication" (Ford, King, & Hollender, 1988).

CONFIRMING AND DISCONFIRMING COMPLAINTS

In some cases we have not been able to reach a final conclusion on the relative truthfulness of two versions of what happened. Differences between accounts may, in fact, reflect honest differences in memories of events.

Although we find ourselves developing beliefs about the relative honesty of one person vs. another, we have learned that there is no reliable way to judge truthfulness by examining the reaction of either the client or the therapist. Clients vary dramatically in how much trauma they feel. Some clients are stylistically predisposed to exaggerate and some have a knack for not looking credible even when they are telling the truth. We know of some cases in which licensure boards rejected complaints because of the client's style of telling a story. Even the reactions of professionals are difficult to predict or judge. We were surprised once by a friend and colleague whose defensive reaction made him look guilty. When we processed the complaint later with him it turned out that there were aspects of the situation of which we were not aware that enraged him and thus exaggerated his difficulty in dealing with the complaint.

In confirming a case, we look for one or several of the following:

1. Admission by the Therapist: Either a frank admission that the entire allegation is correct or admission to a great many key details.

2. Multiple Cases: Several clients who do not know or never have spoken to each other tell stories with great similarity in detail.

3. Evidence: Letters or tapes of sessions or phone calls that verify the client's account; pieces of evidence that confirm an improper amount of intimacy, such as expensive gifts that can be traced, photos of the two together, and the like; and witnesses, such as roommates, who testify to the involvement.

4. Knowledge of the Therapist: Knowing of marks on or unique characteristics of the therapist's body may confirm at least some sort of nude encounter, and intimate details of the therapist's home or personal life also tend to confirm inappropriate intimacy.

5. Diary and Other Contemporaneous Records: Despite the possibility of fabrication, a diary or evidence that the relationship when on-going was known to another person, supports a client's story.

It is difficult if not impossible to ever prove a denial, nevertheless therapists at times have successfully challenged a client's allegations by some of the following measures:

1. Admission by the Client: Clients admit to exaggeration or in a few instances, fabrication.

2. <u>Witnesses</u>: An event, in a complaint, occurred in front of other people (e.g., in group, in day treatment) who are able to speak to the accuracy of an account.

3. <u>Evidence</u>: Therapists produce letters or other evidence to challenge client allegations of not meeting to discuss things or of the therapist's failure to clarify professional boundaries, etc.

4. <u>Notes</u>: Contemporaneous case notes that provide an explan-ation of events, and although they certainly can be doctored in a self-serving fashion, verify the therapist's version of at least some events.

5. <u>Consultation</u>: Ethical therapists often obtain consultation on troublesome situations; sometimes the consultant has participated in a session with the therapist and client in an attempt to clear things up.

The remainder of this chapter addresses and describes various types of false or misleading complaints.

MISUNDERSTANDING BY FOLLOW-UP HELPER

People who interview clients with complaints may err by not specifying what it is the client is reporting. Statements that "he was sexual with me" or "he had sex with me" can mean anything from "he looked at me in a strange way...I think he might be interested in me" to "we had sexual intercourse." A touch on the knee becomes a touch on the leg, and later becomes a touch on the thigh. An allegation can be like the "telephone game" children play in which each person whispers a message or phrase into the ear of the person next to him/her; and by the time the story gets around the circle it bears no resemblance to the original. Two examples follow:

<u>Case 1</u>: A professional serving on a Board of Directors was asked why she served on the Board of an outfit that permits sex with clients. She was shocked and began inquiries. The original allegation by a client was that things "had gotten sexual" with her counselor. Her subsequent therapist assumed that meant sexual intercourse. Had he inquired, he would have learned that she and her counselor had a seductive verbal exchange while on a field trip. There was no touching or even solicitation for sex.

<u>Case 2</u>: A young child said that the professional who did a diagnostic assessment on her had been "sexual with her." She meant that she had been asked about sexual contact with someone in the household. By the time the confusion was cleared up, an investigation was underway into child sexual abuse by the evaluator.

We also know about a case of a teacher, not a therapist, in which a criminal charge of sexual misconduct was made after an inept police officer conducted very brief interviews with several kids. All the reported touch occurred in an open classroom with other kids and another teacher watching, which made the charge questionable on the face of it. The teacher was acquitted and the jurors indicated that they felt him to be totally innocent.

MISINTERPRETATION OF LOOKS, WORDS, OR TOUCH

It should be noted at the outset that therapists are responsible for being careful with looks, words, and touch to avoid alarming or confusing clients. In some cases a therapist has been careless or not used good judgment and the interpretation of events is overblown.

Sometimes a therapist manages the situation poorly and the client believes in the possibility that he is out to seduce her. Also, clients sometimes over-interpret touch as part of a sexual seduction.

Some examples:

Case 3: A client claimed that her therapist had tried to seduce her and now was avoiding her and not willing to face the charge. When we called him he was glad to have the opportunity for a meeting with consultants. What emerged was that she greatly exaggerated and read considerable meaning into his innocuous acts and had been harassing him ever since.

Case 4: A young woman seeing a counselor reported that she felt he was trying to seduce her, citing the fact that he had quickly offered to drop his fees, had shifted appointments to a vacant office in the evenings, and at the last session had hugged and kissed her. A processing session revealed that she was his first client, he felt very inadequate to the task, and he feared losing her as a client, thus when she showed resistance to the fees, he lowered them; and when time was an issue, he scheduled evening appointments (even though he was uneasy about the vacant office). A brief hug and kiss came about when, in the last session, on the way out of the room she told him that it had been a very helpful session. He was so overwhelmed by gratitude, he impulsively kissed her. There was a seduction of sorts, but it was not sexual. (This is not to say that he did not have problems; in fact we counseled him out of the field.)

Case 5: A somewhat disturbed adolescent with multiple problems was in an adolescent treatment center. He had a history of exposing himself. He told a staff member that a consultant had touched him in some ways that were bad, implying something sexual. The subsequent investigation ended with the filing of charges of criminal sexual misconduct. The professional was acquitted when the adolescent's account of the touch was presented in considerable detail and did not appear to represent sexual misconduct.

It is important to note here that even psychotic clients often are able to give very accurate accounts of what went on with a therapist. Despite a history of psychosis and an emotional breakdown during the trial, Julie Roy won her civil suit over Dr. Renatus Hartogs when a number of other women came forward and told similar stories (Freeman & Roy, 1982). Serious disorder and psychosis do not, in themselves, indicate that a story should be treated as less than credible.

MISTAKEN IDENTITY

Although rare, we have had cases of mistaken identity. Sometimes the follow-up professional assumes he or she knows the initial therapist who is being referred to and even passes a rumor about the person; later, the follow-up therapist learns that the assumption was incorrect. Anne List (Ch. 16) noted that she made such a mistake. The authors of this chapter, upon hearing an allegation about a man named _____, with degrees in two related professional fields, who was young and had hair of a particular color, felt it could be only one person—someone about whom we had already received a complaint. Some time later we learned we were wrong: there were two professionals who were alike on these details.

Sometimes clients will mention a past therapist but not be able to remember his or her name. They and the follow-up consultant will run through names of people known to the consultant and, sometimes, will end up picking a name only to learn, later, that it was not the right person.

We had one instance of a client making an absolutely false allegation on her own; and it was a clear case of mistaken identity.

<u>Case 6</u>: A therapist phoned an agency director and indicated that a female client he was seeing, who was not willing to identify herself, was alleging that Dr. X, a therapist at the agency, had fondled her breasts and genitals when he had seen her for therapy two years earlier. Dr. X denied the charge and was devastated by it. He had no idea who could have made the complaint.

Communication went back and forth for two months until eventually we got a complete account of what allegedly happened. When a processing session was set up the client changed her story considerably. However, now that her identity was known and Dr. could check his records, he found that she had seen a local therapist who was known for sexual contact of the type she recounted. When she described the therapist as wheeling a "big black desk chair on rollers" over to touch her it was noted that Dr. X did not have such a chair but the previous therapist did. It is virtually certain that she had confused the two therapists. Meanwhile, this two-month nightmare took quite a toll on Dr. X.

Another unusual case involved an allegation by a client that the therapist had phoned late one night and talked sexually on the phone. This was about six months following termination. The client gave somewhat circumstantial arguments for why it was the therapist in question. The phone caller never identified himself and the therapist in question has a somewhat nondescript voice. Although no one can prove it was a case of mistaken identity, we believe that it was.

EXAGGERATION OR DISTORTION BY CLIENT

In several cases the clients, perhaps inadvertently, left out some key details of the story—details that somewhat changed our assessment of it. Usually they related to statements or directions by the therapist as opposed to actions.

Situations also arise in which there are indications that the client has exaggerated part of the story. These are cases in which the client has added more details to the original story, or he or she claims more contact than in the original story. When challenged, some clients back off, although this behavior does not necessarily acknowledge that the story was embellished. Sometimes, if there was considerable seductive interplay in the therapeutic relationship, the client may feel that he or she won't be taken seriously unless more sexual touching, for example, is alleged. Such seduction, however, is a serious problem in its own right and should be treated as such.

PERSONAL RATHER THAN PROFESSIONAL RELATIONSHIPS

Therapists sometimes use as a defense the fact that their relationship with the client was personal and not professional. It is important to note that occasionally a complaint is made by a friend or family member who initially may make the relationship sound like a professional one.

We have had several cases in which someone strongly implied that he or she had been abused in a professional relationship. After careful questioning we learned that a personal relationship was at issue. In some cases, allegations by family or friends may relate to the question of professional impairment although not to client abuse per se—for example, charges of criminal sexual assault in the home or community.

APPARENT FABRICATION

We have had local cases of children and adolescents admitting that they had lied, even in serious criminal cases, about alleged sexual contact with teachers and mental health professionals. In other cases the complaint was made to a third party who reported it, at which point the client disavowed it. In some instances clients have admitted to grudges against a therapist. In one case we have no idea of why the complaint was made. Some examples follow:

Case 7: A woman made a number of allegations against a therapist, including the use of age regression hypnosis to take advantage of her. When confronted on this charge by a psychiatrist who did not believe it, the client admitted to being outraged that the therapist had terminated with her, that she was "out to get" him, and that the allegations were not true.

Case 8: A therapist, after discovering that a client had been lying to him for several years and was a pathological liar, referred the client to a colleague. When this therapist asked for permission to obtain records, the client refused, claiming that she and the first therapist had had sex. Mandated reporting forced the new therapist to report the charge to a Board which then charged the therapist, although the client steadfastly refused to be involved in a complaint. Eventually it was concluded that the allegation was a fabrication.

Case 9: A client charged that 12 years earlier a therapist she had been seeing had had two-hour orgies with her in his office on Saturday mornings. She insisted that the sessions ran over and that this was because of the orgies. Another staff member who received supervision immediately after this client's appointment, and who was often in the vicinity, indicated that a number of points in the story were impossible. Furthermore, if the story were true it would be strange for the therapist to have referred the client to a psychiatrist who took a dim view of client abuse. After a processing session, the psychiatrist felt strongly that the story was fabricated.

Case 10: A chronically mentally ill, borderline client got drunk one night and propositioned a female therapist, who turned him down. He went to the Board of Directors of the program and claimed that she had had sex with him. When the Board abruptly fired her, the client was shocked and admitted that he had made the story up, even retracting it in writing. Unfortunately, she lost her job and her reputation was badly damaged by rumors. It was also very damaging for the client who felt quite guilty, became very depressed, and committed a serious criminal act.

Case 11: While in an adolescent psychiatric unit, a delinquent adolescent told an attorney that he had been sexually assaulted by a staff member. When an attempt was made to follow-up on the allegation, the client changed his story and indicated that it wasn't "sexual assault" but, rather, "sexual insult," which took the form of a vulgar comment.

THE HOSTILE AND AGGRESSIVE CLIENT WITH AN AGENDA

In this category we include some clients who are fairly strong individuals but who have axes to grind, and some very vulnerable and disturbed individuals; both types were out to get their therapists. It should be noted that in a number of these cases at least some errors in judgment were made by the therapists, but the client's characterizations of these errors seem to have been blown far out of proportion. It also should be noted that attempting to assist such clients as an advocate can put one in line to be the subject of the next grievance.

Case 12: A client with a history of sexual victimization by a previous therapist was being set up for another victimization by a new counselor. She then consulted a psychologist about the relationship with the new counselor. The psychologist tried to prevent the victimization by pointing it out and attempting to get her to terminate the relationship. The client became angry about the pressure being applied and got into a power struggle with the psychologist, charging her with professional misconduct and attempting to file a civil suit and licensure complaint.

Case 13: A male client claimed that his female therapist had been very seductive with him; when he attempted to deal with it she terminated him abruptly, being unwilling to deal with him. After obtaining a release, we spoke with her. She indicated that he had tried in every way possible to personalize their relationship, and then began hanging around her house and peeking in windows. When he did not stop this behavior she terminated him. Upon being confronted with this information, the client admitted all of it. He then began coming to another agency for help, always demanding a young and attractive female therapist. Eventually he became angry at one of us and filed a complaint with a regulatory board.

Case 14: A lesbian woman was being seen for an evaluation and some short-term counseling. Her lover, Ms. X, was invited to participate in two sessions as a "significant other." A month or so later, after the client had terminated the counseling and also broken off the relationship with Ms. X, the latter and the therapist ended up in contact. Ms. X asked if they could go out. The therapist indicated that they should not because of the past professional relationship. Ms. X allegedly said that there was no transference and she really had not been a client. Foolishly, the therapist agreed to go out. They ended up in a short relationship. When the therapist broke off with Ms. X, she labeled it "exploitation" and complained. The regulatory board decided that it was not a case of sexual exploitation per se, although the therapist had been careless and needed some supervision.

Fortunately, despite angry words, harassing phone calls, and unwarranted complaints to boards, clients rarely assault their therapists. The few such assaults are unpredictable and are not related to therapist characteristics (Guy & Brown, 1989; Reid & Kang, 1986).[2] Sadly, individuals with axes to grind burn up a great deal of the time and energy of

---

[2] The staff of psychiatric hospitals, including nurses and psychiatrists, do experience some violence by patients, and this may be on the increase. Turner (1984) reported that there was a 27% increase in assaults and a 33% increase in rapes of medical care staff during the period 1977-80. A recent study of psychologists found that 49% had been threatened by a client, whereas 39% had been physically attacked, most commonly during training or the first few years of practice (Guy & Brown, 1989). Methods to manage violent patient behavior (e.g., see Moran, 1984) and approaches to the treatment of staff victims of violence (e.g., see Lenehan & Turner, 1984) are available.

advocates and boards and reduce the resources available to people with more serious cases of abuse. It is important to recognize that even careful and ethical therapists can be the subject of complaints when small things are misinterpreted or blown out of proportion.

SELF-DEFENSE FOR THERAPISTS

Gutheil (1989, p. 599) noted that all of the cases he examined, whether the accusations were shown to be true or false, were "clinically mismanaged in important ways, most commonly through failure to attend to boundaries and to the patients' need for clarity." He warns that "...the impulse to make an exception—especially with patients with borderline personality disorder—no matter how plausibly rationalized, is suspect and should set off red flags of caution" (p. 601). He further suggests:

> From a preventive viewpoint, the clinician encountering a transference that becomes eroticized would do well to begin regularly presenting the case to a colleague, supervisor, or appropriate consultant. In addition to providing valuable input and perspective, such consultation opens the case up and avoids the dangerous insularity of the treatment dyad that often promotes boundary violations. Not only does this approach prevent the illusion that the dyad is encased in a magic bubble from forming but—through this very openness—may also offer some possible defense against false accusations of sexual misconduct. (Gutheil, 1989, p. 601)

A recent Wisconsin study (Brigham, 1989) found that 71% of psychologists surveyed felt that state and national psychological associations had not effectively reduced the risk of unfounded complaints of sexual misconduct by therapists. Despite their fears, there was only one "defensive office practice" aimed at reducing the risk of "frivolous sexual misconduct complaints" which was endorsed by a majority of respondents—maintaining detailed notes (63%). Only 16.6% indicated that they would refuse to see clients that they perceived as "potentially seductive or receptive to sexual overtures" (Brigham, 1989, p. 69).

It is surprising that only 63% said they kept "careful notes," given the fact that this is easily done and a part of good clinical practice. When we encounter a therapist who claims he or she was falsely accused and find clinical notes lacking or inadequate we inform them that they wll have serious problems defending themselves or appearing credible. Unfortunately, Brigham did not include seeking consultation as an option, but it is noteworthy that in response to being asked about "other" preventive measures, only a few psychologists volunteered it. (Brigham, 1989, p. 70) Again, the use of a consultant would appear to be a very basic method of handling a difficult situation and safeguarding oneself against a false complaint. When we examine cases and find that the therapist, despite admissions that the therapy relationship was troubled, or claims that the client was seductive or sexually aggressive, did not utilize a consultant. For example, one psychotherapist admitted kissing a client during three or four sessions, but claimed that she had grabbed him and kissed him on each occasion with no encouragement from him. The fact that these events were not recorded in the case notes and that he had taken no clearcut action to put a stop to the behavior, plus the fact that he had not sought any sort of consultation in the case, led a licensure Board to decide to prosecute the case.

The best self-defense for a therapist is to practice ethically and carefully. Keep good records and obtain supervision or consultation regularly. When psychotherapy relationships are troubled, obtain consultation and document it; consider inviting a consultant to a session. Fortunately, false and exaggerated complaints of sexual misconduct by therapists appear to be rare at present so they are not a major threat.

The careful interviewing of clients about their complaints about former therapists will prevent most of the problems associated with false or misleading charges, since many result from misunderstandings.

PART III

TREATMENT OF THE VICTIM

In Chapter 12, Luepker presents a framework for ascertaining the therapy needs of victims. She discusses individual, family, and group treatment options. (See Ch. 7 for suggestions of follow-up therapy with adult victims.) For additional information on the individual treatment of victims, see Oder (1986) who described the treatment of a young man who was sexually involved with his male psychiatrist; Frederick (1986), who discussed children who are sexually abused by professionals; and the lengthy and invaluable discussion of treatment issues for adult victims of therapists by Pope & Bouhoutsos (1986) and Pope & Gabbard (1989).

Milgrom describes in Chapter 13 the development more than a decade ago of the first support group for clients sexually exploited by their psychotherapists. We believe it to be the first group of its type anywhere in the world. The chapter adds an historical perspective to this manual as well as illustrating how one goes about starting such a group. Well before there was any professional support for addressing the problem of client-therapist sex, Milgrom was proving the need for and efficacy of groups as a treatment modality for abused clients.

Her pioneering effort led directly, several years later, to the development of short-term group services by Luepker and her colleagues at the Minneapolis Family & Children's Service, a United Way agency. Luepker, in Chapter 14, describes the model she developed and led over a 9-year period.

In Chapter 15, List captures the experience of participating as a co-leader in one's first victim group. List is quite open about her inner struggles and the stresses of working with such a group. She also pictures some of the demands placed on group leaders from a subjective viewpoint.

In contrast, Milgrom comments objectively in Chapter 16 about the use of interns, like List, to co-lead victim groups. Of special interest is her examination of the decision-making process that a supervisor goes through in deciding whether the assignment is a reasonable one for an intern.

We favor both the short-term structured group approach and the workshop approach at WICC. It must be noted, however, that other useful models are described elsewhere in the literature. For example, Kaufman and Harrison (1986) describe longer-term, open-ended group therapy for victims which was modeled on other types of victims' groups and met for 18 months. When Dr. Harrison visited WICC, several years ago, we were impressed with both her dedication and the similarity of experiences between participants in her groups and ours. Yet it sounded as if her group was a one-shot experiment that evolved when, at a given time, both she and Kaufman included a number of victims of the same therapist in their individual caseloads.

Another model is the Post-Therapy Support Group at UCLA. Pope and Bouhoutsos (1986) originated the program in 1982, with 7 or 8 groups conducted from 1983 through the Spring of 1988 (Parelman, 1989). The program no longer exists. Observations of group co-leaders are given by Sonne, Meyer, Borys, and Marshall (1985) and Borys, Meyer, Falke, and Sonne (1986), Sonne (1989), and Parelman (1989). Pope and Bouhoutsos and Sonne et al. provide the best description of the groups.

Therapists in a number of states are now using the Luepker model. Some come to Minnesota for training or consult with her by telephone or at workshops. Currently she conducts the groups in a private practice setting; the agency where she was employed formerly and where most of the groups were held, is still offering the treatment. With two groups in operation in a small metropolitan area some difficulties arise in finding enough referrals at any given time. There is the advantage, of course, of offering alternatives to clients. Milwaukee also has two groups in operation, one led by professionals, the other, by a consumer.

It is hard to overstate the importance of having a group available. Beyond the direct benefits to the participants, the very existence of the group, as Milgrom points out, reassures and encourages abuse victims and, at the same time, makes a statement to the community about this problem that must be taken seriously.

CHAPTER 12

CLINICAL ASSESSMENT OF CLIENTS WHO HAVE BEEN SEXUALLY EXPLOITED BY THEIR THERAPISTS AND DEVELOPMENT OF DIFFERENTIAL TREATMENT PLANS

Ellen T. Luepker

When I began to develop clinical services in 1979 for clients who had been sexually exploited by therapists, I felt distinct concerns about venturing into this uncharted area. (See Ch. 14.) By listening to those early clients, however, I learned what their experiences meant to them and, in consequence, how to assess and treat the problems they had faced. Subsequently, I have logged over 1,000 hours providing various types of clinical services (group, individual and family treatment, assessment, consultation, and referral) to more than 100 clients, in conjunction with the services provided by their advocates. These past and present clients are mostly women who requested help for problems related to boundary violations by therapists. The assessment and differential planning techniques I have learned to use with this specific population are discussed here. I hope that this review will help other therapists and counselors to feel more confidently prepared in their responses to the special requests for help from this hitherto unidentified and underserved group.

The goals of assessment are (a) to clarify the immediate needs of the client who has suffered exploitation, (b) to determine how the client views her/his exploitation, and (c) to determine how the exploitation affects current functioning. Concurrently, potential resources should be identified. Clinicians can assess such problems most accurately by understanding the unique meaning of the exploitation and its effect on the clients' current functioning within the context of other dynamically interrelated "layers" of life experience. Figure I illustrates therapy abuse as one of several layers of interacting life experiences. I frequently draw such a diagram for the client.

The purpose of professional intervention is to assist clients to obtain relief from the problems stemming from the exploitation in order to enable them to return to and re-address those problems for which the clients sought help. Clients with therapy abuse problems may be referred to the clinician for specific help for problems stemming from the therapy abuse or they may be in therapy for other reasons and the information on the sexual exploitation emerges in the context of work on the other problems. In either case, the clients typically are experiencing the following:

- Distrust of self.
- Distrust of their perceptions of reality.
- Distrust of therapists.
- Shame and/or responsibility for the therapy abuse
- Mixed feelings/confusion about the previous therapist.
- Mourning various kinds of losses.
- Difficulties putting thoughts and feelings into words.
- Thoughts of suicide.
- Fear of seeking professional help.

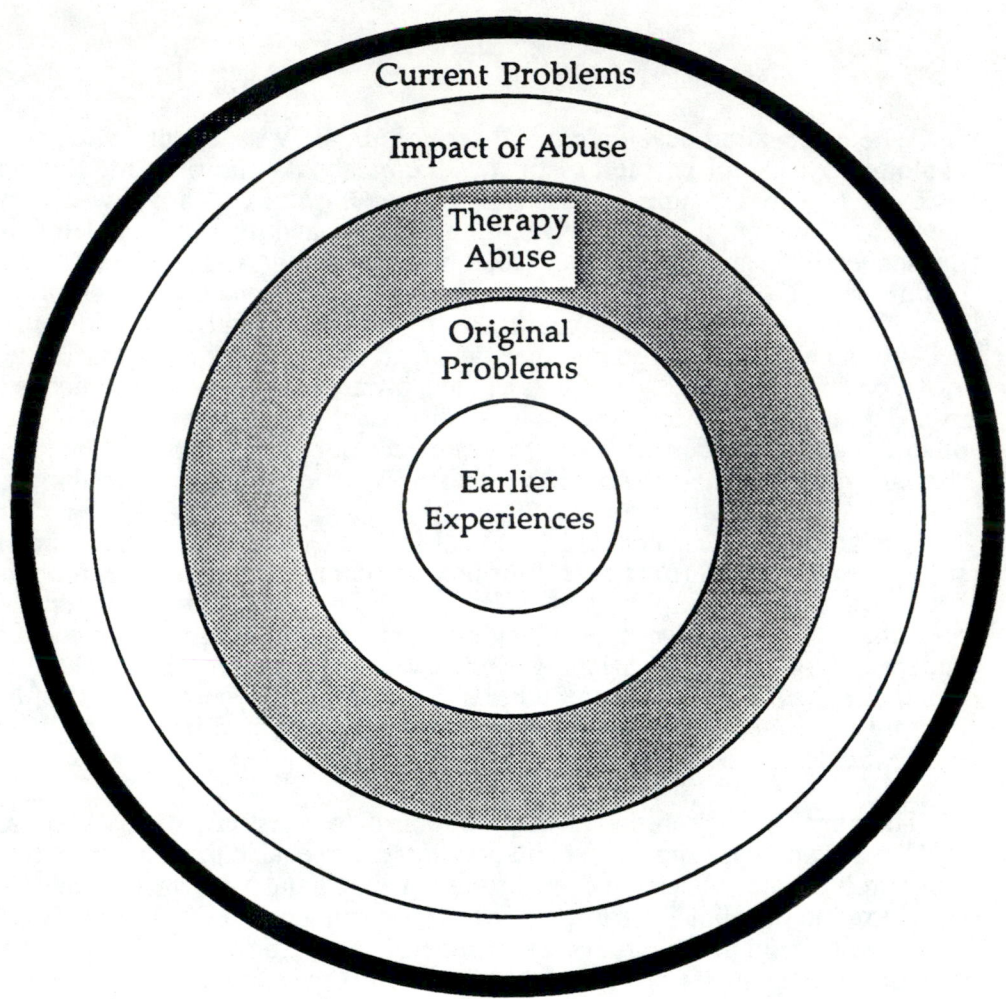

Figure 1: Diagram Used With Clients

It is helpful if therapists who work with sexually exploited clients must have the following attributes to deal with such clients:

- Patience.
- Ability to proceed slowly at the optimum pace for each client.
- Ability to respect each client's unique style of resolving problems.
- Ability to act quickly when crisis intervention is indicated.
- Ability to listen carefully and to avoid taking a position that may sabotage a client's ability to clarify her/his thoughts and feelings.
- Ability to obtain consultation in order to maximize objectivity and avoid professional isolation.
- Ability to use a flexible range of modalities as indicated, either concurrently or at different junctures, in the client's process of resolving problems.

MULTIFACETED TRANSFERENCE ISSUES

Previously exploited clients typically enter a follow-up professional relationship experiencing a multitude of confused feelings. If they experienced sexual involvement with the former therapist, or other kinds of boundary violations, clients did not obtain the help they were seeking then. Instead, they experienced a betrayal by the therapist whose capacities to help they had trusted or idealized to some extent. Such clients, therefore, may approach a subsequent therapist with considerable distrust; and they may wonder if these subsequent therapists will repeat the kind of misconduct that had victimized them earlier.

Because of the issues of secrecy and isolation, clients may find it difficult to put these thoughts into words. They may have little trust in their feelings and in their perception of reality. It is important, therefore, that the follow-up clinician assist these clients to verbalize any thoughts or concerns that may stem from the earlier experiences with the exploitative therapist. The clinician can help by acknowledging the adaptive value of distrust as an important survival technique. Finally, clients will also bring to follow-up clinicians any usual transference issues that relate to previous life experiences.

MULTIFACETED COUNTERTRANSFERENCE ISSUES

Clinicians are challenged in a parallel manner to understand and monitor their own complex countertransference issues when they work with such clients. Typically, professionals who are new to such work may feel inadequate. They may feel angry at the exploitative therapists and guilty that clients have been exploited by members of the therapist's professional "family." They may strive to show clients that they are "better" therapists than the exploitative persons. They may even try to compensate for the client's past damage. (See discussions of countertransference in Chs. 7, 14, and 15.) If these natural reactions are verbalized and/or acted out to the point where they interrupt a client's need to resolve her or his feelings, they may threaten to undo the therapeutic stance necessary to help the clients. Finally, because each client is unique, therapists must monitor their usual countertransference reactions to specific types of clients, diagnoses, and situations.

ASSESSMENT TASKS

Clinicians must articulate assessment questions as clearly and specifically as possible to avoid erroneous assumptions about clients (see Ch. 7). All layers of a client's life experiences should be taken into consideration during the assessment interview (see Fig. 2). The therapist should move the client backward in time from immediate needs, to the therapy abuse, and finally to earlier life experiences and how they may be related to the therapy abuse itself (see Fig. 3). The assessment interview should explore the following:

- Current problems, needs, suicide risk.
- Specific history of therapy abuse (who did what to whom, when, and how).
- Meaning of the therapy abuse to the client.
- Neglect/exacerbation of original problems by therapy abuse.
- Previous functioning and earlier life history.
- Relation of earlier life themes to therapy abuse as perceived by the client.
- Identification of intervention needs and resources.

Even when the sexual exploitation appears not to play a significant role in the client's current problems and specific intervention is not required, clients usually appreciate being asked about their experiences and having the opportunity to verbalize what happened. Although professionals may be anxious about harming clients with inquiries into past sexual abuse, including abuse by past therapists, such inquiries, in my experience, are not harmful. Conversely, avoiding such inquiries may prove harmful because clients, if they are not asked, may never reveal their stories and thus never have the opportunity to resolve the problems stemming from the therapy abuse.

Listening carefully is especially important with clients whose own needs have been given second place to those of a therapist. During assessment interviews, clinicians need to avoid "leading" words that may reveal their biases in a way that cuts off the client's freedom to explore all feelings about previous therapy experiences. For example, although I publicize my own services as directed to helping clients who have been "exploited" by their therapists, I usually do not use the words "exploitation" or "abuse" in initial interviews. Instead, my purpose is to explore what clients have felt and experienced in past therapy. Clients typically have mixed feelings toward an exploitative therapist. Discussion of their positive feelings is as important as discussion of their negative feelings. The use of leading phrases or labels during the interview, however, may have the effect of sabotaging the client's freedom to express all their feelings.

Another issue that may threaten a clinician's ability to maintain a nonjudgmental attitude is the clinician's legal duty to report therapy abuse. When clinicians are required by state law to report alleged therapy abuse, they also must try to respect a client's need for privacy and control. One way to achieve this end is to warn clients of the clinician's legal duty to report the alleged therapy abuse if clients reveal abusive therapists' names.

Although clients with whom I have worked state that they value the protection afforded by such laws, mandated reporting can place clients in the position of having to confront their previous therapists before they feel strong enough to do so. This may weaken the client's control of his or her situation. Often, clients are altruistically motivated to protect others. Therefore, it can be useful to explain two points: (1) when therapists are/have been involved sexually with one client, they usually are/have been involved sexually with several other clients, and (2) the reporting laws are designed to protect clients. Sometimes, when the client does not feel strong enough to endure participation in the complaint process, he/she will request that the clinician report the alleged abuse without revealing the client's identity. This solution may be one way to protect a client's need for privacy, but it handicaps ethics committees and licensing boards in taking action on the complaints. Consequently, clinicians must also explain this fact to clients.

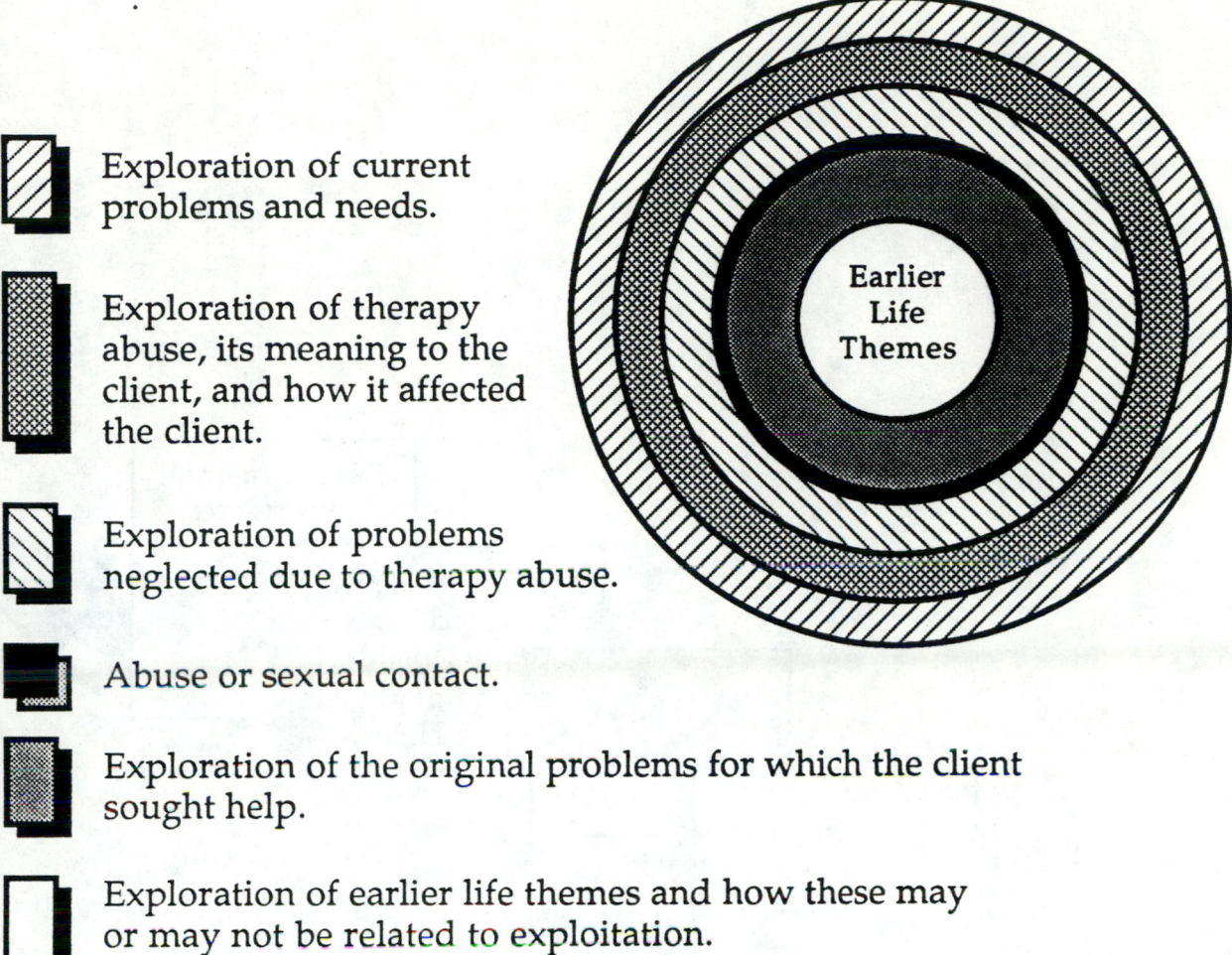

Exploration of current problems and needs.

Exploration of therapy abuse, its meaning to the client, and how it affected the client.

Exploration of problems neglected due to therapy abuse.

Abuse or sexual contact.

Exploration of the original problems for which the client sought help.

Exploration of earlier life themes and how these may or may not be related to exploitation.

In general, assessment moves from the outer layer inward, with awareness that layers of life experience are constantly interacting in a dynamic process.

Figure 2: Layers of a Client's Life Experience

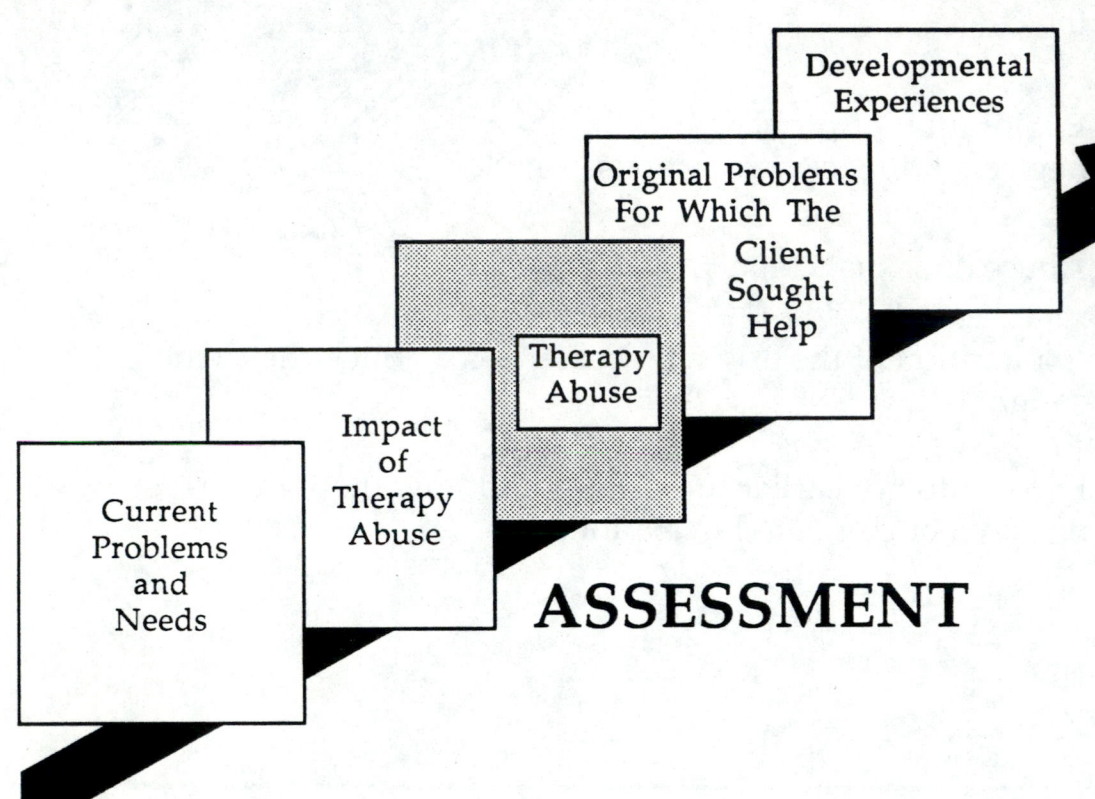

Figure 3: The Assessment Process

ASSESSMENT INTERVIEW SCHEDULE

The following assessment interview schedule may be a resource to therapists in evaluating the following points: The specific nature of therapy abuse; the effects of therapy abuse on client's current functioning; and the relationship of therapy abuse to other factors in the client's life experience.

Identifying information:

- name, address, telephone number, employment status, living arrangements, referral source.

Presenting problems:

- problems for which client is now seeking help;
- which of these are most troublesome to the client?
- are there suicidal thoughts or potential, or other emergencies?

History of therapy abuse: Step-by-step "anatomy" of the previous treatment relationship:

- presenting problems for which the client originally sought help;
- duration of original problems;
- precipitating events that led the client to seek help;
- how did the client choose that particular therapist?
- how did the client initially feel about the therapist?
- in what ways was the therapist helpful or not helpful initially?
- how did the client feel about the therapy as it proceeded?
- at what point did the sexual involvement begin?
- what exactly transpired?
- by whom was it initiated?
- client's feelings about sexual involvement at various phases in this experience;
- what was happening to other important relationships during the sexual involvement with the therapist; e.g., with peers, friends, family?
- what was happening in other life tasks; e.g., work, school, parenting?
- has sexual involvement ended?
- at what point did the sexual involvement end?
- how did it end, by whom was the ending initiated?
- at what point did the client feel the therapy ended?
- has therapy been terminated? If so, in what way did termination happen?
- what feelings does the client have about ending sexual involvement with the therapist?
- what feelings does the client have about ending therapy?
- if there has been no termination of therapy and/or sexual involvement, what specifically is the nature of continued contacts?
- how does the client feel about continued contacts?
- in addition to the sexual involvement, were there any other ways that the client served the therapist's needs; e.g., secretarial work, acting as confidant for therapist's own problems, etc.?
- if so, what were they?
- what has happened to the original problems for which the client had sought help?
- what else can the client say that can help describe what she/he experienced?

Client's current and previous life status and themes:

- living arrangements;
- financial status;
- work functioning;
- school functioning;
- friendships and relationships with family;
- physical health status, including alcohol/drug use;
- previous emotional/mental/social problems;
- previous treatment history;
- are there any ways in which the client feels that the sexual involvement/boundary problems with the therapist might be related to earlier life experiences?

Client expectations and goals:

- what goals or expectations does the client have in seeking help?
- if the client sees no need for help related to the therapy abuse, but wishes other kinds of help for other problems, inquire about what the goals are;
- if the client sees a need for help for problems stemming from the therapy abuse, ask the client to be as specific as possible about goals; e.g., such goals may include one or all of the following: reduction of isolation; clarification of confusing, mixed feelings; clarification of what options for action, if any, the client may wish to take; advocacy support in making a complaint to an appropriate ethics committee or licensing board; resolution of problems with spouse or family members, support to endure stresses of litigation, etc.;
- what kinds of feelings does the client have in seeking help; e.g., any hopeful, positive anticipation as well as any fears about the helping process?

Interview observations:

- take careful note of the client's mental status.
- level of distress and agitation.
- ability to discuss problem.
- eye contact.

Making the diagnosis:

- some, not all, clients suffer from post-traumatic stress disorder;
- the most common diagnoses made for clients specifically seeking help for problems stemming from exploitation by therapists are the adjustment disorders or post-traumatic stress disorder and dissociative disorders; some, in addition, suffer from major depression;
- it is important to ascertain and keep in mind the original diagnosis for which the client had previously sought help and/or other underlying diagnosis, even if the client will not be specifically treated at this time for this diagnosis.

Making the treatment plan: The treatment process, like the assessment process (Fig. 3) often moves back in time as it explores earlier layers of experience.

- review together with the client the specific problems for which the client is now seeking help; his/her goals, and options; e.g., consultation, advocacy, some form of treatment;

- discuss the procedures involved in whatever intervention appears most useful;
- discuss expected length of treatment at time treatment is recommended;
- when the client is in different types of treatment or advocacy simultaneously, obtain informed written consent for collaboration between the therapists and/or advocate and explain importance of step;
- obtain informed written consent for any other consultation needed by the therapist for assessment or intervention phases; and
- put treatment plan into writing to give client the opportunity to later review progress (often clients are pleasantly surprised to see tangible evidence of progress when they can compare their initial goals to outcome). See Figure 4 for example of written treatment plan.

INDICATIONS FOR AND COMMENTS ON DIFFERENT TREATMENT MODALITIES

Consultation:

- For clients who may benefit from an opportunity to tell their story of therapy abuse in order to clarify whether problems have resulted from this experience and, if so, the kinds of resources or options for action that are available to assist with such problems.Sometimes individual therapists find it beneficial to refer clients for consultation with another therapist to obtain an objective opinion for the referring therapist and client.

Advocacy:

- For clients who have begun the process of filing a complaint; clients who wish to file a complaint, or clients who wish to confront previous therapists with how they feel about past therapy experiences. Such clients usually find the support of an advocate advantageous. (See Ch. 26.)

The clinician can help by explaining why, usually, no client should be expected to take such action alone; thus the client is referred to an advocate if it is inappropriate for the clinician to assume the advocacy role.

Whenever possible, it is beneficial to separate the functions of therapy from those of advocacy so the therapist can maintain maximum objectivity.

Individual Treatment:

- For clients who are suicidal, impulsive, in crisis, or clinically depressed (such clients usually require individual care in the initial stages of treatment).

- For clients who believe they can benefit most from a one-to-one opportunity to clarify their thoughts and feelings about the therapy abuse (the individual treatment may be offered as the only treatment modality, as the first step prior to entering group therapy, or as an adjunct to group or family therapy).

- For clients who need treatment but do not feel sufficiently isolated to need a group.

- For clients who need treatment but who fear group therapy because they perceive group members may be critical of their feelings toward their previous therapist or

INDIVIDUALIZED TREATMENT PLAN

NAME: __Jane Doe__ DIAGNOSIS: Adjustment Disorder with   REASONS: Psychosocial stressor
  Mixed Emotional Features   within past 2 months of onset;
INTAKE DATE: __January 20, 1986__   doesn't meet criteria for PTSD
   or Depressive Disorder
TERMINATION DATE: December, 1987   DSM III or
  ICD-9-CM Code: __309.28__
TYPE: _Mutual Agreement_

PROBLEMS	OBJECTIVES	PROCEDURES	TIME	OUTCOME
During college years client in sexual relationship with pastoral counselor. As a result, several friendships interrupted. Secretive nature of relationship with counselor exacerbated her isolation. Grieving loss of relationships with others. Distrusting her ability to understand what happened to her. Distrusting herself, and capacity to form enduring, satisfying, intimate relationships. Disillusionment and loss of trust in God and in the church. Confusion regarding career direction.	To clarify feelings about the exploitative experience. To clarify options for action, if any, she would like to take. To become "unstuck," gain sense of self, be able to start over. To grieve losses resulting from interruption due to relationship with pastoral counselor. To reduce isolation. To clarify career directions. To regain confidence in self.	(1) Individual therapy initially because she does not feel ready to start a group and because not enough clients are available to form a group. (2) Participation in group when ready/ available—ten sessions— with other clients who have been sexually exploited by their therapists. (3) Family session requested post-group. (4) Individual therapy indicated post-family session.	3 months – 2 years	Has clarified confusing, mixed feelings about therapist. Feels more objective, confident in ability to understand what happened to her. Feels less confused, less despairing. Has done considerable grief work to mourn multiple losses: loss of peer & family relationships; interruption to identity development, interruption to career development. Has clarified & worked through fears regarding ability to form intimate, enduring relationships. Has obtained support from friends & family. Has initiated legal action to gain control & protect others. Has developed self-confidence. Has not yet clarified ultimate career goals but has decided to suspend church-related commitments.

_____I have participated in the above treatment plan and agree to cooperate with the plan offered.

*Date:_January 27, 1986_____

__/s/ Ellen Luepker, ACSW_____   __/s/ Jane Doe_____
Staff Signature   **Client Signature**

*Additions/Revisions to Treatment Plan:
     February 1986: Group Therapy
     May 1986: Family Therapy
     June 1986: Individual Therapy

Figure 4: Individualized Treatment Plan Example

attempt to "sway" them to feel or do what they neither feel nor want to do. (Such clients view individual therapy as providing an opportunity to clarify their thoughts and feelings at a slower pace than they imagine would be possible in group and/or family therapy.)

• For clients in group therapy who find they need additional opportunity to focus on issues being stirred up in group therapy.

• For clients following participation in group therapy who wish to focus on the personal problems for which they had originally sought help.

In my experience, it is beneficial to separate the functions of an individual or family therapist from that of a group therapist whenever possible in order to minimize disruption to the group process.

Therapy/Support Groups:

• For clients who feel isolated because of their therapy abuse and, therefore, feel they could benefit from meeting other persons who have had similar experiences.

• For clients who are having difficulty putting into words what they feel about their experiences and who feel that hearing others speak of comparable experiences may assist them in the clarification of their own feelings.

• For clients who may be experiencing shock or disbelief, or who feel "numb" about their past therapy experiences (in some instances, such clients may benefit most initially from listening to others until, eventually, they can put into words what they experienced).

• For clients who feel it would be helpful to see how others cope with problems stemming from therapy abuse in order to develop their own coping techniques.

• For clients who may feel fearful of re-engaging in another one-to-one professional relationship (such clients may feel that a group provides a "safer" treatment modality in that they can observe the therapist from a greater distance in the safety of numbers).

Group treatment may be contraindicated for clients who have histories of serious childhood neglect/abuse and impulsive behavior, or who, in general, have serious difficulty functioning. If such clients are in group treatment, concurrent individual treatment should be arranged at the outset to provide necessary support and crisis intervention.

Family or Relationship Treatment: (See discussion of needs of secondary victims in Chs. 21 and 22.)

• For clients and family members/significant others who have become estranged from each other due to the distractions and/or secretive nature of the therapy abuse.

• For clients and/or family members or significant others (a) to obtain information on therapy abuse problems and their effects upon clients and families; (b) to discuss their respective experiences in order to resolve problems that stem from the stresses to their relationship brought about by the therapy abuse; and (c) to clarify realistic and satisfying ways in which to relate to one another, and (d) to obtain support and information regarding legal and/or complaint processes.

The timing of this type of intervention is an important consideration. Exploited clients usually require the opportunity to clarify for themselves what they feel about their exploitative experience before they are able to consider family members' or significant others' feelings and needs. This delay may be frustrating for spouses or others who may feel further abandoned while their spouses obtain help for themselves. Family members or significant others may need their own opportunities for support and information in such cases, in order to decrease their own isolation and confusion. The spouses'/significant others' groups described in Chapter 22 are examples of separate intervention. Separate individual or family therapy that is educative and supportive is another option.

USEFULNESS OF MULTIPLE MODALITIES AND PROVIDER COLLABORATION

It is common for clients to need various intervention modalities either concurrently (see Case #1 that follows) or at different junctures in the process of resolving the problems stemming from therapy abuse (see Cases #2 and #3). Advocacy frequently may be beneficial either concurrent with or after treatment; in some instances it may be the only intervention required.

Collaboration and clear communication between providers is necessary. In my experience, clients have never complained of "too much" collaboration but, in one instance, a client became anxious when she felt her individual and group therapists held differing views on her situation and were not communicating sufficiently.

ILLUSTRATIONS OF DIFFERENTIAL TREATMENT IMPLEMENTATION

Case #1:

The story of "Nancy" illustrates interventions in which concurrent individual and group treatment (with separate treatment providers) were used together with advocacy. This assisted the client to address the therapy abuse problems in the context of earlier life experiences. She could then re-address and resolve those problems which had been neglected and exacerbated because of the therapy abuse.

Nancy was a single, 34-year-old graduate student and foster parent to two teenage boys. She was referred by her individual therapist, Dr. P., for group treatment because her former therapist had become involved sexually with her by kissing her. Nancy had ceased treatment with the former therapist and had transferred to Dr. P. The latter was uncertain how the therapist's sexual behavior had affected Nancy. She noted that Nancy devalued herself as a woman. Dr. P. wanted Nancy to have an opportunity to discuss her previous therapy experiences with other clients who had experienced similar problems.

During the group intake interview the group therapist observed that Nancy had a pleasant appearance and was intelligent and articulate. Nancy spoke in a detached, intellectualized manner about the sexual seduction by her former therapist, whom she had seen for nearly three years for counseling about her foster son's emotional problems. The therapist also had been treating the foster child. Nancy did not appear to be in emotional distress. Her stated goals for the group were, "I need to identify more with women; I'm not feeling connected with other women." Although Nancy readily agreed with Dr. P.'s referral to the specialized group for clients who had experienced sexual abuse in their previous therapies, her specific goals for being in such a group were unclear.

Significant family-of-origin history included her feelings that she could not rely on her mother for support and that she had grown up without a father because he had been seriously and chronically physically ill from her childhood on.

As the group sessions unfolded, the other group members perceived Nancy as competent and doubted that she needed anything from the group. When she began to tell her story, however, she revealed that currently she was working on her third dissertation topic, having been unable to complete and/or sustain interest in the previous two topics. She doubted that she would complete this topic as well. She also spoke of having relied heavily on her former therapist as an important parenting ally and that she had been forced to terminate her work with him abruptly at the point when he became sexual with her. She expressed sadness in losing his support. She also felt anger at his inappropriate behavior. Almost as an aside, she noted that he had become seductive just at the moment she had developed enough trust in him to reveal her most vulnerable problem: that nearly 18 years earlier she had been unable to obtain support from an adoption worker who had promised to accompany her and support her when she gave up her baby for adoption, and she had felt abandoned and alone when she had watched her baby being carried away by strangers. Nancy expressed sadness when she spoke of her baby's adoption, and gradually realized that in addition to the loss of the therapist, she had lost the opportunity to discuss with him those unresolved earlier losses.

With these insights, Nancy began to express more emotion and other group participants felt more "connected" to her. She expressed eagerness to use her individual therapy sessions to discuss these insights and her unresolved feelings about her baby's adoption. She used group sessions to continue to discuss her mixed feelings about her former therapist and her concerns with his intrusive, self-serving actions which had interrupted the work that was important to her.

Nancy gradually became aware of themes of "unfinished" business and various ways in which tasks in her life had been left "hanging." She also noticed that the familiar theme of not being able to rely upon others pertained not only to the experience with the former therapist but also to earlier life experiences with her parents and the later experiences with her baby's father and the adoption worker. She began to feel that her current sense of detachment from her dissertation and her consequent inability to complete it, her inability to say good-bye to her baby in the way she had wanted, and the recent miscarriage of her previous therapy were all somehow related. Nancy continued to consider these insights in both her individual and group therapy.

Previously, Nancy had attempted to confront her former therapist with her feelings about his sexual advances. She had told him she felt he had betrayed her trust. However, she was disappointed by his insincere response and his inability to empathize or assume responsibility for the negative effect of his behavior. Therefore, although she had not intended to take any further action, she recognized that by not making a formal complaint to the Board of Examiners she was leaving her therapy problems unfinished. Additionally, because another group member had been involved sexually with the same therapist, other patients appeared to be at risk and a formal complaint would have the effect of protecting others from similar exploitation.

The group therapist referred Nancy to an advocate to discuss the complaint process. Following this consultation, Nancy decided to reach closure for herself and do what she could to protect others by filing a complaint. She obtained help from the advocate to write and file the complaint. Hers and others' complaints initiated Board action which ultimately resulted in the therapist losing his license to practice.

While Nancy dealt further with her feelings about the therapist's exploitation and continued to work on the unresolved grief issues in her individual therapy, her depression lifted and she appeared more animated and related more to other members of the group. She eventually completed her dissertation and decided to contact the adoption agency about the possibility of locating the child she had given up for adoption so she could meet this daughter if the child wished to meet her biological mother.

In summary, through specialized help for therapy abuse, Nancy was able to identify the meaning of the abuse in her current functioning. She identified the issues that had been neglected and exacerbated by the abuse. She became able to address the therapy abuse more powerfully. Finally, she felt able to address the problems in her earlier life experience whose resolution had been delayed by the abuse. This intervention resulted in Nancy's feeling much more in charge of herself, less isolated, and better able to complete important life tasks.

Case #2:

The story of "Rene" illustrates the importance of setting priorities in timing and focus during therapy. Different treatment modalities were provided by one therapist, in conjunction with advocacy. These modalities were employed at various junctures in the client's resolution of her problems. The case also exemplifies how the therapy abuse problems were dynamically interrelated to other current and past life experiences. It illustrates treatment focus on immediate life crises, moving back in time to the therapy abuse and to the earlier problems that had been neglected and exacerbated because of the therapy abuse.

Rene was a 43-year-old divorced mother of three teenage children. She was living alone and was employed as a secretary. Her eldest child was in college and the other two children lived with their father in his home, a few blocks away from Rene's apartment. Her problems included depression, suicidal ideation, feeling upset about past sexual involvement with a therapist, health problems, concerns with her daughter's use of alcohol, financial problems, and lack of career plans. Rene had consulted with WICC staff about the problems related to sexual involvement with her therapist and they referred her for individual therapy to deal with the immediate issues of depression and suicidal ideation and, eventually, with the problems stemming from the therapy.

At the intake interview, Rene stated that her feelings of shame about herself and her inability to "face" her former therapist, arose more acutely in the context of current powerlessness. The precipitating event that had led her to seek consultation from WICC regarding the problems with her former therapist was her ex-husband's recent refusal to allow her to meet routinely with him and their children for breakfast, which had been their custom since the divorce several years earlier. As a result, she was feeling disenfranchised as the mother of her children. She felt that she was on the "outside" and was helpless to deal with her fears regarding her daughter's self-destructive behavior.

Significant background history included Rene's sexual abuse by a maternal uncle, her mother's inability to protect her from this abuse, and her father's alcoholism.

Rene's current feelings of helplessness in dealing with concerns about her daughter were arousing painful memories of her own mother's inability to protect her.

The initial intervention focused on Rene's regaining control over her immediate family situation. She was able to clarify what she needed to regain her co-parenting role and was able to talk with her ex-husband about the problems that had led to the rupture of their cooperative parenting. She was then able to discuss with him her concerns with their daughter's alcohol use and to develop a plan with him for working together to address these concerns. In addition, the therapist referred Rene to a physician to deal with her immediate physical symptoms, and she obtained some symptom relief following medical treatment.

After Rene gained some control over her immediate crisis and was no longer suicidal, the therapist helped her to focus on problems stemming from the therapy abuse. Rene stated that she had been in treatment for several years. She and the therapist had terminated therapy to live together when they became mutually attracted. The point at which the therapist suggested they terminate therapy in order to live together was the point at which Rene was dealing with her feelings regarding childhood sexual abuse by her uncle and with the divorce from her husband. Her therapist was separating at the same time from a chronically ill wife. She lived with her therapist for approximately one year, during which time she stated she felt uncomfortable because she never felt his "equal" given her perception that he continued to treat her as his patient. She had continued to feel that he had greater power than she, in part because his responses to her were usually derived from information he had gathered in the context of their treatment relationship.

Rene's work on therapy abuse problems was interrupted by the sudden onset of her mother's terminal illness and the need to take turns with her siblings to care for the mother, who lived in another state. After her mother's death, Rene used individual therapy for support to discuss her childhood incest experience and the recent efforts to confront her uncle about his sexual abuse. She, her sisters, and female cousins had successfully met with the uncle after her mother's funeral to confront him with what he had done to them. Although untimely and unwelcome, Rene's mother's death had created the opportunity to resolve the earlier sexual abuse.

Subsequently, Rene made use of two time-limited groups to clarify her feelings for her previous therapist and for what their relationship had meant to her. Rene appreciated the support of other group members and she began to feel less isolated. She gained sufficient confidence in herself to proceed with her goal of being able to "face" her former therapist.

The group therapist referred her to an advocate for consultation on options and techniques for confronting the former therapist to discuss her feelings. The advocate arranged the meeting in which Rene confronted the therapist with her negative feelings about his interrupting her therapy to act upon their mutual attraction. She was able to tell him that this had felt like a recapitulation of her childhood incest, which had been the problem for which she was seeking his help. She confronted him with the fact that his actions also had interrupted work on feelings regarding her divorce. She later obtained support from the advocate to make a complaint to the director of the therapy institute with which the therapist had been associated, resulting in Rene's feeling less ashamed of herself and better able to "hold her head up."

Following termination of group treatment, Rene continued to be seen individually for periodic support on such matters as financial and career planning. Her entire course of treatment lasted approximately 15 months. Telephone follow-up one year later revealed that she had maintained her self-esteem, control over her life, and was developing options for her career.

As a result of this multimodality intervention, which addressed several familiar themes in interrelated life experiences, starting first with immediate crises and then moving backward to the therapy abuse and earlier childhood problems, Rene was able to develop the self-esteem, control, and power over her life that she had longed to have for many years.

Case #3:

The story of "Jane" illustrates the use of individual, group, and family therapy with the same provider at different junctures in the treatment process, in conjunction with an attorney's legal assistance to resolve problems stemming from therapy exploitation. It illustrates Jane's ability then to re-address those identity issues for which she had originally sought help but which had been neglected and exacerbated by the sexual exploitation.

Jane was 24-years-old, single, a graduate theology student, and employed as an elementary school teacher. She was referred by a friend who had participated in a treatment group for clients who had been sexually exploited by their therapists. Jane was cautious about the prospect of seeing another therapist and, although she knew of the availability of the therapist's group for clients with problems such as hers, she did not feel ready to participate in a group. She was feeling in "shock" and overwhelmed by her recent recognition of how destructive the relationship with a priest, her college counselor, had been. She stated she needed an opportunity to clarify her thoughts and feelings about that experience.

When Jane was seen for assessment, she appeared consumed with grief. She stated that she had sought help from the pastoral counselor during her second year of college because of problems in a hostile-dependent-sexual relationship with a female student advisor. The pastoral counselor initially had helped her to separate from this destructive relationship but then became sexually seductive. Jane acknowledged that initially she was relieved that she had sexual feelings for a man because she had been extremely anxious that she might be lesbian. However, the ensuing relationship with him over the next three years became increasingly destructive to her.

Immediately prior to seeking help, Jane had developed an awareness of her extreme isolation from peers and family and uncomfortable dependence on the counselor. Her awareness had been precipitated by her move to the metropolitan area following her recent graduation from college. After the move, she had had an opportunity to observe other competent women who were leading independent lives and realized then how badly she wanted to feel differently. Also, her contacts with the priest had been interrupted because his Diocese had sent him to another state for sex abuse treatment. Jane knew that the Diocese had been aware of his sexual involvement with other women students, but not of his sexual involvement with her. Jane's earlier life history included the fact that she was the youngest of several children raised on a farm in an intact family. She described her family life as relatively "problem-free," although her mother seemed to have some difficulty discussing sexual information with her. Jane was a hard-working conscientious young woman who had been an above-average student. She had enjoyed singing in the church choir throughout her life. She described herself as having been in "awe" of priests during her childhood and that she had long hoped to have a career within the church.

During the initial phase of individual therapy, Jane used her sessions to grieve multiple losses; for example, how entangled with and dependent upon the pastoral counselor she had become to her own detriment, and how alone she felt as a result. She also used the sessions to clarify which friends and family members she could trust to tell about the secretive relationship in order to reduce her isolation.

When Jane felt ready to enter a group and enough clients emerged to form one, she began to participate in a 10-session group. Her goals were to reduce her isolation further by talking with others who had experienced similar therapy problems. She also wanted to learn how others coped with such problems.

In the group, Jane began to feel less isolated. Through talking about her own experience and listening to others, she discovered how the therapist's inconsistent responses to her had exacerbated her dependence upon him. She also became interested in other group members' thoughts about taking various types of action to help them feel more in control. Since Jane was aware that other college students had become sexually involved with the same pastoral counselor, she decided legal action would be one way to regain power for herself and protect others from a similar fate. The group therapist referred her to an advocate for consultation regarding this option and the advocate subsequently referred her to an attorney.

Following termination of the group, Jane resumed individual therapy where she continued to focus on understanding how the pastoral counselor had gained so much control over her. She also requested a family session to help her and her parents talk together about her impending lawsuit. She was concerned that her mother would "not be strong enough" to cope with what had happened to her because her mother had become tearful following Jane's telling her about the plans for litigation.

In the family session, the therapist briefly provided some general background information regarding the prevalence of client sexual exploitation and its effects upon clients and their families. She then helped Jane's parents to describe their own responses to hearing about their daughter's sexual involvement with the college pastoral counselor. She helped them all consider specific ways to cope together as a family and as individuals with stresses during the upcoming lawsuit, including the prospect of their daughter's possible public exposure in the media. As a result of this session, Jane and her parents felt less isolated from one another and better able to talk together about the abuse and lawsuit without worrying about each other's capacity to speak about such matters.

Following the family session, Jane continued to use her individual therapy to explore the problems which had been neglected, exacerbated, or caused by the priest's sexual exploitation:

- Feelings about her relationship with the student advisor; concerns about having had a same-sex relationship.

- Dilemmas related to how to express anger when she feels dependent in relationships with other women.

- Concerns about being able to trust while developing an intimate relationship with a man.

- Grief related to feeling betrayed by God.

- Grief related to feeling a need to give up her theology graduate studies, participation in church services/church choir due to her traumatic disillusionment in God and the church.

- Feelings of "awe" of priests and the role of these feelings in creating vulnerability to exploitation.

- Flashbacks and nightmares related to the sexual exploitation.

- Stress related to litigation.

Jane initially felt very uncomfortable about her grief and anger toward the church. She gradually became more accepting of her feelings and of her needs within the context of friendships, intimate relationships, and relationships with persons in authority. She became more confident in asserting herself. With the support of an understanding, creative liturgist, Jane decided to craft a ceremony within the church which would acknowledge and put to rest the losses she had incurred.

Like other women exploited by clergy, Jane's problems and losses related to the sexual exploitation were extensive, and required long-term help. After two years, Jane continues to make effective use of individual therapy for support in litigation and help with developmental issues; e.g., relationships with parents, fiance, and career goals. Her use of multiple treatment modalities has helped her obtain clarity regarding her past and present life experiences, to grieve multiple losses, to gain confidence in herself, and to establish more realistic, satisfying relationships with others.

CONCLUSIONS

In sum, work with clients requires the following:

- Nonprejudicial, open-minded assessment that specifically explores the therapy abuse itself and its meaning in the context of a client's unique life experiences.

- Multiple treatment and advocacy strategies to be used differentially, depending upon the client's unique needs at various stages in the resolution of therapy abuse problems.

- Specialized help that initially addresses any immediate crises and then the therapy abuse in order to free clients to re-address those problems that were neglected and/or exacerbated by the therapy abuse.

In the process of clarifying the meaning of the therapy abuse in the context of total life experience, such clients can realize unprecedented opportunities for growth.

CHAPTER 13

THE FIRST GROUP FOR CLIENTS SEXUALLY EXPLOITED BY THEIR THERAPISTS: A TWELVE-YEAR RETROSPECTIVE

Jeanette Hofstee Milgrom

The Walk-In Counseling Center (WICC) started, in the fall of 1976, a therapy/support group for clients who had been sexually exploited by their counselors and therapists. By then, staff members had gained some experience working with individual clients who had sought assistance after being exploited by a previous therapist. Therefore, when one woman came in requesting that WICC sponsor a group, staff members decided to take the step.

ANNOUNCING THE GROUP

WICC sent announcements of the group to particular staff persons at other mental health/social service agencies during the summer of 1976. When some professionals saw the announcement of the group they were incredulous and suspicious in their responses. Others felt it was a joke. Still others thought the group was WICC's way of warning professionals not to get sexually involved with clients, or considered the problem such an isolated one there never would be enough clients to form a group.

Nevertheless, the group started in late September 1976 with three clients and two co-therapists, myself and Donna Witthaus, a clinical psychologist who was a WICC volunteer. Subsequently, two more women joined the group.

FORMAT AND STRUCTURE OF THE GROUP

The group ran for 16 consecutive weekly sessions with a total of 5 members, but no more than 4 active ones at any time, and an average of 3 in attendance. Each session was two hours long; by meeting in the early evening employed women were able to attend. Group discussion was the primary format; some role-play of anticipated situations and recommending or lending helpful books augmented the discussions.

The "up-front" announcement that the group was expressly designed for clients who had been sexually abused by therapists overcame the main barrier to free discussion. Inasmuch as every client in the group had had a similar experience, all were able to get down to business almost immediately and to share with each other their experiences and the effects of those experiences.

COMPOSITION OF THE GROUP

All group members were women. The composition of the group was similar to that of subsequent groups in its variety of individuals and their stories. The women varied in socio-economic background, marital status, psychological make-up, and other demographics. Their stories regarding the former therapists also differed a great deal although their reactions were similar. The exploitative therapists represented various professions: psychiatry, psychology, and the clergy. I remember that my reaction to learning about a clergy sexually exploiting a client/counselee was one of shock; it was hard for me to conceive of someone "next to God" behaving in this way.

BENEFITS TO GROUP MEMBERS

The group participants expressed how the group helped them: Their feelings of isolation diminished; they no longer felt that they were the only person who had been victimized by a therapist; and they were able to get through the week better and to concentrate on their jobs or studies because they knew they could focus on the issue of the sexual exploitation at the weekly sessions. As a group, they were able to laugh with rather than at each other and to share their sometimes bizarre stories. They created a great deal of humor to help themselves to cope with a great deal of pain.

The women expressed improvement in their self-concepts as they got to know, like, and respect each other. After all, if they respected a member who had been involved in a similar situation then they themselves might be deserving of respect. Group members were so motivated to keep going throughout the Christmas holiday season that they chose not to take a break.

REACTIONS OF GROUP FACILITATORS

The two co-therapists, 10 years later, met again to look back at their outstanding impressions.

One remembered, predominantly, feeling the grief and pain expressed by the group members. The other mostly remembered feeling great anger toward the therapists who had abused these women. Both remembered the group members as emotionally vulnerable; romantic; yearning to have a relationship with a man (the therapist) who needs them; and blaming themselves for what had happened.

The therapists' behaviors that were reported by the group members included immature expression of sexuality—like a child molester—as well as sexual dysfunction; financial exploitation (e.g., having clients do office work for no pay, although, at the time, the woman saw it as an honor rather than exploitation); and multiple victimization. Much as the women hated to admit it to themselves, some had become aware that they weren't the "special" clients they had been led to believe they were and that the therapist was involved with other clients also.

My involvement with this group was a great challenge. I had had extensive experience working with groups of all kinds of clients with a multitude of problems. In many instances I had been the first person to initiate a new type of group in a particular agency. Yet, this first group for sexually exploited clients required all the skill, energy, good judgment, and willingness to take risks that I could muster up.

ENDING THE GROUP

The group was terminated in early January 1977. One member had discontinued earlier because her husband was unaware of the situation and her attendance became problematic. Another member subsequently felt that she had finished. A third member moved out of town and a fourth was about to have a baby. In addition, one meeting had to be cancelled because of an early January Minnesota snowstorm. The time had come, evidently, to end the group.

OBSERVATIONS AND RECOMMENDATIONS

Based on the 12-year retrospective of this first group and what was learned from subsequent similar groups, here are some observations and recommendations that we made in 1977 that still seem accurate today.

Although now we might do things differently, given our subsequent experience with exploited clients and groups, I do not believe we made major mistakes with that first group. If I were to take a different approach today it would be (a) to be much more direct with clients and (b) to be much less hesitant in asking about what specifically went on, and what, if anything, the clients wanted to do about it. But the climate was different at that time and the more direct approach might not have been acceptable to clients.

Having co-facilitators/co-therapists is highly desirable if not absolutely necessary. Working with clients/group members who are highly distressed is very demanding and difficult especially when the issues are as complex as those of women who have been sexually exploited by therapists. Also, it is less intimidating to clients (who already have been exploited) to meet with two group leaders rather than one because it helps to diffuse the authority.

Limiting the size of the groups makes a lot of sense. Small groups are best because (a) each member is likely to want and need a lot of time and attention, and (b) participation in a group at any one time is the choice of only a subset of the population in a given community. For some sexually exploited clients, a group may be held too early; they are not yet ready to seek help. For some it is too late; they are beyond the point of wanting help. And some exploited clients cannot or will not participate in a group, ever. But there is always a small number of clients who want and can use a group <u>now</u>. Therefore, whatever one's previously conceived notion of the proper or desirable size of a group, the notion should be reconsidered. A group of 3-6 clients, with an average attendance of 2-4 may seem like a very small number—and indeed it is—but this size may be of the greatest benefit to the participants and just about the right size for the group leaders to deal with.

Having group facilitators who are experienced clinicians/therapists as well as experienced group leaders is certainly recommended. Clinical skills are needed to deal with clients' problems, such as depression and suicide potential. Group-work skills are needed to provide optimal opportunity for group members to support each other and to learn from each other; this is different from doing individual therapy in a group.

In conclusion, a group experience is a valuable and unique opportunity for sexually exploited clients. And even though the group may well demand a great deal from the group facilitator(s), it can simultaneously be very rewarding to see clients help each other and to make great progress in dealing with a devastating chapter in their lives.

CHAPTER 14

TIME-LIMITED TREATMENT/SUPPORT GROUPS FOR CLIENTS WHO HAVE BEEN SEXUALLY EXPLOITED BY THERAPISTS: A NINE YEAR PERSPECTIVE

Ellen T. Luepker

In discussions of the unethical sexual behavior of therapists with clients, the legal and professional aspects of these relationships have received considerable attention. Less is known, however, about the negative effects of such behavior on clients.

Sexually exploited clients largely have been ignored by the therapeutic community just as victims of incest were until recently. The tragedy of some of the reported situations challenges professionals. For example, during an intake interview a young woman revealed that she had to appear in court the following day to sign papers relinquishing parental rights and giving up her baby for adoption. The prospect would be difficult under any circumstances but her situation was even worse: The child had been conceived with her therapist and she had no supportive friends or family nearby. These facts made scheduling a future group or individual session seem insufficient so a group leader accompanied her to court and helped her through this event.

Victims of therapist sexual exploitation, like victims of incest, often suffer alone or in silence. The isolation intensifies their confusion, guilt, sense of shame, and feelings of responsibility. They do not know who is to blame—the therapist or themselves. Family, friends, and community respond defensively by denying that such events could happen. They discount the occurrences and even blame the victims for retaliations if they report the experiences. Even worse, although their need for professional help may be even greater than it was earlier, they now distrust therapy and therapists because the problems for which they originally sought help were neglected and new ones have been added.

One way to assist these clients is through time-limited treatment and support groups. The sessions offer them an opportunity to discuss their situation with persons who have been similarly exploited and to end the isolation they feel. I review in this chapter my clinical experiences with 57 women who participated in group therapy during the years 1980 - 1989. The account of my experiences and observations, I hope, will stimulate further understanding of the problems and unique needs of such exploited clients in the context of a practical treatment model.

PLANNING AND DEVELOPMENT

The groups were initially developed in a private, nonprofit, United Way-funded family service agency and continued in a private practice outpatient, mental health clinic. Planning for the groups was done at the request of and with consultation from the Walk-In Counseling Center (WICC).

The two functions of therapeutic intervention (by "facilitators") and advocacy were separated from the outset. Advocacy, provided by WICC staff members, assisted clients in pursuing complaints to licensure boards or ethics committees, conducting processing sessions with the former therapists, or finding competent attorneys. This division of responsibilities has proven invaluable; freed from most advocacy responsibilities for clients, group facilitators enjoyed greater freedom in therapy sessions to objectively help clients to discuss their wide-ranging feelings without feeling pressured to take action.

All groups were time-limited. They met once a week for 2-12 weeks and consisted of 3-5 members per group. The groups meeting for the shorter periods were those that had fewer members. Group length also varied as a function of clients' needs or the leaders' time availability. The sessions lasted for 1-1/2 hours for the smaller groups and 2 hours for groups of 4-5 members. The optimal length for the groups was 10 sessions.

The fees for clients seen at the family service agency were set according to their ability to pay, determined by the agency's sliding-fee scale. Clients seen at the private clinic paid the clinic fees out of pocket or with insurance reimbursements. Flexible payments over time were necessary because of the economic/occupational disequilibrium frequently resulting from the problems associated with the exploitation.

Access to co-therapists and consultation was crucial to minimize the facilitators' professional isolation and maximize their objectivity. This support is usually useful in therapy situations but it was especially important in work with this population because threats to a leader's objectivity is inherent when one is a member of the "professional family" in which the exploitation occurred. Co-facilitators were available for all but two groups and they participated in most of the intake interviews.

GOALS AND OBJECTIVES

The primary goal of the groups was to offer clients the opportunity to free themselves enough from the problems associated with the exploitation to be able to re-address the problems for which they had originally sought help. The time-limited format reflects the philosophy that the victimization experience can be short-circuited so that one can move on in life, and that significant help toward this end can be obtained in the brief therapy format.

The group objectives follow:

1. To explore and clarify in a confidential setting one's feelings about the previous therapist and the sexual exploitation.

2. To explore and clarify what, if any, action one wishes to take.

3. To reduce one's isolation.

4. To explore earlier family of origin/other significant relationships and to identify how they may have contributed to the exploitative therapy experience.

5. To obtain consumer information on appropriate psycho-therapy and its availability.

6. To identify and use alternative responses to the exploitation.

INTAKE INTERVIEWS

All prospective clients were scheduled for intake interviews with one or both facilitators. The purpose of these interviews is to assess clients' presenting problems and goals and to inform them about the group so they can decide whether it may be useful. In light of the clients' histories, facilitators tried to provide as predictable a structure as possible from the beginning. Therefore, they announced to each client what she could expect in the intake interview, tried, whenever possible, to have both co-therapists present at intake so the clients could meet both, and give as much information as possible to help clients to anticipate what they could expect in the group sessions.

The following information was obtained in the intake interview:

1. Reasons for seeking help from the group;

2. Personal goals in the group;

3. History of previous treatment with the exploitative therapist, including:

    a. original presenting problem,
    b. general nature of that therapy,
    c. what was experienced as useful/not useful,
    d. how the treatment ended, and
    e. client's feelings about all that;

4. Other treatment history;

5. Current life situation, including:

    a. current problems in functioning,
    b. support system,
    c. areas of strength;

6. Pertinent family of origin/school/work/relationship history;

7. General health history; and

8. Concerns with entering group.

In addition, group facilitators have provided clients with the following group rules during the intake interview:

1. Group leaders do not use touch; communication in therapy is limited to words.

2. Clients are encouraged, but not forced, to talk about whatever is on their minds.

3. Discussion need not be limited to thoughts on the previous therapy as issues of current importance to clients usually are related in some way to the exploitation.

4. Clients are expected to arrive on time, attend regularly, absent themselves only for unavoidable reasons that, whenever possible, should be announced to the group in advance in order to provide the necessary continuity for the most useful group process.

5. Communication between members outside group sessions is to be shared with the group to facilitate group process.

6. Clients are encouraged to provide feedback about what is needed, useful, or not useful in the group sessions.

The group facilitators also explained the usefulness of the leaders' collaboration with WICC staff members. Initially, the leaders obtained signed consent for collaboration only when clients had seen WICC staff members. Subsequently, however, it became clear that routine consultation with WICC staff members enhanced the services to all clients. Therefore, leaders decided to obtain routine permission for regular work with WICC staff consultants, regardless of whether the client was active with WICC. In order to coordinate treatment services, leaders also obtained signed consent for collaboration with the individual therapists clients might be seeing.

REFERRAL SOURCES

Most clients in the groups were referred from the Twin Cities metropolitan area but some came from towns within a 120-mile radius. About one-half were referred by the Walk-In Counseling Center; others, by professionals in social service agencies, mental health clinics, sexual assault centers, private practice, the Board of Medical Examiners, and the Minnesota Task Force on Sexual Exploitation of Clients by Therapists and Counselors. Some clients were referred by friends who had participated in previous groups.

REASONS FOR REFERRAL

Discomfort about the previous therapy relationship and the wish to feel better were the primary reasons for seeking group services. This discomfort usually arose in the context of unsatisfying personal and/or employment relationships and feelings of low self-esteem.

CLIENT CHARACTERISTICS

All group members were women ranging in age from 22-55. In marital status they were equally divided among separated/divorced, married, and single. Most had obtained at least some college education. Occupations ranged from professional (30%), managerial (10%), clerical/trade (30%), housewives and/or unemployed (20%), to students (10%).

Previous histories and functioning included the following features:

About 30% of the group members were victims of childhood sexual abuse—approximately the same level of prevalence in the general population as estimated by researchers (Kinsey, 1983; Russell, 1983).

Nearly all described "tense" or difficult family situations, including such problems as incest, alcoholism, divorce, emotional and/or physical abuse, poor communication, and either extremely distant or intrusive parents. Clients from the more severely disturbed families reported feeling depressed, suicidal, paranoid, and phobic prior to seeking help from the exploitative therapist.

Seven members had been hospitalized for psychiatric reasons prior to the sexual involvement with their previous therapists. Eleven clients required psychiatric hospitalization at some time after the onset of sexual activity and/or termination of therapy with the exploitative therapists; of the eleven, ten had no prior history of psychiatric hospitalization.

These clients originally had sought help for a variety of concerns, including vocational, marital, and family problems, relationship issues, and their own and/or spouses' chemical dependency. Two clients had been high school students at the time of the sexual exploitation and seven had been college/university students. All stated they had felt "vulnerable," "depressed," or "anxious" when they sought help from the exploitative therapist.

With one exception, the characteristics of the group members are representative of both the agency's and clinic's respective general client populations. The one exception is the high prevalence of psychiatric hospitalizations, which is higher than the prevalence in either the agency's or clinic's respective general populations.

CHARACTERISTICS OF ABUSING THERAPISTS

All but two of the abusing therapists were male and practicing primarily in the professions of psychology, psychiatry, social work, and alcohol/drug abuse. Some were pastoral counselors or ministers and/or priests serving as counselors. Over half the therapists worked in private practice settings, equally divided between solo and group practices; the rest practiced in more public settings, such as agencies, hospitals, high schools, colleges, universities, and churches.

BOUNDARY PROBLEMS IN THE PREVIOUS THERAPY

In the previous therapy, all but two clients experienced various types of overt sexual contact with their therapists. Nearly half had engaged in sexual intercourse and others participated in fondling, kissing, erotic embraces, and oral sex. One of two clients who had not been sexually involved with their therapists had felt troubled by his sexual involvement with other patients. One had been disturbed by his and other patients' negative reactions when she expressed concern with his behavior; for the other, the involvement had been a fantasy. The fact that it had been but a fantasy emerged only after several group sessions.

Inappropriate nonsexual behaviors usually had occurred as well. For example, one client did her therapist's shopping for his wife; another shopped and performed other services for the therapist's children, and many had acted as consultants for the therapist's personal problems.

Some group members had anticipated marriage with their therapists in the future, an expectation based on dating, intimate conversations that included future plans for the relationship, and remarks that had led the clients to believe they were important to their therapists. Some clients had taken vacations and/or lived for a time with their therapists.

Two chemically dependent clients had been fondled by their therapists in exchange for pills. Three others had smoked marijuana with their therapists. Five clients had been either hypnotized and/or sedated with medication prior to the therapist's sexual advances. Three clients had financially supported their therapists. One client had become impregnated by her therapist while she was a resident in a chemical abuse treatment half-way house.

PRESENTING PROBLEMS AT INTAKE

Presenting problems for which clients sought group services typically included discouragement about current relationships, low self-esteem, and a sense of personal stagnation—all linked by clients to the exploitation. For example, several women who had difficulties raising their children felt that these difficulties were exacerbated by guilt about the relationships with their previous therapists. They felt that their marriages had ended in divorce because they had become distracted by those relationships. They blamed themselves for depriving their children of their fathers, which, in turn, made parenting more difficult.

Others described different kinds of disruptions of important relationships because of distractions stemming from involvement with their therapists. They felt lonely and isolated. Those involved with therapists who had a cult-like or popular following described the pain of being ostracized by the therapist's loyal followers or associates.

Some thought they already had mastered or "buried" the problems associated with the exploitative relationships but sought help after experiencing a resurgence of painful feelings. The resurgence often disrupted important personal and/or work relationships, or caused difficulties in the progress of subsequent therapy. All clients described symptoms of either adjustment disorders or post-traumatic stress disorder.

All clients reported varying degrees of distrust at intake. The facilitators acknowledged the suspicion as understandable and adaptive, given their experiences. In addition, the clients reported varying degrees of readiness to separate emotionally from the previous therapist. In part, the degree of readiness was related to the passage of time since the last contact with the therapist; the nature of the termination, or the lack thereof, also played a major role.

All group participants at intake described feeling very isolated and of there being few or no persons with whom they could discuss their conflicted feelings about the previous therapy. They hoped the group could help to reduce this isolation. Nearly all expressed shame and guilt about the relationship with the therapist and felt responsible for what happened; that is, they believed that what happened was their "fault." All had intense and wide-ranging feelings about their therapists: anger; a sense of having been "betrayed" or "ripped off"; sadness over help not received; frustrations over new problems resulting from the exploitative relationship and its distractions; a sense of having received something worthwhile from the therapists; and fear of "hurting" the therapist in his personal/professional life.

Many participants who had hoped for an enduring relationship with their therapists expressed feelings of sadness, disappointment, rejection, jealousy, and a wish for renewed contact, even as late as the time of group intake. Most clients described having had a "gut feeling" that what had happened was not right, and they expressed frustration with themselves for their "poor judgment" and "naivete." Even though they understood that they had felt needy and vulnerable in that relationship, they berated themselves as having been "dumb" for becoming sexually involved with the therapists. Several clients reported feeling emotionally "numb" whereas others reported fears that their feelings toward the previous relationship would resurface, and several expressed confusion at not knowing what they felt. Grief and despair were typical responses expressed at intake.

Also, at the time of intake, most clients expressed the need to be believed by the facilitator(s) and to be able to speak in confidence about their problems. Many worried that the facilitator(s) or other group members would judge them critically for proceeding too slowly and/or ineffectually in resolving their problems. In response, the facilitators emphasized that they believed the accounts, that information is kept in confidence (except for the reports mandated by law), that every client proceeds in her own way and at her own pace, and that judgments are not made regarding the actions, if any, group clients take. Leaders also reiterated the group's purpose: to help clients to explore their unique solutions, however the solutions vary among group members. The test of a solution is whether it feels "right" to the client.

In addition, immediate treatment needs also were assessed at intake and appropriate action and/or referrals made. For example, when clients appeared suicidal, appropriate arrangements were made for immediate individual assistance. Occasionally, clients not already in individual treatment requested individual in addition to group treatment. Facilitators made referrals to individual therapists, preferring not to see clients themselves in concurrent individual treatment because it had the potential of interrupting the group process. Sometimes clients requested individual assistance from a facilitator during a several week waiting period prior to the first group session. The assistance worked well when it was anticipated that the client would not suffer from interrupting the individual therapy when she entered the group.

REASONS FOR NOT JOINING GROUPS

In addition to the 57 group participants, one or both facilitators interviewed an additional 20 women who wished to explore the possibility of participating in the groups but did not join for the following reasons: (a) Several had friends/family with whom they could discuss the exploitation and therefore did not feel isolated enough to need the group, (b) individual therapy was the preferred modality when the client was uncomfortable with groups or the exploitation was not the central issue requiring attention at that time, (c) in two cases, one leader felt she had a conflict of interest because of indirect associations with the client's former therapist which she believed could impair her objectivity. The leader explained this situation and referred the women to WICC for the exploration of alternative services. (d) For one woman, the exploitation, based on strong evidence, very likely was only a fantasy; hence she was deemed not appropriate.

Of the total 77 women interviewed, only two (2.6%) appeared to have fantasized the exploitation. The stories of the others were supported by various kinds of evidence, such as acknowledgements by the therapists themselves that the exploitation had happened and/or similar complaints from other clients about the same therapist.

GROUP THEMES

CONCERNS WITH CONFIDENTIALITY

All clients felt it imperative that everyone in the group keep what was said in strict confidence. Although this need is present in any treatment group, fears of retaliation by the previous therapist and intense guilt over the involvement heightened the need for the assurance of confidentiality and privacy. Some members were involved in litigation and for legal reasons, were obliged not to discuss publicly their involvement with the previous therapists. In one group, a member prepared a written contract for everyone to sign, pledging confidentiality; in other groups, the agreement was verbal.

INITIAL COHESION

Group members expressed relief initially when they realized that they were not the only ones who had experienced sexual exploitation by a therapist. Sharing their feelings of anger, distrust, and sadness added to the reassurance. When groups comprise members with similar problems cohesion develops rapidly; because it offers a false sense of security, group facilitators proceeded cautiously. They informed members that they had a sense of closeness and relief in being with others who had had similar experiences, but the feeling should not be mistaken for the deeper sense of trust that takes more time to develop.

COUNTERTRANSFERENCE ISSUES

The countertransference experienced by facilitators was the wish to be "better" therapists than those with whom the clients had encountered problems. Initially, the facilitators imagined that they would do everything right and that group members would finally see models of truly helpful therapists. Sometimes this countertransference fantasy was promoted by the clients themselves who wanted the facilitators to undo the disasters of the previous therapy. The facilitators' fantasies soon eroded, however, when it has became clear that what group members actually wanted was to see the facilitators as imperfect and to be able to point it out. This need is illustrated in the following account, as is the therapists' temptation to be overaccommodating and to overstep boundaries in the wish to compensate for a client's past pain.

Anne, age 33, arrived at the agency for her intake interview feeling furious at the co-facilitators. She had originally sought vocational counseling with Mr. B. Instead of focusing on her vocational concerns, however, he asked about her sexual practices and offered specific advice. She was confused. When she expressed this confusion to him, she felt that Mr. B. "gave up" on her. As a result, she felt abandoned, became depressed, and was subsequently hospitalized for psychiatric reasons. In the hospital she felt unable to talk about the events that prompted her admission.

While speaking during the intake interview, Ann sat angrily in a corner, not looking at the facilitators. She stated emphatically that she was interested in joining the group but she refused to pay for further therapy, given that the damage to her was caused by the first therapy. Ann was trying to hold the facilitators responsible for what had happened previously and to punish the prior therapist through punishing them. The facilitators were empathic with Ann's feelings and were tempted to waive her fee. Nonetheless, they adhered to the agency policy that clients pay what they can. Although they could appreciate her feelings they could not make up for the hurts she had experienced elsewhere. Ann was furious with their decision but she decided to join the group and to pay the required fee.

Another countertransference issue is the facilitators' anger and discomfort when they listen to group members recount their experiences. The facilitators' occasional over-identification with these clients sometimes became an obstacle to their facilitating further discussion. All group members were aware of how hard it is to talk about what happened, yet how necessary it was to be able to do so. They directly asked the facilitators for more help with this task. The facilitators found it helpful to have regular consultation and to talk together after each group session. These meetings minimize the likelihood that the facilitators' own feelings would become inadvertent obstacles to the group.

Still another countertransference issue that threatened to become a barrier to effective work with these clients was the facilitators' fear of harassment or accusations of libel. This fear is useful in understanding the clients' similar fears. It is sobering to learn that the fears are realistic because some clients actually were threatened by their therapists and/or the therapist's associates when they pursued complaints to licensure boards or filed legal charges.

GRIEF WORK

All group members had experienced a profound loss as a consequence of the exploitative relationship with their previous therapists. In many cases, the therapists had offered them the hope that sexual involvement would help to solve their problems. For many clients the therapists' sexual advances raised their hopes that they were indeed lovable, interesting, and desirable. For some there had been a greater degree of sexual response than in other relationships. Therefore, when the involvement ended, not only did clients undergo the loss of hope that therapy would be helpful but, also, a loss of enhanced self-esteem and sexual pleasure. Many experienced a traumatic disillusionment with the therapist whom they had idealized. In addition, involvement with the therapist had distracted them from establishing and working on satisfying relationships with other persons. When cut off from their therapists, many clients became aware of how isolated they had become and how much time had been irrevocably lost.

Because of these losses, grief issues were a common theme in the groups. The participants needed to conclude the old relationships with the therapists in order to begin new ones with other people. The following case illustrates one woman's grief process and how it facilitated a more effective and satisfying relationship with her children.

Marilyn initially had been referred to her previous counselor for help with marital problems. Her husband was an alcoholic. She hoped that her marriage would improve if she obtained information and guidance on problems connected with alcoholism. Her counselor told her that she could be a "better wife, mother, employee, and friend" if she cooperated in some heavy petting with him. She cooperated because she believed him. Thus, she became distracted from the problems in her relationship with her husband. When she began to distrust the helpfulness of this approach, questioned the counselor, and finally threatened to speak with others on the staff about their conduct in therapy, he accused her of "playing one of her crazy games."

At first Marilyn appeared to be in an initial stage of mourning. She seemed disbelieving as she described the events of her therapy and her subsequent divorce. She wondered if the loss of her marriage was related to the therapy. When she recognized the seriousness of her situation, she turned to WICC for advocacy services. She wished to make a complaint against the counselor and his agency. Later she decided to file a formal charge of unethical conduct against the counselor through a licensure board.

Marilyn decided to join our second group when her first group ended because she was anxious about the upcoming litigation. In this second group she described feelings of pervasive anxiety and anger. She was tearful as she spoke of feeling responsible for her divorce and her children's loss of their father. She went on to describe her difficulties in setting limits for her teenage children. She related this to her guilt. The group helped Marilyn to set limits for her children and thereby to gain more control in her relationship with them which, in turn, helped her to feel more successful.

As part of grieving, it is as important for group members to talk about their affectionate feelings toward the former therapists as it is to talk about their anger and distrust. Clients benefitted from discussing positive aspects of the relationship as well as their hopes and fantasies. (See Ch. 7 and Ch. 12.)

RELATION BETWEEN EARLY LIFE EXPERIENCES AND EXPLOITATION

Clients explored various factors that contributed to their vulnerability in being exploited in therapy, including the relation between earlier life experiences and the exploitation. Clients welcomed such a discussion because it helped them to feel less confused, more organized, and better able to prevent future exploitation. It also helped them to clarify the issues that must be addressed following termination of the groups. Examples of the importance of such exploration are the following accounts:

Peg had been involved with a cult leader-type therapist with whom she had lived and whom she had financially supported. The therapist had also persuaded her to recruit her physically ill younger sister to live with him, threatening that the sister "otherwise would die." Peg realized that her childhood experiences had contributed to her vulnerability to exploitation by this therapist. Specifically, she had experienced her father as "spineless," i.e., unavailable emotionally during her childhood. She also never had mourned another sibling's suicide nor resolved her feelings of responsibility for that death. She recognized that (a) her longing for a "strong" man who would protect and care for her and (b) her disproportionate sense of responsibility for not saving her dead sister had contributed to her joining this therapist and bringing her sister into his cult, for which she felt responsible. Peg recognized the need to work through these unresolved issues upon termination of the group.

* * *

Deb had been verbally abused by one therapist and sexually abused by another in an in-patient chemical abuse treatment program. She had sought help for alcohol abuse and her sexual promiscuity. She had felt paralyzed and confused when these therapists admonished her, blamed her for her promiscuity, and when one became sexual with her. She gradually realized that earlier life experiences in which her parents either had ignored, minimized, or discounted her feelings of both physical and emotional discomfort had caused her to lose her sense of reality and, therefore, to become more vulnerable to exploitation. In group discussions, Deb gradually learned to trust her own reality, even when another group member had a different perception. Following termination of the group she was able with advocacy help to confront her former therapists and to enter individual treatment to work on the unresolved family-of-origin issues.

BETRAYAL BY PROFESSIONALS ASSOCIATED WITH THE THERAPIST

All the women in the groups reported a sense of betrayal by other personnel with whom the former therapists were associated, and/or by the persons who initially had referred them. Several group members wondered why personnel associated with the therapists had not been aware of what had been going on or, if they had, why they had not attempted to stop it. Other women who had complained to referring physicians or counselors felt that their concerns had been discounted. An example follows:

Jean was referred to Dr. A. by her female psychotherapist, Ms. N., who stated her belief that a male therapist was a better choice, given Jean's history of incest with her father. Jean expressed misgivings about this referral; she pointed out that Dr. A. had been placed on probation by a licensure board two years earlier for improper sexual contact with his patients. She feared that Dr. A. would make sexual advances toward her. Ms. N. reassured Jean that Dr. A. would be helpful and that he had personally told Ms. N. that he had "once had a problem, but this had resolved itself." When Dr. A. initiated hugging during a therapy session with Jean, she made an appointment with Ms. N., to complain. Ms. N. replied, "Dr. A. is the most intrusive therapist I know, but he works miracles." Ms. N. encouraged Jean to return to Dr. A., which she did.

Jean cried as she talked about Ms. N.'s inability to protect her. As a result of her work in the group, Jean decided to make an appointment with Ms. N. to tell her how she had felt about the dismissal of her concerns with Dr. A.

This sense of betrayal by professionals associated with an exploitative therapist is analogous to the feelings children have about the mother's not knowing and not stopping incestuous involvement between daughter and father, even when the mother is aware of its occurrence. Many women described this betrayal as even more painful than the sexual exploitation itself.

A number of women in the groups felt betrayed by the mental health professions in general for not better policing the field. In 1984, when the Minnesota State Legislature created the Task Force for Sexual Exploitation of Clients by Psychotherapists, some group members' sense of despair about betrayal diminished. It was as if the legislature represented the symbolic caring and protective mother needed in the incestuous family. The spirit of group discussions became more hopeful as clients kept each other informed about the status of the proposed legislation to protect clients from exploitation.

CONCURRENT INDIVIDUAL THERAPY

All group members who were in concurrent individual therapy stated that they derived significant benefit from this arrangement. Some clients were especially in need of concurrent individual therapy because of their on-going needs for crisis management. In no instance was there a conflict between group and individual therapy.

HUMOR

Many clients expressed delightful humor in group sessions to the surprise of the facilitators. Humor was a significant healing feature in a number of the groups, especially through jokes about therapy or therapists. Laughter relieved tension and pain for many group members.

REALITY TESTING

A predominant theme in all the groups was distrust of one's own reality testing. Most women had a sense that "something was wrong" in the relationships with their previous therapists, but they had distrusted these doubts. Subsequently, some women also distrusted their decisions not to pursue the complaint options available to them through legal or professional organizational channels, comparing themselves unfavorably to group members who had chosen to pursue complaints. A major function of the group sessions was to encourage the clarification of feelings and to support trust in one's unique feelings, judgments, and decisions.

GUILT

Another major need expressed in the groups was to talk about feelings of guilt and responsibility for allowing or initiating the sexual relationships with their therapists.

Several clients had been attracted to their therapists and believed that these feelings had encouraged or caused the sexual involvement. Some had felt relieved initially when the sexual involvement had sidetracked them from problems they were afraid to face, such as alcohol and drug abuse, unhappy marriages, and the like. Group members asked for considerable help in sorting out these feelings and experienced relief in knowing that others felt a similar sense of responsibility for what happened.

Facilitators were uncomfortable at first with how tenaciously clients held to their perceptions of responsibility for having been exploited in therapy. Although group participants appreciated explanations of their previous therapists' professional responsibility to put clients' needs before their own, such explanations did not reduce the sense of responsibility for what happened. It became clear to me that by holding on to the perception of responsibility for what happened, the women were able to feel more in control of preventing it from reoccurring.

NEED FOR EDUCATION

Another major need expressed by all the group members was to clarify what is appropriate or ethical treatment. The facilitators often were asked to repeat that it is inappropriate for therapists to act out sexual attraction, even though the therapist as well as the client may have such feelings. Group members frequently referred to the paper by Schoener, Milgrom & Gonsiorek (1983) that spells out the therapist's responsibility for setting limits in relationships.

Confusion over "what is therapy anyway?" also was expressed. Specifically, group members were confused about whether therapy is supposed to be an actual re-enactment of earlier family experience. Those women who had been told by their exploitative therapists that the relationship with the therapist would help them to "work through" their earlier child-parent relationships were particularly confused. They needed to learn that effective therapy cannot literally re-enact earlier relationships but, rather, can clarify and sometimes solve the problems derived from verbalizing their important thoughts and feelings. A therapist must provide boundaries so that earlier feelings can be re-awakened, identified, and discussed in order to help clients to form more satisfying relationships.

Facilitators had opportunities to model the use of boundaries within the therapeutic relationship. The following account is an example:

In the final minutes of the last session, Rosemary spontaneously invited the group to her home for a party planned for sometime in the near future. Group members were interested and pleased by her invitation. However, the facilitators were uncomfortable; they felt that the boundaries of the therapeutic relationship would become blurred in such a social setting. One facilitator stated that although she appreciated the invitation, she considered it inappropriate for her to socialize with clients. She said that she would, however, be pleased to meet with the group members for a follow-up session should they wish to have another group meeting. The participants were satisfied by this answer and decided to request a follow-up session a few months later.

TAKING ACTION

All participants used the sessions to explore the various possibilities for action and whether any action would be beneficial. Most decided to take some type of action in order to feel more in control and to protect other clients from abuse by their therapists. The activities ranged from processing sessions with the therapist with an advocate/facilitator present; complaints to professional ethics committees; to complaints to licensing boards; civil lawsuits; complaints to other professionals.

Most participants experienced relief from taking charge through such action. However, the group facilitators noticed that risks are involved. Those clients who had more time to distance themselves emotionally from their therapists and had ample opportunity to clarify their mixed feelings about the exploitative experience were able to pursue such actions more easily than clients who only recently had terminated the exploitative relationship. Although most clients suffered from some kind of "let down" after completing a complaint or legal action, clients who took complaint/legal action soon after ending the relationships with their therapists appeared to be much more vulnerable to depression and suicide risks. Therefore, group discussions included anticipation of the risks inherent in taking action and preventive strategies for the necessary support.

EFFECTS ON SIGNIFICANT OTHERS

Another group theme was how significant others were affected by the exploitation. Married women who had become distracted from their marriages during the relationships with their therapists requested help to deal with their husbands' anger, sense of betrayal, and the like. In response to the concerns of several women in one group, I arranged with a colleague to offer a spouses' support group (described in Ch. 22). Unmarried women who had become estranged from friends and their families used the group to clarify whom it would be helpful to tell about their experiences and how it could be accomplished. I met with various women and their family members to help in the process of talking about the exploitation and what it meant to their relationships. (See Ch. 21 and Ch. 22.)

OUTCOME

As a result of group treatment, almost all the clients experienced the following outcomes:

1. Reduction of isolation and feeling of relief in discovering some universality in their experiences and feelings.

2. Relief in having a confidential opportunity to share their experiences with others.

3. Clarification of mixed feelings about the previous therapist.

4. Clarification of options for complaints and/or other actions.

5. Opportunity to mourn.

6. A clearer understanding of how to become a more effective consumer of mental health services.

Group members also increased the trust in their own feelings and then used this new strength to establish more effective relationships with others. As a result of the group, most women were able to re-address the problems for which they had originally sought help. One client said, "The problems for which I originally sought help have been 'on hold' for all these years. As a result of the work in the group I feel I can now move forward." This sense of becoming "unstuck" to varying degrees was experienced by nearly all participants.

DISPOSITION AT TERMINATION OF GROUP

Six clients who needed further work on the goals they had set for themselves joined the next group. In at least one case, however, a client applied for participation in a subsequent group but was refused admittance because it was not deemed to be beneficial.

Upon termination of their work in the groups, the majority of participants who felt able to re-address the problems for which they had originally sought help chose to continue in some other kind of counseling, that is, individual, couple, group, or family. Some asked me or other facilitators to become their individual or family therapist; others sought help from other providers. Some women renewed their interest in defining career goals and obtained career counseling. A woman who had struggled with low self-esteem since childhood because of a serious learning disability gained enough confidence to obtain psychological testing and consultation. Several clients, who were not already using WICC advocacy services, sought consultation/advocacy from WICC on their decisions to hold processing sessions with former therapists and/or to pursue complaint or litigation options for action. Several women's attorneys asked me to provide expert testimony in their civil or criminal cases.

SUMMARY

This chapter is a review of my 9-year clinical experience with 57 participants in either one or two of a total of 17 time-limited groups. These women had experienced problems as the result of sexual exploitation by therapists. At the time the women sought the group services, all reported feeling "stuck" at the developmental stage at which they had originally sought help from the exploitative therapists; at the same time they were experiencing new problems, feelings of extreme isolation, and the inability to move forward in their lives.

Group treatment assisted all these women to reduce their isolation, clarify the mixed feelings about their experiences, and decide what options, if any, they wished to take. Most then were able to re-establish more satisfying relationships with others and to re-address the problems for which they had originally sought help.

I observed several parallels between these women's experiences and the experiences of children of incest. The most remarkable were the needs for validation of feelings about the experiences and for protection from abuses in both types of unequal power relationships. The relief experienced as a result of a) being able to talk freely with others about their problems and experiences, b) the state's establishment of a task force and enactment of civil and criminal legislation, c) our availability to provide information, referrals, and/or expert testimony highlighted the need for validation and protection.

The division of therapeutic and advocacy tasks between the facilitators and WICC staff members, and the facilitators' regular consultation with each other and the WICC staff during the group tenure, provided the support necessary to minimize the potential of countertransference issues to obstruct effective work with this unique client population. Some women noted that leaders' collaboration with each other and other professionals served as valuable role models to them as they strove to find ways to reduce their own isolation.

Follow-up research is needed to learn about the on-going experiences of these women, the long-term effects of this kind of exploitation, and the efficacy of different types of intervention.

CHAPTER 15

A First Experience In Co-Facilitating A Group For Victims

Anne List

During a social work field placement at the Walk-In Counseling Center, I served as a co-facilitator in two 10-week therapy groups for clients who had been sexually exploited by a counselor, psychotherapist, or clergyperson. I had had little prior group treatment experience and no prior experience with this particular group of clients. By presenting my impressions I hope that other persons will gain a perspective on and be encouraged to undertake this type of work. This chapter is based in part on notes made after each session.

Before the groups began I reviewed the available literature, watched some videotapes, and discussed my concerns with my supervisor, Jeanette Milgrom, and my co-facilitator, Ellen Luepker. Both had conducted such groups previously. This background material, however, gave me little preparation for the particulars of these group experiences.

The literature offers little information on effective treatment groups for women who have been sexually exploited by therapists, counselors, ministers, priests, and others. I learned from Luepker and Milgrom's experiences that some of these women had symptoms and needs that are similar to those of women who have been raped or physically assaulted or who have experienced incest. The diagnostic category most frequently mentioned was that of post-traumatic stress disorder (PTSD); several clients reported symptoms of nightmares, fears, feelings of being "cut off" from significant others, startle reactions when in situations that are reminiscent of the sexual exploitation, flashbacks, feelings of being brainwashed, and an inability to trust.

LEADERSHIP

Each of the groups in which I worked had only four members but we felt it very useful to have two facilitators. One rationale was the teaming of an inexperienced therapist with one who has more experience, for training purposes. Other reasons included (a) providing the security of a second therapist with whom clients could check things out, given their distrust of therapist; (b) providing the two co-facilitators with mutual support and readily available feedback to enhance our understanding of these clients' complex situations; and (c) providing the opportunity to so interact with each other that we could model various behaviors for the group.

Initially, for me one of the most difficult aspects of facilitating these groups was trying to feel comfortable and to balance my role as learner with Ellen's role of experienced group leader and teacher. It was helpful to check out my perceptions and alternative ideas with her outside of group sessions in order to become comfortable enough to spontaneously offer my observations in the group itself. Although I wished to be primarily an observer in the initial group sessions, I grew into more of an active facilitator. I realized that I could contribute to the group when I paid attention to the group process as well as the unspoken, nonverbal cues of clients.

INTAKE INTERVIEWS

My schedule permitted me to be present for all but three of the intake interviews which I conducted with Ellen. One prospective client did not learn of our group sessions until after the first group had started. We interviewed her with the explicit understanding that she would be added to the group if it was acceptable to group members, but if it was contraindicated, she could join the second group. We interviewed a total of 11 clients for the two groups. Of these, 8 elected to participate; the other 3 did not so choose. We and they felt that the problems stemming from their sexual exploitation were not so central to their lives so they decided they needed other services.

In the intake interviews, all eight prospective clients demonstrated high levels of anxiety and varying degrees of depressive symptoms. Two clients were on medications for these symptoms. Three prospective clients for the first group showed extreme fright and distrust. They also had considerable difficulty speaking during the intake interviews.

The intake interviews gave all the women the opportunity to hear what the group could offer and to decide whether the experience was what they were searching for. We explained that the purpose was to deal with the exploitation by providing support and help in dealing with the mixed emotions of anger, shame, guilt, and the like. The secondary goal was to help the women to explore their options of the type of action to take, if any. We encouraged them to explore what it was they wanted to get out of the group and to set their own goals. We also gave referrals to individual therapists as needed and encouraged clients to "shop around." Clients such as these (because of their previous exploitation) are distrustful of professionals.

The intake procedure was the most anxiety-provoking and unsettling experience for me. Listening to the clients' stories, I was aware of my feelings of anger and even horror. After the first two intakes, conducted back-to-back, I was exhausted. I wanted so badly for these women to be angry—to be furious—about what had happened to them.

THE FIRST GROUP: NOTES

The first session of the first group started out with lots of nervousness and anxiety for everyone, including me. We wondered what would transpire: Would their expectations be met? Would they find support? My own question was: How can I help this group of women who have been so totally devastated by one of my "own kind"? When the individual stories began to pour out, so did the tears. The raw pain that threatened to fill the entire room was soon, to my surprise, short-circuited via humor. Various comments were made by group members about diabolical ways to avenge themselves on the exploiters. The sense of relief in turning their tragic situations into humor was enormous. While feeling relieved, I also recall feeling useless. These women were in the group to meet each other, to find out they weren't alone, and to find support for their situation. It was unclear to me what I could offer this group.

The second session, in contrast, was low energy and gloomy. I think the group members had expectations that once the group began they would feel an immediate sense of relief and the worst would be behind them. Perhaps preparing them a little more for what would happen (i.e., this problem will be very painful to work on and old and uncomfortable feelings may surface) would have been helpful.

In the third session the fears that came out included wondering if they would ever be able to trust again—themselves or others; suspecting other people's intentions; and not feeling comfortable with physical closeness. Additional group themes included having never learned to say no, set limits, or express anger.

Another predominate theme in the third session was anger: at the exploiters, the world, and themselves. The question—"How did I get myself into this mess?"—emerged. Some group members expressed the idea that they had grown up believing that everyone was trustworthy, so the idea of letting others earn their trust was novel. Again the mixed feelings embodied in their original attraction as opposed to their current rejection of the exploitative therapists surfaced. In addition, the members expressed their ambivalence about attending the group because the discussions made them remember what had happened.

After this session my impressions were those of relief and surprise. The group members had been more active in questioning each other's story and providing support. The group process had begun to work.

At the fourth session a new member joined; she proved to be much more disruptive than was anticipated because she was potentially suicidal. Although the two facilitators had consulted the initial participants and found them unanimous in wanting another member, when she appeared, the old members were cordial but a little hesitant to disclose their stories one more time. The new member was extremely agitated, wringing her hands nervously.

I was myself worried at this stage; I wondered whether I had made a mistake in taking on this role. Later, I learned that Ellen also was anxious, given the suicide potential of the new member and its disruptive effects on the others.

This fourth session was particularly painful but it ended on a somewhat hopeful note. After observing the other group members, the new client felt she could "make it through this since the other group members had survived." In turn, I think it gave the others the chance to see just how far they had progressed. Although no one else was actively suicidal at this stage the new member reawakened frightening memories of their own suicidal thoughts and their struggles to overcome the compelling temptation to end it all.

A later session's theme again was one of anger. One client directed her anger at her parents; she felt that they had not prepared her adequately for adult life, and had given her little education or support for her emerging sexuality. Another client became angry at the whole group; she felt that support for her was lacking and that no one was listening to her story. She was angry at her boyfriend, parents, attorney, exploiter, and others. This client ended up leaving the room because she felt so hopeless and too frightened to deal with her anger in the group. All clients struggled with idealizations of the previous relationships, and the broken promises that had followed. It seemed important to reassure clients continually that their situations were unique and differed from each other's; but they were also urged to note common threads when they emerged.

In the first group two participants required considerable crisis management. Ellen collaborated with the suicidal client, her psychiatrist, and her individual therapist to jointly develop a protection plan. Also, during one week, we had to take turns being on call for another member who was feeling depressed but was too distrustful to see an individual therapist.

THE SECOND GROUP: NOTES

The second group I co-facilitated was an entirely different experience. Consequently, it deserves some comment on the group process and on my own experience. The suicidal client who, by now, was no longer at risk for suicide, elected to join this group in order to complete the work she had been unable to do in the first group given the acute nature of her symptoms. In this group the daily functioning of the members was much less impaired than that of the members of the first group. The members of this group as individuals were able to express their thoughts and feelings more freely; and as a group they were better able to identify and work on the relation between past history and exploitative therapy relationship. The group was stable and cohesive; members did not require our help for crisis management. More of the actual therapeutic work was done by the group members themselves. Often, when a group member made a comment, I thought, "That's what I would have said, only not as well." The group members were very supportive of each other.

Most spouses of this group's members elected to participate in a group facilitated by one of Ellen's colleagues. The purpose of the parallel group was to enable its members to deal with their own hurt feelings about the marital disruptions caused by the sexual exploitation.

In summarizing this second group experience, the members found that not only had the group helped them to clarify their situations but, also, to increase their ability to express caring, vulnerability, and compassion. There was a general feeling that they had progressed in learning to trust oneself and others, and "to make connections" with other members of the group and significant others outside. A healing process unfolded as the sessions proceeded. Ellen indicated that this group had been more typical than the first one I had co-led.

COMMON THEMES

One of our main goals as facilitators was to empower group members to take charge of themselves and their lives. We hoped to accomplish this goal by encouraging the clients to pay attention to their "gut feelings" and to trust in their instincts again. Common themes in both groups were, "Why did I let this happen?" and "How responsible am I for what happened?" Thus clients talked about their "not having trusted their gut feelings that something was wrong" or "not having used their protection meters." They asked themselves what had happened to their instincts for survival (or "protection meter") while they were getting involved in such destructive relationships. Most stated that they had assumed that they would be safe in seeking out help and hence had left their inner doubts or "protection meters" outside the door.

One technique Ellen and I used in the group was to assist members to clarify the dilemma of "saying no" in similar situations, and to visualize themselves as using alternatives to going along with the expectations of others when those expectations felt uncomfortable. In retrospect, it could have been very useful for the first group to have spent more time explicitly exploring alternatives in the event such situations arose again.

Group members later reiterated to each other the goals they had established in the intake sessions: wanting to know they "weren't alone"; "hearing others' stories"; and being able to trust themselves and others again. For most members the lack of trust included not wanting/not enjoying being touched by anyone and being suspicious of people who were nice to them. All were interested in learning to trust themselves, to feel less self-doubt, and to reduce the stress associated with this problem. In clarifying their feelings about what had happened to them, most were able to decide on a course of action toward further recovery. Some decided they wanted to confront their exploiters eventually, either in person, by letter, or through a legal process, in order to feel more in control and to protect others.

INTERVENTIONS

One of the most useful intervention concepts, for this group of clients, was the co-therapists' modeling of appropriate behaviors, for example, limit-setting or, "It's OK to say no." For the first group in particular, I felt a need to be a model of what a "perfect" therapist does or, perhaps more appropriately, what a good therapist doesn't do. My expectations got in the way at first because I feared offending a group member or "saying the wrong thing." Ellen and I made it clear to both groups that we did not touch clients: no hugs, hand-holding, and the like. We also modeled respecting what group members said even if we didn't always agree with them. We used very little self-disclosure; these women had a common history of knowing too much about their previous helpers.

A couple of opportunities arose to model disagreement between co-therapists but I felt too much the neophyte to do so. In looking back I realize it might have been helpful to the group. We also modeled making mistakes and then discussing them. For example, during one intake I blundered in assuming that I knew at which clinic this client had been exploited. When I recognized my mistake I apologized to her. Several women had believed that people in the helping professions are unable to acknowledge errors, and they stated that our acknowledging and discussing our mistakes was helpful and therapeutic.

As a group therapy student I was inhibited, especially in the early sessions, by the fear of saying the "wrong" thing. This feeling was intensified by working with clients who previously had experienced abuse at the hands of the helping professions and I did not want to risk causing further damage. However, just as they learned to trust in themselves to express what they were feeling, I too began to trust in my "gut reaction" when working therapeutically; and I found that most often I was correct in my assumptions. Nevertheless, by being open to errors and criticism and to owning up to my imperfections, I could better illustrate that therapists too are fallible.

The most effective use of modeling was by the group members themselves. When some members were in the process of "fighting back," either through litigation or other means, their actions modeled possibilities for members who never had considered such actions. Toward the end of the group sessions, one member's anger toward Ellen and Ellen's acceptance and nonretaliatory response became an effective model for other members to voice their own concerns. In the instance of the suicidal group member, modeling may have had a negative and contagious effect in that at the next session two more group members talked about their suicidal thoughts.

Reflecting back on the group process in both groups, I think it is of utmost importance to genuinely hear how a client experienced the exploitative relationship. For me, this sometimes meant pushing down "should be" thoughts: that the client "should be" progressing faster, or "should be" angry, and so forth. Traumatic events first need to be recalled and then, perhaps, re-lived through expressions of thoughts and feelings more than once. With empathy, compassion, and understanding, I learned that facilitators can help group members to move into the next stage of resolving the feelings engendered in such a situation. Once group members get in touch with these wide-ranging feelings, they are better able to come to terms with what occurred. Their anger can be used productively. The final stage may be one in which clients look at their own vulnerability: How did I get involved with this person? How can I protect myself in the future?

My primary feeling when I first came into contact with these clients was anger. I was angry at therapists who compounded their clients' problems and left them with worse problems than the ones for which they originally sought help. In the early sessions, I was hesitant to confront the clients because they seemed very fragile. Part of this, I believe, had to do with my beginner's fear of group therapy, that is, the fear that the group easily could turn its rage on me.

Despite the intense and, at times, very difficult group experiences, there were many benefits for me. At the end of the group, several members were pleased with the comparison between their original problems and their feelings at the end of the group. One member who had made great progress seemed ready to tackle the world. Other group members' fear levels had lowered so much they felt secure enough to enter individual therapy or to pursue complaint options with assistance from an advocate. It was exciting for me to be part of the process that helped to establish their ability to trust again in themselves and others and to provide "a light in the darkness." I also became more aware of my own strengths and vulnerabilities as a therapist. More than many types of therapeutic experiences, these groups caused me to trust my own resources as a therapist.

CHAPTER 16

INTERNS AS GROUP LEADERS

Jeanette Hofstee Milgrom

The question of having graduate-level interns function as group leaders is an important one. Before employing interns in the delivery of services, especially group therapy, to sexually exploited clients, the following factors should be considered.

In general one looks for experienced therapists to work with clients who are often severely traumatized, but we have found that less-experienced counselors also can be productive under certain conditions. In the case of Anne List, author of the preceding chapter ("A First Experience in Co-Facilitating a Group for Victims"), the situation was as follows:

In my roles as List's internship supervisor and the overseer of the consultation and training activities at WICC, I had to judge the reasonableness of having her co-facilitate the group with Luepker as the senior therapist. List had no broad experience with this clientele or working with groups. She did, however, have other relevant professional experience coupled with personal maturity; during her previous six months at WICC she had been exposed to the issue of the sexual exploitation of clients. Additionally, she read up on working with groups, viewed videotapes of clients and others discussing sexual exploitation by therapists, and discussed group process as well as participating in the intake interviews with Luepker; these activities helped to prepare List for the group experience. List, in retrospect, felt that nothing could have totally prepared her for working with this particular group, however.

Important factors in this arrangement, which is an apprenticeship model, are as follows:

1. Have a very experienced senior group therapist who likes to teach and takes time to do so.

2. Have a supportive working/learning environment for the "apprentice"/intern.

3. Have other staff members immediately available to the intern when needed for decompression and reality testing.

Under these circumstances the employment of a student intern to co-facilitate a group can be mutually beneficial. The intern can gain valuable experience and grow professionally. The senior group facilitator benefits by gaining fresh perspectives, having the opportunity to serve as a mentor, and having a co-leader in a situation in which otherwise the group may have to be conducted solo. Group members also benefit, given the advantages of having two leaders instead of one, with the added perspective that this arrangement may bring to the group. Last but not least, it is important to continue to expand the number of practitioners who work in this domain and not to have this experience limited to a small group of highly trained and experienced "old guard."

Ellen Stewart, psychology intern from September 1988 to June 1989, subsequently co-led three groups with Luepker with the same benefits as noted by List.

For a somewhat different approach to the use of graduate students to lead groups of victims of client/therapist sex, see the description of the Post-Therapy Support Groups at UCLA (Pope & Bouhoutsos, 1986; Borys, Meyer, Falke & Sonne, 1986).

PART IV

WORKSHOP APPROACHES

Schoener describes in Chapter 17 the value of special meetings or workshops for victim/survivors of sexual exploitation by therapists at professional conferences on the issue. Victims often attend professional workshops but are disappointed by the neglect accorded them and their personal issues. Schoener makes the case that these "mini-conferences" within the larger format are easily conducted and pay big dividends.

Chapter 18, by Estelle Disch, is one of the few in this volume which is not based on work at WICC. Her contribution was solicited because we regard her workshop approach as exciting and useful. It is an approach that can be duplicated by other professionals in other places.

The workshops have a number of advantages over groups as a method of breaking down isolation. First of all, for clients who fear or distrust psychotherapy, workshops are educational in part and do not require on-going involvement, which reassures persons who are afraid of being "sucked back into therapy." Second, it often is easier for a group of people to commit themselves to a single day or a weekend rather than an on-going group. Third, when clients are widely dispersed geographically, a workshop may be far more practical than a group that meets regularly. It is even possible for people to come from different states to attend a workshop.

The workshop approach also can serve as a trial run or "warm-up" for a possible on-going group, either led by professionals or self-help. This possibility is noted by Disch.

CHAPTER 17

WORKSHOPS AND CONFERENCES FOR PEOPLE WHO HAVE BEEN SEXUALLY INVOLVED WITH COUNSELORS OR PSYCHOTHERAPISTS

Gary Richard Schoener

From the very first time they were offered, workshops and conferences that focus on client/therapist sexual involvement have attracted the victims. Even conferences aimed exclusively at a professional audience have drawn victim/survivors of exploitations who attend because of their personal experiences rather than for the more traditional needs of continuing professional education.

A surprising number of people who work in the mental health field themselves have had bad experiences with therapists, and some also have been sexually exploited. The disclosures were first made in the Report of the American Psychological Association's Task Force on Sex Bias and Sex-Role Stereotyping (APA, 1975), which was based on self-reports by women psychologists. Studies of harmful psychotherapy experiences in which mental health professionals were themselves the clients have also noted, among the negative experiences reported, sexual involvement with the therapist (Grunebaum, 1985, 1986). Last but not least, in the national survey of psychiatrists by Gartrell, Herman, Olarte, Feldstein, and Localio (1986), 1.6% of the 1,233 respondents reported having been sexually involved with their own therapists.

Conferences aimed at a broader audience invariably attract former clients who have been sexually exploited by their therapists. When workshops on sex between client and therapist were held in Madison, Wisconsin, in February 1985 and Milwaukee, Wisconsin, in September 1985, a number of victim/survivors attended. Some of them already knew other victim/survivors or had been working on the issue; thus they were able to network and to obtain support during and after these conferences.

When the Minnesota Task Force on Sexual Exploitation by Counselors and Therapists planned the first large-scale national conference on sexual exploitation by counselors and therapists, which was dubbed, "IT'S NEVER OK," there was a concern that some victims who would attend were not already in support networks. The planners hoped that these participants would identify themselves and that some informal networking would be possible.

The conference took place June 5-6, 1986, with about 240 participants from throughout the United States, with some coming from as far away as Puerto Rico and Sweden. (See Appendix AA for program.) In addition to the formal presentations, hour-long small group discussions were scheduled with facilitators who had been involved in the Task Force.

Unfortunately, the highly professional nature of the conference and the fact that professionals outnumbered victim/survivors led a number of the latter to feel an acute need for more support. One victim, who was in training to become a professional, had an unsettling encounter with a group facilitator and she brought this experience to the attention of presenters, including myself. When she had revealed in the small group discussion that she was there because she'd been victimized, the facilitator reacted in what she perceived as an agitated fashion and quickly warned her that these groups were for discussing conference content—not personal experiences. She was surprised and dismayed by this comment.

A number of the people who had suffered bad experiences at the hands of their therapists had been in contact with WICC by phone or mail earlier, and I had spoken with many of them. Thus I decided to offer myself and the facilities of the WICC for an impromptu "mini-conference" on the Saturday after the formal program ended (June 7, 1986).

Other WICC staff members were not available so I had the task of picking up the victims at hotels and ferrying them to the conference center. Most had spoken to each other during the conference so there was some degree of trust and acceptance. Given the conference setting (an older home) and its quiet, homey atmosphere (nothing was scheduled there for that day), the people seemed able to share with each other quite easily. The group, which varied in size over time, began with about nine persons and myself.

We started by trying to identify personal agendas by discussing first the individual reactions to the conference. This led to considerable discussion of many issues during which people made clear references to their situations and to what brought them to the conference. Each ended by sharing something of her personal story and the problems she was still facing relative to the abuse. Some were in the middle of litigation, some were considering it, and some were struggling with continued depression or other problems.

Somewhere around midmorning we informally broke into a few subgroups, partly because people needed a break and partly because some people asked if they could consult with me privately. This arrangement seemed to work out remarkably well; people were careful not to take up too much time and to provide support to each other.

By late morning the participants decided that they would like to take me up on my offer to show some videotapes. We viewed a tape of the CBS *Sixty Minutes* program entitled "Fifty Minutes" (CBS, 1978), two local media exposes of sexual abuse in residential mental health programs, and tapes of several local interview programs on the topic. These had quite an impact on some persons. Seeing and hearing other people tell stories of their abuse was moving. Some participants were both heartened and upset to see the breadth of coverage Minneapolis and St. Paul media have given the topic and expressed regret that in their home towns the issue is still kept under wraps. Several people were put in touch with the isolation they had been feeling.

Although I had committed myself to being available, only through the morning, when the session was still going strong around noon I decided to go on all day. I found the discussion stimulating, the perspectives on the conference useful and, very frankly, I found the mutual support expressed by the participants, inspiring. I too gained energy from the group.

Several people needed to catch planes. We worked out ways of getting individuals back to their hotels or off to the airport. Amidst the periodic good-byes, those who remained continued to talk. I delivered the last people to their destinations at almost 5 p.m.; from my perspective the day had been well-spent. Subsequent calls and letters from the participants reaffirmed this—they too had found it useful.

Afterwards I received considerable feedback on how valuable this impromptu conference had been; to some participants it had been of greater use than the formal conference. This reaction was a bit of a surprise because everyone agreed that the planned conference was first rate. I stayed in touch with a number of the participants and learned that several of them had maintained contact with each other, including, in one instance, providing important support during a crisis.

When Sylvia Diamond of the Association of Psychologically Abused Patients in Ft. Worth, Texas (see Ch. 31) began planning the 2nd National Conference on Psychotherapy Abuse, I suggested on the basis of my earlier experience that a second companion conference be planned just for victim/survivors. The conference was held on February 27, 1987; the informal gathering of abuse victims was held in Sylvia's living room the next day. I played only a very limited role in this meeting because I spent so much time talking with one person about the processing session I had done with her and her ex-therapist the day before.

The informal meeting was somewhat facilitated by Drs. Linnda Durré and Jacqueline Bouhoutsos, well-known figures in the field who, like myself, had spoken at the conference. Other participants included Sylvia Diamond, the conference organizer, and Bill Cliadakis, head of the National Committee for Preventing Psychotherapy Abuse, a consumer group (and a contributor to this book—see Ch. 30). People basically took turns telling their stories and asking for input on issues of concern to them. The meeting lasted about 3 hours and could have gone on longer. The group never got to watch the videotapes several of us had brought, although some people stayed and watched some of them.

Based on this experience, I feel quite strongly that conferences on the topic of client/therapist sex or related issues must anticipate and plan for the needs of persons who have been victimized. It is highly likely that some victims[1] will attend conferences and that the experience will be enhanced for them by the opportunity to process the conference afterwards. I cannot stress enough how useful the workshop approach is in terms of helping to diminish the sense of isolation most victims have. The mutual support possible at such gatherings is powerful and invaluable.

I also have been struck by how much such conferences of victims almost run themselves. People are generally considerate of each other and do not require a great deal of structure after sharing the experience of a formal conference. An added benefit may be the networking that is possible at more intimate gatherings.

---

[1]Some professionals who attend are typically there because they've been victimized. Virtually every professional group to whom I have spoken on the topic of therapist-client sex has included at least one victim.

CHAPTER 18

ONE DAY WORKSHOPS FOR FEMALE SURVIVORS OF SEXUAL ABUSE BY PSYCHOTHERAPISTS

Estelle Disch

Since 1984 I have been running workshops for female survivors of sexual abuse by psychotherapists. The idea for them emerged when an intern at the therapy center where I work asked me to co-lead a survivors' group with her. Both of us also are survivors: she of a female therapist, I of a male. Assuming a high level of mistrust of therapists among the survivors of this abuse, we decided to run a one-day, sliding-fee-scale workshop. We hoped that this carefully organized, focused workshop would minimize survivors' hesitancy to discuss the issue of exploitation with therapists. I also assumed that people who do not want a therapy group may find a one-day workshop helpful.

So far I have led or co-led five workshops following the same format we developed in 1984. I plan to continue offering these workshops once or twice each year.

GOALS

The primary purpose of the workshops is to help survivors to feel less alone and less to blame by providing a forum for them to share their similar experiences. Each participant gets equal time to give a brief version of her story and then is helped to consider what, if anything, she wants to do in response to the abuse.

Participants in the workshops I have led so far report that they do in fact feel less alone, less crazy, less to blame, and less ashamed after spending six hours with other women who have experienced similar abuse. And most women have left the workshops knowing what they want to do next.

ADVERTISING

All the workshops have been preceded by a mailing to about 150 agencies and individuals who have expressed an interest in this work. In addition, I have placed ads in *Sojourner*, a Boston-based women's newspaper with national circulation. The ads included a small-print listing in the "Calendar" as well as a 2" x 3" display ad in the "Therapy" listings. The titles of the workshop read more or less as follows:

Survivors of Sexual Malpractice

For Women Who Have Been Sexually Abused
or Seduced in Psychotherapy:

All ads included date, time, place, and a reference to either the sliding-fee-scale or the availability of scholarships. Two examples of the mailed notice are included in Appendix T.

CLIENTELE

Between four and eight participants came to each workshop. The age range was 25 to 58. About 80 percent had been abused by male therapists and over half knew themselves to be incest survivors. About 80 percent were in their twenties when the therapist abuse occurred, and the abuser was often 10 to 20 years older than the client. The overt sexual activity usually began within the first two years of therapy. The average gap between the occurrence of the abuse and the telling of the story in the workshop was about 10 years (a range of 6 months to 25 years).

Participants expressed a range of responses to the abuse. A few were still deeply in love with the therapist and felt profoundly rejected and confused; they wondered what had happened to make the therapist give up what had seemed to be such an important, deep relationship. Others were ready to put the experience behind them; they were more or less adjusted to what had happened but needed a place to tell their stories. Others were unclear about how they felt and they came to the workshop for help to clarify their feelings. And about 40 percent were filing or about to file some sort of complaint: in court, with licensing boards, with professional associations, with agencies, or directly to the therapist him/herself.

The abuses suffered by the women included a range of behaviors: repeated intercourse over many years while the patient was heavily medicated in the office; "serious" love relationships at the end of and following therapy, often lasting for several years; a one-time visit to a hypnotist who touched the client in a sexual way while she was in trance; a highly seductive but nonphysical therapy relationship; and so forth. Some clients had ended important relationships in order to develop the relationship with the therapist, only to find that the therapist was not willing to do the same.

HOW THE WORKSHOPS ACTUALLY WORKED

The structure of the workshop always is described to participants ahead of time. People are asked to bring bag lunches and are told that there will be unstructured time during lunch with the leader(s) present. They are told that time in the morning will be dedicated to remembering one's experience with the therapist (via a visualization process), and then to telling a brief version of that experience. I announce that time will be divided equally among participants. Typically each person has at least 15 minutes to tell her story with a minimum of interaction with others.

Participants are told that following the lunch break they will be asked to do another visualization in which they will be invited to identify future actions open to them and to consider whether they want to take any of the possible courses of action. Again, time is equally divided to give each participant the opportunity to explore where she is now with the issue and what next steps, if any, she wants to take. During each person's turn in the afternoon, the group as a whole is invited to help the person think through what she wants to do, and to develop strategies for action, if appropriate.

Each workshop has, in fact, closely followed this format. I am a strict timekeeper; I make sure that each person gets her share of group attention and I stick closely to the verbal contract I made with participants on how the day will be structured. I do not stop to "do therapy" with anyone although I may suggest that someone work on a particular issue with her current therapist, if she has one. The one variation in structure occurred in a four-person workshop when one woman came in crying, ready to start, and the others asked to skip the opening visualization and just begin telling their stories. I agreed. The workshop seemed to work more or less like all the others, nevertheless.

Participants in these workshops have been incredibly open about the details of their stories despite the profound humiliation, guilt, and self-hatred that almost always accompanies this abuse. Most seem very amenable to—in fact relieved by—the limits built into the structure; it seems to help to create a feeling of safety.

Two outcomes have been obvious at the end of each workshop: (a) There is a profound sense of relief and camaraderie. People feel less isolated, less ashamed, less crazy, less "dumb." They often exchange addresses and phone numbers. (b) Almost everyone leaves with a clear sense of what she wants to do next, even if her next step is to let go of the issue and to move on.

FOLLOW-UP SESSIONS

I have run no-fee, two-hour follow-up sessions about a month after the workshop three times. The decision to have a follow-up session depends upon whether participants are geographically close enough to attend and whether the group is interested in doing so.

I invited participants from prior workshops to the second and third follow-up sessions I held which allowed people to meet a few new survivors. About four or five persons came to each follow-up session. The structure of these meetings was informal. Each person checked in about where she was with the issue and discussed any requests she might have of the others present.

During the second follow-up session, a group of people decided to form an open, leaderless support group for survivors that would meet about once a month. The goals of the group were: (a) to provide on-going contact and support among survivors; (b) to welcome new survivors into the structure; and (c) to accumulate and share resources and information relating to sexual abuse by therapists. All three goals were met over the year and a half that the group existed. At the end of that time, the needs of some participants changed, leaving the group too small to continue because new people had not joined in large enough numbers to fill the places of those leaving.

I attended the support group twice to observe and support what the group was doing. My sense is that most of those attending got a lot of help of various types ranging from swapping articles and books to attending each other's hearings. Most participants had therapists at the time and used the group as a support without looking to it for therapy.

RECOMMENDATIONS FOR OTHERS USING THIS MODEL

I find this workshop model both effective and viable, with or without the follow-up sessions. Some suggestions for anyone wanting to run similar workshops follow:

1. If a survivor of sexual abuse by a therapist is not available to run the workshop, try to find a co-leader who is a survivor so that participants don't get caught in a "you-us" struggle with the leaders. Lacking a therapy abuse survivor, an incest or sexual harassment survivor is a possible alternative. And, lacking the latter, the leader(s) should anticipate some power struggle inasmuch as they represent the group to which abusers belong.

2. I recommend female leaders given that most abusers are male.

3. Leaders should be well informed about the issue of sexual abuse by therapists, particularly about complaint options, both official and unofficial.

4.   Leaders should be prepared to hear shocking, enraging stories. I take a few notes while each participant tells her story in order to keep the details straight. Hearing six or eight such stories in one morning can be very heavy.

5.   Leaders should have a good, supportive supervision structure so that they do not have to carry the information alone.

6.   Leaders should make clear contracts with participants about limits to confidentiality. I usually say that I don't want to know a therapist's name unless the client is willing for me to use the information if I need to for ethical reasons. For example, if the name of an abuser comes up as a possible referral in some other context, I need to feel free to say something like, "I have good reason to believe that you should not see that therapist." It is also important to say what you plan to do with the information if the identity of the therapist becomes obvious to you in the course of the person's story, even if the therapist's name has not been mentioned. This is particularly important in small communities. And in states where the reporting of sexual abuse by therapists is mandatory, this legal obligation of the leader must be made explicit to the participants before they sign up for the workshop.

7.   Keep to the schedule, both in content and time frame. The last thing such a group needs is sloppy workshop boundaries.

8.   Keep the group small. I think eight is as large as a 6-hour workshop should accommodate. I do not recommend lengthening the workshop to include more people.

9.   Use a sliding-fee scale if at all possible.

10.   Warn people ahead of time that it is helpful to have support after the workshop. Many people have left the workshops much angrier or otherwise upset than they expected to be, and they needed people to talk with.

STRUCTURE

10 Minutes	Ground Rules. Confidentiality and its limits. Schedule described. Leader keeps time. Not a therapy group. Introduction of leader(s). I briefly tell my own abuse story and explain why I do this work.
10-15 Minutes	Guided Imagery Exercise—Review the Relationship. I ask people to close their eyes if they feel comfortable doing so and then I lead them in a brief relaxation exercise focusing on slowing down. Then I ask them to drift backwards in time to the point at which they first met the therapist, noticing why they wanted therapy, noticing how the relationship began, then moving forward in time to the point where the therapy relationship began to feel or be sexual, tracing the rest of the relationship up to the present.
1 1/2—2 Hours	Participants get equal time to tell their stories. Leader keeps time, gives each person a two-minute warning. Leader limits interaction if others interrupt a lot. Questions from others should be limited to clarifying questions only; no problem-solving or "me too" stories.

1 Hour | Bag Lunch and Open Discussion. Leader is present. Often people ask each other questions, share resources.

15 Minutes | Guided Imagery—Confronting the Therapist. Relax. Imagine that you assemble a support team to accompany you, and go with that team to a place where you can confront the therapist. Notice how you feel in the therapist's presence...imagine saying or doing anything you would like to say or do to the therapist. Then imagine saying or doing something that you might realistically do. Consult with your support team or your wise inner voice to decide what, if anything, you actually want to do in real life in response to the abuse you've received.

1 1/2—2 Hours | Participants get equal time to discuss their next steps. The whole group talks with each person—problem-solving, helping the person to clarify what she wants to do.

15 Minutes | Evaluation of Workshop. Each person is invited to tell briefly how the workshop was for her. People often exchange addresses and phone numbers at this point. A follow-up session is scheduled if people are interested and if they live within commuting distance.

PART V

SOME SPECIAL SITUATIONS

Issues that do not fit into other parts of this volume are discussed in these five chapters. The three topics that are examined are not connected logically; instead, they elaborate on themes discussed elsewhere.

Chapter 19 by Schoener and Milgrom probes the issue of psychotherapy cults. Although interest in cults has been growing over the past decade (Temerlin & Temerlin's classic article on psychotherapy cults appeared in 1982), the topic tends to be ignored in the literature. If anything, however, the number and variety of such cults has increased over the years.

Schoener and Milgrom's discussion of sexual exploitation by pastors and pastoral counselors in Chapter 20 complements the earlier exposition by the Rev. Marie Fortune (Ch. 6). In addition to examining special aspects of this type of exploitation, Chapter 20 provides resources for readers who are interested in studying the issue more intensively.

The significant others, friends, or family members of clients who have been sexually exploited by therapists often are secondary victims of the offenses. Chapter 21 by Milgrom looks at the nature of the effects—usually indirect but, nevertheless, painful—on these victims.

In both Milwaukee and Minneapolis, support groups have been organized for the spouses and significant others of client-victims; these groups are described in Chapter 22 by Luepker and O'Brien. At least one therapist in Minnesota has specialized in counseling couples of whom one member has been sexually exploited by a therapist.

Although the literature on victims of client-therapist sexual exploitation has been accumulating fairly rapidly since the mid-1970s, the problems of secondary victims still receive scant attention. The single exception, until recently, was Milgrom's (1981) paper which has been privately circulated by the Walk-In Counseling Center. Since then, other investigators have made contributions. The effect on the family and friends of the victim of sexual exploitation by a clergyman is described in Baker's (1984) book, *Beyond Forgiveness*, and Pope and Bouhoutsos (1986, p. 68) presented a short section, "Effects on Significant Others." Schoener and Milgrom (1986, pp. 156-57) also devoted a couple of pages to secondary victims; they are, however, noteworthy largely because the editor of the book insisted on retaining the discussion despite serious space limitations.

Other investigators have reached beyond sexual exploitation by therapists. Burgess & Hartman (1986, pp. 29-36), for example, described the effect on parents of child molestation by a physician in the chapter, "The Good Deed Undone"; and in the subsequent chapter they chronicled the effect on a husband and cousin of the sexual exploitation of an adult woman by a physician. Burgess (1986, pp. 77-78), in a chapter on gynecologist-patient sexual abuse, described the trauma to family and friends when the abuse was disclosed. She also discussed the different reactions of husbands to such abuse and their effects on the wives. Reactions ranged from anger to minimalization to rationalization.

In our experience, the reactions of not only spouses but, also, families and friends vary markedly; sometimes the family and friends even have a profound role in determining the degree to which the primary victim will recover.

Chapter 23 focuses on still another issue: sexual exploitation of trainees by their therapy supervisors. This problem has been compared to that of therapist-client sex although the authors, Conroe and Shank, limit their observations to some specific situations. In another recent article Sanderson (1989b) found an even closer parallel between therapist-client and supervisor-supervisee sex. It has also been argued that this problem may contribute to the incidence of sexual exploitation of clients by therapists, although the linkage is difficult to document.

Other authors (Edelwich & Brodsky, 1982; White, 1987), also note the parallels but treat the relationships quite differently. It is not clear, in fact, how psychotherapy supervision in general differs greatly from other types of training or employment-related supervision. Certainly within these contexts sexual harassment is unlawful and improper. However, the definition of "sexual exploitation" is problematic. Are there actually no circumstances in which such a relationship may be deemed consensual? What happens after the supervisory relationship ends: Is a romantic or sexual relationship still impossible? Does a trainee have no responsibility whatsoever for the relationship with the supervisor? After all, the trainee is within months of going out into professional work and, presumably, to being bound by the same code of ethics.

Perhaps the most obvious aspect of supervisor-supervisee sexual relationships is that like therapist-client sex the various psychotherapy fields have failed to come to grips with it and to make clear rules regarding its propriety.

CHAPTER 19

PSYCHOTHERAPY CULTS

Gary Richard Schoener
and
Jeanette Hofstee Milgrom

Temerlin and Temerlin (1982), in their classic article, "Psychotherapy Cults: An Iatrogenic Perversion," presented the first, and to date, only discussion of the special problem of psychotherapy cults. According to the Temerlins,

> ...psychotherapy may be misused to produce cults. These psychotherapists produced cults by failing to maintain professional boundaries with their patients: they treated their friends, students, lovers, relatives, employees, and colleagues, and brought them together to form cohesive, psychologically incestuous groups, of which they were the leader. They did not consider their patients' idealization of them to be a transference, to be understood as part of the treatment, but used it to encourage submission, obedience, and adoration, as in religious cults. (Temerlin & Temerlin, 1982, p. 131)

They indicated that patients become true believers with totalitarian patterns of thought, increased dependency, and paranoid thinking. In addition, "Both therapist and patient became trapped in a closed system which encouraged mutual exploitation and corruption" (Temerlin & Temerlin, 1982, p. 131). They presented the following characteristics of cult members:

1. Leader is a therapist with charismatic, authoritarian, dominating personality; narcissistic, grandiose and paranoid features.

2. Followers are patients who idealize their therapist. Consider her/him a genius. S/he is supreme authority.

3. Patients are, or become, "True Believers," accepting the therapist's theory and therapy as valid, true and superior to all others. This belief is encouraged, and rational-empirical research is discouraged.

4. Followers joined by becoming patients of the therapist in periods of transition when identity and security needs greatest, as in graduate school. Followers alienated from other professionals.

5. Members organize their lives around their therapist, who is consulted on all aspects of personal or professional life. Little social or professional life outside of group.

6. Group cohesive, considered an elite professional family. Members consider themselves superior to other professionals. Therapist keeps love, veneration and allegiance directed toward self. Idealizing transference not analyzed.

7. Group suspicious, fearful and hostile toward other professionals. Therapist controls or interprets for members all contact with other professionals. Dependence and submissiveness increase; critical thinking decreases. (Temerlin & Temerlin, 1982, p. 134)

Their characterization of the manner of entry into these psychotherapy cults bears a marked similarity to that described in the literature on pseudoreligious cults. For example, MacCollam in *Carnival of Souls* (1979) described the recruitment by other members of the cult through reinforcement and integration of personal goals to concur with those of the cult, strong peer pressure, and the presentation of commitment and service as key elements. Deutsch (1983), in "Psychiatric Perspectives on an Eastern-Style Cult," described a path that followed the search for acceptance, relief of guilt, feeling free, being good and loving, and the development of purpose.

The cult leader assumes a "teacher" role. Torrey (1986) noted that even in ordinary therapy this element is present and, in fact, has spiritual overtones:

The therapist-client relationship is simply one species of the teacher-student genre, which is universal: the teacher imparts specialized knowledge to the student, thereby strengthening him or her, and for this knowledge the student is supposed to be eternally grateful. A psychotherapist in this sense is analogous to a guru and has overtones of spiritual preceptor as well as instructor. (p. 71)

In both therapy and pseudoreligious cults, other characteristics of cult leaders and the group processes, which play such an important role, are strikingly similar.

Within the destructive cult, the leader's need for self-aggrandizement creates a setting that covertly sponsors regression and overtly creates an ideology that justifies the institutionalization of regression. Many individuals enter cults at times when the continuities in their lives are placed in question. Cults exaggerate their concerns and provide an institutional framework in which these needs are met. (Halperin, 1983, p. 233)

Another characteristic of both pseudoreligious and psychotherapy cults is the tenacity of affiliation to the cult leader. When the leader is challenged by persons in the mainstream, is revealed to be dishonest or unprofessional, or begins to deteriorate emotionally, followers continue their attachment, often draw closer, and ignore the mounting evidence. Deutsch (1980), in a fine article on the "Tenacity of Affiliation to a Cult Leader—A Psychiatric Perspective," noted that members of the cult used denial, rationalization, and increased idealization to deal with growing manifestations of the guru's emotional deterioration.

PSYCHOTHERAPY BROADLY VIEWED

Much has been written about the personality cults surrounding Freud and his followers. The various ideological factions that grew up in psychoanalysis also have some cult-like elements which have been examined (e.g., Lothane, 1983).

During the 1960s and 1970s a number of therapy movements, or "mass therapies," arose, partly in response to the growth of notions (often fostered by these movements) that therapy could do much more than just deal with psychiatric disorder. Rosen (1977) in his interesting book, *Psychobabble,* examined many such groups and the shifting expectations of therapy and noted that "psychotherapeutic and spiritual objectives have increasingly merged and blurred" (p. 207). Conway & Siegelman (1978, p. 57) also concluded,

Except for the religious component, virtually all the mass therapies use the same basic techniques.

Here the individual is drawn into an intense group setting or therapeutic session in the hope of having some life-changing breakthrough.

The growth of therapeutic approaches to drug and alcohol problems over the past 20 years created a number of movements that, at times, appear cult-like. Synanon, for example, was widely labeled a cult (e.g., Rebhan, 1983, "The Drug Rehabilitation Program: Cults in Formation?"). When Gary Schoener visited Synanon in 1972 it already had all the features of a cult. At the time, it was referred to as a "third community approach," a term coined to avoid calling it a cult. During the visit it became clear that Synanon no longer could simply be referred to as a "therapeutic community treatment program." Its clients were no longer clients but, rather, members of an alternative and very insular society.

Therapeutic communities and other residential treatment programs that did not become cults still exhibited many of the characteristics. Ponsor, Soler, and Abod (1976) described the abuse of women in drug treatment programs in the New Haven, Connecticut area— abuse that occurred in the context of treatment programs with many cult-like features.

Stylistically different but also cult-like at times, are some of the programs that grew up in the Midwest and supposedly were based on the philosophy of alcoholics anonymous. Some of these groups began to claim they could treat almost any problem an individual might have using a single approach, called a "12-step" method. Some groups drifted out of the mainstream, became very insular and incestuous, and became psychotherapy cults under a guru. Their adherents failed to note the inconsistency of having a guru while adhering to a supposedly self-help, nonprofessional philosophy.

The focus by the mid- to late-1970s on services for victims or members of disadvantaged groups, such as gays, lesbians or incest victims, led occasionally to the formation of small, insular, and often quite paranoid cults. Some, ironically, employed very abusive and sadistic treatment approaches including, at times, physical assault. Here again, the desire to find approaches that were different and directed to the needs of a given subgroup led people far afield. When the adherents were challenged, they justified the approaches with jargon and statements that the clients' pain and problems were so great drastic means were needed to "cure" them.

At the other end of the spectrum, perhaps, are therapy movements with high public visibility, such as the Center for Feeling Therapy in southern California. Mithers (1988) examined the origins of the organization and its charismatic founders, and even analyzed their TV and radio talk show appearances ("When bad shrinks make good talk show guests," p. 79; and "How the publishers and talk shows were fooled," p. 83). During public hearings,

...patient after patient recounted instances of sex with therapists, of being hit, kicked, punched, ordered to strip, called "dead," "insane," of being told how often to have sex and with whom, where to live and work, how much to weigh, what to eat, what to think, what to feel....What had happened? On the surface most people saw a new psychotherapy promising happiness, fulfillment and utopian community. In reality there were 350 people who had spent up to ten years of their lives in what administrative law judge Robert A. Neher called an "almost gothic maelstrom." (Mithers, 1988, p. 78)

SOME CULT TYPES

Temerlin and Temerlin (1982) should be read for some useful examples. The following illustrative cases are drawn from our experience nationally and are not necessarily Minnesota-based cults. Some have since broken up. Some details have been altered to avoid identifying any one group.

1. A psychotherapist had a tight-knit group of clients whom he saw in both individual and group therapy. Although he was not well-known in the professional community, these clients idolized him. His groups applied considerable peer pressure so that when someone tried to leave the group he or she was pursued and pressured. After a woman client whom the psychotherapist had sexually exploited drifted away and started to file charges, a number of the clients harassed her.

2. A drug abuse counselor developed her own program of outpatient therapy in which a highly idiosyncratic approach was developed. She virtually demanded that all spouses and significant others belong to the group and also receive individual counseling. She led people to believe that they could not make it on their own and pushed them to develop harsh confrontational styles of relating that pushed family and friends away.

3. A male paraprofessional counselor operating on his own in people's homes provided group and individual work. Clients who tried to pull away or to leave the group were pursued and confronted by group members. The therapist introduced clients to each other for dating purposes. It was virtually impossible to stay in the therapy unless one's spouse or significant other was also involved.

4. A well-known psychotherapist who lectured and taught a great deal set up a clinic and then a training program. His trainees all had to get therapy from one of the senior staff members in the program, and they were charged full fee so that they would run up large bills. They could pay off the bills by working for free. When the therapist began to use intrusive physical approaches and also to behave in a sexual manner to clients these behaviors were overlooked by staff members, trainees, and the board.

As in pseudoreligious cults, it is not easy to draw the line between cult and religion or, in this case, cult and legitimate therapy. There are cult-like private practices that some persons would call cults and others would simply term "a bit incestuous" or "a bit ingrown." The therapist described by Plasil (1985) in *Therapist* is an authoritarian, highly disturbed, and controlling professional who has a small group of his clients tightly tied to him. Particularly striking is the description of an episode in which the group members sit stunned while the therapist has a violent confrontation with a client (pp. 106-110).

The label is less important than some of the cult-like traits. Clients who are members of these groups often are more difficult to work with because they do not find it easy to leave the group.

WORKING WITH CLIENTS

We have heard from a number of clients over the years who have been members of what either they or we termed "psychotherapy cults." The clients come to us alleging sexual exploitation by the cult leader, various other boundary violations, and a great deal of manipulation of their lives. In some cases they had loaned money to the guru and realized subsequently that they were not likely to see their money again.

Like youthful members of pseudoreligious cults, they often had given money, gifts, or valuable personal possessions to the leader. Invariably they had alienated friends and family or, in some instances, successfully recruited them into the cult. Although clients in psychotherapy cults often have wasted their own resources, it is far less common for them to use up family resources. They have less guilt than is usually the case with people who have come out of pseudoreligious cults. Both, however, may feel quite guilty about having recruited friends and family members (especially siblings) into the cult. When we interviewed them it was usual for the recruits to be still involved in the cult.

Unlike the young people studied by Singer (1979), who reported an average age of 23, and Levine (1984 a, b), whose subjects ranged in age from 18 to 26, our clients tended to be much older. Nonetheless some appeared, in Levine's (1984 a, b) terms, to have made a "radical departure" from their family's values whereas others simply sought to obtain help for personal problems. The latter were seeking neither identity nor an alternative life philosophy, only help for depression or anxiety.

Most problems that these ex-members of pseudoreligious cults struggled with were, for example, extreme indecisiveness, slipping into altered states, blurring of mental activity, and fear of the cult (Singer, 1979) which, to a lesser extent, are characteristic of clients who have left psychotherapy cults. None whom we interviewed could be accurately diagnosed as having an "Atypical Dissociative Disorder (300.15 in the DSM-III)," a disorder common among ex-members of pseudoreligious cults (Golper, 1983).

These members of psychotherapy cults had given up less of their lives to be accepted in the cult, possibly because they were older when they entered the group and had more of an established adult identity and lifestyle. However, their family relationships often were damaged as well as friendships, and sometimes they went through divorces. Such disrupted relationships may not be easily repaired. Sometimes the client either gave up a job or alienated employers or co-workers to such a degree they lost their jobs or irreparably damaged the relationships.

When family members and friends observe the apparent deterioration or losses in these areas of life, they may attempt various methods of intervention. "Deprogramming" was tried in some cases with which we were involved although we advised against it. We sometimes gave to families copies of Singer's (1979) and Levine's (1984b) articles, carefully noting the differences between what is described therein and what the family was dealing with. We advised reaching out with honest feedback, and if that did not work to back off and withdraw financial support. We noted, as did Levine (1984 a, b), that in about 90% of the cases a cult member is likely to leave on her/his own within about 2 years.

Ironically, some long-term psychoanalytic patients seem to be locked into therapy longer than many people involved in psychotherapy cults (e.g., "Prisoners of Psychotherapy" by Terri Minsky, 1987). One is reminded of the sardonic humor in the movie *Annie Hall* by Woody Allen (1977):

"You see an analyst?"
"Just for 15 years."
"Fifteen years?"
"Yeah, uh, I'm gonna give him one more year and
then I'm going to Lourdes."

In fact, in some cases, psychoanalytic patients may see about as much of their psychoanalysts as members of psychotherapy cult members see of their therapists. In the average week some cult members have one individual session plus perhaps two group sessions. In other cases, of course, there is much more involvement, including actually living with the therapist and extensive socialization with other group members.

INTERVENTION

Clients who have been sexually exploited in a psychotherapy cult have often made the decision to exit the group because they discovered that the therapist or guru had exploited other people as well. It is quite common, therefore, for people to leave in groups, or for one person's departure to trigger that of several others in a domino effect.

When one or more people leave, those who remain pull tightly together and make efforts to draw the defectors back into the group using phone calls, letters, or personal confrontations. Hence, clients need assistance in deciding how to handle these encounters.

In many instances it is possible to pull together a small group of ex-cult members who can support each other in moving on. On several occasions we have held group meetings of some clients from the same group. This procedure can be very helpful because of the difficulty of crossing from the tightly knit cult back to earlier personal and family relationships which have been ruptured or damaged.

One common intervention relates to what Singer (1979, p. 80) calls "the agonies of explaining." The clients have difficulty explaining to others why they got involved in such a group and why they adopted what may have been strange ways of relating to other people. For example, it is difficult to explain the rationale behind hostile and contentious encounters with family and friends. We often helped clients to develop a plan of reaching out to old friends and family and apologizing for abusive behavior.

As in the pseudoreligious cults (Singer, 1979, p. 80) there may be guilt about the deceptive practices related to involvement with the cult. Frequently a client has a problem with the jargon he/she learned to use and which must be dropped if one is to be able to communicate with other people and to re-enter ordinary everyday relationships. Use of jargon becomes second nature and is not easy to stop. Clients in Ellen Luepker's support groups (see Ch. 14) commented that participating in a support group helped them to become free of the jargon.

A WARNING

Both the client who is breaking away and an advocate or therapist who assists the client may become targets for the cult. Typically, defectors will receive phone calls or even be visited by other members of the group. These other members and the cult leader will use pathological terms to describe the client's departure from the group, often covering the expressions with a syrupy sweet icing of self-proclaimed concern and caring. The departure is interpreted as a self-destructive act. Fortunately, most clients already have seen this behavior enacted with other former members and may themselves have participated in it, so it comes as no surprise.

When you or former members file charges, strangers may appear and ask why you are persecuting this therapist. The cult leader may try to set up a confrontation on his or her turf—usually one to which you cannot say "no" because, often, it is a session with a spouse. You need to be prepared for the cult leader's presentation and defense of reasonable picture. It is important to challenge the nonsense without getting into a fight or trying to convince the leader that he/she is wrong.

Cult leaders usually are hampered in filing counter charges to retaliate because they tend to be outside the mainstream of the profession. Temerlin & Temerlin (1982) warned against the proclivity of some of the groups or gurus to sue, and it is worth keeping this fact in mind. In our experience, however, they rarely have done so.

On the other hand, former clients often find it difficult to sue for a variety of reasons. First of all, those therapists sometimes lack any sort of malpractice coverage. Second, many of their harmful behaviors are not easily shown to be malpractice. If sexual exploitation or physical violence have occurred, a case is easier to make.

Furthermore, it is difficult to file complaints against many cult leaders: some are not professionals; those that are professionals are sometimes not members of a professional association or they think nothing of resigning from it; and most of their adherents refuse to testify. In some circumstances adherents are even willing to fabricate evidence or to perjure themselves to protect the "master."

OUTCOMES

Most psychotherapy cults with which we have dealt have lasted about 3 - 5 years. A number of the leaders have been charged with having sex with clients and have been disciplined by a Board and/or sued. Those cults that have not been put out of business have lost members and are somewhat destabilized.

The clients often lost a great deal in terms of alienation from family and friends. In the cases in which the therapist was not licensed and the abuses were difficult to deal with in a civil suit, clients often ended up quite frustrated at their inability to change the situation or to obtain redress.

It is clear that unless our field does a better job of defining what is and what is not psychotherapy, clients will have difficulty in identifying a charlatan.

CHAPTER 20

SEXUAL EXPLOITATION BY CLERGY AND PASTORAL COUNSELORS[1]

Gary Richard Schoener
and
Jeanette Hofstee Milgrom

Our concern with the sexual exploitation of clients by clerical and pastoral counselors came about through our efforts to help the victims. In recent years, however, we also have assisted various church organizations and several seminaries, and we have evaluated clergypersons who have sexually exploited clients or parishioners. Some of this work was noted in the *Legislative Report* (1985) of the Minnesota Task Force on Sexual Exploitation by Counselors and Therapists, and discussed in *Sexual Assault and Abuse, A Handbook for Clergy and Religious Professionals* (Milgrom & Schoener, 1987).

Meanwhile, during the past several years, an ever-increasing number of newspaper stories, many of them given large headlines, have been devoted to cases of alleged sexual exploitation by clergypersons. These stories typically have focused on civil suits or criminal charges brought against clergy for sexual involvement with minors, or civil suits by adult women or their husbands against clergy who have seduced them. Recently, criminal charges were brought against a minister for the sexual exploitation of an adult woman in Minnesota where criminal statutes prohibit such behavior (see Ch. 43, Case 7).

Our file of clippings on sexual abuse by clergy contains predominately stories concerning sexual abuse of children. The accounts are from throughout the United States and concern clergy of a great many faiths. They describe sexual abuse of virtually every imaginable type perpetrated against children of all ages and both sexes. Some examples of headlines may be useful here:

"Pastor accused of having sex with girl, 15" (Phelps, 1983)

"Church is quiet on sexual accusation against its pastor" (McCoy, 1984)

"When priests molest children—A Louisiana case unveils the shame (Sawyer, 1985)

"Byzantine Catholic priest pleads guilty to sexually abusing boys" (Zack, 1987)

"Ramsey judge mulls punitive damages in sex case—Suits allege 20 years of priest's sexual abuse of boys" (Oaks, 1987)

"Priest fired due to charge of sex assault" (Dunbar, 1988)

---

[1]Rev. Marie Fortune provides an excellent overview of this topic in Chapter 6. She has contributed greatly to bringing the problem of sexual exploitation by clergy and pastoral counselors out into the open by extensive public speaking and contributions to serious discussions on this issue (Washington Council of Churches, 1984). Her book, *Keeping the Faith* (Fortune, 1987), which is aimed at women who are abused by family members, may be quite helpful to women who are abused by clergy. Her most recent book, *Is Nothing Sacred? When Sex Invades the Pastoral Relationship* (Fortune, 1989), is essential reading.

"Judgment day for a Harlem minister?" (Salholz, 1988)

"Don't Tell Anybody...You'll get in trouble and so will I, a three part series (Ehlert, 1988)

The recently published *Betrayal of Trust: Clergy Abuse of Children* (Gaylor, 1989) contains numerous accounts from the news media of clergy abuse of children. It was published by the Committee to Protect Children From Abusive Clergy. Appendix BB, "Child Sexual Abuse Within the Catholic Church," by Kathe Starke, provides an overview of this topic.

Sexual exploitation of adults has received considerably less press attention, but it too has been the subject of newspaper stories (see for example Gaylor, 1989, pp. 69-71) and a number of local and national TV shows. Ann Landers (1986c) published a letter from "More Than I Needed to Know in Panama City," who learned on his honeymoon that his wife had slept with five men who were at their wedding including the minister who married them. Among other things, Landers advised:

And for heaven's sake, tell Sally to keep her mouth shut. The minister doesn't need the publicity.

Landers (1986d) withdrew this advice when she published a followup letter from "Disappointed in Detroit:"

For 32 years I was married to a minister who was protected by people who also kept their mouths shut. In the meantime, my husband was taking advantage of young women to whom he should have been ministering. If people had not remained silent, he would have been removed from his job. The net result was that he caused irreparable harm to all of those who believed he was a servant of God.... (p. 6C)

Landers (1989b) recently published a letter from "A Crushed Christian in California" who indicated that an associate pastor began courting her as soon as he learned of a recent large insurance settlement she had received. As soon as she married him he began dominating her life, frequently citing "God's will" as a rationale for his pronouncements. She wrote:

Using "God" to control, manipulate, bully, and extort is cruel and sadistic. My emotional scars wlil take years to heal and I may never fully trust a minister or church again. (p. 7E)

Little is available in the way of incidence/prevalence data. Blackmon (1984) surveyed 300 clergy in southern California from four denominations—Assembly of God, Episcopal, Presbyterian, and United Methodist. Thirteen percent reported that they had had sexual intercourse with a parishioner. Kuchan (see Ch. 3) reports Wisconsin data in which counselors reported having received a total of 73 complaints of sexual exploitation by clergy during the years 1982 through 1984. While this was well below the 221 for psychiatrists and 127 for psychologists during the same period, it was higher than that for non-psychiatric physicians (36) and marriage counselors (23).

Bradshaw (1977), in an article entitled "Ministers in Trouble: A Study of 140 Cases Evaluated at the Menninger Foundation," noted:

Like psychotherapists in other disciplines, the minister who has not taken special training is poorly prepared to handle the hazards of transference and countertransference processes in the pastoral counseling situation. Many of the men felt it was "therapeutic" to become intimate with their clients and thus could not avoid very personal contact with women parishioners. Their actions triggered off reactions by their spouses and their own consciences. Other psychotherapists have access to consultation on difficult situations, but many ministers do not ever seek expert guidance in the matter of treating women of their congregations. (p. 238)

Bradshaw (1977, pp. 238-39) describes the case of a minister who "...had a fleeting affair with a parishioner after counseling her for an emotional problem," resulting in "...a marked loss of self-esteem and increased guilt feelings which he attempted to handle with alcohol abuse." He further notes:

Several other ministers in our sample handled their guilt feelings, and subsequent loss in their self-esteem from having an affair with a counselee, by "arranging" to get themselves caught or otherwise exposed. Some even made confessions to family or parishioners with the naive expectation that they would be praised and adulated for this bit of truthful behavior! (p. 239)

Our work with victims, clergypersons, and religious institutions has led us to reach some conclusions that may be of some use in examining sexual exploitation by clerical or pastoral counselors. A great many similarities to abuse by other types of counselors and therapists can be identified but there are also some differences, especially when the exploitation occurs in a church or religious setting. We discuss these differences from the perspective of definitional problems, the victim, the perpetrator, and the church or religious body.

DEFINITIONAL PROBLEMS

Sexual involvement with minors is clearly as unethical and illegal for clergy as it is for any adult but sexual exploitation of adults is a more confusing issue.

When religious professionals such as priests and nuns take vows of celibacy or chastity sexual contact with any adult violates church roles or sacred vows. The exact definition of what is included in these vows, however, is usually lacking. Consequently, some clergypersons rationalize that certain types of contact are permissible even though they clearly are sexual. Lay people also tend to be unclear about such definitions so clergypersons sometimes are able to make authentic-sounding arguments to justify exploitative behavior.

Adultery is a sin in most religions. Even if clergy are permitted to marry, therefore, sex with someone other than one's spouse is a serious offense. Also, in many creeds, sex outside of marriage is prohibited.

For these reasons sexual involvement with a parishioner or counselee may be examined in clerical circles in terms of general rules about sexual conduct rather than the sexual exploitation of a client by a counselor. Furthermore, because pastoral work often takes place in settings other than a counseling office, it is not easy to define what a counseling relationship consists of in a religious setting. Instead of regular counseling sessions, for example, counseling may take place in the clergyperson's residence, the parishioner's home, a hospital room, or at a retreat.

It may seem reasonable to assume that the generally tighter strictures regarding sexual contact permits counselees to have an easier time recognizing abuse; in fact, this does not seem to be the case. For one thing, unclear standards on physical contact and the setting in which counseling is provided blurs the potential distinction between professional standards and the definition of personal relationships. Terms like "Christian love" and "sharing" may confuse everyone involved about what is happening. Last but not least, the unspoken belief that the clergyperson is acting on behalf of God may create a sense of security in the righteousness of his or her actions.

Intimacy in the pastoral, or pastoral counseling, relationship can be very confusing to both parties. Madden (1976), in an article on "Meaningful Pastoral Intimacy," wrote:

> Pastoral intimacy is often, and perhaps primarily, allowed or authorized out of an individual need for blessing and affirmation. In other words, the intention of the parishioner in admitting the pastor into the intimate space is bound up in his or her hope or expectation of being affirmed in some way. The inner door is not opened to the minister just to pass the time of day. That can be done on the sidewalk or front porch without the risk of exposure of some part of one's inner space.

> If persons allow pastoral intimacy in the hope of pastoral affirmation, it becomes very important that pastors remain aware of why doors are being opened for them. For example, if a parishioner is seeking more to be affirmed than to affirm, he will most likely come off with bad feelings following intimate contact— so will the parishioner.

> Pastoral intimacy also carries a "no-sex" contract. This does not preclude the presence of sexual stimulation in pastoral intimacy, but traditionally intimacy is more easily granted to the "holy man" because holiness and sexuality are thought to occupy opposite ends on the spectrum. The holy man did not seem to have sexual feelings, while sexual man was assumed to be without holiness. (p. 37)

Rolfe (1985), in an article, "The Destructive Potential of Psychological Counseling for Pastor and Parish," discusses some of the difficulties inherent in the pastor playing a psychotherapeutic role. He notes that such activities compete with other pastoral duties and with the needs of the clergyman's family. He further asserts:

> The clergy are the only professional group involved in counseling who regularly mix counseling with friendship and thus systematically destroy their own credibility and then relegate themselves to positions of isolation. (p. 64)

THE VICTIM

Clients or parishioners who are sexually exploited vary as broadly as do victims of other types of counselors and therapists. Some are very dependent and/or have relatively serious emotional difficulties whereas others are relatively healthy and functioning well. The effect of the sexual contact is also variable.

Groups of persons within many church settings are potentially highly vulnerable because they lack experience in adult romantic or sexual relationships. They include parishioners who are highly constricted in their life experience as well as nuns. Sometimes when such persons seek to broaden their life experience, or when nuns, for example, decide to move into the secular world, they are particularly disadvantaged in judging other people's motives and the propriety of certain types of interpersonal behaviors.

Fortune (1989) raises concern about a misnaming of the problem of clergy-parishioner sex by saying that both are vulnerable. She writes:

...although the pastor is <u>at risk</u>, it is only the parishioner who is <u>vulnerable</u>. (p. 121)

Rutter (in press), in his book, *Sex in the Forbidden Zone*, also addresses some of the unique features of the clergy-parishioner relationship:

The power of the pastor over the congregant is tremendously enhanced by his authority, if he wishes to exercise it, to describe to a woman her status with God. (p. 38)

Two problems often are greater for victims of clergy than for victims of other counselors. First of all, they tend to blame themselves for corrupting a presumably "pure" clergyman and often become markedly disenchanted with religion or confused about issues of sin and guilt. Beyond acquiring the normal distrust of authority figures, they also may suffer a loss of faith—a damage to their spiritual side.

Second, many such victims feel extremely isolated, fearing that others in the church hierarchy or congregation will blame them for what happened. When, in fact, they are so accused, which sometimes happens, the parishioner may assume all responsibility and blame. This experience leads to considerable loss of self-esteem and, possibly, the loss of a support network. For someone whose social support network is intertwined with the church, this blow can be devastating. Baker (1984) provided an account of this sort of social context; although the victims were believed, Baker's exposition clearly indicated the devastating potential of the context had the church sided with the pastor. Fortune's (1989) *Is Nothing Sacred? When Sex Invades the Pastoral Relationship*, provides an excellent analysis of these issues.

Nathaniel Hawthorne's *The Scarlet Letter*, published in 1850, and thought by many to be the first American psychological novel, focused on the mistreatment of a young woman made pregnant by a highly respected clergyman who largely escaped the community's wrath. Fortune (1989) cites the non-fictional case of eminent preacher Henry Ward Beecher, who in the 1870s was sued by the husband of parishioner Elizabeth Tilton with whom he had a sexual affair. Not only did Beecher weather the storm, but Victoria Woodhull was jailed for publishing the story of the involvement in 1872. The parishioner has good reason to expect rough treatment in such situations, whereas the clergyman will often be given the benefit of the doubt. In the case Fortune (1989) describes, the minister/perpetrator, who was a multiple offender, was given a standing ovation when he left the church (p. 82).[2]

The impact of sexual exploitation on parishioners who have been victimized by clergy was studied by the Minnesota Interfaith Committee on Sexual Exploitation by Clergy (1989), which published a list of common long-term effects on the victim that included:

---

[2] Olsen (1989) describes a very similar series of events in the case of a physician/perpetrator who was shielded by church leaders and the congregation, and afforded the luxury to tell his story from the pulpit.

•extreme anger at the violation of sacred trust
•crisis in one's faith and spiritual life
•grief over the loss of the relationship with the clegyperson and faith community
•fragmentation of self: the mind shuts down the heart, splits off the spirit, and alienates the body
•fear of being disbelieved, blamed, ostracized (p. 8)

The remainder of the list included symptoms common to victims of therapists such as low self-esteem.

A variety of resources may be of assistance to victims of clergy. Fortune (1989) reports having given a group of victims the book *Sexual Violence: The Unmentionable Sin* to read. Some have found the book *Sexual Assault and Abuse: A Handbook for Clergy and Religious Professionals* (Pellauer, Chester, & Boyajian, 1987a) quite helpful, especially the chapter on "Resources for Ritual and Recuperation" (Pellauer, Chester, & Boyajian, 1987b). Several clients have recommended *Rebuilding Your Broken World* (MacDonald, 1988), although we found the author's vague references to his own unnamed transgressions distracting. Fortune's (1989) *Is Nothing Sacred? When Sex Invades the Pastoral Relationship* and *Sexual Exploitation by Clergy: Reflections and Guidelines for Religious Leaders* (Minnesota Interfaith Committee on Sexual Exploitation by Clergy, 1989) have both been helpful to local victims.

THE PERPETRATOR

We have seen the same range of personality types among clergypersons as those described by Schoener and Gonsiorek in Chapter 32. A clergyperson may put forth far-reaching rationalizations to justify the sexual contact, such as providing the counselee or parishioner with self-serving definitions of celibacy or the boundaries of "Christian love."

By the same token, many well-intentioned clergy are poorly prepared for the counseling role. Thus they lack an understanding of the importance of professional boundaries. Rassieur (1976), in *The Problem Clergymen Don't Talk About*, provides an excellent although dated introduction to this issue and offers useful practical advice to clergy and their spouses. The book was ahead of its time when published and is still unique. He provides a variety of examples of pastoral attraction to counselees (pp. 70-87) and discusses problems in the pastoral role and closeness of the work which can set the stage for sexual intimacy. He also lists factors which tend to mitigate against sexual involvement with counselees: marital satisfaction; fear of social consequences; self-image as a pastor; theological and moral constraints; and supportive social relationships. He recommends a value framework to help guide the pastoral counselor and advises, as others have earlier (e.g., Pattison, 1965), that the pastoral counselor obtain professional consultation. A more recent contribution by McDowell (1989) described the pastor's moral defenses in situations where there are temptations of sex with a parishioner.

More than two decades ago Pattison (1965), in "Transference and Countertransference in Pastoral Care," provided an excellent overview of these phenomena for ministers. He wrote in part:

> Sexual transferences are common. The woman who overvalued and idealized her father may overestimate the pastor and regard the pastor's wife as a rival. (p. 197)

*****

Some people become defensive when their sexual impulses are stimulated and they fear the expression of the impulses. Thus the pastor may provoke negativism to a warm intense personal approach which the parishioner experiences as sexually stimulating. So the pastor is well advised to refrain from physical contacts as well as intimate gestures which may provoke unwanted sexual fantasies or frightened withdrawal. (p. 197).

*****

The pastor who is afraid of his own sexuality may deny his erotic feelings in situations where he should be aware that he is responding in a sexually provocative or reactive fashion. Often pastors find women accusing them of improper advances while the pastor protests his innocence. Had the pastor recognized his own impulses he might have avoided playing into a mutual sexual distortion of the relationship. (p. 199)

It has become apparent, in the years since Pattison's article was published, that a number of the pastors who protested their innocence were in fact guilty of sexual misconduct with parishioners. However, the scenario which Pattison describes can also occur.

Malony (1989), while noting that ministers may be especially vulnerable to sexual transgressions with counselees, argued that popular belief to the contrary, the ministry is "not as stressful as had been presumed" (p. 50). However, others (e.g., Pellauer, 1987) argue that the ministry is a high stress profession characterized by overcommitment and "workaholism." Clergy and their spouses both experience a number of stressors, although studies have shown that they rate the relative importance of stressors somewhat differently (e.g., Gleason, 1977). Even when in training ministerial candidates are aware of pastoral burnout:

Burnout in pastoral ministry has been occupying the attention of an increasing number of writers. Students in the seminary read these materials with keen interest and, at times, deep personal concern. They are already aware of what it is like to feel overextended in the seminary and wonder how they will escape burnout in the parish. (Harbaugh & Rogers, 1984, p. 99)

Hulme (1989), in a recent contribution, although noting that some ministers are "sex addicts," places considerable faith in education, marriage care groups, and spiritual growth as preventive measures. He wrote:

The protection that clergy and the congregations have in this unsupervised ministry is the commitment of the clergy to their calling, the accepting attitude of the clergy toward their own sexual passions, and the wholesome respect of the clergy's responsibility for their own actions. (p. 191)

As with psychotherapists from professions such as psychiatry and psychology (see Ch. 32), narcissism has been identified as a problem among some clergy and pastoral counselors. Bradshaw (1977, p. 236) reported that 39 out of 140 clergymen evaluated at the Menninger Clinic "...were considered narcissistic personalities." One author has even argued that narcissistic character disorders "...are prevalent among members of the clergy precisely because the profession provides strong reinforcement for such personality problems." (Meloy, 1986, p. 50) Meloy (1986) argues that the pattern of transient sexual partners characteristic of narcissistic pathology is actually a form of autoeroticism, and that clergy whose sexual outlets are limited to masturbation thus have a sanction for self-love.

Merrill (1985) quoted Jim Smith, the head of the counseling staff at the Family Life Center in a Dallas church, and listed the following warning signs:

•Finding you look forward to someone's visit—thinking, "Let's see, what shall I wear today?"
•Rearranging your schedule to accommodate a certain appointment; "bumping" someone else.
•Meeting in less-than-standard locations: for lunch, at her home, and so on.
•Nurturing fantasy.
•Being secretive with your spouse about what's happening. (p. 105)

Like professional university graduate and medical schools, seminaries rarely provide much in the way of useful guidance on dealing with sexualized or romanticized counseling relationships. The problem is even more serious for clergypersons who operate in situations with fewer clear-cut boundaries and without professional supervision.

Like the mental health professions, religious institutions do little or no screening of individuals who may have difficulty handling the professional role. In addition, the lack of sexual outlets as well as the inattention to sexual issues in many denominations frequently add to the hazards of the role.

There is little if any incentive for clergypersons to self-report their exploitative behavior. Having chosen the ministry as a lifelong profession they have security as long as they remain a minister or priest; should they fall out of grace, however, they chance losing all their security. Typically, few alternative occupations are available to them.

Until relatively recently the careers of clergypersons who were caught were seldom endangered. The clergy were rarely prosecuted criminally for child sexual abuse; and if they were, the penalties were often light. If complaints were made by adults, the clergy often were moved to new parishes where they continued in their pastoral role. Now, suddenly, clergypersons find themselves targets of lawsuits and criminal actions as well as of church discipline.

THE CHURCH OR RELIGIOUS BODY

Churches, religious organizations, and denominations tend to be ill-equipped to deal with complaints of this type. Sexual impropriety is a serious charge and constitutes such a danger to the church body that the tendency in the past has been to discount the reports or to cover them up. All that has been changed by the growth in the number of complaints and the willingness of some parishioners to "go public."

Baker (1984) in *Beyond Forgiveness* provided a dramatic account of how a church body faced the serious charges of sexual exploitation that were leveled at their pastor. Whether the theology cited or the eventual resolution agrees with a reader's views is immaterial; the account itself is useful because it is realistic and reveals the social and political context in which such matters may occur. He provides a graphic description of his reaction to learning that the allegations of sexual misconduct by the pastor were true:

When he finished, I replaced the phone, sat in stunned disbelief for a few moments, and then laid my head on my desk and cried. (p. 11)

The impact on the church body of such revelations is often devastating, with many "secondary victims" (Fortune, 1989, p. 45).

The church or religious body, of course, has immense power to help to heal the victim's wounds or to exacerbate the victim's pain. Some religious groups discount victims and exclude them, even to the extent of attacks by other members of the parish and innuendos in sermons. Although such behaviors are often devastating to the point of prompting the victim to denounce his or her religion, they also may backfire and result in lawsuits against the church. When children have resulted from sexual liaisons and church organizations have collaborated to hide the clergyman from a paternity suit, the issue attracts public attention. A recent Donahue (1988) television show focused on this very issue.

Rev. Fortune, in Chapter 6, calls for the development of clearer ethical codes and better complaint procedures for victims of pastoral counseling and we heartily agree. Frankly, many church bodies seem unclear about the seriousness of such charges and about their liability to deal with them. In some instances we have advised victims to take their attorney along when they meet with church officials; we know on the basis of our experience that the presence of an attorney tends to get attention. In Minnesota there is little question that the specific listing of clergy in statutes dealing with criminal and civil liability of psychotherapists is helpful.

Fortune (1989) proposes a plan of action aimed at countering the obstacles created by church myopia, a lack of realization of the power of the pastor, and the fact that churches operate like families. She advises that the following actions by the church body will lead to healing for all involved:

       1. Truth telling...
       2. Acknowledging the violation...
       3. Compassion...
       4. Protecting the vulnerable...
       5. Accountability...
       6. Restitution...
       7. Vindication...   (pp. 114-8)

The Minnesota Interfaith Committee on Sexual Exploitation by Clergy (1989) lists common responses by the family or congregation to sexual exploitation by clergy as:

•attempts to maintain normalcy at all costs
•attempts to avoid confrontation of the behavior
•efforts to maintain a good family image by not talking to outsiders about the family or congregational needs and inadequacies, including sexual exploitation
•fear of disintegration of the family or congregation
•feelings of helplessness, inadequacy, or unacceptability
•shocked disbelief, anger, and rage
•inability to deal with the conflict and anger in helpful ways
•feelings of betrayal and abandonment
•denial
•blaming the victim
•faith and spiritual crisis (p. 9)

The report also makes some useful suggestions for prevention.

To their credit, a number of churches and religious groups have begun to address this issue. A local seminary asked a psychologist to assist the screening committee in better identifying applicants with possible sexual-impulse control problems. Other seminaries are adding course material on the issue of sexual exploitation. The Archdiocese of St. Paul and Minneapolis has sponsored several well-designed conferences aimed at bishops, priests, and other church personnel on the topic of sexual abuse in its many forms. It has also publicized its policies and procedures regarding responses to situations in which pastors are accused of sexual misconduct (Roach, 1988).[3] A number of other church groups have called our center for consultation on developing resources to assist them in such cases, and some are utilizing the hiring procedures we suggest (see Ch. 37 and Appendix C).

The Minnesota State Task Force on Sexual Exploitation by Counselors and Therapists (Sanderson, 1989) gave special attention to the problem of the clergy. The group set up an interfaith task force to examine the problem of the sexual exploitation of counselees by clergy and pastoral counselors.

This discussion group, which became the Minnesota Interfaith Committee on Sexual Exploitation by Clergy, continued its work long after the Task Force had ended, releasing in 1989 its final report entitled Sexual Exploitation by Clergy: Reflections and Guidelines for Religious Leaders.[4] Beyond the recommendations concerning intervention and prevention, which are likely to affect church organizations, the continued work of this group has helped stimulate broader discussion in the local religious community. A local Episcopalian publication, for example, has published articles on sexual exploitation by clergy and on boundaries in the pastor/parishioner relationship (Moss, 1988a,b) written by a member of the Committee. During the first half of 1989 the Evangelical Lutheran Church in America sponsored a local workshop on this topic with Schoener as a presentor.

Nationally, however, the picture is dismal. The pioneering changes in Seattle, Washington, and in Minnesota (described in Rev. Fortune's work and here) are not readily visible elsewhere, although at least two protestant denominations (Evangelical Lutheran Church in America and the United Church of Christ) are developing policies and procedures. Church officials in other states sometimes telephone or write or visit Rev. Fortune or our center for assistance. Far more religious groups, however, are still trying to avoid responsibility or to deny the problem.

Consumer advocacy groups such as the Association of Psychologically Abused Patients in Ft. Worth, Texas, and Stop Abuse by Counselors (Stop ABC) in the State of Washington (see Ch. 31) continue to encounter cases of sexual misconduct by clergy where the church or denomination fails to take responsibility for the problem. Good Tidings, a self-help group which specializes in assisting women who become infatuated with or romantically involved with Roman Catholic priests has assisted many women and some priests during the past five years (see Ch. 31). The Walk-In Counseling Center continues to receive requests for assistance from both clients/parishioners and from church bodies and denominations in Minnesota and elsewhere. It is clear both locally and nationally that a great variety of religious organizations and their memberships are facing many of the same challenges as the health care delivery system and mental health professions.

---

[3] Appendix BB presents these policies and discusses the Archdiocese's approach to sexual abuse of children.
[4] Currently available at a cost of $5.00 from Chaplain John Martinson, Abbott-Northwestern Hospital, 2700 Chicago Avenue S., Minneapolis, Minnesota 55407.

CHAPTER 21

SECONDARY VICTIMS OF SEXUAL EXPLOITATION BY COUNSELORS AND THERAPISTS: SOME OBSERVATIONS

Jeanette Hofstee Milgrom

Devastating as the effects of sexual exploitation may be on the client-victim, the impact is not limited to her or him alone. Those persons close to the client (spouse, children, parents, friends, etc.) also may be, and often are, affected variously. The same holds true for the spouse, family, friends, colleagues and clients of the therapist-perpetrator and for the agency or clinic with which the therapist is associated. For purposes of this article, however, the focus is only on those secondary victims who surround the exploited client.

Virtually nothing appears in the literature regarding secondary victims of sexual exploitation. Rape and sexual assault centers recognized this problem (as it pertains to rape victims) some time ago, as is evident in the handout "Significant Other Support/Secondary Victims" (1986), used by the Sexual Violence Center in Minneapolis; it describes the feelings of significant others and suggests how to respond to the victim and to take care of oneself. This handout stresses some of the complexities of the issue. A secondary victim must assist or support the victim and take care of him/herself simultaneously by finding a balance. Similarly, the primary victim of sexual exploitation must take care of him/herself but often has other adult responsibilities (e.g., child care, job duties, financial obligations, etc.) that require simultaneous attention and energy.

The following observations regarding various secondary victims are based largely on the experience gained in working directly with various sexually exploited clients, and directly or indirectly with a number of spouses, family members, and friends of the clients.

WHEN THERE ARE NO APPARENT SECONDARY VICTIMS

The situations of greatest concern are those in which there seem to be no secondary victims. The reason may be that a client had invested her/himself totally in the relationship with the therapist to the exclusion of family members and friends over a long period of time. In some cases clients break away from a cult-like therapy situation which had alienated them from family, friends, and employers, usurped their financial resources, taught them a different language, and conditioned them to meet all their needs within the context of the group. Another instance is the case in which the former therapist was also the client's priest or minister; here, the client's religious/spiritual world usually collapses, as does the social life associated with the church.

In such situations clients may feel extremely lonely and isolated, as if they were on an island far from the rest of humanity. It is likely that these clients will be severely depressed and possibly suicidal. Consequently, cases in which there are no apparent secondary victims paradoxically tend to be the most destructive for primary victims because they also have lost their significant others and their support systems.

EFFECTS ON SPOUSES AND PARTNERS

Effects on spouses, boyfriends, or lovers vary. In some cases clients have decided not to inform partners of the sexual involvement with the therapist; they may be afraid the spouse will divorce them, that he or she may try to take legal action, or even that the spouse may physically attack the therapist. If the partner is not informed, the relationship is affected by the client's hiding a secret. The secrecy may necessitate covering up subsequent therapy sessions, payment of fees, or private meetings with the therapist. Emotional distance, confusion, and suspicion are likely to develop, and sometimes the spouse or another close relative may find out anyway. One husband stated he was glad when he finally found out about the sexual contact between the therapist and his wife; it enabled him to understand his wife's moods and behavior which had made no sense to him earlier.

When clients inform the spouse or partner, the latter may respond with a variety of reactions ranging from anger, hurt, and shame to confusion, concern, and ambivalence. Some husbands have not wanted to deal with the issue and have told their wives never to mention it again. Other members of heterosexual as well as lesbian couples have been very supportive and protective of the exploited partner. In these cases it is important to help the partner avoid an overprotective stance, which may involve discouraging the victim from taking action and thus limiting the victim's options. On the other hand, the partner may become overly involved in filing charges or taking other action, causing the victim to feel obliged to go along with it. Both partners often need help to prevent the fall-out from the exploitation by the therapist from permeating their relationship to the degree that it is the primary topic of discussion between them.

Clients frequently have made the initial contact with the therapist because of marital or relationship problems. Thus, when the therapist involves the client sexually, insult is added to injury.

Whether the breakdown of the client's primary relationship came first or it was caused in part by the client's involvement with the therapist, the client as well as the spouse/partner are under considerable stress in having to deal with two issues at once.

Spouses/partners often need and want an opportunity to share their feelings and reactions with a counselor; one or a few sessions may be necessary. In deciding which counselor to see, the partner's preference should be taken into account. If a male counselor was the perpetrator, a male partner may prefer to talk with a male counselor or, he may prefer to talk to a female counselor. A lesbian partner may prefer a lesbian counselor although in some cases, she may feel more comfortable with a straight female counselor. Another consideration is confidentiality. In the initial individual contact with the partner, the counselor should be someone other than the client's/victim's counselor. The emphasis here must be primarily on the partner's needs rather than on those of the client/victim, otherwise the two may compete for attention.

More long-term couple counseling may follow at some later date but usually it is not appropriate until each partner has had a chance to deal with the crisis and to express individual feelings and reactions.

EFFECTS ON FORMER SPOUSES

Sometimes former spouses enter the picture, for example, when a woman client has been in a long-term sexual relationship with a therapist that began prior to a divorce. The former husband may be called upon to provide certain information or data (e.g., cancelled checks for therapy fees, or dates of certain events). Former husbands often respond with more detachment than do current spouses. In a number of instances, they have been supportive of their former wives and helpful in providing information requested. The revelation of the exploitation may in fact confirm their prior suspicions.

EFFECTS ON SIBLINGS

Not infrequently sisters (and sometimes their spouses) have seen the same counselor or therapist and have become involved with him/her to various degrees. (It is common for people to refer family or friends to a particular therapist.) In the case of therapy cults, many family members and friends may be involved. The dynamics among siblings become very complex and are quite similar to those seen in cases of incest between a parent and multiple children. In this situation, it is hard to say who is the primary victim and who the secondary.

Exploited siblings sometimes may function as an impromptu mutual support group for one another and re-establish the family closeness that had been disrupted by the divisive behavior of the exploitative counselor. However, their involvements and reactions also may vary and their support needs may lead to different follow-ups.

Siblings who were not involved with the exploitative counselor are also affected. Often a sister or brother is the first to notice something has gone awry; she or he may suffer greatly from watching the effects on the victim and attempt to help her/him see the light. Later in the process the victim may reject the sibling. For example, a woman client who had been exploited by a male therapist subsequently found herself unable to tolerate men, including the brother to whom she had been very close.

EFFECTS ON PARENTS

Parents may be affected in a number of ways. In some instances, the therapist has (further) alienated the client from parents, possibly to increase the therapist's power over the client by destroying his or her support system. In other cases, parents may blame themselves for what happened; they may feel that in some way they were responsible and wonder where they went wrong. In addition to worrying about the cause of the sexual exploitation, parents often have to deal with the effects. Their adult child may be severely dysfunctional as a result, in part, of the sexual exploitation. Parents may need to drive the client/victim to subsequent therapy sessions and, sometimes, to pay for the therapy. The client may be unable to manage living independently and therefore moves back to the parent's home. The client may be so traumatized by the sexual exploitation and the system's lack of response that (s)he now expects to be treated with kid gloves by parents and others.

In these situations parents may need some assistance to clarify issues, set limits, and take care of themselves as well as care for the exploited daughter or son.

EFFECTS ON CHILDREN

Children also may suffer to a considerable extent from the effects of sexual exploitation of the parent. Even though this parent may be very committed to the children, and the care of the children is the last thing to go, there are situations in which a parent's resources are completely depleted and (s)he has little to give the children.

1. <u>Young Children</u>: Exploited clients at times are barely able to give their young children the physical care they need. Peanut butter sandwiches may be all a mother can come up with at mealtime. Severe depression may result in a mother's inability to get herself out of bed, a not uncommon symptom. It is important to ask the sexually exploited client about the care of young children and to help arrange for substitute care if necessary.

In addition to the physical care, the emotional care may be minimal. A parent who is sexually involved with a therapist may invest a lot of emotional energy in this relationship for the duration. Then when the relationship is terminated, a great deal of energy often is taken up dealing with the aftermath. Meanwhile, the children have had to live in a situation in which one or both parents were emotionally absent for a period of sometimes many years. Although some children seem to cope remarkably well, it stands to reason that others can be assumed to be adversely affected.

2. <u>Adolescents</u>: Adolescents suffer in different ways. If the sexually exploited parent does not inform the teenagers of what is going on, the family lives with a secret. The teenager may not be able to make sense of the parent's unexplained absences or mood swings. If the teenagers are told, or find out for themselves, they are faced with a number of issues. To the extent that they are in the process of defining themselves as sexual human beings they may become quite confused. Teenagers may feel embarrassed about the parent's illicit sexual contact. Many teens are extremely self-conscious and fearful of what neighbors or peers may say of domestic problems. This is enough of a reason for some exploited parents to decline filing a lawsuit, or to legally restore their maiden names prior to bringing suit.

Teenagers in this predicament may act out by running away from home and/or by getting involved with drugs. They often need some kind of help, which they may find in Alateen or other teen support groups.

When the young child or adolescent is the primary client, the adult/parent may be brought in on an adjunctive basis and subsequently be sexually exploited by the therapist. In these situations, the exploited parent wonders what the therapist did with the child, and feels guilty for having taken the child to the therapist in the first place.

3. <u>Adult Children</u>: Sexually exploited clients often share their stories, retroactively, with adult children. The effect, usually, is that these children (who now may be lawyers and doctors) stick up for the exploited parent and, in the case of a lawsuit or other action, assist the parent in a supportive and helpful manner.

EFFECTS ON FRIENDS AND ROOMMATES

Many friendships have been put to the test by the issue of sexual exploitation. Some friends or roommates just do not understand what is going on and blame the victim. However, many friends do understand and sincerely try to help the exploited friend. Like siblings, they may find out about the exploitative relationship early on. The client/friend may be secretive about the therapy sessions, or may think and talk about the "wonderful" therapist all the time. Then, when the relationship is discontinued, the exploited friend may be totally preoccupied with the aftermath. In either stage the victimized client has very little to offer friends, roommates, and housemates. The friends may feel frustrated because they are unable to make the client/friend realize that (s)he is being exploited or because (s)he seems to take forever trying to get over it. Friendships sometimes have to be resumed in the future and social and emotional needs may have to be met by others. Still, friendships that survive all this (and many do) are very valuable indeed.

EFFECTS ON MISCELLANEOUS OTHERS

The effects on the groups of people discussed so far are the most obvious but the fall-out of sexual exploitation hits many others also. Co-workers and bosses often have to deal with the exploited person's difficulties in concentrating on the job and on her or his emotional absence[1]. Fellow church group members may be puzzled by the sudden disappearance of the exploited member and may feel rejected (see Chs. 6 and 20). If a relative referred the victim to the therapist she or he may feel guilty subsequently or may minimize the negative effects. In a group for victims of rape or incest, a member may suddenly realize that she, too, was exploited by a therapist in the past. Other clients of the same therapist may hear of the allegations and feel troubled, confused, betrayed and hurt. Former clients of the therapist may feel the same. Clients whose therapy is forcibly interrupted because the therapist lost his or her license, or is otherwise ordered to discontinue practicing, may be angry and feel abandoned. And so the side effects and after effects of sexual exploitation go on and on.

INTERVENTION

Follow-up therapists should be mindful of the possible effects of sexual exploitation on the people who surround the primary client. Although these people may be able to provide valuable support to the exploited person, they may need support and assistance in turn from someone other than the primary client.

An assessment of the safety of the client, spouse, and children is the first point of order. If the client or spouse is suicidal, a referral to an emergency or crisis service should be made. If the client is unable to adequately care for the children, supportive help should be arranged by contacting a relative or a community resource such as a crisis nursery. In this process, one must strike a balance between being intrusive and ignoring the obvious. One must be sensitive to clients' and families' rights to privacy, nevertheless one must not fail to act as a resource person in responding to the complexity of issues and needs resulting from the sexual exploitation.

Referral to a support group for friends and families of persons sexually exploited by therapists is helpful if such a group can be started and maintained. Like other types of victimization (rape, incest) a group helps to lessen isolation and promotes self-esteem. Groups for families of rape victims have been initiated but seem to be less than successful in maintaining attendance. Groups for incest victims, perpetrators, and families appear to have worked out well; however, in many cases attendance may have been court ordered. Groups for friends and families of persons exploited by therapists can provide a valuable service (see Ch. 22).

Confidentiality must be guarded carefully in these situations. The follow-up therapist must be informed on the laws that mandate reporting sexual exploitation and, in turn, must inform the exploited client of them.

The client may talk to the follow-up therapist about the sexual exploitation in some detail. Usually, the client's partner or spouse knows few facts. This may be one reason for

---

[1] A recent study by Brigham (1989), discussed in Chapter 2, found significant anxiety in therapists connected with knowledge of reports of sexual misconduct by others.

referring the spouse who requests services to a different person in the same agency or, perhaps, to a different agency if one is available. Because confidentiality issues are complex, one must be mindful of all the factors, particularly since clients and their families already have been betrayed and their trust level is very low.

Victims of sexual exploitation were ignored for far too long; now, however, they are being recognized and listened to. Secondary victims, such as spouses, children, friends, and family members also need recognition and support. It is up to follow-up counselors and therapists to provide this support or referrals to other resources with the competence and concern these secondary victims deserve.

CHAPTER 22

SUPPORT GROUPS FOR SPOUSES

Ellen T. Luepker
and
Michael O'Brien

The persons victimized by therapists also include family members and spouses (see Ch. 21). The usefulness of family or couple therapy when clients are able to undergo joint counseling is discussed in Chapter 13. The present chapter focuses on examples of support services provided in Minneapolis and Milwaukee for spouses. Information about the Milwaukee group was obtained through an interview with a group member and interviews with the group therapist.

The first support group for spouses that we know about originated in Milwaukee in January 1988. Another group was formed in Minneapolis two months later. Both groups have been offered in small, private, state-licensed mental health clinics. Both group leaders have extensive group leadership experience. Both leaders observed that the groups have been extremely beneficial to participants in managing their victimization. Although there are some differences between the groups, the themes, processes, and management of the group processes have been strikingly similar. Both leaders feel that enough has been learned about the efficacy of their respective groups to draw conclusions and make recommendations.

DESCRIPTION AND COMPOSITION OF THE GROUPS

The Milwaukee men's group was planned to be on-going. It meets three times a month. The leader limited the size of the group to five persons. Membership has included seven men; two of them have participated since the group's inception. Group size has averaged four members. Sessions attended by participants range from six to continuous involvement from inception. The participants are spouses of women who either had experienced childhood incest or, during their marriages, sexual abuse by counselors or, in one case, a clinical supervisor.

The Minneapolis group, in contrast, was planned at the outset to be brief and time-limited. It included one intake interview and three group sessions within a two-month period. The group comprised only men whose wives had been sexually exploited by their counselors: two women had been exploited during the marriage; one prior to the marriage.

The Milwaukee group's men's ages have ranged from 31-55 with most from their mid-30s to mid-40s. All have been in professional or managerial positions. All but one have children and all but one have been in first marriages. The length of these marriages has ranged from 7-30 years, and the average has been 15 years.

The Minneapolis group participants were in their mid-to-late 30s. Like the Milwaukee group participants, all were in either professional or managerial positions. All had children and two were in first marriages; one in a second marriage. Length of marriages ranged from 5-12 years.

In both groups, all the men showed strong commitment to their marriages.

GROUPS' FORMATION

Two men who had met as a result of their wives' acquaintance formed the Milwaukee group. They recognized their need for information and support and interviewed professionals in their search for a group facilitator. They expressed a need for a professional facilitator to provide a "sense of safety" so they would not lose control of tumultuous feelings. Of those professionals they interviewed, some lacked interest or expertise in the role. However, the men found a clinical social worker, Charles Smithers, MSW,[1] who, they felt, would be a good facilitator and who was interested in the subject.

The Minneapolis group, in contrast, was proposed by Luepker in response to learning of husbands' despair, impatience, and isolation from their wives who were in her women's group (see Ch. 14). Luepker felt that a men's group could provide support to the husbands and reduce pressure upon the women, who needed an opportunity to explore and resolve their problems at their own pace. The women described the group as a resource, whereupon husbands promptly called Luepker's colleague, O'Brien, a clinical psychologist, for intake appointments.

GROUP PURPOSE

The purpose of both the Milwaukee and Minneapolis groups was the following: (a) to provide opportunity to clarify and ventilate feelings in a confidential atmosphere; (b) to reduce isolation; (c) to receive support from other men going through similar feelings/situations; (d) to receive and share information related to sexual abuse dynamics and victimization; (e) to receive information about and explore options for action.

GROUP THEMES

1. Isolation:

Like the women victims, all the men were experiencing extreme isolation. Several factors contributed to the feeling. They lacked information regarding the dynamics of sexual abuse and how it affected them as secondary victims. They had few, if any, persons with whom they could freely discuss their wide-ranging feelings. Few, if any, others had enough knowledge of sexual abuse to understand their complex experiences and feelings. Most, therefore, felt stranded. Their marriages were the primary, if only, forum through which they could attempt to work through their confusion and feelings.

2. Confusion and Ambiguity:

All the men felt confused regarding the dynamics of sexual abuse. They were particularly confused about the extent of their wives' role in the abuse. It was easier for the men whose wives had been sexually abused in childhood to view the abuse as the perpetrators' responsibility; but the men whose wives had been sexually exploited during the marriage by professionals were extremely confused about whether their wives had had an "affair" or whether the sexual involvement truly had been out of their control. Their confusion over whether their wives had had a choice was excruciatingly painful. As one

---

[1]Charles Smithers, MSW, clinical social worker, is co-director of Wellspring Clinical Associates, Wauwatosa, Wisconsin.

put it, "It would have been a lot easier to understand and accept if my wife had been raped; then I would know whom to blame."

The men's confusion over their wives' responsibility parallel many women victims' own confusion regarding their responsibility in the victimization (see Ch. 14).

3. Anger and Rage:

All the men felt anger; it often bordered on feelings of rage toward the perpetrators. The men whose wives had been exploited during the marriage felt the most intense anger. All had on-going, explicit fantasies of violent retributions against the perpetrators. One, for example, had fantasized hiring someone to kill the perpetrator. Only one, however, attempted to act upon his violent fantasies. This man drove his car dangerously close to the car of the exploitative therapist's wife and shouted obscenities relating to her husband's behavior toward his wife. He had intended his harassment to disrupt the therapist's family life in the way his own life had been disrupted by the therapist.

In addition to anger at the perpetrators, all felt angry at their wives for what they perceived as the women's role in becoming involved sexually. Again, the men whose wives had been sexually exploited by professionals during their marriage felt the most anger. Their anger at the women for the perceived responsibility appears to parallel many women's own self-blame for and struggles with the responsibility for what had happened (see Ch. 14).

4. Loss and Grief:

All the men described numerous kinds of losses. All, for example, had experienced some dysfunctions in the sexual relationships with their wives which they felt was related to the sexual abuse. A common type of loss for the men whose wives had been exploited by professionals during the marriage was the loss of their dreams for their marriages. The sense that "something had been spoiled" in the marriages was pervasive. All experienced loss in their wives' preoccupations in working through their own victimization which, as a result, had been disruptive to the marriage. Two women who had lived with the exploitative professional had left the men and their children alone for several months.

Many men also described painful losses in their self-esteem. Some questioned, for example, whether they had done something to create an unfavorable marriage which, in turn, had made their wives more vulnerable to becoming involved sexually with professionals. The need to grieve numerous losses, therefore, was a prominent theme in the men's groups just as it was in the women's groups (see Ch. 14).

5. Helplessness, Frustration, and Impatience:

All the men experienced considerable feelings of helplessness, frustration, and impatience. Many felt despair about the lack of response and inability of the legal or professional systems to provide substantial remedies for them and/or protection to potential victims. For example, some felt dismayed upon learning that an exploitative therapist whose license had been suspended had resumed his practice. The exploitative therapist had telephoned many of his former clients and did not seem to show understanding of or remorse for the harm he had caused his clients. In another instance, an exploitative therapist had moved to Canada to set up practice there after having been found guilty of sexual exploitation of clients in his own state. The feeling that "someone's got to stop him" was also a pervasive theme in the women's groups (see Ch. 14).

GROUP PROCESS

Like the women's groups described by Luepker (Ch. 14) the participants in both the Milwaukee and Minneapolis men's groups experienced intense, immediate cohesion. All were extremely relieved to find others who had experienced similar problems and to have the opportunity to speak freely with others in a knowledgeable, nonjudgmental atmosphere to reduce their extreme isolation and to find an outlet for their feelings.

The men in both groups used the leaders and one another to clarify the dynamics of sexual abuse to reduce their confusion and sense of ambiguity. In instances of professional abuse, they assisted one another in efforts to avoid self-blame. They helped one another to understand that their wives had been in less powerful positions and, therefore, had had diminished capacity for making decisions in their own best interest.

Expression of feelings in both groups was intense. The men talked of struggling to support their wives and to offer forgiveness, love, and patience, even while they were feeling anger and mistrust. They used the group to describe intense wishes for retribution. They offered each other understanding and support in these dilemmas.

MANAGEMENT OF GROUP PROCESS

Both leaders provided a structured, safe opportunity to obtain information and support, and to ventilate strong feelings. Both offered intake interviews to discuss needs and mutual expectations. The Milwaukee therapist required abstinence from alcohol/drugs prior to or during a group session. The Minneapolis therapist required abstinence from alcohol/drugs during the entire duration of the two-month group. Both leaders experienced the group participants as more ready/needy for opportunities to talk than participants in any other type of group they had previously led. Both leaders found their primary role was to provide information and help participants find enough time in each session to say what they needed to say.

The Milwaukee group leader found his past experience in leading groups for divorced/separated men to be helpful in dealing with the men's issues of confusion, anger, loss, and grief. The Minneapolis group leader's extensive experience with groups of male and female sexual abuse victims and sexual abuse perpetrators assisted him in helping his group participants to understand the dynamics of sexual abuse victimization.

RECOMMENDATIONS

Both group leaders concluded that group support services for spouses are a necessary component to providing help to individuals who are victimized sexually by counselors and recommend their continued availability. Such groups provide a unique opportunity not found elsewhere to reduce isolation, clarify feelings, obtain support in dilemmas, and to develop options for action. The groups acted like a "pressure cooker valve," not only for the men but, also, for their overburdened marriages.

The Minneapolis group leader recommends, however, a longer time-limited group (for example, ten to twelve sessions or an on-going group) rather than a brief, time-limited format. He recommends that whenever a time-limited group for spouses is offered, it ideally should be planned to coincide with a time-limited women's group. Both leaders recommend limiting the number of participants to a maximum of five or six, owing to the amount of time needed by each participant to say all that demands to be said.

CHAPTER 23

SEXUAL INTIMACY IN CLINICAL SUPERVISION: UNMASKING THE SILENCE[1]

Ray M. Conroe
and
Janet A. Schank

Sexual intimacy between clinical supervisor and supervisee harms supervisees both personally and professionally. It retards learning, creates self-doubt, and arouses feelings of anger, shame, and resentment. The supervisee is not an "equal partner" in supervision. Rather, she or he[2] is in a position of lesser power and, as a result, under undue pressure when a supervisor makes sexual requests, overtures, or demands.

The literature on clinical supervision treats the topic of sexual involvement inadequately. There are available some data on the frequency of supervisor and supervisee involvement and some observations on its harmful effects. The literature, however, minimizes the problem's prevalence and magnitude.

Our concern with the avoidance of discussing supervisor-supervisee sexual involvement prompts our attention to the issue. Thus, in this chapter we combine observations found in the existing literature with our personal experiences as supervisor and supervisee. We look at the ways in which sexual intimacy impedes supervision, the dynamics that may lead to such involvement, the ethical issues that are inherent in supervisor-supervisee intimacy, and the actions that may reduce the risk of sexual involvement and remedy the involvement, should it occur. Our purpose is to broaden readers' understanding of the problems associated with supervisor-supervisee sexual intimacy and to stimulate others to think about and write on the issue.

Before proceeding we must define what we mean by <u>clinical supervision</u> and <u>sexual intimacy/involvement</u>. <u>Clinical supervision</u> is used here to signify the instruction, direction, and feedback provided to a supervisee as part of an organized learning experience. The supervisor is the professional designated to oversee the supervisee's work. The supervisee may use the clinical experience to fulfill degree or certificate-granting requirements in a college, university, professional school, or clinical institution (e.g., a psychoanalytic institute or family therapy training center).

Our definition does not specifically include two common forms of clinical supervision: administrative and consultative.

The first, administrative supervision, encompasses the supervision of a professional's clinical work, whether voluntary or required. Here the power relationship between

---

[1] An earlier version of this chapter, "Sexual Harassment in Clinical Supervision of Students: An Overview and Suggested Guidelines," was prepared in March 1986 for the Task Force on Sexual Exploitation by Counselors and Therapists, Minnesota Department of Corrections. We would like to thank the following people for their contributions to the paper or for their feedback prior to this revision: Annette Brodsky, Maria Brown, Valerie DeMarinis, Raina Eberle, Dorothy Loeffler, Jeanette Hofstee Milgrom, Patricia Mullen, Barbara Sanderson, Gary Schoener, and William L. White.

[2] Given the preponderance of male supervisor and female supervisees, the order of personal pronouns for supervisors is <u>he or she</u> and <u>him or her</u> and for supervisees, <u>she or he</u> and <u>her or him</u>.

supervisor and supervisee varies greatly. In some instances, the supervisor has considerable administrative and clinical authority over the supervisee. Much of what is discussed in this chapter is applicable to such situations. In other instances, however, the supervisor and supervisee interact primarily as co-workers. Edelwich and Brodsky (1982) and White (1986) address the sexual dilemmas arising in colleague-to-colleague relationships in considerable detail.

The second form of supervision that is not discussed directly is consultative supervision. Here "supervision" is arranged with someone outside the agency who consults on difficult cases or clinical issues but does not actually oversee a consultee's work. Again, the power differential between supervisor and supervisee varies with the situation. (See Ch. 4 in which the topic is explored in depth.)

The terms sexual intimacy and sexual involvement are used interchangeably. They refer to any overt actions or indirect gestures of a sexual nature communicated either verbally or physically by a supervisor to a supervisee, or vice versa. Such gestures and actions are inappropriate in and of themselves because they violate those supervisor-supervisee boundaries that facilitate learning. They do not require proof of concrete harm, such as receiving an unfavorable evaluation because of refusing a supervisor's sexual advances, to be considered detrimental.

Our definition of sexual intimacy/sexual involvement does not encompass all boundary violations that may occur between supervisor and supervisee. For instance, a supervisor's tapping a supervisee's shoulder during their first meeting may be intrusive even if no sexual intent is involved. Judging from the work on therapists' sexual exploitation of clients, however, it is apparent that sexual involvement between persons in positions of unequal power renders greater harm than other boundary violations. Thus, the topic warrants special attention.

SUPERVISION AND CLINICAL LEARNING

Until recently mental health professionals largely took clinical supervision for granted. They spent considerable time doing it, and they acknowledged its importance, yet they devoted little time to writing and thinking about it (Hess, 1987).

But the situation changed drastically over the last 10 years. A host of publications have appeared on the topic (e.g., see *The Counseling Psychologist,* Vol. 10, no. 1, 1982 & Vol. 11, no. 1, 1983; and *Professional Psychology: Research and Practice,* Vol. 18, no. 3, 1987) and conferences, workshops, and presentations on supervision have become commonplace. In addition, a journal entitled *The Clinical Supervisor* has appeared.

What these publications and presentations tend to show is that supervising is a systematic endeavor. Certain supervisor qualities, such as accessibility, supportiveness, teaching skill, and ability to provide constructive feedback have been found to contribute to good as opposed to poor supervision (Allen, Szollos, & Williams, 1986, Carifio & Hess, 1987). The pivotal nature of the supervisor-supervisee relationship in promoting supervisee learning and development has been recognized (Hess, 1987). For example, proponents of a developmental model of clinical training (e.g., Skovholt & Ronnestad, 1986; Stoltenberg, 1981) examined the interaction between supervisor and supervisee which occurs as the trainee moves from dependency and imitation to autonomy and self-direction. Numerous observers (see review by Worthington, 1987) have posited specific supervisory behavior that is consistent at each supervisee level of development, with a progression toward less structure and greater reciprocity.

Advocates of a process-oriented view of supervision (e.g., Doehrmann, 1976; Ekstein & Wallerstein, 1972; Mueller & Kell, 1972) have focused on the dynamics of the supervisory relationship and its effect on the supervisee's work with clients. These investigators, through their examination of parallel process, have shown the effects of the interplay between supervisor and supervisee on the interactions of supervisee and client. Doehrmann aptly observed that the supervisor-supervisee relationship is more than a simple adjunct to treatment. It has a direct, major, though somewhat intangible, bearing upon the supervisee-client relationship and upon the entire treatment process. Thus, two different supervisors can impart the same set of skills to a supervisee, yet one supervisor may have a harmful effect and the other a salutary one, depending upon the nature of the relationship and upon the adequacy of boundary formed. Boundaries should be firm enough to allow the supervisor to set appropriate limits and to provide necessary feedback but open enough to allow the supervisee to explore even the most sensitive personal issues as they arise in counseling and supervision.

SEXUAL INTIMACY IN SUPERVISION: AN OVERVIEW

Prevalence

Mary was one of four students accepted in a one-year graduate internship program at a highly regarded mental health clinic. Jim, her supervisor, was well-known in the community for innovative, high-quality work. Mary was eager to be supervised by him. She looked forward to the weekly group supervision sessions Jim had with the interns. As supervision progressed, Mary enjoyed being praised by him and feeling somehow "special." She began staying after the supervision sessions, at Jim's request, to discuss her cases further. Mary felt vaguely uncomfortable at times when the conversation became increasingly personal. At the same time, she was pleased that she was developing a more collegial relationship with a man she had respected for so long. She sometimes wondered if their relationship should be so "friendly"; but she decided it must be all right because her "highly regarded" supervisor was the one encouraging the familiarity.

Jim began calling Mary at home to talk about matters only tangentially related to work. One night, when they were alone after supervision, he put his arms around her and kissed her. When Mary resisted Jim's advances, he angrily accused her of having encouraged his interest and "leading him on." He told Mary that, if she did not want "more of a relationship" she would have to find a new supervisor.

This hypothetical case illustrates how a highly regarded supervisor violated the boundaries of his relationship with a supervisee who wanted very much to work with him, and how the boundary violation resulted in the ultimate deterioration of the supervisory relationship. The literature suggests that this kind of interaction happens all too frequently. In separate studies conducted with members of the American Psychological Association's (APA) Division of Psychotherapy and Division of Clinical Psychology, investigators found that supervisors became sexually involved with supervisees. In a study by Pope, Levenson, and Schover (1979) 17% of the female respondents acknowledged overt sexual contact with educators who were clinical supervisors. In an investigation by Glaser and Thorpe (1986) 31% of the respondents reported receiving clear sexual advances from educators, of whom 26% were clinical supervisors.

The preceding case also exemplifies the fact that sexual intimacy in supervision usually involves a male supervisor and female supervisee. The reverse may also occur (Pope et al.,

1979; Rozsnafszky, 1979), although at a lower rate of incidence. Pope et al. (1979), for example, found that only 3% of male trainees reported contact with clinical supervisors as opposed to 17% of female trainees. Similarly, same-sex involvements are possible although they too are less likely (Brodsky, 1986). From an ethical standpoint what is critical is not the gender of participants but, rather, the power differential between them because of their respective roles. That differential in and of itself creates the potential for sexual exploitation (Glaser & Thorpe, 1986; Pope et al., 1979).

IMPACT OF SEXUAL BOUNDARY VIOLATIONS ON THE SUPERVISORY RELATIONSHIP

Sexual involvement between supervisor and supervisee constitutes a violation of the letter and intent of existing ethical principles and legal standards. For instance, a psychologist/supervisor who engages in or makes overtures for such involvement risks violating the American Psychological Association's (APA) *Ethical Principles of Psychologists* (1981). They prohibit a psychologist/supervisor from exploiting professional relationships with supervisees "sexually or otherwise" and from condoning or engaging in sexual harassment (Principle 7d), and they warn practitioners to avoid dual relationships that may impair professional judgment or increase the risks of exploitation (Principle 6a). "The Code of Ethical Principles for Marriage and Family Therapists" (1985) of the American Association for Marriage and Family Therapy (AAMFT) stated in part (in Principle 4.1): "sexual harassment or exploitation of students, employees, or supervisees is prohibited." The Code was recently revised, and effective Aug. 1, 1988, Section 4.1 carries the following prohibition: "Sexual intimacy with students or supervisees is prohibited." Marriage and family therapists also are cautioned to "make every effort to avoid dual relationships" with students, employees, and supervisees, including "close personal relationships" (AAMFT, 1988).

A supervisor also may face sexual harassment proceedings under Federal and state civil rights laws, institutional codes, or civil litigation under common law relating to malpractice or other types of negligence (Cnudde & Nesvold, 1985; Dziech & Weiner, 1984; Pope, Schover, & Levenson, 1980). In addition, the supervisor can be considered negligent and held legally liable if a supervisee is sued by a client for unethical conduct of any type, including sexual involvement. Such liability exists even if the alleged violation was never reported directly to the supervisor (Slovenko, 1980).

Supervisee/student perceptions of the harm and ethical dilemmas involved in sexual intimacy with a supervisor are highlighted by Pope et al. (1979) and by Glaser & Thorpe (1986). Of the respondents in the Pope et al. study, 77% hypothesized that such involvements are not beneficial. In Glaser & Thorpe's work, 95% of their sample judged sexual contact to be coercive, unethical, and significantly harmful to a working relationship. Among respondents who had actually engaged in intimacy, Glaser & Thorpe found increased concern over time with the coerciveness of the involvements and the damage to the working relationship. Finally, they noted "very negative reactions" to the supervisees who had declined unwanted sexual advances which took the form of indirect and direct punitive damage.

Glaser & Thorpe (1986) cautioned readers against drawing premature conclusions from their complex data. However, they question the consenting nature of supervisee-supervisor sexual involvement, seeing it as "[varying] in character from the naive and gonadal to the informed and cortical" (Glaser & Thorpe, 1986, p. 49). They perceived the experience of many of their respondents as constituting "grossly unethical and harmful exploitation" (Glaser & Thorpe, 1986, p. 49).

Peterson (1984) and Schank and Johnston (1986) expressed similar sentiments regarding the exploitative nature of supervisor-supervisee sexual involvement. Both voiced grave concern with the danger that the supervisee's learning needs would become secondary and subservient to the supervisor's personal needs in the relationship, and they questioned whether the supervisee's involvement in such a relationship can be truly considered consensual.

Sexual intimacy severely compromises the supervisor-supervisee relationship. From a developmental perspective, it retards the supervisee's ability to individuate and to acquire those skills that are necessary to become an autonomous professional. The supervisor no longer is an appropriate role model because he or she, in essence, sanctions the violation of boundaries with persons in positions of lesser power to meet personal needs—whether those individuals be supervisees, subordinate staff, or clients (Pope et al., 1979). In addition, the supervisor places the supervisee in a "double-bind" by outwardly promoting autonomy but inwardly fostering dependency. Given such circumstances, it would not be surprising if the supervisee were tentative in seeking professional and personal independence.

From a process prospective, sexual intimacy, of both an overt and covert nature, greatly restricts discussions during supervision. Brodsky (1980) cited an example of a female supervisee who, fearing her supervisor's sexual advances, could not freely discuss pertinent information regarding a particular client's sexuality; she was afraid the discussion of the client's sexuality might lead to a parallel discussion of her sexuality. Thus her ability to explore how transference might be affecting the client was greatly diminished.

A supervisee also faces significant personal losses as a result of sexual involvement with the supervisor. Glaser & Thorpe (1986) reported that many of their respondents who, as students, declined sexual overtures faced punitive damages from educators, and that a few even considered leaving graduate studies because of the situations.

The profession needs to acknowledge and address the reality of a population of women (and, to a lesser extent, men) of unknown numbers who, after gaining keenly competitive admission to doctoral studies in psychology, take leave of that effort and goal not through lack of ability or diligence but through disgust, dissuasion, and disuse. The numbers need not be large for that to be an appalling and shameful situation. (Glaser & Thorpe, 1986, p. 50)

Even if such dire consequences do not occur, a supervisor still loses objectivity in evaluating a supervisee's work. Under the best of circumstances, the supervisor must rely on subjective, ambiguous measures of highly complex, personal behaviors to assess a supervisee's clinical performance (Doehrman, 1976). When physical attraction and acceptance or refusal of sexual overtures become additional criteria, evaluation is even more subjective and potentially harmful.

The professional community largely has denied the potential damage of sexual contact between supervisor and supervisee. The latter has been viewed as a mature, psychologically stable individual who enters a relationship based on free accord (Brodsky, 1980). Some people have argued that, given the lack of an adequate definition of good supervision, one cannot definitely state that sexual contact would be harmful. In addition the community has maintained a "conspiracy of silence" that allows the practice to continue unnoticed.

We believe that the professional community must end the conspiracy and must place squarely on the supervisor the responsibility for maintaining appropriate boundaries and monitoring both his or her behavior and that of the supervisee. Sexual involvement in supervisory relationships must be viewed as forbidden, regardless of who initiates it! The supervisor must be willing to acknowledge his or her feelings of attraction for a supervisee and to seek appropriate consultation when those feelings become problematic. He or she needs "to establish with clarity and maintain with consistency, unambiguous ethical and professional standards regarding appropriate and inappropriate handling of those feelings" (Pope, Keith-Spiegel, & Tabachnick, 1986, p. 157).

The same can be said of overtures by supervisees for whatever reason they occur. The supervisor is ultimately responsible for responding in a manner that puts such advances into proper perspective. That perspective should allow dealing with the supervisee's overtures as part of supervision. However, more drastic measures, such as transferring the supervisee to another supervisor or terminating the internship, may be required.

Whatever the outcome, the fact-finding process must be fair and discussion with the supervisee must be open and humane. Emphasis should be placed on doing that which is helpful for the supervisee, such as helping to arrange for personal counseling, in addition to that which is necessary programmatically. Decisions on what to discuss, how to discuss it, and what action to take should be made only after consultation with superiors, colleagues, and appropriate faculty from the supervisee's educational institution.

CONTRIBUTING FACTORS

The most productive approach to examining contributory factors is through the application of a multideterminant model to the supervisor-supervisee relationship. In this model, the boundary violation that occurs when the supervisor and supervisee become involved sexually may be related to a number of personal factors, stressors, and situational variables; and any given factor may play a greater or lesser role depending on the situation. If either or both persons, whether in or out of the context of the professional relationship, face demands that they find overwhelming, their reaction may be to seek intimacy during supervision and thus decrease their respective ability to complete tasks germane to that relationship (Brodsky, 1986; Edelwich & Brodsky, 1982; Maslach, 1986; White, 1986).

Personal Factors

When looking at the factors that lead a supervisor and supervisee to become sexually involved one must consider the stress produced in their respective personal lives and in the clinical environment in which they interact (Maslach, 1986). Brodsky (1986), in her discussion of psychologists who are sexually exploitative, specifically looked at characteristics that put psychologists and the people they see professionally at risk for sexual intimacy. Her observations, as well as those of other investigators, offer useful information on how naiveté, situational vulnerability, and characterological impairments heighten both supervisor and supervisee's risk for sexual involvement.

NAIVETE. Several researchers, in both direct reference to supervision (Pope et al., 1980) and by implication (Brodsky, 1986) question the supervisor and supervisee's judgment in becoming involved with each other on the basis of romantic or passionate love. They see one or both such individuals as naive and unsophisticated and as unsure of the degree to which their respective roles in supervision fosters their romantic attachment. The supervisor may be young, inexperienced, and unaware of the actual influence he or she has on the supervisee. The latter may share a similar naiveté because of a lack of personal experience or of exposure to professional settings.

The supervisor and supervisee may terminate their working relationship and become lovers or spouses. If that relationship proves satisfactory, they may not see as problematic the development of their attachment during supervision. However, it is when the relationship deteriorates that the former supervisee may recognize the degree to which the former supervisor took advantage of her or his personal needs as they were projected in supervision (Brodsky, 1986).

SITUATIONAL VULNERABILITY. In a sexual liaison based on situational vulnerability, a supervisor or supervisee experiences a momentary lapse in judgment that leads him or her to seek companionship from the other (Schoener, 1986a). Oftentimes, trouble coping with an "unusual" stressor, such as a failing marriage, the death of a loved one, or a general feeling of despondency, may cause one to feel especially lonely or needy. He or she then may turn to the person who seems the most understanding or comforting, regardless of whether the person is appropriate, given the nature of their prior relationship (Glaser & Thorpe, 1986; Schoener, 1986).

If both parties are relatively well functioning and stable, they likely will remain involved for a relatively brief, isolated period. Someone—perhaps the initiator—will realize that the behavior is inappropriate, will express regret, and gently will seek to terminate the relationship (Schoener, 1986a). However, situational vulnerability may be the basis for on-going exploitation if the person from whom comfort or attention is sought is manipulative by nature in such situations to meet his or her own ends.

CHARACTEROLOGICAL IMPAIRMENT. The two distinguishing features of characterological impairment are (a) the relation to long-standing difficulties and unresolved conflicts; and (b) the repetitive, indiscriminate forming of sexual contacts (Brodsky, 1986; Rozsnafsky, 1979; Schoener, 1986). Such liaisons reflect a typical pattern of behavior as opposed to a one-time indiscretion. Involvement in a series of relationships is common. Conscious or unconscious manipulation of relationships to meet personal needs, such as power, prestige, status, or tangible reward, is prominent. Attempts by the other person to terminate the involvement may be met by intimidation and/or dependent, demanding entreaties.

The most common form of characterological impairment seems to be the narcissistic personality disorder. Supervisors who exhibit this pattern have been given a variety of labels: "charismatic" (Brodsky, 1986), "Super Guru" (Rozsnafsky, 1979), and cult leader or "High Priest/Priestess" (Temerlin & Temerlin, 1982; White, 1986). All demonstrate a self-centered exploitation of others with little remorse or guilt (Schoener, 1986a).

Jim, our hypothetical supervisor, fits this category. He has developed a rather grandiose style. He exercises considerable latitude in supervision and allows for little if any questioning about what is or is not appropriate. He seeks people, who for one reason or another, are especially vulnerable because they are likely to feel "honored" to be one of his supervisees, given his reputation for providing nurturance and sense of importance. He thereby establishes a climate in which the transition from a professional to a personal/sexual relationship is relatively easy (Brodsky, 1986; Temerlin & Temerlin, 1982). Should the person with whom Jim becomes involved muster sufficient strength to terminate the relationship or should that individual finish the internship and move, she or he will be replaced almost immediately.

Several investigators describe the supervisee equivalent of Jim. That individual looks at supervision as a "business exchange" (Pope et al., 1980). She or he may trade sexual "favors" for tangible "assets": e.g., a glowing letter of recommendation for a prestigious job. She or he also may see sexual involvement as a form of conquest of a highly regarded individual and even as a means of bringing about the supervisor's downfall.

A supervisor who allows himself or herself to be coerced sexually indeed does risk loss of prestige, respect, and maybe, even, job. Questions also can be raised about his or her competency as a supervisor, given the failure to set proper limits and to assess the situation adequately (Brodsky, 1986). (The matter of supervisor responsibility when facing supervisee sexual advances is discussed in ensuing sections.)

Three other forms of characterological impairment are worth noting, although admittedly, they are not as prominent as the one just described (Schoener, 1986a). In some instances the supervisor or supervisee, because of long-standing emotional difficulties, makes work the focus of his or her life and either knowingly or unknowingly mixes personal needs with professional involvements. The pattern established is similar to a topic discussed in the section on environmental stressors. However, here, the person rather than the environment is isolated so he or she demonstrates similar behavior, regardless of setting.

The second major form of characterological impairment is represented by the supervisor or supervisee who forms liaisons as a manifestation of compulsive sexual behavior (Schoener, 1986a). The behavior is indiscriminate, in that it may be directed at anyone of a given gender regardless of position, and is intractable in that it is not easily controlled by the individual.

Another form of sexual involvement is impulsive, unpredictable, and self-damaging; it also is a manifestation of poor social judgment or a disturbed thought process (Schoener, 1986a). Individuals displaying such behavior usually are assessed as having a borderline personality disorder, paranoid grandiosity, or a thought disorder. This form occurs only rarely but it is noteworthy because of the significant damage that may be inflicted on someone who becomes involved with such a person.

Environmental Factors

How does a given work environment affect the probability of supervisor-supervisee sexual involvement? To answer the question we begin by describing the characteristics of a setting in which such involvement is likely to take place and then proceed to trace the likely evolution of that setting. Our brief overview is drawn especially from White's (1986) systems approach to professional burnout in which burnout is seen as "a breakdown or disruption in the reciprocal relationship between the individual and the organization—a relationship that affects and is in turn affected by broader systems outside the organization" (White, 1986, p. 26).

We acknowledge in this discussion that people assume roles in given settings based upon personal disposition. Thus the charismatic leader seeks a position in which he or she can exercise unquestioned authority with little outside accountability. On the other hand roles evolve over time based on the organization's collective needs and its unique dynamics (White, 1986). Therefore, it is important to hold personal characteristics of the supervisor and supervisee constant while we look at environmental factors.

In his description of the "enmeshed organizational family," White (1986) listed specific features of a setting in which the risk of supervisor-supervisee sexual intimacy is great. Dziech and Weiner (1984) in their analysis of academic institutions and Temerlin & Temerlin (1982) in their portrayal of psychotherapy cults offered additional insights into the attributes of such a milieu. The characteristics are as follows:

1. Low boundary permeability between the agency and the outside professional and social world, creating an "us versus them" mentality.

2. Diffused authority and unclear goals combined with rigid organizational control.

3. Excessive demands for time and emotional commitment to the agency combined with an emphasis on loyalty, rather than performance.

4. Extreme levels of group cohesion and mutual dependence creating an atmosphere in which professional and personal needs become enmeshed.

5. Formation of "insider-outsider" cliques with accompanying divisiveness, discord, and lack of trust.

White (1986) believed that burnout results from the progressive closure of the organizational system, starting with professional closure, proceeding to social closure, and ending with sexual closure. Professional closure frequently begins when an agency cuts ties to the outside community during a period of initial organization, reorganization, or internal conflict. The organization becomes "an overprotective parent" sheltering its members from a threatening, hostile world.

Remember Jim, our hypothetical supervisor who suffers from a characterological disorder? It is quite possible that his clinic went through the progressive closure process. Thus, Jim in his leadership role, became a "protector." In addition, through his agency's turning inward, Jim was able to maintain his previously earned reputation as a supervisor with no further accountability to outside sources, such as university faculty members or students.

During social closure, members begin meeting more of their social needs within the organization system, with a progressive deterioration in the boundary between personal and work life. The ability of the agency to accomplish tasks necessary for its survival declines as well. Thus one would not be surprised to see Jim enticing Mary, our hypothetical intern, into believing that she is someone "special" and into entering more of a collegial relationship, which extends beyond the agency. The supervision of Mary suffers as a result.

In the final phase, that of sexual closure, sexual contact starts between group members. Those liaisons generally do not stem from feelings of physical attractiveness but, rather, from other needs, such as power, physical nurturing, money and position, or co-conspiracy. Group dynamics are altered in the process and increase the probability of disruptive interpersonal relationships, staff extrusion, and personnel turnover. Marriage and other intimate relationships likely dissolve. The agency's mission becomes severely damaged by the formation of staff cliques and the spreading of rumors and gossip.

Thus Mary faces the risk of being manipulated by Jim if she responds to his overtures. Any outside relationship she has will be jeopardized as she becomes more enmeshed in the agency. The nature of supervision with Jim is likely to change radically, with little attention paid to the significant issues Mary may be encountering in her work with clients. Finishing her internship and leaving the agency may become difficult because of the strong ties Jim has formed with her. Should Mary refuse Jim's overtures, she risks ostracism and premature termination of her internship.

PREVENTIVE AND REMEDIAL STEPS

What can be done to prevent supervisor-supervisee sexual intimacy and to remedy such involvement should it occur? The literature on the topic is fragmentary and incomplete. No one source gives a comprehensive overview.

To rectify this inadequacy we present material we have collected and then we offer our insights on four specific issues: (a) codes of professional practice, (b) grievance procedures, (c) education and training programs, and (d) boundary maintenance in supervision. On the basis of this discussion steps can be taken to deal with the problem by the supervisor, the supervisee, professional organizations, service agencies, and educational institutions. Each has a unique responsibility for preventing its occurrence.

Codes of Professional Practice

White (1986) offered a sound rationale for establishing a code of professional practice. He viewed such a code as a mechanism to establish behavioral boundaries within which adherents are expected to operate and to which they can be held accountable. By opening standards of conduct to public scrutiny, the code legitimizes and mandates professional boundary transactions and reduces institutional isolation and elitism.

White's (1986) observations apply to standards promulgated by professional organizations, clinical training sites, and educational institutions alike. The existing standards established by organizations of professionals who provide psychotherapy explicitly prohibit therapist-client sexual involvement but ignore (except for the AAMFT Code) or are less clear about supervisor-supervisee sex.

The codes of the American Medical Association, American Psychiatric Association, and National Association for Social Work do not address the issue. The code of the American Psychological Association (1981) explicitly prohibits sexual exploitation and sexual harassment of students and trainees. It also cautions psychologists to avoid "dual relationships"; one can assume they would include being both the lover and supervisor of a trainee. Although sexual harassment has a commonly accepted definition (and is specifically defined in Principle 7d of the APA code), sexual exploitation is defined in neither code. Furthermore the *Casebook on Ethical Principles of Psychologists* (APA, 1987) offers no examples of sexual exploitation. The code is unnecessarily vague in this area. Only the AAMFT code, as revised in 1988, explicitly prohibits sex with supervisees and students.

Like Glaser and Thorpe (1986), we advocate an explicit statement prohibiting educator/student and supervisor/supervisee sexual and romantic relationships, and a clear statement on the responsibility of educators or supervisors to remove themselves from positions of responsibility if a sexual relationship is contemplated. It is important that the code take note of the dangers of exploitation in such a situation.

The available literature (Cnudde & Nesvold, 1985; Dziech & Weiner, 1984) documents a growing recognition among colleges and universities of the need for a sexual code of conduct. We are not aware of comparable documentation regarding clinical training sites, although we know that the Veterans Administration has a Policy Statement on and Definition of Sexual Harassment.

Every educational institution and training agency should develop a code of sexual conduct that elucidates its commitment to protecting the welfare of employees and consumers, as well as students at supervision sites. Evidence suggests that the existence of written codes does indeed induce compliance and deters potential violations (Dziech & Weiner, 1984). No student should be placed in a site that does not have a code. Indeed, written policies and procedures regarding sexual conduct should be required of any agency seeking accreditation from a professional organization or other regulating body. Both the educational institution and the clinical facility should be aware of each other's guidelines and, to the extent possible, should act cooperatively in handling inquiries, complaints, and grievances.

We propose some guidelines for the development of a code of sexual conduct and for its dissemination. These suggestions may be useful both to agencies and institutions that are thinking of developing a code and to those who want to revise existing statements. We are especially indebted to Schank and Johnston (1986) and Dziech and Weiner (1984) for their ideas on the topic.

Our recommendations are as follows:

1. The code contains an explicit statement of both policies and procedures. The statement of policy reflects what is being regulated: sexual involvement between supervisor and supervisee. A statement of policy not only should prohibit sexual harassment, as defined by existing federal and state statutes but, also, should strongly discourage even seemingly consenting relationships, recognizing the potential for exploitation that exists in the power differential between supervisor and supervisee. The statement of procedure outlines how inquiries and complaints are to be handled. It should be comprehensive so that someone considering a grievance will know precisely what to do, where to go, and whom to see. The statement should outline the grievance process from inquiry about the process and filing of a complaint, through hearing, and any appeal. It also should list possible sanctions when someone is found to be in violation of the code. Both informal and formal means of resolution should be emphasized because most often a complainant seeks the cessation of the disruptive behavior and protection against retaliation, rather than punishment of the offender.

2. The code should be developed, discussed, and approved by the institutional body as a whole—whether that be faculty members, administrative staff, clinical personnel, and students themselves. The standard should be adopted only after a reasonable degree of consensus has been obtained. The evaluation of policy and procedures should be on-going; updating and reformulation should take place as necessary.

3. The standards should be published in both an agency/institution handbook and a student field manual. It should be readily accessible to anyone. The code should be reviewed in depth with new employees and students during orientation and should be re-disseminated and re-discussed periodically. Larger settings should consider publishing a list of the number of cases handled and of their resolutions to make people aware that action is being taken, even if names and details cannot be disclosed.

Grievance Procedures

To direct attention to the process undertaken by a student who fears being or may have been sexually exploited by a supervisor, let us begin by looking at Mary, our hypothetical supervisee, and how she responded to Jim's sexual advances.

Mary talked to another intern at the clinic about her problems. She was surprised and confused by that person's reaction. Rather than being supportive, the other intern was distant and uninvolved. She told Mary that the issue was between Mary and Jim and that she did not want to discuss it any further.

During her weekly on-campus supervision group, Mary tried talking about her difficulties. The other students listened but offered no support. They challenged Mary to look at her role in fostering Jim's sexual advances. They maintained that, since Mary was recently separated and attractive, she must have encouraged Jim's attention. The group's faculty supervisor did not enter into the discussion at all. Mary later discovered that he had been censured for having been sexually involved with a female graduate student a few years earlier. Very discouraged and questioning her own perceptions and judgment, Mary decided to let the matter lapse. She subsequently received an "Incomplete" for her internship, based on Jim's vague assessment of her as not being able to "induce sufficient growth" in clients. Mary became discouraged to the point of considering leaving graduate school.

This scenario demonstrates the pressure and dilemmas that a supervisee who wants to take action may encounter. Not only did Mary have to face her own feelings of shame and guilt, but, also, the resistance from her peers and faculty members who, for their own reasons, feared upsetting the status quo. Mary was left isolated and confused. The external repercussions for her were heavy in that she received an "Incomplete"; the internal repercussions were equally as pronounced in that she was left feeling she had gotten what she deserved. She had no opportunity to work through her feelings.

The reactions of supervisees like Mary to sexual overtures is documented in that portion of Schank and Johnston's (1986) study dealing with graduate students in social work who reported having been sexually harassed during their field placements. Schank and Johnston found that 78% said they discussed the matter with family and/or friends, and 33% also acknowledged that they talked with other field agency staff members and students. Surprisingly, 67% of affected respondents said they confronted the harasser about the incident(s). Yet no one talked to a faculty field coordinator or to any other university-based person, and no one left or changed field placement because of the incident. Only 10% were aware of existing procedures for sexual harassment complaints at the agency, university, or National Association of Social Workers. The common reasons given for not disclosing the incident to faculty members were the fear of jeopardizing their placements and/or receiving a bad grade, possible repercussions, and personal embarrassment.

The pattern exhibited is similar to that illustrated by Mary. She was willing to make some initial attempts to explore the matter with others but, because of her lack of knowledge or feelings of fear, embarrassment, and discouragement, she decided against further action. Some additional deterrents for supervisees may be the relatively brief period of the clinical placement and the geographic isolation associated with a "captive" field setting away from the university. One may just want to "live through" the experience because it will last no more than six months to a year or to "make the best" of the situation because the physical, emotional, and monetary expense involved in staying in contact with the home institution may seem prohibitive. We respect people's concerns but we also caution them to examine the emotional residue if they do not bring the matter to closure.

Mary was sitting in the department lunch room one day when she was joined by Janice, a student in her program. Janice told of hearing what had happened to Mary in the supervision group and of feeling angry and concerned. She spoke of some summer work she had done at the university's equal opportunity office and suggested that Mary talk to someone there. Sensing Mary's resistance, given her prior experiences, Janice offered to go with her. After lengthy discussion, Mary agreed. Almost instantly, she began feeling relieved of the burden she had been carrying inside. Tears and feelings of rage toward those who had neglected and abused her followed.

In the rest of this section we present some suggested guidelines for filing and hearing complaints and for imposing sanctions. Again, we draw upon Dziech and Weiner (1984) and Schank and Johnston (1986). In addition we incorporate material provided by P. Mullen (personal communication, August 13, 1987) of the Office of the Director of Equal Opportunity and Affirmative Action and by D. Dale Jones (personal communication, August 13, 1987) of the Minnesota Women's Center (both at the University of Minnesota) and by Schoener and Milgrom (Milgrom, 1986; Schoener & Milgrom, 1984) based on their work of processing therapist sexual misconduct complaints. Our proposals are as follows:

1. Complaints by students/supervisees must be taken seriously. Alleged offenders obviously are considered innocent until proven guilty. However, equal regard and respect must be given to the claimant and to the trauma she or he may have experienced in the reported incidents and in the current process of making a complaint. Students must be reassured that they will not be penalized for taking action.

2. Ideally an academic department should have a complaint processing mechanism (e.g., an internal ethics or professional standards review committee) that is easily accessible to students/supervisees. This committee should be separate from the department hierarchy, having its own operational guidelines. It must be flexible enough to be a "safe sounding board" for students who wish support, counsel, and advice without necessarily filing a formal complaint; yet it must have sufficient authority to investigate grievances and recommend appropriate action.

3. In the absence of a departmental procedure, the most appropriate body for students/supervisees to take their concerns to is their college or university's equal opportunity office. In the case of programs for which even this does not exist, complaints may go to a comparable state or local agency. Complainants hopefully will be in direct contact with individuals with some expertise in sexual exploitation claims and with direct responsibility for implementing the educational institution's policies and procedures. We believe that these resources should be used in instances where the training site is or is not campus-based.

Admittedly, the role of the departmental committee or the equal opportunity office in either case is different. They can recommend direct sanctions against offenders in campus-based sites but they have far less authority at off-campus facilities, except where the alleged offender either has a regular or adjunct faculty appointment. In those cases, sanctions such as a reprimand, termination of appointment for cause, or criminal investigation can be recommended, even if the individual receives no salary. When the alleged offender has no university affiliation, the departmental committee or equal opportunity office can serve as a support and/or advocate; the exact nature of the assistance provided depends on what the particular agency policies and procedures allow, should the student decide to take action through the training facility. It can also work with the student's department to decertify the agency as a clinical placement to insure that the student is not penalized academically or financially because of the experience, and to arrange a suitable alternative placement.

4. When working with a student/supervisee, the representative from the departmental committee or equal opportunity office should follow a systematic procedure: inform the student what the screening procedure involves and, if necessary, supply the student with a copy of the sexual conduct code. The committee member or officer should then invite the student for an initial interview. To prepare for it the student should be asked to assemble information on dates, nature, any witnesses, and perceived consequences of the alleged incidents. The initial interview assessment should focus on what brought the student to seek assistance at this time, how the student defines the problem, and what the student is requesting of the interviewer. A careful assessment also must be made of the student's level of functioning in regard to whether any significant vulnerability is present, what types of support the student may require, and what kinds of interventions the student may be able to handle during the complaint process. The interviewer should then work with the student to explore the options available, ranging from doing nothing to arranging for a processing session to filing a civil suit for damages or a criminal complaint. If more formal action seems warranted, the interviewer should institute the mechanisms specified within the policies and procedures as quickly as possible. On-going attention should be given to how the student reacts to the stress involved, and referrals should be made to counseling and support services, when deemed necessary for that individual's health and well-being.

5. The fact that the educational institution has a mechanism for handling complaints of improper sexual contact in no way exempts the training facility from having one also. Indeed, whether or not mandated by law, every clinical agency should have policies and procedures in place. A given training facility should act with due speed if a student/supervisee wishes to file a complaint under its auspices. University involvement should be invited to the fullest possible extent without jeopardizing the agency's procedure for a fair hearing and resolution. Every effort should be made to counteract negative effects from the student/supervisee not having been affiliated for as long a time period or not being as integral a part of organizational functionings as the supervisor.

Let us look at what ultimately happened to our hypothetical student:

Mary took Janice's advice. She arranged to see Sally, an officer at the university's equal opportunity office. After several interviews, Mary decided she did not wish to file charges through Jim's agency or to make a formal complaint through the professional organization to which he belonged. The entire situation had taken its toll on her to the point that she was now receiving personal counseling. Mary questioned her ability to handle any additional stress.

Mary and Sally met with the department's director of clinical training who decided that Jim's agency should no longer be used for placement given its history of lackadaisical response to past charges. The director met with her counterpart in the agency and with the facility's executive director and informed them of her decision. That meeting was followed by written notification.

Several months later Mary was accepted in another internship. She approached that new situation cautiously. However, after a few weeks, she found the atmosphere was more conducive to learning than her previous placement had been. Boundary issues were addressed more directly in supervision and professionalism was demonstrated in the services provided to clients. Still Mary felt guilty and uneasy about what had happened. Indeed she never talked to her new supervisor and to the other interns about the situation. Mary did not realize the profound effect that Jim's behavior had upon her until she read an article on boundary issues in supervision several years later.

Training

Training, both of persons entering and already in the field, is vital to developing and maintaining job-related skills; to recognizing issues that may affect job performance; and to knowing what the standards of conduct are, how to seek resolution and redress if aggrieved, and what sanctions might be imposed were the standards to be violated. Pope et al. (1986) believe the best way to prevent such violations is through formal training at both the graduate and continuing education levels, rather than relying upon some organization to impose external penalties. They see personal ethics and a regard for the welfare of others as more compelling reasons for refraining from inappropriate intimacies than fear of negative consequences.

Sadly, both Glaser and Thorpe (1986) and Pope et al. (1979) suggested that the actual is far below the ideal. Glaser and Thorpe (1986) found that only 12% of their sample received any graduate training that addressed sexual contact between educators and students and only 22% of the respondents reported receiving what they thought was "thorough" training on sexual intimacy in clinical practice. Pope et al. (1979) noted that educators already in the field are very reluctant to seek confidential consultation regarding matters of sexual intimacy even though they may be experiencing considerable fear, guilt, and conflict. They assert that this reluctance stems in part from the anxiety that students who are their actual or potential sexual partners will soon become colleagues in the same profession and from the difficulty in acknowledging and accepting their sexual attractions in light of the profession's prevailing silence.

Glaser and Thorpe (1986) observed a need for housekeeping. Both students and practitioners must be better informed on the issues, no matter how disconcerting the knowledge may be. The following guidelines, based on recommendations by Pope et al. (1986) and Schank and Johnston (1986), propose ways to bolster preventive efforts.

1. Training on sexual attraction and sexual intimacy must be integral to the graduate curriculum. The approach must acknowledge the value of honest and open discussion of one's sexual feelings toward clients, supervisees, etc. Those feelings should be differentiated from actual sexual contact. The role of both personal and environmental stressors in precipitating such liaisons must be explored, using models like that developed by White (1986). Relevant research should be presented, with ample discussion of the validity and generalizability of findings and of areas of further exploration and replication. Training must be thorough. It cannot be limited to a one-hour lecture set apart from the "regular" curriculum. Rather, it must be integral to all courses and training.

2. Similar training should be made available to practitioners and educators already in the field through workshops, discussions, consultations sponsored by professional organizations, university offices of continuing education, and agencies

themselves. Once again the on-going nature of such training must be stressed. Educators and practitioners must be consistently encouraged to seek consultation any time they see sexual feelings toward a client or a student/supervisee interfering with their work. The stigma for doing so must be removed.

3. Both students and educators must be sensitized to issues of sexual exploitation. Written materials should be developed and disseminated prominently, widely, and frequently. Items addressed should include institutional/agency policies and procedures on sexual conduct, cues for identifying sexually exploitative behavior, ways of confronting such behavior should it occur, and available resources for support and complaint resolution. Seminars and other educational programs should be scheduled regularly with attendance being compulsory. No student should be allowed to begin training and no professional should be allowed to begin work without a thorough orientation to the topic.

4. Those who in any way may be involved in assessing and handling complaints of sexual exploitation must be trained thoroughly in their work. Dealing with such grievances is a specialized task for which one is not equipped automatically through generic professional training. Persons so involved must be well-versed both in legal and administrative precedents of affirmative action and in equal opportunity as well as the interpersonal skills and strategies necessary to deal with such matters in an effective, humane way. With regard to the latter, we heartily recommend the work of Schoener, Milgrom, and Gonsiorek (Milgrom, 1986; Schoener & Milgrom, 1984; Schoener & Milgrom, 1986; Schoener, Milgrom & Gonsiorek, 1983) on dealing with complaints of sexual misconduct by therapists.

Boundary Maintenance

We have come full circle to an initial concept, "Good supervision involves good boundary maintenance." The implications of this statement, with special but not exclusive emphasis on supervisor-supervisee sexual involvement, are as follows:

1. All professionals functioning as clinical supervisors should receive special training for that role and should participate in activities, such as workshops and consultation groups, that help them to maintain and enhance their clinical and supervision skills. They should seek consultation immediately if they think personal and/or professional problems are interfering with their judgment in supervision. Colleagues who note such difficulties should make every effort to confront the individual and to offer whatever assistance seems appropriate.

2. Students in their own way should be trained in how to be supervised. Before beginning a clinical placement, they should be given an orientation by their academic department in which they discuss topics such as what constitutes good and poor supervision, how to set limits with supervisors, and how to solicit and provide feedback regarding supervision.

3. All clinical training should be organized to the extent that it has specific goals, objectives, and training strategies; a designated training coordinator; ample and varied supervision; a clear statement of student rights and responsibilities and an explicit procedure for negotiating and resolving conflicts and for terminating student participation if necessary; and a clearly-defined method for evaluating and discussing student performance and soliciting student feedback thereof (Bobbitt, Conroe & Loeffler, 1985).

4. At the initial contact, supervisee and supervisor should openly discuss respective expectations, training strategies, and desired outcomes. They should arrange for periodic review of supervisee performance and of supervision itself, both person-to-person and in writing.

5. The supervisor should carefully monitor how he or she interacts with the supervisee throughout the process. Questions such as "Whose needs are primarily being met by what I am doing: mine or the supervisee's?" and "Is what I am doing within the realm of supervision?" should be asked continually. The supervisor must be ever-mindful of his or her evaluative function vis-a-vis the supervisee by posing the question, "Is what I am doing in any way compromising my ability to evaluate the supervisee objectively and to provide negative feedback even to the point of termination if need be?" Self-disclosure should be considered important and indeed vital. Again the aim of such disclosure should be kept in mind. Talking about one's own difficulties as a supervisee may help the supervisee to put her or his issues into perspective, but talking about one's mental or relationship problems serves no useful function. Inordinate prying into the supervisee's personal life should be avoided. Personal issues should be examined only when they affect the supervisee's work with clients or on his or her ability to relate during supervision or during the field placement in general. A distinction must be made between doing therapy and doing supervision, with appropriate referral for the former arranged if deemed necessary. A regular time and a specific professional site should be arranged for supervision. The supervisee should be afforded the opportunity for informal, as-needed consultation within prescribed limits.

Social contact both inside and outside the agency is desirable to the extent that it does not detract from the supervisory relationship. One special supervisee should not be singled out for a party invitation or for company during coffee breaks. When examining one's motives for extending a social invitation, one might wish to ask, "If this supervisee was the most physically unattractive person I knew but as competent as X, would I still consider inviting him or her?" Finally, careful forethought must be given to any physical touch by either party—looking at rationale, type of contact, and anticipated effect on each party.

6. Extreme caution must be exercised when addressing poor supervisee performance or unethical behavior. A well-defined, explicit procedure for dealing with such instances should be established. On-going coordination between agency and university departments must exist if the best possible outcome is to be achieved (Holloway & Roehlke, 1987). Students should be aware of their obligation to bring to the attention of the agency training director any knowledge they have of incompetent behavior or unethical conduct by a supervisee or supervisor. Protection from retribution must be afforded persons who make such reports.

CONCLUSION

Our views on supervisor-supervisee sexual involvement, augmented by the relevant literature, are presented in this chapter. Rather than weighing pros and cons, we have stated flatly that such intimacy is inappropriate and destructive. We have looked at contributing factors, ethical implications and preventive and remedial steps in the context of the responsibility borne by a supervisor to monitor and control his or her sexual behavior and to respond professionally to a supervisee's sexual advances.

Supervisees are in a vulnerable position. One can argue that from an emotional standpoint they are not as vulnerable as psychotherapy clients. This statement is indeed true in most instances, though it is important to keep in mind that most therapists have at one time or another themselves been clients (Chance, 1987). The distinction is therefore not a clear one.

Supervisees stand to lose a great deal by becoming sexually involved with a supervisor or by having to contend with a supervisor's sexual advances. They face potential loss of time, money, skills and knowledge acquisition, and even career. They may become the object of rumor and gossip; encounter enormous pressure from other students, agency staff, or faculty members to maintain silence; and may be ostracized if they fail to do so. They are subject to trauma, self-doubt and loss of self-esteem, shame, guilt, sheer emotional exhaustion, and discouragement, as well as to the feeling that they "got what they deserved." They are in an unequal relationship with their supervisor, a position that continues even after supervision is terminated. They may see themselves as having little recourse to complaint and grievance because of inadequate knowledge of resources or because such resources do not exist or are woefully inadequate. For these reasons and, we suspect, many more, supervisees must be afforded the maximum protection possible of the right to a beneficial clinical learning experience. They also must be accorded fair hearing when they are bringing a complaint or when they themselves are of concern because of alleged incompetent or unethical behavior.

The time has come to take the topic of supervisor-supervisee sexual involvement out of a secondary status. No further books, monographs, or articles published on professional sexual misconduct, on supervision, or on internships/field placements should appear without affording the subject its due; otherwise, the literature will continue to contribute, in its own way, to the "conspiracy of silence."

PART VI

POST-TERMINATION RELATIONSHIPS

The two chapters in this section focus on an area of considerable controversy in the field of psychotherapy: sexual and romantic relationships with <u>former</u> clients.

In 1983 the Ladd Company released *LOVESICK*, a film starring Dudley Moore as Dr. Saul Benjamin; it was billed as a comedy about a psychotherapist who falls in love with a client. Dr. Benjamin very abruptly terminates the professional relationship hoping to legitimize the budding romance. He then consults a senior psychoanalyst, played by John Houston, for advice, and is confronted with the challenge: "At what point did she stop being your patient?... after you screwed her?... before?... during?" In the background, in one episode, the shade of Sigmund Freud (played by Alec Guiness), asks: "Haven't you read my paper on countertransference?"

Although the film was not a successful comedy, it is fascinating to professionals because the entire film focused on a therapist trying to deal with his infatuation with a client.

Chapter 24 of this book presents an overview by Schoener of the legal and ethical issues in sexual relationships between therapists and former clients. He also examines some of the risks to therapists and clients.

In Chapter 25, Gonsiorek and Brown examine the ethical dilemmas in more depth, and they weigh several possible solutions. They then propose a set of standards to map the ethical boundaries of relationships with former clients.

CHAPTER 24

SEXUAL INVOLVEMENT OF THERAPISTS WITH CLIENTS AFTER THERAPY ENDS: SOME OBSERVATIONS[1]

Gary Richard Schoener

Historically, there has been disturbingly little debate in the psychotherapy professions over sexual involvement with clients following termination of the professional relationship. I have scanned workshop and conference offerings up until 1986 in vain looking for any discussion of this issue. Furthermore, conceptual articles and research on the subject have been virtually nonexistent until the past three years.

Post-therapy personal and sexual relationships between client and therapist are rarely discussed by practitioners, even in private. When the issue comes up someone invariably mentions a colleague, often one of some prominence, who married an ex-patient (Brodsky, 1982). On rare occasions some mention is made of such relationships in the public media; for example, the former chair of a Psychiatric Society ethics committee made a point of telling a reporter that he had married a former patient (Newland, 1980).

In the earliest study of client/therapist sex, Kardener, Fuller, and Mensh (1973) did not separate out relationships after termination of therapy. A subsequent study, Holroyd & Brodsky (1977) asked about such relationships but only those within 3 months of therapy termination. More recently, Gartrell, Herman, Olarte, Localio, and Feldstein (1986) found, in a large self-report survey of psychiatrists, that 69% of the respondents acknowledged having had sex with clients after termination. Among the latter, 18% reported the occurrence within a month of termination and 63%, within 6 months.

The demographic characteristics of psychiatrists who began sexual contact with clients during therapy did not differ from those who initiated it after termination (Gartrell et al., 1986), nor were there differences in the number of repeat offenses or in the characteristics of their most recent sexual relationship with a client.

However, 81% of the respondents who began the relationship after termination reported that they were in love with the clients—just about double the number of those who began the sexual relationship prior to termination. For example, a married male psychiatrist claimed post-termination involvement with 12 clients. At the time he completed the questionnaire he was still involved with one client, who, he said, he was in love with; he said he had begun the relationship within days of the termination of therapy (Gartrell et al., 1986).

Pope, Tabachnick, and Keith-Spiegel (1988) discussed a survey in which the respondents were 456 members of Division 29 (Psychotherapy) of the American Psychological Association. Although 88.2% claimed they never had had sex with a former client, 10.5% said it had happened "rarely," 0.4%, "sometimes," and 0.2%, "very often." Akamatsu (1988), who surveyed a sample of the same size from Division 29, received 395

---

[1]This chapter is an updated revision of an early paper of the same title that I presented at the annual convention of the American Psychological Association, August 24, 1986 (Schoener, 1986). A second version was published in the *Minnesota Psychologist* in the Winter of 1987 (Schoener, 1987).

replies, of whom 11% reported sex with former clients (14.2% of male and 4.7% of female therapists).

Both studies asked respondents to rate on a 5-point scale the ethicality of sex with a former client, although different descriptors were used for some of the points. Pope et al. (1988) received the following replies to their question:

Unquestionably not ethical	50.2%
Ethical under rare circumstances	34.4%
Don't know/Not sure	7.2%
Ethical under many circumstances	3.9%
Unquestionably ethical	3.3%

The responses given to Akamatsu (1988) differed somewhat:

Very unethical	44.7%
Somewhat unethical	23.9%
Neither ethical nor unethical	22.9%
Somewhat ethical	3.7%
Very ethical	4.7%

The difference between the two sets of data illustrates how much the manner in which the question is asked influences the responses.

Akamatsu (1988) also asked respondents what factors should be taken into account in determining the ethicality of the situations; the following responses were given.

Item	N
Time since termination	76
Transference issues	22
Length of therapy	21
Nature of therapy	20
Nature of termination	19
Freedom of choice	16
Whether exploitation occurred	14
Mental health of the client	13
Whether therapy will be reactivated	13
Whether there is harm to client welfare	12

When asked about an appropriate time interval between termination of therapy and beginning an intimate relationship, 37.8% answered no time limit is appropriate and 18.7% checked off "Other"; most of these respondents indicated that time had to be considered along with other factors. Among the respondents who proposed a specific interval, the distribution was as follows:

Immediately after termination	1.0%
After 1 month	1.3%
After 3 months	3.1%
After 6 months	8.5%
After 1 year	16.3%
After 2 years	7.5%
After 3 years	5.7%

(Akamatsu, 1988)

Conte, Plutchik, Picard, and Karasu (1989) report a survey of practicing psychotherapists on the faculty of the Dept. of Psychiatry of a medical school. The 101 respondents consisted of 74% psychiatrists, 22% psychologists, and 4% social workers. They were asked to rate various behaviors on whether they were grounds for malpractice or were unethical, inappropriate, or acceptable. The results permit a comparison of attitudes concerning sex during therapy and sex following its termination:

	Grounds for Malpractice	Unethical	Inappropriate	Acceptable
Having sexual contact with a patient while the patient is still in treatment	80.2%	19.8%	0	0
Terminating treatment for the purpose of having sexual contact with a patient	37.0%	52.0%	10.0%	1%
Having sexual contact with a patient after proper termination of long-term treatment	14%	50%	31%	5%
Having sexual contact with a patient after proper termination of brief therapy	14%	53%	27%	6%
Having sexual contact with a patient you have seen only once or twice for or twice for consultation	28%	43%	24%	5%
Terminating treatment for the purpose of marrying a patient	8.2%	41.8%	40.8%	9.2%
Marrying a patient after proper termination of brief therapy	3.1%	33.7%	42.9%	20.4%
Marrying a patient you have seen once or twice for consultation only	4.1%	28.9%	43.3%	23.7%
Marrying a patient after proper termination of long-term therapy	2%	27.6%	40.8%	29.6%
Having sexual contact with a patient's spouse while the patient is still in treatment	56%	39%	5%	0
Having sexual contact with another member of a patient's immediate family the patient is still in therapy	31%	50%	17%	2%
Having sexual contact with the patient's spouse after completion of the patient's therapy	25.7%	53.5%	19.1%	1%
Having sexual contact with another member of a patient's immediate family after completion of the patient's therapy	15.2%	38.4%	35.4%	11.1%

(Conte, et al., 1989, pp. 34-35; Conte, Personal Communication, July 6, 1989)

Significant differences were found between psychoanalysts and other therapists concerning marriages to clients and former clients, with the psychoanalysts reporting such conduct as less acceptable.

I am indebted to Dr. Conte for providing me with this fascinating data, some of which was not reported in her published study. One of the most interesting findings of this study is that the respondents differentiated little between situations involving clients who were seen for consultation or brief therapy versus long-term therapy. This runs counter to my expectations and to the model proposed by Gonsiorek and Brown in Chapter 25. Secondly, contact with a former client for the purpose of marriage is seen as far more acceptable than contact for sex alone. It is also surprising to find that having sex with a patient's spouse after completion of the patient's therapy is seen as <u>less</u> acceptable than having sexual contact with the patient. Last but not least, the wide range of opinions concerning sex with another member of the patient's immediate family after termination is confusing.

Borys (1988) surveyed a large national sample of psychologists, psychiatrists, and social workers. Of 871 practitioners, only 4 (0.46%) acknowledged having sex during therapy, and 40 (4.6%) acknowledged having sex following termination. The latter group was broken down into various professions; respondents who indicated that they had no opportunity for such conduct were not included:

	Sexual contact after termination	
	No Clients	Few Clients (N=40)
Psychiatrists	93%	7%
Psychologists	88.1%	11.9%
Social Workers	98.4%	1.6%

(Borys, 1988, pp. 205-7)

Because the sample is small (only 40) the differences between groups should be viewed with caution.

THE DEBATE

Despite these four surveys and the 15 years of professional debate over client-therapist sex, little still is known about post-termination sexual or romantic relationships between clients and therapists. The earliest in-depth examination of the issue of which I am aware is a chapter, "Intimacies with Former Clients" in *Sexual Dilemmas for the Helping Professional* (Edelwich & Brodsky, 1982). Major treatment is not given to the issue in recent major contributions (e.g., Brodsky, 1986; Burgess & Hartman, 1986; Pope & Bouhoutsos, 1986). However, in one of the cases cited by Pope & Bouhoutsos (1986) post-termination sex is central.

A number of recent contributors to the debate have pushed the American Psychological Association to develop clearer standards on post-termination sexual involvement between psychologists and therapy clients (Akamatsu, 1988; Brown, 1988; Gabbard & Pope, 1988; Gottlieb, Sell, & Schoenfeld, 1988).

Gabbard and Pope (1988) presented the best argument to date for holding sex with former clients to be always "unacceptable." They focused on the long-term continuation of transference after termination, citing follow-up studies done by Buckley, Karasu, and

Charles (1981); Calef and Weinshel (1983); Carlson (1986); Norman, Blacker, Oremland, and Barrett (1976); Oremland, Blacker, and Norman (1975); and Pfeffer (1963). Gabbard and Pope argued that the idealization of the therapist, which need not be limited to transference, may have an important effect on the long-time benefits of therapy. In addition, they raised the question of continuing professional responsibilities to the client, citing a finding by Harlaub, Martin, and Rhine (1986) that two-thirds of supposedly "successfully analyzed patients" came into contact again with their analysts during the 3-year period after termination.

Hartlaub, Martin, & Rhine (1986, p. 901) reported that 60.6% of patients of psychoanalysts (50% of the men, 70% of the women) had recontacted their analysts within three years of termination. Examining 55 instances of recontact by a total of 43 former patients, only 7.3% of which were planned at termination, the types of recontact reported were:

Telephone call, letter, card	36.4%
Brief office contact	27.2%
Psychotherapy	12.7%
Further psychoanalysis	1.8%
Referral to someone else	5.5%
Student in seminar, workshop	1.8%
Other	7.3%

The reasons for recontact by the 43 former patients were determined to be:

Reworking termination issues	39.5%
Reworking of issues raised in first analysis but knowingly left unresolved	14%
Activation of life circumstances of previously latent issue	18.6%
Continuation of issues previously unrecognized by analyst (countertransference, inexperience, etc.)	4.7%
Other	23.3%

On the other side of the argument is an article in the Oklahoma Law Review by Phyllis Coleman (1988); she proposed a "No harm, no foul" rule for post-termination relationships. Her focus was predominantly on psychiatry and on the issue of transference, arguing that "when therapy has been properly terminated and the transference resolved...there is no longer a therapeutic power relationship that can be abused." She further argued that total resolution of the transference is not necessary, since "transference exists in any relationship, the former patient needs only to have a more objective, realistic view of the psychiatrist." She raises the possibility of a positive side to such relationships without presenting data to support her argument (p. 43).

Her basic stand is that sex with a former client should not be malpractice per se; it should require a showing that the therapist mishandled transference, causing harm to the client. It is unclear, in this light, why Coleman sees little virtue in the Minnesota statute (see Appendix N) which provides that one of two conditions must be met during the 2-year period following termination for malpractice to be proved.[2]

---

[2] The two conditions are that there was therapeutic deception (client was led to believe that sex was part of therapy) or that the client was so emotionally dependent as to be unable to resist the therapist's advances.

Although Coleman does not provide a good explication of the constitutional issues involved, any absolute rule against a romantic relationship following the termination of the professional relationship may impinge on the constitutional rights of both client and therapist. Given that a number of therapists have entered long-term relationships or marriages with former clients, in which both parties claim to be happy and healthy, an absolute rule against such relationships might have difficulty passing a test of constitutionality.

There has been some debate over the years concerning the resolution of transference, and its continuation after the termination of therapy. Beyond the discussions cited by Gabbard and Pope (1988) it is worth noting a discussion reported by Hurn (1973) which occurred at a meeting of the American Psychoanalytic Association in 1972. While it is noted that ideally the transference neurosis is resolved during the termination phase of therapy, transference reactions are observed to exist longterm. One panelist is quoted as remarking: "hopefully, transference neuroses are dissolved, although transference reactions disappear only with death" (p. 190).

The complexity of analyzing post-termination contacts, and of the continuing power of the therapist, even after a "successful analysis" which was properly terminated according to accepted standards, can be found in a clinical case example presented by Hartlaub, Martin & Rhine (1986) of a woman in her mid-twenties in which "The relinquishing of her romantic wishes toward the analyst presaged a long and emotion-laden terminal phase..." and who "...terminated feeling tenderly toward the analyst..." (p. 907):

About one year after termination, she wrote the analyst a brief note informing him that she was doing well and that she was marrying a nice man whom she loved very much. The analyst wrote her back saying he was pleased to hear the good news..."

Two years later, she telephoned to make "one appointment." She came in proudly carrying her newborn son, and tenderly cared for him during the session. She said she wanted the analyst to see how well she was doing as a woman, wife, and mother: She was pleased with the outcome of their work and she thought he would be too. He said that he was. She reviewed some of the important dynamics... and how she still occasionally struggled with them but was no longer "a prisoner of them." She thanked the analyst for his help and left. (p. 907)

About four and one-half years later she again called for an appointment, stating she had had a loss in her family and was depressed, but not grieving as she knew she should be. During the session she spoke of the importance of this individual, of how unexpected and painful the loss had been and finally broke down sobbing. The analyst said little other than to empathize with her pain. She requested "a couple of more sessions" to help her with this. The following Monday, however, she telephoned to say she had been able to open up to her husband about her feelings, that he had finally expressed his grief over the loss, and that—since they were both, now, helping each other through "this rough time," she no longer felt the need for those other meetings with the analyst. He replied that he was pleased to hear this. (p. 908)

Since 1986 a somewhat intense debate has been going on among psychologists over the proposal to change the code of ethics to explicitly forbid client/therapist sex after therapy terminates. The debate has ranged from discussions of primarily sexual relationships to broader discussions of romantic and even social relationships.

The two opposing positions in this debate were voiced by well-known practitioners at the American Psychological Association convention in 1986. Dr. Karen Machover, certainly one of the "grande dames" of practicing psychotherapists, argued that clients, like children, mature and reach adulthood and thus, after termination, should be treated as consenting adults. Although she did not specifically argue _for_ post-therapy sexual relationships, she held social relationships to be unquestionably permissible, nor did she rule out romantic or sexual involvements. Dr. Laura Brown, a contributor to this volume and a national figure in her own right, picked up on Dr. Machover's metaphor, arguing that although children grow up and even end up taking care of their parents in their old age, children and parents still do not engage in sex.

This large-scale debate is not, at this time, occurring in psychiatry; thus, the data collected by Gartrell et al. (1986) is very revealing regarding the beliefs and attitudes voiced by their respondents. Although 98% affirmed their belief that sex between client and psychiatrist is always inappropriate prior to termination, 29.6% felt that such contact sometimes could be appropriate after termination and 8.5% had no opinion. In addition, 17.4% believed that the stance of the American Psychiatric Association permits sex with clients following termination (Herman, Gartrell, Olarte, Feldstein, & Localio, 1987).

The written comments by psychiatrists who responded to a self-report survey conducted by Herman and associates displayed the same variation in views that was seen in the debate among psychologists. Some said that it was never OK, even after termination. One respondent proposed a 6-month grace period after termination during which sex is prohibited; others, a 6-24 month "gray zone" and then no restrictions after 2 years. However, the range of time limits proposed varied dramatically. Some respondents suggested professional consultation to decide if the psychiatrist and client could get involved whereas others espoused the view that it is OK if they fall in love (Herman et al., 1987).

> Many respondents also indicated a belief that, while casual sexual contacts with a patient could not be condoned even after termination, such contacts could be countenanced if both patient and therapist were seeking marriage or a serious love relationship. (Herman et al; 1987)

Rigby-Weinberg (1986) made a similar point about committed lesbian relationships that follow therapy termination. In fact, marital relationships between therapists and former clients are often noted when arguments are made against creating an absolute prohibition against such relationships.

It is worth noting that although we have considerable anecdotal information on therapists married to ex-clients, empirical data are lacking. Such marriages, however, are known in other cultures.

> Occasionally in other cultures a male therapist may accept a female client as his wife in lieu of a fee. This is found, for instance, in Nigeria. Although it is not rare in Western therapy for a therapist to marry his or her patient—some nationally known therapists have done it—presumably it is not in lieu of a fee. (Torrey, 1986, p. 41)

Somehow, if love, marriage, or a committed relationship results it is accepted as a measure of the propriety or ethics of a post-termination relationship; but it makes little sense: first because it has an "ends justifies the means" sound to it and second because it is difficult to conceptualize how to judge the situation. What should be the criterion—that a couple got married? that they stayed married? or that they lived together in a committed relationship for X years?

The Walk-In Counseling Center has become involved in this debate because we are consulted by both clients and therapists who are trying to sort out the propriety of such relationships or to deal with the consequences of them. We, too, have respected colleagues who are married to past clients, in some cases apparently quite happily. (See Chapter 11 in which Case 15 illustrates a post-termination dilemma.)

A SORRY STATE OF AFFAIRS: THE ETHICS CODES

Until August 1, 1988, no code of ethics in a mental health profession provided a clear standard for sex with clients after therapy. The American Association for Marriage and Family Therapy added the following sentence to section 1.2 of the "AAMFT Code of Ethical Principles for Marriage and Family Therapists": "Sexual intimacy with former clients for two years following the termination of therapy is prohibited" (AAMFT, 1988). Although no definition of termination is given, the standard is clear-cut.

The codes of ethics for each of the other psychotherapy professions tend to be in agreement: they are silent on the issue of post-therapy sex. The possible exceptions are the codes for psychiatry and clinical social work.

The psychiatric code itself is not specific. However, the companion booklet of "Opinions..." includes one case that raises the issue as follows:

Question: A psychiatrist begins a sexual relationship with a former patient a few weeks after the termination of treatment with this patient. Is this unethical?

Answer: 'Sexual activity with a patient is unethical.' This is because '...the necessary intensity of the therapeutic relationship may tend to activate sexual and other needs and fantasies on the part of both patient and therapist, while weakening the objectivity necessary for control.'

A psychiatrist is exploiting his patient by not helping him or her to see that his or her affection for him is a projection of feelings to another person at another point in time. Is the exploitation any less 'a few weeks after termination of treatment?' A few months? A few years? The District Branch ethics committee's investigation should be able to settle the issue not simply on the basis of time span, but on the basis of the committee's determination of the extent to which this was exploitation of the therapeutic relationship. (Dec. 31, 1975) (APA, 1983, p. 13)

Furthermore, in December of 1988 the Assembly and Board of Trustees of the American Psychiatric Association ratified some new wording which has been added to Section 2, Annotation 1, of the code:

Sexual involvement with one's former patients generally exploits emotions deriving from treatment and therefore almost always is unethical. (APA, in press)

In psychiatry we can say that a standard of sorts has been established: if the post-termination relationship is seen as "exploitative," it is considered unethical, possibly regardless of time span. However, criteria for determining the extent of exploitation are not articulated and time is not absolutely ruled out as a criterion. My experience in licensure-related disciplinary hearings involving psychiatrists where the code is referred to have convinced me that clear decision making is not possible as long as it is the only standard in psychiatry.

The other possible exception, clinical social work, has a code of ethics that dates from 1976; it was published by the Committee on Professional Standards of the National Federation of Societies for Clinical Social Work. The Federation consists of 27 state societies made up of social workers who are engaged in clinical work, especially psychotherapy. The October 1985 revision of the "Code of Ethics" states in part as follows:

II. RESPONSIBILITY TO CLIENTS

***

c) Clinical social workers use care to prevent the intrusion of their own personal needs into relationships with clients. They recognize that the private and personal nature of the therapeutic relationship may unrealistically intensify clients' feelings toward them, thus increasing their obligation to maintain professional objectivity. Therefore, specifically:

***

3. Clinical social workers do not initiate, and should avoid when possible, personal relationships or dual roles with current clients, or with any former clients whose feelings toward them may still be derived from or influenced by the former professional relationship.

Thus, although the Code does not contain an explicit prohibition against participation in sexual or romantic relationships with former clients, it appears to prohibit initiation by the therapist of a personal relationship with a former client whose feelings may still be a product of the professional relationship. It is not clear how the term "avoid when possible" should be interpreted in this context. Furthermore, instead of referring to transference or continued emotional dependency on the therapist, the code refers to feelings "derived from or influenced by the former professional relationship." Frankly, it is difficult to imagine any situation in which a former client's feelings were not, in part at least, related to the past therapy relationship.

Since 1986 the Ethics Committee of the American Psychological Association has engaged in an intense debate on the topic of sexual involvements with former clients. Input has been sought and received from psychologists throughout the U.S. and Canada. A proposal to make sex with a former client never permissible passed in the Ethics Committee in a lopsided vote, but a member resigned as a result (Dawes, Gottlieb, Pope & Hall, 1986). Some arguments against the "it's never OK" approach were very similar to those advanced by Riskin (1979) in a *California Law Review* article, although that article focused exclusively on sex that occurred during therapy.

Given the intense debate and complexity of the matter, the American Psychological Association decided not to change the Code of Ethics in 1986 but to continue study and discussion of the issue. An update on the progress of this discussion reported that the Ethics Committee was still debating the matter, but the Committee was cited as recommending the following approach to adjudication of such cases (APA Monitor, June 1987):

1. If, upon examination, it seems that the treatment ended in order to give the appearance of compliance with the ethical proscription against the psychologist-client intimacies, the committee will find that behavior a clear violation of Principle 6.a. Such terminations are seen as subterfuge.

2. If... the treatment appears to have ended without elements of duplicity concerning possible later sexual contact, no such violation of 6.a. would be found." However, it leaves open the possibility that "Such behavior may be found not to be consistent with the highest standards of the profession (General Principle 1) ...." (p.45)

Unfortunately, the new *Casebook on Ethical Principles of Psychologists* (APA, 1987) does not contain an example of the adjudication of post-termination sexual involvements.

As is noted in Chapter 27, the code of ethics of the Minnesota Chemical Dependency Association (MCDA) specifically prohibits sexual relationships with former clients within one year of termination of service (MCDA, 1985). Personnel policies and internal codes of conduct in a number of Minnesota's drug and alcohol abuse treatment facilities have also contained such prohibitions. However, the Code of Ethics of the National Association of Alcoholism and Drug Abuse Counselors (NAADAC, 1987) is silent on post-termination relationships as is the code for employee assistance counselors utilized by the Association of Labor-Management Administrators and Consultants on Alcoholism (ALMACA, 1988).

POLICING OF THE PROFESSIONS—ETHICS COMMITTEES AND LICENSURE BOARDS

Licensure Boards rely heavily on existing codes of professional ethics. Most licensure laws for the various professions that provide psychotherapy services refer to existing codes or allow their regulatory Boards to rely on them. Therein lies the rub. Since existing ethics codes do not address the issue, the regulatory bodies are hampered in dealing with such cases.

In our experience over the past 15 years we have observed that such cases tend to be troublesome for Boards and, also, to be handled inconsistently from state to state and even within the same state. For example, we know of one situation in one state in which a psychology licensure body declined to prosecute a case but a medical licensing body prosecuted a post-termination case against a practitioner licensed in both fields. Presumably the same evidence was examined but different conclusions were reached regarding whether to prosecute the case.

State associations in medicine, nursing, psychiatry, psychology, and social work are all affiliated with major national organizations. Thus it is not practical for them to develop their own codes of practice; furthermore, such codes would have dubious authority. Licensure and regulatory Boards, however, can undertake the task given that their authority flows from state law.

We have no way of knowing whether or how many state Boards are currently attempting to further define the rules for post-therapy sexual or social contact between client and therapist.

The Board of Psychological Examiners in the State of Florida passed an amendment to the Board Rules on December 21, 1986; it addresses client-therapist sex in some detail (see Appendix R). This amendment also makes special note of the post-termination situation; it states in part as follows:

The effects of the psychologist-client relationship endure after psychological services cease to be rendered....

For the purposes of determining the existence of sexual misconduct... the psychologist-client relationship is deemed to continue in perpetuity. (Biedermann, 1987)

So, for psychologists in Florida, sexual activity or making requests for sex from ex-clients is never OK. To date, all the cases handled under this new rule have been settled by stipulation or other means so no legal test has been made of this rule (Biedermann, 1987). Obviously, it could be open to constitutional challenge in terms of its potential impingement on the right of free association of client, therapist, or both.

In 1988 the Colorado Legislature enacted House Bill No. 1026. It provided for extensive amendments to Article 43 of title 12, Colorado Revised Statutes, 1986. The revised statute provides for uniform disciplinary procedures for psychologists, clinical social workers, marriage and family therapists, and licensed professional counselors. It reads, in part,

(1) A person practicing psychotherapy under this article is in violation of this article if he:

*****

(q) Has engaged in sexual contact, sexual intrusion, or sexual penetration, as defined in section 18-3-401, C.R.S., with a client during the period of time in which a therapeutic relationship exists or <u>for up to six months after the period in which such a relationship exists</u>;

[Col. Rev. Statutes, 12-43-704-1 (q)]

The Minnesota Board of Psychology debated this issue for a number of years. In 1981 it sought input from psychologists in the state on the development of some means of policing post-therapy relationships. The lively debate that followed examined proposals covering a range of potential solutions:

1. Simple <u>Prohibition</u>: It's never OK.

2. Prohibition for a certain <u>time period</u>, with proposals ranging from 6 months to 5 years.

3. Requiring written notice of termination and written referral to another practitioner before commencing a personal relationship.

4. Requiring and obtaining consultation from another mental health professional before undertaking such a relationship.

Constitutional questions, especially interference with the right of association, were raised, particularly in regard to absolute prohibition. There was considerable disagreement about the time period options. The time period approach, or requiring termination to be carried out in a certain fashion, was regarded as perhaps actually legitimizing post-therapy sexual relationships. Also, the system was regarded as easy to manipulate so the rules could be used to defend exploitative activities.

When the new Code of the Minnesota Board of Psychology was approved on August 7, 1982, it was silent on the issue, even though the language was improved on sexual misconduct and reporting sexual abuse of clients by psychologists. However, in the revised rules adopted on July 14, 1989, Subp. 8., Sexual Contact with a Client, was expanded to address the post-termination situation:

...A psychologist must not engage in sexual intercourse or other physical intimacies with a former client for a period of two years following the date of the last professional contact with the client, whether or not the psychologist has formally terminated the professional relationship.

As this book goes to press the State of California is on the verge of passing Senate Bill 1004, which will become Section 729 (1989) of the Business and Professions Code which will forbid any professional licensed under the code (e.g., psychologist, psychiatrist, social worker, marriage and family therapist, etc.) to have sexual contact with a former patient "if the professional relationship was terminated primarily for engaging in those acts unless the client has been "referred... to an independent and objective psychotherapist, recommended by a third party psychotherapist" (personal communication, Barry Brokaw, Aug. 23, 1989). The bill originally contained a 6-month "cooling off period," but that has been dropped. Although this bill may be further altered by debate on the Assembly floor so that this language is tentative, it is not clear how it will protect consumers in that the standard it uses is less restrictive than that in several of the existing professional ethics codes. Furthermore, it could easily be read to imply that post-termination sex is acceptable as long as the client received a referral to another therapist from an independent therapist. (There seems to be no requirement that this third party have full knowledge of the situation and evaluate it.)

It is entirely possible that states other than Colorado and California and professional regulatory bodies other than the Florida Board of Psychological Examiners have or are in the process of developing rules, guidelines, or tests for dealing with post-termination sexual or romantic relationships.

In a survey (April 1984) of state psychological association ethics committees and state licensure boards for psychologists, several state bodies reported that they had developed guidelines. Two ethics committees and one state board used a formal one-year waiting period. One ethics committee had an informal standard of a 6-month wait, and one state board had some sort of "greater than one year" standard. Additionally, one ethics committee responded that it would never be OK and one requires, informally, a 2-year wait plus consultation "by both parties with a neutral professional before a sexual relationship may be initiated" (Sell, Gottlieb, & Schoenfeld, 1986, p. 505).

This study found that the use of time elapsed since termination as a defense, in and of itself, did not lead to the dismissal of any case (Sell, Gottlieb, & Schoenfeld, 1986). However, this finding does not rule out the possibility that the time lapse since termination played a role in the decision to dismiss or to apply some lesser remedy in a case. Furthermore, the fact that a psychologist claimed there had been a determination does not mean the Board believed there had been one, so disciplinary action may result simply from the Board's refusal to believe the psychologist's claim that there had been a termination or his statement of how much time had elapsed since termination.

In a follow-up study, the same investigators (Gottlieb, Sell, & Schoenfeld, 1988) found that only a single case reported by any of the 48 psychology licensure Boards that responded to a survey involved exoneration of a psychologist for admitted sexual contact with a former client. No Board had established a standard that would "allow a sexual relationship to take place between a psychologist and client after a specified time had elapsed after termination" (p. 460). Unfortunately, it is unclear from the study whether factors other than the passage of time might lead to the differential treatment of such cases or whether lesser penalties are granted when the sexual involvement followed termination.

WHAT WE TELL THE PUBLIC

None of the professions that provide psychotherapeutic services have done much to educate the public in general or consumers in particular on post-termination relationships with therapists. Given the lack of clarity in the field, this neglect is not surprising.

The outstanding consumer brochure, "Making Therapy Work For You" (Appendix Z), was developed by the Wisconsin Coalition on Sexual Misconduct by Psychotherapists and Counselors. It focuses entirely on the on-going therapeutic relationship; it does not deal directly with sex with former clients.

"Women and Psychotherapy," a consumer handbook prepared by the American Psychological Association Task Division of the Psychology of Women and the Task Force on Consumer Issues in Psychotherapy of the Association for Women in Psychology, mentions the topic in an interesting fashion (Federation of Organizations for Professional Women, 1981):

> Occasionally a client may terminate therapy with the therapist in order to engage in sexual relations. You should realize that it is difficult to overcome the initial power relationship of the therapy situation. You may find that you end up feeling betrayed and hurt by the situation (p. 19).

The handbook is otherwise very clear about sexual contact in therapy and about exploitative therapists, but here it seems to focus only on the situation in which the client is attracted and gives only a mild warning; it does not take a clear stand on the propriety of such relationships.

Even the recently developed booklet, "It's Never O.K.: A Handbook for Victims and Victim Advocates on Sexual Exploitation by Counselors and Therapists" (Public Issues Workgroup, 1988) does not explicitly discuss sexual involvement after termination of the professional relationship.

The subject, however, does receive discussion, as does the issue of termination, in the book, *How to Find a Good Psychotherapist: A Consumer Guide* (Striano, 1987). Although cost factors would limit broad distribution of the book in waiting rooms, having a copy available for a client to page through would be useful.

The popular press has rarely discussed the post-termination relationship. For example, Bowen Northrup's series, "Psychotherapy Under Analysis," in the *Wall Street Journal*, devoted a lengthy article to abuses by therapists (October 29, 1986); client/therapist sex was discussed but the post-therapy dilemma was not mentioned. The rare exceptions are articles providing case histories centering on post-termination sex or romance. One such article mentioned an Ann Arbor psychiatrist whose suspended license was reportedly reinstated after he testified "that his sexual relationship with the woman did not begin until after therapy had been terminated" (Amy Smith, 1985). The story went on to note that she received a $180,000 settlement in a civil suit and, subsequently, that she committed suicide.

THE MINNESOTA SOLUTION

Before examining current legal solutions to the problem, I must note that a major discussion of this issue was held at the 50th Anniversary meeting of the Minnesota Psychological Association in May 1986 and that it was the topic of a survey by the Ethics Committee of the MPA (Gross, 1986).

The Minnesota Task Force on Sexual Exploitation by Counselors and Psychotherapists discussed the issue at length. The Wisconsin Coalition on Sexual Misconduct by Psychotherapists and Counselors also has been working diligently to define solutions. However, Wisconsin Act 275 (Appendix G), enacted April 15, 1986, which redefined sexual exploitation of a client by psychotherapists as a felony (previously, it was a first-class misdemeanor) and which created a specific cause of civil action against a therapist, does not provide for criminal prosecution unless the sex occurred, "during any on-going therapist-patient or therapist-client relationship...."[3] The new criminal law in Colorado (see Appendix L) does not specify that the sex must occur during an on-going professional relationship, nonetheless, it appears to focus on sex prior to termination.

Over the past several years the number of professional workshops on therapist/client boundaries has increased. WICC staff members and other persons with expertise in this arena also have received many requests for inservice training on this topic, and I do regular seminars for graduate students in local graduate training programs.

THE NEW LAWS IN MINNESOTA

Criminal: In 1985 the Minnesota Legislature passed Chapter 297 Minnesota Laws 1985 (see Appendix H) which amended the Minnesota Criminal Sexual Conduct Code (609.341-609.351) to make a psychotherapist's sex with clients third- or fourth-degree criminal sexual conduct, a felony. Under two circumstances sex with a former patient is in violation...

1. when the "...former patient is emotionally dependent upon the psychotherapist" (given that consent may be a defense, the legislative intent was to cover situations in which the emotional dependency renders the patient unable to give full consent). The legal definition of "emotionally dependent" is "that the nature of the patient's or former patient's emotional condition and the nature of the treatment provided by the psychotherapist are such that the psychotherapist knows or has reason to know that the patient or former patient is unable to withhold consent to sexual contact or sexual penetration by the psychotherapist."

2. when the sex "occurred by means of therapeutic deception" (meaning, "a representation by a psychotherapist that sexual contact or sexual penetration by the psychotherapist is consistent with or part of the patient's treatment").

It should be noted that there is no time limit for former patients, unlike the civil statute discussed in the following section. So, theoretically, at least, if a prosecutor can prove

---

[3]In the matter of a civil suit, things seem less clear because the statute [Section 895.70 (2)] indicates that the sexual contact must be with a "therapist who is rendering or has rendered...." I do not know what the legislative intent was, but it may well include post-therapy sex. To date, no cases have been filed that would test this proposition.

beyond a matter of reasonable doubt that the client was too dependent, even years later, to withhold consent, a conviction may be possible.

Maximum penalties are 10-20 years in prison and fines of $10,000-$20,000. The Sentencing Guidelines Commission suggests that for third-degree conduct (with penetration) the first offense can be a prison term. Probation is recommended for the first offense with fourth-degree (no penetration) conduct, however. Charges have been brought in at least eight cases since the law has been on the books (August 1, 1985), but only one involved post-termination sex.

In this case, discussed in Chapter 43 (see, also, Schoener, 1988b), a psychologist was acquitted of criminal sexual conduct charges when the state prosecutor could not convince a jury that the former client was so emotionally dependent that she was unable to withhold consent for the sex. It is impossible to generalize from a single case with unique facts, but there is obviously a much higher standard of proof required to make a matter criminal as opposed to unprofessional. The psychologist had his license to practice suspended.

Civil: In 1986 the Minnesota Legislature passed Chapter 372 Minnesota Statutes (see Appendix N) which created a cause of action against a psychotherapist, his/her current employer, and his/her past employer for sexual exploitation of clients and former clients.

This statute sets a time limit. Subdivision 3 of Section 1 defines "former" patient as "...a person who was given psychotherapy within two years prior to sexual contact with the psychotherapist." It uses the same standards as the criminal law regarding the conditions under which a former client is included: (a) emotional dependency; and (b) therapeutic deception. (Section 43.93 of the California Civil Code, reproduced in Appendix O, uses the same standards; an Illinois statute, reproduced in Appendix CC, has a one-year period.)

The Minnesota civil statute has a 5-year statute of limitations, much longer than the 2 years for medical malpractice. This law became effective August 1, 1986. I am not aware that a suit for damages for alleged post-termination sex has been filed to date. However, even without such a statute a client may sue for damages based on a post-termination romance.[4]

Reporting: The likelihood of the discovery of sexual involvements with clients in Minnesota has increased dramatically, not only because of the community-wide education efforts of the State Task Force but, also, the statutes or rules that require reporting (see Appendix K).

> VULNERABLE ADULTS ACT: Passed in 1982 as Minnesota Statute 626.557, this act mandates reporting abuse of vulnerable adults. Although the original language suggested it would cover psychotherapy outpatients, and one can make such a report using the law to provide some protection against suit by the person being reported, in practice the act is aimed at inpatients and clients of residential treatment programs. It has resulted in reports of sexual involvements in these

---

[4]For example, Smith & Bisbing (1988) cite unpublished cases: Dawson vs. Fink and Lovelace vs. York-Adams Mental Health Program; and Gabbard & Pope (1988) cite Whitesell vs. Green. In the recent New York case of Noto v. St. Vincent's Hospital, Manhattan State Supreme Court Justice Michael Dontzin ruled that a patient can sue a psychiatrist for a post-treatment affair, citing as part of his reasoning the Minnesota and California civil statutes which deal with post-termination sexual relationships with psychotherapy clients (Pinsley, 1989). The reader is referred to Chapter 43 for further discussion of these statutes as well as the Illinois statute which also addresses post-termination relationships.

settings, including some situations of post-discharge sexual liaisons. Numerous other states have similar laws.

BOARD OF PSYCHOLOGY, CODE OF CONDUCT: Psychologists licensed in Minnesota are required to file a complaint with the Board when they have "reason to believe that another psychologist" has had "sexual contact with a client." The only exception allowed is information obtained when psychologists in question are in professional relationships with offenders. Should an offender be a friend and reveal an offense in a casual conversation, or a therapist-client relationship is discovered in a social situation, or an offense is revealed at a staff meeting, a psychologist should make a report (Board of Psychology, 1982).

MEDICAL PRACTICE ACT: In a 1985 supplement to Chapter 147 Minnesota Statute sweeping changes were made in the Medical Practice Act. All licensed health professionals (including psychologists) are now required to report within 30 days any conduct by a physician that may result in discipline or that indicates possible medical incompetence. This mandate includes, of course, "engaging in sexual conduct with a patient or in any verbal behavior which is seductive or sexually demeaning to a patient." The only exception allowed is if you are a physician treating the physician in question and the latter has voluntarily limited her or his practice or withdrawn from practice so that clients are not at risk! Reporting, by the way, is also required by all health care facilities, insurance companies, etc. (Breviu & Meyerle, 1985).

MARRIAGE & FAMILY THERAPISTS, SOCIAL WORKERS, AND UNLICENSED MENTAL HEALTH PRACTITIONERS: Appendix K gives the reporting requirements for Licensed Marriage and Family Therapists, Licensed Social Workers, and Unlicensed mental health service providers (for the description of this group see Appendix U). These requirements are modeled after those in the Medical Practice Act and specifically require reporting of professionals who engage in sexual contact with a client or former client.

The Minnesota reporting requirements go far beyond those of most other jurisdictions. For example, in 1987 California passed statutes protecting professional organizations that deal with complaints of misconduct (see Appendix O) and requiring mental health professionals to provide and discuss with clients a brochure outlining complaint options (see Appendix P), but it has no statute requiring the reporting of sex between an adult client and a therapist. In fact, handing out the brochure is mandated only for situations in which the client has had sex with a previous psychotherapist during the course of treatment; it appears to be optional if the sex occurred following termination.

Colorado also requires informing clients that sexual intimacy is never appropriate and that it should be reported, nevertheless, psychotherapists are not required to report if clients do not grant permission (Article 43 of title 12, Colorado Revised Statutes, as amended 1987—see Appendix L). Wisconsin Act 380 (see Appendix W) requires psychotherapists to ask as soon "as practicable" if the client wants the therapist to make a report to the licensing board. It allows for a report that does not identify the client if he or she prefers not to be identified, even though the anonymity may make it impossible for the Board to act on the complaint.

RISKS FOR PROFESSIONALS

In Minnesota needless to say, a psychotherapist would be foolish to begin a sexual involvement with an ex-client, especially within two years of termination, given the risk of criminal prosecution, civil suit, licensure-related action, or adverse impact on employability. The risks for professionals performing related functions, such as psychological testing and evaluation are less clear. The prudent professional should be wary, however.

Even the time period of two years is very problematic. When does therapy actually end? Was a follow-up phone call six months later a psychotherapeutic intervention? Was that brief, impromptu follow-up consultation in private during a chance social meeting a continuation of the psychotherapy relationship?

Whether, with hindsight, the laws will turn out to be good or bad, right now in Minnesota the situation in relation to post-therapy sex is much clearer.

AND MORE RISKS

1. The civil statute, Chapter 372 Minnesota Statutes (Appendix N), creates a cause of action against employers who fail to ask past employers about an applicant's sexual misconduct with clients. Under this statute one may also sue a past employer for failing to pass on such information when it is requested. (The statute protects the past employer from suit if the failure to pass on the information is done in good faith.) If this standard becomes a common practice nationally, it may be that complaints will follow an offending therapist throughout his/her career.

2. As with typical child abuse reporting situations, the mandated reporting of therapist-client sex is required even if the events already have been reported by somebody else. In a recent situation, the wife of a psychiatrist was the subject of a proposed referral. During the referral process, the prospective therapist was told in passing that the wife was a former patient of the psychiatrist. The psychotherapist, although turning down the referral for various reasons, still had a duty to report the psychiatrist because (a) the relationship may have started during their previous professional relationship (which terminated many years earlier); and (b) even if it began after termination it could still be cause for discipline.[5]

AND SOME RISKS YOU NEVER DREAMED OF

1. When the relationship, even if it ends in marriage, does not work out the psychotherapist, who previously appeared all-powerful, may find him or herself the subject of civil suit, criminal charges, blackmail, or other punitive actions. The story about the relationship may sound very different when it is told from a different perspective. For example, in one case a lesbian therapist (A) attended two sessions with another lesbian therapist (B), who was sitting in to discuss the death throes of her relationship with the primary client. The relationship between the client and B ended and the client terminated therapy. About a month later B called A and suggested a social contact. A said this proposal made her very uncomfortable because she and B had had a professional relationship. B ridiculed the idea of any transference having occurred, pointing to her limited involvement as a "significant other" in only two sessions. So, A and B got involved. After several months the relationship did not work out and B made a complaint that she was "exploited." Although it was pointed out that when she was asked in detail about this charge she emphasized the technical grounds and did not claim that A had had power over her.

---

[5]Some states do have statutes of limitation, but many do not.

2. <u>Pregnancy</u>. It should be no surprise, but often is, that heterosexual involvements may lead to pregnancy. Pregnancy, as is usually the case, can result from the intention of one or both parties, contraceptive failure, or carelessness. Some cases I know of are reminiscent of adolescents who do not carry birth control devices as a way of denying an interest in sex, despite the obvious fact that sex may occur.

In some instances the female client (we have not dealt with pregnant female therapists thus far) may choose an abortion or the therapist may pressure her to have one. Beyond the costs involved, the procedure can leave emotional scars. In other situations the child is carried to term but then is given up for adoption, either immediately or within a few weeks, when the mother finds she cannot handle the situation. The therapist may have little or no say in the matter. And in still other situations the female client may bear the child and raise it. If the therapist denies paternity she is likely to sue him. Therapists are paying paternity costs in a number of cases. Developing a plan for visitation and raising the child can be quite complex in such cases.

Although in many instances therapists have attempted to deny paternity and do not want visitation rights, in a few cases they have sought to marry the client or, in the case of one married therapist, to gain visitation rights. In a case in Alaska a therapist admitted paternity but was denied access to the newborn child by the mother, an ex-client. He went to court and the judge ruled that he could have only supervised visitation, and even that was contingent on his obtaining professional help for himself (Sullivan, 1986).

Had this situation occurred in Minnesota or Wisconsin, where client/therapist sex is classified as a type of sexual assault, it is possible that the therapist would have been denied visitation, just as rapists are denied access to children who result from the rape.

RISK-TAKING BY PSYCHOTHERAPISTS

Having conducted both formal evaluations as well as sessions with therapists to process the development of their sexual or romantic relationships with clients, I have been struck by how many therapists are incredibly naive about their personal relationships. The fact is that ordinary romantic relationships often do not work out, and during the process of separation or divorce the parties often behave badly toward each other. Some people, whether clients or not, sometimes start out with passive and vulnerable behavior but end up being tough or dominant. Many therapists seem flabbergasted when relationships with ex-clients do not work out and clients turn on them; apparently the therapists are unprepared for the dynamics of either a typical romantic relationship or a client's recognizing that he or she has been victimized.

SOME ISSUES WORTHY OF THOUGHT

1. <u>Who is a client</u>?

First of all, at what point does a person become a client? After the first phone call? after an interview? or at some other point? Many professionals equate "client" status with the opening of a case file. In fact, however, client status probably is reached when a person considers herself or himself a client.

Second, what sort of interactions are professional enough to make someone a client? If a therapist does an unplanned crisis intervention on a social acquaintance at a party, and then talks to the acquaintance the next day to follow-up or make a referral, is the acquaintance a client?

Third, when a parent or family member talks as a "significant other" with a therapist on the telephone, is this person a client? Does the person become a client if he or she attends a single session as a "significant other"? The same questions can be asked in regard to roommates, friends, or others who may play a role in the evaluation or treatment of an individual.

Last but not least, is any client in your program, facility, or clinic everybody's client, or only the client of her or his primary therapist? Many residential treatment programs consider each client to be everybody's client.

2. Who is a Therapist?

In Minnesota any staff person of a residential treatment program for minors is considered to be a counselor, even the janitor. In any program, clinic, or facility it is essential to define the rules for all staff members. If the program offers "team" or "milieu" treatment, it can be argued easily that all staff members are therapists for all clients.

Furthermore, when one is involved in facilitating the helping process, such as making and/or following-up on referrals (e.g., as in Employee Assistance Programs or Impaired Practitioner Programs), is one a therapist of sorts? Do the same rules apply?

What about peer support or self-help groups? Even though, technically, a "peer" is the leader, nonetheless, a "therapist"? What about an Alcoholics Anonymous sponsor? In the early days an informal rule required AA sponsors to be of the same sex as the person being sponsored.

3. What is Therapy?

Minnesota laws relating to client/therapist sex not only have created a very broad definition of who is a therapist but, also, of what is therapy. For example, the Minnesota Criminal Sexual Conduct Code, as revised August 1, 1985, Section 609.341, Subdivision 17, defines "psychotherapy" as "the professional treatment, assessment, or counseling of a mental or emotional illness, symptom, or condition." Note that it includes assessment; and note also that the problem being addressed need be only a symptom or condition in the "mental" or "emotional" realm. (See Appendices G, L, M, O, and W for other definitions.)

To what degree is an educational or support group considered "psychotherapy"? Even a college class in which students learn about group therapy through experiences as part of a group may, in fact, be considered therapy clients. The same may be true regardless of whether fees are paid or the contact is somewhat informal, as when a student visits with a professor after class to discuss and get support for some personal problems.

What about groups or programs aimed at weight loss? cessation of smoking? Can clients in those groups be considered psychotherapy clients, even if the focus is predominantly educational?

4. When Does Therapy End?

Many therapists believe that their personal definitions of the point of therapy termination is all that matters. Those who work in programs or agencies may see termination as the closing of a case file.

First of all, what actual events must take place between client and therapist to make for a termination of the relationship?

There is remarkably little definition of termination in the professional literature. In an article entitled "Termination Criteria in Psychotherapy: A Comparison of Private and Public Practice," DeBerry and Baskin (1989), note the absence of clear criteria for termination in psychotherapy, although noting that there is some agreement in the literature that it is ideally a mutually shared process between client and therapist. Their study found significant differences in the reasons for termination of psychotherapy comparing private practice with a public clinic.

Regardless of what happens in that last session with the client, what happens if the therapist stresses that the client can re-contact him or her for more therapy at a later date? Given that the therapist still maintains files on the client and the client can return at any time, shouldn't the person still be considered a client? Examining this reality led Linda Biedermann, Director of the Florida Board of Psychological Examiners to suggest that the client be considered a client for as long as the professional records are maintained by the therapist (Biedermann, 1987).

What about follow-up contacts? If any are pre-arranged, whether for a visit, phone call, or mail, it can be argued that the therapy has not terminated. Even if they are not pre-arranged, any follow-up, whether part of the therapist's routine, related to a crisis the client is experiencing, or a chance meeting, may well revive the relationship.

Last but not least, we have family doctors and lawyers whose clients we remain even though we may not see them for many years and may have nowhere near as intense relationships with them, why do we believe that the therapy situation is any different? Ironically, many therapists pride themselves on the degree to which the client internalizes the therapist's directions and remembers them long after therapy ends, and how the continued influence of the therapist's words may sustain the client through crises. Clients who are fearful that they cannot make it on their own are sometimes told, "Don't worry, I'm always available."

KEY FACTORS IN EVALUATING A POST-TERMINATION RELATIONSHIP

Generally, we warn both therapist and client about the pitfalls of a personal or romantic relationship. Relationships are difficult enough as it is without adding the extra baggage of a past professional relationship. Even under the best circumstances it is unwise and risky. It has already been noted that for Minnesota-based psychotherapists and, at present, for psychologists in Florida, the risks are extreme.

Edelwich and Brodsky (1982) do a good job of listing the common rationalizations of therapists who seek to justify post-termination relationships with clients. It is good to be familiar with these before consulting to therapists in such situations. They also provide the topics for discussions of ethical and policy considerations such as: Compromise of the therapeutic process and gains; Denial of future therapeutic help; and "Corruption of the personal relationship" due to the power inequity and intimate knowledge of things revealed in therapy (Edelwich & Brodsky, 1982). On the other side, their discussion of the "exceptional instance" is equally worthy of review.

Having provided consultation to therapists and their clients as well as testifying in licensure and civil actions, we have had to articulate issues that need to be examined in weighing the risks and proprieties of post-termination relationships. Bear in mind that the question asked is not always "Is sex OK?" but, more likely, "Can we see each other socially?" or "Is romance permissible?" The following list contains some of the factors we consider:

1. <u>What was the length and level of therapeutic involvement</u>?

Typically, longer term therapy and intensive therapy create a power inequity that lasts longer—possibly even forever. By contrast, a crisis or brief therapy relationship may leave little or no lasting dependency or power inequity.

2. <u>How much transference, dependency, or power inequity remains after termination</u>?

To what degree is the therapist seen as an ordinary man or woman, or is the client seen as an ordinary man or woman? How strong was the transference? The stronger it was during the therapy, the less likely it has been resolved completely. In cases in which the therapist was seen more as a technician who was a helper in problem solving there may have been little or no transference.

3. <u>Personality variables and therapy style</u>.

Very dependent clients or those with chronic disorders can be vulnerable long after therapy terminates. When either the therapist or client is in a vulnerable position due to a recent loss, or because of longer term loneliness, social isolation, or difficulties in trusting others, one or both are at risk. Minnesota statutes focus on the client's continuing dependency but the therapist's continuing dependency on the client is also a common issue. Therapy styles can influence personality variables to worsen the situation, for example, when a dependent client becomes even more dependent on a "god-like" therapist or boundaries are not maintained in a therapy that emphasizes the supposed lack of a power differential between the two.

4. <u>Has there been therapeutic deception</u>?

Has a romantic or sexual relationship been presented as a part of or as consistent with therapy? Was it stated or implied that sex is commonly or generally accepted, or is acceptable under "certain circumstances"? Did the therapist cite a required time interval, or indicate that it was OK as long as the client was referred to another therapist? One type of therapeutic deception is that when the therapist tells the client that it will be OK as long as they get a pro forma or cursory consultation from another professional. Another type is that when the therapy style has involved considerable touch, self-disclosure by the therapist, or other elements that can be calculated to bring about intimacy.

5. <u>Was there an actual termination</u>?

This area is difficult because professional standards are woefully lacking. We usually ask how and when the decision to terminate was made. When it was made, was it mutual? What progress had been made on the client's original presenting complaint or the subsequent problems that emerged? What problems remain? How will they be dealt with? What sort of discussion was there of the treatment itself, the client's progress, the reasons for terminating at this time, and what the future holds? To what degree has either client or therapist mentioned possible re-initiation of therapy? (Some short-term therapy approaches emphasizing that the client can always return for more treatment can be problematic.) Last but not least, is there an indication that either party wanted to terminate so that a social, romantic, or sexual relationship could start?

6. <u>Who initiated post-termination contact</u>?

Here one must carefully examine the situation because not infrequently one or both parties have done things to set up a "chance" meeting. Therapists can make comments that invite contact, even by suggesting that the "good" client who is appreciative will not "be a stranger." Whenever a therapist initiates social contact the situation is suspect. For example, when Dr. Jones telephones out of the blue he/she is still "Dr. Jones" and not just "Mr./Ms. Jones." The client is still getting a call from the therapist, not just from another person. After all, the call could be some sort of a follow-up for professional reasons. Therapists who use their appointment books as a dating register are out of line, no matter how much time has elapsed after the termination of therapy.

7. <u>Has there been discussion of the pros and cons of such a relationship</u>?

Have the two parties talked about what they are up to: their intentions? the risks involved? how they would know if they were getting into trouble? A frank discussion of these and other questions should occur prior to consulting a neutral party to examine the proposed relationship.

8. <u>Has consultation been obtained</u>?

Have the two parties discussed their intentions with, for example, close friends, therapists, or supervisors? Have they met with an outside consultant of sufficient independence who can challenge what is going on, and provided him/her with sufficient information for a thorough review of the situation? An off-the-cuff or "quickie" consult with a friend just is not enough. If there has been a formal consultation, check with the consultant to verify the extent and quality of her/his information base and the events that transpired. We have heard some distorted accounts of the results of such consultations when we relied on the account of the therapist or client.

9. <u>The legal context, professional setting, and local standards</u>.

Has the therapist completely reviewed his/her vulnerability given the possible criminal and civil liability, reactions of colleagues and others, and effects on other clients? It is worth remembering that all psychotherapists are expected to behave somewhat as good role models, and that clients and the public at large develop their understanding of proper boundaries by observing the actions as much as the words of therapists.

SOME FINAL THOUGHTS

1. The issue of post-termination contact with clients is complex and even more difficult to deal with in a small or minority community. Gonsiorek and Brown address some of these issues in more detail in Chapter 25.

2. Post-therapy romances or sexual relationships are hazardous for the client, the professional, and the field of psychotherapy. Legal trends suggest that the risks of such relationships are increasing.

3. Persons thinking of working in the field should note that being a psychotherapist (as opposed to a business person) may preclude making social or romantic contacts during the course of one's work. If you do not want to observe these limitations you should enter some other field.

4. Psychotherapy is a much more difficult business than the model we typically learn in graduate or medical school. Our own vulnerabilities put us at risk in many types of situations.

5. There is a need for consultation on professional boundary issues to be more readily available in most communities. At WICC we get numerous calls from professionals seeking such consultation. Many callers told us that they have tried to get it from colleagues but found that the colleagues were muddled about the issues, or that disapproval was the only response, or that they feared disciplinary action or disapproval for even raising the issues.

6. The psychotherapy field must define the parameters of sexual relations between therapists and clients after therapy for both practitioners and consumers of the services. The current lack of clarity is appalling. Ignorance is not bliss. It is the breeding ground for disaster for the therapist, the client, and the field itself.

CHAPTER 25

POST THERAPY SEXUAL RELATIONSHIPS WITH CLIENTS

John C. Gonsiorek
and
Laura S. Brown

The Ethics Committee of the American Psychological Association in recent years has been engaged in a complex and protracted debate over whether to designate as unethical sexual and romantic relationships between therapists and their former clients. The deliberations are still continuing and opinions are still being sought in and given by all sectors of the field of psychology. Many groups (e.g., the Board of Professional Affairs, the Committee on Professional Practice) have taken a clear stance against such relationships but others have called for caution or expressed outright disagreement with the proposed change. The protracted nature of the discussion among psychologists illustrates the complexity of the issue.

Several questions are the focus of attention. (a) On what clinical grounds may such relationships be called unethical? (b) Is it legally possible to ban such relationships when the contractual relationship is no longer in place? (c) Is there evidence of harm to clients and former clients from the questioned practices that would justify making such an ethical judgment?

Only psychology, of all the mental health professions, is approaching the complex issues in an organized and serious manner (the Feminist Therapy Institute's recently published ethical code bans such post-termination relationships outright, however). Unfortunately, avoidance, denial, and insensitivity to the critical issues tend to be the common response of the helping professions. The problem is a skeleton in the closet of too many therapists. The stereotype of the psychoanalyst who marries his former patient is one with many kernels of truth, and the collective discomfort of mental health professionals with this issue is reflected in the general lack of attention paid to it until very recently.

We outline, in this chapter, the major themes of the problems as we have conceptualized them, and we try to address both clinical and legal concerns. We then generate a series of decision-making rules that we suggest be used by therapists to guide their behavior when the primary goal is the client's welfare rather than simply obedience to the letter of the law.

Another introductory point is important. We have worked together on this paper for about 18 months, and have developed a set of rules which we both endorse. However, we remain in respectful disagreement with each other about the reason for endorsement. We offer our differing opinions as an example of the remarkable complexity of this issue, and of the importance of working together to find common ground and workable solutions.

Brown believes that although there have been proposals to make sexual contact with a former client a violation of ethical codes or state statutes (for instance, in Florida, clients are considered to remain clients in perpetuity for purposes of sexual contact), she is not hopeful that such changes will either occur on a broad scale, or hold up to the inevitable constitutional challenges to their enforcement. She advises against romantic and sexual relationships with all former clients and believes them to be high-risk situations for all involved, notwithstanding the many "exception to the rule" stories that are told when this issue is raised among professionals. However, given the reality of the situation, e.g., that legal and ethical bans will not be feasible given the current understanding of therapist and client as having a fiduciary relationship that ends at termination, she suggests that our decision-making guidelines, if followed by a therapist considering such a post-termination relationship, should lead to the same conclusion, e.g., that such a relationship is harmful to all involved and should be avoided. She would hope that simply saying "no" would suffice; however, this is not enough, given legal complexities and state-to-state variability.

Gonsiorek, on the other hand, believes that the constitutional problems with a total ban involve substantive philosophical and political issues about the nature of psychotherapy which must be balanced against the overriding principle of acting with the client's welfare in mind. He believes that situations which satisfy the decision-making rules do exist, and may—and occasionally do—pose no harm to clients and no violation of the ethical imperatives of mental health professionals. He cautions, however, that such situations are in a clear minority, and that the demands of the proposed rules are—and should be—considerable.

Our differences may involve varying perspectives of gender, although individuals of all genders fall on all sides of this issue. Probably more relevant is professional context. Brown does primarily long-term psychotherapy, in a context where such practice is expected and normative. Gonsiorek does primary goal-oriented therapy in a community where such practice is expected and normative. Our different professional prospectives have likely colored our beliefs about this issue. Nevertheless, we have found—or rather created—an area of agreement.

For Brown, then, the proposed decision-making rules are the best current compromise, given a belief that post-therapy sexual involvements with clients are always unsound, but that this opinion must co-exist with competing principles in a legal context. For Gonsiorek, the proposed decision-making rules are, in fact, the best current principles, given that both the need to protect clients and the need to respect the rights of all parties are part of ethical decision making. We are, in any case, in agreement on the viability and usefulness of our proposed rules.

STATEMENT OF THE PROBLEM

1. The Clinical Problem:

The emotional "contract" between therapist and client carries meaning beyond that of a legal contract in which responsibilities terminate when the services have been rendered. Therapy, clinically, is differently construed. Most theories of psychotherapy give a central role to the relationship between therapist and client; it is the agent for change. Although some more recent approaches to psychotherapy have de-emphasized the importance of the relationship, it is still difficult to find a school of psychotherapy that does not grant some importance to it. Most ethical codes in the helping professions pay homage to the existence of that special relationship by defining certain actions by a therapist as likely to do harm to a client, given that implicit relationship "contract."

The special, unusual, and emotionally significant nature of the relationship between therapist and client is usually defined by the term "transference." We use the term in the remainder of this paper to characterize symbolic aspects of a client's feelings about the client-therapist relationship. Similarly, we refer to the therapist's symbolic responses to the client by the term "countertransference." We recognize that we are using these terms in a very broad, generic, and nonprecise manner that goes beyond their classic psychoanalytic definitions. It is because of what occurs in this transferential relationship that sexual contacts between therapists and current clients are deemed to be unethical. There is a risk that the client will be harmed.

Clinically, the problem of post-termination relationships centers in part on the extraordinary difficulty of determining when a transferential relationship can be deemed resolved or ended. One commentator (Hall, 1984, p. 11) noted that, "The half-life of transference exceeds that of plutonium," suggesting that an end may be long in coming, if at all. In the transferential relationship, the therapist's power is greater than the client's in various ways, even in those approaches to psychotherapy in which the equalization of power is an explicit goal of the process. Thus, we have another way of framing the problem: It is difficult to determine when or if the power relationship has become genuinely equal. The clinical assumption is that in the context of greatly unequal power sexual contact risks damage to the less powerful person. Such a power differential is not merely symbolic; a number of real-world and observable phenomena (e.g., the therapist is paid for participating in the relationship with the client; the therapist is perceived as expert and her/his opinions are given greater credibility than are the client's) attest to this power imbalance. Legally, in fact, the relationship between therapist and client is viewed as a fiduciary one with the therapist deemed to have the greater power and responsibility (see Schutz, 1982, Chapter 1).

Psychodynamic psychotherapies have always emphasized the meaning and importance of transference but the issue of how power is distributed in psychotherapy has become less clear as treatment methods have diversified. It may be possible currently to use a continuum of variation in depth and emotional intensity to describe psychotherapeutic approaches that range from classical psychoanalysis to long-term psychodynamic therapy, short-term psychodynamic therapy, family therapy, systems theory, cognitive-behavioral, and behavioral therapies, to brief, goal-oriented counseling and situations that are primarily or purely evaluative, educational, or informative and referral-oriented.

At one pole the relationship between client and therapist is the core and heart of the therapy process. The treatment is likely to be long-term, exploratory in nature, anxiety-producing, potentially regressive, possibly psychologically intrusive, and resting on the profound power differential between a client who shares his/her every fantasy and a therapist whose personal life remains largely unknown. The symbolic parental aspects of the therapist-client relationship may become extremely important.

At the other pole the relationship is all but ignored and the therapist is seen as a giver of information or as a consultant to a client addressing certain limited issues. The power differential is minimized although it is still present in the designation of the therapist as "expert." There is little opportunity for exploration of in-depth issues or emotional regression. The therapist's skill and knowledge, not the relationship, are the crucial elements. Currently, this entire range of services in all its diversity can be subsumed under the heading "mental health," and thus all are within the purview of our discussion.

Once there are answers to the questions of whether and to what degree transference and a power differential exist within a therapist-client relationship, however, new complexities emerge. Even if it is possible to determine with some confidence that a particular relationship between the client and the therapist has terminated both legally and clinically, the possibility that the client may need to return to the therapist for future therapy clouds the issue. Many schools of therapy do not conceptualize a point of cure. Even for those that do, it is not unheard of for a client to return for help to address a new life issue, to cope with a current crisis, or to follow up on the previous work. In such a situation transference may wax and wane but never entirely die out.

A further complication exists in using termination as the decision-making variable to enter a sexual relationship with a client; it may be, in fact, duplicitous behavior by some therapists. Such persons "officially" terminate therapy in order to initiate sexual or romantic relationships with clients and yet retain the appearance of ethical behavior. Such duplicity can be either overt or covert. The therapist may inform a client, "I would love to have a relationship with you but cannot because we are client and therapist." The implicit message is that the client should initiate termination to free the therapist to pursue the romance and avoid the appearance of premature termination. The therapist may "declare" the client terminated or "cured" in order to be free to initiate the sexual relationship; the ostensible justification for such a termination is that the client is finished with therapy.

Such duplicitous situations raise many complex clinical and ethical questions. Certainly one may be concerned with the standard of care offered by a therapist who plans to terminate the overt therapeutic relationship in order to initiate sex, because such a termination is based on the therapist's narcissistic needs rather than the good of the client. Such a termination is often pro forma only; the client is offered few or no opportunities for the emotional resolution of therapy issues before he or she is plunged into a relationship in which the therapist's romantic or sexual needs—not the client's needs—are often primary. One such therapist, prior to making love to a client, even had her write a letter stating that they had terminated therapy. Furthermore, the therapy is likely to have been "contaminated" for some time prior to the exploitation. The therapist's suggestion to terminate may represent only the tip of the iceberg of manipulating the client to satisfy the therapist's sexual and emotional needs during the course of therapy.

Many professionals agree that it is clearly improper to terminate therapy solely to pursue a sexual or romantic relationship with the client although such behavior is not explicitly prohibited by any professional ethics code (except for the Feminist Therapy Institute code). The psychiatric code does not specify this situation but it has an accompanying casebook that may be construed as speaking to this issue. Thus there is a legal loophole through which duplicitous or unethical therapists can slide. In an attempt to deal with such possibilities the American Psychological Association's Ethics Committee recently stated that termination of therapy with the intent to pursue a sexual relationship is an ethical violation equivalent to sexual relations with a current client. However, the debate still continues over the propriety of such relationships, when the intention is unconscious, denied, or nonexistent.

One perspective on this issue is that sexual relationships with former clients simply should be banned. This suggestion, although appealing, becomes problematic when the full range of definitions of "therapist" and "client" is examined. Should the ban apply when psychological testing was the only service rendered? When there was only medication management, no "talk therapy?" To structured, time-limited group therapies that were primarily educational in nature? To telephone contacts that were solely for information and referral?

For the therapist who works as an organizational consultant the questions are even more complex. Are all members or employees of the organization deemed to be clients? Do public educational activities fall under the rubric of therapy? It is relatively simple to imagine a long list of situations that are common among and normative for therapists in which a total ban on post-termination relationships appears problematic in the extreme. On the other hand, our experience has demonstrated that an equally long list of horror stories relate to therapists who have actively abused the transferential relationship and power differential in order to sexually exploit a former client, yet have managed to present a plausible explanation for why the behaviors were allowable.

The total ban also has been criticized on clinical grounds. In one argument, based on a humanistic perspective, a total ban implies that therapists are always and forever magically powerful superhumans and that clients are never "persons" but, rather, always in the box of "patient" (Machover, 1986). Another related argument is that a ban restricts the rights and freedoms of former clients in a manner that is unfair and disrespectful of the growth and change they experienced in therapy (Dawes, 1986). Some supporters of such a ban have argued that a parallel model and precedent for post-therapy restraints on therapist behavior is found in the continuing requirement for confidentiality after termination. The counter argument finds in this model the assumption that harm will befall the client from the post-termination sexual relationship; the assumption is seen as "infantilizing," as demeaning the client's adulthood and humanity in the post-termination situation. On the other hand, the assumption of harm is reasonable and nonpejorative in the confidentiality situation. These humanistic arguments are closely linked to the legal questions of how and whether such a total ban would abridge the constitutional right of freedom of association between two individuals who no longer have a professional or fiduciary relationship.

One commonly proposed solution to this problem is that sexual relationships with clients be banned for a specified period of time post-termination; in fact, some therapists appear to believe that such a rule is already in place to judge by their statements in post-termination relationships that they waited out the required time period! For example, in a recent survey of psychologists reported by Pope, Tabachnik and Keith-Spiegel (1987, p. 996) 96.1% of respondents were of the opinion that "engaging in sexual contact with a client" is "unquestionably not ethical," but only 50.2% believed that "becoming sexually involved with a former client" is "unquestionably not ethical." The length of this proposed period varies; the usual suggested range is between six months and two years. The time variation itself suggests a major problem with this proposed solution. That is, it is difficult to determine how long it should take for transference and power differentials to disappear, which is the rationale, ostensibly, for the waiting period. In addition, time-related proposals carry the implication that sexual relationships with former clients generally are permissible after the designated time period, thus encouraging involvements that may be clearly and frankly damaging, given the facts of a particular case.

This brief overview indicates that the discourse has raised more counter arguments and questions clinically than it has provided clarity. We conclude, therefore, that the confusion stems from the inherently faulty assumptions of the discourse. At least one assumption of the discourse is that there is only one answer to the question; or that all clients, therapists, and therapy relationships are alike. Another faulty assumption is that it is always possible to ascertain when a client becomes an ex-client. Prior to discussing our remedies to this question, however, it is important to review first the legal and administrative responses. This review is crucial because whatever consensus may be generated among mental health professionals also must stand the test of functioning well in the complicated realm of administrative, civil, and criminal law; their assumptions on reality and the nature of relationships often are quite different from those in psychotherapy.

2. Legal and Administrative Responses: Current State

National data are lacking on the responses of professional regulatory boards, except for psychology licensure boards, to post-treatment relationships between therapists and clients. Sell, Gottlieb and Schoenfeld (1986) reported that whether or not such relationships were prohibited by laws or ethics codes, many psychology licensing boards have found psychologists to be "in violation even when they claimed that the therapeutic relationship had already been terminated" (p. 505).

Finally, recent research on the work of state licensing boards (Gottlieb, Sell, and Schoenfeld, 1988) suggests that time since termination is not a factor in determining attitudes of such boards toward post-termination relationships, with one board finding a psychologist is in violation for a relationship begun four years post-termination. Although the other facts surrounding this case are not given in the Gottlieb article, the message is clear that waiting to act may not be considered a mitigating factor by those bodies who evaluate and adjudicate such post-termination relationships.

State licensing boards have responded to the problem on a case-by-case basis because they have resisted establishing a clear overall standard (except for the Florida Psychology Board; recently it specifically put a total ban on post-treatment relationships. (See Ch. 24, for further discussion.) Our experiences bear out this conclusion. Gonsiorek testified at a rule-making hearing for a state licensing board some years ago and suggested that, at the very least, sexual interaction with former clients within six months of termination be treated as sexual contact during therapy. The board rejected the idea on the grounds that they had no authority to regulate post-therapy situations and that such a ban would be unconstitutional. However, this same board has responded to complaints about post-therapy situations as if they were the same as sexual contact during therapy. Thus the administrative response has tended to be one of ambivalence and confusing double messages to both therapists and aggrieved clients.

Such a situation creates as many problems as it resolves. Therapists are held to a covert standard, and case-by-case decision making risks arbitrary, capricious, and biased applications of law. The same offense behaviorally may result in very different consequences for different individuals. Keith-Spiegel and Koocher (1986) pointed out that mental health professionals tend to prescribe more stringent punishments for the same ethical offenses committed by colleagues they dislike than by those they respect; the potential is great for the occurrence of such unfair treatment. This kind of capriciousness by licensing boards and ethics committees also contributes to an adversary relation between mental health professionals and their ethics and regulatory colleagues. Rather than being regarded as positive sources of quality control and consultation, ethics committees and licensing boards that operate without or in violation of clear standards are considered dangerous watchdogs to be tricked and bypassed when possible.

In four states (Wisconsin, Minnesota, North Dakota, and Colorado) sexual activity between client and therapist has been specifically criminalized. Two other states (New Hampshire and Michigan) have older criminal statutes that pertain more generally to the exploitation of patients by physicians and may be construed to apply to client-therapist sexual contact. Only the Minnesota statute specifically addresses post-therapy situations. This statute (see Appendix H) makes sexual activity with a former client a felony in two instances: (a) when the "former patient is emotionally dependent upon the psychotherapist," and (b) when the sexual activity "occurred by means of a therapeutic deception." Clearly, this legislation attempts to address the clinical issues of transference reactions and power differentials that persist post-therapy. Schoener (1986) believes that the Wisconsin statute may be open to interpretation as criminalizing post-therapy relationships, although this nuance remains to be tested in court.

Minnesota's civil code also provides for dealing with post-therapy situations. In 1986, the state legislature enacted a statute holding that a former client may have a civil cause of action against a therapist if sexual contact occurred between them within two years after the termination of psychotherapy. This civil statute uses the same wording as the criminal statute regarding therapeutic deception and emotional dependency. Thus, a client suing for damages related to sexual involvement during a two-year post-termination period would have to prove that one of the two situations existed.

Although none of the laws has been tested in court on such questions as constitutionality (an important concern of people who would prefer not to explicitly ban post-termination relationships), it is noteworthy that the laws speak to the clinical issues of transference (emotional dependency) and power differential (therapeutic deception). They appear, therefore, to provide a model for common ground and shared discourse between mental health and legal personnel. (See Ch. 24 for details of the implications of recent legislative and administrative rulings on post-therapy situations.)

Unfortunately, recent contributions in legal theory have done little to elucidate the issues. Coleman (1988) reviewed the legal principles that govern sexual activity between psychiatrists and their former patients. Her analysis and conclusion are both problematic for several reasons. First, she restricts her discussion of the problem to the narrow area of psychoanalytic practice by psychiatrists, which accounts for only a small percentage of psychotherapy practiced today. Second, her assumptions about what occurs in therapy reflect deep misunderstandings of that process. In particular, she relies on the incorrect notion that termination is marked by a full resolution of the transference relationship, which she also incorrectly believes to be always eroticized. This last belief is the basis for her argument that sex with former patients should be allowed on the grounds that transference will no longer be present. She assumes there is a clear demarcation between times when transference is present, and times when it is not, and seems to believe that a failure to completely eradicate transferential dynamics is equivalent to a failure of therapy. This article is an excellent indicator of the failure to adequately comprehend the nature of psychotherapy, and underscores the problems in attempting to deal with an issue that combines elements of psychotherapy ethics and legal requirements.

SPECIAL ISSUES FOR CONSIDERATION

1. Overlapping Roles and the Small-World Problem:

Much of the previous discussion is based on assumptions about the nontherapy social relationships of clients and therapists which may not be true in certain specific settings and for some groups of practitioners. One assumption is that it is relatively simple for therapists and their current or former clients to maintain social distance, and that it is unlikely the two groups will meet spontaneously outside the therapy office. However, this assumption does not extend to certain groups. They include rural psychotherapists; recovering alcoholism or other substance-abuse counselors who are in 12-Step programs attended by clients; and ethnic or sexual minority therapists who work with members of their own group.

For such therapists, social distance from clients may be impossible and, in some cases, undesirable to attain. They must constantly negotiate issues of overlapping professional and personal boundaries, often in public, and with little prior warning or time to reflect on the best course of action. Further, given that confidentiality requirements simultaneously exist, therapists may not be able to give socially appropriate reasons for withdrawing from certain situations. It is common for ethnic and sexual minority therapists to have case loads with significant numbers of members of their own groups. The reason, in part, is the perception by the clients that their "own kind" will serve them better and have greater empathy with the realities of shared oppression; and, in part, a reflection of the desire to support the work of members of one's own group. In rural areas where only one or two therapists may be in practice, almost anyone can be a client or former client. Among racial or ethnic minorities, minority psychotherapists are often part of the community's educated elite. In the gay and lesbian communities, psychotherapists may be accorded more respectability and greater access to power in the larger society than are other members. In small towns, higher educational level is often a factor. In such settings, in addition, there is also often real or perceived pressure on the therapist, as a prominent member of a reference group, to participate visibly on community boards and committees.

Thus, a therapist who identifies with a specific group is constantly confronted with what are referred to in ethics codes as "dual relationships" in which he or she is both therapist and fulfilling another role; sexual relationships with clients always have been seen as a subset of dual relationships, which also are generally considered to be unethical or, at least, problematic. Berman (1985) suggested the term "overlapping relationships" to refer to the unavoidable aspects of certain sociocultural contacts in which therapists and their clients live.

In organized psychology over the last decade the theoretical principle of dual relationships has evolved as a major touchstone for decisions on the boundaries of client-therapist relationships. The principle is that a psychologist should make every effort to avoid dual relationships with clients. At first glance, this principle makes considerable sense and appears to be very useful for actualizing the principle that psychotherapists always act in the general welfare of their clients. Dual relationships, at least in the initial articulation of the concept, were generally viewed to include romantic, sexual, business, and other clearly complicating interactions with clients.

A reasonable application of the dual relationship concept rapidly becomes obscure in post-therapy situations, however. First of all is the general problem in determining when therapy ends. Few professionals disagree that sexual, romantic, business, and other relationships with clients are improper and can lead to the exploitation of the client, especially if the therapist is unscrupulous or the client suspends normal personal judgment because of trust in the therapist. We would like to note, in addition, if only in passing, that such activities are also unwise because they may equally lead to the exploitation of the therapist who, too, may suspend normal personal judgment. But where are the limits? In the same place for clients as for ex-clients? Is it improper to be waited on in a department store by a client or an ex-client? Is it improper to buy a work of art that happens to be produced by a client or ex-client? What about a house? It is improper to buy one's stationery from a business that is partially owned by a client or ex-client? With a little imagination one can generate all sorts of situations in which either the client or ex-client potentially may be exploited by some kind of involvement; and one can also generate situations in which strict prohibitions against such involvement constrict the activities of both parties, but particularly those of the therapist, to an increasingly absurd degree, particularly as the nature of the dual relationship becomes more removed and tenuous.

In minority communities, it is common for a therapist to find her/himself attending cultural or social events with current or former clients, or serving with them on the board of a local rights group or community service organization. In a small town, a client may ring up purchases at the supermarket or be the only available physician to treat one's children in an emergency. Chemical dependency counselors speak of steering clients away from their favorite AA meetings because of a feeling that their private spaces will be invaded. Additionally, many members of minority groups enter professional training with the stated goal of serving their communities, which are still notoriously underserved. They feel that— and they are—needed in their own groups by whom they are often seen as role models and community leaders.

Thus, the risk of encountering a former client long after the termination of therapy and of entering into a romantic relationship is heightened for such therapists. Ironically, because of their minority and sometimes marginal status in professional communities, such persons are also at greater risk for the kind of capricious and unfair treatment by regulatory groups in the current context of confusion regarding post-termination relationships. This seems particularly to be the case when the post-termination relationships are between same-gender individuals.

Further, in minority groups that are oppressed economically, socially, or both, practitioners often find that the standard application of traditional psychotherapeutic procedures may introduce biases that are racist, sexist, homophobic, or class related. Therefore, minority psychotherapists more often synthesize derivations of traditional psychotherapies to bring them more in line with the needs of minority populations, such as various kinds of support groups, educational services, and larger community interventions. In other words, the tendency is for minority psychotherapists, at least in some communities, to include in the mix of services they offer more contributions from the educational, goal-directed end of the spectrum.

We would argue that it is both naive and insensitive to respond to the complicated boundary situations that often result in a dictum that minority and small-town psychotherapists and alcohol and substance abuse counselors simply should absent themselves from these activities. The idea is tantamount to suggesting that such psychotherapists avoid participating in the life of the community. To do so often will be seen as a disparagement of the community and hence will be correctly viewed as a social and political statement. At the same time, there is often a greater potential for abuse by minority and small-town psychotherapists precisely because they often have these additional and powerful roles in their communities.

Therefore, in order to develop for post-termination relationships an ethical rule that can be clearly and fairly applied, the special needs and conditions of therapists working in geographical or sociocultural "small towns" must be addressed. For the question of post-termination romantic or sexual relationships, the whole problem of post-therapy, nonsexual dual or overlapping relationships must be better understood and addressed also.

The introduction of the dual relationship concept into a discussion of post-therapy sex may seem an unnecessary complication. Yet the issue must be addressed because of the apparent naivete with which some licensing boards have made the banning of dual relationships a part of their deliberations without considering the limits of this concept and what are its legitimate and problematic applications. A simple ban on dual relationships neither informs nor encourages a therapist who must overlap roles with current or former clients simply, for example, to get dry cleaning done. It is important to articulate the concept because its strict application rapidly evolves into overt economic and political implications for minority psychotherapists, such as prohibiting them from participating in the economic, social, and political life of their communities. Thus the discussion is relevant here because the principle is often seen as the basis for determining which behaviors by psychotherapists are improper or exploitive.

2. Bias and Inconsistency in Response to the Problem of Sexual Exploitation:

After so many decades of professional neglect of clients who have been sexually exploited, it may seem misguided to worry about justice for the therapists who have exploited them. Many professional ethics committees and state licensing boards are taking a long, firm—even if overdue—stance on the exploitation of clients and even to view sexual contact with ex-clients as a comparable act. Yet, professional ethics codes do not offer a clear statement on post-therapy relationships and licensing boards rarely make a clear rule about the conduct. Further, few guidelines have been formulated within which ethics committees and licensing boards are required to operate to respond to unethical behavior. Essentially, it is also their prerogative to work on a case by case basis.

The result is that ethics committees and licensing boards appear to be responding to ethical violations not only with greater rigor but, also, with greater inconsistency. The same unethical behavior may have very different consequences, depending on the current composition of an ethics committee or a licensing board; the political pressures operating on the board when they make their decision (e.g., recent publicity about board actions; criticism of previous leniency), whether the unethical behaviors involve same-sex or opposite-sex situations; the reputation of the offending psychotherapist; and a host of other variables.

The net result of the wide latitude given to ethics committees and licensing boards, coupled with the pressures they face, tends to reproduce a microcosm of the biases inherent in our society. In other words, psychotherapists who may be unpopular because of their sexual orientation, racial or ethnic minority status, theoretical orientation, political connections, and the like, are apt to be treated with greater severity than are therapists who more resemble the majority of the population, who are well connected politically and who are viewed as working in the mainstream of their profession. Granted that such concerns have little legitimate place in discussions of the proper solution to post-therapy sexual situations, nevertheless they cannot be overlooked in terms of pragmatic solutions to the issue. In other words, any reasonable solution to the post-therapy sexual situation should incorporate basic concepts of justice and fair play; it should not be capricious, arbitrary, inconsistent, or unduly vulnerable to political manipulation or the vicissitudes of societal prejudices.

We must note, however, that there is a reasonable and proper use of a licensing board's discretionary powers, such as fine tuning their responses to the particulars of an unethical situation. For example, it might include responding to the overly sadistic treatment of a client or to the co-existence of other ethical violations, and the like. This kind of fine tuning, though, is not the same as responding to variables that are external to the unethical situations at hand. (See Gonsiorek & Schoener, 1987, for a discussion of licensing board responses.)

PROPOSED CONCEPTUAL FRAMEWORK FOR A TEMPORARY SOLUTION

In reviewing the issue, it quickly becomes apparent that until now no clear and certain solution has been found to the question of how to respond ethically or legally to post-termination romantic and sexual relationships between therapists and former clients. Intuitively, one can sense considerable potential for harm to the people in such a relationship, but so far there are both clinical and legal obstacles to making a definitive statement within the context of an ethics code.

Thus, in this section, we draw upon our preceding explication of the issue to suggest a decision-making model, one that reduces the risk of harm to vulnerable clients, increases thoughtfulness and self-care by the therapists, and still respects the legal and clinical realities of the arguments against a total ban. This decision-making model takes into account the variations in types of therapy, definitions of "therapist" and "client," and factors that can increase or intensify a transferential relationship with its inherent power imbalance.

Our model makes a very rough distinction between two types of therapy; for the sake of simplicity we refer to them as "Type A" and "Type B." Type A therapy is defined for our purposes as psychotherapy in which the transferential relationship plays a primary or central role in the process; in which there exists a clear and objectively determinable power differential between client and therapist; in which therapy is long term (e.g., more than one year); and in which therapy is regressive in nature, that is, the client comes to consciously or subconsciously perceive the therapist in a parental or powerful authority role. Type B therapies, on the other hand, are short-term (e.g., less than one year); they offer few opportunities for the development of a transferential relationship or overtly minimize transference; they tend to be structured or problem focused; and they do emphasize power differentials. Clearly, these two groupings do not describe all types of therapy and many approaches fall somewhere between. However, for the very tentative and initial purposes of our proposed model, this typology is useful.

Based on these types, we make the following proposals:

I. Sexual contact with former clients who have received Type A therapy is always and forever prohibited.

This restriction reflects what appears to be the area of greatest consensus in the debate. However, it leaves open a question with which we continue to have grave concern: Can a post-therapy sexual relationship with certain kinds of clients **ever** be considered proper? In response to this question, which raises the issue of the variability of clients and therapists, we offer the second proposal.

II. Post-termination sexual contact with severely disturbed clients always will be considered unethical and improper, regardless of the type of service rendered. Clients with a history of childhood physical and sexual abuse, regardless of degree of current disturbance, also shall be included in this prohibition.

The principle in this restriction is that for certain clients the power differential or symbolic/transferential aspects of the relationship are such that the power differential almost always will continue after therapy, and any post-termination sexual contact almost always will be exploitative. In our experience, two groups are at the highest risk for damage from post-termination relationships. Among the severely disturbed, we include persons with diagnoses of any sort of psychosis, low-functioning personality-disordered individuals, and any others who, because of intensity or chronicity of a problem, are likely to remain in need of the therapist's services and thus, remain vulnerable, isolated, emotionally dependent, or manifesting poor reality testing on judgment abilities. Survivors of childhood abuse are included because, in our clinical experience, such persons represent the bulk of clients who are sexually exploited by therapists. Their early experiences leave them particularly vulnerable to further sexual exploitation, regardless of their ability to function in settings outside of therapy.

III. It is never permissible for the therapist to initiate post-termination romantic contact.

When the therapist contacts the client, he or she is always still a "therapist," by virtue of being in a powerful position vis a vis the definition of the relationship and because the client likely assumes that it is his or her former therapist who is phoning. If the therapist is still in a powerful position, the client may accede to the request or suggestion of social or romantic contact. When a client describes receiving such a phone call from a therapist, one must ask whether the call came from <u>Mr</u>. Jones or <u>Dr</u>. Jones—normally the response is "Hello <u>Dr</u>. Jones."

It is worth noting in this context that therapists do at times phone terminated clients in order to do follow-up or to obtain long-term feedback on outcome. Such follow-up calls are by and of themselves not ethically problematic. Rather, it is when they are used as a stratagem to entrap a former client into a planned romantic or sexual relationship that they become evidence of error.

IV. Sexual contact with a client (other than those excluded in Proposal II) who has received Type B services always will be considered unethical if it occurs within two years after termination of therapy. Sexual contact with any client who has received Type B therapy will continue to be prohibited if any of the following conditions pertain: (A) the therapist at some time has told the client to return to therapy at a later date or (B) if any other than incidental social contact occurred during the two-year period. It is always the responsibility of the therapist in such a situation to obtain an independent objective consultation to evaluate whether all these criteria have been met. The application of this principle in no way implies any necessary propriety of post-termination relationships after the two-year waiting period; rather, it suggests how to evaluate and avoid possible risks of harm.

This third proposal, although complex, allows for the possibility of a genuinely "innocent" and nonexploitative post-termination involvement. If, for example, the therapist genuinely provided only a Type B service that was clearly terminated **and** no or merely incidental contact has occurred for at least two years, then if the parties randomly meet each other completely apart from the professional situation **and** there are no implicit or explicit expectations of a professional relationship, **if** they wish to pursue the possibility of a romantic relationship at that time **and** the therapist seeks consultation from an objective colleague who is not a friend, then **perhaps** the relationship should not be prohibited. Our requirement for consultation here is not meant to imply a request that the relationship receive some sort of "seal of approval"; rather, we wish to emphasize the <u>degree</u> to which the therapist bears a special responsibility to act in the best interest of all parties in making certain that the relationship is not potentially harmful and unethical.

V. Any mental health services that cannot clearly and easily be defined as Type B shall be considered to be Type A for purposes of this model.

We stress here our general principle that the welfare of the client is paramount. When there is any possibility of risk or harm to a former client, the most stringent standards should apply.

VI. Rules for ethical action in nonsexual post-therapy overlapping or dual relationship situations should be formulated apart from rules regarding sexual contact. The preceding proposals should not be considered necessarily to apply to nonsexual post-termination contacts between therapists and former clients.

Although many concepts relating to sexual relationships may be applicable to certain other types of post-termination relationships (e.g., business relationships, close friendship relationships), our preceding discussion demonstrates that for some therapists overlapping post-therapy roles are unavoidable. They are complex situations and deserve further study and consideration so that guidelines for ethical behavior, when unavoidable overlap occurs, can be developed. We believe that such guidelines can clarify the goals and rationales of ethics codes for all therapists, not simply for those who must function in small-community settings.

VII. Ethical and regulatory groups should develop a clear, written standard regarding post-therapy sexual or romantic relationships with clients and apply it consistently. Case by case determinations in the absence of written standards or the application of "unwritten rules" are unethical and unacceptable. Further, it is imperative that various ethical and regulatory groups develop common standards. Diverse responses from such groups are confusing to clients and the public, as well as to many professionals.

It is our belief that in most cases, post-termination sexual relationships are probably unethical and harmful to clients. However, current practices by ethical and regulatory groups invite arbitrary and capricious behavior by such groups and risk violation of the legal rights of offending therapists. The best encouragement for ethical action by the community of mental health professionals is to clearly model ethical ways of thinking and acting by our ethics committees and licensing boards in all their activities.

CONCLUSION

The question of how to approach post-termination romantic and sexual relationships between therapists and former clients is a difficult one. The arguments on all sides in many ways are a reprise of the discussions held over a decade ago when the American Psychological Association first explicitly banned sexual contact between therapists and current clients. The statistics suggest that as many as 10% of all therapists engage in such relationships, and many do so more than once (Bouhoutsos, Holroyd, Lerman, Forer and Greenberg, 1983; Gartrell, Herman, Olarte, Feldstein and Localio, 1986). The issues are not esoteric but, rather, real and painful aspects of psychotherapy practice and the experience of being a psychotherapy client. Our seven proposals, although tentative, offer some preliminary guidelines for ethical decision making by a therapist who is in doubt of the appropriateness of his/her actions. Our discomfort with post-termination relationships is apparent. In our experience most tend to violate our proposed decision-making rules and to bring further harm and pain to already vulnerable and wounded individuals. On the other hand, it is important that professional ethics codes maintain a delicate balance between the protection of vulnerable clients and the civil and legal rights of both clients and therapists. A simple, "Thou shalt not" does not suffice for a problem that is so complex in nature.

PART VII

Advocacy, Complaints, And Processing Sessions

Milgrom, in Chapter 26, delineates the role of advocate. Many therapists shy away from this role because they want to be more of a "pure" therapist. Unfortunately, other qualified advocates often are not available and thus a client is left to fend for him or herself.

Yet advocacy is often very helpful to a client, and sometimes plays a more important role in recovery from abuse and exploitation than follow-up psychotherapy (see Ch. 7). When therapists are unwilling to take on the tasks and try to stay completely clear of complaint processes, the message they inadvertently communicate to the client is that they do not either fully believe the client or support punitive action against the exploitative therapist (presumably because they don't think it's all that serious a case of abuse). This tacit message in many instances confuses and troubles the client.

The "Wheel of Options" is a useful illustration of the range of alternatives that are possible for a therapist-advocate. Some clients have found it very reassuring.

Various complaint options are examined in more detail by Schoener in Chapter 27. Readers will still have to do homework on state and local laws and regulations to properly advise clients. The chapter covers not only complaint options but, also, some fundamentals of helping clients to explore their goals vis `a vis taking action. It also reviews the ethics codes of various psychotherapy professions with regard to language relevant to sexual contact between therapist and client.

The model of the "processing session" developed at the WICC is presented in Chapter 28 by Schoener and Milgrom. A processing session is a meeting, facilitated by an outside consultant, that involves a client with a grievance and a therapist who is the subject of the grievance. The procedure was developed as a way of helping clients to confront therapists with questions on or accusations of sexual exploitation; the model, however, is useful for other types of complaints as well.

CHAPTER 26

ADVOCACY: ASSISTING SEXUALLY EXPLOITED CLIENTS THROUGH THE COMPLAINT PROCESS[1]

Jeanette Hofstee Milgrom

The most consistent and unique role played by the Walk-In Counseling Center in Minnesota over the past 14 years has been as a provider of advocacy services (see Ch. 1). WICC staff have acted as advocates for many hundreds of clients who had been or were being sexually abused by prior therapists. This chapter is based on the accumulated experience. It is addressed to those persons in the helping professions who provide counseling/therapy and who may need to take an advocacy role when a sexually exploited client comes to their attention. Many counselors and therapists may not be familiar with this role and, initially, may feel uneasy about taking it on. Fortunately, the advocate does not have to go it alone; assistance, support, and resources can be found along the way.

The term "advocacy" means different things to different people. In this chapter the word is used to denote the active assistance of a client in formulating, filing, or processing a complaint against a previous therapist who engaged in unethical or unprofessional conduct toward the client.

To correct the power imbalance in the therapist/client relationship, the advocate assists the sexually exploited client in restoring the balance by putting her/his weight on the client's side of the scale and beginning the reckoning process. The goal of advocacy is to empower the client and to promote the healing process.

THE ADVOCACY ROLE

The advocacy role includes many components for which basic counseling skills are critical, such as being able to communicate, to empathize, and to establish a relationship with a client.

Some skills are particularly important. They include clinical assessment of a depressed and sometimes suicidal client, and crisis intervention skills, especially when the trauma is recent. The client must be told that in cases of sexual exploitation the therapist is always responsible, no matter who initiated what. Clients may not be ready to accept this statement if they have strong feelings of guilt and loyalty toward the abusing therapist but an advocate's failure to inform the client of this fact may prolong her or his confusion.

Establishing trust with a client whose faith in counselors/therapists has been badly shaken requires special effort. It is important to accept the clients' reluctance to work with helpers following the exploitative experience and to actually commend them for not blindly trusting the helpers. As in other counseling situations, clients must be told how the

---

[1] An early version of this paper was prepared in April 1986 with the participation of the Workgroup on Therapeutic Issues of the State Task Force on Sexual Exploitation of Clients by Counselors and Therapists. It has been available as a monograph from WICC. A second and edited version of the monograph, "Advocacy: The Process of Assisting Sexually Exploited Clients," is included in *It's Never OK: A Handbook for Professionals on Sexual Exploitation by Counselors and Therapists* (Sanderson, 1989), published by the State of Minnesota.

The complaint options described here are discussed in more depth in Ch. 27.

information they share with the advocate will be used, that is, what records will be kept, who will have access to the information, and what mandatory reporting, if any, will take place.

Exploited clients need and often want very clear professional boundaries by the advocate and/or follow-up therapist. Having been badly served by the offending therapist who may have simultaneously played the roles of friend, counselor, lover, spouse and/or parental figure, the client certainly does not need a repetition of this sort of confusion.

One other matter to be mindful of is timing, that is, how rapidly to encourage the client to move in a complaint process. One can err in either direction. Expecting the client to take major action too soon is likely to backfire and have the opposite result, whereas passively going along with the client's postponement of action tends to prolong her or his agony unnecessarily.

THE ADVOCACY PROCESS

The advocacy process consists of a series of basic steps that may vary in detail from case to case.

1. Awareness that victimization may have occurred

Some clients may express their concern or complaint directly. Other clients may give indirect clues, such as maintaining a physical distance from the follow-up counselor or refusing to make eye contact. These behaviors may reflect great distrust, depression, and low self-esteem. It is important to ask the client about any problem in past professional relationships, including the possibility of abuse by a counselor. This question is no different from asking a client about possible family violence and chemical or sexual abuse. Questioning does not hurt the client whereas overlooking the possibility of previous abuse may deprive the client of an opportunity to reach a resolution.

When the client initially tells the story one should not assume that he or she will manifest particular reactions (see Ch. 7). People react differently to experiences of victimization. For example, sexual intercourse may seem like a more serious abuse than erotic talk or suggestive behavior. Yet the latter may be more confusing to the client. It is important to help each client to arrive at a personal definition of her or his problem.

2. Assessment and crisis intervention

Understanding a client's experience of sexual exploitation and her or his emotional response to it is the advocate's first task. The experience may range from a relatively mild upset over some minor infraction of ethical boundaries by the former therapist to major distress stemming from extremely serious and damaging sexual exploitation.

Some clients may be able to relate their stories in chronological order and to include a great many details whereas other clients may be less articulate and/or too embarrassed to share a coherent picture of the occurrence. The advocate should ask all questions necessary to clarify what took place. For example, if the client reports in somewhat general terms that she/he has been abused, the advocate may need to ask what it was the previous counselor said or did that made the client feel that way.

The advocate's or follow-up therapist's function is to assess the client's immediate life situation and needs:

What else is going on in the client's life?
What is the client's family/marital situation?
How stable are the client's job/financial arrangements, health, and social support system?
How serious is any anxiety or depression evidenced by the client?

Inasmuch as the client may be in crisis the advocate's or follow-up therapist's first task may be crisis intervention. Before exploring possible courses of action on a complaint further, the client may need medical treatment (e.g., medication, hospitalization) or physical protection (e.g., move out of an abusive situation) or protection from harassment (e.g., an unlisted telephone number to prevent contact with the former therapist).

It is quite likely that a client is telling the truth about what he or she experienced even when events may be confused or accuracy is in question. The client's consistency in telling the same story and her or his truthfulness in other areas in which corroboration is possible can help to develop a complaint.

When a client is actively psychotic, hallucinating, or otherwise out of touch with reality, it may be difficult to assess whether the report of sexual exploitation is based on fact. Referring the client to a psychiatrist for evaluation and possible medication is in order in such an event although the client retains the option of pursuing the complaint later when she/he is stabilized. If the client's story is consistent after recompensating, it is reasonable to assume that the sexual exploitation indeed happened.

A client may be a habitual liar and may have fabricated the story. Even in this instance the advocate or follow-up therapist has a responsibility to continue probing, even to question appropriate other persons needed to clarify what happened in the therapeutic relationship and to work toward a resolution that is in the best interest of the client as well as anyone else involved.

Another problem may be the client's exaggeration or misunderstanding. A client may report as sexual abuse a counselor's putting his/her hand on the client's arm or knee. The problem in this case may be the poor judgment and/or inexperience of a counselor who is trying too hard to be helpful rather than one who is intentionally exploitative. Even if the behavior is not exploitative it still may have caused the client to feel distressed. More investigation is needed to address this issue.

3. Exploring the options

Exploring the options with the client is the next phase (see Fig. 1). It is the advocate's responsibility to maintain current information on various complaint options, resources, procedures, and the like. Information may be obtained from such professional organizations as the National Association of Social Workers (NASW), the State Psychiatric Society, or the State Psychological Association and from regulatory bodies (see the section on "support and resources for the advocate" at the end of this chapter). The choice of an option should correspond closely to what the client basically wants to accomplish and to the sort of effort or risks he/she is willing to undertake. It may be helpful to ask the client what, in fantasy or imagination, she/he ideally would like to achieve and then to translate it into realistic possibilities. The client's goals generally are a combination of the following:

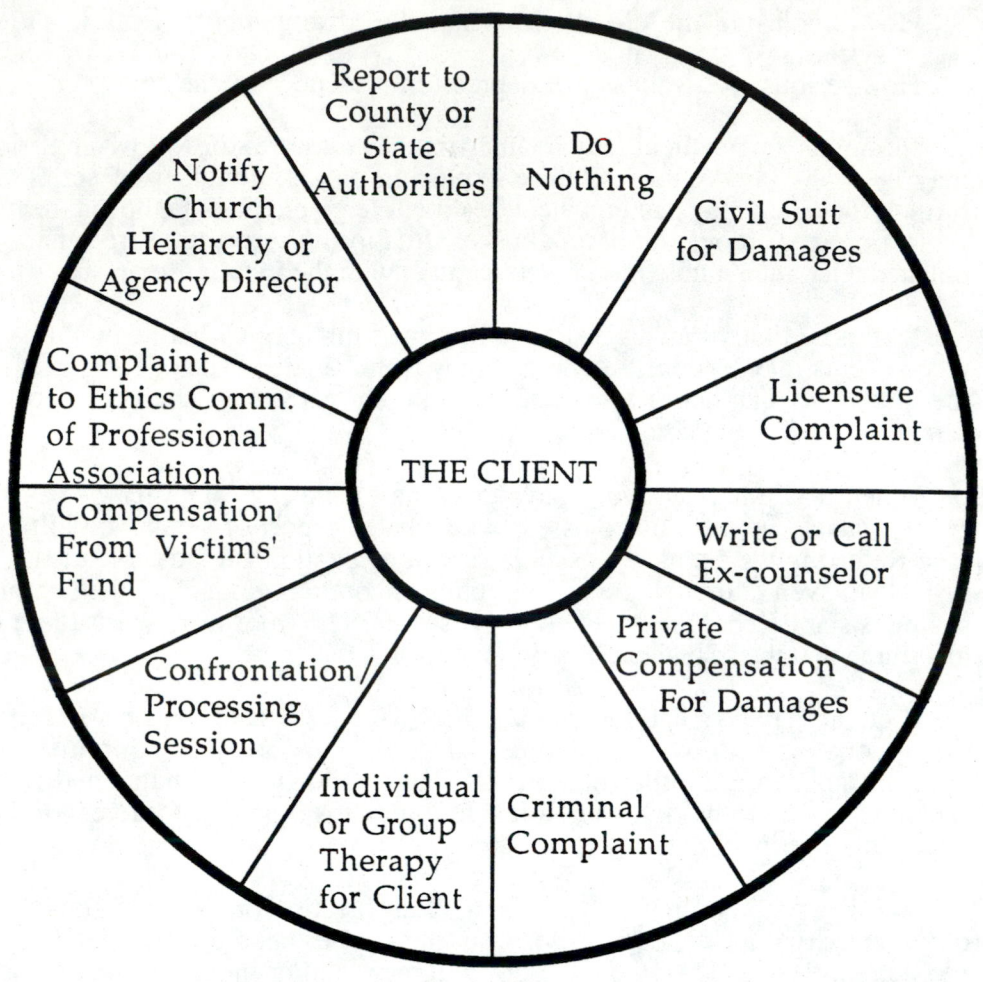

FIGURE 1.: "WHEEL OF OPTIONS

This "Wheel" does not imply random selection, Rather, it suggests that there is no linear heirarchy, and that a combination of choices may be appropriate.

(a) In all cases the action taken should provide clients with the opportunity to **stand up** for themselves, to communicate to the former therapist, if only indirectly, that the sexual exploitation was not OK, and that it hurt the clients. It is a way for clients to "take back their power."

(b) Clients often are concerned with the likelihood of the exploitative counselor hurting future clients, and they want to minimize that possibility.

(c) Clients sometimes seek monetary compensation for the damage done, restitution of fees paid, or cost of subsequent therapy.

(d) The goal of both the client and the advocate is in all cases to arrive at a resolution that permits clients to put the abuse behind them and go on with their lives.

The question at this stage of advocacy is which option or combination of options is most likely to accomplish the goals of this particular client as effectively and efficiently as possible, in a manner that is consistent with what the client can tolerate emotionally, financially, in terms of possible public exposure, and other considerations.

It is worth remembering that many clients believe they brought the abuse on themselves. Also, many clients believe that their options are limited to either doing nothing, or suing, with nothing in between. Communicating to the client a range of options and allowing the client to decide which one(s) to pursue may empower the client. If the client is considering legal action, an appropriate attorney should be contacted before taking any other action.

The crucial guideline is that the client must make the decision on which option(s) to take. If the follow-up counselor/advocate has a strong bias in one direction or another, he/she should inform the client of this bias. However, whatever the advocate's bias it must be subservient to the client's choice and best interest. The advocate should keep in mind the client's vulnerability and tendency to follow the recommendations.

4. Initiating action

Assisting the client to initiate the chosen action is the next task. Some clients obviously need more help than others. It may suffice to give the client a telephone number to contact in some cases but in others it may be appropriate to take some steps on behalf of the client. In most cases it is necessary that the client write down the story of what happened. Clients who have poor verbal/writing skills may need direct help in putting together a complaint. They often experience considerable difficulty in writing out their stories, and may want the advocate's opinion of the product. Keep in mind that a client often re-lives the traumatic events in the process of writing the account. It can be helpful to ask the client to state a time line or deadline for completing the account.

5. Continuing support

After the process has been initiated and the complaint filed, it may be weeks, months, or years until the complaint is acted on. Supportive contact with the client during this period is important because the client is likely to have ups and downs, and often is not able or allowed to speak with other people about the situation. It helps if the client has access to the advocate and can touch base periodically.

6. Preparing the client for the event

When the date of the "action" (e.g., hearing before an ethics committee or board of examiners; confrontation session with the former therapist; civil or criminal suit; etc.) approaches, it is important to prepare the client as well as possible for the event. Preparation includes letting the client know what to expect in terms of proceedings, time frame, people present, and physical layout (an attorney would do this in case of a lawsuit). To lessen the client's anxiety, it may be helpful to role play the anticipated situation with a client or to "walk through it."

When a meeting or processing or confrontation session is scheduled with the former therapist, it is important to discuss the client's expectations ahead of time and to point out her or his unrealistic expectations, such as an apology from the former therapist or a promise she/he will never do it again (the client may have no way of evaluating the therapist's sincerity); or an understanding of the former therapist or of what happened (it may be impossible to make sense out of nonsense).

Often a great deal of energy is invested in dealing with the victimization and the complaint process. Clients tend to experience a low ebb after it is all over, and it is good to help them to plan for the day or night after the session(s), so they can activate their support systems, and think of future activities or how to revive old interests.

7. The advocate's presence at the event

It may be appropriate for the advocate to be present at the session or hearing. In some situations (e.g., a confrontation/processing session with the former therapist) it may be imperative for the advocate to be there to lessen the power imbalance between the client and the former therapist (see Ch. 28).

In other instances it may be more appropriate for the advocate to meet with the client before or after the hearing.

8. Termination and follow-up

After the hearing or meeting a short "debriefing" session is likely to be very helpful to the client. It is at this session that the advocate may want to ascertain and communicate to the client whether this contact is the last, whether to follow-up in a few days or weeks, or whether to ask the client to contact the advocate. Clear termination of the role as advocate is necessary, particularly in view of the client's prior ambiguous experience in which boundaries between a professional relationship and a social/sexual relationship were vague or nonexistent and client status was ill-defined.

ADVOCACY AND/OR THERAPY

Some clients need therapy subsequent to experiencing sexual exploitation and some need advocacy. Most clients are best served by a combination of the two, either simultaneously or consecutively.

Advocacy and therapy can go hand-in-hand. Ideally, being supported by two different persons—one as the advocate and one as the therapist—may be the most productive arrangement for a client for a number of reasons. For example, the client is less likely to perceive the therapist as omnipotent. Advocate and therapist can keep in touch (with the client's permission) and inform each other of important developments and problems in the client's life or situation. However, it may not always be possible for two different persons to assume these roles; in smaller communities (e.g., rural areas, ethnic minority, or gay/lesbian communities) a therapist also may have to function as an advocate and vice versa if a client is unable or unwilling to go beyond this particular community. In this situation, it may be helpful to differentiate the roles for the client.

Problems for the Advocate

Although there are definite rewards in functioning as an advocate for sexually exploited clients, some potential problems are inherent in assuming this role. They are like the opposite sides of the same coin.

The advocate often sees dramatic progress in the client. Starting as a badly wounded individual, the client may proceed through a stage of courageously facing difficult challenges and then advance to a state of strength and renewed integrity. This change is rewarding for the advocate. This is the point at which the advocate should terminate the contact. Termination requires sound professional judgment by the advocate.

Stress and burnout may be integral to functioning as an advocate as it is with any work with victims in crisis. The advocate's workload may be erratic because clients often need the advocate on short notice, and the advocate must be immediately responsive and available.

Some counselors/therapists are uncomfortable with the advocacy role, either they do not know how to function in this capacity or they choose not to function in a dual therapist/advocate role. If the latter, other advocacy resources should be sought for the exploited client.

Given that in cases of sexual exploitation of clients the perpetrator/wrongdoer is another counselor, the follow-up therapist may be tempted not to listen to the client's story or to overlook the possibility that a colleague may have committed infractions or to redefine the incident or situation as the client's emotional problem. Because the client may well need counseling or therapy for prior or subsequent problems, one should keep in mind that in cases of sexual exploitation by counselors, this _is_ the client's primary problem and other things come later.

Inasmuch as the advocate is dealing with the client on matters of a very private nature, the advocate must maintain a balance between being afraid to ask about them and pressuring the client for unnecessary details. The advocate should avoid voyeurism as well as timidity.

Even if it is appropriate for the advocate to be appalled by the client's sexual exploitation by another counselor/therapist, the advocate should not, in turn, victimize the client again by "using" her or him to fight the advocate's own cause. Should this temptation arise, the advocate must keep in mind that it is the particular client's best interests that must be given primacy.

To summarize, human service workers who, on occasion, take on an advocacy role, must be aware of their individual allergic reactions to certain types of abuses, counselors, and clients. When in doubt, they should seek advice.

SUPPORT AND RESOURCES FOR THE ADVOCATE

Support for the advocate can be found or created. The minimum support is one other professional (a superior, colleague, agency director, or consultant) who is available both to ventilate to and to consult with on how to proceed. Sharing with another professional one's indignation, frustration, successes and failures as an advocate is not only desirable for the role but, also, it is actually necessary in order to avoid or deal with the problems described earlier.

Another way to deal with the problems inherent in advocacy work is to build a professional network. Establishing contact with other therapists, lawyers, agency administrators, professional organizations, regulatory agencies (such as licensure boards), or Adult Protective Services, can be most helpful to advocates.

Additionally, locating and using referral resources for the client helps to serve the client in a comprehensive manner and to take some of the burden off the advocate's shoulders. These resources may include but not be limited to the local/regional mental health center, family service agency, sexual assault center, therapists in private practice, and self-help groups, such as Alcoholics Anonymous or Al-Anon.

In conclusion, functioning as an advocate for clients who have been sexually exploited by a previous counselor or therapist is often rewarding, sometimes stressful, always interesting and challenging, and seldom the same from case to case.

CHAPTER 27

FILING COMPLAINTS AGAINST THERAPISTS WHO SEXUALLY EXPLOIT CLIENTS

Gary Richard Schoener

Three earlier versions of this paper (Schoener, 1977, 1978, 1979), all entitled "Filing Complaints of Unethical or Unprofessional Conduct Against Counselors and Psychotherapists," were written in response to requests from both clients and therapists who sought guidance on how to file complaints against sexually exploitative therapists. (See Appendix X for Schoener, 1979.) Some of the information in those papers was useful in any jurisdiction (e.g., information from professional ethics codes) but the instructions on filing a complaint applied only to Minnesota.

For this reason, the information is organized differently in this chapter. It is meant to serve as a companion article to Chapter 26 on "Advocacy.". Nevertheless, the format of the earlier version (Schoener, 1979) may be of interest to professional organizations, task forces, or consumer advocacy groups who are interested in preparing guides to filing complaints in their state.

In this chapter the literature relating to professionals in the role of direct reporter or client advocate in therapist sexual misconduct cases is reviewed. Following sections deal with the professional as a direct reporter; assisting the client to take action; complaint options; and issues specific to various psychotherapy professions.

THE PROFESSIONAL AS A REPORTER OR CLIENT ADVOCATE

For some time there has been some discussion in the professional literature on the failure of psychotherapists to report colleagues who engaged in sexual misconduct with clients (e.g., Davidson, 1977; Stone, 1982). It has become an almost universal theme in the public media reports on this issue as well as in the writings of consumer advocates (see Ch. 30).

Vinson (1984) interviewed 30 members of California's licensing boards and professional organizations of therapists, who estimated that a miniscule 1-2% of all cases of therapist-client sex are brought to licensure board attention. Data from Wisconsin (see Ch. 3) leads one to a similar conclusion. From our experience in Minnesota we are certain that a great many cases go unreported, although the large-scale statewide educational effort begun in 1984 (see Ch. 42) and the mandatory reporting laws and rules have improved the situation dramatically.

Pope, Keith-Spiegel, & Tabachnick (1987), surveyed a group of psychologists who are practicing therapists on ethical behavior. The participants were asked to compare their likely actions with what they felt would be the right course of action in dealing with ethical infractions by themselves or others. The results showed that in a number of areas these practitioners would not take proper corrective action. Using a similar format, Bernard and Jara (1986) found that a full 50% of clinical psychology graduate students did not believe that they would intervene to the extent required by professional ethics if they knew a colleague was sexually exploiting a client. (A similar percentage reported that they would not intervene in a case of an alcoholic colleague to the degree they felt was required.)

When Bernard, Murphy, and Little (1987) asked practicing clinical psychologists to respond to the hypothetical scenarios used by Bernard & Jara (1986), their results showed that a full one-third would not respond as they should to a case of sexual misconduct by another practitioner. A lesser percentage (25%), however, said that they would take less action in a case of alcoholism or problem drinking than the ethics code requires. The authors concluded,

> This is even more puzzling when one considers that although the problem-drinking/alcoholism scenario requires that the reader interpret the Ethical Principles as they apply to impaired psychologists, sexual intimacies with patients are flatly described as unethical. Perhaps we are more tolerant of sexual misconduct than of chemical dependency, but the reasons for this discrepancy remain obscure. (p. 491)

Noel (1986) surveyed a random sample of 1000 members of Division 12 (Clinical Psychology) of the American Psychological Association. Of the 405 members who responded, the following information was obtained (pp. 82-83):

> 83.6% reported that they had been told about a psychologist who was alleged to have been sexually intimate with a client;
> 36.4% of the reports came from clients and
> 50.7% of the reports came from colleagues;
> 34.8% of study participants had encouraged a client to report the offense to the ethics committee of a state psychological association, and
> 10.8% had assisted a client in making the report;
> 9.4% had encouraged a client to take legal action, and
> 3.5% had assisted the client;
> 1.1% had filed an ethics complaint without the client's permission;
> 5.7%—21 of the respondents—surprisingly enough, had attended some sort of mediation session with the client and psychologist.

These data either may be encouraging or discouraging, depending on how they are interpreted. One would need to know far more about the individual cases to judge whether the psychologist's assistance was appropriate. Noel's respondents indicated that they would be more likely to report cases in which the frequency of the sex or the acts themselves (e.g., sexual intercourse as opposed to kissing) were more intrusive. Formal training in professional ethics or human sexuality also increased the likelihood that a psychologist would report sexual exploitation (p. 2).

Psychiatry too has had problems with the reporting of sexual misconduct by follow-up psychotherapists. Grunebaum, Nadelson, and Macht (1976), in an earlier survey of members of the Massachusetts Psychiatric Society found a number of instances of unreported sexual activity between therapist and client, in some instances because of the client's refusal and of confidentiality.

> When the lack of reporting was the psychiatrist's decision, it was explained in two ways: Frequently, the offending psychiatrist was seen as neurotic, disturbed, or old, and thus excused; and, more often, the event had occurred some time ago or in another part of the country, or involved a non-physician. (Grunebaum, Nadelson, & Macht, 1976, p. 7)

In another survey, almost a decade later, Rynearson, Stewart, & Bachman (1984) reported that 50% of the Fellows in the Southern Psychiatric Association took no action in cases of sexually involved physicians (including psychiatrists) and patients.

A large national survey of psychiatrists by Gartrell, Herman, Olarte, Feldstein, and Localio (1987) found that 65% of the respondents had treated clients who had been sexually involved with previous therapists but only 8.2% filed a report of misconduct. Even more disturbing is the fact that these 920 therapists knew of 3031 cases of misconduct; the overall reporting rate, therefore, may have been considerably lower than 8.2%. Only 4.9% of those (N=754) who had not filed complaints volunteered explanations for the failure to act so it is difficult to know whether we can generalize from these data. The rationales given by this small subset of psychiatrists are worth noting, however (percentages are calculated from the data presented by Gartrell et al., 1987, p. 290).

      41% Client had already reported it
      19% Client refused permission
      14% Psychiatrist considered it "hearsay"
       8% Psychiatrist feared retaliation by the perpetrator
       5% Didn't believe the client
       5% Psychiatrist asked the client to omit the perpetrator's name
      2.7% Contacted the perpetrator directly
      2.7% Psychiatrist learned that the perpetrator had entered treatment
      2.7% Psychiatrist expressed regret at not having reported.

Discussions of the sexual exploitation of clients by therapists has been minimal in the social work literature. Russell (1984, p. 72) was chagrined to find that only 5 of the 111 social workers who responded to her survey were "sufficiently familiar with their professional code to quote the specific statement about sexual contact between worker and client...." A more encouraging picture emerged in relation to taking action on the reported sexual misconduct of therapists, however. Of the social workers who had encountered client complaints, 48% assisted clients in reporting the abuse; another 3% reported it on their own; and 12% had taken supervisory action (Russell, 1984, p. 48). Social workers who had not encountered a case reported that if they did they would assist the client in confronting or reporting the perpetrator (46%), or would report it themselves (25%). Again, these numbers are either encouraging or discouraging depending on one's viewpoint (Russell, 1984, p. 50).

In sum, the data from these three major psychotherapy professions, indicate that many professionals are unlikely to file complaints against colleagues, and there is reason to believe that a large number are unlikely to assist a client in filing a complaint about sexual misconduct by a previous therapist. These data are quite consistent with experience at WICC in dealing with state and national clients. In a larger number of cases clients have received little or no encouragement in and often no support for filing complaints. A follow-up therapist's lack of knowledge about complaint options and procedures or an unwillingness to serve as an advocate have led countless clients to regard filing a complaint as a useless action.

Sadly, many clients who lack support do not file complaints. Vinson (1984) found that 6 of the 7 clients in her sample who filed complaints did so after contact with a supportive professional (a police officer investigating harassment by the former therapist in one case; subsequent therapists in two cases, and in 3 cases the psychiatrists in the hospitals where the clients were treated after suicide attempts). Vinson (1987) also reported the positive effect of taking action, such as filing a complaint. Our experience at WICC concurs. We have observed clinically that taking action is often a very important part of recovery.

In discussing with therapists their avoidance or reluctance to assist clients, we have identified the following five issues:

1. Lack of Belief in the Mechanisms:

Many therapists fear that the available complaint mechanisms may prove harmful to their clients. They are quick to cite the inadequacies of professional ethics committees and licensure boards. In my view these mechanisms can be made to work quite well when they are used. Furthermore, in our experience with a great many clients we find that they are able to handle the inadequacies of these mechanisms if they are forewarned. Furthermore, many clients indicate that making the complaint is very therapeutic, regardless of the outcome.

2. Lack of Knowledge About Complaint Alternatives:

Many therapists have little knowledge of how the licensure board or ethics committee of even their own profession works, let alone those of other professions. When confronted with a situation requiring such knowledge they often are not sure how to get the information, and so they tend to avoid involvement in the complaint process.

3. Concern About Negative Impact on the Therapy:

Some clinicians express concern about the effect making a complaint might have on their psychotherapy with the victimized client. This is not surprising since similar concerns play a major role in clinicians' failure to report child abuse despite mandatory reporting laws (Kalichman, Craig, & Follingstad, 1989). A number of recent studies have found that a substantial percentage of psychologists are unwilling to break confidentiality to report child abuse (e.g., Haas, Malout, & Mayerson, 1986; Kalichman, Craig, & Follingstad, 1988; Pope, Tabachnick, & Keith-Spiegel, 1987).

4. Unsure of Professional Boundaries or the Advocacy Role:

Many therapists are uncomfortable outside their defined traditional professional role. They also may have clear realistic concerns with professional boundaries, especially when a client complains about boundary violations committed by a previous therapist. Instead of seeking consultation to help sort out these issues the professional simply may try to limit his or her role without examining the consequences to the client, or the message that such avoidance may give about the professional's view of the complaint.

5. Worry That the Allegations Are Not True or May be Exaggerated, or That the Complaint May Destroy the Career of the Subject of the Complaint:

These fears are related in that they center on concerns with how the complaint will be judged and the outcome of that judgment. Ironically, the same professional may end up making "quiet inquiries" about the matter, which sends rumors along the professional grapevine to which a response is not possible. If a client is serious about pursuing a complaint, he or she should be assisted in doing so. All complaints deserve a hearing, whether they are deemed valid and whether one has total confidence in the outcome.

6. Fear of Retaliation by the Alleged Perpetrator:

It is important to recognize that even if one is careful and ethical, only assists the client, and never claims to have knowledge of or belief in the accuracy of the charges, the professional being accused may retaliate. Furthermore, the most serious examples of retaliation we have seen have been instituted by perpetrators who eventually were proved guilty of multiple offenses. Although in our experience such retaliation is quite rare, some examples worth noting are as follows:

Case 1: Psychiatrist who was the subject of multiple allegations of sexual misconduct sued therapists working with the complainants to challenge his admitting privileges at several hospitals. Those therapists lost time from work in depositions and had out-of-pocket expenses for legal consultation and representation.

Case 2: A psychologist, the subject of a number of allegations, sued the clients and the persons who assisted them, alleging slander. Again, costs were incurred before the suits were dropped. (Temerlin & Temerlin, 1982, described this danger with psychotherapy cults.)

Case 3: Upon learning that a particular therapist was assisting a client who might file a charge, a perpetrator of some prominence began passing rumors that the therapist was guilty of unprofessional conduct. (In such situations the rumors are often similar to the allegations about the perpetrator.)

Case 4: When an analytic trainee, herself a victim of a well-known analyst, found other victims and filed a complaint, the analyst convinced a professional body that the trainee was disturbed and managed to have her stripped of her trainee status. She eventually won, but only after considerable stress and expenditure. (We know of other instances in which a person was prevented from getting a job because of behind-the-scenes maneuvering.)

Fear of retaliatory suits led the Ethics Committee of the California Psychological Association to stop hearing complaints early in 1986, supposedly because the $250,000 liability coverage available to them was insufficient (Pope, 1987). Actually, however, such suits are rare.

DIRECT REPORTING

Over the past two decades the reporting of various types of abuse mandated by statutes has created many exceptions to what once was nearly absolute confidentiality in professional relationships. All human service professionals must determine, in their own workplaces and jurisdictions, what reporting duties apply to them.

It is absolutely essential that a practitioner forewarn the persons who speak to them or apply for professional services of such reporting duties. The prudent practitioner asks a client, colleague, or friend to stop telling a story until such warning can be given. It is critical to keep in mind that many reporting mandates do not specify that the information be learned in a professional context. Some examples of reporting duties follow:

Child Protection Statutes:

Although the statutes vary, every state requires the reporting of abuse or suspected abuse of minors. Most, if not all, psychotherapists are mandated to make such reports. The mandate becomes an issue when the alleged abuse is of a child or adolescent.

Adult Protection Statutes:

Approximately three-quarters of the states have some sort of protection for adults who are deemed to be vulnerable by virtue of mental or emotional disability. These statutes may refer to a condition or diagnosis and/or the type of facility in which they are receiving care. For example, in Minnesota patients in state-licensed residential or hospital programs or persons who are clients of a community mental health center are all covered by a Vulnerable Adults Act (see Appendix J). Such acts mandate the reporting of abuse, and protect the professional who makes a good faith report.

Licensure Statutes:

A professional practitioner may be mandated to report abuse as a condition of his or her own license. For example, in Minnesota a psychology license carries with it the obligation to report cases of therapist/client sex, when the therapist is a psychologist, to the Board of Psychology unless the information is obtained from the perpetrator in the context of his or her obtaining professional services. Also, the Minnesota Medical Practice Act requires all licensed health professionals to report a variety of misconduct (including sexual exploitation) to the Board of Medical Examiners. The law licensing social workers and marriage and family counselors (Minnesota Statutes Chapter 347; see Appendix K) includes the same provision although a report need not be made if the licensed practitioner is treating the perpetrator and the perpetrator's practice has been restricted so the public is deemed not to be at risk.

Special Reporting Statutes:

Several states are considering the passage of statutes that would require all psychotherapists to report the sexual abuse of clients. Wisconsin considered such a statute initially but then opted for one in which the follow-up therapist is obligated to ask a victim of sexual contact by a previous therapist if he or she wants the therapist to report the offense to a licensure board or district attorney (see Appendix W). If the client withholds permission, no report is made. The statute is silent on the issue of information received from therapist-perpetrators. California also considered mandatory reporting but opted for an amendment to the Business and Professions Code requiring professionals to disseminate information to victims (see Appendix P). This amendment too is silent on the issue of information received from a perpetrator.

Reporting Requirements Within an Organization:

If the practitioner works for an organization, there may be duties which arise as a condition of employment which require reporting of certain situations to a superior.

Normally, one advantage of statute-mandated reporting is that it protects the reporter against suits or licensure complaints when the report is made in good faith. A person making such a report should be sure to cite the statute.

ASSISTING THE CLIENT

The cornerstone of any assistance to a client who is involved in or considering taking some sort of action on a complaint is to provide some structure for decision making.

Turning the process into a series of steps can be very helpful. It is important, at the outset, to ascertain what decisions the client already has made and the precise actions in which they would like help. Furthermore, clients sometimes want to take a particular type of action, such as a licensure complaint, without understanding what it entails or examining other courses of action. The following guidelines may help the client to arrive at a decision on the optimal course of action:

Defining the Situation:

Many clients are not clear about the profession, if any, to which a former therapist belongs. Even if they are clear on this question the clients may not know if the therapist is a member of a professional association or holds the license (or licenses) required to practice. The clients often are unclear about the ownership of a clinic or the therapist's employer. Sometimes, during an initial discussion with a client, we phone a licensure board or professional association to check on such items, largely because it is easy to do. It is pointless to discuss complaint options without first ascertaining these basic facts.

Defining Goals:

The various goals and their relative importance must be defined before looking at complaint options. Each complaint option has a different capacity for meeting certain goals or needs of the client. The common goals are as follows:

1. EXPRESS FEELINGS: Ironically, direct feedback to the therapist or at a processing session is the most effective avenue. Licensure complaints and civil suits allow for little such expression.

2. TO SPEAK OUT, HOPING FOR VALIDATION: One never can be sure of the response when one tells a story publicly. Ethics Committee complaints can bring feedback from other professionals, but civil suits or complaints to the media provide, potentially, a broader forum. Plasil (1985), after her civil suit was settled out of court, wrote *Therapist* out of such a need.

3. COMPENSATION FOR DAMAGES: Clients vary on whether they seek compensation for certain costs (e.g., legal fees, and follow-up care) or for overall damages, including pain and suffering. In some cases the National Association of Social Workers Committee on Inquiry can bring about a payment for damages; and in a few states victim compensation funds are available. The primary method of obtaining compensation for costs or damages is either civil suit or a direct negotiated settlement.

4. TO PROTECT OTHERS: Licensure and criminal complaints may accomplish the protection but so too may a complaint to an employer or, in some circumstances, a civil suit (e.g., the civil suit destroys someone's practice through bad publicity). Sometimes there is a related goal of getting help for the therapist, something more difficult to attain. Clients need to know that in many such cases help is not possible or would not protect clients, or is unlikely to work without formal sanctions. Civil suits are not a good means to bring about the goal of protection, although we have had several negotiated settlements with healthier therapists which have included an evaluation and therapy.

5. TO EMBARRASS OR PUNISH OTHERS: Clients sometimes want to challenge or embarrass the persons who have defended the perpetrator or failed to act in response to a complaint. Many civil suits against therapists' employers result from

discounting a client's complaint. Sometimes ethics complaints or complaints to funding bodies also are aimed at this goal as, of course, are reports to the press.

6. FOR "JUSTICE": Sometimes clients have a more nebulous concern with "justice." They are angry that the profession tolerates or does little to discipline impaired practitioners. They often envision being able to put key officials on the spot, not realizing that in many civil suits and licensure complaints this aim cannot be achieved.

Defining Client Fears And Limitations:

Important as goals are those elements that the client fears or does not want to happen. Just as each complaint option has some potential benefits for the client or society, it also has some associated costs either predictable or possible. A few common limitations follow:

1. UNWILLINGNESS TO TAKE ON THE THERAPIST: Either because of actual or magnified fears of retaliation, or a desire to protect the therapist, some clients are not willing to take any sort of adverse action against the therapist or to authorize an advocate to do so.

2. CONCERN WITH PERSONAL OR FAMILY EXPOSURE: Fear of publicity or fear of embarrassment about things that may be made public during a trial may trigger this concern. Obviously, criminal complaints and civil suits carry high risks for disclosures. Licensure complaints vary from state to state. In some, they are closed and private but in others they are open.

3. FEAR OF BEING PUT DOWN: Some clients fear being cross-examined, either literally or figuratively. Thus, for them, testifying is quite dangerous, and this sense of danger may extend even to making a complaint to a professional body.

4. TIME-RELATED ISSUES: Many clients want any complaint to be over quickly. The time element in civil suits and licensure complaints can be quite problematic. The length of a complaint process has a practical implication for clients who desire to put the situation behind them. Clients who already resent time lost in their lives owing to the relationship with the perpetrator do not want to invest any more time and seek a speedy resolution. Only direct complaints to the therapist or his/her employer can run their course quickly.

Defining Support Needs:

Clients' needs for support and assistance vary considerably. Some clients need help to compose a complaint letter. In such instances we read various drafts and make suggestions for the wording or organization. Others need support to arrange or hold a confrontation; and they may ask for someone to accompany them when they go to make a complaint. Still others need preparation, such as a brief supportive discussion, before giving testimony. Many need and benefit from a supportive debriefing after they give testimony. In some instances they require a support person or advocate to be present during a hearing. The NASW procedure for hearing complaints by a Committee on Inquiry provides for the presence of an advocate to assist the complainant. It is important to ascertain a client's needs for support and to help him or her to plan for those needs to be met by friends, family members, advocates, or a professional.

COMPLAINT OPTIONS

1. Direct Feedback to the Therapist:

This option sometimes is the first step and, in other cases, the only step a client is willing to take. It is quick, direct, and private. It has the advantage of providing for the direct expression of feelings. The disadvantage is that it accomplishes little else.

Direct feedback is possible by letter or phone call. In one case a client elected to tape record a phone call, in case it did not go well, to be able to process it with a subsequent therapist. In other cases clients have used tape recorders to obtain "proof" for a subsequent complaint or civil suit.

2. Confrontation or Processing Session:

A direct personal confrontation can be made by a client alone, although few clients undertake it. Again, it has the advantage of being private and quick, and most perpetrators will agree to it. Clients sometimes take a friend, advocate, or therapist along at such confrontations.

A similar option is a processing session or mediation (see Ch. 28). It provides for the sorting through of what happened and goes beyond a simple confrontation. However, this option, although many therapists will agree to it, cannot guarantee much beyond a discussion and expression of feelings. It may lead to further intervention but there are no guarantees unless the perpetrator's supervisor or employer is present.

3. Complaint to Supervisor or Employer:

This type of complaint requires more exposure by the client. However, it can be set up relatively quickly and in many situations, may lead to very quick intervention. It does not preclude remedies, such as licensure complaints. The role of an experienced advocate or another professional in such complaints often is not only to keep things honest but, also, to provide suggestions on how the complaint may be evaluated. Many organizations have no process for dealing with such complaints. The presence of an advocate may make an employer uneasy but it often helps the dynamics of the situation. When an attorney goes along as an advocate, the effect may be a bit chilling because of the implied threat of a lawsuit. In recent years, however, we have recommended to clients who are approaching religious organizations to consider using an attorney, despite the added costs, because her/his presence seems to help to bring about a more serious response to the complaints.

4. Complaint to Place of Professional Affiliation:

Even when the perpetrator's major employment is a solo private practice, he or she may have other affiliations, usually the hospital at which a psychiatrist has privileges. Here, a complaint can be made to a Chief of Service, Medical Director, or Administrator.

In other situations a practitioner is in some sort of association with other professionals, perhaps through sharing office space. The other professionals may have some influence over the perpetrator. Consultation affiliations are another possible place to complain. Last but not least are teaching affiliations and faculty appointments; they are other potential avenues of complaint.

The arrangements for such complaints can be made quickly and have the potential of bringing about some intervention. Given that they challenge some of the practitioner's income, source of referrals, or general reputation, they may bring about a strong reaction from the perpetrator.

5. Complaint to a Funding Agency:

When a therapist is employed by an organization that seems reluctant to take the complaint seriously or to take effective action, a complaint can be made to a funding agency, such as government or United Way. The action will not necessarily provide for direct intervention but it can lead to an investigation. Here, the potential for public exposure is somewhat greater than for a complaint to the place of employment.

6. Report to the Ethics Committee:

If the practitioner in question belongs to a professional association or society, a complaint can be filed with the ethics committee of that organization. The various professions are discussed separately in the last section of this chapter.

In most instances a call to the professional organization reveals whether the person is a member. If the person is not a member of a state organization, he or she may be a member of the national organization. Some professionals are members of several organizations. Keep in mind, however, that many professionals are not members of their relevant organizations. Check before exploring this option, therefore. Sometimes a professional lets membership lapse or purposely resigns because of a pending complaint.

Ethics committees range from the very informal to those that hold quasi-legal proceedings with attorneys present. Procedures vary markedly as do the time frames for the evaluation of a complaint. All ethics committees are dominated by, if not exclusively composed of, other professionals.

Unlike licensure boards, ethics committees cannot restrict practice. Their major sanctions are dropping a person from membership in the association or society and/or censuring them. Only one, the Committee on Inquiry of NASW, has the potential for imposing heavy sanctions, such as ordering (but not compelling) restitution, taking away an accreditation (the ACSW), and publicizing its actions. (Other ethics committees at times also publicize their actions.) In recent years, being dropped from membership in a professional association has carried with it another negative outcome: possible loss of coverage under the association's malpractice insurance policy. Inasmuch as such insurance is increasingly difficult to obtain, a practitioner may end up having to practice without coverage.

7. Report to County or State Authorities:

In addition to reports to the practitioner's licensure board, (discussed in the next section), other complaint vehicles may apply in a given case. Note that various types of questionable practice may get reported along with the sexual exploitation. Options include the following:

CHILD PROTECTION: When the victim is a minor.

ADULT PROTECTION: When the victim fits the definition of a vulnerable adult or other protected group.

REGULATORY AGENCY: Facilities and programs are often licensed by an office in a state health department or department of human services. Examples are residential treatment programs, nursing homes, and mental health clinics. The agencies have the power and authority to close a facility if unsafe conditions or abuse of clients are found.

Some investigatory procedures used by these state and county agencies are time consuming and complex. Consumers are frequently disappointed with the result, for example, to issue some sort of warning to the facility. Health code and housing code violations may be grounds for closing a program but not, sometimes, mistreatment of clients.

8. Complaints to Board that Licenses the Practitioner:

Many psychotherapists are licensed by the government of the state(s) in which they practice. Psychiatrists must be licensed as physicians in all the states. The 50 states and the District of Columbia and Puerto Rico regulate the practice of psychology, but only 37 states and the District of Columbia regulate the practice of social work. A much smaller number of states license or regulate marriage and family counselors, and some states have a certification process for drug abuse or alcoholism counselors. Nurses must be licensed in all states.

Licensure laws typically require a practitioner to follow the accepted code of ethics for his or her profession; the ethics code may contain a code of conduct of some sort also. Although licensure laws and codes of conduct vary from state to state, the sexual exploitation of clients by therapists is explicitly or implicitly forbidden in virtually all jurisdictions. For example, in the case of licensed psychologists, 12 states specifically prohibit sex with clients in their codes of conduct, and 42 have adopted the APA ethics code that specifically forbids it. The only exception is Nevada; it has proposed the addition of this prohibition to the licensure statute (Hall, 1986).

By and large filing a licensure complaint requires some work by the client and can lead to the client's being subjected to cross examination in a hearing. Furthermore, many licensure Board actions take at least a year if they go to a formal hearing. Boards have the advantage of providing for public protection. The process used by Boards vary from state to state and even within states. For example, the hearings of the medical licensing board may be closed whereas those of the psychology licensing board may be open to the press and public. Unfortunately, good national overviews are not available, except in the case of psychology for which an invaluable overview was provided by Hall (1986) in "Issues and Procedures in the Disciplining of Distressed Psychologists."

Investigation of a given state's disciplinary procedures for a specific profession requires contacting the Board and obtaining written material and explanations of their procedures. Hall (1986) outlined the typical process:

1. The board or licensure agency receives a complaint. This complaint may be placed over the phone initially, but a written complaint must be signed prior to investigation.

2. The charges are investigated by the state investigators.

3. The board may attempt to resolve the charges informally through correspondence, a conference, or a consent order.

4. Failing an informal resolution, the board initiates formal proceedings.

5. A formal notice of hearing is sent to the accused.

6. The board or hearing officer (or both) conducts the hearing.

7. The board makes a determination (or recommendation) on the basis of the hearing and, in some jurisdictions, on the basis of the hearing officer's recommendations.

8. Sanctions are determined and imposed, or in certain states, recommended and reviewed by an internal administrative review process and then imposed.

9. Judicial review is available through the county, district, or state courts. (p. 279)

The following key issues may affect the process and what is required of the client (as complainant):

ARE THE HEARINGS OPEN OR CLOSED?

In some states the formal hearing is always open whereas in others it must be closed. In still others, although it is open, the hearing may be closed to protect the privacy of one or both parties. Furthermore, in some states permitting closed hearings, they can be opened under certain circumstances.

This provision may be the single most important one to many clients who are considering making a complaint; most want to avoid any publicity and, especially, the loss of personal privacy, which may come about in giving testimony.

In contrast, the closed hearing provides a unique opportunity to testify without personal public exposure of the type that occurs in a civil suit or criminal action.

WHAT IS THE HISTORY OF APPEALS?

Either the state or the practitioner may appeal an action of the Board to a court. Commonly, Boards request the judge in the appellate court to seal the records and, in many jurisdictions, this is done. But, the client needs to know the risks of an appeal and whether the case may then become public.

HOW COMMON ARE HEARINGS IN THIS TYPE OF CASE?

A few years ago Wand (1984) surveyed psychology licensing boards and found that one-third had held no hearings at all in a given year. It is useful to know how likely a hearing is for a given type of case.

TYPE OF HEARING:

All states hold quasi-judicial hearings with witnesses under oath and some rules of evidence. At least four common patterns of decision making relate to hearings:

1. Hearing conducted by the Board that acts as both judge and jury.

2. A hearing officer presides over the hearing, functioning like a judge, with Board members serving as jury.

3. A hearing officer conducts the hearing and issues findings of fact and recommendations, and the Board reviews the record and determines the sanctions.

4. The hearing officer has total authority over the hearing and makes the determination.

Obviously, in the first two types a number of people may be present for the hearing, whereas the last two may be somewhat private. (The rules of evidence vary as does the burden of proof on the Board, but these technical items usually mean little to people other than attorneys.)

ACTIONS WITHOUT A HEARING:

In most instances it is possible for an accused practitioner to meet informally with Board representatives to argue his or her case. Sometimes charges are dropped at this point, which frustrates complainants.

Furthermore, accused practitioners may plead guilty to some of or all the charges and accept some sanctions by signing a "consent order." As in plea bargaining, the result may be a lesser sanction, but it allows the Board and the practitioner to avoid a costly hearing. Clients' reactions to this practice vary, often depending on the outcome. For some it is a relief that the action was prompt and they did not have to testify. For others it is frustrating, because either they never had an opportunity to confront the practitioner with their testimony or they felt that the sanctions were inadequate.

These possibilities may vary somewhat from year to year depending on the Board's resources and number of complaints it is processing. When a formal hearing is required a case may take a full year or more to process.

EMERGENCY LICENSE SUSPENSION:

Although many Boards may obtain a court order to prevent a practitioner from doing something, usually the order is used to prevent someone from practicing illegally. (Hall, 1986). In some states a Board can suspend a license on an emergency basis to protect the public, even without a full hearing. In Minnesota, for example, a physician accused of sexually touching several patients had his license suspended by the Board on an emergency basis.

REHABILITATION AND RE-ENTRY INTO THE FIELD:

Unfortunately, rehabilitation standards for therapists who have exploited clients sexually are rarely referred to in licensure statutes or regulations. The standards for assessing such practitioners are not uniform. Nor are assessments always conducted. In some instances, a Board may simply ask the practitioners to "get psychotherapy" from an approved therapist. (For an alternative model, see Ch. 32.) Standards for the restoration of licenses also are lacking; indeed, most statutes and regulations do not even specify a mandatory waiting period let alone criteria for the restoration. A client who files a complaint only in terms of expectations needs to be apprised of what is likely to happen to the perpetrator and, thus, is sometimes disappointed by what seems to be the failure of the board to protect the public.

It is important to note that in cases of sexual exploitation by therapists, bringing the situation to the attention of a licensure Board may result in actions that are related to issues other than the sex, although the disciplinary consequences to the practitioner in terms of protecting the public are the same. Some examples follow:

1. Action against a practitioner for misrepresenting title, credentials, licensure status, etc.

2. If other complaints are under investigation, or if the practitioner is already on probation, a single complaint of less serious offenses still may play a role in decisive action.

3. Even if the Board fails to discipline the therapist or invokes mild sanctions, future complaints are likely to result in more decisive action.

4. In many cases the Board ends up taking action on unprofessional conduct or action that is related to practitioner impairment, which is a part of the complaint. Common examples are discipline for violations of confidentiality; mis-prescription of medications; use of drugs or alcohol with a client; etc.

9. Appeal for Compensation to a Fund for Victims:

CRIME VICTIMS ASSISTANCE:

In states such as Wisconsin and Minnesota which have criminalized sexual misconduct by therapists or in other states if the victim is a minor and a criminal proceeding ensues, compensation for the victim may be provided by crime victim assistance. (In Minnesota, crime victim assistance funds were employed to fund a statewide series of workshops aimed at training people to serve victims of sexual misconduct by therapists.)

For example, an adolescent in Minnesota who was sexually abused by a therapist appealed for compensation to cover the costs of the therapy she received to deal with the consequences. She received full funding for this follow-up therapy, even though the therapist was never charged or tried for the abuse, on the basis of the argument that she was in fact a victim of a crime.

COMPENSATION FOR INJURY OR MALPRACTICE:

Some states recommend or require that persons who have been injured by professional incompetence or malpractice appeal to a victim's compensation panel prior to filing a civil suit. For example, in Wisconsin, clients who charged several psychiatrists with harming them through sexual abuse used this procedure.

Beyond such mechanisms, there are in some states funds created by members of the legal profession to compensate victims of legal malpractice. It may be time for the various psychotherapy professions to consider doing the same thing. It will, at the very least, give all professionals in the field a vested interest in policing members and protecting consumers. At present, however, I am not aware of such a fund for any of the psychotherapy professions.

10. Private Compensation for Damages

In several cases of which we are aware clients approached attorneys to start some action against a therapist for sexual misconduct. Because the statute of limitations had long since run out and there was no good argument for extending the statute of limitations (e.g., the client was well aware that she had a cause of action and simply chose to do nothing), and the client did not want to risk publicity, a novel solution was undertaken.

The client's attorney approached the therapist and/or his employer (where there was one), presented the charges, and asked for specific compensatory actions and payments. This settlement was to be a private matter between the therapist and client; thus, any payments would be made by the therapist (or his/her employer) personally rather than by the insurance company. In these situations, the therapist or employer was motivated by the fear of publicity or the loss of license and reputation, and sometimes, in part, by the desire to make amends. The following case is an example:

Client demanded in excess of $20,000 to cover the return of her original therapy fees and several thousand dollars to cover the portion of her follow-up therapy that dealt with the sexual exploitation, and that the therapist submit to an in-depth evaluation and follow-through with any treatment recommendations. (The therapist not only had a good reputation but, also, the client believed that her case was likely singular, based on a private investigation.) In exchange, the client would agree to keep the matter private and not to complain to the practitioner's professional association or any other body. She also requested her legal fees; they were minimal because the matter was concluded quickly.

The practitioner agreed, submitted to the evaluation, and followed through on the treatment recommendations; both the evaluator and provider of treatment reported to the client's attorney in regard to compliance. The evaluation and treatment plan were probably more sophisticated than those required by licensure boards and professional associations.

Although the financial consequence for the practitioner was substantial (greater in fact than a malpractice suit would have been because in such a suit the practitioner would have had to pay only the deductible), the protection of a fine professional reputation was deemed worth the cost. The practitioner also reported that the evaluation and treatment had been very helpful and of considerable benefit. (Note that the practitioner was comparatively healthy and was genuinely remorseful; all indications were that the sexual involvement was a singular occurrence, a one-time loss of control and objectivity.) The client reported satisfaction with the outcome.

In some jurisdictions an evaluating or treating therapist would have to make a report to the licensing Board so such an arrangement would not be possible there. A client, however, would not be prevented from simply asking for compensation for damages and to forego requiring some sort of evaluation or treatment. The example used here involves evaluation and supervision of treatment by independent practitioners; if an employer is involved he or she may be asked to agree to supervision, practice limitation, and oversight of rehabilitation, for example. Again, it is important to note that in some jurisdictions the employer is a mandated reporter, consequently such an undertaking would have to be reported to the licensure board. We do not advocate this procedure as an alternative to a civil suit or a licensure complaint; it is merely presented as an innovative solution that several clients and their attorneys considered meritorious for them.

11. Civil Suit:

A person damaged through the actions or negligence of another person has the right, under common law, to file a civil suit for damages. One may file a suit alleging intentional acts, such as sexual assault, an action that is called an intentional tort. Such a suit is rarely used against therapists owing to the fact that their insurance coverage invariably excludes intentional acts.

Hence the most common type of suit filed against an exploitative therapist is a negligence tort—specifically, malpractice. Hogan (1979) listed the four elements which a plaintiff must prove in a malpractice action:

1. a legal duty existed between the practitioner and the injured party;

2. the practitioner was derelict in that duty (either through an act that should not have occurred or through an omission);

3. the patient or client suffered harm or injury of some sort; and

4. the harm or injury was directly and proximately caused by the professional's dereliction of duty.

Given that case law is constantly developing, the following texts were helpful to us in the past: Dawidoff (1973), *The Malpractice of Psychiatrists*, and Cohen (1979), *Malpractice*; they are now out of date. The best reference currently available is Joseph Smith (1986), *Medical Malpractice Psychiatric Care*. It contains a lengthy chapter on sexual exploitation and is highly recommended.

Clients' experiences of such a trial are given in Freeman & Roy (1976) and Walker & Young (1986). Bates & Brodsky (1988) provide perspectives from both a client and an expert witness. Last, although it is not a sexual exploitation case, an accused therapist's view of and experience in a trial can be found in Charles & Kennedy (1985), *Defendant*.

Clients who are considering a civil suit may have to meet with several different attorneys or firms before finding one who (a) has had experience with such cases; (b) inspires their confidence; and (c) is willing to take their case. Check to see whether there is a charge for the first visit to discuss the case (usually, there is not). Most attorneys are willing to take such cases on a contingent fee basis, meaning that they receive a proportion of the award if the case is won and thus, a client's costs are minimal.

Obviously one is best off with an attorney who is experienced with such cases or, at least, who specializes in malpractice. However, a qualified attorney may not be available nearby or may turn down the case. Some attorneys who are new to this area of case law end up doing a fine job, especially when they obtain consultation.

A client's primary question may be whether the attorney will believe her/him and is willing to take on a powerful professional. The aspects in which an attorney is immediately interested, however, are as follows:

1. STATUTE OF LIMITATIONS:

When was the last professional contact with the therapist? When did the client know something was wrong with the treatment? In many jurisdictions the statute of limitations for medical malpractice is only 2 years, for example, and it begins running when the plaintiff knows he or she has a cause of action. Although ways around the statute of limitations can be found in some cases, problems in this area are the common reasons that attorneys turn cases down.

2. COVERAGE AND "DEEP POCKETS":

What insurance was in force at the time of the malpractice? The major psychotherapy professions have $25,000 limits on sexual abuse cases, although the limit can be circumvented at times. What sort of policy does the therapist's employer have? Does the therapist have substantial personal resources? The client is not expected to have this information, nevertheless the answers are critical to the conduct of the case.

3. PROOF OF CLIENT STATUS:

Does the client have payment receipts or some other way of verifying he/she was a client?

4. PROOF OF THE MISCONDUCT: Generally, there is no question that overt sexual contact is malpractice. Four states (Wisconsin, Minnesota, Illinois, and California) even have statutes that so declare. If the therapist denies the behaviors alleged, does the client have evidence to support his/her version of the events? For example,

a. a diary or notes written at the time;
b. testimony from friends or others who were told at the time;
c. photographs or other records of contact outside the office;
d. evidence of an out-of-town trip or stay in a motel; evidence of "dates" in a bar or restaurant;
e. intimate knowledge of the therapist's residence, personal life, or unique characteristics of his/her body;
f. gifts, letters, or other evidence of romantic involvement; and
g. witnesses to contacts outside the office; social or sexual contact.

5. HARM OR INJURY:

The client must try to describe the harm and injury that were suffered as a result of the malpractice, and how they can be distinguished from pre-existing problems or from harm and injury suffered elsewhere (see Ch. 10). Although the therapist's behavior was outrageous, the client's personal strengths may have prevented major damage. Remind clients that malpractice actions are suits for damages, not trials of the degree of wrongdoing by the therapist. Furthermore, punitive damages are typically awarded only when actual damages have been demonstrated.

Overall, the case represents a business decision for many attorneys. They have to estimate the likelihood that they will not only prevail in the case but that the amount awarded to the client will make it worthwhile. A $25,000 award, of which the attorney's contingency fee is $8,333 (1/3) to $10,000 (40%), does not begin to cover the time and costs in most cases. Even if an attorney takes on a case out of principle, the client still must realize that it is a business decision.

The major advantage of a civil suit is that it can recover damages for the client and have a profound effect on the therapist, even if the award is paid by an insurance company. The major disadvantages are that if the suit goes to court considerable personal exposure and loss of privacy may result, not to mention abusive and intrusive cross-examination.

Furthermore, the case may take 2 years to get into court and then another year or two if the decision is appealed. For the client, the effect is essentially that he/she is still essentially involved with the therapist.

An added problem arises if an offer to settle is made. The client who may have hoped for the opportunity to publicly accuse the therapist may have to trade it away for a settlement. In addition, a settlement usually does not require the therapist to admit guilt or to answer for his/her behavior. Last but not least, the plaintiff must usually agree not to discuss the case and, therefore, may not make an ethics or licensure complaint. Some clients feel quite guilty about accepting these provisions, as if they took the money in exchange for compromising public safety.

12. Criminal Complaint:

Local prosecutors vary markedly in their approach to sex offenses in general, and in their view of therapist sexual misconduct. Which criminal sanctions are employed in the case, consequently, depend as much on the local prosecutor as it does on the wording of statutes. Quite a variety of criminal complaints are possible, depending on the situation.

SPECIAL STATUTES: Wisconsin, Minnesota, North Dakota, and Colorado have criminalized a therapist's sexual involvement with clients (see Appendices G, H, L, and DD). The statutes classify it as a special type of criminal sexual misconduct. A number of other states have considered criminalization in recent years.

SEX DURING MEDICAL EXAMINATION: Statutes in five states (Colorado, Michigan, New Hampshire, Rhode Island, Wyoming) provide that a physician who engages in sexual activity with a patient during "medical treatment or examination" is guilty of criminal sexual misconduct. Although one may assume that this provision applies only to physicians, including psychiatrists, an analysis by Bliss (1986) noted that in the New Hampshire case of State v. VonKlock, 433 A.2d 1299 (1981), a school psychologist was charged under this statute.

MISDEMEANOR BY A LICENSED PRACTITIONER: Some states (e.g., Texas, Hawaii, Florida) have provisions in their licensure laws for some health professionals allowing for a charge of sexual misconduct by a prosecutor after the state licensing authority has found that the licensee has engaged in misconduct with a client. These provisions do not appear to be used with much frequency, but may represent an additional course of action following a licensure action in a state which hasn't created a felony statute like Minnesota, Wisconsin, Colorado, or North Dakota. The new Section 729 added to California's Business and Professions Code in 1989 makes sexual contact wiht the client of a psychotherapist (see Section 728 of the Code in Appendix P for definition) a misdemeanor for the first offense, and either a misdemeanor or felony for subsequent offenses. It appears that such a case might be prosecuted locally without an action of the licensure board.

PERSONS IN AUTHORITY: A Wyoming statute (see Appendix F) provides for a charge of sexual assault in the second degree if "The actor is in a position of authority over the victim and uses this position of authority to cause the victim to submit" (Wyo. Stat. Ann., Criminal, 6-2-303, p. 43). The definition for "position of authority" is given as:

...that position occupied by a parent, guardian, relative, household member, teacher, employer, custodian or any other person who, by reason of his position, is able to exercise significant influence over a person. (Wyo. Stat. Ann., 6-2-301, p. 39)

It would seem that one could easily argue that a psychotherapist be considered in a position of authority. It is likely that this sort of language can be found in the statutes of other states which, although not previously used to prosecute psychotherapists, might permit such an action.

WRONGFUL REPRESENTATION STATUTES: Some states (e.g., Michigan Comp. Laws 750.90.) have laws, some that date back to the turn of the century and are rarely used, which make it a felony for a person to have sex with a woman during medical treatment by representing it as necessary or beneficial to her health. Although a rarer situation, some states have laws that provide criminal penalties for anyone who enters a health facility and has sexual contact with a patient after falsely misrepresenting her/himself as a physician.

CONSUMER FRAUD: In a few instances it has been possible to successfully charge a therapist with consumer fraud by arguing that it is fraudulent to engage in sex with clients as part of therapy. A local case involved a hypnotherapist and counselor who had engaged in sex with literally hundreds of women clients, several of whom filed complaints. The local country attorney was determined to do something about the situation. A policewoman was sent in wired for sound; the tape and transcript revealed that the therapist turned the talk to sex within minutes of starting the interview. I was called in as an expert. I examined the transcript, interviewed several victims, and executed an affidavit that, in short, (a) that sex was not part of the professional service the therapist in question claimed to offer; (b) sex in this context was usually harmful to consumers; (c) it was my professional opinion that the sexual contact, in fact, had been harmful to the women complainants whom I had interviewed; and (d) the talk about sex on the transcript was not the taking of a sexual history, treatment planning, or treatment itself; therefore, I assumed it to be fraudulent. The judge issued a restraining order and the therapist closed his office and left town eventually. Pursuit of such a case along these lines probably requires multiple victims and an interested prosecutor. It has the advantage of being very fast and of not exposing the victims because they need not be named in the complaint nor appear in court.

CRIMINAL SEXUAL MISCONDUCT (RAPE): Even without the special statutes described earlier, under certain circumstances the police and prosecutors may be willing to charge a case under existing criminal sexual misconduct statutes if any of the following situations exist:

1. Victim is a Minor: See, for example, Burgess & Hartman (1986).
2. Anesthesia is Used: See, for example, Mertz (1986).
3. Electroconvulsive Shock is Used: In one case a psychiatrist had sex with a hospitalized, depressed woman, and then sent her down for ECT. The act was discovered by accident (the ECT erased her memory of it) and a criminal prosecution ensued.
4. Drugs are Used: Several psychiatrists have been charged with the use of drugs (e.g., sodium amytal, nembutal) to render clients partially conscious so that sexual advances can be made. In at least one such case the police treated it as a rape.
5. Hypnosis: See, for example, Perry (1979) and Hoencamp (in press) as well as Chapter 43.
6. Force and Threats of Harm: On occasion therapists use force or threats to coerce patients into sexual contact. These are obviously chargeable as rape.

See Smith and Bisbing (1988, pp. 83-89) for a sampling of case law.

INSURANCE, MEDICAID, OR MEDICARE FRAUD: Unethical therapists sometimes engage in other illegal acts in addition to having sex with their clients. Proof of fraud in connection with their billing practices may be a more effective way of putting them out of business than other type of charge. Furthermore, client exposure in many such cases is minimal. Some clients appreciate this approach because personal exposure is not required and the fact that their main concern is protecting others; thus they do not care how or why the therapist is put out of business. In addition, conviction of billing fraud also opens the door to licensure-related discipline. (See Case 8 in Ch. 43.)

INCOME TAX FRAUD: A client once remarked to us, "If the IRS could get a hood like Al Capone maybe they'd be up to nailing. . ." a particular therapist. The client further noted that unlike licensure boards, the IRS would see that "He can't get away by running across a state line...." Therapists, especially those in psychotherapy cults take a great many cash payments and may not report their income accurately on tax returns. If a group of patients is willing to file a report with the IRS and to cooperate with the investigation, action may be taken.

13. The News Media:

Some clients who lack either an alternative course of action or are concerned predominantly with alerting potential victims, may choose to contact the news media. Needless to say, this is high risk owing to the danger of a defamation action and the unpredictability of the press. However, especially with unlicensed therapists, no other option for taking action may be possible.

PSYCHOTHERAPISTS' ETHICAL CODES

Although the specificity with which they are addressed and the rationales vary, all codes of ethics for the various psychotherapy professions forbid sexual contact with clients. All codes of conduct developed in connection with licensure laws also forbid sexual contact with clients.

Modern ethics codes for the various psychotherapy professions probably have their origins in the code of medical ethics that was itself descended from the Code of Hammurabi, compiled around 2000 BC, and the Hippocratic Corpus, which dates back to the 4th or 5th Century BC. In the section of the Hippocratic Corpus entitled, "The Physician," the intimacy of the physician-patient relationship is described thus:

The intimacy also between physician and patient is close. Patients in fact put themselves into the hands of their physicians, and at every moment he meets women, maidens and possessions very precious indeed. So towards all these self-control must be used. Such then should the physician be, both in body and in soul. (Trans. by W.H.S. Jones, cited in Reiser, Dyck, & Curran, 1977, p. 5)

The original Greek version of the "Oath," usually referred to as the Hippocratic Oath, although there is reason to believe that it was not authored by Hippocrates, states in part:

". . .and I will abstain from all intentional wrong-doing and harm, especially from abusing the bodies of man or woman, bond or free. (Trans. by W.H.S. Jones, cited in Reiser, Dyck, & Curran, 1977, p. 5)

When the "Oath" was rewritten for Christian physicians some years later, this section read as follows:

> ...with purity and holiness I will practice my art.... Into whatever house I enter I will go into them for the benefit of the sick and will abstain from every voluntary act of Mischief and Corruption and further from the seduction of females or males, of freemen and slaves.... (Braceland, 1969, p. 236)

During the Middle Ages, the treatise "De Cautelis Medicorum," thought to have been authored by Arnald of Villanova, read in part:

> Let me give you one more warning: Do not look at a maid, a daughter, or a wife with an improper or a covetous eye and do not let yourself be entangled in woman affairs for there are medical operations that excite the helper's mind; otherwise your judgment is affected, you become harmful to the patient and people will expect less from you. And so be pleasant in your speech, diligent and careful in your medical dealings, eager to help. And adhere to this without fallacy. (Braceland, 1968, p. 236)

Concern about physicians taking sexual advantage of their patients through the misuse of mesmerism (hypnosis) was voiced in 1784 by a Commission of Inquiry headed by Benjamin Franklin, which, in a secret report to the French King, Louis XVI, stated:

> ...the danger exists...since the physician can, if he will, take advantage of his patient...Even if we ascribe to him superhuman virtue, since he is exposed to emotions which awaken such desires, the imperious law of nature will affect his patient, and he is responsible, not merely for his own wrong-doing, but for that he may have excited in another (Franklin, de Bory, Lavoisier, Bailly, Majault, Sallin, d'Arcet, Guillotin, & Le Roy, 1965, p. 6)

Perry (1979) notes that at "...the time the report was written... medical doctors enjoyed a bad reputation in the eyes of a significant segment of the lay public. (p. 188)

There follows in the rest of this section a brief examination of current codes of ethics in use by the major professional organizations for each psychotherapy profession. State associations may have their own codes and a number of licensure boards have codes of conduct also. Individual organizations that employ psychotherapists may have their own codes as well. In the following discussion I focus specifically on the language relevant to a therapist's sexual involvement with clients and I ignore other portions of the codes. Copies of the codes were obtained from the various professional organizations.

It is worth noting that recently Gorlin (1986) published a volume containing the ethics codes for a large number of professions. The professions are listed alphabetically. Technically, these codes apply only to members of the professional organization that developed them. They may be used in legal proceedings to provide some definition of proper practice, however.

ALCOHOLISM, CHEMICAL DEPENDENCY, AND DRUG ABUSE COUNSELORS

Until recently, there were no commonly accepted national ethics codes in this diverse field. Trade organizations in a number of states have ethics codes, although many lack detail. In states such as Minnesota the credentialing board for practitioners is a voluntary one, nevertheless it has an active ethics committee that hears cases. Its ethics code is vague, but sexual contact with clients is regularly disciplined.

Although in states such as Minnesota there are a growing number of fee-for-service independent practitioners, most counselors of this type are employed by an agency or facility, most of which have internal ethics codes.

The Minnesota Chemical Dependency Association (MCDA) has an excellent code of ethics. Standard 61 in that code reads,

> A practitioner should have no personal, business, sexual or social relationship with a client or former client within one year after termination of service, except a casual social relationship. (MCDA, 1985)

This standard is followed by a comment:

> No exception to this standard should be made on the basis of actual or perceived invulnerability of a particular client. (MCDA, 1985)

Principles 1 and 2 of the code require the practitioner to do nothing to encourage client dependency, and to actively discourage it, except "as is clearly essential to the provision of services" (MCDA, 1985).

In *Ethics for Addiction Treatment Professionals*, Bissell and Royce (1987) discuss social contacts with clients, noting that entering into a dating or sexual relationship with a client is forbidden, and suggesting that relationships with former clients are questionable.

The National Association of Alcoholism and Drug Abuse Counselors (NAADAC), which has more than 11,000 members (of the estimated 24,000 alcohol and drug abuse counselors nationwide), published a Code of Ethics in 1987 (NAADAC, 1987), which states in part:

> 9.d. The alcoholism and drug abuse counselor should not engage in any type of sexual activity with a client (p. 16)

In an article which accompanied the Code, Lubben (1987) indicates that state association chapters will be responsible for its implementation. He indicated that NAADAC would serve only as an appeal body for the enforcement process, only reviewing issues of due process. It is unclear whether NAADAC will handle complaints in cases where the state has no enforcement mechanism. To contact NAADAC:

Chair, Ethics Committee, NAADAC
3717 Columbia Pike, Suite 300
Arlington, Virginia 22204
(703) 920-4644

The National Association of Addiction Treatment Professionals has a membership of 700 hospitals and other providers of treatment. The memberships are corporate. The code of ethics is currently being revised. To obtain more information:

National Assn. of Addiction Treatment Professionals
2082 Michelson, Suite 101
Irvine, California 92715
(714) 476-8204

There is also an American College of Addiction Treatment Administrators at:

840 N. Lake Shore Drive
Suite 1103W
Chicago, Illinois 60611
(312) 943-0544

While this group does not have a code and does not deal with treatment professionals, it does have standards for administrators in such programs.

BIOFEEDBACK TECHNICIANS

Health care professionals of many types use biofeedback technology. However, some persons offering biofeedback are technicians and many belong to the Biofeedback Society of America. The society's "Ethical Principles of Biofeedback" (revised and adopted March 11, 1987) reads in part,

F. Protection of Client Rights and Welfare

3. Inappropriate physical contact with clients is one which often leads to litigation; therefore, caution and common sense are required. Sexual intimacies with clients are prohibited. In addition, touching and massage require client permission and are restricted to those body areas considered appropriate for touch or massage within the realm of "common practice" for one's professional discipline. Touching of sensitive body parts, such as the breasts or genitals is not acceptable in biofeedback practice, with the exception of a medical exam or medical treatment provided by a licensed medical practitioner. (Biofeedback Society of America, 1987)

"Sexual exploitation of patients" is the first item on a list of "Grounds for Discipline." To file a complaint, write or call,

Ethics and Disciplinary Committee
Biofeedback Society of America
10200 W. 44th Ave., Suite 304
Wheat Ridge, CO 80033
(303) 422-8436

CLERGY AND PASTORAL COUNSELORS

Various religious groups are beginning to address the problem of clergy sexual involvement with clients (or parishioners; see Chapters 6 and 20). Although written codes are often lacking, it is generally understood that clergy should not have sex with counselees. Where priests are celibate, as in the Roman Catholic Church, any sexual contact would seem prohibited. Rules of conduct may be promulgated by the denomination or the specific institution itself. Complaints go to the church or the denomination. (See Chapter 6 for more information.)

PROFESSIONAL COUNSELORS AND GUIDANCE COUNSELORS

In any large community, many people call themselves "counselors." They have various backgrounds and, at times, belong to some sort of professional counseling trade association. The major national organization is the American Association for Counseling and Development (formerly, the American Personnel & Guidance Association). The "Ethical Standards" approved by the Executive Committee, January 17, 1981 reads in part,

Section A: General

8. In the counseling relationship the counselor is aware of the intimacy of the relationship and maintains respect for the client and avoids engaging in activities that seek to meet the counselor's personal needs at the expense of the client.

Section B: Counseling Relationship

11. ...Dual relationships with clients that might impair the member's objectivity and professional judgment (e.g., as with close friends or relatives, sexual intimacies with any client) must be avoided and/or the counseling relationship terminated through referral to another competent professional.

Some members of the American Association for Counseling and Development, as well as other persons who refer to themselves as "counselors" or "professional counselors," also are members of psychological associations and subject to their codes of ethics.

The American Association for Counseling and Development has more than 55,000 members in the United States, as well as members in over 50 other countries. They can be contacted at:

American Association for Counseling and Development
5999 Stevenson Avenue
Alexandria, Virginia 22304-3303
(703) 823-9800

EMPLOYEE ASSISTANCE COUNSELORS

There are an estimated 10,000 employee assistance counselors in the United States, more than 5,600 of whom belong to the Association of Labor-Management Administrators and Consultants on Alcoholism, Inc. (ALMACA). The ALMACA Code of Ethics was approved in revised form on April 10, 1988 and was published in *The ALMACAN* (ALMACA, 1988). It is also available in the form of a brochure. The Code specifically states that "ALMACA members ...do not engage in sexual conduct with clients..." (ALMACA, 1988, p. 24). Local ALMACA Chapters are expected to deal with complaints, but if there is no local chapter or if the local is unable to resolve a matter in a satisfactory fashion, a complaint can be sent to:

National President
ALMACA
4601 N. Fairfax Drive, Suite 1001
Arlington, Virginia 22203
(703) 522-6272

Since 1987 the Employee Assistance Certification Commission (EACC) has been certifying employee assistance professionals. As of June 1989 3,606 have been certified. The Code of Professional Conduct for Certified Employee Assistance Professionals (CEAP) states in Section II.F.4. that the CEAP will "Not engage in sexual conduct with clients." (EACC, 1988, p. 2) Copies of the code and procedures and other information can be obtained from:

Employee Assistance Certification Commission
ALMACA
4601 N. Fairfax Drive, Suite 1001
Arlington, Virginia 22203
(703) 522-6272

HYPNOTHERAPISTS

As was noted earlier in this chapter, concerns about the misuse of hypnosis to seduce clients dates back to at least the 1780s. The debate has been largely focused on the issue of the role of hypnosis in seduction or coerced sexual contact (see, for example, Conn, 1972; Perry, 1979; Laurence & Perry, 1988). Conn (1972), for example, in the same article in which he notes that seduction occurs in other therapeutic settings "without the use of hypnosis" and contends "...that hypnosis does not facilitate seduction" (p. 75), cites two cases of women who were seduced by their hypnotists. After positing masochistic psychodynamics, Conn (1972) concluded that:

The two patients were not passive "victims," but were actively seeking masochistic sexual relationships with omnipotent parent surrogates. (p. 75)

Orne (Personal Communication, June 23, 1989), who previously questioned (e.g., Orne, 1972) whether hypnosis could compel compliance with sexual demands made by a therapist, now believes that in the context of a psychotherapy relationship, hypnosis may facilitate seduction the way alcohol does, enhancing the effects of transference. However, regardless of whether hypnosis per se facilitates seduction or exploitation, it is clear that sexual contact with clients occurs in some hypnotherapy contexts (for examples see Conn, 1972; Hoencamp, In Press; Kline, 1972; Perry, 1979; Venn, 1988).

In contrast, most of the more than 7,000 members of the American Council of Hypnotist Examiners are not in licensed professions so the organization does have a code of ethics. Section 10 of the Code states, "A hypnotist should avoid dual relationships with clients which might impair professional judgment or increase the risk of client exploitation" (American Council of Hypnotist Examiners, undated). Sexual contact with clients is not explicitly mentioned.

The Association to Advance Ethical Hypnosis, with about 1,200 members worldwide, many of whom are not members of other health professions, has a code of ethics and a formal Ethics and Standards Committee. However, it does not address the issue of sexual contact with a client.

If a hypnotherapist or hypnotist is not a member of another health profession, then one should ascertain if he or she is a member of a professional organization and file a complaint accordingly. A reference librarian can help to locate the address and phone number of any organization to which a hypnotherapist may belong.

MARRIAGE AND FAMILY COUNSELORS AND THERAPISTS

Many practitioners who refer to themselves as marriage or family counselors are not members of a professional organization; others, however, may be psychologists and social workers who simply specialize in this area of work. Only eight states license or regulate the practice of marriage and family counseling.

A growing number of marriage and family counselors belong to the American Association for Marriage and Family Therapy, which has affiliates in most states and three regional associations. The Association's code of ethics has been modeled on the code of the American Psychological Association. The language relating to sex between therapist and client mirrors that of the APA code. The "Code of Professional Ethics" reads in part,

1.2 Marriage and family therapists are cognizant of their potentially influential position with respect to clients, and they avoid exploiting the trust and dependency of such persons. Marriage and family therapists therefore make every effort to avoid dual relationships with clients that could impair their professional judgment or increase the risk of exploitation. Examples of such dual relationships include, but are not limited to, business or close personal relationships with clients. Sexual intimacy with clients is prohibited. Sexual intimacy with former clients for two years following the termination of therapy is prohibited.

2.3 Marriage and family therapists do not use their professional relationship with clients to further their own interests. (American Association for Marriage & Family Therapy, 1988)

Ethics complaints are passed from state and regional associations to the national organization; it is easier, therefore, to send a complaint directly to the national office. Its address is currently,

American Association for
Marriage and Family Therapy
1717 K Street NW, Suite 407
Washington, D.C. 20006

The AAMFT has a Judicial Council; it is the body to which a final appeal goes.

MEDICINE

The Oath of Hippocrates and other earlier medical writings were discussed earlier in this chapter. A separate section, which follows, deals with psychiatrists. Until quite recently sexual contact with patients was not discussed in *The Principles of Medical Ethics*, although ethics committees and licensure boards of physicians have disciplined them for having sexual contact with patients. In 1989 a section was added to the *Current Opinions, Council on Ethical and Judicial Affairs, American Medical Association* as follows:

8.14 Sexual misconduct in the practice of medicine violates the trust the patient reposes in the physician and is unethical. (AMA, 1989, p. 34)

Since sexual misconduct is not defined, it is unclear what specifically is prohibited. Complaints about physicians can be made to the local county medical society, the state medical association, or the American Medical Association (AMA). The AMA is located in Chicago and its phone number is:

(312) 645-5000

PSYCHIATRIC NURSING

Nurses in psychiatric settings have been providing individual, family, and group therapy for some time and, over the past two decades, there has been a growing involvement of nurses in the provision of outpatient psychotherapy. Although many nurses practice in medical clinics, a growing number are in independent practice or practice in association with non-medical psychotherapists.

The "Code for Nurses With Interpretative Statements," issued by the Committee on Ethics, American Nurses' Association (1985 Edition), does not address the issue of sex between therapist and client. It does, however, have an excellent section outlining the ethical duty of nurses to protect clients through aggressive advocacy and the challenge of questionable practice. Section 3 of the code states,

> 3. The nurse acts to safeguard the client and the public when health care and safety are affected by incompetent, unethical, or illegal practices of any person.

The subsections in this part of the code provide detailed instruction on the importance of challenging misconduct and taking aggressive action.

Complaints relative to unethical conduct by nurses should be made to the state Nurses' Association. Normally, the "Practice Council" handles such complaints. The national headquarters of the American Nurses' Association is currently located at

2420 Pershing Road
Kansas City, Missouri 64108

PSYCHIATRY

All psychiatrists are physicians and are licensed as physicians; thus they are subject to the "Principles of Medical Ethics." In 1973 the American Psychiatric Association published "The Principles of Medical Ethics With Annotations Especially Applicable to Psychiatry." This publication went through a major revision in response to the revised "Principles of Medical Ethics" published in 1980 (the first revision since 1957 of that code). The "Annotations..." (APA, 1985) reads in part,

Section 1:

1. The patient may place his/her trust in his/her psychiatrist knowing that the psychiatrist's ethics and professional responsibilities preclude him/her gratifying his/her own needs by exploiting the patient. This becomes particularly important because of the essentially private, highly personal, and sometimes intensely emotional nature of the relationship established with the psychiatrist....

Section 2:

1. The requirement that the physician conduct himself with propriety in his/her profession and in all the actions of his/her life is especially important in the case of the psychiatrist because the patient tends to model his/her behavior after that of his/her therapist by identification. Further, the necessary intensity of the therapeutic relationship may tend to activate sexual and other needs and fantasies on the part of both patient and therapist, while weakening the objectivity necessary for control. Sexual activity with a patient is unethical.

In December 1988 the Assembly and Board of Trustees of the American Psychiatric Association approved an addition to the "Annotations...," further elaborating on Section 2, Annotation 1:

Sexual involvement wiht one's former patients generally exploits emotions deriving from treatment and therefore almost always is unethical.   (APA, in press)

Complaints about psychiatrists can be made to the county or state medical society or the District Branch of the American Psychiatric Association (APA), usually called the state Psychiatric Society. Approximately 70% of U. S. psychiatrists are APA members (Korran, Fenton, and Taintor, 1986) Further information about the procedures used by these ethics committees can be obtained from the societies. The code or other information can be obtained from:

American Psychiatric Association
1400 K Street NW
Washington, D.C. 20005

PSYCHOLOGISTS

Many psychologists belong to the American Psychological Association or their state psychological association, all of which subscribe to the American Psychological Association's "Ethical Standards of Psychologists." There is also a companion "Casebook on Ethical Standards of Psychologists." The 1981 revision of the code states in part,

Principle 6: Welfare of the Consumer

a. Psychologists are continually cognizant of their own needs and of their potentially influential position vis-a-vis persons such as clients, students, and subordinates. They avoid exploiting the trust and dependency of such persons. Psychologists make every effort to avoid dual relationships that could impair their professional judgment or increase the risk of exploitation. Examples of such dual relationships include, but are not limited to, research with and treatment of employees, students, supervisees, close friends, or relatives. Sexual intimacies with clients are unethical....

Principle 7: Professional Relationships

d. Psychologists do not exploit their professional relationships with clients, supervisees, students, employees, or research participants sexually or otherwise. Psychologists do not condone or engage in sexual harassment. Sexual harassment is defined as deliberate or repeated comments, gestures, or physical contacts of a sexual nature that are unwanted by the recipient.

Complaints can be filed with the Ethics Committee of either the state association or the American Psychological Association (APA), if the psychologist is a member. Approximately 73% of doctoral level psychologists in the U. S. are APA members. (Stapp, Tucker, & VandenBos, 1985) Information can be obtained from the state association or

American Psychological Association
1200 Seventeenth St. NW
Washington, D.C. 20036

State licensing boards may have additional codes of conduct for psychologists.

SEX THERAPISTS

This group was omitted from earlier versions of this chapter in order to avoid confusing sex therapy with psychotherapy. Because some sex therapy makes use of "sexual surrogates," some psychotherapists have told clients that they are doing "sex therapy" as a way of justifying sexual contact. However, the "Code of Ethics" (1980) of the American Association of Sex Educators, Counselors and Therapists (AASECT) specifically forbids sex with clients as well as forbids the sex therapist to act as a sexual surrogate:

SECTION III: Welfare of the Client

7. It is unethical for the therapist to engage in sexual activity with a client.

8. Procedures involving nudity of either the client or the therapist or observation of client sexual activity go beyond the boundaries of established therapeutic practice and may be used only when there is good evidence that they serve the best interests of the client....

14. Although controversial, the use of partner surrogates in sex therapy may be an ethically permissible way of establishing a therapeutic environment, when conducted in a responsible manner. If partner surrogates are to be used at all, it should be understood that the partner surrogate is not a sex therapist; surrogates should understand that their role is not that of either sex therapist or psychotherapist; and sex therapists working with partner surrogates must exercise diligence and concern for protecting the dignity and welfare of both the surrogate and the client. (AASECT, 1980)

Complaints should be made to the national ethics committee. At present AASECT's address is:

American Association of Sex Educators,
Counselors & Therapists
11 Dupont Circle NW
Washington, D.C. 20036

SOCIAL WORK

The major social work organization, the National Association of Social Workers (NASW), has state chapters that are very closely affiliated with the national organization. A detailed complaint procedure is described in the publication, "NASW Policy and Procedures for the Adjudication of Grievances." The "Code of Ethics" (1980 version) states in part,

II. The Social Worker's Ethical Responsibility to Clients

4. The social worker should avoid relationships or commitments that conflict with the interests of clients.

5. The social worker should under no circumstances engage in sexual activity with clients.

NASW, perhaps, has the most formal procedure for hearing a grievance. It even includes a provision for the use of an advocate, usually a member of NASW, by the complainant. The ethics committee is called the "Committee on Inquiry." Once the committee decides on sanctions, they must be approved by the officers of the chapter. NASW has a greater range of sanctions than any other professional group, including a recommendation for restitution if there are damages, suspension of the ACSW (Academy of Certified Social Workers) credential, and publication of the findings and penalties. Major sanctions require approval from the national Board of Directors of NASW.

In addition to the NASW Chapters, 27 states have Clinical Social Work Societies that are part of the National Federation of Societies for Clinical Social Work. Their membership consists of social workers engaged in psychotherapy and other types of clinical practice. The Federation developed its own code of ethics in 1976 (revised October 1985). The code states in part,

I. General Responsibilities of Clinical Social Workers:

e) Clinical social workers do not exploit their professional relationships sexually, financially, or for any other personal advantage. They maintain this standard of conduct toward all who may be professionally associated with them, such as clients, colleagues, supervisees, employees, students, and research participants.

II. Responsibility to Clients:

c) Clinical social workers use care to prevent the intrusion of their own personal needs into relationships with clients. They recognize that the private and personal nature of the therapeutic relationship may unrealistically intensify clients' feelings toward them, thus increasing their obligation to maintain professional objectivity. Therefore, specifically....

2. Clinical social workers do not engage in or condone sexual activities with clients.

3. Clinical social workers do not initiate, and should avoid when possible, personal relationships or dual roles with current clients, or with any former clients whose feelings toward them may still be derived from or influenced by the former professional relationship.

Complaints against clinical social workers can be made in states that have societies to which the social worker belongs. All ethics cases are heard at the state level.

For information on the ethics codes or procedures for making a complaint, contact the state association or chapter or

National Association of Social Workers
7981 Eastern Avenue
Silver Spring, Maryland 20910

National Federation of Societies
for Clinical Social Work
2101 L Street N.W.
Washington, D.C. 20037

CONCLUSION

However ethics codes may vary, it is unethical for any therapist to have sexual contact with a client. It is also universally considered grounds for challenging a therapist's right to maintain a license.

Under some circumstances sexual contact with clients is a criminal offense: either a type of criminal sexual misconduct or fraud. It is also grounds for the client to sue for damages.

Persons seeking to support or provide advocacy to clients who have been sexually exploited by a therapist must have sufficient knowledge of the complaint options to assist the client in choosing the one(s) that is consistent with the client's goals while minimizing stress to the client.

Unfortunately, the professional community has a relatively poor track record in assisting clients who have been abused. It is hoped that the background information provided by this article and the conceptual and practical framework provided by Milgrom on "Advocacy" (Ch. 26) will encourage more advocacy activities by professionals.

CHAPTER 28

PROCESSING SESSIONS

Gary Richard Schoener
and
Jeanette Hofstee Milgrom

BACKGROUND

The concept of a face-to-face meeting between a client who claimed to have been sexually exploited and the former therapist who had engaged in the exploitation began developing in 1975, although it was not until June of 1978 that we had an opportunity to try it out. Our interest in face-to-face encounters between clients and their former therapists arose out of our recognition that this might provide a vehicle for meeting two needs commonly expressed by clients: (a) the need to confront the therapist or to give him feedback about the effects of the exploitation; (b) the desire to understand the therapist's motivation for his actions.

The term "processing session" was chosen because it correctly reflects the goal of such meetings: the discussion of the exploitation within the context of a review of the past therapist-client relationship which was exploitative. Its goal is to further understand how the professional relationship became exploitative. This goes beyond simply making a complaint, or of providing some sort of mediation toward a resolution of the client's grievances. At the time we were aware of no models for direct confrontation between former client and therapist that were moderated by a third party; complaints were handled indirectly, through a formal complaint, or not at all.

During 1975, a situation arose in which there seemed to be good reason to hold a direct meeting with a psychotherapist who allegedly had had sexual contact with a client. The client had no desire for any more contact with the therapist, however, and was interested only in filing formal charges. The sex had been imbedded in the therapy and the client did not care why; she simply felt that the therapist was disturbed and exploitative.

Because the client was not interested and we could envision no gain for her, we did not suggest a direct three-way meeting. The therapist in question had heard we were assisting at least one client in making a complaint and tried to apply some pressure on us. We wanted a direct meeting to clear the air as well as to confront this therapist, but his licensure board asked us not to. However, when he phoned and asked for such a meeting, one of us went to his clinic to meet with him and one of his professional colleagues. The meeting was useful in clarifying our position and giving some feedback to the colleague.

While not a classic processing session, this served to "break the ice" and to provide experience in moving beyond discussions with the client alone and to opening the door to discussions with both client and therapist.

During 1975 and 1976 WICC handled several complaints in which the client had a very strong desire to confront the therapist and/or obtain an explanation of why he did what he did. For various reasons a direct meeting with the therapist, facilitated by one of us, did not seem appropriate. During 1977 we also had some possibilities for meetings but either the client or we decided against them.

In June 1978 a young woman came in with an allegation of a sexual relationship with a therapist in which a processing session seemed to have great potential utility. In July 1978, therefore, we held what was to become the first of more than two dozen such sessions with different clients and therapists.

THE FIRST "PROCESSING SESSION"

The complainant was the young woman we first saw in June 1978. She alleged a long-term therapy relationship with a reasonably well-known local therapist who was many years her senior. She said that a sexual relationship developed during therapy and that all sexual contacts occurred in the office. The therapist's practice setting was a highly regarded local social service agency. It seemed an unlikely setting for such a relationship because office doors at the agency were not locked, receptionists occasionally interrupted sessions, and there was good team supervision in practice.

The therapist was hard-working and his involvement with professional activities went beyond the office; for example, he did volunteer work at several sites in the community. He expressed strong feelings about the exploitation of clients by therapists and had taken an aggressive stand within the agency to cut off referrals to a local practitioner who was rumored to engage in sex with clients.

Our client seemed quite credible. She had struggled for a long time to break free of the relationship which was her first sexual experience. It was a very confusing relationship because the therapist was in the role of a very caring father-figure who, while pushing her to grow and become independent, was her secret lover. Thus she had done no dating and had stayed locked into the relationship. To further complicate things, the client had delayed coming to us for about two years because she knew we had had an association with him.

We discussed the possibility of a session with the client; after weighing a number of alternatives we decided it should be held at WICC. The client agreed that both of us should be present and that she would not need an additional advocate. It was also decided to ask for the therapist's administrative supervisor to be present because one of our major goals was to make sure that the therapist got help and that other clients were not put at risk. She wanted the therapist to hear about the effect on her of this sexual exploitation and to find out, if possible, why it happened, that is, what were his motives.

We decided on a format in which she would tell her story and the rest of us would ask questions only to clarify things. We would then ask the therapist to react and to give us his memory of events, to the degree that it differed from hers. Then we would do our best to explore what happened and why. We discussed the unlikelihood of her achieving closure in a single session, even a session scheduled for a good two hours.

The client was instructed to show up early so we could make sure she was settled down before we began, and we also asked her to allow a half hour or so afterward to debrief her.

One of us phoned the therapist. We indicated that Ms. _____, his former client, had come in with some serious concerns with their relationship which she wanted to discuss with him and his supervisor. He readily agreed and the meeting was arranged after calls to him and his supervisor.

The processing session went as planned. The client told her story with minimal interruption. The therapist acknowledged that the story was essentially accurate although he added a few details and comments; the client agreed with some but not with others. He made a sincere and tearful apology; he said he wished he could undo it all somehow. At the time, he said, he was very needy and the relationships with both his wife and his young daughter were troubled; however, he did not use the information as an excuse for his conduct. He explained that somehow he had been able to erect an internal defense that allowed him to conduct the sexual relationship and, at the same time, to feel strongly that it was ethically unacceptable to have sex with a client. He volunteered that this had been the only instance of sexual involvement with a client in his career.

During the debriefing the client indicated that it had been very helpful to finally be able to tell her story and to confront him. However, she still felt angry and frustrated, and she was not fully convinced that there had not been other victims. She also felt that his attempt at a dynamic explanation had fallen far short. We agreed on all points and assured her that we would follow up on the case with his supervisor. We were confident the agency would take some action.

During the processing session the supervisor had listened intently but said little, respecting the format that called for the session to focus on the client's achieving some greater resolution of what had happened. After our initial revelation of the allegations to both the therapist and his supervisor, the therapist submitted his resignation. Wisely, the supervisor delayed acceptance of it, feeling that it was important to probe the situation further before taking some sort of quick solution. These were the days of quick resignations and agreements to keep things under wraps: an approach that not only did not resolve problems but curtailed opportunities to learn from the experiences. The supervisor contacted us subsequently to see if we could set up another session with everyone but the client present. He also applied some pressure on the therapist to reveal any other such relationship. He admitted to three.

In the subsequent meeting with the therapist, the supervisor, and the two of us, we learned that the therapist had sought help on his own for having sexually exploited clients. Even after some lengthy discussion, however, it was abundantly clear that he could not explain his behavior. Both we and the supervisor felt that on the face of it there was a significant question of whether he could be rehabilitated. Given the fact that he was only a few years from retirement we wondered, assuming that his situation was theoretically treatable, if he would ever be able to resume practice.

Subsequently, his supervisor decided to accept his resignation. The therapist left the field and found some relatively menial work for a period. Eventually he managed to obtain part-time consultation in a local residential facility where he worked with hard-core male drug addicts. In our last contact with him he expressed considerable regret for all that had happened and indicated that the processing session had helped, in its own way, to cleanse the wound and relieve him of some guilt. The double life he had led at times had taken its toll.

The client stayed in touch with us off and on over the subsequent several years. She felt that the session had helped to take care of a piece of old business and that the agency response had been appropriate and that future clients were protected. Although she felt good at having taken action, her personal struggles to improve her self-esteem and to develop an adult lifestyle with romantic relationships with peers had a long ways to go.

The therapist's departure from the agency where he had been employed for so many years led to tension among the staff members. A consultant was brought in to facilitate a session in which he and they said their goodbyes, expressed their disappointments, sought meaning in the disaster, and searched for clues to prevent similar incidents.

THE LITERATURE

In *Responding Therapeutically to Clients Who Have Been Sexually Involved With Their Psychotherapists* (Schoener, Milgrom, Gonsiorek, 1981), we noted that a "processing session" with client and therapist may be a helpful intervention for a client seeking to deal with sexual exploitation by a therapist. When this paper was revised in Spring 1983 (Schoener, Milgrom, & Gonsiorek, 1983) we expanded it and added an outline of what such a session should cover.

We wrote a paper devoted entirely to this topic a year later (*Processing Complaints of Therapist Sexual Misconduct*) which Schoener presented at the Annual Meeting of the American Psychiatric Association in Los Angeles, May 7, 1984. However, because the APA audience had little or no knowledge of WICC's overall work with the sexual exploitation of clients by therapists, a major portion of the paper was background information.

The processing session was described by us again in more recent papers but without much detail. (Schoener & Milgrom, 1986; Milgrom & Schoener, 1987). Even in conference presentations that are available on tape the processing session has been described only briefly (Fleming, Luepker, Nye, & Schoener, 1982). When we are contacted by people who are considering doing such a session, the material we have been able to send them has been inadequate so considerable phone consultation has been required.

Fortunately, a set of colleagues who decided to conduct some similar sessions wrote about the process. Bouhoutsos and Brodsky (1985) described, in useful detail two sessions that were aimed more at mediating a grievance (e.g., they compared it to divorce mediation) than was our typical session, nonetheless the similarity is unmistakable. This contribution is helpful reading because of the detailed description of the actual session, but each author wrote a subsequent conceptual account of "mediation" (Brodsky, 1986; Pope & Bouhoutsos, 1986). Brodsky (1986) reported that "The California State Ethics Committee is now experimenting with incorporating mediation sessions into their procedure for handling sexual intimacy complaints" (p. 168). She expressed the hope that many cases could be handled at this level if the procedure is institutionalized, comparing it to divorce mediation.

In a recent workshop the mediation and processing session approaches were compared (Bouhoutsos, Brodsky, & Schoener, 1988). Mediation is predominantly aimed at the ventilation of feelings about specific abusive acts by the therapist and arriving at some agreement as to what actions the therapist will agree to in terms of amelioration of damages or voluntarily undertaking rehabilitation. By contrast, the processing session is aimed at discovering the dynamics of the abusive relationship and at reaching a better understanding of what went wrong. The two would be very similar in a situation in which the client asked for a processing session to discuss some specific complaints, and where the client made some specific demands of the therapist at the end.

It is conceivable that a mediation session could be held following a processing session in a situation where the client had decided to not seek formal or official sanctions. If the client is clear about what he or she wants to ask of the therapist regarding remediation, then a mediation type approach would make the most sense. If the goal is understanding the relationship and why it became exploitative, then a processing session approach would be best. When the client has decided to take no action via formal complaint channels, mediation seems a reasonable option. The processing session is sometimes an "end" in itself, but is often followed by the client taking some further action through formal channels.

In any event, we hope that other investigators will write on this topic and that a variety of examples, or even different models, will find their way into the literature.

THE WICC MODEL OF THE PROCESSING SESSION

The processing session is conceptualized as an event during which the client confronts the therapist with complaints about the treatment process for any or all of the following purposes:

1. To regain some measure of control and mastery after an explosive experience.

2. To air complaints about the therapy or the therapist's behavior.

3. To ask for whatever explanations the therapist cares to offer about his/her behavior.

4. To attempt to gain an understanding of the evolution of a romantic or sexual relationship in therapy.

5. To give the therapist feedback, in front of others, on the effect of his/her conduct in the attempt to provide some accountability.

The processing session evolved and continues to evolve as primarily a clinical tool. It is a method of helping the client to gain understanding and closure as well as to ventilate feelings.

When a client asks "Why did he do it?" or "Why me?" we can venture guesses before or after a processing session. Nevertheless, we point out that the therapist is the only one who actually knows, and it is possible that he will give some sort of answer if we ask directly.

All such sessions to date (two dozen or so) have been instigated at the client's request. We would be glad to do one at a therapist's request but typically we do not see therapists until after they have been named on a formal complaint. At that point it is often too late for such a session. In several situations therapists consulted us about clients who were harassing them when they felt they had been rejected by the therapists. The clients purportedly believed that the therapists had a personal interest in them although there was neither sexual activity nor romantic involvement between them. In both cases a processing session did not seem a good idea.

WHEN TO DO A SESSION

One needs to be reasonably sure that a client is emotionally stable enough to handle an encounter with the therapist. It is also important that the client him/herself wants to do such a session, that the client is not simply agreeing in order to please you. There are times when a processing session to clear the air would be convenient for the therapist in question but not necessarily for the client.

Beyond emotional stability, the client's goals should be attainable. When a client has unrealistic goals it is better to hold off and to seek other options. For example, when the boundary issues are subtle and you are not at all sure of exactly what happened, the client is likely to be disappointed if he or she is fixated on a profuse apology from the therapist. Clients sometimes expect that the contact will "clean things up" and they may fantasize that afterward they will be able to have a relationship with the therapist. Others describe a therapist who sounds as if he were either psychotic or sociopathic and, despite everything one says, the clients fixate on either an apology or a meaningful explanation, neither of which is likely to be forthcoming.

WHEN NOT TO DO A SESSION

Beyond the reservations noted in the preceding section, there are additional reasons to avoid a session. One example is when the client and therapist already have told their story as part of some complaint or informal procedure and the two stories are so far apart that there is no common ground. We have had only one such case; we decided that a processing session would be very hard on the client.

When legal proceedings are underway attorneys usually forbid the parties to talk about the case; thus both the client and the therapist's attorneys probably will veto plans for a processing session. We have never allowed attorneys to be present at the sessions and if we felt that the motivation for a session was simply to gather data for entrapment, we doubt that we would be willing to facilitate it.

If it seems clear that the therapist will refuse to attend or if geographical distance presents insurmountable obstacles to a meeting it is best to point out these obstacles and not to resort to a processing session.

A final reason not to do a session is if, given the client's needs and concerns (see following section), a better option is available.

OPTIONS TO OUR STANDARD MODEL

Like the "Wheel of Options" (see Ch. 26), several options are available to process a complaint with the therapist. Sometimes the client's desire for privacy (i.e., limiting personal exposure) leads to a personal discussion with the therapist without others being present. In other cases, whether there has been a prior confrontation between client and therapist and the client no longer wishes to participate, he/she empowers us to meet with the therapist and his/her supervisor to attempt to arrange for greater resolution of the situation.

Four examples of alternatives requested by clients which we have supported are as follows:

1. Phone Confrontation:

This situation involved a client with high needs for privacy and a therapist who was unlikely to agree to a processing session. The client felt that the therapist was a bit crazy, and we agreed; both she and we felt a session would add little to our understanding.

She wanted to phone and confront him, but was hesitant that there would be no way to process the call if it went badly. She decided to tape the phone call. If all went well she would erase the tape; if it didn't, she would bring it in and we would listen to it with her and discuss what happened.

The phone confrontation went well so she erased the tape.

2. Face to Face Without a Facilitator:

A woman who had been sexually exploited some years earlier by an older therapist who worked for a county wanted an opportunity to give him feedback in a nonthreatening situation. He was about to retire (a matter of weeks) and she had no desire to mess that up. Because he was retiring other clients would not be at risk.

She was afraid that if we were involved in the session it would be more difficult for her to both confront him and get him to hear her out.

One of us helped her to plan the encounter, met with her beforehand, and drove her down to his office; then we met with her afterward to process what had happened. The client felt that the meeting had gone very well and that she had done what she wanted to do.

3. Face to Face With a Third Party Present:

In one case a client and her husband set up a meeting with the clergyman who had sexually exploited her. They ended up having a meeting in a park. In another situation, a woman was accompanied by a woman friend who was acting in the role of an advocate to help confront a chemical dependency counselor who had abused her.

4. Without the Client:

In one situation, during a prior confrontation between the client and therapist, a little dispute over the facts arose. The client felt that she had carried out the confrontation she needed and that she had heard her therapist's reaction to the degree she wanted. She felt that she knew as much about the situation as she wanted.

Although she would have been glad to meet with the therapist's employer if it were absolutely necessary, she preferred not to. She asked if we would be willing to pursue such a meeting and to help the employer set up a plan of action. After obtaining her written permission, we phoned and set up a meeting with the therapist and his employer. The client was pleased with our action and content to get only brief feedback on how the session had gone.

The "standard model" we mentioned earlier involves one of us (or some other neutral facilitator), the client, the therapist, and, often, someone who oversees the therapist's work.

SETTING UP A PROCESSING SESSION

1. The Initial Contact:

Although, theoretically, a client can contact the therapist to set up a session, in all cases thus far we have contacted the therapist. It involves phoning and informing the therapist that his or her client, _____, asked our assistance to set up a meeting with the therapist to talk over the issues or concerns left hanging from the psychotherapeutic relationship. The goal of such a session is to air these concerns and to provide the opportunity to discuss what happened as each person remembers it. We serve as a facilitator.

2. <u>Those Who Say No</u>:

The majority of therapists with whom we have dealt have agreed to come in for a session. One stayed away on the advice of his attorney and another delayed for a while, whereupon the client's attorney questioned the undertaking on the grounds that she should either sue or have a processing session. By this time she was fed up and decided to forego the session. We also have had a therapist who refused to cooperate; he said that it would only feed into the client's fantasies and perpetuate her attachment to him. (Seduction and seductive game-playing were charged in this case, not overt sexual involvement.) It is noteworthy that several other therapists, after discussing and thinking over the risks of perpetuating the client's attachment (and even harassment), decided that there was nothing to lose in having a session.

3. <u>Background Information</u>:

We have, typically, in addition to describing the processing session over the phone, mailed the therapist some of our publications on the topic of client/therapist sex. The most useful was "Processing Complaints of Therapist Sexual Misconduct" (Schoener & Milgrom, 1984). In retrospect, it would have been more helpful clearly to have offered an article that went into the topic in far more detail.

WHO SHOULD BE PRESENT

The normal processing session has one facilitator, usually one of us, who also functions to support the client. Both the client and therapist are also present. Beyond the three parties, it is a judgment call of who else, if anyone, should be present.

The key issue is to decide whether the involvement of a given person would enhance the likelihood of the session's accomplishing its goals. Another perspective, on the negative side, is the degree to which a given person may complicate things. An additional concern is how many people one can involve before things get too crowded and the client and/or therapist feel overwhelmed or intimidated.

Historically, most of our sessions have involved either the basic three players (one of us, the client, and the therapist), or four persons: the additional person has been an agency director or clinical supervisor.

Other possible additional participants are: (a) the client's current therapist; (b) a friend or advocate working with the client; (c) the therapist's therapist; (d) a colleague of the therapist; or (e) several persons with administrative authority over the therapist.

The largest group we have had to date numbered six persons: the basic three plus three officials from the therapist's place of employment. We have had only a few requests for an attorney to be present and we vetoed this idea in each case; we felt that an attorney would be in the way. According to our experience to date, even with the large groups things have run smoothly; those in an advocacy or support role were relatively quiet and helped to keep the focus on the client and therapist.

ARRANGEMENTS

The client has a major role in deciding on the details. It is important that he or she take responsibility for planning the event. Some key issues that must be dealt with follow:

1. <u>Site</u>: Clients typically prefer the neutrality of an office at WICC as opposed to that of the therapist or his supervisor. All but one of the sessions we facilitated in Minnesota took place at our center. The one exception was held in the office of the client's new therapist. In a session done in another state, a colleague graciously allowed us to use his office.

2. <u>Format</u>: The format discussed later in this chapter is the one we use commonly. However, before making a decision we discuss the options with the client and then decide what the most effective format will be. Sometimes, the detailed retelling of the story by the client is unnecessary which means that the session can focus instead on one or two items.

3. <u>Length of Time</u>: Usually we ask the client to come in 15 minutes to 30 minutes ahead of time in order to get comfortable. We review the plan for the session and discuss any anxieties. Being present when the therapist arrives seems to empower the client. In general we ask participants to allow two hours for the session, and we suggest that they schedule their day loosely so if we run over they will not have to leave abruptly. We ask the client to allow an additional half-hour or more for debriefing with us afterwards. Debriefing involves a review of the session and the client's feelings about it. If a follow-up discussion with the therapist is indicated it usually is at a later time or date, and typically by phone call.

4. <u>Additional Sessions</u>: A second processing session is a theoretical possibility but we have never conducted one. We focus on getting as much done as possible in one session.

GROUND RULES

Ground rules should be specified, spelled out, and agreed to by all parties when arrangements are made for the session. Everyone should be reminded of them before the session begins. The following items should be clarified in the rules.

1. <u>Your Role</u>: We stress that we will be present in a professional role—as consultants—to help, to the best of our ability, the parties to clarify and better understand the nature of the client's grievance. Stressing that we are performing a professional service assures confidentiality and places our services within the scope of typical professional liability insurance coverage.

2. <u>Limits of Privacy</u>: Prior to the session, we define our view of the proceedings as confidential and privileged. We distinguish the persons we have brought to the session as client(s) or as advocates for or adjuncts to the client(s). If the persons present did not have professional roles there is the possibility that the session would not be regarded as private and, therefore, not privileged. However, we clearly state that a court order could compel us to testify at some future date. The other parties present must speak for themselves and make their own pledges of how the information will be treated. The therapist and representatives of his/her agency by occupation usually are bound by confidentiality also. Local statutes and standards relating to the information must be clarified and the participants must be reminded of any mandatory reporting.

3. <u>Stopping the Session</u>: Provision should be made to recess for a few minutes or to discontinue the session if any party becomes too upset to continue. You must

reserve the right to terminate the session at any point if you feel that it is going too badly to continue. (In practice we never have had to abort a session although during several sessions it was important to take breaks. On several occasions we have had to be firm about ending on time when the discussion grew repetitive.)

MAKING THE SESSION GO WELL

Many intangibles doubtless enter into making a session go well. Some relate to the client and therapist and how they deal with the situation whereas others relate to the facilitator's ability to judge when to intervene to get things back on track or to move ahead.

First the facilitator must examine his or her attitudes toward various aspects of the situation. It is important to believe that a face-to-face meeting to confront the therapist factually and professionally is preferable to backstabbing or using the professional grapevine to "get even" with him. We view processing sessions as a professional service not only to the client but, also, to the therapist. Second, it is essential that the facilitator recognize that honest differences may occur in the memory of events and that one can be misled by hearing only one side of a story. The affirmative approach, however, is that it is instructive and challenging to try to reconstruct such events by reviewing them with the actual participants. (Much of what we do as therapists focuses only on a client's version of events.)

If the facilitator develops strong feelings of anger or disapproval toward the therapist the proper conduct of the session may be difficult. The role of the facilitator is to achieve the purpose of the session—to give the client the opportunity to tell his or her story and to get a reaction from the therapist—not to lecture the therapist or to reveal him as an exploiter.

Anxiety levels and defensiveness usually are high in all participants during a session and it is not easy to prevent them from getting in the way. The facilitator's best tool for dealing with them is her or his confidence that the session will do some good. The structure of the sessions that we use and that is described here tends to reduce not only anxiety but defensiveness also. The reason is that the format takes us well into the session before the facts or allegations that can be challenged are related. Furthermore, throughout the session we try to use neutral language as much as possible and to stress the tenuous nature of each party's memory of events with such qualifying terms as "according to your memory" or "in your perceptions."

PREPARING THE CLIENT[1]

1. Decide on the major goals for the session so that the main issues will be covered.

2. Discuss ways of illustrating or presenting the major concerns so they will be clear.

3. Clarify the facilitator's role, and the length of the session.

4. Discuss options for handling rough spots, such as time-out periods.

5. Talk about possible outcomes of a session—helpful/not helpful—and give examples of each.

---

[1]The authors acknowledge the input of Ms. Ronda Dee of Dallas, Texas, who helped to outline those factors that should be clarified so the client's expectations for the sessions will be realistic.

6. Emphasize that the session is an end in itself, and that it may not change anything.

7. Make it clear that the session may be of help even if all issues are not covered and there is no agreement on some.

8. Clarify that follow-up will be possible, and what the facilitator's role will be after the processing session.

9. Make it clear that the client may get quite emotional and that old patterns of relating to the therapist may show themselves during the session.

10. Have a clear plan for feedback from the participants.

11. Plan for what will happen after the session.

THE CONTENT OF THE SESSION

We indicated earlier that the format of a session varies with the individual situation. However, we usually start with the client's account of the events and we suggest that it be interrupted only when clarification is necessary. To forearm the client for this experience we instruct him or her to prepare the account in advance so it can be presented in an organized fashion. The following items may be included in the account.

1. How the client originally chose to see this therapist
   a. prior meetings
   b. what the client knew of the therapist beforehand

2. The initial presenting complaint, and the initial therapeutic contract; first impressions of the therapist

3. The general course of therapy and the changes in the therapeutic contract

4. Step-by-step account of boundary breakdowns, as identified in prior discussions with us, including:
   a. Breaking or changing of rules (e.g., after hours visits; change in fees, home phone calls)
   b. Signs of "special status" (e.g., gifts; therapist using client for support; excessive self-disclosure by therapist; excessive praise)
   c. Either party's feelings of attraction; how they were acknowledged or became apparent
   d. Seduction or eroticizing of the therapy through comments, focus, choice of apparel, etc.
   e. General physical contact and touching; erotic or sexual contact

5. Romantic feelings that were expressed or hinted at; promises or expectations of romance, marriage, etc.

6. Description of attempts to terminate the personal or professional relationship

7. Post-termination contact, direct or indirect; current contact and feelings toward each other

8. Effects on the client at the time and currently

While some processing sessions have covered the relationship in this detail, typically they focus on some key issues. In fact, in some cases when we asked clients to "start at the beginning" they responded, "we all know that, let's get to the point." Thus the outline presented above would rarely be covered in its entirety.

The therapist, in some sessions, describes his/her memory of events concurrent with the client's accounts. Most often, however, we ask the therapist to present her or his interpretation of what happened when the client has finished. When events are in dispute, we test the limits by trying to find ways to bring the two stories closer together. For example, if the client claims the therapist said something and the therapist denies it, we query both to see if, although they may disagree on the exact wording some similar terms may have been used. We also discuss practical matters, such as how the therapist and client should handle incidental future social encounters, and the like.

We end the session by summarizing first, those areas in which the two agree on what happened, and second, the areas of disagreement. Each party is told that after the session they may discover additional memories or insights through reflection. In our experience the stories often turn out to be markedly similar, something that does not happen when legal action begins. We emphasize the need to have this session be the termination of the relationship—that each person needs to put it behind her or him.

FOLLOWUP

A debriefing of the client is conducted immediately after the session and a follow-up discussion usually is held within a week or so. Some clients treat the processing session as an end in itself whereas others go on to file licensure complaints or civil suits. A few remain fixated on the therapist and even after a processing session have trouble moving on in their lives.

Follow-up with the therapist and his/her employer often occurs. In the case of a private practitioner, it may be with the therapist's partners in the practice. Sometimes WICC staff members are asked to provide organizational consultation or to give the agency or clinic a referral to a consultant.

EXAMPLES OF USEFUL SESSIONS

1. A seduction unraveled: A female client described a gradual process of seduction, with the therapist being exceptionally accommodating regarding fees, sessions shifted to evening hours in a deserted office, and, finally, a sudden hug and kiss at the end of a session.

The counselor, quite experienced in work with drug and alcohol abusers, was a bit out of his depth in a mental health setting. When the client offered resistance, he was willing to bend rules to keep her coming back. He was quite uncomfortable seeing her in a deserted office, but it was the only one open to him in the evening.

The brief hug and kiss followed a session in which nothing was accomplished; the client, however, suddenly said the session was very helpful and she wanted to come back the following week. The therapist's lack of experience and need for approval were significant enough so that we advised him to change jobs, which he did. The session revealed that a seduction was going on, but it was not a sexual seduction.

2. <u>An apology</u>: In a number of sessions a therapist was able to offer a sincere apology to the client and to provide some explanation for his or her conduct. This was useful for the client's reality testing.

3. <u>A stopping point for harassment</u>: In several cases the client had been somewhat relentlessly harassing the therapist over a lengthy period. After the session this pursuit of the therapist, via mail and phone, diminished and eventually ended altogether.

EXAMPLES OF NOT-SO-USEFUL SESSIONS

1. <u>The Silent Therapist</u>: In one instance a woman therapist, who had consulted with an attorney, took notes during the session, which intimidated the client. The therapist was silent, basically listened to the client's story, and then pretty much refused to comment. Little was accomplished. (Extensive note-taking is atypical and we were not prepared for its very negative effects. We have not yet been asked about audiotaping a session and would probably try to discourage it.) Nevertheless, in this instance, some gains resulted from the session. The client received support and validation from another participant who was in a position of authority over the therapist. She saw the therapist as manipulative and unwilling to take responsibility, tumbling her from a pedestal.

2. <u>The Unfinished Session</u>: In two cases in which the issue was not overt sexual involvement but, rather, romantic involvement or talk and some poor therapeutic boundaries, the client focused on endless details to such an extent the key issues were never identified and resolved. In both it would have been useful to have done even more preparation. Gains were made but they were small ones.

EFFECT OF THE NEW CRIMINAL LAW

After August 1, 1985, sexual involvement with clients and former clients opened the therapist to criminal charges. Thus it is not surprising to find that therapists are far more reluctant to participate in processing sessions. However, in our experience some therapists still are willing to take part in the process. If a therapist consults an attorney first one would expect him/her to be advised to avoid disclosures.

EFFECT OF MANDATORY REPORTING

Mandatory reporting of rules and laws may be expected to have less of an effect on a therapist's willingness to attend a processing session. In Minnesota, for example, if one hears from a client an allegation of sexual misconduct by a therapist, one is obligated to take some action whether or not the therapist ever confirms the allegations. For example, if the perpetrator is a psychologist, another psychologist is obligated to report the exploitation to the Board of Psychology; if he/she is a physician, any licensed health professional is obligated to report the perpetrator to the State Board of Medical Examiners.

FINAL NOTE

The success of the processing session seems to derive from the fact that it is predominantly nonadversarial. Purely adversarial processes often fail to develop an understanding of what actually happened. They leave the neutral participants with two versions of the truth; they rarely have a place for apologies; and they tend to drag on for long periods of time, thus leaving the client's business unfinished. Their goal is punishment, protection of the public, or compensation for damages, rather than an understanding of what happened.

PART VIII

SELF-HELP AND CONSUMER APPROACHES

The goal of this Part is to report on the related work and ideas of other writers. At the WICC we have provided support and assistance to consumer and self-help efforts but their very nature differentiates them from the attitudes and interests of professionals.

Ironically, consumers, many of whom have been victimized by therapists, have played an important role in influencing our work and the professional and legal accomplishments in Minnesota, yet we have no specialized consumer advocacy group in Minnesota that deals with victims of therapist-client sex. Some people have speculated that the activism of the professional community in seeking consumer input has filled what would normally be a vacuum.

Chapter 29 is the text of a speech given more than a decade ago by a consumer advocate, Mary Tambornino. It is as relevant today as it was in 1975 and still challenges the professional community. For a number of years all professional volunteers at the WICC were given copies of the speech to read as part of their orientation.

Chapter 30 by Cliadakis is of more recent vintage. It illustrates what a determined researcher outside the profession can do to document the problems of professional regulation that most practitioners in the various therapy professions tend to ignore. Its author founded the National Committee for Preventing Psychotherapy Abuse, one of the few consumer groups to focus on sexual exploitation by therapists. The paper is reproduced just as it was submitted with its own reference section at the end.

Chapter 31 by Schoener is an overview of some of the organized self-help and consumer efforts around the country which have sought to address the issue of sexual exploitation of clients by therapists. The work of these groups often have had a dramatic effect in the cities in which they are located. Their work, not infrequently, has included activities outside their home state. This chapter also examines coverage of the therapist-client sex issue in advice columns and consumer-oriented guides to therapy.

CHAPTER 29

ACCOUNTABILITY AND CONSUMERISM

Mary Tambornino

The following is the text of a presentation by Mary Tambornino (previously Mary Work) on December 4, 1975 at a workshop titled "Professional Development: Surviving as a Psychologist." The workshop was held at the Marriott Inn, Bloomington, Minnesota and was co-sponsored by the Minnesota Psychological Association and the Department of Conferences of the University of Minnesota. Ms. Tambornino was, at that time, a staff person of the Mental Health Association, a consumer advocacy group, and Vice President of the Board of Directors of the Walk-In Counseling Center, Inc.

This paper is reprinted with a few brief introductory remarks excluded with Ms. Tambornino's permission. It was copywritten in 1975 and cannot be used without the written permission of the author.

****

What I am going to speak to you about this morning is accountability and consumerism. My credentials for addressing this topic are that I am a consumer; and, I am a professional advocate for other consumers. I work for the Mental Health Association of Minnesota. This is part of a national organization advocating mental health services. Our concerns are not only that services and care be available when needed or wanted, but that those services maintain the individual rights and dignity of persons whether they are there voluntarily or involuntarily.

Accountability has two definitions according to Webster's New Collegiate Dictionary, 1975 Edition. The first is: "Subject to giving an account: Answerable." The second definition is: "Capable of being accounted for: Explainable." It is to the first definition I would like to address myself. The second I hope is already true.

To whom are you answerable? You have three publics: your clients, the general public, and each other. I suspect also that one underlying concern of this conference is that you soon expect a fourth—the courts.

You have a responsibility to your clients to make certain that all the cards are on the table. Not just your office hours, fees, policies, or missed or cancelled appointments, or 'after hours calls.'

You have a responsibility to maintain the dignity of your clients. A person coming to a psychologist for help probably does not arrive at the decision to seek you out easily or lightly. Most likely he or she suffered considerable emotional pain before arriving in your office. There are several factors in that pain and in that delay. Not the least of which is wondering what will happen; am I "sick enough;" am I too "sick;" how long will it take; what will it cost; and what will he do. Other seldom discussed concerns are also crucial: What are your credentials? Where did you get them? What does that mean? These questions are not new to you, I hope. What may be a new thought is that you have an obligation to deal with them frankly and directly. Some clients will ask your qualifications—some will question the validity of your degree. Clients are being encouraged to be particular. They are purchasing your skill. They should make certain it is adequate.

It used to be—in the olden days—about 10 years ago—that the patient did not question the doctor; he only did as he was told. This is destructive to the healing process. The more informed one is, the more one is able to participate in the business at hand.

Disconcerting as it may be to be 'sized up'—allow it to happen. When the client does not initiate the exploration, you do so. It is not hard to anticipate what a client wants to know. Make a list—actual or mental of these questions and make certain that they are answered.

When asked, answer in plain language. Language is a communication device. Language can also be used to maintain or build barriers. Do not use language as a means to separate yourself from your client.

I sometimes have the odd feeling the professionals fear that speaking plainly and directly will somehow dissipate their knowledge and skill. The truth is that nothing is more gratefully received than openness and frankness.

The reason the consumer movement is stressing the appropriateness of interviewing the therapist is a need to improve the balance between client and therapist. Too often the client is made to feel that even though the information he or she has about their physical or emotional state is crucial to the healing process, somehow they are not important.

The need to find reasons for things exists in all of us. I have identified two that pertain to this. One is pride. After all, you have spent time, energy and money perfecting your skills. You do not acquire a special glow to show the world your achievement. What can happen instead is adaption of an attitude of superiority. An attitude that lets the client know he or she is less than you. Resist the temptation.

Remember the client spent time, energy, and probably money perfecting the behavior presented to you. The expenditure—and that talent may very well be equal.

The other is familiarity. The professional can easily forget that while he or she may do this frequently, the client only does it once, or if more than once, at least sporadically.

Several years ago when the young son of a good friend of mine broke his leg, the child was rushed to the hospital. The orthopedic surgeon arrived and examined the child and the X-rays. With little explanation, and without anesthetic, he set the youngster's leg. This youngster was four years old. You can imagine the scream he let out, and the ensuing uproar. His parents were startled and angry. The child's agony did not last long, and the leg was set and cast.

Because I knew the physician involved I was called that evening and asked "What the hell goes on?" I said I didn't know but I would find out. The explanation was logical, simple, and short: No anesthetic was used on this youngster because it was not a complicated break and more important—with a child that young, the risk of using anesthesia was far greater than the pain involved in setting it without anesthetic. With a child that age it is hard to tell what has been eaten and when. In the course of this explanation the doctor also said to me, "Mary, I set bones all the time. It is easy to forget that parents don't have children with broken bones all the time."

What I am suggesting to you is that this same need for explanation is true in a relationship between a psychologist and a client. It is easy to skim over what is familiar to you, and forget that it is not familiar to your client. Simply, and bluntly—don't forget.

©Mary Tambornino (1975)

Psychologists are answerable to the public. You are given respect on slim evidence of your reliability. Three letters, Ph.D., carry a lot of weight. The public assumes that you have them whether you do or not.

They imply professionalism. Please do not use your credibility in one area to gain credence in another. I do not suggest that you stick to psychology and leave the world to the rest of us. That would be a bore for you, the public and me. I encourage you to display your brilliance—or your dullness—in the public arena. Just do not expect special treatment or credibility because of your training.

The public also expects you to act within but up to the limits of your skill and training. They expect you to define the limits. This should be contained in a code of ethics. The code should reflect a concern for the public. Too often the professionals appear to protect themselves against the requirements and expectations of the public. The result is no straight answers, deteriorating relationships—and diminishing trust. The public expects you to state clearly what you can do, can't do, will do and won't do. They expect you to develop a code of ethics, and to adhere to them. If your code in Minnesota is not up to date, make it so. If it does not deal with the current issues within or threatening to your profession, make it do so. In any case, whatever the code contains, adhere to it without equivocation.

Admittedly some problems facing your profession are difficult to deal with. Standards are hard to set. That doesn't mean avoid them. It means that the best, fairest, sharpest, and most demanding members of the profession to be conscripted to prepare standards.

Once you have done that, prepare the mechanism for enforcing them.

Once you have done that, enforce them.

This leads to the third area, or what I have chosen to call the third area of your accountability. And that is—to your colleagues. You owe it to each other to maintain and strengthen your professionalism. To maintain and to strengthen the positive images that the public has of psychologists. You also owe it to each other to chip away at the less than positive images the public has of psychologists—and of psychology—and of mental health care generally.

Mental health care—mental illness, treatment, psychology, etc. etc., all are shrouded in mystery and fear. The fear is not always negative—it is often a positive fascination. Just as often though it shows up in a public skepticism. This is expressed through the cynical comments: "Their children are impossible;" "Their marriages don't last;" "They are all crazy themselves."

I will resist the temptation to speculate on the accuracy of these remarks. They are beside the point anyway.

The point is that you cannot afford the luxury of supporting this skepticism. You cannot tolerate less than professional behavior by each other. It is in the manner of things that the 'good guys' do a good job, and even more than a competent job—a skillful and creative job. The bad guys hit the press.

You owe it to each other, and to yourselves to limit, if not eliminate the bad guys.

You are the only ones who can. I can speak to you for a few minutes about what the consumer expects of you. But in the last analysis, you must police yourselves.

©Mary Tambornino (1975)

The public has no control. On the contrary the only role the public can play is in reaction to the fact that you don't do it yourselves. Therefore, the control is still in your hands. I ask that you exercise it wisely. Even more important, I ask that you exercise it.

The prospect is of course that if you do not do it, it will be done for you. The courts are one route. This process has already begun. The issues in a court suit are seldom confined to professional conduct per se. Rather, they are brought, and orchestrated on the basis of expectations of conduct.

The discussion of accountability seems more urgent in light of the new vulnerability of psychologists. Because of licensing for example, you have and will become more visible to the public, therefore more vulnerable. However, it is not new. The only thing new is the discussion about it. And, the need to take responsibility for it.

What are you accountable for? Your behavior—just like the rest of us.

Two areas of concern to me. One is the surfacing discussion of sexual relationships between therapists and clients. If this is now becoming a topic of discussion in the public arena, it has been simmering within the profession for a long time. As a consumer—and an advocate—and a woman—I am angry that it has not been dealt with. I am angry that you are forcing the public to deal with your problem.

For a problem it is—the boundaries of it are exploitation, power, dishonesty, sexism, and ethical failure.

I view sexual relationships between therapists and client as rape. Rape is a power play. In this instance it does not have physical violence or force as a base, but subtle coercion. Somehow the client is made to feel that this submission is integral to the healing process.

It is exploitation because it trades on the insecurity and the trust of the client.

It is dishonest because it does not appear as a healing method available to all who may need it. If it were truly appropriate, the recipient of the sexual ministrations of the therapists would not only be the young, attractive female.

It is sexist because it continues and supports the view that women have less need to be taken seriously.

Last, it is unethical. Even if it is therapeutic, how do we establish your credentials. How do we know if you are acting within, or up to the limit of your training. Indeed, did you take any training. How does the client know that you are the best person to be delivering this type of therapy.

It also indicates to me a paucity of ability and talent. I hope your professional organization establishes and enforces strict prohibitions against it.

The other area of concern is in continuing your professional growth. Do not succumb to the impulse to continue a treatment philosophy just because you have always used it.

Explore new avenues. New insights. Incorporate them. Discard them. Remain alive in your professionalism.

©Mary Tambornino (1975)

Continuing education is a dull phrase to explain what I mean. Some of you will do this for your own renewal—or refreshment. Some of you will need the impetus of a requirement for licensure. In either case, the result should be similar—a broad, seasoned, current, knowledge available to your clients, the public and each other.

Which brings us full circle to what accountability is all about. You are ultimately accountable to yourself, for yourself. Policing your profession and your personal professionalism is up to you. It is not a defense against public scrutiny, involvement, or concern. It is a positive obligation. One that will allow you to maintain and sustain your integrity, and that of your clients. Psychologists are still at the point where you can cash in on the positive aspects of accountability. I think that the point will not hold for long. In view of some of the court decisions and some of the things that have been discussed here this morning by Mr. Wilson, it appears that if you don't do it, someone else will do it for you.

Just for the honor of the thing...you ought to do it yourselves.

Thank you...

CHAPTER 30

Sexual Abuse Of Clients In Psychotherapy: A Non-Professional Perspective[1]

William C. Cliadakis

ABSTRACT: An examination of New York State's disciplinary actions against licensed psychologists who sexually abuse clients indicates very poor results in protecting the public. Social workers have a much lower total number of incidences of abuse per professional than psychologists. The mental health professions have played a prominent role in resisting reform despite efforts by some therapists, and women in particular. Sexual abuse is not the most common form of therapy abuse, occurring in less than one in ten complaints reported. Other less-publicized categories can be equally devastating. Two NCPPA[2] populations largely sampled from the New York metropolitan area indicate a higher percentage of psychiatrists sexually abusing clients than other therapists. Regional differences of abuse by therapists are indicated. Necessary reforms are suggested to provide greater accountability and public protection.

There have been only two actions taken by the New York State licensing boards against psychologists or social workers who had sexually abused their clients for the period from December 14, 1979 to early 1985, a period of more than four years. The number of actions taken against psychiatrists that had sexually abused clients in New York State is not known since the medical licensing board and the Office of Professional Medical Conduct do not separate psychiatrists from other M.Ds. However, for the period between February 1979 to December 1981 there were only two actions taken against all M.Ds. involved in sexual abuse. Therefore, statistically it is unlikely that any action was taken against a psychiatrist that sexually abused a client.

Returning to the population of licensed psychologists and social workers, there were 5,566 licensed psychologists in New York State at the beginning of 1983 and 20,990 licensed social workers in early 1984. (Psychiatrists in New York State would number approximately 5,500 or the same as licensed psychologists if we assume 9%, or slightly higher than the national rate, of the 60,186 licensed M.Ds. that are psychiatrists.) Both sexual abuse actions involved psychologists while none involved social workers.

For psychologists, of the 14 actions taken by the licensing board, two (14%) were for sexual abuse, two (14%) were for driving while intoxicated, four (29%) for medicaid and insurance fraud, fee splitting and income tax evasion, two (14%) for breach of confidentiality, three (21%) for criminal activity outside of the professional role (one for criminal trespass and assault, one for statutory rape of an underage woman, one for false testimony as a professional witness) and one (7%) for inducing a client into investing into a mutual business.

---

[1] This paper was presented at the 62nd Annual Meeting of the American Orthopsychiatric Association, New York, April 24, 1985.

[2] National Committee for Preventing Psychotherapy Abuse (NCPPA)

Eliminating actions taken against licensed psychologists that were not connected with their professional activity and were not client oriented, there were only five disciplinary actions taken against psychologists dealing with the abuse of clients. Further, considering only meaningful disciplinary actions, meaning omitting superfluousness such as censure, probation, reprimand, nominal fines and required supervision under another therapist, there were only three material disciplinary actions regarding the abuse of clients for the period between May 1980 and January 1984.

In summary, this is the per annum equivalent basis of one material disciplinary action per year for every 6,800 psychologists. With respect to actions taken against psychologists committing sexual abuse, this is equivalent to one action per annum for every 10,200 psychologists. It should be noted that in the two actions on sexual abuse, one involved other forms of abuse (breach of confidentiality of two clients and verbal abuse) and both cases involved several clients that charged abuse.

Comparing New York State disciplinary actions against psychologists with material actions against psychologists in Minnesota for example, there were nearly six times the number of material actions taken in Minnesota as there were in New York (one in 6,800 in New York vs. one in 1,200 in Minnesota). On a tentative basis Minnesota would rank in the top quarter of the most effective state licensing systems in protecting the public from therapy abuse, and New York may rank in the top third (Cliadakis, 1984). Interestingly, New York State licensing officials view themselves as being near the top of the list in protecting the public. Much of this perception seems to result from the idea that New York's unique Board of Regents system makes the state more responsive to the needs of its public. However, the record does not bear this out, nor is it true that there is more than token public membership participation in the decision making regarding disciplinary action of mental health licensed professionals even after the Board of Regents process.

SOCIAL WORKERS:

In contrast to actions taken against psychologists, there have been only two disciplinary actions against social workers for the three years ending in 1984. The two actions included one for abandonment and one for intoxication. Neither action taken was material. Evidently, the regulatory bodies do not consider abandonment as a meaningful form of abuse. In contrast to the equivalent of one action annually for every 6,800 psychologists, social workers show less than one material action for every 63,000 professionals (none in three years).

COMPARISONS OF ACTIONS TAKEN FOR PSYCHOLOGISTS, SOCIAL WORKERS AND M.Ds.:

It is difficult to explain the large difference in material actions taken against psychologists and social workers. There is virtually no literature on the subject. It appears doubtful that differences in objectivity of the licensing board members would account for such a large variance. A small part of the difference may be explained by the gender difference of the two populations. The percentage of male professionals is greater among psychologists than for social workers. Male professionals are involved in a greater relative percentage of abuse. Of the 14 psychologists involved in disciplinary action, 12 were males and only two were female. Male psychologists outnumber females approximately 3-1/2 to 1. Among disciplinary actions against M.Ds. where the gender of the first name was identifiable, 94% were males. However, there is a much higher percentage of males among M.Ds. and psychiatrists than there is among psychologists and social workers. I suspect an important contributor to the variance may be the fact that social workers are probably more closely supervised, and in general, have less opportunity to abuse patients in a private practice setting behind closed doors. Another theory to explain the variance is tied to the greater imbalance of power in the therapy relationship between professional and client that may exist between the more highly credentialled psychologist and psychiatrist in comparison to that of the social worker. The other area that needs to be explored is the nature of the personality of the individual psychologist, social worker and psychiatrist abuser of clients. This behavioral pattern approach is considered in, Task Force on Sexual Exploitation by Counselors and Therapists (Sanderson, 1985), although character comparisons of abusive psychologists, psychiatrists and social workers have yet to be covered.

IS TWO TOO FEW TO ACCEPT?

Only few facts exist. Using the following set of error-laden assumptions, it may be projected that the extent of actions taken relative to the incidence of sexual abuse could be used as a guide for further study. Using an extrapolation of the two cases in New York State for the overall U.S. population, we would come up with 27 actions taken against psychologists for all 50 state licensing boards. The APA estimates there are 33,000 clinical psychologists in the United States. The Holroyd & Brodsky (1977) study reported that 10.9% of the male Ph.Ds. in psychology acknowledged sexually abusing clients and an additional 2.6% acknowledged sexual intercourse within 90 days after termination of therapy. Assuming here that there is 'questionable' objectivity and that in most cases the sexual intercourse precipitated the termination, it is reasonable to combine the two figures for a total of 13.5%. However, one has to be suspect of a study based on an abuse population of only 35 psychologists, subject to pressure on the individual professionals to lie given the consequences of what they may admit to and which excluded categories such as erotic contact within ninety days and does not consider the probable underreporting of male victims and homosexual victims.

Using the 72% figure for male psychologists in California (Bouhoutsos, 1983) as a nationwide percentage for psychologists, this results in a figure of 23,760 male psychologists in the U.S. Applying the 13.5% figure for sexual abuse of clients to male psychologists results in a figure of 3,210 abusive male psychologists. If we also add the smaller figure for sexual abuse by female psychologists of 1.9% plus 0.3% within 90 days, or a total of 2.2%, this results in an additional total of 200 sexually abusing psychologists. Combining the two genders, this results in a total of 3,410 sexually abusive psychologists in the United States. Coming back to the original extrapolated figure of 27 for projected cases of actions taken by all state psychology licensing boards for the three-year, eight-month period referred to, action by the state licensing boards is taken in one out of every 126 incidents of sexual abuse by psychologists. However, as indicated earlier, there is good reason to believe that the Holroyd and Brodsky percentages are understated. Furthermore, there are other studies, while more limited in nature and also more qualified because they are directed at specific populations, that suggest a higher percentage of sexually abusive therapists. These include the unpublished Forer study which found 17% of male Ph.D. psychologists in private practice admitted to having had sexual intercourse (not just erotic contact) with clients (Bouhoutsos, 1983), the Pope, Levenson, and Schover (1979) study that indicated that 25% of the recent graduate psychology students had sexual contact with their supervisors or professors and the Masters and Johnson finding that three out of every seven of their female clients that went through their program had been sexually abused by prior therapists not as part of clinical treatment.

In summary, we speculate that one in 200 actions by state licensing boards may be a realistic ratio of actions taken. However, it would not be surprising if the figure turned out to be only one in 250. Settling on one in 200, the trickiest part of this calculation may be in attempting to match corresponding periods of time. The time span of the two actions taken in New York State for sexual abuse by a psychologist is May of 1980 to January 1984, or three years and eight months.

The only comparisons to fall back on are the uncertain figures from the Bouhoutsos (1983) study. Forty-nine percent of the sexual relationships were reported to have begun after 1973. There is no indication when the sexual relationships may have terminated or exactly when the survey was completed. Presumably, that was late in 1978. Also, there is a problem in adjusting the time frame of the two New York cases for the three-year statute of limitations that applies to nonmedical mental health professionals. Further hypothesizing that 35% to 40% would be appropriate to apply to the one in 200 ratio of actions taken which were selected, then one in 70 to 80 would be the ratio of actions taken under the corresponding time frame. This is equivalent to actions taken of 1.25% to 1.43% of the total hypothetical figure for sexual abuse of clients committed by psychologists. This percentage range would seem to be inadequate on the part of the state licensing boards. Placing it in the context of New York State, there would be 575 sexually abusive psychologists in New York State (541 males and 34 females). Approximately 200 to 230 would correspond to the time frame of the two actions taken against psychologists abusing clients. This represents one action taken for every 70 to 80 occurrences within that time frame.

It is suggested that the percentage of actions taken by the New York State licensing board and for other states is too low, especially since state licensing boards generally only have to indicate a preponderance of evidence, rather than 'beyond a reasonable doubt' as is the case in criminal proceedings. How low? For the professional who denies the problem exists and insists that this exercise is nonsense, then the figures are too high. But, for the client who must relive this excruciating experience, then the figures are too low. It seems that the critics claiming exaggeration should take the initiative in developing objective studies which disprove a serious problem.

PROFESSIONAL ATTITUDES RELATIVE TO SEXUAL ABUSE BY THERAPISTS:

The women's movement has been in the forefront in pressing for a solution to the problem. Most women, both therapists and clients, would state that it is a sexist issue and that reform in this area continues to be impeded by traditional sexist attitudes that are clearly demeaning to women. The specifics do not have to be elaborated on. They are well covered in the women's literature. Dr. Bouhoutsos stated that she had great difficulty in receiving approval and funding to conduct the California Task Force Study on Sexual Intimacy Between Patients and Therapists. The recent actions of the American Psychiatric Association's Board of Trustees were so negative toward investigating the extent of sexual abuse among psychiatrists that Dr. Judith Herman, Chairperson of the Women's Committee stated that she was "very disappointed" in the Board's action relating to sexual abuse because they had "turned their backs on victims" (*Psychiatric News*, 1/4/85). She and other members of the Women's Committee are undertaking their own independent survey following the APA's rejection of a survey. Attempts by consumer groups to reach out to professional organizations in resolving conflicts of interest issues have been received apathetically. Neither APA organization has even token representation of public members on their ethics committees, their principal investigating bodies. Failure of the principal mental health organizations to make the names of professionals found guilty of misconduct available to the public places the public at risk and is a violation of professional conduct on the highest level. Clients wishing to file complaints with the National Association of Social Workers are required to sign an oath of secrecy before the association will accept them. How can such attitudes instill trust in professionals whose principal tool requires full disclosure and trust?

©William Cliadakis (1985)

Reflecting this less than objective attitude is the following tabulation of cases investigated in 1983 by the American Psychological Association. Note that there are almost as many complaints involving profession-oriented issues as there are involving patient abuse (Mills, 1984).

APA CASES UNDER INVESTIGATION BY TYPE IN 1983

CLIENT-ORIENTED ISSUES

30 sexual intimacy, dual relationship, exploitation, etc.
 2 practicing outside competence
 1 'controlling' client
_3 breach of confidentiality
36

PROFESSION-ORIENTED ISSUES

6 failure to respect other professionals
4 authorship controversies
4 grading abuse or violation of student rights
1 misuse of media
9 misrepresentation/sensationalism in advertising or public statements
8 failure to correct misrepresentation
_1 lack of cooperation with the committee
33

Another indication of the ineffectiveness of professionals at self-policing is the following table in which there were only 11 material actions by the American Psychological Association out of 70 dispositions completed in 1983 (Mills, 1984). Although in many respects not comparable, note that the percentage of convictions for criminal charges in Manhattan, New Orleans and Washington, D.C. were very much higher (*New York Times*, 12/11/83).

APA CASE DISPOSITIONS VS. CRIMINAL COURT CONVICTIONS

APA CASE DISPOSITIONS 1983

22 cases closed with no sanction
11 reprimand
19 censure
_7 formal charges recommend dropping
59 (84%)

 6 resignation with stipulations
 4 recommend expulsion to board
_1 void membership
11 (16%) (meaningful actions)

70 Total

CRIMINAL COURT CONVICTIONS

MANHATTAN 100 cases	NEW ORLEANS 100 cases	WASHINGTON 100 cases
92 charges filed	53 charges filed	83 charges filed
60 pursued	45 pursued	49 pursued
57 guilty pleas	37 guilty pleas	42 guilty pleas
3 trials (2 guilty, 1 acuit.)	8 trials (6 guilty, 2 acquit.)	7 trials (5 guilty, 2 acquit.)
59% guilty	43% guilty	47% guilty

©William Cliadakis (1985)

SEXUAL ABUSE COMPARISONS WITH OTHER PSYCHOTHERAPY ABUSE:

Sexual abuse in psychotherapy, although the most publicized and the category with the most professional literature, is not the most common form of psychotherapy abuse.

A preliminary survey conducted by the National Committee for Preventing Psychotherapy Abuse in May 1982 (Cliadakis, 1984) indicated that sexual abuse ranked fifth, behind dependency, misdiagnosis with failure to rectify, abandonment, and wrong medication, in that order. The population included 33 individuals with 64 reported incidents of abuse involving 52 psychotherapists. The population of clients, including several therapists who also had been abused as clients, had responded to a local print ad on psychotherapy abuse, which was followed by an invitation to two meetings on the subject. No emphasis whatsoever was placed on sexual abuse. Five-eighths of the preliminary survey participants were women and nearly five-eighths had an education at the graduate school level. Dependency and misdiagnosis were tied for the most common complaint at 25% each. Abandonment was third at 19% followed by wrong medication, fourth at 17%. There were also two complaints of ECT (electroshock). Relative to all complaints of abuse, sexual abuse accounted for slightly less than one in every ten complaints. On a less systematic basis than the questionnaire study, NCPPA has encountered nearly 35 clients reporting sexual abuse by therapists out of a total population of about 300, or a ratio slightly more than one out of nine.

It cannot be said that sexual abuse is more devastating than other categories of therapy abuse. The incident of abuse itself, rather than the category of abuse, seems to have a different impact on different abuse victims. One rule of thumb, which seems to be supported by the findings in the Feldman-Summers and Jones (1984) paper, is that the greater the vulnerability of the client and the greater the feeling of exposure, the more the impact on the victim. With respect to sexual abuse, the feeling of betrayal/abandonment appears to be the most prevailing reaction, with the sexual act itself having only minor effects. Of all the other categories of therapist/client abuse, we sense that abandonment may be the most parallel to the pain that many sexually abused clients experience.

Reconstructing a population of 28 sexually abused clients, the following therapist/client gender breakdown was derived:

THERAPIST/CLIENT GENDER RELATIONSHIP

male therapist/female client	21	(77.8%)
female therapist/male client	2	(7.4%)
male therapist/male client	3	(11.1%)
female therapist/female client	1	(3.7%)
	27	(100.0%)
male orderly/female client	1	
	28	

Of the 27 clients, two conceived a child as a result of the abuse. Two of the 27 clients were raped (one was statutory and the other occurred under the administration of drugs; in the case of the 28th victim, she was raped by a hospital orderly). Four of the women clients indicated no effect whatsoever. Also of interest, the two male clients abused by female therapists reported devastating experiences, although one involved merely touching and the other involved sex therapy with a surrogate other than the therapist. Evidently, male clients are not immune from the devastation of an intimacy encounter.

Another point of interest is the professional category of the abusing therapist. The questionnaire replies came up with four psychiatrists named as sexual abusers out of an identifiable five. Surprisingly, there was only one psychologist named. Another population group gathered through call-ins and other referrals consisted of 34 individuals with 38 abusive therapists including 14 psychiatrists, five psychologists, two MSWs, three 'other' categories and nine therapists 'unknown'. There was also a large number of psychiatrists involved in sexual abuse of clients. Eight of 15 (53%) therapists categorized as sexually abusive were psychiatrists, four (27%) were psychologists, one (7%) was an MSW and two (13%) were 'other'; six were 'unknown', for a total of 21 sexually abusing therapists.

There is, however, a disproportionately high number of psychiatrists among the total population of therapists for the client population of the two groups. In the questionnaire group, 45% of the 51 identified therapists were psychiatrists and 53% of 15 were psychiatrists in the second group. Perhaps the nature of the client population, their very high educational level and the prevalence of psychoanalysts (most of which are M.Ds./psychiatrists, and male) and their high concentration in the New York metropolitan area might explain part of this high concentration. Interestingly, other mental health protection groups are picking up very different patterns. The Seattle-based group, Stop Abuse by Counselors, has received a high percentage of complaints (with the focus on women's groups and sexual abuse) from unlicensed, obviously less credentialled, therapists. NCPPA has been picking up almost the opposite. Paradoxical as the opposing positions may seem, both positions may be largely correct. Evidently, there are regional differences. There is a concentration of traditional, highly credentialled therapists in the East. Psychoanalysts are virtually nonexistent in Texas. The Texas-based Association of Psychologically Abused Patients indicates there are a lot of abusive pastoral counselors in the South. There is no literature on this subject. The subject needs to be further developed.

CONCLUSION—AND WHAT NEEDS TO BE DONE:

No one knows how many victims of sexual abuse there are. Other categories of therapy abuse are less sensational but just as damaging and criminal. Yet few professionals do anything about it. In fact, professional mental health organizations not only continue to be complacent; their record is obstructive.

What needs to be done is to contact a nationwide direct survey of the public along the lines of a Kinsey-Pomeroy type survey. A blue ribbon committee made up of consumers and professionals with a demonstrated record of having protected clients should be selected to monitor the survey. Quarterly meetings should be provided for the public to meet at state licensing board offices to educate the public on the need for reform in the state licensing systems and to make such licensing boards sensitive to protecting the public. Disciplinary bodies should be required to take affirmative action rather than to sit back passively and do nothing until a group of clients, all abused by the same therapist, places the evidence on the laps of the licensing boards. Licensing boards should be persuaded to reform archaic procedures controlled by the professions. The composition of the state licensing boards should be placed in a balance that would be more equitably representative of the needs of the public. A suggestion for fair play is use of a combination of one-third 'traditionalist' mental health professionals, one-third public members with a demonstrated record of protecting the public in the mental health field, and one-third professional members who also have such a record. With this type of reform and public representation, there should be greater accountability, a removal of a large number of abusers from the profession, an improvement in the image of the profession, and less emotional damage to victims of psychotherapy abuse.

©William Cliadakis (1985)

REFERENCES:

Bouhoutsos, J., Holroyd, J., Lerman, H., Forer, B., and Greenberg, M. (1983). Sexual intimacy between psychotherapists and patients. *Professional Psychology: Research and Practice, 14*, pp. 185-196.

Cliadakis, W. C. (1984). A preliminary study by the NCPPA of 34 abused psychotherapy clients. NCPPA, 60 W. 57th St., New York, NY 10019. (Unpublished)

Cliadakis, W. C. (1984). State licensing boards: An effective means of consumer redress in psychotherapy?. NCPPA, 60 W. 57th St., New York, NY 10019. 28 pp. (Unpublished)

Feldman-Summers, S., and Jones, G. (1984). Psychological impacts of sexual contact between therapists or other health care practitioners and their clients. *Journal of Consulting and Clinical Psychology, 52, (6)*, pp. 1054-61.

Holroyd, J., and Brodsky, A. (1977). Psychologists' attitudes and practices regarding erotic and nonerotic physical contact with patients. *American Psychologist, 32*, pp. 843-849.

Mills, D. H. (1984). Ethics education and adjudication within psychology. *American Psychologist, 39, (6)*, pp. 669-675.

Pope, K.S., Levenson, H., and Schover, L. (1979). Sexual intimacy in psychology training—results and implications of a national survey, *American Psychologist, 34, (8)*, pp. 682-89.

Psychiatric News. APA moves to discourage sexual misconduct in therapy. January 4, 1985, p. 17.

Sanderson, B. (1985). Task Force on sexual exploitation by counselors and therapists. Minnesota Department of Correction Legislative Report.

CHAPTER 31

SELF-HELP AND CONSUMER GROUPS

Gary Richard Schoener

According to an old Yiddish proverb, if you want to assess the quality of health care, "Don't ask the doctor; ask the patient."[1] We had adopted this principle long before we came across the proverb. Our efforts to respond to the victims of therapist-client sexual contact owe much to the input of the victims who were our clients (see Chs. 1, 7, & 13). They played a key role in bringing about legislative changes (see Chs. 41 & 42); they attended and made presentations at professional workshops on the subject; and they have written scholarly papers for publications or professional forums (e.g., Ch. 30; Linda J., 1987; Siegel, 1988).

The problem of sexual exploitation of clients by psychotherapists gave rise, during the 1980s, to a number of self-help and consumer groups (discussed later in this chapter). Earlier consumer movements in the mental health arena focused predominately on hospitalization and the treatment of seriously mentally ill patients. Although, in some instances, persons associated with local chapters of the National Association for Mental Health spoke out about or worked on the problem of therapist-client sex (see Chs. 29 & 42), the association and its local chapters have not attended to this issue. The liberation movement of former psychiatric patients, which gained considerable strength during the 1970s and continues to be a major force today, tends to focus on the use of restraints, psychotropic medications, and electroconvulsive shock (Chamberlin, 1979; Franklin, 1987).

Before discussing these self-help and consumer efforts, let's examine, first, how therapist-client sex is dealt with in advice columns and other literature directed to the general public, and then how it is treated in various consumer guides to psychotherapy.

ADVICE COLUMNS AND OTHER RELATED LITERATURE

Advice columns like "Dear Abby" and "Ann Landers" periodically print letters from readers on the subject of therapist-client sex. The frequency of such published letters increased during the 1980s: the period that saw the growth of self-help and consumer efforts directed at this problem.

For example, in a column of April 12, 1981, "Not Guessing in Missouri" wrote to Ann about a TV show that featured several victims of sexual exploitation by therapists. Ann labeled such therapists "despicable" and advised all victims to write to their local medical societies and to the appropriate national associations. Ann said, "I urge you women to come forward and speak out. Name names, places and dates. A favorite ploy of these vermin is to claim the patient is fantasizing" (Landers, 1981).

On Nov. 1, 1985, Ann published a letter from "Boiling in the Midwest"; it told of sexual abuse by a psychologist which led to his being forced to leave the state but, shortly afterwards, setting up practice in a nearby state (Landers, 1985a). Two weeks later Ann's column contained a letter from a "New Orleans Reader" who reported the humiliation and

---

[1] Auden & Kronenberger, 1981, p. 214.

anger she suffered from the violation of confidentiality by a therapist; Ann recommended a complaint to the relevant professional organization (Landers, 1985b).

On Dec. 10, 1985, Ann published a letter from Senator John Glenn referring to the ease with which therapists move from state to state to avoid the consequences of abusing clients. Senator Glenn described the bill he was sponsoring to establish a national computer system to track "unfit health care providers such as the psychologist" referred to in the earlier letter (Landers, 1985c).

In her June 27, 1986, column entitled, "Fondling by therapist is out of line," Ann printed a letter from "Concerned in California" who asked, "Is it considered ethical for a male psychologist to fondle and explore a female patient's body as 'a necessary part of the relaxation technique'?" Ann's response characterized such behavior as "worse than unprofessional... [and] immoral, indecent, unethical, exploitive... and totally unacceptable by any and all standards." She urged that the behavior be reported to the American Psychological Association (Landers, 1986a).

A letter from a reader identified as "Torn Asunder in California" described a marital conflict that started with a husband's anger when he learned that his wife's therapist had asked her to strip naked "as a symbol of shedding [her] inhibitions." Ann labeled the therapist "a lowdown snake" and advised a report be made to the local licensing authority as well as the American Psychological Association (Landers, 1986b).

A fascinating series of letters appeared in Ann's columns during 1988. In one column, "Therapists, go forth and heal thyselves," the former wife of a therapist who had lost his license for becoming sexually involved with several patients, warned readers of sexual advances by therapists and of the early symptoms—the therapist's talking about his personal problems (Landers, 1988a). Some time later, however, "Renewed in Sunshine Valley" took Ann to task for her "strong stand... against therapists touching patients sexually." This reader claimed that her psychiatrist brought her out of a depression and gave her "a sense of personal worth by kissing, fondling and making love" to her. Ann responded:

I asked a psychotherapist, who prefers to remain anonymous, to respond to your statement. This is what he said:

We know that some disturbed people have profited from the extraction of teeth, from shock therapy, from tonsillectomies, from brain concussions and from spankings. But to recommend any of the above as modalities for treating depressed individuals would be ridiculous.

For a therapist to engage in sexual activities with a patient could be so destructive and potentially damaging that it is best to rule it out altogether. Therapists should not be left to decide which patients would benefit and which would be harmed.

Even if the woman who wrote believes that she was made well by sharing intimacies with her doctor it would be foolhardy to use her experience as the basis for deciding this issue. Therapists often have a unique power by virtue of the fact that they represent the caretaker, the parent, the true authority. To abuse that power would be the ultimate travesty. (Landers, 1988b)

A letter from "Getting Well in Pa." was published 3 months later. The writer was a woman with a Ph.D. in psychology who had been sexually exploited by her therapist; she felt that Ann's response to the previous reader had "missed the mark" because it didn't mention filing charges. Ann agreed (Landers, 1988c).

Advice columns have also addressed, in recent years, the problem of sexual contacts with clergy. For example, in Diane Crowley's syndicated column from the *Chicago Sun Times* a reader wrote about a growing romantic and sexual attraction between herself and her parish priest (Crowley, 1987). In 1986, Ann Landers printed a letter from a reader who claimed that on their honeymoon his wife confessed to having slept with five men who had attended their wedding—an usher, two guests, the photographer, and the minister. Part of Ann's reply was, "And for heaven's sake, tell Sally to keep her mouth shut. The minister doesn't need the publicity" (Landers, 1986c). Several months later Ann printed a letter from "Disappointed in Detroit" which took her to task for this advice.

> For 32 years I was married to a minister who was protected by people who also kept their mouths shut. In the meantime, my husband was taking advantage of young women to whom he should have been ministering. If people had not remained silent, he would have been removed from his job. The net result was that he caused irreparable harm to all of those who believed he was a servant of God, including his wife and children. (Landers, 1986d)

Ann agreed and characterized that earlier advice as "a dog."

Ann Landers also has discussed sexual exploitation by physicians other than psychiatrists. For example, a recent letter writer, "Ben Herndon, M.D., from Corona, California," questioned Ann's challenge to the medical profession in the case of Dr. Kook Been Ahn, a gynecologist convicted of raping a patient on the examining table.

> Why don't the decent, caring physicians out there ride herd on these sleazy leeches who are a disgrace to the profession? (Landers, 1989a)

In such cases, Dr. Herndon wrote, the medical profession could do nothing and that it is "a problem for the legislators." Ann responded, in part,

> Even though the decent, caring physicians don't have police power, they could be much more diligent about seeing to it that pressure is brought to bear on colleagues who are a disgrace to the profession. Surely you honorable doctors can band together and figure out how to get the state licensing boards to throw out the rotten apples. If some board members routinely look the other way, use your power to throw those bums off the board. How about putting some lay people on those boards? That would certainly make it less incestuous and more objective.

> I don't buy into the concept that the good guys can't do anything about this appalling situation. That's a cop-out. Your profession is being tarnished by scum and you don't need "police power" to get rid of them. There are other ways and you'd better find them. (Landers, 1989a)

Thanks to Ann Landers, the discussion of sexual abuse by professionals has been kept alive in her columns for at least a decade and doubtless has informed many millions of readers about the problem. Although WICC has corresponded with Abigail Van Buren, author of "Dear Abby," on this topic, fewer interchanges on this topic have appeared in her columns.

CONSUMER-ORIENTED MAGAZINE ARTICLES

Articles about psychotherapy are published relatively frequently in various magazines. For example, *Newsweek* examined short-term therapies, although it may have added to consumer confusion by the pictures of "Quick Fixes," such as massage and use of a sensory deprivation tank (Gelman, Kasindork, King, & Miller, 1986); and the *Utne Reader* (reprints from "the best of the alternative press") included in one issue a cover story on "Psychotherapy" (*Utne Reader*, 1987). Neither of these two articles noted the dangers of sexual exploitation, although they did discuss problems with psychotherapy.

U.S. News and World Report (Goode, 1987, p. 102) published a reasonably lengthy article on psychotherapy, including advice on how to select a therapist. The author warned readers, "[if]... the therapist does or says anything that smacks of sexual innuendo, don't go back," and then suggested that unprofessional conduct be reported. The *Wall Street Journal* published a series by Bowen Northrup (1986) entitled, "Psychotherapy Under Analysis"; in the last installment, "Psychotherapy Faces a Stubborn Problem: Abuses by Therapists," considerable attention was given to the sexual abuse of clients.

In *American Health*, an article entitled, "Should You Keep Your Therapist" presented an approach to choosing and evaluating a therapist and stated in part,

Maybe as many as 7% of patients are actually <u>harmed</u> by psychotherapy, estimates T. Byram Karasu, a New York psychiatrist who heads the American Psychiatric Association's National Commission on Psychiatric Therapy. The dangers range from sexual involvement (an absolute taboo under all circumstances, even after therapy has ended)[1] to loss of trust due to breaches in patient-therapist confidentiality. Then there's what Karasu says is the most common trap of all: "establishment and habituation of unnecessary dependence on the therapist."

---

[1] Sexy Clients: In a rigorous study of this problem, the February issue of the prestigious *American Psychologist* reports that 87% of psychotherapists (95% of the men, 76% of the women) have been sexually attracted to their clients. 63% feel guilty, anxious or confused about it. About half say they've had no training for this human situation; only 9.4% of male therapists and 2.5% of female therapists have acted upon their urges. (Squires, 1986, p. 76)

Warnings about sex in the psychotherapeutic relationship appeared during the 1970s in several popular magazines (see Ch. 2 for some of the interchanges on the propriety of such conduct). Confusion between sex therapy (e.g., Masters & Johnson's work) and sexual exploitation within the psychotherapeutic relationship was common. In *Psychology Today* Koch and Koch (1976) warned readers about sex therapy, noting the lack of regulation in that field. The authors stated, "What does tend to improve the ethics of therapists is a fat malpractice suit...," and they cited Roy vs. Hartogs, although Hartogs was a psychiatrist and not a sex therapist. After noting that the American Psychiatric Association forbids therapist-client sex, they wrote,

The 40,000 psychologists who belong to the American Psychological Association will find nothing in the APA's code of ethics to condemn sexual activity with patients. At their 1975 convention, the APA could not even pass a resolution condemning such activity. (Koch & Koch, 1976, p. 37)

Johnathan Black's article "Pelvic Therapy" appeared in the Dec. 11, 1978, issue of *New Times* magazine. He cited a number of lawsuits against therapists, quoted professionals that sex is unethical in therapy, and presented research findings. Unfortunately, he stated inaccurately that a 1973 study (presumably Kardener, Fuller, & Mensh, 1973) found that 51%[2] of psychiatrists reported having sexual intercourse with their patients (Black, 1978, p. 52). Black went on to review the Shepard case and provided, as a sidelight, an interesting followup on the Roy vs. Hartogs case (see Ch. 2 for both cases).

> So where has Hartogs been? In prison? Slashing his naughty wrists? In South America? No, when this reporter visited him early this year (on a consultation, as a patient), the doctor was director of New York's Stress Coping Institute— essentially a one-man operation—and was carrying on a busy private practice in a modest, somewhat dingy office in Manhattan. His waiting room featured several threadbare couches and one of the most bizarre pictures ever to grace a therapist's outer sanctum. Six sinister baboons oversee a shark tank in which two ferocious hammerheads are busy dismembering a tiny screaming man. One of the man's legs, spouting blood, protrudes from the shark's jaw; a huge bloody hole is visible in the man's chest, from whence his heart has been wrenched. There was nothing quite so forbidding in Hartogs' small, dimly lit office, and it was not hard to see how Julie Roy—or any woman—might have succumbed to the doctor's impressive European accent, cordial manner and eminence grise. (Black, 1978, p. 55)

Black's article clearly indicated that seduction by therapists is common, that it is unethical, and that a growing number of therapists are being sued or subjected to disciplinary action as a result. His treatment of the topic provided a warning to potential consumers.

Other articles addressing the public presented a more confusing message, however, and may have inadvertently encouraged fantasies or less helpful attitudes among consumers. For example, Elizabeth Ames, in "What Your Shrink Really Thinks of You" (*New York* Magazine, April 7, 1980), wrote of the controversy over how frequently psychotherapists are sexually aroused by their patients:

> No one denies that they do. Freud himself admitted it. The conflict focuses on when and how often therapists experience erotic feelings. An eminent psychiatrist and analyst, Georgetown University psychiatry professor Harold Searles, writes that "with every one of my patients who has progressed to... a thoroughgoing cure, I have experienced romantic and erotic desires to marry... the patient." Yet others insisted they were rarely attracted to patients and emphatically rejected this idea. Scoffed Jack Schnee, president-elect of the American Psychiatric Association's Queens district branch, "That's esoteric and absolutely unnecessary. These feelings could occur—but they need not occur." (Ames, 1980, p. 42)

The article actually has a number of disturbing elements in it, not the least of which is the statement in bold print on its first page: "If you are the YAVIS type—young, attractive, verbal, intelligent, and successful—he may actually like you. He could even love you" (p. 41). Ames seems to extoll the virtues of being "The Good Patient," noting that it helps to be responsive, attractive, verbal, intelligent, or famous. She presented one measure of responsiveness:

---

[2]The correct figure is 5%.

Yet many therapists, men and women, say that patients, if responsive, <u>become</u> attractive to them. When they feel they are becoming sexually attracted to a patient, they sometimes consider this an indication of progress. (p. 45)

Furthermore, after describing problems in therapy caused by the therapist feeling that the client is obnoxious or boring, Ames noted that

Georgetown's Harold Searles, in an article entitled "The Patient as Therapist to His Analyst," asserts that he, for one, believes it's a natural part of therapy for a patient to help his therapist overcome such problems. (p. 45)

And in bold print on the same page appears the eye-catcher,

A Good Patient: If you're young, attractive, verbal, intelligent, <u>and</u> successful, he'll love you.

The cover of *Savvy* ("The Magazine for Executive Women") for June 1981 listed as one of its features, "Trapped in Therapy? The Dangerous Appeal of the Lonely Shrink." One article, "Therapy's Tender Trap: The Analyst As Fantasy Lover," discussed not only sex between therapist and client but the seductive elements in all psychotherapy (Whittington, 1981). Beyond overt sexual activity between therapist and client, Whittington wrote of "the interminable flirtation and romantic dalliance which characterizes all too many of the transactions between male psychiatrists and female patients, ...a problem far more frequent, and more hazardous to the average neurotic person seeking psychiatric help" (p. 52). He also described how mutual erotic attraction "increasingly becomes a reciprocal dependency for emotional gratification," leading to "the problem of interminable therapy, which Freud recognized early" (p. 54).

Another article in the popular press dealt with the problem of interminable therapy. "Prisoners of Psychotherapy," by Terri Minsky, is the cover story in the August 1987 issue of *New York*. It was on the newsstands during the convention (held in New York that year) of the American Psychological Association and mentioned with derision in several sessions. Interestingly enough, the article does not mention erotic interplay or attraction as a reason that therapy becomes interminable.

Other major magazine articles during this same period focused specifically on sexual exploitation by physicians or therapists. For example, "Doctors, Patients, & Sex," by Rita Rooney, was published in the June 1986 issue of *Ladies' Home Journal*. The author focused on sexual exploitation by various kinds of physicians, including psychiatrists. After noting that "sexually abusive doctors provide little warning before they act," Rooney suggested that consumers be alert to some "warning signs":

• A physician who offers constant flattery, telling you how beautiful you are, or a doctor who initiates inappropriate touching.

• A physician who makes frequent sexual innuendos, talks a great deal about sex or tells you sexually explicit jokes.

• A physician who suggests that he give you the last appointment of the day or one just before his secretary's lunch.

• A physician who doesn't ask a nurse to be present during a gynecological exam or any other situation requiring you to disrobe. But be aware that the presence of a nurse does not guarantee safety. It was one doctor's pattern to have a nurse present, busy taking notes, as he stood with his back to her, molesting the patient on the table.

• A physician who is overeager to make house calls. While there are still some valid reasons for doctors to see patients in their homes, those reasons are few. Be wary of a doctor who says he doesn't mind stopping by your house on his way home. (Rooney, 1986, p. 159)

Rooney interviewed a number of physicians, most of whom denied that their colleagues exploited clients in this manner. She quoted Dr. James Semmens, who has taught human sexuality to medical students at two different medical schools; he said that "it is the female patients who more often make sexual advances toward their doctors.... In class we talk about the seductive woman patient, warning students to assert themselves rather than being drawn into an affair." The doctor is further quoted as knowing of no medical school programs "that teach students how to deal with their own sexual feelings or that explore attitudes toward women generally" (Rooney, 1986, p. 161).

In September 1988 *Glamour* published "Patient-Therapist Sex" by Claudia Dreifus, an award-winning interviewer and political journalist. Therapist-client sexual involvement was the sole focus of the article, and it included interviews with clients who had been sexually exploited by their therapists as well as with professionals who had studied the problem.

The "Behavior" section of *Time* has questioned the value of all psychotherapy. Leo (1983) in "Lemons from a Shady Dealer" described the reluctance of former clients to criticize their therapy and in "A Madness in Their Method" described emotional disturbances in therapists (Leo, 1985). This article focused on the book, *Madness and Cure* (Langs, 1985), which described manipulation and abuse by therapists:

One male therapist caustically rebuked a female patient for not trying to seduce him. A respected psychoanalyst had an affair with the lover of one of his patients, then lied about it, announcing that the patient was projecting his unresolved Oedipal fantasies upon an innocent therapist. Two female therapists behaved seductively to female patients, and one of them conducted a session while lying in bed in her nightgown. (Leo, 1985)

Problems among impaired practitioners are discussed in a lengthy article, "Wounded Healers," in *The Atlantic Monthly* of January 1989. According to the author, "The 'helping professions', notably psychotherapy and the ministry, appear to attract more than their share of the emotionally unstable" (Maeder, 1989, p. 37). An unnamed clinical psychologist is quoted by Maeder as claiming that

Every patient who comes in to his office who has had a previous experience with a therapist has some kind of horror story to tell, about some major failing on the therapist's part, including, quite often, sexual abuse, verbal abuse, things that cross the boundary of mere bad technique and come pretty damn close to the criminal. (Maeder, 1989, p. 38)

In addition to national publications, some local magazines have focused on therapist-client sex or discussed the problem in articles on psychotherapy. One Minneapolis example, "Sex and the Therapist," a cover story in *MPLS Magazine* (Sundstrom, 1977), helped several victims to come forward and is still used as reading material for victims in the Twin Cities Metropolitan area.

NEWSPAPER ARTICLES AND SERIES

We have received newspaper clippings dealing with therapist-client sex from publications all across the country. They have included accounts of civil suits against therapists, licensure actions, criminal actions, and other issues related to psychotherapy.

In the twin cities of Minneapolis and St. Paul, we have had continuing newspaper coverage of the therapist-client sex issue, often through reports of disciplinary actions or civil suits. Several in-depth stories also have been published in local newspapers, such as the companion articles, "Behind Closed Doors—Therapist Affair Can Betray Trust, Traumatize Client," and "Therapist Can Be As Troubled As Patient," in the *St. Paul Pioneer Press & Dispatch* of Jan. 6, 1985 (Baker, 1985a & b).

Sam Newlund, a staff member of the (Minneapolis) *Star and Tribune*, has written many pieces on this topic, for example, "Study: Therapists Flout Sex Ban" (Newlund, 1986). The newspaper published an editorial on the problem ("Sexual Exploitation and Therapy Don't Mix") on June 8, 1986, in which there was expressed the hope that "the pressure and publicity will be sustained" from the national conference on therapist-client sex which had met in Minneapolis the preceding week (see Appendix AA). A week later the same paper published a lengthy article by Kim Ode entitled, "Sexual Exploitation by Therapists is Hidden Problem" (Ode, 1986).

The *Star and Tribune* editorial of June 8, 1986, read as follows:

Sexual Exploitation and Therapy Don't Mix

No one need be surprised or shocked to find that nearly 90 percent of professional counselors sometimes feel sexually attracted to their clients. That figure was reported, without alarm, to a conference in Minneapolis last week. It comes from a survey of practitioners in professions like psychology, psychiatry and marriage counseling. We would worry more—about the honesty and mental health of those professionals—if 90 percent said that in counseling conversations touching people's intimate lives the counselors were never touched by inappropriate digressions of the mind and eye.

Eyebrows should be raised, however, by how often such digressions develop into deliberate and dishonorable advances. The broad survey of helping professions found 7 percent of counselors acknowledging sexual activity with clients. A separate survey limited to psychiatrists brought similar findings, also reported to the conference here. More than 6 percent of a large national sample said they had initiated or encouraged contact with patients to "arouse or satisfy sexual desire."

It does not blunt the edge of that statistic to learn that most of this activity occurred when the patients were no longer in therapy, and that relatively few of the offending psychiatrists felt strongly troubled by their behavior. Indeed, these survey revelations suggest that counselors' sex with clients is rationalized as often as it is regretted. The professions affected should be alarmed. To face up to, not gloss over, self-destructive behavior is perhaps the most common reason people seek counseling help. The last thing they need is to be exploited and further hurt by self-deceiving therapists.

The small minority of sexual exploiters poses large dangers to clients and to professions that depend on personal trust. Laws like Minnesota's prohibiting such abuse need to be backed by publicity and peer pressure. Both methods were used by the counselors and therapists who conducted last week's conference on sexual exploitation within their professions. We hope the pressure and publicity will be sustained.

The conference referred to in the editorial was "It's Never OK" (see Appendix AA). It is likely that such editorials are seen by more readers than are the average news stories, and they have the potential to exert a major influence on readers.

The Twin Cities media have given excellent coverage to cases in which lawsuits, criminal charges, or licensure actions have been filed against psychotherapists. It is a rare month that passes without at least a short article on the subject. Recently, for example, a lengthy series of articles by Bob Ehlert in the (Minneapolis) *Star Tribune* examined the sexual abuse of young people by clergy through an in-depth examination of a recent case (Ehlert, 1988a, b, & c).

Whenever an in-depth report or headline story on therapist-client sexual abuse is published, WICC receives inquiries or new complaints. There is little doubt that the magazine, newspaper, and television stories and programs help consumers to recognize exploitation.

In recent years the publication of new studies has been reported in many major newspapers around the country. For example, the publication of survey data on psychiatrists by Gartrell, Herman, Olarte, Feldstein, and Localio (1986) led to articles in many newspapers and, even to some on-going debates. After reading the research results and interviewing Dr. Gartrell, Darrell Sifford, a columnist for the *Philadelphia Inquirer*, wrote a column that led, some time later, to a second column—"When Sex Enters the Picture of Psychiatrists and Patients"—detailing a debate that had erupted in response to the first column (Sifford, 1987).

Dan Allegretti of the Madison, Wisconsin, *Capital Times*, wrote a two-part series on therapist-client sex: "Doctor, You Raped Me—A Patient's Horror Story" and "Sexual Exploitation by Therapists" (Allegretti, 1985a & b). The *Philadelphia Inquirer* has covered the subject of therapist-client sex on a number of occasions, including a lengthy story, "Attacking Health-Care Sexual Abuse," by Fawn Vrazo and Donna Shaw (June 23, 1985). Lois Blinkhorn (1984a & b) wrote a major article on this issue for the *Milwaukee Journal*; it's title was "The Psychiatrist and the Patient—Sometimes a Professional Relationship Gets Personal." The *Kansas City Star* published a major piece on therapist client sex ("When the Patient Becomes a Victim") (Rix, 1986); and the Walker vs. Parzen case was described in a lengthy article ("The Final Analysis") by Jeannette De Wyze (1983) in the San Diego *Reader*.

The Chicago Tribune accorded this issue front page space in 1983 with the article, "Therapy Patients Victims of Sexual Abuse" (Emmerman & Gaines, 1983); its "On the Law" column publicized the three civil suits filed against Dr. Jules Masserman, a prominent Chicago psychiatrist, under the title, "Shocking Detour on Road of Fame" (Warren, Possley, & Tybor, 1987).

Our files contain numerous clippings from other publications but, perhaps, the most impressive is the three-part series written by Steve Smith and Barbara Laker for the *Dallas Times Herald*, which appeared on May 20, 21, and 22, 1985. The title for the series was

"Sex and Therapists," and together the articles are the longest treatment of this issue we have yet seen in a newspaper (Smith, 1985a, b, c, d, e, f; Laker, 1985a, b, c; Smith & Laker, 1985). It combined a discussion of local cases with national statistics, models for helping clients, a discussion of self-help and consumer issues, and related topics.

THE ANTI-THERAPY MOVEMENT

Although it is beyond the scope of this chapter, it is worth noting that a small subgroup within the general consumer movement simply opposes psychotherapy, arguing that it often does not help and that the potential harm (e.g., from sexual exploitation) is demonstrably too dangerous.

One of the best-known spokespersons for this position is Jeffrey Masson. His book, *Against Therapy* (Masson, 1988), is an all-out assault on psychotherapy. In television appearances he has attacked psychological testing, electroconvulsive shock, and psychoactive drugs, as well as psychotherapy. One of his major charges against psychotherapy is sexual exploitation of clients.

CONSUMER GUIDES TO THERAPY

Early books, such as *A Consumer's Guide to Psychotherapy* (Wiener, 1975) typically did not devote much if any space to the issue of sexual contact with clients. In fact, those books at times were overly optimistic about the degree to which misconduct would result in a therapist's being cast out of the profession. Wiener (1975, p. 125) for example, wrote,

> Those therapists of irrational thoughts, erratic deeds, or defective character are likely to be eliminated after several years in the same community.

The Health Research Group of Public Citizen, Ralph Nader's consumer organization, published *Through the Mental Health Maze, A Consumer's Guide to Finding a Psychotherapist, Including a Sample Consumer/Therapist Contract* (Adams & Orgel, 1975). The possibility of sexual contact between therapist and client is not raised in this otherwise remarkable work. Ironically, the authors suggested that a prospective client ask if the practitioner makes house calls; they reported that in the questionnaire survey preceding the book, 30% of the psychiatrists, 30% of the psychologists, and 50% of the social workers who returned questionnaires indicated that they did indeed make house calls (Adams & Orgel, 1975, p. 27)! Today house calls by a psychotherapist would be viewed as quite suspicious.

Jean and Jim Erwin's book, *How to Choose and Use the Right Therapist for You*, placed heavy reliance on the Nader book. Nevertheless, they were aware of the possibility of exploitative behaviors.

> In the sexual area, any action or demand on the part of the therapist that violates standard concepts of morality should be challenged directly. Any sexually suggestive physical contact or any erogenous stroking between the therapist and the client/patient is strictly out of line. There is no place for overt sexual activity in a psychotherapy relationship. (Erwin & Erwin, 1978, p. 99)

In *A Complete Guide to Therapy*, Kovel (1976, p. 233) warned against sex with the therapist and indicated that it "is no rarity... and no mystery either, considering the intensity of infantile sexual wishes locked up in neurosis and their inevitable mobilization by treatment."

Friedman, Gams, Gottlieb, & Nesselson (1979) relied on Chesler's (1972) work in their book, *A Woman's Guide to Therapy*. They discussed the "sexual power" a therapist has, indicating that the "power the therapist can have over the 'patient's' mind is even greater for the woman in therapy (especially with a male therapist) than for the man" (p. 32), and they noted further that this power "has all too often extended into a sexual power as well" (p. 33). Although they cited none of the available survey data, they gave some examples from *Women and Madness* (Chesler, 1972) and included a chapter from Nancy Caughran's (1973) book, *Radical Psychology*, in which she described how her psychotherapist attempted to seduce her and how she regained her power by confronting him on it.

By the 1980s a new generation of consumer guidebooks came into being; some of them devoted considerable attention to the dangers of seduction by therapists. *Women and Psychotherapy—A Consumer Handbook* was produced by the umbrella organization, Federation of Organizations for Professional Women (1981). They acknowledged that they had drawn their ideas in part from some earlier therapy guides aimed at women:

> *A Consumer's Guide to Non-Sexist Therapy*, published by the National Organization for Women, New York Chapter; *Guidelines for Women Seeking Psychotherapy*, developed by the Cleveland Women's Counseling Center; the *Therapy Information Packet* distributed by Women in Transition of Philadelphia; and the *Women's Guide to Therapy: Off the Couch*, by the Goddard-Cambridge Program in Social Change. (Federation of Organizations for Professional Women, 1981, Acknowledgements)

I do not know how much circulation each of these source books received outside the localities in which they were produced, or the manner in which each one dealt with the client-therapist sex issue. The *Handbook* flatly stated,

> ...it is clearly unethical for the therapist to engage in any kind of sexual relationship or erotic contact with his or her client as part of treatment or outside of regularly scheduled meetings. This holds true even if you like the therapist and agree to the sexual contact.
>
> *****
>
> Occasionally a client may terminate therapy with the therapist in order to engage in sexual relations. You should realize that it is difficult to overcome the initial power relationship of the therapy situation. You may find that you end up feeling betrayed and hurt by the situation. (p. 19)

Besides focusing on this problem of therapist-client sex more than the guides to therapy available earlier, this *Handbook* provided some discussion of sex following therapy termination.

Other consumer guides produced during the same period for local or national distribution covered this topic with far less specificity. For example, *Mental Health Services in Minnesota—A Guide for Referring Professionals and Consumers*, produced by the Mental Health Interdisciplinary Interest Group (1981), indicated only that professionals are expected to "avoid sexual, romantic, or business relationships with clients" (p. 17). A one-page handout, undated, developed during the 1980s by the Minnesota Council on Family Relations and entitled "What You Need to Know to Be A Responsible Client" presented a strict view of "Sexual Behavior" among the five key "Rules for Professionals."

Counselors and therapists should not, under any circumstances, be involved with you in sexual intercourse, nor in other behaviors such as touching your breasts or genitals. Counselors and therapists should not "date" you, nor behave with you in a "dating" manner.

Your Questions: Do you ever kiss, touch or hold clients as part of your work? Have you ever been disciplined for sexual misconduct by the state board or your fellow professionals? (Minnesota Council on Family Relations)

Ironically, this one-page handout provides more guidance for therapists than much longer works available locally and nationally.

Fischer's *Choosing a Psychotherapist*, for example, first published in 1983, stated only the following:

Note: It is strictly unethical under any circumstances for a psychotherapist to engage in any kind of sexual relationship or erotic contact with a client/patient. If this happens to you, immediately report the incident to both the Ethics Committee of the appropriate professional association and the State Licensing Board. (Fischer, 1986)

Aftel and Lakoff's (1985) book, *When Talk is Not Cheap*, gave only brief mention of sexual feelings toward a therapist:

If you have brought up these sexual feelings (as you should), your therapist should be able to discuss them and not act on them or make fun of them. (p. 88)

Making Therapy Work (Bruckner-Gordon, Gangi, & Wallman, 1988), a 263-page guide to "choosing, using, and ending therapy" contains only a very brief discussion of therapist-client sex:

YOU AND YOUR THERAPIST ARE SEXUALLY INVOLVED

No therapeutic justification exists for a therapist's having a relationship that involves overtly sexual behavior with a client. A sexual relationship exploits a client and is unethical as well as illegal. (For further discussion of appropriate physical contact, see page 105.) (p. 162)

Unfortunately, the "discussion of appropriate physical contact" reference is quite brief, and while some rules for evaluating it are presented there is no discussion of specific types of touch save for a repeat of the prohibition against sexual touching. The same is true for the section on social contact outside of therapy (pp. 103-4) which does not attempt to clarify what sorts of therapists' "...policies about socializing with clients..." might be inappropriate.

Although I did not review all consumer guides to psychotherapy, it seems fair to say in general that most provide little discussion of therapist-client sexual activity, and that such topics as sex after the termination of psychotherapy are rarely discussed. The same has been generally true of guides to obtaining therapy for children and adolescents, which are addressed to parents. This should be no surprise. It is pointed out in Chapter 9 that the abuse of children and adolescents by therapists only recently has been acknowledged. A noteworthy exception is the recently published consumer's guide for parents, *Your Child's and Adolescent's Mental Health—A Resource Guide for Parents*. It states, in part,

Inappropriate Behaviors

Any sexual behavior such as uncomfortable touching, unwanted remarks, or other intimate actions by your therapist is absolutely off-limits. Such behavior is unethical and against the law.

If you observe, or if your child reports to you, unnecessary touching by the therapist, too much talk about sexual matters, or actions that seem unusual and do not fit within the treatment plan, you should take the following steps:

  • Discuss the situation with your child and with the therapist to make sure that you understand what has happened.

  • If, after this discussion, you are not satisfied that the therapist's actions are appropriate, report the matter to a supervisor in the therapist's agency or to the ethical practices board. (Telephone numbers can be obtained from First Call for Help listed at the back of this guide.)

  • Discuss your concerns with another mental health professional or contact the appropriate professional organization or licensing board. (Again, obtain the number from First Call for Help.) (Mental Health Assn. in Hennepin County, 1988, p. 8)

Fortunately, during the past year I became aware of two additional consumer guides that include considerable discussion of therapist-client sexual involvement. Both guides were written by Dr. Judi Striano, a psychotherapist. Her books incorporate input from consumers with information from the professional literature and from interviews with professionals. The first, *How to Find a Good Psychotherapist—A Consumer Guide* (Striano, 1987) devotes nearly six pages to the issue. *Can Psychotherapists Hurt You?* (Striano, 1988), has entire chapters on psychotherapy cults and psychotherapist-client sexual involvement. I hope that future consumer guides will follow Striano's lead and incorporate research data as well as examinations of the problems and dangers in psychotherapy.

CONSUMER GUIDES THAT ARE FOCUSED ON THERAPIST-CLIENT SEX

Part of the stimulus for the production of *Women and Psychotherapy—A Consumer Guide* (Federation of Organizations for Professional Women, 1981), discussed in the preceding section, was the problem of therapist-client sex. Some consumer guides that focused specifically on this problem were published a few years later.

In 1986 the Wisconsin Task Force on Sexual Misconduct published *Making Therapy Work for You* (see Appendix Z). This brochure provided consumers with some guidelines for evaluating therapy and counseling experiences as well as a list of licensure boards for reporting misconduct. The brochure examined aspects of the therapeutic relationship other than sexual contact and advances which spell trouble for the consumer.

The following year "If Sex Enters Into the Psychotherapy Relationship" was developed under the auspices of the Committee on Women in Psychology (American Psychological Association, 1987). It provides nine pages of discussion of key issues surrounding the topic of sex in the therapy relationship.

The Minnesota Task Force on Sexual Exploitation by Counselors and Therapists (see Ch. 42) developed a Public Education Work Group in 1984 which was given the task of educating consumers on the prevention of therapist-client sex. Thus, in early 1988, the State of Minnesota published the brochure for consumers on therapist-client sex entitled "It's Never OK" (Minnesota Dept. of Corrections, 1988). A few months later the State published a 36-page booklet, *It's Never OK: A Handbook for Victims and Victim Advocates on Sexual Exploitation by Counselors and Therapists* (Public Education Work Group, 1988). Minnesota criminalized sex between therapist and client in 1985 (see Chs. 42 & 43), so funds for this free booklet were provided through the U.S. Department of Justice, under the Victim of Crime Act of 1984. This booklet provides a useful list of "warning signs":

In evaluating the counseling experience, before there are any blatant inappropriate suggestions, there may be some clues to lack of professionalism or misuse of power such as:

- the counselor avoiding or refusing to give information about credentials, licensing, or experience;

- the client having a feeling that something is wrong during therapy, despite attempts to clarify or discuss this with the counselor;

- the client having the feeling that therapy is giving in personally to the counselor, rather than engaging in a learning process; and

- the counselor suggesting any mutual activity that is uncomfortable.

In many cases, sexual contact is preceded by actions which may be inappropriate or unprofessional, such as:

Behavior which may feel sexual:

- telling dirty jokes;

- undressing during therapy;

- ogling (eyeing up and down); or

- discussing the therapist's sex life.

Giving client "special" status by:

- scheduling after-hours appointments or changing fees (when different from normal office procedure);

- making out-of-the-office appointments (when not normal office procedure);

- using the client as a confidant or for personal support;

- giving or accepting major gifts;

- inviting client to social engagements;

- borrowing money or getting involved in business deals with client;

- making secrecy a part of the counseling relationship; or

- using or offering alcohol or drugs during counseling.

If you are concerned about what you are experiencing in counseling, trust yourself. Ask questions of the counselor. If you ever feel intimidated or threatened by your counselor, this may be a warning sign. If your questions or concerns are not answered, talk to the counselor's supervisor, a trusted friend, or a crisis line. (Public Education Work Group, 1988, pp. 8-9)

The booklet also has sections on choosing a counselor and taking action if you have been exploited, using the "Wheel of Options." This "Wheel" was developed by Jeanette Milgrom at WICC (see Ch. 26).

We hope that the pamphlet and booklet developed by the Minnesota Task Force will be given widespread distribution. California plans to develop consumer literature and to distribute it widely, according to the *Report of the Senate Task Force on Psychotherapist and Patients Sexual Relations* (1987) and the legislation that followed (see Appendix P). The Wisconsin Task Force on Sexual Exploitation distributes *Making Therapy Work for You* statewide (see Ch. 41 and Appendix Z). As yet, it is far too early to measure the effect of such publications.

The information made available to the general public by the news media during the 1980s vis à vis therapist-client sexual relationships undoubtedly helped to increase the number of consumer complaints and lawsuits. It also seems to have helped to develop more awareness of the problem among professionals and to provide some impetus for action by professional bodies. During the same period self-help and consumer groups emerged to address the issue, and they have continued to play an important role.

SELF-HELP AND CONSUMER GROUPS

A number of self-help and consumer groups are described in the remainder of this chapter. My purpose is to show how such groups arise and the different effects they may have. I cannot give an unbiased history of their efforts. All, in my opinion, have had a positive influence and have been of help to a number of people—some more than others. All have accomplished a great deal with limited resources. To date they have received scant reference in the professional literature: a few pages in Pope & Bouhoutsos's (1986) book, *Sexual Intimacy Between Therapists and Patients*. The groups are presented in the chronological sequence in which WICC first had contact with them.

Association of Psychologically Abused Patients (APAP)

On May 19, 1982, Sylvia Diamond, Executive Director of APAP, wrote asking if I would serve on the APAP's Board of Advisors. She had listened to audio tapes of a program on Therapist-Client Sex which had been recorded at the 1981 convention of the American Orthopsychiatric Association (see Fleming, Schoener, Luepker, & Nye, 1981). I agreed. Shortly afterward I visited with her and some other APAP members during a trip to the Dallas/Fort Worth area.

Diamond told me that she had been sexually exploited by her therapist, a well-known social worker in private practice. She ended up in a struggle with the therapist. She was very angry at him. At first she could not find an attorney to take her case, which infuriated her. She then found that her therapist and some colleagues who were known to exploit clients had a booth at a local singles fair, so she, too, applied for a booth. The sponsors, however, did not allow her to have one. (In the Dallas/Fort Worth area, a great many large, singles organizations, many sponsored by churches, are in existence. They sponsor fairs, and therapists rent booths in the hopes of drumming up business.)

Unable to participate in the fair, Diamond wrote a leaflet to tell her story. She put one on the windshield of every car in the fair's parking lot. As a result, a woman from the *Wall Street Journal* called her during the Spring of 1982 and put her in touch with Bill Cliadakis of the National Association for Preventing Psychotherapy Abuse.

The original description of APAP read as follows:

The recent upswing in divorce rates and the increasing singles communities in this country has led to a widespread breeding ground for a new type of public enemy number one. He/she is the so-called psychotherapist or counselor, with a fist full of paper credentials who makes a mockery of the profession and leaves a wake of victims as devastated as any major disaster.

Seducers and exploiters of the emotionally hungry or emotionally wounded show no real healing concern for the client's needs. Their thrills of seduction through manipulation is a perversion stemming from greed, boredom, burn-out, or plain moral bankruptcy. It ends for the therapist as another cynical detached incident of a series, while the patient lands in an emotional trash dump, less considerable money paid out in counseling fees.

The mental health profession is ripe for infiltration of frauds who have run from legislation of laws that protect the public from plunder of the vulnerable or helpless. Most states have no consumer statutes, policing, or licensing requirements, except for psychologist and psychiatrist. Anyone can hang out a shingle and call himself a psychotherapist or counselor and can specialize in marriage, family, drug, individual, spiritual, sex or any other specialty they choose without accounting to anyone.

The Association of Psychologically Abused Patients is a recently formed National Organization, headquartered in the Dallas/Fort Worth Metroplex and founded by victims of mental rape. Their primary activity is as a support group and information center to other victims. However, long range goals include helping the mental health field to protect itself against unethical and illegal conduct by individuals, calling themselves counselors, who violate the foundations of sound therapy and destroy the public trust of the profession as a whole.

APAP acts as a referral agency to victims of inadequate or inappropriate treatment. The referrals will be: to qualified therapists who are experienced in the care of patients abused in counseling; to Professional Association grievance committees where complaints may be filed; to attorneys who meet the special needs of a mental malpractice suit; and to individuals who offer support to men and women who have suffered abuse at the hands of a therapist. APAP also publishes a paper of preventive suggestions concerning constructive therapy vs. improper therapy techniques.

We hope you will support APAP and its goals.

APAP is a non-profit organization that has an advisory committee of Mental Health Professionals but its staff and directors are not in the counseling field. It has an open membership for those who wish to contribute to better individual and community mental health care.

APAP is not a policy-making organization. It has no enforcement authority. But it does have the power to provide the public with information that protects the individual from exploitation by counterfeit counselors.

Despite the strident tone of this handout, Diamond and the APAP have always maintained liaisons with the professional community, ranging from its advisory committee of professionals to making referrals to a select group of local professionals when a client needs therapy.

In 1982 APAP spent $200 to run an ad in *Psychology Today*,; it said, "If you've been harmed in therapy, maybe we can help." They received about 2,000 responses—including from 8-10 phone calls per day. The responses came from almost all the states and from a few foreign countries. About one half of the calls involved complaints about medication, and the complainants included at least as many men as women; and about 40%, virtually all women, complained of sexual exploitation. The remaining 10% had such miscellaneous complaints as abandonment by a therapist, rip-off fees, therapists borrowing money from patients, and the like. Only a few crank letters came in.

Dr. June Garrett, a psychologist, provided APAP with an office address and a phone for a year. Although Diamond usually had several volunteers helping her, it is my impression that she always handled the bulk of the calls and correspondence herself. The *APAP News Letter*, which was published sporadically, reprinted or reported on civil suits or regulatory board discipline of psychotherapists around the country. Sometimes the allegations contained in letters to the editor were published, and local therapists who were the subject of complaints found themselves listed in the newsletter.

On February 27, 1987, APAP hosted the Second National Conference on Therapy Abuse, which was titled, "Sex and Psychotherapy—It's Never OK!" It was held at Texas Christian University in Fort Worth. Although the turnout was small, owing, in part, to some last-minute problems with the mailing of the notices, the faculty for the conference included Diamond, Bill Cliadakis of NCPPA, Dr. Jacqueline Bouhoutsos, Dr. Linnda Durrè (neè D'Addario), and myself. An afternoon workshop was held for victims (see Ch. 17) at the conclusion.

APAP also engaged in face-to-face sessions with abusive therapists, going along with clients for confrontations. Despite threats from therapists who resented the notoriety of being mentioned in the APAP newsletter, the organization never has been sued for libel or slander.

Diamond, who formerly ran a private detective agency, has a great feel for the proper use of confrontation tactics, which may account for APAP's charmed life. She is a sensitive and caring person and has a good deal of common sense.

She has been a valuable resource all these years. Although pressed for time currently, she is still willing to provide referrals to Dallas/Fort Worth area therapists, dispense information, and assist in lobbying and work with the news media. Her present address is

Association of Psychologically Abused Patients
P. O. Box 9682
Fort Worth, Texas 76147
(817) 732-6565

Bear in mind that she is limited in the time to answer letters. Currently (Spring 1989) APAP is still in business but because so much of its activities revolve around Diamond, this situation could change.

National Committee for Preventing Psychotherapy Abuse (NCPPA)

On May 24, 1982 Bill Cliadakis, founder of the NCPPA, phoned WICC and spoke with Jeanette Milgrom. This was our first contact with a consumer group addressing psychotherapy abuse. Cliadakis identified himself as a securities analyst with a Wall Street firm.

Holding an MS degree in Geology, Cliadakis has worked as a geologist, researcher, securities analyst, and teacher. His scientific and research backgrounds were quite useful when he began to tackle the problem of psychotherapy abuse (see Ch. 30). He had seen a psychotherapist, with whom he terminated in 1978 after unsuccessful attempts to sort out problems in the psychotherapeutic relationship. In 1979 he co-founded Peer Support, a self-help group active in Manhattan, that provides an alternative to traditional psychotherapy.

While seeking involvement in a consumer group, Cliadakis attended on August 24, 1981, the Ninth Annual Conference on Human Rights and Psychiatric Oppression. He was moved by the experience. With the help of an attorney friend, Sig Geronimo, he registered the NCPPA as a business entity in New York two months later. After attending another conference and deciding that something needed to be done for people who had been victimized in private out-patient therapy, Cliadakis placed the following ad in the *Village Voice* on January 13-19, 1982:

ABUSED BY PSYCHOTHERAPISTS? Stop crime of greatest harm with least recourse. Join activists, share experiences. Empathic peers. Confidential. Free. National Committee for Preventing Psychotherapy Abuse, Suite 4C, 175 W. 93 St, NYC 10025; 663-1392 eves.

The first day the ad appeared the phone was continually busy; a total of 18 or 20 calls came in. That first night *Village Voice* reporter Lin Harris got through, and the next issue of the *Voice* contained an article about the NCPPA entitled, "Group to Fight Psych Hype," in which Cliadakis was quoted as saying, "I want activists" (Smith & Harris, 1982).

The first NCPPA meeting was held February 6, 1982; through June 15 of that year there was a total of 9 meetings. The average attendance was 14; more than 30 people attended two general meetings. Committees were formed for research, public relations, a newsletter, and legal rights. Volume 1, Issue 1 of the *NCPPA Newsletter* was published in October 1982. The stories included the founding of the Association of Psychologically Abused Patients in Fort Worth, information on how to obtain one's psychotherapy records, a book review, a summary of a program at the American Orthopsychiatric convention (see Fleming et al., 1981), and the announcement of the First National Conference on Psychotherapy Abuse and Consumer Protection.

The conference, co-sponsored by the National Self-Help Clearinghouse and the NCPPA, was held at the Graduate Center, City University of New York, on November 15, 1982. I gave one of the presentations. It was at this conference that Cliadakis and Diamond first met. A summary of the conference was published in Volume 2, Issue 1 (February 1983) of the *NCPPA Newsletter*. The third issue (Volume 2, Issue 2), did not come out until March 1984; it consisted primarily of an analysis of how the New York State licensing boards functioned.

The core group of NCPPA dwindled by 1984 and regular support group meetings were no longer held. Cliadakis more and more became the organization's major force; he wrote numerous letters to newspapers, regulatory bodies, professional organizations, and others. He also kept WICC continually informed of his advocacy activities, generating a thick file of clippings and copies of letter exchanges. He pushed for consumer involvement in licensure boards and ethics committees. He provided information to reporters writing articles and referred a great many of them to WICC for further information. The paper he presented at the Conference of the American Orthopsychiatric Association in 1985 is representative (see Ch. 30).

Cliadakis spent many long hours listening to the pain and complaints of former clients who had been abused, and he served an invaluable function by linking up many on an individual basis, which took the place of support groups for some of the people.

About 4 years ago Cliadakis gradually began to focus his work on issues other than just psychotherapy abuse; about 2-1/2 years ago he became involved in problems related to institutionalization and the use of electro-convulsive shock therapy (ECT). In mid-1986 Cliadakis began serving as a mental hygiene editor on the monthly *Gene Crescenzi Forum* on Paragon Cable TV in New York, usually commenting on ECT and institutionalization. In early 1988 he began producing a monthly program for Cable TV entitled *Psychiatry's Dark Side*, which is shown in New York City four times a month. At present, NCPPA still exists on paper but not in fact. Cliadakis carries on his work through

Activists for Alternatives
P. O. Box 20651, Columbus Circle Station
New York, N. Y. 10023
(212) 410-6260

Although occasionally he still refers clients or reporters to places for information or support, his main energies are focused on ECT and the problems of institutionalization.

Stop Abuse by Counselors (Stop ABC)

In the Spring of 1983 Cliadakis put WICC in touch with Shirley Siegel, one of the founders of Stop ABC in Tukwila, Washington (the Seattle area). Over the years I have corresponded frequently with her and, on occasion, we have talked with each other by phone. We have never met. Terry Brady, a WICC psychology intern, visited Shirley on September 4, 1985.

In February 1980, about 5 years after she left an exploitative relationship with a therapist, Siegel began her research into various laws, looking for ways that an exploitative therapist could be reported. Stop ABC was incorporated in June 1981 as a non-profit Washington corporation after a legislator told her that some sort of group or organization was needed to pass a law to regulate counselors.

From the beginning Stop ABC focused on consumer advocacy and legislation, with an emphasis on recruiting people to assist in the lobbying effort. Various obstacles thwarted efforts to run a victim support group. Siegel regularly provides support to people over the phone and in letters. Stop ABC has a number of volunteers who provide support to victims involved in hearings or lawsuits.

Initially, Stop ABC listed 5 phone numbers in different areas; by 1985, however, there were only 3—Siegel's and those of two volunteers who were willing to handle information and referral calls. Stop ABC has 35 or 40 members who paid a $15 annual membership fee and 20 active volunteers, with 50 who were expected to be active during the legislative session and more than 500 who could be called upon to write letters. In addition, a biannual newsletter was sent to about 100 people outside the state of Washington. The annual budget remains about $1,000 a year—all from private contributions, memberships, or the sale of informational materials.

The Mission Statement in use by Stop ABC since 1985 reads as follows:

Stop ABC is an organization actively working to prevent abuse by mental health practitioners through the promotion of community education, research projects, remedial legislation, and improved professional standards. Stop ABC also maintains a supporting network for people who have been victimized by mental health practitioners.

Although the organization never intended to work outside the state, its mailing list now includes 1,500 names and it has become a national clearinghouse. Siegel promptly answers all letters. Stop ABC has a small but growing national list of therapists and attorneys to whom it can make referrals. Siegel and Stop ABC have received broad publicity in the State of Washington (e.g., a two-page newspaper story, "Counselor Abuse" by Rockey, 1984), and she has made appearances on the *Woman to Woman, Donahue,* and *Sally Jesse Raphael* shows on national TV.

Currently, Siegel is hard at work writing a book; a number of her articles have appeared in various publications: "Is Registration the Answer?" in *Psychotherapy Newsletter* (Siegel, 1986); "Stop Abuse!" in *Woman's Newspaper* (Siegel, 1987a); "About Re-Evaluation Counseling..." in *American Mental Health Counselor's Association News* (Siegel, 1987b); and "Laws That Help When Therapists Do Harm" in *Student Lawyer* (Siegel, 1988). She also received national visibility in *Ms.* Magazine (1983). She was a speaker at the 1985 conference of the National Clearinghouse on Licensure, Enforcement, and Regulation (CLEAR). Her major goal is the writing and production of additional consumer education material.

Stop ABC offers, at present, a 33-page printout of their clippings for $5.00, and an organizing packet for persons interested in starting up an advocacy group, for $10.00. Stop ABC requests that anyone writing to them include a self-addressed and stamped envelope. Their address is

Stop ABC
Box 68292
Seattle, WA 89168
(206) 243-2723 between 9AM - 6PM Seattle time

Advocates Against Psychic Abuse (AAPA)

In 1981 Evelyn Walker won a lawsuit against her former therapist, Dr. Parzen, which resulted in the largest reported settlement in a therapist abuse suit. The case is described in the book *A Killing Cure* (Walker & Young, 1986). I wrote to her in the Spring of 1984; her response on June 26, 1984, included a package of clippings and information on joining AAPA.

AAPA was founded in 1983. The Board of Directors consisted of Walker, 2 psychiatrists, a social worker, and an attorney; an Advisory Board included 5 attorneys, 2 psychologists, a psychoanalyst, and a (Ph.D.) marriage, family, and child counselor. Walker's letter indicated that AAPA had added quite a few additional board members, including both "Professionals and Lay-People who are prestigious supporters."

The organization planned to publish a series of consumer-oriented books, although I have seen only a single example: *Advocates Against Psychic Abuse Prevention and Protection Guide*, Volume 1, 1983, Psychiatric and Psychological Mental Health Services (Walker, Shepherd, Hubbard, & Casey, 1983). It is 62 pages in length and covers a range of topics.

I have heard nothing from the group in recent years. My last letter (several years ago) went unanswered. The phone is disconnected and no other listing is available. West Coast colleagues indicate that the group, originally based in San Diego, is defunct. It is not clear how long it actually lasted.

Consumers Against Psychotherapy Abuse (CAPA)

In the Spring of 1985 I had a phone conversation with Peggy Black, who was, at that time, in San Francisco. On May 5, 1985, she wrote me that CAPA had been organized. In August 1985 she made a presentation at the annual convention of the American Psychological Association in Los Angeles as part of a panel on therapist-client sex. After the program I was able to meet with her and some of her co-workers, including Michael Swander who currently heads the group.

Soon after being organized, CAPA hired an attorney to draft some legislation, but it was narrowly defeated in the California State legislature, much to the surprise and chagrin of CAPA. Finally, in 1986, the legislature decided that the matter should be studied by a Senate Task Force on Psychotherapist and Patient Sexual Relations. Black was appointed one of the 10 members of that Task Force—the sole consumer representative (or non-professional, for that matter). Shortly after the March 1987 report of the Task Force she decided to pull out of CAPA to pursue some personal goals. Although at the time three post office boxes were listed, there was little else to the organization.

In early 1988 Swander tried to revive CAPA. He helped to sponsor and provide speakers for a conference (April 9 & 10, 1988) on "Sexual Involvement Between Therapists and Patients." On October 26, 1988, Swander wrote me that although they had had some problems "getting CAPA back in action...we're finally set up and ready to function." However, in a recent conversation he indicated that some of the volunteers had fallen away; that a local (Santa Barbara) therapist who was to set up a support group did not do so; and that the Post Therapy Support Group at UCLA had not been going since last Fall. After considerable deliberation Swander has decided to put CAPA on hold until such time as there are enough people to allow it to function as an information, support, and advocacy group. For the present he will maintain the post office box, but cannot promise to respond to correspondence in a timely fashion. The address is

Consumers Against Psychotherapy Abuse
P. O. Box 2652
Santa Barbara, CA 93120

Consumers Against Sexual Exploitation (CASE)

Our first contact with Jane Rasmussen, who founded CASE, was probably in 1985. Rasmussen has a BA degree in psychology and an M.S. in education, and she has worked as a psychiatric aide. As such she has been quite effective on local and national TV programs on the topic of abuse by therapists.

She had filed complaints against an abusive psychiatrist which resulted in his license being revoked in November 1984. This action was undertaken without a support system. She had approached the Mental Health Association about starting a support group for survivors but became disenchanted with the way the group was run. In 1985 she decided to form CASE as an information support system for survivors of abuse by therapists. Initially the organization met monthly at the YWCA, and a small number of people came for support; eventually the monthly meetings were discontinued.

Rasmussen herself, and several other CASE volunteers, periodically receive calls from people in crisis. They provide immediate support as good listeners and then refer the callers to appropriate resources.

In 1987 Rasmussen published *Couched in Silence: An Advocacy Handbook on Sexual Exploitation in Therapy*, a 44-page book aimed at survivors of therapist-client sex. In my opinion, it is the best guide currently in print for individuals who have been victimized by therapists. It is available from CASE for $7.00.

Consumers Against Sexual Exploitation
5036 N. 56th Street
Milwaukee, WI 53218
(414) 464-5845

I.M.P.A.C.T.

I.M.P.A.C.T. (In Motion—People Abused in Counseling and Therapy) was founded in October of 1988 by three victims of abuse by therapists in Colorado. It focuses its efforts in the Denver-Boulder-Colorado Springs area but is in contact with other groups on a national level. I.M.P.A.C.T. has three goals: 1. to provide a support network and group for people who have experienced physical, sexual, or emotioal abuse by a therapist or clergyman; 2. to serve as an information repository, distributing information to the public, the media, and to local professionals; 3. political activity.

Partly as a result of the efforts of I.M.P.A.C.T. members in 1988 Colorado criminalized sex between therapist and client and there were also some highly publicized abuse cases during 1988 and early 1989. While I.M.P.A.C.T. is a relatively small group and quite new, these successes may be helpful in stimulating its growth. To contact I.M.P.A.C.T., write to:

I.M.P.A.C.T.
323 S. Pearl Street
Denver, Colorado 80209

Good Tidings

Good Tidings, a support group for women who have been in love with Roman Catholic priests, was founded by a woman in Iowa who subsequently moved to Pennsylvania and teamed up with a couple there. Since 1984 the couple, Catherine Grenier and her husband, Joe (who is a former, or non-canonical priest),[3] handle the phone and correspondence. There Good Tidings provides support for women and, at times, priests, who have become infatuated, fallen in love, or become romantically involved. Although they do not consider themselves counselors, they talk on the phone to provide support, approaching the situation from both a practical and spiritual point of view. They normally suggest both counseling and spiritual guidance and make referrals to resources geographically close to the caller. They put priests in touch with other priests who have struggled with this issue. They have also offered hospitality in their home to either the woman or the priest. In other cases the guest has stayed in a local inn or resort and visited. They are located in the scenic Delaware Water Gap area of Pennsylvania.

Good Tidings has contacts with individuals and groups around the country. For example, they use the Core of Resigned Priests United for Service (CORPUS), headquartered in Minnesota, but with representatives in every state. They note that many of the approximately 17,000 married non-canonical priests in the United States met their wives in the course of their pastoral work. It should be noted that the vast majority of the situations Good Tidings becomes involved with are not characterized as abusive or exploitative.

Good Tidings can be reached by phone or mail, with calls possible daytime or evening:

Good Tidings
P. O. Box 283
Canadensis, Pennsylvania 18325
(717) 595-2705

Advocates for Responsible Therapy

In the Spring of 1989 a group in Southern California began organizing a new consumer advocacy group named Advocates for Responsible Therapy (ART). The group's motto is "healing through ART." It expects to incorporate and to have a mailing address and phone number in the near future. At present it can be reached by contacting:

ART
c/o Linda Gifford
285 Midbury Hill Road
Newbury Park, California 91320
(805) 499-7058

Other Groups

From time to time we hear from or read about other groups with a self-help or consumer focus. In 1987 we heard of an attempt to form a group called "Victims of Professionals" in the Philadelphia area. In 1988 we became aware of efforts to organize a consumer group in Indiana.

---

[3] A non-canonical priest cannot function as a parish priest. They have resigned from the priesthood but are not ex-communicated. If laicized by the church they can even be married in the church. Under certain circumstances they can be called upon to perform certain duties such as the sacrament of the sick (last rites).

Self-help and consumer groups tend to come and go (although so do "concerned" professionals). They usually lack funding and are dependent on the volunteer services of a few individuals. They often lack the funds or expertise to set up a non-profit organization, or simply do not wish to get "that organized." It is, therefore, important to give them support whenever possible and, also, to stay in touch to know whether they are in a position to render service.

These groups can provide a type of support which professionals cannot offer and are invaluable when it comes to trying to change laws or affect public opinion. Without "live" victims/survivors to be interviewed, the news media often will say that there "is no story." Sometimes the groups produce useful printed materials, like Jane Rasmussen's *Couched in Silence* (1987). Sadly such materials do not often get the distribution they deserve.

CONCLUSION

Consumer guides and consumer groups can assist in both the prevention and the policing of misconduct by therapists. However important and useful these efforts are, the professional community still must shoulder the principal responsibility for policing the various psychotherapy fields and cleaning up the mess that exploitation leaves behind. Consumers can help, but they cannot do the profession's work.

PART IX

INTERVENTION WITH THERAPISTS

Despite the growing literature on treating clients who have been sexually exploited by therapists and other health professionals, little has been written about interventions with the exploitative therapists. Programs for the assessment and treatment of an "impaired practitioner" focus almost exclusively on drug and alcohol abuse and dependency. Given the deluge of civil suits, rising costs of malpractice insurance, increasing number of criminal actions, and negative publicity directed to various psychotherapy fields over the past two decades, the lack of attention to therapists who generate the problem of sexual exploitation of clients is striking.

Our work at the Walk-In Counseling Center (see Ch. 1) centers far more on client/victims; during the last decade, however, we have become increasingly involved in working with therapists, their employers, and the boards that regulate their work. (Some of these activities are detailed in Part X.)

This section of the book opens with a model for evaluating and developing rehabilitation plans for those treatable therapists who have sexually exploited clients (Ch. 32). In addition to a theoretical framework for planning rehabilitation, it presents a typology of therapists who become sexually involved with their clients.

Carrying our framework further, Chapter 33 discusses the problems of providing psychotherapy for the particular subset of offenders who may benefit from it. Like the preceding chapter, this one also takes the position that many perpetrators may not be treatable, thus challenging the prevalent notion that a referral to long-term therapy will cure the problem and render the perpetrator a safe practitioner.

The last two chapters (34 and 35) in this section focus on the supervision and oversight of the practice of therapists who have a history of sexual exploitation of clients. It is quite common for employers and regulatory boards to require a perpetrator to receive "supervision," but the literature lacks a theoretical framework for providing such supervision let alone considering the practical problems that are involved.

The two chapters in Part X on supervision of therapists are directed to preventing sexual misconduct.

As a final note it's important to remember that the accused practitioner may be just as vulnerable as the client/victim and be at risk for suicide. Dr. Erwin T. Johnson of the Menninger Foundation, in descrbing the effects of malpractice litigation on physicians and their families in a videotape about supportive counseling offered to these individuals, described the physician as "bitter, ashamed, depressed..." and the spouse as "uncertain, anxious, embarassed, worried." The entire family was characterized as "withdrawn...isolated, rejected...brutalized." (Johnson, 1988) These people too need assistance.

CHAPTER 32

ASSESSMENT AND DEVELOPMENT OF REHABILITATION PLANS FOR THE THERAPIST

Gary Richard Schoener
and
John C. Gonsiorek

The concepts in this chapter began taking shape in the early 1980s when regulatory bodies and employers of therapists started looking into appropriate therapies for counselors and psychotherapists who had had sexual contact with clients. We interviewed a number of therapists and the clients with whom they had engaged in sexual activities and, from the extensive descriptions provided by the clients, we were able to categorize the therapists' behaviors.

Some Minnesota professionals began to use these constructs and to cite them in their writings. The first was Schoener. On February 1, 1986, he addressed a memorandum to the Therapeutic Issues Work Group of the Minnesota State Task Force on Sexual Exploitation of Clients by Counselors and Psychotherapists. Subsequently, the model was added to and adopted by the Task Force (Thompson, 1989). This model was developed further in our own publications (Gonsiorek, 1987; Gonsiorek & Schoener, 1989; Schoener, 1986a) and is the basis of the present work. New material, however, makes this chapter the most comprehensive and detailed exposition of the model to date.

Essentially, the model consists of three parts: (a) an assessment of the therapist who has engaged in sexual activities with a client(s) to determine the cause of this behavior and whether he or she is a suitable candidate for rehabilitation; (b) the formulation of a rehabilitation plan, if it is indicated, to help the subject to avoid exploitative sexual behavior in the future; and (c) an assessment of how well the subject has participated in the rehabilitation plan and whether a change in her or him has occurred.

The assumptions underlying this model is that sexual contact between therapist and client in its widely varying forms occurs because of a range of factors; for example, acute or chronic psychopathology, problems in the therapist's personal life, practice style, confusion about professional boundaries, or even situational factors.

THERAPIST CHARACTERISTICS AND DYNAMICS

In contrast to the popular assumptions that therapists who sexually exploit their clients are reasonably ethical and well-trained but temporarily overcome by lust or love, the accounts of such exploitations by victims present an image of severely disturbed, sadistic, and even violent individuals who engage in purposive sexual behavior. Indeed, when one such therapist submitted to psychological testing, the conclusion was that although he appeared to be sociopathic, underneath this appearance he might be psychotic or prepsychotic (Walker & Young, 1986).

According to the professional literature, the typical profile of a sexually involved therapist is speculated to be a middle-aged individual with marital problems who is "burned out" and depressed (e.g., Simon, 1987). Other investigators have cited feelings of omnipotence and grandiosity (Goldberg, 1986; Gorkin, 1987, Guy, 1987; Marmor, 1953) and narcissism (e.g., Kottler, 1986). Only rarely has it been suggested that these traits reflect a character or personality disorder (Kaslow, 1984; Simon, 1987). A few writers have found evidence of masochistic and sadistic tendencies (Guy, 1987; Smith, 1982).

Although some investigators blame traditional societal roles of males and females for sexual exploitation in consulting rooms (Brodsky, 1986; Holroyd & Brodsky, 1977; Zelen, 1985), this hypothesis does not explain situations in which a female therapist is the perpetrator.

Few attempts have been made to study sexually exploitative therapists. One researcher (Butler, 1975; Butler & Zelen, 1977) interviewed a relatively small sample of such therapists who reported recent marital difficulties and feelings of loneliness, vulnerability, and being "needy" prior to the sexual involvement.

What is striking in reviews of the literature is the lack of empirical research using either systematic or clinical-case methodology. Even Butler's work was based on self-reports. The absence of critical examination beyond the type of speculation that dominates the literature does not speak well for the sense of responsibility in the psychotherapy professions. Granted that our findings are not based on systematic studies, nevertheless they are derived from the intensive case studies of other therapists. Furthermore, in many instances the data were collected as a prelude to deciding rehabilitation and/or prevention issues in specific situations where generalities are of little use. Hence, we believe that our data base, however subject to revision it may be, supports the categories derived from it.

CATEGORIES OF SEXUALLY EXPLOITATIVE THERAPISTS

None of the cited theories of causative factors in therapist-client sexual encounters has been particularly useful to us although each describes some aspects of some cases. Thus we developed out of our clinical experiences a classification system based on clusters of kinds of offenders. Some groups may show some dissimilarities but, in general, they form natural groupings because of their commonalities. We also found a few therapists who did not fit into any cluster.

Uninformed/Naive

Many paraprofessionals as well as some professionals who received substandard training are included in this cluster. They genuinely lack knowledge of standards of care in mental health and have no understanding of professional boundaries. They have difficulty distinguishing personal from professional relationships. Some individuals even seem to be quite naive about social conventions in general.

The fact that therapists were led into situations that became sexualized by ignorance rather than a drive to exploit does not reduce the harm done to clients or the risk of future exploitation of clients. Some of this group, even after attempts at remedial education, simply do not have the personal maturity or clinical judgment and sensitivity to engage in counseling or psychotherapy.

Healthy or Mildly Neurotic

Among healthy or mildly neurotic therapists who form a reasonably large chapter, the sexual contact with clients is quite limited or represents an isolated circumstance. They do not engage in the repetitive exploitation practiced by therapists in other categories described below. The therapist typically exhibits clear awareness of the unethical nature of the conduct and is remorseful. These therapists often terminate the inappropriate behavior on their own and sometimes self-report.

Situational stressors are often in evidence. Once the sexual exploitation is disclosed the therapists are often highly anxious and depressed. These moods may lead them to confess their behaviors without regard for legal risks. For many, but not all of this group, the prognosis for rehabilitation is good.

Severely Neurotic and/or Socially Isolated

These therapists have long-standing and significant emotional problems, especially depression, feelings of inadequacy and low self-esteem, and social isolation. Their work tends to be at the center of their lives and most of their personal needs are met in the work setting.

The inappropriate behavior with clients normally begins with excessive emotional and/or social involvement outside the therapy sessions. The growth of intimacy breaks down professional boundaries in the consulting room and leads to seductive game-playing, excessive touching, increased social or business involvements (outside of therapy), and far too much self-disclosure by the therapist.

Situational variables may precipitate an overt sexual involvement, it is true, but the roots of the involvement are in the long-term therapeutic relationships. These therapists may experience guilt and remorse, yet they seem to be less able to terminate the inappropriate behavior than are members of the preceding category, and their guilt tends to lead to self-punitive behavior rather than to constructive change.

Denial and distortion may be used to mask the inappropriate sexual quality of the relationship or behavior. Some of these therapists rationalize that the relationship is not inappropriate and that they truly love the client; they may argue that they too are vulnerable and open or that they are engaging in true intimacy, not just sex. They often vacillate among self-revelation, remorse, defensiveness, and self-justification. Rehabilitation is theoretically feasible with this group but the prognosis is more guarded.

Impulsive Character Disorders

These therapists have long-standing problems with impulse control; some may even have had legal difficulties in other areas of their lives. If there is a long history of inappropriate behavior it may include insurance fraud, sexual harassment of staff members or trainees, or poorly controlled sexual behavior in their personal lives. A number of compulsive sex offenders are found in this category.

Many of these therapists are caught because of the large number of their victims and their poor judgment. While severe consequences are pending they show guilt, remorse, and depression; indeed, they resemble neurotics at such times. However, they rarely have any true appreciation of the effect of their behavior on their victims, and they tend to deny that they have caused any harm. In the midst of denial and minimizing their misconduct, they confess at times in an erratic fashion. Inconsistent and full of surprises as they are, they generally are not candidates for rehabilitation.

Sociopathic or Narcissistic Character Disorder

Many therapists in this cluster manifest some features of the persons in the impulsive character disorders group. They too often have a long history of problems with impulse but the history may be less obvious. They differ, however, in that they tend to be far more deliberate and cunning in their sexual exploitation of clients. Typically, they are cool, calculating, and detached, and they are expert at seducing a range of clients and at covering their tracks.

Unlike the therapists in the preceding cluster who tend eventually to anger colleagues, this group is adept at manipulating colleagues. Even with clear evidence of their misdeeds, one may find oneself almost unable to confront them. Yet there is usually (although well-hidden at times) a long string of victims, from clients who have been exploited to other professionals, third party payers, and the like. Using manipulation and/or well-timed threats, these therapists often manage to convince clients, colleagues, and professional organizations to help them to avoid the consequences of their misdeeds.

When caught they may do a remarkable job of mimicking a healthy therapist who is remorseful, and they may confess to acts—but those that they believe are already known. However, sometimes they slip up and "confess" to the wrong case! After they have exhausted the use of manipulation, their final move, typically, is a fierce and often well-planned legal counterattack. They do not hesitate to damage anyone or anything in the attempt to avoid consequences and, hence, they often out-maneuver ethical professionals, boards, and employers.

Some of these individuals voluntarily seek therapy and may appear to be deeply involved in a rehabilitation effort, but they are not candidates for change. They can manipulate their way through even a structured program, such as one designed for sex offenders.

Psychotic or Borderline Personalities

In this cluster the common denominator is poor social judgment and impaired reality testing. A thought disorder may or may not be in evidence. Some of the borderline personalities found in this group share characteristics with therapists in the uninformed and naive group, except that their poor judgment contrasts with their general intelligence and training. Both borderlines and psychotics may rationalize their behavior in some fashion but the justification is idiosyncratic or even bizarre in comparison with the rationalization of the neurotic or character-disordered person.

Some members of this group have active delusional systems and operate out of psychotherapy cults. They demonstrate considerable variability in the capacity to understand the effects of their behavior on others and to feel remorse. In dealings with authorities, their behavior is unpredictable. Some confess without regard for self-protection whereas others are quite paranoid and engage in fierce battles, quite like sociopaths. Rehabilitation is not likely with this group.

Keep in mind that this group of clusters was formulated on the basis of clinical experience, not systematic research. The formulation may even be considered tentative. Nevertheless these constructs can help ethical professionals to understand the widely varying reasons for the sexual exploitation of clients by therapists. The focus of the evaluation is not to classify an offender into a cluster but, rather, to determine the offender's rehabilitation potential. The evaluation itself offers some guidelines for the determination.

I. ASSESSMENT MODEL

There is presented here an "ideal" methodology for assessing a practitioner or trainee who has had sexual contact with a client(s). Although it may not be possible for some assessors to follow the guidelines exactly in a given situation, we strongly recommend that all the steps be followed.

Thus far requests for the type of evaluation we have devised have come from the following:

1. Licensure boards considering rehabilitation.

2. An attorney representing an accused practitioner.

3. An employer wishing to determine if a staff member can be rehabilitated.

4. An ethics committee of a professional association considering what to require of a member before reinstatement at some future date.

5. A professional training program seeking to evaluate a trainee's need for rehabilitation and/or suitability to continue in the field.

6. Self-referral: a therapist requests evaluation, perhaps following the revelation that he or she has sexually exploited a client.

7. As the result of an agreement reached between a client and offending therapist, after an out-of-court settlement in which the therapist agrees to return therapy fees, pay legal costs, provide some funds for the client's future therapy, and be evaluated and rehabilitated as recommended.

The evaluation model itself consists of four separate steps:

1. Determination of the facts, typically, by whoever is requesting the assessment, and the admission to the main body of facts by the professional to be assessed.

2. The assessment itself, which consists of the following:

   a. Collection of facts plus psychological testing.
   b. Identification of the causes of the misconduct.
   c. Decision on whether rehabilitation sufficient to return the professional to practice is possible.
   d. Development of a rehabilitation plan.

3. Review of the findings and recommendations by whoever requested the assessment and by the professional being assessed; these also may be reviewed by another consultant.

4. Carrying out the final plan of action.

Evaluations sometimes are requested by licensure boards or employers as part of an investigation or determination of fact. We typically refuse such requests because, we explain, the purpose of an assessment is solely to develop a rehabilitation plan. An assessment cannot be made if the professional denies the key elements of the complaint.

When an assessment is completed it is not uncommon for us to be asked about discipline. Our practice is to try to separate discipline from rehabilitation. Discipline or punishment is aimed at maintaining standards and providing a deterrent, and, sometimes, to appease victims or the public. Thus punishment and rehabilitation are distanced from each other; punishment, however, is often helpful in rehabilitation (e.g., Gonsiorek, 1987, 1989).

THE ASSESSORS

An assessment may or may not be a team effort. The assessor, for example, may ask another psychologist to administer projective tests. If the test administrator is highly skilled in the field, the assessor benefits both from her or his expertise and from the ensuing discussion of the results, which is a form of consultation. When a social worker or psychiatrist is the primary assessor, a consulting psychologist should be employed to do the psychological testing. In cases involving training or employment situations those requesting the assessment sometimes are able to collect a good deal of background data and thereby save the assessor time.

The assessor must remain as neutral as possible. His or her task is, first, to develop an understanding of why the misconduct occurred and second, to design a plan to prevent the reoccurrence. If during the assessment it becomes clear that information is being withheld, the assessor must stop the process and make clear that total rather than partial cooperation is essential.

If after conducting the interviews, testing, and other data-gathering activities the evaluator still cannot construct a tenable hypothesis of why the questionable behavior occurred, he or she must not try to develop a rehabilitation plan. It is essential to be able to say, if need be, that rehabilitation does not seem feasible or that insufficient information exists for formulating a plan.

Assessments should not be undertaken by individuals who are biased against returning exploitative professionals to practice. If one believes that professionals who have sex with clients cannot in fact be rehabilitated, then it is pointless to conduct an assessment. At the same time, if one believes that devoting time and money to a career entitles an exploitative professional to pursue it after some sort of obligatory course of therapy, then one should also refrain from conducting assessments.

PAYMENT

We have used two different payment mechanisms:

1. Payment by the practitioner or his/her law firm.

2. Payment by the employer or board (in the case of payment by the latter, the costs may be charged to the practitioner).

Although it is easier to collect fees from a law firm, employer, or board, the question of who pays should not affect the outcome of an assessment. Because of the specificity of our model and the designated requirements of both the assessor and person being evaluated, there is no reason for the assessment to be handled as a typical adverse examination (e.g., when the licensure board pays the bill). In a number of cases one of us has worked for and been paid by the defense but the results have been accepted by the licensure board.

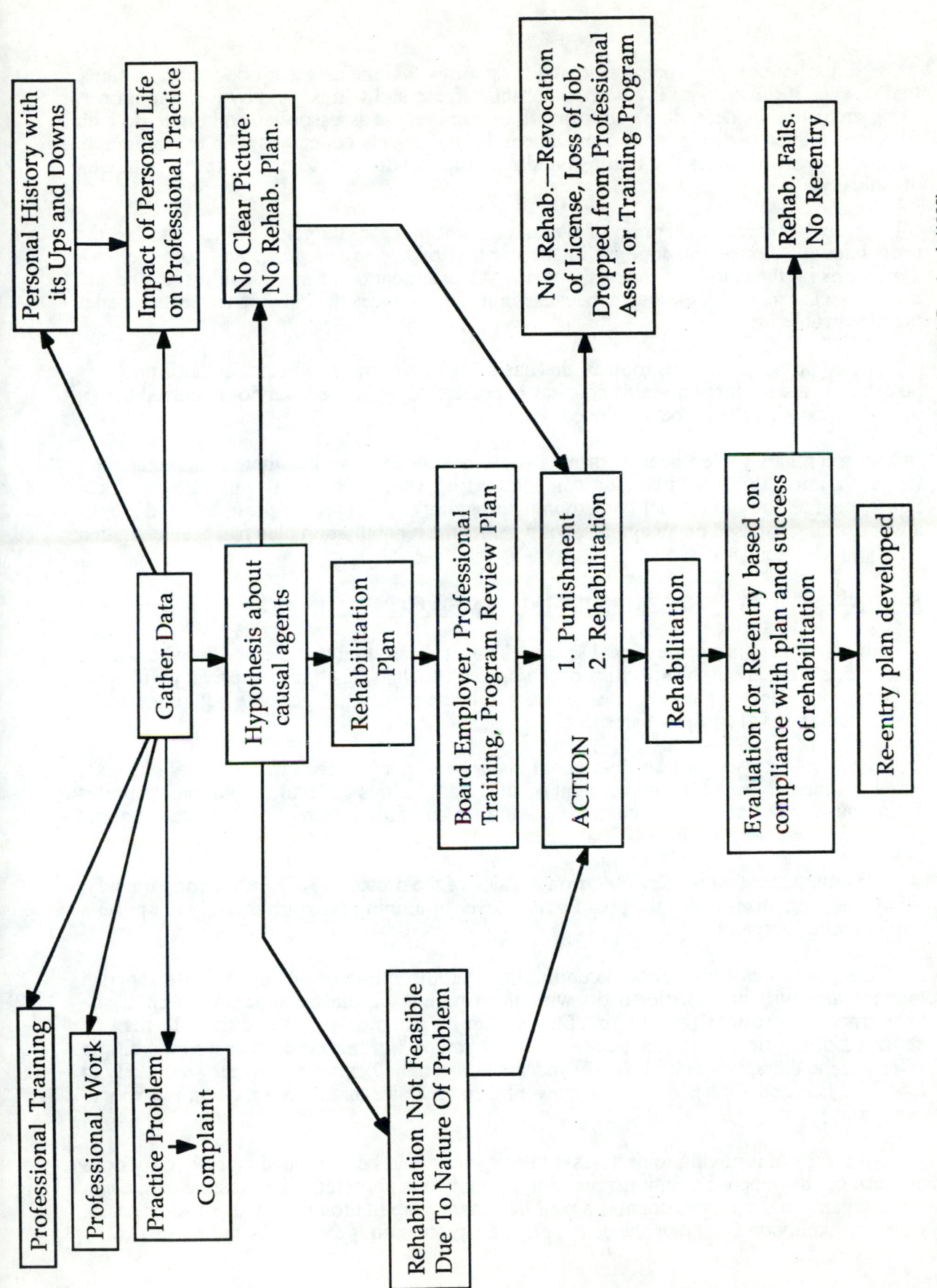

Fig. 1. Overview of assessment process.

Schoener and Gonsiorek (1988)

A practitioner who is being assessed must know that the assessor does not take sides, that is, even if the assessor is a witness for the defense and will be paid by the practitioner, he or she is not the defendant's advocate. Furthermore, the assessor has nothing to do with decisions related to discipline or punishment; his or her only concern is with rehabilitation. An assessor who shades the findings and recommendations in some fashion is behaving unethically.

Figure 1 presents a diagram of the assessment process. Its goals are to examine the professional's sexual misconduct in the context of her or his work and to develop a hypothesis on the causes of the misbehavior. An examination of more than just the sexual misconduct is required, of course, because in many instances the behavior reflects broader practice problems.

The hypothesis of causation is the basis for determining whether rehabilitation is possible. If the evaluation yields no clear hypothesis of why the behavior occurred then a rehabilitation plan cannot be developed.

After a rehabilitation plan is formulated, it must be reviewed. If there is agreement on its provisions, then the plan, or some modified version of it, is put into practice. Subsequent re-entry to the field or a training program, or the return to professional duties in a work setting is based on an appraisal of whether the rehabilitation plan has been complied with and has been successful.

BEGINNING THE ASSESSMENT—INFORMED CONSENT

An assessment is a professional service. Thus it is essential that the person who will be assessed is clear about the specifics of the process, such as, (a) limits of privacy; (b) what data will be collected and what disclosure will be necessary; (c) possible outcomes of the assessment; and (d) cost estimates.

The assessor also must be clear about his or her reporting obligations. He or she must forewarn the subject of the assessment of such possibilities as legal obligations to report child abuse or the abuse of a vulnerable adult, or anything else required by state statute, licensure regulations, or professional ethics.

We emphasize that we tend to err on the side of the protection of clients; consequently, if any question arises we or the board or employer or training program is likely to opt for a conservative alternative.

To repeat an earlier caution, keep in mind that discipline or punishment are separate matters and will have little to do with the findings of the assessment. Even if the assessment determines that the practitioner can be rehabilitated, he or she still may be deprived of the license to practice or of employment. Furthermore, in cases of multiple offenses, the therapists should clearly understand from the beginning that they are likely to lose their licenses. This is in order to prevent their fantasies that the assessment is a way to avoid discipline.

If the subject is paying to be assessed he or she should be cautioned that even if it does not turn out as hoped the findings probably cannot be suppressed. The most he or she can hope to gain from the assessment is a well-designed rehabilitation plan with, in some cases, a greater likelihood that he or she can re-enter the profession if the plan is successful.

PREPARATION FOR THE ASSESSMENT

Releases must be obtained to permit many different items to be examined and a number of individuals to be interviewed. The subject of the assessment must agree to hold the assessor blameless for any damage done by the data gathering (see Appendix E). The following data (among others) are necessary for the assessment:

1. Transcripts and/or videotapes of all depositions or testimony.

2. Written and verbal accounts of information collected during any previous investigation. (Under certain circumstances it may be necessary to interview the complainants.)

3. Results of past diagnostic studies of the therapist, including protocols of psychological tests.

4. Information from past or current therapists from whom the subject of the assessment may have sought help.

5. Information from past and current supervisors and colleagues who have knowledge of the subject's work (usually obtained via interviews).

6. Interview data from the therapist:

   a. Professional training and supervision; practice history, usually reviewed with the therapist's resume.

   b. Therapist's explanation for the activities in question.

   c. Data relevant to assessing the subject's emotional adjustment.

PSYCHOLOGICAL TESTING

It was noted earlier that psychological testing can be done by the principal assessor or by another professional. In fact, consultation with another psychologist on the test results is often quite useful.

The subject must be questioned about his or her familiarity with the various tests proposed for use. If she or he is skilled in the administration of a particular test or very knowledgeable about it, then the assessor should be alert for signs of deception. Bear in mind that a practitioner may try to look either good or bad. Showing some depression, for example, may be calculated to elicit sympathy or to cover up a personality disorder.

Furthermore, sometimes therapists have misleading notions of how a test is scored; such notions need to be addressed before the testing. Most common are inaccurate beliefs about the Rorschach by persons who are not trained in its use (e.g., "seeing anything other than the whole blot as something is indicative of schizophrenia").

A number of subjects have produced highly defensive invalid MMPIs. When they were asked to retake them with a mind-set of more openness and less defensiveness, however, they produced valid profiles. With the Rorschach it is important to try to get enough responses (e.g., at least 3 to 5 per card). Again, this has not been a problem for us. We use the TAT only occasionally, but when we do we insist on sufficiently detailed responses.

Like other types of assessments, psychological testing must be viewed in the context of other data. It should be made clear to the people who request the assessment that no test can rule in or rule out psychopathology in and of itself; therefore, tests should be used only in conjunction with other data.

ISSUES ADDRESSED BY THE MODEL

The issues addressed in the assessment are as follows:

1. exact description of the offense(s); information on other offenses or misconduct;

2. personal adjustment; presence or absence of psychopathology;

3. practice style; clarity about professional boundaries;

4. practice setting; nature of any supervision;

5. nature of clientele served; nature of clients with whom therapist has boundary problems; and

6. miscellaneous special, or situational factors, such as events in the therapist's life.

ISSUE 1: EXACT DESCRIPTION OF THE OFFENSES

At times an accurate description is one of the most difficult items to acquire. It is usually obtained from letters of complaint, reports of investigators, transcripts and videotapes of depositions and testimony, and from the information given by the therapist. In some instances, however, a direct interview with the complainant is essential.

Testimony often may be lacking in detail, and sometimes critical details are left out inexplicably. In one case, for example, the complainant's attorney did a poor job in a civil suit by failing to elicit some damaging data from the client. At other times, the therapist or his or her attorney may withhold data. In one instance a board withheld data because they did not want to let the defense know they had certain information.

Unfortunately, adversary proceedings rarely produce clear pictures of events. It is easier, for this reason, to assess some employment and training program-related situations because then one can sit client and therapist down in the same room and obtain greater clarity (see Ch. 28 on "Processing Sessions").

Going beyond specific offenses, it is critical to understand the context and, in particular, the sequence of behaviors that preceded the sexual contact.

ISSUE 2: PERSONAL ADJUSTMENT OF THE THERAPIST

Earlier in this chapter five broad diagnostic groups were discussed: (a) healthy or mildly neurotic; (b) neurotic/isolated; (c) character disorders; (d) sociopaths and narcissistic character disorders; and (e) psychotics and borderline personalities. Acute distress, marital problems, or other difficulties also may have played a role in the sexual exploitation.

The personal adjustment of the therapist is assessed through past and current psychological testing, information from past or current therapists, interviews with the practitioner, and with professionals familiar with his or her work, and, at times, interviews with a spouse or significant other.

It is important to note here that personal problems unrelated to the offenses charged may be discovered. To the degree that they imply possible impairment of the professional practice they should be addressed in the final report. It is also important to note distress related to the disciplinary proceedings. In a number of our assessments the practitioner's anxiety or depression needed to be addressed if and when they returned to practice.

ISSUE 3: PRACTICE STYLE

The description of the offenses usually raises some initial questions about practice style. This information can be obtained through interviews with the therapist and his or her colleagues. The major area of inquiry relates to professional boundaries: To what degree does the practitioner understand them conceptually? To what degree does he or she maintain them? Some paraprofessionals or poorly trained professionals seem unable to distinguish personal from professional relationships. Furthermore, some therapists have self-serving or ill-advised beliefs about the amount of physical contact that is allowed in therapy relationships.

The use of touch in the therapy practiced by the subject of the evaluation should be examined in connection with the boundary breakdowns. Self-disclosure by the therapist is another frequent source of problem: either in terms of what is disclosed (e.g., its lack of relevance to the client's problems) or in the amount of time spent discussing the therapist's life.

It is important to determine if the therapy in question has a clear therapeutic contract or is process oriented. Does it aim at fostering independence? or is it designed to be long term or even lifelong? Also quite common in situations where therapist-client sex occurs is sloppy diagnostic work.

Last, the assessor must examine how the therapist's personal problems or style of adjustment may have led her or him to develop a therapeutic method that appears to have a theoretical rationalization. Gonsiorek (1987) and Chapter 33 provide useful discussions of the linkage between personal problems and therapeutic approach.

ISSUE 4: PRACTICE SETTING

Are all the services delivered in a professional setting or are there home visits or encounters outside the office? What does the professional office itself look like? How intimate and informal is it? What sort of seating arrangement is provided?

If the setting is private practice, does the therapist have a supervisor or consultant? If so, what is the nature of their arrangement and which cases are discussed? If the practice includes partners, what is the interrelationship, and what are the styles and reputations of the other practitioners?

If the setting is a clinic, agency, or other program, what standards are set for physical or social contact with clients? Are the policies written? How are complaints dealt with? What is the organization's history of sexual complaints?

Sexual exploitation can occur even in very professional settings where it is absolutely forbidden. Nevertheless, the practice setting can contribute to exploitation in a variety of ways.

ISSUE 5: NATURE OF CLIENTELE

Background data on the complaint and interviews with the therapist and, perhaps, his or her colleagues are needed to clarify both the nature of the general clientele the therapist works with and the characteristics of the victim(s). When there is more than one victim it is useful to look for common traits among them.

Although physical appearance sometimes plays a role in the sexual encounters, usually the personality or nature of the client's problem is the common issue. For example, some therapists become overly involved with victims; they bend rules and boundaries to be of help and easily lose their professional perspective. Ironically, although they may set out to do better than previous helpers or to make up for past abuses suffered by the client, they may end up sexually involved themselves, thereby repeating the victimization.

ISSUE 6: MISCELLANEOUS SITUATIONAL FACTORS

Usually, we look for situational variables which may help explain an incident of sexual exploitation. Career changes, marital problems, and the like often are given as explanations or excuses. It is important to determine whether such variables are in fact key elements in what happened. Obviously, many therapists go through divorces or are reminded of someone significant in their lives by a client without having sex with the client. Nevertheless, sometimes there is some unique factor that plays a role. For example, does the client resemble anyone in the therapist's family? Do the therapist and client have life experiences or problems in common? Did some chance social encounter set the stage for the involvement? At times, however, situational factors are not at all relevant.

THE HYPOTHESIS OR FORMULATION

Normally, data are collected until there emerges a hypothesis on why the sexual exploitation occurred. If the evaluator feels "stuck" and has not come up with an explanation, it is worthwhile trying to elicit additional information from the subject by informing her or him that if an explanation is not forthcoming rehabilitation planning cannot begin.

The hypothesis, once it is formulated, can be discussed with colleagues acting as consultants, with the subject, and with other parties in the case. The hypothesis must be presented simply as a tentative explanation and not as an excuse. Some examples of hypotheses follow:

Therapist W: Single client complained, and therapist when confronted seemed upset, confessed, denied there were any others, and promised full cooperation. By chance another victim was discovered, and it became clear that he'd only confessed to what he'd guessed was already known. It turns out that he has victimized others. Hypothesis: He's an exploiter—probably an anti-social personality disorder—rehab. not possible.

Therapist X: Single client complained of seductive behavior and excessive touching. Review suggested a combination of inexperience and a background as an advocate, plus not enough supervision, set the stage. He was remorseful. <u>Hypothesis</u>: Personal style, lack of training were key issues—rehab. possible.

<u>Therapist Y</u>: Single client complained, but there may have been another incident during training. Marital problems and a pattern of isolation with overwork played a role. He and client became infatuated, got involved, considered marriage, and then broke off the relationship. <u>Hypothesis</u>: Neurotic-isolated with severe situational stress and vulnerability—rehab. possible.

<u>Therapist Z</u>: A number of complaints about a psychotherapy cult with poor boundaries between therapist and numerous clients. Only one brief sexual encounter with a male client, but periodic erotic touching of female clients. <u>Hypothesis</u>: Borderline personality disorder with a lack of ability to think in terms of professional ethics—rehab. not possible.

II. REHABILITATION PLAN

With the exception of reports by, for example, Gonsiorek (1987), Schoener and Gonsiorek (1988), and Schoener (1986a), the professional literature to date contains little if any discussion of the issues related to the rehabilitation of a therapist who has sexually exploited clients. Even conceptual discussions of rehabilitation are lacking.

Hall (1986) noted that members of psychology licensure boards in some states favor a rehabilitation approach because psychologists "that lose their licenses may practice under another title, without being subject to a professional conduct code and thus might cause more public harm" (p. 295). A professional society, she went on, may take the same stance, sanctioning the practitioner and requiring some sort of rehabilitation, rather than expulsion. Her observation is consistent with Brodsky's (1986) contention that "Rehabilitation as it is sometimes now practiced serves more as a minor form of punishment, perhaps to expiate the guilt of the offending therapist and, maybe even more, of the sanctioning committee or court" (p. 164).

Other descriptions in the literature of how such complaints are adjudicated by psychology licensure boards (see Sinnett & Linford, 1982) and by psychiatrists (see Stone, 1976) do not describe rehabilitation plans that are based on formal assessments. In a description of the handling of a case by a board, Plaut and Foster (1986) reported on a therapist who had abused several clients; he lost his license for a year and was referred for therapy and supervision; and he agreed to some limitation on his case load. However, no mention is made of a prior assessment nor is the remedy characterized formally as a rehabilitation plan, although it may have been intended as such. Brodsky (1986) discussed a failed rehabilitation during which the therapist allegedly abused a client while under supervision and on probation.

The literature on impaired practitioners focuses almost exclusively on impairment stemming from drug and alcohol abuse and dependency. In one noteworthy exception Brodsky (1986) discussed issues in the rehabilitation of sexually exploitative therapists and raised a number of key questions relating to how one goes about prescribing therapy, re-education, and supervision. Other than our own work, the literature is devoid of models (e.g., Schwebel, Skorina, & Schoener, 1988).

When the literature deals with impairment in trainees and students, it is starkly silent on sexual exploitation. According to Dr. Carol Nadelson, former president of the American Psychiatric Association, "Interventions during the course of medical school and residency training really haven't been adequate to date." Furthermore, "educators for the most part tend to have negative attitudes about emotional problems" (Robertson, 1980, p. 124). In a recent article ("Confronting Professional Impairment During the Internship: Identification, Due Process, and Remediation") by Lamb et al. (1987), scant mention was made of sexual involvement with clients; instead the focus was on procedures that assure due process rather than support rehabilitation strategies. However, Vasquez (1988) recommends our assessment methodology for use with trainees who have had sexual contact with a client.

Sanderson (1989a) suggested that training programs follow the same policies and procedures that are recommended to employers by the Minnesota Task Force on Sexual Exploitation by Counselors and Psychotherapists; they include clear statements on how to evaluate complaints in an employment setting (e.g., Millilo, Shultz, & Couchman, 1989). Save this one contribution the literature lacks discussions of assessment and of setting up rehabilitation plans for employees, although some papers mention the role of the employer (e.g., Plaut & Foster, 1986; Pope & Bouhoutsos, 1986; White, 1986).

From our experience as consultants and expert witnesses, we are led to conclude, consistent with the literature, that many licensure boards, ethics committees, training programs, and employers are deficient in the following:

1. They have no clear procedure for obtaining an independent assessment of a professional or trainee who has had sexual contact with a client.

2. They have no protocol for what should be included in such an assessment.

3. They have no concept of what comprises a rehabilitation plan or how one decides whether rehabilitation is possible.

4. They do not clearly separate punishment consequences from rehabilitation.

5. They have no methodology for re-evaluating a practitioner or trainee who has been rehabilitated or who applies for reinstatement.

6. They do not understand that referrals for psychotherapy and/or supervision should be made prior to comprehensive assessments that are aimed at determining whether these or other interventions have a potential for success.

Beyond the limitations of supervision (discussed in Ch. 34) and Brodsky's (1986) excellent questions on the use of supervision, the literature on outcomes in psychotherapy scarcely argue for its effectiveness as a reliable cure-all. Colleagues who treat psychotherapists that voluntarily seek help have noted, "Although most clinicians probably fall in the 'normal neurotic' range, our ranks also include schizophrenics, borderline, and psychopathic personalities" (Greenberg & Kaslow, 1984). Furthermore, when experienced therapists seek therapy for themselves and hand-pick the provider, a substantial percentage report subsequently that the therapy was not helpful or was actually harmful (Grunebaum, 1986). On the other hand, colleagues experienced in treating therapists who have sexually exploited clients report that these therapists are not easily treated (Gonsiorek, 1987).

Simply stated, our position is that an assessment always should come first, and ideally should be conducted by a party independent of whomever requested the assessment. Licensure boards should evaluate, and give final approval to, a proposed rehabilitation plan only when it has been developed by a skilled external assessor who has conducted the formal assessment.

FORMULATING THE PLAN

The rehabilitation plan should derive from the hypothesis as to why the misconduct occurred. As Figure 1 illustrates, one option is that rehabilitation is not possible. When on occasion, a board or employer requests a rehabilitation plan although our data suggest that rehabilitation is not possible, we uniformly refuse to offer suggestions for treatment unless we have reason to believe that the treatment might work. Even when a board does not feel it has sufficient evidence to sustain a revocation of a license or an employer does not feel he or she can fire the individual, we still refuse to make suggestions if we regard treatment as unworkable.

In rehabilitation plans, setting outcome goals or ways of monitoring and evaluating each aspect of the plan are more feasible than trying to specify an arbitrary time period for the completion of different goals. When a board or ethics committee, for example, suspends a professional for a given period of time, the act should be regarded as a punishment response and not as the period in which rehabilitation is likely to occur.

Some common elements of rehabilitation plans follow:

1. Personal Psychotherapy: Even more important than picking a therapist from a list of approved therapists, perhaps, is defining the purposes of the therapy. What are the goals of this part of the rehabilitation plan? As well as the usual periodic reports to the disciplinary body, we recommend a contract whereby the therapist has both the duty and the right to inform that body if and when the subject exhibits sufficient impairment to place clients at risk.

2. Treatment for Alcoholism or Drug Abuse: Standard methods for monitoring compliance and outcome should be used, including urine screens when they are appropriate.

3. Practice Limitations: Limitations can be either temporary or permanent. They can vary from a prohibition on ever practicing as a therapist again to a prohibition against working with certain types of clients (e.g., women). Practice limitations, of course, only work in settings where they can be monitored.

4. Supervision: This subject is discussed at length in Chapters 34 & 35). The plan should be very specific about what will be reviewed by whom and to what ends. Again, as with personal therapy, we recommend a contract whereby the supervisor can inform the board immediately if the plan does not seem to be working.

5. Further Education or Training: This option is advisable only in the case of an inexperienced and undertrained therapist. We are dubious of the value of requiring enrollment in an ethics course, as a sole intervention, but sometimes substantive courses in basic therapy skills have an effect.

6. Change in Therapy Style: Requiring a change in style is practical only in situations where compliance can be monitored. The common change required is that a therapist not hug clients, or engage in therapies involving physical touch. We emphasize that therapists who have been disciplined must practice according to a very conservative style.

7. Vocational Counseling: A shift within or out of the field may be recommended during or after the counseling. Some plans restrict a practitioner to teaching, evaluation, or other non-therapy work. In other cases leaving the field entirely is considered the best solution. Care must be taken to try to foresee risks should the practitioner enter related fields. For example, if a psychiatrist can no longer practice psychiatry, can he or she retrain for some other area of medicine?

8. Organizational Changes: Particularly in the case of paraprofessionals and young or undertrained professionals, organizational problems may have played a role and require correction. Training, clearer policies, better standards can all help. At other times the subject must leave the current practice setting for one with more or better supervision. If a program or clinic is headed by a guru who teaches a style of practice that is fraught with risks, the subject obviously should move to a different setting.

RE-ENTRY INTO THE FIELD OR ENDING PROBATION

Figure 1 indicates that the final step in the process is an assessment of whether the practitioner is ready to resume professional work. The decision should be based not just on compliance with the rehabilitation plan but, also, on evidence that the plan was successful. The two important questions that must be answered are, to what degree were the goals of each aspect of the plan met? what evidence is there of change? Some examples follow:

CASE 1: A therapist had what was believed to be a single romantic/sexual involvement with a client a number of years earlier. Otherwise he had an excellent reputation. The matter had come to the attention of his employer but was not made the subject of a board action or civil suit; an apology had been given to the client and some compensation paid privately, by the practitioner. The assessment ascertained that some very idiosyncratic factors had contributed to the behavior; for example, the timing in the lives of both participants and the practice style employed by the therapist at the time.

Rehabilitation Plan: Although the practitioner seemed to show proper remorse and good insight to many aspects of the situation, it was decided that additional exploration of the personal dynamics of the involvement were in order. His practice setting and style had already changed dramatically from a long-term intensive approach to a short term, more goal-oriented approach, and his practice was now in a clinic. Individual therapy was the only initial recommendation, consequently.

Outcome: The therapy did generate some additional insight for the therapist to the dynamics of his involvement with the client. It also revealed some personal and marital issues that needed to be addressed. His wife participated in several sessions and helped to set up some goals for their relationship.

Re-Entry: The therapist never actually left the field; it was deemed best for him to practice under peer supervision in his current clinical setting.

CASE 2: This therapist had been reported by the client for involvement in an on-going romantic relationship a short time after the relationship ended. The therapist freely admitted to the relationship but thought that because it was "true love" it was not unethical. No other involvements were known or had been reported. This therapist employed a treatment modality that was psychologically intrusive and involved considerable touch. The therapist earlier had been apprenticed to the originator of this treatment approach and had strong convictions about its efficacy.

The licensure board, without benefit of any outside assessment, prescribed the following rehabilitation plan:

1. A prohibition against the use of the particular treatment approach.

2. Case supervision for a limited time period.

3. Individual psychotherapy; the duration was given a time limit for no apparent reason.

Outcome: The treating therapist was alarmed at the lack of an outside assessment and the seemingly capricious time limit placed on the therapy. He requested that the specifications on the therapy be dropped, but the board refused the request. The treating therapist, with the cooperation of the therapist/perpetrator, made an assessment. The results suggested poor boundaries in a professionally isolated, naive, rigid, and emotionally constricted individual who had both neurotic and narcissistic problems.

The treating therapist, believing that rehabilitation was a possibility, began treatment. The psychotherapy progressed but the original time period required by the board expired. The treating therapist and case supervisor discussed the fact that the therapist continued to justify the now prohibited, intrusive treatment modality. Although he no longer employed it, he still did not seem to understand what had been wrong with it. This led to some confrontation of the therapist/perpetrator and, eventually, to some breakthroughs in therapy. The therapist/perpetrator agreed that the therapy was not complete.

Despite petitions from the persons involved, the board would not stipulate open-ended therapy; nevertheless it allowed an extension of time. Fortunately, the perpetrator decided to continue therapy on his own. The board declared that he had met their condition although neither the perpetrator nor the treating therapist thought that the therapy had been successfully completed.

Re-Entry: Full reinstatement of the license by the board occurred over the objections of the treating therapist and before rehabilitation was completed. Fortunately, the perpetrator voluntarily continued both personal psychotherapy and case supervision until, 10 months later, the treating therapist and supervisor felt that rehabilitation was completed.

CASE 3: The therapist in this case had been reported for sexual contact with a number of clients, almost all of whom he had seen more than 10 years ago. The contact included excessive hugging, kissing, and some touching of breasts and genitals. It was clear that the therapist had previously used a "touchy-feely" style of therapy which he learned during the 1960s. Some elements of this style were still present in his practice; one client complaint was quite recent. The assessment was inconclusive. It raised the possibility of a personality disorder but also noted that the behavior could be explained by poor training and a lack of understanding of both his needs and professional boundaries.

Rehabilitation Plan: The therapist was put on probation and required to do the following:

1. Individual Psychotherapy: Aimed at dealing with some problems identified during the assessment, such as lack of awareness of some personal needs.

2. Case Supervision: Aimed at improving professional boundaries as well as sensitivity to client feedback.

3. Ethics Coursework: Aimed at providing a better conceptual basis for ethical decision making.

Outcome:

1. Therapist actively participated in personal therapy and made some gains; it became clear, however, that he did have a personality disorder that would significantly limit him as a therapist.

2. His participation in supervision was good but he still did not develop much of an ability to function independently after a year.

3. No suitable ethics course was available but individualized instruction was completed; the therapist did quite well and developed a conceptual understanding of ethical principles.

Re-Entry: It was decided that the individual could not engage in solo private practice. He resisted other options and left the field.

CASE 3a: The initial facts of the case, the evaluation results, and the rehabilitation plan are virtually identical with those of Case 3. The outcome and re-entry, however, were as follows:

Outcome:

1. Personal therapy, after some initial power struggles with the therapist, went well. Although self-centered, the therapist did not appear to have a personality disorder. His denial of the role his personal needs had played in his work with clients broke down and he developed some insight as well as what appeared to be a sincere motivation to change his practice.

2. Although at first he resisted case supervision, after initial power struggles with the supervisor he seemed to take responsibility to review his work and his style seriously, and thus he gained from the supervision.

Re-Entry: As with Case 3, it was decided, despite his obvious gains, that he could not engage in solo private practice. He joined a clinic that had good internal discussion of clinical work. (When he applied to join the group, there was full disclosure of his past practice problems and a discussion with his case supervisor on how his new colleagues might identify future practice problems.)

Note on Cases 3 and 3a: The initial assessments or initial reactions to the rehabilitation plans would not have predicted these outcomes, underlining the importance of a final, separate review of progress.

CASE 4: The therapist in this case had sexual contact with several clients, all somewhat recent, which included sexual intercourse. The assessment suggested that the sexual conduct was part of a repetitive pattern, even though only two victims had come forward. However, it was not clear whether the problem was a personality disorder or some sort of neurosis. Prognosis was guarded; rehabilitation, however, was still deemed theoretically possible by the board. The assessor suggested extreme caution.

Rehabilitation Plan: The practitioner's license was suspended pending the outcome of therapy and it was stipulated that if he did get his license back there would be restrictions on his practice; if steps 1 and 2 were completed, he would have to reapply for a limited license. The plan included,

1. Individual psychotherapy;

2. Completion of a sex offender treatment program: Once this step was completed, and pending a favorable recommendation from his therapist, he could reapply for a conditional license; and then,

3. Be prohibited from seeing women clients; and

4. Have on-going case supervision.

Outcome:

1. After 8 months of psychotherapy, and a decision that the only available sex offender treatment program was inappropriate for his needs (probably an accurate assessment), the practitioner tried to obtain assurances that he would get his license back.

2. Failing to get any such reassurance, the practitioner decided to leave the field voluntarily and surrendered his license.

FOLLOW-UP AND EVALUATION

Follow-up and evaluation research should be conducted by all the groups who participate in setting up rehabilitation plans. At present, outcome data are lacking. If an empirical basis is to be created for the rehabilitation potential, then the collection of follow-up and evaluation data is essential

Gartrell, Herman, Olarte, Feldstein, and Localio (1988), in a recent review of this model of assessment and rehabilitation, noted the current lack of outcome data. They also expressed concern with the lack of information on "the efficacy or cost-benefit ratios of the various rehabilitation efforts recommended" (p. 1073).

Thus far, although our follow-up data are limited, no individual whom we assessed to be rehabilitated through our model has been the subject of additional complaints or charges. In a number of instances in which formal assessments were not done and a "rehabilitation plan" was devised by other means, perpetrators have been reported for subsequent offenses, however. In many of these instances the individual was not a likely candidate for rehabilitation in the first place, and the "rehabilitation" was a weak form of punishment. In others, far too much reliance was placed on psychotherapy as a "cure all" and on supervision of whatever sort (see Chs. 34 and 35 for pitfalls) as a safety net.

It is possible in the future that some liability will accrue to licensure boards and others for failures to obtain competent outside assessments and to develop sound rehabilitation plans for offenders. Pope (in press) noted:

It may be that the elimination of bogus rehabilitation efforts and the overly hasty granting of "rehabilitated" status to offending therapists will `be facilitated by malpractice suits filed against those who are less than adequately professional, careful, thorough, and knowledgeable in assessing and rehabilitating offending therapists. (pp. 193-94)

CHAPTER 33

WORKING THERAPEUTICALLY WITH THERAPISTS WHO HAVE BECOME SEXUALLY INVOLVED WITH CLIENTS

John C. Gonsiorek

A number of considerations and issues in the provision of psychotherapy to psychotherapists who have become sexually involved with their clients are described in this chapter. The material, it should be noted, applies only to a subset of such therapists. Using the breakdown of therapist types suggested by Schoener & Gonsiorek (see Ch. 32), almost all the therapist-perpetrators whose treatment is described here fall into the neurotic categories: "mildly neurotic" individuals (isolated exploitation related to situational variables; true remorse of perpetrator) and "neurotic isolated" individuals (overly involved in work and clients; longstanding emotional problems; personally isolated outside of work setting). Some mention is made of other therapist-perpetrator types but only to illustrate certain issues. I do not suggest that my model is necessarily applicable to persons other than neurotic therapist-perpetrator types. The length of treatment in the model varies from 10 to about 30 months.

Another caution: the information on this subject is still tentative at this time. One of the most regrettable and pernicious recent developments in this area has been the emergence of dogmatic, premature, and simplistic guidelines for the assessment and treatment of therapists who sexually exploit clients. They include assuming or asserting that therapist-perpetrators constitute a monolithic group; that certain types of treatment programs or strategies should be required in all cases (e.g., sex offender treatment programs); or the development of understanding or treatment plans based primarily on analogy (e.g., "therapist-perpetrators are just like incest perpetrators").

These views are inappropriate and, in fact, irresponsible on a number of counts. Knowledge about therapist-perpetrators still is in a formative stage; and dogmatic views assert a level of certainty that simply does not exist. Further, acceptable standards of care dictate that individualized assessments and treatment plans be formulated for each client, especially when the individual's problems are incompletely understood.

The content presented here is based on the treatment of about 20 cases and should be viewed as a set of working hypotheses, not final recommendations. I hope that my work will encourage and structure further efforts in the area and will foster a questioning, critical attitude.

PUNISHMENT VERSUS REHABILITATION

The treatment of therapist-perpetrators does not go on in a vacuum. Responses of law enforcement and professional bodies, such as licensing boards and professional ethics committees, either can assist or hinder successful treatment. For example, such bodies may, without careful and independent evaluation, prescribe treatment in such detail that the treating therapist is unable to tailor the treatment plan to the individual; or they may allow the therapist-perpetrator too much leeway in determining his or her own treatment. How then should professional ethics and licensing boards respond to therapists who sexually exploit their clients? I offer some recommendations and the rationale for them in the rest of this section.

The issues of rehabilitation and punishment must be clearly differentiated in dealing with sexually exploitative therapists. Specifically, I recommend two sets of consequences for sexual activity with clients: The first is in the domain of criminal law and uses criminal sanctions; the second is in the area of administrative law and involves the actions of licensing boards or certifying bodies, that is, temporary or permanent suspensions of the perpetrating therapist's license or certification, (or a court order prohibiting practice if the individuals are unlicensed). Further, I suggest that the term of the license suspension be based solely on the severity of the offending behavior. Issues of rehabilitation should not enter into this determination.

I recommend further that this administrative response by licensing boards be uniform and determined by a formula. For example, the boards may set up three or four different levels of temporary or permanent suspension, based on the nature of the offending behaviors. This formula should be used consistently by all licensing boards in a given state. Decisions about prognosis and treatability can be made after this administrative law determination for only those individuals who receive a temporary suspension of their licenses. Individuals whose licenses are permanently suspended (i.e., revoked) may seek psychotherapy for their own understanding and personal resolution of issues, but evaluation relating to the possible continuation of practice is irrelevant.

The rationale for the preceding recommendations is as follows: If sexual exploitation of clients by therapists is to be taken seriously by mental health professions and the public, it is important to establish that certain kinds of exploitation are regarded seriously, and they warrant a serious response, regardless of the motives or psychological status of the perpetrating therapist. This is the same attitude that is taken toward other serious transgressions against society, such as rape and incest. The suggested development of a formula for licensing board responses insures consistency of outcome for all parties and justice for the therapist-perpetrator. Often, an unacceptable level of variability is observed in the responses of licensing boards which stem from sources other than the behavior of the therapist-perpetrator, such as the current composition of the board; publicity about a board's handling of other recent cases; whether the client is the same or opposite sex as the therapist-perpetrators, and the like.

The evaluating or treating therapist must assiduously avoid requests from licensing bodies to help to determine the punishment that is appropriate in a given case. Such requests place the evaluating or treating therapist in an untenable dual relationship with the therapist-perpetrator; it not only compromises the work of the therapist with a therapist-perpetrator but, also, raises serious ethical issues in its own right. It is also unjust to the therapist-perpetrator who is then judged, not only on the offending behavior but on considerably more vague, psychological grounds also.

On the other hand, the evaluating and treating therapists may play a role in the deliberations of licensing bodies, such as helping to determine the appropriate treatment plan for an individual for whom they already had prescribed a temporary suspension. It is important that the evaluating therapist never guarantee therapeutic outcome because the information currently available is inadequate for a prognosis.

Toward the end of therapy, the treating therapist also can help the board to determine the circumstances under which the therapist-perpetrator may re-enter the profession. Although specific prognostic predictions are not appropriate, it is reasonable for the treating therapist to give some indication of the therapist-perpetrator's limitations and vulnerabilities; progress towards therapeutic goals; and how to structure re-entry to optimize her/his chances of successful readjustment for the therapist-perpetrator and to minimize the chances of further exploitation of clients.

It is confusing, inappropriate, and probably unethical for boards to prescribe treatment without the benefit of an outside evaluation. To do so places a board in a dual relationship with the therapist-perpetrator because it cannot take on a therapeutic role at the same time it is acting judgmentally and administering punishment; nor can it develop the most efficacious treatment plan for a perpetrating therapist while it is trying to protect the best interests of the public.

The intent of the foregoing recommendations is to clarify the distinction between punishment and rehabilitation and to provide justice for all parties by reducing the likelihood of unpredictable or arbitrary decisions by licensing boards.

Finally, I suggest that a licensing board's decision to suspend a license on a temporary basis not be viewed as a guarantee that the license will be reinstated. An evaluating therapist has the option to recommend against reinstatement as the result of the evaluation. The treating therapist also has the option of opposing reinstatement as a result of the treatment experience. Thus a board is obligated to weigh the interests of the public versus those of the licensee as it integrates information from the diverse sources.

ASSESSMENT

Although details of an assessment are described in Chapter 32, additional points deserve emphasis here.

There is no inherent problem in the evaluating therapist's becoming the treating therapist if such a move is agreeable to everyone involved. The transition from one role to another, however, may be tricky and even contraindicated in certain situations. Thus the idea always requires careful appraisal.

It must be very clear from the outset that the recommendations following evaluation and treatment are completely separate from the treatment process. When the evaluation is complete both evaluator and therapist-perpetrator have the option of discontinuing the relationship. The therapist-perpetrator may not like the result of the evaluation and, therefore, may not want to be treated by the evaluator. On the other hand, the evaluating therapist may not wish to treat the subject of the evaluation because of a personal antipathy.

The ability to be simultaneously respectful of yet detached from the final outcome and recommendations is an essential quality of the evaluating therapist. He or she must give the therapist-perpetrator two clear and consistent messages: that the therapist-perpetrator will be afforded the respect due any client; and that the unethical behavior is wrong, regardless of whatever extenuating circumstances the therapist-perpetrator may claim. Evaluating therapists must make no guarantees about their ultimate recommendations or about how these recommendations may be received by the licensing board.

The core issue is that the therapist-perpetrator has treated a client abusively. In a misguided attempt to show how improper their unethical behavior was, some evaluating therapists may become overtly or covertly abusive to the therapist-perpetrator. However, the situation is hopelessly compromised if the evaluating therapist treats the therapist-perpetrator abusively.

A consistently respectful stance enhances the evaluation. It is not unusual for therapist-perpetrators who are character disordered (rather than neurotic) to view a respectful stance as an opening for manipulation. They may begin to play out their sociopathic schemes in an increasingly transparent manner. If it happens, the evaluating therapist can understand more accurately how the particular therapist-perpetrator is best categorized.

By not imposing judgment on the therapist-perpetrator, the evaluating therapist maintains maximum flexibility and objectivity. Further, this respectful yet firm stance sets the stage for certain kinds of reactions from the neurotic therapist-perpetrators which are helpful in later stages of their therapy (see section, "Middle Phase of Therapy").

I recommend that the evaluating therapist suspend judgment on the therapist-perpetrator in initial contacts and avoid drawing conclusions until the evaluation is complete. It is not unusual for some neurotic therapist-perpetrators to appear to be suspicious, evasive, and defensive because of advice from their attorneys, distrust of the legal system, or fear. More character-disordered therapist-perpetrators may present themselves in the same manner. The maintenance of a firm ethical stance by the evaluating therapist is very important in such situations. Character-disordered therapist perpetrators often will terminate the evaluation when they understand that the evaluating therapist will not attenuate his or her ethical stance, whereas neurotic therapist-perpetrators are less likely to do so. Professionals who are personally uncomfortable with the prolonged period of ambiguity such an evaluation requires, probably should not serve as evaluators of therapist-perpetrators.

An essential step when the evaluation is completed is for the evaluating therapist to go over the evaluation in detail with the therapist-perpetrator and to ask him or her to carefully consider the recommendations. It may take more than one session for the therapist-perpetrator to absorb the information presented. Frequently, the therapist-perpetrator is panicked or under legal pressure to follow through on the recommendations and may try to do so, consequently, without giving them sufficient consideration. Commonly, therapist-perpetrators desperately seek some sense of direction and, hence, may leap at any clearly formulated treatment plan without actually agreeing with it. In these situations, a time delay of a few weeks is useful to permit the therapist-perpetrator to fully consider the evaluation and the treatment plan.

AGREEMENT WITH THE TREATMENT PLAN

After the assessment, treatment cannot occur unless the treating therapist and therapist-perpetrator agree on the basis of the treatment plan. If the therapist-perpetrator does not agree that unethical behaviors occurred and that these constitute a serious problem, the rationale for initiating treatment is lacking. Without the agreement, it is hard to imagine what therapeutic investment the therapist-perpetrator can have in the treatment process. Further, without agreement, the treating therapist may be cast in the role of a police detective who must ascertain what did and did not occur. The treating therapist, consequently, is forced into a dual relationship that seriously compromises the therapy.

Agreement about the unethical behaviors need not be complete, however. For example, if a therapist admits to engaging in some of the unethical behavior which was reported by a client but not to all the alleged behaviors, the admission may be sufficient, provided the therapist-perpetrator does not in any manner deny that some of his or her behavior was unethical and a serious violation, and the admitted behaviors can serve as the basis for a viable treatment plan. If further revelations of unethical conduct are made, it is important that the therapist-perpetrator acknowledge their seriousness as well. It is important for the treating therapist to recognize that although therapist-perpetrators may not be entirely truthful at this phase, the treating therapist is in no position to make determinations on facts or events that are still obscure. Such determinations are not necessary for treatment to begin.

Ideally, the licensing board has acted upon the evaluator's recommendations before the beginning of treatment. Unfortunately, the backlog of cases that many licensing boards experience does not always permit such promptness. But if the therapist-perpetrator appears highly motivated to initiate the treatment and has a good understanding of and agreement with the treatment plan, or is in considerable psychological crisis, it may not be desirable to delay treatment until licensing-board action occurs. In these cases, the treating therapist ought to make it clear that the treatment plan may require substantial alteration at a later date to fit in with the requirements of the licensing board.

EARLY PHASE OF TREATMENT

This phase of treatment is typically unpredictable. Frequently, therapist-perpetrators are exposed to attention in the media or community forums for their behavior, and they may be in the midst of complex legal proceedings: facing hearings designed to fire them from their jobs; awaiting hearings before licensing boards or ethics committees; answering civil actions initiated by clients; and, in a handful of states, defending themselves against criminal charges. Indeed, they may be thrown into a period of crisis as the series of complex and often unpredictable legal situations develop. Most therapists are naive about the legal system, particularly about the distinctions of criminal, civil, and administrative law, any of which may impinge upon them when they face charges for exploiting clients. Also, many therapists do not understand the adversarial nature of the legal system, and so they personalize this aspect of the procedures.

The treating therapist must be genuinely supportive of therapist-perpetrators during this period of external stress and must direct them to appropriate resources to obtain fair legal representation. As a response to these stresses, the therapist-perpetrators may try to deny, minimize, or rationalize their unethical behavior and to retract early admissions of the innate unethical nature of their behavior. The crucial task of the treating therapist in this phase is to maintain a clear position on the unethical behaviors as, in fact, unethical, and at the same time to express understanding of the stressful nature of these events as well as respect for the therapist-perpetrator's right to legal representation. This situation is the first and, in some ways, the most important opportunity for the treating therapist to model appropriate professional boundaries under very difficult circumstances. If the treating therapist seriously violates professional boundaries, the therapy likely is lost.

This is not to say, however, that the treating therapist must maintain perfect behavior and judgment at all times. In a number of occasions I have temporarily erred by either being insensitive to the stresses or tolerant of denial or minimization, but then I caught myself, explained my perceptions to the therapist-perpetrator, and corrected my stance. This process enables the therapist-perpetrator to observe a treating therapist struggling to maintain an ethical posture and to sort through complex psychological and legal issues. At times this process also may be a very useful role model. Needless to say, the process is a harrowing experience for treating therapists who believe that they must be in control at all times. Such therapists probably ought not to treat therapist-perpetrators.

Typically, the early phase of treatment becomes less volatile when either some legal resolution has occurred or the therapist-perpetrator comes to understand the characteristics of the legal system and loses some of his or her anxiety. The latter is more likely because legal resolution frequently may take years. If new legal dilemmas arise during the course of therapy, as they well may, the therapist-perpetrator may be temporarily thrown back into the emotional turmoil of this early phase.

Given the crisis nature of the treatment in this early phase, its inherent difficulties are somewhat but not totally alleviated if the licensing board has not made an official response to the evaluation and treatment plan before the treatment has started. Much of the work in this initial phase centers on stabilizing the therapist-perpetrator and preparing him or her for further therapeutic work. The middle phase of therapy (see next section) is when most treatment actually occurs. Therefore, it is strongly recommended that a response be sought from the licensing board before the initiation of the middle phase. It probably would be unfair to the therapist-perpetrator to start the middle phase of a therapy that is not satisfactory to the licensing board.

MIDDLE PHASE OF THERAPY

After the therapist-perpetrator has adjusted somewhat to the legal turmoil in his or her life and tolerates the situational anxiety better, the therapy often enters a more intense exploratory phase in which the primary goals of the treatment are addressed. It is recommended that these goals minimally include a detailed understanding and therapeutic working through of (a) the recent and any past unethical behavior; (b) the effects of this unethical behavior upon the clients; (c) the personal history of the therapist-perpetrator; and (d) interrelating the three elements. No universal "psychology of the therapist-perpetrator" probably exists but some common themes may be identified.

The first theme, typically, is something in the therapist-perpetrator's history that has led to boundary problems. For example, there may be overt situations in which the therapist-perpetrator's own boundaries were violated (i.e., physical or sexual abuse); or situations in which her or his boundaries did not fully develop, as in severe emotional deprivation or a cold and emotionally unexpressive family background. In the latter situation, the therapist-perpetrator may have viewed this aspect of his or her history as a problem and have made an attempt to become more emotionally expressive. Often, however, there was no accompanying development of boundaries. Some sort of history of boundary violations or excessively rigid boundaries is common.

A second theme is insensitivity to power dynamics; this often is accompanied by self-esteem problems. Therapists strive to compensate for feelings of personal inadequacy but are insensitive to how powerful they have become. Particularly therapist-perpetrators often are insensitive to their power as therapists; they often are insecure and blind to how powerful is the role they have assumed with their clients. Then they may underestimate the effects of initially minor boundary violations upon the client and may rationalize the early stages of romantic behavior by believing that they are equalizing the relationships with the client through self-disclosure. In fact, such therapists remain very powerful in the eyes of the client.

Any number of other personality characteristics or historical circumstances may be involved in the offending behavior. While a therapist-perpetrator is developing an understanding of how his or her specific history is related to unethical behavior, the therapist-perpetrator in this phase of treatment must understand the immediate life circumstances that led to the expression of his or her vulnerability. The exploration of a variety of areas may require very broad therapy. Although such a diffuse focus may be very fruitful, the treating therapist must make certain that the therapeutic goals are clearly addressed as well.

A particularly crucial therapeutic task during this phase is for the therapist-perpetrator to understand the effect of his or her unethical behavior upon clients. It is not unusual for a therapist-perpetrator to be obtuse in his or her understanding during the early phase of therapy because of, perhaps, involvement in adversarial legal proceedings with former clients. However, the treating therapist should be alert to danger if this lack of sensitivity and empathy prevails and is entrenched during the middle phase of treatment. He or she may want to review the assessment because the therapist-perpetrator's insensitivity may indicate that the diagnosis was not accurate and that this particular therapist-perpetrator is more narcissistic than neurotic in personality structure and, therefore, may be chronically unable to clearly perceive the effect of his or her behavior on others. Therefore, the treatment plan may require revision. Furthermore, the therapist-perpetrator may spontaneously bring up examples of boundary problems, insensitivity to power, other instances of negative effect upon clients, and other issues specific to his or her history which have not been previously discussed. There may be other situations in which the therapist-perpetrator acted in abusive or unethical ways. Typically, he or she will begin to apply what has been learned in the therapy to other relationships and other situations. He or she may begin to see that the problems that led to the unethical behavior have been manifested in other ways; for example, in relationships with a spouse, significant other, children, or professional colleagues.

This phase of therapy is anything but smooth. Rather, it is typically a "two steps forward—one step backward" situation in which the therapist-perpetrators may deny the damaging effects of their behavior upon others. The treating therapist again will have to correct such misapprehensions. There is an on-going interplay between denial and distortion, on the one hand and, on the other, a realistic appraisal of one's effect on other people.

During this phase, interviews with spouses or significant others may be very useful to understand the manifestations of the therapist-perpetrators' problems in different areas. In addition, adjunctive group therapy may elucidate problems in the therapist-perpetrators' interpersonal styles. It can be especially helpful for therapist-perpetrators who remain insensitive to their own power or lacking in understanding of and empathy with the effect of their behavior upon others.

It is crucial to explore the therapist-perpetrator's cognitive understanding of therapeutic work during this period. Frequently, therapist-perpetrators distort their professional theoretical orientations. The distortions, ultimately, stem from their personal problems but are packaged often with plausible intellectual justifications. For example, therapists with a personal history of poor boundaries often gravitate toward highly intrusive and confrontational therapy styles. When questioned about the choice of style, they may offer a justification that sounds very reasonable but, on further exploration, may be based on an attempt to work through their own histories. In addition, therapist-perpetrators often distort their cognitive and theoretical understanding of a chosen therapy style, which then becomes another justification for unethical behavior. For example, a therapist using an intrusive or confrontational form of therapy may minimize or "forget" the contraindications and limitations of the technique. The tasks of this phase of therapy are not complete until a therapist-perpetrator's cognitive understanding of therapeutic work is fully explored and connections between the cognitive distortions and personality problems are made and resolved.

THE BOUNDARY BETWEEN THE TREATING THERAPIST AND THE THERAPIST-PERPETRATOR

A number of reasons indicate the importance of a treating therapist's examination of the boundary between him or herself and a therapist-perpetrator. Attention to this boundary serves a role modeling function for the therapist-perpetrator; other reasons are more directly therapeutic, however. Frequently, therapist-perpetrators have been very lonely much of their lives and have covered up this loneliness with intellectualized defenses. They often (as mentioned earlier) have self-esteem problems. Their ethical violations and subsequent treatment may represent a situation in which they allowed themselves to be more vulnerable to other persons (i.e., the treating therapist) than they have ever been. If the treating therapist has done a good job of maintaining the essential firm and respectful stance (described previously), he or she is likely to take on a very powerful position vis-`a-vis the perpetrator. Frequently, the therapist-perpetrator may begin to idealize the treating therapist. There is a danger, however, that the therapist-perpetrator may not fully integrate the changes made if part of the motivation for doing so is to please the idealized treating therapist. An important goal, then, is to make certain that the integration of changes is relatively independent of the therapist-perpetrator's view of the treating therapist. By doing so, the treating therapist often assists the therapist-perpetrator to develop a more differentiated level of functioning.

One method of accomplishing this goal is to elucidate the boundary between the therapist-perpetrator and the treating therapist by precipitating a disappointment in the idealization. The treating therapist must not create this disappointment in a manipulative, heavy-handed, or "gamey" manner, however. By this time the treating therapist often will have some understanding of an area of disagreement with the therapist-perpetrator (e.g., different perceptions of situations or events or theoretical or other kinds of differences). By focusing on an area of disagreement, the therapist-perpetrator is aided in integrating the possibility that an individual (i.e., the treating therapist) can be positively disposed, helpful, and valuable to the therapist-perpetrator but, at the same time, different and, perhaps, not in agreement with the therapist-perpetrator. It is important not to focus on the disagreement artificially; one should find an unobtrusive area that flows from the therapy material and does not violate or reflect disrespect for the therapist-perpetrator.

The disappointment stemming from the destruction of the idealization can be acute and may create a period of disruption in the therapy. It is important, however, in order to elicit whatever residual self-esteem issues and boundary distortions the therapist-perpetrator may still have. The therapist-perpetrator's remaining ambivalence toward the treatment plan and her or his admissions to the seriousness of ethical misconduct also may be elicited. The goal is to help the therapist-perpetrator to understand what he or she has done without distortion or denial and independent of the support of the therapy relationship.

At times, disappointment over the loss of the idealization may cause a therapist-perpetrator to regress to a level of denial or minimizing that may not have been seen since the earliest phases of treatment. The treating therapist must maintain the ethically firm and yet personally respectful stance described previously. If the therapist-perpetrator does experience some regression during this disappointment process, it is important for the treating therapist not to be punitive but, patiently to assist the therapist-perpetrator to resolve the disappointment and to develop a more differentiated response.

Resolution Phase of Therapy

Before the termination of therapy some time should be spent with therapist-perpetrators in planning the next phase of their careers. If they have been serious about therapy and the supervision requirements that may have been stipulated for regaining their licenses, some opportunity typically will be found for the therapist-perpetrators to do some sort of mental health work. The therapist-perpetrators discussed in this chapter are less likely to have a permanent revocation of their licenses. It is important to help them to understand their personal vulnerabilities and limitations and to begin to make concrete plans for their re-entry into the profession. The re-entry should minimize the possibility that their vulnerabilities and limitations will express themselves again in the exploitation of clients. It is also important that therapist-perpetrators consider the option that mental health work of any sort may not be appropriate for them and to think through clearly what they want to do and why.

In this phase of the treatment, therapist-perpetrators frequently have to come to terms with some painful realities. For example, even though they may have admitted unethical behavior, accepted the punishment, and undergone treatment and supervision, they may never be able to return to the community of their former practice. Realization of this fact may result in feelings of loss and grief; and the therapist-perpetrator will need help to work through the feelings and, just as important, to assess realistically the probability of success in the chosen re-entry path.

Follow-Up

Follow-up appointments for an extended period (i.e., 6-12 months) are desirable. Most of the therapy has been done at this point, of course, but the follow-up appointments have a number of important purposes. They allow the therapist-perpetrator to work through remaining issues, if any, or to address new situations that reflect themes brought up in therapy. If the therapist-perpetrator has shifted her or his career focus, new situations may present different dilemmas for which discussion with the treating therapist can be valuable.

Strains on the Treating Therapist

The strain of working with a therapist-perpetrator may affect the treating therapist in a number of ways. There is much back-and-forth motion by therapist-perpetrators during therapy as they move in and out of denial of the effects of their behavior; this condition can be stressful for the treating therapist. Furthermore, throughout the therapy, the treating therapist may feel (realistically or unrealistically) that the outcome of this case has a greater public dimension than most other cases; consequently, the progress of the therapist-perpetrators may be cherished more than that of other clients.

If a treating therapist does not examine such internally-held attitudes, he or she may avoid confronting the therapist-perpetrator's denial, disabusing him or her of idealization of the treating therapist (discussed earlier), or avoiding the taking of appropriate risks in the therapy. The treating therapist may be overly eager for the therapist-perpetrator to succeed and be unwilling to test out improvement in a manner that temporarily may disrupt the therapy.

Another kind of strain on a treating therapist may occur when therapist-perpetrators feel the legal consequences of their unethical behavior, and the legal system's response is not consistent. Even with the clearest procedures, some aspects of the legal system's actions remain unpredictable. Justice may not always be done or, at least, not done to the satisfaction of the treating therapist. The latter must then be careful not to collude with the denial and minimization of the therapist-perpetrator, even if both feel that the therapist-perpetrator was treated unfairly. In other words, if the legal system responds unfairly to a therapist-perpetrator, it does not change the fact that the therapist-perpetrator inflicted unethical and damaging acts upon his or her client.

During treatment, information may arise that substantially changes the treating therapist's understanding of the therapist-perpetrator and the treatment plan. I want to emphasize that not all new information on other abuses demands a change in treatment. For example, if a therapist-perpetrator admits to involvement with six clients with whom he has had major sexual contact and then admits in the course of therapy that he made passes to others, this information need not drastically change the treatment plan.

The treating therapist should not compromise her or himself by being the only person who possesses serious information on the therapist-perpetrator's behavior. If the treating therapist uncovers new information of a serious nature, he or she should follow the mandated reporting requirements that have been laid down. However, when these requirements are in flux—as they are currently—they may not be adequate for the situations that arise. The treating therapist may request the therapist-perpetrator to report the information to the appropriate licensing board. If the therapist-perpetrator does not comply, the treating therapist has the option of declaring the original treatment plan no longer viable (because of the new information). If, after stating that the therapy cannot move forward until the therapist-perpetrator makes such a self-report and the therapist-perpetrator still refuses, the treating therapist then has the option of terminating therapy. Another method of handling this situation involves obtaining, at the beginning of therapy, releases of information allowing the treating therapist to contact the relevant licensing agency in the event substantive new information is revealed. In many situations, however, I believe there is more therapeutic benefit if the therapist-perpetrators self-report. Granted that a change in the data base for the therapist-perpetrator is manageable, it is also stressful.

I strongly recommend that treating and evaluating therapists develop a support system of peers for consultation and support. Further, treating and evaluating therapists should be thoughtful and deliberate in deciding how many cases they want to take on. Careful monitoring of one's stress level and countertransference reactions are crucial.

ADMINISTRATIVE ISSUES

As a general policy I recommend that copies of relevant correspondence with licensing bodies, administrative agencies, attorneys, and similar bodies be given directly to therapist-perpetrators. This recommendation coincides with data privacy laws; it also helps to maintain a clear boundary between the treating therapist and the therapist-perpetrator by spelling out the treating therapist's role vis-`a-vis the various agencies.

I also recommend at the beginning of treatment that therapist-perpetrators sign an informed consent document in which they agree to the nature and course of the therapy to be offered. At a minimum, this document should indicate that the therapy is likely to be anxiety provoking, of long duration, and may result in recommendations that effectively will prohibit the therapist-perpetrator from ever practicing again. It also may be wise to include in this document an account of how the treating therapist will respond to information that substantially changes the initial treatment plan (as described above).

Finally, the treating therapist and therapist-perpetrator should have a clear understanding on the payment of fees. More so than in other therapeutic situations, delay in payment may reflect ambivalence or disengagement from treatment. Hence delays should be promptly challenged and resolved. The simplest way of handling the situation is for the treating therapist to require full payment at the time of service.

WHEN NOT TO TREAT

A number of situations are possible in which the treatment described here is contraindicated or, at least, should be viewed with considerable caution. Because this treatment is exploratory and anxiety-provoking, it is not likely to be appropriate for therapist-perpetrators who are psychotic or borderline.

Nor is this therapy model always appropriate for therapist-perpetrators who are primarily character disordered. Many such individuals may self-select out of therapy during the assessment or early stages. They often will not admit their unethical actions or will consistently minimize the effect of their actions upon clients. In such cases, treatment should not proceed because the agreement on goals for a viable therapeutic contract is insufficient.

In some situations there may be little if any accord between the client's allegations and the therapist-perpetrator's admissions. If it is unclear to the treating therapist whether the therapist-perpetrator is lying, then treatment is inadvisable because a basis for a therapeutic contract cannot be established.

The response to severely character-disordered therapist-perpetrators who are not candidates to resume practice should be legal, not therapeutic. The licensing board should make it clear that resumption of practice will never be a possibility. Nevertheless such therapist-perpetrators may pursue treatment for personal reasons.

WHO CAN FUNCTION AS EVALUATORS AND TREATING THERAPISTS?

The combination of a firm ethical stance and respect toward the therapist-perpetrator has been emphasized throughout this chapter. A number of additional qualities also are important to evaluate and treat therapists. They include a fairly high tolerance for ambiguity because ethics cases may remain uncomfortably vague for long periods of time. The treating therapists should be able to maintain a goal-directed focus to minimize ambiguity and to make certain that the therapist-perpetrator resolves issues and accomplishes goals directly related to the unethical behavior, regardless of what other personal problems may emerge.

Therapists who have strong political viewpoints on the behaviors of their peers are likely to err in the direction of being either disrespectful of or not firm enough about ethical matters. To treat therapist-perpetrators a therapist should have a fairly high tolerance for interaction with the legal system and its unpredictability and he or she should be adept at rendering testimony. Further, the therapist should be comfortable working within a "legal mindset;" that is, assuming that anything said or done may be challenged in a legal arena.

Unfortunately, when a therapist works in this area he or she can expect to face both overt criticism and covert undermining from colleagues who may be ignorant of or insensitive to the exploitative nature of sexual contact with clients, or who may be aligned with certain therapist-perpetrators. Hence any therapist who is highly vulnerable to political pressure from a therapist-perpetrator's allies because of the nature of the work setting probably is not in a position to do this sort of work.

Whenever a therapist works in this area he or she must be able to resist the temptation of media attention. No matter how sensational or important a case or how much the therapist-perpetrator client may want publicity, the evaluating or treating therapist should avoid all public statements, except those that have a clear therapeutic purpose and are supported by a properly constituted release of information. Given that the evaluation and treatment of therapist-perpetrators are scarcely out of the tentative stage, a treating and evaluating therapist is obligated to be cautious and circumspect in general comments to the media and not to use the role as a route to self-aggrandizement.

Finally, I have observed that therapists with a dynamic of under-control versus over-control in their personality structures find it difficult to act as evaluators or therapists for therapist-perpetrators; often they are too trusting when they should be more challenging in working with therapist-perpetrators; when this trust is disappointed, they are often too punitive.

FINAL COMMENTS

I want to re-emphasize that the model described here is directed to the treatment of therapist-perpetrators who are more or less neurotic and probably is not applicable to other types. I also must caution readers against taking the phase format of the therapy too literally. The concept of phases in this context is more of a convenient vehicle for discussing the various phenomena that occur in treatment than an accurate portrayal of the process. There is very much a "back and forth" aspect in the treatment, and it has been noted frequently in different sections.

Finally, I want to remind readers of the overall context in which sexual exploitation of clients by therapists occurs. Until very recently perpetrating therapists were held to few systems of accountability and client-victims had little recourse to the profession or the courts. The most common outcome for clients was to be discouraged from complaining by most institutions; and if a complaint was made, little or no action was taken. In recent years, increased knowledge of victimization has led licensing boards and ethics committees of professional associations to display greater sensitivity and receptivity. Legal changes in civil law, and, in a few states, criminalization of the sexual exploitation of clients by therapists, as well as the strengthening of administrative procedures, have given complaining clients greater recourse. It remains to be seen whether these measures will prove as effective as they are intended to be, nevertheless the general movement is to give clients greater recourse and to hold therapists to greater accountability.

In the past a client rarely filed a false complaint against a therapist; such a client would have had severe reality-testing problems. In fact, therapists working in this area for a long period of time (e.g., Schoener and Milgrom) have reported that, prior to these changes, the few clients who made false complaints often were psychotic or borderline psychotic. With the system becoming more equitable, however, this relatively simple predictability may be substantially altered. It is conceivable that the future may hold an increase in false or exaggerated complaints against therapists. Another, and perhaps more cynical, interpretation is that in the past it was highly unlikely that character-disordered clients would file false complaints because there was no gain to be had; and it was highly likely that character disordered therapists would be exploitative because consequences were so limited. If this balance shifts as a result of the recent changes to assure accountability and justice, the process of investigating clients' complaints about therapists is likely to become considerably more difficult and complex.

CHAPTER 34

SUPERVISION OF THERAPISTS WHO HAVE SEXUALLY EXPLOITED CLIENTS

Gary Richard Schoener

Before reading this chapter, first read Chapters 38 and 39: "The Role of Supervision and Case Consultation in Primary Prevention" and "The Role of Supervision and Case Consultation: Some Notes on Sexual Feelings in Therapy."

We have little collective experience bearing on this issue and the professional literature is sorely lacking in both research and theories on the subject. Hall (1986) made some reference to supervision when discussing rehabilitation plans for those impaired psychologists who are disciplined by licensure boards.

Nielsen, Peterson, Shapiro, and Thompson (1989) have written the only article to date focusing on this topic; it is entitled "Supervisory Approaches in Cases of Boundary Violations and Sexual Victimization by Therapists." The authors conceptualize five levels of boundary violations of which two involve overt exploitation of the client; further, the authors note that the crossing of boundaries is commonplace and, in fact, integral to treatment. Boundary violations, which are often accompanied by shame and guilt, have several facets that should be recognized: (a) they constitute double binds; (b) they usually involve secrets; and (c) they usually involve the crossing of "generational" lines (e.g., the therapist abandons the role of helper or "parent" and looks to the client for support; or the therapist begins to take too much ownership of changes in the client's life).

THE GREAT CHALLENGE

Unlike the supervision of trainees or inexperienced clinicians, the supervision of therapists who have sexually exploited clients most often means overseeing one's peers or, even, clinicians with more experience than the supervisor. In addition, the professional challenge is greater because these supervisees have demonstrated practice problems, almost always have caused harm to clients, and often are in the professional or public spotlight for misdeeds. Even if the public or the profession does not know that they have abused clients, and they have sought out supervision on their own, there is still the possibility that their misdeeds eventually will become known.

Last but not least, all the legal liabilities described by Slovenko (1980) are present and perhaps heightened, given that the supervisor knows for a fact that the therapist is at risk. Without established standards for supervisors, how does one meet the test of exercising "due care," which Slovenko (1980) defined as that "degree of diligence, care and skill that ordinarily prudent [psychotherapy supervisors] would exercise under similar circumstances in like position."[1]

SOME PROBLEMS AND OBSTACLES TO CONSIDER

---

[1] In a recent case in Texas, the parents of a mentally handicapped girl sued a supervisor appointed by the psychology licensure board to supervise a psychologist with a history of sexual contact with clients, after the psychologist being supervised abused their daughter. An out of court settlement was reached. (Barbara Bailey, personal communication, Aug. 18, 1989)

If a therapist voluntarily approaches a supervisor to request his or her services and reveals an episode of sexual contact with a client, the first issue that must be faced is the mandatory reporting required of the supervisor. In Minnesota, if a therapist is a physician and the supervisor is a licensed health professional or the director of a health care facility, a report must be made to the Board of Medical Examiners. The same is required of health professionals who learn of abuse while supervising a licensed social worker or marriage and family therapist. If the abuse involved a minor or occurred in a hospital or residential facility, a report is also required under child or adult protection statutes.

A second issue, one of even greater importance, is the need to obtain sufficient background information on which to base the decision of whether to undertake the responsibility.

The majority of supervisory situations are not voluntary. Usually an employer of a therapist, a professional ethics committee, or a licensure board orders, or requires, that supervision be obtained. In such circumstances it may be possible to gain more leverage than if one is approached "voluntarily," but not necessarily. The following sections explore a number of these obstacles.

SOME KEY TERMS

Chapter 39 explores the implications of the terms "supervision" and "case consultation." The reader is advised to review this discussion before proceeding further.

At a meeting of the Professional Standards Committee of the Minnesota Chapter of the National Association of Social Workers, Sept. 15, 1988, a lengthy discussion was held of the problems inherent in the use of the term "supervision," given the broad range of meanings assigned to it in mental health work. It was suggested that the term practice monitor be considered instead of "supervisor" to designate someone who is overseeing the work of a practitioner who has been found in violation of the standards of professional practice. The practice monitor would supervise with considerably more authority than the typical clinical supervisor because he or she would be able to require the discussion of any and all cases and to examine clinical notes and records.[2]

For the purpose of the following discussion, the term "supervisor" is used for the sake of simplicity.

REFERRALS FROM LICENSURE BOARDS

Myron Stocking, M.D., a Minneapolis psychoanalyst who has undertaken the supervision of some therapists under licensure board order, mirrored the comments of other professionals in similar roles when we recently discussed the problems inherent in this role. First of all, he and I have observed that disciplinary orders for supervision sometimes are given in cases in which the practitioner has an apparent character disorder.

---

[2] The psychology licensure board in Texas is in the process of developing plans to use monitors where disciplinary orders call for supervision of a practitioner. The practitioner will pay the board who will in turn pay the monitor. The monitor will be expected to travel to the practitioner's office and to examine client records, and will be paid for these activities as well as for meetings with the practitioner. The monitor will have detailed information on the case from the board and the arrangement will be described in a contract signed by the practitioner, monitor, and the board chair. (Barbara Bailey, personal communication, Aug. 18, 1989)

Obviously it is naive to think that a character-disordered therapist can be controlled through the type of supervision ordered (which actually is case consultation because the supervisor has no legal authority over the practitioner).

Without the authority to review records, compel discussion of all cases, or make direct client contact, true supervision is impossible. Given the nature of the offense, Dr. Stocking suggested that supervision should be "client-oriented, not consultee-oriented." Furthermore, when supervisors interview the practitioner and raise serious questions on whether he or she is amenable to supervision, it is not uncommon for them to get a response from the Board such as, "He's impossible...we don't know what to do with him either...better this than nothing!"

Frankly, unless the therapist who is to be supervised is in the healthy or neurotic categories (see Ch. 32), there is serious question of whether supervision can be expected to do much—especially supervision that is actually case consultation. Even with the healthier groups, if supervision is to be successful, it is essential that the supervisee and supervisor form an alliance.

Let us review some of the pitfalls in the typical referral for supervision:

1. Lack of Standards for Rehabilitation: Hall (1986) reported that in only two states, Texas and Utah, do the laws or regulations pertaining to psychologists contain specific reference to rehabilitation criteria. She reprinted the Texas guidelines that direct the Board to specify "the focus of the supervision," whether all or specific areas will be the subject of supervision, the amount of weekly contact required, etc. (Hall, 1986)

2. Lack of a Hypothesis of Why the Misconduct Occurred: The type of evaluation described in Chapter 32 is extremely rare nationally. Even when a diagnostic work-up has been done on the offending therapist there is rarely enough of a comprehensive study to allow for a hypothesis of why the behavior occurred. Even when a thorough evaluation is done, it sometimes does not produce a clear understanding. Without the evaluation it is difficult to put together a rehabilitation plan and to specify precisely what the supervision is supposed to accomplish.

3. Questions on Whether Rehabilitation is Possible: Therapist-perpetrators who fall into the three most serious categories (see Ch. 32) are not in fact candidates for rehabilitation. Our track record with psychotics and borderlines, sociopaths, and character disorders is quite poor in terms of bringing about significant change. Such individuals should lose their licenses or have their practices severely limited.

4. Existence of More Serious Problems Than Those Known to the Board or Contained in the Disciplinary Order: We have been involved in cases in which a board prosecuted only one of numerous sexual misconduct offenses by a given therapist; and we also have examples of therapists who are generally incompetent or broadly impaired but were charged with only a single violation of confidentiality or a minor instance of sexual contact. A therapist's potential danger to clients may or may not be indicated by the act or acts that led to a complaint. However, it has been our experience that the remedies proposed by boards tend to follow a criminal court model of more serious consequences for more serious acts.

5. Lack of a Specific Supervision Plan: It is critical that the plan for supervision be specific about what is to be supervised and how the supervision is expected to bring about a change. In our experience these specifics almost always are absent.

6. <u>Supervisor Has No Actual Authority, and Is In Fact a Case Consultant Only</u>: The fact that the supervisor is a "friend of the Board" and must file reports with the board in no way makes up for a lack of authority to compel the production of records, to choose which cases are discussed, and to have direct client contact if it is deemed necessary.

7. <u>Board Ignores Supervisor's Recommendation</u>: If the regulatory board does not follow the supervisor's recommendations that someone should not be permitted to practice independently, the rehabilitation plan is completely undermined.

8. <u>The Supervision is Used in Place of Revocation or Practice Restriction</u>: Therapists with serious problems, in my experience, come to light as a consequence of close scrutiny; they may constitute enough of a risk to vulnerable clients so that supervision alone does not protect the clients. The issue may not be whether or not they will again engage in sexual misconduct but, rather, that the services they render to clients will be substandard or incompetent. Many victims of sexual exploitation by therapists are harmed more by incompetent therapy than by the sex itself. Furthermore, as is described in more detail in Chapter 32, some therapists need significant practice limitations. Ironically, regulatory boards that deal with misuse of medications (e.g., Medicine, Nursing) not infrequently require impaired practitioners to abandon independent practice and to practice under supervision in some sort of facility. For example, a local physician of excellent reputation was sent away for in excess of a year to practice under supervision in another state after he became self-addicted to painkillers. Yet Boards seem reluctant to write the same orders for psychotherapists, despite the near impossibility of supervising most individuals in independent practice.

DIFFICULTY OF THE ROLE

Under the best of circumstances it is difficult to supervise someone who is ordered into supervision. Most therapists have never been in the role of sharing responsibility with a body like a licensure board, which is somewhat akin to the role of a parole agent. Training and experience prepares therapists to work for a client or supervisee who, presumably, is involved with them on a voluntary basis. Their duty then is to the supervisee.

The demands of the supervisory role are discussed by Kaslow (1986), Stefanson (1989), and Gonsiorek (Ch. 33). Although these authors all refer to doing therapy on an impaired practitioner, the same dynamics are often present.

THE MYTH OF THE DIRECT OBSERVER:

A number of licensure boards have used disciplinary orders that include a requirement for an observer to be present when a practitioner renders professional services. Some psychotherapists, for example, have been required to have a second person present when interviewing women clients. Some of the pitfalls of this approach follow:

1. This measure does not prevent incompetent or harmful practice—it eliminates only overt sexual activity.

2. In some circumstances, more circumscribed sexual touching has occurred, even with a witness present.

3. The person chosen to sit in on sessions invariably is a subordinate practitioner or trainee—not someone who is likely to challenge substandard therapy.

4. Such orders are often limited to solo visits with women, although the same seductive games can be played when a couple is seen.

5. When the practitioner is in independent practice, there is no way to oversee this arrangement and to make sure that exceptions are prevented.

(For further discussion, see Ch. 36).

SO, YOU REALLY STILL WANT TO SUPERVISE AN IMPAIRED PRACTITIONER...

Nevertheless, good professionals should be encouraged to undertake this work, because it is important. The following suggestions may be of help:

1. Examine the assessment work that has been done, demand copies of all records; and hold personal discussions with Board personnel and outside evaluators. If the assessment has not been done adequately, demand that it be done. Then, make your own determination that the plan is, in fact, appropriate. If it is not, turn it down and give the Board feedback.

2. Clarify what leverage you will have and what the limits of the supervision are. Make clear to the Board, or whomever you are dealing with, that you will require:

   a. Authority to communicate with the Board at any time and to withdraw if the supervision is not working.

   b. Authority to compel production of records or to inspect them on site, with reasonable notice.

   c. Authority to determine which cases are reviewed and to compel supervision of a sufficient period of time to allow for such review.

   d. Authority to participate in client interviews or to interview clients separately.

3. Meet with the practitioner and discuss his or her views of the supervision and the disciplinary order. Obtain his or her explanation of the misconduct. Present your requirements and obtain agreement to them. This agreement should then be written and signed.

4. When supervising follow your "gut" instincts and do not hesitate to examine or challenge even small departures from what you believe to be the standard of care. Take the position that whether he/she likes it or not, having been the subject of a complaint puts the therapist, at least for a time, under a microscope. In fact, it is useful to make clear that it is to the therapist's advantage to be under a microscope, both to make sure of not getting in trouble again and because he or she is potentially a "sitting duck," having already been the subject of a complaint. Even a bogus complaint could now be quite dangerous.

5. If you believe that the practitioner also could benefit from psychotherapy, you can write a supervisory directive. Although many Boards make almost knee-jerk referrals for therapy in these cases, there may be some in which a referral is

not made but the therapy is later needed. It may focus on a problem that surfaced in supervision or, perhaps, on more recent life stresses.

Overall, it is important to establish that you are keeping an eye out for more than garden variety deviations from practice standards. The handling of boundaries (Nielsen et al., 1989) is obviously important, but so may such things as the early identification of inappropriate clients. A true supervisor can oversee the intake of clients and raise questions about new clients who may be at risk, given the therapist's limitations.

DOCUMENTATION

Bridge & Bascue (1988) have developed a "Supervisory Record Form" to document psychotherapy supervision. According to Bridge (1988) it has received 8-9 months of field testing and requires less than 10 minutes to complete. It was developed out of a concern with protecting liability in the ordinary supervisory situation, but it also enhances supervision. This form can be used as it is or adapted for situations that are discussed in other sections of this chapter.

Figures 1 and 2 are alternative record forms that may be useful to document the supervision of a practitioner who has sexually exploited clients. These forms provide more space for case descriptions. Additional pages (Figure 2) can be used when needed. For a simple review, only a single line or two may be required, but for a troublesome case considerable space may be essential. Figure 3 illustrates a completed form.

Beyond documenting that the supervision took place, this form, like the one developed by Bridge & Bascue (1988), should provide for the organization of supervisory input and allow the supervisor to monitor the supervisee's follow-through.

SUPERVISION LOG

Supervisee: _____   Date: _____   Total Time: _____   Page 1

Session No. _____   of _____

Case Given	Notes Or Tape Used	Description	Recommendations or Direction

_____   _____
Signature   Date

Fig. 1 Supervision Log Form—Page 1

SUPERVISION LOG   Supervisee: _____   Date: _____   Page _____

Session No. _____   of _____

Case Given	Notes Or Tape Used	Description	Recommendations or Direction

_____   _____
Signature   Date

Fig. 2 Supervision Log Form—Additional Pages

SUPERVISION LOG

Supervisee: Dr. Smith

Date: Oct. 6, 1988

Session No. 7

Case Given	Notes Or Tape Used	Description	Recommendations or Direction
J.D.	Reviewed case notes	New Case - Diagnosis seems clear, but some	1) Get releases to speak with prior therapists.
45-yr.-old	and MMPI.	question as to why she's had trouble with past	2) Continue discussion with client of what went
woman		therapists. Dr. S. properly indicated that they	wrong previously.
		need to discuss this further before he takes	
		her on as a client.	
D.F.	----------	Initial Session - Client wanted hypnotherapy.	Did a good job of clarifying needs.
20-yr.-old		(Referred)	
man			
D.Y.	Case notes.	Ongoing Case - making progress on	1) Continue goal-focused approach.
35-yr.-old		Job hunting, giving feedback to landlord,	2) If he still hasn't confronted fiancè this week,
man		but not in confronting fiancè.	suggest role-play practice during next session.

/s/ Gary Schoener

Signature

10/6/88

Date

Fig. 3 Example of Completed Log Form

EXAMPLES OF SUPERVISORY PLANS

Each of the following examples is a skeleton outline of a plan. In each case the supervisor had full authority to examine records, decide which cases to discuss, and to communicate with the Board.

Example 1:   Therapist had an affair with a single client which lasted more than 5 years and was a love relationship. Sexual activity is not a part of therapy. Therapist was not judged to have psychological problems and had settled issues in his personal life. Careful assessment suggested, quite apart from the client complaint, that the therapist was loose in his diagnostic workups and had trouble handling borderline clients. Supervision involved a review of all new cases for appropriateness and periodic reviews of progress of all clients, with more in-depth review of cases involving boundary struggles.

Example 2:   Therapist had affair with client which began in therapy, although it was not presented as therapy. Under periods of personal stress and marital disintegration, therapist engaged in marked overwork and also tended to become somewhat isolated from peers in his private practice clinic, and developing somewhat grandiose ideas about his ability to help anyone. He was quite depressed after the affair surfaced and removed himself from independent practice. Plan involved 2 years of supervised practice at a VA facility with eventual addition of some women clients to his caseload. Supervision focused on his maintaining reasonable work hours, obtaining peer supervision and consultation, and working with his primary supervisor to identify situations in which he took on too much responsibility.

Example 3:   Female therapist became involved with the friend of a client who had participated in one session. Although careless and naive, the involvement did not seem exploitative, but in evaluating the situation it appeared that the therapist was having some problem in both assessment of pathology and handling certain types of boundary problems. Supervision focused on improving her skills in both areas.

Example 4:   Inexperienced male therapist became careless with touch with a client who felt he was being sexually seductive. Evaluation suggested that he was handling case ineptly and that his chemical dependency-related training and experience did not translate well enough into the mental health arena. It was decided that supervision alone would not correct the situation. He was referred for more training and a supervised training placement before attempting work in a private setting (even with supervision).

Example 5:   Male therapist who is gay-identified lost control briefly in a follow-up home visit with a low-intelligence client who exposed himself. He apologized and attempted to make amends. Subsequent evaluation revealed no other evidence of practice problems, but he had become overly interested in this client. Plan was for no out-of-office visits plus supervision of practice that focused on examining the handling of boundaries, especially with clients in whom he became very invested.

Example 6:   Therapist engaged in sexual contact and sexual intercourse with several clients, all of whom were women and victims of abuse. He overly identified with them and exercised very poor boundaries. Plan was for a practice setting or work role that allowed for no therapy with female clients ever, which likely rules out any independent practice or even work in a private clinic. No specific supervision plan except that employer is to be informed of limitation in practice.

It should be noted that in some instances the supervisory plan must take into account the effect of the Board actions and discipline on the practitioner. For example, if the stress of being on trial leads to significant depression, this in and of itself may constitute a significant impairment which supervision may need to address.

Practitioners on trial, or who are returning to practice after a period of license revocation, normally have supervision or consultation needs, regardless of the reasons for the original offense. They often lack confidence and are a bit "gun-shy," and being unsure of themselves they may back away from confrontation. In two recent cases I had to address these issues:

Example 7:   A professional in training had engaged in sexual contact with a client during a stint as a paraprofessional counselor prior to entering graduate school. The complaint caught up with him. Assessment showed that the original issues, which included both personal problems and a lack of understanding of boundaries had been remedied. However, he appeared still to be trying to atone for his earlier sins by being the "perfect" counselor. He needed to loosen up, to be willing to make mistakes, and not to shy away from challenging female clients. These items were the focus of supervision.

Example 8:   A psychiatrist was returning to practice subsequent to more than a year of not practicing after loss of license because of a sexual involvement with a client. He had settled a number of personal problems, completed therapy, and was not judged to have had serious problems in the first place. Supervision was set up to review general client boundaries, and the supervisor was instructed to assist in confidence building. It was suggested, based on a re-review of the case, that at least for a while the psychiatrist would be like a new resident, needing support and direction. However, hopefully, he would quickly develop confidence and regain his skills.

PULLING THE PLUG

Last but not least, the good supervisor also needs to be willing and able to directly challenge a supervisee's competence to practice, or to question the size of a caseload, the characteristics of the practice setting, or whether some practice limitations are in order. If practice is incompetent and clients are receiving substandard care, the simple fact that the therapist is not having sex with any of them does not change the fact that the therapist shouldn't be practicing, or that practice should be limited. If a surgeon's skill is diminished by illness or advancing age his or her colleagues usually do not wait until a patient dies to suggest that practice be limited or abandoned.

Sometimes the extent of a therapist's deficiencies are not known until someone supervises the therapist for a time. Sometimes the supervisory and rehabilitation plan looks great on paper but just plain does not work. Some "naive" therapists turn out to have a basic lack of social judgment, or even an emotional problem that is chronic and interferes with the ability to judge situations. Sometimes a deterioration in personal adjustment, the onset of an emotional illness, or loss of intellectual ability with advancing age lead to a downhill path despite good supervision.

It is more ethical and more humane to both clients and therapist to directly address the limitations that are in evidence and to suggest practice limitations. It is not the supervisor's job to find vocational alternatives...only to give feedback when seeking alternatives is mandatory. Supervision cannot perform magic, and it is not true that "it's better than nothing." Sometimes supervision gives the semblance of propriety and competence when, in fact, these are merely a hollow shell. Hard work, a long career, and the absence of alternatives do not justify putting consumers at risk. If you would not want a friend or family member to see this therapist, just remember that the people who do see him or her for help are somebody else's family and friends.

CHAPTER 35

Problems In The Use Of Direct Observation In Probation Plans For Professionals Who Have Sexually Exploited Clients

Gary Richard Schoener

For a number of years, licensure and regulatory Boards have issued disciplinary orders on the conduct of health professionals who have sexually exploited their clients. For example, an order may forbid a practitioner to see certain groups of clients unless an observer is present. Commonly, a female observer is required to keep an eye on a male practitioner who has had sexual contact with female patients.

The orders are used to take disciplinary actions against chiropractors, podiatrists, dentists, and physicians, including psychiatrists. For some comments on the problems that are created when the orders are directed to therapists, see Chapter 34, "Supervision of Therapists Who Have Sexually Exploited Clients."

Some Obvious Problems

1. The Observer: The observer most frequently is a female nurse or assistant who already is employed by the practitioner, possibly is a friend, and may have testified in his or her defense at the licensure hearing. If the person can be so described in whole or in part, she is not in a good position to be objective. She often can be easily manipulated into bending the rules by not being present all the time. Indeed it is difficult to imagine that she will phone the licensure Board to report an infraction if she thinks it may mean losing her job. The situation is the same if the practitioner's spouse is the observer; it is not unusual for a spouse to work in her husband's office.

2. Lack of Clarity About What is Being Observed: The usual order that I have seen simply commands the practitioner to see to it that someone is in the office to observe. It does not specify what is to be watched for, that is, what behaviors should require some sort of intervention or action.

3. No Clear Authority for the Observer: The request for observation typically is passed to the observer by the practitioner; there is no true conveyance of authority to that person. This problem is serious given that the observer typically is a subordinate professional or a paraprofessional.

4. No Clearly Delineated Courses of Action: If in fact the observer witnesses some troubling conduct, what does she do with that information?

   a. Immediate feedback to the practitioner?
   b. Direct intervention or feedback to the patient?
   c. Call the Board, or its representative?
   d. Call some sort of consultant or supervisor?
   e. Make a written report?

A Partial Solution

Observational plans, under the best of circumstances, are questionable and Boards should think carefully about why a person is sent back to practice if he or she literally must be watched. Furthermore, even if we assume that the observer protects the public, who will protect the public when observation is no longer required?

In practice, at least with psychotherapists, we know of several situations in which the observational approach did not work. These were cases in which the observers later revealed that they had observed some misconduct but had not intervened or reported it. Even if we grant that the misconduct was not so serious as that for which the therapist was disciplined, still it was potentially harmful. When such behavior occurs with an observer present, the harm may be even greater because the client is led to assume that the behavior must be OK if the observer does not question it.

There are, however, some procedures that are likely to make such a plan workable:

1. Assessment: The rehabilitation assessment should be of the type recommended in this manual. It concludes that sexually exploitative behavior is theoretically controllable and unlikely to recur.

2. Clarifying What is to Be Observed: The observational plan should be in writing and should include a number of specifics, such as answers to the following questions:

a. Precisely what transactions/events are to be observed?

b. When does the observation begin and end within the professional service? Does the observer watch the entire session? What about entry and exit to the office?

c. What behaviors are part of the original charge and are clearly unacceptable?

d. What related behaviors are clearly unacceptable?

3. Clarifying the Observer's Responsibility: The observers must be asked specifically whether they are able and willing to take on this difficult responsibility. It should be made clear that if they agree to it and do not do it properly they may be personally liable in the event of a lawsuit. In the case of a nurse or other licensed professional who takes on these duties, it should be made clear that a failure to fulfill this professional commitment will lead to a complaint to her or his licensure Board.

An alternative or addition may be to develop a written contract between the Board and the observer in which the Board pays the observer out of funds collected by the Board from the practitioner on probation.

4. Authority: A face-to-face meeting should be held of the observer, representative(s) of the Board, and the practitioner during which all the details are discussed; and the practitioner should be required to formally authorize the observer to do a thorough job of observing.

5. Delineate Courses of Action: A set of specific hypothetical situations should be presented with clear directions on what the observer is supposed to do in each. Besides addressing responsibilities to intervene to prevent client harm, I recommend that a

consultant or supervisor be assigned to whom the observer can give the information. This should be an easier course of action than a direct report to the Board.

6. Informed Consent: The practitioner must sign an informed consent agreeing to this arrangement, and he or she specifically must agree to hold the observer harmless for acts performed in good faith in connection with the discharge of the duties as observer.

7. Sanctions: The practitioner should be aware that any pressure on the observer or any attempt to subvert the observation process may lead to license revocation. The observer should be forewarned that a failure to faithfully execute this agreed-upon duty may result in a report to his/her licensure Board.

8. Followup: A consultant or representative of the Board should make routine, periodic followups that include interviews with the observers, at regular intervals, describing how things are going.

CONCLUSION

Some regulatory bodies, such as licensure boards, have assumed that clients can be protected from an impaired practitioner if an observer is present. Experience has shown, however, that this approach has serious limitations. Unless the observer knows what to look for and is truly independent enough to make a report if anything is amiss, observation arrangements provide a false sense of security and do not offer consumers sufficient protection. For example, in the case of a psychotherapist who has a history of sexually exploiting female clients, it is not enough to simply require the therapist to have a female observer in the room during sessions.

PART X

PREVENTION

Chapter 36 provides a checklist of actions which can be taken by an administrator or program director to limit the risk of unprofessional conduct (e.g., sexual involvement with a client). The remaining three chapters in the section elaborate on some specific safeguards through hiring and supervision practices.

Chapter 37 details the screening of job applicants. The contents derive from the knowledge that a large percentage of exploiters are repeat offenders and, also, that some exploitation is the result of poor professional skills and poorly maintained professional boundaries.

In Chapters 38 and 39, the potentials of supervision and case consultation to prevent sexual exploitation of clients are explored. The discussions go beyond simply addressing the sexual feelings a therapist may have for a client to focus on alternative means for supervision, at least in theory, to prevent certain abuse scenarios.

The approach to prevention presented in these chapters is a systems approach. Psychotherapists and counselors wishing to reduce the likelihood of becoming sexually involved with a client should: 1. maintain their own personal adjustment; 2. provide services only within their areas of expertise; 3. obtain appropriate consultation; 4. maintain conservative boundaries regarding touch and contacts with clients outside of sessions; 5. maintain treatment contracts which are specific and reviewed periodically; and 6. avoid excessive self-disclosure. Therapists need to be aware of the seductive aspects of psychotherapy as well as common ways in which professional boundaries are not maintained. Clinical mismanagement is a common precursor to sexual relationships with clients (e.g., Gutheil, 1989, p. 599), and also a common factor in false or misleading complaints (see Ch. 11).

The American Psychiatric Association (1986, 1988) has produced two videotapes, *Ethical Concerns About Sexual Involvement Between Psychiatrists and Patients* and *Reporting Ethical Concerns*, which consist of vignettes which form the basis of discussion concerning the handling of some critical situations relative to therapist-client sex. Discussion leader's guides accompany both tapes. Braude (1986) has reported on workshops aimed at helping psychiatrists deal better with these issues.

The Walk-In Counseling Center has done workshops for psychotherapists which focus on professional boundaries for many years. We have developed a number of demonstrations and exercises which help professionals identify seductive aspects of psychotherapeutic relationships and explore issues in maintaining proper boundaries and their own vulnerabilities. These will be the subject of a future manual.

CHAPTER 36

ADMINISTRATIVE SAFEGUARDS

Gary Richard Schoener

The concept of an administrative checklist to help human service programs to do a better job of preventing or intervening in cases of client-therapist sexual involvement originated with my colleague, Jeanette Milgrom. Her survey form, "Sexual Exploitation of Clients: Its Prevention or Remedy... or ...A Look at Whether Your Agency Has Its House In Order," distributed by WICC starting in October 1978, is reprinted in Appendix E. Its creative graphics and numerical rating system were then and still are both eye-catching and useful.

The utility of this approach inspired me to construct a more detailed checklist in 1979, "Administrative Safeguards to Limit Risk of Unprofessional Conduct" (Appendix E), and to put together an accompanying memorandum, "Selected Items from the Supervisor/Counselor Volunteer Application, Walk-In Counseling Center" (Appendix C). The latter was rewritten in October 1986 primarily to reflect changes in the WICC volunteer form (Appendix C). The checklist itself was revised and expanded considerably in September 1986, partly to incorporate changes in Minnesota Statutes and partly to add new items gleaned from our collective experience between 1979-1986. Following all the guidelines in no way guarantees that one can prevent sexual contact between client and therapist or other boundary violations, however.

CONTENT OF THE CHECKLIST

Neither Milgrom nor I drew on the professional literature or research data to construct the checklist, and the use of a rating system in her original checklist had no scientific basis. In fact, I omitted the rating scale in the 1979 checklist because, despite its value as an attention-getter, I feared that its evaluation of the scores might be misleading.

The two most detailed treatments of organizational issues and potential prevention strategies, Edelwich & Brodsky (1982) and White (1986), do not use checklists. However, in the publication prepared by the Minnesota Task Force on Sexual Exploitation by Counselors and Therapists (Sanderson, 1988), a checklist was included; it is based in part on our 1979 checklist but is much more extensive. (See "A Checklist for Employers of Counselors and Therapists" in Sanderson, 1989.).

The content of our checklist was original. The items derived from our post hoc analysis of the many hundreds of our consultations that permitted us to explore the question of what, if anything, might have prevented the sexual involvement of the client by the therapist.

The inclusion of an item simply indicates that it seemed to be an issue in a number of cases or was a recognizable key issue in a few. Thus, the checklist can be regarded as a set of hypotheses generated by a great deal of case experience.

Overall, four items stand out as common problems, and these four have been used in civil suits to support the theory of an employer's liability. They are as follows:

1. Failure to identify potential employees with a history of problems in the sexual or general boundaries area (repeat offenders account for a number of our cases).

2. Failure to take appropriate organizational action in a prior sexual misconduct case in the same agency.

3. Failure to deal with an obviously distressed or impaired practitioner... to tend to one's own "walking wounded."

4. Inadequate practice oversight and supervision: either they are lacking in general or the atmosphere is such that practitioners do not question each other on practice concerns.

USE OF THE CHECKLIST

Copies of previous versions of the Checklist were circulated in professional workshops or sent in response to inquiries; the 1979 version of the Checklist was published in Schoener and Milgrom (1986). Unfortunately, we have had little feedback on its usefulness other than its utilization by the State Task Force (Sanderson, 1989). Some clinic managers and employers have used it to review the safeguards they should have in place and several even filled it out. Some attorneys have used it to review potential areas of liability. Also it has been introduced to civil trials and administrative hearings relative to employment matters.

Our most frequent use of the checklist is as a teaching aid to help both administrators and clinicians to review systematically areas of clinic operations. Although the language is very terse to fit the format, each item is explicated in the narrative that follows the Checklist.

The reader is also referred to Chapter 37 which contains more detail on hiring practices, as well as Chapters 27 and 43 which discuss the civil liability of employers for sexual misconduct by therapists. Supervisory liability is discussed in Chapters 34, 38, and 39. Hospital administrators may want to review Logan's (1989) paper on "The Evaluation of the Impaired Physician," one of the first such contributions to include a discussion of sexual misconduct. Hospital credentialing procedures and peer review are also discussed in chapters by Callahan and Vocke (1989, Krizek (1989), and Miller (1989), which are included in *Legal Implications of Hospital Policies and Practices* (Miller, 1989).

It's Never O.K.: A Handbook for Professionals on Sexual Exploitation by Counselors and Therapists (Sanderson, 1989) has a number of Appendices with sample administrative tools and policies. Appendix BB and the report of the Minnesota Interfaith Committee on Sexual Exploitation by Clergy (see Ch. 20) both contain useful information on administrative safeguards and policies for religious organizations.

ADMINISTRATIVE SAFEGUARDS WHICH LIMIT THE RISK OF SEXUAL EXPLOITATION BY PSYCHOTHERAPISTS— A CHECKLIST

STAFF SELECTION & HIRING: YES   NO

•Does your job application explicitly ask about:

    —Past terminations/resignations?   ___   ___
    —Past ethics complaints?   ___   ___
    —Past licensure complaints?   ___   ___
    —Past lawsuits, whether adjudicated or not?   ___   ___

•When hiring professionals who are licensed or certified,
    do you directly contact licensure boards concerning
    areas of competency, status of the license, and the
    existence (or lack thereof) of complaints?

    —Boards in this state?   ___   ___
    —Boards in states where previously employed?   ___   ___

•Do you check via direct conversation (not just letter
    of reference) with past supervisors about the
    applicant's:

    —Likely strengths and weaknesses working in a
      setting like that of your agency?   ___   ___
    —Willingness to be supervised and to be a team
      player?   ___   ___
    —Any history of complaints by, or problems with,
      other staff (e.g., sexual harassment)?   ___   ___
    —Any history of client complaints?   ___   ___
    —Any concerns they might have about the
      person's ability to perform in your setting;
      any needs for special care or supervision?   ___   ___

                                                             YES   NO

•If you're a Minnesota employer, do you make written
    requests to all employers from the past five years
    concerning their knowledge of sexual contact with
    clients or ex-clients (Minnesota Statutes 148.A)?   ___   ___
•If you're a non-Minnesota employer, do you comply with
    the local standards for the duty of employers as
    spelled out in statute or case law?   ___   ___

STAFF POLICIES:

•Do you have a written policy forbidding:

    —Sexual contact with clients?   ___   ___

	YES	NO

—Sexual contact with ex-clients?

—Romantic involvement with clients?

•Does your policy also provide rules for support staff and other nonclinical personnel?

•Do you have a policy covering sexual harassment of staff and/or romantic involvements between staff members?

•Do you have a written policy for handling complaints of unprofessional conduct such as allegations of sexual contact with clients?

•Do you have a plan or mechanism for the investigation of complaints by clients and others?

  —Do you have outside consultants who can be used to assist in such investigations?

  —Do you have an Ethics Committee or Professional Standards Review Committee which reviews such complaints?

  —Do you have a method for the filing and investigation of complaints against the Director of your program or facility?

COMPLAINT RESOLUTION:

•Are all complaints processed as complaints and taken seriously—not just seen as "transference" or some other therapeutic event?

•Are complaining clients given reassurance and thanked for coming forward, regardless of your initial assumptions about the validity of the complaint?

•Are clients given support and offered help in finding appropriate independent resources?

•Do you have procedures for deciding whether to temporarily suspend a staff member pending the outcome of a review of a complaint?

•Are all staff involved in the investigation of complaints clear about the limits of privacy—e.g., their reporting duties under existing laws and rules (in Minnesota this includes Vulnerable Adults Act, Child Abuse and Neglect reporting, the Medical Practice Act, and the Code of Conduct of the Board of Psychology)?

	YES	NO

•Is some resolution reached on all complaints, or do you allow some of them to remain moot if a staff member voluntarily resigns?   ___ ___

•After you have decided on action relative to a complaint, are the complainants always given feedback as to final disposition?   ___ ___

•When you receive a request for a recommendation for a former staff member which asks about any history of sexual misconduct with clients, do you:

—Automatically pass the information on to a Minnesota employer as is your duty under Minnesota Statutes 148.A?   ___ ___

—With an out-of-state employer suggest that the employer obtain a release from the former staff member permitting you to share all data?   ___ ___

STAFF EDUCATION:

•Are all staff given written copies of policies?   ___ ___

•Is there a new employee orientation at which these are explained and key policies are underlined?   ___ ___

•Are there training sessions on the issue of boundaries in psychotherapy held at least once per year?   ___ ___

•Following an incident of serious misconduct, is a special session held to discuss what can be learned from the incident?   ___ ___

STAFF SUPERVISION/PEER REVIEW:

•Do you have regular clinical supervision or consultation?   ___ ___

•Do you have a professional standards review system?   ___ ___

•Is there an automatic review of:

—Treatment which exceeds the usual length?   ___ ___

—Situations in which excessive dependency is evident such as when clients phone frequently?   ___ ___

—Situations in which seductive behavior is observed by other staff?   ___ ___

	YES	NO
•Is long-term treatment periodically reviewed as to:		
—Treatment goals & progress toward them?	___	___
—Plans for termination?	___	___
•Does your program have an atmosphere which encourages constructive questioning among staff?	___	___
•Are there clear, nonthreatening pathways for making observations/concerns known to management, by:		
—Clinical & program staff?	___	___
—Support staff; billing office?	___	___
•When staff have obvious personal problems or are in distress:		
—Do other staff generally give them feedback?	___	___
—Is there a clear mechanism, which is used, to bring about feedback and encourage seeking help?	___	___
—Are clinical duties ever reviewed in light of obvious personal problems/distress?	___	___
•Are there readily available interventions when therapeutic relationships become romanticized/sexualized:		
—Use of a co-therapist or consultant who may enter a session with the client if need be?	___	___
—Referral in-house, or to another program?	___	___

CLIENTS:

	YES	NO
•Do you provide new clients with information which:		
—Actively seeks to solicit feedback?	___	___
—Identifies an easy-to-use complaint mechanism?	___	___
—Provides any guidelines to evaluating therapy?	___	___
•Is it general staff practice to carefully assess the client's view of any past treatment at your agency or elsewhere?	___	___
•Do you routinely survey consumer satisfaction or outcome?	___	___
•Is a complaining client given the opportunity for a meeting with the therapist, with or without a mediator present?	___	___

NARRATIVE FOR ADMINISTRATIVE SAFEGUARD CHECKLIST

I. STAFF SELECTION & HIRING:

A. Job Application:

Mental health practitioners and administrators of facilities which employ them historically have been quite shy in asking directly about any history of practice problems. As can be seen from the memo "Selected Items from the Supervisor/Counselor Volunteer Application—Walk-In Counseling Center" (Appendix C) and the application itself (Appendix C), WICC seeks this information even of applicants to volunteer status. One needs to set the stage in the written application itself.

It should be noted that the presence of a problem in a person's employment history or training background does not, in and of itself, mean that the applicant should not be hired. It alerts one to areas that need review and discussion.

It is ironic that historically the employers of therapists in some cases have been careless enough to hire someone within a week of her/his having been fired for a serious offense. Beyond practice issues, it is helpful to know if an old complaint may resurface in the future or if the practitioner in question may be the subject of negative publicity in the future.

We often are asked about private practice situations in which job applications typically are not used. We frankly advise private practitioners to conduct the same inquiry of each other, even if the situation is one of two people sharing an office without a formal association of their practices. Just having both your names on the same door at times can lead to potential liability, even if the only risk is a bad press or changing a lease.

B. Direct Contacts With Boards:

If you want to be extra careful, directly check with the relevant regulatory boards and do not rely on the applicant's presumed honesty. People in various professions fabricate degrees and job histories, so misstating a licensure situation is also a possibility.

Note, however, that licensure boards typically give out only the status of a license or presence of disciplinary orders. They do not reveal complaints in process or certain types of informal board actions.

Professional competencies are listed only by some boards. However, the contents of an application for licensure often is public information and can provide a separate check on background and credentials. With the increase in interstate cooperation and communication between licensure boards it will become easier to rely on your local board's determination of fitness to practice.

Please note also that when individuals are licensed by more than one board, one needs to check with both. The same set of facts may lead one board to take disciplinary action and another, to decline taking action. The common dual license is probably psychologist and physician, although MDs, Ph.D.s, and MSWs also may hold licenses as Marriage & Family Counselors in states licensing that field.

C. Direct Contacts With Past Supervisors:

It is widely known that letters of reference rarely contain negative statements about job applicants; in recent years there has been a strong trend toward very conservative practices in relation to personnel data.

The cornerstone of gaining access to more detailed information on applicants is to obtain a very broad release like the WICC Supervisor/Counselor Volunteer Application (Appendix C). Over a decade and a half hundreds of practitioners have signed this release form simply to volunteer at our Center. They no doubt would be willing to sign in order to apply for a paying job.

The one item not on the list of things to ask about is mental and emotional stability. We exclude this because both federal statutes (Chapter 504) and many state statutes have broad prohibitions against discrimination for reasons of mental or emotional disability. However, if problems in these areas directly affected an applicant's work in a past place of employment, I would expect a careful reference check to turn them up. In doubtful cases check with a local attorney on limitations, given your statutes, local case law, and the provisions that specifically apply to your specific facility.

It is helpful when checking references to be clear about your setting and the job in question, such as general duties, supervision or the lack thereof, stress level, common problems in doing the job, and the like. I often ask, near the end, if the person giving the reference would have any qualms whatsoever about hiring the applicant for the type of position I have described. If there is any way in which the job fit might not be good, does the informant have thoughts on issues that should be raised with the applicant?

D. Minnesota Employers (but others take note!):

Minnesota Statutes 148.A (see Appendix N) delineates employer liability in client/therapist sex cases that end up as civil suits. In addition to the usual liability for failing to take appropriate action when an employer knew or should have known that the abuse was taking place, this statute outlines a fairly specific duty vis-`a-vis the checking and giving of references. It also provides some protection for employers who discharge this duty in good faith. The basic duty is to check via letter with past employers on any history of sexual contact with current or former clients, and any history of solicitation for sexual contact. A past employer who, when asked, fails to pass on information on past offenses can be held directly liable for future damages. This theory of liability has been set out in a statute in Minnesota and it may well be part of statutes in other states also.

E. Other Standards:

Be sure that you follow your local standards on the responsibilities of an employer to check references and screen potential employees, as defined by statute or case law. You may want to approach your professional association to ask that appropriate local counsel be hired to study this issue and then to write an article or a set of guidelines, or to hold a workshop on the topic.

II. STAFF POLICIES:

A. Written Policies:

You need written policies on the romantic/sexual involvement of therapists with present and former clients. The policies should be comprehensive and clear. Vague statements on violating "boundaries" or "dual relationships" are not enough.

B. Rules for Support Staff:

It is important that you clarify to whom the rules apply. Furthermore, rules for the support staff also should be addressed. In residential programs the best procedure may be to consider all staff members to be subject to the same rules.

C. Sexual Harassment Policies:

Why would one assume that a staff member who hustles other staff and trainees stops there? Why not clients also? When the genesis of the problem is sexual impulse control or sexual coercion by a neurotic and insecure professional, the primary outward sign of danger may manifest itself first as sexual harassment. We know of agency situations in which tolerance for sexual harassment contributed to the attitude that involvement with a client could be permissible.

D. Complaint Mechanism:

It is a bit late to design a complaint procedure after a complaint is received. The existence of a clear procedure facilitates complaints by both clients and staff members. The procedure should cover all complaints of possible unethical or unprofessional conduct. Not infrequently, sexual misconduct occurs in the context of other sloppy or unprofessional conduct or work.

E. Mechanism for Adjudication of Complaints:

We strongly favor the use of outside consultants to assist in handling most complaints. The effect of the outsider is to take the pressure off the administrative staff, provide support, and insure a more objective review of the complaint. When the consultant participates in interviewing the involved parties, he or she helps by being objective and by being perceived as objective.

A Professional Standards Review Committee (PSRC) or internal Ethics Committee also is helpful. If a serious complaint is filed against a staff member or volunteer at WICC, it is taken to the PSRC which appoints a three-person subcommittee to hear the case. The committee comprises some board members and well-known professionals from outside the agency. Fortunately, the PSRC is only very rarely used at the Center; serving on it is not a great burden.

Last but not least, it is critical that there be a way to file a complaint against the Director or head of your facility. Without it the program is potentially compromised.

III. COMPLAINT RESOLUTION:

A. Complaints are Complaints:

In our experience mental health professionals and health care professionals in general do a poor job of dealing with clients as **consumers**. Regardless of "transference" or other treatment-related phenomena, complaints must be treated as complaints and not as symptoms of a client's pathology, and they must be given some resolution. Many tearful practitioners have sat in my office wishing that they had learned this principle earlier.

B. The Stress of Complaining:

Given the tide of anxiety, concern, and defensiveness that is generated by a complaint, it is not uncommon for the person(s) to whom the complaint is addressed to react in a formal, distant, and legalistic manner and to become so factually oriented that the client's anxiety is heightened. A client's fear or assumption that the complaint will be discounted seems to find confirmation in this behavior. The careful questioning and studied attempt of an administrator to be "neutral" and to maintain a "poker face" comes across to a client as rejection and disbelief.

Persons handling a complaint must be more humane; they must adhere to a variant of the golden rule: to behave in a fashion they would want a member of their families to experience were he/she to be a complainant in a comparable situation. It costs nothing to reassure a complainant with comments such as, "I know this isn't easy," "You've been through a lot," "If these questions get to be too much, let me know and we can take a break," and so on.

Regardless of your belief in the validity of the complaint, you should thank the complainant for coming forward. If you have trouble finding a reason to be thankful, just remember that the complainant could have gone to your funding agency, the local newspaper, or a major TV station. He/she also could have gone to an attorney and tried to sue you off the face of the earth.

C. Don't Forget That They Are Clients:

The fact that someone is filing a complaint in no way changes your professional duty vis-à-vis her/his needs. You should assess the person's stress level and suicidal potential, for example. In addition, you would be wise to offer help in finding an appropriate independent resource. A failure to do so is unprofessional and, indeed, may be actionable as malpractice.

If the client pushes for service at your agency, however, you have a dilemma. If he/she refuses outside options, you would be best off to provide at least temporary service. Ultimately, however, it may be difficult for the complainant to get help in your facility. In situations that develop at inpatient or residential facilities where the clients are often quite vulnerable, extreme caution is urged in the consideration of a transfer. Whether the client stays for a while or is transferred, extra support usually is needed.

D. Temporary Suspension:

Many directors make the mistake of regarding suspension as a double or nothing proposition. In many instances it is proper to put somebody on leave (administrative, health, or even voluntary; i.e., using vacation time) until things can be sorted out. Whether it is a paid leave can be settled later, depending on the outcome of the investigation.

This action signals to the client and to other staff members that you take complaints seriously. It gives the clinician a break from her/his duties; good clinical work is difficult when one is under a cloud. The pressure of being subjected to an investigation can lead to enough distress in and of itself to impair a previously well-functioning professional. Last but not least, it applies a preventive measure if the practitioner is in fact behaving unprofessionally.

A note is in order here, however, on whether the therapist should be abruptly removed from all duties. It is critical to meet and to review her or his caseload and to make sure that any client in crisis is not left in the lurch. In some situations in which we have consulted we have recommended that the therapist continue to meet with one or two clients in his/her caseload, with or without a co-therapist present, depending on the situation.

E. Limits of Privacy:

Complainants, like all persons seeking professional services, must be forewarned of the limits of privacy before they "spill their guts." Some of the reporting duties in Minnesota are elucidated elsewhere in this volume. All states have child protection reporting statutes and many have vulnerable adults statutes (dealing with the mentally ill, mentally retarded, or people in inpatient and residential settings) which mandate the reporting of various types of alleged abuses. The rules under which you or your facility is licensed may include some mandatory reporting also.

F. Complaint Resolution:

For many years the common resolution to a serious complaint was to allow the practitioner to resign and for the matter to be left moot. Ironically, this resolution did not prevent lawsuits; in fact it may have encouraged suits because consumers became outraged when they saw exploitative behavior being swept under the rug.

In Minnesota, the 1986 statute attempts to curtail this vicious cycle by mandating every employer to answer the questions of future employers on past/present sexual contact with clients. Some employers react by asserting that moot or unproven cases need not be reported but I doubt that this will be much of a defense if any practitioner goes on to harm future clients. Most employers who contact us take the position that they now have to get to the bottom of each and every complaint of sexual misconduct so that they can properly do their duty in responding to requests from potential future employers.

This position is not always an easy one to hold to and we do not always reach a clear resolution. However, the situation today still is much better than that of the recent past when (a) an impaired practitioner or clergyman was simply allowed to go on and abuse more people; (b) subtle language and groans or sighs were used to indicate that something was wrong with the applicant; and (c) innuendos or rumors were surreptitiously spread.

G. Feedback to the Complainant:

We know of lawsuits that were filed largely because the employer of a therapist gave no feedback to the complainant. We also know of complainants who have gone to the media simply because they had heard nothing from an employer. One can draw the line in some cases on what you can tell clients, but they must have feedback to know that something is being done.

H. Job References:

With or without Minnesota Statutes 148.A we feel that it is the employer's duty to try honestly to pass along information on past abuses. We obtain a broad release from all applicants to WICC and we ask employers who request information from us to obtain a similar release to be free to share information. If a signed release is returned to us we go ahead and provide the data we have.

IV. STAFF EDUCATION:

A. All staff need to be given copies of the policies.

B. The policies must be explained. We recommend underlining key items and highlighting them in direct discussion with new staff members.

C. Boundary Issues: No policies can do an adequate job of reviewing all the gray areas relative to therapist/client boundaries. As such we recommend at least a yearly training session at which there is adequate time to discuss boundary issues. Jeanette Milgrom on our staff has developed a manual of exercises, and this is the most frequent type of inservice training our Center does.

D. Learning From Experience: When an incident happens, is investigated, and a resolution is reached, it is important that other staff be told something of the matter. Even though personnel matters carry with them some duties of privacy, it is impossible for staff to fully understand or trust policies unless they see them in action.

Furthermore, it is critical that as much as possible be gleaned from bad events so that they are not repeated. This is an ideal time to bring in a consultant and review how all of the policies worked.

V. STAFF SUPERVISION/PEER REVIEW:

A. Supervision/Consultation:

Given the demands of the psychotherapy business, it is hard to imagine that any of us can give optimal care in the absence of supervision and consultation. At WICC we use a team model in which the designated supervisor's cases are also discussed. The consultation and supervision, ironically, are the major reasons cited by the more than 220 therapists who apply each year for volunteer positions.

B. Professional Standards Review:

It is helpful to have some sort of system for reviewing the quality of care, or for reviewing questions of professional practice.

C. Standards for Triggering a Review:

In our post hoc analysis of cases of client/therapist sex, the most common factors which would have, or could have signalled the need for some review of the case are: 1. longer than usual treatment; 2. evidence of excessive dependency, such as frequent phone calls, letters, etc. (usually noticed by support staff); and 3. seductive behavior observed by other staff (again, often by support staff).

D. Periodic Review of Long-Term Treatment:

A large percentage of sexual encounters between client and therapist occur in the context of long-term therapy heavily focused on the client/therapist relationship and personal growth as opposed to the treatment of particular symptoms or resolution of well-defined problems.

We recommend periodic review of treatment which exceeds six months, focusing on treatment goals and progress toward them. The reviewer needs to seek clarification as to whether therapy is going on or the relationship has taken on too many of the trappings of a friendship or other personal relationship. Furthermore, we always ask what the plans are for termination: When will the therapy end?

E. The Right Atmosphere:

We have encountered many situations in fine clinics or programs in which there is in fact peer interaction and on-going consultation or supervision, but in which practitioners really don't "take each other on."

A classic illustration is one situation in which a therapist admitted sexual abuse of a client. One of the other staff said she'd always felt uncomfortable about what she could see of the therapeutic relationship in question. After some discussion it became clear that people were unwilling to share vague questions or impressions—especially when they weren't sure why they felt the way they did. Of course, if a client were to acknowledge such a vague feeling, but didn't have a rational or immediately identifiable basis for it, they would advise discussion and exploration. But with themselves they simply clammed up. Another issue which emerged was that everybody wanted to do their therapy their way and they felt that if they began putting heat on a colleague he might well turn around and begin challenging them.

We recommend that graduate training programs begin the process and that students and trainees be offered coursework which involves actual role-play in giving feedback to and confronting colleagues.

F. Pathways for Internal Complaint/Concern:

When questions or feedback haven't produced much, is there a nonthreatening way for clinical staff to raise concerns with another staff member's functioning, handling of a specific case, etc.? How does the support staff person who has seen something troubling have a way of raising it?

G. The Impaired or Distressed Practitioner:

We have at times been shocked by the degree to which mental health programs fail to deal with obvious mental health problems among their staff. Beyond colleagial support, there needs to be a referral to an appropriate "helper" as well as a review of clinical duties. In psychotherapy we are the "tools" ourselves, and when we develop problems the "tool" may not work well anymore.

H. Interventions:

There need to be readily available resource persons who can be brought in as consultants or co-therapists when relationships become romanticized or sexualized. The atmosphere needs to be such that clinicians feel comfortable in asking for help. Therapists who keep a romanticized relationship a secret and endeavor to find their own way out often wind up mired down.

VI. Clients:

A. Activating the Consumer:

New clients need to be given both written and verbal information on the importance of giving feedback and raising questions about their therapy. There needs to be an easy-to-use way of getting consultation if the client is uneasy about what is happening and their therapist hasn't been able to reassure them.

Consumer handouts may also provide guidelines to assist the client in evaluating therapy. One such example, aimed at the public as well as consumers, was developed by the Wisconsin Task Force (see Appendix Z).

B. Assessing Past Treatment:

As with previously "hidden" problems such as incest, alcoholism and family violence, the more we ask about them the more we find they exist. It needs to be general practice to carefully assess the client's view of past treatment in your program or elsewhere. It is simply incredible how many clients reveal past abuse to a new therapist only after the passage of months or years, largely because the new therapist did not provide the opportunity by simply asking.

C. Consumer Satisfaction/Outcome:

Both consumer satisfaction and outcome studies sometimes produce information about abusive staff members. Each, of course, has utility in its own right, whether or not it ever helps to ferret out a single case of sex between client and therapist.

D. Processing Sessions/Mediation:

A separate paper in this volume deals with "Processing Sessions." In a great many situations, sitting the client and therapist down together to discuss the complaint is very helpful in gaining an understanding of what went on and in helping the client to begin to work it through. Even if it is not used in all cases, this option must be available.

The List Goes On

So much for the checklist. Like its predecessors, it is an attempt to spell out how a prudent administrator can do a better job of dealing with the problem of client/therapist sex. The list ranges from items related to prevention, those aimed at earlier discovery, to those aimed at cleaner resolution.

Professionals in the field must learn from experience; thus the list may need to grow. The current version is twice as long as earlier ones. This does not mean that it is better but that we have tried to identify some other safeguards.

Clearly, many episodes of sexual involvement between client and therapist are symptomatic of other problems in the provision of service. Therefore many of the solutions are aimed at generally improving the quality of services, especially in regard to the degree to which the needs of clients are served.

CHAPTER 37

THE PREVENTION OF SEXUAL EXPLOITATION OF CLIENTS: HIRING PRACTICES

John C. Gonsiorek

A major administrative safeguard (see Ch. 36) is the careful hiring of staff. Minnesota statutes relating to an employer's civil liability for sexual exploitation by a therapist focus on careful hiring as a major duty. The provision is largely based on work at the Walk-In Counseling Center which suggests that many exploitative cases could have been prevented by selective personnel practices. The major purpose of the provision is to detect repeat offenders. Thus there is articulated in this chapter a hiring strategy that also includes screening for any weakness in practice that may lead to a greater likelihood of exploitation.

More than 30 years ago, Schwebel (1955) wrote, "...there are no published data on the kinds of personal qualities that are associated with ethical practice...." Yet, today, the American Psychological Association Task Force on Impaired Psychologists, which Schwebel chairs, is still unable to identify such predictors (Schwebel, Skorina, & Schoener, 1988). Despite considerable research over the past three decades, good predictors of unethical conduct are lacking (e.g., Welfel & Lipsitz, 1984).

The prevention of sexual exploitation by psychotherapists is an important task. However, based on the reports in this book, a very diverse group of therapists apparently engage in the sexual exploitation of clients. Unfortunately, there are no reliably identifiable "types" to screen for. To make matters worse, a large number of therapists, when distressed, may be capable of slipping into high-risk behaviors that lead to unproductive practices or to resisting feedback and supervision; any such conduct, in turn, can lead to sexual involvement with a client.

Within the context of the foregoing observations, there is described in this chapter a process for hiring mental health professionals; its purpose is to reduce the likelihood of engaging an individual who may sexually exploit a client. The process is not meant to substitute for the substantive contents of the chapters on supervision and administrative safeguards. The common element in all these processes is the gatekeeping function they perform. The hiring process is simply the first of many gatekeeping functions. The information provided here supplements the chapters on supervision and administrative safeguards to shape a system of hiring, administration, and supervision that has the greatest probability of reducing adverse experiences for clients and encouraging the productive and ethical practice of psychotherapy.

Many suggestions in this chapter are generally sound principles for hiring health-care professionals and are not simply aimed at sexual misconduct. Indeed, these contents were initially presented at the (June) 1987 annual meeting of the Group Health Association in Seattle, Washington. The emphasis at that time was on hiring mental health professionals who would function well in the goal-oriented treatment setting of an HMO. Much of the material has been revised and supplemented for presentation here.

Appendix X contains an application form that is in use at the Metropolitan Clinics of Counseling in Minnesota. The form was created by me and draws heavily on the application form in Appendix C, the Walk-In Counseling Center's application form for mental health volunteers, the prototype for this intensive screening process. The comments in this chapter refer to items in Appendix X although many also apply to differently numbered items in Appendix C.

DETERMINATION OF APPLICANT QUALITIES

The first step in selecting and hiring clinical staff is to articulate clearly who is being sought. This question must be answered on a number of fronts. First, what is the treatment philosophy and organizational mission of the institution and how do these translate into training backgrounds for desirable staff members? Next, what specific clinical skills are needed now and in the foreseeable future? These two concerns are addressed in other papers not related to this volume (Gonsiorek, Drucker, & Stoebner, 1987; Gonsiorek, Stoebner, & Drucker, 1987). Although the rest of this paper focuses primarily on the use of hiring to screen for ethical and competency concerns, it is important to note that the approach outlined here is comprehensive and addresses other issues as well.

The final area, the determination of applicant qualities, requires screening for competent practice, appropriate professional boundaries, and adherence to professional ethics. I want to emphasize again that the hiring process is only the first of a number of administrative and supervisory gatekeepers to assure these qualities. Sound hiring alone, it should be noted, cannot guarantee them.

HIRING PROCESS

The Application

Using a standardized application form such as that in Appendix C is strongly recommended. Applicants should be asked to complete this form prior to being interviewed. The form should cover a number of specific areas.

One set of questions (1 & 2 in Appendix D) should obtain specific information on education, degrees held, licensure or certification status, and clinically relevant training and experiences. The information provided by the applicant, however, should not be taken at face value.

Check licensure and certification status with the board in the state in which the license or certification is held. Typically, this information is public. In those states that require a listing of competencies, this information also is public. Complaints that result in final board action typically are public; complaints that are in process, however, often are not.

Similarly, information on educational experience should not be accepted without question. Training programs that receive national credentialing from such organizations as the American Medical Association, the American Psychological Association or the National Association of Social Workers benefit from predictability in the training backgrounds of graduates. An increasing number of applicants, however, especially in psychology and counseling related fields, do not come out of such programs. For example, the American Psychological Association does not certify for approval any terminal masters level program, yet there are hundreds of masters level psychology and counseling programs. I am not arguing that these programs are uniformly deficient but, rather, that without a national professional body to certify such programs the evaluation of their graduates is both difficult and uncertain. Applicants from self-designed or unknown programs should receive special scrutiny. In general, if a training program is unfamiliar, do not hesitate to seek more information on it. Again, the reason is not that the applicant is necessarily deficient but that one cannot predict the skill level from a degree program that is an unknown.

It is no secret that a number of "degree mills" operate in mental-health-related disciplines across the country. For varying fees, these mills provide students with very minimal training experiences (usually of the student's design and choosing) for a degree that in name and transcript, may look identical to those of quality training programs.

Answers to questions on previous employment and other training experiences are informative (questions 4 & 5), providing the information is verified. One often can tell a good deal about an applicant by the additional training experience he or she has undergone. Has the individual attempted to broaden his or her clinical experience or remained very focused on a narrow area or particular theoretical orientation? The basic message of this information on training background and job history, however, is that details should be not only collected but, also, systematically verified and evaluated. This information assists in understanding the competency level of the applicant as well as informing how the applicant may fit into the particular job for which he or she is being considered. In other words, the intent of many sections of the application is not only to screen the applicant but, also, to make an efficacious placement.

Another crucial area to assess is references (question 8). In general, written references are useless unless they are negative. In such cases, the comments are noteworthy for their content and for the applicant's poor judgment in submitting them. The majority of applicants have enough common sense to submit written references that are glowing.

Most written references contain little or no useful information for the reviewer. The latter should obtain from the applicant, instead, the names, addresses and phone numbers of two or three supervisors, colleagues, or co-workers and interview these reference sources by telephone. In this way, the evaluator can pose questions that seem most relevant about the applicant's background and how he or she may fit into the particular setting or program seeking the information. The evaluator should be assertive during these telephone interviews, questioning incongruities, hesitations, or mixed messages from the sources and seeking detailed understanding of the applicant's strengths and weaknesses. Many sources of reference are in the habit of giving bland generic statements about people under discussion, hence I encourage evaluators to push the sources to be specific and to show some critical evaluation in their description of an applicant. If the sources are hesitant (many people fear the prospect of litigation) it is advisable to read the applicant's signed statement that informants will not be held liable for statements they may make.

Next, the application should include various questions on the applicant's adverse experiences and history of ethical practice (question 3). These should be specific: Has the applicant's licensure or certification ever been limited, suspended, or revoked in any jurisdiction? Has the applicant ever surrendered a license or been placed on probation? Ask questions on whether any professional employer, hospital, or training program ever has suspended, eliminated, or terminated the applicant's duties or responsibilities. Include questions on whether the applicant has ever been denied membership, renewal of membership, or subjected to disciplinary proceedings by a professional organization.

Questions about malpractice, of course, are important. Have any malpractice judgments or professional liability claims or suits ever been made against the applicant? Is the applicant aware of any existing situation that is likely to result in a claim or suit, a disciplinary proceeding, a change in licensure, or the like? Further, the applicant should be asked whether he or she ever has been convicted of a criminal charge. Depending on the hiring discrimination laws in your particular jurisdiction, broader questions on the applicant's history of legal difficulties or problems also may be included. Finally, ask applicants specifically if they are aware of any physical or mental limitations or conditions that could significantly impair their ability to render patient care.

The point of these questions is not to automatically eliminate applicants. Sometimes licenses to practice are limited or suspended because of situations that may not necessarily justify denial of employment. An increasing number of malpractice suits are nuisance suits that do not reflect a therapist's problems. The proper response to a question answered "yes" in this section is to suspend judgment until more information has been obtained.

This area of questioning on adverse experiences is controversial but it appears to be winning increasing acceptance. Employers may be held liable in civil actions sometimes if they have not adequately screened professional staff members who later behave unprofessionally or unethically with patients and who have a history of such conduct. Chapter 36 ("Administrative Safeguards") details these considerations further. The only limitation of inquiries on adverse experiences should be legal vulnerability to claims of hiring discrimination. This section of the application, consequently, should be developed to provide as much information as is feasible in the particular jurisdiction without creating an untenable vulnerability to such charges.

The many gray areas in civil law make it preferable to err in the direction of risking charges of hiring discrimination rather than of negligent hiring. Both situations involve legal vulnerability, although only one may endanger clients. The legal system as a whole seems to have become much more sensitive to issues of professional impropriety. Health care organizations that make good faith efforts to screen applicants carefully may well receive a more sympathetic ear from the courts than those organizations that do not adequately check for adverse background experiences for fear of incurring charges of hiring discrimination. An attorney knowledgeable in the relevant statutes of one's particular jurisdiction should review this section.

Other questions focusing on special skills and job expectations again serve as much to properly place as to screen an applicant. The general intent of an application is to learn as much about the applicant as can be summarized in writing to gain a well-rounded picture prior to the interview.

Applicant's Signed Statement

A somewhat controversial suggestion is to have each applicant sign a statement to verify the following items:

1. The information on the application is true.

2. The applicant has abided by and will continue to abide by the relevant professional ethics codes or requirements of the licensure or certification body.

3. The applicant understands that if hired, he or she will read the policy manual and guidelines of the agency and will abide by them.

4. The applicant is expected to renew her or his knowledge of policies and procedures and to sign an annual statement attesting to having done so.

5. The applicant authorizes the agency or its representatives to contact representatives and past supervisors, training programs, and employers to obtain information about him or her.

6. The applicant releases from all liability both the evaluating agency and the individuals it so contacts.

7. The applicant agrees to notify the agency, if later employed by it, about any changes in licensure, censure or sanction by professional bodies for adverse experiences that are included in the application.

The purposes of the signed statement are varied: to inform applicants of the agency's procedures and expectations; to notify applicants about the agency's concern with ethical and professional conduct; to reduce the agency's liability in its application procedure; and to facilitate the application process by gaining permission to check references.

Functions of the Application and Signed Statement

An application and signed statement serves various purposes. It is a vehicle for structuring the interview and it is a screening device. Potential applicants who are intimidated by the signed statement, the questions on adverse experiences, the checking of references, and so forth, are likely to be people one would not want to hire. A novelty factor is present for some applicants, particularly for older professionals who never may have been through such a complete screening before. It may be necessary to answer such individuals' questions on the rationale and intent of these procedures.

Furthermore, this application serves the purpose of intimidating individuals who have something to hide. One of its functions, frankly, is to discourage such people from applying. The procedure puts everyone, particularly the applicant, on notice of the value the agency places on competent and ethical practice. Thus, the screening function tends to create a somewhat smaller pool of higher quality applicants who can be further assessed and interviewed.

The Interview

Prior to the interview, the evaluator should review the application and other submitted materials and should telephone the references. The information thus obtained gives a sense of the applicant's strengths and weaknesses before the interview is conducted. Further, the information can be used to shape the particular direction of the interview.

Discrepancies, misunderstandings or incomplete information on the application can be reviewed during the interview. In addition the applicant's congruence with the organization's treatment philosophy and his or her specific clinical skills can be evaluated in detail.

A somewhat unusual experience for many applicants—namely, role plays—also is recommended during the interview. Each evaluator should develop two or three role plays using situations that are relatively typical of the agency's client population. The evaluator should play the role of the client, the applicant that of the therapist. Ideally, the situation should reflect a weak spot in the applicant's training and background which has been inferred from the application and references, and, at the same time capture a client situation typical to the agency. Following the role play, the evaluator should give the applicant feedback and criticism on the handling of the client.

The purpose of the role play is twofold: to obtain an in vivo understanding of how the applicant functions with clients and to obtain a similar understanding of how receptive the applicant is to supervision and feedback. I see the feedback as every bit as important as the role play because receptivity to supervision is just as important a facet to assess as are specific clinical skills. The role play does not merely screen people out, although it may well do that; it helps to achieve a better understanding of the applicant's strengths and weaknesses. Thus, if the applicant is hired, he or she can be placed most thoughtfully within the agency to optimize her or his performance. In addition, appropriate supervisory arrangements and further professional training and development experiences can be identified and made part of the applicant's hiring agreement.

Work Samples and In Vivo Demonstrations

If an individual is being hired to exercise a very specific skill, it is useful to ask for an in vivo demonstration of the skill. For example, if you are hiring a psychologist to interpret psychological tests, give the applicant some completed and scored test materials. Allow her or him some time to review the materials and then ask for an interpretation. The review of work samples also is informative although these suffer, if to a somewhat lesser extent, than from the same problem as written references. An applicant generally chooses what places him or her in the most favorable light.

Similarly, it is instructive to pose questions on various ethical dilemmas that are typical to the agency or the client population served. These certainly can include direct questions on how the applicant would handle sexual feelings toward clients, knowledge and understanding of ethics codes related to sexual exploitation, and the like. Include questions in other areas that are related to client welfare. Many licensing boards and certification bodies, for example, report that the most frequent complaints about therapists involve confidentiality and proper record keeping. Obtaining information on the applicant's knowledge base and attitudes toward areas of ethical concern that are not directly related to sexual exploitation is crucial. Keep in mind that the core issue in sexual exploitation is that it is exploitative. The sexual aspect is merely the vehicle for that particular exploitation. Evaluating other kinds of ethical concern can be informative about the applicant's potential for exploitation. By incorporating these suggestions in the interview, the general propriety of the applicant's boundaries and level of ethical practice, as well as the specifics of sexual exploitation, can be reasonably estimated.

FINAL COMMENTS

Unquestionably, these proposed procedures require a very questioning and critical attitude toward the screening of mental health professionals as well as greater effort by the evaluator and greater openness from the applicant. Hundreds of professionals willingly undergo this process simply to volunteer at the Walk-In Counseling Center in Minneapolis. A major managed mental health system in the Twin Cities area uses a very similar procedure. Most applicants in both settings have a positive response to the agency upon going through this procedure. They perceive that the consideration given them is thoughtful and thorough, and that the agency has high standards with which they are proud to be affiliated if they are accepted. This procedure is offensive to those professionals who are protective of their professional prerogatives and who feel that a degree and license make them above questioning. Such individuals, I believe strongly, are at a higher risk for unethical practice and it is advisable to screen them out.

Use of the proposed procedures makes it more likely that one's clinical staff will be well trained and competent practitioners who function ethically and responsibly. Their skills will be better understood. Therefore, they can be placed more carefully in the agency and their performance will be optimized. They are more likely to be productive and satisfied with their employment and to have fewer adverse experiences with clients. This application procedure feeds into the development of supervisory structures and inservice training programs. It is the first gateway that informs and directs the later administrative and supervisory gateways. It is not fool-proof but it provides a structure for evaluating elements that may have been overlooked should adverse experiences occur.

Further, the procedures give applicants a powerful message about the seriousness with which the agency considers professional competence and ethics. These procedures help to create a group culture in which competence and professional standards of practice are valued and taken seriously. Most important, these procedures make it more likely that clients will be well served and protected from adverse experiences. It does not guarantee this outcome, of course, but does increase its likelihood. The likelihood can be added to by giving the same attention to the other gatekeeping functions—administrative safeguards and supervision—and also making them as thoughtful and vigorous as possible.

CHAPTER 38

THE ROLE OF SUPERVISION AND CASE CONSULTATION IN PRIMARY PREVENTION

Gary Richard Schoener
and
Ray M. Conroe

The focus of this chapter is the role of supervision and case consultation in the primary prevention of sexual exploitation of clients by counselors and psychotherapists. By primary prevention we mean the prevention of the first episode. Both supervision and case consultation also may be instrumental in preventing recurrences of the problem (see Ch. 34) as well as incompetent therapy and other types of unprofessional conduct. The emphasis here, however, is on the prevention of sexual contact and/or romantic involvement.

Our presentation deals in part with practical suggestions that derive from feedback from therapist-perpetrators who have been interviewed subsequent to the filing of complaints, and on the post-hoc analysis of numerous situations of therapist-client sex. Instead of a detailed plan for action, we present what we hope is a useful set of guidelines.

DEFINING TERMS

In the mental health field, the term "supervision" has a great many meanings. It is used to refer to purely administrative responsibility in situations in which clinical consultation is obtained from someone else, either inside or outside the agency. It is used to describe the teaching-related management of trainees in internships, field placements, and residencies (see Ch. 23). It is applied to the privately arranged (and usually purchased) consultation of a senior colleague by therapists, individually or in groups, to review selected case material. Last but not least, the term is used to refer to certain types of third-party billing arrangements in which practitioners are only reimbursed if they are "supervised" by certain other types of practitioners (e.g., a social worker supervised by a psychiatrist).

When "supervision" is required for practice under certain licensure statutes, third-party reimbursement contracts, or the statutory standards for a licensed or certified facility, the term can be explicitly (and legally) defined in terms of nature and length of supervisory sessions, proximity of a supervisor to a supervisee when services being billed are rendered, and so on.

Several observers (Kaslow, 1986; Rodgers, 1988) have noted that the strict definition of supervision assumes that both supervisor and supervisee deem the supervisor to have control over and responsibility for the treatment provided. The supervisor can determine what spot-checks should be made of the supervisee's work, what material reviewed, and what standards for handling cases, enforced.

By contrast, "case consultation," although it also includes the review of case material and the application of an outside perspective on the handling of a case, does not imply that the consultant has control over or responsibility for the treatment provided. Kaslow (1986) has been one of the few authors to distinguish the two over the years.

In our view, much of what is called "supervision" is and always has been case consultation. When private practitioners arrange for outside "supervision" they actually are purchasing case consultation. Neither they nor the "supervisor" assumes that the latter is responsible for the treatment.

The purpose of this discussion so far is to focus attention on the need to define the supervisor/supervisee contract and to alert persons considering the supervisory role to some potential liabilities that are discussed in the next section.

For the sake of simplicity, we use the term supervision to refer both to true supervision and to voluntary case consultation arrangements that also are commonly referred to in the field as "supervision."

LEGAL ISSUES

Hassenfeld and Sarris's (1978) article, "Hazards and Horizons of Psychotherapy Supervision," is an early but still useful discussion of some liability issues in the supervision of psychotherapy. Slovenko (1980) examined the legal issues in psychotherapy supervision to provide what is to date the only in-depth discussion of legal issues for the supervisor in the literature.

Slovenko discussed the concept of "vicarious liability" or "imputed negligence" in which an employer or supervisor may be held liable for damage to a client even though he or she had no direct role in the treatment, did nothing to encourage the harmful practices, and even did all that was possible to prevent it. It should be noted that the case law related to the vicarious liability of employers (and, therefore, potential supervisors) is constantly changing and vary somewhat in principles and standards from state to state.

A client who is damaged and brings a civil action will try to hold as many people liable as possible in order to recover maximal damages. Under the "deep-pocket" theory, his or her attorney will proceed against the therapist's employer, supervisor(s), and even a professional organization to which the therapist may belong.

In the case of supervision by, or under the aegis of an employer, one key concept is that the conduct of the therapist should be within the "scope of employment." The considerable case law on this concept in any jurisdiction usually deals with situations outside the domain of psychotherapy.[1]

Slovenko (1980) suggested that one might question how liable supervisors actually are given that the few lawsuits filed against psychotherapists relate specifically to therapy, and vicarious liability is a secondary liability built upon the liability of the therapist/supervisee. Nevertheless he noted that the growing attention at the time he was writing to the harm done by some psychotherapy was creating a growing liability.

Currently, the number of suits has multiplied and articles have proliferated on the topic of harmful psychotherapy. In addition, the literature is growing on the topic of

---

[1]For example, in two Minnesota cases, Marston and Williams versus Minneapolis Clinic of Psychiatry and Neurology, filed December 23, 1982, in the Minnesota Supreme Court, the key precedent case utilized by the court was Lange versus National Biscuit Company (297 Minn. 399, 211 NW 2nd 783 1973), which dealt with an assault by a biscuit company employee on a man he met in a grocery store. There were no psychotherapy or even health care-related precedents.

psychotherapy supervision; the possibility of direct liability for negligent supervision, therefore, seems possible. The argument might be that the supervision did not meet the standard of care for supervision, resulting in harm to the client as a result of the actions of both supervisor and therapist/supervisee.

The following examples are a few of the situations cited by Slovenko (1980) which might lead to the finding that a supervisor was negligent. Although the word "trainee" is used in some instances, the same arguments could be used for a practicing professional who is a supervisee.

1. The trainee takes relevant notes during the therapy, the supervisor does not study these notes and does not realize that the notes indicate a therapy method other than that offered or available.

2. Written progress notes are inadequate or do not support the treatment plan.

3. The trainee and patient (or trainee and supervisor) have a conflict of personalities and yet the treatment continues.

4. The trainee becomes socially involved with the client, but cleverly hides the involvement from the supervisor. The supervisor should have known by more complete supervisory sessions. (p. 463)

The last point is of particular interest in light of Bennett's (1986) report of the civil suit against an inexperienced therapist in private practice who sexually exploited a client and then left the state to avoid a courtroom appearance. His "supervisor," who was unaware that this client was being treated by the inexperienced therapist and who, therefore, was not "supervising" the case, nonetheless was sued.

Although it does not offer fail-safe protection, it seems prudent for professionals, who provide case consultation without true authority over the treatment, to call themselves "consultants" rather than "supervisors." Further, it is useful to examine the arguments made in civil suits that the employer of a therapist, or the therapist's supervisor, bear responsibility for the damages to a client by the sexual exploitation of a therapist. Inasmuch as many such cases are settled out of court, one cannot poll a jury on the factors they consider critical. Some examples follow of theories of supervisor liability that have resulted in decisions against supervisors:

1. Supervisor (or employer) should have known that the treatment had gone amiss because the written notes had deteriorated badly.

2. Supervisor would have noted treatment problems had the notes been examined.

3. Based on what the supervisor was told, he/she should have examined the transference/countertransference problems more closely by:

   a. holding a more complete discussion with the therapist;
   b. requesting tapes of several sessions; and
   c. asking to sit in on a session and talking directly to the client.

4. The supervisor should have known that the therapist was at risk to exploit either this client or this type of client because of the therapist's personal problems

   a. that were known to the supervisor; and

b. which the supervisor should have seen.

5. The supervisor ignored or did not react adequately to some sort of unusual event, such as, the client showing up in scant clothing, apparently sleepwalking, at the therapist's home or clinic.

6. The supervisor knew of, but did not take into account, the therapist's past problems of maintaining professional boundaries.

7. A colleague or support staff person had raised some vague concerns with what was going on in the case and the supervisor failed to make further inquiries.

8. A previous complaint or grievance was not adequately assessed; or, no effort was made to track down rumors of supposed unprofessional conduct by the therapist.

9. The supervisor's judgment was impaired by virtue of a romantic and/or sexual relationship with the supervisee, or because the supervisor has a therapeutic relationship as well as a supervisory one with the supervisee.[2]

Cormier and Bernard (1982), in an article on clinical supervisors' ethical and legal responsibilities, suggested that it may be advisable for a clinical supervisor to make an independent assessment of potentially dangerous clients. It is possible that a supervisor might be wise, in a given situation, to visit directly with client and therapist to help sort out a dispute between them.

As a result of our growing understanding of supervision and of the development of standards and models, supervisors should become better informed given that they may be held legally accountable for the mastery of a field's developing technology. It is also incumbent upon professional training programs that, if they have not already done so, they develop programs to train supervisors. In organizations in which supervisors have had no formal training, the possibility should be considered of some sort of continuing professional education in supervision.

In their recent book, *Supervising Counselors and Therapists*, Stoltenberg and Delworth (1987) wrote:

Most important, it is vital that the supervisor be well trained, knowledgeable, and skilled in the practice of clinical supervision. The supervisor should be cognizant of crucial legal issues and should examine his or her work with these questions in mind.

The next three sections focus on the development of supervisory skills.

TRAINING IN SUPERVISION

---

[2] While in theory having such a dual relationship should not, in and of itself, provide evidence of negligence in the supervision of a given case, it could contribute significantly to such an argument. It should be noted that we are aware of unpublished cases in which a claim was made by a supervisee for damages which resulted from sexual relationships with a supervisor. In one case the supervisee was both a client and supervisee; in the other, the supervisee was just a supervisee. Bernard (1987) warns of such dual relationships.

Many mental health professionals provide some supervision or case consultation during their careers although little training in this critical function is offered in graduate or medical school (Borders & Leddick, 1987; Styczynski, 1980).

At WICC we have separate criteria for volunteer supervisors and counselors, although we use a peer supervision model in which the supervisor functions largely as a team leader. Throughout the 1970s clinicians were prepared for the role of supervisor by serving as assistants to supervisors or by co-supervising a team. In 1981 our Clinic Director, Dr. Robert Wiley, designed a Supervisory Training Program that combined didactic presentations with discussion groups and an apprenticeship. Eight trainees completed this 9-month program and received certificates. Since then subsequent clinic directors have continued the program with some annual revisions and, typically, a smaller number of trainees. The program has continued to get good reviews over the years from clinicians who are grateful for the chance to develop and sharpen supervisory skills.

WICC also has trained the staff members of other programs in setting up, receiving, and providing supervision and case consultation. We have at times used videotapes of one of our own team supervision sessions to illustrate aspects of our process as well as pitfalls in the practice of supervision.

The transition to the supervisory role is discussed at some length by Styczynski (1980) but this issue, in general, is given scant treatment in the literature. We hope that the introduction of journals like *The Psychotherapy Supervisor* and the new *Journal of Training and Practice in Professional Psychology* will help to remedy the situation. Several graduate training programs offer courses in supervision but the courses are rarely available to psychotherapists in training. At least one national organization, the American Association for Counseling and Development, has attempted to remedy the situation through the publication of the *Handbook of Counseling Supervision* (Borders & Leddick, 1987).

MODELS OF SUPERVISION

Kaslow (1986) argued that everyone in private practice should make arrangements for supervision/consultation on a regular or an on-call basis, citing in part the following potential uses:

1. the depth and breadth of their knowledge and clinical experience and gaps in same;

2. need for a sounding board for verification and critique;

3. periodic need to recognize and work through transference and countertransference issues;

4. the need to expand one's assessment and treatment repertoire and refine one's skills;

5. to counter professional isolation and the stress associated with carrying the burden of hearing problems for many hours per week without access to a therapeutic support and discussion system. (p. 148)

It is noteworthy, in this regard, that during WICC's nearly two decades of existence, far and away the most frequently cited reasons for volunteering by mental health professionals has been our team approach that offers collegial support and feedback. Therapists seem to be quite willing to put in these additional clinical hours each week in exchange for the chance to network and to remedy professional isolation.

Kaslow's (1986a) *Supervision and Training: Models, Dilemmas, and Challenges*, and Hess' (1986a) *Psychotherapy Supervision: Theory, Research, and Practice*, are very informative on the various models of supervision; they also discuss supervision for group therapists and models and methods in use in psychoanalytic, client-centered, rational-emotive, and behavioral therapy.

Cade, Speed, and Seligman (1986) wrote an interesting article on "Working in Teams: The Pro's and Con's." Strosahl and Jacobsen's (1986) article, "Training and Supervision of Behavioral Therapists," and Wessler and Ellis's (1986) "Supervision in Rational-Emotive Therapy" also interest us. A number of chapters in the Hess (1986a) book focus on supervision in different types of settings.

Several investigators have discussed their theories on and observations of developmental stages in a supervisor/supervisee relationship. Friedman & Kaslow (1986), examined therapists in training and identified six stages in the supervision process when they looked at the development of professional identity in psychotherapists. Hess (1986b), in "Growth in Supervision: Stages of Supervisee and Supervisor Development," reviewed and charted different models in the literature. Stoltenberg and Delworth (1987) applied a developmental model to both supervisors and supervisees.

Last but not least, Abroms (1977) explored the boundary between supervision and psychotherapy. His model of supervision assumes considerable responsibility by the supervisor, and he recommended on-site visits with clients and therapists by the supervisor during the treatment process. These visits provide a check on possible mistaken diagnosis and reassures the client that a senior clinician is helping to oversee her or his care (Abroms, 1977). This examination of supervision as "metatherapy" reminds us not only of the danger that supervision may drift into being therapy, but, also, that in true supervision the supervisor acts somewhat as a co-therapist.

SUPERVISION METHODS

The excellent texts by Kaslow (1986a), Hess (1986a), and Stoltenberg and Delworth (1987) cited earlier offer useful and detailed discussions of the many methods of supervision.

Empirical research on factors that affect the quality of supervision has focused entirely on the supervision of trainees. In their summary of the research literature, Matarazzo and Patterson (1986) concluded that the relationship between supervisor and trainee is critical. Students who experience warmth, empathy, and support show more empathy with their clients and are more effective at the end of their practice.

In a study entitled "Doctoral Students: Comparative Evaluations of Best and Worst Psychotherapy Supervision," Allen, Szollos, and Williams (1986) summarized their findings as follows:

Good supervisors modeled respect of both their and their trainees' differences in values, experiences, and personal privacy. From this non-intrusive and pluralistic base, they provided useful, theory-based conceptual frameworks for understanding psychotherapeutic processes; taught practical skills; and encouraged trainees to experiment with using novel strategies. Good supervisors also were tolerant of mistakes, provided clear and direct feedback, and confronted supervisees' resistances in an atmosphere of safety. They also invested more time in the process and monitored the psychotherapeutic activities of their charges by some means other than trainees' self-reports. Finally, they were open to feedback about their own styles of relating. (p. 97)

Bad supervisors were more difficult to define, but a majority were "characterizable as disinterested or inept, and a minority as authoritarian or exploitive" (Allen, Szollos, & Williams, 1986, p. 98).

What is quite striking about the data from this very interesting study is that virtually no differences were found between "best" and "worst" supervision in terms of reliance on the various tools of supervision (e.g., co-therapy, videotape, audiotape, etc.) with the possible exception of verbal reports; more reliance was put on them in the supervision rated as poorer.

So, whether we look at trainees, a group that has been subjected to some empirical study, or practicing clinicians who have not been studied, there are no data to suggest that particular methods of supervision (see following outline) lead to better supervisory experience.

Although verbal report is by far the most used source of information in the supervision of practicing professionals, students who have been surveyed indicate that audiotapes are the most frequent source of data for monitoring clinical transactions (Allen, Szollos, & Williams, 1986; Hess & Hess, 1980). Verbal reports by trainees were the secondary source for about 2/3 of the situations, it was the primary data source only 14% of the time. Videotapes were used 44% of the time, live observations by the supervisor, 13%, and co-therapy with the supervisor, 10% of the time (Allen, Szollos, & Williams, 1986).

In traditional hierarchical supervision, group supervision, peer supervision, or case consultation, the following methods (and variations that are not included here) are useful:

1. Self-report by the therapist from memory notes.

2. Examination of notes or treatment records.

3. Audiotapes of sessions.

4. Videotapes of sessions.

5. Live observation, through a one-way mirror or by a supervisor in the room, with or without the capability of direct input to the supervisee.

6. Co-therapy, either on-going or on a consultative basis.

7. Role play of events in the session.

In practice, it is rare for supervisors to examine entire audio or videotapes of sessions; to conserve time supervisees typically are asked to present selected segments. Obviously, live observation and co-therapy are also labor intensive and do not allow for the supervision of many cases at one time. Furthermore, it is often difficult, in practice, for supervisors to review entire tapes, given the time required to do so. Certainly such reviews are not possible with more than a few cases in any caseload. A recent article raised concerns about the intrusion into privacy inherent in training supervision, arguing for limited intrusion (Betcher & Zinberg, 1988).

THE SUPERVISORY CONTRACT

Given the legal liabilities in supervision and the confusion over its form and meaning, it is critical that a clear supervisory contract be established. Although contracts often are inadequate, even in organizational settings where they should be easier to establish, they are an even greater challenge in private practice settings. Kaslow (1986b) treated this issue in "Seeking and Providing Consultation in Private Practice." She suggested examining a potential supervisee's training and credentials, theoretical orientation, flexibility, personality compatibility, maturity, and the like but offered no suggestions for how to do so. She also recommended a short trial period of three to four sessions; specifying a contract period, frequency and length of sessions, and cost and time of payment; and defining goals and expectations for both parties at the outset and reviewing them periodically.

We recommend going beyond Kaslow's advice on the subject, however, and investigating the backgrounds of supervisee candidates in the same way that we screen volunteer applicants at WICC (see Ch. 36). Given both the legal liabilities outlined by Slovenko (1980) as well as our own experience in screening about 1,000 applicants over the past 18 years, it is important to be quite careful in examining the vulnerabilities of a supervisee that are revealed by her or his practice history. Goal setting of the type described by Borders and Leddick (1987) can also be quite helpful.

DOCUMENTATION AND ASSESSMENT OF SUPERVISION AND OF SUPERVISEES

Only recently has concern been voiced in the professional literature regarding the formal assessment of the supervision process and of supervisee progress. Robiner, Bobbit, and Fuhrman (1988) recently reported on their efforts to develop the Minnesota Supervisory Inventory (MSI), an instrument for assessing psychology trainees. In a pilot test of the MSI, the authors mailed 350 protocols to 40 internship sites. Although the inventory requires less than 20 minutes to complete, only 14 were returned.

Borders and Leddick (1987, pp. 20-22) have reprinted a "Counseling Practicum Interview Rating Form" and a form for "Assessment of Supervisee Developmental Level," both developed by other authors.

Bridge (1988) reported on the field-testing of a "Supervisory Record Form" that is designed to document supervision in order to provide for both accountability and, possibly, some protection from liability. It is hoped that supervision would be enhanced by the use of this form by providing for more organization and continuity in supervision. The form is published (Bridge & Bascue, 1988) and available to anyone who would like to test its applicability to a given setting.

Schoener discusses accountability and documentation in the supervision of therapists who have sexually exploited clients in Chapter 34. Even if exploitation has not occurred accountability and documentation are still relevant to supervision or case consultation. Record keeping like that proposed by Bridge & Bascue (1988) helps to keep supervision focused so that when a supervisee's vulnerabilities emerge, follow through and corrective learning may prevent future problems.

THE LITERATURE ON SUPERVISION ISSUES RELATIVE TO THE PROBLEM OF SEXUAL EXPLOITATION OF CLIENTS BY THERAPISTS

Until quite recently scant attention was given in the literature to the topic of supervising therapists who have sexually exploited clients. Some references do not refer specifically to sexual involvement although they note the effect of happenings in the therapist's personal life and/or countertransference on events in therapy. For example, Racher (1957) describes the supervision of an analytic candidate in which a number of the patients in treatment with the candidate suddenly began getting divorces. After careful examination it appeared that the marital problems of the candidate, previously unknown to the supervisor, had subtly affected his treatment.

Hess and Hess (1980) mentioned the dilemma of young male therapists who overlooked a client's seductive behavior. They also discussed some of the gender-related issues in the psychotherapy of adolescents which relate in part to sexual issues.

Edelwich and Brodsky (1982) covered the supervisor's role in a relatively short section of their book, *Sexual Dilemmas for the Helping Professional*, but focused mainly on general supervisory issues.

In a paper describing a model for teaching and evaluating a course on gender and psychotherapy for psychiatry residents, Rieker and Carmen (1983) described stages that the residents went through, one of which involved a redefinition of professional and personal identities:

Concerns about the quality of supervision and other professional relationships were prevalent during this stage and were made concrete through a group of readings about erotic countertransference and sex between therapist and patient. Participants were uniform in their reports that supervisors rarely addressed erotic or other countertransference feelings. These reports are consistent with resident feedback over the last five years of teaching this course and with recent literature on countertransference. Residents described receiving both overt and covert messages from supervisors that this material was 'taboo,' For example, a male resident was told by his supervisor that this was irrelevant and he should get on with the work of treating the patient. The more covert message was that this material was inappropriate for supervision and belonged in personal psychotherapy. Participants wondered whether there might be a connection between inadequate models for identifying and working through countertransference and the sexual abuse of psychotherapy patients. Invariably, the class in which this was discussed ran late and participants were intensely involved and self-revealing. They were relieved to have finally had an opportunity to openly explore these issues and to develop models for contracting with supervisors and patients. (p. 414)

Hess (1986b) described the case of a trainee "whose own needs to seduce prompted him to secure a caseload of divorced women and schedule them for evening sessions. [The trainee's] narcissism provoked him to tell the supervisor who then became professionally responsible for the clients' welfare" and directly intervened in the situation, even though it meant breaking confidentiality to do so.

Friedman and Kaslow (1986) reported that although trainees tend to be quite guarded in supervision—at least at first—eventually they usually mention hostile or sexual feelings toward their clients. Charney (1986) described his shame in having an erection in a session with an 8-year-old girl; nevertheless he shared the experience with his supervisor who provided both reassurance and insight.

Moldawsky (1986) described how he, an experienced therapist, did not recognize the erotic feelings that underlay his anxiety until consultation with a colleague brought them into the open:

> I recall an experience from my practice, when an attractive woman was sending me signals that she was very interested in a sexual affair with me. Before I actually 'read' the signals, I only became aware that I was anxious in my work with her. One Sunday morning, I called a colleague, who consented to talk with me. We poured some coffee and I began a case presentation. I reviewed the case and we discussed the patient's hopes and desires related to me. I became aware of erotic fantasies about her. This time, in my friend's presence, I let the fantasies flow over me, and as I contemplated them I relaxed. My anxiety was clearly that I would act on them, fulfill forbidden wishes (and all that meant to me personally), and destroy my professional role. (p. 130)

In an interesting article entitled, "What Do Therapists Worry About: A Tool for Experimental Supervision," Charney (1986) characterized falling in love with a patient as "an almost sure sign of a real deficit back home," but noted that a supervisor may not be in a position to know about the problems in home life. He further noted,

> However, love need not be either romantic or sexual; it can be any of a variety of forms of longing and needing and looking forward to and paying too much attention to a patient because they are giving the therapist something the latter needs for his/her own life, such as getting gratitude or admiration.

> If one can listen, the true inner voice within will flag the therapist with some form of worry about holding on to the patient too much, over-scheduling too many sessions or too frequently, looking forward too much to sessions, being too friendly, avoiding confrontations, or delaying steps in the process of preparation for and actual termination/separation.

> Many, if not all, therapists move into some special attraction and perhaps even "love affair" at one or more times in their work, and the responsibility of the therapist is to work his/her way out... as early and as artfully as possible, including sometimes sharing the problem responsibly with the patient. (pp. 26-27)

As a final piece of advice, Charney added the following:

Here is an exercise:

Write down the name of each of your cases and ask yourself: what about this case really worries me?

Perhaps you might want to go over the list with your supervisor, or with a consultant you seek out. (p. 27)

David Rice (1986) provided an interesting discussion of the issues in supervising co-therapy, noting that sexual attraction between co-therapists is quite important to deal with but it rarely is brought up in supervision. It may emerge as a by-product of case discussion, however. This topic is of interest to us because of a related problem—that of a supervisor who actively encouraged intimacy between co-therapists whom he supervised; he instructed them to touch each other, go out on dates (despite the fact that each was married), and otherwise to develop considerable personal intimacy. Unresolved intimacy issues of attraction between co-therapists must be brought into the open and resolved.

Guy (1987) discussed the potential value of supervision in cases of impaired therapists who are at risk to clients.

Somewhat surprisingly, recent books and articles that have focused on therapist-client sexual involvement have made scant reference to the role of supervision in prevention, with one noteworthy exception: Thompson, Shapiro, Nielson, & Peterson's (1989) "Supervision Strategies to Prevent Sexual Abuse by Therapists and Counselors." This article is highly recommended as a resource. The authors use the concept of "mirroring": emphasizing process dynamics in which the supervision mirrors the psychotherapeutic relationship. The authors examined trust, the supervisor's role of being in charge, countertransference, and the importance of boundary maintenance in the supervisory relationship. In regard to content and themes in supervision, the focus was on limit setting, the role and power of the therapist versus the client, the importance of maintaining a task orientation, and countertransference. Issues of gender and sexuality, family of origin, and unresolved problems from previous therapy and/or supervision were discussed in relation to countertransference.

Although not highlighted in this contribution, one of the authors, Minna Shapiro, who has been speaking on this topic for many years, has always emphasized the importance, in supervision and consultation, of "making the invisible visible." Whatever the issues or dynamics, she recommended bringing them out in the open so they could be examined and understood, and so that they would not continue to have the power that many latent dynamics tend to have.

THEORETICAL MODELS OF PREVENTION

Before discussing the potential role of supervision in the prevention of therapist-client sexual involvement, it is essential to examine our theories of causality. Again, we must reiterate that we have no clear-cut empirical evidence on the genesis of therapist-client sexual relationships. Our hypotheses derive from our analyses, post hoc, of data presented by both clients and therapists on how their sexual involvement developed. Processing sessions on and evaluations of therapists provided an in-depth look at more than 30 cases, and these likely have influenced our thinking more than the 1,000 or so cases on which we have only data from clients.

Why does sexual involvement between therapist and client occur? Basically, it is the result of either an intentional act by the therapist or an unintended consequence of the therapist's being unable to maintain proper professional boundaries in the psychotherapeutic relationship. The inability to maintain boundaries can result from a personality flaw, the style of therapy, the unique challenges presented by the case, or the therapist's vulnerability that is generated by life events.

This multideterminant model can be outlined as follows:

1. THERAPIST PATHOLOGY: (see Ch. 10 on Assessment)

   a. Psychotic or borderline therapists
   b. Sociopathic or narcissistic character disorders
   c. Compulsive sex offenders
   d. Neurotic, insecure, and sometimes socially isolated therapists

2. DISTRESSED PRACTITIONER: situationally impaired, needy, vulnerable, or desperate because of problems or deficits in personal or professional life.

3. UNWISE TREATMENT PRACTICES:

   a. Poorly trained and naive therapists
   b. Styles of therapy that bring about enmeshment
   c. Treatment outside one's area of competence
   d. Drift from professional to personal role

4. UNIQUE THERAPIST VULNERABILITIES/COUNTERTRANSFER-ENCE PROBLEMS: therapist unable to maintain proper boundaries with a particular type of client, or a type of case situation.

The next section refers back to this theoretical model as it relates supervisory practices to methods of responding to these hypothesized causal agents.

PREVENTION THROUGH SUPERVISORY ACTIVITIES

1. IDENTIFICATION OF POTENTIAL EXPLOITERS:

In the case of highly pathological therapists, about all the supervisor can do is to recognize the situation and attempt to get the therapist to move out of the therapist role. In many cases the risk of sexual exploitation is a less serious problem than a whole host of other professional issues, such as incompetence.

   a. Psychotics: These people are rarely supervised. The ones we have seen tended to be at the grandiose paranoid end of the spectrum. The major issue for supervisors is to realize that a few of these highly disturbed individuals do get into the field. You need to trust your diagnostic instincts and to question their ability to do clinical work. Supervision probably cannot prevent trouble.

   b. Borderline: Here the therapists appear at first to be naive about professional boundaries but, on careful inspection, it becomes clear that they have chronic problems judging and maintaining boundaries. Many gravitate toward fringe therapies, especially those that emphasize loose boundaries. Here again supervision alone cannot guarantee acceptable practice.

   c. Sociopaths: A few sociopaths manage to get into the field. With the training they receive they are usually quite good at looking "healthy" and using manipulative tricks to get their own way. They will often choose therapy styles that enable them to exploit individuals and situations. When caught in an unprofessional act they often confess to what they have been caught at, have to get help, and deny that it has ever happened before. Supervision cannot keep them from exploitation.

d   <u>Narcissistic Character Disorders</u>: Similar comments to those about sociopaths apply to this group except that they are likely, at times, to show signs of distress. The diagnostic distinction here is of little relevance because of the action the supervisor needs to take. They are not able to function adequately, even with supervision.

e.   <u>Compulsive Sex Offenders And Other Impulse Control Disorders</u>: Again, sadly, some of these types manage to get into the psychotherapy fields. They are typically spotted by noting impulsive behavior in various domains. The sex offenders are not infrequently found to be sexually harassing or pursuing colleagues, trainees, or even supervisors. Why assume they stop with staff? Clients are often more accessible.

f.   <u>Neurotic and Needy</u>: Therapists who are overinvested in doing therapy and who have little going for them at home have the potential to become overly involved with clients whom they see for long terms. Unlike the preceding five categories, they may benefit from therapy and/or supervision in terms of avoiding trouble.

With supervisees in the first five categories described earlier in Chapter 32, the supervisor needs to confront each with his or her limitations. Examples of deficiencies are more useful than are diagnostic formulations. If the supervisee is still in training it may be possible to direct him or her to a career change. With the "neurotic and needy" group a frank discussion of vulnerabilities and weaknesses should be followed by a plan for supervision that will assist the supervisee and protect clients.

2. DISTRESSED PRACTITIONERS:

Even the healthiest of therapists may become quite vulnerable and needy as the result of situational factors. A decaying marriage, a divorce, or a death in the family may leave a therapist quite needy. Overinvolvement with clients may follow. Some ways for supervisors to spot this situation follow:

a. Use your clinical expertise to spot symptoms of distress (e.g., anxiety, depression) and follow up with some questions on what's going on; examine the need for therapeutic help.

b. Make an arrangement, as part of the supervisory contract, which requires the supervisee to inform you of key life events or general level of distress (with care, there will be no drift into personal therapy).

c. Be alert to changes in the style of therapy practiced or in what's happening to clients, and be willing to ask about possible issues in the therapist's life that may be exerting an influence (e.g., clients seeking divorces when the therapist has marital problems).

Here there are a number of actions the supervisor can take to prevent trouble:

a. Refer the supervisee to a therapist or support group.
b. Identify and acknowledge the distress.
c. Examine the treatment consequences of the situation and follow up with a plan for reducing them. Examples:

(1) limit certain types of clients or situations;
(2) insist on intensive supervision or co-therapy with difficult clients.

3. UNWISE TREATMENT PRACTICES:

Unwise treatment practices such as the following examples:

a. routine hugging of clients;
b. face-to-face hugs of clients;
c. therapy conducted in other than a professional office or setting;
d. excessive touching of clients;
e. holding adolescent or adult clients on one's lap;
f. socializing with clients;[3]
g. excessive self-disclosure by the therapist;[4] and
h. attempting to directly affect clients' lives by setting clients up on dates with each other, having business deals with them, etc.

It is important to note that these factors may be issues in and of themselves, or may be symptoms of therapist pathology. Sometimes the condition becomes apparent when despite repeated efforts by the supervisor a change in behavior never occurs. Supervisory intervention may be needed in several areas:

A. Poorly Trained and Naive Therapists: Some unlicensed practitioners have little or no training in maintaining professional boundaries. They get themselves into situations in which personal intimacy develops. A few lack the necessary intelligence to do therapy. At the very least, they should not be engaged in independent practice. Others need some coursework, or the supervisor should assign readings and conduct discussions on the basics of the professional relationship. Again, this factor is not always easy to separate from certain types of psychopathology. The major test is whether the supervisee can develop good judgment.

B. Therapy Style: The supervisor must be willing to challenge therapeutic styles that encompass potential boundary violations; for example, therapies that involve a considerable amount of touch, or "bonding," "lifelong parenting

---

[3] Borys (1988) studied a sample of therapists who had been sexually involved with clients and was able to use reported social involvements with clients to discriminate between erotic and non-erotic practitioners. The items on her scale included becoming friends with a client following termination, inviting clients to a clinic or office open house, going out to eat with a client after a session, inviting clients to a personal party or social event, and disclosing details of current personal stresses to a client (p. 77). It should be noted that 91% of the erotic practitioners had sex with a former, rather than current, client so these may be correlates rather than predictors (p. 153).

[4] Psychotherapist self-disclosure in therapy has emerged as an issue requiring considerable scrutiny. One of the boundary issues noted by Borys (1988) was disclosure of details of current personal stresses to client (p. 77). Recent articles on the role of therapist self-disclosure (Mathews, 1988) and criteria for therapist self-disclosure (Simon, 1988) are worthy of study. Mathews (1988) quotes an experienced woman therapist voicing concerns that self-disclosure "...can burden the patient with unnecessary worries about me." (p. 527) Our own belief is that judicious self-disclosure can be a useful tool in therapy, but that any therapist self-disclosure should be brief, closely connected with a key issue in therapy, and consist of past events. It should never involve current problems of the therapist, unless it is necessary for the client to know, for example, that the therapist is ill.

contracts," or vague goals that make it difficult for both therapist and client to maintain distance.

A given therapist may be unable to handle the therapy and to maintain professional boundaries. For example, one very experienced therapist we evaluated was infatuated with women clients and he hugged them at the end of group. The clients could handle the hugs, in most cases, but he could not.

Some agencies and programs include programmatic elements that set the stage for trouble. For example, a half-way house program that doesn't have recreational therapists and requires the psychotherapists to take clients out for social activities may put them at risk. Therapists or programs that allow home visits in times of client crisis may not be prudent in today's situation.

Last but not least, some therapists are interpersonally very seductive and need feedback on the trait. Role plays with role reversal can be quite helpful in spot-lighting this behavior in its most blatant form. The more subtle bending of rules for particular clients is less easily seen at first but also must be addressed. One way to highlight this infraction is to have the supervisee do an exercise in which he or she, singly or as part of a supervision or training group, identifies how to seduce a client.

C. Therapeutic Drift: Review therapy goals periodically and ask about plans for eventual termination to identify the gradual drift that eventually transforms a professional relationship into a more personal one. The supervisor can explore the therapist's desire for a more personal relationship and how the client is trying to make the relationship more personal.

D. Treatment Outside One's Area of Competence: The practice may signal a desire to be all things to the client, and may be a correlate of excessive involvement and intimacy. It may also signal trouble because a therapist who has drifted outside of his/her area of expertise is more likely to lose control and is less likely to obtain consultation if trouble develops in the therapeutic relationship.

E. Spotting Boundary Violations: Be alert for boundary breakdowns or risky behavior and make the supervisee aware of these issues. Breaking rules for the client (special fee reductions, special appointment times), overlooking agency policies, bending rules, extending treatment, socializing with the client outside of therapy, setting the client up with dates, etc., should be noted and discussed. The supervisor may need to be firm because therapists often offer numerous rationalizations on how this problem is not at all a major one.

4. UNIQUE VULNERABILITIES:

Goin and Kline (1976), in "Countertransference: A Neglected Subject in Clinical Supervision," reported a study in which they reviewed videotapes of supervision sessions. They found that in most supervisory sessions countertransference, which they defined broadly as therapists' conscious and unconscious reactions to the patient, was neglected. Given their broad definition of the concept, the findings are even more disturbing.

One of the most important contributions a supervisor can make is to help a supervisee to identify and discuss her or his feelings toward a client. These can range from true countertransference phenomena (as defined within psychoanalysis), to an intense need to help certain types of clients (e.g., victims), to emotional or sexual attraction to a client or types of clients. Some areas that require attention follow:

a. Sexual or Emotional Attraction to the Client: These attractions need to be identified and discussed openly in supervision. There should be an initial assessment of whether the feelings are strong enough to compromise the therapy, and whenever these feelings re-emerge or become more intense, they should be discussed again.

b. Over-Identification With Certain Types of Clients: Some therapists over-identify with certain types of clients, such as abuse victims, and lose their boundaries with them. Sometimes the contrast between the work with one type of client and all others is dramatic. The solution can range from more intensive supervision of such cases to a prohibition of seeing the particular clients.

c. Identity Issues in the Sexual Preference Area: Therapists going through crisis or change in sexual preference may be very drawn to clients who are having similar experiences. Sometimes they will project the attraction on to clients. Here again the supervisor should work with the supervisee to examine the action to take. Some therapists who have had a particularly difficult time "coming out" as gay or lesbian over-identify with young people struggling with the same issues.

d. Divorce/Loss: Therapists who have experienced the recent loss of a significant relationship or whose personal or family relationships are deteriorating may over-identify with clients whom they see as going through the same situation. The supervisor may note excessive self-disclosure, excessively long sessions, or other signs of over-involvement. A determination must be made, on a case by case basis, of the degree to which the therapy is being damaged.

e. Family Dynamics: We have seen several situations in which a client was remarkably similar to a deceased wife or an absent and rejecting daughter. In some cases there was an actual physical resemblance as well as some personality similarities. Therapists in these cases became overly involved in the parent role and then ended up allowing the intimacy to lead to a frankly incestuous sexual involvement. Unresolved anger toward family members also can lead to intimacy with clients: either as a way to have an illicit relationship without having a true affair, or in conjunction with sadistic impulses and a need to dominate. This area is the most difficult for the supervisor to ferret out because, typically, the history variables are not known to the supervisor.

SOME GENERAL SUGGESTIONS FOR SUPERVISORS

In summary here are our suggestions for intervening:

1. Screen your supervisees carefully.

2. Develop a clear contract with your supervisees: be careful to use the term "supervisor" only when you are one; otherwise use the term "consultant."

3. Trust your instincts: if something seems wrong, clarify it with your supervisee.

4. Remember that some people in the field are quite pathological: do not leave your diagnostician's cap at home.

5. Discuss any sign of distress you see in the supervisee.

6. Deal with countertransference: ask about feelings toward the client and about personal referents.

7. Re-examine the treatment contract and the client's progress periodically.

8. If the situation becomes very troubling or confusing, suggest that you sit in on or observe a session.

9. Consider examining treatment records, especially in cases in which trouble has arisen.

10. Be alert to seductive behavior and boundary problems in therapy and deal with them early in the proceedings.

DEVELOPING BETTER SKILLS

It is also critical for supervisors to continue to expand their knowledge of and skills in the art of supervision. Some suggestions follow:

1. Attend workshops on psychotherapy supervision.

2. Keep abreast of the developing literature in psychotherapy supervision and in the area of sexual involvement between therapists and clients (as well as other boundary violations). It will help you to do your best job.

3. Develop a support or consultation group with other supervisors. They can give you useful support and consultation for your work as a supervisor.

4. Try to evaluate your supervision: Obtain feedback, periodically, from your supervisees; tape a supervisory session and have peers critique it.

5. Consider putting together a training program for supervisors, perhaps in conjunction with a local training program or with a group of colleagues. Designing such a program can be a terrific learning experience for you and it will help people who are trying to develop supervisory skills.

6. If one of your or someone else's supervisees gets into trouble, do a post hoc review and analysis with your colleagues to see what can be learned from the situation.

7. When you acquire a new idea or insight, please write to us so that we can continue to learn and to expand our understanding of this frontier.

CHAPTER 39

THE ROLE OF SUPERVISION AND CASE CONSULTATION: SOME NOTES ON SEXUAL FEELINGS IN THERAPY

Gary Richard Schoener

To expand upon the discussion of "The Role of Supervision and Case Consultation in Primary Prevention" (see Ch 38), this chapter examines in more detail the issue of a therapist's sexual feelings toward clients as revealed during consultation or supervision.

BACKGROUND

The concept of eroticized transference has been discussed in psychoanalytic writings for many years. Freud (1958), in his article "Observations on Transference Love," noting that the phenomenon was common in psychoanalysis and quite important, described it in terms of

> ...the case in which a woman patient shows by unmistakable indications, or openly declares, that she has fallen in love, as any other mortal woman might, with the doctor who is analyzing her. This situation has its distressing and comical aspects, as well as its serious ones. (p. 159)

Freud saw these impulses as "most dangerous" and characterized them as "highly explosive." (p. 171) He advised analysts, who he envisioned might be struggling with their own desires, that

> It is...just as disastrous for the analysis if the patient's craving for love is gratified as if it is suppressed. The course the analysis must pursue is neither of these; it is one for which there is no model in real life. (p. 166)

Although the literature has focused on attraction experienced by female clients for male therapists, Savitt (1969) described an attraction to a male therapist by a bisexual male client. Blum (1973) provides a good overview of the concept of eroticized transference as it evolved in the psychoanalytic literature. More recently, Person (1985), in an article, "The Erotic Transference in Women and in Men: Differences and Consequences," provided a useful examination of erotic transference in the four possible therapist-client dyads (e.g., male-female, male-male, female-female, female-male). Far more has been written about the client's feelings for the therapist than those of the therapist for the client.

Struggles with highly charged countertransference including sexual feelings appear to date back to the beginnings of psychotherapy. Langs (1982; *The Psychotherapeutic Conspiracy*), in the chapter, "First Therapeutic Conspiracy," observed that Breuer's treatment of Anna O. was marked by highly charged feelings and he commented, "It may be speculated that both patient and therapist felt overwhelmed by sexual and aggressive impulses, fantasies, and perceptions of each other to a point where they felt that termination was the only recourse" (p. 74).

Langs noted that early analysts failed to deal with some of these issues directly, for example, Freud's lie to Frau Emmy von N. (Langs, 1982). He illustrated the failure to fully grasp the effect of boundary intrusions on clients with Freud's ignoring Frau Emmy's anxiety during body massages (Langs, 1982). Furthermore, there are indications that early analysts engaged in intimate contact with clients. Freud, for example, wrote to Ferenczi (Dec. 13, 1931) about Ferenczi's kissing clients (Jones, 1953), an issue that gave Freud some concern.

RECENT LITERATURE

Gorkin (1987) directed attention to therapists' reactions to patients.

It is worth noting that, in spite of the burgeoning interest in countertransference issues, scant attention has been paid in the literature to the therapist's sexual feelings and fantasies towards patients.

...it is more comfortable nowadays for a therapist to fantasize throwing a patient out of the office than it is to imagine joining the patient on the couch. (p. 108)

His section on varieties of sexualized countertransference is the only attempt in the literature so far to deal with this topic in any depth. One of his examples is that of sexual feelings toward a young boy (Gorkin, 1987). Many years earlier, Christ (1964) described countertransference problems with a psychotic child. (See Chapter 9 for further discussion of sexual feelings toward child clients.)

Another recent book, Slakter (1987), all but ignores sexualized countertransference, although the author posed an interesting question related to this issue:

What happens if the analyst, outside the context of an interpretation, reveals to the patient that he has seductive fantasies about him or her? This is not something analysts readily admit to. (p. 213)

In Slakter's example a female client feels angry and betrayed after a male analyst acknowledges that he is so strongly attracted to her that his feelings interfere with treatment and thus he must refer her to another therapist.

In *101 Common Therapeutic Blunders*, Robertiello and Schoenewold (1987) give many examples of scenarios in which the therapist failed to handle sexual feelings appropriately in therapy. Failure to deal properly with seduction is described in some cases (pp. 23-6; 55-57; 175-79); falling in love, in several (pp. 41-43, 62-63); and sexual teasing (pp. 50-51) in one.

SEXUAL ATTRACTIVENESS

Only rarely do clients choose a therapist because of sexual attraction. In the majority of psychotherapeutic relationships that we have examined, the client either was referred to the therapist or sought him/her out because of good reputation. Vinson (1984), in her studies of sexual relationships between client and therapist, found that all her subjects chose their therapists on the basis of a referral, a recommendation, an advertisement, or an assignment by an intake worker.

Among our more than 1,000 cases of therapist-client sexual involvement we encountered only a handful of clients who pursued a therapist because they felt an attraction; they were exceptions.

In one of the few studies of preferred counselor characteristics in which respondents were asked about sexual attractiveness, McQuary (1964) found that sexual attractiveness in a counselor was not one of the characteristics desired by clients.

McClernan (1972), in his doctoral dissertation, "Implication of Sexual Attraction (Feeling) in the Counselor-Client Relationship," found that about 30% of his client-respondents and a full 70% of his counselor-respondents indicated feelings of sexual attraction. The breakdown is as follows:

> 6.5% of clients and 13.5% of therapists reported strong sexual feelings
>
> 11.5% of clients and 16.5% of therapists reported noticeable sexual feelings
>
> 11.5% of clients and 40% of therapists reported mild sexual feelings (p. 57)

This investigator also found that 43 of the 59 subjects who felt sexual feelings noted them at the onset of the counseling relationship, 8 subjects noted them around the middle of counseling, and 6, at the end. In 57 of 59 cases, the feelings that were noticed persisted to the end of the counseling relationship (McClernan, 1972, p. 66).

Interestingly enough, 43% of the clients and 17% of the counselors could not cite a specific stimulus for the feelings of attraction. Physical beauty was cited by 73% of the counselors but only 20% of the clients, yet it was the stimulus cited most frequently by both. Clients also cited sharing (13.5%), discussion (8%), and closeness (5%). Counselors cited sharing (7.5%) and discussion (3.5%). No counselor cited transference, but two clients did (3.5%).

One must not overgeneralize from these data. Had they been collected on a private practice population receiving psychotherapy instead of a student population receiving on-campus counseling from young counselors the results might have been very different. Further, it should be noted that all the clients were women and all the counselors, men. Only three clients were not Caucasian (McClernan, 1972)

Milgrom informally has asked a large number of clients whether they believed that they would have been attracted to their therapist had they met socially instead of in a professional relationship. Most (about 9 out of 10) responded that they would not have: the therapist "wasn't their type," was too old, or wasn't physically attractive.

We have not systematically surveyed these factors in our client population, but our impression is that sexual feelings between therapist and client result from many different determinants. Two early studies of clients sexually exploited by therapists (Belote, 1974; D'Addario, 1977) concluded that the female clients tended to be physically attractive, but this result appears to us to reflect a sampling bias. Our much larger and more diverse sample of clients includes a great many women who would not fit into the stereotypes suggested by those early studies.

Obviously beauty and attractiveness are in the eye of the beholder. One can argue, consequently, for an operational definition of attractiveness that holds that therapists must find clients attractive if they became sexual with them. However, this conclusion ignores possible aggressive impulses or other sorts of needs. Smith (1984), for example, described very sadistic behaviors by some therapists.

AWARENESS OF SEXUAL ATTRACTIVENESS

We know little about a therapist's perception that a client is attractive to her or him except that at times the therapist is aware of it and at other times, not. We have examples of very experienced therapists who failed to recognize the attraction yet experienced the anxiety related to it (Moldawsky, 1986).

We also know little about the therapist's perception that he or she is attractive to a client. Our clinical experience suggests that here too therapists may be out of touch with their feelings and use considerable denial or rationalization about what is going on.

Pope, Tabachnick, and Keith-Spiegel (1987) reported the results of their survey of 1,000 psychologists who are members of APA Division 29 (Psychotherapy); 456 responses were received. Participants were asked to rate the occurrence in their practice of the following behaviors:

Being sexually attracted to a client (question was asked twice):

Never	9.2%	9.2%
Rarely	38.8%	39.5%
Sometimes	43.9%	41.0%
Fairly Often	5.5%	6.1%
Very Often	1.3%	0.9%

Engaging in sexual fantasy about a client:

Never	27.0%	
Rarely	46.3%	
Sometimes	22.4%	
Fairly Often	2.4%	
Very Often	0.7%	(pp. 996-97)

When asked how often they tell a client, "I'm sexually attracted to you," they responded:

Never	78.5%	
Rarely	16.2%	
Sometimes	3.5%	
Fairly Often	0.2%	
Very Often	0.2%	(p. 995)

In sum, about 90% have been attracted to a client, 72% have engaged in sexual fantasies about a client, but only slightly less than 20% ever revealed this fact to a client. (Percentages total slightly less than 100% because of missing data).

It is significant that although in the majority of cases physical attractiveness is likely to be noted early in the therapy relationship, it also may develop later on in response to increased emotional closeness, transference/countertransference, or even a change in appearance. Weight loss, weight gain, change of hairdo, improved grooming, and other factors may directly influence physical attractiveness (Eigen, 1973).

Some of the following factors may come up in supervision at times and indicate the influence of feelings of attraction by the client, the therapist, or both:

1. Unexplained anxiety on the part of either.

2. An unexplained impasse in treatment.

3. Struggles over fees or other aspects of the therapeutic contract.

4. Increased mention of attire, grooming, or other aspects of the client's physical appearance.

5. Client questions about therapist's attire, the layout of the office, the propriety of late appointments.

6. Bringing up client/therapist sex as a professional issue without a clear context.

7. Avoiding talk about the case; shifting from a concern with the case to cavalier comments on how well it is going.

Supervisors routinely should ask supervisees about feelings for clients. Most of the time the question may yield nothing significant nevertheless it should be routinely considered. Obviously, a defensive reaction to any such inquiry signals the need for more careful examination.

One final note is in order. Because sexual feelings toward clients are sometimes not revealed until several years into a therapy relationship, it is possible that they may not develop until later in therapy in some cases. Furthermore, sexual attractiveness may change over time and although not a factor at first in a given relationship, it may become one (Eigen, 1973).

OTHER SIGNS OF SEXUAL ATTRACTION

Other than the feelings a therapist reports to a supervisor, or those that emerge during case discussion, many precursors of sexual involvement may never be revealed in supervision. The bending of rules for a client, exchanges of gifts, and other signs of growing intimacy often are censored by the therapist. The supervisor or case consultant simply does not hear of them, often because the therapist keeps the supervision focused on other cases.

Vinson (1984, pp. 91-95) asked her sample of 28 clients (of which 6 were males) if retrospectively they could identify hints that sex might enter the therapy relationship. Her subjects reported as follows:

9 (6 women, 3 men) could remember no precursors

9 mentioned seductive behaviors, ranging from an arm around the waist or "lingering touch on the thigh," to holding sessions outdoors, doing errands, or having drinks together after the sessions

8 mentioned comments by their therapists, ranging from "You are really beautiful" to queries about whether they found the therapist attractive

3 felt that <u>body language</u> was an issue, from leaning forward in the chair to gazing at the client's body

<u>Asking probing questions about sex</u> was another indicator.

In the survey by Pope et al. (1987) cited earlier, respondents reported the following:

	<u>Hugging a client</u>	<u>Kissing a client</u>
Never	13.4%	70.8%
Rarely	44.5%	23.5%
Sometimes	29.8%	4.4%
Fairly Often	7.7%	0.2%
Very Often	4.2%	0.4%

Given the likelihood that few if any of these behaviors or activities will be brought up in supervision or consultation, it is critical to explore carefully any that are. In some of our organizational consultation work we have learned that both peers and supervisors often overlook the few clues they get that something may be out of line. Any reference to contacts outside of therapy sessions, excessive phone calls, bending rules for the client, sexual jokes, or excessive exploration of sexual issues should trigger further inquiry. It cannot be emphasized enough how important it is for the supervisor or consultant to take his or her "gut" instincts seriously. If something feels wrong, maybe it is.

SEX IS NOT THE PROBLEM

This book and, to some degree, this chapter focus on the prevention of therapists' sexual involvement with clients, yet we believe that the actual incidence of sexual contact is far lower than that of a more troublesome problem: unrecognized or unresolved sexual attraction within the psychotherapeutic relationship. Dealing with this issue may help us to address the broader problems of the effect of seductive game-playing as well as of stalled or ineffective therapy linked to sexual attraction.

1. <u>Seductive Game-Playing</u>:

More than 20 years ago Scheflen (1965) described what he termed "quasi-courting" behavior in psychotherapy which involves activities common to early courtship. Veague (1974), in order to study "Quasi-Courting in the Clinical Interview," directly observed therapeutic encounters. The phenomenon was not observed in the intake interviews at an adult outpatient mental health unit but it was observed in 54% of 36 sessions in the aftercare unit.

Although the behaviors described by Scheflen and Veague seem something less than what one would normally term "seductive," it is noteworthy that one of the therapists interviewed by Veague (1974, p. 108) "described himself as being 'sexy, but not seductive' with the client," seeing "quasi-courting as a means to get in touch with that spark of libido"—that "empty, borderline, suicidal and depressed patients...still have."

Whether one agrees with Veague (1974, pp. 108-9) that these subtle behaviors may be used successfully to facilitate treatment, one must agree with her warning that the "therapist's behavior could be interpreted as being more seductive than intended and the encounter might increase the patient's anxiety."

Certainly the interplay of even more overt seductive game-playing by therapist or client may be quite disruptive in therapy and become an issue in and of itself, distracting both client and therapist from the original presenting complaint. Eigen (1973), in his very useful article, "The Call and the Lure," recounts the seductive interplay between himself and a female client during a year of therapy. He described therapy as depending on "undoing the seductive sidesteps and compromises we are more prone to in daily life" (p. 197), which makes one wonder whether a supervisor could have helped Eigen to sort out his feelings toward the client. At least in this case, according to Eigen, the client made considerable progress and was able to terminate and move on. By contrast, we have interviewed many clients who feel that their time and money were wasted in therapy because of the seductive interplay that dominated the picture.

Beyond seductive behavior by the therapist, the handling of seductiveness by the client is an important issue for the supervisor to examine. For example, Fuchs (1975) described a conference speaker's presentation of

...the case of a seductive, flirtatious young woman who came to him after having had a liaison with a former analyst. As she unfolded her story, she edged closer to him. He became aware of her knee touching his. (p. 174)

The speaker informed the audience that this led to his acute discomfort; and he told the client that "such physical contacts would not be accepted" (Fuchs, 1975, p. 174). Fuchs himself, he said would have taken a different course of action:

My own view is that in the context of the session it would have been far more effective for this therapist to have interpreted the woman's deep fear, not her manipulativeness, at that point. Sexual bids on the part of patients are usually covers for hidden fear, resentment, and doubt. Interpreting them as defensive ploys against anticipated rejection, and thus a product of the frustration of their love needs, I find to be more acceptable to patients and the most fruitful response. (p. 174)

Gareffa and Neff (1975), in their interesting article entitled "Management of the Client's Seductive Behavior," described seductiveness by male clients with female therapists, including subtle examples and one that was not so subtle:

He talked of his wife's 'hot little pants.' He talked about sex incessantly... 'we wore each other out'. He suggested that he should perhaps get a girlfriend—purely for sex. As he talked about his last encounter with his wife, he had a quite obvious erection.(p. 119)

Obviously, such seduction is an expression of aggressive impulses, a defense against intimacy, an attempt to keep the therapist off-guard, or a general desire to subvert therapy. It may or may not indicate how the client relates in everyday life and may or may not represent sexual interest per se.

2. Stalled or Ineffective Therapy:

Beyond the disruption inherent in on-going seduction during therapy (by either party), sometimes therapy is stalled or rendered ineffective by a failure to discover or deal with underlying feelings of attraction. Some therapists (e.g., Gareffa & Neff, 1974) claim that this failure is acceptable and can facilitate progress in therapy but I believe that it is more likely to negatively affect progress or outcome of therapy. When therapy is stalled without obvious reason, the supervisor should check carefully for unexpressed feelings of attraction to the client, and instruct the therapist to inquire about the client's feelings.

SUPERVISORY INTERVENTION

The first step in intervention obviously is to discuss the issue at length, even if it means extending the length of time available for supervision, until the matter is fully examined. The supervisor must ask direct questions about what is going on. Do not fail to inquire about contacts outside the sessions, phone calls, letters, and the like. If there are letters, ask to read them. Examine case notes of sessions; if they are not adequate, demand that accurate and detailed notes be kept.

Consider direct observation, videotaping or audiotaping, or a visit to and participation in a session with the client. Intruding on the relationship may anger the client but, in some instances, it is essential and may be reassuring to the client. Depending on the situation, and to reduce the likelihood of alarming the client, the intrusion can be explained as part of a supervisory review. However, some situations demand complete honesty with the client; then the supervisor simply states clearly what are the concerns that has brought about this intervention.

An assessment must be made of how salvageable the situation is and which of the available options is best. The following examples of options should be considered:

1. Continued therapy with tight supervision of the therapist.

2. Continued therapy with tight supervision plus personal therapy for the therapist (see Pope, 1987, "Preventing Therapist-Patient Sexual Intimacy: Therapy for a Therapist at Risk").

3. Co-therapy with the supervisor or some other therapist.

4. Transfer of the client to another therapist.

Should the therapist and/or client resist these interventions, more drastic action will be required. In one such situation in which I was a consultant, the employer was left with no choice but to fire the therapist and to try to explain things to the client and her family, both of whom were outraged at the supervisor's intervention. Even after the boundary problems were explained to them they insisted that the therapy was very helpful and maintained that it should continue. Further intervention was not an option.

Under certain circumstances one may have a mandate to report the incident to a regulatory body; or one may feel an ethical duty to intervene even if it means breaking confidentiality. Hess (1986) described a situation in which he found such action necessary.

Client welfare must be the main consideration in developing the plan. If, for example, it seems that the therapist, under tight supervision, may be able to continue working with the client, the quality of the therapy that will be rendered should be considered carefully. If performing as a therapist is likely to represent a major struggle for the therapist and the prediction is that therapy will therefore take longer, then one may have to decide on ethical grounds that this arrangement is not proper because the client is being penalized for the therapist's inadequacies.

PART XI

INTERVENTION WITH ORGANIZATIONS

One of the questions that is implicit in several preceding chapters is the degree to which an organizational environment contributes to the ease with which some therapists sexually exploit clients. Even when a therapist's personal pathology is the key determinant of whether one or more clients will be abused the precipitant for the abuse that occurs may well be found in the culture and setting of the organization.

Schoener and Milgrom, in Chapter 40, relate the kinds of organization consultation they have conducted in relation to therapist-client sexual exploitation. Their case descriptions go a long way in identifying those aspects of organizations and group practices that lead to and permit the exploitation to occur without being brought to light.

CHAPTER 40

Organizational Consultation Relative To Therapist-Client Sexual Involvement

Gary Richard Schoener
and
Jeanette Hofstee Milgrom

Since early 1971 the Walk-In Counseling Center has provided consultation and training to many other human service organizations. Most of these organizations have had little to do with the issue of sex between therapist and client; they are best characterized as non-traditional or "alternative" (see Glasscote et al., 1975) and include such services as hotlines, free medical clinics, and drug abuse programs. In some instances, however, the consultation has focused on situations involving sexual contact or propositions by counselors; for example, a phone counselor who set up a meeting with a client and engaged in sex (Schoener, 1974).

During the late summer of 1976, WICC announced the first victim support group for women who had been sexually exploited by their therapists (see Ch. 13), which attracted the attention of local mental health professionals. In March 1977 notices of a second group were circulated and we presented a workshop on the topic, "Eroticism in Therapy," in which sex between therapist and client was discussed. A major local magazine article (Sundstrom, 1977) further showcased WICC's work on this issue later that year.

The result of this growing visibility was telephone calls and letters from other organizations asking WICC for assistance in dealing with client complaints of sexual exploitation by counselors and therapists. In the decade that followed WICC staff members consulted with more than 100 organizations on events and issues related to sex between therapist and client. This work has included quite a variety of activities:

1. Case Consultation:

    a. Regarding the handling of a client complaint.

    b. Regarding the handling of possible client abuse reported by another professional.

    c. Regarding a self-disclosure of sexual misconduct by a staff member.

    d. Regarding evaluation of the impaired practitioner, including development of a supervision or rehabilitation plan.

2. Staff Training:

    a. Planning staff training subsequent to the discovery of an incident of sexual misconduct by a staff member.

    b. Training aimed at explaining existing ethical and legal standards relative to contact with clients, including mandated reporting of misconduct.

    c. Training administrators and supervisors in regard to administrative safeguards; prevention.

    d. Training supervisors and administrative staff regarding the boundaries of the professional relationship:
      (1) Training relative to identified problems.
      (2) Generic training on professional boundaries.

3. Organizational Consultation:

    a. Coaching Board, administrator, or supervisory staff members on the handling of incidents, subsequent to a troublesome event, such as the discovery of a case of sexual exploitation by a staff member.

    b. Review of administrative safeguards; the development of a plan to institute further safeguards.

    c. Conducting a processing session for the staff, with or without a staff member who has sexually exploited a client, to assist in the healing process for the organization itself.

4. Investigation and evaluation of overall agency functioning following either a number of complaints, or a complaint that implicates a number of staff members.

We have conducted two such procedures and in both cases the evaluation was requested and sanctioned by the board of the program and a funding agency. Both situations involved a team of people; both were "unofficial"; both yielded a written report; and in both cases the outcomes were total programmatic overhauls.

The remainder of this chapter focuses largely on item 3.c. above: consultation to help an organization through the healing process after an incident of sexual exploitation has been discovered. Much of what we bring to case consultation situations is covered elsewhere in this manual. Chapter 36, "Administrative Safeguards," provides a good deal of background for much of the organizational consultation we do. Staff training is the subject of a future manual by WICC; it will expand and update our existing work on this topic (Milgrom, Gaskill, & Powell, 1985). However, until now we have not discussed in any publication our assistance to organizations during the period of healing after an incident had surfaced and been dealt with.

BACKGROUND: THE LITERATURE

Edelwich and Brodsky (1982) discussed various organizational issues that relate to sex between therapist and client but they offered only very general advice. Even our own recent writings on the subject (Schoener & Milgrom, 1986) have dealt only with organizational follow-up of processing sessions and administrative safeguards to limit the risk of sexual exploitation of clients.

Milillo, Shultz, & Couchman (1989), in "Strategies for Organizational Intervention With an Agency Where Sexual Exploitation Has Occurred," discuss the use of a consultant from outside the organization to help to evaluate and review a complaint. The authors assumed that a consultant is given a very broad mandate, and they presented an ideal case in which the consultant is able to address a great variety of problems in the organization which are aimed, if necessary, at transforming the organization into the healthier model outlined in a companion paper by Shultz, Milillo, Couchman, and Lundin (1989). Both articles are well worth reading. However, it should be noted that rarely if ever have we, as consultants, been given the mandate to cover the amount of territory that their model assumes. We want to note also that in some situations organizational problems play a very minor role and there is little justification for a total program overhaul.

William L. White (1978, 1979, 1986), in an extraordinary series of contributions culminating in *Incest in the Organizational Family* (1986) examined organizational issues that are related to staff burnout, among them, loss of boundaries and sexual involvement with clients. Because White was struck by the high burnout rate among human service workers, he examined this phenomenon from the perspective of organizational ecology, especially that of closed organizational systems. Most of the organizations with which we have worked regarding the sexual abuse of clients have not been so dysfunctional as those described by White; nevertheless his overall model is still quite useful for anyone considering undertaking such a consultation role.

White's (1986) guidelines and cautions for opening up closed systems are particularly valuable, as is his advice on promoting health and productivity in the organization. Although the book devotes only a few pages to the sexual exploitation of clients by counselors, the overall framework it provides is quite useful. At a workshop in Minneapolis in the Fall of 1986, White applied his analysis of organizational issues to the problem of sexual exploitation of clients by professional helpers, and we hope that he will produce some articles on the subject.

IMPEDIMENTS TO SUCCESSFUL CONSULTATION

A number of factors can reduce the potential for a successful consultation. (a) If there is significant disagreement over the hiring of a consultant or the choice of a given consultant, cooperation can be very difficult to obtain. (b) If those in administrative or supervisory roles are unwilling to make most of the facts known within the organization a broad discussion of the events in question will be difficult. (c) If there is significant disagreement over the facts of the case among the investigators, discussion of it will be difficult. Of greater importance, probably, is the fact that a thorough investigation has been made and most of the attainable facts are known.

THE DANGER OF DEFAMATION

One great difficulty in discussing staff problems broadly within any organization is the risk of defamation, especially slander. In most communities the growing incidence of civil suits against employers has led to guardedness on information about employees and former employees. This attitude has affected responses to reference checks as well as responses to requests by other employees to discuss the details of disciplinary actions and resignations.

Yet there is broad agreement that human service agencies should learn from their experience and that it is important to bring problems of client abuse and exploitation out into the open (White, 1986; Milillo et. al., 1989). At the same time, staff discussions of these events leave open the possibility that information will spread into the community and damage the former staff member.

It is important to obtain legal advice in order to be familiar with the definition of defamation and with measures to reduce the risk of defaming a person. In addition, staff members should be forewarned to keep information in-house and not to discuss it outside the organization. This imperative cannot be emphasized enough. It is part of the covenant between staff members and an organization, in our view, that in exchange for openness the staff agree to maintain strict privacy about the information.

Obviously, considering the dangers of defamation, it is not difficult to argue that no person should be given any information. In fact, one may be given this advice by an attorney and one may choose to follow it. However, everyone who has written on this topic, including us, indicates that it is important to review incidents of sexual exploitation of clients with other staff members so they can learn from the incident and, it is hoped, prevent future incidents. Some arguments for doing so, despite the dangers of defamation, follow:

1. Defamation may occur even if no review takes place because rumors proliferate within an organization. Other staff members usually get wind of what is going on, but if they are not given facts you have the classic context for the development of rumors as well as greater potential for prolonged discussions and gossip.

2. If at least some true facts are shared, exaggerated versions of events are less likely to circulate.

3. If the administration shares information in a deliberate fashion it can make a straightforward demand for privacy and can caution employees against defamation.

4. Given the nature of human service organizations, sharing information is the way to maintain the staff's healthy functioning (White, 1986; Milillo, Shultz, & Couchman, 1989).

5. It is difficult to fully investigate or understand an incident of sexual exploitation, especially in regard to learning how to prevent future incidents, without talking to the staff about what happened and obtaining their observations and/or additional information.

6. It is difficult to fully apprise staff members of the agency's rules on professional boundaries and the consequences for breaking these rules without discussing actual incidents. Staff members judge the situation by what they observe more than by what they read in ethics codes. (This is not to suggest that periodic teaching using hypothetical examples cannot accomplish nearly the same ends, but real situations are much more likely to have an effect.)

Obviously, administrators and Boards must weigh the options in any given situation and make a judgment call on which risks they wish to take. White warns us that when past events have not been fully discussed and resolved they leave dangerous "ghosts" behind (White, 1986). Schoener's "Administrative Safeguards" (Chapter 36) as well as previous versions of the Checklist (Schoener, 1979, 1986) included the following item under the section on staff education:

Following an incident of serious misconduct, is a special session held to discuss what can be learned from the incident?

SITUATIONS IN WHICH THE CONSULTANT WILL HAVE LIMITED IMPACT

The effect of exposing the sexual exploitation of a client by a staff member may have various effects, depending on the circumstances. In the examples that follow the staff members are resistant.

At one extreme is the situation in which other staff members are active accomplices in the abuse or engage in abuse themselves. In such instances the exposure of the abuse puts everyone at risk and the common response is to hide one's complicity and obtain legal consultation on "damage control."

Case 1: A practitioner working in a small private clinic receives a complaint from a client alleging sexual abuse by a male practitioner. Prior to this complaint, there had been rumors about such misconduct. When the complaint is brought to the attention of the head of the clinic she expresses concern but in the end takes no action. It later turns out that she is having a lesbian relationship with one of her own clients. The only consultation obtained was from an attorney on how to handle the client who made the complaint.

If one is called upon to provide consultation in such a circumstance, which is unlikely, the reluctance to face the issue should be apparent early in the consultation relationship. The best that can be done is to confront the people who are involved and to withdraw from the case to prevent oneself from being used.

Another type of situation is that in which other members of the clinic or program are not necessarily abusing clients but are engaged in behaviors that show poorly defined professional boundaries. Typically, they are quite defensive.

Case 2: A well-known practitioner is caught having sex with a client. In an effort to intervene in the relationship, which the client does not want to break off, and to provide feedback to the other members of the practice, consultants meet with the group. They are concerned but characterize the behavior as "acting out"; they are clear that it should not be repeated. Yet they do not raise questions about or even reveal that other members in the practice also engage in considerable physical contact with clients. Thus the consultant and the members never explore the high-risk nature of their practices.

In this case a consultant sometimes can bring about some awareness of practice problems; the common result is that the more self-aware clinicians eventually leave the practice. We have here a classic case in which an in-depth evaluation of the offender (like the one described in the preceding chapter) provides a format for revealing broader problems. Typically, in this situation we get a quick admission of guilt, a quick denunciation by other staff members, and then a quick referral for therapy as a solution.

Then there are situations in which a key staff member is accused of sexually abusing a client and he/she either denies it or minimizes the nature of the complaint. Other staff members are unwilling or unable to consider the possibility that the allegations are true; or a few persons know the truth but hide it.

Case 3: A clinic's staff becomes aware of the allegations made against the top therapist, who is a sort of guru. Because details are not known, the focus of discussions within the clinic is what to do about the "outsiders"—the clients and professionals—who are trying to ruin the clinic. Yet staff members have witnessed some questionable touching of clients by the particular therapist and even heard what appeared to be orgasmic groans coming from his office. The consultation that is sought, however, is on the question of "what to do about" the various "outsiders" who are raising questions.

Case 4: A facility employs a therapist who has been charged publicly with abuse of clients. When other staff members are questioned they emphasize the therapist's denial of the charges to them. Nevertheless, they are uneasy about the situation and ask for consultation.

In this sort of situation the consultant may be able to perform several valuable functions: (a) The consultant can point out what appears to be going on: that people are focused on protecting the staff member rather than on getting to the bottom of the situation. (b) The consultant can point out the potential legal dangers in taking sides rather than in trying to seriously evaluate the complaint. If those inside the program or clinic are unable to step back and be objective, perhaps an outside consultant can. (c) The consultant can point out the risks to their reputations that everyone faces and the importance of taking complaints seriously instead of rushing to the defense of a friend. For the consultant it means sometimes cutting through the fears of disaster other staff members may have by pointing out that if the worst is true, they are better off discovering it for themselves; they would be in a better position to separate themselves from the misconduct and to make plans for what to do after the matter is settled.

Overall, in all the foregoing situations, the consultant may be limited in the freedom to remedy the situation. However, even if the contact is necessarily brief, the constructive feedback and reality testing provided by the consultant may have some positive effect.

INVESTIGATING MULTIPLE COMPLAINTS AND ORGANIZATIONAL BREAKDOWN

In some instances a Board of Directors or funding agency employs a consultant to assess multiple complaints, some involving sexual misconduct, that stem from a mental health or chemical dependency treatment program. In such cases the program staff may prefer not to invite in outside consultants or to provide information, but they have little choice in the matter.

Before undertaking such an examination, it is important to organize a consultation team and, also, to set aside quite a bit of time. This sort of consultation tends to require far more time than one estimates.

Although the details of such a consultation are beyond the scope of this chapter, a useful outline of the procedure can be given here.

1. Consultant obtains a clear mandate from the board and/or funding agency.

2. Consultant holds an initial meeting with the director or key staff members of the facility, emphasizes the importance of total candor, and sets up the initial parameters of the proposed study.

3. Consultant meets with staff members and clients (in the case of a residential program); the director and/or board representatives also are present. Consultant explains what is going to happen.

4. If the program is not residential, clients are informed by letter or other means that an evaluation is underway and their input is needed; they are assured of confidentiality.

5. Consultant conducts staff interviews individually in private; notes or tapes are confidential; and the importance of honesty is stressed. Consultant asks for leads to other persons (e.g., clients or ex-staff members) who may have important information.

6. When a tentative formulation or conclusion has been reached, consultant discusses it with key staff members and invites feedback.

7. Consultant discusses findings with the board and makes recommendations on sharing the information.

8. Consultant prepares, if requested, a written report. Sometimes several reports are needed—in-depth analyses for the board and more general summaries for public consumption.

9. Consultant must be prepared for challenges to the reports and recriminations.

The two large-scale consultative evaluations in which we participated had very different outcomes. In one, the funding agency and the board concurred that the program needed to be dismantled and rebuilt. Staff members were terminated and the program was redesigned. Since then the program has reopened and is doing a fine job in the community.

In the other instance, the funding agency's response was to give the program tighter supervision; but the faults were not corrected, however, and funding was withdrawn. The program's board had protected key staff members and never brought about the overhaul required. Although the consultants had helped to expose many problems, the key staff members continued to engage in bad management practices. Despite the many abuses that were eliminated, some remained, and the program was shut down after charges of fraudulent billing practices were initiated.

Consultation can be carried out also in a stepwise fashion with an initial evaluation of the situation and preliminary report; the board then can decide whether to authorize further work or whether enough evidence has been discovered to warrant closing the program or making major management changes.

A very useful reference for persons who consider undertaking the role of consultant is William White's (1986) *Incest in the Organizational Family*. A consultant must keep in mind that his or her professional duty is to the clients who may be at risk. When client safety is at stake it may be necessary to recommend some sort of protective action even before all of the facts are sorted. By the same token, a consultant must be careful about making recommendations: clients may have difficulty adjusting to sudden changes; special supports may be necessary for clients who have particular difficulty handling the changes; and clients who are tightly tied to given staff members may act out destructively, either spontaneously or with the staff member's encouragement. The behavior may be an attempt to subvert intervention and keep an incestuous system intact (see Appendix A).

CONSULTATION TO THE "OPEN" ORGANIZATION

Sexual exploitation of clients occurs in the best of clinics, hospitals, treatment programs, and human service organizations. It occurs in programs with excellent internal supervision, clear ethics codes, and fine reputations. Even when organizational issues contribute to the exploitation, many organizations are very open to consultative input and they try to learn from their mistakes to prevent a reoccurrence. The remainder of this chapter deals with providing consultation to organizations that are trying to cope with the aftermath to discovering the sexual exploitation of a client.

Effect on Organization of Sexual Exploitation of Client:

Milgrom's chapter on "Secondary Victims" (Ch. 21) reviews the effect of sexual exploitation on persons who are not directly involved in the abusive relationship. A number of issues commonly arise among other staff members with revelations of sexual exploitation:

1. SHOCK AND SURPRISE: When the exploitative therapist was formerly seen as a fine practitioner, other staff members are frankly bewildered by the revelations. They sometimes report a feeling of emotional numbness (not unlike clients who are victims) and even some sense of disorientation.

2. CONFUSION: Staff members may be in a state of disbelief and confusion about how such a thing could have happened. It may relate to the particular therapist or the refusal to believe, for example, that anybody would have sex inside the clinic in an unlocked office during regular office hours.

3. ANGER AND A SENSE OF BETRAYAL: Anger and a sense of betrayal are common, with a number of referents:

   a. That the perpetrator served as an exemplary mentor.

   b. That a client was harmed and the profession was disgraced.

   c. That the perpetrator's actions may have damaged one's reputation, the clinic, or the organization.

   d. That an administrative nightmare has been created and the remaining staff will have to pick up the pieces.

4. GUILT OR SHAME: These feelings may be a response to hindsight whereby the staff member feels he or she had clues to what was going on but ignored them. The feelings may be tied also to a belief that somehow staff members should have known; or some to mistaken notions of complicity.

5. VULNERABILITY: A sense of vulnerability is tied frequently to a belief that other clients or the professional community will blame everyone for the situation. A more practical concern is that one will be asked questions at a professional meeting or workshop.

6. CONCERN FOR THE PERPETRATOR: It can be painful and even frightening to watch the ruination of a respected colleague's career. There is usually some concern that the perpetrator is at risk for suicide or other serious consequences.

7. CONFUSED FEELINGS ABOUT THE PERPETRATOR: Confused feelings are usual. They are problematic in most situations because one may be asked for help or support by this colleague. In addition, one may have a social relationship with this colleague or see her or him at professional gatherings or even on the street.

Other staff members may end up depressed and their clinical work may be impaired somewhat by the stress of events. After-hours meetings, discussions, phone calls, and the like add to a busy schedule. Requests to hold the matter private may mean that one cannot consult the outside professional colleagues who usually provide support. One also may be torn between duty to a friend and strong feelings of anger about what has happened. When the accused person is a key staff member or even the major figure in the practice, one suddenly may be faced with having to make difficult career choices.

CONSULTATION TASKS

The major tasks of the consultation are to provide means of dealing with the troubling feelings, especially the anger and the sense of betrayal, shock, or confusion. Confusion about the situation must be cleared up and feelings of guilt, explored. Collective guilt is not a particularly constructive feeling; it can be diminished by an assessment of anything that might make a difference in the future and a frank examination of the degree to which the event was or was not preventable.

It is important to discuss what should and can be done vis-`a-vis the welfare of the perpetrator. A forum should be provided to discuss feelings associated with friendships and social relationships with the perpetrator. Staff members need support to step back and make personal decisions on handling their individual relationships.

Practical problems and risks to the organization must be discussed. It is important to reach conclusions on what limits will be agreed upon in terms of sharing any information about the situation. If the events are public, there should be discussions of what to tell other clients about the situation and how to describe the perpetrator's current relationship with the organization or clinic.

In some instances it is possible and useful to arrange for the perpetrator's departure from the facility under the guidance of a consultant. There can be advantages for everyone involved if the leave-taking occurs at a single staff meeting: the air can be cleared and goodbyes, whether angry, caring, or both, can be said.

The following three cases illustrate three very different situations and three very different consultation methodologies:

Case A: A therapist working within a medical clinic was found to have had sex with a client, much to the shock of the physicians. The outside consultant held several lengthy phone conversations with a key physician and sent him reading material. The physicians also obtained legal consultation from their attorney and discussed the situation with a therapist who, at times, consulted to the clinic.

All the advice and feedback apparently dovetailed quite well; the physicians were able to sort through their feelings and to make decisions on the actions to take. They discharged the therapist and arranged for transfers of clients to other qualified practitioners. A key factor in the situation was that despite their trust in and close relationship with the perpetrator, he had worked quite independently and they were neither overseeing his work nor in a good position to judge it. The final consultative input centered on the future hiring of a therapist to work in the practice and a discussion of safeguards, but the physicians leaned toward referring out for such services.

Case B[1]: Following a client complaint, a therapist working in a community agency was found to have had sex with several clients. The staff members of the agency were shocked, in part because it was hard to believe that the sex occurred during regular hours in an unlocked office and, in part, because the therapist appeared to have a deep commitment to ethical practice and was outspoken on the subject of therapists who exploit their clients.

The therapist was an older practitioner, only a few years short of retirement, and had few financial resources. His only career had been in mental health work. He had resigned and it had been decided to accept his resignation. At the time there had been no publicity or threats of it, and no suits had been filed, nevertheless staff members felt angry and betrayed and there was also a sense that the agency had been damaged. There was a sense of sadness about the damage done to clients. Last but not least, many staff members expected to encounter the perpetrator in social settings and were not sure how to react.

A meeting was held at the agency for all clinical staff members, the perpetrator, the director and assistant director, with a consultant. The agency decided to exclude receptionists and support staff.

During the meeting the perpetrator apologized to everyone and said goodbye. Staff members had varying reactions but a number expressed anger and a sense of betrayal; they said that they appreciated the apology but it was not enough. Others shared their concern for the welfare of the perpetrator. There was some attempt to discuss and identify how the acts themselves had escaped everyone's notice, and the perpetrator was asked both why the exploitation happened and what might have prevented it. There were no major discoveries in this regard, except the recognition that several staff members had felt uncomfortable about the perpetrator's style of working with clients. Admittedly, erotic involvement had not been suspected. These staff members decided that in the future they would be more direct when they had such vague feelings of discomfort. A discussion of staff members' reluctance, in peer supervision, to bring up such feelings followed and resulted in some staff members resolving to be tougher on each other in peer supervision.

The therapist left the agency, never to return. He took a job outside human services.

Case C[1]: An outpatient program with several branch offices and a large staff had two unrelated incidents of sexual misconduct by two different staff members over a period of several years. The clinic administrator decided that the program should process staff feelings about the incidents and re-examine them to ascertain what could have been done differently. They also wanted to look at the possibility of a problem in their overall structure which had contributed to there having been two incidents.

Several discussions were held with the consultant; middle management staff had been involved in planning the consultation. After a review of the incidents and the situation, it was decided that the best approach would be a two-day workshop for all professional and support staff members. The program closed down for those two days.

---

[1]This case also is described in Chapter 28 on "Processing Sessions," but in that chapter the focus is on the needs of the client.

The workshop began with a review of the two incidents, a sharing of information, and the identification of both the misinformation that had been fed by the rumors and the deficiencies in internal communication about the two incidents. Each incident was then reviewed in terms of what information or observations may have led to earlier discovery had they been noted and communicated. The need to establish clearer pathways for the communication of such observations by the support staff (e.g., receptionists, billing clerks) was established. Feelings about how the administration handled these events were expressed; this ventilation appeared to clear the air and to re-establish some trust that had been lost.

The remainder of the workshop focused on understanding sexual exploitation in therapy with an emphasis on prevention. The need to focus treatment on clear goals and the risks of longer term models of therapy were explored. Exercises related to professional boundaries were conducted. A separate discussion with the support staff was held by one consultant.

After this 2-day workshop, one consultant was available on a retainer basis for telephone calls from the administrator or middle management. A number of calls were made for the review of or coaching on several situations that arose. One middle manager decided that he was not well suited for that role and returned to being a therapist again.

It is important to note in these three cases that it was the consultant who judged the organizations to be reasonably healthy, basically, and that the requests for consultation were sincere efforts to take responsibility for the situation. In all three cases the desire to learn from the experience and to prevent a reoccurrence was genuine; in all three cases the organizations essentially followed at least 90% of the recommendations. Also, in all three cases although additional actions could have been taken, including suggestions for the future, the consultants tried to limit their interventions to what was requested as well as to what they thought could be digested in the time frame available.

In the process of the large-scale consultative evaluations described in an earlier section of this chapter, large group meetings were used to enable the ventilation of staff feelings and, at the end, to explain and discuss the evaluators' findings. It is important to note, however, that such structured meetings are quite different from the intensive staff retreats which some organizations request and some consultants are willing to facilitate. We also use retreats at times but the situations typically would differ from those described here. We share White's (1986) concern with the destructive potential of retreats on an organization whose resources already are depleted. It is both ironic and sad that many counselors and therapists, because of their styles of approaching problems, gravitate toward an intensive, therapy-styled retreat to deal with such problems, and to preferring a consultant who is a therapist rather than skilled in organizational consultation.

Geographical considerations and time also affect the planning of consultation. If an organization is out of town or out of state our choice of a mode of consultation differs from that for the same problem in the Twin Cities. Many contacts may have to be over the phone, and some work may have to be carried by on-the-spot consultants. A trip to the facility may be essential to accomplish a number of goals and to make the most effective use of time while controlling costs.

Last but not least, the degree of urgency is an issue. Like the intervention with victims described elsewhere in this manual (Chs. 7 and 12), the assessment of the level of crisis and impending events is critical to planning the consultation. An urgent situation often requires prompt intervention. Furthermore, just as a client's motivation to look at a broad range of personal problems often diminishes after a crisis has passed, so too do organizations sometimes lose interest in a thorough self-examination or overhaul when the pressure is off. All the consultant can do then is to point out what remains to be done and to remind the organization that, having had one incident, more can be expected in the future should exploitation reoccur. After experience with the problem of sexual exploitation of a client, an organization is expected to take all possible preventive measures; it is judged more harshly if another incident does occur.

PART XII

THE COMMUNITY APPROACH

Therapist-client sex, although essentially a professional issue, nevertheless requires a strong community commitment to help stamp out its continuance.

Both Minnesota and Wisconsin have enacted measures against this form of exploitation although the community action in each state took a radically different form. Schoener describes the genesis of the legislative activities in the two states in Chapter 42. In Chapter 41 Andrew Kane discusses the Wisconsin Coalition on Sexual Misconduct by Psychotherapists and Counselors and makes suggestions for putting together such an organization.

It is beyond the scope of this section of the book to examine developments elsewhere. However, task forces and coalitions are beginning to form in a number of states, either within a given professional group or as the joint action of several groups. Three such community undertakings worthy of note are in California, Pennsylvania, and Massachusetts.

In California, no single organization took the lead. The number of professionals who published in the area of therapist/client sex provided the impetus. Their lobbying and the work of Senator Diane Watson in the California State Senate led to the approval and funding of a Senate Task Force on Psychotherapist and Patient Sexual Relations; it functioned from October 1986 to February 1987. The Task Force had only 10 members but it received statewide publicity by interviewing a number of specialists during 12 hours of public hearings in two cities. The Task Force recommended against criminalization but advised improvements in the civil statutes and in administrative procedures. Although it recommended passage of a "mandatory reporting law," the actual proposal made reporting voluntary. The Task Force also recommended a statewide education program and protection for the professional societies that process complaints of sexual misconduct (California Legislature, 1987).

In Pennsylvania, an interdisciplinary group of professionals and consumers founded the Association Against Client Exploitation by Professionals. This organization has carried on considerable public education as well as client advocacy. Its members also assisted the state legislature to consider a bill to criminalize sexual exploitation by therapists.

Since 1987 the Massachusetts Psychological Association Task Force to Improve Professional Standards has been examining the problem of therapist-client sexual intimacy. In 1989 the state legislature created a special committee to investigate the issue.

Chapter 43 reviews the use, thus far, of the new laws in Minnesota that have criminalized sex between client and therapist or provided for mandatory reporting of sexual exploitation by therapists. It also examines statutory changes related to therapist-client sex in a number of states.

CHAPTER 41

THE WISCONSIN COALITION ON SEXUAL MISCONDUCT BY PSYCHOTHERAPISTS AND COUNSELORS: A REPLICABLE MODEL[1]

Andrew W. Kane

When the Wisconsin Psychological Association held its semi-annual conference in April 1983 on the topic, "Sexual Abuse: In the Home, In the Professional Office, In the Business Office, and In the School," no one expected the Association to continue to deal with these problems individually or collectively. Something happened, however, to bring one of the topics to center stage and make it the focus of a major undertaking by the Association.

One presentation at the W.P.A. meeting was by a member of the State Psychology Examining Board. He went through the stages of filing, investigating, prosecuting, and adjudicating complaints made to the Board and indicated probable outcomes as a result of what took place at each level. Then a hand went up, and a woman stood.

She said, in measured tones, "I speak from the standpoint of the victim, that has never been listened to." She went on to describe the numerous problems in the Board's handling of her case, the slap-on-the-wrist given the perpetrator, and the ensuing psychological, financial, and other damages that she, the victim, had suffered.

After the conference I spoke with her at some length. Two months later, she interviewed me as a potential therapist and then therapy began with me in October 1983. I learned in great detail how the abuse by the system was, in some ways, as bad or worse than the abuse by the therapist. Thus, through her revelations at the conference and the follow-up in therapy, she was the catalyst for what was to become the Wisconsin Coalition on Sexual Misconduct by Psychotherapists and Counselors. She has remained one of its driving forces ever since.

As President of the Wisconsin Psychological Association, I was in a position to lead the discussion of a W.P.A. role to improve the state of affairs so no other victim need go through what she did. That discussion led to a call for volunteers for a Task Force to study the subject and to make recommendations for action. The Task Force was fully constituted by June 1984 when it held its first meeting, and it has met monthly ever since. The initial members were several psychologists, the attorney and administrative assistant for the Psychology Examining Board, and my patient. The Chair was a former Chairman of the Psychology Examining Board.

The first several months were spent ascertaining the current status of the problem and the systems in place to address it. Each of us had to learn about the procedures of making a complaint—whether to a district attorney, a licensing board, or a professional ethics committee—in terms of what was supposed to happen and what did happen. We had to become conversant with the needs of victims, the nature of perpetrators, and how current

---

[1][Based in part on a presentation at the meeting of the American Psychological Association, New York, New York, August 28, 1987. Updated through March, 1989.]

laws and administrative codes addressed each. And we had to learn how the various systems might be affected.

By the end of 1984 we were ready to expand our membership. Thus, we invited representatives of every mental health profession and related group in Wisconsin to a meeting in January 1985. Every group except psychiatry responded (later they sent someone for a period of time). While remaining a Task Force of the Wisconsin Psychological Association, the group had tripled its membership and was ready to try to influence the system.

Part of our success stemmed from the number of concerned organizations that found at least one member who was interested in our work, willing to give up half of the first Monday each month to attend a two-hour meeting, and possibly to do some committee work between meetings. The Task Force was also fortunate in that employers were willing to give people time away from work for a good cause or even to urge an employee to contribute the time. It is the commitment of numerous people from various professions that has enabled the Task Force/Coalition to succeed.

One result of the united commitment has been that virtually all questions have been decided by consensus. We have taken the time to discuss all sides of issues that arise; the result is that almost everyone accepts one or another solution before too long. This practice has helped to maintain the cohesiveness of the group and has kept us from losing sight of the reason for our existence.

The primary task of the enlarged group was to establish a set of goals and objectives on which we could work together, it was adopted by the Task Force on July 1, 1985. The items range from the global goal to "prevent future occurrences of sexual misconduct by psychotherapists" to specifics; improving the definition of "psychotherapy" in the state statutes, changing the civil statute of limitations on when malpractice actions could be commenced, and preparing pamphlets and other materials to educate the professions and the general public. We have continued to work on those goals and objectives for more than three years. We publish an annual update on our progress and pick up additional goals and objectives as we proceed. We are now in the process of defining a new set of goals and objectives for the coming year or two. (see Appendix W for the June 1988 review.)

A major undertaking was a survey of mental health professionals in Wisconsin. Our questionnaire asked whether the professional had had someone in therapy or counseling between 1982 and 1984 who had had sexual contact with a therapist or counselor. Nearly 1,600 responses were received which included 655 reports of sexual misconduct. These are not discrete cases, however; we know that some victims saw more than one therapist/counselor and some perpetrators had multiple victims. The survey was not as rigorous as we would have liked but, in retrospect, it clearly demonstrated that there are many more cases of sexual misconduct in Wisconsin than can be discerned by looking at the relative handful of reports to licensing boards and professional ethics committees. One attempt to survey victims was not successful; only two forms were returned out of the more than one thousand mailed to therapists/counselors. Several victims reported to us that it was too traumatic to fill out the form, even years after the events and after a lot of therapy. After newspapers reported on our therapist survey, a few victims called for information on where to go for help; that was, perhaps, the most important result of the survey. (A report on the survey is in Ch. 3.)

Many changes that we sought and still seek must be accomplished through legislative acts. For example, a law passed in 1983 (see Appendix G) makes it a misdemeanor for a "therapist"—defined as "a physician, psychologist, social worker or other person providing psychotherapy services"—to "intentionally [have] sexual contact with a patient or client during any treatment, consultation, interview or examination." It sounded good but was nearly unenforceable because of the clause, "during any treatment...," which district attorneys took to mean during a scheduled session for which a fee was charged. To the best of my knowledge, only two cases were ever prosecuted under that statute: the first was never adjudicated because the alleged perpetrator died during surgery shortly before the trial. The second is underway as of March 1989. The local and appeals courts ahve indicated that "consent" is not an issue under the misdemeanor statute, and that question is being appealed to the State Supreme Court by the alleged perpetrator. If it concurs, then the misdemeanor trial is expected to commence.

With help from legislators, their staffs, and attorneys, we recommended more than a dozen revisions in the law: changing the penalty from a misdemeanor to a felony; changing the time period from "during any treatment" to "during any on-going therapist-patient or therapist-client relationship"; specifying that "consent is not an issue"; adding nurses, chemical dependency counselors, clergy, and any "other person who performs or purports to perform psychotherapy" to the list; and extending the civil statute of limitations from 3 to 15 years. The first case we are aware of being prosecuted under the new felony statute is underway as of March 1989, with the trial to take place sometime this year.

A legislator came to us for help in writing legislation to mandate the reporting of sexual misconduct by a past therapist or counselor if it has been made known to a subsequent therapist or counselor. The resulting law went into effect May 3, 1988; according to its provisions, a therapist/counselor who has reason to believe that a patient/client has been sexually exploited by another therapist/counselor must ask the victim if he/she wants the current therapist to report that exploitation. The report is made without identifying the victim unless the latter consents to the release of his/her identify. When the victim's consent is given, the therapist must, within 30 days, report the allegations to the State Department of Regulation and Licensing (if the alleged perpetrator is licensed) or to the district attorney for the county in which the misconduct is alleged to have occurred. Failure to file a report is punishable as a misdemeanor. Therapists who file such reports are presumed to act in good faith, makes them immune from civil or criminal liability.

One of the Task Force's most important actions was the production of a pamphlet, "Making Therapy Work For You," which informs patients/clients on how to distinguish therapist/counselor activities that are okay from those that are not or may not be okay. (See Appendix Z.) Few people entering therapy have any idea of what to expect, and few are willing to trust their gut feelings that something is wrong. We are aware of more than 25,000 copies of the pamphlet which have been printed by various groups following our printed request to "please reproduce without prior consent." The State Office of Mental Health indicated that it is planning to send perhaps 100 copies to each state-certified mental health clinic (with a request to reprint at their own expense when the supply runs out), which will double the number in print. Thus, our message is being carried far and wide at no cost to us but with great benefit to actual and potential victims.

We have periodically published position papers on germane topics. The most recent are, "Model Policy Statements and Guidelines Regarding Sexual Conduct by Staff" [of organizations], and "Guidelines for the Rehabilitation and/or Discipline of Therapists (Counselors) Who are Guilty of Sexual Exploitation of Clients (Patients)." Copies have gone to the Psychology and Medical Examining Boards and to all the professional organizations in Wisconsin of which we are aware, as well as other groups. Following the practice with all our publications, reprinting and borrowing the text without prior consent is invited.

From the beginning, we have kept the media informed of our activities. Starting with the few reporters some of us knew, we have expanded the list of outlets each time we are called with a question by someone new or we see a story in print that addresses our issues. At present, we mail our monthly agenda and minutes to about 20 people in the media, apprising them of what we are doing. Thus a few stories a year are prompted on matters related to our work and public education is accomplished at minimal cost with maximal coverage.

We also put people in or out of Wisconsin on the mailing list by request or if we want them to know of our work. Our mailing list has grown, consequently, to about 283 as of March 1989, and the exchange of information permits each of us to learn from the other's experience.

STIMULATION OF RESEARCH

An indirect product of the Coalition is the doctoral dissertation done by the representative of the Wisconsin School Psychologists Association, Richard Brigham. Entitled "Psychotherapy Stressors and Sexual Misconduct: A Factor Analytic Study of the Experience of Nonoffending and Offending Psychologists in Wisconsin," the dissertation provides a substantial amount of intriguing data. It was my privilege to chair his dissertation committee. Brigham's (1989) abstract reads, in part:

> The present study investigated feelings of personal stress, and, by extension, vulnerability, that offending and non-offending licensed psychologists from the state of Wisconsin experience regarding the impingement of the issue of sexual misconduct on their practices. Surveys were received from 41.4% of licensed psychologists and those licensed for the private practice of school psychology in Wisconsin as of January 8, 1988. [Some] 4.4% of the respondents (6.5% of male licensed psychologists and 3.5% of males licensed for the private practice of school psychology) acknowledged sexual intimacies with present or former patients/clients. [No females acknowleged sexual contact.] Data about feelings of stress, paticularly when compared with recent findings regarding other stressors associated with professional practice, challenge the prevailing view that psychologists are indifferent to the sexual misconduct of colleagues. These findings [also] indicate significant and positive relationships between personal misconduct history and stress associated with potential legal/financial consequences of misconduct."

A total of 785 licensed psychologists and 176 people licensed for the private practice of school psychology were sent surveys. Usable responses were received from 324 licensed psychologists, 55 licensed for the private practice of school psychology, and 12 licensed for both, a total of 391 people. Twenty-eight percent were females, 72% males. Nearly 82% of the total sample had doctoral degrees. Fifty-three percent of the respondents indicated their primary work setting was private practice, 41.9% indicated it was in an institutional setting. The survey was 10 pages long and contained 153 items.

A report of a sexual relationship with a previous therapist (Mean = 3.91, S.D. = 1.73) was tied with "receiving phone calls from patients/clients at home" (Mean = 3.92, S.D. = 1.56) as the second-most stressful patient behavior, exceeded only by suicidal gestures by patients/clients (Mean = 4.95, S.D. = 1.56). It should be noted that on the seven-point scale, "suicidal gestures" would be ranked as "moderately stressful," while the other stressors would fall between "mild" and "moderate." "Those who reported being licensed for the private practice of school psychology experienced significantly more stress than clinical psychologists on nearly one-half of the stressful patient/client behaviors."

Further, reports of sexual misconduct on the part of a colleague was the most stressful aspect of therapeutic practice (Mean = 3.87, S.D. = 1.74), surpassing "excessive workload" (Mean = 3.81, S.D. = 1.78). Media coverage of sexual misconduct ranked sixteenth on this list, and the criminalization of sexual misconduct in Wisconsin (in 1984) ranked 31st (last).

In spite of high rankings of some sexual-misconduct-related issues, however, the legal, financial and public relations consequences of misconduct are not even slightly stressful for the majority of the respondents. Only for those respondents who had personally engaged in misconduct was there a significant relationship on these variables. "This data would suggest," Brigham indicates, "that in comparison to a wide range of psychotherapy stressors, with the exception of colleagues personally known to these psychologists, the misconduct of professionals is not experienced personally as stressful or as a negative and stressful reflection on the rest of the professional community." For those psychologists who do know the perpetrator, Brigham suggests, there may be a need for an "opportunity to deal with the feelings of stress, anger and grief in a more organized and systematic manner than presently exists."

The only stressor variable which differentiated offending and non-offending respondents was on the legal-financial-public relations consequences of misconduct. On all other comparisons, there was no significant difference. This raises a question about the accepted hypothesis that some combination of personal stress/burnout and stresses of therapeutic practice contribute heavily to sexual misconduct by many perpetrators.

Respondents who reported as effective "their training for dealing with seductive patient/client behaviors experienced less stress with factors labeled defensive styles, eroticized transferences, and professional doubt," as well as seductive heterosexual or homosexual behavior. "Those who rated as effective their training for dealing with their own attraction to patients/clients experienced less stress with factors labeled eroticized transference, dysthymic affect and therapeutic relationship." Only 35% of perpetrators (vs. 57% for the total sample) "reported satisfaction with their training's assistance in learning how to deal with their responses to patient/client sexual material." There was no difference, however, in the reports by the two groups regarding the adequacy of their training in dealing with their own attraction to patients/clients.

Respondents were asked about the expected effect of a legislative proposal (now law) which would mandate reporting of sexual misconduct by a therapist/counselor. While "56.5% projected increases in the ...prosecution of offenders, ...37% argued that innocent therapists would be subject to increased frivolous complaints...." Even so, this item ranked only 18th on the list of therapeutic stressors (Mean = 2.4, S.D. = 1.6, "mildly" stressful).

The primary "defensive office practice followed for the purpose of reducing risk of frivolous sexual misconduct complaints" was "maintaining detailed notes," endorsed by 63% of the respondents. A poor second was seeing patients/clients only when a secretary was in the outer office (30.7%).

In sum, Brigham's study provides some data on sexual misconduct by clinical vs. school psychologists, and provides strong evidence that psychologists are signficantly affected when a patient/client reports sexual misconduct by a previous therapist or when a report of sexual misconduct by a colleague is received. Perpetrators were not found to be different from non-offenders on any variable not specifically related to the consequences of misconduct. Perpetrators felt less-well-trained than non-offenders in dealing with their responses to patient/client sexual material, but the difference was not significant. Finally, most of the psychologists in the study maintained detailed notes in order to reduce their risk of a frivolous misconduct complaint, but no other defensive behavior stood out.

It is our hope that other researchers will be interested in doing studies on questions generated by Brigham's dissertation and Coalition activities, adding to our knowledge base regarding the incidence and prevalence of sexual misconduct by professionals and the means of prevention and intervention.

BECOMING A COALITION

As the work of the Task Force has progressed since January 1985 when non-psychology organizations were first invited to meet with us, a sense of ownership has grown among the various groups. The movement began to become more than a Task Force of the Wisconsin Psychological Association. When the majority of groups indicated the desire for this development and indicated their willingness to split the cost of the organization, a governance agreement was drafted and eventually adopted. Dues were set at $100 minimum per year (most groups pay exactly $100) and we became in May 1987 the Wisconsin Coalition on Sexual Misconduct by Psychotherapists and Counselors. The membership comprises the following organizations:

> *Alliance for the Mentally Ill of Wisconsin; American Association of Marriage & Family Therapists; American Association of Sex Educators, Counselors & Therapists; Madison Campus Ministry; Mental Health Association in Milwaukee County/in Wisconsin; Milwaukee Psychiatric Hospital; National Association of Social Workers—WI Chapter; Wisconsin Association of Outpatient Mental Health Facilities; Wisconsin Nurses Association; Wisconsin Psychological Association; Wisconsin School Psychologists Association; Wisconsin Society of Clinical Social Workers.

The two relevant licensing boards—Psychology and Medicine—have been invited to send staff and/or Board members to meetings on an ex-officio basis. All the meetings are open; some of our best contributions come from people who are not officially members/delegates but who are interested and who care.

We are at present discussing membership with the State Bar Association and the Wisconsin Dental Association in the hope that they also will join with us. We know that members of every profession have crossed the line and sexually assaulted some patients/clients. If the two organizations do affiliate, our name likely will be amended to read, "...Sexual Misconduct by Professionals."

A great disappointment to us was the Wisconsin Psychiatric Association's rejection of our invitation to join; it is the only mental health group to do so. They cited their desire to handle the problem within their profession through an ethics committee. Prior to our move to a Coalition structure, they had indicated, informally, that they could not participate in a task force run by the state psychological association. Inasmuch as the current Chair of the Coalition is a psychologist, the same objection may prevail. Without their contribution, the coalition seems incomplete.

A major advantage for the Task Force/Coalition is its independence. There have been a few tense moments when we wanted to say something that made some people on the Psychological Association's Council uncomfortable, but the Association never attempted to limit our work or our voice. With the greater independence of a Coalition, there is less likelihood of limitations being imposed on our work. It is unlikely that we could have achieved as much in as short a period had we been a governmental body or dependent on governmental funds for our work. W.P.A. still offers very limited staffing and other assistance, in addition to money, and thus it maintains a more substantial financial commitment than the other organizations.

THE CURRENT[2] AGENDA OF THE COALITION

1. In January 1988, we began publishing the names of adjudicated perpetrators. The adjudication could be by a court, by a licensing board or a professional ethics committee/organization, etc. As of March 1989, we have documentation of 28 adjudicated cases in Wisconsin. We anticipate adding in the near future the results of settlements in civil cases and any other relevant information which is in the public record regarding sexual misconduct cases.

2. We developed a position paper on "gag orders," in which a victim promises never to say a word about sexual misconduct by a given therapist/counselor in return for a cash settlement in a civil lawsuit. We hope to get legislators to forbid this process, on the basis that it interferes with protection of the public and is usually seriously detrimental to the victim, preventing him/her from working through the psychological consequences of the exploitation.

3. We are about to propose to all the professional organizations in the state that they assess each of their members a small amount to help victims of professionals get needed therapy and other assistance.

4. We have assembled a list of more than 40 therapists who have indicated a willingness to provide therapy for victims. In part to expand the list, and in part to try to increase the resources for victims in the northern half of the state, we'll be conducting a training workshop for therapists in the northern half of the state late in 1989.

5. We've started three special funds, and are soliciting donations to those funds: (a) To facilitate communication among victims and between victims and the Coalition; e.g., by paying for long-distance calls from victims and between victims; (b) To foster public professional education; e.g., through paying mileage so victims and professionals can speak on the subject at various forums, for production of brochures, etc.; (c) To generally support the work of the Coalition, to be used for necessary ongoing expenses. As of March 1989 we've collected $1,048 for these purposes, to supplement the dues paid by the member organizations.

6. We hope to get the legislature to modify the Victims Compensation requirements so that victims of therapists and counselors can qualify for financial assistance to pay for psychotherapy, replace lost wages, etc.

7. We are continuing to identify organizatiosn which <u>should</u> have an interest in our work, either because their professional members may engage in exploitative behavior or because their members may become victims of exploiation (e.g., the Alliance for the Mentally Ill and women's groups), and invite them to join the Coalition.

---

[2] Draft 1989-1990 agenda

8. We will continue to disseminate our pamphlets and position papers, our model ethics codes, and our recommendations for reforming the legal and administrative systems, as part of our attempt to eliminate sexual misconduct by psychotherapists and counselors.

9. To increase the independence of the Coalition, to qualify for tax exempt status (501(c)(3)), and to insulate the member organizations in case someone sues the Coalition (e.g., because we published the name of an adjudicated perpetrator), we have begun the process of becoming a nonprofit, nonstock corporation.

10. We are planning to activate a Speakers Bureau, which will offer both educational and public-relations activities.

11. In part because of some recent cases, we plan to enter discussions with religious organizatiosn regarding concerns about how they deal with alleged and adjudicated perpetrators.

12. An attorney is drafting a "Guide for Victims" which goes through the steps involved in filing a complaint wiht a licensing board, an ethics committee, and/or a district attorney, as well as the steps involved in filing a civil lawsuit for malpractice. There will be an emphasis on the problems which may develop for the victim in the course of pursuing each of those options, so that they can prepare for the problems rather than being caught by surprise.

13. We will try to get the State to require that malpractice policies cover sexual misconduct by therapists, so that victims will be able to recover damages.

14. We will try to identify what guidelines are now used by licensing boards for relicensure of individuals who have surrendered licenses or who have had their licenses revoked, and, if necessary, try to facilitate improvements in those guidelines to better protect the public.

INGREDIENTS FOR A SUCCESSFUL COALITION (not in priority order)

1. A lead group to finance initial costs and provide staffing (paid or volunteer). The Wisconsin cost was about $500 the first year; $1,000 the second; $1,400 the third; and $2,000 the fourth and fifth. With incorporation, the budget will increase by $1,500-$2,000 to cover the cost of liability insurance.

2. A group of committed individuals who will attend meetings, divide up the work, and pursue other committed individuals and groups to join the effort.

3. A workaholic Chair and/or a small, highly committed central committee who will do anything no one else is willing or able to do, from drafting documents to putting out mailings.

4. A survey of state mental health professionals or other means of demonstrating that there is a problem in your state that should be addressed.

5. At least one victim. She (given that most are female) should be someone who has gone through the process of complaining to a licensing board and has conducted a civil lawsuit against the offending therapist. No one is in a better position to communicate to the whole group the trauma involved in sexual misconduct and its aftermath. The group needs

that special education to appreciate what must be done if their work is to be successful. It is beneficial to have more than one victim because each will have something significant to contribute.

6. A cooperative effort by professional groups, state licensing or certification authorities, and victims. Given that many questions which arise will involve legal issues, a lawyer is needed at nearly all meetings. [We have been fortunate in having had the lawyer for the Psychology Examining Board at most of our meetings the first year and occasionally since then, and in having had private attorneys at the majority of our meetings.] It is essential that "turf" issues be avoided so that the purpose of the Coalition is not lost.

7. Legislators willing to learn about the problem, take an active interest, and sponsor legislation to remedy identified problems. They need not be official Coalition members but do need to get mailings and to be on call for needed consultation and action.

8. Good media contacts, so that work of the Coalition is reported accurately, without sensationalizing it.

9. Acknowledgement by everyone involved that the Coalition has a singular purpose: the elimination of abuse by professionals and the provision of assistance to their victims. Any issues that do not fall under these headings do not belong on the Coalition agenda. When side issues become a focus of discussion or activity they are divisive.

In summary, every state has the capability to start a coalition of professionals who are united on this issue. It is not terribly expensive, and does not involve an extraordinary amount of time. Mental health professionals should be at the organizational forefront; some of our colleagues are part of the problem and our ethics make it imperative that we become part of the solution.

CHAPTER 42

LEGISLATIVE MODELS FOR DEALING WITH THERAPIST/PATIENT SEX: MINNESOTA AND WISCONSIN[1]

Gary Richard Schoener

In 1984 Wisconsin became the first state to criminalize sex between therapist and client, making it a class A misdemeanor. A year later the Minnesota legislature passed a statute classifying sex between therapist and client a felony, and the following year Wisconsin upgraded its statute to follow suit. This chapter examines developments in Minnesota and Wisconsin in the context of programs that address the problem. Without the contextual background it is impossible to fully understand or evaluate the legislation and regulations that are on the books. *It's Never O.K.: A Handbook for Professionals on Sexual Exploitation by Counselors and Therapists* (Sanderson, 1989) provides a much more detailed description of events in Minnesota.

WISCONSIN

Although I have consulted in Wisconsin and provided workshops there on the issue of sex between client and therapist, I have only second-hand knowledge of the activities that led up to the legislation; they are largely based on interviews with key figures.

Representative James Rutkowski, an attorney who chairs the Committee on Judiciary, Wisconsin State Assembly, recalled seeing an episode of the Phil Donahue show in the early 1980s that featured Linda D'Addario, a psychologist from southern California, and several alleged victims of sexual abuse by therapists. He corresponded with Dr. D'Addario and began an issues file on the topic (Rutkowski, 1985).

In 1983 Dr. Barry Siegel, a psychiatrist, was tried in Milwaukee for the alleged sexual abuse of clients. He pleaded guilty to disorderly conduct and received a year's probation. John DiMotto, head of the Sensitive Crimes Unit, Milwaukee County Attorney's Office, prosecuted the case; he was quoted by the press as saying that a specific law against such behavior was needed. This incident and subsequent newspaper stories impressed Representative Rutkowski and he decided to try to do something for the victims who had been speaking out (Rasmussen, 1982; Rosenberg, 1982; Rutkowski, 1985).

In 1983 representative Rutkowski introduced Assembly Bill 321. It classified sexual intercourse between a therapist and client as a class D felony, and sexual contact between the two as a Class A misdemeanor. The original bill required the sex to occur during an on-going therapist-client relationship and provided that consent between the two not be an issue. As a result of considerable debate the bill became silent on consent and more specific about the situations covered. It limited its applicability to sex that occurs "during any treatment, consultation, interview, or examination" (1983 Wisconsin Act 434). The newly created Section 940.22, Wisconsin Statutes, was enacted May 9, 1984, and published May 17, 1984. It reads in part,

---

[1] An earlier version of this paper, with the same title, was presented by the author at the annual convention of the American Psychological Association in 1985.

(2) Any person who is or who holds himself or herself out to be a therapist and who intentionally has sexual contact with the patient or client during any treatment, consultation, interview or examination is guilty of a Class A misdemeanor. (See Appendix G.)

"Therapist" is defined as a physician, psychologist, social worker, or other person providing psychotherapy services. The definition of "psychotherapy" is based on Section 455.01(6) Wisconsin Statutes: "the use of learning, conditioning methods and emotional reactions in a professional relationship to assist persons to modify feelings, attitudes and behaviors which are intellectually, socially or emotionally maladjustive or ineffectual."

Penalties for a Class A Misdemeanor is 9 months in jail and/or up to a $10,000 fine. Wisconsin lacks a Sentencing Guidelines Commission so actual sentences may vary quite a bit.

The first case to be tried in Wisconsin under the 1984 Statute was State of Wisconsin vs. D. Roger Henneman (85-CM-204) in Circuit Court, La Crosse County. Charges were brought in early 1985 against Henneman, a doctor of divinity and psychotherapist, for alleged sex with a female client. Henneman challenged the constitutionality of the Wisconsin law and briefs were filed in June; oral arguments were scheduled for August 5, 1985, and then rescheduled for August 26, 1985. On August 5, 1985, Henneman died during open heart surgery and the case became moot; the constitutional issues are undecided (Roesler, 1985-a, 1985-b).

During 1985 Representative Rutkowski studied the work of Minnesota's Task Force and examined possible changes in Wisconsin's statutes, given the growing feeling in the community that stiffer penalties were needed (Riepenhoff, 1985).

The Wisconsin Psychological Association (WPA) played a major role in the subsequent developments. In April 1983, at a conference on all types of sexual abuse, a client spoke out angrily about sexual abuse by her psychotherapist. This complaint was the stimulus for WPA president Andrew Kane to set up a Task Force on Sexual Misconduct by Psychotherapists (see Ch. 41). The Task Force, chaired by Gordon Polder, Ph.D., had its first meeting in June 1984. Its initial charge was to identify therapists and attorneys who might serve as resources to victims and the development of means and methods for early identification of the "distressed psychotherapist"; to examine consent within the therapeutic relationship; to define termination of a therapeutic relationship; and to examine the policies and procedures of the WPA Ethics Committee and the Psychology Examining Board (Kane, 1984).

WPA surveyed its members to ascertain how many cases of client-therapist sex they had seen in their practices, and they publicized the findings through the press. It was clear from the number of cases cited that few had been reported to regulatory bodies and that a disproportionate number involved psychiatrists (Rosenberg, 1984).

When his term as WPA President ended, Kane took over the chair of the Task Force. As of April 1985, its membership included five other psychologists, a representative from NASW, a physician, a psychiatrist, a social worker (MSW) representing the Wisconsin Association of Outpatient Mental Health Facilities, a victim advocate, an attorney representing the Psychology Examining Board, a clergyman, a nurse, and the Executive Director of the Mental Health Association in Milwaukee County (Wisconsin Psychological Association, 1985). By late August 1985, a victim survey was sent out amidst broad publicity to attempt to locate victims throughout the state and the findings were reported (Kuchan, 1985; see Ch. 3).

Another key to developments in Wisconsin has been the work of many citizens, especially that of two victims who have been active in the public arena. In Wisconsin, as in Minnesota, the public testimony of victims has been a strong spur to change. Sally Fogelberg serves on the WPA Task Force and her story and views have been reported in the press several times (e.g., Allegretti, 1985). Jane Rasmussen, who was employed at the Milwaukee YWCA, also has become known through newspapers (Rasmussen, 1982). She and I appeared together on the "AM Chicago" TV program on June 28, 1985. Rasmussen helped to coordinate a major regional conference on sexual abuse of clients by therapists, held in Milwaukee September 13 and 14, 1985. A support group was developed for victims, led by Karen Robinson, RN, of the Milwaukee Mental Health Association, which resulted in hearing from more victims and contributed to efforts to bring about change.

Meanwhile, the WPA Task Force broadened its goals and undertook the task of strengthening Wisconsin Statute 940.22 (Appendix G), including broadening its scope and upgrading the exploitative behavior to a felony. The Task Force also created a data base for further analysis of the problem and to increase reporting of offenses; change the statutes relating to civil suits; create funding for training, employing a victim advocate, and setting up a Victims' Compensation Fund; educate professionals and the public about the problem; facilitate interaction of licensing Boards, district attorneys, and ethics committees; and to further define a number of difficult concepts, such as post-termination situations (Task Force, 1985). It has an exceptionally strong presence in Wisconsin and is likely to continue to influence events there (e.g., *Milwaukee Journal*, 1985). (See Ch. 41 for more details on the history and accomplishments of the Task Force.)

MINNESOTA

Formal efforts in Minnesota to deal with the problem of client-therapist sexual involvement date back to 1974, and legislative actions clearly grew out of the various community efforts that were underway. Understanding the context of the events clarifies why Minnesota was able to make major legislative strides on the issue so quickly. The different factors are examined separately.

Work With Victims:

The role of WICC is described in Chapter 1. Services to victims at WICC and elsewhere in the Twin Cities played a major role in stimulating action.

As in Wisconsin, local media coverage, with testimonials by victims, played a role in spurring legislative action. A major magazine article (Sundstrom, 1977) was followed by a CBS Sixty Minutes piece (1978) and a large number of newspaper articles. A major TV investigative piece about a residential program (I Team, 1983) was followed by major newspaper stories (Kohl, 1984) and another TV expose (I Team, 1984) about a psychiatric treatment center for adolescents, the Wilson Center.

The Vulnerable Adults Act:

In 1982 the Minnesota legislature passed the Reporting of Maltreatment of Vulnerable Adults Act, Statute 626.557. Like the child abuse reporting laws, it required persons in a range of professions to report the abuse of adults deemed vulnerable and unable to protect themselves. The law focused on clients of licensed facilities. Although it was broad in language, the rules for applying the law (e.g., Levine, 1983) and explaining it to the public, (e.g., Minnesota Dept. of Public Welfare, 1984) seemed to delimit its effect.

In practice, enforcement units were reluctant to handle cases of outpatient mental health clients who were abused. Because the facilities covered had to be licensed, psychiatric units in hospitals and many residential facilities were covered, but community mental health centers, which were not licensed, and private practitioners, who were not considered facilities, were not covered. Ironically, some clinics and outpatient chemical dependency programs were covered. The law brought forth more reporting of sexual and other abuse of clients, but they were largely those that occurred in residential programs. The law is most useful in situations involving developmentally disabled, elderly, and chronically mentally ill persons in residential facilities.

Board of Psychology:

Effective August 7, 1982, the Minnesota Board of Psychology, the State's licensing authority for psychologists, adopted new Rules of Conduct; they contain a provision with far-reaching consequences:

10. A psychologist shall file a complaint with the board when the psychologist has reason to believe that another psychologist is or has been engaged in conduct which violates C.11., failure to report suspected abuse of children or vulnerable adults, or E.8., sexual contact with a client. (emphasis added)

The only exception is when information is obtained in the course of a professional relationship with a client, who is the offending psychologist. Without this exception a perpetrator would be likely to avoid consulting another psychologist for help. In at least one case, however, I know of a psychologist who filed such a report despite the fact that the client had refused to do so.

Board of Medical Examiners:

The Board, which licenses physicians and, therefore, psychiatrists, has made even more sweeping changes in its rules and operations. In 1986 the Medical Practice Act was amended so that physicians now are required to cooperate fully with any investigation of their practices. In addition to the usual sanctions of censure, suspension, or revocation of license, the Board may impose a civil penalty of up to $10,000 per offense and order the physician to provide volunteer professional services under supervision at a designated facility.

The 1985 Legislature also amended Section 214.10 of Minnesota Statutes 1984 to add a number of special requirements for health-related Boards (including the Board of Medical Examiners and Board of Psychology). The requirements are detailed for holding the Boards accountable for a practitioner's continued contact with the complainant while the complaint is being processed. Sex-related cases always must be referred for further investigation and summaries of their disposition must be included in reports to the legislature. Procedures must be created for establishing good working relations among Minnesota Licensure Boards and between them and those in other states. Last but not least, all health institutions and insurance companies are required to report malpractice claims and all disciplinary actions against physicians to the Board of Medical Examiners.

The 1986 amendments to the Medical Practice Act cite earlier mandated reporting by any licensed health professional or head of any health institution, of any conduct that may result in Board discipline. The only exception allowed is information obtained while a physician is treating the offender and the physician believes that the offender has limited his or her practice so the public is not at risk. Offenses included in the list are, for example, sexual contact with patients and use of sexually demeaning language. The statute, as amended, completely protects any professional who reports physician misconduct or impairment in good faith. In a 2-year period, consequently, after some negative media coverage and a State Senate Committee on Health hearing, the Board of Medical Examiners did a thorough overhaul of its licensing statute, office procedures, and, even, staff.

<u>The Task Force on Sexual Exploitation by Counselors and Psychotherapists</u>:

Minnesota has a longstanding tradition of programs for victims of sexual and physical abuse. Various sexual assault programs have received complaints over the years from victims of sexual exploitation by psychotherapists as have some county attorneys. In most cases county attorneys were unable to prosecute. Among the many people who testified at a hearing on November 12, 1984, before the Task Force were six people who had been abused by the same therapist in one county, and the county authorities who spoke of their frustration in trying to find grounds to prosecute the offender. In one instance a county attorney resorted to charging a therapist with consumer fraud for having sex with clients, leading a judge to issue a restraining order (Newlund, 1980).

Peggy Specktor, Director of the Minnesota Program for Victims of Sexual Assault, wrote a paper on the problem in 1983 (Specktor, 1983). She is one of those rare individuals who is concerned with victims and has program knowledge as well as the ability to operate effectively in political arenas. Thus she soon set about the task of implementing her recommendation that such a task force be formed. As a result, the Legislature enacted a bill which became Chapter 631, Laws of Minnesota, 1984; it mandates the Commissioner of Corrections to form a task force on sexual exploitation by counselors and therapists. The Task Force was housed in the Minnesota Program for Victims of Sexual Assault; Barbara Sanderson, a psychotherapist, was hired as its Coordinator. She was to prove as adept as Specktor. She put together and masterfully managed a statewide effort, including the Task Force of 25 people who represent a range of groups, professionals, victims, clergy, attorneys, and others. Work groups included another 31 people with diverse backgrounds, and 9 more of us served as consultants. An additional 40 people testified at the public hearing or sent in testimony.

Work groups were organized to study Public Education; Professional Education; Criminal and Civil Statutes; Professional Regulation; and Victim Issues. Three legislators, including Senator Donna Peterson, who wrote several Task Force bills, were ex-officio Task Force members.

On March 15, 1985 the Task Force issued its Legislative Report (Sanderson, 1985). It contained both background information and legislative proposals. The bills submitted covered the following areas:

—Administrative Law Changes   —Unregulated Psychotherapists
—Civil Law Changes   —Criminal Law Changes
—Statewide Education Plan

The Civil Law Changes did not get out of committee that session because of one of our few miscalculations. The Administrative Law Changes bill was dropped when the Board of Medical Examiners came up with a far-reaching bill of its own and the Task Force supported their bill instead. The Statewide Education Plan and Unregulated Psychotherapist bill were combined and were passed. This bill extended the life of the Task Force for another year; required the Commissioner of Corrections to establish a program to prevent sexual exploitation by psychotherapists; and established a legislative study commission on the regulation of psychotherapists.

The Criminal Bill, Senate File 1003, became Chapter 297 Minnesota Laws 1985. This bill made it a felony for a psychotherapist to have sexual contact with a client. When there is penetration, the charge is in the third degree and is punishable by a sentence of not more than 10 years in prison and a fine of up to $20,000. This provision covers situations in which the therapist uses deception (e.g., claims that the sex is part of treatment) or the sex occurs during a psychotherapy session. Consent is not a defense. If the person abused is a former patient who is so emotionally dependent on the former therapist that he or she is unable to give effective consent, a charge also may be made but consent is a defense. (See Appendix H.)

The law provides for charging fourth-degree criminal sexual conduct when there is sexual contact without penetration; it carries a maximum penalty of 5 years in prison and a $10,000 fine. The same other provisions are in effect.

The law also holds that a patient's personal or medical history is not admissible except when (a) relevancy is proved in a pretrial hearing; (b) the court finds the history to be relevant and the probative value of the history to outweigh its prejudicial value; (c) the court allows only specific information that is relevant, not the entire history.

The Minnesota Sentencing Guidelines Commission has ruled that the third-degree offense (with penetration) shall have presumptive sentencing, which means a mandatory prison sentence for the first offense unless a judge wants to argue a special case. The sentence for a first conviction, however, is 23-25 months. In the case of the fourth degree (no penetration), probation may be ordered for the first offense with no presumptive sentencing until the third conviction. So, to sentence an offender to a prison term the judge would have to argue for a special case. The commission does not deal with the fine; imposing a fine is completely at a judge's discretion (see Appendix I).

The Task Force organized itself for its second year (1985-86) with Work Groups in the following areas:

—Clergy Issues   —Therapeutic Issues   —Institutional Abuse
—Public Education   —Training Institutions   —Administrative Procedures
—Civil & Criminal Law   —Professional Training   for Employers and
                                                          Professional Organizations

Again, as in its first year, many individuals, from consumers to professionals, participated in the work. Under the able staffing of Barbara Sanderson, the Task Force continued to be incredibly productive.

As a result of its lobbying activities the 1986 legislature passed Chapter 372 Minnesota Laws 1986 which created Chapter 148A Minnesota Statutes (see Appendix N) under which a psychotherapist can be sued for sexual contact with clients. The definitions of "psychotherapist" and sexual contact are quite similar to those in the criminal statute. It has a 3-year statute of limitations, one year more than the medical malpractice statute. It permits suits related to sexual relationships, which began at anytime during the two years following therapy termination, if it can be shown that the therapist employed "therapeutic deception" (led the client to believe that the sex was a part of, or consistent with therapy) or knew, or had reason to know, that the client was sufficiently "emotionally dependent" to be unable to withhold consent for the sex. (The implications of this aspect of the law are analyzed in Ch. 24.)

During this same period a Task Force met to consider the problem of unlicensed psychotherapists. After considerable debate the 1987 legislature passed a bill creating licensure boards for Social Work and Marriage and Family Counseling. A board was also created to study the problem of the remaining groups of unlicensed psychotherapists to determine the sort of regulation that would best serve the public interest.

Meanwhile, in 1986 the Task Force successfully organized "It's Never O.K.": the first major national conference on sex between therapist and client. (See Ch. 17 and Appendix AA) It attracted a very large audience from around the country and was rated as highly successful by participants. There was an overwhelming concensus for such a conference to be held again in 1987 and then every two years.

The Task Force spent the remainder of 1986 and the first half of 1987 working on various worthwhile projects. A series of workshops was held around the State of Minnesota to train advocates and professionals on working with victims of exploitative therapists. A large manual for professionals, *It's Never O.K.* (Sanderson, 1989), was put together and a pamphlet for consumers and consumer advocates was published with the same title. As for the idea of another national conference, Ms. Sanderson asked a coalition which was developing in Pennsylvania if it would sponsor the second national conference, which it agreed to do.

At present the Task Force no longer exists. (Although Ms. Sanderson continued for a time in a related role at the Department of Corrections, she is now a private consultant.) The Task Force's influence has been dramatic. In a 3-year period it carried out many measures aimed at earlier intervention and the prevention of therapist-client sex.

Unfortunately, it is too early to judge the effects of this work. Given the risks, difficult though it may be to believe, some therapists still sexually exploit clients in Minnesota. There is no way to judge if the incidence has gone down. At the very least the attention of the psychotherapy professions has been captured, and several therapists have been tried for sexual misconduct with clients (see Ch. 43). Furthermore, employers of therapists have dramatically altered their hiring practices since the passage of Chapter 148.A. Minnesota Statutes (see Appendix N).

CONCLUSION

The genesis of legislative action in Wisconsin and Minnesota differed but in both states the combined efforts of legislators, professionals, and consumers led to the development of some creative legislative approaches, and they began the long process of collecting data and developing broad solutions to the complex problem of client-therapist sex. The effect of the legislation itself remains to be seen. Certainly, the visibility given the problem should help to protect consumers and the very existence of the criminal laws may act as a deterrent in some instances. The occupational hazards to therapists who seek to exploit clients have been increased.

CHAPTER 43

THE NEW LAWS

Gary Richard Schoener

Legal approaches to therapist-client relationships easily generate sufficient discussion to make a volume the equal of this one in size. My purpose in looking at relevant laws, however, has not been to present an exhaustive study but, rather, enough of an overview to suggest the range of possibilities. Thus, in preceding chapters, the discussion is confined to some complaint options (Ch. 27), implications of relationships with former clients (Ch. 24), administrative safeguards (Ch. 36), employers' responsibilities (Ch. 37), and the legislative models on the books in Wisconsin and Minnesota (Chs. 41 and 42). Other relevant chapters are those on assessment of psychological damages (Ch. 10), false and misleading complaints (Ch. 11), and the four chapters in Part 9 dealing with the assessment and rehabilitation of therapists who have had sexual contact with clients.

In this chapter I review a group of statutes that were enacted by state legislatures during the past six years when further attempts were made to protect consumers from exploitative or impaired therapists. Thus, we will examine statutes related to civil causes of action; statutes that criminalize sex between therapist and client, and statutes that are related to mandatory reporting or to the provision of consumer information relative to therapist-client sexual relations.

Two excellent volumes offer a broader discussion of these and other legal topics: They are Joseph Smith's (1986) *Medical Malpractice: Psychiatric Care*, and Smith and Bisbing's (1988) *Sexual Exploitation by Health Care and Other Professionals*.

A broader overview of the social policy implications of changes in Minnesota statutes can be found in "Sexual Abuse of Patients by Therapists: Strategies for Offender Management and Rehabilitation" by Gartrell, Herman, Olarte, Feldstein, Localio, and Schoener (1989); this article is an updated version of Gartrell, Herman, Olarte, Feldstein, and Localio (1988).

STATUTES AND CIVIL SUITS

Civil suits against therapists for sexual contact with clients have a long history under common law; typically, they have been filed as negligence torts (malpractice). Occasionally, a suit may charge an intentional tort (e.g., Smith, 1986, pp. 303-4), but the drawback in such a cause of action is a significant one: professional liability insurance does not cover intentional acts. Smith and Bisbing (1988) review the issues and history of civil litigation and give a synopsis of reported cases.

Suits alleging damages from sexual contact have been filed against attorneys, chiropractors, clergy, dentists, educators, judges, medical specialists, psychiatrists, psychologists, and social workers (Smith & Bisbing, 1987; 1988). I have attended dozens of workshops on the topic of such suits and repeatedly heard the warning that, unlike medical malpractice cases more broadly considered, in therapist-client sex cases the plaintiff (client) nearly always prevails. According to Smith and Bisbing (1987):

A review of civil cases shows that the only decisions in which a defendant was successful were those in which there was a technical, rather than factual, defense.

In one case the statute of limitation had run out, and in two others the wrong cause of action had been pled. (p. 67)

Beginning in the late 1970s sex between therapist and client emerged as a common cause of action against psychotherapists. Trent (1978), for example, identified sexual contact with patients as one of a list of causes of action against psychiatrists. As of May 1, 1985 the American Psychiatric Association insurance plan sought to exclude coverage for claims that arose out of allegations of sexual misconduct by the therapist; the plan continued to cover the cost of defense, however (Simon, 1985). That same year, Besharov's (1985) survey of malpractice claims against social workers who were insured under the NASW policy showed that sexual contact with clients was the number one cause of such claims against social workers.

The *Monitor*, a monthly publication of the American Psychological Association, reported suits against female therapists (Turkington, 1984) as well as a proliferation of sexual malpractice cases in the early 1980s (Fisher, 1985). From 1976 to 1986, sexual intimacy with clients was the most frequent cause of suits against psychologists insured under the American Psychological Association's policy; the suits accounted for 44.8% of all monies ($7,018,165) paid in response to claims (Pope, 1987).

Even without special statutes, we find that civil actions against psychotherapists were not only possible but, also, not uncommon. One might ask, then, why special legislation was considered. In Minnesota and other states where such statutes have been contemplated or passed, the major objectives have been two-fold: First, to specify sexual involvement as a cause of action by defining the involvement as malpractice; thus the statutes eliminate the need to prove that sex with a psychotherapy client is malpractice. Second, the laws have sought to limit cross-examination and exposure of the plaintiff's sexual history when sexual damages are claimed. The Minnesota statute also sought to make the statute of limitations longer than that for medical malpractice, to clarify when sex with a former client is actionable; and to establish standards of responsibility for employers (insofar as direct liability is concerned).

Minnesota

The statute passed by the Minnesota legislature in 1986, which became effective August 1, 1986, is reproduced in Appendix N. Much of it parallels Minnesota's new criminal statute (passed the previous year; see Appendix H), which is discussed later in this chapter. Some noteworthy features of both statutes follow:

1. "Psychotherapy" is defined broadly to include any "professional treatment, assessment, or counseling of a mental or emotional illness, symptom, or condition."

2. A very broad definition of "Psychotherapist" also is defined broadly to include "a physician, psychologist, nurse, chemical dependency counselor, social worker, member of the clergy, or other person whether or not licensed by the State, who performs or purports to perform psychotherapy."

3. The definition of "sexual contact" is very broad.

4. Sexual exploitation of former clients is a cause for action if the plaintiff can prove that the sex occurred as a result of either "emotional dependency" or "therapeutic deception."

5. Limitations were set on discovery of the client's sexual history.

The civil statute differs from the criminal statute (see Appendix H) in several sections:

1. Under the civil statute, <u>requests by the therapist</u> for any of the long list of types of sexual contact are also considered "sexual contact" and, thus, are actionable; under the criminal law physical contact must occur.

2. The civil statute limits liability for sexual contact to a two-year period following the termination of therapy; the criminal law places no such restriction. Thus, in theory, at least, if sex with a former client was initiated more than two years following termination of therapy, it might be criminal but it would not be actionble in terms of civil damages.

In addition, the civil statute defines the responsibilities of the employer of a psychotherapist as well as of the former employer; an employer is required to make inquiries of current or past employers of the psychotherapist (within the last five years) about their knowledge of the therapist's sexual contacts with patients or former patients. If an employer receives such an inquiry and knows of the occurrence of sexual contacts, then he may be liable for damages if he does not reveal his/her knowledge provided that this failure can be shown to be "a proximate and actual cause of any damages sustained."

Since this law has been in effect for less than three years it is difficult to assess its effect on civil suits against psychotherapists. Civil suits take a long period of time to unfold; thus it will be some time before the effect of this law can be weighed. However, this statute has had several dramatic and almost immediate effects from the date of its passage:

1. Employers had to construct letters of inquiry to be sent to past employers of applicants for psychotherapy and counseling positions.

2. Hiring processes had to be revised to identify all of an applicant's employers within the past five years (including part-time positions and jobs of short duration), and to provide procedures for mailing letters of inquiry and monitoring their return.

3. Employers had to decide how to evaluate any information received relative to alleged past sexual contact.

4. Employers had to develop procedures for dealing with and responding to inquiries on employees' sexual conduct with patients.

5. Employers had to struggle with the decision on what constitutes knowledge of the occurrence of sexual contact and, especially, what to do about situations in which a full investigation did not occur (often because the employee resigned) or because a definitive finding could not be reached.

Insofar as the law was designed to short-circuit the problem of repeat offenders who are able to move from job to job because of the conspiracy of silence that often surrounds such incidents, the impact was immediate. Also, for the first time employers were given a clear incentive to pass on negative information to future employers and afforded some protection, if the disclosure was done in good faith. Prior to the passage of this statute, the fear of a suit by a former employee greatly outweighed an employer's concerns with future liability for damages to a future client. In many instances employers also had an incentive to conduct thorough investigations (often with the assistance of outside consultants), in order to arrive at a finding regarding the allegations, even if the employee resigned, because future inquiries would require the employers to have formed an opinion on whether sexual contact had occurred.

Unfortunately, many employers of psychotherapists have not educated themselves sufficiently about the problem of sexual contact to use the broader range of administrative safeguards which are possible (see Chs. 36 and 37). For example, an employer may fully send out inquiries but not necessarily make better background checks; this employer, consequently, may at times miss learning of other problems in the job applicant's work history which might portend future client abuse or, at least, provide grounds for carefully supervising the therapist's work. In addition, a surprising number of employers seem not to realize that "sexual contact" includes requests for sexual contact (see the WICC letter of inquiry in Appendix D). Far more employers know of allegations of sexual advances than of actual sexual contact because sometimes an accused staff member will admit to seductive acts but deny actual sexual contact.

Traditional health care facilities relatively quickly began sending out inquiry letters prior to hiring psychologists, social workers, and psychiatrists, but churches and some social service organizations have been far slower in following the procedure to hire pastors or social services personnel who, although at times they may counsel individuals with emotional symptoms or conditions, are not typically thought of as "psychotherapists." The use of the term "psychotherapist," in fact, has led to confusion. Furthermore, the situation regarding the screening of volunteers remains unclear. WICC, whose volunteer counselors and supervisors are all traditional mental health professionals, treats all volunteers like prospective employees.

Given that cases have been brought against clergy, nurses aides, and bachelors-level paraprofessionals, a prudent administrator should err on the side of over-inclusion in considering whether a particular job might be construed as a "psychotherapist" position under the statute's broad definition.[1]

Furthermore, the statute has led a number of employers to review policies relating to social or romantic relationships with former clients. In hospitals and residential facilities, especially those treating chemical abuse and dependency, policies often forbade such contact for a year following treatment termination. Many of these establishments have been advised subsequently to forbid such conduct for a two-year period following termination; of course, a surprising number of facilities still have not re-examined their policies.

The major problem area for employers of therapists has been decision-making concerning the handling of requests for information on past sexual contact with clients. I average a call a week from an employer seeking guidance in the handling of these requests. Some examples will help to illustrate these difficulties:

---

[1]This may be further confused by the fact that the Board of Unlicensed Mental Health Practitioners has exempted some types of counselors from its registration requirements. For example, advocates working in rape and sexual assault programs and in shelters for abused women are exempted. However, the work done by these practitioners fits easily into the broad definition of "psychotherapy" provided in both the civil and criminal statutes, so we hope programs which employ such individuals will continue to do such background checks prior to hiring. Chemical dependency counselors were also exempted, but since they are specifically identified as psychotherapists in the statutes, this is less likely to cause confusion. The Board itself (see Appendix V) was established to provide some regulatory oversight of the thousands of unlicensed counselors, therapists, and psychotherapists who previously engaged in fee-for-service counseling work without any public accountability.

1. Following the departure of an employee, the employer learns of alleged sexual misconduct with a client that may have occurred several years before. Shortly thereafter, the employer receives a request for information from a prospective employer and is faced with the dilemma of knowing of a complaint which has never been discussed with the former employee, the validity of which is unknown.

2. A new Executive Director, or Director of Personnel, in reviewing the personnel records of a former employee, finds that there was a past complaint of sexual misconduct which was not carefully investigated, and about which a final conclusion cannot be reached. This may or may not involve some sort of informal agreement to drop the investigation in exchange for a resignation by the staff member. When requests are received from prospective employers there is a dilemma as to whether to respond in the affirmative that there is a history of sexual contact with clients.

3. Some eight months after a therapist has been employed, the employer learns of an allegation of sexual misconduct with a client in a former job. An inquiry reveals that the former employer had known about the allegation but had chosen to ignore it when the staff member resigned. This had not been revealed when the reference check had been done during the hiring process. The current employer now has the task of investigating an old incident to determine whether there is any current risk to clients.

4. A request for information is returned to a prospective employer with a check-mark in a box apparently signifying past sexual contact with a client. However, the scant notes on the form state that the applicant engaged in "boundary violations with a client." A followup call to the former employer who had completed the form revealed that the incident referred to did _not_ involve an allegation of sexual contact, although it did involve several contacts with a former client of the facility who had phoned the staff member for assistance in a crisis.

5. A former employer alters the language on the request for information, crossing out "sexual contact with a client," and writing in "alleged sexual involvement with a client," along with a notation to the effect that the allegation was investigated and rejected based on "inconsistent and inaccurate facts." The prospective employer who receives the form then has to obtain further information to determine whether the former employer had rejected the allegations for understandable reasons.

The solution to the vast majority of such dilemmas is for the prospective employer to request that the applicant provide an authorization similar to that utilized by WICC (see Appendices C and X) permitting a more detailed background check. The former employer who receives a request and does not feel able to adequately respond due to a lack of resolution in a case can suggest to the prospective employer that such a release be obtained. None of these options, however, provide a solution for the situation in which there was a failure to properly investigate and reach a conclusion about a serious allegation of sexual misconduct.

Wisconsin

Appendix M reproduces the 1985 Wisconsin Act 275 which took affect on April 30, 1986. (This same Act upgraded the criminal charge for sexual exploitation in psychotherapy from a Class A misdemeanor to a Class D felony.) Like Minnesota's statute, a wide range of individuals, including clergy and unlicensed practitioners, are defined as "therapists." The defined range of activities covered in the Wisconsin Act includes "psychotherapy, counseling or other assessment or treatment of or involving any mental or emotional illness, symptom or condition." Like Minnesota's statute it provides for possible limitation on the admissibility of a complainant's sexual history.

The Wisconsin statute does not define the duties of a therapist's employer or the circumstances under which an employer may be held liable for a therapist's behavior. It does not define the post-termination period during which sexual contact may be actionable but it seems to leave the door open to suits for sexual involvement with former clients through the clause "...therapist who is rendering <u>or has rendered</u> to that person psychotherapy...." (The same Act amends the criminal statutes to cover sex during an on-going therapist-patient relationship.)

A three-year statute of limitations is written into the Wisconsin law. Nevertheless, it provides a basis for extending the statute of limitations, as follows:

If a person entitled to bring an action under § 895.70 is unable to bring the action due to the effects of the sexual conact or due to any threats, instructions or statements from the therapist, the period of inability is not part of the time limited for the commencement of the action, except that this subsection shall not extend the time limitation by more than 15 years.

The section addresses a major problem in these cases: for various reasons clients often do not come forward for several years, and may have difficulty even then in undertaking such a suit. The absence of a comparable provision is a serious flaw in the Minnesota law. The statute of limitations is one of the major obstacles in sexual exploitation cases.

The original language of the proposed Minnesota statute contained a requirement that professional liability insurance policies for psychotherapists cover sexual exploitation; but lobbying by insurance companies led to this section being discarded, however. Certainly, the cap on damages or the attempts to exclude sex cases from coverage under various professional liability policies have affected the number of civil suits which have been filed. However, it is noteworthy that the American Psychological Association's Insurance Trust reports that sexual misconduct is still the number one cause of action, even though the overall costs of such cases are down (personal communication, Margaret Bogey, April 4, 1989).

California

In 1987 the California Legislature enacted Section 43.93 as an amendment to the Civil Code (see Appendix O); it provides for a cause of action against a psychotherapist for sexual conact with a patient or former patient. Like the Minnesota and Wisconsin statutes, discovery of the plaintiff's sexual history is limited. Like Minnesota, the statute defines a two-year period following termination of therapy during which sexual contact can lead to liability; unlike Minnesota, however, it does not require a plaintiff to show either emotional dependency or therapeutic deception during this period. One of the grounds for action is "therapeutic deception," but it is unclear why the inclusion of this term was considered necessary because there appears to be strict liability during the period the patient was receiving psychotehrapy and for two years afterwards. Similar to Wisconsin, the statute does not distinguish sex occurring during a session from sex that occurs outside the office:

> It is not a defense to the action that sexual contact with a patient occurred outside a therapy or treatment session or that it occurred off the premises regularly used by the psychotherapist for therapy or treatment sessions.

The California statute appears to give "sexual contact" a more limited definition than do either Wisconsin or Minnesota. It also uses a more limited definition of "psychotherapist:"

> "...a physician and surgeon specializing in the practice of psychiatry, a psychologist, a psychological assistant, marriage, family, and child counselor intern, an educational psychologist, an apprentice social worker, or clinical social worker."

This listing would exclude a large number of counselors and therapists, such as chemical abuse and dependency counselors, clergy, unlicensed counselors, and other persons who purport to offer therapy but are not licensed or trainees in the various types of therapy and counseling.

Illinois

In 1988 the Illinois legislature passed Chapter 70 on Sexual Exploitation by Psychotherapists (see Appendix CC) which took effect on January 1, 1989. It is patterned after Minnesota's civil statute but contains several differences:

1. The definition of "psychotherapy" is narrowed. It "does not include counseling of a spiritual or religious nature, social work, or casual advice given by a friend or family member."

2. Post-termination sex is prohibited only for one year (the period is 2 years in Minnesota and California), but, as in Minnesota, a plaintiff must show either emotional dependency or therapeutic deception.

3. Employer liability appears to be limited to situations in which the employer "fails or refuses to take reasonable action...." Background checks and hiring practices are not issues under this statute.

(A recent review of state statutes by attorney Linda Jorgenson[2] provided me with the Illinois statute and found no additional statutes relating to civil liability for sexual exploitation of a client.)

One key aspect of the Minnesota statute, insofar as it relates to the responsibilities of employers of psychotherapists, is the protection it provides for an employer or former employer who responds in good faith to a written request by another employer or prospective employer for a therapist's history of sexual contact with clients. Specifically, it states,

---

[2] Personal communication May 4, 1989, Spero & Jorgenson, Attorneys at Law, Cambridge, Massachusettes.

148A.03(d) No cause of action arises, nor may a licensing board in this state take disciplinary action against a psychotherapist's employer or former employer who in good faith complies with section 3.

This paragraph is intended to protect an employer who, in compliance with the responsibility as outlined, responds to an inquiry in good faith and transmits information that the subject of the inquiry has had sexual contact with a client. The obvious risk for the employer is a suit for defamation by the former employee. It was not assumed that this paragraph would protect an employer against all causes of action by former employees— only for causes of action growing out of the release of information on sexual involvement with patients in response to the written request. It is meant to short-circuit the cycle of silence that commonly protects repeat offenders who, when they are accused, quietly resign and move on, and the former employer agrees to keep the matter private or fears telling the full story to prospective employers because of the possible consequences.

This matter was discussed with legislators because this section of the law was based, in part, on WICC's organizational consultation work in which we found that a number of repeat offenders had continued to find employment. However, subsection 148A.03(d) received little legislative debate and its exact intentions never were clearly delineated in what discussion did occur; thus the legislative intent was unclear. We were unaware of this fact until the publication of the Minnesota Supreme Court decision in the case of Hazelden Foundation vs. Patricia L. Meleen (see Appendix EE) on January 31, 1989.

During the hearings, Hazelden Foundation, a chemical dependency treatment facility, had cited this section of the statute as barring a suit by a chemical dependency counselor who had been discharged following the investigation of a complaint by a former client who had alleged that she had had sex with the counselor immediately after her discharge from the aftercare program. The former employee sued Hazelden Foundation, alleging "wrongful termination of employment, defamation, negligence, intentional and negligent infliction of emotional distress, and violation of her civil rights." So, the claims went far beyond simply responding to a request by a prospective employer for information about past sexual contact with clients.

Presented with this broad question, the court found as follows (see Appendix EE for the full decision):

We hold that the immunity language in section 148A.03(d) does not bar a suit by a psychotherapist employee against a former employer for wrongful termination of employment, defamation, negligence, intentional and negligent infliction of emotional distress, and violation of civil rights. Evidence that the employer acted reasonably and in good faith under the statute can be presented as a defense to these claims under the common law rules for each cause of action. Such potential findings, however, do not automatically act as a bar against a psychotherapist employee commencing an action against the employer.

If our holding is inconsistent with the intent of the legislature, we invite it to amend the statute in the current legislative session to explicitly include claims by a psychotherapist employee against a former employer within the protection of section 148A.03(d).

This finding was based, in part, on agreement with respondent Meleen's argument that the statute bars only a cause of action brought by a former patient, and that the statute provides a cause of action for a patient or former patient and does not explicitly discuss suits by a psychotherapist against an employer.

Donna Geck (1989), legal counsel to the Minnesota Psychological Association, warned,

> The Court's ruling is not a good one for psychologists. The sexual exploitation statute puts certain requirements on employers of psychologists. By holding that the immunity provisions of the statute apply only to suits by patients or former patients, the Court has effectively put psychologist employers in a box. They must comply with the terms of the statute to avoid a lawsuit by a patient or former patient, yet in so doing they will have potential legal exposure to their own former employee. The Court suggests the answer to the dilemma: an amendment to the statute. Persuasive lobbying on the part of psychologists may be the means to speedily achieve such an end. (p. 4)

The foregoing discussion and inclusion of Appendix EE are designed to help persons considering such statutes to avoid this pitfall. In retrospect it is not surprising that during so many discussions and debates which led those of us who were involved in the lobbying effort to feel clear about our goals and intents, no one noted that the statutory language, in fact, lacked clarity.

CRIMINAL LAWS

Considerable confusion is found in the psychotherapy literature over the existence of specific statutes that criminalize therapist-client sex. Simon (1985) claimed that "...15 states have passed statutes making sex with a patient a criminal offense" (p. 50), followed a year later by Pope's (1986) assertion that "...at least 15 states have passed legislation making therapist-patient sex illegal..." (p. 565). Neither author identified the 15 states nor provided a reference for the statement. Unfortunately, other authors (e.g., Hotelling, 1988, p. 235) have repeated this "15-state" figure, citing one of these two authors and another asserted "about one-third of the states have made therapist-patient sexual relations illegal" (Gabbard, 1989, p. xi). However, Bliss (1986) and Smith and Bisbing (1988) never found more than a few such statutes. At present only four states have passed specific statutes that criminalize sex between psychotherapist and client, and a few other states have older statutes that prohibit sex during treatment by health care professionals under certain circumstances.

Before reviewing these statutes, some comments on the prosecution of therapists under existing laws is in order. (See Ch. 27 for further information on criminal charges against therapists.) A historical note may be helpful by way of introduction:

> At common law, the crime of rape was generally limited to unlawful carnal knowledge of a woman forcibly and against her will. However, as rape became a modern social issue, most states amended their rape laws to extend rape offenses to include non-forcible, consensual sexual acts. Minors, the drugged or unconscious and the seriously mentally- and emotionally-impaired were added to the list of protected victims and the elements of force and consent were removed for those victims. These exceptions to the conventional requirements of force or consent were based upon the premise that the aforementioned victims were incapable of intelligent, informed consent. Accordingly, the majority of the States agreed that sexual activity with these victims was so contrary to public policy and morals that proof of an act in itself was sufficient. To date, 37 states. . . provide criminal penalties for those who engage in sexual acts with individuals who suffer from serious mental defects. (Bliss, 1986, pp. 12-13)

Smith (1986) argued that without special statutes it is difficult to bring a charge of rape against a psychotherapist and offered a useful historical perspective.[3]

Early American jurisprudence recognized several situations in which intercourse with a patient under the pretext of medical treatment was rape.[4] For example, intercourse with a patient against the patient's objections, even if such objections were feeble or slight, or if the act was committed by surprise or without the patient's knowledge, were considered sufficient to sustain a finding of rape.[5] This first set of circumstances shares a common thread in that the patient in no way gave his or her consent, either explicit or implied, to the sexual act with the doctor. The lack of consent, including those situations in which intercourse was engaged in over the patient's objections, tends to closely approximate circumstances generally associated with a traditional criminal rape.

Smith (1986) went on to observe that while, in theory, rape may be charged if a therapist misleads a client into believing that sex is part of treatment, courts have held that unless there is clearcut fraud, the act does not constitute rape. (This conclusion should be differentiated from the charge of consumer fraud, which is discussed in Ch. 27.) The charge of fraud can lead to a court's granting injunctive relief by prohibiting the behavior, but not necessarily finding that rape or sexual assault occurred.

I noted in Chapter 27 that physicians, psychologists, psychiatrists and others have been convicted of statutory rape after sexually exploiting clients or patients who are minors. (See Smith & Bisbing, 1988, for examples of such cases.)

Some cases in which medication was used to tranquilize patients and render them unable to resist have led to rape charges. I know of such a case in which Nembutol was used to help a patient to relax so she could remember early life events, after which her psychiatrist had sexual intercourse with her. Smith and Bisbing (1988, pp. 83-89) cite a number of such cases that reached appellate courts.

Stone (1976) cited an unnamed case involving a psychiatrist who was convicted of rape after a combination of electroconvulsive shock therapy and medications rendered his patients nearly helpless to his sexual advances.

Although there is an absence of published American cases where a therapist was charged with rape of a client due to the use of hypnosis (see Smith & Bisbing, 1988), Perry (1979) reported on an Australian case and Hoencamp (in press) reported on a Dutch case where hypnotherapists were charged with rape of their clients. Hypnosis has also played a role in rape cases in which the victim was a minor (Orne, Personal Communication, June 23, 1989), and Kline (1972) reports treating a graduate student in

---

[3]Reprinted from *Medical Malpractice: Psychiatric Care* by Joseph T. Smith, copyright 1986 by McGraw-Hill, Inc. Reprinted by permission of Shepard's/McGraw-Hill, Inc. Further reproduction is strictly prohibited.

[4] Annot, 70 ALR2d 824, 1-3 (1960)

[5] Eberhart v. State, 134 Ind 651, 34 NE 637 (1893); Pomeroy v. State, 94 Ind 96 (1883); State v. Ely, 144 Wash 185, 194 P 988 (1921); Commonwealth v. Morgan, 162 Pa Super 105, 56 A2d 275, revd on other grounds, 358 Pa 607, 58 A2d 330 (1948). (Smith, 1986, pp. 296-97)

psychology who was fearful of prosecution in connection with his sexual abuse of a young boy which had occurred after he had hypnotized the boy.[6]

In addition to the possibility of prosecution for the rape of a patient who is a minor, or of a patient where capacity to resist advances is diminished through the use of drugs, ECT, or hypnosis, five states (Colorado, Michigan, New Hampshire, Rhode Island, and Wyoming) have statutes defining physician-patient sex as rape when it occurs during medical examination or treatment. A discussion of these statutes is beyond the scope of this chapter because they apply only to physicians. The relevant section of Michigan's criminal sexual conduct statute (see Appendix F) is illustrative of the approach taken by these laws:

...The actor engages in the medical treatment or examination of the victim in a manner for purposes which are medically recognized as unethical or unacceptable. (Michigan Comp. Laws. 750.520b (1)(d)(i))

In an analysis of the Michigan statute to ascertain whether it could be used to charge a psychotherapist who is not a physician with criminal behavior under the given conditions, Bliss (1986) noted,

In 1956, the Attorney General issued an opinion which... stated that social workers, psychologists and others dealing with counseling and other non-medical emotional therapy are not practicing medicine....

Additionally, one Michigan District Court Judge specifically rejected the application of this portion of the statute to a non-physician psychologist, stating, in dicta, that the section would only apply to medical doctors. (p. 18)

Bliss (1986) went on to discuss a prosecution under the New Hampshire statute (see Appendix F) which contains language similar to that of Michigan's. A court held that a school psychologist counseling a client could be prosecuted under this New Hampshire statute. In this case (State v. VonKlock, 433 A.2d 1299 [1981]), the court based its ruling on the fact that the legislature had not limited "medical treatment or examination" to physicians, and that the State's Medical Practice Act described the practice of medicine as including the treatment of "mental... ailment" (Bliss, 1986, p. 20).

Some states also have statutes, some of them quite old, which make it a crime for a person to engage in sexual intercourse under the pretext of a medical examination or treatment (e.g., see in Appendix F Michigan Comprehensive Laws, Sect. 750.90). Bliss (1986) was able to find only one appellate court decision relating to this statute—People v. Williams (208 Mich 586 [1919]). The case was not only quite old but "...neither reports the facts nor clearly states the statute's use and application" (p. 22). He concluded that the statute probably was rarely used. It is worth noting that the statute is not only limited to

---

[6] A discussion of the degree to which hypnosis can be used to compel sexual contact where there is no true consent is beyond the scope of this article. Kline (1972) reported an interesting case:

A 56-year-old physician was seen in therapy because of mounting concern and anxiety in relation to his own utilization of hypnosis and the hypnotic relationship to manipulate patients sexually. He had been doing this for some years, and when first seen was concerned only over the fact that in a number of instances there had been serious complications when others found out about the relationships. His seeking help in this connection was not out of a sense of guilt or ethical concern, but rather a desire to avoid this type of compulsive behavior which was threatening him with exposure, malpractice suits, and embarassment. (p. 85)

The reader is referred to excellent reviews of the debate provided by Orne (1972) and Laurence and Perry (1988).

"medical treatment" but, also, to "sexual intercourse," thereby excluding other types of sexual contact and probably excluding non-physicians. Going still farther afield, some statutes make it a crime to impersonate a physician in order to have sexual contact with a client, but we have yet to encounter a charge of sex between therapist and client involving such a set of facts.

A number of licensure laws in various states (e.g., Florida, Texas) allow for the prosecution of sexual misconduct as a misdemeanor once a licensure board has determined the practitioner's guilt. This may require a referral to a local prosecutor for a trial, or may be a penalty the licensure board itself can dictate. For example, Chapter 453, Hawaii Revised Statutes (Medicine & Surgery), in Section 13, allows the Board to penalize an offending physician with a fine of up to $500 or imprisonment up to 6 months.

Wyoming has a statute in its criminal code, 6-2-303, defining sexual assault in the second degree as including situations in which "The actor is in a position of authority over the victim and uses this position of authority to cause the victim to submit" (see Appendix F). The definition of "position of authority" is included in 6-2-301:

> ...that position occupied by a parent, guardian, relative, household member, teacher, employer, custodian or any other person who, by reason of his position, is able to exercise significant influence over a person.

This description, and the inclusion of "teacher," would seem to readily apply to a psychotherapist, although it is not evident whether the law has been used to prosecute psychotherapists. It is likely that some other states have similar language, so a review of statutes related to sexual misconduct in your state is adviseable.

THE NEW CALIFORNIA STATUTE

As this book goes to press the California Legislature is in the process of passing a bill, which is expected to be signed by the governor, to create a new Section 729 to be added to the Business and Professions Code. Originally it proposed adding Section 268 to the Penal Code, but this was stricken in favor of including it with the licensure laws. As such, it resembles the statutes described previously which provide for penalties when sexual misconduct is committed by licensed practitioners.

A document dated August 24, 1989, and entitled, "SB 1004 Floor Statement," states in part:

> SB 1004 would make it a criminal offense, punishable as a misdemeanor for a psychotherapist (psychiatrist, psychologist or marriage counselor) to have sex with a patient. Repeat violators would be prosecuted as wobblers. (Note: "wobblers means that they can be treated like felons and given time in state prison.)

> Currently it is unlawful for counselors or therapists to engage in sex with a client/patient. But the penalty is only either revocation or suspension of license.

> The state Board of Behavioral Science Examiners oversees these professionals. It now has over 100 sex complaints which it is investigating. Sixty cases have resulted in administrative hearings, and there have been 40 recent revocations of licenses. Most of these people have engaged in sex acts with multiple patients. There are state administrative hearings going on right now involving two prominent psychiatrists in San Diego, who each face accusations by six separate women

patients who allege their therapist engaged them in sexual activity. One of the therapists is accused of also __branding__ two women patients with hot metal devices on or about their genitalia, and one of the devices bore his initials.

The bill itself makes "sexual exploitation by a psychotherapist a public offense," and uses the same definition of "psychotherapist" as Section 728 of the code (see Appendix P). The first violation is a misdemeanor, but no punishment is prescribed, whereas subsequent offenses carry the following punishment:

> ...imprisonment in the county jail for a period of not more than one year, or a fine not exceeding one thousand dollars ($1,000), or both, or by imprisonment in the state prison, or a fine not exceeding five thousand dollars ($5,000), or both.

Although the original bill prohibits sexual activity with a former client for six months following termination, that provision has been stricken. The current bill, as passed by the Senate, forbids sex with a former client only "when the relationship was terminated primarily for the purpose of engaging" in sex. Even this is permissible if the psychotherapist has referred the patient or client to an independent and objective psychotherapist, recommended by a third-party psychotherapist, for treatment." So, even a termination aimed at having sex, something forbidden by all major professional ethics codes, would be legally permissible in California as long as a referral of the client has been made. If this becomes law in its current form, which is expected, California will have become the first state to have provided for legitimization of post-termination sex, going in the opposite direction of all of the professions.

CRIMINALIZATION OF SEX BETWEEN THERAPIST AND CLIENT

Thus far, to our knowledge, only four states have passed statutes criminalizing sex between therapist and client; they are Colorado, Minnesota, North Dakota, and Wisconsin.[7] These statutes can be found in appendices L, H, DD, and G respectively. Wisconsin passed the first statute, and later passed a revised statute; both are included in Appendix G. For a comparison of the contents of the four statutes see Figures 1 and 2.

Chapters 41 and 42 of this volume recount the passage of the Wisconsin and Minnesota statutes. Consumer pressure brought about the passage of the Colorado statute in 1988; some of those consumers went on to develop a consumer advocacy group (see Ch. 31). I do not know the events that led to the passage of the North Dakota statute. California and Pennsylvania have seen several attempts to criminalize sex between therapists and patients but none has been successful, and many other state legislatures have seen the introduction of at least one such bill.

Criminalization was first achieved in Wisconsin on May 9, 1984, with a misdemeanor statute that took effect on May 18, 1984. Both Chapters 41 and 42 discuss a case prosecuted under this statute which became moot when the defendant died. Two years later, Wisconsin made sex between therapist and client a felony. The new statutory language (see Appendix G) was introduced via an act (see Appendix M) that went into effect on April 30, 1986. As a consequence, cases in which the sexual contact occurred between May 18, 1944, and April 30, 1986, were tried under the misdemeanor statute; it

---

[7]Attorney Linda Jorgenson, of Spero & Jorgenson (Cambridge, MA) recently informed us that North Dakota had enacted the statute criminalizing sex between a therapist and client. Given the number of legislatures in other states that are considering such statutes, it would not be surprising if they, too, had acted. If so, Jorgenson was unaware of such actions as of May 4, 1989.

had a more limited definition of "Therapist" and also applied only to sex occurring during a "treatment, consultation, interview or examination." Some cases were brought under the earlier statute even after April 30, 1986, but since then, of course, the new statutory language rules.

The Wisconsin law has been challenged constitutionally, starting with the first case brought under it (see Chs. 41 and 42). The law apparently has emerged successfully from such challenges, and so, too, has the principle that consent still can be offered as a defense. However, a review of these challenges will have to await an analysis by the Wisconsin colleagues who have kept us informed of cases over the past five years. Suffice it to say that there have been a number of prosecutions under the statutes in Wisconsin.

Both the North Dakota statute (see Appendix DD), which became effective March 23, 1987, and the Colorado statute (see Appendix L), which became effective July 1, 1988, are relatively new. I have no information on prosecutions brought under them but I hope colleagues in those states or others will publicize the use of these laws.

Figure 1 compares the statutes of the four states (Colorado, Minnesota, North Dakota, and Wisconsin) on a number of dimensions. I do not compare the statutory penalties in each state because they follow state sentencing guidelines. Minnesota's complex guidelines (see Appendix I) are probably less relevant than the actual sentences that are handed down (the sentences are discussed later in this chapter). Minnesota's statute is the only one providing penalties for sex with a former client, an issue that is addressed in detail in Chapter 24.

The Colorado statute does not specify where the sexual contact must take place; it specifies only that the perpetrator be a psychotherapist and the victim, a client. Wisconsin's first statute required, as does North Dakota's recent statute, that the sexual contact with the patient or client occur "...during any treatment, consultation, interview, or examination." When Wisconsin amended the statute in 1986, it broadened this requirement to include any sexual contact

> "...during any ongoing therapist-patient or therapist-client relationship, regardless of whether it occurs during any treatment, consultation, interview or examination...."

In contrast, Minnesota's statute provides for three different situations in which sexual contact can be a felony:

1. If the victim is a client and the sex occurred during a psychotherapy session. (Consent is _not_ a defense.)

2. If the victim is a client, or former client, and the sex occurred by means of therapeutic deception. (Consent is _not_ a defense.)

3. If the victim is a client or former client, and the victim was unable to withhold consent due to emotional dependency on the psychotherapist. (Consent _is_ a defense.)

So, like the North Dakota and Wisconsin statutes, the Minnesota statute makes sex that occurs during a session a felony, and consent is not a defense. However, if the sex occurs outside a session, or follows the termination of therapy, the State must show either emotional dependency or therapeutic deception. The Colorado statute has the same

	COLORADO	MINNESOTA	NORTH DAKOTA	WISCONSIN
Definition of "psychotherapist" or "therapist"	"any person who performs or purports to perform psychotherapy," whether or not licensed or certified	"physician, psychologist, nurse, chemical dependency counselor, social worker, clergy, whether or not licensed by the state, who performs or purports to perform psychotherapy"	Same as the Minnesota definition except for addition of "psychiatrist"	Same as Minnesota [earlier statute used "physician, psychologist, social worker or other person providing psychotherapy services"]
Definition of "psychotherapy"	"treatment, diagnosis, or counseling in a professional relationship to assist individuals or groups to alleviate mental disorders, understand unconscious or conscious motivation, resolve emotional, relationship, or attitudinal conflicts, or modify behaviors which interfere with effective emotional, social, or intellectual functioning"	"the professional treatment, assessment, or counseling of a mental or emotional illness, symptom, or condition"	"diagnosis or treatment of a mental or emotional condition, including alcohol or drug addiction"	"use of learning, conditioning methods and emotional reactions in a professional relationship to assist persons to modify feelings, attitudes and behaviors which are intellectually, socially, or emotionally maladjustive or ineffectual"

Figure 1: Definitions of "psychotherapist" and "psychotherapy" used in the criminal statutes of the four states which have criminalized therapist-client sexual contact.

definition of "therapeutic deception" as does Minnesota, although the reasons for its inclusion in the Colorado statute are unclear to me.

There is considerable feeling in Minnesota that at least during the ongoing therapeutic relationship there should be no requirement that the State prove either therapeutic deception or emotional dependency. If the sex occurs outside the office, or outside a professional encounter, the effect is the same as that occurring inside the office. Insofar as the post-termination case is concerned opinion is mixed; some people favor a strict time period and others favor retaining the current language until the law has been further tested. Thus far only one post-termination case has been prosecuted.

MINNESOTA CRIMINAL PROSECUTIONS TO DATE

As of the end of May 1989 we know of eight prosecutions under Minnesota's criminal statute. There may have been others we don't know about because some cases have been given little or no publicity, especially those that have been plea-bargained. Three of the eight therapists charged have been psychologists; the other five have been various types of unlicensed practitioners, including clergy. In hope of maximizing the deterence potential of the criminal statute, I have written a series of articles on these prosecutions for the *Minnesota Psychologist* (Schoener, 1988a, b; 1989a, b, c). However, the newsletters of other mental health and counseling professions have not published similar articles so it is not uncommon to find some Minnesota professional audiences that are unaware of these prosecutions.

Physician's Weekly (1987) published an interesting "Point/ Counterpoint" on the question: "Is the Minnesota sex-abuse law unfair to psychiatrists?" Dr. Joseph Westermeyer, then-President of the Minnesota Psychiatric Society, responded:

YES. From our point of view the main thing wrong with Minnesota's strict new law against sexual contact between therapists and their clients is that it splits psychiatrists from our real colleagues—other physicians.

Our relationship to society should be primarily as physicians. Medicine is our major discipline. We shouldn't be grouped with other mental-health professionals who don't share our problems, and don't share the collegiality we have with other physicians. We should be under the same regulations as other physicians.

Whether intentionally or not, lumping us in with the other mental-health professions seems designed to create a rift between psychiatrists and other physicians. I don't think it will succeed, but it has the potential to aggravate old wounds. (p. 1)

I was asked to respond to Dr. Westermeyer's comments, and did so as follows:

NO. This law does not create a rift between psychiatrists and other physicians, because the rift already exists. The law's purpose has nothing to do with interprofessional rivalries. Its purpose is to protect society. (p. 1)

I further noted that a non-psychiatric physician practicing psychotherapy would be treated identically under the law, but it was understandable that the State was distinguishing the average physician-patient relationship from the psychotherapeutic relationship.

Other than this single example, I am not aware that any other professional publication has raised questions about the criminal statute. All psychotherapy professions including psychiatry were represented on the State Task Force (Sanderson, 1985; 1989), and all helped to draft the criminal statute.

The cases that have been tried thus far have generated many private discussions among prosecuting attorneys relative to the need to prove either "emotional dependency" or "therapeutic deception" when the therapist-patient sex occurs following termination or outside the therapeutic setting. Following the acquittal of James Nevers (case number 4 which follows), in which the State failed to prove "emotional dependency" although the sex had occurred only a few days after termination, it was suggested that the statute be changed so that a strict time limit be used rather than "emotional dependency." In the Dutton case (number 7 which follows), in which the sex occurred during the course of therapy but the client was not completely certain that it had occurred during specific counseling sessions, a number of people including the victim (see Appendix DD) have suggested that it should not have been necessary to prove "emotional dependency" or "therapeutic deception." This would not have been necessary, for example, in the other three states which have similar laws.

Unfortunately, there is no system for locating such prosecutions in Minnesota. Some cases have escaped media attention. At present the eight cases which follow are the only ones I can locate:[8]

THE CASES

Case 1: State of Minn. vs. Richard Kent Sanford

In March 1986 a complaint was filed against Sanford, a psychologist who was employed as a mental health worker in Faribault County Social Services, alleging that in counseling sessions from May 15, 1985 until October 1985, he "made repeated sexual contact with her [the patient] by touching her in the breast and genital areas," including vaginal penetration in later sessions. The complaint also stated that two former patients reported that he had made "suggestive sexual gestures and invitations to them," and another former patient alleged "sexual gestures." Sanford was charged with two counts of criminal sexual conduct in the third degree, and one in the fourth degree.

According to the prosecutor, in exchange for dismissal of two of the counts, Sanford pleaded guilty to one of the third degree counts, with the understanding that the sentence would not exceed one year and one day in prison, a lowered departure from the sentencing guidelines. (Letter from Joel R. Welder, June 21, 1988.)

Sentencing took place on July 7, 1987; the judge stated in part,

> You took a chance and you lost, and I am willing to bet that if you hadn't have lost now you would have continued taking those chances until you did lose, and for that I think you should go to prison.... You have no one to blame, absolutely no one to blame but yourself. (Transcript p. 14)

---

[8]I am indebted to Mary Theisen and Janet Newberg, both Assistant Attorney Generals, for assistance in tracking down materials on these eight cases. Phil Villaume, a defense attorney, also helped, and Assistant Faribault County Attorney Joel R. Welder provided the sentencing transcript in the Sanford case, while Tim Fox, Assistant Wilkin County Attorney, provided information on the French case.

The judge further noted that Sanford was "...not going to like where [he's] going... and what [he's] going to be doing...," and ended with the Statement:

> You're a young man, you've got a lot of time left and a lot of time to make a good life for yourself. You've got to go through the fire, and that's what you are going to do. (Transcript p. 15)

This case is noteworthy largely because the conduct in question occurred both before and in the few months following the effective date of the law, which was August 1, 1985. It also included the sentence of more than one year in state prison.

Case 2: State of Minnesota vs. Alfred Joseph O'Connor

O'Connor was a 71-yr.-old chemical dependency counselor, with a Ph.D. in French literature, who counseled clients out of his home in Apple Valley, Minnesota (Dakota County). He was charged with the sexual assault of a young client by whipping him on the hands, feet, and buttocks while the client was nude, allegedly to help cure him of a drinking problem. The original four counts of 4th-degree criminal sexual conduct included an alleged attempt to assault an Apple Valley police officer acting as an undercover agent.

After a plea bargain that included dropping all but one of the counts, O'Connor was sentenced on August 31, 1987, to 30 days in jail in the Dakota County jail and five years probation (*Star Tribune*, 1987b). This case serves as a reminder that in Minnesota, as in many other states, criminal sexual conduct involves the intent to satisfy either sexual or aggressive impulses.

Case 3: State of Minnesota vs. Charles Hurtado Silva

This case was the first to attract major media attention (Brunswick, 1987a, b, c), largely because Silva was reputed to be a "guide" for Shirley MacLaine's widely publicized psychic experiences. The charges, which were filed on May 5, 1987, in Hennepin County, included two counts of 3rd-degree and one count of 4th-degree criminal sexual contact. One of the two complainants had paid $50 for a consultation on both health and career issues; she received a "reading" for these problems and then what Silva termed a "healing": she lay down on a bed and he touched her sexually, at which point she left abruptly.

A second woman had traveled with Silva to Minneapolis, at his expense, in response to his promises that he would help her with some emotional difficulties. Despite his assurances that he was not interested in sex, he made sexual advances to her, characterizing them as "praying" together (Brunswick, 1987a).

On August 19, 1987, after spending more than three months in Hennepin County jail, Silva pleaded guilty in Hennepin County District Court to two counts of criminal sexual conduct. Judge Jonathan Lebedoff sentenced him to three years probation. A news story (Brunswick, 1987b) indicated that another similar charge, which had been filed in Madison, Wisconsin, was dropped as part of the plea bargain, and Assistant County Attorney Gail Baez remarked that this case would have been difficult to try because of the victims' vulnerability. Although the 43-yr.-old Silva alleged that he had been in the United States for 26 years, he is a citizen of Peru; the U.S. Immigration and Naturalization Service was informed of the conviction in hopes that he would be deported. Nonetheless, two months later he was back in Minneapolis giving lectures. He was again interviewed and quoted as follows:

"I am a Latin American womanizer," he said. "I do come on to women but I know the difference when a woman says, 'no,' and when a woman says, 'no, but don't stop.'"

Said Silva: "I don't want this to sound sexist, but I do come in contact with a lot of beautiful women. I do not have to use any kind of thing about being a psychotherapist to find women." (Brunswick, 1987c, p. 4A)

The Silva case is important in that it established that the very broad definition of both "psychotherapy" and "psychotherapist" used in the statute allowed for the prosecution of a range of counselors who offered various types of "counseling." It should be noted, however, that the final guilty plea was to the use of force or coercion to obtain sex, even though the original charges had been brought under the sections dealing with sexual exploitation by a psychotherapist.

Case 4: State of Minnesota vs. James Clive Nevers

Nevers, a 36-year-old psychologist, was arrested at his place of work, a medical center in Las Vegas, on August 3, 1987. A complaint had been filed on July 30, 1987, by the Minnesota Attorney General's Office charging Nevers with criminal sexual conduct for having had sex with a former patient in Alexandria, Minnesota (*Star Tribune*, 1987a).

According to the complaint, filed on July 30, 1987, an adult female client was seen at Douglas County Hospital. She had been diagnosed as "depressed, with a dependent personality," and as "male dependent." She saw Nevers for psychotherapy beginning in July of 1986. She "developed a crush" on him and told him of the crush during their second session. By late August, she was thinking about him all the time. After she gave him an envelope containing poems she had written, Nevers allegedly told her that he could no longer be her therapist and offered to refer her to another therapist, which she refused. A formal termination took place on September 8, 1986. It was followed by a succession of evening phone calls, allegedly initiated by Nevers. They set up a date for September 12, 1986, and went to Never's apartment where they had sexual contact, including intercourse. The sexual relationship allegedly continued for approximately three weeks. During that time Nevers allowed the victim to read psychological reports on other clients, and told her not to tell anyone of their relationship or to see another therapist. When he was interviewed on May 21, 1987, Nevers admitted that she was a former patient of his and that he had had sexual intercourse with her. He was charged with criminal sexual conduct in the third degree.

The case was prosecuted by the Medicaid Fraud unit of the Attorney General's Office, in part because the abuse took place in a Medicaid-funded facility. Given that the sexual contact occurred after termination of therapy, and there was no dispute over the fact of termination, the State had to prove beyond a matter of reasonable doubt that the client was "emotionally dependent" to the degree that she was "unable to withhold consent to sexual contact or sexual penetration" by the psychotherapist; the sex had occurred only four days after termination. According to the prosecutor, the jurors saw Nevers as alone, divorced, impaired, and quite vulnerable, and the client as having a crush on him. The State was not able to prove "emotional dependency," as defined in the statute, to the jury's satisfaction (Kurt Erickson, personal communication, July 20, 1988). On March 17, 1988, Nevers was found "not guilty."

The Minnesota Board of Psychology, however, suspended his license on June 3, 1988, and issued the following press release:

At its regular meeting on June 3, 1988, the Minnesota Board of Psychology suspended the license of James Nevers, Licensed Psychologist, formerly of Alexandria. Nevers consented to the suspension.

For the purpose of issuing the Order, Nevers admitted that he dated and had sexual contact with a female client after telling her she had "graduated" from therapy, and had shown her MMPI reports on other clients who she claimed she could identify even though the clients' surnames were blocked out.

Nevers also admitted to having a social relationship with another female ex-client, to discussing therapy issues with her while seeing her socially, and allowing her to live with him for five days.

In addition to the above, the admissions included a social relationship with a female client, with the mother of a child client, and with a family to whom he provided therapy, and failure to report physical abuse of one daughter by the father of that family.

The suspension remains in effect until Nevers is able to demonstrate to the Board that he has been evaluated by the Sexual Perpetrator Treatment Program at the University of Minnesota, has successfully completed a sexual perpetrator program if recommended as a result of the evaluation, has engaged in therapy, has abstained from alcohol and other mood-altering drugs for a period of one year and participated actively in a chemical dependency rehabilitation program.

This case is the only one so far involving sex with a former patient; the psychologist's actions were deemed to be unprofessional (by the Licensure Board; he was not a member of any professional organization) but not criminal. "Emotional dependency" has been an issue in only two other instances: the Dutton case (number 7) in which it was proven, and the French case (number 6), in which it was admitted in the plea. In the Dutton case "therapeutic deception" also was charged. It is my view that we will need considerably more case experience with the "emotional dependency" issue and with post-termination cases before any conclusions can be reached about this aspect of the Minnesota statutes.

Case 5: State of Minnesota vs. Gordon Allen, aka Rocky Allen

Gordon "Rocky" Allen was a 63-year-old chemical dependency counselor who had been employed to do outreach, counseling, and referral work for Stevens County Social Services Department for 15 years. In March of 1988 he was charged with three counts of criminal sexual conduct in the 4th degree for touching an adult female client's breasts through her clothing. The trial was delayed while Allen challenged his termination by Stevens County; he argued Veteran's preference. A hearing was held before three hearing officers and the County's decision was upheld, so his firing was sustained.

Allen went on trial in January of 1989. On January 24 a jury found Allen guilty on all counts. A key element in the trial was the testimony of five Spreigl witnesses: former women clients whose testimony was ruled admissible to establish prior conduct similar to that alleged by the complainant. They testified to improper physical contact or sexual conversation. On May 19, 1989, Judge Davison sentenced Allen to five years probation and ordered him to pay a fine of $1,105. Conditions of probation included a prohibition against counseling women; should he violate probation in any way, he must serve 120 days in the County jail.

Allen was the second chemical dependency counselor to be convicted under the statute and, also, the second case in which sexual intercourse or penetration had not been alleged. It was only the second jury verdict.

Case 6: State of Minnesota vs. Phillip Lorenzo French

Phillip French was a psychologist who served as a consultant to several chemical dependency treatment programs. He had done at least two evaluations of the complainant, an adult woman. She claimed that their meetings were counseling sessions. He said they weren't and that the sexual contact was in the context of a friendship. She made appointments and saw him at his place of work, and these were listed on the main calendar and in his appointment book although the sessions were never billed. A search warrant was executed and a file which he had was found, which further added to the State's case. There was some dispute about whether their meetings had been counseling sessions. The sexual intercourse had occurred at her house, away from the counseling office.

French was arraigned on December 30, 1988, in Wilkin County. He pled guilty to one count of criminal sexual conduct in the 3rd degree. On March 13, 1989, Judge Bruce N. Reuther sentenced him to 24 months in prison (as recommended by the sentencing guidelines) and a fine of $345. The victim was present at the sentencing and given an opportunity to speak, but she declined. The transcript of the sentencing reveals that after French indicated that he had come to see that his conduct was wrong, Judge Reuther said,

> ....I don't intend to lecture at any length, but I simply have to say that in this Court's judgment, and I think that of your association and your peers and those of us at the other end of the line here, are strongly stacked against you in that.
>
> We all feel that there should never have been any question in your mind but that the situation was in your control and if it wasn't it should have been, and that it--the victim was never at fault and no matter how much she may have persisted, as you used that term, you were the one that was and should have remained at all times in control. And... it was inappropriate to be involved with a patient, a former patient, a prospective patient, whatever, sexually.
>
> To have arrived at that conclusion now is fine, and I don't mean to rub it in, but it's obviously a little late. But, how you could with all of the publicity that appears in professional magazines, in the common Sunday supplements, in magazines, and everything that everyone reads now, professional, lay, or whatever, how anyone could have concluded that sexual activity between a psychologist and a patient of any degree is appropriate is inexplicable as far as the Court is concerned.
>
> For you to have told the Court as you did when you pled guiilty that you now have arrived at that conclusion is obviously not sufficient. You should never have arrived at any other conclusion legally or professionally, and persistence, whether that's an accurate characterization or not, neither explains nor excuses that activity on the part of a doctor. (Transcript, pp. 8-9)

French thereby became the first psychotherapist to receive the full sentence as recommended by the Minnesota Sentencing Guidelines (see Appendix I). Although I have written an account (Schoener, 1989b) for the *Minnesota Psychologist*, this case escaped statewide media coverage. The trial took place in Breckenridge, far from the traditional coverage of our major media. If the law is to have the effect of deterence, however, broader visibility is necessary. The lack of media attention to this case is particularly tragic in view of the broad publicity given to the Dutton case in which the judge departed downwards from sentencing guidelines and made unfortunate statements during sentencing.

Case 7: Robert Eugene Dutton

On January 25, 1988, charges of 3rd- and 4th-degree criminal sexual conduct were brought against Robert Eugene Dutton, a former minister and counselor, in Nicollet County. He had been removed from his ministry, based on these charges, after a hearing before the Committee on Discipline of the Christian and Missionary Alliance. At the time the charges were brought he was working as a used car salesman (Crawford, 1988a).

The victim sought discussion of the Scriptures in her early meetings with Dutton, but these led to counseling sessions related to her self-esteem problems and the unresolved grief over the deaths of her father and a newborn infant. According to the complaint, Dutton began to control more and more of her life and eventually convinced her to leave town with him. Both of them left their families and went off to live together, although she returned to her family after a few months.

Because the victim could not specifically state which sexual acts took place during specific counseling sessions, the State charged that the sex occurred as a result of emotional dependency and therapeutic deception. As such, this case involved more expert testimony than had occurred in previous cases. On December 8, 1988, after four hours of deliberation, the jury convicted Dutton of four counts of criminal sexual conduct.

Dutton was sentenced by Judge Noah Rosenbloom to only 90 days in jail with work-release privileges, far below the 32 months in prison requested by the State under the sentencing guidelines. The judge prohibited Dutton from counseling and gave him 5 years on probation and fined him $300, the minimum fine allowed. This fine was far below the $14,384 the State requested for restitution to the victim and her husband, and the $6,288 requested to reimburse the victim's insurance company for the costs of therapy to deal with the incident. Judge Rosenbloom also appeared at times to blame the victim, citing the fact that she was guilty of adultery, which generated letters to the editor, including one from a juror; these letters took issue with the judge's remarks. Both Ellen Luepker and I filed complaints with the Minnesota Board on Judicial Standards after reviewing the transcript of the sentencing, but the Board made a finding of "no judicial misconduct" (letter from Roberta K. Levy, April 7, 1989). Appendix FF contains reactions by the victim to some of these events.

Unlike previous cases, this case received extensive media coverage, especially in southern Minnesota, during both the trial and the debate that followed the sentencing (e.g., Crawford, 1988a,b,c,d,e,f,g,h,i; 1989a,b,c,d,e; McAuliffe, 1989; Peterson, 1988; Schultz, 1988a,b,c,d,e,f,g; 1989). After the sentencing, I filed a formal complaint on February 13, 1989, with the Board on Judicial Standards against Judge Noah Rosenbloom as did Luepker; this complaint received publicity (Chandler, 1989) and led one newspaper to accuse Ellen Luepker and me of using "unfair tactics" for publicizing the complaint (Journal, 1989). The same newspaper printed a lengthy letter to the editor from me responding to these charges (Schoener, 1989d). The State's appeal of the sentence also was given considerable publicity (Crawford, 1989e; Prince, 1989). A local TV station, WCCO-TV (1989) and a Nashville, Tennessee, TV station, WSMV-TV (1989) did special programs on the case. So, this was by far the most publicized local case.

Meanwhile, oral arguments were heard by the Minnesota Court of Appeals on May 18, 1989, in the appeal filed by the Attorney General's Office to challenge the low sentence. On July 19, 1989 the Minnesota Court of Appeals upheld Dutton's light sentence, citing the findings of a presentence investigation and sex offender evaluation as well as the lack of a prior record and the fact that Dutton was remorseful. However, Appeals Court Judge Marianne Short was critical of Judge Rosenbloom's comments concerning the victim, writing that:

> ...I disagree with the trial court's consideration of the victim's capabilities in sentencing respondent.
>
> During sentencing, the trial court opined that this case involved "clearly a two-sided involvement," that the victim "was clearly infatuated during this whole affair" and that "she was equally guilty of adultery and she suffers no legal penalty." The trial court stated that the victim was "not a condemned victim, but to a large point she has a large element of responsibility for what happened." Finally, the trial court commented that "the victim has certain educational training and related intellectual capacity equal to or exceeding those of the defendant."
>
> The legislature has clearly set forth its intent that patients and former patients are to be protected from sexual encounters with their counselors or therapists. Minn. Stat. 609.344, subd. 1(i) and (j), and 609.345, subd. 1(i) and (j) (1988). The unique psychotherapist-patient relationship gives rise to an emotional vulnerability irrespective of age, intelligence or education. Id. Therefore, the trial court's consideration of the victim's capabilities was wholly improper. (State of Minnesota, Court of Appeals, 1989, p. SC-2)

The Office of the Attorney General decided to appeal the action of the Appellate Court to the Minnesota Supreme Court, and an appeal was filed on August 17, 1989. Meanwhile, Dutton appealed his conviction to the Court of Appeals on August 24, 1989. (Mary Theisen, personal communication, August 28, 1989).

Case 8: State of Minnesota vs. Gregg S. Rochester

Gregg Rochester is a psychologist in private practice who was convicted earlier of seven counts of insurance fraud on September 15, 1988, in St. Louis County. In the original complaint, Rochester also was charged with one count of criminal sexual conduct in the 3rd-degree, and one in the 4th degree, for having had sexual contact and sexual intercourse with an adult female client. The trial on those charges initially was scheduled for February 6, 1989, and then was rescheduled for April 10, 1989.

In this case the State successfully argued for the inclusion of Spreigl evidence, that is, the testimony of three former clients who also would testify to some of the same behaviors. The Nevers and Allen cases provided some of the precedents cited in the argument (Response Memorandum, March 28, 1989, Court File No. 88-10040).

On the opening date of the trial, April 10, 1989, Rochester waived his right to a jury trial and the right to cross-examine witnesses, and indicated that he was not guilty. St. Louis County Judge Joseph Scherkenback then found him guilty. A sentencing hearing was set for May 18, but the anticipated testimony and debate did not materialize. The judge took the matter under advisement and moved sentencing to May 25. It was learned during the following week that instead of the 41 months in prison, which Rochester believed would be his maximum sentence when he waived rights to a trial, the sentencing guidelines called for a 54-month sentence.[9] On May 25, 1989, Judge Scherkenback gave Rochester the option of having the conviction on the criminal sexual conduct charges vacated. Rochester took the option and the judge sentenced him to 41 months in state prison on the conviction for insurance fraud last year, and he was taken into custody for transportation to state prison.[10] After less than two months in prison, Rochester decided to enter a plea, and on July 20, 1989, as part of a plea bargain, he pled guilty to one count of criminal sexual conduct in the fourth degree. Judge Scherkenback sentenced him to 54 months in prison, with the term to be served consecutively with the 41 months for fraud. (Janet Newberg, Personal Communication, July 24, 1989.) Unfortunately, the final verdict and sentence received no mention in the major Twin Cities newspapers.

Summing up, of the eight cases we know of thus far, seven resulted in conviction and only one may generate an appeal. No jurisdiction has more than one case, so it appears that the law has reasonably broad acceptance in the state given the number of prosecutors who have been willing to file charges under it. It is far too early to tell what sort of a deterent effect the law has had. The lack of consistent news media coverage has undermined that intent of the law thus far. Even my articles in the *Minnesota Psychologist* only reach psychologists who are members of the association, and none of the psychologists tried so far have been members.

The California Senate Task Force on Psychotherapists and Patients (sic) Relationships (1987) recommended against criminalization in California for a number of reasons. After citing the potential benefits of criminalization, the report stated,

> The realities of the judicial system would make therapist-patient sexual relations extremely difficult to prosecute. Commonly these cases involve little physical evidence and depend instead on the credibility of a distraught victim against a sophisticated and articulate professional. It is unlikely that overworked district attorneys' offices would energetically pursue these complex and difficult cases, given the large felony workload most offices bear. (p.9)

As of this time of writing, the Minnesota experience suggests that these cases are not so difficult to prosecute nor so lacking in interest to prosecuting attorneys as the California Task Force believed.

MANDATED REPORTING AND CONSUMER EDUCATION

A variety of approaches are available to the mandated reporting of sexual misconduct by psychotherapists, even in a single state like Minnesota. Some states have considered mandatory reporting but ended up enacting statutes requiring therapists to inform consumers who allege a previous victimization of the avenues for action.

In 1987 California added two sections to its Business and Professions Code (see Appendix P); they require the state to develop an informational brochure for victims of sexual exploitation by therapists and their advocates. Section 728 of the Code reads as follows:

---

[9]Those who do not understand the confusion should examine the guidelines in Appendix I. They get complicated when one has "criminal justice points," that is, a prior conviction.

[10]If Rochester was tried and convicted, he could have been sentenced for up to 97 months; even if the time served was concurrent, it could have meant an extra 56 months in prison for him.

New Laws — Page 561

(a) Any psychotherapist or employer of a psychotherapist who becomes aware through a patient that the patient had alleged sexual intercourse or alleged sexual contact with a previous psychotherapist during the course of a prior treatment, shall provide to the patient a brochure promulgated by the department which delineates the rights of, and remedies for, patients who have been involved sexually with their psychotherapist. Further, the psychotherapist or employer shall discuss with the patient the brochure prepared by the department.

(b) Failure to comply with this section constitutes unprofessional conduct.

Potentially this law is useful. Section 728 accomplishes Recommendation #20 in the California Senate Task Force Report (1987, p. 31) but it falls short of the mandatory reporting that was recommended:

RECOMMENDATION #8

It is the recommendation of the task force that any licensed psychotherapist or employer who becomes aware that his or her patient had sexual intercourse or sexual contact with a previous psychotherapist during the course of a prior treatment, must seek the patient's consent to file a written report and, with or without the patient's consent, provide certain information to the appropriate licensing authority. Failure to comply with these requirements should result in a civil liability. (p. 17)

In 1988 Wisconsin passed a law (see Appendix W) requiring each therapist to ask victims of sexual exploitation by therapists for permission to report, and that given the client's permission, a report be made either to the licensing authority or a district attorney if the therapist/perpetrator is unlicensed. Failure to report is a Class A misdemeanor. The language of the statute is as follows:

940.22 (3) REPORTS OF SEXUAL CONTACT. (a) If a therapist has reasonable cause to suspect that a patient or client he or she has seen in the course of professional duties is a victim of sexual contact by another therapist or a person who holds himself or herself out to be a therapist in violation of sub. (2), as soon thereafter as practicable the therapist shall ask the patient or client if he or she wants the therapist to make a report under this subsection. The therapist shall explain that the report need not identify the patient or client as the victim. If the patient or client wants the therapist to make the report, the patient or client shall provide the therapist with a written consent to the report and shall specify whether the patient's or client's identity will be included in the report.

(b) Within 30 days after a patient or client consents under par. (a) to a report, the therapist shall report the suspicion to:

1. The department, if the reporter believes the subject of the report is licensed by the state. The department shall promptly communicate the information to the appropriate examining board.

2. The district attorney for the county in which the sexual contact is likely, in the opinion of the reporter, to have occurred, if subd. 1 is not applicable.

(c) A report under this subsection shall contain only information that is necessary to identify the reporter and subject and to express the suspicion that sexual contact has occurred in violation of sub. (2). The report shall not contain information as to the identity of the alleged victim of sexual contact unles the patient or client requests under para. (a) that this information be included.

In Minnesota, a variety of reporting standards are found in a number of statutes and rules; unfortunately, they are not completely consistent with each other. First of all, Minnesota passed a Vulnerable Adults Act (see Appendix J) in 1980 and it was amended in 1982, 1983, and 1985. A number of other states ahve similar statutes that require the reporting of the abuse of certain persons with emotional or mental impairment or disability. In Minnesota, a "vulnerable adult" is any person over the age of 18 who is a resident of or inpatient at any of a number of facilities, "except a person receiving outpatient services for treatment of chemical dependency or mental illness." Somewhat ambiguously, the act also includes persons who are "...unable or unlikely to report abuse or neglect without assistance because of impairment of mental or physical function or emotional status." Although the definition of "abuse" includes "any sexual contact between a facility staff person and a resident or client of that facility," it should be borne in mind that outpatients typically are not included.

As a result, the Vulnerable Adults Act has led to the increased reporting of sexual exploitation which occurs in residential or inpatient settings but had had virtually no effect on the reporting of the sexual abuse of outpatients—by far the most frequest reports we receive.

In 1982 the Minnesota Board of Psychology adopted new Rules of Conduct that contained a provision mandating the reporting of allegations of sexual misconduct by psychologists under certain circumstances. When the Medical Practice Act was amended in 1986 the Board of Medical Examiners, which licenses physicians, wrote a somewhat different law requiring reporting. Then, to further complicate things, the law that licenses social workers and marriage and family therapists, which was passed in 1987, contained still a different standard for mandated reporting of sexual misconduct by therapists (see Appendix K). These various requirements are compared in Figure 2.

The act licensing social work and marriage and family therapists contains language quite similar to the Medical Practice Act, but on careful reading it does not limit reporting if the information was obtained in the course of providing therapy to the perpetrator.

If the information was obtained in the course of a client relationship, the client is another regulated individual, and the treating individual successfully counsels the other individual to limit or withdraw from practice to the extent required by the impairment, the board may deem this limitation of or withdrawal from practice to be sufficient disciplinary action.

The purpose of this section is unclear to me; I can only assume that it is meant to provide the basis for diversion programming.

The Medical Practice Act changes in 1986 inadvertently provided limits on reporting for physicians only rather than all health professionals. This was not intentional; it was a detail overlooked by a number of people who lobbied for the bill, including me. The goal of this exception and that in the Rules of Conduct adopted by the Board of Psychology was to avoid closing off avenues of help-seeking by impaired practitioners. It is worth noting that the physician who decides not to report a colleague to the Board is taking a risk because one would assume that there is civil liability in deciding incorrectly that the impaired physician has limited his or her practice sufficiently to prevent any danger to the public.

	Board of Psychology	Board of Medical Examiners	Social Work and Marriage & Family Therapy Boards
Who is mandated to report?	psychologists licensed by the Board	physicians and all licensed health professionals; employers; medical societies; insurers; self-report required	same as Board of Medical Examiners
What must be reported (beyond disciplinary actions and malpractice judgments)	sexual contact with a client; child abuse or abuse of a vulnerable adult	any conduct that may constitute a basis for disciplinary action by the Board, including engaging in sexual conduct with a patient or in any verbal behavior that is seductive or sexually demeaning	any conduct that may constitute a basis for disciplinary action by the Board, including evidence of incompetence (sex not specifically mentioned)
Exceptions	when information has been obtained in the course of a professional relationship with the psychologist in question	physicians treating the impaired physician don't have to report if they believe he/she is limiting his/her practice to the extent required by the impairment	none in the statute

Figure 2: Mandatory reporting under licensure statutes.

The Executive Director of the Board of Psychology, Lois Mizuno (personal communication, July 22, 1988), believes that the combination of this reporting requirement and the Patient's Bill of Rights have greatly contributed to the receipt of complaints by the Board. She also indicates that a larger number of complaints are now coming from other psychologists. Prior to the reporting rule, few client abuse complaints came in from psychologists. Mizuno (letter of April 25, 1989) reported recently that from March of 1980 to the present, 43 reports were made by licensed psychologists about alleged sexual contact with clients on the part of other licensed psychologists. (An additional twelve mandated reports were made of failures to report abuse of children and vulnerable adults.) For the biennium July 1, 1986 through June 30, 1988, 189 written complaints of all types were received, of which 52 concerned sexual contact with clients. Of this 52, 24 were reports from psychologists.

Richard Auld, Assistant Director for Discipline, Board of Medical Examiners, feels that the 1985 amendments to the Medical Practice Act, which included mandatory reporting, had a dramatic effect (personal communication, June 14, 1989). Sexual misconduct cases are the third most common complaint against physicians. Both mandatory reporting and the requirement that the Board publicize its disciplinary actions have led to an overall increase in reports in general, and an increase in reports from the professional community. Figure 3 illustrates this.

Figure 3: Complaints to the Board of Medical Examiners on Yearly Basis

7/1/86 - 6/30/87 Actual	7/1/87 - 6/30/88 Actual	7/1/88 - 6/30/89 Estimated[11]	7/1/89 - 6/30/90 Estimated	7/1/90 - 6/30/91 Estimated
505	687	960	1,339	1,853

(personal communication, Richard Auld, June 14, 1989)

It should be noted that the number of physicians licensed in Minnesota has remained, and is expected to remain, roughly constant at just above 13,500 during all five years displayed in Figure 3. There are about 1,000 - 1,500 new physicians licensed each year, and about the same number deleted from the roles due to retirement or migration.

John Breviu, an Assistant Attorney General who is one of the Board's prosecutors, and who played a major role in the design of the revised statute, notes that the increased staffing of the Board has led to more disciplinary actions, which in turn has led to more visibility, which has helped generate a larger number of complaints (personal communication, June 15, 1989). The receipt of an increased number of complaints has permitted earlier identification of some repeat offenders, which has in turn led to an increase in the number of emergency license suspensions sought by the Board. At least one involved multiple sexual contacts with patients.

We are aware of some problems related to mandated reporting, but virtually all can be traced to one of two issues:

---

[11]Note: This estimate is on target as of June, 1989, or may be low.

1. Confusion about the requirements, largely due to the fact that they vary from Board to Board and profession to profession.

2. Failure to forewarn clients of possible reporting duties prior to obtaining reportable information.

Certainly for persons like us who see a great many victims a good deal of care is required to forewarn clients when beginning an interview. However, the fears that are voiced about mandated reporting by and large have not been realized because in most cases clients seem to appreciate their new therapist taking a stand and making a complaint. In fact, the very act of reporting is often quite helpful in building trust.

CONCLUSION

It is indicated in Chapter 42 that Minnesota has opted for a number of legal approaches to the problem of sex between psychotherapists and clients. Each statutory change was designed to address part of this complex problem. The reader is referred to Sanderson's (1989) comprehensive report on the Minnesota approach — *It's Never O.K.: A Handbook for Professionals on Sexual Exploitation by Counselors and Therapists*. The Wisconsin approach is detailed in Chapter 41 and Appendix Z. The California approach can be found in the *Report of the Senate Task Force on Psychotherapist and Patients Sexual Relations* (California Legislature, 1987).

In Minnesota, mandatory reporting appears to have increased the number of complaints filed and there is little evidence of problems associated with this reporting. The civil statute has had a dramatic effect on the checking of background references on potential therapist-employees; this, in turn, has made therapists acutely aware of the risks of sexual contact with clients. The effect of the criminal law as a deterrent cannot be measured, but it certainly has led to more clarity in the minds of both professionals and the public that sex with clients is "never O.K."

All of these legal changes notwithstanding, the implementation of administrative law, such as licensure statutes, is not easy. Even Minnesota's hard-working licensure Boards find themselves unable to deal effectively with some complaints and end up the subject of news media attacks for slowness or inadequate sanctions. Sometimes even when a Board wins in a contested hearing, community pressure or the actions of an appellate court undermine the action.[12] In the case of Anderson vs. Love, a recent civil suit brought against a psychologist for sexual misconduct, a Ramsey County judge ruled that sexual contact was not malpractice. Last, the aforementioned criminal case against Robert Dutton, while it led to a conviction, subjected the victim to unnecessary abuse by the trial judge, something the Minnesota Board on Judicial Standards refused to censure (letter from Roberta K. Levy, April 7, 1989). We have a long way to go, even in Minnesota.

---

[12]The Minnesota Supreme Court, in an opinion filed June 9, 1989, in the Matter of the Disciplinary Action Against the Dentist License of Joseph H. Wang (C6-87-1337) overturned an action taken by the Board of Dentistry based on the testimony of 3 women who claimed sexual touching or improper advances, citing, among other things, that his behavior might have been misinterpreted for cultural reasons.

CHAPTER 44

RESPONDING TO SEXUAL EXPLOITATION OF CLIENTS BY THERAPISTS: FUTURE DIRECTIONS

John C. Gonsiorek

"Conclusion" is not the appropriate word for this chapter. The term implies a finality or sense of coherence that is premature, given that we are still in the initial stage of understanding the sexual exploitation of clients by therapists. On the other hand, the term "summing up" might be more appropriate, given that the chapter is directed to identifying the future pitfalls and the areas that need particular development or research or are the possible source of future dangers. To examine these topics, I have, for the sake of convenience, organized the contents by topical areas.

VICTIMS OF SEXUAL EXPLOITATION BY PSYCHOTHERAPISTS

This area, nevertheless, is the only one for which any true conclusions can be offered. We know clearly and unequivocally that most clients experience adverse consequences from sexual exploitation by their psychotherapists. These effects may range from the most devastating and debilitating to the merely annoying but still negative.

Further elucidation is needed to understand the variables that produce the greater and lesser degrees of adverse consequences. We have some impressionistic information: the length of the sexual exploitation, the degree to which other boundaries were violated or other kinds of intrusiveness occurred, the bizarreness of the exploitative behaviors, and other aspects of the situation *per se* are all likely to be relevant in predicting the degree of adverse experience. Client variables, such as the amount of psychological distress, degree of vulnerability, history of past abuse, and similar variables are also likely to play a role. What would be helpful is to obtain further understanding of the kinds of situations and clients that generate greater and lesser degrees of vulnerability.

Although treatment of client-victims of sexually exploitative therapists is discussed in this volume, the work is still too new to draw firm conclusions about outcomes. Impressionistic information from the authors of this manual suggests that whereas many clients benefit from therapy, others do not; indeed, the latter appear to sustain irreparable damage. Then there are those victims who refuse further therapy and whose outcomes remain unknown. It is possible that advocacy or assistance provided to clients in formulating and pursuing complaint options provides equal or greater help than subsequent therapy. Differences between male and female victims appear to exist but how strong and reliable they are remains an open question. Finally, much work remains to be done before predictable patterns of what treatments work with what kinds of client victims can be described with any confidence.[1]

The exploited client often is not the only victim. Spouses, significant others, family members, and friends become secondary victims and may suffer impaired relationships

---

[1] We believe strongly that client-victims require services that are carefully individualized to their experiences and needs. Services that assume monolithic victim experiences, and that are based on victimological theory, and not on a thorough assessment of each individual client are apt to repeat the victimization.

with the primary victim. They also may suffer economic consequences resulting from the adverse affects on the primary victim's ability to work or the costs associated with legal action or obtaining further therapy. Emotional incapacitation or disruption in the victim's sexual functioning may take its toll on and affect significant others. Thus secondary victims also may need therapy and support services.

THERAPIST-PERPETRATORS

A number of chapters deal with attempts to assess and treat exploitative therapists. Outcome studies, however, are nonexistent. We have only impressionistic information on the kinds of therapists who have the capacity to be rehabilitated and on how effective the rehabilitation is.

The typology of offenders (see Ch. 32) is a combination of offender characteristics and offender behavior. The schema is based on what the authors observed in over a thousand cases processed by the Walk-In Counseling Center. Yet it is still too early to ascertain whether therapists' characteristics or behaviors are more important in classifying them and it is certainly too early to have any confidence in understanding or predicting treatment outcomes for offenders. The fact that they are a diverse group complicates outcome research considerably.

LEGAL ENVIRONMENT

Clearly, more states will follow Wisconsin, Minnesota, North Dakota and Colorado in criminalizing sexual behavior between clients and therapists. What is unclear, however, is the specific activities that will be criminalized, how they will be conceptualized legally, how effective the statutes will be. In general, states tend to diverge on the specifics of such legislation so making comparisons on the effectiveness of different statutes is problematic.

Civil statutes in general are in great need of improvement. Chapters 42 and 43 in this volume describe some changes in the Minnesota civil statutes that are directed to greater equity for client-victims. It is important in the development of civil statutes, that the focus be broader than simply sexual exploitation. The overriding issue is the exploitative treatment of clients in general. What we need is a broader consumer fraud approach to creating civil remedies for inappropriate behavior by therapists. Remedies for sexual exploitation should be regarded simply as one subset of this more inclusive approach.

In a number of jurisdictions, there has been raised the question of restitution by the community to the victim. Indeed, the principle of compensating victims is established in some places already. This raises a number of interesting and complex issues regarding sexual exploitation by psychotherapists. Who is responsible for the restitution: the community as a whole? or the mental health professions? Mental health professionals have seen repeatedly that legal remedies produce unintended consequences, and that the legal system follows a different logic from that of the mental health professions. Suffice it to say that legislative remedies will substantially alter the face of mental health practice.

"Perfect" laws are never created and applied forever. Consequently we must take a more reasonable approach to legislative remedies by making a best guess now and amending statutes as experience informs us on the strengths and weaknesses of the particular legislation.

LICENSURE AND ETHICS CODES

Professional ethics codes may uniformly prohibit sexual contact between client and therapist but they diverge greatly in the sophistication with which they approach this issue. The American Psychological Association (APA) ethics code is probably the most complex in its development. Currently the organization is tackling the issue of post-therapy sexual relationships with clients without much consensus but with considerable creativity and intellectual ferment. The sophistication that has been displayed in the APA's struggle with this particular issue may well serve as a model for all psychotherapy professions in the struggle to deal equitably with sexual and other exploitations of clients. Ensuing modifications of ethics codes, we must hope, will be more similar than different because widely divergent solutions would be an embarrassment to all the professions. However, the mental health professions differ in their history and mission and, hence, some diversity is likely.

The standards of licensure and certification boards display a comparable lack of coherence at present. Given the statutory authority of such bodies, however, this inconsistency is the greater problem. The same act committed by the same therapist upon the same clients may well result in widely differing outcomes by different licensing bodies in the same state. In the small number of cases that we have seen in which professionals are licensed by more than one body, such divergence is the rule, not the exception. This inconsistency makes all licensing bodies lose credibility. Great care must be taken to make certain that client victims are not further victimized by those structures created to protect them. This can occur directly, by poor treatment of complainants, or indirectly, by ineffectiveness and inconsistency.

The chapters in this volume detail the unacceptable diversity of outcomes for therapists whose cases are handled by licensing boards. Specifically, those therapists who try to be open and forthcoming with a licensing body, who plead guilty and freely disclose their inappropriate activities, tend to be treated more harshly than those therapists who fight all charges against them, plead not guilty, and resist any attempt at accountability. The latter should not receive lesser consequences.

Currently, licensing boards operate with powerful disincentives for therapist cooperation during investigations of serious ethical issues. It is not reasonable to expect a therapist to behave in a "professional" manner if a licensing board has a history of not adhering to basic concepts of justice and fair play. If licensing and certification bodies do not remedy this situation, the future is likely to hold an extraordinary amount of bitter and lengthy legal struggles. When more and more therapists refuse to cooperate with even the most minimal investigations, and, instead, take a legalistic and adversarial stance to protect themselves, the limited resources available to licensing bodies will rapidly be exhausted and we will see our ethics codes become de facto unenforceable. The solution is to work for the institutionalization of basic concepts of equitable and fair justice in the administrative law structures of licensing boards so we can dispense with the excesses of case-by-case determination. It is ironic that excessive case-by-case determination shares with offending therapists a similar lack of accountability and belief in the omniscience of the more powerful member of the dyad.

A number of chapters outline useful ideas for licensing and certification bodies. Gonsiorek and Schoener (1988) have written specifically on this issue. It is recommended that licensing boards, at least those within a given state, move toward maximum consistency in establishing and administering a core code of conduct, processes of adjudication, and setting penalties. It is unrealistic to expect various licensing and certification bodies not to vary on details given that the professions they regulate vary. Yet, because all licensing bodies share a common mission to protect the public, we should be able to expect greater consistency from them than from ethics committees.

Finally, states vary in the degree to which they license practitioners of psychotherapy. Psychiatrists, doctoral-level psychologists, and nurses are licensed in all states and social workers in many, but there is considerable variability in the licensing of marriage and family counselors, chemical dependency counselors, and masters-level psychologists. This state of affairs not only confuses the public but, also, it deprives consumers of avenues of complaint against some types of practitioners. The controversies surrounding the licensing of these other practitioners would require a volume of its own. For our purposes, we recommend that states decide who is qualified to practice psychotherapy, and then license all qualified practitioners, while effectively restraining unqualified ones from doing so. Psychotherapy practitioners who operate in a grey area, where they are unlicensable but unrestrainable, are unaccountable, and hence a danger to the public, which has no clear recourse against such persons.

PREVENTION AND TRAINING

A number of studies on the amount of sexual exploitation and harassment endured by psychology graduate students clearly suggest a tradition of tolerance for exploitation within the mental health disciplines. This broad issue is inseparable from that of the sexual exploitation clients. We can surmise from the complex ramifications of sexual exploitation of clients that primary prevention is the better course.

The meager amount of time and effort expended in training future professionals on ethical issues is a disgrace. Many professionals go through entire training programs without any formal training in ethics. Courses that do mention ethical issues tend to do so in abstract fashion, and fail to recognize the practical issues. For example, it is not unusual for ethics courses to focus on professional codes but to ignore entirely state licensing board codes, mandated reporting requirements, and the like. The solution is for each profession to develop a vigorous curriculum for teaching professional ethics and to revise it as experience is accumulated and laws are changed.

Beyond training in ethics, there is a serious need for training and practice in the handling of such problem situations as confronting colleagues, dealing with complaints, providing supervision, and the like. Both research and experience demonstrate that a thorough knowledge of ethical principles does not in itself guarantee that a professional will act ethically: practical behavioral experience must supplement the knowledge base.

Similarly, it is the responsibility of professional associations to organize and conduct regular seminars on ethics and professional boundaries for professionals already in the field. Few programs of this nature exist; when they are presented they tend to be relatively unsophisticated and to focus heavily on legal liability and the avoidance of malpractice suits, and less on the core issues of proper and ethical treatment of clients and the maintenance of proper professional boundaries.

Professional associations and interdisciplinary groups also should develop task forces and impaired-practitioner programs. Such programs that exist tend to focus very heavily on alcoholism and drug problems but to ignore other problems. None deal with sexual activity with clients. Although this situation is somewhat understandable historically, at present, this narrow focus is no longer justifiable.

Another aspect of prevention relates to the broader issue of consumer complaints. Some states have established clients' bills of rights but these usually include only vague standards for the handling of complaints. The psychotherapy professions, the regulatory bodies for the professions, and treatment facilities must begin adopting and publishing standards for the handling of consumer complaints.

Finally, consumer education has an important role in preventing sexual exploitation of psychotherapy clients. The better informed clients are on professional ethics and appropriate professional conduct the more likely they are to properly identify and respond to a therapist's inappropriate conduct. The news media can be very helpful in educating consumers as can handouts to clients, such as "Making Therapy Work for You," the pamphlet in Appendix Z. Unfortunately, many professionals oppose requirements to hand out such pamphlets because they consider it more important to retain the mystique of psychotherapy.

BASIC DEFINITIONAL PROBLEMS WITHIN THE PSYCHOTHERAPY FIELD

Probably no other area in health care offers such diverse treatments and theoretical perspectives under the aegis of what is believed to be a discipline as does mental health. Part of the problem with the exploitation of clients stems from some very basic questions in understanding the nature of psychotherapy. In recent years we have seen a greater acceptance of standard diagnostic practice (at least as compared to the distinctly antidiagnostic and iconoclastic views of the 1960s and early 1970s) but we cannot say the same for treatment. So-called schools of therapy continue to diverge in a chaotic and unpredictable fashion. Outcome research, when available at all, is found for only the most "traditional" therapies. Most newly developed therapies are essentially untested. Despite decades of empirical evidence to the contrary, most clinicians act as if their clinical judgment alone is sufficient to determine the efficacy of treatment.

More germane to our discussion, therapy styles vary enormously in regard to the nature of the boundary between therapist and client—from reserved detached distances to intrusive violations. Each stance has its own theoretical explication and most are seemingly reasonable within their own terms. The sum total, however, is that the field as a whole does not seem to know what constitutes psychotherapy or proper professional boundaries. It is not surprising, then, that some critics maintain that all therapy is harmful (Masson, 1988).

Not surprisingly, given this confusion, there is little unanimity in appreciating the issues of control and power between client and therapist. Mental health practitioners tend to avoid addressing the cultural and political context in which they operate and play a powerful role. Remedies to the problem of sexual exploitation or any exploitation of clients by psychotherapists are based on an implicit and explicit philosophical and political viewpoint that clients have rights and that therapists are accountable. Basic as this notion may sound, most theories of mental health practice seem neither receptive to nor clear on even these basic concepts in a meaningful and substantive manner.

PROBLEMS AND PITFALLS FOR THE FUTURE

1. Ignoring contextual factors. Until very recently, sexual exploitation of clients by therapists existed in a context in which therapists had greater rights, therapists rather than clients were believed, and effective remedies did not exist for clients. Our operational experience in this context supports the truth of most allegations of sexual exploitation by

psychotherapists. However, it is difficult to know whether our initial observations of the truth of most reports are intrinsic, related to contextual factors, or both.

Another way to state this observation is that in an inequitable system, character-disordered therapists have no reason to put checks on their behavior and character-disordered clients are unlikely to obtain any benefit from filing false complaints. In a system that is more equitable, neither proposition would necessarily hold. Please note that we do not state that greater equity in legal and ethical codes will necessarily produce greater false complaints; rather, we hold that the relatively simple predictability that we have observed in the one thousand or more cases processed by the Walk-In Counseling Center may be, to an unknown degree, influenced by contextual variables. We suggest, essentially, that an open mind be kept and careful observations continue to be made. This is akin to stating that observing or remedying a phenomenon changes it. It is a truism in many branches of science. It will be relevant here.

2. Premature certainty. Virtually all aspects of sexual exploitation of clients by psychotherapists are in a very early stage of understanding. Thus, sweeping and final theoretical conclusions as a rule, are inappropriate, grandiose, and detrimental to more explorations. Ironically, the mind set that embraces such premature decisiveness is the same omniscient, arrogant position that leads to disregarding client rights in the first place.

A comparison can be helpful here. Recent decades have seen an explosion of theory and practice styles about victims and perpetrators of sexual abuse of minors by adults. It can be safely stated that this is an area in which the data base is smaller than in other forms of psychotherapeutic endeavor, yet the fervor of belief by practitioners and theoreticians is considerably higher than in the more traditional and well-established kinds of psychotherapy practice. We have a situation, consequently, in which everyone who is involved begins to lack credibility.

In a similar manner, we have seen a small but alarming number of individuals working in the area of sexual exploitation of clients move prematurely to rigid dogmatic assertions about the nature of perpetrators, what is best for victims, and so on. In general, these viewpoints tend to assume a monolithic consistency in regard to victims or perpetrators and then to prescribe rigid, unvarying treatment standards or theoretical interpretations to all. The behavior of some prematurely decisive individuals appears to be economically driven. Labeling an entire diverse class of individuals as "co-dependents," "sex addicts," "chronic victims," or "sex offenders" primarily makes sense when one is trying to fill slots in "programs" for such conditions. The issue of sexual exploitation of clients by psychotherapists cannot be effectively handled with a mind set that is arrogant or closed. Otherwise, new kinds of insensitive exploitative treatments will be developed and perpetrated upon both client-victim and therapist-perpetrator.

The current state of affairs is one in which a variety of educated guesses is available. Individuals working in the area are encouraged to pursue their opinions but to show primary concern with the welfare of the client (whether a client-victim or a therapist-perpetrator) and to carefully report and describe what has worked and what has not worked. Many areas of sexual abuse treatment already have attracted some "media hounds" whose main interest appears to be self-aggrandizement with minimal attention to slowly accumulating observational evidence and empirical data. Such behavior is unethical every bit as much as the sexual exploitation of clients. If individuals who work in the area cannot behave in an ethical fashion, they have nothing to offer and hence become part of the problem.

We conclude with the admonition to view our observations as a set of working hypotheses that require further observation, description, refinement, and eventually (and perhaps most important) empirical testing. Other workers in this area of study who have observed far fewer than our one thousand and more cases seem overly quick to draw conclusions with an air of certainty and finality. We are like the geographers of old, far from a geodesic survey map of this territory and, thus, given the current state of knowledge must draw our map by hand. We urge the readers of this book to share our sense of caution.

REFERENCES/BIBLIOGRAPHY

Abramowitz, S.I., and Abramowitz, C.V. (1976). Sex role psychodynamics in psychotherapy supervision. *American Journal of Psychotherapy, 30*, pp. 583-592.

Abramowitz, S.I., Abramowitz, C.V., Roback, H.B., Corney, R.T., and McKee, W. (1976). Sex-role related countertransference in psychotherapy. *Archives of General Psychiatry, 33*, pp. 71-73.

Abroms, G.M. (1977). Supervision as metatherapy. In F. Kaslow (Ed.), *Supervision, Consultation, and Staff Training in the Helping Professions* (pp. 81-99). San Francisco: Jossey-Bass.

Adams, C.A. (1987, June). Sex with patients. *Trial,* pp. 58-61.

Adams, S., and Orgel, M. (1975). *Through the Mental Health Maze*. Washington, D.C.: Health Research Group.

Aftel, M., and Lakoff, R. (1985). *When Talk Is Not Cheap*. New York: Warner Books.

Akamatsu, T.J. (1988). Intimate relationships with former clients: National survey of attitudes and behavior among practitioners. *Professional Psychology: Research and Practice, 19,* pp. 454-458.

Allegretti, D. (1985, Feb. 20). "Doctor, you raped me!" A patient's horror story. *Capital Times,* pp. 1, 7. (a)

Allegretti, D. (1985, Feb. 21). Sexual exploitation by therapists. *Capital Times,* p. 39. (b)

Allen, G. J., Szollos, S.J., and Williams, B.E. (1986). Doctoral students' comparative evaluations of best and worst psychotherapy supervision. *Professional Psychology: Research and Practice, 17*, pp. 91-99.

Allen, W. (1965). *What's New Pussycat?* Film.

Allen, W. (1977). *Annie Hall*. Film. The screenplay can be found in W. Allen (1982) *Four Films of Woody Allen*, pp. 3-109. New York: Random House.

ALMACA. (1988). The ALMACA code of ethics. Arlington, VA: Author. (a)

ALMACA. (1988). Professional conduct. *The ALMACAN, 18 (12),* pp. 19-26. (b)

Allport, G.W. (1954). *The Nature of Prejudice*. Cambridge, MA: Addison-Wesley.

American Assn. for Marriage & Family Therapy. (1985). AAMFT code of ethical principles for marriage and family therapists. Washington, D.C.: Author.

American Assn. for Marriage & Family Therapy. (1988). AAMFT code of ethical principles for marriage and family therapists. Washington, D.C.: Author.

American Assn. of Pastoral Counselors. (1981). Code of ethics. Washington, D.C.: Author.

American Assn. of Sex Educators, Counselors, & Therapists. (1980). Code of ethics. Washington, D.C.: Author.

American Medical Assn. (1989). *Current Opinions — The Council on Ethical and Judicial Affairs of the American Medical Association*. Chicago, IL: Author.

American Psychiatric Assn. (1979). Opinions of the ethics committee on the principles of medical ethics with annotations especially applicable to psychiatry. Washington, D.C.: Author.

American Psychiatric Assn. (1981). Principles of medical ethics with annotations especially applicable to psychiatry. Washington D.C.: Author.

American Psychiatric Assn. (1985). Principles of medical ethics with annotations especially applicable to psychiatry. Washington, D.C.: Author.

American Psychiatric Assn. (1986). Ethical concerns about sexual involvement between psychiatrists and patients. (Videotape and discussion guide.) Washington, D.C.: Author.

American Psychiatric Assn. (in press). Principles of medical ethics with annotations especially applicable to psychiatry. Washington, D.C.: Author.

American Psychiatric Assn. (in press). Reporting ethical concerns. (Videotape and discussion guide.) Washington, D.C.: Author.

American Psychoanalytic Assn. (1983). Principles of ethics for psychoanalysis and provisions for implementation of the principles of ethics for psychoanalysis. New York: Author.

American Psychological Assn. (1975). *Report of the Task Force on Sex Bias and Sex Role Stereotyping in Psychotherapeutic Practice.* Washington, D.C.: Author.

American Psychological Assn. (1977). *Ethical Principles of Psychologists* (revised edition). Washington, D.C.: Author.

American Psychological Assn. (1981). *Ethical Principles of Psychologists* (revised edition). Washington, D.C.: Author.

American Psychological Assn. (1987). *Casebook on Ethical Principles of Psychologists.* Washington, D.C.

Anderson, W. (1986). Stages of therapist comfort with sexual concerns of clients. *Professional Psychology: Research and Practice, 17,* pp. 352-56.

Anthony, B. (1982). Lesbian client—lesbian therapist: Opportunities and challenges in working together. In J. Gonsiorek (Ed.), *Homosexuality and Psychotherapy: A Practitioner's Handbook of Affirmative Models.* New York: Haworth Press.

Apfel, R., and Simon, B. (1986). Sexualized therapy: Causes and consequences. In A.W. Burgess and C.R. Hartman, *Sexual Exploitation of Patients by Health Professionals* (pp. 143-51). New York: Praeger.

Asher, J. (1976). Confusion reigns in APA malpractice plan. *American Psychological Association Monitor, 7,* pp. 1, 11.

Associated Press. (1983, March 8). Ex-counselor sentenced in sexual conduct case. *Minneapolis Star & Tribune,* p. 3B.

Associated Press. (1987, Dec. 19). Priest convicted in sex case involving children in Brainerd. *Minneapolis Star & Tribune,* p. 18A.

Associated Press. (1989, July 19). Appeals court upholds jail term for ex-minister. (Minneapolis) *Star Tribune,* p. 8D.

Association for Clinical Pastoral Education. (1980). Standards, procedures and guidelines. Washington, D.C.: Author, pp. 41-42.

Auden, W.H., and Kronenberger, L. (1981). *The Viking Book of Aphorisms*. New York: Viking Press.

Bach, G. (1966). The marathon group: Intensive practice of intimate interaction. *Psychological Reports, 18*, pp. 995-1002.

Bailey, B. (1989). Personal communication, August 18, 1989. (Chair elect, Texas board of licensure of psychologists.)

Bajt, T.R., and Pope, K.S. (1989). Therapist-patient sexual intimacy involving children and adolescents. *American Psychologist, 44*, p. 455.

Baker, A. (1985, Jan. 6). Behind closed doors—therapist affair can betray trust, traumatize client. *St. Paul Pioneer Press & Dispatch*, pp. G-1, G-14. (a)

Baker, A. (1985, Jan. 6). Therapist can be as troubled as patient. *St. Paul Pioneer Press & Dispatch*, p. G-1. (b)

Baker, D. (1984). *Beyond Forgiveness: The Healing Touch of Church Discipline*. Portland, OR: Multnomah Press.

Baldick, T.L. (1980). Ethical discrimination ability of intern psychologists: A function of training in ethics. *Professional Psychology, 11*, pp. 115-121.

Barnhouse, R.T. (1978). Sex between patient and therapist. *Journal of the American Academy of Psychoanalysis, 6*, pp. 533-546.

Bass, A. (1988, Sept. 22). Therapist survey: Sex with ex-clients OK. *The Boston Globe*, p. 6.

Bates, C., and Brodsky, A. (1988). *Sex in the Therapy Hour*. New York: Guilford Press.

Baum, O.E. (1969-70). Countertransference. *Psychoanalytic Review, 56*, pp. 621-637.

Beck, A.T. (1970). Role of fantasies in psychotherapy and psychopathology. *Journal of Nervous and Mental Disease, 150*, pp. 3-17.

Belote, B. (1974). *Sexual Intimacy Between Female Clients and Male Therapists: Masochistic Sabotage*. Unpublished doctoral dissertation, California School of Professional Psychology, Berkeley.

Benedek, E.P. (1977). Training the female resident to be a psychiatrist. *American Journal of Psychiatry, 134*, pp. 1244-1248.

Berman, A., and Cohen-Sandler, R. (1983). Suicide and malpractice: Expert testimony and the standard of care. *Professional Psychology: Research and Practice, 14*, pp. 6-19.

Bernard, J. (1987). Ethical and legal considerations for supervisors. In L.D. Borders and G. Leddick (Eds.) *Handbook of Counseling Supervision*. Alexandria, Virginia: Assn. for Counselor Education and Supervision.

Bernard, J.L., and Jara, C.S. (1986). The failure of clinical psychology graduate students to apply understood ethical principles. *Professional Psychology: Research and Practice, 17*, pp. 313-315.

Bernard, J.L., Murphy, M., and Little, M. (1987). The failure of clinical psychologists to apply understood ethical principles. *Professional Psychology: Research and Practice, 18*, pp. 489-491.

Berne, E. (1964). *Games People Play.* New York: Grove Press.

Berquist, L. (1987, May 25). "Patient A" says two therapists sexually abused her. *The Milwaukee Sentinel,* p. 5.

Berstein, A. (1974). The genital psychoanalyst. *Psychoanalytic Review, 61,* pp. 257-67.

Besharov, D.J. (1985). *The Vulnerable Social Worker: Liability for Serving Children and Families.* Silver Spring, MD: National Assn. of Social Workers.

Betcher, R.W., and Zinberg, N.E. (1988). Supervision and privacy in psychotherapy training. *American Journal of Psychiatry, 145,* pp. 796-803.

Bettelheim, B. (1983). Scandal in the family. *New York Review of Books, 30 (11),* pp. 39-44.

Beutler, L.E., Crago, M., and Arizmendi, T.G. (1986). Therapist variables in psychotherapy process and outcome. In S.L. Garfield and A.G. Bergin (Eds.), *Handbook of Psychotherapy and Behavior Change,* pp. 257-381. New York: Wiley.

Bindrim, P. (1972). A report on a nude marathon: The effect of physical nudity upon the pattern of interaction in the marathon group. In H. Gochras and L. Schultz (Eds.), *Human Sexuality and Social Work,* pp. 205-220. New York: Association Press. (Previously published in 1968 in *Psychotherapy: Theory, Research and Practice, 5 (3),* pp. 180-87.)

Bissell, L., and Royce, J. (1987). *Ethics for Addiction Professionals.* Center City, MN: Hazelden Foundation.

Black, J. (1978, Dec. 11). Pelvic therapy. *New Times,* pp. 52-58.

Blackmon, R.A. (1984) *The Hazards of Ministry.* Unpublished doctoral dissertation. Fuller Theological Seminary, Fullerton, California.

Blinkhorn, L. (1984, April 29). The psychiatrist and the patient—sometimes a professional relationship gets personal. *Milwaukee Journal,* p. G-1. (a)

Blinkhorn, L. (1984, April 29). In Wisconsin, help is available for patient. *Milwaukee Journal,* p. G-2. (b)

Bliss, J. (1986). *Sexual Exploitation by Therapists: Criminal, Civil and Administrative Remedies.* Unpublished paper, Michigan Dept. of Licensing and Regulation.

Blum, H.P. (1973). The concept of eroticized transference. *Journal of the American Psychoanalytic Association, 21,* pp. 61-76.

Boas, C.V.E. (1966). Some reflections on sexual relations between physicians and patients. *Journal of Sex Research, 2,* pp. 215-18.

Bobbitt, B.L., Conroe, R., and Loeffler, D. (1985, Fall). Thoughts on guidelines for graduate-level training sites in professional psychology. *Minnesota Psychologist,* pp. 9-10.

Boice, Robert, and Myers, Patricia E. (1987). Which setting is healthier and happier, academe or private practice? *Professional Psychology: Research and Practice, 18,* pp. 526-529.

Borders, L.D., and Leddick, G. (1987). *Handbook of Counseling Supervision.* Alexandria, Virginia: Assn. for Counselor Education and Supervision.

Borys, D.S. (1988). *Dual Relationships Between Therapists and Client: A National Survey of Clinicians Attitudes and Practices.* Unpublished doctoral dissertation, University of California at Los Angeles.

Borys, D.S., Meyer, C.B., Falke, R.L., and Sonne, J.L. (1986). Dynamics of treatment groups for victims of sexual misconduct. In A.W. Burgess and C.R. Hartman (Eds.), *Sexual Exploitation of Patients by Health Professionals,* (pp. 178-184). Boston: Praeger.

Boswell, Philip. (1987). Why all this fuss about sexual misconduct? *Florida Psychologist, 38 (3),* pp. 21-24.

Bouhoutsos, J.C. (1984). Sexual intimacy between psychotherapists and clients: Policy implications for the future. In L. Walker (Ed.), *Women and Mental Health Policy,* (pp. 207-227). Beverly Hills, CA: Sage.

Bouhoutsos, J.C. (1985). Therapist-client sexual involvement: A challenge for mental health professionals and educators. *American Journal of Orthopsychiatry, 55,* pp. 177-182.

Bouhoutsos, J., and Brodsky, A. (1985). Mediation in therapist-client sex: A model. *Psychotherapy, 22,* pp. 189-193.

Bouhoutsos, J., Brodsky, A., and Schoener, G.R. (1988). Processing and mediation: New tools for therapist-client boundary problems. Workshop presented at the convention of the American Psychological Assn., Atlanta, GA.

Bouhoutsos, J., Holroyd, J., Lerman, H., Forer, B., and Greenberg, M. (1983). Sexual intimacy between psychotherapists and patients. *Professional Psychology: Research and Practice, 14,* pp. 185-196.

Braceland, F. (1969). Historical perspectives of the ethical practice of psychiatry. *American Journal of Psychiatry, 126,* pp. 230-237.

Bradshaw, S.L. (1977). Ministers in trouble: A study of 140 cases evaluated at the Menninger Foundation. *Journal of Pastoral Care, 31 (4),* pp. 230-41.

Branch, (1969, April). Men of good conscience. *Psychiatric News,* p. 2

Braude, M. (1986). Workshops in patient-therapist sexual relationships. In A. Burgess and C. Hartman (Eds.), *Sexual Exploitation of Patients by Health Professionals,* (pp. 93-96). New York: Praeger.

Breitling, M. (1984). Correspondence with Rev. Marie Fortune, Feb. 27, 1984.

Brevieu, J., and Meyerle, K. (1985). Summary of changes to the Minnesota Medical Practice Act. *Minnesota Medicine, 68,* pp. 785-92.

Bridge, P. (1988). A model for documentation of psychotherapy supervision. Paper presented at the convention of the American Psychological Assn., Atlanta, GA.

Bridge, P., and Bascue, L. (1988). A record form for psychotherapy supervision. In P. Keller and S. Heyman (Eds.), *Innovations in Clinical Practice, 7.* Sarasota, FL: Professional Resource Exchange.

Brigham, R.E. (1989). Psychotherapy stressors and sexual misconduct: A factor analytic study of the experience of non-offending and offending psychologists in Wisconsin. Unpublished doctoral dissertation, Wisconsin School of Professional Psychology, Milwaukee, WI.

Brodsky, A.M. (1977). Countertransference issues and the female therapist: Sex and the student therapist. *Clinical Psychologist, 30,* pp. 12-14.

Brodsky, A.M. (1980). Sex role issues in the supervision of psychotherapy. In A.K. Hess (Ed.), *Psychotherapy Supervision: Theory, Research, and Practice*, (pp. 509-522). New York: John Wiley.

Brodsky, A.M. (1985). Sex between therapists and patients: Ethical gray areas. *Psychotherapy in Private Practice, 3*, pp. 57-62.

Brodsky, A.M. (1986). The distressed psychologist: Sexual intimacies and exploitation. In R.R. Kilburg, P.E. Nathan, and R.W. Thoreson (Eds.), *Professionals in Distress: Issues, Syndromes and Solutions in Psychology*, (pp. 153-171). Washington, D.C.: American Psychological Assn.

Brown, L. (1984). The lesbian feminist therapist in private practice in her community. *Psychotherapy in Private Practice, 2*, pp. 9-16.

Brown, L. (1986). Harmful effects of post-termination sexual and romantic relationships between therapists and their former clients. Paper presented at the annual convention of the American Psychological Assn., Washington, D.C.

Brown, L. (1988). Harmful effects of post-termination sexual and romantic relationships between therapists and their former clients. *Psychotherapy, 25*, pp. 249-55.

Bruckner-Gordon, F., Gangi, B., and Wallman, G. (1988). *Making Therapy Work.* New York: Harper & Row.

Brunswick, M. (1987, May 6). Charges filed against psychic lecturer. (Minneapolis) *Star Tribune*, p. 4B. (a)

Brunswick, M. (1987, Aug. 20). Psychic lecturer pleads guilty to criminal sexual conduct. (Minneapolis) *Star Tribune*, p. 12M. (b)

Brunswick, M. (1987, Oct. 19). Guru focuses on pyramids, dismisses his jail sentence. (Minneapolis) *Star Tribune*, p. 4A. (c)

Buckley, P., Karasu, T.B., and Charles, E. (1981). Psychotherapists view their personal therapy. *Psychotherapy: Theory, Research and Practice, 18*, pp. 299-305.

Buell, A. (1988, Oct. 5). Mein arzt wollte mich mit sex heilen. *Quick, 41*, pp. 84-86.

Burgess, A.W. (1981). Physician sexual misconduct and patients' responses. *American Journal of Psychiatry, 138*, pp. 1335-1342.

Burgess, A., and Hartman, C. (Eds.). (1986). *Sexual Exploitation of Patients by Health Professionals.* New York: Praeger.

Burgess, A., Hartman, M.P., McCausland, M., and Powers, P. (1984). Response patterns in children and adolescents exploited through sex rings and pornography. *American Journal of Psychiatry, 141*, pp. 656-62.

Burnstein, D. (1986). Sexual malpractice litigation. In A. Burgess and C. Hartman (Eds.), *Sexual Exploitation of Patients by Health Professionals*, (pp. 49-60). New York: Praeger.

Butler, S. (1975). Sexual contact between therapists and patients. Unpublished doctoral dissertation, California School of Professional Psychology, Los Angeles.

Butler, S., and Zelen, S. (1977). Sexual intimacies between psychotherapists and their patients. *Psychotherapy: Theory, Research, and Practice, 139*, pp. 143-144.

Cade, B., Speed, B., and Seligman, P. (1986). Working in teams: The pros and cons. In F. Kaslow (Ed.), *Supervision and Training—Models, Dilemmas and Challenges* (pp. 105-118). New York: Haworth Press.

Calef, V., and Weinshel, E.M. (1983). A note on consummation and termination. *Journal of the American Academy of Psychoanalysis, 31,* pp. 643-650.

California Legislature. (1987). *Report of the Senate Task Force on Psychotherapist and Patients Sexual Relations*, prepared for the Senate Rules Committee ($4.50/copy from Joint Publications, State Capitol, Box 90, Sacramento, CA 95814).

California State Psychological Assn. (1981). Task force report. Los Angeles: Author.

Callahan, M., and Vocke, D. (1989). Current legal developments in medical staff credentialing disputes. In R.D. Miller (Ed.), *Legal Implications of Hospital Policies and Practices* (pp. 81-96). San Francisco: Jossey-Bass.

Carifio, M.S., and Hess, A.K. (1987). Who is the ideal supervisor? *Professional Psychology: Research and Practice, 18,* pp. 244-250.

Carlson, R. (1986). After analysis: A study of transference dreams following treatment. *Journal of Consulting and Clinical Psychology, 54,* pp. 246-252.

Carotenuto, Aldo (1982). *A Secret Symetry: Sebina Spielrein Between Jung and Freud.* New York: Pantheon Books.

Carotenuto, Aldo (1984). *A Secret Symetry: Sebina Spielrein Between Jung and Freud* (with commentary by Bruno Bettelheim). New York: Pantheon Books.

Casement, P. (1982). Some pressures on the analyst for physical contact during the reliving of an early trauma. *International Review of Psychoanalysis, 9,* pp. 279-86.

Caughran, N. (1973). Psychiatry as rip-off. In P.M. Brown (Ed.), *Radical Psychology* (pp. 490-92). New York: Harper & Row.

CBS News. (1978, Feb. 19). Fifty minutes. Segment of TV news show, *Sixty Minutes.* New York: CBS.

Chamberlin, J. (1979). *On Our Own—Patient Controlled Alternatives to the Mental Health System.* New York: McGraw-Hill.

Chance, P. (1987, September). When therapists need help. *Psychology Today,* p. 17.

Chandler, Kurt. (1989, Feb. 18). Judge faces complaint for scolding victim. *Minneapolis Star Tribune.*

Charles, S., and Kennedy, E. (1985). *Defendant.* New York: Free Press.

Charney, I. (1986). What do therapists worry about: A tool for experiential supervision. In F. Kaslow (Ed.), *Supervision and Training—Models, Dilemmas and Challenges,* (pp. 17-28). New York: Haworth Press.

Chesler, P. (1972, June 19). The sensuous psychiatrist. *New York,* pp. 52, 54, 56, 59-61. (a)

Chesler, P. (1972). *Women and Madness.* New York: Avon Books. (b)

Christ, A.E. (1964). Sexual countertransference problems with a psychotic child. *Journal of Child Psychiatry, 3,* pp. 298-316.

Christensen, C.W. (1961). The occurrence of mental illness in the ministry: Psychotic disorders. *Journal of Pastoral Care, 15*, pp. 153-59.

Christensen, C.W. (1963). The occurrence of mental illness in the ministry: Psychoneurotic disorders. *Journal of Pastoral Care, 17*, pp. 1-10.

Clements, C.D. (1987). The transference: What's love got to do with it? *Psychiatric Annals, 17 (8)*, pp. 556-563.

Cnudde, C.F., and Nesvold, B.A. (1985). Administrative risk and sexual harassment: Legal and ethical responsibilities on campus. *Political Studies, 33*, pp. 780-789.

Cohen, R.J. (1979). *Malpractice: A Guide for Mental Health Professionals*. New York: Free Press.

Coleman, P. (1988). Sex between psychiatrist and former patient: A proposal for a "no harm, no foul" rule. *Oklahoma Law Review, 41 (1)*, pp. 1-52.

Collins, D.T., Mebel, A.K., and Mortimer, R.L. (1978). Patient-therapist sex: Consequences for subsequent treatment. *McLean Hospital Journal, 3*, pp. 24-36.

Conn, J. (1982). Is hypnosis really dangerous? *International Journal of Clinical and Experimental Hypnosis, 20 (2)*, pp. 61-79.

Conroe, R., Schank, J., Brown, M., DeMarinis, V., Loeffler, D., and Sanderson, B. (1989). Prohibition of sexual contact between clinical supervisors and psychotherapy students: An overview and suggested guidelines. In B. Sanderson (Ed.), *It's Never O.K.: A Handbook for Professionals on Sexual Exploitation by Counselors and Therapists*, pp. 125-131. St. Paul, MN: Minnesota Dept. of Corrections.

Conte, H., Plutchik, R., Picard, S., and Karasu, T. (1989). Ethics in the practice of psychotherapy: A survey. *American Journal of Psychotherapy, 43*, pp. 32-42.

Conway, F., and Siegelman, J. (1978). *Snapping*. Philadelphia: Lippincott.

Corday, R.J. (1967). Limitations of therapy in adolescence. *Journal of Child Psychiatry, 6*, pp. 526-38.

Cormier, S., and Bernard, J.M. (1982). Ethical and legal responsibilities of clinical supervisors. *Personnel and Guidance Journal, 60*, pp. 486-91.

Cottingham, F.H. (1966). The challenge of authentic behavior. *Personnel and Guidance Journal, 45*, pp. 328-36.

Cox, C. (1987). Descent into hell. *City Pages, 8 (338)*, pp. 6-10. (a)

Cox, C. (1987). Taking care of the doctor. *City Pages, 8 (339)*, pp. 6-9. (b)

Crawford, S. (1988, Jan. 27). Woman brings sex charge against ex-minister. *Mankato Free Press*, p. 11. (a)

Crawford, S. (1988, Nov. 29). Jury being picked for Dutton trial. *Mankato Free Press*, p. 15. (b)

Crawford, S. (1988, Nov. 30). Dutton trial begins today. *Mankato Free Press*, p. 13. (c)

Crawford, S. (1988, Dec. 1). Woman's dependency on Dutton described *Mankato Free Press*, p. 9. (d)

Crawford, S. (1988, Dec. 2). Woman tells of her relationship with ex-minister. *Mankato Free Press*, p. 13. (e)

Crawford, S. (1988, Dec. 3). Woman finishes testimony in trial of minister-therapist. *Mankato Free Press*, p. 3. (f)

Crawford, S. (1988, Dec. 7). Expert: Dutton's counseling was "inappropriate." *Mankato Free Press*, p. 13. (g)

Crawford, S. (1988, Dec. 8). Dutton contradicts woman's testimony. *Mankato Free Press*, p. 9. (h)

Crawford, S. (1988, Dec. 9). Ex-minister convicted of exploitation. *Mankato Free Press*, p. 1. (i)

Crawford, S. (1988, Dec. 19). Dutton trial breaks new legal ground. *Mankato Free Press*, p. 1. (j)

Crawford, S. (1989, Jan. 6). Dutton exploitation trial broke new legal ground. *Mankato Free Press*, p. 1. (a)

Crawford, S. (1989, Jan. 10). Dutton's attorneys ask for acquittal or new trial. *Mankato Free Press*, p. 1. (b)

Crawford, S. (1989, Feb. 7). Dutton gets 90 days; Judge also blames victim. *Mankato Free Press*, p. 1. (c)

Crawford, S. (1989, Feb. 18). Second complaint to be filed against New Ulm judge. *Mankato Free Press*, p. 1. (d)

Crawford, S. (1989, Feb. 21). State to appeal Dutton sentence. *Mankato Free Press*, p. 11. (e)

Crowley, D. (1987, Oct. 19). When "friend" is priest, problems of love don't allow for having it all. (Minneapolis) *Star Tribune*, p. 8C.

Cummings, N.A., and Sobel, S.B. (1985). Malpractice insurance: Update on sex claims. *Psychotherapy*, *22*, pp. 186-88.

D'Addario, L. (1977). *Sexual relationship between female clients and male therapists.* Unpublished doctoral dissertation, California School of Professional Psychology, San Diego.

Dahlberg, C.C. (1970, Spring). Sexual contact between client and therapist. *Contemporary Psychoanalysis*, pp. 107-124.

Dahlberg, C.C. (1971). Sexual contact between patient and therapist. *Medical Aspects of Human Sexuality*, *5*, pp. 34-56.

Daniels, A.K. (1971). Descriptions of ethical problems presented by psychiatrists. Unpublished paper. San Francisco, CA: Scientific Analysis Corporation. Cited in B. Belote (Ed., 1974), *Sexual Intimacy Between Female Clients and Male Therapists: Masochistic Sabotage*, pp. 4-5. Unpublished doctoral dissertation, California School of Professional Psychology, Berkeley.

Davidson, V. (1977). Psychiatry's problem with no name: Therapist-patient sex. *American Journal of Psychoanalysis*, *37*, pp. 43-50.

Dawes, R.M. (1986). The philosophy of responsibility and autonomy versus that of being one-up. Unpublished paper presented at the convention of the American Psychological Assn., Washington, D.C.

Dawidoff, D. (1973). *The Malpractice of Psychiatrists.* Springfield, IL: C.C. Thomas.

DeBerry, S., and Baskin, D. (1989). Termination criteria in psychotherapy: A comparison of private and public practice. *American Journal of Psychotherapy, 43,* pp. 43-53.

Denham, T.E., and Denham, M.L. (1986). Avoiding malpractice suits in pastoral counseling. *Pastoral Psychology, 35 (2),* pp. 83-93.

Dept. of Public Welfare. (1984). People who need people—What the Minnesota Vulnerable Adults Reporting Act means to you. Pamphlet. St. Paul, MN: Author.

Derosis, H., Hamilton, J., Morrison, E., and Strauss, M. (1987). More on psychiatrist-patient sexual contact. *American Journal of Psychiatry, 144,* pp. 688-89.

Deutsch, A. (1980). Tenacity of affiliation to a cult leader—a psychiatric perspective. *American Journal of Psychiatry, 137,* pp. 1569-73.

Deutsch, A. (1983). Psychiatric perspectives on an eastern-style cult. In D. Halperin (Ed.) *Religion, Sect, and Cult* (pp. 113-29). Littleton, MA: John Wright-PSG, Inc.

Deutsch, C.J. (1984). Self-reported sources of stress among psychotherapists. *Professional Psychology: Research and Practice, 15,* pp. 833-845.

Deutsch, C.J. (1985). A survey of therapists' personal problems and treatment. *Professional Psychology: Research and Practice, 16,* pp. 305-315.

De Wyze, J. (1983, Jan. 13). The final analysis. *The Reader,* (Minneapolis, MN), pp. 1-6.

Diaz, K. (1989, July 21). Doctor questions board's standards—challenges rules against doctors, patients having sex. *Minneapolis Star Tribune,* p. 3B.

Doehrman, J.J.G. (1976). Parallel processes in supervision and psychotherapy. *Bulletin of the Menninger Clinic, 40,* pp. 9-104.

Donahue TV Show Transcript. (1980). Sex and the psychiatrist, #12160. Cincinnati, OH: Multimedia Program Productions, pp. 1-29.

Dreifus, C. (1988, Sept.). Patient-therapist sex. *Glamour*, pp. 286-90.

Dreyfus, A.E. (1967). Humans: A therapeutic variable. *Personnel and Guidance Journal, 45,* pp. 573-78.

Dunbar, B. (1988, April 30). Priest fired due to charge of sex assault. *The Burlington Free Press* (Vermont), pp. B-1.

Dunn, M.E., and Dickes, R. (1977). Erotic issues in co-therapy. *Journal of Sex and Marital Therapy, 3,* pp. 205-211.

Durre, L. (1980). Comparing romantic and therapeutic relationships. In K.S. Pope (Ed.) *On Love and Loving: Psychological Perspectives on the Nature and Experience of Romantic Love* (pp. 228-43). San Francisco: Jossey-Bass.

Dziech, B.W., and Weiner, L. (1984). *The Lecherous Professor: Sexual Harassment on Campus.* Boston: Bean Press.

EACC (1988). Code of professional conduct for certified employee assistance professionals (CEAP). Arlington, VA: ALMACA.

Edberlein, L. (1987). Introducing ethics to beginning psychologists: A problem-solving approach. *Professional Psychology: Research and Practice, 18*, pp. 353-59.

Edelwich, J., and Brodsky, A. (1982). *Sexual Dilemmas for the Helping Professional*. New York: Brunner/Mazel.

Ehlert, B. (1988). Don't tell anybody...you'll get in trouble and so will I. *Minneapolis Star Tribune*. Series: Dec. 11, pp. 1E, 4E-5E; Dec. 12, pp. 1E, 4E-5E; Dec. 13, pp. 1E, 4E-5E.

Ehrenberg, O., and Ehrenberg, M. (1986). *The Psychotherapy Maze*. Northvale, N.J.: Jason Aronson.

Eigen, M. (1973). The call and the lure. *Psychotherapy: Theory, Research and Practice, 10*, pp. 194-97.

Ekstein, R., and Wallerstein, R.S. (1972). *The Teaching and Learning of Psychotherapy* (Second Edition). New York: International Universities Press.

Eldridge, N.S. (1987). Gender issues in counseling same-sex couples. *Professional Psychology: Research and Practice, 18 (6)*, pp. 567-72.

Ellis, A. (1975, Oct. 21). Personal communication to Gary Schoener.

Emmerman, L., and Gaines, W. (1983, May 1). Therapy patients victims of sexual abuse. *Chicago Tribune*, p. 1.

Erwin, J., and Erwin, J. (1978). *How to Choose and Use the Right Therapist for You*. Kansas City: Sheed, Andrews, and McMeal.

Farber, B.A. (1983). Psychotherapists' perceptions of stressful patient behavior. *Professional Psychology: Research and Practice, 14*, pp. 697-705.

Farber, B.A., and Heifetz, L.J. (1981). The satisfactions and stresses of psychotherapeutic work: A factor analytic study. *Professional Psychology: Research and Practice, 12*, pp. 621-629.

Farber, B.A., and Heifetz, L.J. (1982). The process and dimensions of burnout in psychotherapists. *Professional Psychology: Research and Practice, 13*, pp. 293-301.

Federation of Organizations for Professional Women. (1981). *Women and Psychotherapy—A Consumer Handbook*. Washington, D.C.: Author.

Feist, J. (1968). Neurotic-symbiotic counseling relationships. *Personnel and Guidance Journal, 47 (1)*, pp. 63-67.

Feldman-Summers, S., and Jones, G. (1984, Sept.). Psychological impacts of sexual contact between therapists or other health care practitioners and their clients. *Journal of Consulting and Clinical Psychology, 52*, pp. 1054-61.

Ferenczi, S. (1955). *Final Contributions to the Problem and Methods of Psychoanalysis*. New York: Basic Books.

Fine, R. (1965). Erotic feelings in the psychotherapeutic relationship. *Psychoanalytic Review, 52*, pp. 30-37.

Finney, J.C. (1975). Therapist and patient after hours. *American Journal of Psychotherapy, 52*, pp. 30-37.

Finkelhor, D. (1985). *Sexually Victimized Children*. New York: Free Press.

Fischer, S.C. (1986). *Choosing a Psychotherapist*. (Revised, Third Edition). Waterford, Michigan: Minerva Press.

Fisher, K. (1983, May). Pro bono. *APA Monitor*, pp. 16-17.

Fisher, K. (1985). Charges catch clinicians in cycle of shame, slip-ups. *APA Monitor, 16*, pp. 6-7.

Fitzgerald, F.S. (1933). *Tender is the Night*. New York: Charles Scribner's.

Fitzgerald, L.F., Weitzman, L.M., Gold, Y., and Ormerod, M. (1988). Academic harassment: Sex and denial in scholarly garb. *Psychology of Women Quarterly, 12*, pp. 329-340.

Fitzgerald, L.F., Shullman, S.H., Bailey, N., Gold, Y., Omerod, M., Richards, M., Sweckler, J., and Weitzman, L. (1988). The incidence and dimensions of sexual harassment in academia and the workplace. *Journal of Vocational Behavior, 3*, pp. 152-175.

Flescher, J. (1953). On different types of countertransference. *International Journal of Group Psychotherapy, 3*, pp. 357-372.

Fleming, P. D., Luepker, E. T., Nye, S. G., and Schoener, G.R. (1982). Treatment services/legal issues for clients who have been sexually involved with psychotherapists. Presentation at the Annual Meeting of the American Orthopsychiatric Assn., San Francisco, California, April 2, 1982. Info Medix, Garden Grove, CA. (Audiotape)

Ford, C.; King, B., and Hollender, M. (1988). Lies and liars: Psychiatric aspects of prevarication. *American Journal of Psychiatry, 145*, pp. 554-62.

Forer, B.R. (1969). The taboo against touching in psychotherapy. *Psychotherapy: Theory, Research and Practice, 6*, pp. 229-231.

Forer, B.R. (1980, Feb.). The therapeutic relationship: 1968. Paper presented at the annual meeting of the California State Psychological Assn., Pasadena.

Fortune, M. (1987). *Keeping the Faith: Questions and Answers for the Abused Woman*. New York: Harper & Row.

Fortune, M. (1989). *Is Nothing Sacred? When Sex Invades the Pastoral Relationship*. San Francisco: Harper & Row.

Franklin, B., deBory, G., Lavoisier, A.L., Bailly, J.S., Majault, S., D'Arcet, J., Guillotin, J., and LeRoy, J.B. (1965). Secret report on mesmerism or animal magnetism. In R.E. Shor and M.T. Orne (Eds.), *The Nature of Hypnosis: Selected Basic Readings*. New York: Holt, Rinehart, & Winston. (Original work published 1784).

Franklin, N. (1987). The ex-psychiatric patients' liberation movement. *Utne Reader, 20*, pp. 44-45.

Franks, R.D. (1980). The seductive patient. *American Family Physician, 22*, pp. 111-114.

Franks, R.D. (1981, Jan. 30-Feb. 15). How to manage the seductive patient. *Modern Medicine*, pp. 79-83.

Frederick, C. (1986). Post-traumatic stress disorder and child molestation. In A. Burgess and C. Hartman (Eds.), *Sexual Exploitation of Patients by Health Professionals* (pp. 133-142). New York: Praeger.

Freeman, L., and Roy, J. (1976). *Betrayal*. New York: Stein and Day.

Freud, S. (1958). Observations on transference-love (Further recommendations on the technique of psychoanalysis). In J. Strachey (Ed. & Trans.), *The Standard Edition of the Complete Psychological Works of Sigmund Freud* (Vol. 12, pp. 158-71). London: Hogarth Press. (Original work published 1915).

Freud, S. (1958). Introductory lectures in psychoanalysis. In J. Strachey (Ed. & Trans.), *The Standard Edition of the Complete Psychological Works of Sigmund Freud*, (Vol. 16). London: Hogarth Press. (Original work published in 1917).

Freund, K., and Langevin, R. (1976). Bisexuality in homosexual pedophilia. *Archives of Sexual Behavior*, *5*, pp. 415-23.

Friedman, D., and Kaslow, N. (1986). The development of professional identity in psychotherapists: Six stages in the supervision process. In F. Kaslow (Ed.), *Supervision Training—Models, Dilemmas and Challenges* (pp. 29-50). New York: Haworth Press.

Friedman, S., Gams, L., Gottlieb, N., and Nesselson, C. (1979). *A Woman's Guide to Therapy.* Englewood Cliffs, N.J.: Prentice Hall.

Fuchs, L.L. (1975). Reflections on touching and transference in psychotherapy. *Clinical Social Work, 3 (3)*, pp. 167-176.

Fulero, S.M., and Wilbert, J.R. (1988). Record-keeping practices of clinical and counseling psychologists: A survey of practitioners. *Professional Psychology: Research and Practice, 19*, pp. 658-660.

Gabbard, G. (1989). *Sexual Exploitation in Professional Relationships.* Washington, D.C.: American Psychiatric Press.

Gabbard, G., Menninger, R., and Loyne, L. (1987). Sources of conflict in the medical marriage. *American Journal of Psychiatry, 144 (5)*, pp. 567-572.

Gabbard, G., and Pope, K. (1988, May). Sexual intimacies after termination: Clinical, ethical, and legal aspects. *The Independent Practitioner (Division 42 Newsletter)*, pp. 21-26.

Gaines, B. (1972, Sept.). Sex on the couch: Analysts and their patients. *Cosmopolitan*, pp. 152-55, 166.

Galper, M. (1983). The atypical dissociative disorder: Some etiological, diagnostic, and treatment issues. In D. Halperin (Ed.), *Religion, Sect and Cult* (pp. 353-68). Littleton, MA: John Wright-PSG.

Gareffa, D.N., and Neff, S.A. (1975). Management of clients' seductive behavior. *Smith College Studies of Social Work, 44*, pp. 110-24.

Garfield, S., and Bergin, A. (1986). *Handbook of Psychotherapy and Behavior Change.* New York: John Wiley.

Gartrell, N., Herman, J., Olarte, S., Feldstein, M., and Localio, R. (1986). Psychiatrist-patient sexual contact: Results of a national survey, I: prevalence. *American Journal of Psychiatry, 143*, pp. 1126-1131.

Gartrell, N., Herman, J., Olarte, S., Feldstein, M., and Localio, R. (1987). Reporting practices of psychiatrists who knew of sexual misconduct by colleagues. *American Journal of Orthopsychiatry, 57*, pp. 287-295.

Gartrell, N., Herman, J., Olarte, S., Feldstein, M., and Localio, R. (1988). Management and rehabilitation of sexually exploitive therapists. *Hospital and Community Psychiatry, 39*, pp. 1070-1074.

Gartrell, N., Herman, J., Olarte, S., Feldstein, M., Localio, R., and Schoener, G.R. (1989). Sexual abuse of patients by therapists: strategies for offender management and rehabilitation. In R.D. Miller (Ed.), *Legal Implications of Hospital Policies and Practices* (pp. 55-66). San Francisco: Jossey-Bass.

Gay, P. (1988). *Freud: A Life for Our Times*. New York: W.W. Norton.

Gaylor, A.L. (1988). *Betrayal of Trust: Clergy Abuse of Children*. East Orange, N.J.: Committee to Protect Children From Abusive Clergy, Survival Associates.

Gechtman, L. (1989). Sexual contact between social workers and their clients. In G. Gabbard (Ed.), *Sexual Exploitation in Professional Relationships*, pp. 27-38. Washington, D.C.: American Psychiatric Press.

Gechtman, L., and Bouhoutsos, J. (1985, Oct.). Sexual intimacy between social workers and clients. Paper presented at the annual meeting of the Society for Clinical Social Workers, Universal City, California.

Geck, D. (1989). Immunity provision of sexual exploitation statute are limited. *Minnesota Psychologist*, *38*, pp. 1, 4.

Gelman, D., Kasindorf, M., King, P., and Miller, M. (1986, May 26). Quick-fix therapy. *Newsweek*, pp. 74-76.

George, J.C. (1985). Psychotherapist-patient sex: A proposal for a mandatory reporting law. *Pacific Law Journal*, *16*, pp. 431-459.

Gerson, A. (1989). The anatomy of a malpractice case. *The Independent Practitioner, 9 (3)*, pp. 23-24.

Gilbert, L.A. (1987). Female and male emotional dependency and its implications for the therapist-client relationship. *Professional Psychology: Research and Practice, 18 (6)*, pp. 555-61.

Glaser, R.D., and Thorpe, J.S. (1986). Unethical intimacy: A survey of sexual contact and advances between psychology educators and female graduate students. *American Psychologist, 41*, pp. 43-51.

Glasscote, R.M., Raybin, J.B., Reifler, C.B., and Kane, A.W. (1975). *The Alternate Services: Their Role in Mental Health*. Washington, D.C.: Joint Information Service.

Gleason, J.J. (1977). Perception of stress among clergy and their spouses. *Journal of Pastoral Care, 31 (4)*, pp. 248-51.

Goin, M.K., and Kline, F. (1976). Countertransference: A neglected subject in clinical supervision. *American Journal of Psychiatry, 133 (1)*, p. 41.

Goldberg, C. (1986). *On Being a Psychotherapist*. New York: Gardner Press.

Goleman, D. (1987, November 19). When do therapist's actions cross over the line? *New York Times*, p. 16.

Gonsiorek, J. (Ed.). (1982). *Homosexuality and Psychotherapy: A Practitioner's Handbook of Affirmative Models*. New York: Haworth Press.

Gonsiorek, J. (1987). Intervening with psychotherapists who sexually exploit clients. In P. Keller and S. Heyman (Eds.) *Innovations in Clinical Practice: A Sourcebook*, *Vol. 6* (pp. 417-27). Sarasota, FL: Professional Resource Exchange.

Gonsiorek, J. (1989). Working therapeutically with therapists who have become sexually involved with clients. In B. Sanderson (Ed.), *It's Never O.K.: A Handbook for Professionals on Sexual Exploitation by Counselors and Therapists* (pp. 81-90). St. Paul, MN: Minnesota Dept. of Corrections. (a)

Gonsiorek, J. (1989). Sexual exploitation by psychotherapists: Some observations on male victims and on sexual orientation concerns. In B. Sanderson (Ed.), *It's Never O.K.: A Handbook for Professionals on Sexual Exploitation by Counselors and Therapists* (pp. 95-99). St. Paul, MN: Minnesota Dept. of Corrections. (b)

Gonsiorek, J., and Schoener, G.R. (1987). Assessment and evaluation of therapists who sexually exploit clients. *Professional Practice of Psychology, 8 (2)*, pp. 79-93.

Goode, E. (1987, Sept. 28). For a little peace of mind. *U.S. News and World Report*, pp. 98-102.

Gorkin, M. (1987). *The Uses of Countertransference*. Northvale, N.J.: Jason Aronson.

Gorlin, R.A. (Ed.) (1986). *Codes of Professional Responsibility*. Washington, D.C.: Bureau of National Affairs.

Gottlieb, M.C., Sell, J.M., and Schoenfeld (1988). Social/romantic relationships with present and former clients: State licensing board actions. *Professional Psychology: Research and Practice, 19*, pp. 459-462.

Gray, J. (1985, Sept.). What to do if your patient makes a pass. *Medical Economics*, pp. 83-84.

Greenbank, R.K. (1965). Management of sexualized counter-transference. *Journal of Sex Research, 1*, pp. 233-38.

Greenberg, S., and Kaslow, F.W. (1984). Psychoanalytic treatment for therapists, residents and other trainees. In F.W. Kaslow (Ed.), *Psychotherapy With Psychotherapists*, pp. 19-32. New York: Haworth Press.

Greenson, R.R. (1967). *The Technique and Practice of Psychoanalysis, Vol. 1*. New York: International Universities Press.

Gross, S. (1986). Ethics: Post-therapy social interaction/intimacy followup. *Minnesota Psychologist*, Summer issue, pp. 20-21.

Groth, A.N., Hobson, W.F., and Gary, T.S. (1982). The child molester: clinical observations. In J. Conte, and D.A. Shore (Eds.), *Social Work and Child Sexual Abuse* (pp. 129-44). New York: Haworth Press.

Grunebaum, H. (1983). A study of therapists' choice of a therapist. *American Journal of Psychiatry, 140*, pp. 1336-1339.

Grunebaum, H. (1985). Helpful and harmful psychotherapy. *Harvard Medical School/Mental Health Letter, 1 (10)*, pp. 5-6.

Grunebaum, H. (1986). Harmful psychotherapy experiences. *American Journal of Psychotherapy, 40 (2)*, pp. 165-176.

Grunebaum, H., Nadelson, C.C., and Macht, L.B. (1976). Sexual activity with the psychiatrist: A district branch dilemma. Unpublished paper presented at the annual convention of the American Psychological Assn., Miami, Florida.

Gutheil, T. (1989). Borderline personality disorder, boundary violations, and patient-therapist sex: Medicolegal pitfalls. *American Journal of Psychiatry, 146,* pp. 597-602.

Guttman, H.A. (1984). Sexual issues in the transference and countertransference between female therapist and male patient. *Journal of the American Academy of Psychoanalysis, 12,* pp. 187-97.

Guy, J. (1987). *The Personal Life of the Psychotherapist.* New York: John Wiley.

Guy, J.D., and Brown, C. (1989). Psychologist as victim: A discussion of patient violence. Unpublished paper presented at the annual convention of the American Psychological Assn., New Orleans.

Guy, J.D., and Liaboe, G.P. (1986). The impact of conducting psychotherapy on psychotherapists' interpersonal functioning. *Professional Psychology: Research and Practice, 17,* pp. 111-114.

Haas, L.J., Malouf, J.L., and Mayerson, N.H. (1986). Ethical dilemmas in psychological practice: Results of a national survey. *Professional Psychology: Research and Practice, 17,* pp. 316-321.

Hall, J.E. (1986). Issues and procedures in the disciplining of distressed psychologists. In R.R. Kilburg, P.E. Nathan, and R.W. Thoreson (Eds.), *Professionals in Distress: Issues, Syndromes, and Solutions in Psychology* (pp. 275-299). Washington, D.C.: American Psychological Assn.

Hall, J. E. (1987). Gender-related ethical dilemmas and ethics education. *Professional Psychology, Research and Practice, 18 (6),* pp. 573-79.

Halperin, D. (1983). *Religion, Sect, and Cult.* Littleton, MA: John Wright-PSG. (a)

Halperin, D. (1983). Group processes in cult affiliation and recruitment. In Halperin, D. (Ed.), *Religion, Sect, and Cult,* (pp. 223-34). Littleton, MA: John Wright-PSG. (b)

Hamilton, J., and DeRosis, H. (1985). Report of the women's committee to the Washington Psychiatric Society—Results of questionnaire on sexual abuse between physicians and their patients. Washington, D.C.: Washington Psychiatric Society.

Handelsman, M.M. (1986). Ethics training at the master's level: A national survey. *Professional Psychology: Research and Practice, 17,* pp. 24-26. (a)

Handelsman, M.M. (1986). Problems with ethics training by "osmosis." *Professional Psychology: Research and Practice, 17,* pp. 371-372. (b)

Hare-Mustin, R.T. (1974). Ethical considerations in the use of sexual contact in psychotherapy. *Psychotherapy: Theory, Research and Practice, 11,* pp. 308-310.

Harbaugh, G.L., and Rogers, E. (1984). Pastoral burnout: A view from the seminary. *Journal of Pastoral Care, 38 (2),* pp. 99-106.

Harlaub, C.H., Martin, G.D., and Rhine, M.W. (1986). Recontact with the analyst following termination: A survey of 71 cases. *Journal of the American Psychoanalytic Assn., 34,* pp. 895-910.

Hassenfield, I.N., and Sarris, J.G. (1978). Hazards and horizons of psychotherapy supervision. *American Journal of Psychotherapy, 32,* pp. 393-401.

Hays, J.R. (1980). Sexual contact between psychotherapist and patient remedies. *Psychological Reports, 47,* pp. 1247-54.

Heimann, P. (1950). On countertransference. *International Journal of Psychoanalysis, 31,* pp. 81-84.

Hellman, I.D., Morrison, T.L., and Abramowitz, S.I. (1986). The stresses of psychotherapeutic work: A replication and extension. *Journal of Clinical Psychology, 42,* pp. 197-205.

Hellman, I.D., Morrison, T.L., and Abramowitz, S.I. (1987). Therapist flexibility/rigidity and work stress. *Professional Psychology: Research and Practice, 18,* pp. 21-27.

Herman, J.L., Gartrell, N., Olarte, S., Feldstein, M., and Localio, R. (1987). Psychiatrist-patient sexual contact: Results of a national survey, II: Psychiatrists' attitudes. *American Journal of Psychiatry, 144,* pp. 164-169.

Hess, A. (1986). Growth in supervision: Stages of supervisee and supervisor development. In F. Kaslow (Ed.), *Supervision and Training—Models, Dilemmas and Challenges* (pp. 51-68). New York: Haworth Press.

Hess, A.K. (1987). Advances in psychotherapy supervision: Introduction. *Professional Psychology: Research and Practice, 18,* pp. 187-88.

Hess, K. and Hess, A. (1980). Supervision of psychotherapy with adolescents. In K. Hess (Ed.), *Psychotherapy Supervision: Theory, Research and Practice* (pp. 306-22). New York: John Wiley.

Hesselberg, G. (1987, May 4). Seduced: psychiatrist's abuse shreds patient's life. *The Wisconsin State Journal,* pp. 1, 8.

Hoencamp, E. (in press). Sexual abuse and the abuse of hypnosis in the therapeutic relationship. *International Journal of Clinical and Experimental Hypnosis.*

Hogan, B. (1979). *The Regulation of Psychotherapists, Vols. I, II, III, & IV.* Cambridge, MA: Ballinger Publications.

Holloway, E.L., and Roehlke, H.J. (1987). Internship: The applied training of a counseling psychologist. *The Counseling Psychologist, 15,* pp. 205-60.

Holroyd, J.C., and Bouhoutsos, J.C. (1985). Biased reporting of therapist-patient sexual intimacy. *Professional Psychology: Research and Practice, 16,* pp. 701-709.

Holroyd, J.C., and Brodsky, A.M. (1977). Psychologists' attitudes and practices regarding erotic and nonerotic physical contact with patients. *American Psychologist, 32,* pp. 843-849.

Holroyd, J.C., and Brodsky, A.M. (1980). Does touching patients lead to sexual intercourse? *Professional Psychology, 11,* pp. 807-811.

Horst, E.A. (1988). *Dual Relationships Between Psychologists and Clients.* Unpublished Master's Plan B paper, Dept. of Psychology, University of Minnesota.

Hospital & Community Psychiatry, (1977). No-red-tape counseling for clients alienated from traditional services, *28 (11),* pp. 843-45.

Hotelling, K. (1988). Ethical, legal, and administrative options to address sexual relationships between counselor and client. *Journal of Counseling and Development, 67,* pp. 233-37.

Howells, K. (1981). Adult sexual interest in children: Considerations relevant to theories of etiology. In M. Cook and K. Howells (Eds.), *Adult Sexual Interest in Children* (pp. 55-94). London: Academic Press.

Hubble, M.A., Noble, F.C., and Robinson, S.E. (1981). The effect of counselor touch in a counseling session. *Journal of Counseling Psychology, 28,* pp. 533-535.

Hulme, W.E. (1989). Sexual boundary violations of clergy. In G.O. Gabbard (Ed.), *Sexual Exploitation in Professional Relationships,* pp. 177-191. Washington, D.C.: American Psychiatric Press.

Human Behavior. (1975, Nov.). Healing in the hay? p. 38.

Hurn, H. (1973). On the fate of transference after the termination of anlysis. *Journal of the American Psychoanalytic Association, 12,* pp. 182-92.

I Team. (1983, June). Homestead Homes. Television special. Minneapolis: WCCO-TV.

I Team. (1984, Dec.). Wilson Center. Television special. Minneapolis: WCCO-TV.

Ishida, Y. (1974). Physician-patient sexual relations. *Medical Aspects of Human Sexuality, 8,* p. 103.

Jacobson, A., and Richardson, B. (1987). Assault experiences of 100 psychiatric inpatients: Evidence of the need for routine inquiry. *American Journal of Psychiatry, 144 (7),* pp. 908-913.

Johnson, E. (1988). *Family Stress During Malpractice Litigation.* Videotape available from the American Medical Assn. Auxilliary, Chicago, Illinois.

Johnson, K. (1989, Aug. 15). It's over: '77 rape case dropped. *USA Today,* p. 3A.

Jones, E. (1953). *The Life and Work of Sigmund Freud, Vol. 1.* New York: Basic Books.

Jorgenson, L. (1989). Psychiatrist malpractice: The furor over patient-therapist sexual contact—A survey of the law. Unpublished paper. Cambridge, MA: Spero and Jorgenson, Attorneys at Law.

Kalichman, S., Craig, M., and Follingstad, D. (1988). Mental health professionals and suspected cases of child abuse: An investigation of factors influencing reporting. *Community Mental Health Journal, 24,* pp. 43-51.

Kalichman, S., Craig, M., and Follingstad, D. (1989). Factors influencing the reporting of father-child sexual abuse: Study of licensed practicing psychologists. *Professional Psychology: Research and Practice, 20,* pp. 84-89.

Kane, A.K. (1984, June 4). Memo to Wisconsin task force on sexual misconduct by therapists.

Kane, A.K. (1985, Jan. 7). Needs of victims. Memo to Wisconsin task force on sexual misconduct by therapists.

Kane, A.K. (1988). The Wisconsin coalition on sexual misconduct by psychotherapists and counselors: A community effort. In M. Schwebel, J. Skorina, and G. Schoener (Eds.), *Assisting Impaired Psychologists: Program Development for State Psychological Associations* (Appendix P, pp. 1-6). Washington, D.C.: American Psychological Association.

Kane, H. (1974). *A Kind of Rape.* New York: Dell.

Kaplan, A. (1975). Sex in psychotherapy: The myth of Sandor Ferenczi. *Contemporary Psychoanalysis, 11,* pp. 175-87.

Kaplan, D. (1972). On transference, love and generativity. *Psychoanalytic Review, 58,* pp. 573-79.

Kaplan, H.S. (1977). Training sex therapists. In W.H. Masters, V.E. Johnson, and R.D. Kolodny (Eds.), *Ethical Issues in Sex Therapy and Research* (pp. 182-205). Boston: Little, Brown.

Kardener, S.H. (1974). Sex and the physician-patient relationship. *American Journal of Psychiatry, 131*, pp. 1134-36.

Kardener, S.H. (1976). Characteristics of "erotic" practitioners. *American Journal of Psychiatry, 133*, pp. 1324-25.

Kardener, S.H., Fuller, M., and Mensh, I. (1973). A survey of physicians' attitudes and practices regarding erotic and non-erotic contact with clients. *American Journal of Psychiatry, 130*, pp. 1077-1081.

Kaslow, F. (1984). *Psychotherapy with Psychotherapists*. New York: Haworth Press.

Kaslow, F. (1986). *Supervision and Training—Models, Dilemmas and Challenges*. New York: Haworth Press. (a)

Kaslow, F. (1986). Seeking and providing consultation in private practice. In F. Kaslow (Ed.), *Supervision and Training—Models, Dilemmas and Challenges*. New York: Haworth Press. (b)

Kaufman, P.A., and Harrison, E. (1986). Open-ended group therapy for victims of therapist sexual misconduct. In A.W. Burgess and C.R. Hartman (Eds.), *Sexual Exploitation of Patients by Health Professionals*, pp. 173-177. New York: Praeger.

Kavoussi, R.J., and Becker, J.V. (1987). Psychiatrist-patient sexual contact. *American Journal of Psychiatry, 144*, pp. 1249-1250.

Keith-Spiegel, P., and Koocher, G.P. (1985). *Ethics in Psychology: Professional Standards and Cases*. New York: Random House.

Kelley, T. (1987, May 25). Therapists can abuse their power. *Milwaukee Sentinel*, pp. 8, 9.

Kilburg, R.R., Nathan, P.E., and Thoreson, R. (1986). *Professionals in Distress: Issues, Syndromes, and Solutions in Psychology*. Washington, D.C.: American Psychological Association.

Kinsey, A. (1953). *Sexual Behavior in the Human Female*. Philadelphia: Saunders.

Kitchener, K. (1988). Dual role relationships: What makes them so problematic? *Journal of Counseling and Development, 67*, pp. 217-221.

Kline, M.V. (1972). The production of anti-social behavior through hypnosis: New clinical data. *International Journal of Clinical and Experimental Hypnosis, 20 (2)*, pp. 80-94.

Klopfer, W.G. (1974). The seductive patient. In W.G. Klopfer and M.R. Reed (Eds.), *Problems in Psychotherapy*. New York: John Wiley.

Kluft, R.P. (1989). Treating the patient who has been sexually exploited by a previous therapist. *Psychiatric Clinics of North America, 12 (2)*, pp. 483-500.

Koch, J., and Koch, L. (1976, March). Sex therapy: Caveat emptor. *Psychology Today*, p. 37.

Kohl, L. (1984, Oct. 21). Chief psychiatrist is sex allegation target. *Sunday Pioneer Press.*, p. 1.

Kohrman, R., Fineberg, H., Gelman, R., and Weiss, S. (1971). Technique of child analysis: Problems of countertransference. *International Journal of Psychoanalysis, 52*, pp. 487-97.

Korran, L.M., Fenton, W.S., and Taintor, Z. (1986). The nation's psychiatrists: 1983 survey. Washington, D.C.: American Psychiatric Press.

Kottler, J. (1986). *On Being a Therapist*. San Francisco: Jossey-Bass.

Krizek, C.R. (1989). Addressing the problem of the impaired physician. In R.D. Miller (Ed.), *Legal Implications of Hospital Policies and Practices* (pp. 11-20). San Francisco: Jossey-Bass.

Kutz, S.L. (1986). Defining "impaired psychologist" (letter to the editor). *American Psychologist, 41*, p. 220.

Laker, B. (1985, May 21). State regulation does very little to protect public. *Dallas Times Herald*, p. 1D. (a)

Laker, B. (1985, May 21). Texas state regulatory boards: What they are and what they do. *Dallas Times Herald*, p. 4D. (b)

Laker, B. (1985, May 21). Kinds of licensed therapists in Texas. *Dallas Times Herald*, p. 5D. (c)

Laliotis, D., and Grayson, J. (1985). Psychologist heal thyself: What is available for the impaired psychologist? *American Psychologist, 40*, pp. 84-96.

Lamb, D., Presser, N. Pfost, K., Baum, M., Jackson, V., and Jarvis, P. (1987). Confronting professional impairment during the internship: Identification, due process, and remediation. *Professional Psychology: Research and Practice, 18 (6)*, pp. 597-603.

Landers, A. (1981, April 12). Intimate treatment no legitimate therapy. (Minneapolis) *Star Tribune*.

Landers, A. (1985, Nov. 1). Unethical therapists can flee punishment. *The Star Ledger*. (a)

Landers, A. (1985, Nov. 14). Ann Landers column. (Minneapolis) *Star Tribune*. (b)

Landers, A. (1985, Dec. 10). Senator sponsors bill to curb charlatans *Milwaukee Journal*. (c)

Landers, A. (1986, June 27). Fondling by therapist is out of line. (Minneapolis) *Star Tribune*, p. 7C. (a)

Landers, A. (1986, Oct. 23). Undress the therapist tells her: She's advised to avoid him, report him. (Minneapolis) *Star Tribune*. (b)

Landers, A. (1986, Sept. 11). He's shocked by bride's account of sex life. (Minneapolis) *Star Tribune*, p. 9C. (c)

Landers, A. (1986, Dec. 17). Bride should blow whistle on minister she slept with. (Minneapolis) *Star Tribune*, p. 6C. (d)

Landers, A. (1988, May 12). Therapists, go forth and heal thyselves. (Minneapolis) *Star Tribune*, p. 10E. (a)

Landers, A. (1988, Aug. 19). Sex with psychiatrist helped, woman says. (Minneapolis) *Star Tribune*, p. 4E. (b)

Landers, A. (1988, Nov. 7). Sex isn't a legitimate part of therapy. (Minneapolis) *Star Tribune*, p. 4E. (c)

Landers, A. (1989, Feb. 12). Doctors should "cure" the bad practitioners among their ranks. (Minneapolis) *Star Tribune*, p. 5E. (a)

Landers, A. (1989, Aug. 17). "Associate pastor" fleeced her of insurance money. *(Minneapolis) Star Tribune*, p. 7E. (b)

Landis, C.E., Miller, H.R., and Wettstone, R.P. (1975). Sexual awareness training for counselors. *Teaching of Psychology*, 2, pp. 33-36.

Lange, E.T., and Hirsh, H.L. (1981). Legal problems in intimate therapy. *Medical Trial Techniques*, 28, pp. 201-208.

Langs, R.J. (1982). *The Psychotherapeutic Conspiracy*. New York: Jason Aronson.

Lanyon, R. (1986). Theory and treatment in child molestation. *Journal of Consulting and Clinical Psychology*, 54 (2), pp. 176-82.

Laurence, J.R., and Perry, C. (1988). *Hypnosis, Will, & Memory: A Psycholegal History*. New York: Guilford Press.

Lehrman, N. (1960, June). The normality of sexual feelings in pastoral counseling. *Pastoral Psychology*, p. 49. (a)

Lehrman, N. (1960). The analyst's sexual feelings. *American Journal of Psychotherapy*, 14, pp. 545-49. (b)

Len, M., and Fischer, J. (1978). Clinicians' attitudes toward and use of body contact or sexual techniques with clients. *Journal of Sex Research*, 14, pp. 40-49.

Lenehan, G.P., and Turner, J.T. (1984). Treatment of staff victims of violence. In J.T. Turner (Ed.), *Violence in the Medical Care Setting* (pp. 251-60). Rockville, MD: Aspen Systems Group.

Leo, J. (1983, May 23). Lemons from a shady dealer. *Time*, p. 60.

Leo, J. (1985, Sept. 30). A madness in their method. *Time*, p. 78.

Lerman, H. (1984). Sexual intimacies between psychotherapists and patients: An annotated bibliography of mental health, legal and public media literature including relevant legal cases. Committee for Women, Division of Psychotherapy, American Psychological Assn. and Association for Women in Psychology.

Levenson, J.L. (1986). When a colleague practices unethically: Guidelines for intervention. *Journal of Counseling and Development*, 64, pp. 315-317.

Levine, L. (1983). Reporting maltreatment of vulnerable adults in licensed facilities. Informational bulletin #83-2, Jan. 17, 1983—12 MCAR 2.010. St. Paul, MN: Minnesota Dept. of Human Services.

Levine, S. (1984). *Radical Departures: Desperate Detours to Growing Up*. New York: Harcourt, Brace, Jovanovich. (a)

Levine, S. (1984, Aug.). Radical departures. *Psychology Today*, pp. 21-27. (b)

Lief, H.I. (1978, Feb.). Sexual survey #7: Current thinking on seductive patients. *Medical Aspects of Human Sexuality*, pp. 46-47.

Linda, J. (1987, Nov.). Therapist sexual exploitation of a patient—the patient's perspective. *Register Report*, 14, pp. 13-14.

Linsley, J. (1989, Feb. 9). Farmington assault case dismissed. *St. Paul Pioneer Press Dispatch*, p. 1.

Little, M. (1951). Countertransference and the patient's response to it. *International Journal of Psychoanalysis*, 32, pp. 32-40.

Logan, W.S. (1989). The evaluation of the impaired physician. In R.D. Miller (Ed.), *Legal Implications of Hospital Policies and Practices* (pp. 33-53). San Francisco: Jossey-Bass.

Lothane, Z. (1983). Cultist phenomena in psychoanalysis. In D. Halperin (Ed.), *Religion, Sect, and Cult* (pp. 199-221). Littleton, MA: John Wright-PSG.

Lowry, T.S., and Lowry, T.P. (1975, July). Ethical considerations in sex therapy. *Journal of Marriage and Family Counseling*, pp. 229-36.

Lubben, P. (1987). Ethics. *The Counselor, 5*, p. 12.

Luepker, E.T. (1989). Sexual exploitation of clients by therapists: Parallels with parent/child incest. In B. Sanderson (Ed.), *It's Never O.K.: A Handbook for Professionals on Sexual Exploitation by Counselors and Therapists*, pp. 15-17. St. Paul, MN: Minnesota Dept. of Corrections.

Luepker, E., and Retsch-Bogart, C. (1985). Group treatment for clients who have been sexually involved with their psychotherapists. In A. Burgess and C. Hartman (Eds.), *Sexual Exploitation of Patients by Health Professionals* (pp. 163-172). New York: Praeger.

MacCollam, J. (1979). *Carnival of Souls*. New York: Seabury Press.

MacDonald, G. (1988). *Rebuilding Your Broken World*. Nashville, TN: Thomas Nelson.

Madden, M. (1976). Meaningful pastoral intimacy. *Pastoral Psychology, 25 (1)*, pp. 34-38.

Maeder, T. (1989, Jan.). Wounded healers. *The Atlantic Monthly*, pp. 37-47.

Malony, H.N. (1989, May). Clergy stress: Not so bad after all? *Ministry*, pp. 8-9.

Marmor, J. (1953). The feeling of superiority: An occupational hazard in the practice of psychotherapy. *American Journal of Psychiatry, 110*, pp. 370-373.

Marmor, J. (1970). The seductive psychotherapist. *Psychiatry Digest, 31*, pp. 10-16.

Marmor, J. (1972). Sexual acting-out in psychotherapy. *American Journal of Psychoanalysis, 32*, pp. 3-8.

Marmor, J. (1976). Some psychodynamic aspects of the seduction of patients in psychotherapy. *American Journal of Psychoanalysis, 36*, pp. 319-23.

Marmor, J. (1977). Designated discussion of The Ethics of Sex Therapy." In W.H. Masters, V.E. Johnson, and R.D. Kolodny (Eds.), *Ethical Issues in Sex Therapy and Research* (pp. 157-61). Boston: Little, Brown.

Maslach, C. (1986). Stress, burnout and workaholism. In R.R. Kilburg, P.E. Nathan, and R.W. Thoreson (Eds.), *Professionals in Distress: Issues, Syndromes and Solutions in Psychology* (pp. 53-75). Washington, D.C.: American Psychological Association.

Maslow, A. (1965). *Eupsychian Management: A Journal*. Homewood, IL: R.D. Irwin.

Masson, J.M. (1985). *The Assault on Truth*. New York: Penguin Books.

Masson, J.M. (1988). *Against Therapy—Emotional Tyranny and the Myth of Psychological Healing*. New York: Atheneum.

Masters, W.H. (1974, Nov.). Phony sex clinics—medicine's newest nightmare. *Today's Health*, pp. 22-26.

Masters, W.H., and Johnson, V.E. (1966). *The Human Sexual Response*. Boston: Little, Brown.

Masters, W.H., and Johnson, V.E. (1970). *Human Sexual Inadequacy*. Boston, MA: Little, Brown.

Masters, W.H., and Johnson, V.E. (1975, May 6). Principles of the new sex therapy. Paper delivered at the annual meeting of the American Psychiatric Association, Anaheim, California.

Masters, W.H., and Johnson, V.E. (1976). Principles of the new sex therapy. *American Journal of Psychiatry, 133*, pp. 548-53.

Masters, W.H., Johnson, V.E., and Kolodny, R.D. (1977). *Ethical Issues in Sex Therapy and Research*. Boston: Little, Brown.

Matarazzo, R.G., and Patterson, D.R. (1986). Methods of teaching therapeutic skill. In S.L. Garfield and A.G. Bergin (Eds.), *Handbook of Psychotherapy and Behavior Change*, pp. 821-839.

McAuliffe, B. (1989, Feb. 7). Ex-minister given 90 days for sexual misconduct. (Minneapolis) *Star Tribune*, p. 3B.

McCartney, J.L. (1966). Overt transference. *Journal of Sex Research, 2*, pp. 227-37.

McClernan, J. (1972). *Implications of Sexual Attraction (Feeling) in the Counselor-Client Relationship*. Unpublished doctoral dissertation, University of Southern Mississippi.

McCoy, J. (1984, Feb. 13). Church is quiet on sexual accusation against its pastor. *Seattle Post-Intelligencer*, p. C-2.

McDowell, L. (1989, May). The dynamics of ministerial morality. *Ministry*, pp. 4-6.

McEnroe, P. (1983, July 14). Two men charged with criminal sexual conduct against patient. (Minneapolis) *Star Tribune*, p. 3B.

McKneely, D. (1987). *Touching: Body Therapy and Depth Psychology*. Toronto: Inner City Books.

McQuary, J.P. (1964, March). Preferred counselor characteristics. *Counselor Education and Supervision*, pp. 145-148.

Medlicott, R.W. (1968). Erotic professional indiscretions, actual or assumed and alleged. *Australian/New Zealand Journal of Psychiatry, 2*, pp. 17-23.

Mehl, L.G. (1977). The occupational rehabilitation of psychiatrically hospitalized clergymen. *Journal of Pastoral Care, 31 (4)*, pp. 243-47.

Meloy, J.R. (1986). Narcissistic psychopathology and the clergy. *Pastoral Psychology, 35 (1)*, pp. 50-55.

Menninger, K. (1958). *Theory of Psychoanalytic Technique*. New York: Basic Books.

Mental Health Association in Hennepin County. (1988). *Your Child's and Adolescent's Mental Health—A Resource Guide for Parents*. Minneapolis: Author.

Mental Health Interdisciplinary Interest Group. (1981). *Mental Health Services in Minnesota—A Guide for Referring Professionals and Consumers*. Minneapolis: University of Minnesota Health Sciences Center.

Merrill, D. (1985). *Clergy Couples in Crisis*. (a)

Merrill, D. (1985, Nov. 8). The sexual hazards of pastoral care. *Christianity Today*, p. 105. (b)

Mertz, A.W. (1986). Sexual abuse of anesthetized patients. In A.W. Burgess and C.R. Harman (Eds.), *Sexual Exploitation of Patients by Health Professionals*, pp. 61-65. New York: Praeger.

Metro Goldwyn-Mayer. (1970). *Pretty Maids All In A Row*. Film.

Milgrom, J.H. (1978). Sexual exploitation of clients: Its prevention or remedy; or A look at whether your agency has its house in order. Minneapolis: Walk-In Counseling Center (Reproduced in Appendix E).

Milgrom, J.H. (1981). Some observations regarding secondary victims of exploitation of clients by therapists and counselors (memorandum). Minneapolis: Walk-In Counseling Center.

Milgrom, J.H. (1986). Advocacy: Assisting the sexually exploited client through the process (memorandum). Minneapolis: Walk-In Counseling Center.

Milgrom, J.H. (1989). Advocacy: The process of assisting sexually exploited clients. In B. Sanderson (Ed.), *It's Never O.K.: A Handbook for Professionals on Sexual Exploitation by Counselors and Therapists*, pp. 29-34. St. Paul, MN: Minnesota Dept. of Corrections.

Milgrom, J.H., Gaskill, W., and Powell, R. (1985). Staff-resident relationships and boundaries—Presenter's outline. Monograph. Minneapolis, MN: Walk-In Counseling Center.

Milgrom, J.H., and Schoener, G.R. (1987). Responding to clients who have been sexually exploited by counselors, therapists, and clergy. In M.D. Pellauer, B. Chester, and J.A. Boyajian (Eds.), *Sexual Assault and Abuse: A Handbook for Clergy and Religious Professionals*. San Francisco: Harper & Row.

Milgrom, J.H., and Schoener, G.R. (1989). Assisting victim-survivors of client-therapist sex. In B. Sanderson (Ed.), *It's Never O.K.: A Handbook for Professionals on Sexual Exploitation by Counselors and Therapists*, pp. 9-14. St. Paul, MN: Minnesota Dept. of Corrections.

Milillo, M., Shultz, J., and Couchman, J. (1989). Strategies for organizational intervention with an agency where sexual exploitation has occurred. In B. Sanderson (Ed.), *It's Never O.K.: A Handbook for Professionals on Sexual Exploitation by Counselors and Therapists* (pp. 141-45). St. Paul, MN: Minnesota Dept. of Corrections.

Miller, A. (1987). *For Your Own Good*. New York: Farrar, Straus, & Giroux.

Miller, R.D. (1989). *Legal Implications of Hospital Policies and Practices*. San Francisco: Jossey-Bass. (a)

Miller, R.D. (1989). Recent developments in antitrust: Challenges to medical autonomy. In R.D. Miller (Ed.), *Legal Implications of Hospital Policies and Practices* (pp. 69-80). San Francisco: Jossey-Bass. (b)

Milwaukee Journal. (1985, July 11). Task force takes steps to end client sex abuse, p. 1.

(Minneapolis) *Star Tribune*. (1984, March 14). Wisconsin psychiatrist charged with 7 more counts of sexual assault, p. 6B.

(Minneapolis) *Star Tribune*. (1986, June 8). Sexual exploitation and therapy don't mix. Editorial. (a)

(Minneapolis) *Star Tribune*. (1986, Aug. 6). Psychologist's license restricted after sexual contact with boy, 16. p. 3B. (b)

(Minneapolis) *Star Tribune.* (1987, Aug. 5). Psychologist to be returned to state to face sex charge, p. 8B. (a)

(Minneapolis) *Star Tribune.* (1987, Sept. 1). Therapist sentenced for whipping patient, p. 3B. (b)

Minnesota Council on Family Relations. (Undated). What you need to know to be a responsible client. Minneapolis: Author.

Minnesota Department of Corrections. (1988). It's Never O.K. (Consumer brochure). St. Paul, MN: Minnesota Dept. of Corrections.

Minnesota Interfaith Committee on Sexual Exploitation by Clergy. (1989). *Sexual Exploitation by Clergy: Reflections and Guidelines for Religious Leaders.* Minneapolis, Minnesota: Author. (Available for $5.00 from John P. Martinson, Director, Abbott-Northwestern Counseling Center, 2545 Chicago Ave. S., Suite 309, Minneapolis, MN 55404.)

Minnesota Psychologist. (1986). Minnesota Psychological Association guidelines for the practice of psychology in child sex abuse cases. Winter issue, pp. 1, 17-19.

Minsky, T. (1987). Prisoners of psychotherapy. *New York, 20 (34),* pp. 34-39.

Mintz, E.E. (1967). Time-extended marathon groups. *Psychotherapy: Theory, Research and Practice, 4 (2),* pp. 65-70.

Mintz, E.E. (1969). Touch and the psychoanalytic tradition. *Psychoanalytic Review, 56,* pp. 365-66.

Mithers, C. (1988, Aug.). When therapists drive their patients crazy. *California Magazine,* pp. 76-85, 135-36.

Mizuno, L.E. (1988, June 13). News release. Minneapolis: Minnesota Board of Psychology.

Moisan, J.M. (1987). Sins of the secular priesthood: Civil liability for the sexual seduction of patients. *Medical Trial Technique Quarterly, 33,* pp. 440-57.

Moldowsky, S. (1986). Psychoanalytic psychotherapy supervision. In K. Hess (Ed), *Psychotherapy Supervision: Theory, Research and Practice* (pp. 126-35). New York: John Wiley.

Money, J., and Lamacz, M. (1987). Genital examination and exposure experienced as nosocomial sexual abuse in childhood. *The Journal of Nervous and Mental Disease, 175,* pp. 713-21.

Moran, J.F. (1984). Teaching the management of violent behavior to nursing staff: A health care model. In J.T. Turner (Ed.), *Violence in the Medical Care Setting* (pp. 231-49). Rockville, MD: Aspen Systems.

Moss, S. (1988). Clergy and parishioners must respect boundaries. *Soundings, 10 (6),* pp. 6-7. (a)

Moss, S. (1988). It's Never O.K. *Soundings, 10 (6),* p. 7. (b)

Ms. (1983, Jan.). When the therapist is the problem, p. 19.

Mueller, W.J., and Kell, B.L. (1972). *Coping with Conflict: Supervising Counselors and Psychotherapists.* New York: Appleton-Century-Croft.

Murase, T., and Johnson, F. (1974). Naikan, morita and western psychotherapy. *Archives of General Psychiatry, 31,* pp. 121-28.

Murray, J., and Abramson, P.R. (1983). An investigation of the effects of client gender and attractiveness on psychologists' judgments. In J. Murray and P.R. Abramson (Eds.), *Bias in Psychotherapy* (pp. 129-67). New York: Praeger.

National Association of Alcoholism and Drug Abuse Counselors. (1987). Code of Ethics. *The Counselor*, *5*, pp. 12-16.

National Association of Social Workers. (1980). *NASW Policy Statements: Code of Ethics*. Washington, D.C.: Author.

Nemiroff, G. (1983, Sept.). Psychiatric malpractice: This case is about power. *Communiquèlles*, *9*, pp. 3-14, 18.

Newberger, C.M., and Newberger, E.H. (1986). When the pediatrician is a pedophile. In A.W. Burgess and C.R. Hartman (Eds.), *Sexual Exploitation of Patients by Health Professionals*, pp. 99-119. New York: Praeger.

Newlund, S. (1980, Sept. 11). Hypnotist sued for consumer fraud. *Minneapolis Tribune*, p. 1B. (a)

Newlund, S. (1980, Oct. 14). Women sexually used by their male therapists trying to undo damage. *Minneapolis Tribune*, p. 1A. (b)

Newlund, S. (1986, June 6). Therapists flout sex ban. (Minneapolis) *Star Tribune*, p. 3B.

Nielson, L., Peterson, M., Shapiro, M., and Thompson, P. (1989). Supervision approaches in cases of boundary violations and sexual victimization by therapists. In B. Snaderson (Ed.), *It's Never O.K.: A Handbook for Professionals on Sexual Exploitation by Counselors and Therapists*, pp. 55-68. St. Paul, MN: Minnesota Dept. of Corrections.

Noel, M.M. (1986). *Sexual Misconduct by Psychologists: Who Reports It?* Unpublished doctoral dissertation. Antioch-New England Graduate School, Keene, N.H.

Norcross, J.C., and Prochaska, J.O. (1986). Psychotherapist heal thyself: I. The psychological distress and self-change of psychologists, counselors, and lay persons. *Psychotherapy*, *23*, pp. 102-14. (a)

Norcross, J.C., and Prochaska, J.O. (1986). Psychotherapist heal thyself: II. The self-initiated and therapy-facilitated change of psychological distress. *Psychotherapy*, *23*, pp. 155-68. (b)

Norman, H., Blacker, K., Oremland, J., and Barrett. (1976). The fate of the transference neurosis after termination of a satisfactory analysis. *Journal of the American Psychoanalytic Association, 24*, pp. 471-498.

Northrup, B. (1986, Oct. 29). Psychotherapy faces a stubborn problem: Abuses by therapists. *Wall Street Journal*, pp. 1, 18.

Nursing Ethics. (1974). *Nursing, 4 (9)*, pp. 43-44.

Oaks, L. (1987, Nov. 18). Ramsey judge mulls punitive damages in sex case—suits allege 20 years of priest's sexual abuse of boys. (Minneapolis) *Star Tribune*, p. 3B.

OB-Gyn News. (1976, Jan.). Therapist as sex partner better than "surrogate," p. 11.

Oberdorfer, D. (1982, July 2). Counselor denies trip with girl, 12. (Minneapolis) *Star Tribune*, p. 3C.

Obholzer, K. (1982). *The Wolf-Man Sixty Years Later*. New York: Continuum.

O'Byrne, B. (1970). Civil liability of doctor or psychologist for having sexual relationship with patient. *American Law Reports, 33*, pp. 1393-1396.

Ode, K. (1986, June 14). Sexual exploitation by therapists is hidden problem. (Minneapolis) *Star Tribune*, p. 1C.

Oder, F.E. (1986). Observations on a case of patient sexual abuse. In A.W. Burgess and C.R. Hartman (Eds.), *Sexual Exploitation of Patients by Health Professionals*, pp. 45-48. New York: Praeger.

Oldham, R.L., Burgoyne, R.W., and Yamamoto, J. (1978). Comparative experience with erotic behavior. *Journal of Operational Psychiatry, 9 (2)*, pp. 17-22.

Olsen, J. (1989). *Doc—The Rape of the Town of Lovell*. New York: Atheneum.

Orne, M.T. (1972). Can a hypnotized subject be compelled to carry out otherwise unacceptable behavior? A discussion. *International Journal of Experimental and Clinical Hypnosis, 20 (2)*, pp. 101-117.

Pakdaman, H. (1982). The prevalence of sexual intimacy between therapists and their clients. Unpublished doctoral dissertation, U.S. International University, Los Angeles.

Parelman, A. (1989). Group psychotherapy as an approach to "righting the wrong." Unpublished paper presented at the annual convention of the American psychological Assn., New Orleans.

Parry, K. (1987, April 16). Ex-child-care counselor faces sex charges involving patient. (Minneapolis) *Star Tribune*, p. 5B.

Patten, S.B., Gatz, Y.K., Jones, B., and Thomas, D.L. (1989). Post-traumatic stress disorder and the treatment of sexual abuse. *Social Work, 34*, pp. 197-203.

Pattison, E.M. (1965). Transference and countertransference in pastoral care. *Journal of Pastoral Care, 19 (4)*, pp. 201.

Pellauer, M.D. (1987, Feb. 16). Sex, power, and the family of God. *Christianity and Crisis*, pp. 47-50.

Pellauer, M.D., Chester, B., and Boyajian, J.A. (1987). *Sexual Assault and Abuse: A Handbook for Clergy and Religious Professionals*. San Francisco: Harper & Row. (a)

Pellauer, M.D., Chester, B., and Boyajian, J.A. (1987). Resources for ritual and recuperation. In M.D. Pellauer, B. Chester, and J. A. Boyajian (Eds.), *Sexual Assault and Abuse: A Handbook for Clergy and Religious Professionals* (pp. 223-247). San Francisco: Harper & Row. (b)

Pelletier, C.S., and Settin, J.M. (1988). The distressed psychologist: Survey and action. Unpublished report, Distressed Psychologists Committee, Maine State Psychological Assn.

Perry, C. (1979). Hypnotic coercion and compliance to it: A review of evidence presented in a legal case. *International Journal of Clinical and Experimental Hypnosis, 27 (3)*, pp. 187-218.

Perry, J.A. (1976). Physicians' erotic and non-erotic physical involvement with patients. *American Journal of Psychiatry, 133*, pp. 838-840.

Person, E.S. (1985). The erotic transference in men: Differences and consequences. *Journal of the American Academy of Psychoanalysis, 13 (2)*, pp. 159-80.

Peterson, C. (1988, Nov. 8). Dutton case goes to trial—prosecution rests Tuesday, Dec. 6. *St. Peter Herald*, p. 1.

Peterson, M. (1984). Boundary issues in field instruction. Unpublished paper.

Phelps, D. (1983, June 14). Pastor accused of having sex with girl, 15. (Minneapolis) *Star Tribune*, p. 1B. (a)

Phelps, D. (1983, March 25). Boys sexually abused by doctor get $240,000 in malpractice suit. (Minneapolis) *Star Tribune*, p. 3B. (b)

Phillips, E.L. (1982). *Stress, Health, and Psychological Problems in the Major Professions* (pp. 297-313). Lanham, MD: University Press of American.

Physician's Weekly (1987, April 27). Point/Counterpoint: Is the Minnesota sex-abuse law unfair to psychiatrists? *Physician's Weekly*, *4 (16)*, p. 1.

Pinsley, E. (1989, Jan. 17-23). Patient can sue doctor over post-treatment affair. *Manhattan Lawyer*, p. 4.

Plasil, E. (1985). *Therapist*. New York: St. Martin's Press.

Plaut, S.M., and Foster, B.H. (1986). Roles of the health professional in cases involving sexual exploitation of patients. In A.W. Burgess and C. Hartman (Eds.), *Sexual Exploitation of Patients by Health Professionals* (pp. 15-18). New York: Praeger.

Ponsor, L., Soler, E., and Abod, J. (1976). The A-B-C's of drug treatment for women. *STASH Capsules, 8 (5)*, pp. 1-4. Madison, WI: Student Assn. for the Study of Hallucinogens.

Pope, K.S. (1986, June). New trends in malpractice cases and changes in APA liability insurance. *The Independent Practitioner (Division 42 Newsletter)*, pp. 23-26.

Pope, K.S. (1987). Preventing therapist-patient sexual intimacy: Therapy for a therapist at risk. *Professional Psychology: Research and Practice*, *18*, pp. 624-628.

Pope, K.S. (1987, May). Sex with patients: New data, standards, and liabilities. *The Independent Practitioner (Division 42 Newsletter)*, pp. 15-20.

Pope, K.S. (1988). How clients are harmed by sexual contact with mental health professionals: The syndrome and its development. *Journal of Counseling and Development*, *67*, pp. 222-26.

Pope, K.S. (in press). Rehabilitation of therapists who have been sexually intimate with a patient. In G. Gabbard (Ed.), *Sexual Exploitation in Professional Relationships*. Washington, D.C.: American Psychiatric Press.

Pope, K.S., and Bajt, T.R. (1988). When laws and values conflict: A dilemma for psychologists. *American Psychologist*, *43*, pp. 828-829.

Pope, K.S., and Bouhoutsos, J. (1986). *Sexual Intimacy Between Therapists and Patients*. New York: Praeger.

Pope, K.S., and Gabbard, G.O. (1989). Individual psychotherapy for victims of therapist-patient sexual intimacy. In G.O. Gabbard (Ed.), *Sexual Exploitation in Professional Relationships*, pp. 89-100. Washington, D.C.: American Psychiatric press.

Pope, K.S., Levenson, H., and Schover, L. (1979). Sexual intimacy in psychology training: Results and implications of national survey. *American Psychologist*, *34*, pp. 682-689.

Pope, K.S., Keith-Spiegel, P., and Tabachnick, B.G. (1986). Sexual attraction to clients: The human therapist and the (sometimes) inhuman training system. *American Psychologist*, *41*, pp. 147-158.

Pope, K.S., Schover, L.R., and Levenson, H. (1980). Sexual behavior between clinical supervisors and trainees: Implications for professional standards. *Professional Psychology, 11*, pp. 157-62.

Pope, K.S., Tabachnick, B.G., and Keith-Spiegel (1987). Ethics of practice: The beliefs and behaviors of psychologists as therapists. *American Psychologist, 42*, pp. 993-1006.

Prince, P. (1989, Feb. 22). Humphrey to appeal minister's sentence. (Minneapolis)*Star Tribune*, p. 1B.

Psychiatric News (1985, May 3). APA's ethics procedures upheld as fair in federal court.

Public Education Work Group (1988). *It's Never O.K.: A Handbook for Victims and Victim Advocates on Sexual Exploitation by Counselors and Therapists*. St. Paul, MN: Minnesota Dept. of Corrections.

Quinn, F. (1988). Ethical considerations for employee assistance professionals. *The ALMACAN, 18 (6)*, pp. 20-22.

Quinn, S. (1988). *A Mind of Her Own*. Reading, MA: Addison-Wesley.

Rachner, H. (1957). The meaning and uses of countertransference. *Psychoanalytic Quarterly, 26*, pp. 303-57.

Raimo, A.M. (1985). Therapist-patient sex: Legal and ethical implications. *American Journal of Forensic Psychology, 3*, pp. 13-33.

Randall, J. (1985). *Through the Door*. New York: Stein & Day.

Rappaport, E.A. (1956). The management of an eroticized transference. *Psychoanalytic Quarterly, 23*, pp. 515-529.

Rappaport, E.A. (1959). The first dream in an eroticized transference. *International Journal of Psychoanalysis, 40*, pp. 240-45.

Rasmussen, J. (1987). *Couched in Silence: An Advocacy Handbook on Sexual Exploitation in Therapy*. Milwaukee, WI: Author.

Rasmussen, J. (1982, Sept. 12). Protecting their own. *Milwaukee Journal*, letter to the editor.

Rassieur, C. (1976). *The Problem Clergy Don't Talk About*. Philadelphia: Westminster Press.

Rebhan, J. (1983). The drug rehabilitation program: Cults in formulation? In D. Halperin (Ed.), *Religion, Sect, and Cult* (pp. 187-198). Littleton, MA: John Wright-PSG.

Redlich, F.C. (1977). The ethics of sex therapy. In W.H. Masters, V.E. Johnson, and R.D. Kolodny (Eds.), *Ethical Issues in Sex Therapy and Research* (pp. 143-157). Boston: Little, Brown.

Redlich, F.C., and Pope, K.S. (1980). Ethics of mental health training. *Journal of Nervous and Mental Disease, 168*, pp. 709-714.

Reich, A. (1951). On countertransference. *International Journal of Psychoanalysis, 32*, pp. 25-31.

Reich, W. (1945). *Character Analysis*. New York: Orgone Institute.

Reid, W. H., and Kang, J.S. (1986). Serious assaults by outpatients or former patients. *American Journal of Psychotherapy, 40 (4)*, pp. 594-599.

Reiser, S.J., Dyck, A.J., and Curran, W.J. (1977). *Ethics in Medicine—Historical Perspectives and Contemporary Concerns.* Cambridge, MA: MIT Press.

Renshaw, D.C. (1977, December). The seductive patient. *J.C.E. Psychiatry,* pp. 41-44.

Renshaw, D.C. (1985). When sex abuse is falsely charged. *Medical Aspects of Human Sexuality, 19,* pp. 116-24.

Rice, D. (1986). Supervision of cotherapy. In F. Kaslow (Ed.), *Supervision and Training—Models, Dilemmas and Challenges* (pp. 119-142). New York: Haworth Press.

Rieker, P., and Carmen, E. (1983). Teaching value clarification: The example of gender and psychotherapy. *American Journal of Psychiatry, 140 (4),* pp. 410-415.

Riepenhoff, R.M. (1985, Feb. 17). Harsher rules urged for abusive therapists. *Milwaukee Journal, Part 2,* p. 3.

Rigby-Weinburg, D.N. (1986). Sexual involvement of women therapists with their women clients. Unpublished paper presented at the eleventh national conference of the Association for Women in Psychology.

Riskin, L. (1979). Sexual relations between psychotherapists and their patients: Toward research or restraint. *California Law Review, 67,* pp. 1000-1027.

Rivera, G. (1988, Sept. 12). Therapy sex abuse. *Geraldo ,* Television Program.

Rix, H. (1986, Oct. 19). When the patient becomes a victim. *The Kansas City Star,* p. 1J, 4J.

Roach, J.R. (1988, Jan. 31). Archbishop explains diocesan policies to combat sexual abuse. *St. Paul Pioneer Press,* p. 3G.

Robertiello, R. (1975). Iatrogenic psychiatric illness. *Journal of Contemporary Psychotherapy, 7,* pp. 3-8.

Robertiello, R., and Schoenewold, G. (1987). *101 Common Therapeutic Blunders.* Northvale, N.J.: Jason Aronson

Robertson, J. (1980). *The Impaired Physician: Building Well-Being.* Chicago: American Medical Association.

Robiner, W., Bobbitt, B., and Fuhrman, M. (1988, Aug.). Development of the Minnesota Multiphasic Supervisory Inventory (MMSI): An instrument for assessing psychology trainees. Paper presented at the convention of the American Psychological Assn., Atlanta, GA.

Robinson, W.L., and Reid, P.T. (1985). Sexual intimacies in psychology revisited. *Professional Psychology: Research and Practice, 16,* p. 512-520.

Robitscher, J. (1980). *The Powers of Psychiatry.* Boston: Houghton Mifflin.

Rockey, L. (1984, March 25). Counselor abuse. *Seattle Times,* p. F-1, F-5.

Rodgers, D.A. 91988). Proposed AASPB board position. Unpublished paper. Montgomery, AL: American Assn. of State Psychology Boards.

Roesler, K.A. (1985, March 27). Personal communication. Assistant District Attorney, La Crosse County. (a)

Roesler, K.A. (1985, Aug. 8). Letter to G. Schoener. .(b)

Rolfe, D.J. (1985). The destructive potential of psychological counseling for pastor and parish. *Pastoral Psychology, 34 (1),* pp. 61-68.

Romeo, S. (1978, June). Dr. Martin Shepard answers his accusers. *Knave,* pp. 14-38.

Rosen, R.D. (1977). *Psychobabble.* New York: Atheneum.

Rosenberg, N.D. (1982, Aug. 15). Society refuses to open records in sex abuse suit. *The Milwaukee Journal,* p. 10.

Rosenberg, N.D. (1984, Oct. 22). Poll finds 110 cases of therapist-client sex. *The Milwaukee Journal.*

Rosenberg, N.D. (1988, June 6). Law cracks down on therapists. *The Milwaukee Journal,* p. D-1.

Rozsnafszky, J. (1979). Beyond schools of psychotherapy: Integrity and maturity in therapy and supervision. *Psychology: Theory, Research and Practice, 16,* pp. 190-198.

Russell, D. (1983). Incidence and prevalence of intrafamilial and extrafamilial sexual abuse of female children. *Child Abuse and Neglect, 7,* pp. 133-146.

Russell, R. (1984). *Social Worker's Awareness of and Response to the Problem of Sexual Contact Between Client and Helping Professional.* Unpublished masters thesis, University of Washington.

Rutkowski, J. (1985, Aug. 9). Personal communication. (Author was Chair, Committee on Judiciary, Wisconsin State Assembly.)

Rutter, P. (in press). *Sex in the Forbidden Zone: When Therapists, Doctors, Clergy, Teachers and Other Men in Power Betray Women's Trust.* Los Angeles: Jeremy P. Tarcher.

Rynearson, R.R., Stewart, W.L., and Bachman, B.A. (1984, March). Physician-patient sexual relationships. *Physician and Patient,* pp. 13-19.

Sadoff, R. (1975). *Forensic Psychiatry: A Practice Guide for Lawyers and Psychiatrists.* Springfield, IL: Charles C. Thomas.

Salholz, E. (1988, May 30). Judgment day for a Harlem minister? *Newsweek,* p. 40.

Sanderson, B. (Ed.) (1989). *It's Never O.K.: A Handbook for Professionals on Sexual Exploitation by Counselors and Therapists.* St. Paul, MN: Minnesota Dept. of Corrections. (a)

Sanderson, B. (1989). Issues for institutions that train counselors and therapists. In B. Sanderson (Ed.), *It's Never O.K.: A Handbook for Professionals on Sexual Exploitation by Counselors and Therapists* (pp. 103-114). St. Paul, MN: Minnesota Dept. of Corrections. (b)

Sanderson, B. (1989). Similarities between counseler-client sexual contact and professor-student sexual contact in counselor training programs. In B. Sanderson (Ed.), *It's Never O.K.: A Handbook for Professionals on Sexual Exploitation by Counselors and Therapists* (pp. 115-123). St. Paul, MN: Minnesota Dept. of Corrections. (c)

Saretsky, L. (1977). Sex-related countertransference issues of a female therapist. *Clinical Psychologist, 30,* pp. 11-12.

Saul, L.J. (1962). The erotic transference. *Psychoanalytic Quarterly, 31,* pp. 54-61.

Savitt, R. (1969). Transference, somatization and symbiotic need. *Journal of the American Psychoanalytic Association, 17,* pp. 1030-1054.

Sawyer, K. (1985, June 24). When priests molest children—a Louisiana case unveils the shame. *The Washington Post National Weekly Edition,* p. 7.

Scheflen, A.E. (1965). Quasi-courtship behavior in psychotherapy. *Psychiatry, 28 (3),* pp. 245-257.

Schoener, G.R. (1974). The chronic caller. *STASH Capsules, 6 (6),* pp. 1-3. Madison, WI: Student Assn. for the Study of Hallucinogens.

Schoener, G.R. (1976). The heterosexual norm in chemical dependency treatment programs: Some personal observations. *STASH Capsules, 8 (1),* pp. 1-4. Madison, WI: Student Assn. for the Study of Hallucinogens.

Schoener, G.R. (1977). The "Heterosexual Norm" revisited. Monograph. Minneapolis, MN: Walk-In Counseling Center.

Schoener, G.R. (1979). *Filing Complaints of Unethical or Unprofessional Conduct Against Counselors and Psychotherapists* (monograph). Minneapolis, MN: Walk-In Counseling Center.

Schoener, G.R. (1979). *Administrative Safeguards to Limit the Risk of Unprofessional Conduct.* Minneapolis, MN: Walk-In Counseling Center.

Schoener, G.R. (1986, Sept.). *Assessment and Development of Rehabilitation Plans for the Counselor or Therapist Who Has Sexually Exploited Clients.* Paper presented at the Sixth National Conference of the National Clearinghouse on Licensure, Enforcement, and Regulation, Denver, Colorado.

Schoener, G.R. (1988, May). Prosecution of therapists for sexual contact with clients. *Minnesota Psychologist,* pp. 6-7. (a)

Schoener, G.R. (1988, Sept.). Prosecution of therapists for sexual contact with clients—some additional thoughts and followup information. *Minnesota Psychologist,* pp. 8-10. (b)

Schoener, G.R. (1988, Nov.). Sexual involvement with clients after termination of psychotherapy: An update. *Minnesota Psychologist,* p. 5. (c)

Schoener, G.R. (1989, Jan.). Sex between therapist and client: Another update. *Minnesota Psychologist,* p. 14. (a)

Schoener, G.R. (1989, March). Trials of psychotherapists for criminal sexual conduct: The continuing saga. *Minnesota Psychologist,* p. 12. (b)

Schoener, G.R. (1989, July). Trials of psychotherapists for criminal sexual conduct: Another update. *Minnesota Psychologist,* pp. 9-10. (c)

Schoener, G.R. (1989, March 1). Apology requested (letter to the editor). *The Journal* (New Ulm, MN), p. 4A. (d)

Schoener, G.R., and Gonsiorek, J.C. (1988). Assessment and development of rehabilitation plans for counselors who have sexually exploited their clients. *Journal of Counseling and Development, 67,* pp. 227-232.

Schoener, G.R., and Milgrom, J.H. (1984, May). *Processing Complaints of Therapist Misconduct.* Paper presented at the Annual Meeting of the American Psychiatric Assn., Los Angeles, California.

Schoener, G.R., and Milgrom, J.H. (1986). A Walk-In Counseling Center approach to therapist sexual misconduct. In A.W. Burgess and C.R. Hartman (Eds.), *Sexual Exploitation of Patients by Health Professionals* (pp. 152-162). New York: Praeger.

Schoener, G.R., Milgrom, J.H., and Gonsiorek, J.C. (1976). *Dealing therapeutically with clients who have been sexually involved with their psychotherapists* (monograph). Minneapolis, MN: Walk-In Counseling Center.

Schoener, G.R., Milgrom, J.H., and Gonsiorek, J.C. (1981). *Responding therapeutically to clients who have been sexually involved with their psychotherapists* (monograph). Minneapolis, MN: Walk-In Counseling Center.

Schoener, G.R., Milgrom, J.H., and Gonsiorek, J.C. (1983). *Responding therapeutically to clients who have been sexually involved with their psychotherapists* (monograph). (Revised). Minneapolis, MN: Walk-In Counseling Center.

Schoener, G.R., Milgrom, J.H., and Gonsiorek, J.C. (1984, Winter). Sexual exploitation of clients by therapists. *Women and Therapy. 3 (3/4)*, pp. 63-69. Also in Carol Mobray (Ed.), *Women & Therapy*, New York: Haworth Press.

Schover, L.R. (1981). Male and female therapists' responses to client sexuality: A source of bias in treatment? In J. Murray and P.R. Abramson (Eds.), *Bias in Psychotherapy* (pp. 256-284). New York: Praeger.

Schultz, J.S., Millilo, M.D., Couchman, J.G., and Lundin, S.C. (1989). Using administrative procedures to prevent sexual exploitation by counselors and therapists. In B. Sanderson (Ed.), *It's Never O.K.: A Handbook for Professionals on Sexual Exploitation by Counselors and Therapists*, pp. 137-139. St. Paul, MN: Minnesota Dept. of Corrections.

Schultz, L.G. (1975, Sept.). Survey of social workers' attitudes and use of body and sexual psychotherapies. *Clinical Social Work Journal*, *3*, pp. 90-99.

Schultz, L.G.,and McGrath, J. (1978). Developing seduction management skills through the use of video vignettes. *Journal of Humanities*, *5*, pp. 70-78.

Schultz, T. (1988, Nov. 30). Dutton sexual conduct trial begins today. *The Journal* (New Ulm, MN), p. 3A. (a)

Schultz, T. (1988, Dec. 1). Testimony opens in Dutton trial. *The Journal* (New Ulm, MN), p. 1. (b)

Schultz, T. (1988, Dec. 1). Dutton case may set legal precedent. *The Journal* (New Ulm, MN), p. 1. (c)

Schultz, T. (1988, Dec. 2). Alleged victim in Dutton case testifies. *The Journal* (New Ulm, MN), p. 1. (d)

Schultz, T. (1988, Dec. 7). Counselors testify in Dutton case. *The Journal* (New Ulm, MN), p. 2. (e)

Schultz, T. (1988, Dec. 8). Dutton takes stand. *The Journal* (New Ulm, MN), p.1. (f)

Schultz, T. (1988, Dec. 9). Dutton convicted on sex charges. *The Journal* (New Ulm, MN), p. 1. (g)

Schultz, T. (1989, Feb. 7). Dutton sentenced. *The Journal* (New Ulm, MN), p. 1.

Schwebel, M. (1955). Why? Unethical practice. *Journal of Counseling Psychology*, *2*, pp. 122-28.

Schwebel, M., Skorina, J., and Schoener, G.R. (1988). *Assisting Impaired Psychologists—Program Development for State Psychological Associations.* Washington, D.C.: American Psychological Assn.

Scruggs, S. (1986). Sexual intimacy in psychotherapy: A review and analysis of the empirical literature and theoretical assumptions. Unpublished doctoral research paper, Rosemead School of Psychology, La Mirada, California.

Seagull, A.A. (1972). Should a therapist have intercourse with patients? *Proceedings, 80th Annual Convention, American Psychiatric Assn.,* pp. 855-56.

Searles, H.F. (1959). Oedipal love in the countertransference. *International Journal of Psychoanalysis, 40,* pp. 180-90.

Searles, H.F. (1977). *Countertransference and Related Subjects.* New York: International University Press.

Sell, J.M., Gottlieb, M.C., and Schoenfeld, L. (1986). Ethical considerations of social/romantic relationships with present and former clients. *Professional Psychology: Research and Practice, 17,* pp. 504-508.

Serban, G. (1981). Sexual activity in therapy: Legal and ethical issues. *American Journal of Psychotherapy, 35,* pp. 76-85.

Sgroi, S.M. (1982). *Handbook of Clinical Intervention in Child Sexual Abuse.* Lexington, MA: Lexington Books.

Shank, B.W., and Johnston, N. (1986, March). SExual harassment: An issue for classroom and field educators. Paper presented at the annual program meeting of the Council on Social Work Education, Miami, Florida.

Shearer, L. (1981, Aug. 23). Sex between patient and physician. *Parade,* p. 8.

Shepard, M. (1971). *The Love Treatment: Sexual Intimacy Between Patients and Psychotherapist.* New York: Peter H. Wyden.

Shepard, M. (1972, April). The love treatment: The pros and cons of patient-therapist sex. *Forum,* pp. 18-25. (a)

Shepard, M. (1972). *A Psychiatrist's Head.* New York: Peter H. Wyden (Republished as *Memoirs of a Defrocked Psychoanalyst)* (b)

Shepard, M. (1975). *Fritz.* New York: E.P. Dutton.

Shimberg, B. (1986, Spring). Sexual abuse by therapists a powder keg issue. *The Psychotherapy Newsletter, 4 (1),* pp. 1-4.

Shor, J., and Sanville, J. (1974). Erotic provocations and dalliances in psychotherapeutic practice: Some clinical cues for preventing and repairing therapist-patient collusions. *Clinical Social Work Journal, 2,* pp. 83-95.

Shortt, S.E.D. (Ed.) (1982). *Psychiatric Illness in Physicians.* Springfield, IL: Charles C. Thomas.

Siassi, I., and Thomas, M. (1973). Physicians and the new sexual freedom. *American Journal of Psychiatry, 130,* pp. 1256-57.

Siegel, S. (1986, Spring). Is registration the answer? *Psychotherapy Newsletter, 4 (1),* pp. 4-6.

Siegel, S. (1987, March). Stop abuse. *Woman's Newspaper* (Princeton, N.J.) No. 60, p. 1, 4, 5, 7-8. (a)

Siegel, S. (1987, Oct.). About re-evaluation counseling... *American Mental Health Counselors Association News, 11 (2),* p. 9. (b)

Siegel, S. (1988). Laws that help when therapists do harm. *Student Lawyer, 17 (4),* pp. 32-38.

Simon, R.I. (1985, May). Sexual misconduct of therapists: A cause for civil and criminal action. *Trial, 21,* pp. 46-51.

Simon, R.I. (1987). *Clinical Psychiatry and the Law.* Washington, D.C.: American Psychiatric Press. (a)

Simon, R.I. (1987). A clinical philosophy for the (unduly) defensive psychiatrist. *Psychiatric Annals, 17,* pp. 197-200. (b)

Singer, M. (1979, Jan.). Coming out of the Cults. *Psychology Today,* pp. 72-82.

Singer-Kaplan, H. (1974). *The New Sex Therapy.* New York: Brunner/ Mazel.

Sinnett, E.R., and Linford, O. (1982). Processing of formal complaints against psychologists. *Psychological Reports, 50,* pp. 535-544.

Slakter, E. (Ed.). (1987). *Countertransference.* Northvale, N.J.: Jason Aronson.

Skovholt, T.M., and Ronnestad, M.H. (1986). Optimal and alternative stages of counselor/therapist development. Unpublished manuscript.

Slovenko, R. (1980). Legal issues in psychotherapy supervision. In K. Hess (Ed.), *Psychotherapy Supervision: Theory, Research and Practice* (pp. 453-473). New York: John Wiley.

Smith, A. (1985, Feb. 24). The abusive therapist—three case histories. *The Ann Arbor News,* pp. F-1, F-12.

Smith, H., and Harris, L. (1982, Jan. 20-26). Group to fight psych. hype. *The Village Voice, 27 (4),* p. 1.

Smith, J.T. (1986). *Medical Malpractice—Psychiatric Care.* Colorado Springs, CO: Shepards/McGraw Hill.

Smith, J.T., and Bisbing, S.B. (1987, Dec.). Sexual Exploitation of patients. *Trial,* pp. 65-70.

Smith, J.T., and Bisbing, S.B. (1988). *Sexual Exploitation by Health Care and Other Professionals, (2nd Edition).* Potomac, MD: Legal Medicine Press.

Smith, S. (1984). The sexually abused patient and the abusing therapist: A study in sadomasochistic relationships. *Psychoanalytic Psychology, 1,* pp. 89-98.

Smith, S. (1985, May 20). Guilt lingers, lives damaged after "therapy." *Dallas Times Herald,* p. 1C. (a)

Smith, S. (1985, May 20). One woman's five-year hell of drugs, sex. *Dallas Times Herald,* p. 1C. (b)

Smith, S. (1985, May 21). Patients' complaints seldom put therapists in jail. *Dallas Times Herald,* p. 1D. (c)

Smith, S. (1985, May 22). Sexual overtures often test counselors' ethical resolve. *Dallas Times Herald,* p. 1F. (d)

Smith, S. (1985, May 22). Angry woman unites clients abused by their therapists. *Dallas times Herald*, p. 1F. (e)

Smith, S. (1985, May 22). How to avoid pitfalls of hiring professional help. *Dallas Times Herald*, p. 1F. (f)

Smith, S., and Laker, B. (1985, May 20). Epidemic of abuse devastates patients, hurts the profession. *Dallas Times Herald*, p. 1C.

Sonne, J.L. (1989). An example of group therapy for victims of therapist-client sexual intimacy. In G. Gabbard (Ed.), *Sexual Exploitation in Professional Relationships*, pp. 101-113. Washington, D.C.: American Psychiatric Press.

Sonne, J., Meyer, C.B., Borys, D., and Marshall, V. (1985). Clients' reactions to sexual intimacy in therapy. *American Journal of Orthopsychiatry, 55*, pp. 183-189.

Spector, P. (1983). *Sexual Exploitation by Therapists: Perspectives, Problems, and Public Policy*. Unpublished paper, Humphrey Institute for Public Affairs, University of Minnesota.

Squires, S. (1986, June). Should you keep your therapist? *American Health*, pp. 72-77.

Stapp, J., Tucker, A.M., and VandenBos, G.R. (1985). Census of psychological personnel: 1983. *American Psychologist, 40*, pp. 1317-1351.

State of Minnesota, Court of Appeals. (1989). Unpublished opinion in appeal of State of Minnesota, appellant, vs. Robert Eugene Dutton, Respondent. C8-89-680. Filed July 18, 1989. Office of Appellate Courts, St. Paul, Minnesota.

Stefanson, A. (1989). Countertransference issues for therapists working with sexually exploitative therapists. In B. Sanderson (Ed.), *It's Never O.K.: A Handbook for Professionals on Sexual Exploitation by Counselors and Therapists*, pp. 91-93. St. Paul, MN: Minnesota Dept. of Corrections.

Stoltenberg, C. (1981). Approaching supervision from a developmental perspective: The counselor complexity model. *Journal of Counseling Psychology, 28*, pp. 59-65.

Stoltenberg, C., and Delworth, U. (1987). *Supervising Counselors and Therapists*. San Francisco: Jossey-Bass.

Stone, A.A. (1976). The legal implication of sexual activity between psychiatrist and patient. *American Journal of Psychiatry, 133*, pp. 1138-41.

Stone, A.A. (1983). Sexual misconduct by psychiatrists: The ethical and clinical dilemma of confidentiality. *American Journal of Psychiatry, 140*, pp. 195-97.

Stone, L.G. (1980). *A Study of the Relationships Among Anxious Attachment, Ego Functioning, and Female Patients' Vulnerability to Sexual Involvement with their Male Psychotherapists*. Unpublished doctoral dissertation, California School of Professional Psychology, Los Angeles.

Stone, M.H. (1975). Management of unethical behavior in a psychiatric hospital staff. *American Journal of Psychotherapy, 29*, pp. 391-401.

Stone, M.H. (1976). Boundary violations between therapist and patient. *Psychiatric Annals, 6*, pp. 8-31.

Stoner, C., and Parke, J. (1977). *All God's Children*. New York: Penguin.

Striano, J. (1987). *How to Find a Good Psychotherapist—A Consumer Guide.* Santa Barbara, CA: Professional Press.

Striano, J. (1988). *Can Psychotherapists Hurt You?* Santa Barbara, California: Professional Press.

Strosahl, K., and Jacobson, N. (1986). Training and supervision of behavior therapists. In F. Kaslow (Ed.), *Supervision and Training—Models, Dilemmas and Challenges* (pp. 183-206). New York: Haworth Press.

Styczynski, L. (1980). The transition from supervisee to supervisor. In K. Hess (Ed.), *Psychotherapy Supervision: Theory, Research and Practice* (pp. 29-40). New York: John Wiley.

Sullivan, M. (1986). Personal communication, May 24, 1986, re: Norman Moore vs. Connie Poor, 3AM-84-12139, 3rd Judicial District, Anchorage, Alaska.

Summit, R.C. (1985). The child sexual abuse accommodation syndrome. *Child Abuse and Neglect, 7.*

Sundstrom, I. (1977, October). Sex and the therapist. *MPLS Magazine,* pp. 39-41, 79-83.

Tardiff, K. (1984). Violence: The psychiatric patient. In J. T. Turner (Ed.), *Violence in the Medical Care Setting* (pp. 33-55). Rockville, MD: Aspen Systems.

Task Force on Sexual Exploitation by Counselors and Therapists. (1985). *Legislative Report.* St. Paul, MN: Minnesota Dept. of Corrections.

Task Force on Sexual Misconduct by Psychotherapists. (1985). Goals. Adopted July 1, 1985. Milwaukee: Wisconsin Psychological Assn.

Tauber, E.S. (1979). Countertransference reexamined. In L. Epstein and A.H. Feiner (Eds.), *Countertransference* (pp. 59-70). New York: Jason Aronson.

Taylor, B.H., and Wagner, N.W. (1976). Sex between therapists and clients: A review and analysis. *Professional Psychology, 7,* pp. 593-601.

Temerlin, M.K., and Temerlin, J.W. (1982). Psychotherapy cults: An iatrogenic perversion. *Psychotherapy: Theory, Research, and Practice, 19 (2),* pp. 131-141.

Tennov, D. (1975). *Psychotherapy: The Hazardous Cure.* New York: Abelard-Schuman.

Thompson, P., Shapiro, M., Nielsen, L., and Peterson, M. (1989). Supervision strategies to prevent sexual abuse by therapists and counselors. In B. Sanderson (Ed.), *It's Never O.K.: A Handbook for Professionals on Sexual Exploitation by Counselors and Therapists,* pp. 19-26. St. Paul, MN: Minnesota Dept. of Corrections.

Torrey, E.F. (1986). *Witchdoctors and Psychiatrists.* Northvale, N.J.: Jason Aronson.

Tower, L.E. (1956). Countertransference. *Journal of the American Psychoanalytic Association, 4,* pp. 224-255.

Trent, C.L. (1978). Psychiatric malpractice insurance and its problems: An overview. In W.E. Barton and C.J. Sanborn (Eds.), *Law and the Mental Health Professions* (pp. 101-117). New York: International University.

Turkington, C. (1984, December). Women therapists not immune to sexual involvement suits. *APA Monitor, 14,* p. 15.

Tymchuk, A.J., Drapkin, R.S., Ackerman, A.B., Major, S.M., Coffman, E.W., and Baum, M.S. (1979). Survey of training in ethics in APA-approved clinical psychology programs. *American Psychologist, 34,* pp. 1168-1170.

Tymchuk, A.J., Drapkin, R.S., Major-Kingsley, S., Ackerman, A., Coffman, E., and Baum, M.S. (1982). Ethical decision-making and psychologists' attitudes towards training in ethics. *Professional Psychology, 13,* pp. 412-421.

Ulanov, A.B. (1979). Follow-up treatment in cases of patient-therapist sex. *Journal of the American Academy of Psychoanalysis, 7,* pp. 101-110.

Utne Reader. (1987, March/April). Psychotherapy, pp. 24-47.

Valiquette, M. (1989). *Les sèquelles psychologiques de l'intimitè sexuelle en psychothèrapie.* Unpublished doctoral dissertation. Department of Psychology, University of Montreal.

Van Hoose, W., and Kottler, J. (1985). *Ethical and Legal Issues in Counseling and Psychotherapy, 2nd Ed.* San Francisco: Jossey-Bass.

VandenBos, G.R., and Stapp, J. (1983). Service providers in psychology: Results of the 1982 APA Human Resources Survey. *American Psychologist, 38,* pp. 1330-1352.

Vasquez, M. (1988, Aug.). Ethics training and monitoring in internship settings. Paper presented at the 96th annual conference of the American Psychological Assn., Atlanta, GA. (a)

Vasquez, M. (1988). Counselor-client sexual contact: Implications for ethics training. *Journal of Counseling and Development, 67,* pp. 238-241. (b)

Vasquez, M., and Kitchener, K. (1988). Introduction to special feature. *Journal of Counseling and Development, 67,* pp. 214-216.

Veague, P. (1974). Quasi-courting in the clinical interview. *Smith College Studies in Social Work, 44,* pp. 101-109.

Venn, J. (1988). Misuse of hypnosis in sexual contexts: Two case reports. *International Journal of Clinical and Experimental Hypnosis, 36 (1),* pp. 12-18.

Vinson, J.S. (1984). *Sexual Contact with Psychotherapists: A Study of Client Reactions and Complaint Procedures.* Unpublished doctoral dissertation, California School of Professional Psychology.

Vinson, J.S. (1987). Use of complaint procedures in cases of therapist-patient sexual contact. *Professional Psychology: Research and Practice, 18,* p. 159-64.

Voth, H.M. (1972). Love affair between doctor and patient. *American Journal of Psychotherapy, 26,* pp. 394-400.

Vrazo, F., and Shaw, D. (1985, June 23). Attacking health-care sexual abuse. *The Philadelphia Inquirer,* p. G-1.

Wagner, N. (1972). *Ethical Concerns of Medical Students.* Unpublished paper presented at the 1972 western workshop of the Center for the Study of Sex Education in Medicine, Santa Barbara, CA.

Walker, E., and Young, T.D. (1986). *A Killing Cure.* New York: Henry Holt.

Walker, E., Shephert, G., Hubbard, B., and Casey, D. (1983). *Advocates Against Psychic Abuse— Prevention and Protection Guide—Vol. 1.* Psychiatric and Psychological Mental Health Services. San Diego: Advocates Against Psychic Abuse.

Wand, B. (1984). Financial resources and the regulatory activities of professional licensing bodies in psychology. *Professional Practice of Psychology: Legal, Regulatory and Licensure Issues, 5 (1),* pp. 41-50.

Warren, Possley, and Tybor. (1987, Jan. 6). Shocking detour on road of fame. *Chicago Tribune,* p. 1E.

Washington Council of Churches. (1984). *Sexual Contact by Pastors and Pastoral Counselors in Professional Relationships.* Seattle, WA: Author.

Watterson, D.J. (1982). Psychiatric illness in the medical professional: Incidence in relation to sex and field of practice. In S.E.D. Shortt (Ed.), *Psychiatric Illness in Physicians,* pp. 19-35. Springfield, IL: Charles C. Thomas.

WCCO-TV. (1989, Feb. 6 and 7). Sexual malpractice. A television special. Minneapolis, Minnesota.

Webb, C. (1987). *Forgive Me.* New York: Putnam-Berkeley.

Weber, M. (1972, Jan.). Should you sleep with your therapist? The raging controversy in American psychiatry. *Vogue,* pp. 78-79.

Weiner, M.F. (1978). *Therapist Disclosure: The Use of Self in Psychotherapy.* Woburn, MA: Butterworths.

Welfel, E., and Lipsitz, N. (1984). The ethical behavior of professional psychologists: A critical analysis of the research. *The Counseling Psychologist, 12 (3),* pp. 31-40.

Werrbach, J., and Gilbert, L.A. (1987). Men, gender stereotyping, and psychotherapy: Therapists' perceptions of male clients. *Professional Psychology: Research and Practice, 18 (6),* pp. 562-566.

Wessler, R., and Ellis, A. (1986). Supervision in rational-emotive therapy. In K. Hess (Ed.) *Psychotherapy Supervision: Theory, Research and Practice,* pp. 181-191. New York: John Wiley.

West. (1969). Ethical psychiatry and biosocial humanism. *American Journal of Psychiatry, 126,* pp. 228-29.

White, W.L. (1978). *A Systems Response to Staff Burn-Out.* Rockville, MD: HCS, Inc.

White, W.L. (1979). *Incest in the Organizational Family: The Unspoken Issue in Staff and Program Burn-Out.* Rockville, MD: HCS, Inc.

White, W.L. (1986). *Incest in the Organizational Family: The Unspoken Issue in Staff and Program Burn-Out.* Rockville, MD: HCS, Inc.

Wichman, L. (1989, Aug.). Sex-sick shrinks. *Hustler,* pp. 32-34, 42, 92, 96-97, 104.

Widiger, T.A., and Rorer, L.G. (1984). The responsible psychotherapist. *American Psychologist, 39,* pp. 503-515.

Wiener, D. (1975). *A Consumer's Guide to Psychotherapy.* New York: Hawthorn Books.

Wilbert, J.R., and Fulero, S.M. (1988). Impact of malpractice litigation on professional psychology: Survey of practitioners. *Professional Psychology: Research and Practice, 19,* pp. 379-82.

Wisconsin Psychological Assn. (1985). Task Force on Misconduct by Psychotherapists— Membership List.

Wolff, W. (Ed.) (1956). *Contemporary Psychotherapists Examine Themselves.* Springfield, IL: Charles C. Thomas.

Wood, B., Klein, S., Cross, H.J., Lammers, C.J., and Elliot, J.K. (1985). Impaired practitioners: Psychologists' opinions about prevalence and proposals for intervention. *Professional Psychology: Research and Practice, 16,* pp. 843-50.

Worthington, E.L. (1987). Changes in supervision as counselors and supervisors gain experience: A review. *Professional Psychology: Research and Practice, 18,* pp. 189-208.

Wright, R.W. (1981). Psychologists and professional liability (malpractice) insurance: A retrospective review. *American Psychologist, 36,* pp. 1485-1493.

Wright, R.W. (1985). Who needs enemies. *Psychotherapy in Private Practice, 3,* pp. 111-118.

WSMV-TV. (1989). Untitled series on abuse by health professionals. Nashville, TN.

Wynn, K. (1977). If you can survive treatment you can survive anything! The inside dope. In Division of Substance Abuse, State Dept. of Health, California, *Human sexuality and drug treatment: A closer look.* Sacramento, CA.

Yates, A., and Musty, T. (1988). Preschool children's erroneous allegations of sexual molestation. *American Journal of Psychiatry, 145 (8),* pp. 989-992.

Zack, M. (1987, May 8). Byzantine Catholic priest pleads guilty to sexually abusing boys. (Minneapolis) *Star Tribune,* p. 1B.

Zelen, S. (1985). Sexualization of therapeutic relationships: The dual vulnerability of the patient and therapist. *Psychotherapy: Theory, Research and Practice, 23,* pp. 178-185.

Zicherman, V. (1984). Sociocultural considerations in the emergence of sexual feelings in male patients seeing female therapists. *Journal of the American Academy of Psychoanalysis, 12,* pp. 545-551.

Ziskin, J. (1984). Malingering of psychological disorders. *Behavioral Sciences and the Law, 2,* pp. 39-49. (a)

Ziskin, J. (1984). *Coping with Psychiatric and Psychological Testimony, Vols. I and II, (3rd Ed.).* Venice, CA: Law and Psychology Press. (b)

APPENDIX A

The Incest Analogy: A comparison of the Incest Dynamic in the nuclear
family with that in the Organizational Family

Reprinted with permission from:

White, William (1986) *Incest in the Organizational Family*

   pp. 84-88
   published by:

   Lighthouse Training Institute
   702 West Chestnut
   Bloomington, Illinois 61701
   (309) 827-6026

Do not reproduce without permission of William White.

THE INCEST ANALOGY

To those readers not familiar with the family dynamics seen in cases of consummated incest, the author's use of the incest analogy may be both confusing and offensive. This analogy was not chosen out of flippancy or poor taste. The author's contention is that the process of organizational closure described in this book directly parallels the family dynamics often noted (in the professional literature and in my clinical experience) in cases of consummated incest. It was by comparing my clinical work counseling incest victims and their families with my consulting work with organizations that I noted the similarity in group dynamics. In the space below, I have charted a number of these similarities, some of which will be explored in greater detail in the chapter.

AREA OF COMPARISON	INCEST DYNAMIC IN THE NUCLEAR FAMILY	INCEST DYNAMIC IN THE ORGANIZATIONAL FAMILY
Degree of closure	Family members restricted from outside transactions	Professional and social closure precede sexual closure
	Social closure often precedes consummation of incest	Same
	Outside world viewed as evil and threatening	Same
	Over-protection of family members; e.g., no dating or boyfriends of daughters; victims treated with hostility and jealousy	Outside intimate partners of organizational family members may be treated with hostility and jealousy
	Closure may be secondary to family stigma; e.g., alcoholism, psychiatric illness, etc.	Closure may be related to stigma....
	Inherent message that all needs of family members can be met inside family	Same
Family Image	Preoccupation with looking good on the outside	Same
	No talk rules; distrust talking to outsiders about family	Same
	Incongruence between external image and internal emotional reality	Same
Timing of Incest	Father-daughter incest is often preceded by or concurrent with deterioration in husband-wife sexual relationship	Sexual relationships between organizational family members often preceded by deterioration in outside marital/intimate relationships

Type of Relationship	Father aggressor may try to establish pseudo-marital relationship with daughter; e.g., courting behavior, daughter's interest in boyfriends seen as infidelity or unfaithfulness	Pseudo-marital relations may be established as part of sexual relations

Problems in outside relationships played out in incestuous relationship |
Restraining Agent	Lack of an effective restraining agent, e.g., physical absence or illness of mother in case of father-daughter incest	Lack of an effective restraining agent, e.g., absence of anyone with sufficient power to check supervisor as sexual aggressor
Distortion of Sexual Culture	Violation of intimacy barriers	Same
	Breakdown of sexual privacy and distance	Same
	Consummation of incest last stage of this breakdown	Same
Value System	Value system not sufficient to restrain sexual contact	Same
	Where value system is present, there may be incestuous dynamic without consummation of incest	Where value system is present, there may be professional and social closure without sexual closure
Individuation	All aspects of the incestuous dynamic violate the victim's need for individuation, e.g., personal and sexual safety at home to begin the process of meeting needs and establish identity separate from family	Adults may regress from the emotional ingrown atmosphere of the closed organizational family thus reversing their process of individuation; identity and self-esteem needs are all tied to the emotional life of the organization
	Aggressor dominates life of the victim—emotional suffocation	Same
Sequential victimization	In father-daughter incest, sons may mimic the behavior of the father and also become sexually aggressive with the victim	Sexual relationships in the closed organizational family rarely occur in isolation; the pattern usually involves multiple concurrent and/or sequential sexual relationships between organizational members
Response of non-partici-pants	First denial—"conspiracy of silence"	Same
	Rage, shame, jealousy	Same
	Identification with aggressor or victim	Same

| Extrusion | Incest increases the extrusion of individual family members from the family | Same |
| | Sons who challenge the sexual supremacy of their fathers are extruded from the family | Staff who challenge the sexual supremacy of supervisory/ management staff are extruded from the organizational family |

The above are just a few of the parallels between the incestuous dynamic in nuclear and organizational families that will be explored in this chapter. One of the most important aspects of this discussion is that the meeting of sexual needs inside the boundary of the family is the last stage in the progressive closure of both nuclear and organizational families. Our concern is not simply with the sexual activity at the end of this continuum. The entire process of closure— each progressive step of this incestuous dynamic—can have powerfully debilitating effects on nuclear and organizational family members and the overall health of these systems regardless of whether the stage of sexual intimacy has been reached.

APPENDIX B

Schoener, Gary (1979)   "Filing Complaints of Unethical or Unprofessional Conduct Against Counselors and Psychotherapists"

Filing Complaints Of Unethical Or Unprofessional Conduct Against Counselors And Psychotherapists

April 1979

By: Gary Schoener, Licensed Psychologist
and Executive Director,
Walk-In Counseling Center, Inc.

Introduction

This paper is designed to assist clients, therapists, administrators, and other concerned persons who are exploring the possible filing of complaints related to sexual involvement between a client and psychotherapist or counselor. Many of the mechanisms discussed would also be appropriate for situations in which other types of unprofessional or unethical conduct are at issue.

The first and most important responsibility when confronted with such a situation is to assist the client in obtaining appropriate support and/or therapeutic help. As much as the filing of a complaint may help protect other clients as well as assist the client who is complaining to resolve his/her feelings about the situation, it is important not to coerce clients into filing such complaints. Suggestions for working therapeutically with such situations is contained in another paper: "Dealing Therapeutically With Women Who Have Been Sexually Involved With Their Psychotherapists" (available from the Walk-In Counseling Center, Inc.).

The first three sections of this paper deal with: Types of Complaints and Remedies, Third Party Complaints, and Some Words of Warning. Most of this paper is devoted to specific procedures for filing complaints about different types of practitioners. Please note that some of this information may change over time and should be double-checked before assuming it to be completely accurate. Procedures, for example, change with changes in law or regulation. Practitioner groups covered are:

pp. 5-6	Chemical Dependency & Drug Abuse Counselors
pp. 6-7	Clergy/Pastoral Counselors
pp. 7-8	Marriage & Family Counselors
pp. 8-10	Psychiatric Nurses/Nurse Therapists
pp. 10-14	Psychiatrists
pp. 14-16	Psychologists
pp. 16-17	Social Workers

Types of Complaints and Remedies

1.   .Personal Complaint to Counselor/Therapist: A client, concerned person, or attorney may ask to discuss the situation with the counselor/therapist or write a letter of complaint. While this rarely does any good at times it is the only possible vehicle for complaint—e.g., the case of an unlicensed "counselor" who is not a professional who is doing private practice independently of any clinic or agency.

In situations where seductiveness rather than actual sexual involvement is alleged and where the therapist/counselor is basically a healthy person who is inexperienced, careless, or who had poor insight about his/her behavior, a meeting with the client and another professional can be helpful and useful. It is best, however, when combined with #2 below, which is possible in agencies and clinics.

2. Complaint to Supervisor: If the counselor/therapist works in an agency or clinic and has a supervisor for his/her clinical work, a complaint can be directed to the supervisor. We have had a number of successful meetings involving the client, the therapist whose work is being questioned, his/her supervisor, and one of our staff.

   This has the advantage that it can bring about closer supervision of work and provide for quicker response than any other remedy. It does not, and should not, preclude other remedies, such as ethics and licensure complaints.

3. Complaint to Administrator or Employer: If there is no supervisor, if the supervisor is unresponsive, or for other reasons it may be useful to lodge a complaint with the Director, Administrator, Board of Directors, etc.

4. Complaint to a Funding Body: If satisfaction is not obtained from a complaint to program staff or if the behavior in question appears to be agency policy complaints may be made to the body which funds the program (e.g., the mental health or chemical dependency division of county or state government; a private foundation; Dept. of Public Welfare; etc.).

5. Complaint to a Regulatory Agency: If the situation is as with #4 above, if the program/agency is licensed or certified, a complaint can be filed with the regulatory agency. For example, the Dept. of Public Welfare licenses chemical dependency programs and some mental health programs and group homes; the State Dept. of Health licenses nursing homes.

6. Ethics Complaint: Complaints of unethical conduct can be filed with ethics committees of professional organizations insofar as they exist. Most, unfortunately, do not have very strong sanctions available to them.

7. Licensure Complaint: When a professional is licensed or certified, or applying for such status, a complaint to the appropriate licensing body can result in sanctions, including the loss of the right to practice within the state.

8. Civil Suit: If other remedies don't work and/or if the client wishes redress for damages, and if the client does not fear publicity, a civil suit is a possibility. These generally take the form of malpractice suits which require proof that the professional had a duty to perform vis a vis the client (including the fact that the person was clearly a client), that he/she failed to perform this duty, and that damages resulted. This remedy has serious drawbacks including the problem that it often takes years of frustration and may result in public exposure once the suit is filed. If it gets to court there may be further exposure, and even if the client is successful, appeals can drag it out for additional time.

9. Criminal Complaint: Under certain circumstances therapists who sexually exploit clients have been criminally charged and successfully prosecuted. While Masters and Johnson have suggested that such behavior should be prosecuted as rape, we do not know of instances where this has happened, although assault has been charged along with criminal sexual misconduct. Thus far we know of cases which have either occurred in a hospital or

residential setting or where the client is a minor. The use of medication, shock therapy, or hypnosis has been cited as coercive behavior in those settings.

We know of no situation in which a therapist has been charged with prostitution for having sex with clients, although in at least one case an alleged prostitute has used the defense that she was providing "therapy," and some alleged houses of prostitution call themselves "counseling centers."

10. Complaint to the News Media: While not to be recommended and risky under the best of circumstances, on occasion complaints have been made to the news media and brought about useful outcomes possibly unobtainable through other means. An example would be a situation in which a client's story was told by a reporter, without identifying those involved, as part of an article on sexual exploitation of clients, which leads agencies to review their policies in this regard and alerts consumers to the parameters of ethical professional behavior. Another example would be the investigation of a large and powerful drug abuse treatment program which had become an isolated, armed, cult.

In most cases, the media's proper role, and the one they prefer to play, is to publicize the actions of a public or professional body or court which has reviewed a case and issued findings. In addition, it is critical for professionals and professional organizations to utilize the news media to reach consumers with information about professional practices and ethical issues.

THIRD PARTY COMPLAINTS

As will be clear from the sections to follow, complaint procedures are complicated and can be quite threatening to clients, especially to those who have been "wounded" by unethical professionals. Contrary to popular fiction, therapists who exploit clients not infrequently pick on clients who have relatively serious problems and who are not good at taking care of themselves under the best of circumstances. Clients and professionals both are often fearful or distrustful of the available complaint mechanisms, often assuming that professionals will "stick together and cover up."

When clients are fearful or reluctant, a concerned professional or agency can start the ball rolling for both the client and the professional body by filing what we've termed a "third party complaint." Although formal action usually must await an actual complaint from the client, in some instances preliminary investigation can occur when a complaint is filed by someone other than the client.

Such a complaint takes the form of a letter which outlines, for example, the case of Ms. X or Mr. Y, giving as much detail as can be done without violating confidentiality. We have done this on occasion, after obtaining the client's permission, and found that seeing a copy in print has served as encouragement to clients to be willing to talk on the phone with a professional or attorney representing a licensure board. Usually such contact proves to be reassuring and leads to face-to-face meetings and the filing of a complaint. Even if the client never comes forward, the Board may have other complaints on file against the same professional and the information may aid in the investigation.

In some instances clients have told us that had such a step-wise procedure not been utilized, they would never have had enough courage to file a complaint. Some have indicated that in retrospect one of the major barriers they faced was the difficulty in spelling out the details and presenting them in a fashion which would clearly describe their experiences. Our initial letter helped organize their allegations, making it easier for them to write out their eventual complaint letter.

At present clients must often take substantial risks, real or perceived, when making a complaint, for little in the way of possible tangible gain, so professionals should lend all the assistance they can. It is our responsibility to help clean up our own field in any way possible. Beyond the obvious need to protect clients and to prevent additional mental health problems which may be caused by unethical practitioners, our own ability to practice and our own malpractice insurance will be in jeopardy should the present trends continue. Last but not least, many clients report that filing a complaint did more for their personal growth and recovery than even follow-up therapy.

Do not, however, confuse assistance and advocacy with investigation or "police work." While 41 out of 42 cases our center has handled at the date of this writing were eventually corroborated by other exploited clients or the therapist himself, we always try to avoid making a judgment about the truthfulness of a client's story. That is for a professional body or licensure board to determine. Your role is to see that the story is heard where it needs to be heard.

SOME WORDS OF WARNING

There are many situations in which the client, advocate, concerned person, and/or therapist should consider obtaining legal consultation before proceeding with a complaint.

Raising questions about a counselor/therapist's competence or performance can lead to damages such as loss of job, reputation, clients, agency funding as well as mental distress and marital or relationship disruption. While most therapists prefer to avoid untoward publicity, they too can sue for damages based on slander, libel, interference with their right to contract or do business, etc. While in most situations acting in good faith and speaking or writing the truth is a defense, such is not always the case. Even if one successfully defends oneself against such a suit, the legal fees can impose a severe penalty on the well-meaning crusader. Furthermore, the only defense in such a suit may be the testimony and cross-examination of a client who has sought to avoid publicity and exposure. Countersuit for suits with malicious intent is difficult, and you could end up winning the suit and still being out the $10,000 in fees.

Do not promise, or yourself expect, justice. There are many pitfalls in legal proceedings. If there is a lone client complaining, even if he/she is convincing, the odds are stacked in favor of the therapist.

Both verbally and in notes, learn to use the words "alleged" and "claimed" to accurately reflect the fact that you are not independently verifying things about which you lack first-hand knowledge. No matter how believable a client is or how many negative things you have heard on the "grapevine" about the therapist involved, his/her story is still a set of allegations.

You do not have to assert the correctness of the client's story or how believable it is...only that it is important that the proper body or institution hear it and respond to it. Don't be apologetic—an agency or professional should be grateful that you are willing to bring any complaint to their attention directly rather than having it result in rumors on the "grapevine" or unspoken distrust.

CHEMICAL DEPENDENCY AND DRUG ABUSE COUNSELORS

At present the closest things to professional organizations in this field are the Minnesota Chemical Dependency Association (MCDA) and Minnesota Association of Counselors on Alcoholism (MACA). Quite recently, the MCDA has formally accepted a code of ethics which has also been adopted by MACA, although many of those working in the field do not seem to know of its existence. While it is good to see the field finally develop some sort of a code, it is far less adequate than any other existing code and specifies little which would be useful in setting standards of conduct or identifying unethical conduct. Sexual involvement with clients is not addressed, nor is seductive behavior mentioned. It is unfortunate that the authors of the code did not make any apparent uses of previously developed codes.

This code of ethics has been published in connection with the newly developed certification procedure for "Chemical Dependency Practitioners" and is available in the "Certification Manual for Chemical Dependency Practitioners." This credentialing is voluntary and has no foundation in law at present, although the State Dept. of Health is developing a Rule requiring registration of chemical dependency counselors which may simply incorporate the procedure developed by MCDA and MACA. This Rule could be in effect as early as November of 1979 if it is approved. At present there are no committees for processing complaints or procedures for making a complaint, although such committees are expected to be developed at some time in the future. For information, contact:

Certification: Chemical Dependency Practitioner
Credentialing Board
P. O. Box 4457
St. Paul, MN 55104

or: Riley Goodwin, MCDA credentialing coordinator
646-7231

Registration: Larry Wood
Manpower Division, MN Dept. of Health
717 Delaware Street S.E.
Minneapolis, MN 55440
296-5532

Many treatment facilities are licensed by the State, but there are no rules forbidding sex with clients, although members of the review committees have indicated privately that sex with clients "has no place in treatment programs." At present contracts written by the State do not forbid sex with clients. (The latter is mentioned because several years ago the State of California's Substance Abuse Division took a public stance against such behavior and added language to contracts with treatment programs forbidding it.)

There has been some concern about the vulnerability of clients in the alcoholism field as evidenced by the traditional avoidance within Alcoholics Anonymous (AA) of having male sponsors for female members and vice versa. A study of a large drug abuse treatment system funded by the Drug Abuse Council in 1974 documented widespread exploitation of women including the use of coercive tactics to bring about sex between clients and counselors as well as between clients. Our center has received a number of complaints from clients of local programs and practitioners.

Until procedures are established for filing complaints to a certification committee or registration board (assuming one is established), complaints are only possible to the program itself, to a funding body, or to the Division of the Dept. of Public Welfare which licenses programs (assuming that the program is licensed).

Unfortunately, the growing number of chemical dependency counselors in private practice are immune from the sort of complaint which can be made to or about an agency.

CLERGY/PASTORAL COUNSELORS

Members of the clergy do a considerable amount of counseling and are not infrequently found among the staff of community mental health centers and hospitals. Some have professional degrees in addition to their divinity degrees so that complaints can go through professional channels.

In the case of a clergyman working in a church, synagogue, or cathedral, complaints of sexual involvement with counselees or church-body members may be handled as either a disciplinary issue within the church denomination or as possible violations of the clergyman's contract with the church body.

Various statements of ethical principles exist within different religious denominations. Some deal with sexual involvement with counselees. Many Christian seminaries utilize a text which contains a case of unethical conduct involving a relationship between a clergyman and a church member (i.e. Casebook on Church and Society by Keith Bridston & Fred Foulkes).

In the case of a clergyman working within a religious institution, a complaint can be filed with:

1. THE GOVERNING BODY OF THE INSTITUTION: for instance, the Church Council in a Christian Church, the Board of Directors of a Synagogue, etc.

2. THE BODY RESPONSIBLE FOR MINISTERIAL STANDING OR THE ORGANIZATION IN WHICH THE CONGREGATION HAS MEMBERSHIP: for instance, the Pastoral Relations Committee of the United Presbyterian Church, Committee on Church and Ministry of the United Church of Christ, etc.

Within the past three years we are aware of one clergyman who lost his position due to alleged sexual misconduct with counselees in the Twin Cities area. We are also aware of the case of a divinity school graduate doing private counseling who was confronted about such behavior but against whom no action was possible since he was not connected to either an agency or church.

MARRIAGE AND FAMILY COUNSELORS:

Unfortunately, the use of the terms "marriage counselor" and "family counselor" is widespread and does not necessarily mean that the counselor is a member of the American Association of Marriage and Family Counselors, the recognized professional association in this area of work.

Of the 7,000 or so members of the American Association of Marriage and Family Counselors, most are psychologists or social workers. However, some are ministers or other types of counselors. Membership in the association requires a specified amount of professional training and supervised experience and is a sort of certification in and of itself. A branch of the association, the Upper Midwest Association of Marriage and Family Counselors, covers Minnesota and the two Dakotas. While Marriage and Family Counselors are licensed in some states, their efforts to develop licensure in Minnesota have not yet been successful, so only the sanctions of the professional association exist. The association's current "Code of Professional

Ethics" is being revised and has grown far beyond its original four pages. It forbids sexual involvement with clients:

> Marriage and family counselors attempt to avoid relationships with clients which might impair their professional judgment or increase the risk of exploiting clients. Examples of such relationships include: treatment of family members, close friends, employees, or supervisees. <u>Sexual intimacy with clients is unethical</u>. (emphasis added)

I. <u>Upper Midwest Assn. of Marriage & Family Counselors</u>:

This professional organization is run by an Executive Committee and has a standing Committee on Ethics. Since the chairman of the national Committee on Ethics and Professional Practices, Gene Burke, is a Minnesotan, he serves as chair of the local committee also.

If a complaint is made he carries on an informal discussion with the parties involved. If he feels that the complaint is a serious one which justifies formal action, he refers it to the Committee on Ethics and Professional Practices of the American Assn. of Marriage and Family Counselors (which he chairs). Only the national association takes action.

    Contact: Gene Burke, Chairman   347-2210
                 Committee on Ethics and Professional Practices
                 American Assn. of Marriage & Family Counselors
      c/o   Psychiatry Dept.
                 Hennepin County Medical Center
                 701 Park Avenue South
                 Minneapolis, MN 55415

II. <u>American Association of Marriage and Family Counselors</u>:

The Committee on Ethics and Professional Practices has handled several cases of sexual misconduct with clients in the past several years, although none were from Minnesota. When a complaint is received, the committee and its legal counsel decide how to proceed in order to establish the facts and guarantee due process.

The committee recommends action to the Executive Committee of the Board of Directors of the association which can: 1. reprimand; 2. suspend or remove membership; 3. remove the person's status as a supervisor of other marriage & family counselors (under the association's credentialing process). However, the association does not make such action public or contact places where the counselor works or teaches, although the Committee on Ethics is currently considering recommending to the Board that such action may be advisable in some cases.

PSYCHIATRIC NURSES:

Nurses in the psychiatric setting have been taking over more and more therapeutic duties over the past decade. In addition to their traditional nursing practice role, registered nurses on psychiatric inpatient units often provide individual, family and/or group therapy. Registered nurses with master's degrees in psychiatric nursing are providing psychotherapy on an outpatient basis in both public and private mental health clinics. In terms of education, a growing number of nurses are obtaining a masters degree in psychiatric nursing.

The only existing code of ethics for nurses, the "Code for Nurses With Interpretative Statements" of the American Nurses Association, does not address sexual involvement between nurse and client. Ironically, it does, however, have an excellent section requiring that nurses play the role of an advocate and challenge unprofessional conduct of other professionals. Section 3 (pp. 8-9) reads:

"3. The Nurse Acts to Safeguard the Client and the Public When Health Care and Safety are Affected by Incompetent, Unethical, or Illegal Practice of Any Person." (Note: see especially Section 3.1 Role of Advocate, 3.2 Initial Action, and 3.3 Follow-up Action.)

So, although representatives of the Minnesota Nurses Association and Board of Nursing have stated that sexual involvement between nurse and client is unethical and unprofessional, it does not receive mention in any formal code of ethics or rules of conduct.

I. Nursing Practice Council, Minnesota Nurses Assn.:

The state constituent of the American Nurses Assn. is the Minnesota Nurses Assn. Its Council on Nursing Practice handles concerns over practices and reports of infractions of the "Code for Nurses" developed by the American Nurses Assn.

Most complaints come from other professionals, including nurses, and not from clients directly. The council, after receiving a complaint, investigates and develops further information on the case, and may work with various governmental agencies which regulate health care delivery in various settings (e.g., Dept. of Public Welfare for State Hospital-related situations).

The Council on Nursing Practice is appointed by the Board of Directors of the Minnesota Nurses Assn. It functions as a part of the Department on Nursing Practice of the Association. There is also a Commission on Economic and General Welfare which is elected by the Association membership. It has the responsibility for the overall direction and activities of the Economic and General Welfare Program. Recently, when the Commission believed the charges were unjustified, it acted to write a letter and provide staff support for a nurse who had been accused of sexual misconduct with a client. The activities of the Commission on Economic and General Welfare are separate from those of the Minnesota Nurses Assn.

To file a complaint or obtain more information:

Contact: Ruth Hass, RN, Assoc. Exec. Dir.   646-4807
or Chairperson, Council on Practice
Minnesota Nurses Association
Griggs-Midway Building, Suite N 377
1821 University Avenue
St. Paul, MN 55104

II. Board of Nursing:

This Board is a state agency responsible for the licensing of nurses (including psychiatric nurses) in the State of Minnesota. Under current state law, all nurses must be licensed. The 11 member Board includes both nurses and representatives of the public at large. The Board exists to protect the public and its disciplinary proceedings are legal actions in which the State of Minnesota is a party representing the public, not the profession. By law the Board can withdraw a license to practice nursing in this State.

To file a complaint the client contacts the Board of Nursing and speaks with a staff member who then sends out a complaint form by mail. This must be filled out and notarized and returned. Staff then examine the complaint and if they feel the Board of Nursing has jurisdiction, it's sent to the assistant attorney general who represents the Board (currently Terry O'Brien who is also counsel for the Board of Psychology).

After any investigation which is necessary, a conference is held between the Board and its counsel and the nurse about whom the complaint has been made (the respondent) and his/her attorney. A single member of the Board represents the Board, and this person is usually a nurse. If resolution cannot be reached in this informal conference, then the case is heard by the State Board of Hearing Examiners (see p. **15** on Board of Psychology for description).

The Board has a number of sanctions available: 1. censure;2. restriction of practice; 3. suspend from practice; 4. revocation of license. The Board is authorized to publicize its findings but is hesitant about this at present since standards for doing this haven't been set up.

The Board of Nursing has handled three cases of sexual misconduct during the past year. For information or to file a complaint:

Contact: Kimi Hara, RN, Assistant Director   296-5493
          Board of Nursing
          Suite 350, 717 Delaware St. SE
          Minneapolis, MN 55414

PSYCHIATRISTS:

All psychiatrists are physicians and as such, many take the Oath of Hippocrates, which states in part:

Into whatever houses I enter I will go into them for the benefit of the sick and will abstain from every voluntary act of mischief and corruption; and further from the seduction of females or males, bond or free.

The American Medical Association, a private professional organization of physicians, has published a booklet entitled "Opinions & Reports of the Judicial Council" (80 pages). In 1978 the American Psychiatric Assn., a private professional organization of psychiatrists, published a 19-page booklet entitled "The Principles of Medical Ethics With Annotations Especially Applicable to Psychiatry." The annotations to Section I (page 4) of the Code read in part:

1. The patient may place his/her trust in his/her psychiatrist knowing that the psychiatrist's ethics and professional responsibilities preclude him/her from gratifying his/her own needs by exploiting the patient. This becomes particularly important because of the essentially private, highly personal, and sometimes intensely emotional nature of the relationship established with the psychiatrist.

2. The requirement that the physician "conduct himself with propriety in his professional and in all actions of his life" is especially important in the case of the psychiatrist because the patient tends to model his/her behavior after that of his/her therapist by identification. Further, the necessary intensity of the therapeutic relationship may tend to activate sexual and other needs and fantasies on the part of both patient and therapist, while weakening the objectivity necessary for control. Sexual activity with a patient is unethical.

Besides the licensure Board, complaints can be pursued through two professional channels since a psychiatrist is both a psychiatrist and a physician.

I. <u>Ethics Committee, Minnesota Psychiatric Society</u>:

The Minnesota Psychiatric Society is a branch of the American Psychiatric Association. Its Ethics Committee investigates complaints of unethical conduct made against psychiatrists who are members of the society. It only has jurisdiction over its own members. Complaints can initially be made by phone but must eventually be made in writing.

Once a complaint is received, the local ethics committee conducts a preliminary investigation. If they feel it warrants action, they pass it on to the American Psychiatric Association in Washington, D.C. which studies the case and decides whether or not to pursue it. Once they decide to pursue it, both parties are notified. Sanctions available are censure and/or removal from membership in the association and society. Over the past five years, 3 or 4 psychiatrists have been removed from membership in the Minnesota Psychiatric Society. The society feels that sexual involvement with clients is a serious breach of professional ethics and refers all such cases on to the State Board of Medical Examiners.

Contact: Ms. Patricia Rowe, Executive Secretary   698-1971
           Minnesota Psychiatric Society
           1770 Colvin Avenue
           St. Paul, MN 55116

II. <u>Medical Ethics Committee, County Medical Society</u>:

Since each county in the state has its own Medical Society, all of which are affiliated with the American Medical Association, the Hennepin County Medical Society will be utilized here for purposes of illustration.

If a psychiatrist is a member of the Hennepin County Medical Society, and most are, the Medical Ethics Committee can investigate any complaints. It has no jurisdiction over non-members. After a complaint is received the Executive Vice president conducts an investigation. If enough evidence is found to warrant a hearing, the Chairperson of the Ethics Committee conducts a hearing utilizing the Society's legal advisor and a court reporter, with witnesses under oath. This hearing attempts to determine the facts of the case and afterwards the chairperson recommends a course of action to the Board of

Directors of the Hennepin County Medical Society. The Board can censure and/or suspend or expel the psychiatrist from membership in the Society.

When such action is taken, the County Medical Society contacts the State Board of Medical Examiners as well as all hospitals with which the psychiatrist is connected and informs them of the action taken. Furthermore, the Hennepin County Medical Society has formal memos of agreement with most area hospitals providing for exchanges of information when either or both take disciplinary action. (A hospital can remove admitting privileges for a psychiatrist who admits to an inpatient service or otherwise limit the psychiatrist's practice at the hospital.)

The Senator North Amendments (Minn. 147.23) to the Medical Practice Act require hospitals to report to the Board of Medical Examiners any decision to withdraw the right to practice or limit the practice of any physician. The Medical Practice Act also requires insurance companies to report malpractice settlements with physicians. In addition, the clerk of the district court is required to report all commitment proceedings against physicians which result in commitment to an institution or guardianship.

The Hennepin County Medical Society has an Impaired Physician Committee which sets up treatment plans for physicians who have mental health or chemical dependency problems.

Over the past several years the Society has had complaints of alleged sexual misconduct by psychiatrists brought to its attention, but in all cases they were not members of the Society so they could not be disciplined. The Society referred these cases on to the State Board of Medical Examiners.

To make a complaint contact the staff of the county medical society. For example, in Hennepin County:

Contact: Mr. Thomas Hoban, Exec. Vice President   375-0000
or   Mr. Douglas Shaw, Exec. Asst.
Hennepin County Medical Society
20 South Washington Avenue
Minneapolis, MN 55401

III. Credentialing Committee of a Hospital:

Where unprofessional behavior by a psychiatrist has occurred within a hospital setting, or occurs in conjunction with treatment in a hospital, a complaint can be made to the hospital itself.

While in the hospital the patient may enlist the aid of a patient advocate or patient grievance committee. Once one has left the hospital, these vehicles can still be of help.

In private hospitals, staff privileges are reviewed by a credentialing committee periodically. Minor complaints are noted and placed in the physician's file in most cases. However, with serious complaints such as those involving sexual misconduct, action is usually taken immediately rather than waiting for the regular review process.

Complaints can be made to the administrator or chief executive officer, to the President or Chief of Medical Staff, or to the Credentials Committee. Typically there is a special investigative committee, often called something like the "Tissues and Procedures Committee," which investigates isolated incidents, and which may be a subcommittee of either the Credentials Committee or the Executive Committee of the Medical Staff. After receipt of a complaint an investigation is conducted and a hearing held. A psychiatrist can lose his hospital privileges or have his practice in a hospital restricted. When such action is taken, the county medical society is automatically notified.

While this mechanism has seldom been used with complaints about sexual involvement between psychiatrist and client, it has the advantage of being quick. Loss of hospital privileges can be a serious sanction.

IV. State Board of Medical Examiners:

This Board is a state agency responsible for the licensing of physicians (including psychiatrists) in the State of Minnesota. Under current state law all physicians must be licensed. The Board's membership includes physicians as well as members of the lay public. The Board exists to protect the public and its disciplinary proceedings are legal actions in which the State of Minnesota is a party representing the public, not the profession. By law the Board can withdraw the grant of a license to practice medicine in the State of Minnesota if the physician is proved guilty of unprofessional conduct which includes "any departure from the minimal standards of acceptable and prevailing medical practice" (Medical Practice Act, 147.021 Minn. Statutes).

The Attorney General of Minnesota assigns a Special Assistant Attorney General to represent the Board and professional investigators are used.

When a complaint is received, it is forwarded to a panel of three Board members which is chaired by the Secretary/Treasurer of the Board. The panel changes every six months, but each panel follows each case through to its conclusion. If the panel feels that the complaint warrants further action, it is sent to the attorney for review, and the attorney authorizes an investigation. Once the results of the investigation are complete, the entire file is again reviewed by the panel to determine whether or not there is probable cause to believe that the licensee was engaged in activities which constitute grounds upon which action can be taken. If it feels there are such grounds, the panel authorizes a conference with the psychiatrist.

A conference is generally held with the Board's attorney, the panel, the psychiatrist being charged and his/her attorney. The charges and their seriousness are discussed along with what action by the Board seems appropriate. If an understanding can be reached at this point it is incorporated into a written stipulation which outlines the alleged (but not necessarily admitted) facts and includes a proposed disciplinary order. The psychiatrist must then accept these terms or go into a formal hearing.

The Office of Hearing Examiners conducts a formal hearing in situations where the situation is contested. A Hearing Examiner presides and rules on legal motions and evidentiary questions. The psychiatrist becomes the "respondent" and is present along with his/her attorneys, the hearing examiner, a court reporter, the counsel for the Board, and whichever witness is testifying. There is no jury. Witnesses are cross-examined. Witnesses are not, under current rules, permitted to be personally represented by counsel or to have friends or supporters present. At the conclusion the Hearing Examiner reaches a recommended decision which is sent along with the transcript of the hearing to the Board of Medical Examiners.

The Board renders the final decision. It can go along with the recommendation of the hearing examiner or reach its own decision. In one recent case it did overrule the

Hearing Examiner. It has the final legal authority, although the respondent (psychiatrist) can appeal the decision in District Court. Its decision is made public, although the transcript and data which might identify clients remains confidential. If the case is appealed, the Board requests that the judge of the District Court seal the administrative records to protect client confidentiality. In a recent case this request was granted although it should be noted that when there is an appeal privacy cannot be guaranteed.

The Board can: 1. Remove or suspend a license to practice in the state; 2. Restrict a psychiatrist's practice (e.g., require supervision of all therapy; disallow individual therapy, etc.); 3. Require personal therapy prior to reinstatement of license; 4. Public censure; etc.

In the past 10 years, five cases of sexual involvement between physician and client have been settled (4 in past 3 years). In four of the cases the physician lost his license; in one probation was granted. The outcomes of these cases were publicized. Several other cases are currently under investigation.

Contact: Mr. Arthur Poore, Executive Secretary   296-5534
            State Board of Medical Examiners
            717 Delaware Street SE, Room 352
            Minneapolis, MN 55414

PSYCHOLOGISTS:

The American Psychological Association publishes *Ethical Standards of Psychologists* (8 pages) and a *Casebook on Ethical Standards of Psychologists* (86 pages) giving examples of cases of alleged unethical conduct and how they were adjudged by the APA (including cases of both homosexual and heterosexual involvement with clients). The code specifically forbids sex between client and therapist under Principle 6—Welfare of the Consumer (*Ethical Standards of Psychologists* [1977 Revision], p. 6):

a. Psychologists are continually cognizant of their own needs and of their inherently powerful position vis a vis clients, in order to avoid exploiting their trust and dependency. Psychologists make every effort to avoid dual relationships with clients and/or relationships which might impair their professional judgment or increase the risk of client exploitation. Examples of such dual relationships include treating employees, supervisees, close friends or relatives. <u>Sexual intimacies with clients are unethical</u>. (emphasis added)

I.   Ethics Committee, Minnesota Psychological Association:

The Minnesota Psychological Association (MPA) is a private organization of psychologists which is affiliated with the American Psychological Association (APA) and utilizes the APA's code of ethics. The Ethics Committee of MPA can investigate complaints against any psychologist who is a member of APA but not MPA, the complaint would have to be forwarded to the APA, but MPA could assist in this process.

MPA's Ethics Committee has handled three cases of alleged sexual involvement with clients during the past six years. Once a complaint is received the committee undertakes whatever investigation seems necessary and then sets up a meeting with the psychologist whose practices are under question. The current chairman of the Ethics Committee has been in that position for more than eight years.

When the Ethics Committee reaches a decision, it makes a recommendation to the Board of Directors of MPA, which has the power to: 1. Censure; 2. Suspend or remove from membership in MPA; 3. Pass the complaint on to the APA for possible removal of membership; 4. Forward the complaint to the Board of Psychology (see below).

Contact: William Schofield, Ph.D.   373-1905
            Chairman, Ethics Committee, MPA
            Bos 393 Mayo Hospital
            Minneapolis, MN 55455

II. Board of Psychology:

This Board is a state agency responsible for the licensing of psychologists engaged in the private practice (fee for service) of psychology. Under current state law not all psychologists need to be licensed (e.g., those working in public agencies don't), although many are and all private practitioners must be. Membership on the Board includes psychologists and public members ("consumer" representatives). The Board exists to protect the public and its disciplinary proceedings are legal actions in which the State of Minnesota is a party representing the public, not the profession. By law the Board can withdraw the grant of a license to engage in the private practice of psychology in the State if a violation of the Psychology Practice Act (Minn. Statutes 148.88-.99) can be proven. The Board's powers and duties have thus been defined by the state legislature.

The Attorney General assigns a Special Assistant Attorney General to represent the Board and professional investigators are also available.

When a complaint is received it is reviewed by the Board's Executive Secretary. It is then forwarded to the Board's attorney for review as to whether the alleged facts, if true, provide the Board with jurisdiction to proceed. Once this determination is made, the attorney initiates an investigation. Once the results of an investigation are complete, it is referred to the Board's Ethics Panel which consists of both psychologists and public members, which reviews the file. The panel can recommend to the Board what step should be taken next. If the case seems solid, the Board may authorize a conference with the psychologist in question.

A conference is generally held with the Board's attorney, the Ethics Panel, the psychologist and his/her counsel. They discuss the charges, their seriousness, and what action by the Board seems appropriate. If an understanding can be reached at this point it is incorporated into a written stipulation which outlines the alleged (but not necessarily admitted) facts and includes a proposed disciplinary order to which the psychologist agrees. The full Board reviews the stipulations and may accept or diminish the severity of the sanctions. If the psychologist refuses the Board's offer, the case goes to formal hearing.

The Office of Hearing Examiners conducts a formal hearing which is presided over by a Hearing Examiner who rules on legal motions and evidentiary questions. The psychologist becomes the "respondent" and is present along with his/her attorneys, the hearing examiner, a court reporter, the counsel for the Board, and whatever witness is testifying. No jury is present and witnesses are cross-examined. Witnesses are not now, under current rules, allowed to be personally represented by counsel or have friends or supporters present. At the conclusion the Hearing Examiner reaches a decision which is sent along with the transcript of the hearing to the Board of Psychology.

While it is the intention of the Board of Psychology to keep all proceedings confidential, the Board lacks the protection afforded the Board of Medical Examiners by the Medical Practice Act. At present the Board has as its only protection the argument that its work is a "quasi-legal proceeding" and that it is therefore private under Minnesota's Open Meeting Law (as one of the classes of meetings which is exempt). An emergency classification has been obtained which may run out on June 30, 1979, making such meetings private. However, this makes for a weak argument when one enters an appeal process and so again confidentiality can't be guaranteed. Furthermore, about 1 1/2 years ago a hearing examiner opined that evidence against the professional should be "clear and convincing," not just the "preponderance of evidence," and Hearing Examiners have informally indicated that this is the new standard and that two separate complaints may be necessary to prove a case.

The Board of Psychology renders the final decision. It can go along with the recommendation of the Hearing Examiner or reach its own decision. It has final legal authority, although the psychologist can appeal the decision in District Court. The final decision is made public, although the Board would make every effort to keep the transcript (and identities of the clients) confidential.

The Board can: 1. Remove or suspend a license; 2. Restrict or attach conditions to a psychologist's practice (e.g., forbid him/her to do psychotherapy; require supervision, etc.); 3. Require personal therapy prior to reinstatement of a license; 4. Issue a public censure.

Over the past several years the Board of Psychology has made public actions it took against two psychologists who were allegedly sexually involved with clients. Other cases are under investigation. The Board has never taken a case of sexual involvement to a formal hearing before a Hearing Examiner.

Contact: Ms. Harriett Hartungs, Executive Secretary   296-5419
          Board of Psychology
          717 Delaware Street SE, Room 343
          Minneapolis, MN 55414

SOCIAL WORKERS (updated Dec. 1979):

The National Association of Social Workers (NASW) publishes "NASW Standards for Social Work Personnel Practices" (39 pages) which contains a "Code of Ethics" (2 pages) plus a publication on "NASW Policy and Procedures for the Adjudication of Grievances" (13 pages). However, the NASW News of July 1979 published a much longer revised code of ethics which represents the "most extensive revision of the code since its adoption by the fledgling association in 1969" according to an editorial in the NASW News, Nov. 1979. One of the major changes in the code is for the first time to specifically proscribe sexual activities with clients. While the final version of the code is not yet published, the proposed code, under Section II, reads:

4. The social worker should avoid relationships or commitments that conflict with the interests of clients.

5. The social worker should under no circumstances engage in sexual activities with clients.

Although Social Workers are licensed in some states are attempting to introduce licensure in Minnesota, currently they are not licensed in Minnesota so that the only avenue of complaint is via the professional organization—NASW and its Minnesota Chapter.

I. <u>Committee on Inquiry, Minnesota Chapter of NASW</u>:

This committee of seven members has jurisdiction over all social workers who are members of NASW. If a social worker is not a member of NASW it has no jurisdiction.

The NASW complaint procedure is spelled out in great detail in "NASW Policy and Procedures for the Adjudication of Grievances." It is impressive, but unfortunately aimed primarily at complaints within agencies rather than client complaints. For example, there is a stipulation that complaints must be filed within 30 days of the occurrence, except in situations where the committee decides that the situation is "exceptional" and "provided it has only recently come to the complainant's attention." The Minnesota committee has been quite flexible in handling sex-related cases, so locally these procedures have not presented a real problem.

A formal set of complaint guidelines are available from the NASW which urge the complainant to press the complaint through other channels first. The complainant is required to document attempts to deal with the situation, to submit a list of possible witnesses and/or sources of information which would substantiate his/her claims, and indicate in what way the "Code of Ethics" was violated.

A hearing should be held within 45 days of the receipt of the complaint. The complainant may not be represented by an attorney but may bring an NASW member to aid in the presentation of the case. Considerable burden is placed on the complainant to present the case, and the social worker who is being charged with unethical conduct is present and may be sitting in close proximity. A final report and recommendation for action should be completed within 45 days of the hearing.

The final report, which does not contain the names of the complainant or the accused, is submitted to the officers of the chapter for review. If they don't agree with the recommendations they can send the report back to the committee for reconsideration, but they can't reverse its decision. If the committee decides not to change its report, then it stands as the final decision. An appeal process is spelled out in the "procedures."

The committee may recommend: 1. Restitution by the accused if harm was done; 2. Censure by the chapter; 3. Censure by the national Board of Directors; 4. Suspension of membership in NASW and/or ACSW (Academy of Certified Social Workers); 5. Permanent exclusion from NASW and/or ACSW membership; 6. Publication of the findings and penalties imposed. Approval of the national Board of Directors of NASW is required when recommendations 4, 5, or 6 are considered.

In the past two years the Committee on Inquiry, Minnesota Chapter of NASW, has received two complaints of alleged sexual misconduct by social workers. One social worker was dropped from membership in NASW, ACSW, and was censured publicly, both in the NASW newsletter and to the general public via a press release.

Contact: John H. Graf, ACSW   226-8835 (NASW)
                Chairman, Committee on Inquiry   348-3553 (work)
                NASW—Minnesota Chapter
                22 N. Dale Street
                St. Paul, MN 55102

II. Committee on Inquiry, NASW (national):

This committee would have jurisdiction over a social worker who was an NASW member but who did not belong to the Minnesota Chapter. Its procedures are identical to those described above for the Minnesota Chapter. It has more staff plus legal counsel. It can be contacted through the assistance of the Minnesota Chapter.

APPENDIX C

Memorandum on "Selected Items from the
Supervisor/Counselor Volunteer Application,
Walk-In Counseling Center"

and

Counselor/Supervisor Volunteer Application

SELECTED ITEMS FROM THE SUPERVISOR/COUNSELOR VOLUNTEER APPLICATION

Walk-In Counseling Center

1) All Past & Present Licensure & Certification is requested, and then applicants must answer:

    *Has disciplinary action of any sort ever been taken against you by a licensing board, professional association, or educational/training institution?
    NO___   YES___

    *Are there complaints pending against you before any of the above-named bodies?
    NO___   YES___

    *Have you ever had a civil suit brought against you relative to your professional work or is any such action pending?
    NO___   YES___

2) All Training & Clinically Relevant Experience is requested, and applicants must answer:

    *Have you ever been asked to resign or been terminated by a training program or employer?
    NO___   YES___

    If "YES" attach an explanation to the end of this volunteer form.

3) Past supervisors are contacted by phone and besides being asked about skills, abilities, limitations of the applicant in a setting like ours, are asked about any questions the supervisor has about the applicant's professional judgment, ethics, or any reservations they might have about their work. We read them the "STATEMENT OF APPLICANT" which follows to indicate that providing us with such information should not leave them liable.

STATEMENT OF APPLICANT (must be signed and dated)

All information submitted by me in this application is true to the best of my knowledge. I understand that any significant misstatement in, or omission from, this application may be cause for denial of appointment as a volunteer or cause for dismissal from the volunteer staff.

By applying for appointment to the volunteer staff of WICC, I acknowledge that I have the responsibility to read the "Ethical Guidelines at Walk-In Counseling Center" and other WICC rules and regulations. I agree to act in accordance with these ethical guidelines and any other rules or regulations adopted by WICC.

I authorize the Walk-In Counseling Center, its staff, and their representatives to consult with persons or institutions with which I have been associated with and others, including past and present employers, who may have information bearing on my professional competence, character, and ethical qualifications. I release from liability all representatives of WICC for their acts performed in good faith and without malice in connection with evaluating my application and my credentials and qualifications, and I release from liability all individuals and organizations who provide information to WICC in good faith and without malice concerning my professional competence, ethics, character, and other qualifications.

I understand and agree that I will notify WICC of any changes in my job or training status, licensure, censure or sanction by professional bodies, or any other information relating to my ability to perform as a volunteer at WICC.

_____   _____
Name (Please Print or Type)   Date

_____
Signature

We have the name printed or typed because some references want a copy of this signed pledge for their records and it made it easier to simply Xerox this page of the application. Since we began using this pledge approximately 900 applicants have signed it and we have had no refusals. Some of the benefits have been:

*People have commented that they feel that this gives a clear message as to the high standards we try to maintain.

*Past supervisors who act as references report feeling more comfortable about commenting on the applicant, especially as regards his/her deficiencies.

*University training programs which have recently tightened up on information they are willing to give out will accept this release as sufficient to permit disclosure, thus saving everyone time and expense and needlessly delaying applications.

*Some clinics have begun using it to screen job applicants for employment as professionals.

Furthermore, because we contact Licensure Boards directly and Supervisors directly, we suspect that we are far more likely to learn of past concerns or problems.

Also, pursuant to the duties outlined in Minnesota Statutes Chapter 148A. Section 3 which became effective 1 August, 1986, a written inquiry is sent to the applicant's past employers (of past five years) requesting information concerning the occurrence of sexual contact with clients or former clients.

WALK-IN COUNSELING CENTER
2421 Chicago Avenue South
Minneapolis, MN 55404
870-0565/-0566/-0574

**COUNSELOR/SUPERVISOR
VOLUNTEER APPLICATION**

(Return to Clinic Director, Jim Ayers)

DATE_____

NAME_____   SEX_____

ADDRESS_____   ZIP_____

PHONE (Office)_____   (Home)_____

CURRENT EMPLOYMENT_____
　　　　　　　　　　(Agency/Company)　　　　　　　(Position/Title)
****

1. PAST WICC INVOLVEMENT

　　a. Have you ever volunteered at WICC previously? YES___   NO___

　　b. Have you ever <u>applied</u> at WICC previously, but not volunteered?

　　　　YES___   NO___   (If "yes", please attach an explanation. Include date of application
　　　　　　　　　　　　　　　　and reasons for not having volunteered.)

2. DEGREES HELD AND/OR EXPECTED

　　<u>Institution</u>　　　　　<u>Major Field</u>　　　　　<u>Degree</u>　　　　　<u>Year</u>

　　_____

　　_____

　　_____

3. LICENSURE STATUS

　　a. Have you ever been licensed or certified?　　　YES___   NO___

　　b. Type (e.g., Licensed Psychologist, ACSW)_____

　　_____

　　State Where Held_____

　　Expiration Date_____

　　Areas of Competency or Professional Practice for which Licensed/ Certified_____

　　_____
　　__

/_/ Check if you hold more than one licensure or certification and list on the back of the last page.

c. Has disciplinary action of any sort ever been taken against you by a licensing board, professional association, or educational/training institution?

NO___   YES___

d.   Are there complaints pending against you before any of the above-named bodies?

NO___   YES___

e. Have you ever had a civil suit brought against you relative to your professional work or is any such action pending?

NO___   YES___

Note: IF YOU HAVE ANSWERED "YES" TO 3c, d, OR e, PLEASE ATTACH AN EXPLANATION.

4. TRAINING AND CLINICALLY RELEVANT EXPERIENCE

Practicum Placement, Internship and other Supervised Clinical Experience

Agency (include client populations & treatment modalities)	Approximate Dates	Hours

5. RELEVANT JOB EXPERIENCE

a. Current & Past Employment in Mental Health Related Settings (List most recent first.)

Name of Agency & Description (Job Titles, Setting, Duties & Dates)

_____

_____

_____

_____

_____

_____

b. Have you ever been asked to resign or been terminated by a training program or employer?

NO___   YES___   (If "yes", attach an explanation.)

c. Experience as Clinic Supervisor

<u>Description</u> (Setting, Type of People Supervised,   Approximate
Client Population, Treatment Modalities)   ___Hours___

_____

_____

_____

_____

> NOTE: In accordance with Minnesota Statute 148A., we are obliged to contact your employers over the last five years and ask whether they have knowledge of your having sexual contact with clients. Complete the attached yellow sheet. Please note that paid internships are considered a form of employment.

6. GENERAL INFORMATION

a. Relevant Present and Past Volunteer Work

<u>PROGRAM</u>	<u>ACTIVITIES</u>	<u>DATES</u>

b. Areas of Special Expertise (e.g., sexual abuse counseling, chemical dependency counseling, sign language, foreign language)

_____

_____

_____

_____

7. EXPECTATIONS REGARDING WICC

Why do you want to volunteer at WICC? How did you learn of/become acquainted with WICC? What do you expect from this experience?

_____

_____

_____

_____

_____

8. REFERENCES

Give the names, agency/institution affiliations and phone numbers of 3 people who are familiar with or who have supervised your clinical work within the last 5 years.

<u>Name</u>	<u>Agency/Institution</u>	<u>Phone</u>

9. AVAILABILITY TO VOLUNTEER AT WICC:

__Counselor: Does crisis intervention, short-term (10 sessions or less) counseling, referral, and follow-up.

__Supervisor: Oversees and is responsible for team functioning, reviews therapeutic work, leads case conference, and does some counseling and referral.

NOTE: Monday and Wednesday afternoon teams meet once a week and Friday afternoon teams once every other week, 12:45-5:00 p.m. Evening teams meet Monday, Tuesday, Wednesday and Thursday (once every-other-week) 6:45-11:00 p.m. Return sessions are often necessary on intervening weeks.

10. CONSULTATION/TRAINING VOLUNTEER OPPORTUNITY—Contact Jeanette Milgrom, Director of Consultation & Training.

11. PRIVATE PRACTICE REFERRALS—WICC volunteers in private practice who wish to receive WICC referrals may be eligible for listing in the rolodex on the receptionist's desk. For further information, contact Jim Ayers, Clinic Director.

<u>PLEASE SEE "STATEMENT OF APPLICANT" ON FOLLOWING PAGE.</u>

STATEMENT OF APPLICANT: (Please read this carefully before signing.)

All information submitted by me in this application is true to the best of my knowledge. I understand that any significant misstatement in, or omission from, this application may be cause for denial of appointment as a volunteer or cause for dismissal from the volunteer staff.

By applying for appointment to the volunteer staff of WICC, I acknowledge that I have the responsibility to read the "Ethical Guidelines at Walk-In Counseling Center" and other WICC rules and regulations. I agree to act in accordance with these ethical guidelines and any other rules or regulations adopted by WICC.

I authorize the Walk-In Counseling Center, its staff and representatives to consult with persons or institutions with which I have been associated and with others, including past and present employers, who may have information bearing on my professional competence, character, and ethical qualifications. I release from liability all representatives of WICC for acts performed in good faith and without malice in connection with evaluating my application and my credentials and qualifications. I also release from any liability all individuals and organizations who provide information to WICC in good faith and without malice concerning my professional competence, ethics, character, and other qualifications.

I understand and agree that I will notify WICC of any changes in my job or training status, licensure, censure or sanction by professional bodies, or any other information relating to my ability to perform as a volunteer at WICC.

_____   _____

Name (Please print or type)   Date

_____

Signature

APPENDIX D

1. Form for volunteer applicant to list past employment

2. Letter to past employer

3. Applicant release form ("Statement of Applicant")

4. Feedback form for past employer to indicate whether there is
   a history of sexual contact or solicitation for sex with past clients.

WALK-IN COUNSELING CENTER
2421 CHICAGO AVENUE SOUTH
MINNEAPOLIS, MN 55404

Volunteer
Applicant _____
                          (Name)

MN. Law (Statutes 148A., effective 8-1-86) requires WICC to make written inquiry to past employers in the mental health field regarding psychotherapists' possible sexual misconduct with clients.

Please list below all current and past employment in the mental health field (part-time, temporary & fulltime) and all paid internships (including post-doctorals) during the past 5 years. (List chronologically, most recent first, etc.)

☐ Not applicable. I have had no employment or paid internships in the last 5 years. _____
                                    (Signature)

		Date Letter Sent	Returned	Date Follow-up Letter Sent	Returned

WALK-IN COUNSELING CENTER
2421 CHICAGO AVENUE SOUTH
MINNEAPOLIS, MINNESOTA 55404
    870-0565, 870-0566

Re: _____

Dear Personnel Director:

The person named above is applying to be a volunteer counselor at our Center. We are in need of specific information before we can complete the screening process.

On August 1, 1986, Minnesota Statute 148.A went into effect. That law imposes liability on a current employer of a psychotherapist if that employer fails to inquire of the therapist's other employers about sexual contact between the therapist and clients or former clients. Since our volunteers perform job duties comparable to paid positions, we are bound by the Statute.

The definition of what constitutes sexual contact is on the back of this sheet. Please note that the definition includes requesting sexual contact with a client as well as actually <u>making</u> sexual contact.

We are liable if we do not seek such information, whether or not we have reason to believe sexual contact has occurred. Past and other current employers also are liable if they (a) know of the occurrence of sexual contact; (b) receive a specific written request about whether sexual contact has ever occurred; and (c) fail or refuse to disclose the requested information. Conversely, employers who in good faith comply are not subject to civil suit or to action by any Minnesota state licensing board.

We therefore are asking you to complete the enclosed form and return it as as quickly as possible. Please note that we include a signed form from the applicant releasing you from any liability should you provide information in good faith about areas like past sexual contact with clients or former clients.

Please feel free to contact me if you have any questions. Thanks for your cooperation.

Very truly yours,

                                           Enclosed: -return envelope
                                                   -signed "Statement of
                                                          Applicant"
James Ayers, Ph.D.   -Form to be returned
Licensed Consulting Psychologist
Clinic Director

MINNESOTA STATUTES

Chapter 148A

Section 1.[148A.01] [Definitions.] in part reads:

<u>Subd. 7.</u> (SEXUAL CONTACT) "Sexual Contact" means any of the following, whether or not occurring with the consent of a patient or former patient:

(1) Sexual intercourse, cunnilingus, fellatio, anal intercourse or any intrusion, however slight, into the genital or anal openings of the patient's or former patient's body by any part of the psychotherapist's body or by any object used by the psychotherapist for this purpose, or any intrusion, however slight, into the genital or anal openings of the psychotherapist's body by any part of the patient's or former patient's body or by any object used by the patient or former patient for this purpose, if agreed to by the psychotherapist;

(2) kissing of, or the intentional touching by the psychotherapist of the patient's or former patient's genital area, groin, inner thigh, buttocks, or breast or of the clothing covering any of these body parts;

(3) kissing of, or the intentional touching by the patient or former patient of the psychotherapist's genital area, groin, inner thigh, buttocks, or breast or of the clothing covering any of these body parts if the psychotherapist agrees to the kissing or intentional touching.

"Sexual contact" includes requests by the psychotherapist for conduct described in clauses (1) to (3).

"Sexual contact" does not include conduct described in clause (1) or (2) that is a part of standard medical treatment of a patient.

Page 5

STATEMENT OF APPLICANT: (Please read this carefully before signing.)

All information submitted by me in this application is true to the best of my knowledge. I understand that any significant misstatement in, or omission from, this application may be cause for denial of appointment as a volunteer or cause for dismissal from the volunteer staff.

By applying for appointment to the volunteer staff of WICC, I acknowledge that I have the responsibility to read the "Ethical Guidelines at Walk-In Counseling Center" and other WICC rules and regulations. I agree to act in accordance with these ethical guidelines and any other rules or regulations adopted by WICC.

I authorize the Walk-In Counseling Center, its staff and representatives to consult with persons or institutions with which I have been associated and with others, including past and present employers, who may have information bearing on my professional competence, character, and ethical qualifications. I release from liability all representatives of WICC for acts performed in good faith and without malice in connection with evaluating my application and my credentials and qualifications. I also release from any liability all individuals and organizations who provide information to WICC in good faith and without malice concerning my professional competence, ethics, character, and other qualifications.

I understand and agree that I will notify WICC of any changes in my job or training status, licensure, censure or sanction by professional bodies, or any other information relating to my ability to perform as a volunteer at WICC.

_____   _____
Name (Please print or type)   Date

_____
Signature

(Revised 8/86)

NAME OF PSYCHOTHERAPIST*:_____

EMPLOYER:_____

ADDRESS:_____

EMPLOYED FROM:_____ TO _____ STILL EMPLOYED _____ _____
                                                     YES   NO

POSITIONS WHILE EMPLOYED:_____
                         _____

*NOTE: The law defines "psychotherapist" as "a physician, psychologist, nurse, chemical dependency counselor, social worker, member of the clergy, or other person...who performs or purports to perform...treatment, assessment or counseling of a mental or emotional illness, symptoms, or condition." In short, a very broad range of people and activities are included. Any past work of a human services nature is of interest.

___We have no record or knowledge of sexual contact as described in the statute.

___We do have record or knowledge of such contact.

    ___A written report on the matter is enclosed.

    ___We have no written reports on the matter.

Who may we contact for further information on this matter?

NAME:_____

TITLE:_____

PHONES: _____

ADDRESS:_____

    _____

    _____

PERSON COMPLETING FORM: NAME:_____
                    (Please print)
            SIGNATURE_____
            TITLE:_____
            DATE:_____

Please return to Jim Ayers, Clinic Director of Walk-In Counseling Center, in the enclosed envelope.

APPENDIX E

ADMINISTRATIVE SAFEGUARDS CHECKLIST:

1978 version: "Sexual Exploitation of Clients: Its Prevention or Remedy; or A Look at Whether Your Agency Has Its House In Order" (Milgrom)

1979 version: "Administrative Safeguards to Limit Risk of Unprofessional Conduct" (Schoener)

1986 version: "Administrative Safeguards Which Limit the Risk of Sexual Exploitation By Psychotherapists—A Checklist" (Schoener)

SEXUAL EXPLOITATION OF CLIENTS:
ITS PREVENTION OR REMEDY

or

A Look at Whether Your Agency Has Its House in Order

DOES YOUR AGENCY: YES   NO

• Check staff references thoroughly at the time of hiring?   _____ _____

• Give new staff members written materials which include the
  expectations of the agency, as well as its ethical stance, and
  which explicitly prohibit sexual/erotic behavior with clients?   _____ _____

• Offer an open, non-punitive atmosphere which promotes
  staff communication? Does it encourage and model
  assertiveness and early confrontation among staff?   _____ _____

• Provide individual/group/peer supervision or
  consultation, or make it readily available?   _____ _____

• Offer alternatives in cases where counselor-client
  relationships threaten to become sexualized (alternatives
  such as co-therapy, transfer of client, etc.)?   _____ _____

• Have clearly spelled out policies and procedures for
  dealing with undesirable staff behavior of any nature,
  with undesirable staff behavior of any nature
  and implement them?   _____ _____

• Discuss the phenomenon of eroticism in therapy
  in staff meetings or in-service training sessions?   _____ _____

• Survey your client population to actively solicit
  feedback from clients about the quality of service
  received? Do you take notice of this feedback?   _____ _____

• Do you ask new clients who make vague negative
  comments about a previous counselor what went
  wrong? Do you consider the possibility that your client
  may have "run away" from a sexualized relationship
  with a previous counselor?   _____ _____

• Do you believe that the problem of sexual
  exploitation of clients actually exists, and that it
  occurs with some frequency?   _____ _____

Number of YES Answers	Assessment	Prescription
10	Terrific	Keep it up!
7-9	Not Bad	Can use some in-house spring cleaning
4-6	In need of overhaul, reconditioning	Bring in an outside expert.
0-3	Severe condition	Bring in the exterminator to prevent condemnation.

ADMINISTRATIVE SAFEGUARDS TO LIMIT RISK
OF UNPROFESSIONAL CONDUCT

Gary Schoener, 1979

STAFF SELECTION & HIRING: YES   NO

•Does your job application explicitly ask about:

    — Past terminations/resignations?   _____ _____

    — Past ethics complaints?   _____ _____

    — Past lawsuits, whether adjudicated or not?   _____ _____

    — Past licensure complaints?   _____ _____

•When dealing with licensed or certified practitioners,
    do you directly contact licensure boards concerning
    areas of competency, existence of complaints, and
    whether the license is in force without limitations:

    — Boards in this state?   _____ _____

    — Boards in states where previously employed?   _____ _____

•Do you check via direct conversation (not letter, or in
    addition to letter) with past supervisors to ask about:

    — General professional strengths & weaknesses?   _____ _____

    — Any concerns or past complaints which might
      relate to special problems, vulnerabilities, or the
      need for tight supervision in some circumstances?   _____ _____

STAFF POLICIES:

•Do you have a written policy forbidding:

    — sexual involvement with clients or other
      unprofessional conduct?   _____ _____

    — sexual involvement with ex-clients?   _____ _____

•Do you have written policy for handling complaints
    of unprofessional conduct?   _____ _____

•Do you have a peer review system/process?   _____ _____

•Do you have a Professional Standards Review
    Committee or Ethics Committee which reviews
    concerns or complaints?   _____ _____

<u>STAFF SUPERVISION & CONTINUING EDUCATION</u>:   <u>YES</u>   <u>NO</u>

•Do you have agency inservices or staff meeting
       discussions on the issues of eroticism in
       psychotherapy at least once a year?   _____ _____

•Do you have regular clinical supervision?   _____ _____

•Does your program have an atmosphere which
       encourages non-punitive confrontation and
       constructive questioning among staff?   _____ _____

•Does your agency offer readily available alternatives
       when therapeutic relationships become sexualized
       to the point that they are dysfunctional:

        — Referral in-house or to another program?   _____ _____

        — Use of a co-therapist or consultant in the sessions   _____ _____

•Is it general staff practice to carefully evaluate past
       treatment with thorough assessment of client's
       complaints & negative impressions of past therapists? _____ _____

<u>CLIENTS</u>:

•Do you hand out a sheet of information or have staff
       read standardized information to new clients which:

        — Actively seeks to solicit feedback & complaints
          about the service   _____ _____

        — Gives clients a specific vehicle for making a
          complaint known (e.g., procedure, contact person) _____ _____

•Do you survey your client population periodically to
       obtain consumer satisfaction or outcome data and
       followup on negative feedback?   _____ _____

•Are all complaints processed as complaints and taken
       seriously—not just seen as "transference" or some
       other therapeutic event?   _____ _____

•Are complaining clients and therapists who are being
       complained about given a chance to confront each
       other with a mediator present?   _____ _____

•After you have decided on action relative to a complaint,
       are the complaining client(s) always given feedback
       as to outcome?   _____ _____

MISCELLANEOUS:

•Are therapist's doors locked?   _____ _____

•Is there review of long-term treatment or treatment which
    exceeds usual length of treatment; and/or situations
    in which clients phone the therapist a great deal?   _____ _____

<u>ADMINISTRATIVE SAFEGUARDS WHICH LIMIT THE RISK</u>
<u>OF SEXUAL EXPLOITATION BY PSYCHOTHERAPISTS—</u>

<u>A CHECKLIST</u>

Gary Schoener, Licensed Psychologist
September, 1986

<u>STAFF SELECTION & HIRING</u>:   <u>YES</u>   <u>NO</u>

•Does your job application explicitly ask about:

    — Past terminations/resignations?   ____ ____

    — Past ethics complaints?   ____ ____

    — Past licensure complaints?   ____ ____

    — Past lawsuits, whether adjudicated or not?   ____ ____

•When hiring professionals who are licensed or certified,
    do you directly contact licensure boards concerning
    areas of competency, status of the license, and the
    existence (or lack thereof) of complaints?

    — Boards in this state?   ____ ____

    — Boards in states where previously employed?   ____ ____

•Do you check via direct conversation (not just letter
    of reference) with past supervisors about the
    applicant's:

    — Likely strengths and weaknesses working in a
      setting like that of your agency?   ____ ____

    — Willingness to be supervised and to be a team
      player?   ____ ____

    — Any history of complaints by, or problems with,
      other staff (e.g., sexual harassment?)   ____ ____

    — Any history of client complaints?   ____ ____

    — Any concerns they might have about the person's
      ability to perform in your setting; any needs
      for special care or supervision?   ____ ____

•If you're a Minnesota employer, do you make written
    requests to all employers from the past five years
    concerning their knowledge of sexual contact with
    clients or ex-clients (Minn. Statutes 148.A)?   ____ ____

STAFF POLICIES: YES   NO

•Do you have a written policy forbidding:

    — Sexual contact with clients?   _____   _____

    — Sexual contact with ex-clients?   _____   _____

    — Romantic involvement with clients?   _____   _____

•Does your policy also provide rules for support staff
    and other non-clinical personnel?   _____   _____

•Do you have a policy covering sexual harassment of
    staff and/or romantic involvements between staff
    members?   _____   _____

•Do you have a written policy for handling complaints
    of unprofessional conduct such as allegations of
    sexual contact with clients?   _____   _____

•Do you have a plan or mechanism for the investigation
    of complaints by clients and others?   _____   _____

    — Do you have outside consultants who can be
      used to assist in such investigations?   _____   _____

    — Do you have an Ethics Committee or Professional
      Standards Review Committee which reviews such
      complaints?   _____   _____

    — Do you have a method for the filing and investi-
      gation of complaints against the Director of your
      program or facility?   _____   _____

COMPLAINT RESOLUTION:

•Are all complaints processed as complaints and taken
    seriously—not just seen as "transference" or some
    other therapeutic event?   _____   _____

•Are complaining clients given reassurance and thanked
    for coming forward, regardless of your initial
    assumptions about the validity of the complaint?   _____   _____

•Are clients given support and offered help in finding
    appropriate independent resources?   _____   _____

•Do you have procedures for deciding whether to
    temporarily suspend a staff member pending
    the outcome of a review of a complaint?   _____   _____

	YES	NO
•Are all staff involved in the investigation of complaints clear about the limits of privacy—e.g., their reporting duties under existing laws and rules (in Minnesota this includes Vulnerable Adults Act, Child Abuse and Neglect reporting, the Medical Practice Act, and the Code of Conduct of the Board of Psychology)	____	____
•Is some resolution reached on all complaints, or do you allow some of them to remain moot if a staff member voluntarily resigns?	____	____
•After you have decided on action relative to a complaint, are the complainants always given feedback as to final disposition?	____	____

•When you receive a request for a recommendation which asks about any history of sexual misconduct with clients, do you:

	YES	NO
— Automatically pass the information on to a Minnesota employer as is your duty under Minn. Statutes 148.A?	____	____
— With an out-of-state employer suggest that the employer obtain a release from the ex-staff member permitting you to share all data?	____	____

STAFF EDUCATION:

	YES	NO
•Are all staff given written copies of policies?	____	____
— Is there a new employee orientation at which these are explained and key policies are underlined?	____	____
•Are there training sessions on the issues of boundaries in psychotherapy held at least once per year?	____	____
•Following an incident of serious misconduct, is a special session held to discuss what can be learned from the incident?	____	____

STAFF SUPERVISION/PEER REVIEW:

	YES	NO
•Do you have a regular clinical supervision or consultation?	____	____
•Do you have a professional standards review system?	____	____

•Is there an automatic review of:

	YES	NO
— Treatment which exceeds the usual length?	____	____
— Situations in which excessive dependency is evident such as where clients phone frequently?	____	____

	YES	NO

— Situations in which seductive behavior is
observed by other staff?

•Is long-term treatment periodically reviewed as to:

— Treatment goals & progress towards them?

— Plans for termination?

•Does your program have an atmosphere which
encourages constructive questioning among staff?

•Are there clear, non-threatening pathways for making
observations/concerns known to management, by:

— Clinical & program staff?

— Support staff; billing office?

•When staff have obvious personal problems or are
in distress:

— Do other staff generally give them feedback?

— Is there a clear mechanism, which is used, to
bring about feedback and encourage seeking help?

— Are clinical duties ever reviewed in light of
obvious personal problems/distress?

•Are there readily available interventions when therapeutic
relationships become romanticized/sexualized?

— Use of a co-therapist or consultant who may
enter a session with the client if need be?

— Referral in-house, or to another program?

CLIENTS:

•Do you provide new clients with information which:

— Actively seeks to solicit feedback?

— Identifies an easy-to-use complaint mechanism?

— Provides any guidelines to evaluating therapy?

•Is it general staff practice to carefully assess the
client's view of any past treatment at your agency
or elsewhere?

	YES	NO
•Do you routinely survey consumer satisfaction or outcome?	____	____
•Is a complaining client given the opportunity for a meeting with the therapist, with or without a mediator present?	____	____

APPENDIX F

Criminal Statutes: New Hampshire, Michigan, and Wyoming

CRIMINAL STATUTES

NEW HAMPSHIRE

*632-A:2   Aggravated Felonious Sexual Assault.

A person is guilty of class A felony if he engages in sexual penetration with another person under any of the following circumstances:

> VII. When the actor engages in the medical treatment or examination of the victim in a manner or for purposes which are not medically recognized as ethical or acceptable.

*N.H. Rev. Stat. Ann. Section 632-A:2 Part VII (Supp 1977, 1986)

MICHIGAN

Under Michigan's Criminal Sexual Conduct statute, first degree sexual conduct may be charged when:

> (i) ...The actor engages in the <u>medical treatment</u> or examination of the victim in a manner or for purposes which are medically recognized as unethical or unacceptable. (emphasis added)

Michigan Comprehensive Laws 750.520b (1) (d) (i)

*750.90   Sexual intercourse under pretext of medical treatment.

> Sec. 90. SEXUAL INTERCOURSE UNDER PRETEXT OF MEDICAL TREATMENT—Any person who shall undertake to medically treat any female person, and while so treating her, shall represent to such female that it is, or will be, necessary or beneficial to her health that she have sexual intercourse with a man, and shall thereby induce her to have carnal sexual intercourse with any man, and any man, not being the husband of such female, who shall have sexual intercourse with her by reason of such representation, shall be guilty of a felony, punishable by imprisonment in the state prison not more than 10 years.

*Mich. Comp. Laws Ann. Section 750.90 (Supp 1984-85)

WYOMING

Under Wyoming's statutes covering "offenses against the person," Sexual Assault in the Second Degree may be charged if sexual contact occurs in situations where:

*6-2-303

a. (vi) The actor is in a position of authority over the victim and uses this position of authority to cause the victim to submit; or

(vii) The actor inflicts sexual intrusion in treatment or examination of a victim for purposes or in a manner substantially inconsistent with reasonable medical practices.

*6-2-301 Definitions

a. (iv) The actor is in a position of authority means that position occupied by a parent, guardian, relative, household member, teacher, employer, or custodian or any other person who by reason of his position is able to exercise significant influence over a person.

APPENDIX G

CRIMINAL STATUTES: WISCONSIN

1. Wisconsin Act 434, passed in 1983, creating 940.22 of Wisconsin statutes; which made it a Class A misdemeanor for a therapist to have sexual contact with a client.

2. 940.22 as amended in 1985, and 940.225 as amended in 1985, which made sexual contact with a client a felony instead of a misdemeanor, and which expanded the definition of "Therapist."

3. Definition of psychotherapy—Wisconsin Statutes 455.01(6).

STATE OF WISCONSIN

Date of enactment: May 9, 1984

1983 Assembly Bill 321

Date of publication: May 17, 1984

1983 Wisconsin Act 434

AN ACT *to create* 940.22 of the statutes, *relating to* sexual contact between a therapist and patient and providing a penalty.

The people of the state of Wisconsin, represented in senate and assembly, do enact as follows:

SECTION 1. 940.22 of the statutes is created to read:

940.22, Sexual exploitation by therapist.

(1) In this section:

    (a)   "Physician" has the meaning designated in s. 448.01(5).
    (b)   "Psychologist" means a person who practices psychology, as described in s. 455.01(5).
    (c)   "Psychotherapy" has the meaning designated in s. 455.01(6).
    (d)   "Sexual contact" has the meaning designated in s. 940.225(5)(a).
    (e)   "Therapist" means a physician, psychologist, social worker or other person providing psychotherapy services.

(2) Any person who is or who holds himself or herself out to be a therapist and who intentionally has sexual contact with a patient or client during any treatment, consultation, interview or examination is guilty of a Class A misdemeanor.[1]

•940.22. Sexual exploitation by therapist

(1) In this section:

    (a) "Physician" has the meaning designated in s. 448.01(5).
    (b) "Psychologist" means a person who practices psychology, as described in s. 455.01(5).
    (c) "Psychotherapy" has the meaning designated in s. 455.01(6).
    (d) "Sexual contact" has the meaning designated in s. 940.225(5)(a).
    (e) "Therapist" means a physician, psychologist, social worker, <u>nurse. chemical dependency counselor, member of the clergy</u> or other person..., <u>whether or not licensed by the state. who performs or purports to perform</u> psychotherapy...

(2) Any person who is or who holds himself or herself out to be a therapist and who intentionally has sexual contact with a patient or client during any <u>ongoing therapist-patient or therapist-client relationship. regardless of whether it occurs during any</u> treatment, consultation, interview or examination, is guilty of a <u>Class D felony. Consent is not an issue in an action under this subsection.</u>

•940.225. Sexual assault

(2) Second degree sexual assault. Whoever does any of the following is guilty of a Class C felony:

---

[1]Section 991.11, WISCONSIN STATUTES 1981-82. Effective Date of acts. "Every act and every portion of an act enacted by the legislature over the governor's veto which does not expressly prescribe the time when it takes effect shall take effect on the day after its date of publication as designated" by the secretary of state [the date of publication must be within 10 working days from the date of enactment].

(b) Has sexual contact or sexual intercourse with another person without consent of that person and causes injury, illness, disease or impairment of a sexual or reproductive organ, or mental anguish requiring psychiatric care for the victim.

•Wisc. Stat. Ann. Sections 940.22(2) & 940.225(2)(b) (Supp 1985)

•In Wisconsin, "psychotherapy" is defined by Wisconsin Statutes 455.01(6):

Psychotherapy means the use of learning, conditioning methods and emotional reactions in a professional relationship to assist persons to modify feelings, attitudes, and behaviors which are intellectually, socially, or emotionally maladjustive or ineffectual.

APPENDIX H

CRIMINAL STATUTE: MINNESOTA

Minnesota Criminal Sexual Conduct Code

August 1, 1985

Indicates portions of the code that specifically relate to psychotherapist/ client sexual abuse; however, any part of the code may be used in prosecuting a sexually abusive psychotherapist.‖

609.341 DEFINITIONS.

Subdivision 1. For the purposes of sections 609.341 to 609.351, the terms in this section have the meanings given them.

Subd. 2. "Actor" means a person accused of criminal sexual conduct.

Subd. 3. "Force" means the infliction, attempted infliction, or threatened infliction by the actor of bodily harm or commission or threat of any other crime by the actor against the complainant or another, which causes the complainant to reasonably believe that the actor has the present ability to execute the threat, and also causes the complainant to submit.

Subd. 4. "Consent" means a voluntary uncoerced manifestation of a present agreement to perform a particular sexual act.

Subd. 5. "Intimate parts" includes the primary genital area, groin, inner thigh, buttocks, or breast of a human being.

Subd. 6. "Mentally impaired" means that a person, as a result of inadequately developed or impaired intelligence or a substantial psychiatric disorder of thought or mood, lacks the judgment to give a reasoned consent to sexual contact or to sexual penetration.

Subd. 7. "Mentally incapacitated" means that a person is rendered temporarily incapable of appraising or controlling his conduct due to the influence of alcohol, a narcotic, anesthetic, or any other substance administered to that person without his agreement, or due to any other act committed upon that person without his agreement.

Subd. 8. "Personal injury" means bodily harm as defined in section 609.02, subdivision 7, or severe mental anguish or pregnancy.

Subd. 9. "Physically helpless" means that a person is (a) asleep or not conscious, (b) unable to withhold consent or to withdraw because of a physical condition, or (c) unable to communicate nonconsent and the condition is known or reasonably should have been known to the actor.

Subd. 10. "Position of authority" includes but is not limited to any person who is a parent or acting in the place of a parent and charged with any of a parent's rights, duties or responsibilities to a child, or a person who is charged with any duty or responsibility for the health, welfare, or supervision of a child, either independently or through another, no matter how brief, at the time of the act.

Subd. 11. "Sexual contact" includes any of the following acts committed without the complainant's consent, for the purpose of satisfying the actor's sexual or aggressive impulses, except in those cases where consent is not a defense:

(i) the intentional touching by the actor of the complainant's intimate parts, or

(ii) the touching by the complainant of the actor's, the complainant's, or another's intimate parts effected by coercion or the use of a position of authority, or by inducement if the complainant is under 13 years of age or mentally impaired, or

(iii) the touching by another of the complainant's intimate parts effected by coercion or the use of a position of authority, or

(iv) in any of the cases above, of the clothing covering the immediate area of the intimate parts.

Subd. 12. "Sexual penetration" means sexual intercourse, cunnilingus, fellatio, anal intercourse, or any intrusion however slight into the genital or anal openings of the complainant's body of any part of the actor's body or any object used by the actor for this purpose, where the act is committed without the complainant's consent, except in those cases where consent is not a defense. Emission of semen is not necessary.

Subd. 13. "Complainant" means a person alleged to have been subjected to criminal sexual conduct, but need not be the person who signs the complaint.

Subd. 14. "Coercion" means words or circumstances that cause the complainant reasonably to fear that the actor will inflict bodily harm upon, or hold in confinement, the complainant or another.

Subd. 15. **Significant relationship.** "Significant relationship" means a situation in which the actor is:

(1) the complainant's parent, stepparent, or guardian;

(2) any of the following persons related to the complainant by blood, marriage, or adoption: brother, sister, stepbrother, stepsister, first cousin, aunt, uncle, nephew, niece, grandparent, great-grandparent, great-uncle, great-aunt; or

(3) an adult who jointly resides intermittently or regularly in the same dwelling as the complainant and who is not the complainant's spouse.

Subd. 16. "Patient" means a person who seeks or obtains psychotherapeutic services.

Subd. 17. "Psychotherapist" means a physician, psychologist, nurse, chemical dependency counselor, social worker, clergy, or other person, whether or not licensed by the state, who performs or purports to perform psychotherapy.

Subd. 18. "Psychotherapy" means the professional treatment, assessment, or counseling of a mental or emotional illness, symptom, or condition.

Subd. 19. "Emotionally dependent" means that the nature of the patient's or former patient's emotional condition and the nature of the treatment provided by the psychotherapist are such that the psychotherapist knows or has reason to know that the patient or former patient is unable to withhold consent to sexual contact or sexual penetration by the psychotherapist.

Subd. 20. "Therapeutic deception" means a representation by a psychotherapist that sexual contact or sexual penetration by the psychotherapist is consistent with or part of the patient's treatment.

609.342 CRIMINAL SEXUAL CONDUCT IN THE FIRST DEGREE

Subdivision 1. **Crime defined**. A person is guilty of criminal sexual conduct in the first degree if he engages in sexual penetration with another person and if any of the following circumstances exists:

(a) the complainant is under 13 years of age and the actor is more than 36 months older than the complainant. Neither mistake as to the complainant's age nor consent to the act by the complainant is a defense;

(b) the complainant is at least 13 but less than 16 years of age and the actor is more than 48 months older than the complainant and in a position of authority over the complainant, and uses this authority to cause the complainant to submit. Neither mistake as to the complainant's age nor consent to the act by the complainant is a defense;

(c) circumstances existing at the time of the act cause the complainant to have a reasonable fear of imminent great bodily harm to the complainant or another;

(d) the actor is armed with a dangerous weapon or any article used or fashioned in a manner to lead the complainant as to reasonably believe it to be a dangerous weapon and uses or threatens to use the weapon or article to cause the complainant to submit;

(e) the actor causes personal injury to the complainant, and either of the following circumstances exist:

(i) the actor uses force or coercion to accomplish sexual penetration; or

(ii) the actor knows or has reason to know that the complainant is mentally impaired, mentally incapacitated, or physically helpless;

(f) the actor is aided or abetted by one or more accomplices within the meaning of section 609.05, and either of the following circumstances exists:

(i) an accomplice uses force or coercion to cause the complainant to submit; or

(ii) an accomplice is armed with a dangerous weapon or any article used or fashioned in a manner to lead the complainant reasonably to believe it to be a dangerous weapon and uses or threatens to use the weapon or article to cause the complainant to submit;

(g) the actor has a significant relationship to the complainant and the complainant was under 16 years of age at the time of the sexual penetration. Neither mistake as to the complainant's age nor consent to the act by the complainant is a defense; or

(h) the actor has a significant relationship to the complainant, the complainant was under 16 years of age at the time of the sexual penetration, and:

(i) the actor or an accomplice used force or coercion to accomplish the penetration;

(ii) the actor or an accomplice was armed with a dangerous weapon or any article used or fashioned in a manner to lead the complainant to reasonably believe it could be a dangerous weapon and used or threatened to use the dangerous weapon;

(iii) circumstances existed at the time of the act to cause the complainant to have a reasonable fear of imminent great bodily harm to the complainant or another;

(iv) the complainant suffered personal injury; or

(v) the sexual abuse involved multiple acts committed over an extended period of time.

Neither mistake as to the complainant's age nor consent to the act by the complainant is a defense.

Subd. 2. **Penalty**. A person convicted under subdivision 1 may be sentenced to imprisonment for not more than 20 years or to a payment of a fine of not more than $35,000, or both.

Subd. 3. **Stay**. Except when imprisonment is required under section 609.346, if a person is convicted under subdivision 1, clause (g), the court may stay imposition or execution of the sentence if it finds that:

(a) a stay is in the best interest of the complainant or the family unit; and

(b) a professional assessment indicates that the offender has been accepted by and can respond to a treatment program.

If the court stays imposition or execution of a sentence, it shall include the following as conditions of probation:

(1) incarceration in a local jail or workhouse; and

(2) a requirement that the offender complete a treatment program.

History: *1985 c 24 s 5; 1985 c 286 s 15*

609.343 CRIMINAL SEXUAL CONDUCT IN THE SECOND DEGREE.

Subdivision 1. **Crime defined.** A person is guilty of criminal sexual conduct in the second degree if he engages in sexual contact with another person and if any of the following circumstances exists:

(a) the complainant is under 13 years of age and the actor is more than 36 months older than the complainant. Neither mistake as to the complainant's age nor consent to the act by the complainant is a defense. In a prosecution under this clause, the state is not required to prove that the sexual contact was coerced;

(b) the complainant is at least 13 but less than 16 years of age and the actor is more than 48 months older than the complainant and in a position of authority over the complainant, and uses this authority to cause the complainant to submit. Neither mistake as to the complainant's age nor consent to the act by the complainant is a defense;

(c) circumstances existing at the time of the act cause the complainant to have a reasonable fear of imminent great bodily harm to the complainant or another;

(d) the actor is armed with a dangerous weapon or any article used or fashioned in a manner to lead the complainant to reasonably believe it to be a dangerous weapon and uses or threatens to use the dangerous weapon to cause the complainant to submit;

(e) the actor causes personal injury to the complainant, and either of the following circumstances exist:

(i) the actor uses force or coercion to accomplish the sexual contact; or

(ii) the actor knows or has reason to know that the complainant is mentally impaired, mentally incapacitated, or physically helpless;

(f) the actor is aided or abetted by one or more accomplices within the meaning of section 609.05, and either of the following circumstances exists:

(i) an accomplice uses force or coercion to cause the complainant to submit; or

(ii) an accomplice is armed with a dangerous weapon or any article used or fashioned in a manner to lead the complainant to reasonably believe it to be a dangerous weapon and uses or threatens to use the weapon or article to cause the complainant to submit;

(g) the actor has a significant relationship to the complainant and the complainant was under 16 years of age at the time of the sexual contact. Neither mistake as to the complainant's age nor consent to the act by the complainant is a defense; or

(h) the actor has a significant relationship to the complainant, the complainant was under 16 years of age at the time of the sexual contact, and:

(i) the actor or an accomplice used force or coercion to accomplish the contact;

(ii) the actor or an accomplice was armed with a dangerous weapon or any article used or fashioned in a manner to lead the complainant to reasonably believe it could be a dangerous weapon and used or threatened to use the dangerous weapon;

(iii) circumstances existed at the time of the act to cause the complainant to have a reasonable fear of imminent great bodily harm to the complainant or another;

(iv) the complainant suffered personal injury; or

(v) the sexual abuse involved multiple acts committed over an extended period of time.

Neither mistake as to the complainant's age nor consent to the act by the complainant is a defense.

Subd. 2. **Penalty.** A person convicted under subdivision 1 may be sentenced to imprisonment for not more than 15 years or to a payment of a fine of not more than $30,000, or both.

Subd. 3. **Stay.** Except when imprisonment is required under section 609.346, if a person is convicted under subdivision 1, clause (g), the court may stay imposition or execution of the sentence if it finds that:

(a) a stay is in the best interest of the complainant or the family unit; and

(b) a professional assessment indicates that the offender has been accepted by and can respond to a treatment program.

If the court stays imposition or execution of sentence, it shall include the following as conditions of probation:

(1) incarceration in a local jail or workhouse; and

(2) a requirement that the offender complete a treatment program.

History: *1985 c 24 s 6; 1985 c 286 s 16*

609.344 CRIMINAL SEXUAL CONDUCT IN THE THIRD DEGREE.

Subdivision 1. **Crime defined.** A person is guilty of criminal sexual conduct in the third degree if he engages in sexual penetration with another person and any of the following circumstances exists:

(a) the complainant is under 13 years of age and the actor is no more than 36 months older than the complainant. Neither mistake as to the complainant's age nor consent to the act by the complainant shall be a defense;

(b) the complainant is at least 13 but less than 16 years of age and the actor is more than 24 months older than the complainant. In any such case it shall be an affirmative defense, which must be proved by a preponderance of the evidence, that the actor believes the complainant to be 16 years of age or older. If the actor in such a case is nor more than 48 months but more than 24 months older than the complainant, he may be sentenced to imprisonment for not more than five years. Consent by the complainant is not a defense;

(c) the actor uses force or coercion to accomplish the penetration;

(d) the actor knows or has reason to know that the complainant is mentally impaired, mentally incapacitated, or physically helpless;

(e) the complainant is at least 16 but less than 18 years of age and the actor is more than 48 months older than the complainant and in a position of authority over the complainant, and uses this authority to cause the complainant to submit. Neither mistake as to the complainant's age nor consent to the act by the complainant is a defense;

(f) the actor has a significant relationship to the complainant and the complainant was at least 16 but under 18 years of age at the time of the sexual penetration. Neither mistake as to the complainant's age nor consent to the act by the complainant is a defense; or

(g) the actor has a significant relationship to the complainant, the complainant was at least 16 but under 18 years of age at the time of the sexual penetration, and:

(i) the actor or an accomplice used force or coercion to accomplish the penetration;

(ii) the actor or an accomplice was armed with a dangerous weapon or any article used or fashioned in a manner to lead the complainant to reasonably believe it could be a dangerous weapon and used or threatened to use the dangerous weapon;

(iii) circumstances existed at the time of the act to cause the complainant to have a reasonable fear of imminent great bodily harm to the complainant or another;

(iv) the complainant suffered person injury; or

(v) the sexual abuse involved multiple acts committed over an extended period of time.

(h) the actor is a psychotherapist and the complainant is a patient of the psychotherapist and the sexual penetration occurred during the psychotherapy session. Consent by the complainant is not a defense;

(i) the actor is a psychotherapist and the complainant is a patient or former patient of the psychotherapist and the patient or former patient is emotionally dependent upon the psychotherapist; or

(j) the actor is a psychotherapist and the complainant is a patient or former patient and the sexual penetration occurred by means of therapeutic deception. Consent by the complainant is not a defense.

Neither mistake as to the complainant's age nor consent to the act by the complainant is a defense.

Subd. 2. **Penalty.** A person convicted under subdivision 1 may be sentenced to imprisonment for not more than ten years or to a payment of a fine of not more than $20,000, or both.

609.344 CRIMINAL CODE OF 1963

Subd. 3. **Stay.** Except when imprisonment is required under section 609.346, if a person is convicted under subdivision 1, clause (f), the court may stay imposition or execution of the sentence if it finds that:

(a) a stay is in the best interest of the complainant or the family unit; and

(b) a professional assessment indicates that the offender has been accepted by and can respond to a treatment program.

If the court stays imposition or execution of sentence, it shall include the following as conditions of probation:

(1) incarceration in a local jail or workhouse; and

(2) a requirement that the offender complete a treatment program.

History: *1985 c 24 s 7; 1985 c 286 s 17; 1985 c 297 s 6*

609.345 CRIMINAL SEXUAL CONDUCT IN THE FOURTH DEGREE.

Subdivision 1. **Crime defined.** A person is guilty of criminal sexual conduct in the fourth degree if he engages in sexual contact with another person and if any of the following circumstances exists:

(a) the complainant is under 13 years of age and the actor is no more than 36 months older than the complainant. Neither mistake as to the complainant's age or consent to the act by the complainant is a defense. In a prosecution under this clause, the state is not required to prove that the sexual contact was coerced;

(b) the complainant is at least 13 but less than 16 years of age and the actor is more than 48 months older than the complainant or in a position of authority over the complainant and uses this authority to cause the complainant to submit. In any such case, it shall be an affirmative defense which must be proved by a preponderance of the evidence that the actor believes the complainant to be 16 years of age or older;

(c) the actor uses force or coercion to accomplish the sexual contact;

(d) the actor knows or has reason to know that the complainant is mentally impaired, mentally incapacitated, or physically helpless;

(e) the complainant is at least 16 but less than 18 years of age and the actor is more than 48 months older than the complainant and in a position of authority over the complainant, and uses this authority to cause the complainant to submit. Neither mistake as to the complainant's age nor consent to the act by the complainant is a defense;

(f) the actor has a significant relationship to the complainant and the complainant was at least 16 but under 18 years of age at the time of the sexual contact. Neither mistake as to the complainant's age nor consent to the act by the complainant is a defense; or

(g) the actor has a significant relationship to the complainant, the complainant was at least 16 but under 18 years of age at the time of the sexual contact, and:

(i) the actor or an accomplice used force or coercion to accomplish the contact;

(ii) the actor or an accomplice was armed with a dangerous weapon or any article used or fashioned in a manner to lead the complainant to reasonably believe it could be a dangerous weapon and used or threatened to use the dangerous weapon;

(iii) circumstances existed at the time of the act to cause the complainant to have a reasonable fear of imminent great bodily harm to the complainant or another;

(iv) the complainant suffered personal injury; or

(v) the sexual abuse involved multiple acts committed over an extended period of time.

(h) the actor is a psychotherapist and the complainant is a patient of the psychotherapist and the sexual contact occurred during the psychotherapy session. Consent by the complainant is not a defense;

(i) the actor is a psychotherapist and the complainant is a patient or former patient of the psychotherapist and the patient or former patient is emotionally dependent upon the psychotherapist; or

(j) the actor is a psychotherapist and the complainant is a patient or former patient and the sexual contact occurred by means of therapeutic deception. Consent by the complainant is not a defense.

Neither mistake as to the complainant's age nor consent to the act by the complainant is a defense.

Subd. 2. **Penalty.** A person convicted under subdivision 1 may be sentenced to imprisonment for not more than five years or to a payment of a fine of not more than $10,000, or both.

Subd. 3. **Stay.** Except when imprisonment is required under section 609.346, if a person is convicted under subdivision 1, clause (f), the court may stay imposition or execution of the sentence if it finds that:

(a) a stay is in the best interest of the complainant or the family unit; and

(b) a professional assessment indicates that the offender has been accepted by and can respond to a treatment program.

If the court stays imposition or execution of sentence, it shall include the following as conditions of probation:

(1) incarceration in a local jail or workhouse; and

(2) a requirement that the offender complete a treatment program.

History: *1985 c 24 s 8; 1985 c 286 s 18; 1985 c 297 s 7*

609.346 SUBSEQUENT OFFENSES.

Subdivision 1. **Definition; conviction of offense.** For purposes of this section, the term "offense" means a completed offense or an attempt to commit an offense.

Subd. 2. **Subsequent offense; penalty.** If a person is convicted of a second or subsequent offense under sections 609.342 to 609.345 or sections 609.364 to 609.3644 within 15 years of the prior conviction, the court shall commit the defendant to the commissioner of corrections for imprisonment for a term of not less than three years, nor more than the maximum sentence provided by law for the offense for which convicted, notwithstanding the provisions of sections 242.19, 243.05, 609.11, 609.12 and 609.135.

Subd. 3. **Prior convictions under similar statutes.** For the purposes of this section, an offense is considered a second or subsequent offense if, prior to conviction of the second or subsequent offense, the actor has been at any time convicted under sections 609.342 to 609.345 or sections 609.364 to 609.3644 or under any similar statute of the United States, or this or any other state.

History: *1975 c 374 s 7; 1978 c 723 art 1 s 16; 1981 c 273 s 4; 1984 c 588 s 9; 1984 c 655 art 1 s 77*

609.347 EVIDENCE.

[For text of subds 1 to 5, see M.S.1984]

Subd. 6. (a) In a prosecution under sections 609.342 to 609.346 involving a psychotherapist and patient, evidence of the patient's personal or medical history is not admissible except when:

(1) the defendant requests a hearing prior to trial and makes an offer of proof of the relevancy of the history; and

(2) the court finds that the history is relevant and that the probative value of the history outweighs its prejudicial value.

(b) The court shall allow the admission only of specific information or examples of conduct of the complainant that are determined by the court to be relevant. The court's order shall detail the information or conduct that is admissible and no other evidence of the history may be introduced.

(c) Violation of the terms of the order is grounds for mistrial but does not prevent the retrial of the defendant.

History: *1985 c 297 s 8*

609.3471 RECORDS PERTAINING TO VICTIM IDENTITY CONFIDENTIAL.

Notwithstanding any provision of law to the contrary, no data contained in records or reports relating to complaints or indictments issued pursuant to sections 609.342, clause (a) or (b); 609.343, clause (a) or (b); 609.344, clause (a) or (b); 609.345, clause (a) or (b); or 609.3641 to 609.3644, which specifically identifies the victim shall be accessible to the public, except by order of the court. Nothing in this section authorizes denial of access to any other data contained in the records or reports, including the identity of the defendant.

History: *1985 c 119 s 1*

APPENDIX I

Sentencing Guidelines as Modified Aug. 1, 1985

with Commentary on Recommended Sentencing

for Therapists who are Convicted of Sexual Exploitation of Clients

SUMMARY INFORMATION ON MINNESOTA'S SENTENCING GUIDELINES

The purposes of the guidelines are to 1) reduce sentencing disparity for those convicted of felonies; 2) establish proportionality in sentencing by recommending harsher sanctions for serious person offenders and property offenders with lengthy criminal history records; 3) provide certainty and truth in sentencing so that it is known what period of time will be served when sentence is pronounced; and 4) coordinate sentencing practices with the correctional resources made available by the legislature.

The Minnesota Sentencing Guidelines Commission was created by the Legislature in 1978 to establish sentencing guidelines which define:

1. when state imprisonment of a felon is appropriate, and

2. a fixed sentence for felons who are imprisoned in state facilities based on reasonable offense and offender characteristics.

The sentencing guidelines apply to persons convicted of felonies committed on or after May 1, 1980. Guidelines replace the old indeterminate system where judges pronounced symbolic sentences and the parole board determined actual durations. Guidelines are presumptive with respect to who should go to prison and the length of the sentence. Felons imprisoned in state prisons under the guidelines serve the sentence pronounced by the judge, reduced by good time. Judges can depart from the guidelines if there are substantial and compelling circumstances associated with the case. Either the defendant or the county attorney may appeal any sentence to the Appeals Courts.

The recommended guideline sentence is based on two factors: the primary factor is the severity of the conviction offense and the secondary factor is the criminal history score of the offender.

The Commission ranked all Minnesota felony offenses into ten levels according to the severity of the offense. These ten severity levels comprise the vertical axis of the sentencing guidelines grid. By law, First Degree Murder is excluded from the guidelines and continues to have a mandatory life sentence. The Commission continues to rank felony offenses as they are created or amended by the state legislature. (A full listing of offenses in the various severity levels is contained on pages 33 through 40 of the sentencing guidelines.)

The criminal history index measures the offender's prior record, and the score on that index comprises the horizontal axis of the sentencing guidelines grid. The index consists of four measures of prior criminal record: (1) the number of prior felony sentences; (2) a limited measure of prior misdemeanor/gross misdemeanor sentences; (3) a limited measure of the prior serious juvenile record; and (4) "custody status", which indicates if the offender was on probation or parole status when the current offense was committed.

The recommended guideline sentence is found in the cell of the sentencing guidelines grid where the offender's criminal history score and the appropriate severity level intersect. For cells above and to the left of the solid line, the guidelines recommend a stayed sentence unless the conviction offense carries a mandatory minimum sentence. For cells below and to the right of the solid line, the guidelines recommend imprisonment in a state prison. The number in the cell is the recommended length of the prison sentence in months.

For offenders given stayed sentences, the judge may set probationary conditions including fines, restitution, treatment, community work orders, or confinement in a county jail or workhouse for a period up to one year. At present, there are no guidelines for judges to use when setting conditions of a stayed sentence or the length of probation.

Those imprisoned under the guidelines will serve the prison sentence pronounced by the judge, reduced by one day for every two days of good behavior. All offenders must serve a period of supervised release equal to the amount of good time earned. Thus, on a 60 month prison sentence an offender would serve 40 months in prison, and 20 months on supervised release subject to conditions set by the Commissioner of Corrections. If the offender violates those conditions, the supervised release may be revoked and the offender returned to prison.

The current Commission consists of 11 members: one justice from the Supreme Court, one judge from the Court of Appeals, two district court judges, a prosecuting attorney, a defense attorney, a probation officer representative, a law enforcement representative, the Commissioner of Corrections, and two citizen representatives, one of which is a crime victim. The current Chair of the Commission is Dan Cain, one of the citizen representatives.

Second, the Commission modifies the guidelines each year. The major area of modification is the ranking of crimes created or amended by the legislature. Modifications are also made in response to case law and to problems identified by the monitoring system.

Third, the Commission provides information and training on sentencing guidelines to criminal justice groups, the legislature, and other interested organizations.

For Further Information Contact:

Minnesota Sentencing Guidelines Commission
51 State Office Building
St. Paul, MN 55155
Phone: (612) 296-0144

II. Mandatory Minimum Provisions for Second or Subsequent Sex Offenders.

A. *Statutory Provisions*

1. Minn. Stat. § 609.346 establishes a three year mandatory minimum sentence for any second or subsequent completed or attempted criminal sexual conduct or intrafamilial sexual abuse offense that occurred within 15 years of the current offense.

2. The definition of second or subsequent is unique to this provision. For the purposes of sex offenses, an offense is considered a second or subsequent offense if, prior to conviction of the second or subsequent offense, the offender had already been convicted of a criminal sexual conduct or intrafamilial sexual abuse offense.

C. *Presumptive Sentences*

1. The presumptive duration for second or subsequent sex offenses is 36 months or the cell time, whichever is greater.

2. Although the Supreme Court decision authorized stays of execution for second or subsequent sex offenses, the presumptive disposition for second or subsequent sex offenses is still imprisonment. A stay of execution for such a case constitutes a dispositional departure and written reasons which specify the substantial and compelling nature of the circumstances and which demonstrate why the disposition selected is more appropriate, reasonable, or equitable than the presumptive duration are required (See <u>Minnesota Sentencing Guidelines and Commentary, Revised August 1, 1984</u>, II.E.03.)

In the sentencing guidelines grid which follows, Criminal Sexual Conduct in the Third Degree which involves a therapist exploiting a client with penetration [609.344 subd. 1(h)(i)(j)] is rated as level 7. Some other types of 3rd degree conduct are rated only as level 5. Criminal Sexual Conduct in the Fourth Degree involving a therapist exploiting a client without penetration [609.345 subd. 1(h)(i)(j)] is rated as level 6.

IV. SENTENCING GUIDELINES GRID
Presumptive Sentence Lengths in Months

Italicized numbers within the grid denote the range within which a judge may sentence without the sentence being deemed a departure.

Offenders with nonimprisonment felony sentences are subject to jail time according to law.

CRIMINAL HISTORY SCORE

SEVERITY LEVELS OF CONVICTION OFFENSE		0	1	2	3	4	5	6 or more
Unauthorized Use of Motor Vehicle Possession of Marijuana	I	12*	12*	12*	13	15	17	19 *18-20*
Theft Related Crimes ($2500 or less) Check Forgery ($200-$2500)	II	12*	12*	13	15	17	19	21 *20-22*
Theft Crimes ($2500 or less)	III	12*	13	15	17	19 *18-20*	22 *21-23*	25 *24-26*
Nonresidential Burglary Theft Crimes (over $2500)	IV	12*	15	18	21	25 *24-26*	32 *30-34*	41 *37-45*
Residential Burglary Simple Robbery	V	18	23	27	30 *29-31*	38 *36-40*	46 *43-49*	54 *50-58*
Criminal Sexual Conduct 2nd Degree (a) & (b)	VI	21	26	30	34 *33-35*	44 *42-46*	54 *50-58*	65 *60-70*
Aggravated Robbery	VII	24 *23-25*	32 *30-34*	41 *38-44*	49 *45-53*	65 *60-70*	81 *75-87*	97 *90-104*
Criminal Sexual Conduct 1st Degree Assault, 1st Degree	VIII	43 *41-45*	54 *50-58*	65 *60-70*	76 *71-81*	95 *89-101*	113 *106-120*	132 *124-140*
Murder, 3rd Degree Murder, 2nd Degree (felony murder)	IX							
Murder, 2nd Degree (with intent)	X							

COMMENTARY ON SENTENCING OF PSYCHOTHERAPISTS
WHO SEXUALLY ABUSE CLIENTS

By Gary Schoener

Minnesota is one of the states which utilizes a Sentencing Guidelines Commission. Relevant sections of these Guidelines are on the pages which follow.

The Minnesota State Task Force on Sexual Exploitation by Counselors and Psychotherapists successfully argued that to have a deterrent effect the sentencing guidelines for a psychotherapist convicted of criminal sexual conduct with a client needed to be serious ones. In particular, it was argued that there needed to be a prison term for the first offense.

The relevance of these guidelines are that judges are obligated to either follow them in their sentencing, or to explain their deviation from them. In other words, if the sentence they give in a specific case is either harsher or more lenient, they must justify it.

Please note that the sentencing guidelines do not make any recommendation regarding fines, so the judge can use complete discretion in this area. A therapist convicted of Criminal Sexual Conduct in the 3rd degree (with penetration) may be fined up to $20,000, whereas one convicted of Criminal Sexual Conduct in the 4th degree (sexual touching, but no penetration) may be fined up to $10,000.

The Sentencing Guidelines Commission ruled that the first offense with 3rd degree Criminal Sexual Conduct would have presumptive sentencing—meaning a mandatory prison sentence for the first offense. The sentence for the first conviction would be 24 months if the therapist has no criminal history. In the case of 4th degree Criminal Sexual Conduct (assuming no criminal history), there would be probation for up to five years, with stayed sentence of 21 months (meaning a 21-month sentence if they violate probation) with the first offense, but presumptive sentencing of 36 months in prison with the 2nd conviction. (Minn. Sent. Guidelines Commission, 1985a & b).

It should be noted that the sentence for a 4th degree conviction is more severe than that for intrafamilial sexual abuse.

STATE OF MINNESOTA
SENTENCING GUIDELINES MODIFICATIONS
EFFECTIVE AUGUST 1, 1985

C. Presumptive Sentence: The offense of conviction determines the appropriate severity level on the vertical axis. The offender's criminal history score, computed according to section B above, determines the appropriate location on the horizontal axis. The presumptive fixed sentence for a felony conviction is found in the Sentencing Guidelines Grid cell at the intersection of the column defined by the criminal history score and the row defined by the offense severity level. The offenses within the Sentencing Guidelines Grid are presumptive with respect to the duration of the sentence and whether imposition or execution of the felony sentence should be stayed.

The line on the Sentencing Guidelines Grid demarcates those cases for whom the presumptive sentence is executed from those for whom the presumptive sentence is stayed. For cases contained in cells below and to the right of the line, the sentence should be executed. For cases in cells above and to the left of the line, the sentence should be stayed, unless the conviction offense carries a mandatory minimum sentence.

When the current conviction offense is burglary of an occupied dwelling (Minn. Stat. § 609.582, subd.1 (a)) and there was a previous adjudication of guilt for a felony burglary before the current offense occurred, the presumptive disposition is Commitment to the Commissioner of Corrections. The presumptive duration of sentence is the fixed duration indicated in the appropriate cell of the Sentencing Guidelines Grid. <u>Similarly, when the current conviction offense is sale of a severity level VI drug or sale of cocaine and there was a previous adjudication of guilt for a sale of a severity level VI drug or sale of cocaine before the current offense occurred, the presumptive disposition is Commitment to the Commissioner of Corrections. The presumptive duration of sentence is the fixed duration indicated in the appropriate cell of the Sentencing Guidelines Grid.</u>

Every cell in the Sentencing Guidelines Grid provides a fixed duration of sentence. For cells below the solid line, the guidelines provide both a presumptive prison sentence and a range of time for that sentence. Any prison sentence duration pronounced by the sentencing judge which is outside the range of the presumptive duration is a departure from the guidelines, regardless of whether the sentence is executed or stayed, and requires written reasons from the judge pursuant to Minn. Stat. § 244.10, subd. 3, and section E of these guidelines.

Modifications to <u>Offense Severity Reference Table</u>

VIII ~~Intrafamilial Sexual Abuse 1 - 609.3641~~

Criminal Sexual Conduct 2 - 609.343 (c), (d), & (f)<u>, & (h)</u>
Criminal Sexual Conduct 3 - 609.344 (c)<u>,</u> & (d)<u>, & (g)</u>
VII   <u>Criminal Sexual Conduct 3 - 609.344 (h), (i), & (j)</u>
~~Intrafamilial Sexual Abuse 2 - 609.3642, subd. 1 (2)~~
~~Intrafamilial Sexual Abuse 3 - 609.3643, subd. 1 (2)~~

Criminal Sexual Conduct 2 - 609.343 (a)<u>,</u> & (b)<u>, & (g)</u>
Criminal Sexual Conduct 4 - 609.345 (c)<u>,</u> & <u>(d), & (g)</u>
VI   <u>Criminal Sexual Conduct 4 - 609.345 (h), (i) & (j)</u>
~~Intrafamilial Sexual Abuse 2 - 609.3642, subd. 1 (1)~~
~~Intrafamilial Sexual Abuse 4 - 609.3644, subd. 1 (2)~~

Criminal Sexual Conduct 3 - 609.344 (b)<u>,</u> & (e)<u>, & (f)</u>
V   ~~Intrafamilial Sexual Abuse 3 - 609.3643, subd. 1 (1)~~

Criminal Sexual Conduct 4 - 609.345 (b)<u>,</u> & <u>(e), & (f)</u>
IV   ~~Intrafamilial Sexual Abuse 4 - 609.3644, subd. 1 (1)~~

II   Negligent Fires (damage greater than $10,000) - 609.576 (b) ~~(4)~~ (3)

COMMENTARY MODIFICATIONS
EFFECTIVE AUGUST 1, 1985

II.A.02. The date of the offense is important because the offender's age at the time of the offense will determine whether or not the juvenile record is considered, ~~and~~ the date of the offense might determine whether a custody status point should be given~~.~~<u>, and the date of offense determines the order of sentencing with multiple convictions.</u> For those convicted of a *single offense, there is generally no problem in determining the date of the offense. For those convicted of multiple offenses* <u>*when theft and damage to property aggregation procedures are*</u> <u>*used for sentencing purposes or when multiple offenses are an element of the conviction*</u> <u>*offense, the following rules apply:*</u> ~~*the following rules should apply in determining the date of the offense:*~~

> ~~*a. The date of the most severe offense should be used. If there are two or more convictions of equal severity, and none of a higher severity, the earliest of the offenses should be used to establish the date of the offense.*~~

> <u>*a.*</u> *If offenses have been aggregated under Minn. Stat. § 609.52, subd. 3(5), or § 609.595, the date of the earliest offense should be used as the date of the* <u>*conviction*</u> *offense.*

> <u>*b. If multiple offenses are an element of the conviction offense, such as in Subd. 1 (h) (v) of first degree criminal sexual conduct, the date of the earliest offense should be used as the date of the conviction offense.*</u>

<u>*If the date of the offense is not specified in the complaint and cannot be ascertained with certainty, the judge shall establish the relative order of events, based on the information available, to determine whether or not the juvenile record is to be considered, whether or not a custody status point is to be assigned, and the order of sentencing.*</u>

If the date of offense established by the above rules is on or before April 30, 1980, the sentencing guidelines should not be used to sentence the case.

II.A.04. *Incest was excluded because since 1975, the great majority of incest cases are prosecuted under the criminal sexual conduct statutes.* ~~*and more recently, under the intrafamilial sexual abuse statutes.*~~ *If an offender is convicted of incest under Minn. Stat. § 609.365, and when the offense would have been a violation of one of the criminal sexual conduct statutes* ~~*or intrafamilial sexual abuse statutes*~~, *the severity level of the applicable criminal sexual conduct* ~~*or intrafamilial sexual abuse*~~ *statute should be used. For example, if a father is convicted of incest for the sexual penetration of his ten year old daughter, the appropriate severity level would be the same as criminal sexual conduct in the first degree* ~~*or intrafamilial sexual abuse in the first degree*~~. *On the other hand, when the incest consists of behavior not included in the criminal sexual conduct* ~~*or intrafamilial sexual abuse*~~ *statues (for example, consenting sexual penetration involving individuals over age 18) that offense behavior is excluded from the Offense Severity Reference Table.*

<u>**II.A.06.** *When felony offenses are inadvertently omitted from the sentencing guidelines, judges should exercise their discretion by assigning an offense a severity level which they believe to be appropriate. A felony offense is inadvertently omitted when the offense appears neither in the Offense Severity Reference Table nor in the list of offenses in II.A.03, which are excluded from the Offense Severity Reference Table.*</u>

II.B.101. *The basic rule for computing the number of prior felony points in the criminal history score is that the offender is assigned one point for every felony conviction for which a felony sentence was stayed or imposed before the current sentencing. In cases of multiple offenses occurring in a single behavioral incident in which state law prohibits the offender being sentenced on more than one offense, the offender would receive one point. The phrase "before the current sentencing" means that in order for prior convictions to be used in computing criminal history score, the felony sentence for the prior offense must have been stayed or imposed before sentencing for the current offense. When multiple current offenses are sentenced on the same day before the same judge, sentencing shall occur in the order in* *which the offenses occurred. <u>The dates of the offenses shall be determined according to the procedures in II.A.02.</u>*

<u>II.B.108. A felony sentence imposed for a criminal conviction treated pursuant to Minn. Stat. Ch. 242 (Youth Conservation Commission and later Youth Corrections Board, repealed 1977) shall be assigned one felony point in computing the criminal history score according to procedures in II.B.1.</u>

<u>II.B.204. When three months is added to the cell duration as a result of the custody status provision, the lower and upper durations of the sentence range in the appropriate cell are also increased by three months.</u>

<u>II.B.205. When the conviction offense is an attempt or conspiracy under Minn. Stats. §§ 609.17 or 609.175 and three months is added to the cell duration as a result of the custody status provision, the following procedure shall be used in determining the presumptive duration for the offense. First, three months is added to the appropriate cell duration for the completed offense, which becomes the presumptive duration for the completed offense. The presumptive duration for the completed offense is then divided by two which is the presumptive duration for those convicted of attempted offenses or conspiracies. No such presumptive sentence, however, shall be less than one year and one day.</u>

II.B.302. The Commission placed a limit of one point on the consideration of misdemeanors or gross misdemeanors in the criminal history score. This was done because with no limit on point accrual, persons with lengthy, but relatively minor, misdemeanor records could accrue high criminal history scores and, thus, be subject to inappropriately severe sentences upon their first felony conviction. <u>With the exception of offenses with monetary thresholds</u> ~~T~~the Commission limited consideration of misdemeanors to those which are misdemeanors under existing state statute, or ordinance misdemeanors which substantially conform to existing state statutory misdemeanors. This was done to prevent criminal history point accrual for misdemeanor convictions which are unique to one municipality, or for local misdemeanor offenses of a regulatory or control nature, such as swimming at a city beach with an inner tube. The Commission decided that using such regulatory misdemeanor convictions was inconsistent with the purpose of the criminal history score. In addition, several groups argued that some municipal regulatory ordinances are enforced with greater frequency against low income groups and members of racial minorities, and that using them to compute criminal history scores would result in economic or racial bias. <u>For offenses defined with monetary thresholds, the threshold at the time the offense was committed determines the offense classification for criminal history purposes, not the current threshold.</u>

<u>II.C.07. The term "sale" as it relates to presumptive imprisonment for second or subsequent sale of a severity level VI drug or sale of cocaine encompasses all elements of Minn. Stat. § 152.09 subd. 1 (1) which reads "Manufacture, sell, give away, barter, deliver, exchange or distribute; or possess with intent to manufacture, sell, give away, barter, deliver, exchange or distribute, a controlled substance."</u>

II.F.05. Minn. Stat. § 624.74 provides for a maximum sentence of three years or payment of a fine of $3000 or both, for possession or use of metal-penetrating bullets during the commission of a crime. Any executed felony sentence imposed under Minn. Stat. § 624.74 shall run consecutively to any felony sentence imposed for the crime committed with the weapon, thus providing an enhancement to the sentence imposed for the other offense. The extent of enhancement, up to the three year statutory maximum, is left to the discretion of the Court. If, for example, an offender were convicted of Aggravated Robbery with use of a gun and had a zero criminal history score, the mandatory minimum sentence <u>and the presumptive sentence</u> for the offense would be 36 months<u>:</u> ~~with a presumptive sentence of 54 months;~~ if the *offender were also convicted of Minn. Stat. § 624.74, Metal-Penetrating Bullets, the Court could, at its discretion, add a maximum of 36 months, without departing from the guidelines.*

II.F.06. *The criterion that crimes must be against different persons for permissive consecutive sentencing is designed to exclude consecutive sentences in two types of situations. One type involves multiple offenses against a victim in a single behavioral incident such as burglary with a dangerous weapon and aggravated robbery with bodily harm. The requirement of different victims is also intended to exclude consecutive sentences in domestic abuse and child abuse situations when there are multiple incidents perpetrated against a victim over time. Assault, criminal sexual conduct, ~~intrafamilial sexual abuse,~~ and incest are the conviction offenses most frequently found in domestic abuse and child abuse cases. Multiple incidents against a victim typifies these types of situations. In fact, t~~he intrafamilial sexual abuse~~ one criminal sexual conduct provision~~s~~ delineates multiple incidents as an element of the offense. The high severity rankings assigned to offenses that tend to involve very young victims reflect the understanding that multiple incidents generally occur in these kinds of situations. The Commission believes that a uniform policy reflected in high severity rankings provides the best approach in sentencing these cases. Permissive consecutive sentences would result in enormous disparity based on varying charging practices of prosecutors and discretionary judicial decisions.*

<u>APPENDIX J</u>

Minnesota Vulnerable Adults Act

VULNERABLE ADULTS ACT

Minnesota Statutes 626.557

(This material is the complete and current Act. Material included is from the original Act passed in 1980 and amendments passed in 1982, 1983, and 1985.)

626.557 REPORTING OF MALTREATMENT OF VULNERABLE ADULTS

Subdivision 1. PUBLIC POLICY. The Legislature declares that the public policy of this state is to protect adults who, because of physical or mental disability or dependency on institutional services, are particularly vulnerable to abuse or neglect; to provide safe institutional or residential services or living environments for vulnerable adults who have been abused or neglected; and to assist persons charged with the care of vulnerable adults to provide safe environments.

In addition, it is the policy of this state to require the reporting of suspected abuse or neglect of vulnerable adults, to provide for the voluntary reporting of abuse or neglect of vulnerable adults, to require the investigation of the reports, and to provide protective and counseling services in appropriate cases.

Subdivision 2. DEFINITIONS. As used in this section, the following terms have the meanings given them unless the specific context indicates otherwise.

a. "Facility" means a hospital or other entity required to be licensed pursuant to sections 144.50 to 144.58; a nursing home required to be licensed to serve adults pursuant to section 144A.02; an agency, day care facility, or residential facility required to be licensed to serve adults pursuant to sections 245.781 to 245.812; or a home health agency certified for participation in Titles XVIII or XIX of the Social Security Act, United States Code, title 42, sections 1395 et seq.

b. "Vulnerable adult" means any person 18 years of age or older:

 1. who is a resident or inpatient of a facility;

 2. who receives services at or from a facility required to be licensed to serve adults pursuant to sections 245.781 to 245.812, except a person receiving outpatient services for treatment of chemical dependency or mental illness;

 3. who receives services from a home health agency certified for participation under Titles XVIII or XIX of the Social Security Act, United States Code, title 42, sections 1395 et seq. and 1396 et seq.; or

 4. who, regardless of residence or type of service received, is unable or unlikely to report abuse or neglect without assistance because of impairment of mental or physical function or emotional status.

c. "Caretaker" means an individual or facility who has responsibility for the care of a vulnerable adult as a result of family relationship, or who has assumed responsibility for all or a portion of the care of a vulnerable adult voluntarily, or by contract, or agreement.

d. "Abuse" means:

 1. any act which constitutes a violation under sections 609.221 to 609.223, 609.23 to 609.235, 609.322, 609.342, 609.343, 609.344, or 609.345;

2. non-therapeutic conduct which produces or could reasonably be expected to produce pain or injury and is not accidental, or any repeated conduct which produces or could reasonably be expected to produce mental or emotional distress;

3. any sexual contact between a facility staff person and a resident or client of that facility; or

4. the illegal use of a vulnerable adult's person or property for another person's profit or advantage, or the breach of a fiduciary relationship through the use of a person or a person's property for any purpose not in the proper and lawful execution of a trust, including but not limited to situations where a person obtains money, property, or services from a vulnerable adult through the use of undue influence, harassment, duress, deception, or fraud.

e. "Neglect" means:

1. failure by a caretaker to supply the vulnerable adult with necessary food, clothing, shelter, health care, or supervision;

2. the absence or likelihood of absence of necessary food, clothing, shelter, health care, or supervision for a vulnerable adult; or

3. the absence or likelihood of absence of necessary financial management to protect a vulnerable adult against abuse as defined in paragraph (d), clause (4). Nothing in this section shall be construed to require a health care facility to provide financial management or supervise financial management for a vulnerable adult except as otherwise required by law.

f. "Report" means any report received by a local welfare agency, police department, county sheriff, or licensing agency pursuant to this section.

g. "Licensing agency" means:

1. the Commissioner of Health, for facilities as defined in clause a. which are required to be licensed or certified by the Department of Health;

2. the Commissioner of Human Services, for facilities required by sections 245.781 to 245.813 to be licensed;

3. any licensing board which regulates persons pursuant to section 214.01, subdivision 2; and

4. any agency responsible for credentialing human services occupations.

Subdivision 3. PERSONS MANDATED TO REPORT. A professional or his delegate who is engaged in the care of vulnerable adults, education, social services, law enforcement, or any of the regulated occupations referenced in subdivision 2, clause g.3. and 4., or an employee of a rehabilitation facility certified by the Commissioner of Economic Security for Vocational Rehabilitation, or an employee of or person providing services in a facility who has knowledge of the abuse or neglect of a vulnerable adult, has reasonable cause to believe that a vulnerable adult is being or has been abused or neglected, or who has knowledge that a vulnerable adult has sustained a physical injury which is not reasonably explained by the history of injuries provided by the caretaker or caretakers of the vulnerable adult shall immediately report the information to the local police department, county sheriff, local welfare agency, or appropriate licensing or certifying agency. The police department or the county sheriff, upon receiving a report, shall immediately notify the local welfare agency. The local welfare agency, upon receiving a report, shall immediately notify the local police department or the county sheriff and the appropriate licensing agency or agencies.

A person not required to report under the provisions of this subdivision may voluntarily report as described above. Medical examiners or coroners shall notify the police department or county sheriff and the local welfare department in instances in which they believe that a vulnerable adult has died as a result of abuse or neglect.

Nothing in this subdivision shall be construed to require the reporting or transmittal of information regarding an incident of abuse or neglect or suspected abuse or neglect if the incident has been reported or transmitted to the appropriate person or entity.

Subdivision 3a. REPORT NOT REQUIRED.

a. Where federal law specifically prohibits a person from disclosing patient identifying information in connection with a report of suspected abuse or neglect under this act, that person need not make a required report unless the vulnerable adult, or the vulnerable adult's guardian, conservator, or legal representative, has consented to disclosure in a manner which conforms to federal requirements. Facilities whose patients or residents are covered by such a federal law shall seek consent to the disclosure of suspected abuse or neglect from each patient or resident, or his guardian, conservator, or legal representative, upon his admission to the facility. Persons who are prohibited by federal law from reporting an incident of suspected abuse or neglect shall promptly seek consent to make a report.

b. Except as defined in subdivision 2, paragraph d., clause 1., verbal or physical aggression occurring between patients, residents, or clients of a facility, or self-abusive behavior of these persons does not constitute "abuse" for the purposes of subdivision 3 unless it causes serious harm. The operator of the facility or a designee shall record incidents of aggression and self-abusive behavior in a manner that facilitates periodic review by licensing agencies and county and local welfare agencies.

c. Nothing in this section shall be construed to require a report of abuse, as defined in subdivision 2, paragraph (d), clause (4), solely on the basis of the transfer of money or property by gift or as compensation for services rendered.

Subdivision 4. REPORT. A person required to report under subdivision 3 shall make an oral report immediately by telephone or otherwise. A person required to report under subdivision 3 shall also make a report as soon as possible in writing to the appropriate police department, the county sheriff, local welfare agency, or appropriate licensing agency. The written report shall be of sufficient content to identify the vulnerable adult, the caretaker, the nature and extent of the suspected abuse or neglect, any evidence of previous abuse or neglect, name and address of the reporter, and any other information that the reporter believes might be helpful in investigating the suspected abuse or neglect. Written reports received by a police department or a county sheriff shall be forwarded immediately to the local welfare agency. The police department or the county sheriff may keep copies of reports received by them. Copies of written reports received by a local welfare department shall be forwarded immediately to the local police department or the county sheriff and the appropriate licensing agency or agencies.

Subdivision 5. IMMUNITY FROM LIABILITY.

a. A person making a voluntary or mandated report under subdivision 3 or participating in an investigation under this section is immune from any civil or criminal liability that otherwise might result from the person's actions, if the person is acting in good faith.

b. A person employed by a local welfare agency or a state licensing agency who is conducting or supervising an investigation or enforcing the law in compliance with subdivisions 10, 11, or 12 or any related rule or provision of law is immune from any civil or criminal liability that might otherwise result from the person's actions, if the person is acting in good faith and exercising due care.

Subdivision 6. FALSIFIED REPORTS. A person who intentionally makes a false report under the provisions of this section shall be liable in a civil suit for any actual damages suffered by the person or persons so reported and for any punitive damages set by the court or jury.

Subdivision 7. FAILURE TO REPORT.

a. A person required to report by this section who intentionally fails to report is guilty of a misdemeanor.

b. A person required by this section to report who negligently or intentionally fails to report is liable for damages caused by the failure.

Subdivision 8. EVIDENCE NOT PRIVILEGED. No evidence regarding the abuse or neglect of the vulnerable adult shall be excluded in any proceeding arising out of the alleged abuse or neglect on the grounds of lack of competency under section 595.02.

Subdivision 9. MANDATORY REPORTING TO A MEDICAL EXAMINER OR CORONER. A person required to report under the provisions of subdivision 3 who has reasonable cause to believe that a vulnerable adult has died as a direct or indirect result of abuse or neglect, he shall report that information to the appropriate medical examiner or coroner in addition to the local welfare agency, police department, or county sheriff or appropriate licensing agency or agencies. The medical examiner or coroner shall complete an investigation as soon as feasible and report the findings to the police department or county sheriff, the local welfare agency, and, if applicable, each licensing agency.

Subdivision 10. DUTIES OF LOCAL WELFARE AGENCY UPON A RECEIPT OF A REPORT.

a. The local welfare agency shall immediately investigate and offer emergency and continuing protective social services for purposes of preventing further abuse or neglect and for safeguarding and enhancing the welfare of the abused or neglected vulnerable adult. Local welfare agencies may enter facilities and inspect and copy records as part of investigations. In cases of suspected sexual abuse, the local welfare agency shall immediately arrange for and make available to the victim appropriate medical examination and treatment. The investigation shall not be limited to the written records of the facility, but shall include every other available source of information. When necessary in order to protect the vulnerable adult from further harm, the local welfare agency shall seek authority to remove the vulnerable adult from the situation in which the neglect or abuse occurred. The local welfare agency shall also investigate to determine whether the conditions which resulted in the reported abuse or neglect place other vulnerable adults in jeopardy of being abused or neglected and offer protective social services that are called for by its determination. In performing any of these duties, the local welfare agency shall maintain appropriate records.

b. If the report indicates, or if the local welfare agency finds that the suspected abuse or neglect occurred at a facility, or while the vulnerable adult was or should have been under the care of or receiving services from a facility, or that the suspected abuse or neglect involved a person licensed by a licensing agency to provide care or services, the local welfare agency shall immediately notify each appropriate licensing agency, and provide each licensing agency with a copy of the report and of its investigative findings.

c. When necessary in order to protect a vulnerable adult from serious harm, the local agency shall immediately intervene on behalf of that adult to help the family, victim, or other interested person by seeking any of the following:

   1. a restraining order or a court order for removal of the perpetrator from the residence of the vulnerable adult pursuant to section 518B.01;

   2. the appointment of a guardian or conservator pursuant to sections 525.539 to 525.6198, or guardianship or conservatorship pursuant to chapter 252A;

   3. replacement of an abusive or neglectful guardian or conservator and appointment of a suitable person as guardian or conservator, pursuant to sections 525.539 to 525.6198; or

4. a referral to the prosecuting attorney for possible criminal prosecution of the perpetrator under chapter 609.

The expenses of legal intervention must be paid by the county in the case of indigent persons, under section 525.703 and chapter 563.

In proceedings under sections 525.539 to 525.6198, if a suitable relative or other person is not available to petition for guardianship or conservatorship, a county employee shall present the petition with representation by the county attorney. The county shall contract with or arrange for a suitable person or nonprofit organization to provide ongoing guardianship services. If the county presents evidence to the probate court that it has made a diligent effort and no other suitable person can be found, a county employee may serve as guardian or conservator. The county shall not retaliate against the employee for any action taken on behalf of the ward or conservatee even if the action is adverse to the county's interest. Any person retaliated against in violation of this subdivision shall have a cause of action against the county and shall be entitled to reasonable attorney fees and costs of the action if the action is upheld by the court.

Subdivision 10a. NOTIFICATION OF NEGLECT OR ABUSE IN A FACILITY.

a. When a report is received that alleges neglect, physical abuse, or sexual abuse of a vulnerable adult while in the care of a facility required to be licensed under section 144A.02 or sections 245.781 to 245.812, the local welfare agency investigating the report shall notify the guardian or conservator of the person of a vulnerable adult under guardianship or conservatorship of the person who is alleged to have been abused or neglected, unless consent is denied by the vulnerable adult. The notice shall contain the following information: the name of the facility; the fact that a report of alleged abuse or neglect of a vulnerable adult in the facility has been received; the nature of the alleged abuse or neglect; that the agency is conducting an investigation; any protective or corrective measures being taken pending the outcome of the investigation; and that a written memorandum will be provided when the investigation is completed.

b. In a case of alleged neglect, physical abuse, or sexual abuse of a vulnerable adult while in the care of a facility required to be licensed under sections 245.781 to 245.812, the local welfare agency may also provide the information in paragraph (a) to the guardian or conservator of the person of any other vulnerable adult in the facility who is under guardianship or conservatorship of the person, to any other vulnerable adult in the facility who is not under guardianship or conservatorship of the person, and to the person, if any, designated to be notified in case of an emergency by any other vulnerable adult in the facility who is not under guardianship or conservatorship of the person, unless consent is denied by the vulnerable adult, if the investigative agency knows or has reason to believe the alleged neglect, physical abuse, or sexual abuse has occurred.

c. When the investigation required under subdivision 10 is completed, the local welfare agency shall provide a written memorandum containing the following information to every guardian or conservator of the person or other person notified by the agency of the investigation under paragraph (a) or (b): the name of the facility investigated; the nature of the alleged neglect, physical abuse, or sexual abuse; the investigator's name; a summary of the investigative findings; a statement of whether the report was found to be substantiated, inconclusive, or false; and the protective or corrective measures that are being or will be taken. The memorandum shall be written in a manner that protects the identity of the reporter and the alleged victim and shall not contain the name or, to the extent possible, reveal the identity of the alleged perpetrator or of those interviewed during the investigation.

d. In a case of neglect, physical abuse, or sexual abuse of a vulnerable adult while in the care of a facility required to be licensed under sections 245.781 to 245.812, the local welfare agency may also provide the written memorandum to the guardian or conservator of the person of any other vulnerable adult in the facility who is under guardianship or conservatorship of the person, to any other vulnerable adult in the facility who is not under guardianship or conservatorship of the person, and to the person, if any, designated to be notified in case of an emergency by any other vulnerable adult in the facility who is not under guardianship or conservatorship of the person, unless consent is denied by the vulnerable adult, if the report is substantiated or if the investigation is inconclusive and the report is a second or subsequent report of neglect, physical abuse, or sexual abuse of a vulnerable adult while in the care of the facility.

e. In determining whether to exercise the discretionary authority granted under paragraphs (b) and (d), the local welfare agency shall consider the seriousness and extent of the alleged neglect, physical abuse, or sexual abuse and the impact of notification on the residents of the facility. The facility shall be notified whenever this discretion is exercised.

f. Where federal law specifically prohibits the disclosure of patient identifying information, the local welfare agency shall not provide any notice under paragraph (a) or (b) or any memorandum under paragraph (c) or (d) unless the vulnerable adult has consented to disclosure in a manner which conforms to federal requirements.

Subdivision 11. DUTIES OF LICENSING AGENCIES UPON RECEIPT OF REPORT. Whenever a licensing agency receives a report, or otherwise has information indicating that a vulnerable adult may have been abused or neglected at a facility it has licensed, or that a person it has licensed or credentialed to provide care or services may be involved in the abuse or neglect of a vulnerable adult, or that such a facility or person has failed to comply with the requirements of this section, it shall immediately investigate. Subject to the provisions of chapter 13, the licensing agency shall have the right to enter facilities and inspect and copy records as part of investigations. The investigation shall not be limited to the written records of the facility, but shall include every other available source of information. The licensing agency shall issue orders and take actions with respect to the license of the facility or person that are designed to prevent further abuse or neglect of vulnerable adults.

Subdivision 11a. DUTIES OF PROSECUTING AUTHORITIES. Upon receipt of a report from a social service or licensing agency, the prosecuting authority shall immediately investigate, prosecute when warranted, and transmit its findings and disposition to the referring agency.

Subdivision 12. RECORDS.

a. Each licensing agency shall maintain summary records of reports of alleged abuse or neglect and alleged violations of the requirements of this section with respect to facilities or persons licensed or credentialed by that agency. As part of these records, the agency shall prepare an investigation memorandum. Notwithstanding section 13.46, subdivision 3, the investigation memorandum shall be accessible to the public pursuant to section 13.03 and a copy shall be provided to any public agency which referred the matter to the licensing agency for investigation. It shall contain a complete review of the agency's investigation, including but not limited to: the name of any facility investigated; a statement of the nature of the alleged abuse or neglect or other violation of the requirements of this section; pertinent information obtained from medical or other records reviewed; the investigator's name; a summary of the investigation's findings; a statement of whether the report was found to be substantiated, inconclusive, or false; and a statement of any action taken by the agency. The investigation memorandum shall be written in a manner which protects the identity of the reporter and of the vulnerable adult and may not contain the name or, to the extent possible, the identity of the alleged perpetrator or of those interviewed during the investigation. During the licensing agency's investigation, all data collected pursuant to this section shall be classified as investigative data pursuant to section 13.39. After the licensing agency's investigation is complete, the data on individuals collected and maintained shall be private data on individuals. All data collected pursuant to this section shall be made available to prosecuting authorities and law enforcement officials, local welfare agencies, and licensing agencies investigating the alleged abuse or neglect. Notwithstanding any law to the contrary, the name of the reporter shall be disclosed only upon a finding by the court that the report was false and made in bad faith.

b. Notwithstanding the provisions of section 138.163:

1. all data maintained by licensing agencies, treatment facilities, or other public agencies which relate to reports which, upon investigation, are found to be false may be destroyed two years after the finding was made;

2. all data maintained by licensing agencies, treatment facilities, or other public agencies which relate to reports which, upon investigation, are found to be inconclusive may be destroyed four years after the finding was made;

3. all data maintained by licensing agencies, treatment facilities, or other public agencies which relate to reports which, upon investigation, are found to be substantiated may be destroyed seven years after the finding was made.

Subdivision 13. COORDINATION.

a. Any police department or county sheriff, upon receiving a report shall notify the local welfare agency pursuant to subdivision 3. A local welfare agency or licensing agency which receives a report pursuant to that subdivision shall immediately notify the appropriate law enforcement, local welfare, and licensing agencies.

b. Investigating agencies, including the police department, county sheriff, local welfare agency, or appropriate licensing agency shall cooperate in coordinating their investigatory activities. Each licensing agency which regulates facilities shall develop and disseminate procedures to coordinate its activities with

i. investigations by police and county sheriffs, and
ii. provision of protective services by local welfare agencies.

Subdivision 14. ABUSE PREVENTION PLANS.

a. Each facility, except home health agencies, shall establish and enforce an ongoing written abuse prevention plan. The plan shall contain an assessment of the physical plant, its environment, and its population identifying factors which may encourage or permit abuse, and a statement of specific measures to be taken to minimize the risk of abuse. The plan shall comply with any rules governing the plan promulgated by the licensing agency.

b. Each facility shall develop an individual abuse prevention plan for each vulnerable adult residing there. Facilities designated in subdivision 2, clause b.2. or clause b.3. shall develop plans for any vulnerable adults receiving services from them. The plan shall contain an individualized assessment of the person's susceptibility to abuse, and a statement of the specific measures to be taken to minimize the risk of abuse to that person. For the purposes of this clause, the term "abuse" includes self-abuse.

Subdivision 15. INTERNAL REPORTING OF ABUSE AND NEGLECT. Each facility shall establish and enforce an ongoing written procedure in compliance with the licensing agencies' rules for insuring that all cases of suspected abuse or neglect are reported promptly to a person required by this section to report abuse and neglect and are promptly investigated.

Subdivision 16. ENFORCEMENT.

a. A facility that has not complied with this section within 60 days of the effective date of passage of temporary rules is ineligible for renewal of its license. A person required by subdivision 3 to report and who is licensed or credentialed to practice an occupation by a licensing agency who willfully fails to comply with this section shall be disciplined after a hearing by the appropriate licensing agency.

b. Licensing agencies shall as soon as possible promulgate rules necessary to implement the requirements of subdivisions 11, 12, 13, 14, 15, and 16, clause a. Agencies may promulgate temporary rules pursuant to sections 14.29 to 14.36.

c. The Commissioner of Human Services shall promulgate rules as necessary to implement the requirements of subdivision 10.

Subdivision 17. RETALIATION PROHIBITED.

a. A facility or person shall not retaliate against any person who reports in good faith suspected abuse or neglect pursuant to this section, or against a vulnerable adult with respect to whom a report is made, because of the report.

b. Any facility or person which retaliates against any person because of a report of suspected abuse or neglect is liable to that person for actual damages and, in addition, a penalty up to $1,000.

c. There shall be a rebuttable presumption that any adverse action, as defined below, within 90 days of a report, is retaliatory. For purposes of this clause, the term "adverse action" refers to action taken by a facility or person involved in a report against the person making the report or the person with respect to whom the report was made because of the report, and includes, but is not limited to:

1. discharge or transfer from the facility;

2. discharge from or termination of employment;

3. demotion or reduction in renumeration for services;

4. restriction or prohibition of access to the facility or its residents; or

5. any restriction of rights set forth in section 144.651.

Subdivision 18. OUTREACH. The Commissioner of Human Services shall establish an aggressive program to educate those required to report, as well as the general public, about the requirements of this section using a variety of media.

Subdivision 19. PENALTY. Any caretaker, as defined in subdivision 2, or operator or employee thereof, or volunteer worker thereat, who intentionally abuses or neglects a vulnerable adult, or being a caretaker, knowingly permits conditions to exist which result in the abuse or neglect of a vulnerable adult, is guilty of a gross misdemeanor.

(The 1985 amendments in chapter 150 and chapter 293 are effective August 1, 1985. This material compiled July, 1985.)

APPENDIX K:

LICENSURE-RELATED

REPORTING REQUIREMENTS IN MINNESOTA.

Health care professionals in Minnesota, by virtue of being licensed, are mandated reporters of sexual misconduct by other health care practitioners. These mandates are contained in various licensing statutes, or in one case, in the Rules of Conduct established by a board of licensure.

PSYCHOLOGY: The Rules of Conduct, adopted by the Minnesota Board of Psychology on August 7, 1982 (7 MCAR § 10.008 Rules of Conduct.) contain the following reporting mandate:

10. A psychologist shall file a complaint with the board when the psychologist has reason to believe that another psychologist is or has been engaged in conduct which violates C.11., failure to report suspected abuse of children or vulnerable adults, or E.8., sexual contact with a client. This requirement to file a complaint does not apply when the belief is based on information obtained in the course of a professional relationship with a client who is the other psychologist. Nothing in this rule relieves a psychologist from the duty to file a report as required by Minn. Stat. § 626.556 or 626.557, reporting abuse of children and vulnerable adults.

[Minn. Stat. § 626.557 is contained in Appendix J. Sections C.11. and E.8. referred to above are presented below.]

C.11. In the course of professional practice, a psychologist shall not violate any law concerning the reporting of abuse of children and vulnerable adults.

[Section 8 below was changed in rules adopted July 14, 1989. New language is underlined]

E.8. A psychologist shall not engage in sexual intercourse or other physical intimacies with a client, nor in any verbal or physical behavior which is sexually seductive or sexually demeaning to the client. Physical intimacies include handling of the breasts, genital areas, buttocks or thighs of either sex by either the psychologist or the client. A psychologist must not engage in sexual intercourse or other physical intimacies with a former client for a period of two years following the date of the last professional contact with the client, whether or not the psychologist has formally terminated the professional relationship.

MEDICINE (INCLUDING PSYCHIATRY):   The Medical Practice Act, as amended in 1985 (Minn. Stat. 147), contains the following reporting mandate:

147.111 [REPORTING OBLIGATIONS.]

Subd. 1. [PERMISSION TO REPORT.] A person who has knowledge of any conduct constituting grounds for discipline under § 147.01 to 147.33 may report the violation to the board.

Subd. 2. [INSTITUTIONS.] Any hospital, clinic, prepaid medical plan, or other health care institution or organization located in this state shall report to the board any action taken by the institution or organization or any of its administrators or medical or other committees to revoke, suspend, restrict, or condiction a physician's privilege to practice or treat patients in the institution, or as part of the organization, any denial of privileges, or any other disciplinary action. The institution or organization shall also report the resignation of any physicians prior to the conclusion of any disciplinary proceeding, or prior to the commencement of formal charges but after the physician had knowledge that formal charges were contemplated or in preparation. No report shall be required of a physician voluntarily limiting his or her practice at a hospital provided that the physician notifies all hospitals at which he or she has privileges of the voluntary limitation and the reasons for it.

Subd. 3. [MEDICAL SOCIETIES.] A state or local medical society shall report to the board any termination, revocation, or suspension of membership or any other disciplinary action taken against a physician. If the society has received a complaint which might be grounds for discipline under § 147.01 to 147.33 against a member physician on which it has not taken any disciplinary action, the society shall report the complaint and the reason why it has not taken action on it or shall direct the complainant to the board of medical examiners.

Subd. 4. [LICENSED PROFESSIONALS.] A licensed health professional shall report to the board personal knowledge of any conduct which he or she reasonably believes constitutes grounds for disciplinary action under § 147.01 to 147.33 by any physician, including any conduct indicating that the physician may be medically incompetent, or may be medically or physically unable to engage safely in the practice of medicine. No report shall be required if the information was obtained in the course of a physician-patient relationship if the patient is another physician and the treating physician successfully counsels the other physician to limit or withdraw from practice to the extent required by the impairment.

> [NOTE: Subd. 5 provides requirements for quarterly reports from all malpractice insurance carriers, and Subd. 6 reports from the District Court.]

Subd. 7. [SELF-REPORTING.] A physician shall report to the board any action concerning himself or herself which would require that a report be filed with the board by any person, health care facility, business, or organization pursuant to subdivisions 2 to 6.

****

147.121. [IMMUNITY.]

Subd. 1 [REPORTING.] Any person, health care facility, business, or organization is immune from civil liability or criminal prosecution for submitting a report to the board pursuant to § 147.111 or for otherwise reporting to the board violations or alleged violations of § 147.021. All such reports are confidential and absolutely privileged communications.

****

147.131. [PHYSICIAN COOPERATION.]

A physician who is the subject of an investigation by or on behalf of the board shall cooperate fully with the investigation. Cooperation includes responding fully and promptly to any question raised by or on behalf of the board relating to the subject of the investigation and providing copies of patient medical records, as reasonably requested by the board, to assist the board in its investigation. The board shall pay for copies requested. If the board does not have written consent from a client permitting access to his or her records, the physician shall delete any data in the record which identifies the patient before providing it to the board....

****

The grounds for disciplinary action are listed in 147.021, subdivision 1. The grounds are very broad Two that are of relevance to physician-patient sex are:

(t) Engaging in conduct with a patient which is sexual or may be reasonably interpreted by the patient as sexual, or in any verbal behavior which is seductive or sexually demeaning to a patient.

(u) Failure to make reports as required by 147.111 or to cooperate with an investigation by the board as required by 147.131.

SOCIAL WORK, MARRIAGE AND FAMILY THERAPY, AND UNLICENSED MENTAL HEALTH SERVICE PROVIDERS: These three groups were regulated beginning in 1987 through the creation of a new law, Minnesota Statutes 148B. This law has requirements for institutions, professional societies, and insurance carriers, as well as self-reporting which are virtually identical to that required by the Medical Practice Act. However, one section differs slightly:

148B.07 [REPORTING OBLIGATIONS.]

Subd. 4 [REGULATED INDIVIDUALS AND LICENSED PROFESSIONALS.] A regulated individual or a licensed health professional shall report to the appropriate board personal knowledge of any conduct that the regulated individual or licensed health professional reasonably believes constitutes grounds for disciplinary or adverse action under this chapter by any regulated individual, including conduct indicating that the individual may be medically incompetent, or may be medically or physically unable to engage safely in the provision of services. If the information was obtained in the course of a client relationship, the client is another regulated individual, and the treating individual successfully counsels the other individual to limit or withdraw from practice to the extent required by the impairment, the board may deem this limitation of or withdrawal from practice to be sufficient disciplinary action.

APPENDIX L

CRIMINAL STATUTE: COLORADO
(passed 1988)

AN ACT

1988

SENATE BILL NO. 17.

BY SENATORS Martinez, DeNier, McCormick, Gallagher, Lee, and Mendez: also REPRESENTATIVES Tebedo, Kopel, Armstrong, Bowen, Dambman, P. Hernandez, Lawson, Mutzebaugh, Neale, Owen, Paulson, Philips, Ratterree, Webb, and S. Williams.

CONCERNING SEXUAL ASSAULT ON CLIENTS BY PSYCHOTHERAPISTS.

Be it enacted by the General Assembly of the State of Colorado:

SECTION 1. Part 4 of article 3 of title 18, Colorado Revised Statutes, 1986 Repl. Vol., is amended BY THE ADDITION OF A NEW SECTION to read:

18-3-405.5. Sexual assault on a client by a psychotherapist. (1) (a) Any actor who knowingly inflicts sexual penetration or sexual intrusion on a victim commits aggravated sexual assault on a client if:

(I) The actor is a psychotherapist and the victim is a client of the psychotherapist; or

(II) The actor is a psychotherapist and the victim is a client and the sexual penetration or intrusion occurred by means of therapeutic deception.

(b) Aggravated sexual assault on a client is a class 4 felony.

(2) (a) Any actor who knowingly subjects a victim to any sexual contact commits sexual assault on a client if:

(I) The actor is a psychotherapist and the victim is a client of the psychotherapist; or

(II) The actor is a psychotherapist and the victim is a client and the sexual contact occurred by means of therapeutic deception.

(b) Sexual assault on a client is a class 1 misdemeanor.

(3) For the purposes of subparagraph (I) of paragraph (a) of subsection (1) and subparagraph (I) of paragraph (a) of subsection (2) of this section, consent by the client to the sexual penetration, intrusion, or contact shall not constitute a defense to such offense.

(4) As used in this section, unless the context requires otherwise:

(a) "Client" means a person who seeks or receives psychotherapy from a psychotherapist.

Capital letters indicate new material added to existing statutes; dashes through words indicate deletions from existing statutes and such material not part of act.

(b) "Psychotherapist" means any person who performs or purports to perform psychotherapy, whether or not such person is licensed by the state pursuant to title 12, C.R.S., or certified by the state pursuant to part 5 of article 1 of title 25, C.R.S.

(c) "Psychotherapy" means the treatment, diagnosis, or counseling in a professional relationship to assist individuals or groups to alleviate mental disorders, understand unconscious or conscious motivation, resolve emotional, relationship, or attitudinal conflicts, or modify behaviors which interfere with effective emotional, social, or intellectual functioning.

(d) "Therapeutic deception" means a representation by a psychotherapist that sexual contact, penetration, or intrusion by the psychotherapist is consistent with or part of the client's treatment.

SECTION 2. <u>Effective date—applicability</u>. This act shall take effect July 1, 1988, and shall apply to acts committed on or after said date.

SECTION 3. <u>Safety clause</u>. The general assembly hereby finds, determines, and declares that this act is necessary for the immediate preservation of the public peace, health, and safety.

Ted L. Strickland
PRESIDENT OF
THE SENATE

Carl B. Bledsoe
SPEAKER OF THE HOUSE
OF REPRESENTATIVES

Joan M. Albi
SECRETARY OF
THE SENATE

Lee C. Bahrych
CHIEF CLERK OF THE HOUSE
OF REPRESENTATIVES

APPROVED_____

Roy Romer
GOVERNOR OF THE
STATE OF COLORADO

APPENDIX M

CIVIL STATUTE: WISCONSIN

1985 Wisconsin Act 275

STATE OF WISCONSIN

1985 Assembly Bill 776

Date of enactment: April 15, 1986

Date of publication: April 29, 1986

1985 Wisconsin Act 275

AN ACT *to renumber* 972.11(3); *to amend* 940.22(1)(e), 940.22(2), 949.03(1)(b) and 972.11(1); *to repeal and recreate* 901.04(3); and *to create* 893.585, 895.70, 939.74(4), 971.31(12) and 972.11(3) of the statutes, relating to sexual exploitation of a client by a therapist, statutes of limitation and providing a penalty.

The people of the state of Wisconsin, represented in senate and assembly, do enact as follows:

SECTION 1. 893.585 of the statutes is created to read:

893.585 Sexual exploitation by a therapist. (1) Notwithstanding ss. 893.54, 893.55 and 893.57, an action under s. 895.70 for damages shall be commenced within 3 years after the cause of action accrues or be barred.

(2) If a person entitled to bring an action under s. 895.70 is unable to bring the action due to the effects of the sexual contact or due to any threats, instructions or statements from the therapist, the period of inability is not part of the time limited for the commencement of the action, except that this subsection shall not extend the time limitation by more than 15 years.

SECTION 2. 895.70 of the statutes is created to read:

895.70 Sexual exploitation by a therapist. (1) DEFINITIONS. In this section:

(a) "Physician" has the meaning designated in s. 448.01(5).

(b) "Psychologist" means a person who practices psychology, as described in s. 455.01(5).

(c) "Psychotherapy" has the meaning designated in s. 455.01(6).

(d) "Sexual contact" has the meaning designated in s. 940.225(5)(a).

(e) "Therapist" means a physician, psychologist, social worker, nurse, chemical dependency counselor, member of the clergy or other person, whether or not licensed by the state, who performs or purports to perform psychotherapy.

(2) CAUSE OF ACTION. Any person who suffers, directly or indirectly, a physical, mental or emotional injury caused by, resulting from or arising out of sexual contact with a therapist who is rendering or has rendered to that person psychotherapy, counseling or other assessment or treatment of or involving any mental or emotional illness, symptom or condition has a civil cause of action against the psychotherapist for all damages resulting from, arising out of or caused by that sexual contact.

(3) PUNITIVE DAMAGES. A court or jury may award punitive damages to a person bringing an action under this section.

(4) CALCULATION OF STATUTE OF LIMITATIONS. An action under this section is subject to s. 893.585.

SECTION 3. 901.04(3) of the statutes is repealed and recreated to read:

901.04(3) HEARING OUT OF THE PRESENCE OF A JURY. Hearings on any of the following shall be conducted out of the presence of the jury:

(a) Admissibility of confessions.

(b) In actions under s. 940.22, admissibility of evidence of the patient's or client's personal or medical history.

(c) In actions under s. 940.225, admissibility of the prior sexual conduct or reputation of a complaining witness.

(d) Any preliminary matter if the interests of justice so requires.

SECTION 4. 939.74(4) of the statutes is created to read:

939.74(4) In computing the time limited by this section, the time during which an alleged victim under s. 940.22 is unable to seek the issuance of a complaint under s. 968.02 due to the effects of the sexual contact or due to any threats, instructions or statements from the therapist shall not be included.*

SECTION 5. 940.22(1)(e) of the statutes is amended to read:

940.22(1)(e) "Therapist means a physician, psychologist, social worker, nurse, chemical dependency counselor, member of the clergy or other person providing, whether or not licensed by the state, who performs or purports to perform psychotherapy services.

SECTION 6. 940.22(2) of the statutes is amended to read:

940.22(2) Any person who is or who holds himself or herself out to be a therapist and who intentionally has sexual contact with a patient or client during any ongoing therapist-patient or therapist-client relationship, regardless of whether it occurs during any treatment, consultation, interview or examination, is guilty of a Class A misdemeanor D felony. Consent is not an issue in an action under this subsection.

SECTION 7. 949.03(1)(b) of the statutes is amended to read:

949.03(1)(b) The commission or the attempt to commit any crime specified in s. 346.63(2), 940.01, 940.02, 940.05, 940.06, 940.07, 940.08, 940.09, 940.19, 940.20, 940.201, 940.21, 940.22, 940.225(1) to (3), 940.23, 940.24, 940.25, 940.26(2), 940.28, 940.29, 940.30, 940.305, 940.31, 940.32, 943.02, 943.03, 943.04, 943.10, 943.20, 943.32 or 944.12.

SECTION 8. 971.31(12) of the statutes is created to read:

971.31(12) In actions under s. 940.22, the court may determine the admissibility of evidence under s. 972.11 only upon a pretrial motion.

SECTION 9. 972.11(1) of the statutes is amended to read:

972.11(1) Except as provided in subs. (2) and (3) to (4), the rules of evidence and practice in civil actions shall be applicable in all criminal proceedings unless the context of a section or rule manifestly requires a different construction. No guardian ad litem need be appointed for a defendant in a criminal action. Chapters 885 to 895, except ss. 804.02 to 804.07 and 887.23 to 887.26, shall apply in all criminal proceedings.

SECTION 10. 972.11(3) of the statutes is renumbered 972.11(4).

SECTION 11. 972.11(3) of the statutes is created to read:

972.11(3)(a) In a prosecution under s. 940.22 involving a therapist and a patient or client, evidence of the patient's or client's personal or medical history is not admissible except if:

1. The defendant requests a hearing prior to trial and makes an offer of proof of the relevancy of the evidence; and

2. The court finds that the evidence is relevant and that its probative value outweighs its prejudicial nature.

(b) The court shall limit the evidence admitted under par. (a) to relevant evidence which pertains to specific information or examples of conduct. The court's order shall specify the information or conduct that is admissible and no other evidence of the patient's or client's personal or medical history may be introduced.

(c) Violation of the terms of the order is grounds for a mistrial but does not prevent the retrial of the defendant.

---

* Section 991.11, WISCONSIN STATUTES 1983-84: **Effective date of acts**. "Every act and every portion of an act enacted by the legislature over the governor's partial veto which does not expressly prescribe the time when it takes effect shall take effect on the day after its date of publication as designated" by the secretary of state [the date of publication may not be more than 10 working days after the date of enactment].

Appendix N

CIVIL STATUTE: MINNESOTA

Chapter 372 Minnesota Statutes 1986

S.F. No. 1619

AN ACT

CHAPTER No.
372

relating to civil and criminal actions; providing acause of action for sexual exploitation; providing new procedures for enforcing restitution orders; amending Minnesota Statutes 1984, section 609.135, by adding a subdivision; proposing coding for new law as Minnesota Statutes, chapter 148A.

BE IT ENACTED BY THE LEGISLATURE OF THE STATE OF MINNESOTA:

Section 1. [148A.01] [DEFINITIONS.]

Subdivision 1. [GENERAL.] The definitions in this section apply to sections 1 to 6.

Subd. 2. [EMOTIONALLY DEPENDENT.] "Emotionally dependent" means that the nature of the patient's or former patient's emotional condition and the nature of the treatment provided by the psychotherapist are such that the psychotherapist knows or has reason to believe that the patient or former patient is unable to withhold consent to sexual contact by the psychotherapist.

Subd. 3. [FORMER PATIENT.] "Former patient" means a person who was given psychotherapy within two years prior to sexual contact with the psychotherapist.

Subd. 4. [PATIENT.] "Patient" means a person who seeks or obtains psychotherapy.

Subd. 5. [PSYCHOTHERAPIST.] "Psychotherapist" means a physician, psychologist, nurse, chemical dependency counselor, social worker, member of the clergy, or other person, whether or not licensed by the state, who performs or purports to perform psychotherapy.

Subd. 6. [PSYCHOTHERAPY.] "Psychotherapy" means the professional treatment, assessment, or counseling of a mental or emotional illness, symptom, or condition.

Subd. 7. [SEXUAL CONTACT.] "Sexual contact" means any of the following, whether or not occurring with the consent of a patient or former patient:

(1) sexual intercourse, cunnilingus, fellatio, anal intercourse or any intrusion, however slight, into the genital or anal openings of the patient's or former patient's body by any part of the psychotherapist's body or by any object used by the psychotherapist for this purpose, or any intrusion, however slight, into the genital or

anal openings of the psychotherapist's body by any pat of the patient's or former patient's body or by any object used by the patient or former patient for this purpose, if agreed to by the psychotherapist;

(2) kissing of, or the intentional touching by the psychotherapist of the patient's or former patient's genital area, groin, inner thigh, buttocks, or breast or of the clothing covering any of these body parts;

(3) kissing of, or the intentional touching by the patient or former patient of the psychotherapist's genital area, groin, inner thigh, buttocks, or breast or of the clothing covering any of these body parts if the psychotherapist agrees to the kissing or intentional touching.

"Sexual contact" includes requests by the psychotherapist for conduct described in clauses (1) to (3).

"Sexual contact" does not include conduct described in clause (1) or (2) that is a part of standard medical treatment of a patient.

Subd. 9. [THERAPEUTIC DECEPTION.] "Therapeutic deception" means a representation by a psychotherapist that sexual contact with the psychotherapist is consistent with or part of the patient's or former patient's treatment.

Sec. 2. [148A.02] [CAUSE OF ACTION FOR SEXUAL EXPLOITATION.]

A cause of action against a psychotherapist for sexual exploitation exists for a patient or former patient for injury caused by sexual contact with the psychotherapist, if the sexual contact occurred:

(1) during the period the patient was receiving psychotherapy from the psychotherapist; or

(2) after the period the patient received psychotherapy from the psychotherapist if (a) the former patient was emotionally dependent on the psychotherapist; or (b) the sexual contact occurred by means of therapeutic deception.

The patient or former patient may recover damages from a psychotherapist who is found liable for sexual exploitation. It is not a defense to the action that sexual contact with a patient occurred outside a therapy or treatment session or that it occurred off the premises regularly used by the psychotherapist for therapy or treatment sessions.

Sec. 3. [148A.03] [LIABILITY OF EMPLOYER.]

(a) An employer of a psychotherapist may be liable under section 2 if:

(1) the employer fails or refuses to take reasonable action when the employer knows or has reason to know that the psychotherapist engaged in sexual contact with the plaintiff or any other patient or former patient of the psychotherapist; or

(2) the employer fails or refuses to make inquiries of an employer or former employer, whose name and address have been disclosed to the employer and who employed the psychotherapist as a psychotherapist within the last five years,

concerning the occurrence of sexual contacts by the psychotherapist with patients or former patients of the psychotherapist.

(b)   An employer or former employer of a psychotherapist may be liable under section 2 if the employer or former employer:

(1)   knows of the occurrence of sexual contact by the psychotherapist with patients or former patients of the psychotherapist;

(2)   receives a specific written request by another employer or prospective employer of the psychotherapist, engaged in the business of psychotherapy, concerning the existence or nature of the sexual contact; and

(3)   fails or refuses to disclose the occurrence of the sexual contacts.

(c)   An employer or former employer may be liable under section 2 only to the extent that the failure or refusal to take any action required by paragraph (a) or (b) was a proximate and actual cause of any damages sustained.

(d)   No cause of action arises, nor may a licensing board in this state take disciplinary action, against a psychotherapist's employer or former employer who in good faith complies with section 3.

Sec. 4.   [148A.04]   [SCOPE OF DISCOVERY.]

In an action for sexual exploitation, evidence of the plaintiff's sexual history is not subject to discovery except when the plaintiff claims damage to sexual functioning; or

(1)   the defendant requests a hearing prior to conducting discovery and makes an offer of proof of the relevancy of the history; and

(2)   the court finds that the history is relevant and that the probative value of the history outweighs its prejudicial effect.

The court shall allow the discovery only of specific information or examples of the plaintiff's conduct that are determined by the court to be relevant. The court's order shall detail the information or conduct that is subject to discovery.

Sec. 5.   Minnesota Statutes 1984, section 609.135, is amended by adding a subdivision to read:

Subd. 1a.   [FAILURE TO PAY RESTITUTION.]   If the court orders payment of restitution as a condition of probation and if the defendant fails to pay the restitution ordered prior to 60 days before the term of probation expires, the defendant's probation officer shall ask the court to hold a hearing to determine whether or not the conditions of probation should be changed or probation should be revoked. The court shall schedule and hold this hearing and take appropriate action before the defendant's term of probation expires.

Sec. 6.   [148A.05]   [ADMISSION OF EVIDENCE.]

In an action for sexual exploitation, evidence of the plaintiff's sexual history is not admissible except when:

(1) the defendant requests a hearing prior to trial and makes an offer of proof of the relevancy of the history; and

(2) the court finds that the history is relevant and that the probative value of the history outweighs its prejudicial effect.

The court shall allow the admission only of specific information or examples of the plaintiff's conduct that are determined by the court to be relevant. The court's order shall detail the information or conduct that is admissible and no other such evidence may be introduced.

Violation of the terms of the order may be grounds for a new trial.

Sec. 7.   [148A.06] [LIMITATION PERIOD.]

An action for sexual exploitation shall be commenced within five years after the cause of action arises.

Sec. 8.   [EFFECTIVE DATE; APPLICATION.]

Sections 1 to 7 are effective August 1, 1986, and sections 1 to 7 apply to causes of action arising on or after that date.

Passed the House of Representatives March 14, 1986; passed the Senate March 15, 1986; Signed by Governor Rudy Perpich March 19, 1986; Filed by Secretary of State March 19, 1986.

APPENDIX O

CIVIL STATUTES: CALIFORNIA

1. Chapter 1474, 1987 (Section 43.93 of Civil Code)

2. Chapter 1169, 1987 (amendment to Section 43.7
of the Civil Code)

Senate Bill No. 1406

CHAPTER 1474

An act to add Section 43.93 to the Civil Code, relating to psychotherapy.

[Approved by Governor September 30, 1987. Filed with
Secretary of State September 30, 1987.]

LEGISLATIVE COUNSEL'S DIGEST

SB 1406, Watson. Psychotherapy: sexual exploitation.

Existing law makes no provision for a cause of action based specifically upon sexual contact by a psychotherapist.

This bill would provide such a cause of action, as specified. With specified exemptions, evidence of the plaintiff's sexual history would not be subject to discovery or admissible as evidence.

The people of the State of California do enact as follows:

SECTION 1. Section 43.93 is added to the Civil Code, to read:

43.93. (a) For the purposes of this section the following definitions are applicable:

(1) "Psychotherapy" means the professional treatment, assessment, or counseling of a mental or emotional illness, symptom, or condition.

(2) "Psychotherapist" means a physician and surgeon specializing in the practice of psychiatry, a psychologist, a psychological assistant, marriage, family and child counselor, a registered marriage, family and child counselor intern, an educational psychologist, an apprentice social worker, or clinical social worker.

(3) "Sexual contact" means the touching of an intimate part of another person. "Intimate part" and "touching" have the same meanings as defined in Section 243.4 of the Penal Code. For the purposes of this section, sexual contact includes sexual intercourse, sodomy, and oral copulation.

(4) "Therapeutic relationship" exists during the time the patient or client is rendered professional service by the therapist.

(5) "Therapeutic deception" means a representation by a psychotherapist that sexual contact with the psychotherapist is consistent with or part of the patient's or former patient's treatment.

(b) A cause of action against a psychotherapist for sexual contact exists for a patient or former patient for injury caused by sexual contact with the psychotherapist, if the sexual contact occurred under any of the following conditions:

(1) During the period the patient was receiving psychotherapy from the psychotherapist.

(2) Within two years following termination of therapy.

(3) By means of therapeutic deception.

(c) The patient or former patient may recover damages from a psychotherapist who is found liable for sexual contact. It is not a defense to the action that sexual contact with a patient occurred outside a therapy or treatment session or that it occurred off the premises regularly used by the psychotherapist for therapy or treatment sessions. No cause of action shall exist between spouses within a marriage.

(d) In an action for sexual contact, evidence of the plaintiff's sexual history is not subject to discovery and is not admissible as evidence except in either of the following situations:

(1) The plaintiff claims damage to sexual functioning.

(2) The defendant requests a hearing prior to conducting discovery and makes an offer of proof of the relevancy of the history, and the court finds that the history is relevant and the probative value of the history outweighs its prejudicial effect.

The court shall allow the discovery or introduction as evidence only of specific information or examples of the plaintiff's conduct that are determined by the court to be relevant. The court's order shall detail the information or conduct that is subject to discovery.

Senate Bill No. 545

CHAPTER 1169

An act to amend Section 43.7 of the Civil Code, relating to liability.

[Approved by Governor September 25, 1987. Filed with
Secretary of State September 26, 1987.]

LEGISLATIVE COUNSEL'S DIGEST

SB 545, Watson. Immunity of professional societies.

Under existing law, professional societies, which include, among others, legal, medical, psychological, and engineering organizations, which have at least a majority of the eligible persons or licentiates in the geographic area served by the particular society, are immune from monetary liability, as specified.

This bill would require that a professional society with 100 or more members have only 25% of the eligible persons or licentiates in the geographic area served by the society to qualify for the above-mentioned immunity. Those professional societies with less than 100 members would, however, be required by this bill to have at least a majority of eligible persons or licenciates in the geographic area served by the society to qualify for this immunity.

The people of the State of California do enact as follows:

SECTION 1. Section 43.7 of the Civil Code, as amended by Section 1 of Chapter 669 of the Statutes of 1986, is amended to read:

43.7 (a) There shall be no monetary liability on the part of, and no cause of action for damages shall arise against, any member of a duly appointed mental health professional quality assurance committee that is established in compliance with Sections 4070 and 5624 of the Welfare and Institutions Code, for any act or proceeding undertaken or performed within the scope of the functions of the committee which is formed to review and evaluate the adequacy, appropriateness, or effectiveness of the care and treatment planned for, or provided to, mental health patients in order to improve quality of care by mental health professionals if the committee member acts without malice, has made a reasonable effort to obtain the facts of the matter as to which he or she acts, and acts in reasonable belief that the action taken by him or her is warranted by the facts known to him or her after the reasonable effort to obtain facts.

(b) There shall be no monetary liability on the part of, and no cause of action for damages shall arise against, any professional society, any member of a duly appointed committee of a medical specialty society, or any member of a duly appointed committee of a state or local professional society, or duly appointed member of a committee of a professional staff of a licensed hospital (provided the professional staff operates pursuant to written bylaws that have been approved by the governing board of the hospital), for any act or proceeding undertaken or performed within the scope of the functions of the committee which is formed to maintain the professional standards of the society established by its bylaws, or any member of any peer review committee whose purpose is to review the quality of medical, dental, dietetic, chiropractic, optometric, or veterinary services rendered by physicians and surgeons, dentists, dental hygienists, podiatrists, registered dietitians, chiropractors, optometrists, veterinarians, or psychologists which committee is composed chiefly of physicians and surgeons, dentists, dental hygienists, podiatrists, registered dietitians, chiropractors, optometrists, veterinarians, or psychologists for any act or proceeding undertaken or performed in reviewing the quality of medical, dental, dietetic, chiropractic, optometric, or veterinary services rendered by physicians and surgeons, dentists, dental hygienists, podiatrists, registered dietitians, chiropractors, optometrists, veterinarians, or psychologists or any member of the governing board of a hospital in reviewing the quality of medical services rendered by members of the staff if the professional society, committee, or board member acts without malice, has made a reasonable effort to obtain the facts of the matter as to which he, she, or it acts, and acts in reasonable belief that the action taken by him, her, or it is warranted by the facts known to him, her, or it after the reasonable effort to obtain facts. "Professional society" includes legal, medical, psychological, dental, dental hygiene, dietetic, accounting, optometric, podiatric, pharmaceutic, chiropractic, physical therapist, veterinary, licensed marriage, family, and child counseling, licensed clinical social work, and engineering organizations having as members at least 25 percent of the eligible persons or licentiates in the geographic area served by the particular society.

"Medical specialty society" means an organization having as members at least 25 percent of the eligible physicians within a given professionally recognized medical specialty in the geographic area served by the particular society.

(c) This section does not affect the official immunity of an officer or employee of a public corporation.

(d) There shall be no monetary liability on the part of, and no cause of action for damages shall arise against, any physician and surgeon, podiatrist, chiropractor, or attorney who is a member of an underwriting committee of an interindemnity or reciprocal or interinsurance exchange or mutual company for any act or proceeding undertaken or performed in evaluating physicians and surgeons, podiatrists, chiropractors, or attorneys for the writing of professional liability insurance, or any act or proceeding undertaken or performed in evaluating physicians and surgeons or attorneys for the writing of an interindemnity, reciprocal, or interinsurance contract as specified in Section 1280.7 of the Insurance Code, if the evaluating physician and surgeon, podiatrist, chiropractor, or attorney acts without malice, has made a reasonable effort to obtain the facts of the matter as to which he or she acts, and acts in reasonable belief that the action taken by him or her is warranted by the facts known to him or her after a reasonable effort to obtain the facts.

(e) This section shall not be construed to confer immunity from liability on any quality assurance committee established in compliance with Sections 4070 and 5624 of the Welfare and Institutions Code or hospital. In any case in which, but for the enactment of the preceding provisions of this section, a cause of action would arise against a quality assurance committee established in compliance with Sections 4070 and 5624 of the Welfare and Institutions Code or hospital, the cause of action shall exist as if the preceding provisions of this section had not been enacted.

This section shall remain in effect only until January 1, 1990, and as of that date is repealed, unless a later enacted statute, which is enacted before January 1, 1990, deletes or extends that date.

SEC. 2. Section 43.7 of the Civil Code, as amended by Section 2 of Chapter 669 of the Statutes of 1986, is amended to read:

43.7. (a) There shall be no monetary liability on the part of, and no cause of action for damages shall arise against, any member of a duly appointed mental health professional quality assurance committee that is established in compliance with Sections 4070 and 5624 of the Welfare and Institutions Code, for any act or proceeding undertaken or performed within the scope of the functions of the committee which is formed to review and evaluate the adequacy, appropriateness, or effectiveness of the care and treatment planned for, or provided to, mental health patients in order to improve quality of care by mental health professionals if the committee member acts without malice, has made a reasonable effort to obtain the facts of the matter as to which he or she acts, and acts in reasonable belief that the action taken by him or her is warranted by the facts known to him or her after the reasonable effort to obtain facts.

(b) There shall be no monetary liability on the part of, and no cause of action for damages shall arise against, any professional society, any member of a duly appointed committee of a medical specialty society, or duly appointed member of a committee of a professional staff of a licensed hospital (provided the professional staff operates pursuant to written bylaws that have been approved by the governing board of the hospital), for any act or proceeding undertaken or performed within the scope of the functions of the committee which is formed to maintain the professional standards of the society established by its bylaws, or any member of any peer review committee whose purpose is to review the quality of medical, dental, dietetic, chiropractic, optometric, or veterinary services rendered by physicians and surgeons, dentists, dental hygienists, podiatrists, registered dieticians, chiropractors, optometrists, veterinarians, or psychologists which committee is composed chiefly of physicians and surgeons, dentists, dental hygienists, podiatrists, registered dietitians, chiropractors, optometrists, veterinarians, or psychologists for any act or proceeding undertaken or performed in reviewing the quality of medical, dental, dietetic, chiropractic, optometric, or veterinary services rendered by physicians and surgeons, dentists, dental hygienists, podiatrists, registered dietitians, chiropractors, optometrists, veterinarians, or psychologists or any member of the governing board of a hospital in reviewing the quality of medical services rendered by members of the staff if the professional society, committee, or board member acts without malice, has made a reasonable effort to obtain the facts of the matter as to which he, she, or it acts, and acts in reasonable belief that the action taken by him, her, or it is warranted by the facts known to him, her, or it after the reasonable effort to obtain facts. "Professional society" includes legal, medical, psychological, dental, dental hygiene, dietetic, accounting, optometric, podiatric, pharmaceutic, chiropractic, physical therapist, veterinary, licensed marriage, family, and child counseling, licensed clinical social work, and engineering organizations having as members at least 25 percent of the eligible persons or licentiates in the geographic area served by the particular society. However, if the society has less than 100 members, it shall have as members at least a majority of the eligible persons or licentiates in the geographic area served by the particular society.

"Medical specialty society" means an organization having as members at least 25 percent of the eligible physicians within a given professionally recognized medical specialty in the geographic area served by the particular society.

(c) This section does not affect the official immunity of an officer or employee of a public corporation.

(d) There shall be no monetary liability on the part of, and no cause of action for damages shall arise against, any physician and surgeon, podiatrist, or chiropractor who is a member of an underwriting committee of an interindemnity or reciprocal or interinsurance exchange or mutual company for any act or proceeding undertaken or performed in evaluating physicians and surgeons, podiatrists, or chiropractors for the writing of professional liability insurance, or any act or proceeding undertaken or performed in evaluating physicians and surgeons for the writing of an interindemnity, reciprocal, or interinsurance contract as specified in Section 1280.7 of the Insurance Code, if the evaluating physician or surgeon, podiatrist, or chiropractor acts without malice, has made a reasonable effort to obtain the facts of the matter as to which he or she acts, and acts in reasonable belief that the action taken by him or her is warranted by the facts known to him or her after the reasonable effort to obtain the facts.

(e) This section shall not be construed to confer immunity from liability on any quality assurance committee established in compliance with Sections 4070 and 5624 of the Welfare and Institutions Code or hospital. In any case in which, but for the enactment of the preceding provisions of this section, a cause of action would arise against a quality assurance committee established in compliance with Sections 4070 and 5624 of the Welfare and Institutions Code or hospital, the cause of action shall exist as if the preceding provisions of this section had not been enacted.

(f) This section shall become operative on January 1, 1990.

APPENDIX P

BUSINESS & PROFESSIONS CODE: CALIFORNIA

Chapter 1448, 1987 — Sections 337 and 728,
requiring professionals to disseminate information to victims.

Senate Bill No. 1277

CHAPTER 1448

An act to add Sections 337 and 728 to the Business and Professions Code, relating to psychotherapists.

[Approved by Governor September 30, 1987. Filed with
Secretary of State September 30, 1987.]

LEGISLATIVE COUNSEL'S DIGEST

SB 1277, Watson. Psychotherapists.

(1) Existing law does not require a licensed physician and surgeon, psychologist, clinical social worker, marriage, family, and child counselor, psychological assistant or psychiatric technician to report any misconduct suspected of another licensee.

This bill would require any psychotherapist, as defined, including the above licensees, or employer of a psychotherapist, to provide, and discuss with, a patient a specified brochure whenever the person becomes aware through a patient of sexual intercourse or sexual contact with a patient by or with a previous psychotherapist during the course of a prior treatment.

This bill would make it unprofessional conduct to fail to comply with these requirements.

(2) Existing law does not require the Department of Consumer Affairs to disseminate information for victims of sexual exploitation by any licensee of the Board of Medical Quality Assurance.

This bill would require the department to prepare and disseminate a brochure for victims of psychotherapist-patient sexual contact and the victim's advocates, as specified.

The people of the State of California do enact as follows:

SECTION 1. Section 337 is added to the Business and Professions Code, to read:

337. (a) The department shall prepare and disseminate an informational brochure for victims of psychotherapist-patient sexual contact and advocates for those victims. This brochure shall be developed by the department in consultation with members of the Sexual Assault Program of the Office of Criminal Justice Planning and the office of the Attorney General.

(b) The brochure shall include, but is not limited to, the following:

(1) A legal and an informal definition of psychotherapist-patient sexual contact.

(2) A brief description of common personal reactions and histories of victims and victim's families.

(3) A patient's bill of rights.

(4) Options for reporting psychotherapist-patient sexual relations and instructions for each reporting option.

(5) A full description of administrative, civil, and professional associations complaint procedures.

(6) A description of services available for support of victims.

(c) The brochure shall be provided to each individual contacting the Board of Medical Quality Assurance and their allied health boards or the Board of Behavioral Science Examiners regarding a complaint involving psychotherapist-patient sexual relations.

SEC. 2. Section 728 is added to the Business and Professions Code, to read:

728. (a) Any psychotherapist or employer of a psychotherapist who becomes aware through a patient that the patient had alleged sexual intercourse or alleged sexual contact with a previous psychotherapist during the course of a prior treatment, shall provide to the patient a brochure promulgated by the department which delineates the rights of, and remedies for, patients who have been involved sexually with their psychotherapist. Further, the psychotherapist or employer shall discuss with the patient the brochure prepared by the department.

(b) Failure to comply with this section constitutes unprofessional conduct.

(c) For the purpose of this section, the following definitions apply:

(1) "Psychotherapist" means a physician specializing in the practice of psychiatry or practicing psychotherapy, a psychologist, a clinical social worker, a marriage, family, and child counselor, a psychological assistant, marriage, family, and child counselor registered intern, or social worker apprentice.

(2) "Sexual contact" means the touching of an intimate part of another person.

(3) "Intimate part" and "touching" have the same meaning as defined in subdivision (d) of Section 243.4 of the Penal Code.

(4) "The course of a prior treatment" means the period of time during which a patient first commences treatment for services which a psychotherapist is authorized to provide under his or her scope of practice or which the psychotherapist represents to the patient as being within his or her scope of practice until such time as the psychotherapist-patient relationship is terminated.

APPENDIX Q

Chapter 631, Laws of Minnesota, 1984

The bill which created the Minnesota Task
Force on Sexual Exploitation by
Psychotherapists

Chapter 631
Laws of Minnesota, 1984

relating to occupations and professions; establishing a task force to study the problem of sexual exploitation by counselors and therapists.

BE IT ENACTED BY THE LEGISLATURE OF THE STATE OF MINNESOTA:

Section 1. (TASK FORCE ON SEXUAL EXPLOITATION BY PSYCHOTHERAPISTS.)

Subdivision 1. (CREATION; MEMBERSHIP.) The commissioner of corrections shall appoint a task force to study the problem of sexual exploitation by counselors and therapists. The task force shall consist of not more than 18 members who are broadly representative of the state, including representatives of professional organizations, board of medical examiners, board of psychology, and board of nursing, agencies and individuals offering counseling or therapy services, the legal community, appropriate state agencies, women's organizations, and consumers. The terms, compensation, and removal of members are as provided in section 15. 059.

Sub. 2. (STATE-WIDE PLAN.) The task force shall develop a statewide plan to:

(1) educate the public about the nature and scope of sexual exploitation by counselors and therapists;

(2) educate counselors and therapists, their employers, and training institutions about the consequences of and methods of preventing unethical conduct; and

(3) educate clients and potential clients about their rights, ways to select nonabusive counselors and therapists, and remedies for sexual exploitation by a counselor or therapist.

Sub. 3. (RECOMMENDATIONS.) Based on its findings, the task force shall make recommendations to the legislature by February 1, 1985, on:

(1) the need for a bill of rights for counseling and therapy clients;

(2) the need to improve the procedures and rules of regulatory agencies to minimize trauma for complainants and standardize penalties;

(3) the advisability of prohibiting information concerning the previous sexual conduct of a client or former client in proceedings of regulatory agencies;

(4) the need to create a felony offense for sexual exploitation by a counselor or therapist;

(5) the need for increasing damage awards in civil suits involving sexual exploitation by counselors or therapists;

(6) the need to require rules of professional conduct that prohibit sexual contact with clients and patients and require reporting of known violations;

(7) the need for regulation of all professionals engaging in therapy and counseling; and

(8) the need for other actions to address the problem of sexual exploitation by counselors and therapists.

Subd. 4. (EXPIRATION.) The task force expires on July 1, 1985.

Sec. 2. (EFFECTIVE DATE.)

Section 1 is effective the day following final enactment.

Appendix R

Rules of the Dept. of Professional Regulation, Board of Psychological
Examiners, State of Florida, Chapter 21U-15.004

Sexual Misconduct in the Practice of Psychology

Note especially section (5)(b) in which, for the purposes of determining the
existence of sexual misconduct, the psychologist-client relationship is deemed
to continue in perpetuity.

21U-15.004 Sexual Misconduct in the Practice of Psychology.

(1) In accordance with the intent of Chapter 490, Florida Statutes, to preserve the health, safety and welfare of the public, sexual misconduct as defined herein is prohibited. The Board finds that the effects of the psychologist-client relationship are powerful and subtle and that clients are influenced consciously and subconsciously by the unequal distribution of power inherent in such relationships. Furthermore, the Board finds that the effects of psychologist-client relationship endure after psychological services cease to be rendered. Therefore, the client shall be presumed incapable of giving valid, informed, free consent to sexual activity involving the psychologist and the assertion of consent by the client shall not constitute a defense against charges of sexual misconduct.

(2) It shall constitute sexual misconduct for a psychologist, who is involved in a psychologist-client relationship, to engage, attempt to engage, or offer to engage the client in sexual intercourse or other sexual behavior. Sexual behavior includes, but is not limited to, kissing, or the touching by either the psychologist or the client of the other's breasts or genitals.

(3) It shall constitute sexual misconduct for a psychologist, who is involved in a psychologist-client relationship, to engage the client in verbal or physical behavior which is sexually arousing or demeaning to the client unless:

(a) such behavior is for the purpose of treatment of psycho-sexual disorders or dysfunctions; and

(b) complies with generally accepted professional standards for psychological treatment of the client's specific psycho-sexual disorders or dysfunctions.

(4) It shall constitute sexual misconduct for a psychologist who is involved in a psychologist-client relationship to use the influence inherent in that relationship to induce the client to engage in sexual conduct with a third party unless:

(a) such inducement is consistent with the planned psychological treatment of the client's specific psychological, social, or sexual dysfunctions or disorders; and

(b) treatment is provided in accordance with generally accepted professional standards for psychological treatment.

(5) (a) A psychologist-client relationship exists whenever a psychologist has rendered, or purports to have rendered, psychological services including, but not limited to, psychotherapy, counseling, assessment or treatment to a person. A formal contractual relationship, the scheduling of professional appointments, or payment of a fee for services are not necessary conditions for the existence of a psychologist-client relationship, though each of these may be evidence that such a relationship exists.

(b) For purposes of determining the existence of sexual misconduct as defined herein, the psychologist-client relationship is deemed to continue in perpetuity.

Specific Authority 490.004(5), 490.0111 FS.
Law Implemented 490.0111 FS.
History-New 6/23/82, Formerly 21U-15.04, Amended 12/21/86

APPENDIX S

Sample Group Notice of the type currently utilized by Ellen Luepker, ACSW,
to advertise her ten-session support groups for clients who have been sexually exploited by counselors, therapists, or clergy.

ANNOUNCEMENT   **PLEASE POST**

<u>PARK PLACE CLINIC</u>

TEN-SESSION THERAPY/SUPPORT GROUPS
FOR CLIENTS WHO HAVE BEEN SEXUALLY EXPLOITED
BY COUNSELORS, THERAPISTS, OR CLERGY

PURPOSE: If you have experienced a sexually seductive relationship with a counselor, psychotherapist, or member of the clergy, discussions with other clients in a small group may assist you. In a confidential atmosphere, you can feel less isolated as the group offers an opportunity to clarify your mixed feelings about the experience and to decide what, if any, options for action you may wish to take. These group services are to assist clients to become "unstuck," freer to move ahead in their lives again.

PLACE: The groups will be held in either Park Place Clinic's St. Paul Office (Hanover Building at 480 Cedar) or Minneapolis office (2445 Park Avenue).

COST: $73/intake interview. $40/group session. The clinic is a Rule 29 Minnesota state licensed mental health clinic. It can accept many types of insurance, referrals from HMOs, and welcomes inquiries about fee payment arrangements as needed.

TIME: Starting date and hour of day to be determined.

LEADER: Ellen T. Luepker, M.S.W., A.C.S.W., Licensed Psychologist, received her M.S.W. from Smith College in 1966, and a Bush Fellowship at the University of Minnesota in early childhood education and development in 1977. She is a past president of the Minnesota Society for Clinical Social Work. She has twenty years' clinical experience in child guidance and adult psychotherapy settings. Since 1980, she has provided group therapy services for exploited clients in cooperation with Walk-In Counseling Center of Minneapolis. She formerly served as Special Consultant to the Minnesota Task Force on Sexual Exploitation of Clients by Therapists and Counselors, and has authored professional publications on this topic.

FOR FURTHER INFORMATION/INTAKE APPOINTMENT: Call Ellen Luepker, 870-1081 or 729-0111.

2445 Park Avenue South
Minneapolis, Minnesota 55404
(612) 870-1081

APPENDIX T

Sample notice for One-Day Workshops
run by Estelle Disch, Ph.D., LCSW

Survivors of
SEXUAL MALPRACTICE
for women who have been sexually abused by psychotherapists

ONE DAY WORKSHOP

Many therapists abuse their power in the therapy relationship, often by taking advantage of the client in sexual ways. Ethics codes in all professional therapy organizations condemn sexual contact with clients as outside the boundaries of healthy therapy. In Wisconsin and Minnesota it is now a crime for a psychotherapist to have sexual contact with a client, even if the client consents. This workshop is designed for women who believe that they have been abused sexually in therapy, no matter what form the abuse took and no matter how long ago it occurred. Women attending will have an opportunity to tell their stories and to consider what, if anything, they want to do next in response to the abuse they have suffered. Information will be available regarding post-workshop options, including complaint procedures and other less formal possibilities. People who attend will be expected to keep other participants' stories confidential.

TIME: Saturday, Nov. 21, 1987, 10am to 4pm. Please bring lunch.

Optional Follow-up Session - for anyone who has ever been to one of these workshops: Sat., Dec. 5, 1987, 10am to 12noon.

FEE: Sliding Scale, $25 to $50. Scholarships available.
Limited to 8 participants.

LEADER: ESTELLE DISCH, Ph.D., C.C.S. is a feminist therapist and Certified Clinical Sociologist who is a survivor of sexual abuse by a therapist.

PLACE: **TAPESTRY, INC.**
20 Sacramento Street, Cambridge, MA 02138
(617) 661-0248

Survivors of
SEXUAL MALPRACTICE
for women who have been sexually abused by psychotherapists

Many therapists abuse their power in the therapy relationship, often in sexual ways. Ethics codes in all professional therapy organizations condemn sexual contact with clients as inappropriate and destructive in a therapeutic relationship. In three states, this behavior constitutes a crime. The workshop and group described below are designed for women who believe that they have been abused sexually in therapy, no matter what form the abuse took and no matter how long ago it occurred.

Twelve Session Therapy/Support Group. Nancy Avery, MSW, LICSW, will run a twelve-session group starting in October 1989. The group will help participants grieve their losses, find their anger, and cope with any complaint procedures they might be facing. The focus of the group is on feelings and support as participants work toward understanding the effects the abuse has had on them. Insurance accepted. For more information, or to register call Nancy Avery at (617) 232-5280.

One-Day Workshop. Estelle Disch, Ph.D., CCS, will run a one-day workshop on Sunday, November 5, 1989, from 10am to 4pm. Women attending will have an opportunity to share their therapy abuse experiences and will be helped to consider what, if anything, they want to do next in response to the abuse they have suffered. Information will be available regarding both formal and informal complaint procedures. Sliding fee scale. Scholarships are available for this workshop, provided by survivors who have won settlements. For more information, or to register, call Estelle Disch at (617) 661-4667. Wheelchair accessible.

About the Leaders. Both leaders are Co-Directors of BASTA! Boston Associates to Stop Therapy Abuse. **Nancy Avery** is a lecturer in psychiatry at Harvard Medical School and in private practice in the Boston area. She has worked with survivors of sexual abuse by therapists since 1987. **Estelle Disch** teaches sociology at the University of Massachusetts/Boston and has a private practice in the Boston area. She has worked with survivors of sexual abuse by therapists since 1984, formerly at Tapestry, Inc. in Cambridge, MA.

These services are sponsored by:

BASTA!
Boston Associates to Stop Therapy Abuse
528 Franklin Street
Cambridge, MA 02139
(617) 661-4667 or (617) 232-5280

Basta! means Enough! in Italian and Spanish.

APPENDIX U

SURVEY FORM USED IN WISCONSIN INCIDENCE STUDY

SURVEY OF PSYCHOTHERAPISTS AND COUNSELORS IN WISCONSIN REGARDING SEXUAL CONTACT BETWEEN THERAPISTS AND CLIENTS

The Task Force on Sexual Misconduct by Therapists was formed by the Wisconsin Psychological Association to study the problem of sexual involvement of therapists with clients and to make recommendations on how to control it more effectively. At this stage of its work, the Task Force needs to obtain some estimate of the frequency with which the problem exists in Wisconsin. We ask you, therefore, to assist us in this effort by answering the questions below, a task which should take no more than 10 minutes of your time.

If you do not have exact figures available, give us your best estimates. Even if you have had no cases, please return the form so that we can establish an accurate return rate. Please return the completed survey in the enclosed return envelope within one week of receiving it. Your reply will be kept strictly confidential and will be used for statistical purposes only. Please call Sarah Bowen at WPA (608-251-1450) or Tony Kuchan of the Committee (414-224-7198) if you have any questions.

1. Since January 1, 1982, how many different clients have you seen during each year who have reported having had sexual contact with a previous therapist/counselor?

    1982_____   1983_____   1984_____   None_____   (Please skip to Respondent Information on page 2.

2. During each of these years, how many of these clients were male? How many were female? (Record the appropriate number in each category.)

	Male	Female
1982	_____	_____
1983	_____	_____
1984	_____	_____

3. In each of these cases, what was the training of the therapist? (Record the appropriate number in each category.)

	Psycho-logist	Psychi-atrist	Physician	Social Worker	Marriage Counselor	Clergy	Other
1982	_____	_____	_____	_____	_____	_____	_____
1983	_____	_____	_____	_____	_____	_____	_____
1984	_____	_____	_____	_____	_____	_____	_____

4. In each of these cases, how many of the therapists were male? How many were female? (Record the appropriate number in each category.)

	Male	Female
1982	_____	_____
1983	_____	_____
1984	_____	_____

5. To the best of your knowledge, what was the frequency of the sexual exchange reported in each of the following types of contact? (Report the appropriate number in each category.)

	Inter-course	Fond-ling	Oral Sex	Mastur-bation	Erotic Hugging/ Kissing	Suggestive Looks, Remarks or Behavior	Anal Inter-course	Genital Exposure
1982	_____	_____	_____	_____	_____	_____	_____	_____
1983	_____	_____	_____	_____	_____	_____	_____	_____
1984	_____	_____	_____	_____	_____	_____	_____	_____

6. Please indicate the degree to which you agree with the following statement for each of your reported cases. (Record the number of cases for each opinion category.) "In my opinion, the psychological well-being of this client was seriously and negatively affected by the sexual encounter with his/her therapist."

	Strongly Agree	Agree	Neutral or Uncertain	Disagree	Strongly Disagree
1982	_____	_____	_____	_____	_____
1983	_____	_____	_____	_____	_____
1984	_____	_____	_____	_____	_____

7. If the Task Force wished to contact clients who have had sexual encounters with therapists for the purpose of further study, would you be willing to seek their permission to be contacted; i.e., send them a copy of our request?

    Yes_____   No_____   Yes, but on the condition that_____

    _____

    If you answered "Yes," please provide us with your name and address below so that we can contact you with our request.

    _____

    _____

    _____

8. Comments:

Respondent Information

1. Gender: Male_____   Female_____

2. Years in Practice: 1-2_____   3-5_____   6-10_____   11 or more_____

3. Number of different therapy clients seen per week:

    1-5_____   6-10_____   10-20_____   21-30_____   30 or more_____

Thank you very much for your assistance in our study of this most serious issue.

<u>Appendix V</u>

MINNESOTA STATUTE ON UNLICENSED MENTAL HEALTH
SERVICE PROVIDERS

In 1987, after a two-year study, the State of Minnesota created three new regulatory Boards, thereby licensing social workers, marriage and family therapists, and regulating (without licensure) all other psychotherapists and counselors not previously licensed.

This new law, Chapter 347 Minnesota Statutes 1987, under Article 4, created the Board of Unlicensed Mental Health Service Providers. This appendix contains the portion of this law, now 148B.40-148B.47 Laws of Minnesota, pertaining to the unlicensed practitioner.

The new Board will sunset [sic] on July 1, 1991, after a plan has been worked out as to how to regulate the diverse group of counselors and therapists who are **not** physicians, nurses, psychologists, social workers, or marriage and family therapists. The most populous single subgroup included are chemical dependency counselors.

At present chemical dependency practitioners are certified through a voluntary process under a privately organized certification board. While many work in residential or outpatient facilities, a growing number are in private practice. Unlike other counseling fields, there has been no active movement to petition for licensure, partly due to the fact that third party reimbursement has been available without licensure.

The goal of this new Board is to provide for some regulation and study of the diverse group of people not yet licensed with the expectation that an appropriate form of regulation will be decided upon.

ARTICLE 4   MS 148B.40

BOARD OF UNLICENSED MENTAL HEALTH SERVICE PROVIDERS
    Section 1. [148B.40] [DEFINITIONS.]
    Subdivision 1. [TERMS] As used in sections 1 to 8, the following terms have the meanings given them in this section.
    Subd. 2. [BOARD] "Board " means the board of mental health service providers established in section 2.
    Subd. 3. [MENTAL HEALTH SERVICE PROVIDER.] "Mental health service provider" or "provider" means any person who provides, for a remuneration, mental health services as defined in subdivision 4. It does not include persons licensed by the board of medical examiners under chapter 147; the board of nursing under sections 148.171 to 148.285; or the board of psychology under sections 148.88 to 148.98; the board of social work under article 2, sections 1 to 13; the board of marriage and family therapy under article 3, sections 1 to 11; or another licensing board if the person is practicing within the scope of the license.
    Subd. 4. [MENTAL HEALTH SERVICES.] "Mental health services" means the professional treatment, assessment, or counseling of another person for a cognitive, behavioral, emotional, mental, or social dysfunction, including intrapersonal or interpersonal dysfunctions.
    Subd. 5. [MENTAL HEALTH CLIENT.] "Mental health client" or "client" means a person who receives the services of a mental health service provider.
    Sec. 2. [148B.41] [BOARD OF UNLICENSED MENTAL HEALTH SERVICE PROVIDERS.]
    Subdivision 1. [COMPOSITION.] The board of unlicensed mental health service providers consists of 17 members, including two chemical dependency counselors, two professional counselors, two pastoral counselors, five members representing other identifiable specialties and subgroups of providers subject to filing requirements, and six public members as defined in section 214.02. Within 90 days after the effective date of rules adopted by the board to implement sections 1 to 8, members of the board specified must be mental health service providers who have filed with the board pursuant to section 3.

Subd. 2. [APPOINTMENT.] Members of the board are appointed by the governor and serve under section 214.09.

Subd. 3. [BOARD ADMINISTRATION.] The board shall elect from among its members a chair and a vice-chair to serve for one year or until a successor is elected and qualifies. The members of the board have authority to administer oaths and the board, in session, to take testimony as to matters pertaining to the duties of the board. Six members of the board constitute a quorum for the transaction of business.

Subd. 4. [RULEMAKING.] The board shall adopt rules necessary to implement, administer, or enforce sections 1 to 8 under chapter 14 and section 214.001, subdivisions 2 and 3. The board shall consult with the commissioner of health, the commissioner of human services, and the commissioner of employee relations in the development of rules. The board may not adopt rules that restrict or prohibit persons from providing mental health services on the basis of education, training, experience, or supervision; or that restrict the use of any title.

Sec. 3. [148B.42] [FILING REQUIRED.]

Subdivision 1. [FILING.] All mental health service providers shall file with the state, on a form provided by the board, their name; home and business address; telephone number; degrees held, if any, major field, and whether the degrees are from an accredited institution and how the institution is accredited; and any other relevant experience. An applicant for filing who has practiced in another state shall authorize, in writing, the licensing or regulatory entity in the other state or states to release to the board any information on complaints or disciplinary actions pending against that individual, as well as any final disciplinary actions taken against that individual. The board shall provide a form for this purpose. The board may reject a filing if there is evidence of a violation of or failure to comply with this chapter.

Subd. 2. [ACKNOWLEDGMENT OF FILING.] The board shall issue an acknowledgment of filing to each mental health service provider who files under subdivision 1 and relevant rules of the board, and who is determined by the board to be in compliance with this chapter. The acknowledgment of filing must not be displayed in any manner nor shall it be shown to mental health clients. The acknowledgment of filing shall contain, in bold print, the phrase: "This acknowledgment of filing does not imply or certify in any way that this mental health professional has met any standards or criteria of education or training.

Subd. 3. [NONTRANSFERABILITY.] Acknowledgments of filing are nontransferable.

Subd. 4. [PENALTIES.] Failure to file with the board, or supplying false or misleading information on the filing form, application for registration, or any accompanying statements shall constitute grounds for adverse action.

Subd. 5. [PROVISION OF MENTAL HEALTH SERVICES WITHOUT FILING.] Except as otherwise provided in this chapter, it is unlawful for any person not filing with the board to provide mental health services in this state as defined in section 1, subdivision 4. Any person violating subdivision 1 is guilty of a gross misdemeanor.

Sec. 4. [148B.43] [PROHIBITED USE OF ACKNOWLEDGMENT.]

No mental health service provider may display the acknowledgment received under section 3, subdivision 2, or refer to it in any advertising, on stationary, or in any communication to a client or the public, or otherwise use the fact that the provider has filed with the state as an indication of state approval or endorsement or satisfaction of standards of conduct, training, or skill.

Sec. 5. [148B.44] [PROHIBITED CONDUCT.]

Subdivision 1. [PROHIBITED CONDUCT.] Notwithstanding any law to the contrary, the board may reject a filing or application, or may impose adverse action as described in section 6 against any mental health service provider for failure to comply with the provisions of this chapter. The following conduct is prohibited and is grounds for adverse action:

(a) Conviction of a crime reasonably related to the provision of mental health services. Conviction, as used in this subdivision, includes a conviction of an offense which, if committed in this state, would be deemed a felony without regard to its designation elsewhere, or a criminal proceeding where a finding or verdict of guilty is made or returned but the adjudication of guilt is either withheld or not entered.

(b) Conviction of crimes against persons. For the purposes of this chapter, a crime against a person means violations of the following sections: sections 609.185; 609.19; 609.195; 609.20; 609.205; 609.21; 609.215; 609.221; 609.222; 609.223; 609.224; 609.23; 609.231; 609.235; 609.24; 609.245; 609.25; 609.255; 609.265; 609.26; subdivision 1, clause (1) or (2); 609.342; 609.343; 609.344; 609.345; 609.365; 609.498, subdivision 1; 609.50, clause (1); 609.561; 609.562; and 609.595.

(c) Revocation, suspension, restriction, limitation, or other disciplinary action against the mental health professional's license, certificate, registration, or right of practice in another state or jurisdiction, for offenses that would be subject to disciplinary action in this state, or failure to report to the board that charges regarding the person's license, certificate, registration, or right of practice have been brought in another state or jurisdiction.

(d) Advertising that is false or misleading.

(e) Filing with the board false or misleading statements of credentials, training, or experience.

(f) Conduct likely to deceive, defraud, or harm the public; or demonstrating a willful or careless disregard for the health, welfare, or safety of a client; or any other practice that may create unnecessary danger to any client's life, health, or safety, in any of which cases, proof of actual injury need not be established.

(g) Adjudication as mentally incompetent, or as a person who has a psychopathic personality as defined in section 526.09, or who is dangerous to himself or herself, or adjudication pursuant to chapter 253B, as chemically dependent, mentally ill, mentally retarded, or mentally ill and dangerous to the public.

(h) Inability to provide mental health services with reasonable safety to clients by reason of physical, mental, or emotional illness; drunkenness; or use of legend drugs, chemicals, controlled substances, or any other similar materials or mood-altering substances.

(i) Revealing a communication from, or relating to, a client except when otherwise required or permitted by law.

(j) Failure to comply with a client's request made under section 144.335, or to furnish a client record or report required by law.

(k) Splitting fees or promising to pay a portion of a fee to any other professional other than for services rendered by the other professional to the client.

(l) Engaging in abusive or fraudulent billing practices, including violations of the federal Medicare and Medicaid laws or state medical assistance laws.

(m) Engaging in sexual contact with a client or former client as defined in section 148A.01.

(n) Failure to make reports as required by section 5, or cooperate with an investigation of the board as required by section 7.

(o) Obtaining money, property, or services from a client, other than reasonable fees for services provided to the client, through the use of undue influence, harassment, duress, deception, or fraud.

(p) Undertaking or continuing a professional relationship with a client in which the objectivity of the professional would be impaired.

(q) Failure to provide the client with a copy of the client bill of rights, or violation of any provision of the client bill of rights.

Subd. 2. [EVIDENCE.] In adverse actions alleging a violation of subdivision 1, paragraph (a), (b), or (c), a copy of the judgment or proceeding under the seal of the court administrator or of the administrative agency that entered the same shall be admissible into evidence without further authentication and shall constitute prima facie evidence of its contents.

Subd. 3. [MENTAL EXAMINATION; ACCESS TO MEDICAL DATA.] (a) If the board has probably cause to believe that a mental health service provider comes under subdivision 1, paragraph (g) or (h), it may direct the provider to submit to a mental or physical examination or chemical dependency evaluation. For the purpose of this subdivision every mental health service provider is deemed to have consented to submit to a mental or physical examination or chemical dependency evaluation when directed in writing by the board and further to have waived all objections to the admissibility of the examining physicians', psychologists', or mental health professional's testimony or examination reports on the ground that the same constitute a privileged communication. Failure of a mental health service provider to submit to an examination when directed constitutes an admission of the allegations against the provider, unless the failure was due to circumstance beyond the provider's control, in which case a default and final order may be entered without the taking of testimony or presentation of evidence. A mental health service provider affected under this paragraph shall at reasonable intervals be given an opportunity to demonstrate that the provider can resume the provision of mental health services with reasonable safety to clients. In any proceeding under this paragraph, neither the record of proceedings nor the orders entered by the board shall be used against a mental health service provider in any other proceeding.

(b) In addition to ordering a physical or mental examination, the board may, notwithstanding section 13.42, 144.651, or any other law limiting access to medical or other health data, obtain medical data and health records relating to a mental health service provider without the provider's consent if the board has probable cause to believe that a provider comes under subdivision 1, paragraph (g), (h), or (m). The medical data may be requested from a health care professional, as defined in section 144.335, subdivision 1, paragraph (b), an insurance company, or a government agency, including the department of human services. A health care professional, insurance company, or government agency shall comply with any written request of the board under this subdivision and is not liable in any action for damages for releasing the data requested by the board if the data are released pursuant to a written request under this subdivision, unless the information is false and the person or organization giving the information knew, or had reason to believe, the information was false. Information obtained under this subdivision is private data under sections 13.01 to 13.87.

Sec. 6. [148B.45] [ADVERSE ACTIONS.]

Subdivision 1. [FORMS OF ADVERSE ACTION.] When the board finds that a mental health service provider has violated a provision or provisions of this chapter, it may do one or more of the following:

(1) deny or reject the filing;

(2) revoke the right to practice;

(3) suspend the right to practice;

(4) impose limitations or conditions on the provider's provision of mental health services, the imposition of rehabilitation requirements, or the requirement of practice under supervision;

(5) impose a civil penalty not exceeding $10,000 for each separate violation, the amount of the civil penalty to be fixed so as to deprive the provider of any economic advantage gained by reason of the violation charged or to reimburse the board for all costs of the investigation and proceeding;

(6) order the provider to provide unremunerated professional service under supervision at a designated public hospital, clinic, or other health care institution; or

(7) censure or reprimand the provider.

Subd. 2. [PROCEDURES.] The board shall adopt a written statement of internal operating procedures for receiving and investigating complaints reviewing misconduct cases, and imposing adverse actions.

Subd. 3. [MANDATORY SUSPENSION OR REVOCATION OF RIGHT OF PRACTICE.] The board shall suspend or revoke the right of a provider to provide mental health services for violations of section 4, subdivision 1, paragraphs (a), (b), and (m).

Sec. 7. [148B.46] [MENTAL HEALTH CLIENT BILL OF RIGHTS.]

Subdivision 1. [SCOPE.] All mental health service providers other than those providing services in a facility regulated under section 144.651 shall provide to each client prior to providing treatment a written copy of the mental health client bill of rights. A copy must also be posted in a prominent location in the office of the mental health service provider. Reasonable accommodations shall be made for those clients who cannot read or who have communication impairments and those who do not read or speak English. The mental health client bill of rights shall include the following:

(a) The name, title, business address, and telephone number of the provider.

(b) The degrees, training, experience, or other qualifications of the provider, followed by the following statement in bold print:

THE STATE OF MINNESOTA HAS NOT ADOPTED UNIFORM EDUCATIONAL AND TRAINING STANDARDS FOR MENTAL HEALTH SERVICE PROVIDERS. THIS STATEMENT OF CREDENTIALS IS FOR INFORMATIONAL PURPOSES ONLY.

(c) The name, business address, and telephone number of the provider's supervisor, if any.

(d) Notice that a client has the right to file a complaint with the provider's supervisor, if any, and the procedure for filing complaints.

(e) The name, address, and telephone number of the board and notice that a client may file complaints with the board.

(f) The provider's fees per unit of service, the provider's method of billing for such fees, the names of any insurance companies that have agreed to reimburse the provider, or health maintenance organizations with whom the provider contracts to provide service, whether the provider accepts Medicare, medical assistance, or general assistance medical care, and whether the provider is willing to accept partial payment, or to waive payment, and in what circumstances.

(g) A statement that the client has a right to reasonable notice of changes in services or charges.

(h) A brief summary, in plain language, of the theoretical approach used by the provider in treating patients.

(i) Notice that the client has a right to complete and current information concerning the provider's assessment and recommended course of treatment, including the expected duration of treatment.

(j) A statement that clients may expect courteous treatment and to be free from verbal, physical, or sexual abuse by the provider.

(k) A statement that client records and transactions with the provider are confidential, unless release of these records is authorized in writing by the client, or otherwise provided by law.

(l) A statement of the client's right to be allowed access to records and written information from records in accordance with section 144.335.

(m) A statement that other services may be available in the community, including where information concerning services is available.

(n) A statement that the client has the right to choose freely among available providers, and to change providers after services have begun, within the limits of health insurance, medical assistance, or other health programs.

(o) A statement that the client has a right to coordinated transfer when there will be a change in the provider of services.

(p) A statement that the client may refuse services or treatment, unless otherwise provided by law.

(q) A statement that the client may assert the client's rights without retaliation.

Subd. 2. [ACKNOWLEDGMENT BY CLIENT.] Prior to the provision of any service, the client must sign a written statement attesting that the client has received the client bill of rights.

Sec. 8. [148B.47] [RENEWALS.]

Notwithstanding any other law, the board shall adopt rules providing for the renewal of filing. The rules shall specify the period of time for which a filing is valid, procedures and information required for the renewal, and renewal fees.

Sec. 9. [REPORTS.]

Subdivision 1. [COMMISSIONER OF HEALTH.] The commissioner of health shall review the report of the office under sections 214.001, 214.13, and 214.141. The commissioner shall make recommendations to the legislature by January 15, 1991, on the need for registration or licensure of unlicensed mental health service providers and the need to retain the board of unlicensed mental health service providers.

Subd. 2. [BOARD OF UNLICENSED MENTAL HEALTH SERVICE PROVIDERS.] The board of unlicensed mental health service providers must report on the board's findings and activities to the commissioner of health and the legislature by July 1, 1990. The board shall report to the legislature on or before January 15, 1991, with recommendations on whether providers who are not trained should be allowed to continue to practice.

Subd. 3. [LEGISLATIVE INTENT.] Nothing in this section is intended to require the commissioner of health to delay review of applications for credentialing pursuant to sections 214.13 and 214.141 pending the outcome of the reports required under this section.

Sec. 10. [APPROPRIATION.]

$835,000 is appropriated from the special revenue fund to the office of social work and mental health boards.

Sec. 11. [SUNSET.]

Article 4, sections 1 to 8, are repealed effective July 1, 1991.

APPENDIX W

Wisconsin Act 380, passed in 1987, outlining the
duty to report sexual contact between client and
therapist

STATE OF WISCONSIN

Date of enactment: April 22, 1988

1987 Assembly Bill 929

Date of publication*: May 2, 1988

1987 Wisconsin Act 380

AN ACT *to renumber* 940.22 (1) (a) to (e); *to amend* 939.74 (4), 940.22 (title) and 949.03 (1) (b); **and** *to create* 146.82 (2) (a) 13, 940.22 (1) (title), 940.22 (1) (a), (e), (f) and (h) and 940.22 (2) (title) and (3) to (5) of the statutes, *relating to* reporting alleged incidents of sexual exploitation by a therapist and providing penalties.

The people of the state of Wisconsin, represented in senate and assembly, do enact as follows:

SECTION 1. 146.82 (2) (a) 13 of the statutes is created to read:

146.82 (2) (a) 13. To persons and entites under s. 940.22.

SECTION 2. 939.74 (4) of the statutes is amended to read:

939.74 (4) In computing the time limited by this section, the time during which an alleged victim under s. 940.22 (2) is unable to seek the issuance of a complaint under s. 968.02 due to the effects of the sexual contact or due to any threats, instructions or statements from the therapist shall not be included.

SECTION 3. 940.22 (title) of the statutes is amended to read:

940.22 (title) **Sexual exploitation by a therapist; duty to report.**

SECTION 4. 940.22 (1) (title) of the statutes is created to read:

940.22 (1) (title) DEFINITIONS.

SECTION 5. 940.22 (1) (a) to (e) of the statutes are renumbered 940.22 (1) (b), (c), (d), (g) and (i).

SECTION 6. 940.22 (1) (a), (e), (f) and (h) of the statutes are created to read:

940.22 (1) (a) "Department" means the department of regulation and licensing.

(e) "Record" means any document relating to the investigation, assessment and disposition of a report under this section.

(f) "Reporter" means a therapist who reports suspected sexual contact between his or her patient or client and another therapist.

(h) "Subject" means the therapist named in a report or record as being suspected of having sexual contact with a patient or client or who has been determined to have engaged in sexual contact with a patient or client.

SECTION 7. 940.22 (2) (title) and (3) to (5) of the statutes are created to read:

940.22 (2) (title) SEXUAL CONTACT PROHIBITED.

(3) REPORTS OF SEXUAL CONTACT. (a) If a therapist has reasonable cause to suspect that a patient or client he or she has seen in the course of professional duties is a victim of sexual contact by another therapist or a person who holds himself or herself out to be a therapist in violation of sub. (2), as soon thereafter as practicable the therapist shall ask the patient or client if he or she wants the therapist to make a report under this subsection. The therapist shall explain that the report need not identify the patient or client as the victim. If the patient or client wants the therapist to make the report, the patient or client shall provide the therapist with a written consent to the report and shall specify whether the patient's or client's identity will be included in the report.

(b) Within 30 days after a patient or client consents under par. (a) to a report, the therapist shall report the suspicion to:

1. The department, if the reporter believes the subject of the report is licensed by the state. The department shall promptly communicate the information to the appropriate examining board.

2. The district attorney for the county in which the sexual contact is likely, in the opinion of the reporter, to have occurred, if subd. 1 is not applicable.

(c) A report under this subsection shall contain only information that is necessary to identify the reporter and subject and to express the suspicion that sexual contact has occurred in violation of sub. (2).

The report shall not contain information as to the identity of the alleged victim of sexual contact unless the patient or client requests under par. (a) that this information be included.

(d) Whoever intentionally violates this subsection by failing to report as required under pars. (a) to (c) is guilty of a Class A misdemeanor.

(4) CONFIDENTIALITY OF REPORTS AND RECORDS. (a) All reports and records made from reports under sub. (3) and the disclosure of a report or record under this subsection does not violate any person's responsibility for maintaining the confidentiality of patient health care records, as defined in s. 146.81 (4) and as required under s. 146.82. Reports and records may be disclosed only to appropriate staff of a district attorney or a law enforcement agency within this state for purposes of investigation or prosecution.

(b) 1. The department, a district attorney or an examining board within this state may exchange information from a report or record on the same subject.

2. If the department receives 2 or more reports under sub. (3) regarding the same subject, the department shall communicate information from the reports to the appropriate district attorneys and may inform the applicable reporters that another report has been received regarding the same subject.

3. If a district attorney receives 2 or more reports under sub. (3) regarding the same subject, the district attorney may inform the applicable reporters that another report has been received regarding the same subject.

4. After reporters receive the information under subd. 2 or 3, they may inform the applicable patients or clients that another report was received regarding the same subject.

(c) A person to whom a report or record is disclosed under this subsection may not further disclose it, except to the persons and for the purposes specified in this section.

(d) Whoever intentionally violates this subsection, or permits or encourages the unauthorized dissemination or use of information contained in reports and records made under this section, is guilty of a Class A misdemeanor.

(5) IMMUNITY FROM LIABILITY. Any person or institution participating in good faith in the making of a report or record under this section is immune from any civil or criminal liability that results by reason of the action. For the purpose of any civil or criminal action or proceeding, any person reporting under this section is presumed to be acting in good faith. The immunity provided under this subsection does not apply to liability resulting from sexual contact by a therapist with a patient or client.

SECTION 8. 949.03 (1) (b) of the statutes, as affected by 1987 Wisconsin Act 90, is amended to read:

949.03 (1) (b) The commission or the attempt to commit any crime specified in s. 346.63 (2), 940.01, 940.02, 940.05, 940.06, 940.07, 940.08, 940.09, 940.19, 940.20, 940.201, 940.21, 940.22 (2), 940.225 (1) to (3), 940.23, 940.24, 940.245, 940.25, 940.26 (2), 940.28, 940.285, 940.29, 940.30, 940.305, 940.31, 940.32, 941.327, 943.02, 943.03, 943.04, 943.10, 943.20, 943.32 or 944.12

APPENDIX X

METROPOLITAN CLINIC OF COUNSELING

APPLICATION FOR CLINICAL POSITION

This application was developed by John Gonsiorek, Ph.D., who was serving as a consultant to Metropolitan Clinic of Counseling, an organization which provides mental health and chemical dependency services primarily to HMO enrollees in Minnesota, but which has operations elsewhere in the U.S. This application form was based on the Counselor/Supervisor Volunteer Application of the Walk-In Counseling Center contained in Appendix C.

METROPOLITAN CLINIC OF COUNSELING
APPLICATION FOR CLINICAL POSITION

All items in this application must be completed to be considered for a position with the Metropolitan Clinic of Counseling. A resume does not substitute for this application, although a resume may be attached to provide additional information.

DATE_____

NAME _____

ADDRESS _____ Zip _____

PHONE (office) _____ (home) _____

CURRENT EMPLOYMENT_____
                      (Agency/Company)   (Position/Title)

POSITION FOR WHICH YOU ARE APPLYING: _____

Please describe your therapeutic orientation and the way you prefer to work in treatment.

_____
_____
_____
_____

1. DEGREES HELD OR EXPECTED

| Institution | Major Field | Degree | Year |
Awarded			

2. LICENSURE/CERTIFICATION STATUS (present and past - list each separately)

    a. Level or type (e.g., Licensed Psychologist, ACSW, CD Certificate)

_____

State Where Held_____

Expiration Date_____

Areas of Competency or Professional Practices for which Licensed/Certified

_____

_____

2. b. Level or Type

_____

State Where Held_____

Expiration Date_____

Areas of Competence or Professional Practice for which Licensed/Certified

_____

_____

3. a. Has your license or certification ever been limited, suspended, or revoked in any jurisdiction; or have you ever surrendered your license or certification; or ever been placed on probation by a professional licensing body? NO_____ YES_____ N.A. (Never Licensed) _____ If "YES" attach an explanation to the end of this application form.

   b. Have charges of unprofessional conduct ever been brought against you? NO_____ YES_____ Please identify if any action was taken against you. If "YES" attach an explanation to the end of this application form.

   c. Have you ever been named as a defendant in a malpractice suit? NO____ YES_____ Was judgment ever awarded? NO_____ YES_____ If "YES" attach an explanation to the end of this application form.

   d. Have you ever been convicted of a criminal charge and/or had a judgment against you as a defendant in a civil action within the last three years? (excluding bankruptcy). NO____ YES_____

4. TRAINING AND CLINICALLY RELEVANT EXPERIENCE

   a. Internship and Practicum Placement(s)

Agency	Dates	Approximate Hours

b. Supervised Individual Counseling/Psychotherapy Experience

<u>Description</u> (Setting, Client Population   <u>Approximate Hours</u>
       Treatment Modalities)

_____

_____

_____

_____

c. Other Types of Supervised Counseling/Psychotherapy Experiences

<u>Description</u>   <u>Approximate Hours</u>

_____

_____

_____

_____

5. JOB HISTORY

A. Current or Most Recent Employment in Clinical Setting

Agency/Clinic Name_____ Phone _____

Description (Job Title, Setting, Duties, Dates and length of Employment, Supervisor's name, title, and phone number)

_____

_____

_____

_____

b. Past employment in Clinical Settings (list most recent first) If more space is needed, please attach additional page.

<u>Description</u> (Job Title, Setting, Duties, Dates and length of Employment, Supervisor's name, title, and phone number)

_____

_____

_____

_____

c. Have you ever been asked to resign; or been terminated; or been placed on probation by a training program or employer? NO _____ YES _ If "YES" attach an explanation at the end of this application form.

d. Experience in Providing Clinical Supervision

<u>Description</u> (Setting, Type of People   <u>Approximate Hours</u>
         Supervised, Client Population,
         Treatment Modalities)

_____

_____

_____

_____

e. Experience with short-term, brief, or problem-focused therapy (for the MH applicant only) or please describe your experience in a CD outpatient treatment program (CD applicants only).

<u>Description</u> (Setting, Type of Client   <u>Approximate Hours</u>
         Treatment Modalities)

_____

_____

_____

_____

f. Please describe whatever training you have received in short-term, brief, or problem-focused therapy and assessment techniques.

_____

_____

_____

_____

6. BACKGROUND INFORMATION

a. Please describe any volunteer work, other job history not in mental health, hobbies, or leisure activities that you believe contribute to your knowledge, perspective, or effectiveness as a clinician.

_____

_____

_____

_____

b. Areas of special knowledge (e.g., sign language, foreign languages, knowledge of working with special client populations, knowledge of special therapy techniques, etc.)

_____

_____

_____

---

7. EXPECTATIONS REGARDING METROPOLITAN CLINIC OF COUNSELING

Please explain your reasons for wanting to obtain employment at Metropolitan Clinic of Counseling. Include information on where you learned of MCC, what your expectations are, and how you believe you would fit in at MCC.

_____

_____

_____

_____

8. REFERENCES (no references will be contacted before the interview without your consent)

Give the names, agency/institution affiliations and phone numbers of 3 people who are familiar with or who have supervised your clinical work over the last 5 years.

Name	Agency/Institution	Phone

STATEMENT OF APPLICANT: (Please read carefully before signing)

All information submitted by me in this application is true to the best of my knowledge. I understand that any significant misstatement in, or omission from, this applicatio may be cause for denial of my application or cause for dismissal from the MCC staff.

By applying for appointment to the staff of MCC, I acknowledge that I have the responsibility to read the "Ethics Code" of my profession and licensure status. I agree to act in accordance with these ethical guidelines and any other rules or regulations adopted by MCC. I understand, that if employed or retained, I will be expected to read through the policy manual of MCC and abide by those policies. I further understand that on a yearly basis I will be expected to renew my knowledge of the policies and to sign a yearly statement that I have read through them.

I authorize Metropolitan Clinic of Counseling, its staff and their representative to consult with persons or institutions with which I have been associated and with others, including past and present employers, who may have information bearing my professional competence, character, and ethical qualifications. I release from liability all representatives of MCC for their acts performed in good faith and without malice in connection with evaluating my application and my credentials and qualifications, and I release from liability all individuals and organizations who provide information to MCC in good faith and without malice concerning my professional competence, ethics, character, and other qualifications.

I understand and agree that I will notify MCC of any changes in my job or training status, licensure, censure or sanction by professional bodies or licensing organizations, or any other information relating to my ability to perform as an employee or retained staff member of MCC.

_____   _____
Name (Please type or print)   Date

_____
Signature

APPENDIX Y

Consent Agreements for evaluation of a licensed professional and medical waiver to permit records access for such assessments. These were developed by John Gonsiorek, Ph.D. in consultation with regulatory board staff.

THIS AGREEMENT, between_____ (hereinafter "Licensee") and _____ (hereinafter "Evaluator"), is entered into for the purpose of attempting to provide information to the_____ Examining Board (hereinafter "Board") relating to Licensee's license to practice _____ in the State of_____ and pursuant to which Licensee has furnished Evaluator a Medical Waiver (a copy of which is attached hereto as Exhibit 1),

NOW, THEREFORE, IT IS AGREED:

1. Licensee, at his own expense, shall submit to a complete psychiatric and psychological evaluation by the Evaluator.

2. Licensee understands and agrees that although the evaluation is taking place at the expense of Licensee, the Evaluator is not entering into a physician/patient relationship with Licensee, nor is the Evaluator in any way employed by or an agent of the Licensee, but rather, Evaluator is engaged in the investigation of alleged violations of misconduct. Licensee further understands and agrees that the Evaluator may make findings or conclusions adverse to the Licensee;

3. Licensee agrees to make payment for the time spent by the Evaluator and expenses incurred by the Evaluator in carrying out the evaluation as follows:

a. Licensee shall pay the Evaluator at his usual and customary hourly rate of _____ per hour for Evaluator's time in connection with the evaluation, including review of documents and records, preparing for and meeting with the Licensee and others, and preparing reports to and meeting with the Board or its designees or agents;

b. Licensee shall reimburse the Evaluator for travel and subsistence expenses actually and necessarily incurred by the Evaluator in the same amount and manner as state officers and employees are reimbursed pursuant to the regulations promulgated by the Commissioner of Personnel;

c. Payment shall be made by Licensee within _____ days of the date of billing by Evaluator;

d. The total obligation of Licensee for all payments to and reimbursement of expenses of evaluator shall not exceed _____.

4. This Agreement may be cancelled by the Licensee or the Evaluator at any time, with or without cause, upon written notice to the other party. In the event of such cancellation, the Evaluator shall be entitled to payment for time spent prior to cancellation and for time spent in preparing or completing any report concerning the evaluation.

5. Licensee agrees to indemnify and save and hold the Evaluator, his agents and employees harmless from any and all claims or causes of action arising from the performance of the evaluation by Evaluator or Evaluator's agents or employees. This cause shall not be construed to bar any legal remedies Evaluator may have for Licensee's failure to fulfill his obligations pursuant to this Agreement.

6. Any reports, studies, or other documents received or prepared by Evaluator or his agents or employees in the performance of his duties shall be the exclusive property of the Board and all such materials shall be remitted to the Board by the Evaluator upon completion, termination, and cancellation of this Agreement.

IN THE WITNESS WHEREOF, the parties have caused this contract to be duly executed intending to be bound thereby.

_____   _____
Evaluator   Date   Licensee   Date

MEDICAL WAIVER

I, _____ understand and agree that for purposes of attempting to resolve complaints currently under investigation by the_____ Board, I will undergo a complete psychological evaluation, at my expense, from John C. Gonsiorek, Ph.D. I waive my medical privilege as to any records of information relating to former and current treatment for my physical health, mental and/or emotional health, and any chemical dependency. Records or information he deems appropriate as to my medical training, clinical work, any past or current complaints arising out of my practice of _____ _____, and any post or current civil suits relating to my practice of_____ I understand that Dr. Gonsiorek may question me and others, with my permission, regarding any matter he believes may have bearing on my former and current professional career and work, and any former or existing health and personal adjustment (including marital) problems. I hereby authorize any individual or institution having knowledge, records, or any other information relating to the foregoing to provide that information to Dr. Gonsiorek.

I understand that, for the purpose stated above, Dr. Gonsiorek will administer or order a complete psychiatric and psychological evaluation of me. I agree to cooperate fully with this evaluation. I understand that any significant misstatement, error, or omission as to any information provided to Dr. Gonsiorek may result in the_____ Board issuing a complaint against me which may affect my license to practice_____ in the State of_____. I release Dr. Gonsiorek, his agents, the Board and and its agents, from liability for any of their acts performed in connection with this evaluation.

This waiver is subject to express written revocation at any time except to the extent that action has been taken in reliance on the terms contained herein. Unless written revocation is made, this waiver is revoked upon the conclusion of any proceedings.

_____

Signature   Date

APPENDIX Z

Documents from the Wisconsin Coalition on Sexual Misconduct by Psychotherapists and Counselors:

1. "Making Therapy Work for You" — consumer brochure

2. Statement on Settlement Agreements Calling for Promises of Secrecy by Victims

3. Goals of the Task Force on Sexual Misconduct by Psychotherapists—Status Report: June 1986

4. Goals of the Coalition—Status Report: June 1987

5. Goals of the Coalition—Status Report: June 1988

MAKING

THERAPY

WORK

FOR YOU

The Wisconsin Coalition
On Sexual Misconduct

121 S. Hancock St.
Madison, WI 53703

Resources For Questioning Or Reporting Misconduct

Licensing/Certifying Boards

MEDICAL EXAMINING BOARD
1400 East Washington Avenue
P. O. Box 8936
Madison, Wisconsin 53708
(608) 266-7842

PSYCHOLOGY EXAMINING BOARD
1400 East Washington Avenue
P. O. Box 8936
Madison, Wisconsin 53708
(608) 266-7842

WISCONSIN ALCOHOLISM AND DRUG COUNSELOR CERTIFICATION BOARD
416 East Main Street
Waukesha, Wisconsin 53186
(414) 542-4144

Professional Associations
(Ethics Committees)

WISCONSIN PSYCHOLOGICAL ASSOCIATION
121 South Hancock Street
Madison, Wisconsin 53703
(608) 251-1450

WISCONSIN PSYCHIATRIC ASSOCIATION
P. O. Box 1109
Madison, Wisconsin 53701
(608) 257-6781

NATIONAL ASSOCIATION OF SOCIAL WORKERS (WI Chapter)
6414 Copps Avenue
Madison, Wisconsin 53716
(608) 222-7566

LEGAL: Call your local District Attorney's Office

OTHER: Call your local Mental Health Association

THE WISCONSIN COALITION ON SEXUAL MISCONDUCT

An Open Letter to the New or Prospective Client:

The following "CLIENT/PATIENT GUIDELINES FOR EVALUATING THERAPY/COUNSELING EXPERIENCES" has been prepared by the Coalition on Sexual Misconduct to better inform you of your rights and reasonable expectations in psychotherapy and to alert you to ways of protecting yourself.

Some of these are:

1) You may talk (or not talk) about your therapy to anyone you choose, but the therapist is ethically obligated to maintain confidentiality (with some legal exceptions, see footnote[1])

2) You have the right to ask questions about the therapist's credentials, training, and experience.

3) You are entitled to ask the therapist about the methods of therapy, the techniques used, the duration of therapy, fees, and any other facts about the therapy or therapist relevant to your therapy.

4) You may refuse any technique in therapy which makes you feel unduly uncomfortable.

5) You are always entitled to a second opinion.

6) You have the right to terminate therapy at any time.

The vast majority of therapists practice from an ethical basis, and our expectation is that you grow in the direction you and your therapist have mutually agreed to.

We hope, with you, that you will come out of the therapy experience more skilled in living, more personally empowered, more self-sufficient, more able to trust yourself and your attributes, more able to cope, more able to enjoy life.

Some clients/patients expect to develop a close relationship with the therapist, while others do not; whichever is comfortable for you is all right. HOWEVER, A SEXUALLY INTIMATE RELATIONSHIP IS NEVER RIGHT. There are many ways for a therapist to be human and humane without being sexual. BEING SEXUAL WITH A CLIENT IS A REPORTABLE CRIME.

---

[1] Legal exceptions involve child abuse (Ch. 48, WI Stats)

For your well-being, we want you to know that there are definite therapist attitudes which are considered healthy and growth-producing, and there are definite behaviors considered unethical and/or ILLEGAL. There may also be situations you have a right to question, get a second opinion on, take another look at, get further information about, and address one way or another; these occur whenever you get that "OH-OH" feeling, and for your sake warrant another look. Please read the following guide and use it to aid your continued personal healing and growth.

Sincerely,

The Wisconsin Coalition on Sexual Misconduct

Prepared by: Vilma O. Ginzberg, Clinical Psychologist, and Jan Singer, Psychotherapist

Client/Patient Guidelines for Evaluating Therapy/Counseling Experiences

	OK Attitudes and Behaviors	OH-OH: Take Another Look	NOT OK Attitudes and Behaviors
PROFESSIONALISM (Therapist's credentials and office practice)	—office practices regarding fees and appointments are clear and professional —training and experience are readily shared —therapist skill is devoted to your concerns —therapist maintains confidentiality	—if therapist's behavior seems not professional (being friendly is OK, becoming your friend is not) —if too much attention is on therapist's feelings or problems DON'T SUSPEND YOUR JUDGMENT CLARIFY WITH THERAPIST AND SOMEONE ELSE	—avoiding or refusing information about credentials/licensing —using alcohol or illegal drugs during sessions —indulging in an erotic relationship with you during therapy DISCONTINUE THE RELATIONSHIP CONSIDER ENDING THERAPY CONSIDER A NEW THERAPIST
POWER (Use of therapist's authority and knowledge)	—lets you learn how to deal with your life your way —promotes any and all sources of positive change —supports and encourages your self-confidence and ability to choose your own life path	—if you're uneasy with insistence on drugs as the only treatment possibility —if you can't tell whether you are • giving in to the *therapy*, (the learning *process*) (OK) or • giving in personally to the *therapist* (not OK) CLARIFY WITH THERAPIST GET SECOND OPINION RESPECT YOUR OWN JUDGMENT	—degrading, humiliating, intimidating, shaming or pressuring you • personally/emotionally or socially AND physically/sexually for the purpose of sexual exploitation DISCONTINUE THE RELATIONSHIP TERMINATE THERAPY CONSIDER ANOTHER THERAPIST
RELATIONSHIP (Quality and use of therapist's and client's feelings)	—treats you with respect, care, and dignity —willingly, professionally discusses your feelings for each other —demonstrates how feelings can be safely discussed and understood rather than acted upon	—if therapist suggests any mutual activity which makes you uncomfortable —if you enjoy therapist's attention, but feel it's not right somehow TRUST YOUR INSTINCTS CHECK IT OUT WITH SOMEONE ELSE SUSPEND THERAPY	—using inappropriate erotic comments —touching you sexually —having *any* sexual contact with you, in or out of the office, *with* or *without your consent* END THE RELATIONSHIP TERMINATE THERAPY SEE ANOTHER THERAPIST CONSIDER REPORTING THIS ACTION (see resource list)

Wisconsin Coalition on Sexual Misconduct by Psychotherapists and Counselors

121 South Hancock Street • Madison, Wisconsin 53703 • (608) 251-1450

Approved: November 7, 1988

STATEMENT ON SETTLEMENT AGREEMENTS CALLING FOR PROMISES OF SECRECY BY VICTIMS

By Carol Bartelt, Ruth Ann Guthman, Karen Robinson and Rock Pledl, members of a committee on this issue formed by the Wisconsin Coalition on Sexual Misconduct by Psychotherapists and Counselors.

The following is a discussion of secrecy agreements or "gag orders" by the above individuals, who represent treatment, victim and legal perspectives. An attempt was made to discuss both sides of the issue and to determine whether they would ever be appropriate. No valid reason for approving secrecy pacts could be found. The following is a discussion of the reasons they were felt to be inappropriate.

First, a general definition of secrecy agreements may be useful. They are an accepted part of commercial litigation. Before filing a case, two or more parties may agree to settle a legal dispute. This is generally done following the payment of money. The party receiving the money agrees not to make any public statements about how much was paid, about the wrongful acts that supposedly occurred, about the fact that there was a dispute in the first place, and may even agree to destroy certain documents that the party paying the money does not want exposed. The same thing can be done after a suit has been filed. Sometimes the court enters an order putting the secrecy settlement into effect. Such settlements or orders often contain a punitive sanction for breaking secrecy. For example, the injured party who received $50,000 in the settlement could be required to pay $500,000 as damages to the wrongdoer if the promise of secrecy were ever broken.

Despite the acceptance of secrecy agreements in the commercial context, they have no place in the settlement of cases involving sexual exploitation or other transference-type injuries by therapists, or in cases of incest or other child abuse. One of the common features of the injury itself in these cases is the imposition of secrecy by the perpetrator. It is paradoxical that a legal proceeding initiated in response to an injury of this type could ever be resolved by imposing secrecy on the victim once again. Treatment for various dysfunctions arising in the family (e.g., "Adult Children of Alcoholics") will often focus on breaking the "rule of secrecy" as a therapeutic process. Similarly, treatment of sexual exploitation victims cannot occur in an atmosphere of secrecy.

Subsequent treatment and recovery from sexual exploitation will hopefully result in eliminating or minimizing the power that the perpetrator exercised in harming the victim. Another way of saying this is that the therapeutic relationship out of which this power imbalance arose must be broken down as the victim forms other beneficial relationships. A secrecy agreement formalizes and continues the very power differential which was harmful in the first instance. The victim must always be aware of the agreement and must monitor his or her own words in order to protect the perpetrator's secret or else forfeit a large sum of money. Some secrecy pacts have even forbidden the victim to use the perpetrator's name in subsequent therapy, which both continues the original exploitation and causes additional victimization. The concept of protecting the perpetrator's reputation as a healer at the expense of the victim's recovery is unconscionable.

What of the victim who truly believes that s/he is getting a fair settlement and that the secrecy conditions are not overly harmful? While every victim must have the final word in any settlement decision, the negative impact of a secrecy agreement cannot be assessed in advance. Subsequent treatment and recovery following sexual exploitation by a therapist is a long term (and potentially life-long) process. The reports of victims who have signed secrecy agreements in the past suggest that no one can really evaluate the harm until s/he has lived through the revictimization process that secrecy entails. The victims have not felt it was worth it, and the additional psychological damages have been devastating.

Victims of sexual exploitation may bring legal actions for a variety of reasons, and that is where the commercial litigation example breaks down completely. A victim's major goals may well be self-empowerment and protection of the public. The money obtained by a victim in a civil suit is necessary and well deserved, but other participants in the legal process should not believe that the victim can truly be made whole by money. When it can only be obtained through a new promise of secrecy, additional psychological damage occurs. This is truly adding insult to injury.

The previous sections have focused on the victim's perspective. Secrecy pacts also relate to the role of the lawyer representing the victim and to the interests of the public. In view of the fact that money per se is not the primary goal of most victims, the lawyer in a contingent fee situation will often experience a conflict of interest with his or her own client. Frankly speaking, and putting the treatment interests of the victim aside, secrecy agreements are a good financial arrangement for the attorney working on a contingent fee case because they potentially increase the size of the monetary settlement and, therefore, increase the size of the fee. This conflict should be discussed openly and in light of the lawyer's duty to settle the case only on the client's terms and with the client's consent. Attorneys must recognize that they are capable of revictimizing their sexual exploitation clients in various ways, and that attempting to convince a client to accept a secrecy pact is one of the worst forms. Any settlement decision is a mixed legal/psychological question and the attorney should be certain that the client has access to other professionals necessary to resolve the treatment issues. Further discussion is necessary on the propriety of contingent fee contracts in cases involving emotional injuries where empowerment, protection of the public, and recovery of money are often equal yet competing goals.

Secrecy agreements also obstruct a clear public policy that criminal courts, licensing boards and professional organizations should have access to evidence of secual exploitation in order to protect future victims and deter other professionals from similar acts. American law has evolved the concept of a "private attorney general", an ordinary plaintiff who sues for his or her own injury but achieves a benefit for the public. Every sexual exploitation victim may be seen in this light. Perpetrators try to portray victims who wish to pursue criminal charges, license revocation or other professional discipline as vengeful. The proper word, of course, is "responsible". Surviving victims of drunk drivers want monetary compensation and the conviction and sentencing of the perpetrator. This is a natural consequence of the illegal behavior. No perpetrator should be able to obstruct a criminal, licensing, or ethical proceeding by purchasing the victim's silence.

The public contacts treatment professionals for a variety of reasons and based on a variety of public information. Referrals are made from one professional to another based on known information. Professionals and consumers of mental health services have a right to all available information in order to make the best possible decision in selecting a treatment professional. Every settlement or adjudication has a part ot play in educating the public and the profession about service providers. Even if a particular settlement or adjudication does not suggest that the professional be avoided entirely, it would provide information about danger areas and topics of concern which would be important to the public and referral sources.

Settlements and adjudications also play a part in educating the professions and creating contemporary practice standards. Secrecy agreemeents prevent the natural development of professional standards by restricting information about ethical breaches.

WISCONSIN PSYCHOLOGICAL ASSOCIATION

Affiliated with the American Psychological Association
625 West Washington Avenue • Madison, Wisconsin 53703 • (608) 251-1450

Adopted July 1, 1985

Goals of the Task Force on Sexual Misconduct by Psychotherapists

STATUS REPORT: JUNE 1986

(1) Prevent future occurrences of sexual misconduct by psychotherapists.

STATUS: Ongoing

(2) Increase reporting to licensing boards, professional ethics committees and district attorneys of sexual misconduct by psychotherapists.

STATUS: Ongoing

(3) Create a database for analysis of the incidence, prevalence, and nature of the problem in Wisconsin.

STATUS: Therapist survey completed; analysis will be completed by July 1986. Victim/Survivor survey has had only two responses to date.

(4) Strengthen W.S. 940.22 [AB 321]:

The present statute states: "Any person who is or who holds himself or herself out to be a therapist and who intentionally has sexual contact with a patient or client during any treatment, consultation, interview, or examination is guilty of a Class A misdemeanor."

(a) Should go beyond "during any treatment, ..." so that, e.g., a therapist could not claim that therapy and/or the therapeutic relationship terminated immediately prior to the beginning of the sexual relationship.

STATUS: Accomplished via 1985 Wisconsin Act 275 [AB 776]

(b) Should increase the penalty to a felony:

STATUS: Accomplished via 1985 Wisconsin Act 275

(c) Should change the rules for Victims' Compensation so that victims of sexual assault by therapists will be eligible for compensation:

—eliminate the statute of limitations for these cases, or extend it to at least 10 years, and

—eliminate the requirement that the crime be reported to the police within 5 days;

STATUS: Not yet accomplished

(d) Should protect people (other psychotherapists, physicians, family and friends, etc.) who file a complaint in good faith from civil liability for libel;

STATUS: Not yet accomplished

(e) Should include other professionals who have counseling relationships with people (e.g., marriage counselors, guidance counselors, clergy);

STATUS: Accomplished via 1985 Wisconsin Act 275

(f) Should define "psychotherapy" more broadly than does 455.01(6): "'Psychotherapy' means the use of learning, conditioning methods and emotional reactions in a professional relationship to assist persons to modify feelings, attitudes and behaviors which are intellectually, socially or emotionally maladjustive or ineffectual."

STATUS: Partially accomplished via 1985 Wisconsin Act 275 [AB 776], which does not change the definition of "psychotherapy" but does specify "psychotherapy, counseling or other assessment or treatment" as bases for a civil suit against a therapist.

(5) The civil statute of limitations now provides that actions must be "commenced with the later of: (a) three years from the date of the injury, or (b) one year from the date the injury was discovered ... except that an action may not be commenced under this paragraph more than 5 years from the date of the act or omission."

(a) Malpractice by a psychotherapist should be dealt with in a separate statute from "medical malpractice" [W.S. 893.55], a new statute which applies to all therapists regardless of the type of professional training, and

STATUS: Accomplished via 1985 Wisconsin Act 275 [AB 776]

(b) Should use "3 years" rather than "1 year" from the date the injury was discovered, and

STATUS: Accomplished via 1985 Wisconsin Act 275 [AB 776]

(c) Should use "10 years from the date of the malpractice," rather than "5 years" as the limit on when actions may be commenced.

STATUS: Accomplished via 1985 Wisconsin Act 275 [AB 776] — time extended up to 15 years.

(6) Create funding:

(a) For a "Victim/Survivor" advocate, who will help the victim through the complicated administrative and legal processes, provide supportive counseling, refer for psychotherapy (if needed), and try to assure that complaints are both filed and followed through;

(b) To pay for the psychotherapy needed by most victims of sexual abuse. The Victims' Compensation Fund should pick up where private insurance falls off, to help "victims" become "survivors;"

(c) To train staff of existing sexual assault intervention and treatment programs to deal with the special problems associated with sexual misconduct by psychotherapists;

(d)   To develop a "guide for victims" which goes through the steps involved in filing a complaint wiht a licensing board, an ethics committee, and/or a district attorney, and the steps involved in filing a civil lawsuit for malpractice, with an emphasis on the problems which may develop for the victim in the course of pursuing each of those options (e.g., delays involved in the legal process, limits on the results which may be obtained through each of those courses of action, sources of emotional trauma inherent in each of those processes, and so forth).

STATUS: None of the four objectives have yet been accomplished.

(7)   To educate professionals and the public about this subject:

(a)   To help actual and potential clients/patients and the general public to recognize the varieties of behavior which constitute sexual misconduct by psychotherapists;

STATUS: Partially ongoing, partially accomplished via the "Making Therapy Work for You" pamphlet, newspaper stories, articles in the newsletter of the Mental Health Association in Wisconsin, and so forth.

(b)   To help professionals recognize warning signs in themselves and their colleagues;

STATUS: Partially ongoing, partially accomplished via quarterly information in the Wisconsin Psychological Association newsletters for the past two years, newsletters of other organizations, Madison Campus Ministry workshop in 1985, Wisconsin Psychological Association workshop in April 1986, etc.

(c)   To try to assure that training programs for therapists deal with appropriate ethical issues (including the need for reporting of misconduct by other psychotherapists), including having ethics questions which deal with this subject on exams at schools and for licensing or certification.

STATUS: Not yet accomplished.

(d)   To conduct an awareness program among the general public on this issue.

STATUS: Same as (a), above.

(8) To facilitate the interaction of licensing boards, district attorneys, and professional groups' ethics committees in resolving cases which come to their attention.

STATUS: Not yet accomplished.

(9) To try to define difficult concepts so that they may be incorporated into legal and ethical codes; e.g.,

(a)   How long does a professional relationship last? It clearly goes beyond the official termination of psychotherapy—but how far beyond? Need there be different principles/practices for small towns vs. big cities? Some concrete number of months; e.g., 6 or 12, must be recommended to legislators.

STATUS: Final draft approved June 2, 1986

(b) Can a romance between a therapist and an ex-patient or client EVER be acceptable? What if a therapist really falls in love with a patient/client—how does he/she deal with that dilemma?

STATUS: Same as (a)

(c) How does one balance the need for disciplining the therapist with the belief of the mental health professions that people generally are able to be rehabilitated and should have a chance to change?

STATUS: Draft circulated early 1986; discussion held summer 1986.

(d) How does one distinguish between the perpetrator who can be rehabilitated vs. the perpetrator who is not a candidate for rehabilitation?

STATUS: To be discussed summer 1986

(e) How do we know when rehabilitation has occurred and the person can safely resume practice (and, if relevant, regain professional group membership and/or get re-licensed), and what limitations, if any, should be imposed on that practice?

STATUS: To be discussed summer 1986

(f) Should there be an ethical rule for clinic certification which restricts the employment of people who have been convicted of sexual misconduct with clients/patients?

STATUS: Consensus: Yes, there should.

(g) Should malpractice insurance cover or not cover sexual misconduct by a therapist? Does coverage imply that sexual misconduct can be tolerated? How can a victim win substantial damages in court if the therapist is NOT covered?

STATUS: Consensus: Yes, insurance should—must—cover sexual misconduct, since that is likely the only way a victim can recover damages (including cost of psychotherapy, lost wages, etc.). No, coverage does not imply that sexual misconduct can be tolerated.

(10) To remind therapists that they must report sexual misconduct involving children to the local Department of Social Services—Child Protective Services unit, or to the police.

STATUS: Partially accomplished through organizational newsletters, the 1985 and 1986 conferences cited above, etc.

Other questions raised:

—How can we assure that a settlement in a civil suit does not prevent the victim from reporting any sexual misconduct?

—Can/should there be mandated reporting of sexual misconduct by therapists by later therapists to whom the victims go for help? May this not be counterproductive by forcing the victim into a legal arena well before she is ready to proceed, adding to the burden she is carrying? How do we convey to the victim the tremendous emotional burden involved in pursuing an ethics committee, licensing, and/or civil lawsuit action?

—While there are very few false accusations, they do occur, and in a climate where a few "rape victims" have recanted, this needs to be addressed. How can/should therapists try to assure that they are not the subject of such an accusation?

—Should psychotherapists be requested/required to contribute some money each year to a fund to pay for the psychotherapy needed by victims of psychotherapists, as attorneys now pay $15/year to a similar fund? It could be paid to the relevant professional organization (though not all members of any of the professions are members of a professional organization) to fund treatment for victims of members of that profession, or to a general fund for victims of sexual misconduct by psychotherapists without regard to the discipline of the therapist-perpetrator.

WISCONSIN COALITION ON SEXUAL MISCONDUCT BY PSYCHOTHERAPISTS AND COUNSELORS

121 South Hancock Street • Madison, Wisconsin 53703 • (608) 251-1450

Adopted July 1, 1985

GOALS OF THE COALITION

Status Report: June 1987

(1) Prevent future occurrences of sexual misconduct by psychotherapists.

STATUS: Ongoing

(2) Increase reporting to licensing boards, professional ethics committees and district attorneys of sexual misconduct by psychotherapists.

STATUS: Ongoing

(3) Create a database for analysis of the incidence, prevalence, and nature of the problem in Wisconsin.

STATUS: Therapist survey completed; analysis will be completed by July 1986. Victim/Survivor survey has had only two responses to date.

(4) Strengthen W.S. 940.22 [AB 321]:

The present statute states: "Any person who is or who holds himself or herself out to be a therapist and who intentionally has sexual contact with a patient or client during any treatment, consultation, interview, or examination is guilty of a Class A misdemeanor."

(a) Should go beyond "during any treatment, ..." so that, e.g., a therapist could not claim that therapy and/or the therapeutic relationship terminated immediately prior to the beginning of the sexual relationship.

STATUS: Accomplished via 1985 Wisconsin Act 275 [AB 776]

(b) Should increase the penalty to a felony:

STATUS: Accomplished via 1985 Wisconsin Act 275

(c) Should change the rules for Victims' Compensation so that victims of sexual assault by therapists will be eligible for compensation:

—eliminate the statute of limitations for these cases, or extend it to at least 10 years, and

—eliminate the requirement that the crime be reported to the police within 5 days;

STATUS: Not yet accomplished

(d) Should protect people (other psychotherapists, physicians, family and friends, etc.) who file a complaint in good faith from civil liability for libel;

STATUS: Not yet accomplished

(e) Should include other professionals who have counseling relationships with people (e.g., marriage counselors, guidance counselors, clergy);

STATUS: Accomplished via 1985 Wisconsin Act 275

(f) Should define "psychotherapy" more broadly than does 455.01(6): "'Psychotherapy' means the use of learning, conditioning methods and emotional reactions in a professional relationship to assist persons to modify feelings, attitudes and behaviors which are intellectually, socially or emotionally maladjustive or ineffectual."

STATUS: Partially accomplished via 1985 Wisconsin Act 275 [AB 776], which does not change the definition of "psychotherapy" but does specify "psychotherapy, counseling or other assessment or treatment" as bases for a civil suit against a therapist.

(5) The civil statute of limitations now provides that actions must be "commenced with the later of: (a) three years from the date of the injury, or (b) one year from the date the injury was discovered ... except that an action may not be commenced under this paragraph more than 5 years from the date of the act or omission."

(a) Malpractice by a psychotherapist should be dealt with in a separate statute from "medical malpractice" [W.S. 893.55], a new statute which applies to all therapists regardless of the type of professional training, and

STATUS: Accomplished via 1985 Wisconsin Act 275 [AB 776]

(b) Should use "3 years" rather than "1 year" from the date the injury was discovered, and

STATUS: Accomplished via 1985 Wisconsin Act 275 [AB 776]

(c) Should use "10 years from the date of the malpractice," rather than "5 years" as the limit on when actions may be commenced.

STATUS: Accomplished via 1985 Wisconsin Act 275 [AB 776] — time extended up to 15 years.

(6) Create funding:

(a) For a "Victim/Survivor" advocate, who will help the victim through the complicated administrative and legal processes, provide supportive counseling, refer for psychotherapy (if needed), and try to assure that complaints are both filed and followed through;

(b) To pay for the psychotherapy needed by most victims of sexual abuse. The Victims' Compensation Fund should pick up where private insurance falls off, to help "victims" become "survivors;"

(c) To train staff of existing sexual assault intervention and treatment programs to deal with the special problems associated with sexual misconduct by psychotherapists;

(d)   To develop a "guide for victims" which goes through the steps involved in filing a complaint wiht a licensing board, an ethics committee, and/or a district attorney, and the steps involved in filing a civil lawsuit for malpractice, with an emphasis on the problems which may develop for the victim in the course of pursuing each of those options (e.g., delays involved in the legal process, limits on the results which may be obtained through each of those courses of action, sources of emotional trauma inherent in each of those processes, and so forth).

STATUS: None of the four objectives have yet been accomplished.

(7)   To educate professionals and the public about this subject:

(a)   To help actual and potential clients/patients and the general public to recognize the varieties of behavior which constitute sexual misconduct by psychotherapists;

STATUS: Partially ongoing, partially accomplished via the "Making Therapy Work for You" pamphlet, newspaper stories, articles in the newsletter of the Mental Health Association in Wisconsin, and so forth.

(b)   To help professionals recognize warning signs in themselves and their colleagues;

STATUS: Partially ongoing, partially accomplished via quarterly information in the Wisconsin Psychological Association newsletters for the past two years, newsletters of other organizations, Madison Campus Ministry workshop in 1985, Wisconsin Psychological Association workshop in April 1986, etc.

(c)   To try to assure that training programs for therapists deal with appropriate ethical issues (including the need for reporting of misconduct by other psychotherapists), including having ethics questions which deal with this subject on exams at schools and for licensing or certification.

STATUS: Not yet accomplished.

(d)   To conduct an awareness program among the general public on this issue.

STATUS: Same as (a), above.

(8) To facilitate the interaction of licensing boards, district attorneys, and professional groups' ethics committees in resolving cases which come to their attention.

STATUS: Ongoing

(9) To try to define difficult concepts so that they may be incorporated into legal and ethical codes; e.g.,

(a)   How long does a professional relationship last? It clearly goes beyond the official termination of psychotherapy—but how far beyond? Need there be different principles/practices for small towns vs. big cities? Some concrete number of months; e.g., 6 or 12, must be recommended to legislators.

STATUS: Final draft approved June 2, 1986

(b) Can a romance between a therapist and an ex-patient or client EVER be acceptable? What if a therapist really falls in love with a patient/client—how does he/she deal with that dilemma?

STATUS: Same as (a)

(c) How does one balance the need for disciplining the therapist with the belief of the mental health professions that people generally are able to be rehabilitated and should have a chance to change?

STATUS: Final draft approved June 1987

(d) How does one distinguish between the perpetrator who can be rehabilitated vs. the perpetrator who is not a candidate for rehabilitation?

STATUS: To be discussed summer 1986

(e) How do we know when rehabilitation has occurred and the person can safely resume practice (and, if relevant, regain professional group membership and/or get re-licensed), and what limitations, if any, should be imposed on that practice?

STATUS: Final draft approved June 1987

(f) Should there be an ethical rule for clinic certification which restricts the employment of people who have been convicted of sexual misconduct with clients/patients?

STATUS: Consensus: Yes, there should.

(g) Should malpractice insurance cover or not cover sexual misconduct by a therapist? Does coverage imply that sexual misconduct can be tolerated? How can a victim win substantial damages in court if the therapist is NOT covered?

STATUS: Consensus: Yes, insurance should—must—cover sexual misconduct, since that is likely the only way a victim can recover damages (including cost of psychotherapy, lost wages, etc.). No, coverage does not imply that sexual misconduct can be tolerated.

(10) To remind therapists that they must report sexual misconduct involving children to the local Department of Social Services—Child Protective Services unit, or to the police.

STATUS: Partially accomplished through organizational newsletters, the 1985 and 1986 conferences cited above, etc.

Other questions raised:

—How can we assure that a settlement in a civil suit does not prevent the victim from reporting any sexual misconduct?

—Can/should there be mandated reporting of sexual misconduct by therapists by later therapists to whom the victims go for help? May this not be counterproductive by forcing the victim into a legal arena well before she is ready to proceed, adding to the burden she is carrying? How do we convey to the victim the tremendous emotional burden involved in pursuing an ethics committee, licensing, and/or civil lawsuit action?

　　Note: Representative Young has taken a major interest in this issue, and may be drafting legislation to address the issue during 1987.

—While there are very few false accusations, they do occur, and in a climate where a few "rape victims" have recanted, this needs to be addressed. How can/should therapists try to assure that they are not the subject of such an accusation?

—Should psychotherapists be requested/required to contribute some money each year to a fund to pay for the psychotherapy needed by victims of psychotherapists, as attorneys now pay $15/year to a similar fund? It could be paid to the relevant professional organization (though not all members of any of the professions are members of a professional organization) to fund treatment for victims of members of that profession, or to a general fund for victims of sexual misconduct by psychotherapists without regard to the discipline of the therapist-perpetrator.

Wisconsin Coalition on Sexual Misconduct By Psychotherapists and Counselors

121 South Hancock Street • Madison, Wisconsin 53703 • (608) 251-1450

Adopted July 1, 1985

CHAIR: Andrew W. Kane, Ph.D.
2815 N. Summit Ave.
Milwaukee, WI 53211
(414) 964-6449

GOALS OF THE COALITION

Status Report: June 1988

(1) Prevent future occurrences of sexual misconduct by psychotherapists.

STATUS: Ongoing

(2) Increase reporting to licensing boards, professional ethics committees and district attorneys of sexual misconduct by psychotherapists.

STATUS: Ongoing, but substantially addressed by 1987 Wisconsin Act 380, which requires a current therapist to ask a victim for consent to report a sexual relationship with a previous therapist, and who must report if the victim consents.

(3) Create a database for analysis of the incidence, prevalence, and nature of the problem in Wisconsin.

STATUS: Therapist survey data published September 1986. The Victim/Survivor survey was unsuccessful, as it was too traumatic for most to fill out even after years of therapy. Additional data will be available by early 1989 from research in progress by Richard Brigham, M.S., doctoral candidate at the Wisconsin School of Professional Psychology.

(4) Strengthen W.S. 940.22 [AB 321]:

STATUS: Largely accomplished through 1985 Wisconsin Act 275, which increased the penalty from a misdemeanor to a felony, changed the time period from "during any treatment" to "during any ongoing therapist-patient or therapist-client relationship," and removed "consent" as an issue. It also clearly added other professionals who have counseling relationships with people; e.g., marriage counselors and clergy. These changes met four of our original goals here.

REMAINING NEEDS:
(a) Change the rules for Victims' Compensation so that victims of sexual assault by therapists will be eligible for compensation:

—eliminate the statute of limitations for these cases, or extend it to at least 10 years, and

—eliminate the requirement that the crime be reported to the police within 5 days;

(b) Protect people (other psychotherapists, physicians, family and friends, etc.) who file a complaint in good faith from civil liability for libel;

STATUS: Therapists are protected under 1987 Wisconsin Act 380

(c) Should define "psychotherapy" more broadly than does 455.01(6): "'Psychotherapy' means the use of learning, conditioning methods and emotional reactions in a professional relationship to assist persons to modify feelings, attitudes and behaviors which are intellectually, socially or emotionally maladjustive or ineffectual."

STATUS: Partially accomplished via 1985 Wisconsin Act 275, which did not change the definition but does specify "psychotherapy, counseling or other assessment or treatment" as bases for a civil suit.

(5) The civil statute of limitations now provides that actions must be "commenced with the later of: (a) three years from the date of the injury, or (b) one year from the date the injury was discovered ... except that an action may not be commenced under this paragraph more than 5 years from the date of the act or omission."

(a) Malpractice by a psychotherapist should be dealt with in a separate statute from "medical malpractice" [W.S. 893.55], a new statute which applies to all therapists regardless of the type of professional training, and

STATUS: Accomplished via 1985 Wisconsin Act 275 [AB 776]

(b) Should use "3 years" rather than "1 year" from the date the injury was discovered, and

STATUS: Largely accomplished via 1985 Wisconsin Act 275, which expanded the types of therapists/counselors to whom the statutes apply, and expanded the period of time for filing an action to a maximum of 18 years if the person "is unable to bring the action due to the effects of the sexual contact or due to any threats, instructions or statements from the therapist."

(6) Create funding:

(a) For a "Victim/Survivor" advocate, who will help the victim through the complicated administrative and legal processes, provide supportive counseling, refer for psychotherapy (if needed), and try to assure that complaints are both filed and followed through;

(b) To pay for the psychotherapy needed by most victims of sexual abuse. The Victims' Compensation Fund should pick up where private insurance falls off, to help "victims" become "survivors;"

(c) To train staff of existing sexual assault intervention and treatment programs to deal with the special problems associated with sexual misconduct by psychotherapists;

(d) To develop a "guide for victims" which goes through the steps involved in filing a complaint with a licensing board, an ethics committee, and/or a district attorney, and the steps involved in filing a civil lawsuit for malpractice, with an emphasis on the problems which may develop for the victim in the course of pursuing each of those options (e.g., delays involved in the legal process, limits on the results which may be obtained through each of those courses of action, sources of emotional trauma inherent in each of those processes, and so forth).

> STATUS: (a) through (c) remain unfunded and undone. (d) is being drafted by a volunteer attorney and should be available to the public well before the end of 1988.

(7) To educate professionals and the public about this subject:

(a) To help actual and potential clients/patients and the general public to recognize the varieties of behavior which constitute sexual misconduct by psychotherapists;

> STATUS: Partly ongoing, partly accomplished via our "Making Therapy Work for You" pamphlet, newspaper stories, etc.

(b) To help professionals recognize warning signs in themselves and their colleagues;

> STATUS: Partly ongoing, partly accomplished through regular articles in the Wisconsin Psychologist and other organizational newsletters, organizational workshops, and other means.

(c) To try to assure that training programs for therapists deal with appropriate ethical issues (including the need for reporting of misconduct by other psychotherapists), including having ethics questions which deal with this subject on exams at schools and for licensing or certification.

> STATUS: Not yet accomplished

(d) To conduct an awareness program among the general public on this issue.

> STATUS: Same as (a)

(8) To facilitate the interaction of licensing boards, district attorneys, and professional groups' ethics committees in resolving cases which come to their attention.

> STATUS: Ongoing

(9) To try to define difficult concepts so that they may be incorporated into legal and ethical codes; e.g.,

(a) How long does a professional relationship last? It clearly goes beyond the official termination of psychotherapy—but how far?

> STATUS: Final draft approved June 2, 1986

(b) Can a romance between a therapist and an ex-patient or client EVER be acceptable? What if a therapist really falls in love with a patient/client—how does he/she deal with that dilemma?

> STATUS: Final draft approved June 2, 1986

(c) How does one balance the need for disciplining the therapist with the belief of the mental health professions that people generally are able to be rehabilitated and should have a chance to change?

STATUS: Final draft approved June 1987

(d) How does one distinguish between the perpetrator who can be rehabilitated vs. the perpetrator who is not a candidate for rehabilitation?

STATUS: Final draft approved June 1987

(e) How do we know when rehabilitation has occurred and the person can safely resume practice (and, if relevant, regain professional group membership and/or get re-licensed), and what limitations, if any, should be imposed on that practice?

STATUS: Final draft approved June 1987

(f) Should there be an ethical rule for clinic certification which restricts the employment of people who have been convicted of sexual misconduct with clients/patients?

STATUS: Consensus: Yes, there should be.

(g) Should malpractice insurance cover or not cover sexual misconduct by a therapist? Does coverage imply that sexual misconduct can be tolerated? How can a victim win substantial damages in court if the therapist is NOT covered?

STATUS: Consensus: (a) Yes, insurance should—must—cover sexual misconduct, since that is likely the only way a victim can recover damages (including cost of psychotherapy, lost wages, etc.). (b) No, coverage does not imply that sexual misconduct can be tolerated.

(10) To remind therapists that they must report sexual misconduct involving children to the local Department of Social Services—Child Protective Services unit, or to the police.

STATUS: Partially accomplished through organizational newsletters, the 1985 and 1986 conferences cited above, etc.

Other questions raised:

—How can we assure that a settlement in a civil suit does not prevent the victim from reporting any sexual misconduct?

—Can/should there be mandated reporting of sexual misconduct by therapists by later therapists to whom the victims go for help? May this not be counterproductive by forcing the victim into a legal arena well before she is ready to proceed, adding to the burden she is carrying? How do we convey to the victim the tremendous emotional burden involved in pursuing an ethics committee, licensing, and/or civil lawsuit action?

Note: Representative Young has taken a major interest in this issue, and may be drafting legislation to address the issue during 1987.

—While there are very few false accusations, they do occur, and in a climate where a few "rape victims" have recanted, this needs to be addressed. How can/should therapists try to assure that they are not the subject of such an accusation?

—Should psychotherapists be requested/required to contribute some money each year to a fund to pay for the psychotherapy needed by victims of psychotherapists, as attorneys now pay $15/year to a similar fund? It could be paid to the relevant professional organization (though not all members of any of the professions are members of a professional organization) to fund treatment for victims of members of that profession, or to a general fund for victims of sexual misconduct by psychotherapists without regard to the discipline of the therapist-perpetrator.

<u>Appendix AA</u>

Program for the Conference *IT'S NEVER OK—*
the first national conference on sexual exploitation
by counselors and therapists

Held June 5-6, 1986
Minneapolis, Minnesota

Sponsored by:

Programs for Human Services Professionals,
Continuing Education and Extension,
University of Minnesota

The Minnesota Task Force on Sexual
Exploitation by Counselors and Therapists,
Minnesota Dept. of Corrections

CONFERENCE SCHEDULE

<u>June 5, 1986</u>

8:00 a.m.	Registration
8:30	Welcome and Introduction
9:00	**A Guide to the Issues: No Easy Answers** Barbara Sanderson
10:00	**Break**
10:15	**The Victim's Experience: A Media Presentation** Produced by John Armour and Sharon Satterfield
10:30	**A Victim's Experience: A Personal Story**
10:45	**Sexual Dilemmas for the Helping Professional** Jerry Edelwich
12:15 p.m.	Lunch
1:15	**Sexual Exploitation by Psychiatrists** Nanette Gartrell
2:00	SMALL GROUP DISCUSSIONS: Focusing Your Conference Experiences
3:00	Break
3:15	CONCURRENT SESSIONS I (choose one):

1. **THERAPEUTIC ISSUES: Working With Victims**
   * Emotional, sexual, and relationship issues
   * Recognizing victims among the people you serve
   * Defining your role as counselor or advocate
   * The healing process for victims: individual and group psychotherapy
   * Sexual exploitation in psychotherapy cults
   * The complexities of same sex and opposite sex abuse

   Marie Fortune, Ellen Thompson Luepker, Jeanette Milgrom

2. **ADMINISTRATIVE ISSUES: Legal and Ethical Responsibilities of Employers, Administrators and Organizational Officers**
   * Protecting client and therapist confidentiality
   * Reporting abusive colleagues
   * Reducing the risk of civil liability
   * Threats to individual and institutional licensure
   * Resolving ethical conflicts

   Annette Brodsky, Nanette Gartrell, Sandra Nye

3. **LEGAL AND LEGISLATIVE ISSUES: Criminal Law Remedies**
   - Obstacles to passing criminal legislation
   - Differences between the therapeutic relationship and other professional relationships
   - Sexual penetration, other physical sexual contact, and verbal harassment
   - Deceiving the client about the therapeutic process
   - Consent of the client
   - Abuse outside the office and after termination of therapy
   - Limiting introduction of evidence of victim's personal and medical history

   Jeffrey Kremers, William Neiman, Donna Peterson

5:00   Social Hour with Resource Tables

June 6, 1986

8:30 a.m.   **Organizational Incest: Sexual Exploitation as a Systems Problem**
William L. White

9:30   CONCURRENT SESSIONS II (choose one):

4. **THERAPEUTIC ISSUES: Practice and Supervision of Counseling**
   - Supervision as prevention of sexual exploitation by counselors and therapists
   - Helping counselors set and keep appropriate interpersonal boundaries with clients
   - Sexual attraction and other transference and countertransference issues
   - Supervising therapists who are working with victims
   - The abusing therapist as part of a troubled organization

   Lindsay Nielson, Marilyn Peterson, Minna Shapiro, Peg Thompson, William White

5. **ADMINISTRATIVE ISSUES: Preventing Sexual Exploitation of Clients**
   - Reducing the threat of civil suit for employers and administrators
   - Providing education and supervision for counselors
   - Screening potential employees
   - Model policies and procedures for counselor behavior
   - Prevention strategies for the clergy

   Marie Fortune, Don Horton, Dorothy Loeffler, Pat Mullen

6. **LEGAL AND LEGISLATIVE ISSUES: Civil Law Remedies**
   - Common law and statutory law
   - Actual and punitive damages
   - Therapist liability and employer liability
   - Statute of limitations
   - Limits to discovery and admissibility of evidence of complainant's history

• Malpractice insurance coverage
• Obstacles to passing civil laws
Sandra Nye, Allan Spear, M. Sue Wilson

11:00   Break

11:15   **Education Toward More Competent, Ethical Practice: The Role of Colleges, Training Institutions, and Seminaries**
Annette Brodsky

12:00 p.m. Lunch

Discussion topic tables available

1:00   **The Problem Among the Clergy**
Marie Fortune

1:45   CONCURRENT SESSIONS III (choose one):

7. **THERAPEUTIC ISSUES: Working With Exploitative Counselors and Therapists**
    • Situational and psychological factors that
      result in abuse
    • Defining your role as diagnostician,
      supervisor, or therapist
    • Working therapeutically with sexuality
      and intimacy issues
    • Determining appropriate treatment for
      the perpetrator
    • Making recommendations for restriction
      or curtailment of practice
    • Supevision of restricted practice
    John Gonsiorek, Kenneth Pierre, Gary Schoener,
    Ann Stefanson

8. **ADMINISTRATIVE ISSUES: Procedures for Handling Client Complaints**
    • Reducing the risk of civil suit
    • Creating an internal ethics review committee
    • Model policies and procedures for investigating
      and processing complaints
    • Being respectful of the needs of the
      complaining client and the accused therapist
    • Responding to requests for recommendations
      after an incident has occurred
    Elizabeth Horton, Virginia Marso, Jeanette
    Milgrom, Sue Schaefer

9. **LEGAL AND LEGISLATIVE ISSUES: Administrative Law Remedies**
    • Problems with unregulated counselors and
      therapists
    • Problems related to licensure boards
    • Obstacles to dealing with regulation
    • Difficulties in tracking abusers as they
      move from state to state
    • Sexual exploitation of institutionalized
      clients and the licensing of institutions
    • Obstacles to protecting institutionalized
      clients
    David Jeffreys, Susan Lentz, Daniel McInerney

3:15	Break
3:30	**The Law and Sexual Exploitation** Sandra Nye
4:15	**Where Do We Go From Here?: The Challenge** Gary Schoener
5:00	Adjourn

FACULTY

John Armour, Media Coordinator, Program in Human Sexuality, Family Practice and Community Health, School of Medicine, University of Minnesota

Annette Brodsky, Ph.D., Director of Training/Professor, Psychology Division of the Department of Psychiatry, Harbor Medical Center, University of California Los Angeles Medical Center

Jerry Edelwich, M.S.W., Assistant Professor of Drug and Alcohol Rehabilitation Counseling, Manchester Community College, Manchester, Connecticut; Author of Sexual Dilemmas in the Helping Professions, Bruner/Mazel Publisher, New York, and Burnout: Stages of Disillusionment, Human Sciences Press, New York

Marie Fortune, Rev., Ordained Minister, United Church of Christ; Executive Director of the Center for Prevention of Sexual and Domestic Violence, Seattle

Nanette Gartrell, M.D., Assistant Professor of Psychiatry, Harvard Medical School at Beth Israel Hospital, Cambridge

John Gonsiorek, Ph.D., Psychologist, Director of Psychological Services, Twin Cities Therapy Clinic, Minneapolis

Elizabeth W. Horton, M.S.W., President, Minnesota Society for Clinical Social Work; President Elect, National Federation of Societies for Clinical Social Work, Inc.; Clinical Social Worker in Private Practice, Minneapolis

Donald Horton, J.D., Attorney in Employment Law, Horton and Associates, Minneapolis

David Jeffreys, Ph.D., Executive Director, American Association of State Social Work Boards, Columbia, South Carolina

Jeffrey Kremers, J.D., Attorney, Fox, Carpenter, O'Neill and Shannon, Milwaukee, Wisconsin

Susan Lentz, J.D., Supervising Attorney, Minnesota Mental Health Law Project, Minneapolis

Dorothy Loeffler, Ph.D., Professor, Educational Psychology, Director of Training, University Counseling Services, University of Minnesota; President, Psyche, Inc., Minneapolis

Ellen Thompson Luepker, M.S.W., Clinical Social Worker and Supervisor, Minneapolis Family and Children's Service

Virginia Marso, J.D., Attorney, Schmitt, Johnson, Marso and Janson, St. Cloud, Minnesota

Daniel McInerney, J.D., M.P.H., Assistant Commissioner of Health, Minnesota Department of Health; Assistant Professor, School of Public Health, University of Minnesota

Jeanette H. Milgrom, M.S.W., Director of Consultation and Training, Walk-In Counseling Center, Inc., Minneapolis

Patricia A. Mullen, M.A., Director of the Office of Equal Opportunity and Affirmative Action, University of Minnesota, Minneapolis

Lindsay Nielsen, Psychotherapist, Private Practice,

Minneapolis

William Neiman, J.D., Assistant Hennepin County Attorney, Minneapolis

Sandra G. Nye, J.D., M.S.W., President, Sandra G. Nye and Associates, Attorneys and Consultants, Chicago; Assistant Professor of Jurisprudence in Psychiatry, University of Illinois Abraham Lincoln School of Medicine, Chicago

Donna Peterson, State Senator, 61st Senate District; Vice Chair, Senate Economic Development and Commerce Committee

Marilyn Peterson, M.S.W., Family Therapist in Private Practice, Minneapolis

Kenneth Pierre, Ph.D., Psychologist/Clergyperson, Consultation Services Center of the Catholic Archdiocese of Minneapolis and St. Paul

Barbara Sanderson, M.A., Coordinator, Minnesota State Task Force on Sexual Exploitation by Counselors and Therapists, Minnesota Department of Corrections, St. Paul

Sharon Satterfield, M.D., Associate Professor, Family Practice and Community Health; Director, Program in Human Sexuality, School of Medicine, University of Minnesota

Sue Schaefer, M.A., Psychologist, Private Practice, Minneapolis

Gary Schoener, M.A., Psychologist, Executive Director, Walk-In Counseling Center, Inc., Minneapolis

Minna Shapiro, M.S.W., Private Practice, Minneapolis

Allan Spear, State Senator, 59th Senate District, Minneapolis; Chair, Senate Judiciary Committee; Associate Professor, History, University of Minnesota, Minneapolis

Ann D. Stefanson, M.S.W., Psychologist, Private Practice, Minneapolis

Peg Thompson, Ph.D., Psychologist, Private Practice, St. Paul

William L. White, Director of Training and Consultation, Lighthouse Training Institute, Bloomington, Illinois

M. Sue Wilson, J.D., Attorney, Wilson and Pomerene, Minneapolis

APPENDIX BB

CHILD SEXUAL ABUSE WITHIN THE CATHOLIC CHURCH

Kathe A. Stark

Ms. Stark is the former Administrative Assistant to the President of a construction company who is currently seeking a degree in social work.

This paper was written in 1988 for a class at the University of Minnesota entitled, "Toward an Understanding of Child Sexual Abuse." (The course instructor, Robert W. ten Bensel, M.D., M.P.H., is an internationally known authority on child abuse.) This work is the most thoroughly researched paper or article we have seen on the subject. It was stimulated by a number of highly publicized local cases as well as by the fact that the Archdiocese of Minneapolis and St. Paul was establishing policies and speaking out on these issues.

Footnoted references can be found in the Endnotes at the end of this appendix. Ms. Stark's Appendices have been numbered so as to avoid confusion with the appendices in this volume.

*****

Although examples of child sexual abuse could be cited from many professions, abuse by Catholic priests is a problem across the country. Certainly the Roman Catholic Church has no monopoly on sexual abuse cases, no religious group is immune; but recent criminal and civil charges have brought considerable attention to the problem of child sexual abuse within the Catholic Church that deserve attention. Nationally, more than a dozen Roman Catholic priests have been convicted of child sexual abuse over the past two years and an even larger number have been accused, some estimates reach as high as 400-500. Even L'Osservatore Romano, the Vatican newspaper, was moved to issue a call for action against the "horror, worry and humiliation" of child sexual abuse.[1]

Child sexual abuse involving priests is not a new phenomenon within the Catholic Church. Renaissance history reveals evidence of an awareness of this problem within the Church. During that period the Church took a traditional stance that clerics were the responsibility of the Church and, in theory, were not subject to secular law. The prosecutions that took place were tried in ecclesiastical courts under Cannon Law[2]. The basis of prosecution was that the priest had committed a sin against God, without recognition of the violation of another individual. There appears to be little historical reporting of what the outcomes of these courts were, but the issue of child sexual abuse among clergy remained well hidden until 1985.

The hierarchy of the Church may have felt justified in ignoring the early history of child sexual abuse involving clergy but it could not suppress the revelations in 1985 about pedophilia among priests. A number of cases involving Catholic priests came to light and were examined in depth by the National Catholic Reporter (NCR)[3]. The reports, which focused on the abuse and the Church's response, revealed that priests have been convicted of multiple sexual assaults of children in Louisiana, California, Oregon and Idaho and that charges had been filed in five additional states. The reaction of the Church, in case after case, was equally troubling. The National Catholic Reporter editorialized:

"These are serious and damaging matters that have victimized the young and innocent...But a related and broader scandal seemingly rests with local bishops and a national episcopal leadership that has, as yet, no set policy on how to respond to cases."[4]

The NCR series of reports revealed:

-Frequently local bishops exhibit little concern for the traumatic effects these incidences of sexual abuse have on the children and their families, even though mental disturbances and one suicide have followed the abuse.

-Too often complaints against priests involved in child sexual abuse have been disregarded by the bishops, or the priest is given the benefit of the doubt.

-Only legal threats and lawsuits seem capable of provoking some bishops into taking action against the priest involved.

-In some cases, once identified as offenders, priests have merely been moved to other parishes and have remained in positions of authority.

Denial of the problem was illustrated when a member of the clergy was convicted of sexually abusing 5 children at a Bronx, New York daycare center run by his church. Throughout the judicial process he maintained a remarkable following. Fellow clergymen raised more than $70,000 in defense funds and proclaimed their support even after he began serving a 15-45 year prison sentence. One clergyman quoted as calling the accusations "the worst travesty of justice in the history of the United States," and he used the church newsletter to solicit defense contributions.[5] Where prior knowledge of a clergy's behavior is known, one clergy member said, "We may acquiescence his being transferred, silently closing ranks behind the abuser."[6]

This mode of denial has far-reaching consequences. Recently intercepted correspondence between child molesters suggests that churches and church activities are the ideal place to obtain access to children. Molesters are telling others that churches are afraid to even think about child sexual abuse and that they will not prosecute because they don't want bad publicity. A child molester or pedophile is going to seek out children as a means of sexual gratification. It is only logical that they're going to go to the sources of children.

In 1987 the St. Paul Pioneer Press released the first of several reports of criminal charges being filed against priests and the Catholic Archdiocese of Minneapolis-St. Paul[7]. Again, similar charges were made alleging the Church had prior knowledge, had not taken action but rather transferred the accused to a series of other parishes, and generally showed no concern for the child victims or their families until civil and criminal charges were filed. The Church attempted to deal with the problem internally with no due process for anyone.

IMPLICATIONS

All child sexual abuse is damaging to the child, but sexual abuse by clergy presents some very special issues that further damage the child victim. Archbishop John Roach of Minneapolis-St. Paul wrote that "sexual abuse of a minor or a vulnerable adult is a tragedy. The degree of the tragedy is heightened when the abuser is a priest, minister, teacher, doctor, or anyone who occupies a privileged position in his or her relationship to the families."[8]

The Minneapolis Walk-In Counseling Center reports that victims of sexual abuse by clergy are faced with the additional issues of religion, spirituality, and God. Injuries are spiritual as well as physical and emotional. Their faith in a God has been severely shaken; they often are distrustful of all clergy, and withdraw from all Church-related activities further isolating themselves, as seen in many child sexual abuse victims. They challenge the religion that has played a major role in shaping their beliefs and values as they struggle to integrate these with their losses as a child victim. Children develop their process for moral decision-making implicitly or explicitly through the principles of a framework, like religion, which makes sense to them and to their social group. For children this is their family.

Because a child's sexuality is in the process of development concurrent with physiological, psychological and emotional development, it will be affected by all kinds of experience and much depends upon the context in which this occurs. Because the pain and fear are not simply of physical origin, feelings of guilt and confusion in childhood also may result in later psychological disturbance.

Guilt and shame are common reactions for victims of sexual violence; these feelings are particularly poignant for victims who are sexually inexperienced. For victims who are abused by priests there may be additional feelings of guilt and shame stemming from religious teachings. A report prepared by five Lafayette, Louisiana psychologists involved in the molestations by Rev. Gauthe stated:

"Consider, if you will, the impact on a child (who) is sexually abused during the week, and on Sundays witnesses his parents bowing, kneeling, genuflecting, praying, receiving the sacraments and graciously thanking the priest for his involvement in their lives. Such events (make) him believe such sexual activities have been sanctioned by his parents."[9]

Typically, the children are afflicted with guilt, confusion about their sexual identity, humiliation, fear of rejection by their family members and a loss of religious faith.

Ethics and theology have provided little guidance in understanding the difference between sexual activity and sexual violence for a society faced daily with experiences that reflect the confusion between the two. Christian sexual ethics often have promoted the confusion between sexual activity and sexual violence. Furthermore, Christian ethics have failed to confront the problem of sexual violence itself, thus there has been no mandate for Christians to address this widespread problem.

Too often the teachings of the traditional Church confuse sexual activity with sexual violence. In doing so, they focus on the sexual rather than on the violent aspect and they blame the victim and fail to hold the offender accountable.

Traditional sexual ethics have missed the mark by providing a list of "thou shalt nots" and using guilt as a means to encourage conformity to the rules of the Church. To make responsible ethical choices in the area of sexuality requires information, a willingness to communicate and negotiate, a respect for the other's choices, a sense of self-worth, and a sense of one's own power to consent or withhold consent. The Church has sought to control people's sexual behavior through fear, guilt and regulation.

The Church has not heard about sexual violence because they have not spoken about it. "Silence is not an indication of the absence of the problem; it is itself a loud, orchestrated denial of a problem which certainly exists."[10] Seldom does it occur that the reason the Church does not hear about it is that it has made it clear that they are not prepared to hear or are unavailable to be of assistance.

Silence is perpetuated by shame and confusion. Sexual violence, in most people's minds, has something to do with sex and thus is shameful for the victim. Silence is reinforced by the lack of ethical and theological clarity about sexual violence especially as found in the religious community. It has not provided adequate guidance to its clergy to enable them to deal with sexual violence. Victims remain isolated in their suffering, pastors remain oblivious to their people's needs, society ignores the extent of the problem and responds only occasionally to the most severe situations, and the church continues to misplace its ethical concern and avoids the task before it.

If a woman has accepted the Christian teaching that sexual activity outside of marriage is sinful and that women are temptresses, then she will probably view her victimization as a sexual sin and see herself as being responsible. If a male victim views his rape as sexual activity rather than violence and if he has learned from Christian teachings that any sexual contact with another male is sinful, then he will problably view his victimization by another man as his own sexual sin. Both victims may feel guilty and shamed by the experience because they see the events as sexual, not as violent.

For young girls the message is clear in the all too familiar story of St. Maria Goretti. At age 12, Maria was brutally attacked by a rapist. Although she successfully prevented the rape, her attacker stabbed her to death. As she lay dying, she forgave him. When Pope Pius XII delivered his homily at the canonization of St. Maria Goretti he said:

"From Maria's story carefree children and young people with their zest for life can learn not to be led astray by the attractive pleasures which are not only ephemeral and empty but also sinful."[11]

The Pope seemed to regard rape as "being led astray by attractive pleasures." The belief that rape is sexually pleasurable and that its victim is sinful emerges.

There is a great tragedy in hearing victims quote scripture that was misused in their instruction that now propagate their feelings of guilt, shame, and responsibility for their abuse. Victims recall such instructions as: 1) if you are bad, bad things happen to you; 2) bear the cross you have to bear; 3) if you are a good Christian, God will treat you kindly; and 4) respect and obey your elders. Victimization is seen as a punishment for previous sin, that it is God's way of testing faith and strengthening character. The instruction to respect and obey one's elders presents special difficulty for the child who is being abused because the priest is not only viewed as an individual authority but also as the authority of the Church and the Bible.

Further adding to the confusion and trauma is the Catholic Church's Sacrament of Reconciliation. Founded in their religious instruction the child victim feels responsible for their abuse. They view themselves as the "sinner" who must confess their sin and repent their wrong-doing through the confessional. For those abused by clergy their struggle is made more difficult because they may, in fact, be placed in the position of confessing to the actual abuser and asking his forgiveness. If this priest is a pedophile, confession by the victim may fuel his distorted thinking that the child must have wanted to participate in the sexual activity—that they view it as their sin for participating—absolving the priest from all responsibility for his actions. The child also exposes great vulnerability to the priest during the confession which may increase the likelihood of further abuse and result in terrible confusion for the child. The child has gone to confession and asked for forgiveness, told to "go and sin no more," and yet the abuse continues reinforcing their personal feelings of being bad and evil. Numerous reports have been released where sexual abuse has occurred between a child and the priest within the confessional. In Lafayette, Louisiana a priest suggested that the abused children confess their sins as a gesture meant to remedy the pain. The effect on the victim at this point can only be extremely confusing and further damaging to the child.

Explicit in Catholic instruction is the necessity to forgive those who have inflicted harm. This presents a troublesome dilemma for the abuse victim. In order to be a "good" Christian they should forgive their abuser and yet to forgive is to minimize or deny the wrongfulness of the harm done to them. In addition, victims experience great shame and confusion over their angry feelings because of religious instruction that anger is not a Christian virtue. Secondly, they may be afraid of feeling the anger they have because it is a power that they know can be misused.

The child also may feel great ambivalence about the abuse because they may well have received benefits from the priest in the past. The Church has been a place where the child has learned basic life values and a place to turn to for caring. In the event of sexual abuse the child has looked to the priest for caring and faith, and received betrayal.

The symbolic use of the title "Father" should not be overlooked in understanding the position a priest has in relation to a child. The commandment of "honor thy father" as obedience to the Lord puts the child abuse victim in a state of great confusion. This teaching makes it easier for a priest to take advantage of a child and sexually abuse them. To be "good" they feel that they have no choice but to obey.

THE ROLE OF THE PRIEST

Priests touch people's lives in a way that almost no one else can touch them. The priest's role is one of life-giver and unifier. He is meant to be an enabler of his people. He is meant to nurture their hopes and dreams and as a pastor in a parish, he is meant to be the father of his congregation. In this role he is intended to help create positive memories for his people as any father worth the name.

A priest holds a special role of authority and power which can easily be misused to coerce a sexual encounter. The key elements are power and powerlessness. Not only do priests have access to children, they are authoritarian figures and, often, the objects of hero-worship that eases the road to seduction. The power of a misguided priest can devastate the life of a child. Catholic instruction teaches children that the priest is God's representative on earth and is next to God. As such, the priest is seen in a position of authority and as having more knowledge. The child is emotionally vulnerable because of age, size, naivete, and dependence on adults. A priest who engages in sexual abuse of children has betrayed the trust placed in him and exploits the vulnerability of the child, leaving them feeling betrayed, exploited, guilty and confused.

Having authority does not confer the right to abuse anyone. Authority is first and foremost a responsibility for the well-being of others. Whenever a person who has authority misuses that power to harm another, he then gives up his authority and he should be prevented from harming others.

CHURCH'S REACTION

What the Catholic church is doing to address the issue of child sexual abuse involving its clergy, and the broader issue of all child sexual abuse within congregations, appears to be a closely held secret. Faced with more than 200 cases in the last two years of Roman Catholic priests accused of sexually abusing children, church officials in this country are beginning to talk about the problem, but not within the public eye.

In 1986, Rev. Thomas Doyle, a Domican priest and Canon lawyer who had tried for two years to force the U.S. Catholic Conference to address this issue, made the strongest public statements by a church official. At that time Rev. Doyle said, "It [child sexual abuse] is the most serious problem we in the Church have faced in centuries...when people perceive the Church is covering up, condoning, and stonewalling, they are doubly scandalized."[12] Rev. Doyle went on to explain that the desire to avoid publicity, coupled with "extreme moral judgmentalism in matters of sex" hampered efforts to solve problems with sexual abuse and that "church officials too often did nothing because they feared admitting the problem would lead to a lawsuit."[13]

Rev. Doyle, F. Ray Mouton, a Catholic defense attorney, and Rev. Michael Petersen, a priest and psychiatrist, joined forces. The three prepared a confidential report presented to the National Conference of Catholic Bishops meeting in Collegeville, Minnesota. The proposal included the establishment of a crisis management team to deal with the problem anywhere in the United States. The team would ensure that the offending priest was removed from his duties and institutionalized for long-term therapy. In addition, the team would seek out and contact all parents of victims, encourage them to get professional counseling for their children and offer to pay for it. One goal of the proposal was to "maintain, preserve, and seek to enhance the credibility of the Church as a Christian community."[14]

They warned that the Church's liability during the next 10 years could exceed $1 billion and predicted, accurately, that liability insurance would be rewritten so that it would not cover damages claimed in cases of sexual molestations. The report outlined the devastating effects sustained by child victims and recommended that church officials deal with the child victim, their family, and the public in a straightforward manner.

Although the proposal was discussed at the closed-door meeting, it was not widely distributed, it was never put to a vote, and the crisis management team was not formed. In June, 1986 Mouton resubmitted the proposal to the administration of the U.S. Catholic Conference. Once again the proposal failed. Mouton responded strongly, "This church, which loudly proclaims uniform positions on significant sexual issues relating to the creation of children, did not deem this issue—the sexual abuse of children by its own priests—to be worthy of consideration."[15]

National and local church officials say they haven't adopted a uniform procedure because they believe these cases are best handled by each local diocese. Archbishop John May, President of the National Conference of Catholic Bishops, has said, "We've had meetings with our legal people, our insurance people, our psychological people, usually regionally, and tried to give each diocese all it needs from an educational and doctrinal standpoint."[16] Specifics on what was actually provided to the diocese during these meetings is not part of the public record and local diocesan officials declined to discuss it.

In January, 1988, the National Catholic Reporter editorialized a call for bishops to thoroughly investigate and reveal the situation of child sexual abuse by priests. The editorial also asked the bishops to develop a national policy for victims and to deal with the problem as a moral issue. Twelve diocese and archdiocese are developing written policies to handle the issue of child sexual abuse, including the Archdiocese of Minneapolis-St. Paul. Many diocese, however, have been reluctant to deal with the problem despite multi-million dollar settlements paid to date by the Church across the country.

Despite numerous reports of denial of the problem by church officials, and despite refusal to adopt a national policy, the Church has indirectly and very quietly admitted to having a significant problem with child sexual abuse involving clergy. The Church has established several regional treatment centers to deal with priests who commit molestations. The Servants of the Paraclete order in New Mexico have added a wing to its hospital for pedophilic priests. St. Luke Institute in Maryland was established in 1981 as a psychiatric hospital to treat priests with alcohol and drug addictions and sexual disorders, including pedophilia. Across the country regional diocese and archdiocese have retained psychologists trained in treating pedophilia. This is not the stance of an institution without a problem.

Some archdiocese have begun to address this issue. After the 1985 conviction of Rev. Laughlin, the Portland, Oregon Archdiocese reminded personnel of state laws mandating reporting of child sexual abuse and also set up a panel to evaluate complaints. In June, 1985 the New Jersey diocese established the following procedures and guidelines:

1. Reports of abuse are to be referred immediately to state authorities and diocesan officials.

2. Any accused priest is to be removed from contact with children until the case is resolved.

3. The child victims and their families are to be offered church counseling.

Closer to home, the Archdiocese of Minneapolis-St. Paul has undertaken a concerted effort to address all aspects of sexual abuse within the Church. According to Michael O'Connell, Vicar General, a group effort is being undertaken by clergy, psychologists and lawyers to develop policies and procedures for dealing with sexual abuse which they hope will be adopted by the Church state-wide. The focus is on a seven-phase program including: education, prevention, intervention, evaluation, treatment, restitution, and reconciliation. In January, 1988 the archdiocese issued the adopted policies and procedures for dealing with sexual abuse of minors and vulnerable adults (Appendix I).

Gary Schoener at the Minneapolis Walk-In Counseling Center has worked closely with the archdiocese and has participated in evaluation and treatment of accused priests. In an interview with him, he reported that this archdiocese "is doing more and moving faster on this issue than many, establishing and strictly adhering to policies."[17] Mr. Schoener reported that the aim of the archdiocese is to support the victim, investigate all allegations and assess the perpetrator. Initial assessments are generally done out of town, usually at St. Luke Institute, and then double-checked here to insure treatment and role limitations that are adequate to prevent further abuse.

In the fall of 1987, the Archdiocese in conjunction with Consultation Services Center instituted three separate workshops for priests and other kinds of pastoral ministers. The objective was to inform Catholic leaders of the issues of sexual health in ministry and included a focus on sexual abuse as persons in ministry are involved as perpetrators, concerned leaders, or colleagues. (Definitions used for these workshops are found in Appendix II.) While clergy were not required to attend, over 1,000 persons did respond to the invitation. Three perspectives were included in these workshops:

1. Ethical/Theological — focusing on philosophical, professional, and religious norms for sexual behavior.

2. Pastoral/Psychological — with emphasis on humanistic care, the science of human behavior, individual differences and pathology.

3. Legal/Administrative — highlighting the Minnesota law and the responsibilities of leaders of the Church to be aware and involved.

Included as a portion of these workshops was a confidential questionnaire (Appendix IV) pertaining to sexual issues in ministry. The questionnaire, based on the work of Dr. Nanette Gartrell of Harvard Medical School, was used in an attempt to determine the scope of sexual issues among participants, including child sexual abuse. While results are not accessible to the public, Rev. Michael O'Connell reports that "the scope of the problem is substantial".[18] He added that a very large portion of his time is now consumed with dealing with victims and alleged perpetrators of sexual misconduct, where the victim is still a child as well as where the victim is currently an adult coming forward. Many of these adults are receiving psychiatric/psychological care and have been diagnosed as suffering Post Traumatic Stress and major depression.

In early 1988, the same pastoral ministers engaged in another set of workshops with the objective of involving leaders-ministers in learning more about education, prevention, intervention and confrontation, treatment and care; and restitution and reconciliation as these four areas relate to sexual health, including sexual abuse. Leaders-ministers were brought together to pool specific suggestions for goals and action plans in 12 areas (Appendix III) and to begin to draft policies, procedures and guidelines that have to do with ensuring a sexually healthy environment in church ministry. The goal is to complete a Planning Committee Report by the spring of 1989 which can be submitted to the State's Bishops.

The process being undertaken is a long, complex one which began in 1986. The question arises: What is happening in the meantime?

In January, 1988, Archbishop John Roach wrote a "Viewpoint" article for the St. Paul Pioneer Press which included:

"When faced with a situation of such abuse, we have tried to deal compassionately and justly with the victims, and to do everything we possibly could do to obtain the help necessary for the priest-abuser.

...There is no doubt that the primary victims in all of this are the abused and their families. We must do everything possible to provide whatever care is appropriate for them. I am totally committed to that."[19]

St. Paul attorney, Jeffrey R. Anderson, who has filed several lawsuits against the Church and individual priests on behalf of victims/survivors of child sexual abuse, does not confirm that this commitment to helping the victim is occurring. Mr. Anderson reports that, despite efforts to mediate with church officials on behalf of victims and their families out of the judicial system, "the only results obtained have involved a difficult, lengthy and adversarial court situation that is terribly difficult for the victim who is re-traumatized in the process."[20] As his involvement in cases involving sexual abuse by clergy has increased, Mr. Anderson recommends that victims and their families do not attempt to resolve the matter directly with the Church, that "legal action appears to be the only method of ensuring appropriate action be taken on behalf of the victims." He indicated a procedure involving putting the Church "on notice" that a Jane/John Doe is filing a lawsuit which provides the Church with the opportunity to respond without court action, but that this seldom occurs and civil and/or criminal charges are then filed.

In a recent example, a woman who was sexually abused and raped as a child by a priest confronted the archdiocese in May, 1988. She is receiving psychiatric care for the diagnosis of Post Traumatic Stress Disorder, exhibiting severe depression and anxiety as the memories of the abuse surface. At the meeting in May she had been assured by church officials that the priest involved would be immediately removed from active ministry, that a psychiatric evaluation would be completed to determine what subsequent steps would be taken with the perpetrator, and that she did not need to worry about her costly medical bills because the Church had a responsibility to ensure she was able to continue to receive the necessary care.

Two months later, no substantive action had been taken by the Church, who now requested a consent form be executed to allow her psychiatrist to release information regarding his assessment of her credibility. She complied and a report from the doctor was sent to the Church stating there was "no pathology present to raise doubt as to the allegations made." At the same time, the archdiocese changed their position on providing for her medical care stating they would be willing to pay expenses if she began to see a psychologist they worked with rather than the doctor with whom she had finally begun to trust and work closely with.

In September, 1988 friends of the victim introduced her to an acquaintance, ("NM" used to maintain anonymity), who was recovering from child sexual abuse, in the hope that they could be supportive of each other. During the conversation NM said she would never forget Father "_____", the priest who had abused her and another woman she knew of. Once the name of the priest was mentioned the emotional response was overwhelming as both victims realized they were abused by the same priest. To further exacerbate the situation, NM revealed that she had reported the incident in prior years to church officials. There are now three women, sexually abused by the same priest, in three separate parishes, a complaint had been filed with the church, and yet the priest was still functioning within a parish.

As a group, the three women confronted church officials along with the couple who had witnessed the emotional response that accompanied the realization that the abuse was perpetrated by the same priest. They were assured that there could be no question about the allegations since there were multiple victims and that immediate action would be taken.

At the end of September church officials finally confronted the alleged perpetrator, explained the allegations and gained his cooperation in undergoing a comprehensive evaluation and strict curtailment of his pastoral activities. Again, the victims were assured that restitution was to be provided.

After a 10-day evaluation, the alleged perpetrator had admitted to deviant sexual behavior with the three women but was unable or unwilling to be specific. All three women received a letter from the archdiocese which said they "need" to have each of them interviewed by the same psychologists evaluating the alleged perpetrator to "gain greater clarity and specificity" of the allegations. The impact on the victims was devastating. They felt as though they were disbelieved and that, once again, the trust they had placed in the Church had been betrayed. The "need" for this type of interview would be needlessly traumatic since it required that, to some extent, the victim re-experience the original trauma.

Mr. Anderson reported that despite the sheer number of the women involved, the span of time during which the abuse is to have occurred, and the fact that these women did not have prior knowledge of each other, the Church refused to stand firm on their commitment to aid the victims but, rather, attempted to further traumatize and re-victimize them. A notice was sent to the archdiocese officialls that a civil suit would be filed against both the offending priest and the Church. Mr. Anderson added that "church representatives have only added to the victimization of these individuals through the callousness of their response to the initial complaints. Had they [the Church] shown a caring attitude, none of these women would have had an interest in filing a lawsuit, but it seems to be the only language the Church can understand."[21] In litigating cases Anderson said all lawyers are faced with extremely difficult questions. How can you compensate for the loss of innocence? How can you predict the years of treatment that will be necessary and their costs throughout the lifetime of the victim? What can compensate the victim for the residual effects resulting from the trauma of sexual abuse such as related health disorders, alcohol and drug abuse, or ruined marriages?

With the exception of a few isolated cases, the public has not been made aware of the number of complaints, lawsuits, and out-of-court settlements made by this, or other, archdiocese in cases of child sexual abuse. Archbishop Roach scorned the media coverage of the 1987 case saying, "There is another set of victims, however. They are the vast majority of Catholic priests of this archdiocese and of the United States who must bear the burden of the attendant publicity that is lacking in perspective."[22] A reader responed, "without the level of coverage, neither the new policy nor the attendant Viewpoint article ever would have seen the light of day. The archdiocese has already shown it will not effectively respond to this issue if allowed its privacy."[23]

CONCLUSION

The Catholic church is not much different than society, in general, on the issue of child sexual abuse, but there is the added dimension of religious issues. All child sexual abuse victims must face the problems of dealing with the abuse and its effect, but to face the possibility that the Church does not understand or want to know about the experience leaves the victim feeling further abandoned and betrayed.

The people in power must be held responsible. Victims deserve to receive acknowledgment from the Catholic church for what was done to them, as well as recognition of responsibility that the Church has to the victim to insure they are able to receive the same medical treatment being afforded to the priests who have abused them. Victims/survivors need to know that the Church and the public is outraged by the crimes committed against them. Survivors must know that the Church recognizes the long-term implications to their lives as a result of child sexual abuse, that they may appear to have recovered only to have the issue resurface at a later time with all of the emotional impact of the initial abuse, and that they deserve to receive the help that is necessary during these periods.

The Catholic church must intentionally break its silence on the issue of child sexual abuse. Regardless of arguments against publicity, there is no reason that child sexual abuse should be relegated to silence. "The topic must be brought into public awareness. Deploring child sexual abuse verbally is a modest beginning;" Rev. Robert Schwartz at the St. Paul Seminary, School of Divinity said, "we must take a hard, careful look at the issue of child sexual abuse within the Church and stop moralizing about it."[24] There is a great need to speak openly about the issue, using correct terminology, and to promote awareness. The Church must make it clear that it is a place of refuge and demonstrate the validity of this ideal through direct, compassionate and consistent behavior. The victims of child sexual abuse need guidance that they are not to blame and did not deserve the abuse, that they are good people, and that the sin was not a sin <u>by</u> the victim but, rather, a sin <u>against</u> them. Many victims/survivors have been reluctant to confront the Church, and with good reason. They may never have heard their priest mention anything about abuse or they may have heard something mentioned that made it clear that their experience would not be understood or believed.

Theological messages need to be re-examined. Is there a sexual hierarchy implied? Are sex and sexual violence viewed together? What are the meanings of forgiveness, suffering, and confession? Theological positions must be disentangled from facts.

The Catholic church is an institution of great power—a power that can hurt or heal. The power to heal must be directed toward education of seminarians, clergy, and congregations, and the Church must become strong advocates for prevention. So much depends on their ability to hear the stories of victims and the courage and creativity to respond and change on behalf of the victims.

Reverend Michael O'Connell said, "We have learned a lot about this issue in the last two years and I believe we are doing a much better job now, but we are still learning."[25] The issue of child sexual abuse has emerged as a national issue of overwhelming proportions and the Church is as perplexed as the people in society. "The ability to admit we have a long way to grow speaks of an emerging willingness to change."[26] Such change involves great risks at times but the refusal to change can only continue to inflict great pain and suffering on child victims of sexual abuse within the Church.

While the Church is slowly, cautiously and quietly beginning to acknowledge and discuss the complexity and extent of the problem they have long minimized, it remains to be seen how effective any new methods of dealing with the problem will be. The important thing is to take immediate action responding to all complaints received and, at the same time, protect the rights of everyone, most primarily: to protect the children.

Justice Frances T. Murphy, at a speech on child sexual abuse in 1985, said:

"Children have neither power nor property. Voices other than their own must speak for them. If those voices are silent, then children who have been abused may lean their heads against window panes and taste the bitter emptiness of violated childhoods."[27]

APPENDIX I

ARCHDIOCESAN POLICY OF INTERVENTION
AND TREATMENT OF ABUSE
(Catholic Bulletin, February 4, 1988)

"When considering sexual abuse of a minor or others at risk by a priest, the archdiocese maintains a primary concern for the victim's safety and well-being. Recognizing that the sexual abuse of minors and others at risk can be a disease, and that it has tragic consequences for victims as well as abusers, the Archdiocese of St. Paul and Minneapolis will exercise the following steps in dealing with a priest accused of the sexual abuse of a minor or a person at risk.

1. When a priest has been accused of sexually abusive behavior toward a minor, an appropriate **archdiocesan official will investigate the facts of the case.

2. The archbishop will be informed of all alleged cases and, in the instance of a credible charge he will:

   a. Ensure that the victims receive immediate and on-going pastoral care.
   b. Inform the accused priest of the investigation and temporarily relieve him of his duties; this is to protect the minors or others at risk who are involved.
   c. Ensure that the appropriate police or child protection agency is contacted according to law and direct church authorities to cooperate in the investigation and prosecution of the case.

3. If the civilian and church investigation confirms the accusation, the archdiocese will ensure that the best diagnostic evaluation and treatment resources are made available for the priest.

4. After a priest has cooperatively completed initial treatment, and if the recommendation following that treatment is positive, the priest will enter a four-year supervised aftercare program which will:

   a. Have the archbishop appoint a director/supervisor who will work with the priest in regular accountability meetings.
   b. Establish a supervised transitional living arrangement based on recommendations from the treatment resource.
   c. Design a vocational rehabilitation program of up to four years in non-parish ministry. During this time the priest will participate in on-going treatment, and he will not have a permanent pastoral assignment.
   d. Require that the priest participate in a one-week annual evaluation and therapeutic workshop over this four-year period.
   e. Have all elements of the aftercare program under specific contract between the priest and the archdiocese. Failure to successfully cooperate with this contract will result in the priest's removal from active ministry.

5. Long-term assignment and on-going treatment:
   Four to five years following diagnosis, evaluation, and successful aftercare, the individual priest will be eligible for consideration of a permanent contractual assignment, excluding ministry to minors and others at risk. He will be expected to participate in a regular support group and will report to a supervisor assigned by the archbishop."

** Moderator of the Curia/Vicar General
   Chancellor
   Vicar Bishop

APPENDIX II

DEFINITIONS

Sexual Health

The integration of the somatic, emotional, intellectual, social (and spiritual), aspects of sexual being, in ways that are positively enriching and that enhace human personality, communication and love.

Sexual Abuse

The subjection of a child or vulnerable adult, by any person responsible for their care, to any sexual act which is a violation of the Minnesota Criminal Code.

Education and Prevention

Attitudes and programs that promote healthy sexual behavior for ministers of the church and those in their pastoral care.

Intervention and Confrontation

Policies and procedures which encourage ethical, empathic, effective and efficient methods of receiving data about sexual transgressions, of notifying civil and church authorities, and of instituting appropriate pastoral, psychological and legal action.

Treatment and Care

Assessment, therapy and supportive care for victims/survivors of sexual abuse, for offending ministers, and for all populations directly affected by such violations of sexual boundaries.

Restitution and Reconciliation

Post-trauma pastoral and psychological care for individuals and church communities affected by inappropriate sexual incidents.

APPENDIX III

TWELVE AREAS OF CONCENTRATION

EDUCATION AND PREVENTION
1. Code of Ethics:
Task: Develop a suggested Code of Ethics for ministers to use in responding to sexual issues in ministry. Consider the need for a general Code of Ethics for ministers.

Starter List of Responses:
1. Develop an ethical statement for ministers in the specific area of sexual behavior in ministry.
2. Develop a full Code of Ethics for all ministers like those for physicians, psychologists, social workers and other human service professionals.
3. Develop a mechanism for promulgating and enforcing a Code of Ethics for ministers.

2. Policy Development:
Task: Review the policy that is being prepared for use by all of the diocese of Minneosta. Identify ways to promulgate and use this policy in the Archdiocese.

Starter List of Responses:
1. To offer consultation on the proposed policies regarding education/prevention.
2. To offer consultation on the proposed policies on intervention/confrontation.
3. To offer consultation on the proposed policies regarding treatment/care.
4. To offer consultation on the proposed policies on restitution/reconciliation.
5. To develop proposals for the promulgation and use of the proposed state policies regarding sexual issues in ministry.

3. Curriculum and Public Education:
Task: Suggest curriculum guidelines for instruction in sexual health for ministers and ministers-in-training. Prepare a program for public education concerning sexual issues in the Church.

Starter List of Responses:
1. Develop training programs for ministry candidates in sexual issues in ministry.
2. Develop in-service programs for ministers around sexual issues in ministry.
3. Develop guidelines for healthy touch in ministry situations.
4. Develop a program of education of the people of the Church around sexual issues in ministry.

INTERVENTION AND CONFRONTATION
4. A Minister's Individual Response
Task: Identify behavioral signs of inappropriate sexual behavior in the potential offender and signs of distress in the victim/survivor. Suggest decision-making strategies for intervention.

Starter List of Responses:

1. Develop guidelines for ministers who need to respond to survivors of sexual offenses by ministers.
2. Develop guidelines for ministers who need to identify and respond to colleagues who are at risk or involved in inappropriate sexual behavior.
3. Develop guidelines for ministers who are called upon to advise families, colleagues, or friends of survivors or perpetrators of sexual offenses.
4. Develop guidelines for ministers to use when they are required to confront or intervene in a case of a colleague's inappropriate behavior.

5. Advocacy for Survivors and Offenders

Task: Set up advocacy procedures for both the victim/survivor and the alleged offender so that the rights of both are protected. List data-collecting methods.

Starter List of Responses:
1. Recommend an advocacy structure to be used by victim/survivors in cases of sexual offenses by ministers.
2. Recommend an advocacy structure to be used by ministers who are alleged offenders in cases of sexual offense.
3. Become familiar with advocacy resources already available within the community.
4. Understand the dynamics of advocacy programs as they affect the advocates, the survivors, and the perpetrators.

6. Systems Cooperation

Task: Plan step-by-step intervention and cooperation between Archdiocesan representatives, local agencies, parish or institution leaders, police and other civil authorities, psychological professionals, the victim/survivor and the alleged offender.

Starter List of Responses:
1. Recommend the appropriate cooperation between church and law enforcement bodies when intervention on a minister accused of a sexual offense is required.
2. Recommend cooperative steps that can be taken at this time to meet the needs of victim/survivors of sexual offenses and their communities.
3. Recommend the most beneficial way to disclose the facts of a situation to the affected communities and to the media.
4. Recommend changes in present policies of affected groups that would improve the quality of intervention and confrontation in cases of sexual offenses by ministers.

TREATMENT AND CARE

7. Treatment and Care for Survivors

Task: Identify treatment options for the victim/survivor. Suggest ways that friends, colleagues, and other primary support persons can be of assistance.

Starter List of Responses:
1. Develop an understanding of the needs of victim/survivors of sexual offenses by ministers.
2. Develop guidelines for treatment and care programs for survivors.
3. Develop funding proposals for this treatment and care.
4. Develop guidelines for the inclusion of support persons and groups in the treatment and care of survivors.

8. Treatment and Care of Offenders

Task: Identify treatment options for the alleged offender. Suggest ways that friends, colleagues, and other primary support persons can be of assistance.

Starter List of Responses:

1. Develop an understanding of the treatment and care needs and experiences of ministers who have committed sexual offenses.
2. Develop guidelines for treatment and care programs for offenders.
3. Develop guidelines for aftercare programs for offenders.
4. Develop guidelines for the inclusion of support persons and groups in the treatment and care of offenders.

9. Treatment and Care of Parents/Family/and Others

Task: Reflect on the care needs of those who surround both the victim/survivor and the alleged offender. Identify support systems that provide opportunities for their treatment and care.

Starter List of Responses:

1. Develop an understanding of the effects of sexual offenses in ministry on those near to the survivors and to the perpetrators.
2. Recommend treatment and care possibilities for these persons or groups.
3. Develop funding proposals to make this treatment and care possible.
4. Develop recommendations for the role of church leadership in the treatment and care of these persons or groups.

RESTITUTION AND RECONCILIATION

10. Reconciliation - Person/Community

Task: Review programs in existence and prepare suggestions for personal and public reconciliation in cases of sexual harassment, abuse and exploitation.

Starter List of Responses:

1. Recommend a variety of reconciling experiences that might be helpful for survivors and offenders, separately or together.
2. Recommend public or community experiences that would be helpful in the restoration of trust to communities affected by sexual offenses.
3. Recommend the spiritual resources that could be used in the process of reconciliation and restoration of trust for individuals and groups involved in the trauma of sexual offenses in ministry.

11. Restitution - Money/Jobs/Law Suits

Task: Develop guidelines for just restitution for persons victimized by damaging sexual behavior. Review consequences of civil suits and criminal prosecution for persons and churches involved. Consider justice issues for sexual offenders.

Starter List of Responses:

1. Recommend a standard of just restitution to be used in assessing the appropriate response to persons and communities victimized by sexual offenses...money, jobs, good name, etc.
2. Recommend a standard of just restitution to be used in assessing the civil and criminal and church penalties to offenders in cases of sexual offense by ministers.
3. Recommend guidelines for restitution to be made to third parties affected by sexual offenses by ministers.

4. Recommend guidelines for restitution in cases of false accusation of sexual offenses by ministers.

12. Societal Connections - Laws/Press/Church

Task: Identify public policy issues involving church, press, judicial systems, helping professions, government and the legal profession.

Starter List of Responses:

1. Develop standards of respect to govern the relationship of the major systems involved in dealing with sexual issues in ministry.
2. Make recommendations for changes in the present relationships between the systems.
3. Recommend ways in which the church can take the leading role in the communication needed between systems in this field.

APPENDIX IV

QUESTIONNAIRE ON SEXUAL ISSUES IN MINISTRY

(THIS QUESTIONNAIRE IS AN EFFORT BY PROFESSIONAL MINISTERS TO DETERMINE THE EXTENT OF INAPPROPRIATE SEXUAL CONTACT BETWEEN MINISTERS AND THOSE THEY SERVE. IT IS SIMILAR TO SURVEYS USED WITH OTHER PROFESSIONAL GROUPS. IT IS BASED ON THE WORK OF NANETTE GARTRELL, M.D. OF THE HARVARD MEDICAL SCHOOL.)

<u>Sexual Contact</u> in this questionnaire is defined as sexual harassment, sexual abuse, or sexual exploitation which is intended to arouse or satisfy sexual desire in the minister or the person(s) served.

RESPONDENT DEMOGRAPHICS:

Please provide the following information about yourself:

1. Your Age: _____ Years

2. Your Sex: _____ Female
    _____ Male

3. How many years have you been a minister: _____ Years

4. Have you ever received counseling from a minister: _____ No
    _____ Yes

5. If yes, how many months were you in counseling: _____ Months

6. What is your relationship status: _____ Single
    _____ Celibate
    _____ Married
    _____ Separated
    _____ Divorced

7. What is your sexual orientation (check one) _____ Heterosexual
    _____ Homosexual
    _____ Bisexual

PERSONAL EXPERIENCE OF OTHERS AS VICTIM/SURVIVORS:

8. In your ministry, have you seen persons
    who have sexual contact with a minister   _____ Yes
    in a helping role?   _____ No

9. If yes, how many persons acknowledge   _____ Females
    this to you?   _____ Males

10. In your opinion, what was the effect of this sexual contact between a minister and
    this person:

    _____ Helpful
    _____ Helpful in some cases;
                harmful in others
    _____ Harmful
    _____ No Effect
    _____ Other

11. How many of the involved ministers were:

    _____ Priests
    _____ Teachers
    _____ Youth Ministers
    _____ Pastoral Counselors
    _____ Sisters
    _____ Brothers
    _____ Pastoral Ministers
    _____ Vocation Personnel
    _____ Other Ministers

12. Did you report any of these cases to an authority?

    _____ in the church
    _____ in the government
    _____ to a professional
                association

13. How many cases did you report: _____ Number

PERSONAL EXPERIENCE OF MINISTERS AS PERPETRATORS:

14. Did you, personally, know any ministers
    who have had sexual contact with a   _____ No
    person served?   _____ Yes

15. If yes, how many?   _____ Ministers

16. Have you reported any of these ministers   _____ No
    to a person in authority?   _____ Yes

17. How many reports of this nature have you
    filed?   _____ Number

EXPERIENCE OF SELF AS VICTIM/SURVIVOR

18. Have you ever had sexual contact with a person who has ministered to you?

    _____ No
    _____ Yes

19. If yes, how did you view this contact or the most recent contact if there has been more than one experience.
    (Check all that apply)

    _____ Inappropriate
    _____ Helpful
    _____ Harmful
    _____ Caring
    _____ Exploitative
    _____ Other

20. I have been sexually abused:

    _____ No
    _____ Yes
    _____ Age
    _____ A Family Member
    _____ A Church Minister
    _____ Other (Describe)

_____

_____

21. I have been sexually harassed:

    _____ Yes
    _____ No
    _____ Age
    _____ In church ministry
              employment
    _____ In other employment
              (Describe)

_____

_____

22. I have been sexually exploited:

    _____ Yes
    _____ No
    _____ Age
    _____ A Church Counselor
    _____ Other (Describe)

_____

_____

EXPERIENCE OF SELF AS PERPETRATOR:

23. Have you had sexual contact with one or   _____ No
    more pesons to whom you were ministering?_____   Yes

24. If no, thank you for your participation in this survey.

    If yes, how many of these persons were: _____ Female
                                                        _____ Male

25. Did you ever seek consultation with a
    colleague because of your sexual contact
    with a person to whom you were   _____ No
    offering ministry?   _____ Yes

For Questions 26 and following, please describe your more recent sexual contact with a person to whom you offered ministry:

26. Sex of this person: _____ Female
                                                        _____ Male

27. Age of this person: _____ Years

28. Did this sexual contact occur:
    _____ While your ministry was being offered
    _____ Concurrent with ministry, but outside
           the ministry setting
    _____ After the ministry relationship ceased

29. If after the termination of ministry, how
    long after?   _____ Months

30. The sexual contact consisted of:
    _____ Hugging
    _____ Kissing
    _____ Fondling
    _____ Sitting on Lap
    _____ Disrobing
    _____ Genital Contact
    _____ Verbal Harassment
    _____ Non-Verbal Harassment
    _____ Other
    Specify:_____
    _____

31. Who initiated the sexual contact? (Check one)
    _____ The Other Person
    _____ Yourself
    _____ Both

32. How long did you engage in sexual contact with this person?
    _____ Only one sexual encounter
    _____ Less than 3 months
    _____ 3 to 11 months
    _____ 1 to 5 years
    _____ More than 5 years

33. If the sexual contact has ended, how did this occur? ·
    _____
    _____

34. Did you have strong, positive feelings toward this person (e.g., did you believe yourself to be in love with the person)?
    _____ Yes
    _____ No

35. To the best of your knowledge, do you thing that the person had strong, positive feelings toward you?
    _____ Yes
    _____ No

36. Did your sexual contact change your feelings about this person?
    _____ Yes
    _____ No
    If yes, in what way:_____

37. If ministry continued during the time you had sexual contact with the person, did the sexual contact affect your ministry?
    _____
    _____

38. To the best of your knowledge, did the person view sexual contact as:
    _____ Inappropriate
    _____ Helpful
    _____ Harmful
    _____ Caring
    _____ Exploitative
    _____ Harassing

39. What is the current status of your relationship with this person?
    _____ No contact whatsoever
    _____ Continued ministry, but no sexual
              contact
    _____ No ministry contact, but continued
              sexual contact
    _____ Continued ministry and sexual
              contact
    _____ Married to or in a committed
              relationship with this person
    _____ Other

40. Which one of the following statements most closely reflects your overall feelings about your sexual contact with this person?

_____ I am pleased to have had sexual contact with this person.

_____ I have mixed feelings about having had sexual contact with this person.

_____ I regret having had sexual contact with this person.

41. Did you ever seek consultation with a colleague because of your sexual contact with this person?

_____ No

_____ Yes

THANK YOU FOR YOUR PARTICIPATION IN THIS STUDY

ADDITIONAL
COMMENTS:_____

_____

_____

REFERENCES

1. Crewdson, J., "By Silence Betrayed: Sexual Abuse of Children in America," Little, Brown and Company, 1988.

2. Ennew, J., "The Sexual Exploitation of Children," St. Martin's Press, 1986.

3. Fortune, M.M., "Sexual Violence: The Unmentionable Sin, An Ethical and Pastoral Perspective," The Pilgrim Press, New York, N.Y., 1983.

4. Fortune, M.M., "Keeping the Faith," Harper and Row, 1987.

5. Gallagher, C.A., and Vanderberg, T.L., "The Celibacy Myth, Loving for Life," The Crossroad Publishing Company, 1987.

6. Hechler, D., "The Battle and the Backlash," Lexington Books, 1988.

7. Lader, L., "Politics, Power and the Church," MacMillan Publishing Company, New York, N.Y., 1987.

8. Mead, J.J. and Blach, Jr., G.M., "Child Abuse and the Church: A New Mission," HDL Publishing Company, 1987.

9. Pellauer, M., Chester, Boyajian, J., "Sexual Assault and Abuse: A Handbook for Clergy and Religious Professionals," Harper and Row, 1987.

10. Ruggiero, G., "Boundaries of Eros," Oxford University Press, 1985.

PERSONAL INTERVIEWS

1. "NM", Personal Interview. 10/01/88. (Name withheld upon request)

2. O'Connell, Rev. Michael, Vicar General, Archdiocese of Minneapolis-St. Paul, Personal Interviews, 10/10/88 and 10/25/88.

3. Rocker, Dr. Delore, Consultation Services Center, Personal Interview, 10/10/88.

4. Schoener, Gary, Minneapolis Walk-In Counseling Center, Personal Interview, 10/10/88.

5. Schwartz, Rev. Robert, St. Paul Seminary School of Divinity, 10/13/88.

PERIODICALS

1. Archdiocese St. Paul and Minneapolis Clergy Bulletin, "Sexual Issues in Ministry," October 20, 1987.

2. Catholic Bulletin, "Archdiocesan Policy of Intervention and Treatment of Abuse," February 4, 1988, Vol. 78, #5.

3. Archdiocese St. Paul and Minneapolis Clergy Bulletin, "Policy of Intervention and Treatment of a Priest Accused of Sexual Abuse of a Minor or Others at Risk," January 22, 1988, Vol. XIII, #4.

4. National Catholic Reporter, "Priest Child Abuse Cases Victimizing Families; Bishops Lack Policy Response," June 7, 1985, Vol. 21, #32.

5. National Catholic Reporter, "Pedophile Priest: Study In Inept Church Response," June 7, 1985, Vol. 21, #32.

6. National Catholic Reporter, "Church Still on Trial in Pedophilia Crisis," "Dioceses React to Deepening Dilemma," May 30, 1986, Vol. 22, #32.

7. New York Times, "Roman Catholic Church Discusses Abuse of Children by Priests," May 4, 1986.

8. Psychology Today, "Shattered Innocence," February, 1987, Vol. 21, #2.

9. St. Paul Pioneer Press Dispatch, "Second Sexual Abuse Lawsuit Filed Against Catholic Priest," February 13, 1987.

10. St. Paul Pioneer Press Dispatch, "Troubled Priest 'Two Men in One,'" February 22, 1987.

11. St. Paul Pioneer Press Dispatch, "Church/Viewpoint is Criticized," January 10, 1988.

12. St. Paul Pioneer Press Dispatch, "Archbishop Explains Diocesan Policies to Combat Sexual Abuse," Viewpoint, January 31, 1988.

13. St. Paul Pioneer Press Dispatch, "Archdiocesan Policy," Opinion, February 15, 1988.

14. Time Magazine, "Painful Secrets," July 1, 1985, Vol. 125, #26.

ENDNOTES

[1] Crewdson, J., "By Silence Betrayed: Sexual Abuse of Children in America," 1988, pp. 115-116.

[2] Ruggiero, G., "Boundaries of Eros," 1985, pp. 75-88.

[3] National Catholic Reporter, "Priest Child Abuse Cases Victimizing Families; Bishops Lack Policy Response," 1985, p. A-1.

[4] National Catholic Reporter, "Priest Child Abuse Cases Victimizing Families; Bishops Lack Policy Response," 1985, p. A-1.

[5] Mead, J.J. and Blach, Jr., G.M., "Child Abuse and the Church: A New Mission," 1987, p. 50.

[6] Pellauer, M., Chester, Boyajian, J., "Sexual Assault and Abuse: A Handbook for Clergy and Religious Professionals," 1987, p. 113.

[7] St. Paul Pioneer Press Dispatch, "Second Sexual Abuse Lawsuit Filed Against Catholic Priest," 1987, p. A-1.

[8] St. Paul Pioneer Press Dispatch, "Archbishop Explains Diocesan Policies to Combat Sexual Abuse," 1988.

9 National Catholic Reporter, "Priest Child Abuse Cases Victimizing Families; Bishops Lack Policy Response," 1985, p. A-1.

10 Fortune, M.M., "Sexual Violence: The Unmentionable Sin," 1983, p. 56.

11 Fortune, M.M., "Sexual Violence: The Unmentionable Sin," 1983, p. 68.

12 St. Paul Pioneer Press Dispatch, "Church/Viewpoint is Criticized," 1988, p. 10A.

13 New York Times, "Roman Catholic Church Discusses Abuse of Children by Priests," 1986, p. 14:5.

14 St. Paul Pioneer Press Dispatch, "Church/Viewpoint is Criticized," 1988, p. 10A.

15 St. Paul Pioneer Press Dispatch, "Church/Viewpoint is Criticized," 1988, p. 10A.

16 St. Paul Pioneer Press Dispatch, "Church/Viewpoint is Criticized," 1988, p. 10A.

17 Gary Schoener, Minneapolis Walk-In Counseling Center, Personal Interview, 1988.

18 Rev. Michael O'Connell, Vicar General, Minneapolis-St. Paul Archdiocese, Personal Interview, 1988.

19 St. Paul Pioneer Press Dispatch, "Archbishop Explains Diocesan Policies to Combat Sexual Abuse," 1988.

20 Jeffrey R. Anderson, Attorney at Law, Personal Interview, 1988.

21 Jeffrey R. Anderson, Attorney at Law, Personal Interview, 1988.

22 St. Paul Pioneer Press Dispatch, "Archbishop Explains Diocesan Policies to Combat Sexual Abuse," 1988.

23 St. Paul Pioneer Press Dispatch, "Archdiocesan Policy," 1988.

24 Rev. Robert Schwartz, St. Paul Seminary School of Divinity, Personal Interview, 1988.

25 Rev. Michael O'Connell, Vicar General, Minneapolis-St. Paul Archdiocese, Personal Interview, 1988.

26 Pellauer, M., Chester, Boyajian, J., "Sexual Assault and Abuse: A Handbook for Clergy and Religious Professionals," 1988, p. ix.

27 Hechler, D., "The Battle and the Backlash," 1988, p. 32.

Appendix CC

Civil Statute: Illinois

PSYCHOTHERAPISTS—EXPLOITATION

PUBLIC ACT 85-1254

H.B. 3938

AN ACT concerning sexual exploitation by psychotherapists.

Be it enacted by the People of the State of Illinois, represented in the General Assembly:

[S.H.A. ch. 70, ¶ 801]

§ 1. Definitions. In this Act:

(a) "Emotionally dependent" means that the nature of the patient's or former patient's emotional condition and the nature of the treatment provided by the psychotherapist are such that the psychotherapist knows or has reason to believe that the patient or former patient is unable to withhold consent to sexual contact by the psychotherapist.

(b) "Former patient" means a person who was given psychotherapy within 1 year prior to sexual contact with the psychotherapist.

(c) "Patient" means a person who seeks or obtains psychotherapy.

(d) "Psychotherapist" means a physician, psychologist, nurse, chemical dependency counselor, social worker, or other person, whether or not licensed by the State, who performs or purports to perform psychotherapy.

(e) "Psychotherapy" means the professional treatment, assessment, or counseling of a mental or emotional illness, symptom, or condition. "Psychotherapy" does not include counseling of a spiritual or religious nature, social work, or casual advice given by a friend or family member.

(f) "Sexual contact" means any of the following, whether or not occurring with the consent of a patient or former patient:

(1) sexual intercourse, cunnilingus, fellatio, anal intercourse or any intrusion, however slight, into the genital or anal openings of the patient's or former patient's body by any part of the psychotherapist's body or by any object used by the psychotherapist for that purpose, or any intrusion, however slight, into the genital or anal openings of the psychotherapist's body by any part of the patient's or former patient's body or by any object used by the patient or former patient for that purpose, if agreed to by the psychotherapist.;

(2) kissing or intentional touching by the psychotherapist of the patient's or former patient's genital area, groin, inner thigh, buttocks, or breast or the clothing covering any of these body parts;

(3) kissing, or intentional touching by the patient or former patient of the psychotherapist's genital area, groin, inner thigh, buttocks, or breast or the clothing covering any of these body parts if the psychotherapist agrees to the kissing or intentional touching.

"Sexual contact" includes a request by the psychotherapist for conduct described in paragraphs (1) and (3).

"Sexual contact" does not include conduct described in paragraph (1) or (2) that is a part of standard medical treatment of a patient, casual social contact not intended to be sexual in character, or inadvertent touching.

(g) "Therapeutic deception" means a representation by a psychotherapist that sexual contact with the psychotherapist is consistent with or part of the patient's or former patient's treatment.

[S.H.A. ch. 70, ¶ 802]

§ 2.   Cause of action for sexual exploitation.

(a)   A cause of action against a psychotherapist for sexual exploitation exists for a patient or former patient for injury caused by sexual contact with the psychotherapist, if the sexual contact occurred:

(1)   during the period the patient was receiving psychotherapy from the psychotherapist; or

(2)   after the period the patient received psychotherapy from the psychotherapist if (i) the former patient was emotionally dependent on the psychotherapist or (ii) the sexual contact occurred by means of therapeutic deception.

(b)   The patient or former patient may recover damages from a psychotherapist who is found liable for sexual exploitation. It is not a defense to the action that sexual contact with a patient occurred outside a therapy or treatment session or that it occurred off the premises regularly used by the psychotherapist for therapy or treatment sessions.

[S.H.A. ch. 70, ¶ 803]

§ 3. Liability of employer. An employer of a psychotherapist may be liable under Section 2 if the employer fails or refuses to take reasonable action when the employer knows or has reason to know that the psychotherapist engaged in sexual contact with the plaintiff or any other patient or former patient of the psychotherapist.

[S.H.A. ch. 70, ¶ 804]

§ 4. Scope of discovery. (a) In an action for sexual exploitation, evidence of the plaintiff's sexual history is not subject to discovery except when the plaintiff claims damage to sexual functioning; or

(1)   the defendant requests a hearing prior to conducting discovery and makes an offer of proof of the relevancy of the history; and

(2)   the court finds that the history is relevant and that the probative value of the history outweighs its prejudicial effect.

(b)   The court shall allow the discovery only of specific information or examples of the plaintiff's conduct that are determined by the court to be relevant. The court's order shall detail the information or conduct that is subject to discovery.

[S.H.A. ch. 70, ¶ 805]

§ 5. Admission of Evidence. (a) In an action for sexual exploitation, evidence of the plaintiff's sexual history is not admissible except when:

(1)   the defendant requests a hearing prior to trial and makes an offer of proof of the relevancy of the history; and

(2)   the court finds that the history is relevant and that the probative value of the history outweighs its prejudicial effect.

(b)   The court shall allow the admission only of specific information or examples of the plaintiff's conduct that are determined by the court to be relevant.   The court's order shall detail the information or conduct that is admissible and no other such evidence shall be introduced.

(c)   Violation of the terms of the order may be grounds for a new trial.

[S.H.A. ch. 70, ¶ 806]

§ 6.   Limitation period. An action for sexual exploitation shall be commenced within two years after the cause of action arises.

[S.H.A. ch. 70, ¶ 807]

§ 7.   Application. This Act applies only to causes of action arising on or after the effective date.

Approved: August 30, 1988

Effective: January 1, 1989

APPENDIX DD

Criminal Statute: North Dakota

NORTH DAKOTA — 1987

12.1-20-06.1. Sexual exploitation by therapist — Definitions — Penalty.

Any person who is or who holds oneself out to be a therapist and who intentionally has sexual contact, as defined in Section 12.1-20-02, with a patient or client during any treatment, consultation, interview, or examination is guilty of a class C felony. Consent by the complainant is not a defense under this section. As used in this section, unless the context or subject matter otherwise requires:

1. "Psychotherapy" means the diagnosis or treatment of a mental or emotional condition, including alcohol or drug addiction.

2. "Therapist" means a physician, psychologist, psychiatrist, social worker, nurse, chemical dependency counselor, member of the clergy, or other person, whether licensed or not by the state, who performs or purports to perform psychotherapy.

Source: S.L. 1987, ch. 169 s. 1.

Effective Date.
This section became effective
March 23, 1987.

APPENDIX EE

Hazelden Foundation vs. Patricia L. Meleen
Syllabus and Opinion,
Minnesota Supreme Court

January 31, 1989

STATE OF MINNESOTA
IN SUPREME COURT

CO-88-1599

United States District Court   Popovich, J.
Hazelden Foundation
                    Appellant,
vs.   Filed January 31, 1989
                                                   Office of Appellate Courts
Patricia L. Meleen,
                    Respondent.

SYLLABUS

The statutory bar of Minn. Stat. § 148A.03(d) (1986) does not extend to claims by a former employee, a psychotherapist, brought against the therapist's former employer.

Certified question answered.

Heard, considered and decided by the court en banc.

OPINION

POPOVICH, Justice.

This is a certified question from the United States District Court, District of Minnesota, Fourth Division, pursuant to Minn. Stat. § 480.061 (1986). The following question was certified to this court:

Does the statutory bar of Minnesota Statutes, § 148A.03(d), extend to claims by a former employee, a psychotherapist, for wrongful termination of employment, defamation, negligence, intentional and negligent infliction of emotional distress, and violation of civil rights when those claims are asserted against that therapist's former employer?

We answer the question in the negative.

In the certifying order of July 25, 1988, the following summary of facts gives rise to the certified question:

From June 15, 1983, until June 7, 1987, plaintiff Patricia Meleen was employed as a chemical dependency counselor by defendant Hazelden Foundation (Hazelden), a Minnesota chemical dependency treatment facility. In December 1986, Hazelden was contacted by a former patient whom plaintiff had counseled during his participation in defendant's aftercare program. The patient alleged that plaintiff had sexual contact with him immediately following his departure from the aftercare program.[1] In April 1987, plaintiff was suspended from her job with pay pending the conclusion of defendant's investigation of the patient's allegations. For the purposes of this inquiry, it is assumed that the investigation was conducted in good faith. Based upon this investigation, plaintiff was terminated from her employment with Hazelden on June 3, 1987. On October 16, 1987, plaintiff commenced this action against defendant alleging wrongful termination of employment, defamation, negligence, intentional and negligent infliction of emotional distress, and violation of her civil rights.

In its answer to the complaint, defendant Hazelden asserts that plaintiff's claims are barred by Minnesota Statutes § 148A.03(d).

II.

Minn. Stat. § 148A provides, in pertinent part:

148A.02 CAUSE OF ACTION FOR SEXUAL EXPLOITATION.

A cause of action against a psychotherapist for sexual exploitation exists for a patient or former patient for injury caused by sexual contact with the psychotherapist, if the sexual contact occurred:

(1) during the period the patient was receiving psychotherapy from the psychotherapist; or

(2) after the period the patient received psychotherapy from the psychotherapist if (a) the former patient was emotionally dependent on the psychotherapist; or (b) the sexual contact occurred by means of therapeutic deception.

* * * *

148A.03 LIABILITY OF EMPLOYER.

(a) An employer of a psychotherapist may be liable under section 148A.02 if:

(1) the employer fails or refuses to take reasonable action when the employer knows or has reason to know that the psychotherapist engaged in sexual contact with the plaintiff or any other patient or former patient of the psychotherapist; or

(2) the employer fails or refuses to make inquiries of an employer or former employer, whose name and address have been disclosed to the employer and who employed the psychotherapist as a psychotherapist within the last five years, concerning the occurrence of sexual contacts by the psychotherapist with patients or former patients of the psychotherapist.

(b) An employer or former employer of a psychotherapist may be liable under section 148A.02 if the employer or former employer:

(1) knows of the occurrence of sexual contact by the psychotherapist with patients or former patients of the psychotherapist;

(2) receives a specific written request by another employer or prospective employer of the psychotherapist, engaged in the business of psychotherapy, concerning the existence or nature of the sexual contact; and

(3) fails or refuses to disclose the occurrence of the sexual contacts.

(c)   An employer or former employer may be liable under section 148A.02 only to the extent that the failure or refusal to take any action required by paragraph (a) or (b) was a proximate and actual cause of any damages sustained.

(d)   <u>No cause of action arises, nor may a licensing board in this state take disciplinary action, against a psychotherapist's employer or former employer who in good faith complies with this section.</u>

Minn. Stat. §§ 148A.02, 148A.03 (1986) (emphasis added).

Respondent Meleen argues that § 148A.03(d) ("subdivision (d)"), which bars a cause of action against an employer who in good faith complies with the statute, applies only to a cause of action brought by a former patient, not a former employee. The explicit language of the statute supports respondent's argument. The statute does not discuss suits by a psychotherapist employee against the employer. In fact the statute clearly provides that "[a] cause of action against a psychotherapist for sexual exploitation exists for <u>a patient or former patient</u> for injury caused by sexual contact with the psychotherapist***." Minn. Stat. § 148A.02 (1986) (emphasis added). No mention is made of a cause of action by a psychotherapist employee against the former employer.

In addition, the statute sets forth in section 148A.03 the circumstances under which an employer may be vicariously liable for actions taken by a psychotherapist employee under section 148A.02. Suits under section 148A.02 are limited by the words of the statute to those initialed by "a patient or former patient." Respondent argues that an employer's liability and immunity under section 148A.03 is also limited to those suits as a result of the reference to section 148A.02. Appellant Hazelden argues that the immunity language in subdivision (d) is broad enough to encompass all causes of action brought against an employer, even those initiated by a psychotherapist. However, this intent is not clear from the language of the statute since only suits by patients and former patients against a psychotherapist's employer are explicitly discussed.

The legislative history of this statute does not provide clear guidance as to the intent behind this immunity provision. Our review indicates that subdivision (d) was only discussed at the February 4, 1986, meeting of the Senate Subcommittee on Civil Law. In that discussion the subcommittee hypothesized about the effect of subdivision (d) on suits brought against an employer for release of information protected under the Data Practices Act. <u>See</u> Hearings on Senate File No. 1619, 1986 Minn. Legis., February 4, 1986 (audio tape). A memorandum from senate counsel to members of the Judiciary Committee concludes that the immunity provisions of subdivision (d) would not create any significant changes from the protections already available for employer communications under common law doctrines. Letter from Senate Counsel to Members of the Judiciary Committee (Feb. 12, 1986) (memorandum regarding privileged communications by employers). Neither the discussion by the subcommittee nor the language of the memorandum reflects a clear intent by the legislature to grant full-scale immunity to employers from any suit brought by a terminated psychotherapist employee.

Nor is the title of the act of assistance in descerning the intent of the legislature. The title reads: "An act relating to civil and criminal actions; providing a cause of action for sexual exploitation***." 1986 Minn. Laws ch. 372. The title does not indicate the law provides immunity for any person. This court has previously stated that in construing a statute "courts cannot supply that which the legislature purposely omits or inadvertently overlooks." <u>Wallace v. Commissioner of Taxation</u>, 289 Minn. 220, 230, 184 N.W.2d 588, 594 (1971). <u>See</u> <u>also</u> Minn. Stat. § 645.16 (1986). In this case the legislature gave no indication that suits by a psychotherapist employee against an employer are to be included within the immunity protection of subdivision (d). We cannot assume a legislative intent that is not evidenced by the words of the statute or the legislative history surrounding its enactment.

We hold that the immunity language in section 148A.03(d) does not bar a suit by a psychotherapist employee against a former employer for wrongful termination of employment, defamation, negligence, intentional and negligent infliction of emotional distress, and violation of civil rights. Evidence that the employer acted reasonably and in good faith under the statute can be presented as a defense to these claims under the common law rules for each cause of action. Such potential findings, however, do not automatically act as a bar against a psychotherapist employee commencing an action against the employer.

If our holding is inconsistent with the intent of the legislature, we invite it to amend the statute in the current legislative session to explicitly include claims by a psychotherapist employee against a former employer within the protection of section 148A.03(d).

Certified question answered.

---

[1] In March 1987, following settlement discussions between defendant and the patient, any claims which the patient may have had against Hazelden and its employees were resolved and are not at issue with respect to the question certified herein.

APPENDIX FF

Text of remarks by Judith Janssen,
entitled "A Victim's Perspective"
from the program "Ethics in Practice,"
June 7, 1989, Normandy Inn, Minneapolis
Sponsored by the Minnesota Department of Corrections
[See Case 7 in Chapter 43]

The program was focused on a review of the Task Force's work—especially the criminalization of sex between therapist and client. Mary Theisen, Special Assistant Attorney General, who prosecuted Robert Dutton, the clergyman and counselor who exploited Ms. Janssen, made a presentation entitled, "Criminalization: It's Working." Ms. Janssen then provided her perspective.

The case itself is described in Chapter 43 (Case 7). The audience was quite familiar with the case, but some clarifying notes are in order for the reader:

•the "handbook" mentioned is *It's Never O.K.: A Handbook for Victims and Victim Advocates on Sexual Exploitation by Counselors and Therapists,* a 36-page booklet

•the "Wheel of Options" is in Chapter 26

•the comment near the end about the power of the judge speaking from the bench refers to Judge Noah Rosenbloom's remarks when explaining why he was departing downward from the sentencing guidelines. Part of his stated rationale had to do with the fact that he believed Ms. Janssen was "guilty" of the crime of adultery. (See Ch. 43 for a discussion of this element of the trial.)

Thank you for this opportunity to speak to you, for inviting me to be a part of this special day. I am so pleased to be with you—nervous, but pleased!

I have wrestled with what to share, and how to share. I am not the emotional wreck I was 2 - 3 years ago, thanks in part to the efforts of this Task Force. I can now choose to allow you "up close and personal," or to keep you "out there." That's a new choice for me. Boundaries are new to me.

Not so long ago I was not able to tell what had happened to me, much less understand it. The only words I had, the only understanding, had been given to me by my pastor. You provided me the words to tell what had happened to me, and the understanding that what I'd been told was "good for me, done out of love for me," was in fact a felony. Thank you. You have played a vital part in my recovery.

I frankly don't know all that was required for this legislation to be passed. I do know first-hand what I suffered: the sense of being out of control and powerless; having someone else define for me what was going on, and why it was OK; not knowing where he ended and I began; which were his problems and which mine; losing not only self-respect, but even a sense of self, doubting that I existed apart from him, fearful that I couldn't; and eventually the betrayal of trust and overwhelming guilt. That's where I was 2 - 3 years ago. Because of your efforts I am a recovering victim, able to stand (sort of!) before you today, to thank you and to provide some input.

Even before I became involved in the criminal process I benefitted from your labor. Only recently, as the fog has lifted and the numbness worn off have I become increasingly aware of my journey, and the role your efforts have played. The 4 steps listed on page 10 of your handbook, "It's Never OK" describe that journey.

Those steps are: gaining awareness, considering the wheel of optios, initiating action, and continuing support. The 1st step, gaining awareness, for me meant channelling into Ellen Luepker's victims' group, identifying with other victims, and experiencing support and encouragement in a safe environment. It was there that I realized that people can be intelligent and vulnerable at the same time, and I began to forgive myself for not "knowing better." Obviously, other bright women hadn't "known better," either. Ellen provided publications which helped tremendously to reduce my sense of isolation and to restore my sense of sanity. I had felt so alone, so confused, so "out of it." The client reactions I read validated my feelings and experiences, and made me painfully, yet gratefully, aware that I was not alone. I was relieved to read, and re-read, "Don't expect consistency." Daily, sometimes hourly, I would ask aloud, "What happened? How could this have happened?" My husband and I walked and talked and cried, and I tried desperately to make sense out of nonsense. At the same time I was working on rebuilding my relationship with my family and re-entering the community, constantly checking if friends and family were embarassed to be seen in public with me. Spring of 1987 our then-13-year-old daughter, Monica, wrote a poem to me: "The birds were chirping merrily, the sky was crystal clear, and I was left standing all alone, way over here. The grass was a lovely shade of green, and the bright flowers were all blooming, but right at that minute in time I felt kind of gloomy. I was thinking of you, Mom, and all of the great times that we've shared, and also, all of the painthat you have seemingly always beared. I prayed every night that the pain would be gone the next day, but when I got up and heard you cry, I knew that it hadn't turned out that way. I know that if we keep hoping and trying, that everything will turn out fine, but until then, I'll always wish the pain wasn't yours, but mine." My family suffered, and watched me suffer, through the guilt, shame, self-blame, and sense of responsibility. I anguished and grieved over the abuse, my loss of self and community respect, lost relationships, lost time, lost trust. I asked repeatedly, "What does this say about me?" I was full of fear and paranoia, and distrustful of everyone, especially myself. Gradually I began to realize there were concerned people working on the problem, seeking to increase public awareness; understanding and compassionate toward victims. In group I moved from denial to acceptance of the reality of the exploitation. I was beginning to emerge.

At Ellen's suggestion I met one day with Jeanette Milgrom, who shared with me the wheel of options available to victims, which my husband and I began to prayerfully consider.

Step 3 involved initiating action, and I made a criminal complaint to Don Wersal, Nicollet County Sheriff's Investigator, who not only <u>insured</u> that my complaint was sent to the Attorney General's office, but also took me seriously and believed me.

Then, in May 1987, the Mankato "Free Press" carried 2 articles on Therapeutic Abuse after a local seminar on sexual exploitation. I wept and rejoiced as I read those articles, reminded again that I was not alone, and there were others actively involved in combatting this problem.

For continuing support, in addition to my family and some very loyal friends, I returned to group during the trial, and am grateful for Ellen Luepker's awareness of the need for support during the post-trial phase, and in this case, after sentencing.

I have profited from this Task Force's efforts. Long before I had access to the handbook, your members had been at work behind the scenes, informing, educating, revising, lobbying. I thank you, for providing counseling for abused clients, for providing a legal process, for providing education. Your work has been critical to my resolving this experience.

I do have some reflections, and 2 major concerns I'd like to provide input on. One involves the need to prove emotional dependency when sex occurs during counseling. The second involves the media's need to be sensitive to victims.

I agree with Gary Schoener: "Reporting can be a painful experience, as the complainant's entire emotional history is tossed into the proceedings." My situation was somewhat unique, and I credit the Attorney General's Office, and specifically Mary Theisen, with doing an <u>outstanding</u> job of prosecuting this case. Mary's efforts deserve to be commended. She demonstrated the professionalism and the sensitivity essential to my establishing trust and confidence, not only in her abilities, but in the judicial process.

There is in Scripture an admonition to "count the cost." That is, to envision the best scenario/worst scenario. What is your greatest hope? What is your greatest fear? In this case the reality is that the good was better, and the bad was worse, than I'd anticipated. I'm hoping for future victims that bad might be improved.

I was prepared for the fact that my emotional history would be revealed in the courtroom. Mary had adequately forewarned me. I thought I had counted the cost. However, as I understand it, one objective in prosecuting the exploitation as a felony is to make public the perpetrator's offense to deter others, not to publicize the victim's emotional history to deter other victims from reporting. Although sometimes therapists contend that the sex was permissible because the therapist was in love with the patient, sexual involvement with a client is <u>always</u> a failure of therapy. Even though my pastor said he was in love with me, it wasn't OK. I was there for therapy. Therapy failed, and a felony occurred. That's Never OK.

Consent may not be used as a defense. I was in no shape to consent, or to withhold consent. I quote: "What needs to be proved is only that the activity took place." I agree with Gary Schoener: "One criticism of the new statute is that it should not require proof that the victim was emotionally dependent or under therapeutic deception if the acts occurred while counseling was still occurring. Any sexual interaction is inappropriate if counseling is still going on." My emotional history was tossed into the proceedings. That's painful enough. What's worse is when that emotional history is reported in the local papers.

In counting the cost, I failed to calculate the extensive public exposure, and the toll that would take on me and on my family, who had already suffered considerably. St. Peter is a small town. Even initials are a dead give-away.

The media's coverage included disclosure of my problems. The 1st amendment guarantees freedom of the press, and what occurs during a criminal trial is a matter of public record.

Victims, however, have expressed concern and hesitancy as a result of the detailed coverage of the trial testimony. So much detail of a most personal nature was included. Local papers daily listed 5 specific issues for which I sought help, as well as other intimate details. I checked in with my children every evening during the trial to see that they were OK at school. My husband lost clients. When the verdict was reported my mailman offered me congratulations and his condolences. I had a sense that everyone knew everything, and it took a great deal of courage to grocery shop, pick the kids up after school, go to the Post Office. I temporarily quit attending the Bible Study Fellowship luncheons. The point I'm trying to make is publication of a victim's emotional history will simply deter other victims from reporting. The objective in prosecuting is to deter other therapists from exploiting their patients. I agree with you: "Recommendations should be made to better ensure the protection of the privacy of the client, so that more victims might be willing to risk prosecuting." Perhaps journalists can employ voluntary restraint, so that a balance is achieved between issue coverage and re-victimization. Victim identification is an issue. In "counting the cost" of reporting, victims are concerned about:

-disclosure of emotional history;
-public exposure through media coverage;
-the availability of advocacy. Every county in outstate Minnesota needs to provide advocacy programs.
-a sense of validation. Victims need to know they're not alone, and that their experiences, sad to say, are fairly common. And Christians, calling to accountability, are often accused of being vengeful. There is also the legitimate fear of acquittal, and "What does that say about me?" And there is the fear of comments at sentencing that could prove to be a victim's worst nightmare. Ellen Goodman expressed it best when she said: "the notion that women provoke their own abuse is just that ingrained. Indeed, as often as not, the justice system hands out excuses with sentences." I experienced a terrible set-back after sentencing. A judge speaking from the bench is frighteningly like God speaking from the heavens.

You as a Task Force feel strongly that the justice system needs to understand the issues and dilemmas faced by both victims and therapists. I agree.

There have been countless times during the past few years when I have cried out to the Lord about our ever moving to St. Peter. I can now gratefully acknowledge that it was in Minnesota, afger August, 1985, that the abuse occurred. If this had occurred earlier, or in most other states, I might still be struggling to figure out what had happened. Thanks to the efforts of this Task Force, victims are increasingly aware of the exploitation scenario, and the options available when such occurs. Reviewal and evaluation are good and worthy objectives; your efforts to date warrant recognition, and from me, Judy Janssen, a personal thank-you.